CRITICAL SURVEY
OF
DRAMA

CRITICAL SURVEY

OF

DRAMA

Second Revised Edition

Volume 4

Victor Hugo - John Marston

Editor, Second Revised Edition
Carl Rollyson
Baruch College, City University of New York

Editor, First Editions, English and Foreign Language Series
Frank N. Magill

SALEM PRESS, INC.
Pasadena, California   Hackensack, New Jersey

Editor in Chief: Dawn P. Dawson
Managing Editor: Christina J. Moose
Developmental Editor: R. Kent Rasmussen
Project Editor: Rowena Wildin
Research Supervisor: Jeffry Jensen
Research Assistant: Michelle Murphy

Acquisitions Editor: Mark Rehn
Photograph Editor: Philip Bader
Manuscript Editor: Sarah Hilbert
Assistant Editor: Andrea E. Miller
Production Editor: Cynthia Beres
Layout: Eddie Murillo and William Zimmerman

Library of Congress Cataloging-in-Publication Data

Critical survey of drama / edited by Carl Rollyson.-- 2nd rev. ed.

    p. cm.

Previous edition edited by Frank Northen Magill in 1994.

"Combines, updates, and expands two earlier Salem Press reference sets: Critical survey of drama, revised edition, English language series, published in 1994, and Critical survey of drama, foreign language series, published in 1986"--Pref.

Includes bibliographical references and index.

ISBN 1-58765-102-5 (set : alk. paper) -- ISBN 1-58765-106-8 (vol. 4 : alk. paper) --

1. Drama--Dictionaries. 2. Drama--History and criticism--Dictionaries. 3. Drama--Bio-bibliography. 4. English drama--Dictionaries. 5. American drama--Dictionaries. 6. Commonwealth drama (English)--Dictionaries. 7. English drama--Bio-bibliography. 8. American drama--Bio-bibliography. 9. Commonwealth drama (English)--Bio-bibliography. I. Rollyson, Carl E. (Carl Edmund) II. Magill, Frank Northen, 1907-1997.

PN1625 .C68 2003

809.2′003—dc21

2003002190

First Printing

CONTENTS

VOLUME 4

COMPLETE LIST OF CONTENTS

VOLUME 1

VOLUME 3

VOLUME 4

VOLUME 5

VOLUME 6

VOLUME 7

AMERICAN DRAMA

BRITISH DRAMA

VOLUME 8

EUROPEAN DRAMA

WORLD DRAMA

DRAMATIC GENRES

DRAMA TECHNIQUES

RESOURCES

INDEXES

CRITICAL SURVEY
OF
DRAMA

VICTOR HUGO

Born: Besançon, France; February 26, 1802
Died: Paris, France; May 22, 1885

PRINCIPAL DRAMA

Irtamène, wr. 1816, pb. 1934 (verse drama)

Inez de Castro, wr. c. 1818, pb. 1863 (verse drama)

Cromwell, pb. 1827 (verse drama; English translation, 1896)

Amy Robsart, pr. 1828, pb. 1889 (English translation, 1895)

Hernani, pr., pb. 1830 (verse drama; English translation, 1830)

Marion de Lorme, pr., pb. 1831 (verse drama; English translation, 1895)

Le Roi s'amuse, pr., pb. 1832 (verse drama; *The King's Fool*, 1842, also known as *The King Amuses Himself*, 1964)

Lucrèce Borgia, pr., pb. 1833 (*Lucretia Borgia*, 1842)

Marie Tudor, pr., pb. 1833 (English translation, 1895)

Angelo, tyran de Padoue, pr., pb. 1835 (*Angelo, Tyrant of Padua*, 1880)

Ruy Blas, pr., pb. 1838 (verse drama; English translation, 1890)

Les Burgraves, pr., pb. 1843 (*The Burgraves*, 1896)

La Grand-mère, pb. 1865, pr. 1898

Mille Francs de Recompense, pb. 1866

Torquemada, wr. 1869, pb. 1882 (English translation, 1896)

Les Deux Trouvailles de Gallus, pb. 1881

Théâtre en liberté, pb. 1886 (includes *Mangeront-ils?*)

The Dramatic Works, pb. 1887

The Dramatic Works of Victor Hugo, pb. 1895-1896 (4 volumes)

OTHER LITERARY FORMS

Victor Hugo, one of the titanic figures of nineteenth century literature, produced major works in every genre. He is among the greatest lyric poets in French literature; two of his many novels, *Notre-Dame de Paris* (1831; *The Hunchback of Notre Dame*, 1833) and *Les Misérables* (1862; English translation, 1862), are classics of world literature; and his remaining works are prodigious in their variety and their ambition, ranging from literary criticism, biography, and philosophical reflection to impassioned polemics on social and political issues—notably capital punishment, against which Hugo was a tireless crusader.

ACHIEVEMENTS

Victor Hugo is regarded by many critics as the preeminent figure in nineteenth century French literature. As a playwright, he ranks with Alexandre Dumas, *père*, Alfred de Vigny, and Alfred de Musset as one of the most representative authors of the romantic theater. At least one critic sees him as the essential link between the classical theater of Jean Racine and the modern twentieth century revival. As Molière raised farce to true comedy, so Hugo brought the melodrama to the level of authentic literary drama.

Although Hugo wrote some of the finest plays of the romantic period, especially *Hernani* and *Ruy Blas*, he is best appreciated as a theorist of the theater. The preface to *Cromwell* served as the manifesto of romantic liberation for French drama, calling for the Shakespearean tradition rather than the classical, the abolition of the unities of time and place, and the fusion of the sublime and the grotesque. It is, in fact, for his appreciation and creation of the grotesque that his dramatic theories are best known. He calls for the joyful grotesque of the carnivals, in the manner of Mikhail Bakhtin; the grotesque of the cathedrals; and the revival of the buffoons Scaramouche, Sganarelle, and Harlequin, for "beauty has only one face; ugliness has thousands." His own theater was to produce several buffoons: Flibbertigibbet, Triboulet, and Don César are among the best.

Because Hugo was a great poet, his theater is essentially lyric. He writes with ease, charm, and poetic beauty. His lines are musical, and the Alexandrine carries the tragic and fatal revenge that marks every play or it expresses the delicate love of Hugo's young heroes or heroines. Rapidity of dialogue and quick exchange of wit contribute to the poetic schema as well, for the fragmented Alexandrine and the enjambments that he used and abused become the vehicle for the comic theme that Hugo considered indispensable to drama. Even the dramas in prose, such as *Lucretia Borgia*, *Marie Tudor*, and *Angelo*, *Tyrant of Padua*, have a rhythmic character that makes them unmistakably Hugoesque.

Hugo saw the theater as a vocation and as the best way of influencing the public. In this he resembles Voltaire, although his desire to please makes him the heir of Molière. He was determined to conquer the rigid structure of outdated classical models. He was thwarted by the conservative Restoration government's censure of *Marion de Lorme*, although he had triumphed with *Hernani*. He was thwarted again when *The King Amuses Himself* was banned under King Louis-Philippe. *Hernani* is better known for the furor it provoked than for its intrinsic literary merit, which is also great. Hugo installed his friends Théophile Gautier, Honoré de Balzac, Luis-Hector Berlioz, and Prosper Mérimée in the audience among others in informal attire, so their applause would triumph over the conservatives such as Mme Récamier and Chateaubriand. He succeeded, and the thirty-eight repeated performances of *Hernani* that same year assured the victory of romanticism in the theater.

Essentially a visionary, Hugo saw life in terms of a metaphysical conflict between good and evil. Although a rebel against classicism, he inherited the Greek perception of humanity moving in the grip of destiny. *The Burgraves* has often been seen as an Aeschylean tragedy, the Titans against the gods. Hugo's imagination was limitless, and his theatrical images, whether in staged or closet drama, show the realization of his childhood wish to be *Chateaubriand ou rien* (Chateaubriand or nothing). Although his plots are in many respects dated, his nineteenth century melodramas, his art, and his vision keep alive his immortal heroes and his matchless lyric verse.

Victor Hugo (Library of Congress)

BIOGRAPHY

Born in Besançon, France, *quand le siècle avait deux ans* (when the century was two years old), on February 26, 1802, Victor-Marie Hugo was one of three sons of a future general, Joseph-Leopold-Sigisbert Hugo, and a temperamental mother of Breton origin, Sophie-Françoise Trébuchet. His early years were marked by parental incompatibility and travels to Italy and Spain. His childhood memories of Spain were deep and lasting, and names such as Hernani, Torquemada, and Elespuru originate in this trip, as do the inspirations of many plays and poems. His first verses go back to his early school days in Paris in a private pension from 1815 to 1818, and he began his dramatic experimentations with classical tragedies, comic opera, and melodrama.

From 1819 to 1821, he and his brother Eugène directed a journal, *Le Conservateur littéraire*, with little financial remuneration. His first literary success, *Odes et poésies diverses*, in 1822, brought with it a pension of one thousand francs, which made possible his marriage to his first and great love, Adèle Foucher. Their four children were born before 1831, when his wife's attachment to Hugo's friend and literary colleague, Charles-Augustin Sainte-Beuve, first came to his attention. Crushed, Hugo turned more intensely to the theater, and it was his success with *Lucretia Borgia* in 1833 that was to precipitate his lifelong liaison with the actress Juliette Drouet. Together they traveled to Alsace, Switzerland, and Provence in 1839, and to the valley of the Rhine the following year, which was the inspiration for *The Burgraves*.

The Burgraves, majestic and somber, was a failure on the stage. That same year, Léopoldine, Hugo's favorite daughter, was killed along with her husband of six months in a tragic boating accident on the Seine. Hugo abandoned the theater and turned to politics, particularly in 1848, when he became the spokesperson in the new republic for the democratic and social Left. When Louis-Napoleon took power in his famous *coup d'état* of December 2, 1851, Hugo protested so violently that he was obliged to flee, first to Brussels, then to the Channel Islands of Jersey and, finally, Guernsey, where he lived at Hauteville House from 1856 to 1870.

The years of exile were productive, especially for Hugo's poetic genius. They are the years of *Les Contemplations* (1856), one of the best volumes of his poetry, and *Les Misérables*, his immortal novel. It was at this time that he also returned to the theater, though he never again wrote for the stage. He wanted to produce a theater in freedom, immune from government censure and popular disapproval, and he destined his works for *Théâtre en liberté*, published posthumously in 1886.

The fall of Napoleon III in 1870 allowed Hugo's return to France, which proved disillusioning at first, as the Commune reigned in Paris. Although the 1870's were marred by the death of his two sons and the mental illness of his daughter Adèle, they were also years of triumph. He was elected senator in 1876; his plays *Marion de Lorme*, *Marie Tudor*, and *Hernani*, among others, were revived, and he was everywhere acclaimed. He died on May 22, 1885, and on June 1 was solemnly buried in a national ceremony.

ANALYSIS

Critics divide Victor Hugo's theater into four categories, excluding the plays before *Cromwell*. The first group constitutes his romantic dramas in verse: *Cromwell*, *Marion de Lorme*, *Hernani*, *The King Amuses Himself*, and *Ruy Blas*. Romantic dramas in prose include *Amy Robsart*, *Lucretia Borgia*, *Marie Tudor*, and *Angelo, Tyrant of Padua*. *The Burgraves* and *Torquemada* form his epic theater, while *Théâtre en liberté* is lyric comedy. Although there is a distinct evolution, particularly in the development of the plot after *Cromwell*, and a greater integration of themes after *Ruy Blas*, all of Hugo's plays have definite characteristics that mark them as his own dramatic creations.

After 1830, the role of woman becomes more important, possibly because of Juliette Drouet's influence in Hugo's life. At the same time, the populist theme grows in importance, culminating in the character of Ruy Blas, the man of the people. Hugo usually portrayed royalty in decline or dissipation, and *Ruy Blas* emphasizes this theme. Hugo's earlier works tend to have tragic, melodramatic endings, while in his later works he moves to more human themes, and in *La Grand-mère* and *Mangeront-ils?*, maternal and conjugal love triumph.

The exposition is straightforward and usually takes place in the first few scenes. Even mysteries and disguises are made evident to the audience without diminishing interest. It is obvious, for example, that Lucretia Borgia is Gennaro's mother, and that the masked intruder in *Hernani* is Don Carlos, who will not succeed in winning the beautiful Doña Sol. The exposition usually reveals a trait of character that does not change throughout the play. Hernani personifies Castilian honor; Don Salluste, revenge; Amy Robsart, love. A notable exception is Cromwell, one of the most complex and fully realized characters in Hugo's theater. Acts, or *journées* (days), usually bear the title of a character and reveal the essential message of the section.

Hugo portrays the situation clearly and immediately and proceeds at once to action, which dominates his theater. The action converges on the resolution of the problem and is often produced by melodramatic devices: poison, disguise, hidden stairways, closets, and other such *coups de théâtre*. Poison is Hugo's most common method; he uses it more than all the other romantic playwrights combined; hardly a play is without it. Yet in all cases, the real obstacle that necessitates the tragic resolution is fate, and the melodramatic devices are actually symbols for human powerlessness against the all-pervading destiny that thwarts humankind.

At the center of almost every drama there is a couple, young, handsome, and passionately in love. Their love is pure and fatal: Amy Robsart and Dudley, Doña Sol and Hernani, and Regina and Otbert. In the earlier plays, they form the heart of the drama; later, they are merely accessory.

In contrast to the ideal woman and her valiant hero is the villain. The portrayal of villainy gave Hugo full scope for his delight in the grotesque, and some of his most memorable creations are of this type. The villains in his early plays recall the cloak-and-dagger melodrama, while later types lean more to the demoniac, culminating in Torquemada, as John Peter Houston describes him, "the satanic enemy of Satan." The grotesque is also embodied in the buffoon: the deformed Triboulet or the comic Flibbertigibbet, Cromwell's four fools, or the best and most convincing character, Don César in *Ruy Blas*. Finally, in his later years, Hugo successfully combined the sublime and the grotesque in the chameleonlike Aïrolo in *Mangeront-ils?*, with a Shakespearean touch.

CROMWELL

Of the six verse dramas written before 1830, the two most significant are *Cromwell* and *Marion de Lorme*. The other early verse dramas are tragedies in imitation of classical models, a comic-opera, and a melodrama. None of the six was staged before 1830. *Cromwell*, published in 1827, was unstageable by its very length. It was presented for the first time in 1956, in the Cour Carrée of the Louvre, in an adaptation by Jean Cocteau. *Marion de Lorme* was censored by the conservative government of Charles X but was successfully staged in 1831 at the Théâtre Porte-Saint-Martin.

Cromwell, depicting the vast panorama of a giant historical figure, is the story of a failed attempt to as-

sassinate Oliver Cromwell by both Puritans and Cavaliers. Profiting from a flirtation of Lord Rochester with his daughter Francis, Cromwell succeeds in escaping from his enemies by drugging Rochester and disguising himself as a soldier. In the end, Cromwell thwarts all his enemies by refusing the crown. The play is a complex study of Cromwell's character, and an attempt by Hugo to capture Cromwell's personality from every side. Cromwell is less a depiction of the real historical personage than a fictitious mélange of Julius Caesar and Napoleon Bonaparte, yet Hugo's dramatic creation is his best characterization. The play is written in liberated verse with the introduction of several other important Hugoesque techniques, among them, the characterization of the buffoon.

The significance of the play itself, however, has been overshadowed by that of its preface, the manifesto of romanticism in the French theater. Dividing history into three ages—patriarchal, theocratic, and modern—Hugo develops the concept of the grotesque as particularly appropriate for modern times. In the same way, he sees drama as complete poetry, a combination of comedy and tragedy, with only unity of action as necessary from among the three classical unities. Hugo proclaims liberty of creation and of versification in the drama and urges writers not to choose the beautiful but rather the characteristic. Art for him is divine, and its aim is the imitation of nature and truth.

MARION DE LORME

Both in *Cromwell* and *Marion de Lorme*, Hugo attempted to put these rules into practice. *Marion de Lorme*, shorter and therefore stageable, is the story of a courtesan redeemed by a pure love for Didier, a melancholy hero of unknown origin. He is the unconscious victim of Cardinal Richelieu's edict against duels, as he challenges Marion's former lover, Saverny, to a duel from which both escape, yet for which both are condemned. Marion tries to save Didier by every means, even resigning herself to the diabolic Laffemas. Yet all fails, for the implacable Cardinal Richelieu, who never appears yet who is omnipresent and all-powerful, refuses the pardon granted by the weak-willed Louis XIII. The portrayal of a feeble monarch did not appeal to the Restoration government, but Louis-Philippe's regime permitted it, and the play was a moderate success with Marie Dorval in the leading role.

HERNANI

Hugo's two greatest plays are generally acknowledged to be *Hernani* and *Ruy Blas*. *Hernani* represented the triumph of the romantic theater at the conservative Théâtre-Français, following the famous battle of the winter of 1830, brought about by the efforts of Hugo and his liberal friends. *Ruy Blas* inaugurated the Théâtre de la Renaissance, where Hugo was given complete freedom by the newly married Hélène de Mecklembourg, duchess of Orléans and wife of the heir to the throne.

Hernani has as its theme Castilian honor, not unlike Pierre Corneille's *Le Cid* (pr., pb. 1637; *The Cid*, 1637), of which it has definite echoes. It is set in sixteenth century Spain and portrays three rivals for the brilliant and beautiful Doña Sol: Ruy Gomez, her elderly tutor, who represents both honor and vengeance; Don Carlos, the future Holy Roman Emperor; and Hernani, the bandit seeking revenge on Carlos and a noble in disguise. Don Carlos changes from a comic lover to a noble prince and pardons Hernani, giving him Doña Sol as his bride. Ruy Gomez, while respecting his honor as a host to Hernani, demands Hernani's life in the name of the same honor. At the very moment of their marriage, Hernani and Doña Sol fall victims to Ruy Gomez' vengeance and die poisoned in each other's arms.

RUY BLAS

Ruy Blas is also set in Spain, this time in the seventeenth century, the era of declining empire under King Charles II. It is, in fact, an image of decadence that pervades the entire play, showing royalty by indifference and nobility by corruption and impoverishment. In contrast, Ruy Blas represents the growing role of the people and the social ascension of a simple lackey who aspires not only to political power but also to the love of a queen, Marie-Anne de Neubourg, a young and passionate woman who has been abandoned by her indifferent husband.

Ruy Blas assumes his political role and his pursuit of the queen under the orders of his corrupt master, Don Salluste, who wants revenge against the queen

for her discovery of his liaison. Ruy Blas does so in disguise, taking the name of the impoverished Don César, a picaro type and Hugo's most convincing comic character, whose unexpected return in act 4 causes a comedy of errors. Ruy Blas has become a faithful servant of the queen and a political success, and he has gained her love and esteem when Don Salluste pursues his revenge by snaring the queen in a compromising situation. Ruy Blas confesses his identity and poisons himself rather than expose the queen to dishonor. As a final tribute to his love and a concession to the romantic audience, he dies hearing the queen speak his name.

Both plays are replete with Hugo's melodramatic devices: disguise, ladders, closets, and the ubiquitous poison. Yet the plot is integrated, the heroes are convincing, and the lines are swift and melodic. Ruy Blas's monologue in act 1, Don César's comic wit, as well as the scene of the portraits in *Hernani*, are superb poetry and drama. Especially in *Ruy Blas*, the political portrait of the hero is noble and persuasive.

AMY ROBSART

With the exception of *Amy Robsart*, which was staged in 1828, Hugo's prose dramas *Lucretia Borgia*, *Marie Tudor*, and *Angelo, Tyrant of Padua*, were written between his most successful verse dramas and were staged at the more popular Théâtre Porte-Saint-Martin. Grant sees this change of theater and genre as an effort by Hugo to appeal to the "people" rather than to the "public." All are noticeably inferior to his verse productions, though they are not without merit.

Amy Robsart was a failure on the stage, despite its elegant costumes, designed by Eugène Delacroix. It is set in sixteenth century England and focuses on the love of the pure and passionate Amy for the count of Leicester, favorite of Elizabeth, the queen of England. Amy and Leicester are secretly married, without the knowledge of even Amy's honorable and self-sacrificing father, Hugh. The villain Varney, ancestor of Claude Frollo and Don Salluste, profits from Elizabeth's attraction to Leicester and attempts to seduce the faithful Amy, who is eventually killed despite the efforts of the gentle buffoon Flibbertigibbet to save her. Although the play is exaggerated and melodramatic, it contains Hugo's great characters in embryo:

the ideal heroine, the noble elderly gentleman, the monster-woman, the villain, and the buffoon.

LUCRETIA BORGIA

Lucretia Borgia was designed as a counterpart to *The King Amuses Himself*, Hugo's drama in verse that was censored by Louis-Philippe's government for its portrayal of a dissolute monarch, François I, a portrait not justified by history. The central feature of *The King Amuses Himself* is the redemption of the deformed buffoon Triboulet through his paternal love for his daughter Blanche. *Lucretia Borgia*, on the other hand, set in sixteenth century Venice, is a story of maternal love. Lucretia Borgia, presented by Hugo as more depraved than historical documents admit, has accidentally poisoned her own son, Gennaro, who is ignorant of his parentage, in an effort to avenge an insult made on her by his five companions. The magnificent final act shows a cavernous vault with a solemn procession of chanting monks bearing the coffins for Lucretia's victims. As she dies at the hand of her own son, she finally reveals her identity to him.

MARIE TUDOR

As Hugo exaggerated Elizabeth's sordid character in *Amy Robsart*, he made Marie Tudor into a jealous queen "whose bedroom opened onto the scaffold," an assertion once again contrary to history. In *Marie Tudor*, she plots the death of her unfaithful suitor, Fabiani, who becomes enamored of her cousin Jane. Less tragic in this play, however, Hugo allows virtue to triumph and vice to be punished, as Gilbert, Jane's noble guardian, is saved, and Fabiani is executed.

ANGELO, TYRANT OF PADUA

Like Hugo's other dramas in prose, *Angelo, Tyrant of Padua* also portrays women as its principal figures, despite its title. Hugo intended to present woman in two roles: the woman in society, the faithful yet maligned Caterina; and the woman outside society, the courtesan Tisbe who is redeemed by pure love and self-sacrifice. The tyrant Angelo suspects his wife of infidelity and is about to kill her when Tisbe allows herself to die in order to save Catarina, in whose possession she finds her mother's crucifix. Catarina's rebellion against her husband's tyranny in a powerful speech is particularly significant in the development of Hugo's attitudes toward women.

THE BURGRAVES

The Burgraves, one of Hugo's most powerful creations, was a failure on the stage because of the nature of the play as well as the intrigues of Hugo's rivals and a change in popular taste. The chronicle of a family, it is an epic creation of mythic proportions, recalling the fall of the Titans, and of biblical grandeur, evoking Cain, Nemrod, and Job. Four generations of warriors dwell in the valley of the Rhine, the younger two given over to corruption and vice. The patriarch of the clan, Job, is the mortal enemy of Frederic Barbarossa, discovered to be his brother and formerly his rival for the same woman, Guanhamara. Job atones for his crime by recognizing the power of Barbarossa as the savior of Germany. Patricia Ward proposes that this is Hugo's metaphor for his own belief in the emperor and in the union of France and Germany, as well as for his faith in pardon and redemption.

THÉÂTRE EN LIBERTÉ

After *The Burgraves*, Hugo no longer wrote for the stage but continued to think in the language of drama. He planned a theater in liberty, *Théâtre en liberté*, where he would give free rein to his imagination without fear of governmental or popular criticism. During his years in exile, he composed several fragments around the characters of César de Bazan and Maglia, a Robin Hood character. By 1873, the plays destined for *Théâtre en liberté* were completed, although the work was not published until 1886, the year after Hugo's death.

MANGERONT-ILS?

The finest pieces of this period are *Mangeront-ils?* and *Torquemada*. *Mangeront-ils?* recalls William Shakespeare's *A Midsummer Night's Dream* (pr. c. 1595-1596), and Hugo's Aïrolo is not unlike Puck or Ariel. It is the love story of Lord Slada and Lady Janet, who, pursued by the King of Man, take refuge in a ruined cloister where they are unable to eat. Aïrolo, aided by the dying sorceress Zineb, who wills him her magic plume, saves the lovers in a delightful fantasy in which love triumphs.

TORQUEMADA

Torquemada, on the other hand, is a magnificent and frightful portrayal of the demoniac Inquisitor

Torquemada, who kills for the glory of God. King Ferdinand is the symbol of selfish hedonism; Pope Alexander VI, powerful and corrupt, is balanced by the saintly hermit, Francis of Paula, while Sanche and Rose are Hugo's typical lovers. They save Torquemada from prison, but because he considers their use of an iron cross as sacrilege, he condemns them to death.

Like the grandiose Torquemada, Hugo's visionaries peer with God and Satan into the immense abyss which Hugo himself tried to penetrate during his entire life. His lyric approach to the theater and his concern with the authentic, with destiny, and with good and evil enabled him to rise above convention, placing melodrama on a level with serious artistic endeavor.

OTHER MAJOR WORKS

LONG FICTION: *Han d'Islande*, 1823 (*Hans of Iceland*, 1845); *Bug-Jargal*, 1826 (*The Noble Rival*, 1845); *Le Dernier Jour d'un condamné*, 1829 (*The Last Day of a Condemned*, 1840); *Notre-Dame de Paris*, 1831 (*The Hunchback of Notre Dame*, 1833); *Claude Gueux*, 1834; *Les Misérables*, 1862 (English translation, 1862); *Les Travailleurs de la mer*, 1866 (*The Toilers of the Sea*, 1866); *L'Homme qui rit*, 1869 (*The Man Who Laughs*, 1869); *Quatre-vingt-treize*, 1874 (*Ninety-Three*, 1874).

POETRY: *Odes et poésies diverses*, 1822, 1823; *Nouvelles Odes*, 1824; *Odes et ballades*, 1826; *Les Orientales*, 1829 (*Les Orientales: Or, Eastern Lyrics*, 1879); *Les Feuilles d'automne*, 1831; *Les Chants du crépuscule*, 1835 (*Songs of Twilight*, 1836); *Les Voix intérieures*, 1837; *Les Rayons et les ombres*, 1840; *Les Châtiments*, 1853; *Les Contemplations*, 1856; *La Légende des siècles*, 1859-1883 (5 volumes; *The Legend of the Centuries*, 1894); *Les Chansons des rues et des bois*, 1865; *L'Année terrible*, 1872; *L'Art d'être grand-père*, 1877; *Le Pape*, 1878; *La Pitié suprême*, 1879; *L'Âne*, 1880; *Les Quatre vents de l'esprit*, 1881; *The Literary Life and Poetical Works of Victor Hugo*, 1883; *La Fin de Satan*, 1886; *Toute la lyre*, 1888; *Dieu*, 1891; *Les Années funestes*, 1896;

Poems from Victor Hugo, 1901; *Dernière Gerbe*, 1902; *Poems*, 1902; *The Poems of Victor Hugo*, 1906; *Océan*, 1942.

NONFICTION: *La Préface de Cromwell*, 1827 (English translation, 1896); *Littérature et philosophie mêlées*, 1834; *Le Rhin*, 1842 (*The Rhine*, 1843); *Napoléon le petit*, 1852 (*Napoleon the Little*, 1852); *William Shakespeare*, 1864 (English translation, 1864); *Actes et paroles*, 1875-1876; *Histoire d'un crime*, 1877 (*The History of a Crime*, 1877-1878); *Religions et religion*, 1880; *Le Théâtre en liberté*, 1886; *Choses vues*, 1887 (*Things Seen*, 1887); *En voyage: Alpes et Pyrénées*, 1890 (*The Alps and Pyrenees*, 1898); *France et Belgique*, 1892; *Correspondance*, 1896-1898.

MISCELLANEOUS: *Œuvres complètes*, 1880-1892 (57 volumes); *Victor Hugo's Works*, 1892 (30 volumes); *Works*, 1907 (10 volumes).

BIBLIOGRAPHY

Frey, John Andrew. *A Victor Hugo Encyclopedia.* Westport, Conn.: Greenwood Press, 1999. An encyclopedic reference work dedicated to Hugo. Bibliography and index.

Halsall, A. W. *Victor Hugo and the Romantic Drama.* Buffalo, N.Y.: University of Toronto Press, 1998. A scholarly study of the dramatic works of Hugo. Bibliography and index.

O'Grady, Deidre. *Piave, Boito, Pirandello: From Romantic Realism to Modernism.* Lewiston, N.Y.: Edwin Mellen Press, 2000. A look at the dramatic works of Hugo, Franceso Maria Piave, Arrigo Boito, and Luigi Pirandello. Bibliography and index.

Porter, Laurence M. *Victor Hugo.* New York: Twayne, 1999. A basic biography of Hugo that covers his life and works. Bibliography and index.

Robb, Graham. *Victor Hugo.* New York: W. W. Norton, 1998. This thorough biography of Hugo reveals many previously unknown aspects of his long life and literary career. Bibliography and indexes.

Irma M. Kashuba

DAVID HENRY HWANG

Born: Los Angeles, California; August 11, 1957

PRINCIPAL DRAMA

F.O.B., pr. 1978, pb. 1983

The Dance and the Railroad, pr. 1981, pb. 1983

Family Devotions, pr. 1981, pb. 1983

Sound and Beauty, pr. 1983 (two one-acts, *The House of Sleeping Beauties*, pb. 1983, and *The Sound of a Voice*, pb. 1984)

Broken Promises: Four Plays, pb. 1983

Rich Relations, pr. 1986, pb. 1990

As the Crow Flies, pr. 1986

Broken Promises, pr. 1987 (includes *The Dance and the Railroad* and *The House of Sleeping Beauties*)

M. Butterfly, pr., pb. 1988

One Thousand Airplanes on the Roof, pr. 1988, pb. 1989 (libretto; music by Philip Glass)

F.O.B. and Other Plays, pb. 1990

Bondage, pr. 1992, pb. 1996 (one act)

The Voyage, pr. 1992, pb. 2000 (libretto; music by Glass)

Face Value, pr. 1993

Trying to Find Chinatown, pr., pb. 1996

Golden Child, pr. 1996, pb. 1998

The Silver River, pr. 1997 (music by Bright Sheng)

Peer Gynt, pr. 1998 (adaptation of Henrik Ibsen's play)

Aida, pr. 2000 (with Linda Wolverton and Robert Falls; music by Elton John; lyrics by Tim Rice; adaptation of Giuseppe Verdi's opera)

Flower Drum Song, pr. 2001 (adaptation of Richard Rodgers and Oscar Hammerstein's musical)

OTHER LITERARY FORMS

David Henry Hwang has written a number of screenplays, including *M. Butterfly* (1993), *Golden Gate* (1994), and *Possession* (2001). He has also written for television with scripts that include *My American Son* (1987) and *The Lost Empire* (2001).

ACHIEVEMENTS

David Henry Hwang is the first Asian American playwright to bring specifically Asian and American themes to Broadway and Off-Broadway theater. His plays explore issues of ethnic identity, gender, and imperialism, with often stunning theatrical flair. Within the first decade of his career as a playwright, he staged six major productions in New York and abroad, garnering four Off-Broadway "Best Play" nominations and awards. *M. Butterfly*, his first Broadway play, won both the New York Drama Desk Award and the Tony Award for Best Play as well as a nomination for the Pulitzer Prize in Drama. *Golden Child* was nominated for a Tony Award for Best Play in 1998 and earned an Obie Award for Playwriting in 1997.

BIOGRAPHY

David Henry Hwang was born in Los Angeles on August 11, 1957, the son of Henry Yuan Hwang, a banker, and Dorothy Huang Hwang, a professor of piano. His father grew up in Shanghai, China, and emigrated in the late 1940's to California, where he enrolled in the business program at the University of Southern California. His mother, born in southeastern China, had grown up in the Philippines.

Hwang received his A.B. degree in English from Stanford University in 1979, then briefly taught writing in a high school in Menlo Park, California, before attending the Yale School of Drama in 1980 and 1981. His first play, *F.O.B.*, was performed at Stanford University before being accepted for production at the National Playwrights Conference at Connecticut's O'Neill Theater Center in 1979, when he was twenty-one years old. The following year, Joseph Papp brought it to the New York Shakespeare Festival's Public Theatre, Off-Broadway. It won an Obie Award for the best new play of the season.

Like *F.O.B.*, Hwang's next two plays focused on the Chinese American experience. *The Dance and the Railroad* depicts two nineteenth century immigrants working on the transcontinental railroad, while *Family Devotions* is a bizarre farce set in contemporary California.

His next two plays, jointly titled *Sound and*

Beauty, are stylized one-act plays set in contemporary Japan; they were produced Off-Broadway in 1983. The first, *The House of Sleeping Beauties*, reinvents a novella by Yasunari Kawabata, making the author a character in a version of his own work. The second, *The Sound of a Voice*, involves a conflict between a samurai warrior and a bewitching female hermit whom he intends to kill.

In 1983, Hwang received a Rockefeller playwright-in-residence award and a National Endowment for the Arts artistic associate fellowship. A Guggenheim Fellowship followed in 1984, as did fellowships from the National Endowment for the Arts and the New York State Council on the Arts in 1985. On September 25, 1985, he married Ophelia Y. M. Chong, an artist, from whom he was later divorced.

Rich Relations, produced Off-Broadway in 1986, was his first work not about the Asian experience and his first critical failure, though it recapitulated various themes from his earlier plays. Nevertheless, Hwang has termed this failure exhilarating, freeing him from undue concern about critical reaction.

M. Butterfly, produced in 1988, brought Hwang international renown, a Tony Award for the Best Play of 1988, the Outer Critics Circle Award, and a nomination for the Pulitzer Prize in 1989. Based on a true story of a French diplomat and his Chinese lover who turned out to be not only a spy but also a man, the play explores issues of gender, identity, racism, and political hegemony. The same year, he collaborated with composer Philip Glass on *One Thousand Airplanes on the Roof*, a science fiction work concerning a character who may have been kidnapped by visiting aliens.

In 1992, Hwang's one-act play *Bondage* premiered at the Humana Festival of New Plays at the Actors Theatre of Louisville, Kentucky. Set in a parlor frequented by sadomasochists, its two characters are completely covered in black leather, so that their respective races cannot be discerned.

In 1994, the film *Golden Gate* was released, based on Hwang's screenplay and directed by John Madden. Set in San Francisco in 1952, it depicts the persecution of Chinese Americans by the Federal Bureau of Investigation (FBI) during the Joseph McCarthy era, when they were suspected of having ties to the communist revolution in China. FBI agent Kevin Walker (Matt Dillon) investigates laundryman Chen Jung Song (Tzi Ma), who has collected and sent funds to his and his friends' impoverished relatives in China. Following Song's ten-year imprisonment and subsequent suicide, agent Walker, in disguise, courts the dead man's daughter, who is a law student trying to clear her father's name.

Hwang's play *Golden Child* opened at the Joseph Papp Public Theatre in New York in 1996, directed by James Lapine. Its plot concerned the struggle between tradition and change in a family in

David Henry Hwang

1918 China, when its members encounter a Christian missionary whose values challenge their traditional Confucianism. The play won an Obie Award in 1997.

The Silver River, a "chamber opera" on which Hwang collaborated with composer Bright Sheng, premiered at the Santa Fe Chamber Music Festival in 1997. Based on a beloved Chinese legend, the opera's four characters were intended to be radically different kinds of performers—two "Westerners" and two Chinese, performing in the style of Peking Opera.

In 1998, the Trinity Repertory Company of Providence, Rhode Island, presented Hwang's adaptation and abridgment of Henrik Ibsen's *Peer Gynt* (pb. 1867; English translation, 1892). Described by one reviewer as "Gynt-lite," this version shortened Ibsen's epic drama to two hours (a 50 percent reduction), removing entire scenes and characters while renaming others. It also added pop-culture anachronisms, Freudian symbols, and broad farce.

Hwang next collaborated with Linda Wolverton and Robert Falls in writing the book for the pop musical *Aida*, with music by Elton John and lyrics by Tim Rice. It was first produced in 2000. Like Giuseppi Verdi, whose opera *Aida* premiered in 1871, Hwang and his co-authors drew on a story by nineteenth century Egyptologist Mariette Bey; however, they added characters not present in Verdi's work. These included Mereb, an Ethiopian slave who provides comic relief, and Zoser, who seeks to poison the pharaoh and assume the throne himself.

In 2001, Hwang's radically overhauled version of Richard Rodgers and Oscar Hammerstein's *Flower Drum Song* premiered in Los Angeles, directed by James Longbottom; it was the musical's first major revival since it opened in 1958. During this year Hwang also completed a screen adaptation of A. S. Byatt's novel *Possession* (1990). Now set in a fading Chinese Opera house in Chinatown, the central theme of *Flower Drum Song* is the tension between the older generation's belief in tradition and the younger generation's desire to assimilate into American culture. It also focuses on a young woman's experience after fleeing Mao Zedong's China in 1959.

ANALYSIS

Images of Asians and Asian Americans in modern culture have been relatively rare and often stereotypical; few have been created by Asian Americans themselves. On-screen stereotypes ranged from Charlie Chan (performed by a white actor), an image of wise but humble, ultimately "knowing" inscrutability, to the cook Hop Sing on the television series *Bonanza* (1959-1973). Contact between Eastern and Western cultures had been depicted in such works as David Belasco's *Madame Butterfly* (pr. 1900, pb. 1935, the basis for Giacomo Puccini's opera of the same name), Richard Rodgers and Oscar Hammerstein II's *The King and I* (pr. 1951) and *Flower Drum Song* (pr. 1958), John Patrick's *The Teahouse of the August Moon* (pr. 1953, pb. 1954), and Paul Osborn's *The World of Suzie Wong* (pr. 1958, based on the novel by Richard Mason). Whatever their merits, however, none of these plays offered a genuinely Asian perspective on the events portrayed. By the early 1970's, literature by and about Asian Americans began to emerge; a decade later, its first critically acclaimed and commercially successful playwright was David Henry Hwang. From his earliest plays about the Chinese American experience to his Broadway hit *M. Butterfly* and the subsequent rewriting of *Flower Drum Song*, he has progressively explored issues of ethnic cultural identity, gender roles, the East/West relationship, and the effects of imperialism—and has done so with deftly constructed plots, a number of which incorporate elements of Chinese opera.

F.O.B.

In his introduction to *F.O.B. and Other Plays*, Hwang identified three phases "in attempting to define [his] place in America," and his early plays correspond to these. The first is an "assimilationist" phase, in which one tries to "out-white the whites" in order to fit in with the majority culture. Dale, the central character of his first play, *F.O.B.*, is a second-generation American of Chinese descent who dresses like a "preppy" and particularly disdains Chinese immigrants who are "Fresh Off the Boat," abbreviated "F.O.B." One such, named Steve, is the target of his scorn throughout the play, in part because he reminds Dale of his ancestry, the nonwhite, non-American past that he prefers to ignore, discard, or deny. Steve's cousin Grace, a first-generation Chinese American, functions as an intermediary between the two men, with insight into the plight of both the newly arrived and the all-too-assimilated "A.B.C.'s," meaning "American-Born Chinese." Steve announces himself as the great god Gwan Gung, the Chinese folk hero, the "god of warriors, writers, and prostitutes." Grace tells him that in the United States, Gwan Gung is dead; nevertheless, her contact with Steve reawakens her own fantasy, Fu Ma Lan, a great woman warrior. Dale repudiates both myths, having struggled for so long to overcome his Chinese-ness, but Steve's presence forces him to reexamine his values. Following Dale's attempts to humiliate the immigrant, Steve becomes in monologue the embodiment of "ChinaMan," the immigrant Everyman who helped build the American West, particularly its railroads. Such cultural kinship finally binds Steve and Grace, who transmutes him from dead god to living warrior. Dale is left behind at the end of the play, uncomprehending, unrepentant, and alone.

The Dance and the Railroad

Gwan Gung also figures significantly in *The Dance and the Railroad*, Hwang's second play, a product of his "isolationist-nationalist" phase, in which he wrote primarily for other Asian Americans, having rejected "the assimilationist model" as "dangerous and self-defeating." Set in 1867, *The Dance and the Railroad* is a two-character, one-act play whose characters, Lone and Ma, are workers building the transcontinental railroad but are currently on a nine-day laborers' strike. Although conflicts between white management and Chinese labor underlie the action, personal differences between the characters and the traditions of Chinese opera and culture become increasingly prominent. Lone, a refugee from the Chinese opera, isolates himself from the other workers, practicing his art in solitude on the mountainside, above the strike and commercial toil. Ma, a gullible F.O.B. laborer who believes in the promises of the Gold Mountain in America, ascends in search of Lone, discovers his austere artistic training regimen, and yearns to learn opera to "become" Gwan Gung in

the new land. To learn the discipline that artistry requires, Ma maintains the "locust" position all night, a metaphor for immigrant experience. Finally worthy to study Gwan Gung, Ma rejects doing so and returns to the work below when the strike ends. The play's later scenes are performed in the style of Chinese opera. The actor playing Lone—his namesake, John Lone—had trained with the Peking Opera for eight years; he also directed the play, choreographed it, and provided its music.

Family Devotions

Hwang's third play, *Family Devotions*, is a nine-character farce set in contemporary California. The action centers on three generations of a thoroughly "assimilated" Chinese American family satirically based on Hwang's own; they are visited by their "second brother" Di-gou, a doctor and former violinist who has lived for thirty years under the Communist Chinese regime. His sisters, ardent fundamentalist Christians, are shocked to find out that he is an atheist and that he rejects the legend of See-Goh-Poh, a Christian "Woman Warrior" who allegedly saved his soul at age eight. He, in turn, is baffled by the family's crass materialism and conspicuous consumption and has come to ask his sisters to renounce their faith and return home with him. The first act ends with one of them, Ama, delivering a fiery testimonial from a rolling, neon-lit pulpit as the "Hallelujah Chorus" blares away. In the second act, the sisters and their daughters tie Di-gou to a table, assailing him with the word of God and See-Goh-Poh. He breaks his bonds in a holy fit of possession, speaks in tongues, and exposes See-Goh-Poh as a fraud whose crusade was a ruse to conceal an unwanted pregnancy. As the grotesque exorcism proceeds, the sisters die in their chairs as Di-gou continues his vehement speech. Di-gou and the young child of the family depart, leaving the house a spiritual wreck, torn between the Chinese past and the California present, between myth and reality. The play shows the influence of American playwright Sam Shepard, to whom it is dedicated, but many of its thematic preoccupations—assimilation versus origins, lost ethnic awareness, a core conflict of incompatible values—are recognizably Hwang's own.

THE HOUSE OF SLEEPING BEAUTIES

In the third phase of his writing, Hwang sought to move beyond his personal experience. *The House of Sleeping Beauties* is an adaptation of a novella *Nemureru bijo* (1960-1961 serial, 1961 book; *The House of the Sleeping Beauties*, in *The House of the Sleeping Beauties and Other Stories*, 1969) by Yasunari Kawabata, who is himself one of the play's two characters. The play is set in a brothel where elderly men learn to accept their mortality by sleeping beside comatose, nude, drugged young virgins. In Hwang's version, Kawabata comes there to research a book but becomes spiritually (platonically) involved with Michiko, the elderly proprietress. The play ends with his suicide by self-poisoning, and he is rocked to his final eternal sleep in her lap.

THE SOUND OF A VOICE

The companion piece of *The House of Sleeping Beauties* is *The Sound of a Voice*, a fable of a samurai warrior who goes into a forest to kill a bewitching female hermit but instead falls in love with her. The role of the witch was originally written for an *onnagata*, a male actor specializing in women's parts in Japanese Kabuki theater, but in the initial production it was played by a woman, Natsuko Ohama.

RICH RELATIONS

Rich Relations, produced in 1986, was Hwang's first play with all Caucasian characters and his first critical and commercial failure. Like *Family Devotions*, it lampooned evangelical Christianity, deathbed resurrections, and crass materialism within a suburban Los Angeles family, but it offered little that was new in technique or ideas.

M. BUTTERFLY

M. Butterfly, two years later, was a commercial and critical triumph on Broadway. The play is based on an article that appeared in *The New York Times* about the conviction for espionage of a French diplomat, who aided the Communist Chinese government by turning over embassy documents to his mistress of twenty years, a Chinese opera singer whom he had mistakenly believed to be an extremely modest woman. Hwang, however, sought no additional details from the actual case so as to avoid writing a docudrama; he was struck by the story as an inversion of the plot of the play and opera *Madame Butterfly*, in which a Japanese woman falls in love with a Caucasian man, is spurned, and commits suicide. In Hwang's play, the diplomat, René Gallimard, is the counterpart of Puccini's Westerner, Pinkerton, as he falls in love with opera singer Song Liling, unaware that she is the Chinese counterpart of an *onnagata* and an agent of the Communist government. The role of Song Liling is played by a man (B. D. Wong in the original production), though this fact is not revealed to the theater audience until the beginning of the third act when, in a moment of startling theatricality, Song Liling removes her makeup and changes clothes onstage, dispelling the illusion for the audience before disclosing her true gender and identity to Gallimard in a nude scene near the end of the play.

In many ways, *M. Butterfly* continues the thematic preoccupations that became apparent in Hwang's earlier plays: the use of Chinese opera from *The Dance and the Railroad*, the role for an *onnagata* and the unorthodox sexuality of *The Sound of a Voice*, and the clash of Asian and Western values that recurred in all of his earlier plays. Incorporating both Puccini's music and Chinese opera, *M. Butterfly* also explores issues of gender and racial stereotyping, of dominance and submission (political as well as sexual), and of the morality of the Western presence in Asia. Furthermore, the play audaciously questions the nature of love and illusion, undermining any certainty about the ultimate knowability of another person or, indeed, of the world itself. While that theme is not new in twentieth century literature—having been particularly prominent in Ford Madox Ford's novel *The Good Soldier* (1915), for example, seldom, if ever, has it been presented with such dramatic effectiveness and theatrical flair.

M. Butterfly also marks a considerable advance in Hwang's dramatic technique over the earlier plays, which were chronologically presented on realistic sets. The play begins with a retrospective monologue by Gallimard in his prison cell; many flashbacks to European and Asian locales are introduced throughout twenty-seven brief scenes in three acts. The stylized set, designed by Eiko Ishioka, is dominated by a gently sloping, curved ramp, enabling a flexible use of the stage space. The original title, *Monsieur Butterfly*, was shortened to *M. Butterfly* (at Hwang's wife's suggestion) to seem more mysterious and ambiguous.

Following the phenomenal success of *M. Butterfly*, Hwang worried that whatever he did next would be considered a disappointment; accordingly, following a collaboration with the composer Philip Glass on a work titled *One Thousand Airplanes on the Roof*, he worked primarily on film scripts, including a screen adaptation of *M. Butterfly*. In 1992, his one-act play titled *Bondage* opened in Louisville, Kentucky. *Bondage*, like *The House of Sleeping Beauties*, is set in an exotic brothel: one that caters to sadomasochists, where a dominating female is paid to humiliate a male clientele. The play begins with Terri, the female dominatrix, in a session with Mark; both are covered from head to toe in black leather so that their faces as well as their ethnic identities are concealed from the audience. The play consists of a fantasy game in which their races continually change, further exploring themes of gender, racial, and political stereotyping, as well as intricate power relationships.

TRENDS AND THEMES IN THE 1990'S

In the plays and screenplays that Hwang has written after *Bondage*, two major trends have become increasingly apparent. The first is his ongoing interest in the history of Chinese American experience in the twentieth century; he has consistently articulated this little-known aspect of American history, as in the award-winning *Golden Child*, set in 1918, and in the critically assailed film *Golden Gate*, which was set during the McCarthy era of the 1950's. In each of these works, questions of allegiance are paramount: The desire to preserve centuries-old cultural traditions and family values proves difficult to reconcile with a desire to become assimilated into American culture. Yet, as *Golden Gate* demonstrates in particular, the extent of one's "American-ness" or "Otherness" remains dangerously in question, difficult if not impossible to prove to the satisfaction of those in authority. Like V. S. Naipaul, Salman Rushdie, and Busci Emecheta, among others, Hwang explores the nature of "hybridity," a crosscultural experience that

has drawn increasing attention in postmodern and postcolonial literature.

The second major trend in Hwang's later plays is his boldly transformative use of earlier works, particularly (but not exclusively) Western operas. Puccini's *Madame Butterfly* and Verdi's *Aida* both exemplify what the critic Edward Said has termed "Orientalism," the tendency of European (or American) writers and composers to "invent" an "Orient" that is defined by the "other-ness" of its ways, though such presentation may have little or nothing to do with the actualities of life in those non-Western cultures. Hwang's works are often redactions of these classics, deconstructing some of the cultural assumptions that prevailed when they were first produced. Because *Aida* was a collaboration in which Hwang joined two other writers, a composer, and a lyricist, the extent and nature of his specific contributions to the text cannot readily be ascertained.

FLOWER DRUM SONG

In his revamping of Rodgers and Hammerstein's *Flower Drum Song*, however, both of the trends cited above receive their fullest elaboration since *M. Butterfly*. The original production, which opened in New York in 1958, was not as successful as *South Pacific*, *Oklahoma!*, *Carousel*, or *The Sound of Music*, but it ran for over 600 performances and was made into a film in 1961. Based on a novel by Chin Y. Lee (1957), it told the story of a mail-order bride from China, Mei-Li, who arrived in San Francisco to marry nightclub owner Sammy Fong, who was already in love with Linda Low, a stripper in the club. Although many of its cast members were Asian (including Pat Suzuki as Linda Low and Miyoshi Umeki as Mei-Li), the role of Sammy Fong was played by a Caucasian actor, Larry Blyden, who was made up to appear Chinese. In Hwang's revision of the story, the character of Sammy Fong has been eliminated. The setting is now a traditional Chinese theater that has presented Chinese opera, but is being transformed by the owner's son into a Western-style nightclub, the Club Chop Suey. The father, Master Wang, is rooted in traditional Chinese culture, while his son Ta is attracted to the more modern and Americanized culture that is represented by the nightclub. The characters of Linda

Low and Mei-Li have been retained in Hwang's version, although Mei-Li is now a refugee from Mao's China. The score, though re-orchestrated, retains most of the songs from the original (except "The Older Generation") and restores one that was cut from the original production before its Broadway opening ("My Best Love"). One song ("The Next Time It Happens") from another Rodgers and Hammerstein musical, *Pipe Dream*, was also added. The emphasis on the two styles of theater also allows Hwang to develop the theme of performance and theatricality that also characterized *M. Butterfly*.

OTHER MAJOR WORKS

SCREENPLAYS: *M. Butterfly*, 1993 (adaptation of his play); *Golden Gate*, 1994; *Possession*, 2001 (with Neil LaBute and Laura Jones; adaptation of A. S. Byatt's novel).

TELEPLAYS: *My American Son*, 1987; *The Lost Empire*, 2001.

BIBLIOGRAPHY

Bernstein, Richard. "France Jails Two in Odd Case of Espionage." *The New York Times*, May 11, 1986, p. K7. The original news account on which *M. Butterfly* is based. It recounts the sentencing for espionage of Bernard Bouriscot, a forty-one-year-old French diplomat, and Chinese opera singer Shi Peipeu. During their twenty-year relationship, Bouriscot mistakenly believed Peipeu was a woman. He also believed they had a son, Shi Dudu.

Chen, Tina. "Betrayed into Motion: The Seduction of Narrative Desire in *M. Butterfly*." *Hitting Critical Mass: A Journal of Asian American Cultural Criticism* 1, no. 2 (Spring, 1994): 129-154. Analyzes *M. Butterfly* as postmodern drama, focusing on its relationship with the audience.

Gerard, Jeremy. "David Hwang: Riding on the Hyphen." *The New York Times Magazine*, March 13, 1988, p. 44, 88-89. This biographical profile, preceding the Broadway debut of *M. Butterfly*, focuses on Hwang's crossover from ethnic to mainstream commercial theater with a play that violates conventions of commercial theater in its treatment of sexism, racism, and imperialism, plus its inclusion of Chinese opera, its scandalous plot, and its brief nudity. Hwang comments on the self-doubt that accompanied his sudden fame.

Hwang, David Henry. "Interview with Marty Moss-Coane. Edited with an Introduction by John Timpane." In *Speaking on Stage: Interviews with Contemporary American Playwrights*. Edited by Philip C. Kolin and Colby H. Kullman. Tuscaloosa: University of Alabama Press, 1996. Edited transcript of an interview broadcast on National Public Radio in 1993. Hwang discusses the process of adapting *M. Butterfly* for the screen and discusses his family and childhood in more detail than typically found elsewhere.

_____. "*M. Butterfly*: An Interview with David Henry Hwang." Interview by John Lewis DiGaetani. *The Drama Review: A Journal of Performance Studies* 33, no. 3 (Fall, 1989): 141-153. In this extensive interview, Hwang discusses *M. Butterfly*, Edward W. Said's *Orientalism* (1978), the mutual misperceptions of West and East embodied in Giacomo Puccini's *Madame Butterfly*, and his play's implications about homosexuality, heterosexuality, and fantasy in love. He also suggests that René Gallimard knew—at some level—that his lover was a man. Photographs.

Morris, Rosalind. "*M. Butterfly*: Transvestism and Cultural Cross Dressing in the Critique of Empire." In *Gender and Culture in Literature and Film East and West: Issues of Perception and Interpretation*. Edited by Nitaya Masavisut, et al. Honolulu: University of Hawaii Press, 1994. Discussion of gender issues and the theme of imperialism in Hwang's best-known play.

Pace, Eric. "I Write Plays to Claim a Place for Asian Americans." *The New York Times*, July 12, 1981, p. D4. This biographical profile was published shortly after *The Dance and the Railroad* opened in New York. Among his attributes as a playwright, Hwang discusses his ability to listen to people with opposite views and empathize with both, his interest in myth and legend, and his concern that Chinese American characters be presented not as polemics but as people.

Skloot, Robert. "Breaking the Butterfly: The Politics

of David Henry Hwang." *Modern Drama* 33, no. 1 (March, 1990): 59-66. Skloot discusses the ways in which *M. Butterfly* brings its audience "into complicity with the discovery, dismantling, and re-establishment of theatrical illusion." Though within the limits of "old-fashioned playwriting," it also challenges traditional assumptions about gender politics, cultural politics, and theatrical politics, which are discussed in separate sections of the article.

Street, Douglas. *David Henry Hwang*. Boise, Idaho: Boise State University Press, 1989. This fifty-two-page study, the first book to have been written on Hwang's work, provides a useful introductory overview of his plays through *M. Butterfly* and contains a concise but detailed biography of the playwright. Bibliography.

Weinraub, Bernard. "Fleshing Out Chinatown Stereotypes." *New York Times*, October 14, 2000, section 2, pp. 7, 27. Lengthy interview-based profile of Hwang, emphasizing his reworking of *Flower Drum Song* and its preproduction history.

William Hutchings

I

HENRIK IBSEN

Born: Skien, Norway; March 20, 1828
Died: Christiania (now Oslo), Norway; May 23, 1906

PRINCIPAL DRAMA

Catalina, pb. 1850, revised pb. 1875, pr. 1881 (verse drama; *Catiline*, 1921)

Kjæmpehøien, pr. 1850, revised pb. 1854 (dramatic poem; *The Burial Mound*, 1912)

Norma: Eller, En politikers kjærlighed, pr., pb. 1851 (verse satire)

Sancthansnatten, pr. 1853, pb. 1909 (*St. John's Night*, 1921)

Fru Inger til Østraat, pr. 1855, pb. 1857 (*Lady Inger of Østraat*, 1906)

Gildet paa Solhaug, pr., pb. 1856, revised pb. 1883 (verse and prose drama; *The Feast at Solhaugh*, 1906)

Olaf Liljekrans, pr. 1857, pb. 1902 (verse and prose drama; English translation, 1911)

Hærmænde paa Helgeland, pr., pb. 1858 (*The Vikings at Helgeland*, 1890)

Kjærlighedens komedie, pb. 1862, pr. 1873 (verse comedy; *Love's Comedy*, 1900)

Kongsemnerne, pb. 1863, pr. 1864 (*The Pretenders*, 1890)

Brand, pb. 1866, pr. 1885 (dramatic poem; English translation, 1891)

Peer Gynt, pb. 1867, pr. 1876 (dramatic poem; English translation, 1892)

De unges forbund, pr., pb. 1869 (*The League of Youth*, 1890)

Kejser og Galilæer, pb. 1873, pr. 1896 (2 parts: *Cæsars frafald* and *Kejser Julian*; *Emperor and Galilean*, 1876, 2 parts: *Caesar's Apostasy* and *The Emperor Julian*)

Samfundets støtter, pr., pb. 1877 (*The Pillars of Society*, 1880)

Et dukkehjem, pr., pb. 1879 (*A Doll's House*, 1880; also known as *A Doll House*)

Gengangere, pb. 1881, pr. 1882 (*Ghosts*, 1885)

En folkefiende, pb. 1882, pr. 1883 (*An Enemy of the People*, 1890)

Vildanden, pb. 1884, pr. 1885 (*The Wild Duck*, 1891)

Rosmersholm, pb. 1886, pr. 1887 (English translation, 1889)

Fruen fra havet, pb. 1888, pr. 1889 (*The Lady from the Sea*, 1890)

Hedda Gabler, pb. 1890, pr. 1891 (English translation, 1891)

Bygmester Solness, pb. 1892, pr. 1893 (*The Master Builder*, 1893)

Lille Eyolf, pb. 1894, pr. 1895 (*Little Eyolf*, 1894)

John Gabriel Borkman, pb. 1896, pr. 1897 (English translation, 1897)

Naar vi døde vaagner, pb. 1899, pr. 1900 (*When We Dead Awaken*, 1900)

Samlede verker, hundreaarsutgave, pb. 1928-1957 (21 volumes)

The Oxford Ibsen, pb. 1960-1977 (8 volumes)

The Complete Major Prose Plays, pb. 1978

OTHER LITERARY FORMS

Henrik Ibsen's volume of poetry, *Digte*, was published in 1871; *Ibsen: Letters and Speeches* appeared in English translation in 1964, and *The Collected Works of Henrik Ibsen* appeared between 1906 and 1912 and in 1928.

ACHIEVEMENTS

Henrik Ibsen is widely acknowledged as the father of modern drama, but his significance in literature and history overshadows the influence of his revolutionary stage techniques and his iconoclastic concept of the theater. James Joyce observed of Ibsen, his youthful idol, "It may be questioned whether any man has held so firm an empire over the thinking world in modern times." Despite early disappointments, which led to twenty-seven years of self-imposed exile from Norway, Ibsen at last received the acclaim there that he had been accorded previously throughout Europe, and by the end of his long and immensely productive career, the Norwegian government granted him a state funeral as one of its most illustrious, if controversial, citizens. Ibsen's plays continue to be revived throughout the world, and a steady stream of scholarly books and articles testifies to his popularity among critics and readers who appreciate the therapeutic Northern blasts of Ibsen's message.

The unvarying setting of Ibsen's quest as a creative artist was the human mind. At first, he concentrated, with little success, on Norwegian nationalistic themes and historical subjects, in opposition to the Danish domination of Scandinavian theater. As he probed increasingly profound psychological themes involving the individual and society, his analytic dramas seemed threateningly radical, largely incomprehensible, or simply obscene to European audiences then content with frothy farce or Scribean melodrama. His first plays written from exile in Italy won for him fame, but their critical reception was mixed. Later, his social problem plays found their greatest contemporary acceptance in England through William Archer's devoted translations and George Bernard Shaw's espousal of Ibsen's work as support for his own Socialist theories. In his next stage, Ibsen concentrated on the individual's psychological condition; his last plays, written after his return to Norway, which deal with the conflict between art and life, exhibited his shift to Symbolism and were greeted with enthusiasm by James Joyce and Thomas Mann, who both learned Norwegian solely to read Ibsen's works. Another lonely thinker, Sigmund Freud, wrote a perceptive essay on the Oedipus complex as motivation in Ibsen's *Rosmersholm*. Much of Europe, especially czarist Russia, saw Ibsen's plays as potentially explosive, but by 1935, the prominent critic Johanna Kröner commented, "Through Ibsen's influence, European drama has experienced a powerful renewal and progress."

Ibsen's technical innovations in the theater have become so widely accepted that it is difficult to grasp the intense novelty that they represented to their contemporary audiences. The strongly realistic and even naturalistic stage settings of his mature plays contain a wealth of closely observed detail that requires a corresponding intensity of attention by actors to the individualized behavior of his characters. His tense, crackling interchanges of dialogue, a dramatic shorthand, often seem to omit more words than they include, conveying highly complex states of mind and passions through implication and demanding a high degree of emotional stamina from his actors. As his American translator Rolf Fjelde has observed, the language of Ibsen's finest plays resembles poetry in its compaction and resonance. Above all, as Henry James noted, Ibsen has a "peculiar blessedness to actors . . . the inspiration of dealing with material so solid and so fresh," an attraction that seems as valid for the careful reader as it is for Ibsen's stage interpreter. Though Ibsen's contributions to dramatic theory and form have been outmoded by many of the very dramatists his work inspired, his insight into the human condition has not dated. Ibsen insisted that he not only "described human beings" but also "described human fates." Such fates, springing from deep conflicts in human personalities, provide both solid and fresh material for endless meditation. In scholar Einar Haugen's words, "Ibsen's plays . . . enable people to look beyond the little cares of the day and . . . give them some glimpses of eternity."

BIOGRAPHY

Henrik Johan Ibsen was born on March 20, 1828, to a well-to-do merchant family of Skien, a small town in the county of Telemark in Norway, whose people Norwegian historians describe as "sanguine but often melancholic . . . proud and stiff . . . afraid openly to surrender to a mood," people who have an apparent lack of spontaneity that Ibsen called "the shyness of the soul." The Ibsens lived well, entertaining lavishly, until Henrik was seven, when financial pressures bankrupted his father, and the family was forced to move to an isolated farm. For the next eight years, young Ibsen felt himself an outcast from the provincial, snobbish social clique once eager to savor the family's hospitality. When he was fifteen, Ibsen became apprenticed to an apothecary at Grimstad, a tiny shipbuilding village down the coast, and his poverty was intensified by the necessity of supporting an illegitimate son for the following fourteen years. The boy's mother, a servant of his employer, was ten years older than Ibsen, and there was no thought of marriage. Though he was already writing poetry, Ibsen originally had considered becoming a physician, but the revolutionary fervor in the air in 1848 led him to write *Catiline*, a dramatic treatment in blank verse of the rebellious Roman senator.

After failing his entrance examinations for medicine, Ibsen turned wholeheartedly to literature. In the fearsome struggles that he experienced in the next two decades of his life, Fjelde sees "the seeds of so many of the themes and motifs that found their way into the series of masterpieces composed between Ibsen's forty-seventh and seventy-first years." Having already endured financial ruin and the scorn of "pillars of society," Ibsen next faced the frustrations of an unappreciated author. Selling his painfully financed copies of *Catiline* as scrap paper, he realized only enough funds to buy himself and a friend one decent dinner during his six years as the new Norwegian Theater's stage manager and resident playwright. From 1857 to 1862, he abandoned some of his early bohemianism to become artistic director of the poverty-stricken Norwegian Theater in Christiania (now Oslo), which then was a backward, swampy town whose audiences worshiped the dominant Danish theater. Ibsen wrote eight plays there, all stressing Norwegian history and national spirit; all failed. He had married Suzannah Thoreson in 1858, the Norwegian Theater closed in 1862, and in 1864 they left for the Continent with their only child, Sigurd. Ibsen chose not to live in Norway again for twenty-seven years.

The disillusionment that Ibsen must have felt toward his countrymen is clear in the two verse plays that he wrote in exile, *Brand* and *Peer Gynt*. *Brand* involves an unbending country pastor whose ideal is "all or nothing"; he sets out to reform his society but is destroyed. *Peer Gynt*, a folktale drama, chronicles the escapades of a picaresque rascal who wins forgiveness in a woman's embrace. *Brand* earned for Ibsen fame and a modest stipend from the Norwegian government at the same time that it provoked fiery debate at home and abroad, while *Peer Gynt*, a witty criticism of the relatively comfortable life in eastern Norway, eventually became the one book that most Norwegians would take with them if they had to emigrate, according to the Norwegian literary historian Francis Bull. At the same time, Ibsen was mulling over the implementation of Hegelian idealism in a huge "world-historical" play which evolved into *Emperor and Galilean*, an account of Julian the Apostate that depicts the monumental battle of Christianity against paganism in the fourth century Roman Empire. This ten-act play, impossible to stage, was not accepted by Ibsen's contemporaries and remained largely unappreciated.

Beginning in the 1870's, the second half of his exile, Ibsen moved restlessly from place to place in Eu-

Henrik Ibsen (Library of Congress)

rope: Rome, Austria, Munich, and Dresden. As he went, he constructed a series of twelve major prose plays that he wanted grasped "as a continuous and coherent whole," the "subtly and significantly interconnected dramatic cycle," as Fjelde describes it, on which Ibsen's artistic reputation chiefly rests. For these plays, he not only drew on the bitter disappointments of his own early life in Norway but also wove the most personal experiences of others' anxiety, frustration, and mental anguish into them. By 1891, when Ibsen had somewhat hesitantly returned to Norway to stay, Meyer claims that "Christiania was . . . full of people who regarded themselves as the originals of various characters in his plays," not an unmixed blessing. Whatever their social or psychological antecedents, the characters of Ibsen's great prose cycle represent the complex stresses of the modern world, relentlessly exposing such human failings as hypocrisy, moral cowardice, emotional slavery, and deep frustration in marriage.

The conflict between the demands of his life and his art adversely affected Ibsen's own marriage. Often at least geographically separated, he and his wife gradually drew apart emotionally as well. As he aged, Ibsen became increasingly fascinated with the young, and during a holiday to the Tirol in 1889, he had a brief and hopeless affair with an eighteen-year-old Viennese girl, Emilie Bardach, whom he called "the May sun of a September life." Ibsen subsequently formed emotional attachments to three other young women, among them the pianist Hildur Andersen, whom he described in a phrase from *Peer Gynt* as "My Empire and my Crown!" The young women who dominate his last plays—Hedda, Hilde, Rita, and Irene—share passionate, youthful intensity, but their hopes are defeated by the careers of their would-be lovers. Moreover, none of Ibsen's late involvements developed into a total sexual relationship. As he wrote in his notes for *Hedda Gabler*, "The great tragedy of life is that so many people have nothing to do but yearn for happiness without ever being able to find it." Meyer cites psychiatrist Anthony Storr's diagnosis of Ibsen as technically "an obsessional character": Such creative people "want to create an imaginary world in which everything can be controlled, and want to avoid the unpredictability and spontaneity of real relationships with real people."

Ibsen's attraction to youth, however, was not limited to young girls. His young French male companion, director Aurélian-Marie Lugné-Poë, noted that Ibsen "had an almost obsessive interest in the rising generation" and took pains to become acquainted with Norway's new writers and artists, "the people who understood his plays most clearly." During 1891, the year that he returned to Norway to stay, Ibsen attended a performance of August Strindberg's *Fadren* (pr., pb. 1887; *The Father*, 1912) and a lecture by the thirty-two-year-old Knut Hamsun, author of a pain-filled autobiographical novel of the working class entitled *Sult* (1890; *Hunger*, 1899). Hamsun had already given his lecture elsewhere and attacked Ibsen and his work forcefully, particularly "the inherent stiffness and poverty of his emotional life." Hamsun mistakenly saw merely social significance in Ibsen's work, a position of many later critics, but Ibsen attended not only that lecture but also the second and third of the series, finding confirmation there, Meyer conjectures, "of the conviction he himself had already reached that a writer must explore the uncharted waters of the unconscious," the dark arena that Ibsen chose for his last plays.

At seventy-two, as the new century arrived, Ibsen was failing physically. He suffered the first of a series of strokes on March 5, 1890, and never regained full physical health. He hoped to start a new play and perhaps even to travel, but as his condition deteriorated, he was able only to sit at his window gazing vacantly before him; once the renowned actress Eleonora Duse, whose greatest stage triumphs were in his works, gazed in mute tribute at his wintry silhouette from an icy sidewalk. Toward the end, he told his wife, "You were the eagle that showed me the way to the summit." His last word was "Tvertimod!" ("On the contrary!"), a fitting comment, Meyer observes, "from one who had devoted his life to the correction of lies." His state funeral on June 1, 1906, was attended by an immense crowd, and over his grave, the Norwegian people set a column bearing "the simple and appropriate symbol of a hammer."

ANALYSIS

"To be a poet is, most of all, to see," Henrik Ibsen said, and early in his literary career, he had already recognized the hammer as at once the symbol of creation and of destruction, with mythical overtones of the Old Norse thunder god, Thor, who unflinchingly sacrificed his own hand to bind the wolf Fenris and save his world from the unleashed forces of the underworld. Ibsen's early poem "The Miner" shows his gaze fixed firmly into the depths: "Downward I must break my way . . . break me the way, my heavy hammer, to the hidden mystery's heart." Throughout his literary canon, although he is best known for his prose dramas, the rich poetic vein is never far from the working face of Ibsen's creativity.

The constructions and destructions necessary to the realization of Ibsen's vision fall into two distinct categories on either side of the watershed year of 1875. Fjelde differentiates them in apt architectural metaphor, viewing the earlier romantic group of Ibsen's plays as a diverse old quarter, ranging from Roman villa to Viking guildhalls and even a contemporary honeymoon hotel, while glimpsing immediately beyond a small arid space "what appears to be a model town of virtually identical row houses . . . dark and swarming with secret life."

Whatever the outward style of their construction, at the core, all of Ibsen's earlier plays share a basically romantic orientation. Romanticism had already reached its fiery height in most of Europe by the time Ibsen published his first verse drama in 1850, but like the Northern summer sun, the German-derived glow of romanticism lingered longer in Norway, where the emerging Norwegian state, lately reestablished, was seeking its national identity in its Viking heritage. While reviewing a folkloristic play in 1851, Ibsen presented his own characteristically individual theory on nationalism in literature: "A national author is one who finds the best way of embodying in his work that keynote which rings out to us from mountain and valley . . . but above all from within our own selves." Following that precept at the risk of alienating superpatriots, Ibsen wrote three Viking plays, *Lady Inger of Østraat*, *The Feast at Solhaugh*, and *The Vikings at Helgeland*. In 1862, he made an extensive field trip to gather folklore, which he incorporated with Rousseauistic ideals of the simple natural life in *The Pretenders*, another medieval Viking drama; in the volcanic *Brand*, set in the harsh west fjord country; and in the lighthearted *Peer Gynt*.

An important part of Norway's nationalistic fervor stemmed from its state Lutheranism, in which Ibsen had received a traditionally rigorous grounding as a child, although none of his plays portrays clergymen sympathetically. In *Brand*, Ibsen also seemed to embody Søren Kierkegaard's famous "either-or" in Brand's call for "all or nothing," challenging the institutionalized religion of his day. Haugen has commented that paradoxically "the rascal Peer is saved, but the heroic Brand is sacrificed," seeing therein a reflection of Ibsen's early religious training, similar to his puritanical attitude toward sex and his emphasis on the necessity of confession and atonement for redemption.

The dominant philosophical trend of Ibsen's time and place was the idealism of Georg Wilhelm Friedrich Hegel, who died in 1831. Ibsen's enormous double play, *Emperor and Galilean*, departs from the strictly romantic theories present in his earlier work to take the direction of a Hegelian dialectic conflict between "thesis" and "antithesis," which is resolved by a "synthesis" that itself becomes the "thesis" of a new conflict. Ibsen pits the pagan happiness that he had celebrated in his Viking plays against the spiritual beauty represented by Christ's redeeming sacrifice on the Cross. The failure of Julian the Apostate to bring about the required "third empire," mingling the Christian and the pagan worlds, may be read as Ibsen's rejection, like Kierkegaard's, of the possibility of achieving a synthesis in this life. For Ibsen, duality was inescapable in the human condition, with man caught between what he is and what he should be, between the beastly nature and the divine.

In 1875, midway in his literary career, Ibsen struck an "arid place" where he reluctantly had to concede that the rhyme and meter suitable to romantic drama could no longer convey his explorations of "the hidden mystery's heart." The literary trend in Europe, leading toward the realistic and even naturalistic expression of contemporary social problems, came to Scandinavia principally through the critic Georg Brandes, who had become Ibsen's close friend in 1871. Ibsen's last twelve plays divide neatly into three distinct subgroups of four dramas each, characterized by their dominant thematic elements—social, psychological, and philosophical. This sequence, which Ibsen clearly intended as an organic whole, leads inexorably from social agony to spiritual conflict and at last to an area hitherto unexplored in Ibsen's time, described by Fjelde as an "extraordinary, pre-Freudian sensitivity to unconscious pressures behind the conscious mind—the relationships of motives and conflicts bred in the troll-dark cellar." In each category, Ibsen employed his personal experiences differently. From *The Pillars of Society* to *An Enemy of the People*, the social plays use contemporary settings that might have been encountered on the streets of Christiania and characters caught up in the new industrialized manifestation of the old conflict between what is and what ought to be. Between *The Wild Duck* and *Hedda Gabler*, Ibsen's hammer broke through to a deeper layer of consciousness beyond the social, forcing away the barriers which the individual erects between his self-image and his ideals. Finally, from *The Master Builder* to *When We Dead Awaken*, Ibsen probed the clash between his artistic vocation and his responsibility to those who loved him, using in each play a flawed creative personality who at last realizes that the ultimate height of achievement is denied him because he has not been able to merge love with his art. With the twelve plays of his prose cycle, Ibsen adopted what Fjelde calls "a way of seeing, deceptively photographic on the surface, actually a complex fusion of perspectives, which then became his dramatic method," as, even more significantly, he simultaneously reached the summit and the deepest heart of his own experience of life.

To the theater in particular and to literature in amazing generality, Ibsen bequeathed innovations almost as astonishing in retrospect as they must have been to his contemporaries. He was first to involve ordinary human beings in drama, abandoning the old artificial plots and instead creating scenes that might be encountered in any stuffy drawing room or aching

human heart. He conveyed for the first time in centuries a depth and subtlety of understanding of human character and relationships, especially those of women, evocative of the height of human tragic experience seen previously among the Elizabethans and the Periclean Greeks. He dared to challenge social abuses, knowing their agonizing sting at first hand. He explored the unconscious mind to an extent unmatched until the promulgation of Freud's theories decades later.

THE VIKINGS AT HELGELAND

Before Ibsen gained the summit of his creative efforts he participated in the attempt to create a national Norwegian theater by writing plays based on Norwegian folktales. Ibsen gathered his material for *The Vikings at Helgeland* not from the medieval German epic *The Nibelungenlied* but from a much older work, *The Völsungasaga*, itself a derivation of the Elder Edda containing the story of the Valkyrie Brynhild, who destroys her beloved hero Sigurd because he has betrayed her trust. Ibsen chose to base *The Vikings at Helgeland* on the Icelandic family saga, in which, he said, "the titanic conditions and occurrences of *The Nibelungenlied* and the *Volsung-Saga* have simply been reduced to human dimensions." Yet he saw an insoluble incompatibility between the objective saga and the dramatic form: "If a writer is to create a dramatic work out of this epic material, he must introduce a foreign element. . . ." Ibsen's "foreign element" in *The Vikings at Helgeland* is realism, a rendition of the myth of Brynhild set in tenth century Norway, at the advent of Christianity. The Brynhild-figure is Hjørdis, a merciless visionary, married to Gunnar but in love with Gunnar's close friend, the weak-willed warrior Sigurd, who had won her under the guise of Gunnar and with whom she has had her only satisfying sexual experience. When Hjørdis learns of the deception—Sigurd is married to another woman—she slays her lover, hoping to be united with him in death, but as he dies, Sigurd reveals that his meek wife Dagny has converted him to Christianity. In despair and rage, the pagan Hjørdis hurls herself into the sea. Ibsen's preoccupation in *The Vikings at Helgeland* is not with the fall of mythic goddesses and heroes but with the human tragedy wrought by deliberate falsehood, a theme to which he would often return.

BRAND

Ibsen called *Brand* "a dramatic poem." Brand is a stern young pastor who defies both his church superiors and the self-serving local governmental officials, demanding "all or nothing" in the service of his God. Brand even applies his unbending doctrines to his mother, to whom he refuses to grant forgiveness unless she relinquishes all her property, and to his wife and his child, who die because Brand will not take them to a milder climate. Brand then leads his flock to an "ice church" high in the mountains, where he believes that they will all be closer to God, but, daunted by the painful journey, his people at last stone him and return to their valley far below. Brand is finally moved to tears by a vision of his dead wife shortly before he is buried by a mammoth avalanche, above whose roar he hears a voice proclaim, "He is a God of love." In *Brand*, the story of a man whose tragedy is the negation of love, Ibsen not only used the figure of an acquaintance he had met in Rome, Christopher Bruun, a devout reformer who fought the established church as well as the spirit of compromise, but also drew on his own personality. He remarked in an 1870 letter, "Brand is myself in my best moments."

EMPEROR AND GALILEAN

Emperor and Galilean, the double play that stands between Ibsen's two groups of dramas, ranges over much of the fourth century Roman Empire, interpreting successive phases in the life of Julian the Apostate, who tried to replace Constantine's Christianity with a renewed paganism. In part 1, *Caesar's Apostasy*, the young Julian is disillusioned by Christianity and is influenced by the pagan seer Maximos, who desires a "third empire" uniting classical beauty and Christian ethics. In part 2, *The Emperor Julian*, force proves ineffective in reinstating pagan religious observances; in battle, Agathon, a Christian, slays Julian, who mutters as he dies, "Thou hast conquered, Galilean." Like Cain and Judas, Julian unknowingly changed history in a way he never intended. Ibsen told Edmund Gosse, "The illusion I wanted to produce is that of reality . . . what I desired

to depict were human beings." He also said later that *Emperor and Galilean* contained "more of my own personal experience than I would care to admit." He saw Christianity as removing the joy from human life, his own included, encasing people in an emotional confinement from which only violent action could free them. This play marks Ibsen's "farewell to epic drama" and his adoption of prose as his dramatic medium; Meyer calls it the "forerunner of those naturalistic plays which were shortly to explode . . . like a series of bombs."

A DOLL'S HOUSE

The famous slamming of the Helmer front door in *A Doll House* was the second realistic explosion in Ibsen's bombardment of his society's outmoded thought and repressive lifestyle. Significantly, new translations of the play point out the vital difference between the older title, *A Doll's House*, a house belonging to the "doll" Nora, and *A Doll House*, a complex toy, as Fjelde suggests, that itself is "on trial . . . tested by the visitors that come and go, embodying aspects of the inescapable reality outside." At the beginning, Nora is merely a pretty young wife preparing for Christmas, almost a child herself in her eagerness to please her banker-husband as his "squirrel" and "lark." As Hermann J. Weigand has demonstrated, however, Nora's love of playacting, her readiness to lie, and her desire to show off make her all the more convincing as she reveals that she has secretly borrowed money needed to save her husband from a physical collapse. Worse, the conventions of the day denied women the right to take out loans in their own names, so Nora was forced by circumstances to forge her dying father's signature to the loan. Her creditor, Nils Krogstad, blackmails her to keep his position at Helmer's bank. When Helmer learns of Nora's debt, he selfishly and brutally declares that she is unfit to rear their children. Nora recognizes the falsity of her position and leaves her husband and children, slamming the door on her life as the toy of Helmer, who is himself a toy of society.

In his "Notes for a Modern Tragedy" (1878), Ibsen wrote, "There are two kinds of moral laws . . . one for men and one, quite different, for women." He knew that in his day, "woman is judged by masculine law," and he used for specifics the contemporary real-life tragedy of Laura Kieler, a friend of Ibsen who had taken out a secret loan so that she could travel with her husband to Italy for his health. The loan went bad; she forged a check; and when the bank refused payment, her husband had her committed to a public asylum and demanded a separation, so that her children would not be contaminated by her presence. Kieler grudgingly took his wife back eventually, but Ibsen's use of her sad story in his play placed additional stress on their already difficult relationship, and Laura Kieler resented *A Doll House* fiercely.

Many interpreters narrowly see *A Doll House* as a plea for female emancipation. Nothing seems further from Ibsen's intention. In 1879, he did strongly support equal voting rights for female members of the Scandinavian Club in Rome, but nearly twenty years later, in 1898, when he spoke to the Norwegian League for Women's Rights, he declared, "My task has been the *description of humanity*," as Fjelde notes, putting the issue of women's liberation squarely in the larger context of "the artist's freedom and the evolution of the race in general."

GHOSTS

Ibsen wrote to Sophie Adlersparre in 1882, "After Nora, Mrs. Alving had to come," and he often said that writing *Ghosts* was "an absolute necessity" for him. Mrs. Alving is not simply a Nora grown older, but a character evolved into a vastly more tragic figure. Nora leaves her home, but Mrs. Alving stays with her debauched husband, an irredeemable syphilitic sot. After his death, she builds an orphanage with his fortune and welcomes home their son Oswald, who has been living as an artist in Paris. A villainous carpenter at the orphanage, Engstrand, tries to entice his daughter Regine, Mrs. Alving's maid, into becoming a hostess (and more) in a seamen's hangout he plans to build, and Engstrand convinces Mrs. Alving's pastor, Manders, to speak to Mrs. Alving in that regard. Manders, once Mrs. Alving's lover, though he counseled her to return to her husband, learns not only that Regine is Captain Alving's illegitimate daughter but also that Mrs. Alving has begun to question her religion. As they talk, they overhear an innocent flirtation between Oswald and Regine in

the next room, a "ghost" of a flirtation of years before, when Mrs. Alving overheard her husband and her maid, Regine's mother. After fire destroys the uninsured orphanage, consuming the captain's financial legacy, the ill and exhausted Oswald learns the horrifying truth about Regine's birth and his own inherited venereal disease. Regine consequently leaves to join Engstrand, who blackmails Manders into supporting his new business venture, and Mrs. Alving is left alone with Oswald as he slips into paretic insanity, begging his mother to help him end his life at once.

Ibsen knew that such material could hardly help but inflame Victorian sensibilities. Early in 1882, he wrote, "The violent criticisms and insane attacks . . . don't worry me in the least." As always, Ibsen relished the thrill of the battle, but *Ghosts* aroused more negative sentiment than any of his other plays. Norwegian critics led Europe in dismissing it, Ludvig Josephson calling it "one of the filthiest things ever written in Scandinavia," and Erik Bøgh rejecting it as "a repulsive pathological phenomenon."

Nevertheless, *Ghosts* stimulated the young and the daring. By 1888, some observers noted that the play was comparable to classical Greek tragedy though written about modern people, an opinion still popular today. Whereas in the Greek drama, inexorable Fate brings heroes low, in Ibsen's *Ghosts*, the power of the past devours the central figures. A choice once made must stand, regardless of the consequences, Ibsen is saying, and all the shocks that he delivers to his audience reinforce his basic message. The human choice must be made, in Fjelde's words, "out of the integrity of one's whole being." The ghosts of the past rise to strangle Helene Alving, the hypocritical Pastor Manders, and even the innocent victims of their parents' mistakes, Oswald and Regine. The most powerful of Ibsen's tightly constructed social plays, *Ghosts* also marks an important milestone in dramatic history; according to Meyer, it was "the first great tragedy written about middle-class people in plain, everyday prose."

ROSMERSHOLM

Ghosts of a somber past also haunt the brooding manor house in *Rosmersholm*, the second of Ibsen's psychological dramas and the one that, after *Ghosts*, had the worst contemporary reviews. Among the few who supported it, Strindberg, in a rare tribute to Ibsen, declared *Rosmersholm* "unintelligible to the theatre public, mystical to the semi-educated, but crystal-clear to anyone with a knowledge of modern psychology."

The central problem of *Rosmersholm* is the redemption of a human spirit. A young, liberal-spirited woman, Rebecca West, came to the estate on a western fjord as companion to Rosmer's wife, Beate, and after Beate's suicide stayed on as manager of the household, influencing Rosmer, who feels drawn to her unconsciously. His brother-in-law, the inflexible schoolmaster Kroll, attempts to turn Rosmer back to conservativism, but when he fails, he recalls his late sister's intimations of "goings-on," as does the leader of the radical element, the journalist Mortensgaard. Rosmer tries to quiet the talk by proposing to Rebecca, but she rejects him violently. After Rosmer's sense of guilt at his wife's despair begins to eat at him, Rebecca openly admits her guilt in urging Beate to death, confessing that she had acted out of love for him. As she prepares to leave the estate, she tells Rosmer that her earlier "pagan" will has fallen under Rosmersholm's traditional moralistic spell, which "ennobles . . . but kills happiness." Rosmer and Rebecca pledge their mutual love, savoring one final moment of bliss before, in atonement, they follow Beate into the white foam of the millrace.

Meyer claims that "in this play Ibsen was, for the first time . . . in any play for over two centuries, overtly probing the uncharted waters of the unconscious mind." Ibsen had given the play the working title "The White Horses," after the ghost reputedly seen frequently on the estate, a white horse, the symbol of irresistible unconscious forces driving the individual to excessive behavior, based on a folktale about a water spirit in equine shape that lures its victims into dangerous depths. Ibsen gradually reveals that Rebecca came to Rosmerholm as not only the former mistress of one Dr. West but also, as she learned too late, his daughter. Her Oedipal guilt, as Freud observed in 1914, drove her to dispose of Beate, "getting rid of the wife and mother, so that she might take her place with the husband and father."

Beate's death in the millrace was only the most recent guilt-inspired act of violence that Rebecca, under the refining, "ennobling" influence of Rosmer, found she must expiate. Ironically, Rosmer himself is weak, and his one act of heroism is performed for Rebecca: "There is no judge over us; and therefore we must do justice upon ourselves."

In his advice to a young actress undertaking the role of Rebecca in Christiania, Ibsen wrote, "Observe the life that is going on around you, and present a real and living human being." He also instructed the head of the Christiania Theater that Rebecca "does not *force* Rosmer forward. She *lures* him." His characterization of Rebecca West, who throughout the play crochets an indefinable white garment, calls up mythic overtones of the Norse Norns, spinning out human destiny in some white-fogged eternal night. Ibsen's revelation of man's destiny in *Rosmersholm* is once more in woman's hands, here lightening the eternal dark with one perfect gesture of sacrificial atonement made ironically for an imperfect lover, an echo of the myth of Brynhild that he had treated earlier in *The Vikings at Helgeland* and to which he would return before long.

With *Rosmersholm*, Ibsen left off political themes as motivation in his drama. The men and women of the Ibsen plays that followed became increasingly aware of what Meyer calls "the trolls within, not the trolls without . . . strange sick passions which direct their lives." Ibsen's earlier plays had portrayed men such as Rosmer undone by their involvement with provincial politics, while his later works stress figures, mostly women such as Rebecca, who feel intense passion but who cannot express it and thus become "ennobled" without some salvific act of atonement requiring the emancipation of self-sacrifice.

HEDDA GABLER

In the powerful domestic tragedy *Hedda Gabler*, often considered his most popular play, Ibsen adapted the old myth of Brynhild to startling new uses. Around this time, he wrote, "Our whole being is nothing but a fight against the dark forces within ourselves," and he began to see that the greatest human resource in that struggle, the will, tended to remain undeveloped in women of his day. As the daughter of

General Gabler, Hedda had romantically dreamed of a perfect hero, but her dreams and her physical realization with a man not her equal were quite different. Eilert Løvborg, whose combination of profligacy and brilliant scholarship had originally fascinated her, proved unworthy, and she turned in anger and frustration to mediocre Jørgen Tesman, settling for the weaker man as Hjørdis had done in *The Vikings at Helgeland*. Like Hjørdis, too, Hedda is violently jealous of the gentle girl her first hero seems to prefer. At the opening of the play, Hedda and Jørgen have returned to their bourgeois home and to Jørgen's bourgeois aunts after a wretched six-month European honeymoon. Hedda is suffering from massive ennui already, compounded by a pregnancy she ferociously denies. When she learns that Eilert Løvborg has reformed under the tutelage of ordinary Thea Elvstad, whose lovely curling hair she has always envied, Hedda exacts a horrifying vengeance. She goads Løvborg to drink again; he loses the only manuscript of the monumental book he has composed with Thea's help, and he later comes to his senses in the boudoir of the redheaded Mlle Diana, a notorious *fille de joie*. Jørgen finds Løvborg's manuscript and gives it to Hedda, but when Løvborg, frantic at the loss of his "child," comes to Hedda for help, she denies all knowledge of it. Alone, she burns his book, and after a final conversation, she sends him to a "beautiful" death by handing him one of her father's dueling pistols. Hedda's own moment of despair arrives when she learns that Løvborg has botched his suicide disgracefully. She now is trapped not only with Jørgen, and Thea Elvstad, now Jørgen's scholarly inspiration, and his remaining aunt, but also with a blackmail threat from lascivious Judge Brack. Her only escape is to kill herself and Jørgen's despised unborn child.

The portrayal of Hedda Gabler has challenged actresses throughout the play's history, and critics have read her variously as a frustrated feminist, a remnant of the shattered aristocracy, a sadistic psychopath, and even, as Meyer does, as Ibsen's "Portrait of the Dramatist as a Young Woman." No one-sided interpretation seems adequate. Throughout this play, the most claustrophobic of Ibsen's dramas, Hedda Gabler

moves in a web of complex symbols, trapped at last, according to Haugen, "between a Christian-bourgeois domesticity and a pagan-saturnine liaison." Her father's pistols, symbols of his rank, his avocation, and his personality, represent both Hedda's entrapment and her release, for the pistol found with the mortally wounded Eilert Løvborg at Mlle Diana's establishment catches Hedda in an unthinkable scandal, while the remaining one allows her to make restitution to the only person who matters now to Hedda Gabler—herself.

Hedda Gabler is appropriately the last of Ibsen's psychological dramas. Ibsen often claimed that "Self-realization is man's highest task and greatest happiness," yet, as he expressed it in *Peer Gynt*, "to be oneself is to slay oneself." Hedda Gabler's tragedy is not merely the selfish act of a spoiled, bored woman, but a heroic act to free herself from a domination she cannot accept. Incapable of selfless love for a fatal multitude of reasons, Hedda Gabler at last even ruefully abandons her youthful dream of "vine leaves in his hair," the pagan ecstasy that had aroused her sensuous curiosity toward Eilert Løvborg. Her self-realization allows her one last moment of paradoxical human life, the moment she leaves it, a poetic truth of "hidden and mysterious power," in Martin Esslin's words, "which springs from the co-existence of the realistic surface with the deep subconscious fantasy and dream elements behind it."

THE MASTER BUILDER

Not long after the publication of *The Master Builder*, Ibsen stated, "It's extraordinary what profundities and symbols they ascribe to me. . . . Can't people just read what I write?" Ibsen insisted then, as always, that he only wrote about people's inner lives as he knew them: "Any considerable person will naturally be . . . representative of the . . . thoughts and ideas of the age, so that the portrayal of such a person's inner life may seem symbolic." Having shared experiences, at least to some degree, with many of his characters, Ibsen's last plays, the philosophical garnering of his life's harvest, are in that sense rich in symbol.

The title "Master Builder" has been applied frequently to Ibsen himself in recognition of his mastery of his craft and art, and more perilously, as an identification of the dramatist with the hero of the first of his philosophical plays, Halvard Solness, a talented architect just realizing that he is passing his prime. At the peak of his chosen profession, Solness is gnawed by his wife's unhappiness, a result of his absorption in his work, and obsessed by his strange ability to affect the lives of others, especially his bookkeeper Kaja, by the extrasensory projection of his powerful will. Solness had begun his career with churches erected to the glory of God, though for the last ten years he has defied God by choosing to build only human dwellings. Now Solness is attempting a synthesis, a "third world" of architecture, by building himself a home with a tall spire, like a church. At this difficult moment in his art and life, the passionate young Hilde Wangel enters both. She had become infatuated with Solness ten years earlier when he had daringly hung his last dedication wreath on the tower of her village church. She now urges him to repeat the feat, though he has begun to suffer from vertigo, and, inspired by her youthful ardor, he attempts "the impossible" again. As Hilde waves her white shawl—like Rebecca's, but completed, quivering to unseen harps—Solness plunges to his death.

Critics following William Archer have often played heavily on overt resemblances between Ibsen and Solness. Their ages are similar, their marriages unhappily affected by their devotion to their work, their infatuations with much younger girls notorious. Other commentators stress the resemblance between Solness's three types of building and Ibsen's three types of prose drama. Still others stress the Hegelian thesis-antithesis-attempted synthesis structure of Solness's work and Ibsen's several dramatic versions of that theme. Meyer cites Ibsen's 1898 lecture to students in Christiania, in which he observed that Solness was "a man somewhat akin to me." In an interview, Ibsen also declared that architecture was "my own trade." His "May sun," Emilie Bardach, was unspeakably grieved to have been identified publicly with the vicious Hilde of *The Master Builder*, and conjectures about Solness's marriage injured Ibsen's relations with his own wife. Haugen suggests that *The Master Builder* "involves the Christian-pagan

conflict," since Solness defies God, ceases building churches, and attempts to find his creative outlet solely among "happy human beings." Fjelde convincingly warns against equating Solness's "homes for happy human beings" with Ibsen's *Ghosts* or *Rosmersholm*, and suggests an archetypal reading, in which Solness represents the sacred king who has reached the acme of his powers and must be sacrificed by his own consent to ensure the continued existence of his clan, an impression reinforced, Fjelde claims, when at the close of the play "the young king, Ragnar, brings to the old king, Solness, that ambiguous symbol of victory and death, the ribboned wreath."

Thus, Solness's death, which illuminates the entire play, may be seen on various levels of meaning, as biographically, realistically, symbolically, and mythically significant. *The Master Builder* perhaps more than any other of Ibsen's plays illustrates the immense control that Ibsen could exert over his expressed theme through the limpid prose he used as his dramatic vehicle, which approaches poetry in its compression, imagery, and suggestiveness. Here, too, Ibsen examines not only the workings of the unconscious mind but also mysterious powers beyond ordinary sensory perception, without destroying his chosen naturalistic perspective. Fjelde aptly describes the dramatic method in Solness's tragedy as "Truths beyond, within, outside the self . . . a lyric and seamless unity."

OTHER MAJOR WORKS

POETRY: *Digte*, 1871; *Poems*, 1993.
NONFICTION: *Ibsen: Letters and Speeches*, 1964.
MISCELLANEOUS: *The Collected Works of Henrik Ibsen*, 1906-1912, 1928 (13 volumes).

BIBLIOGRAPHY

Bloom, Harold, ed. *Henrik Ibsen*. Philadelphia: Chelsea House, 1999. A collection of criticism regarding Ibsen's plays. Bibliography and index.
Ferguson, Robert. *Henrik Ibsen: A New Biography*. London: R. Cohen, 1996. A basic biography that covers the life and works of Ibsen. Bibliography and index.

Garland, Oliver. *A Freudian Poetics for Ibsen's Theatre: Repetition, Recollection, and Paradox*. Lewiston, N.Y.: Edwin Mellen, 1998. A Freudian approach to examining the psychology that pervades Ibsen's plays. Bibliography and index.

Goldman, Michael. *Ibsen: The Dramaturgy of Fear*. New York: Columbia University Press, 1999. An analysis of Ibsen's plays with respect to his portrayal of fear. Bibliography and index.

Johnston, Brian. *The Ibsen Cycle: The Design of the Plays from "Pillars of Society" to "When We Dead Awaken."* Rev. ed. University Park: Pennsylvania State University Press, 1992. An examination of some of Ibsen's social plays. Bibliography and index.

Ledger, Sally. *Henrik Ibsen*. Plymouth, England: Northcote House in association with the British Council, 1999. A biographical study of the dramatist Ibsen. Bibliography and index.

McFarlane, James, ed. *The Cambridge Companion to Ibsen*. New York: Cambridge University Press, 1994. A comprehensive reference work devoted to Ibsen. Bibliography and index.

Shepherd-Barr, Kirsten. *Ibsen and Early Modernist Theatre, 1890-1900*. Westport, Conn.: Greenwood, 1997. An examination of Symbolism, modernism and Ibsen, focusing on his reception in England and France. Bibliography and index.

Templeton, Joan. *Ibsen's Women*. 1997. Reprint. New York: Cambridge University Press, 2001. A study of Ibsen's drama that examines his portrayal of women. Bibliography and index.

Theoharis, Theoharis Constantine. *Ibsen's Drama: Right Action and Tragic Joy*. New York: St. Martin's Press, 1996. A critical examination of Ibsen's plays, with special emphasis on the themes of joy and dutiful action. Bibliography and index.

Mitzi Brunsdale

ELIZABETH INCHBALD

Born: Standingfield (now Stanningfield), England; October 15, 1753

Died: London, England; August 1, 1821

PRINCIPAL DRAMA

The Mogul Tale: Or, The Descent of the Balloon, pr. 1784, pb. 1788

I'll Tell You What, pr. 1785, pb. 1786

Appearance Is Against Them, pr., pb. 1785

The Widow's Vow, pr., pb. 1786

Such Things Are, pr. 1787, pb. 1788

The Midnight Hour, pr., pb. 1787 (adaptation of Antoine Jean Bourlin's *Guerra Ouverte*)

All on a Summer's Day, pr. 1787

Animal Magnetism, pr., pb. 1788

The Child of Nature, pr., pb. 1788 (adaptation of Madame de Genlis's *Zélie*)

The Married Man, pr., pb. 1789 (adaptation of Philippe Néricault's *Le Philosophe marié*)

The Hue and Cry, pr. 1791

Next Door Neighbours, pr., pb. 1791 (adaptation of Louis Sebastien Mercier's *L'Indigent* and Néricault's *Le Dissipateur*)

Young Men and Old Women, pr. 1792

Every One Has His Fault, pr., pb. 1793

The Wedding Day, pr., pb. 1794

Wives as They Were, and Maids as They Are, pr., pb. 1797

Lovers' Vows, pr., pb. 1798 (adaptation of August von Kotzebue's *Das Kind der Liebe*)

The Wise Man of the East, pr., pb. 1799

To Marry, or Not to Marry, pr., pb. 1805

OTHER LITERARY FORMS

Elizabeth Inchbald published two novels: *A Simple Story* (1791) and *Nature and Art* (1796). For the 125 plays collected in *The British Theatre* (1806-1809), she provided brief critical prefaces, and she chose the works for the seven-volume *A Collection of Farces and Other Afterpieces* (1809) and the ten-volume *The Modern Theatre* (1811).

ACHIEVEMENTS

Elizabeth Inchbald was a highly successful playwright for her time. Fourteen of her plays ran ten or more nights their first season. In the 1788-1789 season, six of her works were performed, and during the week of March 16, 1790, *The Child of Nature, Such Things Are,* and *The Midnight Hour* were performed at Covent Garden. Her comedies were sufficiently popular to allow her to retire in 1805. When the *Quarterly Review* was begun in 1809, Inchbald was invited to contribute. Though she declined, she did agree to write critical prefaces to the 125 plays in *The British Theatre* and to select the pieces to be included in two other anthologies.

BIOGRAPHY

According to writer Mary Shelley, when Elizabeth Inchbald would enter a room, every man present turned his attention to her, ignoring all other women in the room. This beautiful actress and author was born Elizabeth Simpson at Standingfield, Suffolk, on October 15, 1753, the eighth child and sixth daughter of the Catholic farmer John Simpson and his wife, the former Mary Rushbrook.

At an early age she fell in love with the stage. When she was seventeen, she tried to join the theater in Norwich, where her brother George was acting. She received encouragement but no engagement. On April 11, 1772, she boarded the Norwich Fly, bound for London's playhouses forty miles away. Here, too, she could not gain a foothold. On June 9, 1772, she married the actor Joseph Inchbald, whom she had met the previous year when she visited her married sisters in the English capital. Joseph Inchbald was twice Elizabeth's age, but he had theatrical experience and connections. Their seven-year marriage would be tempestuous, in large part because Elizabeth's beauty gained her many admirers and her independent spirit caused her to reject subservience to her husband. The rebellious Miss Milner of *A Simple Story* is largely a self-portrait.

Through her husband's connections and her own good looks, Inchbald secured positions in various provincial theaters, where she performed such leading roles as Cordelia to her husband's Lear, Desdemona to her husband's Othello, Cleopatra in John Dryden's *All for Love: Or, The World Well Lost* (pr. 1677), and Lady Snearwell in Richard Brinsley Sheridan's *The School for Scandal* (pr. 1777). Such parts may have satisfied her ego, but acting in Hull, Edinburgh, or Dublin paid poorly. After Joseph's sudden death on June 6, 1779, the widowed Inchbald returned to London to try her luck, which now proved better: Thomas Harris of Covent Garden hired her. However, in the metropolis, she received only minor parts, and in 1782, she returned to the provincial theaters of Shrewsbury and Dublin. Her roles were bigger, but her income remained about one hundred pounds a year. In 1783, she went back to Harris.

Her experience had taught her what pleased audiences, and the early 1780's, she began writing plays. Her earliest efforts never saw daylight, but on July 6, 1784, the summer Haymarket Theatre produced her farce *The Mogul Tale*, with Inchbald as Selima. The piece earned her a hundred guineas, as much as a year's salary. The success of her next comedies allowed her to abandon acting in 1789 to concentrate on her writing, and by 1805, she was able to retire. Thereafter, in addition to working on *The British Theatre* and two other anthologies, Inchbald contributed the occasional periodical article. She also devoted much time to writing her memoirs, though on her deathbed she ordered that these be burnt, and they were. Inchbald died on August 1, 1821, and was buried in Kensington churchyard.

ANALYSIS

The latter half of the eighteenth century witnessed the rise of the cult of sensibility. Scottish writer Henry McKenzie, author of the sentimental novel *The Man of Feeling* (1771), claimed that "the stimulation of melancholy feelings" led to "social sympathy" and a sense of "the duties of humanity." The literary heroes of the period are magnanimous, even to their enemies. Novels and plays sought to provoke the tender smile or tear rather than laughter. Though wit was not banished from stage and page, it often was associated with morally ambiguous characters. Elizabeth Inchbald fit squarely into this new cult of sentiment. Because plays were family affairs, dramatists such as Inchbald were careful to exclude ribaldry or questionable morality.

Inchbald's prefaces to the plays in *The British Theatre* expressed her views about comedy. She praised David Garrick's adaptation of William Wycherley's *The Country Wife* (pr., pb. 1675) because Garrick had removed parts that a tasteful person might find objectionable. She condemned Sir George Farquhar's *The Beaux' Stratagem* (pr., pb. 1707) for its licentiousness and John Gay's *The Beggar's Opera* (pr., pb. 1728) because she felt it made vice appealing. She criticized Farquhar's *The Inconstant: Or, The Way to Win Him* (pr., pb. 1702) because it sought only to amuse, and she commended her friend and fellow playwright Thomas Holcroft for combining entertainment with instruction.

As in the Restoration comedies that Inchbald condemned, the battle of sexes looms large in her work. However, where the Restoration heroine defends herself with witty repartee, Inchbald's does so with sentiment. In addition, where the Restoration heroine achieves marriage of equality with a Truewit, Inchbald's weds a moralizer to whom she surrenders her autonomy. Friendly with the radicals William Godwin and Thomas Holcroft, Inchbald even shared their liberal publisher Joseph Robinson. Politically she was liberal and used her plays to advocate prison reform, Jean-Jacques Rousseau's theories of education, and humanitarian forgiveness rather than punishment. Yet unlike Godwin, Holcroft, and Mary Wollstonecraft (from whom Inchbald pointedly distanced herself), she had no quarrel with the existing political or social establishment, nor did she express sympathy with the French Revolution that energized the English radicals. Her plays remain firmly in the sentimental mainstream.

SUCH THINGS ARE

Although Inchbald sets this play in Sumatra, her central concern is prison reform in England. In the play, the benevolent Haswell (based on contemporary philanthropist and prison reformer John Howard) tours the sultan's jail and is appalled by what he sees. The keeper points out a man who remains incarcerated because he cannot pay the costs of the trial that acquitted him. Many are political prisoners. Haswell asks the jailer whether "gentleness, or mercy, [might] reclaim them." The jailer replies, "That I can't say— we never try those means in this part of the world." Inchbald implies that this approach is not used in England either.

Inchbald demonstrates the efficacy of Haswell's method through his encounter with Zedan. When the jailer's torch is extinguished, Zedan steals Haswell's wallet. The money Zedan thus secures will allow him and his companions to bribe their way to freedom. Hardened by ill treatment, Zedan rejoices at the thought of Haswell's chagrin on discovering the theft: "And then the pleasure it will be to hear the stranger fret, and complain of his loss!— O, how my heart loves to see sorrow!—Misery such as I have known, on men who spurn me." Unaware of his loss, Haswell, before leaving the prison, gives Zedan some coins to buy food. Overwhelmed by the stranger's generosity, Zedan confesses his theft and returns the purse. Haswell's action, Zedan says "makes me like not only you, but all the world besides—the love of my family was confined to them alone; but this makes me feel I could love even my enemies."

Conversely, harsh treatment teaches bloody instruction, which being taught returns to plague the inventor. Thinking that his wife, Arabella, has been murdered, the sultan declares that he has avenged the wrongs committed against her and him "with such unsparing justice on the foe, that even the men who made me what I was, trembled to reveal their imposition." Haswell undertakes to purge the sultan's cruelty by taking him to the prison to exercise benevolence in freeing six inmates. The inmates' gratitude, Haswell promises, will give the sultan more pleasure than the suffering he has imposed on them. In prison, the sultan finds his long-lost wife. Reunited with Arabella, the sultan gives Haswell a signet ring, allowing him to free whomever the philanthropist chooses.

Into this serious play, Inchbald introduces some comic touches, chiefly through the obtuse Twineall. Like so many of his dramatic counterparts, he derives from the early seventeenth century comedy of humors created by Ben Jonson, with his name a guide to his character. He is a sycophant, who would bind himself to everyone else through flattery. Meanright, whose name perhaps suggests that he wishes to reform this bad habit, tells Twineall to speak of bravery to Lord Tremor, pedigree to Lady Tremor, and to question the sultan's legitimacy in front of Lord Flint. Lord Tremor, as his name reveals, is a coward; his wife is the daughter of a grocer and niece of a wigmaker; and Lord Flint is fiercely loyal to the sultan. By following Meanright's advice, Twineall engenders humorous embarrassment, until Flint has him condemned to death for treason. At the end of the play, Haswell frees him, though Lady Tremor still wants his head and Lord Flint would have him sent to row in the galleys. Sententious Haswell uses even this comic moment to inculcate a moral: "For shame—for shame—Gentlemen! the extreme rigour you shew in punishing a dissension from your opinion, or a satire upon your folly, proves to conviction what reward you had bestowed upon a *skilful* flatterer." Presumably forgiveness will reform the comic Twineall as it will the other characters.

EVERY ONE HAS HIS FAULT

Like so many of Inchbald's other plays, *Every One Has His Fault* concerns marriage and forgiveness. Sir Robert Ramble has been divorced for five months, but he and his wife continue to harbor an affection for each other that leads to their remarrying at the end of the comedy. Although the Placids' married life belies their name, they, too, reach a truce in the fifth act, and Solus, who has been debating whether or not to wed, decides at last to marry Miss Spinster. Comic playwright Miles Peter Andrews's epilogue opens with witty portraits of unhappy marriages but concludes that whatever the problems of conjugal life, it is preferable to the alternative.

The Placids and Rambles agree to overlook or accept their partners' flaws, thus illustrating the value of forgiveness. The same lesson underlies the plot involving Captain Irwin and Lord Norland. Irwin has married Norland's daughter, Eleanor, against the wishes of both her father and his uncle, Solus. Hence, neither man will help the impoverished couple. Rebuffed by friends and relatives, Irwin declares that the English are worse than the savages he encountered in North America. A savage shares what he has with his fellow savage, "gives him the best apartment his hut affords, and tries to hush those griefs that are confined in his bosom," whereas in London no one will invite him to visit.

As in *Such Things Are*, punishment and cruelty lead to crime. Needing money to feed his family, Irwin robs Lord Norland. Even though Lord Norland's daughter and grandson urge mercy, Norland at first wants to prosecute his son-in-law. Inchbald's greatest creation in this play, Mr. Harmony, effects a happy ending in his customary way: He lies. He has reconciled the Rambles and Placids by telling the wives that their husbands have been seriously wounded in a duel. They rush to their husbands' sides, and even though both men are unhurt, the women recognize their love for their men. Similarly, he announces that Irwin has killed himself. When Lord Norland, Solus, Ramble, and Placid all wish that they had been kind to Irwin, he produces the captain. Everyone is now forgiven, and Lord Norland confesses that mercy gives him greater joy than rigorous justice.

In this, her best play, Inchbald deftly fuses sentiment and humor. The tearful plot involving Irwin is offset by Solus's five-act dithering over whether to marry and Harmony's clever deceptions. The Placids' bickering is also treated with wit at times worthy of Oscar Wilde. When Harmony tells Mrs. Placid that her husband has been wounded, she responds, "Mr. Harmony, if Mr. Placid is either dying or dead, I shall behave with very great tenderness; but if I find him alive and likely to live, I will lead him such a life he has not led a long time."

TO MARRY, OR NOT TO MARRY

In her final play, Inchbald once more illustrates the power of forgiveness. Years before the opening scene, Sir Oswin Mortland had successfully prosecuted Lavensforth, modeled on Indian mogul Warren Hastings. Though the court's judgment against Lavensforth extended only to a hefty fine, he exiled himself, leaving his daughter, Hester, to the care of Ashdale. As the curtain rises, Hester, fleeing an arranged marriage, has arrived at Sir Oswin's house seeking asylum.

A confirmed bachelor, Sir Oswin, unaware of Hester's parentage, more than once resolves to send her back to Ashdale, but each time he relents. At length his kindness prompts her to reveal her identity. Although Lavensforth has sworn to kill Sir Oswin, Sir Oswin has fallen in love with Hester and so cannot reject her despite this information. Also, over time, he has come to doubt the justice of his prosecution and Lavensforth's guilt. When Lavensforth, back in England, summons his daughter, Sir Oswin accompanies her. Near Lavensforth's hut, Lavensforth's faithful servant, Amos, wounds Sir Oswin, and Sir Oswin retires to the nearby shelter. Lavensforth now has his opportunity for revenge, but when Hester relates how Sir Oswin has protected her and has changed his mind about the long-ago trial, the two men are reconciled.

Balancing this sentimental plot is Willowear's matrimonial quest. Ashdale had intended him to marry Hester. Jilted, Willowear proposes to Lady Susan Courtly, and when she, too, refuses him, he woos Sir Oswin's spinster sister, Sarah Mortland. Unlike the typical Inchbald female, Sarah prefers the single life. In the last scene, Willowear seems to have won Lady Susan after all, though she reminds him that she is free to change her mind. Inchbald thus again combines laughing and weeping comedy in a play that advocates humanitarian forgiveness.

OTHER MAJOR WORKS

LONG FICTION: *A Simple Story*, 1791; *Nature and Art*, 1796.

NONFICTION: *The British Theatre*, 1806-1809 (prefaces to 125 plays).

EDITED TEXTS: *A Collection of Farces and Other Afterpieces*, 1809 (7 volumes); *The Modern Theatre*, 1811 (10 volumes).

BIBLIOGRAPHY

Boaden, James. *Memoirs of Mrs. Inchbald*. London: Richard Bentley, 1833. Still the most comprehensive biography, drawing on Inchbald's diaries and the recollections of those who knew her. Includes many of her letters and two of her plays not previously produced or published.

Littlewood, S. R. *Elizabeth Inchbald and Her Circle: The Life of a Charming Woman (1753-1821)*. London: Daniel O'Connor, 1921. A charming biography that draws freely on Boaden. Offers little analysis of Inchbald's writings and contains some factual errors.

Manvell, Roger. *Elizabeth Inchbald: England's Principal Woman Dramatist and Independent Woman of Letters in Eighteenth Century London*. Lanham, Md.: University Press of America, 1987. Examines Inchbald's literary and political theories as she expressed them in her plays, novels, and literary criticism. Includes a useful primary and secondary bibliography as well as excerpts from Inchbald's letters and brief plot summaries of her plays.

Joseph Rosenblum

WILLIAM INGE

Born: Independence, Kansas; May 3, 1913
Died: Los Angeles, California; June 10, 1973

PRINCIPAL DRAMA
To Bobolink, for Her Spirit, pb. 1950
Come Back, Little Sheba, pr., pb. 1950

Picnic, pr., pb. 1953 (expansion of the fragmentary "Front Porch")
Bus Stop, pr., pb. 1955 (expanded version of his one-act *People in the Wind*, pb. 1962)
The Dark at the Top of the Stairs, pr., pb. 1957 (originally as *Farther Off from Heaven*, pr. 1947, pb. 1950)

Four Plays by William Inge, pb. 1958

The Tiny Closet, pr. 1959 (in Italy), pb. 1962 (one
 act)

A Loss of Roses, pr. 1959, pb. 1960

The Boy in the Basement, pb. 1962 (one act)

Bus Riley's Back in Town, pb. 1962 (one act)

Summer Brave, pr., pb. 1962 (revision of *Picnic*)

Summer Brave and Eleven Short Plays, pb. 1962

Natural Affection, pr., pb. 1963

Where's Daddy?, pr., pb. 1966 (originally as
 Family Things, pr. 1965)

Two Short Plays: The Call, and A Murder, pb.
 1968

Midwestern Manic, pb. 1969

Overnight, pr. 1969

Caesarian Operations, pr. 1972

*The Love Death Plays: Dialogue for Two Men,
 Midwestern Manic, The Love Death, Venus and
 Adonis, The Wake, The Star*, pr. 1975

OTHER LITERARY FORMS

William Inge was fundamentally a dramatist. At-lantic/Little, Brown published two of his novels, *Good Luck, Miss Wyckoff* (1970) and *My Son Is a Splendid Driver* (1971). Bantam published his earlier scenario for *Splendor in the Grass* (1961). The manuscript of his final novel, "The Boy from the Circus," was found on a table in his living room after his suicide. The manuscript had been rejected by a New York publisher and returned to him; he had not opened the envelope containing it. His two published novels and his first screenplay are set in Kansas and are populated by the same sort of lonely, frustrated people found in his major dramas.

ACHIEVEMENTS

Although William Inge cannot be said to have advanced the technique of modern drama, as Eugene O'Neill did, he was the first notable American dramatist to write seriously and sensitively about the Midwest, much in the tradition of Theodore Dreiser and Sherwood Anderson among novelists, of Carl Sandburg and Edgar Lee Masters among poets, and of Grant Wood among painters. Inge's first five Broadway plays—*Come Back, Little Sheba, Picnic,*

Bus Stop, The Dark at the Top of the Stairs, and *A Loss of Roses*—are set in the Midwest and examine in believable and accurate detail the pent-up frustrations of living in the sort of midwestern small towns that Inge knew intimately from his childhood and youth. The Liberty of some of his plays is the Independence, Kansas, of his childhood; great irony underlies his choice of that place-name.

The decade beginning in 1950 was a remarkable one for Inge. It is unique for an unknown playwright to emerge on Broadway with the sort of critical and commercial success that *Come Back, Little Sheba* commanded and then to be able to produce in rapid-fire succession three more commercial triumphs. Inge did just this, following the 1950 production of *Come Back, Little Sheba* with *Picnic* in 1953, *Bus Stop* in 1955, and *The Dark at the Top of the Stairs* in 1957. *Come Back, Little Sheba* ran for 190 performances; the next three plays ran for more than 450 performances apiece.

Come Back, Little Sheba won for its author an award from the New York critics as the most promising playwright of the season. *Picnic* won the Pulitzer Prize, a New York Drama Critics Circle Award, and the Donaldson Award, which it shared with Arthur Miller's *The Crucible* (pr., pb. 1953). Even though Inge's next two plays won no awards, they were highly successful. Inge's reputation as a serious dramatist was assured; in addition, his first four full-length plays were made into films that succeeded both critically and commercially.

In 1958, just as Inge crested the wave of popularity to which his first four Broadway plays had brought him, *Four Plays by William Inge* was issued by Random House, which had previously published each of the plays separately. It was followed by Heinemann's British edition in 1960. Inge's next play, *A Loss of Roses*, into whose production the author put a considerable amount of his own money, reached Broadway in 1959 and was rejected by critics and audiences alike. It closed after twenty-five performances, leaving Inge, who was singularly sensitive, severely depressed as well as financially strained.

The failure of *A Loss of Roses* caused Inge to leave New York permanently. At the strong urging of

Elia Kazan, who had become a close friend after directing *The Dark at the Top of the Stairs*, Inge moved to the West Coast and turned his talents to screenwriting. His first attempt, *Splendor in the Grass*, which Warner Bros. produced, again focused on small-town midwestern life and was so successful that it received the Academy Award for Best Original Screenplay of 1961.

Splendor in the Grass was to be Inge's last artistic triumph. He followed it in 1963 with *Natural Affection*, which played on Broadway for only thirty-six performances and was the subject of even harsher criticism than *A Loss of Roses* had received. Hurt and distraught, Inge returned to California, where he worked on screenplays. He also did a final original screenplay, based on one of his one-act plays entitled *Bus Riley's Back in Town*, about which he wrote (in a letter to R. Baird Shuman of May 20, 1965): "As for *Bus Riley*, the picture is a loss. I took my name off it. I haven't even seen the version they are showing."

Inge died a broken and defeated man, convinced that he had nothing more to say. His legacy to American drama is nevertheless great. He dealt with the Midwest as had no American playwright before him. As his close friend Tennessee Williams had focused dramatic attention on the South, so had Inge focused dramatic attention on the Midwest. He created a gallery of memorable characters, particularly female characters, because he understood the female mind remarkably well.

Inge's Broadway successes and his screenplay for *Splendor in the Grass* have secured his position as an American dramatist. Although he generally lacked the pioneering genius and willingness to experiment with form possessed by Eugene O'Neill, Clifford Odets, and Tennessee Williams, Inge still ranks high among the significant contributors to American theater in the twentieth century.

BIOGRAPHY

William Inge's understanding of the female personality is not surprising in view of the fact that he came from an emphatically female-dominated home. As the youngest of Luther Clayton and Maude Sarah Gibson Inge's five children, Inge identified more closely with his mother and sisters than he did with males. His father was a traveling salesman who spent little time at home during Inge's formative years. The young Inge, much dominated by his mother, early developed an interest in acting, largely through his initial school experiences with recitation.

Popular as a teenager, Inge was a cheerleader and was active in his high school's dramatic programs. He enjoyed acting and continued his studies after high school at the University of Kansas, where he majored in drama and frequently acted in university productions. Still provincially midwestern at the time of his college graduation, Inge feared going to New York to pursue his first love, acting, and went instead to George Peabody College for Teachers in Nashville to prepare for teacher certification and to take a master's degree in education. Inge taught high school for one year in Columbus, Kansas, where he surely met numerous teachers such as those he depicts with such accuracy in *Picnic* and students such as those in *Splendor in the Grass*. For the next ten years, except for a crucial three years as art, music, book, and drama critic for the St. Louis *Star-Times*, Inge taught English and drama at the college level, first at Stephens College in Columbia, Missouri, and then at Washington University in St. Louis.

It was the crucial years away from teaching, from 1943 to 1946, that led Inge into his career as a playwright. In his position as a three-year replacement for a friend on the *Star-Times* who had been drafted, Inge interviewed Tennessee Williams, who was resting at his parents' home in St. Louis after the 1944 Chicago opening of *The Glass Menagerie*. A friendship blossomed, and Williams persuaded Inge to do some serious writing. *Farther Off from Heaven*, the prototype for *The Dark at the Top of the Stairs*, was the result, and in 1947, Margo Jones, whom Inge had met through Williams, produced the play in her theater in Dallas. The production was well received, and Inge was encouraged by its success to continue writing. By 1949, he had abandoned teaching in order to devote himself fully to his writing.

During this period, Inge had become a heavy drinker, and in 1948, he joined Alcoholics Anonymous. Through his association with this organization, he came to understand much more about alcoholism and about alcoholics, information that finds its way directly into *Come Back, Little Sheba* in the person of Doc Delaney, the play's frustrated protagonist.

Similarly, Inge, continually beset by depression, self-doubt, and concern about his homosexuality, which he was never able to accept, began a course of psychoanalysis in 1949, and he was in and out of analysis through the 1950's. Although one may question whether psychoanalysis made Inge any better able to cope with his own fears and frustrations, its influences and effects are clearly seen throughout his work, particularly in *A Loss of Roses*, *Natural Affection*, and *Where's Daddy?*

Despite the successes he had known, by 1973 Inge felt that he was "written out," that he had nothing more to say. Although he enjoyed his work in theater workshops at the University of California campuses at Los Angeles and Irvine and was successful in them, he was unable to deal with the artistic frustrations that plagued him, and on June 10, 1973, he took his own life.

ANALYSIS

William Inge understood both the people and the social order of the Midwest, particularly the matriarchal family structure common to much of the area. Inge's midwestern plays reverberate with authenticity. His first four Broadway plays depict their commonplace characters with extraordinary sensitivity, building through accounts of their prosaic lives toward a pitch of frustration that is communicated to audiences with enormous impact. By capturing so deftly this pervasive sense of frustration, Inge presents the universal that must be a part of any successful drama. Audiences left Inge's early plays with an internalized sense of the gnawing isolation and conflict that his characters experienced. This is his legacy to American drama.

COME BACK, LITTLE SHEBA

All Inge's best instincts as a playwright are at work in *Come Back, Little Sheba*, the story of Doc and Lola Delaney, who are twenty years into a marriage that was forced on them when the eighteen-

year-old Lola became pregnant while the promising young Doc was a medical, student. Their hasty marriage was followed by Doc's dropping out of medical school and becoming a chiropractor as well as by the loss of the baby through the bungling of a midwife, to whom Lola went because she was too embarrassed to go to an obstetrician. Lola ends up sterile and, as the action of the play begins, fat and unattractive. Doc has become an alcoholic, but as the play opens, he has been dry for a year.

Come Back, Little Sheba is a study in contrasts. It presents thesis and antithesis but seldom any satisfying or convincing synthesis, which makes it a sound piece of realistic writing. Little Sheba is Lola's lost puppy, who "just vanished one day—vanished into thin air." More than representing a surrogate child, Little Sheba represents Lola's lost youth, and only when Lola stops looking for Sheba is it clear that some resolution has taken place, even though the resolution is not presented as a cure-all for Doc and Lola Delaney's problems.

The play revolves largely around four characters: Doc; Lola; Marie, their boarder; and Turk, the recurring priapic figure whom Inge later used to keep the action moving in *Picnic* and in other of his plays. Marie, although she is engaged to someone else, is having a brief affair with Turk (significantly, a javelin thrower) before the arrival of her fiancé from out of town. Lola is titillated by this tawdry affair and actively encourages it, even though she is planning to fix a special meal for Marie's fiancé, Bruce, when he arrives. Doc, who sees Marie as the daughter he never had, is appalled by the whole misadventure. He falls off the wagon and gets roaring drunk. The dramatic climax of the play is his drunk scene, in which he threatens passionately to hack off all of Lola's fat, cut off Marie's ankles, and castrate Turk, but falls into a drunken stupor before he can accomplish any of these vile deeds and is taken off to the drunk tank. So terrified is he by the drunk tank that he returns home chastened, but not before Lola has attempted to go home to her aging parents, only to be rebuffed when she telephones them with her request that they allow her to come home for a while.

As the play ends, Doc pleads with Lola, "Don't

ever leave me. *Please* don't ever leave me. If you do, they'd have to keep me down at that place [the drunk tank] all the time." Doc and Lola are back together, not for very positive reasons, but rather because neither has any real alternative.

The characterization and the timing in this play are superb; the control is sure and steady. The business of the play is well taken care of early in the action as Lola, a lonely woman unhappy with herself and with what she has become, talks compulsively to anyone who will listen—the milkman, the postman, the next-door neighbor, and Mrs. Coffman, who in contrast to Lola is neat, clean, and well-organized, as a woman with seven children needs to be. Lola tells the audience all they need to know about her history while convincing them of her loneliness by reaching out desperately to anyone who comes into her purview. The resolution for Lola comes in the last act, when she begins to clean up the house, pay attention to her appearance, and write a note for the milkman rather than lurk to engage him in conversation.

Lola's dream sequences, which hold up quite well psychologically, are skillfully used to handle more of the necessary business of the play. The final dream has to do with Turk and the javelin, which Turk has already described as "a big, long lance. You hold it like this, erect." In Lola's dream, Turk is disqualified in the javelin throwing contest and Doc picks up the javelin "real careful, like it was awful heavy. But you threw it, Daddy, clear, *clear*, up into the sky. And it never came down." Inge's exposure to Freudian psychoanalysis certainly pervades the dream sequences.

Inge does not give the audience an upbeat or hopeful ending in *Come Back, Little Sheba*; rather, he presents life as it is. Perhaps Lola has matured a little. Perhaps both she and Doc have gained some insights that will help them to accept their lives with a bit more resignation than they might otherwise have, but nothing drastic is likely to happen for either of them. They will live on, wretchedly dependent on each other. If their marriage lasts, as it probably will, the mortar that holds it together will be dependence more than love. At least Lola has faced reality sufficiently to say, "I don't think Little Sheba's ever coming back, Doc," and to stop searching for her.

PICNIC

Inge's second Broadway success, *Picnic*, started as a fragmentary play, "Front Porch," that Inge wrote shortly after *Farther Off from Heaven*. The original play consisted of little more than character sketches of five women in a small Kansas town. The play grew into *Picnic*, a much more fully developed play, and finally into *Summer Brave*, which is little different from *Picnic* except in the resolution of the Madge-Hal conflict.

Four of the five women in *Picnic* live in one house. They are Flo Owens; her two daughters, Millie, a sixteen-year-old tomboy, and Madge, the prettiest girl in town; and their boarder, Rosemary Sydney, a schoolteacher in her thirties. Madge is engaged to marry Alan Seymour. Their next-door neighbor is sixty-year-old Helen Potts, who also participates in the action of the play. These women are all sexually frustrated; although Madge and Rosemary both have suitors, the relationships are specifically delineated as nonsexual.

Into this tense setting is introduced an incredibly handsome male animal, Hal Carter, who exudes sexuality. As insecure as he is handsome, Hal is down on his luck and has arrived in town looking for his friend Alan Seymour, who might be able to give him a job. Hungry, he exchanges some work in Helen Potts's yard for a meal. He works bare-chested, much to the consternation of the women, whose upbringing decrees that they feign shock at this display but whose natural impulses are in conflict with their conservative upbringing.

Hal, reminiscent of Turk in *Come Back, Little Sheba*, causes chaos, as might be expected. The play focuses on the women, and Hal serves as the catalyst. Inge's ability to draw convincing characters, particularly female characters, is particularly evident in *Picnic*. He maintains his clear focus on the women in the play, using Hal precisely as he needs to in order to reveal these women as the psychologically complex beings they are. Never does the focus slip; never does the control over material and characters waver.

As the action develops toward a climax in the second act, Hal's physical presence more than anything else pushes the conflict to its dramatically necessary outcome. Millie and Rosemary start drinking from Hal's liquor bottle after Hal turns his attention from Millie to her more mature sister. Both Millie and Rosemary are soon drunk. Flo vents her own frustrations by upbraiding the two of them, but not before Rosemary, humiliated that Hal is not available to her and distressed that she finds him so attractive, shrieks at him that he came from the gutter and that he will return to the gutter. This emotional scene heightens Hal's insecurity, which is necessary if the play is to proceed convincingly to a love affair between Hal and Madge, an outcome that seems inevitable.

The screaming fit also forces Rosemary to face reality and to realize that her erstwhile suitor, Howard, is probably her only realistic out if she is not to continue teaching and if she is not to become frustrated and grow old alone. She goes off with Howard and yields to him, after which she asks, then begs him to marry her. In the play's final version, he will go only so far as to say that he will come back in the morning but when he does, Rosemary has already spread the news that she and Howard are going to marry, so that when Howard arrives, everyone congratulates him, and he has no choice but to leave with Rosemary, presumably to marry her. Inge is intrigued by the theme of forced marriage, which recurs in nearly all his major plays, and *Picnic* offers a striking variation on the theme.

Back at the picnic, Alan and Hal have engaged in fisticuffs and Alan has reported Hal to the police, forcing him to leave town in order to avoid arrest. In *Summer Brave*, Hal leaves and Madge stays behind; at the urging of Joshua Logan, Inge changed the ending of the play, so that in *Picnic*, Madge packs her suitcase and follows Hal a short time after his forced departure.

BUS STOP

Bus Stop, despite its popular acceptance, does not have the stature of *Come Back, Little Sheba* or *Picnic*. An expanded version of Inge's one-act *People in the Wind*, *Bus Stop* is set in a small crossroads restaurant between Kansas City and Wichita, where the passengers on a bus are stranded because of a blizzard. Among the passengers is Bo Decker, a twenty-one-

year-old cowpoke from Montana who is traveling with Virgil Blessing, a middle-aged father surrogate (suggestive of Pinky in *Where's Daddy?*), and with a brainless little singer, Cherie, whom he met in a Kansas City nightclub, where she was performing. Bo was pure until he met Cherie, but now, in a comical role-reversal, he has lost his virginity to her and is insisting that she return to Montana with him to make him an honest man. Cherie joins Bo and Virgil, and they are on their way west when the bus is forced by the weather to pull off the road.

Cherie has second thoughts about going to Montana, and after thinking the matter over, she accuses Bo of abducting her and the police become involved in the situation. Bo has a fight with the sheriff. He is humiliated and apologizes to everyone in the restaurant, including Cherie. Before the play is over, however, Bo asks Cherie to marry him, she agrees, and they set out for Montana, leaving Virgil Blessing behind and alone.

The development of *Bus Stop* is thin, and the characterization, particularly of Bo, is not close to the high level reached in *Come Back, Little Sheba* and *Picnic*. Although Bo is similar in many ways to Turk and Hal, he is made of cardboard and lacks the multidimensional elements that make Turk and Hal convincing.

The play is stronger in the presentation of its minor characters, particularly the lonely, frustrated Grace, a middle-aged woman who lives at the small crossroads where the bus has stopped and who works the night shift in the restaurant. She has sex with a truck driver not because she loves him but because he keeps her from being lonely. In the end, she and Virgil Blessing are left alone in the restaurant. The bus has pulled out, and one might think that Grace and Virgil are the answer to each other's loneliness, but Inge does not provide a double resolution in this play. He permits Bo and Cherie to leave on a somewhat optimistic note, much as he allowed Hal and Madge a future in *Picnic*, but he wisely backs off from providing the pat resolution that a romance between Grace and Virgil would have provided, because the psychological motivation for such a relationship has not been built sufficiently throughout the play.

The original play, *People in the Wind*, contained two characters who were not included in *Bus Stop*. They are two older women, apparently both unmarried and seemingly sisters, who are going to visit their niece. It appears that they want the niece to take them in in their old age, but they are not sure she will do so. They are nervous, drinking bicarbonate of soda to calm their stomachs. They represent the fate that can befall people who do not form close family ties early in their lives. In dropping them from *Bus Stop*, Inge was clearly opting to make the focus of the later play love rather than loneliness, which was the central focus of *People in the Wind*.

The Dark at the Top of the Stairs

The Dark at the Top of the Stairs, the finished version of *Farther Off from Heaven*, is Inge's most autobiographical play. In it, the author returns to a plot centering on a family, and this time, it is clearly Inge's own family that he is writing about. Rubin Flood is a harness salesman who travels a great deal, leaving his children, Sonny and Reenie, in a mother-dominated home. The setting is a small town in Oklahoma.

Inge, who had been in psychoanalysis for several years when he wrote *The Dark at the Top of the Stairs*, paid particular attention to the Oedipal elements of the mother-son relationship in this play and in two subsequent plays, *A Loss of Roses* and *Natural Affection*, although not with the success that he achieved in this earlier presentation.

Rubin Flood and his wife, Cora, were married early, propelled into marriage by Rubin's unmanageable libido. The marriage has encountered difficulties, which come to a head when Rubin, having lost his job—a fact he keeps from his wife—discovers that Cora has bought Reenie an expensive dress for a dance given at the country club by the nouveau riche Ralstons. He demands that the dress be returned for a refund, and a heated argument ensues, during which Cora taunts Rubin to strike her. He obliges and then leaves, vowing never to return. In act 2, Cora's sister, Lottie, and her dentist husband, Morris, have arrived for a visit. Cora hopes that she will be able to persuade Lottie to take her and the children in now that

Rubin has abandoned them. In this scene, also, Reenie's blind date for the dance, Sammy Goldenbaum, arrives. A cadet at a nearby military academy, Sammy is meticulously polite and none too secure. His exquisite manners charm Lottie and Morris before he and the pathologically shy Reenie depart for the dance. Once at the dance, Reenie introduces Sammy to the hostess, who is drunk, and Reenie leaves the dance, not telling Sammy she is going. He tries to find her but cannot.

In act 3, Reenie's friend Flirt appears with the news that Sammy took the train to Oklahoma City, rented a hotel room, and killed himself, presumably because the drunken Mrs. Ralston, on discovering that Sammy was Jewish, had asked him to leave the party. Sammy's suicide forces the principal characters to reconsider their lives, and the play ends somewhat on the upbeat. Rubin has returned home. He is tamed, as is evidenced by the fact that he confesses to Cora, "I'm scared. I don't know how I'll make out. I . . . I'm scared," and that he leaves his boots outside, not wanting to dirty up Cora's clean house.

Sonny Flood, who has been an obnoxious child throughout the play, apparently has turned the corner by the end of it. He volunteers to take his distraught sister to the movies, and when his mother tries to kiss him goodbye, he declines to kiss her, giving the audience an indication that his Oedipal tendencies are now coming under control.

Inge tried to do something daring in *The Dark at the Top of the Stairs*, and although he failed, it was a creditable attempt. He juggled two significant conflicts, the Rubin-Cora conflict and the Sammy-society conflict. As the play developed, the conflict involving the suicide was not sufficiently prepared for to be wholly believable. Inge's admitted purpose was to use the suicide subplot to divert the attention of the audience from the conflict between Rubin and Cora, so that they could return to this conflict in the last act with a fresher view.

The suicide subplot has been severely attacked by critics. It is, however, a serious misinterpretation to view the suicide as an event that the author intended to present realistically. It can succeed only as a symbol, serving the useful function of promoting the resolution of the main conflict. This is not to justify the suicide subplot, which is a weakness in the play, but rather to demonstrate the artistic purposes Inge envisioned for it.

LATER PLAYS

None of Inge's later plays achieved the standard of his four Broadway successes. Some of his most interesting work is found in his one-act plays, fourteen of which are available in print. Had Inge lived longer, probably some of the materials in these plays would have lent themselves to further development as full-length dramas; particularly notable are *To Bobolink, for Her Spirit*, *The Tiny Closet*, and *The Boy in the Basement*.

OTHER MAJOR WORKS

LONG FICTION: *Good Luck, Miss Wyckoff*, 1970; *My Son Is a Splendid Driver*, 1971.

SCREENPLAYS: *Splendor in the Grass*, 1961; *All Fall Down*, 1962; *Bus Riley's Back in Town*, 1964.

BIBLIOGRAPHY

Leeson, Richard M. *William Inge: A Research and Production Sourcebook*. Westport, Conn.: Greenwood Press, 1994. A study that focuses on the stage history and production of Inge's works. Contains plot summaries.

McClure, Arthur F. *Memories of Splendor: The Midwestern World of William Inge*. Topeka: Kansas State Historical Society, 1989. The focus is the "regional quality" of Inge's work. Unusual features include photographs and posters from stage and film productions and reminiscences from those who served as models for Inge's characters and from actors who played them.

McClure, Arthur F., and C. David Rice, eds. *A Bibliographical Guide to the Works of William Inge, 1913-1973*. Lewiston, N.Y.: Edwin Mellen Press, 1991. An attempt to "present a complete picture of Inge's work as a teacher, journalist and author." Divided into works by Inge, including his journalistic articles and reviews; biographical information, among them obituaries; critical articles and reviews of Inge's work; and brief chapters on his forays into film and television. Sporadic annotations.

Shuman, R. Baird. *William Inge*. Rev. ed. Boston: Twayne, 1989. An updated version of Shuman's 1965 book, this volume focuses primarily on summarizing and analyzing the plays. Shuman's stated goal is "to present a balanced view of William Inge and . . . show the inroads . . . public expectations make upon the private and creative life" of a sensitive artist. Index, select bibliography.

Voss, Ralph F. *A Life of William Inge*. Lawrence: University Press of Kansas, 1989. A carefully researched "reconstruction" of Inge's life, with numerous photographs, most of Inge at various stages of life. Voss's examination reveals a troubled man whose life was a "pattern" of secrecy, especially concerning his homosexuality and alcoholism. Voss concludes, "'Inge Country' was never just the state of Kansas or the midwestern prairies . . . [but] almost always a troubled state of mind."

R. Baird Shuman,
updated by Elsie Galbreath Haley

ALBERT INNAURATO

Born: Philadelphia, Pennsylvania; June 2, 1948

PRINCIPAL DRAMA

Urlicht, pr. 1971, pb. 1980

I Don't Generally Like Poetry but Have You Read "Trees"?, pr. 1972 (with Christopher Durang)

The Life Story of Mitzi Gaynor: Or, Gyp, pr. 1973 (with Durang)

Wisdom Amok, pr. 1973?, pb. 1980

The Transfiguration of Benno Blimpie, pr. 1973, pb. 1976

The Idiots Karamazov, pr., pb. 1974, augmented pb.

1981 (with Durang, music by Jack Feldman, lyrics by Durang)
Earth Worms, pr. 1974, pb. 1980
Gemini, pr. 1976, pb. 1977
Ulysses in Traction, pr. 1977, pb. 1978
Passione, pr. 1980, pb. 1981
Bizarre Behavior: Six Plays, pb. 1980
Coming of Age in Soho, pr., pb. 1985
Best Plays of Albert Innaurato, pb. 1987
Magda and Callas, pb. 1989
Gus and Al, pr., pb. 1989

OTHER LITERARY FORMS

In addition to his dramatic works, Albert Innaurato has become a regular reviewer of, and commentator on, opera, publishing articles about directors and reviews of recordings in *The New York Times*. He has also written several teleplays, including *Verna, USO Girl* (1978), and *Coming Out* (1989).

ACHIEVEMENTS

Albert Innaurato enjoyed enormous popularity with the simultaneous success of *Gemini* and *The Transfiguration of Benno Blimpie* in 1977. Both plays received Obie Awards. Since then, Innaurato has struggled to fulfill the high expectations of his audience, and none of his subsequent efforts has met the high level of critical acclaim that the earlier plays enjoyed. Innaurato has received Rockefeller and Guggenheim grants and has served as resident playwright at the Circle Repertory Company and The Public Theatre. *Coming of Age in Soho* underwent a widely publicized revision during the course of its Public Theatre production and received a measure of praise, as did his next play *Gus and Al*. Nevertheless, Innaurato continues to be remembered for his first two New York productions, which established his place as an important contemporary dramatist.

BIOGRAPHY

Albert Innaurato was born and reared in Philadelphia, the son of Italian immigrants. The ethnic world of south Philadelphia provides the background for his most successful plays. Though precise autobiographical parallels have not been revealed by Innaurato, the

events and characters in the plays are transformations of his own experiences and acquaintances. His portrayals of Italian American life are sufficiently realistic that Innaurato's opinions about ethnic identity have been sought out by reporters.

Many of Innaurato's plays were begun when he was quite young; a version of *Urlicht*, for example, dates from his late teens. He continued to write prolifically during his undergraduate years at Temple University, where he received his B.A. Many of these early works were lost or destroyed, though some of the titles are known. Innaurato develops scripts rather slowly, so some of the material may eventually surface again in new plays.

Perhaps the most persistent early influence on Innaurato was his taste for opera. He taught himself to play the piano and made some early experiments in operatic composition, but its influence lingers mostly through frequent allusions to opera in plays such as *Gemini* and in the leitmotif structure of the plays, which also feature set speeches designed as arias. Innaurato collects opera recordings and has written about his fascination with the form for *The New York Times*.

After attending Temple University, an experience transposed into *Ulysses in Traction*, the young writer spent a year at the California Institute of the Arts. His education there was unsettling, causing him to question his assumptions about art, politics, and society, and he left the school to return to the East Coast.

During the early 1970's, Innaurato studied playwriting at Yale University under Howard Stein and Jules Feiffer. The discipline of regular writing and constructive feedback seems to have provided an unusually productive routine for Innaurato, who developed his serious dramatic talents in plays such as *Earth Worms*. Feiffer's influence seems important to Innaurato's development as a satirist, too—his concern for grotesque, seriocomic characters who exist beyond social conventions.

Equally important to Innaurato's development at Yale was his association with Christopher Durang. The two young writers shared a virulent anti-Catholicism, most concisely demonstrated in the famous monologue by the title character of Durang's play

Albert Innaurato in 1980. (AP/Wide World Photos)

Sister Mary Ignatius Explains It All for You (pr. 1979). Durang is more important to Innaurato for having collaborated with him on a number of madcap comic satires. The ridiculous mayhem of *Gemini* does not seem eccentric in Innaurato's œuvre when considered in relation to plays such as *The Idiots Karamazov, I Don't Generally Like Poetry but Have You Read "Trees"?*, and *The Life Story of Mitzi Gaynor: Or, Gyp*, all written during the Yale years with Durang. These works also provided the experience with allusion and the manipulation of theatrical conventions that Innaurato used later in *Ulysses in Traction*.

In 1974, Innaurato was graduated from Yale with a master of fine arts degree in playwriting. He had also directed and acted in some of the plays, which even in their student productions featured talented, capable casts. His work was published in Yale's *Theater* magazine and was produced by the Yale Repertory Theatre. Some of his plays also received read-

ings and critical feedback at the Yale summer session, the O'Neill Theater Center's National Playwrights' Conference.

In 1975, Innaurato received a Guggenheim Fellowship and began his career as a full-time playwright. The first production of *Gemini*, at the PAF playhouse in Huntington, Long Island, was so successful that a subsequent production was arranged at the Circle Rep. When this Off-Broadway staging was acclaimed by critics, the play was moved downtown to a small Broadway house where it ran for 1,778 performances. This bona fide hit, following close on the heels of a heralded performance by James Coco as Benno Blimpie, made Innaurato the most talked-about young playwright of the season. His work received especially close scrutiny from the gay press, where Innaurato's theme of sexual confusion was furiously debated.

In the mid-1970's, Innaurato's progress became uneven as he tried to support his playwriting activity through a series of odd jobs, including work as a commentator on opera broadcasts and as a television writer. *Ulysses in Traction* was very coolly received, as were productions of some of the early plays. Innaurato directed the Playwrights' Horizons production of *Passione* in 1980, which was then transferred to Broadway, with Frank Langella supervising the performance. The personal financial and health problems that have slowed Innaurato's production were eventually made public in 1985, during his work with Joseph Papp on the production of *Coming of Age in Soho*. Still, Innaurato seemed to remain committed to dramatic writing and continued to produce new material—two plays in 1989—despite the lack of a major later success and his continuing public statements against the power structure of the critical press in New York. He began writing reviews of theatrical productions and essays on theater in general.

ANALYSIS

Albert Innaurato's plays alternate in their effect from farcical comedy to unrelenting pathos. The consistent aspect of his work is not a matter of genre or formula, but one of theatrical style. Innaurato populates his plays with grotesque misfits, vivid personalities that depart from traditional theatrical types. The settings are drawn from contemporary lower-class dwellings and ground the desires of his sympathetic characters in a run-down atmosphere that predicts their eventual defeat. Actions, too, are frequently grotesque, particularly when the plays' themes combine death, eating, and debased sexuality. Innaurato's vision disturbs and fascinates audiences because he has created new voices for the expression of obsessive concerns, new ways to dramatize important themes through characterization. Innaurato's work is uneven, however, almost equally divided between adeptly constructed scripts that shift cleanly from one scene to the next and plays that diffuse his obsessions into shrill, unfocused energy. If any single work can be said to predict the themes and style of Innaurato's work, it is John Guare's *The House of Blue Leaves* (pr. 1971).

Unlike many young playwrights, Innaurato was given little time to develop; instead, his work was consistently condemned as disappointing. Tangential debate over his portrayals of homosexual characters only tended to fuel the critical fire. Yet in retrospect, Innaurato's achievements are great for such a young writer. Like Tennessee Williams, he developed a personal, slightly grotesque seriocomic style that was rooted in a particular environment. Within this paradigm, he has created a number of good plays, and two outstanding ones: *The Transfiguration of Benno Blimpie* is a kind of miracle of ugliness, and *Gemini* is the sort of popular comedy that also has the power to change public perceptions. If Innaurato has settled into a pattern with the last plays, it is as a writer of competently constructed domestic comedies with unusual characters. This role may be a disappointment to some critics, but with the state of commercial theater in contemporary America, Innaurato is a writer for whom the public can be grateful—one who should be encouraged to continue.

THE TRANSFIGURATION OF BENNO BLIMPIE

The Innaurato hero is usually unhappy, from a depressed family, sexually confused, but in love with beauty. The most concise expression of this character's unhappiness comes in Innaurato's *The Transfiguration of Benno Blimpie*, perhaps his best work. Benno, "an enormously fat young man," narrates his story while seated on a stool apart from the main acting area. Benno's desire for love and beauty, expressed by his passion for great paintings, is contradicted by everything around him. His combative Italian parents ignore and abuse him, his grandfather carries out a sordid affair with a foul young Irish girl, while Benno, eventually raped by a gang of schoolboys, takes solace in eating.

The performance begins with Benno's announcement that he plans to eat himself to death. The plot then proceeds through a series of flashbacks, which establish in turn the cruelty of his parents, the depravity of his grandfather's sexual activity, and the incongruity of his passion for art. Much of the story is narrated by Benno, who remains stationary and participates in the flashback action only vocally, altering his voice to indicate youth while the other actors behave as if a Benno figure were present in the scene. This choice to disrupt the conventional structure of the acting event causes the behavior of the other characters toward the phantom Benno to be more noticeable than usual. When they ignore his needs and requests, or send him away, the audience is conscious of the theatrical parallel that objectifies his rejection. Once Benno's story is complete, Innaurato repeats the first scene; this time, however, Benno adds a gesture with a cleaver, showing that he will literally eat himself—consume his own body until he dies.

WISDOM AMOK AND URLICHT

The economy of construction and unrelenting plot progression in *The Transfiguration of Benno Blimpie* are especially impressive when compared with Innaurato's other early works, such as *Wisdom Amok*, *Urlicht*, and *Earth Worms*. In the first two of these plays, Innaurato's anti-Catholic feelings are so virulent that the plays surrender any pretension of credible mimesis to a free-associative, vengeful attack on the Church. Nothing like reality, the plays also fail to achieve any internal, formal coherence, dissolving instead into a disintegrated barrage of images. In *Wisdom Amok*, there are no sympathetic characters; the action begins with grotesquely disrupted public events, then immerses itself in a sacrilegious madhouse. The power and fascination of charismatic madness were important themes in other plays popular at the time of *Wisdom Amok*'s composition, such as Peter Weiss's *Die Verfolgung und Ermordung Jean Paul Marats, dargestellt durch die Schauspielgruppe des Hospizes zu Charenton unter der Anleitung des Herrn de Sade* (pr., pb. 1964; *Marat/Sade*, 1965), but Innaurato's attempt to explore the plunge of a cleric into insanity and murder sheds no new light on the repressive qualities of religion, nor is his character sufficiently interesting to maintain sympathetic attention. *Urlicht* is slightly more compact, substituting the extravagance of opera for the decadence of the Church but still surpassing credibility with its grotesque extremes of imagery and action.

EARTH WORMS

In *Earth Worms*, Innaurato's work remains diffuse, but the characters evolve along with the dramatic events to create a number of unique, fascinating personalities. The most flamboyant of these characters is Bernard, an aged transvestite and retired English professor who takes the dominant role in the action, performing a Pygmalion-like transformation on the central female. This character, Mary, who reappears in *Passione* as Aggy, is an uneducated young Appalachian woman who becomes mature enough eventually to push the other crippled characters away. Innaurato's trademark of sexual confusion is stamped not only on the professor but also on Arnold, Mary's serviceman husband. He brings her back to his childhood home, now grown filthy and decayed, then abandons her when his guilt over the death of their child overcomes him. These roles and a few others make *Earth Worms* a fascinating play for actors, and its challenges have been met in the professional production by Robert Goldsby at the Berkeley Stage Company.

The anti-Catholic theme is communicated in a different, symbolic mode in *Earth Worms*. Nuns who resemble Furies or the witches from *Macbeth* terrorize the husband and perform actions that reflect back on the play's dramatic events. The most terrifying of these is the surreal dance they perform with the dead infant impaled on a cross. Innaurato's alternation of these horrible symbolic gestures with squalid realistic scenes provides a loose form that supplies striking effects almost at random.

GEMINI

In *Gemini*, Innaurato deals with a similar group of people but shows them at an earlier age, when their environment is less decayed, their dreams still intact. This shift, accompanied by the change into a quick, complex, but more conventionally comic dialogue structure, transforms the same themes and grotesque character images into the material of farce. The audience, no longer directly addressed by a Benno figure, gains some perspective on the action; this distance from the bizarre world of Italian south Philadelphia is at least partially supplied by the introduction of two visitors from Harvard. The consternation of these attractive outsiders at the rude characters and strange twists of action guides the audience's response. In addition, Innaurato finally omits his obsessive, distracting attack on Catholicism, allowing full attention to be focused on the construction of the play itself.

The title character of the play, Francis Geminiani, is probably the most autobiographical hero in the playwright's first group of plays. A young Harvard (not Yale) student whose name symbolizes his split sexual inclinations, Francis acts out his sexual indecision in the playwright's old neighborhood. The hero also loves opera, using the music to express his moods and provide inspiration for important decisions. While Francis, like the playwright, thinks that he is pudgy, the genuinely grotesque traits of Benno Blimpie have been foisted off onto Herschel, a young next-door neighbor who is still childish enough that he arouses more laughter than pathos. In the serious plays, all kinds of sexuality seem disgusting, but in *Gemini* Innaurato introduces Bunny, a robust, tolerant neighbor who finds such humor and pleasure in her sex life that when Francis finally leaves home to work out his sexual preference, either choice on his part would seem to offer a healthy, comfortable conclusion. In *Gemini*, the parents are benevolent and encouraging, if embarrassingly provincial; they want to help Francis answer his questions about social and sexual values. Innaurato reduces his own didactic impulses to the level of a gentle, implied satire, and so raises issues without seeming maudlin or pathetic.

THE IDIOTS KARAMAZOV

One of Innaurato's most striking intellectual skills is his facility for comic allusion. He uses this talent sparingly in most cases, as a way to develop character voices. He has also, however, written whole plays based on allusion. The most successful of these plays is *The Idiots Karamazov*, a lampoon of nineteenth century Russian literature that was written with Christopher Durang at Yale. Apart from Fyodor Dostoevski, the play includes numerous references to Anton Chekhov; perhaps the most amusing moments are those when the two sources are combined, as when the Karamazov brothers enact portions of *Three Sisters*. The rapid-fire flow of allusive material includes many such incongruous turns, as well as several bizarre song-and-dance numbers that help to pace the laughter while providing a measure of relief from the intellectual demands of the dialogue scenes. Apart from the Russian sources, major roles are given to Constance Garnett, the aged "translatrix" whose

wandering mind presides over the play, and feminist writers Anaïs Nin and Djuna Barnes. These last two characters begin to control the action in act 2, when Innaurato's obsessions with death and decay emerge to dominate the play. Unfortunately, the comic effects subside proportionally in this second half of the text, giving way to a kind of enervated morbidity as the corpses pile up. Though it loses some steam at the end, the fantastic complexity and inspired satire of the first act is probably impossible to sustain for two hours. Even a master allusionist such as Tom Stoppard takes time out for weighty issues in the second act of *Travesties*. Unfortunately, however, the serious parts of *The Idiots Karamazov* cannot sustain the attention that the first half attracts.

ULYSSES IN TRACTION

Ulysses in Traction suffers from much the same gradual loss of energy. The first act manages to entertain through a number of devices: a satire of the David Rabe-style Vietnam drama, the gossipy sexual intrigue between cast members, and a world-as-drama-department twist on the *theatre mundi* theme. So long as the clever devices keep coming, the play retains an engaging novelty. In the second act, however, when a race riot outside the theater confines the actors, an introspective group analysis session begins that fails to reveal anything unusual or particularly moving about the selfish characters. Certain biographical parallels are obvious: Chapel University for Temple; Detroit for Philadelphia; a sexually disturbed M.F.A. playwright from Yale. Yet Innaurato seems to push away the personal aspect of the material, instead embracing sentimental abstractions to conclude the action and reconcile the characters. Innaurato's inability to pull political themes into the play, to develop a range of characters sympathetically, or to sustain his formal innovations reveals many of his limitations as a playwright. *Ulysses in Traction* begins with a pretentious premise, adopts a self-righteous tone, and then does not deliver. It has been the least successful of Innaurato's plays in professional production.

PASSIONE

In *Passione*, Innaurato retreats considerably from the challenges of *Ulysses in Traction*, and in doing so constructs one of his most appealing plays. Using familiar elements such as the south Philadelphia setting, Italian song, and vivid, obese characters, Innaurato composes an entertaining domestic play about giving relationships a second chance. This limited theme carries the play because it applies to a number of the characters. Aggy, a self-possessed woman who abandoned her family a decade ago, has returned to her husband's apartment to claim her belongings. Though she brings with her a hard-nosed sister named Sarah and expects no complications, the patient appeals of Berto, her former husband, finally convince her to remain. She also comes to accept her son, who had disappointed her by forsaking professional ambition for the love of a fat girl. Meanwhile, Sarah, strong and hostile, develops feelings for Renzo, a willful friend of Berto. The serious moments are interrupted throughout by the comic antics of Berto's senile father and Francine, a magnetic, robust beauty who works as the fat lady in a children's circus. There is little in the way of intrigue or character development, apart from Aggy's change of heart, and some of the rough-and-tumble action spins out of control, but *Passione*'s modest, conventional goals are well realized. The grotesque has become something cozy and commercial in *Passione*, a fact that perhaps says more about the changing taste of American theater audiences than it does about Innaurato's artistic development. The play is unmistakably Innaurato's, but it is also solidly second-rate.

COMING OF AGE IN SOHO

After *Passione*'s lukewarm reception, Innaurato suffered serious difficulty coming up with new material. He finally emerged from his dry spell with *Coming of Age in Soho*, a play that marks an important shift in several aspects of his work. Rather than Philadelphia, the setting is Soho, where the play's hero, having abandoned a comfortable but sexless marriage to declare his homosexuality, is now coincidentally trying to get over a case of writer's block. Unlike some of the earlier characters, such as Benno, this man, named Beatrice, is openly autobiographical, even if the precise circumstances of the play are fictitious. Innaurato seems to do his best work when he believes that it is both honest and witty, and with Beatrice he invented a strong vehicle for expression.

The play underwent an unusually extreme revision after its first tryouts. The script began with a female composer named Gioconda at its center; she was confronted by an unacknowledged son and his companion, a boy with whom she fell in love. Bartholomew Dante, or Beatrice, was merely the downstairs neighbor who harbored the rejected son. In the revised version, Gioconda was eliminated, the son was attributed to Beatrice, and the other boy's attraction was made homosexual. Many of the lines remained unchanged, and the author/director resumed production with a new confidence in the play.

Some of *Coming of Age in Soho* remains far-fetched, such as the Mafia connections of the former wife, yet the play generates a confident charm without resorting to grotesque images for its effects. The most successful aspect of the play is the character of the son, a German computer whiz whose frank appraisals of foreign situations lend a precocious, fresh tone to the whole work, much like that supplied by the two visitors in *Gemini*. The supporting characters tend to be young and tolerant, rather than old and decayed, so that Beatrice is able to indulge in his introspection in an encouraging atmosphere that is simple rather than barren. Once again, as with *Passione*, the themes are scarcely world-shaking—frequent references to the "health crisis" do not amount to confronting the impact of AIDS—yet the story is engaging and the dialogue articulate.

GUS AND AL

Innaurato's early acclaim caused the critical expectations about his subsequent work to be very high. *Gus and Al* demonstrates the pressure that Innaurato endures from the mostly negative critical response to his later plays, though in this case the press was rather friendly and indulgent in its evaluation of *Gus and Al*. The premise of the piece is that Al, an autobiographical character who lives with a talking gorilla, becomes so depressed over the reviews of his most recent play (presumably *Coming of Age in Soho*) that he tries to electrocute himself. Rather than dying, Al is transported from his contemporary Manhattan apartment to *fin de siècle* Vienna, where he meets one of his heroes, Gustav Mahler, who also suffered from hostile reviews. The artists strike up a friendship, share their impressions of the differences between their times, and become involved in the changes in Mahler's private life that begin to occur when they meet Alma Schindler (who eventually becomes Mahler's wife). Along the way, they also meet Freud, who seems strangely detached and irrelevant, as well as his Italian gardener, who seems insignificant only until Al realizes that this handsome young man is actually his own grandfather, Camillo Innaurato. The beauty and wonder of this encounter eventually bring Al to a new peace of mind, as he tells his grandfather (who cannot at the moment understand) that he loved him. Soon, Al is rescued by his landlady and his pet gorilla, Kafka, who have followed him back in time to report that not all the reviews were bad, after all. *Gus and Al* is probably Innaurato's most whimsical play, yet it succeeds precisely because it accepts in frank terms the subjective process of self-examination and public expression that Innaurato faces when he tries to write a new play for the New York theater. His tentative commitments to the Mahler story allow the charm of his personal voice to emerge more clearly than in any other play. Though Innaurato explained in an interview that he wrote the play to show his "well-upholstered derriere" to critics of his autobiographical technique, the play works because of its many more generous personal qualities; the point of the play, he goes on to say, is really the "struggling to keep going that every artist has always had."

MAGDA AND CALLAS

Innaurato has no built-in outlet for personal expression in *Magda and Callas*, and consequently the play tends to resemble the slightly off-center but still realistic writing of his Italian-American comedies. The only candidate for author-identification is Magda La Selva, an operatic diva, who returns to her mother's south Philadelphia home when she loses her voice. The mother, Nella, who writes romance novels with titles such as *Pasta on the Plains*, and Magda's first teacher, Rosalie, an amateur magician who has real visions, must consider ways to dissuade Magda from suicide. Meanwhile, Magda's teenage daughter, Callas, becomes acquainted with a neighborhood boy, Vito, and they begin a romance based on a com-

mon interest in heavy metal music. Rosalie invites Magda's former husband, Luther, for dinner; Luther, a black musician who was imprisoned for his role in a violent protest, is pleased to meet his daughter, Callas, for the first time, but his current work as a political activist in north Philadelphia has no place for a white former wife, nor does his commitment to politics allow him to respect classical music, which he forced himself to abandon. Any plans for a rebirth of romance between Luther and Magda collapse when his rebukes convince her to attempt suicide by slashing her wrists. At the same time, Nella had conceived another plan for Magda's salvation, inviting an old flame, Vito's father Bey (a policeman with a fear of bloodshed), to dinner as well. When Magda attempts her suicide, Rosalie expends all of her spiritual energy to help Bey overcome his fear of blood. He saves Magda, but Rosalie collapses and dies. A new romance develops between Bey and Magda, the whole group having been redeemed by Rosalie's sacrifice. The play attempts to use an odd mix of materials, from references to the grim realities in north Philadelphia's slums to a serious dramatic use of the spells cast by Rosalie, and the demands on credibility are probably greater than audiences of this otherwise conventional play can withstand. The final effect of Magda's rejuvenation, if disbelief can be suspended, is fairly uplifting. Yet *Magda and Callas* is finally a sloppy, giddy, not-quite-serious play that reads, in its "Plays in Process" publication, more like a draft than a finished work of art. It finds new ways to express many of Innaurato's passions, such as his love of opera or his concerns about the reality of human suffering, but the pieces do not quite fit into a recognizable whole, even though the style of the piece, and some aspects of its form, suggest that they should.

OTHER MAJOR WORKS

TELEPLAYS: *Verna, USO Girl*, 1978; *Coming Out*, 1989.

BIBLIOGRAPHY

Ahearn, Carol Bonomo. "Innaurato and Pintauro: Two Italian-American Playwrights." *Melus*. 15, no. 3 (Fall, 1989): 113. Ahearn examines the ethnic identity conflicts in the works of Innaurato and Joseph Pintauro.

Freedman, Samuel G. "Reshaping a Play to Reveal Its True Nature." *The New York Times*, February 24, 1985, p. B1. This article explains the process of revision that *Coming of Age in Soho* underwent as the gender orientation of the play changed and Beatrice displaced Giaconda as the central character.

Gussow, Mel. *Theatre on the Edge: New Visions, New Voices*. New York: Applause, 1998. Gussow discusses playwrights of modern theater, including Innaurato.

Innaurato, Albert. "An Interview with Albert Innaurato." Interview by John Louis Digaetani. *Studies in American Drama, 1945-Present* 2 (1987): 87-95. Innaurato offers his opinions about the plausibility of several different critical per-

spectives on his work, in addition to describing his major personal concerns.

Rothstein, Mervyn. "For Angry Innaurato, No Self-Effacement." *The New York Times*, March 20, 1989, p. C13. Innaurato explains his anger over the reviews he has received and how *Gus and Al* was conceived to prove to his critics that they were wrong to condemn his autobiographical tendencies.

Ventimiglia, Peter James. "Recent Trends in American Drama: Michael Cristofer, David Mamet, and Albert Innaurato." *Journal of American Culture* 1 (Spring, 1978): 195-204. Favorably compares Innaurato's early plays with the works of two other young writers, Cristofer's *The Shadow Box* (pr. 1975) and the many plays by Mamet that were produced at that time.

Michael L. Quinn

EUGÈNE IONESCO

Born: Slatina, Romania; November 26, 1909
Died: Paris, France; March 28, 1994

PRINCIPAL DRAMA

La Cantatrice chauve, pr. 1950, pb. 1954 (*The Bald Soprano*, 1956)

La Leçon, pr. 1951, pb. 1954 (*The Lesson*, 1955)

Les Chaises, pr. 1952, pb. 1954 (*The Chairs*, 1958)

Victimes du devoir, pr. 1953, pb. 1954 (*Victims of Duty*, 1958)

Le Maître, pr. 1953, pb. 1958 (*The Leader*, 1960)

La Jeune Fille à marier, pr. 1953, pb. 1958 (*Maid to Marry*, 1960)

La Nièce-Épouse, pr. 1953 (*The Niece-Wife*, 1971)

L'Avenir est dans les œufs: Ou, Il Faut de tout pour faire un monde, pr. 1953, pb. 1958 (*The Future Is in Eggs: Or, It Takes All Sorts to Make a World*, 1960)

Amédée: Ou, Comment s'en débarrasser, pr., pb. 1954 (*Amédée: Or, How to Get Rid of It*, 1955)

Jacques: Ou, La Soumission, pb. 1954, pb. 1955 (*Jack: Or, The Submission*, 1958)

Théâtre, pb. 1954-1966 (4 volumes)

Le Nouveau Locataire, pr. 1955, pb. 1958 (*The New Tenant*, 1956)

Le Tableau, pr. 1955, pb. 1963 (*The Picture*, 1968)

L'Impromptu de l'Alma: Ou, Le Caméléon du berger, pr. 1956, pb. 1958 (*Improvisation: Or, The Shepherd's Chameleon*, 1960)

Tueur sans gages, pr., pb. 1958 (*The Killer*, 1960)

Plays, pb. 1958-1965 (6 volumes)

Rhinocéros, pr. in German 1959, pb. 1959, pr. in French 1960 (*Rhinoceros*, 1959)

Les Salutations, pr. 1959, pb. 1963 (*Salutations*, 1968)

Scène à quatre, pr. 1959, pb. 1963 (*Foursome*, 1963)

Délire à deux, pr. 1962, pb. 1963 (*Frenzy for Two or More*, 1965)

Le Roi se meurt, pr. 1962, pb. 1963 (*Exit the King*, 1963)

Le Piéton de l'air, pr. 1962, pb. 1963 (*A Stroll in the Air*, 1964)

La Colère, pb. 1963 (*Anger*, 1968)

La Soif et la faim, pr. 1964, pb. 1966 (*Hunger and Thirst*, 1968)

La Lacune, pb. 1966, pr. 1969 (*The Oversight*, 1971)

L'Œuf dur: Pour préparer un œuf dur, pb. 1966, pb. 1970 (*The Hard-Boiled Egg*, 1973)

Jeux de massacre, pr., pb. 1970 (*Killing Game*, 1974; also pb. as *Wipe-out Games*, 1970)

Macbett, pr., pb. 1972 (English translation, 1973)

Ce Formidable Bordel, pr., pb. 1973 (*A Hell of a Mess*, 1975)

L'Homme aux valises, pr., pb. 1975 (*Man with Bags*, 1977)

Parlons française, pr. 1980

Voyages chez les morts: Ou, Thèmes et variations, pb. 1981 (*Journeys Among the Dead: Themes and Variations*, 1985)

OTHER LITERARY FORMS

Eugène Ionesco was known primarily for his plays. Over the years, however, he published memoirs and fiction worthy of critical attention; most notable are the memoirs *Journal en miettes* (1967; *Fragments of a Journal*, 1968) and *Présent passé passé présent* (1968; *Present Past Past Present*, 1972) and the novel *Le Solitaire* (1973; *The Hermit*, 1974). Successful as a playwright, Ionesco also surfaced occasionally as a theorist of the drama, notably in *Notes et contre-notes* (1962; *Notes and Counter-Notes*, 1964). Several of his better-known plays, including *The Killer* and *Rhinoceros*, were in fact developed from texts originally conceived, written, and published as short fiction; in addition, Ionesco published several highly innovative children's books that prove edifying to the adult reader as well.

ACHIEVEMENTS

Eugène Ionesco is rivaled only by Samuel Beckett as the world's best-known and most influential exponent of experimental drama, and he is credited with the development of new conventions according to which serious drama would henceforth have to be written and judged. A number of his early plays, such as *The Bald Soprano*, *The Lesson*, and *The Chairs*, are already established in the "permanent" dramatic repertory, along with Beckett's *En attendant Godot* (pb. 1952, pr. 1953; *Waiting for Godot*, 1954) and *Fin de partie* (1957; *Endgame*, 1958). Although his work differs sharply from Beckett's, both in concept and in execution, Ionesco is recorded as having welcomed Beckett's 1969 Nobel Prize in Literature as applicable partially to himself, in recognition of a kindred spirit. It is clear that, following the emergence of these playwrights, serious drama will never again be the same.

In 1971, two years after Beckett received the Nobel Prize, Ionesco found his own achievement honored by election to the highly conservative Académie Française, a turn of events that only a short time earlier might have seemed equally unthinkable to the playwright and to the institution. Perhaps it appeared for a time that the ultimate artistic anarchist had

Eugène Ionesco in Copenhagen in 1976. (Hulton Archive by Getty Images)

joined, or become, the establishment; in fact, it was the theater that had changed.

Discovered, according to his own account, by accident, Ionesco's singular approach to dramatic creation ultimately revolutionized the French—and international—stage as thoroughly as the imported work of Luigi Pirandello had a generation earlier. Casting doubt not only on dramatic conventions but also on more fundamental assumptions concerning the nature of language and the nature of humankind, Ionesco's chaotic and tragic vision proved, on reflection, even more anarchic than Beckett's lugubrious pessimism, to which it is frequently compared.

Unlike Beckett, Ionesco mistrusted language to such an extent that it assumes a distinctly minor function in his plays, considerably overshadowed by such visual elements as the gestures and placement of actors. For Ionesco, language was at best the means to an end, certainly never an end in itself. As a result, Ionesco's plays frequently prove unrewarding if they are merely read or considered simply as literature. Arguably, Ionesco's plays are in fact not literature at all, depending as heavily as they do on actors and directors for their completion. Once staged, however, Ionesco's plays turn out to be as profound and intellectually challenging as any drama ever written.

BIOGRAPHY

The writer now known to the world as Eugène Ionesco was born November 26, 1909, as Eugen Ionescu in Slatina, Romania. His father (and namesake) was a Romanian lawyer, and his mother, née Thérèse Ipcar, was the daughter of a French engineer working in Romania. (When fame sought out Ionesco in his early forties, he advanced his publicized birth date to 1912 in an effort to appear younger; as he approached the age of eighty, he reversed his original decision. Many reference sources, however, continue to cite his birth year as 1912 even years after his death at age eighty-four.)

Shortly after Ionesco's birth, his parents moved to Paris, where his father continued the study of law. In 1911 a daughter, Marilina, was born to the couple and in 1912 another son, Mircea, who would die in infancy of meningitis. In 1916 the elder Eugen Ionescu returned to Romania, presumably to take part in World War I, leaving his family in France. It later turned out that instead of serving in the military, he had joined the government police. After the war, even as his wife assumed that he had died in battle, he had used his political power to arrange for himself a convenient divorce and remarriage, adding insult to injury by demanding (and getting) custody of his children by his first wife. Thus it happened that the twelve-year-old Eugène returned with his sister to Romania, where he would continue and complete his studies.

By 1926, Thérèse Ipcar Ionescu had herself returned to Romania, settling in Bucharest where she found work in a bank. Following a dispute with his father and stepmother, young Eugène sought refuge in his mother's apartment, to which his sister had already escaped. By the time he completed his secondary education in 1928, he was living in a furnished room at the home of an aunt, his father's sister. The elder Ionescu, all the while refusing to pay alimony or child support, used his political connections to secure scholarships for his son at the University of Bucharest. Father and son would, however, remain divided on the issue of the son's studies, with the father favoring engineering over literature. Notwithstanding, the future playwright pursued a degree in French and became a regular contributor of poetry and criticism to various literary magazines. In 1934 he created a minor scandal with a volume entitled simply *Nu* (No!), a collection of articles questioning most of the major (Romanian) literary figures and movements of the day.

Married in 1936 to Rodica Burileanu, whom he had met during their student days some six years earlier, Ionesco taught French in various Romanian schools, remaining active as a contributor to literary journals. In 1938, he obtained from the Romanian government a grant to study French literature in Paris. His projected thesis, on the themes of sin and death in French poetry since Baudelaire, would remain unfinished and perhaps unwritten as Ionesco read the writings of such thinkers as Nikolai Berdayev, Gabriel Marcel, and Jacques Maritain. With the declaration of World War II in 1939, Ionesco returned with his wife to Romania, where he taught French at a Bucharest secondary school. Before long, however, he thought better of his move and began trying to get back to France, finally succeeding in May, 1942. A daughter, Marie-France, was born to the Ionescos in August, 1944. For the remainder of the decade, Ionesco earned a meager living on the fringes of literary life, dividing his work among translation, journalism, editorial work, and occasional teaching. During those years, the future playwright recalled, he studiously avoided the theater, dismissing its stock-in-trade as lies or, at the very least, a massive waste of time and energy.

By his own account, Ionesco blundered into playwriting quite by accident when, not long after World War II, he sought to broaden his employment prospects by learning English on his own time, with the help of a popular text-and-record set then readily available in bookstores. As the trained literary scholar and translator applied himself to his task, the seemingly random recital of phrases and phonemes began to make less and less sense. Named characters would, for example, inform one another of their names and relationships, then announce with finality that the floor was down, while the ceiling was up. Ionesco, soon losing all interest in the acquisition of English, began instead to jot down words and phrases as they rearranged themselves in his mind. When he had finished, the result looked rather like the script of a stage play, albeit a play such as had never before been seen or heard. Revised and reworked well into rehearsal, *The Bald Soprano* was eventually performed in May, 1950, at the Théâtre des Noctambules. The author, meanwhile, had begun to frequent avant-garde artistic and dramatic circles in Paris, most notably the Collège de 'Pataphysique, named in honor of the turn-of-the-century playwright Alfred Jarry, author of *Ubu roi* (wr. 1888, pr., pb. 1896; English translation, 1951).

Understandably reluctant at first, Ionesco soon warmed to the task of writing plays, having at last discovered what was evidently his true vocation; by 1952, he had seen two more of his plays in production, with others already written and waiting to be performed. He also found himself at the forefront of

what appeared to be a new kind of theater, soon to be joined by such other middle-aged authors as Samuel Beckett and Arthur Adamov, for both of whom, as for himself, French was essentially an adopted idiom. Incredibly, Ionesco continued to turn out new and baffling plays for years without repeating himself, drawing on a rich store of images and memories that had lain dormant since childhood. Only later did Ionesco's expression begin to seem labored, because, in part, of the consequences of an ill-advised "debate" initiated in the late 1950's by the British critic Kenneth Tynan.

Recalling such controversies of the 1930's as Marxist attacks on Thornton Wilder or Clifford Odets's rebuke of Pirandello for not openly opposing Benito Mussolini in his plays, Tynan's criticism of Ionesco (whose work he had at first championed) centered on the resolute antirealism and seeming "irrelevance" of Ionesco's dramatic expression, implying that the playwright was derelict in his duties as an artist and that such tendencies as his, if allowed to continue, would distract audiences from social and political problems urgently requiring their attention. Ridiculous though such charges may seem in retrospect, they provoked at the time a vigorous debate involving such peripheral figures as Philip Toynbee and Orson Welles. Ionesco, in defense of his art, wisely argued that art should serve no particular political creed but should remain a watchdog to all. Indeed, Ionesco's theater had already projected a profound sensitivity to human suffering, beyond politics in its defense of dignity and its aversion to posturing of any kind. Nevertheless, Ionesco proved to be peculiarly sensitive to the charges leveled against him, allowing at least one of his subsequent plays, *Rhinoceros*, to be interpreted as liberal social satire, presumably a bone thrown to pacify his more antagonistic critics. In fact, *Rhinoceros* is little different from Ionesco's other plays, written before or since, and collapses under the freight of political significance applied to it as if by afterthought.

From the early 1960's onward, Ionesco stressed the primacy of art, both in his plays and in his other writings, opposing in particular the Bertolt Brecht style of Social Realism that had asserted itself on the

Paris stage. As an artist, however, he became increasingly committed to the cause of intellectual and artistic freedom, particularly in Romania and other nations of the eastern bloc. During the 1970's and 1980's, despite increasingly frail health, he took part in a number of international colloquia both literary and political. He died March 28, 1994, at his home on the Boulevard Montparnasse in Paris and is buried in the Montparnasse Cemetery.

ANALYSIS

Although Eugène Ionesco's dramatic art is often traced to such precursors as the plays of Alfred Jarry and Antonin Artaud, it is essentially *sui generis*, springing primarily from nightmarish visions deeply rooted in the author's own mind and experience. In fact, two of his later plays, *A Hell of a Mess* and *Man with Bags*, can be traced directly to nightmares recorded in his autobiographical writings of the mid-1960's. As a boy, he recalled, he frequently attended puppet shows mounted for children in the Jardin de Luxembourg; during the years since, he remained haunted by the reverse relationship of human beings to marionettes, seeing his fellow mortals as puppets pulled by forces unseen and unexplained, prone to violence either as perpetrator or as victim. Puppetry must thus be seen as one of the strongest verifiable influences on Ionesco's theater, as on modern drama in general. Indeed, the grotesquely "flat" characters of *The Bald Soprano*, although immediately drawn from names assigned at random to dialogue in a language textbook, can readily be traced to a deeper, more fecund source in the tradition of the Punch and Judy show.

Critic Martin Esslin hailed Ionesco's theater as a far more effective illustration of Albert Camus's concept of the absurd than Camus himself had ever written for the stage. Forsaking the convenience of rational expression still relied on by Camus, Jean Anouilh, and even Jean-Paul Sartre, Ionesco—in Esslin's view—presents on the stage the absurd in its purest form, more true to life (if less "realistic") by the mere fact of its apparent gratuity. Indeed, it is difficult to imagine a more effective illustration of dehumanizing habit than is to be found among Ionesco's

peculiarly automated characters, whose aspirations (if any) have long since been separated from their lives. When death threatens (as it often does in the later plays), Ionesco's habit-conditioned characters will often proceed as lambs to the slaughter in a manner even more credible than the "philosophical suicide" described by Camus in *Le Mythe de Sisyphe* (1942; *The Myth of Sisyphus*, 1955) as a characteristic human response to the absurd.

Ionesco's memories of puppetry may also account for the strong visual element in his plays, more dependent on gesture and blocking than on the stage set itself, which may range from elaborate to nonexistent. (The most elaborate of Ionesco's stage sets are those that call for enormous quantities of objects, be they household furnishings or eggs, implying that humans are being crowded off the earth by the commodities used for their need or pleasure.) As noted, the spoken text itself is, as a rule, the least significant element of Ionesco's dramaturgy, literally "upstaged" by the posturing and placement of its characters. Dramatically, Ionesco's most effective use of language occurs in its deformation, with "normal" speech replaced either by incongruous banalities or by equally nonsensical monosyllables. Even so, it is possible to imagine certain of Ionesco's plays performed as pure pantomime; *Exit the King*, for example, was originally written in the form of a ballet. Certain critics, moreover, detected in Ionesco's dramaturgy a strong cinematic influence, primarily from silent films and those of the Marx Brothers.

Considered as a whole, Ionesco's work exhibits a number of different styles, each of them uniquely his own. Although it may be tempting to consider those styles as evolutionary stages, such analysis founders on the simple evidence that the styles do not necessarily occur in chronological order. *The Lesson*, for example, would appear at first glance to be more evolved and "later" than it really is.

There is also the matter of the Tynan debate, or London controversy as it has often been called among students of Ionesco's work. During the late 1950's, perhaps because of the debate, Ionesco began writing plays in which, for the first time, he appeared to be saying something specific; critics, noting the trend either with delight or with alarm, observed that his expression was somewhat weaker than in his earlier efforts. Yet, his expression had not really changed; the best of his apparently "didactic" plays, in retrospect, have much in common with the rest of his theater, both earlier and later. *Rhinoceros*, perhaps the weakest of the lot, is a highly typical Ionesco play, hampered mainly by the commonly held assumption of intended specific meaning.

One of Ionesco's more entertaining and edifying styles, although commonly associated with his shorter plays, involves the characters in aimless speech as the stage gradually fills with objects. In one of Ionesco's earliest plays, *The Chairs*, the two main characters keep bringing out chairs to seat an unseen multitude of guests. Although the proliferation of chairs is hardly the main point of the play, Ionesco clearly appreciated the visual effect and would use it again more than once, most notably in *The New Tenant*, in which furniture is carried onstage with difficulty inverse to its weight. At first, the movers struggle under the weight of bric-a-brac and table lamps; with their task well under way, they balance heavy chests delicately on the tips of their fingers. At the end, not only is the stage filled with furniture, but also presumably the streets and highways outside. The title character, who apparently owns all these things, asks only that the landlady turn out the lights as she leaves him; in a rather obvious effort to rediscover the prenatal state, he has long since been hidden from view by his possessions.

Easily appreciated or understood at a preconscious level, yet subject to varied interpretations, Ionesco's imagery has brought to the stage sights and sounds that would tax the ingenuity and imagination of even the most resourceful designers. In a variation on the proliferation theme, for example, the characters of *Amédée* share the stage with a growing corpse that is about to crowd them out of house and home; what usually shows of this monstrosity is a man's shoe, approximately three meters in length, with sock and trouser leg attached. In *Hunger and Thirst*, the furniture must be specially designed so that it will sink into the floorboards as if into mud. In *Exit the King*, similarly, the king's throne must simply vanish from the stage while the curtain remains open. Not all of the headaches fall upon the set designer alone; two of Ionesco's plays call for an "attractive" female character with multiple noses and breasts.

Whether (as is doubtful) Ionesco's dramaturgy was in any way influenced by Camus's speculations on the absurd, his writings, both expository and creative, give evidence of a deep sensitivity and strong moral conscience of the sort commonly associated with *The Myth of Sisyphus* and its author. Although more visceral than cerebral, Ionesco's expression adds up to one of the most deeply humanitarian statements in contemporary literature, haunted by a nagging doubt that humankind will ever assimilate the evident lessons of history. Ionesco's King Bérenger, the Everyman protagonist of *Exit the King*, meets and surpasses in his life and death the anguished declaration of Camus's *Caligula* (1954; English translation, 1948) that men die and are not happy; resuming in his modest person the history of all human endeavor, King Bérenger remains lucid even in his final moments, painfully aware that all has gone for nought. Elsewhere in Ionesco's theater, nearly all forms of human behavior are duly stripped of acculturated meaning, shown to be as absurd and out of phase as they often seemed to Camus himself. In *Jack: Or, The Submission* and *The Future Is in Eggs*, for example, courtship and marriage are reduced to the least attractive stereotypes, characterized by animal noises, obscene rutting gestures, and a quantitative standard for human reproduction. In *Amédée*, the telephone-operator wife "goes to work" at a switchboard in her own apartment while her husband, a writer, labors over the same phrases that have occupied him fruitlessly for years. The theme of repetition, dominant in several plays that end exactly as they began, bears further witness to the apparent futility of all human endeavor. Beneath it all, however, the viewer can perceive a strong nostalgia for lost innocence, or at least for things as they ought to be. In each of his plays, Ionesco seems to be exhorting his audience to "rehumanize" the world before matters get worse than they already are.

Striking in its imagery and resonance, Ionesco's theater remains one of the more durable bodies of work in twentieth century drama. Although uneven in quality, perhaps least effective when the author seemed to have a specific message in mind, his theater is nevertheless sufficiently rich and varied to provide rewarding work for future generations of actors and directors. At the turn of the twenty-first century, the strongest of his plays were in frequent production around the world, performed by professional and amateur actors alike. In retrospect, it appears fortunate that the playwright never capitulated fully to his detractors' stated demands for relevance; his theater, perennially relevant to basic human needs and tendencies, stands as a useful, even necessary mirror through which to study human behavior, both individual and social.

THE BALD SOPRANO

The Bald Soprano, Ionesco's first play, served clear notice of a major new talent and remains his best-known effort and the one most frequently performed. Rivaled only by Beckett's *Waiting for Godot* as a classic of the contemporary drama, *The Bald Soprano* (produced in London as the *The Bald Prima Donna*) is neither the strongest nor the weakest of Ionesco's plays; it is surely, however, among the most memorable.

Set against the stuffy banality of a bourgeois household (Ionesco himself suggested the use of a set prepared for Henrik Ibsen's *Hedda Gabler*, 1890, English translation, 1891), *The Bald Soprano* begins with the dour, machine-voiced Mrs. Smith informing her husband that it is nine o'clock. The grandfather clock, however, has just struck seventeen times. Silent except for the regular clucking of his tongue, Smith puffs on his pipe as he reads the evening paper, held upside down. Mrs. Smith, seemingly oblivious to his lack of interest, continues to discuss the fine English food that they have eaten (including such anomalous dishes as quince-and-bean pie) and tell him the ages of their children. If Mrs. Smith's monologue seems increasingly surreal, the dialogue becomes even more so as Smith, still reading the paper, expresses amazement that the ages of the deceased are routinely printed in the papers, while those of newborns never are. Husband and wife then discuss a recent operation that the surgeon first performed on

himself; even so, the patient died. A good doctor, opines Smith, should die with his patient, just as a captain should go down with his ship. Discussion of an apparent obituary for one Bobby Watson soon elicits the further information that the man has been dead for three years, that he left a truly well-preserved corpse, that his wife (also named Bobby Watson, as are their son and daughter) is unattractive because she is too dark, too fat, too pale, and too thin. All traveling salespeople, it seems, are also known as Bobby Watson, and vice versa.

Before long, the Smiths' maid interrupts to announce the arrival of their invited guests, Mr. and Mrs. Martin. Although introduced as husband and wife, the Martins (in what has since become one of the most famous scenes in contemporary drama) begin speaking to each other with all the tentative awkwardness of a pickup between strangers on a train. Gradually, expressing amazement with each passing coincidence, the Martins discover that they live in the same town, on the same street, in the same building, on the same floor, in the same apartment, and sleep in the same bed. Cleverly mocking every recognition scene known to conventional theater, Ionesco locks the couple in a passionate embrace, only to have the maid announce that the Martins are not husband and wife or even who they think they are, since her daughter and his daughter are not the same person, having eyes of different color on each side of the face.

Once admitted to the Smiths' parlor, the Martins join their hosts in what may well be the most effective parody of social interaction ever portrayed on the stage; all four participants hem and haw, clear their throats, and let one another's conversational gambits drop with a resounding thud. Ionesco's true intentions, however, clearly lie deeper than mere parody, and the conversation soon degenerates into a nightmare of cross-purposes interrupted (and complicated) by the arrival of an even more gratuitous personage, the Fire Chief. The Chief, it seems, is making his rounds in search of possible fires; his arrival, meanwhile, has been preceded by a long discussion of whether the ringing of a doorbell indicates the presence of someone at the door. (The bell in fact sounds three times, at rather long intervals, before the Chief sees fit to show himself.) Once inside, the Chief avails himself of celebrity treatment to regale his hosts with a long, involved, and totally nonsensical story prefaced with the title, "The Head-Cold." The maid, attempting a story of her own, is pushed brutally offstage by the other characters and possibly beaten to death; in any event, she is not seen again.

Once the Chief has left, conversation among the four main characters resumes with a gabble of inapposite proverbs, soon degenerating into nonsense syllables shouted with great vehemence, simulating quite effectively the sounds of a genuine argument among four people. At the end, the syllables assume the regular rhythm of a chuffing locomotive, whereupon the curtain falls. A brief final scene recapitulates the first, with the Martins instead of the Smiths.

In its current and final form, *The Bald Soprano* incorporates many evolutionary changes said to have occurred in the course of production. At first, Ionesco admitted, he had no real idea of how to end the play, having once considered (and rejected) the arrival of armed "police" to clear the house of spectators. Later, he decided on a reprise of the opening scene with the Smiths, replacing them still later with the Martins to reinforce the notion of interchangeability already manifest in the Bobby Watson dialogue. Even the play's title is claimed as an addition, having occurred when an actor playing the Fire Chief in rehearsal misspoke the phrase "*institutrice blonde*" ("blonde schoolmistress") as "*cantatrice chauve*" (roughly, "bald primadonna" or "bald soprano"). Supposedly, the actress playing Mrs. Smith ad-libbed the line, "She still wears her hair the same way," and the hitherto untitled play was on its way. Although such an explanation may well be apocryphal, the fact remains that much of *The Bald Soprano* as it is now known was improvised in production, proving (among other things) the impressive fluidity of Ionesco's developing talent.

THE LESSON

To those spectators falsely conditioned by the nonsense title of *The Bald Soprano*, the action of *The Lesson* may well have come as a rude shock. Although his first play calls for no vocalist, or even any

bald person, *The Lesson* has very much to do with instruction, as seen in its most negative aspects. If knowledge is power, the play seems to be saying, it can also be used as a weapon, either political or sexual.

In fact, there is no evidence that the Professor of *The Lesson* really knows anything—except perhaps, on occasion, the techniques of psychological manipulation. His important-sounding lectures are by turns banal, nonsensical, irrelevant, and self-contradictory; yet the torrent of verbiage that pours forth from his mouth soon reduces his young, strong, confident Pupil to utter helplessness in anticipation of her inevitable death. Mild-mannered and tentative at the outset, the elderly Professor gains such confidence from the sound of his own voice that he is quite plausibly capable of murder, committed with an invisible knife made manifest by words.

Recapitulating the frequent use of nonsense dialogue in *The Bald Soprano*, Ionesco in *The Lesson* at first disorients the spectator with the Pupil who, armed merely with a schoolgirl's book bag, confidently announces her intention to pursue the "total doctorate"; even so, she is shaky on elementary geography and utterly unable to subtract, although she can multiply six-digit numbers in her head. When asked to account for the latter talent, she calmly replies that she has memorized all possible products. As in the earlier play, incipient tragedy is never far removed from comedy, and *The Lesson*, for all its sense of impending doom, is well provided with hilarious moments.

Despite obvious elements of political satire (increasingly evident toward the end of the play), the predominant tone of *The Lesson* is sexual. The Pupil, for all her apparent innocence, is a highly provocative figure only dimly aware of her powers. The Professor, helpless and seemingly tongue-tied in the presence of his acerbic Housekeeper, responds to the Pupil's implicit provocation with increasingly violent and eventually murderous aggression. As the Housekeeper has warned him, "philology leads to the worst"; for Ionesco, "philology" here connotes not a "love of language" but a penchant pursued past the point of addiction. The Professor seems to exist only when, and because, he speaks. Language covers a multitude of probable sins, acquiring hypnotic powers quite beyond the scope of logic. For some, *The Lesson* symbolizes the inherently sexual nature of all teaching, which involves, at least in its intent, an act of penetration. Such an interpretation gathers further momentum from a Sartrean interpretation, whereby the Professor hides inauthentically behind his function in order to brutalize and terrorize a world that has long threatened him.

The Lesson retains such resonance as to resist simplistic attempts at explanation. For all its weaknesses (especially the anticlimactic ending), the play presents an arresting and still original deformation and reformation of human behavior and is one of Ionesco's best-realized expressions of a nightmarish vision.

THE CHAIRS

Initially baffling even to those spectators familiar with *The Lesson* and *The Bald Soprano*, *The Chairs* broke new ground in the development of Ionesco's theater by introducing a poetic element of which his earlier plays had given little indication. Although connected to the earlier plays by nonsense elements, disconnected speech, and disorientation of the spectator, *The Chairs* establishes a thoughtful, elegiac tone that anticipates both *Exit the King* and the best plays of Beckett, whose *Waiting for Godot* was soon to be produced for the first time.

Like *The Lesson*, *The Chairs* vigorously rejects simplistic efforts at interpretation, although on the surface it might be said to be "about" love, marriage, aging, and, above all, the futility of all human endeavor. Both individually and as a pair, the nonagenarian couple with the main speaking parts recapitulate in their behavior all stages of human life, from babyhood to extreme old age. By turns pathetic and ridiculous, frequently sympathetic, the Old Man and the Old Woman represent as effectively as Hamm and Clov, of Beckett's *Endgame*, the human need to "mean something," even against insuperable odds.

Set inside a tower on a remote and sparsely populated island, *The Chairs* presents the old couple in what will be their final moments, as the Old Man prepares to leave his testament for all humanity. The tes-

tament, it seems, is in the form of a speech that the Old Man has prepared from the raw material of his long life, but which he feels unqualified to deliver in his own voice. For the momentous occasion, he has hired a professional Orator, who will deliver the speech to a carefully selected assemblage of invited dignitaries including the Emperor himself.

In time, the distinguished guests begin to arrive, greeted and seated by the delighted and understandably anxious old couple. The audience, however, never sees the guests, who are represented onstage by a rapidly growing number of empty chairs—hence the play's title. Gesturing and grimacing in a worthy parody of Marcel Proust's aristocratic hosts, the old couple continue to seat their invisible audience; the Orator, however, is quite visible, and as soon as the Emperor arrives (unseen), the action is ready to begin. Sure at last that he has not lived in vain, his message about to be delivered, the Old Man leaps to his death from a tower window, followed closely by his wife. When the Orator rises to speak, however, he proves to be a deaf-mute (or at least tongue-tied). Turning at last to an available blackboard, the Orator fares hardly better, managing at best a meaningless gabble of words, letters, and fragments. Lest the spectator, however, leap to the conclusion that the Orator's audience has been hallucinated by the old couple, Ionesco calls in his script for crowd noises that, in production, tend to sound like a cross between applause and howls of derision. The audience, invisible or not, is still in evidence. *The Chairs* remains, like its predecessor, hauntingly enigmatic, reflecting back on the spectator his own attempts to determine the play's meaning.

THE KILLER

Following the belated success of *The Chairs*, Ionesco embarked on the most prolific phase of his career, producing more than a dozen short sketches and one-act plays as well as his first full-length plays, including *Amédée* and *Victims of Duty*. It was also during this period that the author's earliest and best-known work gave rise to the revisionist London controversy, involving (as have many similar disputes in the twentieth century) the social role of the writer as seen from the political Left. By 1958, Ionesco stood persuasively accused (by Kenneth Tynan and others) of shunning his appropriate function in favor of nonsense theater, which is irrelevant by definition. Among the greater of ironies is that Ionesco, a man truly displaced by two world wars, gave evidence even in his earliest plays of a profound social conscience. Nevertheless, his deep-seated mistrust of political extremism on both sides left him peculiarly vulnerable to charges of political indifference. Like George Orwell before him, Ionesco aroused the ire of doctrinaire liberals by rejecting their proposed "solutions" as well as those offered from the Right. In any event, it appears in retrospect that Ionesco may well have taken the criticism very much to heart, much as he professed not to in such documents as *Notes and Counter-Notes*. Toward the end of the 1950's Ionesco's plays seemed to strive increasingly for political relevance, with decidedly uneven results. In the strongest of these efforts, however, Ionesco retained his unique personal stamp with plays that resist any attempt to assign arbitrary political significance. *The Killer*, in particular, functions effectively as satire while going far deeper in its analysis of human aspirations and behavior. While waxing eloquent about the abuses of political power, *The Killer* also has much to say about the simple imperfectibility of human nature and the inevitability of death.

Partially set in a futuristic "Radiant City," probably inspired by the projections of the architect Le Corbusier, *The Killer* marks the first appearance of the protagonist Bérenger, a partially autobiographical Everyman-figure to be featured in several more plays of Ionesco's middle period. Arriving in Radiant City, which is surrounded by several darker neighborhoods, Bérenger is astounded to learn that most common problems and ailments have been banished from the area for good. His guide, the Architect (who also functions as police chief and coroner), explains that nothing has been left to chance, and that even the weather is controlled. Unfortunately, the streets are empty; eventually, the Architect explains to Bérenger that the inhabitants are hesitant to leave their homes for fear of an unknown killer, who lures people to their deaths by promising a glimpse of "the colonel's photograph."

Based on a short story in fact entitled "La Photo du colonel" ("The Colonel's Photograph"), *The Killer* quickly departs from simple satire in its deliberately uncertain distinction between the act of murder and the basic fact of death. If curiosity kills the cat, it doubtless kills people as well; whatever the "colonel's photograph" may indeed be like, it represents, among other things, the irrational element implicit in all human behavior. In French, the play's title suggests an unpaid, hence gratuitous killer, and in many respects the Killer differs little from the conventional figure of the Grim Reaper.

If death is inevitable, *The Killer* is not, however, without distinct political overtones. Employees of the state, it seems, enjoy guaranteed immunity from the Killer's assaults, a fact made painfully evident when Mlle Dany, the Architect's secretary and the woman of Bérenger's dreams, resigns her job only to fall victim soon after to the Killer. Another plainly political element is evident in the person of Mother Peep ("la mère Pipe"), a demagogue and rabble-rouser who has risen to prominence of sorts as keeper of the public geese. Divorced from the context of the play, the masterly scene depicting Mother Peep's rally might well be seen as one of the most powerful parodies of demagoguery and totalitarianism ever portrayed on the stage. Restored to context, however, the scene ultimately provides still further evidence of the absurd, together with the Killer himself. Political satire thus serves, for Ionesco, as the means to an end, rather than as an end in itself.

Motivated primarily by his desire to avenge Mlle Dany's apparently senseless murder, Bérenger sets off on a dogged search for the Killer, often appearing to be the only sane man (or indeed the only human being) in a world turned upside down. After adventures involving several cases of mistaken identity, Bérenger at last comes face to face with his quarry, an apparently feeble, one-eyed individual who, according to Ionesco, may or may not actually appear on the stage, according to the wishes of the individual director. In any case, the Killer has no real lines to speak, serving mainly as foil to Bérenger's impassioned, eloquent (and perhaps overlong) speech in defense of life, liberty, and the human race. As close to lyricism as Ionesco had thus far come in his career, Bérenger's speech in *The Killer* remains a powerful statement in defense of humanity; predictably, however, it falls on deaf ears, and Bérenger, out of options, offers himself freely to the Killer's brandished knife.

More ambitious in scope than any of Ionesco's earlier efforts for the stage, *The Killer* seemed to move his career into a new phase, partially satisfying those critics who had assailed his earlier work for its "irrelevance." It seems likely, however, that such critics may have seen primarily what they wanted to see; despite obvious political overtones, *The Killer* seems far closer to Ionesco's characteristic mode of expression than it may at the time have been supposed. In any case, it was not long before the critics were presented with a new object of study, the well-known and still controversial *Rhinoceros*.

RHINOCEROS

First produced within a year after *The Killer* (to which it is related by the character of Bérenger), *Rhinoceros* remains the best-known and most frequently performed of Ionesco's later plays, quite probably for the wrong reasons. Although decidedly weaker than *The Killer*, *Rhinoceros* is not without its strengths; unfortunately, those strengths tend to be slighted by directors and spectators alike, in favor of those elements providing the play with its apparent "relevance."

Considering the heat generated at the height of the so-called London Controversy, it is perhaps not surprising that Ionesco proved more willing than usual to allow the attachment of literal significance to one of his more ambitious efforts. Unfortunately, the play itself, although up to Ionesco's usual standards, tends to collapse under the weight of "meaning" applied from without.

Last seen in *The Killer* as an eloquent advocate of human nature, Bérenger makes his entry in *Rhinoceros* in a decidedly more passive role, as an easygoing if rather morose fellow who would prefer, when possible, to be left alone. Indeed, he tries as long as possible to go about his business, despite the gathering invasion of rhinoceroses, whose bizarre trumpeting can be heard from the street below. Indeed, the device of the proliferating pachyderms is every bit as

powerful and eloquent as that of a gratuitous murderer in the previous play. Perceived at first as invaders from outside, the pachyderms are gradually seen to be emerging among the populace as well. A certain Mme Boeuf at first flees in terror from a trumpeting beast, only to recognize (somehow) in its voice the accents of her missing husband: She rides happily off on the animal's back in a parody of the traditional recognition scene rivaled only by the Martins of *The Bald Soprano*. Characters around Bérenger begin to talk and act strangely, finding the invaders handsome and their language beautiful, far more so than the "merely" human. It is not long before transformations from man to beast become an hourly occurrence, with the animals taking over local businesses and ultimately the broadcast media. At the time of the play's introduction, Ionesco readily admitted to obvious parallels between "rhinoceritis" and the rise of Nazi Germany from the decadent Weimar Republic. Unfortunately, his acknowledgment served to authorize a fixed interpretation of a play which, in true Ionesco fashion, is in its essence open-ended and fraught with ambiguities.

If staged without preconceptions as to meaning, *Rhinoceros* quickly emerges as one of Ionesco's more unsettling staged nightmares, less effective than *The Killer* but nearly as resonant as *The Lesson*. Unfortunately, deliberate efforts to present *Rhinoceros* as antifascist propaganda rob the play of one of its more haunting qualities, implicit in the characterization of Bérenger.

Quite unlike his earlier avatar in *The Killer*, the Bérenger of *Rhinoceros* is neither eloquent nor potentially heroic. Indeed, one of the major tensions latent in the play as written resides in the passivity of Bérenger, in his anguished uncertainty as to whether he *could* turn into a rhinoceros even if he so wished. His refusal to capitulate, articulated in the final scene and hailed by critics as proof of Ionesco's "message," emerges from the context of the play in accents not of heroism but of desperation. Bérenger alone remains the last human being on earth, less because he will not change than because he simply *cannot*. If viewed with sufficient objectivity, *Rhinoceros* thus emerges as a chilling portrayal of an individual in a society, any society, ostracized by his or her fellows for reasons that cannot be fully comprehended. It is possible that future generations of actors and directors may well discover the latent subtext of *Rhinoceros* and restore the play to its rightful place among Ionesco's more disorienting nightmare visions. In the meantime, *Rhinoceros* remains hampered by its prevalent literal interpretation, far less effective as polemic than such overtly political plays as those of Bertolt Brecht or the later Adamov. Neither fish nor fowl, *Rhinoceros*, as commonly interpreted, can neither swim nor fly. To Ionesco's ultimate credit, however, it remains a better play than it seems.

EXIT THE KING

Rivaled only by *The Killer*, *Exit the King* is perhaps the strongest and best realized of Ionesco's later plays, deserving more frequent revivals than it has received. Deceptively simple both in concept and in execution, *Exit the King* harks back to *The Killer* and *The Chairs* in its portrayal of a royal Bérenger awaiting death. Deftly compressing all of human history into a single life-experience, Ionesco presents a King Bérenger who, during several centuries of life and rule, has invented the airplane and the bicycle, has pseudonymously written all the plays and sonnets attributed to William Shakespeare, and has personally built all the major cities in Western Europe. By now, however, his kingdom is crumbling, its monuments are in ruins, and his rule is crippled by anarchy. The action of the play compresses some twenty years, indicated by Queen Marguerite's assertion that the king will be dead within an hour and a half, at the end of the play.

Inevitably reminiscent of Camus's *Caligula*, whose historically inspired imperial protagonist substitutes his own caprices for those of an incomprehensible natural order, Ionesco's King Bérenger suffers primarily from an awareness of the simple fact that people die and are not happy. Like the Old Man of *The Chairs*, Bérenger has lived and labored in vain; unlike the Old Man, he knows as much, vigorously protesting the unfairness of his fate. Resuming in his person the lives of all who have ever suffered, worked, or dreamed, Bérenger ultimately speaks in his anguish to the futility of all human endeavor

given the eventuality of death, a finality as capricious as the actions of The Killer in the first of the Bérenger plays.

Surprisingly, in the light of its evident ambitions, *Exit the King* genuinely works, both as text and in production. Ponderousness of tone is avoided largely through Ionesco's choice of supporting characters; the king's protracted final moments are witnessed by both of his queens (one young and pretty, the other middle-aged and tart of tongue), a guard, and a Doctor who serves also as Astrologer and Chief Executioner. Among them, the characters provide for a strong infusion of humor, if never "comic relief." The aging Queen Marguerite, clearly descended from Mrs. Smith and from Madeleine of *Amédée*, continues the satire of marriage that runs as an undercurrent through many Ionesco plays; the younger Queen Marie, meanwhile, seems to represent maternal warmth as well as the promise of young love. The Doctor, who has aided and abetted the king in many of his Promethean schemes, frequently provides a perfect foil for the king's thoroughly human grievances. In an evident parody of the political slogan "Every man a king," Ionesco presents a king who is indeed Everyman and whose life will be nullified as well as ended with his death. In the French title, the use of the reflexive construction reinforces the notion that death is a process rather than a mere event; the king, implies Ionesco, is dying—as are all men and women from the moment of their birth.

Exit the King remains among the most eloquent and economical of Ionesco's dramatic statements, surpassing most of his subsequent efforts. *Hunger and Thirst*, for all its innovative brilliance, is sententious and often confused; *Killing Game* reiterates what Ionesco had already said, and said better, in such earlier efforts as *The Killer* and *The Chairs*. Of Ionesco's later efforts, only *Man with Bags* approaches the concise statement and eloquent imagery to be found in such plays as *The Killer* and *Exit the King*.

MAN WITH BAGS

Based in large measure on nightmare visions already recorded in Ionesco's memoirs, *Man with Bags* ironically inverts, intentionally or not, the title and premise of Jean Anouilh's immensely popular 1937 play, *Le Voyageur sans bagage* (*Traveller Without Luggage*, 1959). Anouilh's play, in part a parody of the Oedipus theme, presents an amnesiac war veteran who, reunited with his true family after twenty years and countless false leads, seeks refuge in amnesia against a sordid past that he has no desire to reclaim. Rejecting the obviously valid claims of the Renaud family, the pseudonymous Gaston opts instead for outright fantasy, declaring that he is "washed clean" of his youth, and indeed of his identity. It remained for Ionesco, however, to explore even in his earliest efforts the horrific consequences that result when identity is lost or denied. Whether the individual likes it, identity (especially as retrieved through memory) is the only available proof of his existence. It therefore seemed quite fitting that Ionesco, nearly forty years after *Traveller Without Luggage*, should balance Anouilh's speculative fantasy with a highly convincing rebuttal.

Despite the strong infusion of dream elements in such earlier plays as *The Chairs*, *The Killer*, and *A Stroll in the Air*, *Man with Bags* is the first of Ionesco's efforts to be characterized by its author as a dream play. Ionesco, who, by the time of the play's introduction, was well acquainted with the precepts and procedures of Jungian psychoanalysis, readily conceded that his characters were in fact archetypes and that the play represented an attempt to explore human identity through dreams. No longer known as Bérenger, the autobiographical protagonist is identified simply as "The Man" or "No-man," the latter an obvious recollection of the pseudonym chosen by Odysseus during his encounter with the Cyclops. Another archetype strongly recalled by the protagonist in his adventures and behavior is that of the Wandering Jew. In a succession of scenes shifting wildly in space and time, the man travels resolutely in search of both his ancestry and his identity, accompanied only by the "luggage" of his memory.

Unlike such earlier dream plays as those of August Strindberg and those attempted by the Surrealists, *Man with Bags* abounds in the sharp, seemingly realistic detail to be found in actual dreams. Linked by the preconscious logic peculiar to the dream expe-

rience, the scenes are striking in their imagery and often memorable. In one, for example, an old woman converses animatedly with her long-lost mother; the actress playing the mother is in her young and vibrant twenties, the age at which the old woman last saw her. Political elements such as bureaucracy, war, and oppression are present in abundance, although portrayed (as usual in Ionesco's work) without emphasis, as yet another anomalous fact of life, such as death. As in real dreams, sexual fantasies are juxtaposed with philosophical and political ones. In another memorable scene, the protagonist is propositioned by a married woman and accepts the offer in full view of her apparently willing husband, who agrees to keep an eye on the protagonist's luggage; the assignation then takes place in a public park ominously filled with armed guards. In the final scene, the man pauses to rest on one of his suitcases while the other characters rush about with their own luggage, vigorously pursuing the quest for identity of which the man himself has now grown tired. He does not, however, abandon or drop his own luggage; no doubt he will soon rise to his feet and continue as before. Memories, suggested Ionesco, remain the only proof that people have concerning the fact of their own individual passages through life.

OTHER MAJOR WORKS

LONG FICTION: *Le Solitaire*, 1973 (*The Hermit*, 1974).

SHORT FICTION: *La Photo du colonel*, 1962 (*The Colonel's Photograph*, 1967).

SCREENPLAY: *La Vase*, 1970 (*The Mire*, 1973).

RADIO PLAY: *Le Salon de l'automobile*, 1952 (*The Motor Show*, 1963).

NONFICTION: *Nu*, 1934; *Notes et contre-notes*, 1962 (*Notes and Counter-Notes*, 1964); *Journal en miettes*, 1967 (*Fragments of a Journal*, 1968); *Présent passé passé présent*, 1968 (memoir; *Present Past Past Present*, 1972); *Un Homme en question*, 1979; *Le Blanc et le noir*, 1980; *Hugoliade*, 1982 (*Hugoliad: Or, The Grotesque and Tragic Life of Victor Hugo*, 1987); *La Quête intermittente*, 1988.

CHILDREN'S LITERATURE: *Story Number 1: For Children Under Three Years of Age*, 1969; *Story*

Number 2: For Children Under Three Years of Age, 1970; *Story Number 3: For Children over Three Years of Age*, 1971; *Story Number 4: For Children over Three Years of Age*, 1975.

BIBLIOGRAPHY

Coe, Richard N. *Ionesco: A Study of his Plays*. London: Methuen, 1971. The latest of several volumes written on Ionesco by the same critic beginning in 1961; the present volume includes a translation of the hitherto unpublished short play *The Niece-Wife*.

Esslin, Martin. *The Theater of the Absurd*. Reprint. Garden City, N.Y.: Doubleday, 1968. Esslin's ground-breaking study remains authoritative on Ionesco's theater and on its situation within the context of twentieth-century avant-garde drama.

Gaensbauer, Deborah B. *Eugène Ionseco Revisited*. New York: Twayne, 1996. Replaces an earlier volume (1972) by Allan Lewis in Twayne's World Authors Series; generally sound critical and historical presentation of Ionesco's dramatic canon and its legacy.

Lane, Nancy. *Understanding Eugène Ionesco*. Columbia: University of South Carolina Press, 1994. Published just before Ionesco's death, Lane's study is among the first to take note of Ionesco's corrected birth date and other biographical details; generally sound readings of the major plays.

Nottingham French Studies 35, no. 1 (1996). Edited by Steven Smith. A special Ionesco issue of the journal published by the University of Nottingham, collecting a dozen articles dealing with all aspects of the author's thought and theater. Contributors include David Bradby, Ingrid Coleman Chafee, Emmanuel Jacquart, and Rosette Lamont.

David B. Parsell,
updated by David B. Parsell

DAVID IVES
David Roszkowski

Born: Chicago, Illinois; 1951

PRINCIPAL DRAMA

The Lives and Deaths of the Great Harry Houdini, pr. 1982

Words, Words, Words, pr. 1987, pb. 1994

Sure Thing pr. 1988, pb. 1994

Ancient History, pr. 1989, pb. 1990

Four Short Comedies, pb. 1989

Philip Glass Buys a Loaf of Bread, pr. 1990, pb. 1994

Foreplay: Or, The Art of Fugue, pr. 1991, pb. 1994

The Red Address, pr., pb. 1991

The Secret Garden, pr. 1991 (adaptation from the book, with Greg Pliska)

Variations on the Death of Trotsky, pr. 1991, pb. 1994

All in the Timing, pr. 1993, pb. 1994

The Philadelphia, pr. 1993, pb. 1994

The Universal Language, pr. 1993, pb. 1994

English Made Simple, pr. 1994, pb. 1995

Degas, C'est Moi, pr. 1995, pb. 1997

Don Juan in Chicago, pr., pb. 1995

Land of Cockaigne and English Made Simple, pb. 1995

Mere Mortals, pr. 1997, pb. 1998

Time Flies, pr. 1997, pb. 2000

Babel's In Arms, pr. 1999, pb. 2000

Captive Audience, pr. 1999, pb. 2000

Enigma Variations, pr. 1999, pb. 2000

Lives of the Saints, pr. 1999, pb. 2000

Long Ago and Far Away and Other Short Plays, pb. 1999

Arabian Nights, pr., pb. 2000

Polish Joke, pr. 2000

Time Flies and Other Short Plays, pb. 2001

OTHER LITERARY FORMS

Some of David Ives's first attempts at professional writing were for the film world. He lived in Hollywood early in his career, developing scripts for television movies. He also worked as a staff writer for the Fox network television series *Urban Anxiety* (1990). Later in his career, Ives's reputation made him a popular choice as a writer of stage banter for performers such as illusionist David Copperfield and shows such as *Ira Gershwin at One Hundred: A Celebration at Carnegie Hall* (1997). He has written a humorous regular column, "Endpaper," for *New York Times Magazine*, short fiction for the *Kenyon Review*, and nonfiction for *The New Yorker*. He has also published a children's story, *Monsieur Eek* (2001).

ACHIEVEMENTS

Though David Ives has yet to have a play produced on Broadway, he has become one of the most oft-produced playwrights in the United States, primarily because of the success of his breakthrough work, *All in the Timing* (1993). The Off-Off-Broadway performance of this collection of short plays won a Drama Desk Award, a John Gassner Playwriting Award, and a Best Plays citation for 1993. It was also the most frequently produced play in the season of 1995-1996, thanks to its popularity with colleges and smaller theater companies.

Known for his perfection of the short form as a playwriting vehicle, Ives has had works included in the Best Short Plays series in four different years. The playwright's accessible wit and playful absurdity have made his plays favorites with both actors and theatergoers. Ives has been a major force in turning the ten-minute play into a valid theatrical form.

Though his works since *All in the Timing* have not received comparable critical acclaim, they have continued to prove Ives's mastery of the English language and its comic potential. A consummate comic, Ives has managed to use humor to touch existentially on issues of time, inevitability, communication, and human existence. A prolific writer even before his success with *All in the Timing*, Ives continues to produce a number of new works every year.

BIOGRAPHY

David Ives was born David Roszkowski (a name he would change before he entered college) in Chicago, Illinois, in 1951. He had a blue-collar childhood as the son of a machinist and a secretary and began writing plays at an early age for family and friends. He continued writing as a student at Northwestern University in Illinois, where a few of his early plays were mounted as student productions. He earned a B.A. in English from Northwestern in 1971, then spent a few years doing various jobs such as teaching in West Germany and working in a bookstore. Eventually taking a job as a junior editor at *Foreign Affairs* magazine, Ives moved to New York City and continued to write plays.

After his now-obscure play *Canvas* was produced by a small company in Los Angeles, Ives decided to write plays full time. He entered the prestigious Yale Drama School in 1981, earning his M.F.A. in playwriting three years later. After graduating, he acquired an agent and moved to Hollywood to write for film and television. Unhappy with what he viewed as the frustrating development process of Hollywood, Ives left the West Coast in the late 1980's for New York, where he quickly formed a relationship with the comedy club Manhattan Punch Line. Punch Line originally produced several of the works that eventually became a part of his hit *All in the Timing*, including *Seven Menus*, *Sure Thing*, and *Philip Glass Buys a Loaf of Bread*.

Ives's breakthrough as a playwright came at the age of forty-three, when in 1993 Primary Stages mounted *All in the Timing*, a collection of short Ives comedies. *All in the Timing* was a critical success as well as a popular one, becoming the most-produced play in the United States outside of the works of William Shakespeare in 1995 and garnering him attention from all over the country. *All in the Timing*, with its dense comic dialogue and explorations of time and existence, earned for Ives comparisons to his heroes Stoppard, Pinter, and Samuel Beckett, and marks what is still the pinnacle of his popularity.

Ives's next major opening after this phenomenal success was *Don Juan in Chicago*, a full-length play that received a universally lukewarm reception from critics and audiences. Many critics attributed the faults of *Don Juan* to Ives's being unable to sustain a full-length play, an image he has yet to overcome. His next offering was a return to the winning *All in the Timing* formula—1997's *Mere Mortals* was again a collection of short comedies—establishing this form as Ives's most recognizable *modus operandi*.

His next work, *Lives of the Saints*, was again a collection of short works in which he continued to explore the same themes of time and existence and began to explore his Polish heritage onstage. He would continue this exploration in the full-length play *Polish Joke*.

Ives's success with *All in the Timing* and reputation as a clever wordsmith have made him a popular go-to guy for various theatrical endeavors. He has adapted several musicals for concert performances to take part in the City Center ENCORES! Series and has written stage banter for illusionist David Copperfield and for an Ira Gershwin tribute.

Other Ives occupations since 1993 have included teaching playwriting at New York University and Columbia University, writing short fiction for the *Kenyon Review*, and writing essays for *New York Times Magazine*. His first Broadway production—an adaptation of *Dance of the Vampires*—was set to open in 2002. Ives has married twice, first briefly, and more recently to graphic designer Martha Stoberock.

ANALYSIS

Often considered a Tom Stoppard for audiences with a short attention span, Ives writes plays that are characterized by his smart use of language, as well as his tendency to delve into issues of time and chance. Because his plays—especially *All in the Timing*—have been so widely produced, Ives enjoys a singular popularity unusual for someone with so few full-length plays. Ives's short comedies—variations on the themes of language, communication, and misinterpretation—have done much to validate the ten-minute play as a valid and vibrant form of writing for the stage.

Ives's work, never guilty of being overly serious, has typically relied on some sort of overlying gimmick in form or structure to define the plays' action. The use of a bell to reset the action of a scene, the use of two sets of actors playing the same characters, a

play that recreates language in the form of a Philip Glass composition—these are typical devices in Ives's œuvre. His short plays are usually around just long enough to present their premise, deliver a condensed theme, and not wear out their welcome. His longer works, such as *Don Juan in Chicago*, often lose focus, and the formula is less successful.

For themes, the plays tend to recirculate a few key ideas. Ives often touches on love and human relationships—mostly on their unpredictability and instability—as well as on the mutability and absurdity of language. Ives's characters exist in worlds of strange uncertainty, in which language is the only key to human communication but is flimsy at best and at worst downright incomprehensible. Also central to his body of work has been the exploration of time. In his mind, time is not necessarily experienced as a linear progression but rather as a fugue of repeated sequences and unexpected turns.

ANCIENT HISTORY

Ancient History was one of Ives's first works to be produced in New York, staged in 1989 while the playwright was still writing in obscurity. As a full-length play, *Ancient History* is an anomaly amidst Ives's other works and is also one of the darkest. A pessimistic cautionary exploration into the burdens of the past on human relationships, it is one of very few Ives plays to end on a down note.

Ancient History, like many of his works, features a central male-female couple trying to work out their relationship's place in a larger and crueler world. Self-described as being perfectly matched, exactly alike, Jack and Ruth open the play by extolling the many wonders of their perfect relationship. As the play progresses, as the two are ostensibly planning for a party, they slowly reveal the flimsy foundations of their stated bliss. Though the pair share an absolutely perfect present life together, they are burdened by the lack of shared traditions, and more important, by the lack of a shared future.

As always, Ives is concerned with time—most notably the connection between the transgressions of the past and the possibilities for the future. Though Ruth's Jewish heritage is seemingly not a problem with atheist Jack, the implications of tradition have a far greater effect on Ruth and Jack's relationship than was anticipated.

Ancient History, though considered one of Ives's lesser works, is perhaps his most compelling attempt at traditional character development. Though the two main characters still talk in his typical witticisms, it is not their language that defines them as is the case with other Ives characters. At times, their banter resembles that of George and Martha in Edward Albee's *Who's Afraid of Virginia Wolf?* (pr., pb. 1962). Like the Albee couple, Jack and Ruth use their verbal games to both sustain their relationship and cover up its flaws.

ALL IN THE TIMING

A reading of *All in the Timing* is essential to the understanding of Ives as a writer. *All in the Timing* is a collection of six short Ives plays: *Words, Words, Words*; *Sure Thing*; *Philip Glass Buys a Loaf of Bread*; *Variations on the Death of Trotsky*; *The Philadelphia*; and *The Universal Language*. A showcase of his cleverness, invention, and comic intuition, *All in the Timing* was the first of Ives's works to garner attention from critics in New York.

Among these, *Sure Thing* is probably the most instantly recognizable because of its use of the ringing bell as a theatrical device. In this play, a man and woman meet in a restaurant, then proceed to explore every possible outcome for their simple meeting. When one character makes a blunder that would possibly end the encounter, the bell rings and the scene is reset, giving the character an opportunity to correct the mistake.

Though each of the six ten-minute vignettes that make up *All in the Timing* are self-contained, Ives carries a few key themes and devices throughout the series of shorts. The key connection between the six pieces is the use and flexibility of language—in *All in the Timing*, Ives's characters take joy in bending the rules of language, using language only sometimes for communication. Other times—such as in *Philip Glass Buys a Loaf of Bread* or *The Universal Language*—language exists more for musical effect or even as a obstacle to communication.

The other overall theme of *All in the Timing* is evident in the title. All six pieces deal with time—the illusion of it, the mutability of it, and our ability to rearrange it with the ring of a bell. Characters explore the possibilities of reliving the same moment in time in *Sure Thing* and *Variations on the Death of Trotsky* or become stuck living one moment in time indefinitely, as in the Hamlet-writing monkeys of *Words, Words, Words*. The idea that existence is not settled into linear patterns but rather into clusters of enigmatic loops and fleeting states of mind is key to the understanding of this most popular Ives work.

DON JUAN IN CHICAGO

Most critics considered this full-length play, a followup to *All in the Timing*, to be a disappointment. Most were looking to *Don Juan in Chicago* to decide whether Ives was capable of carrying an entire evening's entertainment on the shoulders of a single plotline, to which the answer was a universal "not really."

A mixture of Faustian myth and the story of the Don Juan character, *Don Juan in Chicago* suggests that the man exalted as the greatest lover of all time was actually living out a pact with the devil, wherein he received immortality only as long as he could bed a new woman every day. Eventually, Don Juan ends up in Chicago, where he must decide if endless sexual conquest in the Windy City is actually a better alternative to eternal damnation. A testament to Ives's optimism, this is perhaps the only retelling of the Faustian myth in which the devil actually forgives the debt and sends everyone involved to heaven.

Ives's attention to language is also present in this work but in a much more pedestrian manner. Much of Ives's experimentation in this work comes in the form of a rhyming Mephistopheles. Although some of the rhyme-humor is quite clever, much of it is mundane and not comparable to the word wizardry that audiences saw in *All in the Timing*. The larger theme is an analysis of mortality versus immortality—again an issue of time—but in this work, Ives failed to connect with audiences expecting *All in the Timing* II.

OTHER MAJOR WORKS

SCREENPLAY: *The Hunted*, 1998.
TELEPLAY: *The Pentagon Wars*, 1998.
CHILDREN'S LITERATURE: *Monsieur Eek*, 2001.

BIBLIOGRAPHY

Grimes, William. "David Ives Quick-Hit Approach to Staging the Human Comedy." *The New York Times*; January 4, 1994, p. C15. Grimes offers a comprehensive biography of Ives's life until 1994, as well as an analysis of *All in the Timing* and other works. He compares Ives's work to those of Eugène Ionesco, Samuel Beckett, and Harold Pinter and interviews Ives regarding his success.

Kanfer, Stefan. Review of *Mere Mortals* by David Ives. *The New Leader* 80, no. 15 (September 22, 1997): 22-24. A review of the presentation of this collection of one-act plays at the John Houseman Theater in New York. The reviewer particularly enjoyed *Time Flies* and *Foreplay*.

Klein, Alvin. "On the Trail of Coherence and Meaning." Review of *Lives of the Saints* by David Ives. *New York Times*, August 29, 1999, p. 10. This review examines *Lives of the Saints*, a group of one-act sketches, performed by Ives Reperatory Company in the Berkshire Theater Festival production.

Zinman, Toby. Review of *Lives of the Saints* by David Ives. *Variety* 373, no. 12 (February 8, 1999): 89. A review of the Philadelphia Theater Company presentation of *Lives of the Saints*. The reviewer finds this collection of one-act plays to be inferior to *All in the Timing*.

Leah Green

J

HENRY JAMES

Born: New York, New York; April 15, 1843
Died: London, England; February 28, 1916

Principal drama

Daisy Miller, pb. 1883 (adaptation of his novel)
The American, pr. 1891, pb. 1949 (adaptation of his novel)
Guy Domville, pb. 1894 (privately), pr. 1895, pb. 1949
Theatricals: Tenants and Disengaged, pb. 1894
The Reprobate, pb. 1894, pr. 1919
Theatricals, Second Series: The Album and The Reprobate, pb. 1895
The High Bid, pr. 1908, pb. 1949
The Other House, wr. 1909, pb. 1949
The Outcry, wr. 1909, pr. 1917, pb. 1949
The Saloon, pr. 1911 (one act), pb. 1949
The Complete Plays of Henry James, pb. 1949 (Leon Edel, editor)

Other literary forms

Henry James was a prolific writer, most lauded for his fiction. His best-known novels, on the intersection of American and European manners and morals, include *The American* (1876-1877), *The Europeans* (1878), *Daisy Miller* (1878), *The Portrait of a Lady* (1880-1881), *The Wings of the Dove* (1902), *The Ambassadors* (1903), and *The Golden Bowl* (1904). He combined his study of mannered society with an evaluation of social and political justice in *The Bostonians* (1885-1886) and *The Princess Casamassima* (1885-1886). In *The Tragic Muse* (1889-1890), he produced his one novel about the theater. James also wrote more than one hundred short stories and tales (now collected in Leon Edel's twelve-volume *The Complete Tales of Henry James*, 1962-1964). James was a perceptive critic of his own fiction as well as that of others. His study *The Art of Fiction* (1884) is a seminal work of its kind. He prefaced many of his novels with long discussions of fiction writing (collected by R. P. Blackmur in *The Art of the Novel: Critical Prefaces*, 1934) and wrote essays on other fiction writers, both contemporaries and predecessors, among them Nathaniel Hawthorne (*Hawthorne*, 1879), Honoré de Balzac, Anthony Trollope, George Eliot, Robert Louis Stevenson, Ivan Turgenev, and Charles Dickens. He also wrote theater reviews and essays on playwrights from William Shakespeare to Henrik Ibsen, which are collected in *The Scenic Art* (1948; Allan Wade, editor). James was a major travel writer of his day, contributing his essays on England and Europe to American publications such as *The Nation*, *Atlantic Monthly* and the New York *Tribune*. After a return visit to the United States, he wrote *The American Scene* (1907), a reflection on American life. He wrote a biography of his sculptor friend, *William Wetmore Story and His Friends* (1903), and completed two volumes of memoirs, *A Small Boy and Others* (1913) and *Notes of a Son and Brother* (1914). An edition of his letters has been edited by Leon Edel (*Henry James Letters*, 1974-1984).

Achievements

Henry James's novels detail the complexities of human relationships. His exploration of consciousness and of narrative viewpoints led, in his more mature works, to the psychological realism for which his novels are chiefly remembered. James's reputation as a dramatist never equaled his reputation as a novelist. James saw five of his plays professionally produced and five others published, but of his fifteen completed plays, none was both produced and published during his lifetime. Most of James's plays became a part of English dramatic literature only in 1949, some thirty-

three years after James's death, when they were collected by Leon Edel in *The Complete Plays of Henry James*. Consequently, James's importance as a playwright stems neither from influential productions nor from timely publications. He is a minor but unique figure in English-language drama, valuable for his ability to treat common turn-of-the-century dramatic themes and forms in an uncommon way. Although he borrowed liberally from the French well-made drama he admired, his plays are best understood as English comedies of manners. James took the British stage tradition of William Congreve, William Wycherley, Sir George Etherege, Oliver Goldsmith, and Richard Brinsley Sheridan, refined its upper-class milieu, and in doing so clarified the comedy of manners' conflation of manners and morals. As James's characters struggle for a livable synthesis of manners and morals, James focuses on understanding the special social skills, limitations, and perceptions of women. James realized the full dramatic potential of his innovative comedy of manners only once, in *The High*

Henry James (Library of Congress)

Bid, a play that stands as an emblem of his successful distillation of the dramatic tradition. Although James's plays often suffer from oblique dialogue, melodrama, and flimsy plots, his dramatic works that came after *The American* are generally more graceful and are often more substantial than is the successful West End fare of such contemporaries as Arthur Wing Pinero and Henry Arthur Jones.

James's theater interests were encouraged by such important figures as actresses Elizabeth Robins and Fanny Kemble, writer and producer Harley Granville-Barker, and playwright George Bernard Shaw; his work was commissioned by the actress Ellen Terry and by producer-managers Augustin Daly, Charles Frohman, Edward Compton, Sir John Hare, and Sir Johnston Forbes-Robertson. James's achievements as a playwright, however, remain limited. Although his plays are stageable (two were successfully produced in London in the late 1960's), his work has found success on television, stage, and screen only through the adaptations of his fiction by other writers. When he first edited James's plays, Leon Edel suggested that they were most important as experiments in the "dramatic method" that enabled James to write his last novels. Many critics join Edel in finding the plays most important as adjuncts to James's fiction.

BIOGRAPHY

Henry James, Jr., was the second of five children born to Mary Robertson Walsh and Henry James, Sr. A friend of Ralph Waldo Emerson and a follower of the Swedish philosopher-theologian Emanuel Swedenborg, Henry James, Sr., advocated a "sensuous" rearing of his children. This amounted to showering his five children with educational opportunities and encouraging them to adopt an individual morality. Although much of the young James's education occurred at home and through extensive foreign travel (his first trip abroad came when he was five months old and was followed by several more stays during his childhood and adolescence), he also had tutors and attended various schools in the United States and in Europe, including Harvard Law School. James's family was of great importance to him throughout his life. He was close to his parents until they died in 1882 and remained close to his siblings—especially William James, his older brother and greatest rival, who gained fame as a psychologist and philosopher, and his only sister, Alice, whom James helped care for during her many long illnesses. The frequent, long, newsy, philosophical letters that passed between James and his brother and sister suggest the interests, love, and concern the three shared.

When James traveled to Europe in 1872 at the age of twenty-nine, he began the first of his extended stays abroad. He lived in the United States only for brief stretches of time after this, settling permanently in Europe in 1875. His preference for foreign residency led him, in 1915, the year before his death, to become a naturalized British citizen. James spent the longest stretches of time in England—both in London, where he set up several residences, and in Rye, Sussex, where he took out a long lease on Lamb House. He also paid lengthy visits to France and Italy. James documented such foreign living in the many travel pieces he wrote for American readers but put it to best use in his fiction and drama, where the American abroad and the clash of American and European manners were his special terrain. During his early years in the United States and abroad, James published stories, reviews, essays, and novels while he developed important literary friendships with William Dean Howells, Henry Adams, Robert Louis Stevenson, Ivan Turgenev, Gustave Flaubert, and Émile Zola.

From the publication of his first novel, *Roderick Hudson*, in 1875, the greatest share of James's life was devoted to his fiction writing. Writing was a daily concern, for most of James's work, even his novels, appeared first in magazines such as *Macmillan's Magazine*, *Century Magazine*, *Atlantic Monthly*, and *Harper's Weekly*, which had demanding deadlines. James's preoccupation with his writing was also an aspect of his concern about money; he appears to have had enough money to live comfortably, but he constantly worried about income and expenses. The course of his career has generally been measured by the fluctuating success of his fiction. James gained his early reputation from novels such

as *The American*, *Daisy Miller*, and *The Portrait of a Lady*, in which he developed his world of cross-cultural confrontations and integration. During the 1880's, however, with the publication of the more overtly political novels *The Bostonians* and *The Princess Casamassima*, James lost public favor. Although production of his stories continued to be prolific, it was in the first decade of the new century, with the publication of his last, long novels—*The Wings of the Dove*, *The Ambassadors*, and *The Golden Bowl*—that he gained his stature as "the Master." James's American tour in 1904, when he returned after a twenty-one-year absence, occasioned *The American Scene*, a volume of essays on his homeland. From 1907 to 1909, James prepared the prefaces and revisions of his life's work for the twenty-four volumes of the New York edition, issued by Scribner's. Although sales of this collected edition disappointed James, his literary reputation had been secured.

While producing novels, stories, travel pieces, reviews, and critical essays, James also managed a full social life. He was a welcome guest at English country-house weekends and a seemingly essential addition to American expatriate households in London, Paris, Rome, Florence, and Venice. His friendships with Americans James Russell Lowell (United States ambassador to Great Britain), Grace Norton and the Curtises (Bostonian socialites), Francis Boott and his daughter Lizzie (Bostonians with European art interests), John Singer Sargent and Edwin Abbey (American artists), and others were cemented by extensive correspondence as well as social visits. Late in life, James traveled and corresponded with American novelist Edith Wharton and was neighbor to H. G. Wells. James's brother and sister, William and Alice, remained James's most life-sustaining connections after their parents died in 1882. James traveled in Europe and to the United States to visit and care for both, and he mourned them deeply when they died (Alice in 1892 and William in 1910). James never married, finding marriage anathema to his art, though he was romantically pursued by Constance Fenimore Woolson, a fellow American writer who was James's close friend from 1880 to her death in 1894. Late in his life, James had close attachments to several of his young admirers, including Jocelyn Persse, Howard Sturgis, and Hendrik Andersen.

James's interest in the theater culminated in the five years from 1890 to 1895, when he considered himself mainly a playwright, but lasted throughout his life. Some of James's most vivid childhood memories include early trips to Broadway and productions of Shakespeare, Dickens, and Harriet Beecher Stowe's *Uncle Tom's Cabin* (1852). As a teenager, he dabbled in playwriting, and one of his first pieces of critical writing was in response to the absorbing performance of an actress. James's several extended stays in Paris in the 1870's convinced him of the vitality of the French theater, and in his essays on the Théâtre Français and on French playwrights such as Victorien Sardou and Alexandre Dumas, *fils*, he displayed his respect for the well-made play he would use as an early model for his own drama. After James completed *The Tragic Muse*, his novel about the London theater, he devoted the next five years of his life to theatergoing and playwriting. Biographer Leon Edel contends that James never wrote with greater intensity. The embarrassment of the opening night of his play *Guy Domville* in 1895 provoked James to declare that he would never write for theater again, but during the remaining years of his life he continued to write plays, attend the theater regularly, and maintain his friendships with actresses, producers, and playwrights. In 1909, James even found himself lobbying the British Parliament for a relaxation of stage censorship.

Some of James's last writings were memoirs of his childhood, in which he recorded his vivid memories of early theater experiences. He continued to write fiction to the last, leaving two unfinished novels at his death. His final years were shadowed by the outbreak of World War I, which James saw as a negation of the world and the art in which he believed. After he had sustained a stroke in 1915, William James's widow, Alice, and her son and daughter, Harry and Peggy, came from the United States to nurse James until his death in February of 1916. The British government bestowed the Order of Merit on James shortly before he died.

ANALYSIS

Henry James's legacy to drama is a perspective on American and British upper- and middle-class social life that no one else could imitate. He brought to his drama the multicultural understanding that was the basis of his best fiction. Onstage, as in a narrative, he tracked turn-of-the-century Americans and their English counterparts through courtship and marriage, leisure and business, money and art. The drama that resulted was not always successful but was an instructive experiment in dramatic style. Concentrating his effort on the creation of a social milieu in which manners function as they should, James offered a world in which morality is not a matter of right and wrong but a negotiating between individual wants and society's needs. The two most important components of the milieu, or atmosphere, in James's plays are the women who are in control and the missions of social and moral salvation on which they embark.

James was influenced by two dramatic traditions—those of the French and the English theaters. James's intimate knowledge of French theater that he acquired in Paris convinced him that the well-made play was the model to imitate. In his earliest plays, he tried to approximate the neat plots, the series of climaxes, and the easy identification of right and wrong he found in the French drama. As James himself showed in his comparative studies of English and French drama, however, the French model could not be translated neatly into English. James had often complained of the crude morality of English theater audiences, going so far as to label its tastes immoral, yet as he practiced his own playwriting skills in the 1890's, it became clear that he was finding the English tradition of the comedy of manners as useful a model as the French tradition of the well-made play. Borrowing from the English tradition both a striving to balance opposites and a stylized concentration on wit, social artistry, and women, James wrote his best plays.

James's theater career is divided in two by the ill-fated production of *Guy Domville* in 1895. In the first part of his career, while still in his twenties, James wrote three short plays, "Pyramus and Thisbe," "Still Waters," and "A Change of Heart," which were published as short stories and suggest his attraction to witty, comic dialogue and romantic plots. These were followed by adaptations of his novels *Daisy Miller* and *The American*, the first commissioned for an American production with Daniel Frohman in 1882 but never produced, and the second commissioned by British manager Edward Compton in 1889 and produced in 1891. Neither adaptation was successful, but James's lifelong desire to write for the theater had been awakened and he went on to spend the five years from 1890 to 1895 consumed by drama.

These years, which Edel has labeled "the dramatic years," are marked in James's letters, notebooks, and life by the great hopes and disappointments tied to the stage. Although James completed at least six plays and parts of several others during these years, only *The American* and *Guy Domville* were produced. When James was hooted off the stage during the curtain call of *Guy Domville* in January of 1895, he pronounced himself done with theater. James's letters of early 1895 are full of his feeling that drama (the written product) must be separated from theater (the onstage product), but, as his later involvement with the theater attests, he could not relinquish the hope of seeing his plays produced. While the second half of James's theater career, after 1895, was not marked by the great energy, commitment, and concentration of the earlier period, the plays of this period are more mature and natural. James wrote an early version of *The High Bid* immediately after the *Guy Domville* debacle and completed four plays after 1895, his best among them.

THE AMERICAN AND THE OUTCRY

The failures in James's plays are of two extremes, represented by his earliest (*The American*) and latest (*The Outcry*) full-length dramatic works. When James adapted his novel *The American* for the stage in 1890, his decision to use the French well-made play as a model led him to simplify the cultural collisions of the story, so that in the play, the cultured French become everything bad and the innocent American Christopher Newman is everything good. James's imitation of his French model also produced superfluous entrances and exits and melodramatic dialogue and confrontations, and necessitated the addi-

tion of a neat, happy ending. Later, James would build a synthesis out of the meeting of European and American morals by borrowing from the comedy of manners, but in this play he offered only a stalemate. By the time of James's last full-length play, *The Outcry* (written in 1909), he had mastered the basics of dramatic construction, but the play is nevertheless a failure, the wit and repartee of its dialogue obscured by oblique references and convoluted thinking. *The Outcry* is too much art and too little life. James's best plays—*The Reprobate*, *Guy Domville*, and *The High Bid*—offer believable social milieus and delightful characters and dialogue.

THE REPROBATE

The Reprobate is the best of the four plays James published in 1894 in his two-volume series, *Theatricals: Tenants and Disengaged* and *Theatricals, Second Series: The Album and The Reprobate*. The play's two main characters, Mrs. Freshville and Paul Doubleday, are former lovers who meet by chance at the Hampton Court villa of Mr. Bonsor. Mrs. Freshville is there chasing a new love, Captain Chanter, although she eventually ends up with a third man, Pitt Brunt. Doubleday lives there as a ward of Mr. Bonsor; Doubleday is the "reprobate" of the title, whose past indiscretions have necessitated his now being closely guarded. In the course of the play he matures, aided by both Mrs. Freshville and his new love, Blanche Amber. The play is the earliest example of James's mastery of dramatic form. The tight construction of the play is suspenseful, not artificial, and melodrama has become a technique James uses to good effect at the end of his acts. James has also adapted the milieu of the comedy of manners successfully. The dialogues are enticing mixtures of wit, innuendo, and manipulation, and the comedy-of-manners emphasis on social decorum and romance is believable.

James also developed, in *The Reprobate*, the controlling female character who would become the hallmark of his drama. Mrs. Freshville assumes control of the play's events from her first entrance, displaying her understanding of her social world as one where a person gains power by knowing how to play social games. Blanche Amber is, in many ways, a younger Mrs. Freshville, just learning how her world operates and practicing her newfound social skills. Together, Blanche Amber and Mrs. Freshville direct attention to the issues of the play as they set out to "save" Doubleday. They teach the overprotected Doubleday that social power lies in an understanding of manners, and they teach him how to use that power. By the end of the play, he has learned his lesson well, and his message is James's: Good, bad, and freedom are relative concepts which must be negotiated in the world of manners. The play's first production came in 1919, in London, after James's death. It received both praise and criticism but established the stage-worthiness of James's delicate brand of manners comedy.

GUY DOMVILLE

Guy Domville is the best known of James's dramas, although it is remembered for its melodramatic stage failure rather than its artistic merits. James wrote the play in 1893 for George Alexander, the popular actor-manager of London's fashionable St. James's Theatre, and worked closely with Alexander and his cast during rehearsals. On the play's opening night, January 5, 1895, however, James was too nervous to watch the production of his own play and spent the evening at a production of Oscar Wilde's *An Ideal Husband* (pr. 1895). In his absence, James's first act met with great approval, but his second act was jeered, and the third merely tolerated. When James returned to the St. James's Theatre, he was encouraged by Alexander to acknowledge the curtain-call applause, completely unprepared for the vicious disapproval and hooting with which the audience greeted him. He left the stage "green with dismay" (in the words of actor Franklyn Dyall) and vowed to friends that he would abandon the theater altogether. The play continued its run for four weeks and did not, in the end, mark the conclusion of James's playwriting career, but James's attitude to playwriting had been irrevocably changed. He would never again write plays in which he made such a personal investment.

As even the first-night audience knew, however, the play had its merits. Although *Guy Domville* is not a comedy of manners, James had created for this serious drama a mannered milieu that had a grace,

charm, and delicacy rare on the English stage. Reviewers including Arthur B. Walkley and George Bernard Shaw, applauded a dialogue that was witty and playful while allowing the characters to discuss the play's serious issues. While the play, like most of James's other plays, has a love interest, that love is a platonic one between Guy Domville, a young man about to enter the Church, and Mrs. Peverel, a widow whose child Guy is tutoring. Instead of detailing this love, James focuses on the choice Guy must make between entering the Church and accepting his family's call to join them in the fast-paced social world. The play is marred by the melodrama of an unbelievable scene in act 2 in which Guy and another character, George Round, feign drunkenness to trick each other, but generally its topics, seriously expressed, are those of James's other plays: the potential artificiality of mannered life, the saving of individual freedom and morality, and the connection between manners and morals. The play is atypical of his work in that it is not a comedy and is not centered on a powerful woman, but it is the first of James's plays in which his central character is portrayed as a social "artist" who masters the "art" of living.

THE HIGH BID

Also in 1895, shortly after the stage failure of *Guy Domville*, James wrote the one-act "Summersoft" for British actress Ellen Terry. Terry never performed the play, but James expanded it to the full three-act play *The High Bid* in 1907 and saw it successfully performed both in Edinburgh and London by Sir Johnston Forbes-Robertson and his company in 1908. The play is James's best because in it he combined the clean dramatic lines that he mastered in his earlier plays with the cultural insights of his last years. The key to the play's success is Mrs. Gracedew, an American widow who uses her position as a cultural outsider to show the play's Britons why their society's traditions and manners are sacred. Mrs. Gracedew comes to Covering End, the family home of Captain Yule, merely to visit, but finds herself obliged to save the majestic home from the greedy Mr. Prodmore. She also saves Prodmore's daughter, Cora, from a bad love match and successfully engineers her own love match with Yule.

Specific structural techniques James had garnered from his long apprenticeship to the well-made play—suspenseful act closings and ups and downs in a character's fortunes—embellish one of the simplest of James's play plots in *The High Bid*. Such simplicity is balanced by the rich comedy-of-manners milieu, with characters aware of decorum and full of politeness and well-timed deference. Because Mrs. Gracedew—as an American—is an outsider to this mannered world, she has learned its ways almost better than the natives. More than any other character, she commands this world of nuance through innuendo and indirection, wit and wordplay. In her, James created his fullest portrait of the social artist and social savior. What Mrs. Gracedew must save is upper-class British society, a mission accomplished in part through her alliance with young Cora, in part by detailing for others, primarily Yule, the ideals of mannered life, which preserve culture and civilization. Although the progressive Yule raises important questions about inequities in this system that Mrs. Gracedew defends, she is successful in her mission: She saves a world in which manners are morals and life is a delicate art, as James himself sought to save the comedy of manners as a viable dramatic form. In a series of letters that he exchanged with George Bernard Shaw in 1907, James defended his dramatic art as a rarefied and complex image of life, valuable precisely because it challenges audiences to strive for the most that they can possibly achieve in life. In *The High Bid*, James created such a dramatic world, where life is an art worth saving.

OTHER MAJOR WORKS

LONG FICTION: *Roderick Hudson*, 1876; *The American*, 1876-1877; *The Europeans*, 1878; *Daisy Miller*, 1878; *An International Episode*, 1878-1879; *Confidence*, 1879-1880; *Washington Square*, 1880; *The Portrait of a Lady*, 1880-1881; *The Bostonians*, 1885-1886; *The Princess Casamassima*, 1885-1886; *The Reverberator*, 1888; *The Tragic Muse*, 1889-1890; *The Spoils of Poynton*, 1897; *What Maisie Knew*, 1897; *The Awkward Age*, 1897-1899; *In the Cage*, 1898; *The Turn of the Screw*, 1898; *The Sacred Fount*, 1901; *The Wings of the Dove*, 1902; *The Am-bassadors*, 1903; *The Golden Bowl*, 1904; *The Outcry*, 1911; *The Ivory Tower*, 1917; *The Sense of the Past*, 1917.

SHORT FICTION: *A Passionate Pilgrim*, 1875; *The Madonna of the Future*, 1879; *The Siege of London*, 1883; *Tales of Three Cities*, 1884; *The Author of Beltraffio*, 1885; *The Aspern Papers*, 1888; *The Lesson of the Master*, 1892; *The Private Life, Lord Beaupre, The Visits*, 1893; *The Real Thing*, 1893; *Terminations*, 1895; *Embarrassments*, 1896; *The Two Magics: The Turn of the Screw and Covering End*, 1898; *The Soft Side*, 1900; *The Better Sort*, 1903; *The Novels and Tales of Henry James*, 1907-1909 (24 volumes); *The Finer Grain*, 1910; *A Landscape Painter*, 1919; *Travelling Companions*, 1919; *Master Eustace*, 1920; *Stories of Writers and Artists*, 1944; *Henry James: Selected Short Stories*, 1950; *Henry James: Eight Tales from the Major Phase*, 1958; *The Complete Tales of Henry James*, 1962-1965 (12 volumes; Leon Edel, editor); *Tales of Henry James*, 1984; *The Figure in the Carpet and Other Stories*, 1986; *The Jolly Corner and Other Tales*, 1990.

NONFICTION: *Transatlantic Sketches*, 1875; *French Poets and Novelists*, 1878; *Hawthorne*, 1879; *Portraits of Places*, 1883; *A Little Tour in France*, 1884; *The Art of Fiction*, 1884; *Partial Portraits*, 1888; *Essays in London*, 1893; *William Wetmore Story and His Friends*, 1903; *English Hours*, 1905; *The American Scene*, 1907; *Views and Reviews*, 1908; *Italian Hours*, 1909; *A Small Boy and Others*, 1913 (memoirs); *Notes of a Son and Brother*, 1914 (memoirs); *Notes on Novelists*, 1914; *The Middle Years*, 1917; *The Art of the Novel: Critical Prefaces*, 1934 (R. P. Blackmur, editor); *The Notebooks of Henry James*, 1947 (F. O. Matthiessen and Kenneth B. Murdock, editors); *The Scenic Art*, 1948 (Allan Wade, editor); *Henry James Letters*, 1974-1984 (5 volumes; Leon Edel, editor); *The Art of Criticism: Henry James on the Theory and Practice of Fiction*, 1986; *The Complete Notebooks of Henry James*, 1987; *Henry James: A Life in Letters*, 1999.

BIBLIOGRAPHY

Bailie, Ronnie. *The Fantastic Anatomist: A Psychoanalytic Study of Henry James*. Atlanta, Ga.: Rodopi,

2000. A look at James and his works from the psychological perspective. Bibliography and index.

Flannery, Denis. *Henry James: A Certain Illusion.* Brookfield, Vt.: Ashgate, 2000. An analysis of illusion in the works of James. Bibliography and index.

Freedman, Jonathan, ed. *The Cambridge Companion to Henry James.* New York: Cambridge University Press, 1998. A reference work that provides extensive information on James's life and literary influences and also details his works and the characters contained in them. Bibliography and index.

Graham, Kenneth. *Henry James: A Literary Life.* New York: St. Martin's Press, 1996. A biography of James that looks at his life and works, examining how the two were intertwined. Bibliography and index.

Greenwood, Christopher. *Adapting to the Stage: Theatre and the Work of Henry James.* Burlington, Vt.: Ashgate, 2000. An analysis of James's dramatic works and of his works that have been adapted for the stage. Bibliography and index.

Moore, Harry Thornton. *Henry James.* New York: Thames and Hudson, 1999. A biography that covers the life and works of James.

Pippin, Robert B. *Henry James and Modern Moral Life.* New York: Cambridge University Press, 2000. A look at the moral message James tried to convey through his works.

Rowe, John Carlos. *The Other Henry James.* Durham, N.C.: Duke University Press, 1998. A biography of James that examines his political and social views and looks at his portrayal of gender and sex roles.

Stevens, Hugh. *Henry James and Sexuality.* New York: Cambridge University Press, 1998. A study of sexuality as it presents itself in James's work, including homosexuality and sex roles. Bibliography and index.

Tambling, Jeremy. *Henry James.* New York: St. Martin's Press, 2000. Provides critical analysis of the works of James. Bibliography and index.

Susan Carlson,
updated by Peter C. Holloran

ALFRED JARRY

Born: Laval, France; September 8, 1873
Died: Paris, France; November 1, 1907

PRINCIPAL DRAMA

Ubu Roi, wr. 1888, pr., pb. 1896 (English translation, 1951)

Ubu cocu, wr. 1888, pb. 1944, pr. 1946 (*Ubu Cuckolded*, 1953)

Ubu enchaîné, pb. 1900, pr. 1937 (*Ubu Enchained*, 1953)

Ubu sur la butte, pr. 1901, pb. 1906 (marionette play; shortened version of *Ubu roi* with songs)

Le Moutardier du pape, pb. 1906 (operetta)

L'Objet aimé, pb. 1909

Pantagruel, pr. 1911 (libretto)

OTHER LITERARY FORMS

Alfred Jarry, in addition to being a playwright, was a literary and art critic, a journalist, a poet, and a writer of science fiction.

ACHIEVEMENTS

Alfred Jarry's contributions to drama cannot fully be evaluated without taking into consideration the state of the theater in the late nineteenth century. Despite the impact of naturalism, the European theater of that time was essentially a commercial enterprise. Devoid of artistic ambitions, superficial and noncontroversial in content, drama was viewed as a commodity or, as one critic put it, an after-dinner entertainment aimed largely at a pleasure-seeking bourgeois audience.

It was against this background that Jarry, who knew perfectly well the European literary heritage and was also a keen observer of his own time, conceived his plays. The famous battle that Victor Hugo's *Hernani* (pr., pb. 1830; English translation, 1830) caused was mild in comparison to the raucous indignation and hatred that was provoked by the performance of *Ubu roi*. Jarry's most vociferous critics took it for an indecent hoax, a political satire, and, worse, a subversive expression of literary anarchism and terrorism composed with the intention of destroying social order. A witness of the first performance later wrote that *Ubu roi* was in fact nothing less than a gun pointed at society.

Such fears, however, were ungrounded. Jarry, who affected a strong contempt for the masses, had nothing in common with the anarchists. His aim was to revolutionize the theater—playwriting, acting, and stagecraft as a whole—and in this he succeeded. Of the many dramatic theories formulated in the nineteenth century and before, it is, without a doubt, Jarry's revolutionary concept of the theater that has had the greatest impact on the philosophy and techniques of modern stagecraft. Antonin Artaud's Theater of Cruelty and Samuel Beckett's, Boris Vian's, Jean Genet's, and Eugène Ionesco's contributions to the Theater of the Absurd are all in one way or another indebted to Jarry.

BIOGRAPHY

Born immediately after the disastrous Franco-Prussian War (1870) and the massacres that ended the Paris Commune (1871), Alfred Jarry belonged to a generation that was deeply affected by France's humiliating defeat and by the political turmoils of the newly created Third Republic. He was of Breton ancestry on his mother's side and developed a strong interest in the legends of Brittany, daring to speak its Celtic language at a time when the government in Paris forbade the use of anything but French. His father, after a rather successful start in business, went bankrupt and eventually became a frequently absent and alcoholic traveling salesman. Jarry's mother, who has been compared to Gustave Flaubert's Madame Bovary because of her eccentric manners, left her

husband while Alfred and his sister were still quite young and went to live with her father, a well-to-do magistrate who had settled in Saint-Brieuc. She was an ambitious person who was determined to preserve family traditions; she closely supervised her children's formal education, which was to her, as to most bourgeois, a status symbol.

In 1888, Jarry's mother decided to move from Saint-Brieuc to Rennes, the former capital of Brittany, so that her son could attend the lycée to prepare himself for the competitive entrance examinations for the École Normale Supérieure and the Polytechnique. Early in school, Jarry was perceived as an unusually gifted and intelligent child, although unruly, mischievous, and sarcastic, with a strong sense of sardonic humor. Because he was short and stocky, his classmates called him Quasimodo, a nickname that, curiously enough, seemed to foreshadow the gross image of Jarry's own infamous character Pa Ubu, with whom he came to identify himself until his death.

At Saint-Brieuc, Jarry's outstanding scholastic achievements had earned for him prizes in Greek, Latin, English, French, German, physics, geography, and mathematics. In Rennes, his intellectual curiosity extended far beyond the prescribed curriculum. He not only studied the great writers of Europe, from William Shakespeare to Pierre Corneille, Voltaire, Hugo, and Johann Wolfgang von Goethe, but he also managed to follow with keen interest the new artistic, philosophical, and scientific developments taking place in his own time. When only eighteen, he was acquainted with Friedrich Nietzsche's work, which had not yet been translated into French. His first poems, sketches, and satires already betrayed his obsession with violence, death, and buffoonery, coupled with strong leanings toward misanthropy and pessimism, at times bordering on nihilism. It was during this period that Jarry, in collaboration with some of his school friends, wrote the first versions of *Ubu roi* and *Ubu Enchained*.

After earning his two baccalaureates, and prompted by his mother, Jarry went to Paris to attend the celebrated Lycée Henry IV. Among his professors was the philosopher Henri Bergson, whose major work, *Essai sur les données immédiates de la conscience* (1889), had a significant impact on the Symbolist school of literature. In 1893, Jarry's mother died. Unable to win admittance to the École Normale Supérieure, he switched his major from the sciences to the humanities. In 1894, however, he failed his examinations for the Licence-ès-lettres at the Sorbonne; thereafter he devoted himself exclusively to writing. In the meantime, he had discovered the artistic world of Paris, in particular the new school of Symbolism, which had a considerable influence on his conception of art and on his fundamental outlook on life. The Symbolists believed in the primacy of the imagination and of the self as the sole and unique reality, outside of which nothing could be shown to exist. With them, as noted above, Jarry shared a contempt for the masses as well as for realism and, especially, for Émile Zola's doctrine of naturalism. Jarry also shared the Symbolists' preference for an autonomous, allusive language, existing in its own right, similar to music and free from the conventional, formal rules governing style and syntax.

Jarry's acceptance of the Symbolists' innovations and ideas, however, was selective. He was fiercely independent and went beyond them to create his own imaginary world and his revolutionary theater of shock. He discovered a kindred spirit in Alfred Vallette, founder and editor of the *Mercure de France* and an unconventional writer. Vallette and his wife, Marguerite—who, under the pen name Rachilde, was widely known as the author of a number of novels centering on psychological aberrations—became a kind of second family for the young Jarry, whose health and financial position were both weak.

Through the Vallettes, Jarry became a familiar figure in the most important Parisian literary circles of the so-called *belle époque*. Remy de Gourmont, a staunch Symbolist; Félix Fénéon, editor of *La Revue blanche*; the Natanson brothers, its proprietors; Léon-Paul Fargue; and Aurélian-Marie Lugne-Poë, director of the Théâtre de l'Œuvre, were among the playwright's friends and acquaintances. Above all, Jarry admired Stéphane Mallarmé's treatment of language conceived as a musical abstraction and as a system of signs.

Because Jarry, like Molière, thought that theater should embrace all forms of art, he paid close attention to the new trends in the field of painting. Félix Vallotton, Édouard Vuillard, Paul Gauguin (himself from Brittany), Henri Toulouse-Lautrec, Pierre Bonnard, and Henri Rousseau, "Le Douanier," were his favorites. What mostly attracted Jarry to these artists was their nonrealistic approach, which eventually evolved into nonfigurative art. This discovery was not to be forgotten; for the production of *Ubu roi*, the costumes, the scenery, the painted props, the use of masks, the characters themselves, as well as the entire stage setting were conceived in terms of abstractions—to the great dismay of the public.

In November, 1894, Jarry was conscripted into the infantry at Laval, his native town. His dislike of military life and regulations was so vehement that he attempted to poison himself by swallowing a dose of picric acid, and as a result he was discharged on medical grounds. This one-year stint in the army inspired one of his best novels, *Les Jours et les nuits: Roman d'un déserteur* (1897; *Days and Nights: Novel of a Deserter*, 1989).

The turning point of Jarry's career came in 1896. The text of *Ubu roi* was published, first in April in *Le Livre d'art* and then in June in *Mercure de France*. In September, the latter published Jarry's groundbreaking essay "De l'inutilité du théâtre au théâtre" (on the futility of the "theatrical" in the theater).

Ubu roi was performed twice in December, and each time the play unleashed the wrath of a public that was totally unprepared and took it for an obscene hoax. In spite of all the jeers and outcries, Jarry had achieved his goal of restoring pure theatricality to the stage, as he saw it, while substituting it for the so-called well-made play and for conventional literature as a whole. This artistic revolution fell into oblivion during Jarry's lifetime, and it was only after World War II that he came to be recognized as the chief forerunner of the Theater of the Absurd.

In 1899, Jarry wrote *Ubu Enchained*, but the play was not performed until 1937. Always obsessed with his outrageous character Pa Ubu, he created the Théâtre des Pantins in 1898 and then the Guignol des Gueules de Bois in 1901, when he performed *Ubu sur la butte* (Ubu on the mound), but these ventures were short-lived.

Although Jarry was a prolific writer, when he died of tubercular meningitis, on November 1, 1907, at the age of thirty-four, he was deeply in debt and destitute. Among his friends who attended the funeral were Vallette, Rachilde, Paul Valéry, Rémy de Gourmont, and Guillaume Apollinaire.

ANALYSIS

Rejecting the notion of theater as a pastime or a didactic vehicle, Alfred Jarry viewed dramatic art as a creative pursuit reserved for an elite who would actively participate in it. In his essay "De l'inutilité du théâtre au théâtre," Jarry revealed in detail his theory of what drama ought to be if it is to survive as a great art form.

Jarry insisted that characters should be walking abstractions more complicated and integrated than those to which audiences were accustomed and who are, on close examination, merely shallow imitations of real human beings. In the same manner, the act of writing could no longer be emphasized, nor a role designed for a particular actor, for the obvious reason that once the actor had retired or was dead, it would be impossible to find an identical replacement. Such a practice, in any case, was a futile exercise, since it did not involve imagination or artistic intuition. Jarry dismissed the plays of Jean Racine on the ground that they were merely a collage of parts written for specific actors and actresses. Viewed from this new perspective, the myth of the star who is an individual speaking for and about himself should be done away with once and for all. More than half a century later, Genet would adopt this idea in *Les Nègres* (pb. 1958; *The Blacks*, 1960) and *Les Paravents* (pr., pb. 1961; *The Screens*, 1962).

Actors are what they are—if not stupid, certainly mortal—therefore it is wrong, Jarry asserted, to make them the center of attraction. Against all established conventions, he asked that they wear masks so as not to distract the audience from the play itself and its message. The use of masks, or the wrapping of the entire body, as in the case of Pa Ubu, is not to be interpreted as a form of travesty or as the embodiment, as in Greek tragedy or comedy, of tears and laughter, of sorrow and joy, but as a reflection of the eternal nature of a character: the Miser, the Waverer, the Covetous Man. Hidden behind a simulacrum, the actors should speak in a monotonous voice like automatons or puppets, in an inarticulate, primitive, and scatological language. Moreover, the stage decor should be heraldic—that is, boldly abstract, not a duplication of life in all its minute detail, as was too often the case with the naturalists. Instead of conventional sets, Jarry recommended the use of painted signs, props, and even unpainted backgrounds.

In Jarry's view, a play basically needs no story, no chronological order, no psychological characterization: What is required above all is action in the spirit of a Punch and Judy show. He argued that the unities of time and space, so important to the theorists of classicism, should be discarded entirely. It does not matter, Jarry said, in what country an action is taking place. Great theater must go beyond the particular to unmask the real nature of humankind, regardless of race, religion, or nationality. Finally, and most important, dramatic art should undergo a perpetual process of evolution, so that, through an unrelenting quest for new forms of expression, it does not become obsolete and mummified.

UBU ROI

These revolutionary ideas are given form in Jarry's masterpiece, *Ubu roi*. Although one can find in it echoes of Corneille's *Cinna: Ou, La Clémence d'Auguste* (pr. 1640; *Cinna*, 1713) and *Horace* (pr. 1640, pb. 1641; English translation, 1656), along with some Racinian overtones, Jarry's first play was largely inspired by Shakespeare's *Macbeth* (pr. 1606). Its story is, in itself, very simple.

Influenced by his wife, Ma Ubu, who is a crafty, vociferous, cantankerous, and miserly woman, Pa Ubu, former king of Aragon, decides to overthrow his benefactor, Venceslas, king of Poland, with the help of Captain Macnure, to whom he promises the duchy of Lithuania. Wasting no time, the plotters massacre the royal family and its friends with the exception of Crown Prince Buggerlas. True to himself, that is, acting, in Jarry's own words, as a perfectly "ignoble being, which is why he resembles (by the lower parts) everybody," Ubu quickly refuses to give Macnure his reward and just as promptly gives the order to slaughter the nobility, the judiciary, and the financiers, in order to levy exorbitant taxes that he will collect himself in a merciless fashion.

Ubu's victory and his tyrannical regime, however, are short-lived when the Czar of Russia, helped by Macnure, stages a war of revenge if not of liberation. As a safety measure, King Ubu sends his wife back to the palace, not so much to protect her as to salvage their possessions. Once there, she decides to steal for herself the treasures of all the former princes of Poland who are buried in the crypt of the cathedral of Warsaw. While inside the sacred grounds, she hears the voice of a ghost emerging from one of the tombs. Frightened, she runs away without forgetting, however, to take with her the royal gold. Pursued by Crown Prince Buggerlas and his loyal men, she is forced to flee into the mountains where eventually she meets her defeated husband hiding in a cavern. Oblivious of their precarious situation, the two cowardly misers proceed to quarrel fiercely over money matters. As Ubu is about to tear his wife apart, Prince Buggerlas discovers their hiding place. In the nineteenth century Romantic novel or melodrama, villains are, as a rule, caught, brought to justice, and punished. Jarry, who felt nothing but contempt for traditional theater, chose a different, quite unconventional ending. Although outnumbered and scared to death, the tyrant and his wife manage to escape without a scratch. In the final scene, the Ubus and their gang are on a boat sailing for France, where they hope the French government will appoint Pa Ubu master of finances in Paris.

Most great playwrights, including Shakespeare, Racine, and Corneille, have borrowed their major characters such as Cleopatra, Caesar, Augustus, Nero, and Attila from either modern or ancient Greco-Roman history. Jarry, however, strongly opposed historical drama and this traditional practice. According to him, a playwright either has to create an original being or else should not be writing drama. Pa Ubu is the exact embodiment of this idea; he cannot be traced back, either in recorded history or in mythology, but is imitated from real life.

The prototype of the antihero, Pa Ubu, totally deprived of feelings and conscience, was one of Jarry's teachers, Félix Hébert, physics master at the Lycée of Rennes. Short-legged, potbellied, looking from the back like an enormous insect, he was, according to some of his former students, incompetent, pompous, unfair, and unable to distinguish the innocent from the offenders who repeatedly played pranks on him in the classroom. In the eyes and minds of these young schoolboys, he was truly a monster. Nicknamed Père Hébert, Père Hébé, Eb, Ebé, Ebou, Jarry immortalized him under the now infamous name of Ubu. On the eve of *Ubu roi*'s opening, Jarry wrote an article in *La Revue blanche*, stating that he did not know what the name Ubu meant, then, interestingly enough, he admitted that it was the accidental distortion of the name of his still-living prototype: Ybex, maybe, the vulture. There is no question that Jarry pictured Ubu as a monster, whom he described in the article as an animal with a piglike face, a nose like the upper jaw of a crocodile, and a cardboard-like shell that makes him, aesthetically speaking, the brother of the most horrible sea creature, the horseshoe crab.

The use of human monsters in world literature goes back to ancient times. One comes across them in Homer's voyages, in legends, fairy tales, medieval stories, and particularly in Dante's *Inferno*. In the Romantic as well as in the English gothic novels, human characters are mutilated, deformed, sinister, and, in some cases, more bestial than beasts. In the works of Victor Hugo (as Jarry well knew), monsters appear in the image of vampires, dwarfs, and gargoyles. Although most of them symbolize Satan, physical and/or moral ugliness, a few are rehabilitated through revelation and their innocence is brought to light. The hunchback of Notre Dame, Quasimodo, is typical of this vision of man caught between the forces of good and evil, between his basest instincts and his loftiest ideals. Feared and cursed by society, Quasimodo at first appears to be as repulsive as a Dantean creature from the *Inferno*. In reality, however, this lonely, disfigured, suffering, tragic character is the essence of innocence, capable of true love and compassion. In his heart dwells an angel of spiritual beauty. In his famous preface to *Cromwell* (pb. 1827; English translation, 1896), Hugo stated that the subject of ugliness had for too long, too conveniently, been ignored and that the time had come to deal with it as an essential part of a work of art. Hugo claimed that there was a kind of ugliness, which was, paradoxically, true beauty and which in turn was antithetical to the superficial, if not hypocritical, notion of beauty advocated by the neoclassical school, whose heroes, although handsome, wealthy, and urbane in their outward appearance, were, in fact, too often possessed by undue pride, haughtiness, vanity, and lust.

This antithesis, dear to the Romantic writers and poets, was both disturbing and at the same time reassuring. Jarry, who was well acquainted with their work, held it in contempt and thought that dualities between black and white, darkness and revelation, the divine and the diabolical, simply did not exist. For this reason it is not surprising that nowhere in *Ubu roi* can an inversion of the images of good and evil be found.

To begin with, the former king of Aragon and his wife are the guests of the royal family of Poland. They are not grateful to their hosts for having offered them political asylum but, indeed, the opposite: They slaughter Venceslas, the queen, and their loyal subjects without ever expressing the slightest remorse. It is obvious that the perpetrator of this *coup d'état* is an old hand at it, and as the dethroned king of Aragon, it is easy to imagine how he governed his people. Like Nero, he embraces his allies not as a gesture of friendship but, rather, to stifle them all the better. Above all, Ubu, the man without either memory or conscience, is a killer who is never killed, never caught and punished for his crimes. Love and friendship are unknown words to him, and the same is true of his wife. Their marriage, too, is a monstrous, unholy alliance founded on greed and pure, undisguised hatred. In fact, Ma Ubu is the exact double of her husband. Each serves as a mirror to the other, which explains why each thoroughly abhors the other. They both swear, plot, betray, plunder, and slaughter to the same degree—so well, indeed, that there is really no difference between them. In this sense they must be viewed as mere mechanical puppets out of a Punch and Judy show. Although in the end the villains are defeated, they escape—unscathed, unscrupulous as ever, and, above all, free to pursue a life of betrayal and crime without punishment. Lady Macbeth and her husband, haunted by the memory of their crime, commit suicide to silence their tormented conscience. Ubu, on the contrary, never dies; he is in a way like the plague, forever present.

UBU CUCKOLDED

Ubu Cuckolded was written in 1888, while Jarry was still attending school in Rennes. It belongs to the second cycle of Ubu and was published for the first time in Geneva in 1944 with the help of the poet Paul Eluard, who owned the manuscript.

A short play without a story in the traditional sense of the word, *Ubu Cuckolded* is based on a series of quick events loosely related to one another. The action takes place in the home of an old, naïve, and kind scientist, Achras. His quiet existence comes to an abrupt end when Ubu and his companion Conscience, covered with spiderwebs, enter. The former king of Poland and of Aragon is now a doctor of pataphysics, the "science of imaginary solutions" (and one of Jarry's dearest inventions). Not to be surpassed by a scientist, Ubu, the eternal usurper, takes possession of Achras's house. The self-invited guest proceeds to explain to his disconcerted host, without any hint of embarrassment, that his wife is deceiving him with an Egyptian named Memnon. Achras exits baffled. Ubu, after consulting Conscience, and in spite of the latter, decides, on the grounds that the scientist is unable to defend himself, to experiment on Achras with his instrument of torture, the stake, on which his wife is to die. Immediately after, Achras is impaled by the Palotins, three henchmen of Ubu, who, armed with a "disembraining machine," kill and plunder for the benefit of their cowardly master.

Entering as unexpectedly as her husband, Ma Ubu arrives and asks to be introduced to her host. Happy to oblige her, the usurper shows her the impaled victim, whereupon she has a nervous breakdown. In the following acts, the henchmen go on their rampage, singing vociferously the praises of their infernal machine:

See, see the machine grind and grind
See, see the brains ground to pieces
See, see the stock-holders tremble with fear
Hurrah! Horns on your arse, long live Pa Ubu!

Ma Ubu deceives her husband with Memnon. Pa Ubu flushes his Conscience down the toilet. Memnon is happy to undergo the same fate because to him it is the only place where he can work. Achras, who was believed dead, comes back to life. To end this repetitive sequence of sadistic events, complete with blood and smashed brains, Jarry uses, of all forms of *deus ex machina*, another monster, a crocodile, which could just as well be a snake, implying that, contrary to traditional comedy, in the final analysis, there is no happy denouement. As the curtain falls, the three henchmen sing:

Fear the master of Phynances
Whatever the weather, wind or frost
He is on his way to strangle with delight his own brothers.

The cuckold theme was by no means new in French literature, dating back to at least the time of Molière and Racine. The manner in which it is treated by Jarry, however, is so radical that *Ubu Cuckolded* must be seen as more than another spoof of bourgeois morality. To begin with, the notions of time and space are entirely rejected. In addition there is no plot. The end is similar to the beginning or the center point, supposing there is one. Actions and decisions succeed one another without any hint of what has gone before. Whether a master or a slave as in *Ubu Enchained*, humankind, in the final analysis, has no memory or conscience. Crime pays and innocence itself is a crime.

Ubu Cuckolded is totally devoid of cohesion and form, and it can be regarded as an antiplay and as a metaphor for the world perceived as a cesspool, ruled by madness, and from which there is no escape. This nihilistic view of man's fate foreshadowed Ionesco's *Tueur sans gages* (pr., pb. 1958; *The Killer*, 1960) and Beckett's Dantean dramas.

OTHER MAJOR WORKS

LONG FICTION: *Les Minutes de sable mémorial*, 1894 (*Black Minutes of Memorial Sand*, 2001); *César-* *Antéchrist*, 1895 (*Caesar-Antichrist*, 1971); *Les Jours et les nuits: Roman d'un déserteur*, 1897 (*Days and Nights: Novel of a Deserter*, 1989); *L'Amour absolu*, 1899; *Messaline: Roman de l'ancienne Rome*, 1901 (*The Garden of Priapus*, 1936); *Le Surmâle: Roman moderne*, 1902 (*The Supermale: A Modern Novel*, 1968); *Gestes et opinions du docteur Faustroll, pataphysicien: Roman néo-scientific, suivi de spéculations*, 1911 (*Exploits and Opinions of Doctor Faustroll, Pataphysician*, 1965); *La Dragonne*, 1943.

NONFICTION: *Almanach illustré du Père Ubu*, 1901 (satiric chronicle); *La Chandelle verte, lumières sur les choses de ce temps*, 1969.

TRANSLATIONS: *La Papesse Jeanne*, 1908 (of Emmanuel Rhoïdès's novel; with Jean Saltas); *Les Silènes*, 1927 (of Christian Dietrich Grabbe's play *Scherz, Satire, Ironie und tiefere Bedeutung*).

MISCELLANEOUS: *Selected Works of Alfred Jarry*, 1965; *Œuvres complètes*, 1972; *Adventures in 'Pataphysics: Collected Works of Alfred Jarry, Volume 1*, 2001.

BIBLIOGRAPHY

Beaumont, Keith S. *Alfred Jarry: A Critical and Biographical Study.* New York: St. Martin's Press, 1984. A biography of Jarry that contains both information on his life and critical analysis of his work. Bibliography and index.

Fisher, Ben. *The Pataphysician's Library: An Exploration of Alfred Jarry's Livres Pairs.* Liverpool, England: Liverpool University Press, 2000. Although not centering on Jarry's dramatic work, this study examines Jarry's concept of pataphysics extensively. Bibliography and index.

LaBelle, Maurice Marc. *Alfred Jarry: Nihilism and the Theater of the Absurd.* New York: New York University Press, 1980. A study of Jarry's works, with emphasis on nihilism and his dramatic works' relation to the Theater of the Absurd. Bibliography and index.

Lennon, Nigey. *Alfred Jarry: The Man with the Axe.* Los Angeles: Panjandrum Books, 1984. A biography of Jarry, covering his life and works. Bibliography and index.

Schumacher, Claude. *Alfred Jarry and Guillaume Apollinaire*. New York: Grove Press, 1985. Schumacher compares and contrasts the works of Jarry and Guillaume Apollinaire. Bibliography and index.

Stillman, Linda Klieger. *Alfred Jarry*. Boston: Twayne, 1983. A basic biography of Jarry, treating his life and works. Bibliography and index.

Jacques Benay

ELIZABETH JOLLEY

Born: Birmingham, Warwickshire, England; June 4, 1923

PRINCIPAL DRAMA

Night Report, pr. 1975, pb. 1995 (radio play)
The Performance, pr. 1976, pb. 1995 (radio play)
The Shepherd on the Roof, pr. 1977, pb. 1995 (radio play)
The Well-bred Thief, pr. 1977, pb. 1995 (radio play)
Woman in a Lampshade, pr., pb. 1979 (radio play)
Two Men Running, pr. 1982, pb. 1995 (radio play)
Paper Children, pr. 1988, pb. 1995 (radio play)
Little Lewis Has a Lovely Sleep, pr. 1988, pb. 1995 (radio play)
The Well, pr. 1992, pb. 1995 (radio play)
Off the Air: Nine Plays for Radio, pb. 1995

OTHER LITERARY FORMS

Elizabeth Jolley's literary reputation is based mostly on her novels and short stories, although it is quite possible that more people have heard her radio plays than have extensively read her other works. The Australian Broadcasting Corporation estimated that up to fifty thousand people were listening each time they aired her plays.

Her novels include *Palomino* (1980), *Mr. Scobie's Riddle* (1983), *Milk and Honey* (1984), *The Well* (1986), *The Sugar Mother* (1988), *My Father's Moon* (1989), *Cabin Fever* (1990), *The Orchard Thieves* (1995), *Lovesong* (1997), *An Accommodating Spouse* (1999), and *An Innocent Gentleman* (2001). *The Well* was adapted to a full-length radio play and also made into a film (2000).

Short stories, many published in journals, appear in the collections *Five Acre Virgin and Other Stories* (1976), *The Travelling Entertainer and Other Stories* (1979), *Woman in a Lampshade* (1983), *Stories* (1984), and *Fellow Passengers: Collected Stories* (1997). "Woman in a Lampshade" appeared as a short story and as a radio drama, and the Australian Broadcasting Commission also dramatized it for television.

ACHIEVEMENTS

Elizabeth Jolley's first radio play, *Night Report*, won the inaugural Soundstage Radio Drama Special Prize (1975) from the Australian Broadcasting Corporation. *Two Men Running* received the Australian Writers Guild Award for original radio drama in 1982.

In addition to numerous honors for individual works, most notably for her novels, Jolley was awarded the Literature Board of the Australia Council Senior Fellowship in 1984. In 1986 the Western Australia Institute of Technology (now Curtin University) conferred on her an honorary doctorate. In 1987, she was named Citizen of the Year in the Arts and Culture and Entertainment and awarded an Officer of the Order of Australia for services to Australian Literature. In 1998 she was named one of Australia's Living Treasures.

Her work has been translated into many languages, including Spanish, German, Dutch, French, and Greek. Her papers, held in the Mitchell Library in Sydney, Australia, include unpublished works: at least two three-act plays for stage, a film script, and numerous radio plays.

BIOGRAPHY

Elizabeth Jolley was born Monica Elizabeth Knight on June 4, 1923, in Birmingham, England, and was raised in a largely German-speaking household. Her British father met her Austrian mother in Vienna in 1919. Although her father was a schoolteacher, Jolley and her younger sister were educated at home by a succession of French and Austrian governesses and by a series of "wireless lessons," radio lectures on specialized subjects. At age eleven Jolley was sent to a Quaker boarding school near Banbury Oxon. At seventeen she began training as a nurse at St. Thomas's Hospital in London, completing her training in Queen Elizabeth Hospital in Birmingham from 1943 to 1946. In 1959 she moved to Western Australia with her husband Leonard Jolley, a university librarian, and with their three children they settled in Perth and for a while lived on a small farm.

Jolley's first public recognition came from radio. Six of her radio plays were produced, and many short stories appeared before the publication of her first novel, *Palomino*, in 1980. Her work began attracting attention in the mid-1960's, and by the early 1980's she emerged as one of Australia's leading authors.

In the 1970's Jolley joined the faculty at Curtin University, in Perth, Western Australia, where she is professor of creative writing and writer-in-residence. When designing its largest theater complex, the university chose to honor Jolley by naming it for her.

ANALYSIS

Elizabeth Jolley is an important writer whose critical reputation keeps increasing. Her radio plays were very popular in Australia when produced by the Australian Broadcasting Corporation from 1975 to 1992, and the audio and scripts deserve to be more accessible to the reading and listening public. Jolley navigates skillfully between the realist tradition and the narrative experiments of postmodern fiction. Her deviation from the historical/biographical style of much fiction changed the direction of Australian literature in the later decades of the twentieth century.

Often comic and with frequently eccentric characters, Jolley's works always have a serious subtext. Major themes explore the effects on individuals of

Elizabeth Jolley (© Miriam Berkley)

differing from social norms, the valuation of the worth of a life, the role of women in a patriarchal society, and the intersection of life and death as individuals confront imminent death. Jolley's long interest in drama and the dramatic form influence all her work. She is particularly alert to the nuances of language and to the speaking voice. Her radio plays and also her novels and short stories emphasize monologue and dialogue. Action is typically structured around single dramatic moments.

NIGHT REPORT

Jolley's first produced radio play, *Night Report*, was highly recommended by all the judges of the Soundstage competition and was immediately accepted for production in the Australian Broadcasting Corporation's Perth studios.

The comic dialogue in the short play is not spoken; it appears in the form of notes written between Night Sister M. Shady and Matron A. Shroud at a dismal hospital for the aged. In her written instructions the Matron is quick to criticize the subordinate nurse rather than accept her own responsibilities. Nurse Shady in turn excuses herself in equally repetitive reports after her night shift. The inane notes between the two reveal the shoddy care the patients receive. The Matron's brother arrives and is admitted to the ward. Soon he is heavily in debt for gambling long into the nights with the other patients and Nurse Shady. A total reversal in the two women's roles ends the play.

Satirical in its portrayal of lack of compassion, the play uses one specific situation to indicate patterns of the larger world. The play eventually became part of the opening of Jolley's novel *Mr. Scobie's Riddle*, and its characters appear in the short story "'Surprise! Surprise' from Matron." Such re-use or elaboration of material and characters is common throughout Jolley's works.

THE PERFORMANCE

Based on a short story of the same title, the setting is a ward in a large psychiatric hospital. The main character is a middle-aged postal carrier, identified only as "Man," who carries on a long monologue about his life, part meditation and part confession. A ward orderly, Michael, occasionally makes an irrelevant comment.

What emerges is a slow revelation of the postal carrier's life and his mental breakdown. However, the "revelation" is more question than answer. What led to his inability to act? How did his relationship with his outgoing wife, always "performing" before her creative writing students, contribute to his sense of inadequacy? Is his guilt from not delivering a letter to an old woman who desperately awaited a letter from her son, or is it from more sinister events? Is it ever possible to present only one answer? What is the purpose of life anyway? His is a tragic monologue, somewhere between a moan and a howl of the frustration felt by character and listener alike.

Unlike Jolley's first play, the script gives precisely detailed instructions for voices, for background sounds in the hospital, and for specific music to be used in the scenes or between scenes. All elements are designed to reinforce each other in the service of dramatic effects. Jolley continued this pattern in subsequent plays.

By this second play she was also including in the script optional cuts ("opt.cut" and "end opt. cut"),

identifying sections that could be omitted according to the time requirements or the editorial decisions of the producers.

THE SHEPHERD ON THE ROOF

The play is based on Jolley's short story of the same name. The title refers to a major symbol in the text: The main character, Mrs. Clark, has noticed that in the afternoons some combination of shadows and features in the roof of a neighbor's house forms an image that looks like a shepherd tending his sheep.

Jolley says that the setting of the play is "somewhere in the mysterious shades between life and death." In the literal sense, Mrs. Clark is at the edge of the road where her car has crashed into trees along a paddock (enclosed field) where she had always wanted to stop, but her husband had always reminded her that it was restricted land. Two young passengers are already dead, though Mrs. Clark keeps saying (thinking) she will help them as soon as she is able to move. The final words of the play are in keeping with the rest of her very moving monologue following the crash:

> I want to walk now and go on walking to the far end. I've never seen what's at the other end of the long paddock. *(pause) (louder)* Are you there Shepherd? Come down off the roof, Shepherd. Are you there my good Shepherd? *(fade)*

THE WELL-BRED THIEF

Originally titled "Dear Neckless, Dear Barbara," the short-story version and the radio script both take the form of letters between two former schoolmates. The supposedly sophisticated Barbara is in England working for a publishing company; Mabel Morgan, whom Barbara insists on addressing as "Neckless" as she called her years ago, still lives in Medulla, Western Australia. Mabel has written a book-length manuscript, which she mails to Barbara. As the exchange of letters painfully reveals, Barbara claims the manuscript as her own, telling the innocent Mabel that it is lost. The play is filled with dramatic irony, as the audience understands more than the characters do, and is brilliant in its economical revelation of character and its depiction of misplaced trust.

WOMAN IN A LAMPSHADE

Atypically, Jolley wrote this play and then developed it as a short story. This is the only play published before the collection *Off the Air: Nine Plays for Radio*. The main character, a woman aged about forty-five, is an egotistical writer who claims to write better when she is wearing a lampshade. She picks up a young man and takes him to her house for a night, not caring about him but using him as inspiration for lines in what she is writing. Traditional values here are indicated by the lack of them. It is a humorous play with an unlikable cast: The woman is predatory and dominating, and she dismisses the young man because she says that he is boring.

TWO MEN RUNNING

Again, Jolley subverts the listeners' expectations. What first appears to be a dialogue between two prisoners is one man's internal monologue, the second "voice" another side of his personality. Enderby "talks" obsessively as he runs but has no words at all for the prison psychiatrist. There are several Oedipal references throughout the play: Enderby had murdered a woman he learns is his own mother. It is a bleak commentary on one of Jolley's frequent topics, the dysfunctional family.

PAPER CHILDREN

While moving between reality and fantasy, Jolley continues to look at families, here the angst and guilt of an Austrian gynecologist, Clara Shultz, who sent her baby daughter to Australia during World War II. In the last moments of Clara's life, she acknowledges that she did nothing to prevent the crimes of the Nazi regime and that it is too late to visit her grown daughter.

LITTLE LEWIS HAS A LOVELY SLEEP

This is Jolley's only play that does not appear in another form or as part of any other work. Miss Vales is a middle-aged baby-sitter for six-year-old Little Lewis, whose rich father is called Big Lewis. The play opens with Miss Vales writing a note to the parents to warn them there is blood under the bathroom door. It then flashes back to a few hours earlier when a man breaks into the house to kidnap the child.

The suspense is equaled by comedy. Miss Vale is still looking for Mr. Right, so when The Intruder

appears, she remembers that the head of the baby-sitting agency, Mrs. Porter, has always reassured her that the right man will show up. She chatters about anything and everything, endlessly quoting clichés from Mrs. Porter, all the while playing hostess, giving the kidnapper several kinds of liquor, then pills for his drunken headache. He ties her up in a chair so she cannot phone anyone when he goes to the bathroom, but she gets loose and heads after him. She sees blood seeping under the door.

She goes to write the note that started the play. What happened to The Intruder? Why is she bothering with a note when the parents will be home soon? All that is clear is that neither she nor The Intruder get what they want.

THE WELL

Written after the successful novel of the same title, the play presents a key section. Miss Hester Harper, about sixty, has raised an orphan, Katherine, now (as the cast description says) aged "sixteen to twenty-two." The vagueness of her age is suggestive of Miss Harper's possessive desire to keep Katherine a little girl who cannot leave her.

As the two return from a rare party, Katherine hits something with the car. Miss Harper gets out and throws what she says is a man's body down into an unused well, supposedly to protect Katherine. She then discovers that a large sum of money is missing from the house and tells Katherine to go down into the well and get it because the man must have stolen it before they came home. Katherine instead speaks of him as a handsome prince who will come out of the well to marry her.

In *The Well*, as in many of her other plays, Jolley portrays problems in family life, dramatically indicates more than the characters understand, blurs boundaries between reality and fantasy, upsets expectations, and gives the listener much to ponder.

OTHER MAJOR WORKS

LONG FICTION: *Palomino*, 1980; *The Newspaper of Claremont Street*, 1981; *Mr. Scobie's Riddle*, 1983; *Miss Peabody's Inheritance*, 1983; *Milk and Honey*, 1984; *Foxybaby*, 1985; *The Well*, 1986; *The Sugar Mother*, 1988; *My Father's Moon*, 1989; *Cabin Fe-*

ver, 1990; *The Georges' Wife*, 1993; *The Orchard Thieves*, 1995; *Lovesong*, 1997; *An Accommodating Spouse*, 1999; *An Innocent Gentleman*, 2001.

SHORT FICTION: *Five Acre Virgin and Other Stories*, 1976; *The Travelling Entertainer and Other Stories*, 1979; *Woman in a Lampshade*, 1983; *Stories*, 1984; *Fellow Passengers: Collected Stories*, 1997.

NONFICTION: *Central Mischief: Elizabeth Jolley on Writing, Her Past, and Herself*, 1992 (Caroline Lurie, editor); *Diary of a Weekend Farmer*, 1993.

BIBLIOGRAPHY

Bird, Delys. Introduction to *Off the Air: Nine Plays for Radio* by Elizabeth Jolley. New York: Viking Penguin, 1995. Bird provides information on the background and the production of Jolley's plays as well as interpretative commentary on major themes.

Bird, Delys, and Brenda Walker, eds. *Elizabeth Jolley: New Critical Essays*. Moss Vale, New South Wales, Australia: Angus and Robertson, 1991. A collection of essays on Jolley's works, produced in conjunction with the University of Western Australia. Bibliography and index.

McCowan, Sandra. *Reading and Writing Elizabeth Jolley: Contemporary Approaches*. South Fremantle, Western Australia, Australia: Fremantle Arts Centre Press, 1995. Critical analysis and interpretation of Jolley's works. Bibliography.

Salzman, Paul. *Elizabeth Jolley's Fictions: Helplessly Tangled in Female Arms and Legs*. Studies in Australian Literature series. St. Lucia, Queensland, Australia: University of Queensland Press, 1993. Although this study focuses on an examination of the themes in Jolley's fiction, these themes are also the subject of her radio plays. Bibliography and index.

Willbanks, Ray. "Elizabeth Jolley." In *Speaking Volumes: Australian Voices, Writers and Their Work*. Austin: University of Texas Press, 1991. An interview with Jolley, largely on her fiction.

Lois A. Marchino

HENRY ARTHUR JONES

Born: Grandborough, England; September 20, 1851
Died: London, England; January 7, 1929

PRINCIPAL DRAMA

Hearts of Oak, pr. 1879, pb. 1885
A Clerical Error, pr. 1879, pb. 1904
The Silver King, pr. 1882, pb. 1907 (with Henry Herman)
Saints and Sinners, pr. 1884, pb. 1891
Wealth, pr. 1889
The Middleman, pr. 1889, pb. 1907
Judah, pr. 1890, pb. 1894
The Crusaders, pr. 1891, pb. 1893
The Dancing Girl, pr. 1891, pb. 1907
The Bauble Shop, pr. 1893, pb. 1893(?)
The Tempter, pr. 1893, pb. 1898
The Masqueraders, pr. 1894, pb. 1899

The Case of Rebellious Susan, pr. 1894, pb. 1897
The Triumph of the Philistines, pr. 1895, pb. 1899
Michael and His Lost Angel, pr., pb. 1896
The Liars, pr. 1897, pb. 1901
The Physician, pr. 1897, pb. 1899
Carnac Sahib, pr., pb. 1899
Mrs. Dane's Defence, pr. 1900, pb. 1905
The Lackey's Carnival, pr., pb. 1900
The Princess's Nose, pr., pb. 1902
Whitewashing Julia, pr. 1903, pb. 1905
The Hypocrites, pr. 1906, pb. 1907
The Evangelist, pr. 1907, pb. 1908(?) (also known as *The Galilean's Victory*)
The Lie, pr. 1914, pb. 1915
Plays by Henry Arthur Jones, pb. 1982 (includes *The Silver King*, *The Case of Rebellious Susan*, and *The Liars*)

OTHER LITERARY FORMS

Henry Arthur Jones, a prolific dramatist, was also an energetic theater critic and polemicist. His prose writings include *The Renascence of the English Drama* (1895), *The Foundations of a National Drama* (1913), and *The Theatre of Ideas* (1915). Jones's polemics are found in his attacks on H. G. Wells and George Bernard Shaw in *Patriotism and Popular Education* (1919) and *My Dear Wells: A Manual for the Haters of England; Being a Series of Letters upon Bolshevism, Collectivism, Internationalism and the Distribution of Wealth, Addressed to Mr. H. G. Wells* (1921, 1922). Jones actively campaigned for the abolition of theatrical censorship. *The Renascence of the English Drama* brings together the essays in which he argues that drama has definite artistic forms, that it is a serious literary genre, and that a national theater should be established. He calls for copyright laws to be reformed and plays printed—at the time, radical ideas meeting with much opposition. *The Foundations of a National Drama* continues Jones's advocacy for the establishment of a national theater, argues for a more intelligent theater, and attacks contemporary theatrical frivolity. Jones believed that art has a social value—that the theater should educate audiences and bring beauty and culture to otherwise impoverished ordinary lives.

ACHIEVEMENTS

Arthur Henry Jones is regarded as one of the most important English dramatists and men of the theater during the last decades of the nineteenth century. *The Silver King*, hailed as a masterpiece of melodramatic stage craftsmanship, ran for 289 performances—a lengthy run by the standards of the time. In subsequent plays, Jones turned his attention to such serious themes as the exposure of hypocrisy and deceit and the depiction of the emerging "new woman." At his best, Jones was a master craftsman, a superb manipulator of theatrical dialogue and writer of problem plays. After the turn of the century and the success of *Mrs. Dane's Defence* in 1900, Jones, while continuing to write prolifically, began merely to rework well-tried formulas and melodramatic successes. Repetitious melodrama, social comedy, and problem plays

made him a theatrical back-number. His energies turned to the attempt to influence the course of subsequent theatrical literature through the dissemination of his ideas in books, pamphlets, and lectures. The 1982 publication by the Cambridge University Press of three of Jones's plays—*The Silver King*, *The Case of Rebellious Susan*, and *The Liars*—demonstrates that he is not an obscure late-Victorian dramatist of merely historical interest. Jones's reputation as a consummate dramatic craftsperson stands secure, as does his place in the English theatrical renaissance of the last decades of the nineteenth century.

BIOGRAPHY

Henry Arthur Jones was born on September 20, 1851, in Grandborough, Buckinghamshire. His background was Nonconformist; his father was a farmer, and his mother was a farmer's daughter. Jones's formal education seems to have stopped at the age of twelve, when he was sent to work for his uncle, who had a draper's shop on the Kentish coast at Ramsgate. Jones stayed for three and a half years in Ramsgate before moving to Gravesend, which was nearer to London, and to another draper's shop. In 1869, he moved into London, where he was to remain for most of his life. Self-educated, he read widely. His favorite authors were John Milton, Herbert Spencer, and Samuel Butler, and his favorite works were about scientific advancements. From Milton—a lifetime obsession—Jones learned verse drama techniques and the interweaving of biblical quotation into the texture of his plays. Scientists, explorers, and doctors often appear in his plays, and he makes frequent use of Spencerian and Butlerian ideas. In his first year in London, Jones wrote several unstaged one-act plays and an unpublished novel. *Hearts of Oak*, the first of his plays to be produced, premiered at the Theatre Royal, Exeter, on May 29, 1879, and the production encouraged Jones to devote his whole energies to drama. *A Clerical Error*, his first London play, was performed in October, 1879. Jones's reputation was secured by *The Silver King*, which opened at the Princess's Theatre on November 16, 1882. The success of this play provoked a dispute over its authorship, which Wilson Barrett, an actor-manager, claimed to

Henry Arthur Jones (Hulton Archive by Getty Images)

share with Jones and Henry Herman. A 1905 legal settlement denied Barrett's claim. *The Silver King* gave Jones some degree of financial security. His experience with Barrett soured Jones's attitude toward the prevailing actor-manager theatrical hierarchy of his day, but *The Crusaders*, his self-financed effort, which was produced in November, 1891, proved to be a disastrous financial failure.

In the 1890's Jones's work met with mixed fortune. *The Masqueraders*, *The Tempter*, *The Bauble Shop*, and *The Liars* succeeded, whereas *The Triumph of the Philistines*, *Michael and His Lost Angel*, *Carnac Sahib*, and *The Lackey's Carnival* aroused controversy and lost money. *Mrs. Dane's Defence*, first performed at Wyndham's in October, 1900, was his last real theatrical success. George Bernard Shaw, writing in his regular *Saturday Review* column, denounced *The Princess's Nose* as morally bankrupt, and another hostile critic, Arthur B. Walkley of *The*

Times of London, was barred from attending the opening of *Whitewashing Julia* in 1903. *The Hypocrites* was warmly received in the United States, but Jones's subsequent American theatrical venture, *The Evangelist*, failed. Deeply troubled by World War I, as were so many of his contemporaries, Jones wasted much energy in publically feuding with H. G. Wells and Shaw. He opposed what he regarded as their lack of patriotism in their opposition to the war. The fledgling film industry purchased and produced several of Jones's plays, but he disapproved of the end products. In 1923, he achieved a modest theatrical success in London with *The Lie* (originally produced nearly a decade before in the United States); this drama was prematurely replaced at Wyndham's by Shaw's *Saint Joan*.

Jones's private life is an enigma. With failing health and lack of success in his late years, he retreated from the theatrical world he loved so much. Jones had married Jane Eliza Seeley, the daughter of an artificial flower manufacturer, in 1875; she died in 1924. They had seven children, three sons and four daughters, one of whom, Doris Arthur Jones, produced in 1930 the official biography of her father, *The Life and Letters of Henry Arthur Jones*. A recurring leitmotif in Jones's drama is the conflict among sexual passion, social duty, and respectability. Such a conflict may well have had a foundation in the secrets of his own carefully guarded private life.

ANALYSIS

In 1894, Henry Arthur Jones called for "a school of plays of serious intention, plays that implicitly assert the value and dignity of human life, that it has great passions and great aims, and is full of meaning and importance." He set out to gain respect for the theater as a serious art form, rejecting the sensational melodrama so prevalent on the English stage. In *The Old Drama and the New* (1923), William Archer, a distinguished, perceptive critic, looked back at the theatrical world of late-Victorian and Edwardian England. For Archer, Jones was a natural dramatist whose chief aim was to criticize life as he saw it and especially to expose philistinism. Jones's chief weakness, in Archer's view, was his inability to free himself from the melodramatic traditions in which he served his theatrical apprenticeship. Jones's work largely falls into two categories: melodrama and comedy of intrigue. "The pity is" writes Archer, "that the world of his imagination is not sunlit but limelit."

Jones was a superb craftsperson and the author of a melodrama to outdo all the others, *The Silver King*, and of two brilliantly constructed plays, *The Liars* and *Mrs. Dane's Defence*. He is remembered as a champion of the serious theater, of the theater of ideas, and as an advocate of theatrical freedom. Jones was largely antagonistic toward contemporary theatrical developments, finding, for example, Anton Chekhov's *Vishnyovy sad* (pr., pb. 1904; *The Cherry Orchard*, 1908) to be the product of "someone who had visited a lunatic asylum." Even though Jones was eclipsed by Pinero, Shaw, and Wilde, his best plays are still appreciated. After all, as Shaw pointed out, Jones possessed "creative imagination, curious observation, inventive humour, originality, sympathy, and sincerity."

THE SILVER KING

The plot of *The Silver King*, Jones's first major success, provides a good illustration of his manipulation of melodramatic form. The play contains dialogue that is natural without being artificial (a quality of Jones's drama at its best), real passion, and some elements of genuine comedy (a quality sometimes lacking in Jones). *The Silver King* has a wronged hero, a persecuted heroine, a ruthless landlord, a snobbish aristocrat, a faithful family servant, a detective, and a Cockney comic. Wilfred Denver loses his money at the races and, while drowning his sorrows in a London pub, is taunted by his wife's former admirer, Henry Ware. Denver publicly swears to kill Ware. Ware's house is broken into by a gang led by the aristocrat Captain Skinner; Denver is chloroformed. Skinner, using Denver's gun, kills Ware, and Denver, believing that he is the murderer, takes a train north from London—the dramatist not missing the opportunity to throw in a scenically lavish but costly railway scene. Denver gets out at the first station and subsequently discovers that the train he was on has crashed. The police believe him to be dead. Going to the United States, he makes a fortune in the Montana silver mines. Returning to England, Denver discovers that his starving, ailing wife and child are to be ejected from Skinner's land without a roof over their heads. Secretly he gives them money and, in the disguise of an idiot, infiltrates Skinner's gang in order to find out what really happened. Justice triumphs in the end. All the ingredients of classic melodrama are here: an exciting plot, a great deal of action, violence, intrigue, a wronged hero and a suffering heroine, a malignant and devious villain of aristocratic origins, asinine police officers, and the triumph of good over evil. Even Matthew Arnold (not an easy critic to please), writing in the *Pall Mall Gazette*, December 6, 1882, thought that Jones had managed to transcend the limitations of his chosen genre: "Throughout the piece the diction and sentiments are natural, they have sobriety, they are literature." In spite of Jones's subsequent attempts to free himself from the shackles of melodrama and to write serious theatrical literature, he is still remembered for *The Silver King*, with its masterly use of well-tried formulas and its invigorating theatricality.

SAINTS AND SINNERS

Saints and Sinners is an example of Jones's early attempts to render contemporary social problems dramatically, to write "plays of serious intention." The plot revolves around a village girl's seduction by a handsome, worldly villain—the Little Emily syndrome. The honest fiancé is forced abroad, returning to claim his girl. Jones's aim in *Saints and Sinners*, as stated in his preface to the published text (in which Jones changed his original ending to a happy one), was to expose the "ludicrous want of harmony, or apparently of even the most distant relation of any sort between a man's religious professions and his actions." Letty, the seduced, is the daughter of a pastor in conflict with his materialistic congregation. Pastor Fletcher opposes the attempt of his deacon, a tanner, to throw the widow of his former partner out of his home. The tanner, Hoggard, makes public Letty's seduction, and Fletcher is forced by his congregation to resign. The 1884 theater audience found Jones's exposure of the congregation's hypocrisy too much and strongly reacted to the play, which had a long but controversial London run. After *Saints and Sinners*,

Jones had a reputation as an unconventional dramatist who daringly exposed folly. *Saints and Sinners* began his fight for theatrical freedom of expression, and he published the play in book form—not standard practice at the time—in order to give its ideas permanence as serious literature.

In the following year, 1885, his one-act play "Welcome Little Stranger" was turned down by the Lord Chamberlain on the grounds that its opening hinted at the mysteries of childbirth. From a modern point of view, Jones's depiction in *Saints and Sinners* of seduction, hypocrisy, and the dichotomy between religious belief and private conduct may appear tame and the Victorian public's outcry surprising. "Welcome Little Stranger" provides insight into Victorian attitudes concerning what was permissible onstage and what was not.

WEALTH AND THE MIDDLEMAN

Two plays of 1889, *Wealth* and *The Middleman*, demonstrate Jones's theatrical attempt to develop serious themes. *Wealth* revolves around the refusal of its heroine to obey her father and marry the wealthy man he has chosen for her. Turned out into the streets for her disobedience, she marries for love and finally is reconciled with her father on his deathbed. In *Wealth*, Jones deals with the conflict between love and wealth, emotion and filial duty. He was tackling a subject that was increasingly to occupy the attention of his fellow dramatists Arthur Wing Pinero, Oscar Wilde, and Shaw: the emerging modern woman and her aspirations. As theater, however, *Wealth* was not a success—it was believed to lack wit. By contrast, *The Middleman* was a stage success and is a very witty play. Humor, love, and social comment are inextricably interwoven into its plot, which has as its focal point a dreamy, exploited porcelain worker turning the tables on his ruthless master. The subplot unites the worker's daughter and the master's son. In terms of the development of Jones's stagecraft, *The Middleman* paved the way for his success with *Judah*; it is with *Judah* that Jones threw off the shackles of melodrama and wrote a genuine problem play.

JUDAH

Reviewing *Judah* in the *Saturday Review*, Shaw objected to it on the ground that it failed to tackle the

issues it raised, merely skirting around them. The play, Shaw wrote, "consists of clever preliminaries; and when the real play begins with the matrimonial experiment of Judah and Vashti, down comes the curtain as usual." *Judah*, with its pervasive biblical allusions, its use of allegory, and its hereditary motif, proved to be too ambitious for its author. The plot is not complicated and centers on a low-church clergyman, Judah, who holds extreme religious beliefs. Judah falls passionately in love with Vashti, a faith healer manipulated by her father into practicing public deceit. Vashti, true to the origin of her name, is torn between loyalty to her father and love. Judah helps her to free herself from her father's deception, and in the final act, after public confession, he resigns his ministry. There appear to be Ibsenite influences at work in the play's treatment of remorse and conscience, even though Jones vigorously denied that he had been influenced by Henrik Ibsen. Contemporary theatergoers were moved by powerful performances in the leading role, but *Judah* is essentially a closet drama, more suited to reading than to theatrical performance.

THE TEMPTER

Jones regarded *The Tempter* as one of his finest efforts. A verse play of ideas in five acts, *The Tempter* concentrates on the conflict between duty and passion. The blank verse drama is set in the fourteenth century, with the Devil setting traps for the other characters, especially for a religious man who, despite himself, falls deeply in love with a rebellious, unhappily married girl. The setting is too ambitious and the play too full of Shakespearean and Miltonic echoes and associations to be successful.

THE MASQUERADERS

Jones returned to the theme of the struggle against temptation in *The Masqueraders*, in which one of the leading characters is a scientist, presented as a high-principled but tempted man, devoted to his work and endeavoring to expand the frontiers of knowledge. One woman (a role played for all its worth by one of the leading ladies of the day, Mrs. Patrick Campbell) is caught between two men: her dissolute feckless husband and the scientist. Eventually, the latter chooses the path of research and goes to Africa, but not before he has given the heroine, who has thrown in her lot with him, financial security. The play's attempt to reveal the unhappiness behind the glitter of seemingly successful lives is interesting, but theatrically it does not succeed.

THE CASE OF REBELLIOUS SUSAN AND THE TRIUMPH OF THE PHILISTINES

Jones's next play, *The Case of Rebellious Susan*, was a box-office success. Set in high society and wittily focusing on the new woman and sexual repression, it tackled adultery and sexual discrimination. The play demonstrates in the character of its heroine, Susan, Jones's remarkable ability to create a character whose ideas are basically not in sympathy with his own. *The Case of Rebellious Susan* and *The Triumph of the Philistines* were partly reactions to Shaw's counsel that Jones should write detailed comedies of manners. In *The Triumph of the Philistines*, Jones returned to his earlier theme of attacking English philistinism and resistance to change.

THE LIARS

In *The Liars*, Jones returned to social comedy, the comedy residing in each character's frantic attempts to cover up the "truth" from the others. Lady Jessica Napean weaves a tangled web in order to divert her jealous husband's suspicion concerning what in effect was an innocent meeting. Edward Falkner, a young explorer in love with Lady Jessica, plans an elaborate and complicated elopement, stopped at the last moment by Sir Christopher Deering. Sir Christopher upholds the traditional social conventions and the wisdom that, in English society, pretenses have to be maintained at all costs. Marriage cannot be destroyed. The young explorer goes on an expedition to Africa. Particularly noticeable in *The Liars* is the superb craftsmanship exhibited in the plotting, which reaches a crescendo of Jamesian elaborateness of deceit in the third act. In the brilliant dialogue of *The Liars*, Jones captures the upper-class spirit of his milieu. Even Shaw remarked, when reviewing the play, that Jones gave a "very keen and accurate picture of smart society." Unfortunately, Jones's play ultimately accepts the very conservative values that it seems to have set out to attack.

MRS. DANE'S DEFENCE

Today, *Mrs. Dane's Defence* is regarded as Jones's masterpiece. It has been praised for its tightness and economy of construction, its strength of characterization, and its superb dialogue—especially in the third act's cross-examination scene between Sir Daniel (Mr. Justice) Carteret and Mrs. Dane. The ending is not without power. Mrs. Dane is forced into exile to Devonshire, "outside the palings." She and Jones accept that "the world is very hard on a woman," but that is the way of the world. There is no attempt at a happy ending. The dramatist accepts what he regards as inexorable social laws. Jones was a superb craftsman, and his skill reached its consummate height in *Mrs. Dane's Defence*. After this play, he churned out another twenty-six full-length plays, variations on anachronistic themes with settings in a time gone forever. *The Lie*, produced in London in 1923 but written and produced in New York nearly a decade before, became a West End hit. Jones tapped his old melodramatic techniques to produce a drama that revolves around two sisters in love with the same man and that deals with illegitimacy and deceit.

OTHER MAJOR WORKS

NONFICTION: *The Renascence of the English Drama*, 1895; *The Foundations of a National Drama*, 1913; *The Theatre of Ideas*, 1915; *Patriotism and Popular Education*, 1919; *My Dear Wells: A Manual for the Haters of England; Being a Series of Letters upon Bolshevism, Collectivism, Internationalism and the Distribution of Wealth, Addressed to Mr. H. G. Wells*, 1921, 1922.

BIBLIOGRAPHY

Booth, Michael R. *Theatre in the Victorian Age*. Cambridge, England: Cambridge University Press, 1991. Contains a discussion of Jones, one of the two most popular writers of melodrama (the other being Arthur Wing Pinero, with whom he is always linked). Examines his interest in the themes of the exploitation of the working class, the conflict between capital and labor, and the struggle between faith and doubt.

Foulkes, Richard. *Church and Stage in Victorian England.* Cambridge, Mass.: Cambridge University Press, 1997. This examination of the relationship between the church and the theater in Victorian England examines, among other plays, Jones's *Michael and His Lost Angel.*

Griffin, Penny. *Arthur Wing Pinero and Henry Arthur Jones.* New York: St. Martin's Press, 1991. A biographical work that examines the lives and literary output of Jones and Arthur Wing Pinero, along with the times in which they lived. Bibliography and index.

Wearing, J. P. "Henry Arthur Jones: An Annotated Bibliography of Writings About Him." *English Literature in Transition, 1880-1920* 22, no. 3 (1979): 160-228. A useful collection of critical reviews, ranging from an appreciation of Jones's contributions to the theater to a dismissal of his work as hopelessly out of fashion. Some critics note that one or two of his plays, however, have enjoyed successful revivals.

William Baker,
updated by Mildred C. Kuner

PRESTON JONES

Born: Albuquerque, New Mexico; April 7, 1936
Died: Dallas, Texas; September 19, 1979

PRINCIPAL DRAMA

The Last Meeting of the Knights of the White Magnolia, pr. 1973, pb. 1976
Lu Ann Hampton Laverty Oberlander, pr. 1974, pb. 1976
The Oldest Living Graduate, pr. 1974, pb. 1976
A Texas Trilogy, pr. 1974, pb. 1976 (includes *The Last Meeting of the Knights of the White Magnolia, Lu Ann Hampton Laverty Oberlander*, and *The Oldest Living Graduate*)
A Place on the Magdalena Flats, pr. 1976, pb. 1984
Santa Fe Sunshine, pr., pb. 1977 (one act)
Juneteenth, pr. 1979 (one act)
Remember, pr. 1979

OTHER LITERARY FORMS

Preston Jones is known only for his plays.

ACHIEVEMENTS

Preston Jones is often labeled a regional playwright, and certainly one of his achievements was his treatment of the American Southwest as a setting for serious drama. His plays capture the idiosyncratic characters, regional language, and unique experience of the rural Southwest at a time of transition for the land and its people. The significance of Jones's work, however, is not limited to his recording of the life of a specific community. The plays are significant commentaries on the way people deal with fundamental human problems: the pain of loneliness, the fear of failure, the effects of time. Like Anton Chekhov, Jones chronicles the passing of a way of life, and he does so with much of the gentle criticism and humorous affection of the Russian playwright. Jones's work also contains an exuberance and rough energy, however, which are uniquely his and are rooted in the language and energy of his characters. Indeed, Jones's discovery of the value to be found in the lives and troubles of the most ordinary of people and of the lyric poetry embedded in their native idiom constitutes his most important theatrical achievement.

BIOGRAPHY

Preston St. Vrain Jones was born in Albuquerque, New Mexico, on April 7, 1936. His father, a former lieutenant governor of New Mexico, had been a professional military man who at one time had hoped for

Preston Jones in 1976. (AP/Wide World Photos)

a career writing Western novels. Jones grew up in New Mexico, attending a Catholic boarding school for boys for a short time before he was graduated from high school in Albuquerque. After a brief period of military service, Jones entered the University of New Mexico, from which he received a bachelor of science degree in speech in 1960. He taught one semester in a high school in Tucumcari, New Mexico, before returning to the University of New Mexico to study drama for a year. During this period, he also spent some time working with the State Highway Department in and around Colorado City, Texas, which later became the model for Bradleyville, Texas, the setting of *A Texas Trilogy.*

In 1961, Jones enrolled in the drama department of Baylor University in Waco, Texas, where he studied with Paul Baker, nationally known as an innovative force in Southwestern theater. Baker quickly be-

came, and remained, a major influence on Jones's life and career; he asked Jones to join the Dallas Theater Center, where Jones continued his studies and worked with the theater's professional company. While there, he married Mary Sue Birkhead, an actress and designer and then assistant director of the Dallas Theater Center. In 1963, the Dallas Theater Center transferred its academic affiliation from Baylor to Trinity University in San Antonio, Texas, from which Jones received a master of arts in drama in 1966. Jones remained in Dallas as a member of the Dallas Theater Center's resident professional company, accumulating experience in all phases of theater, which served him well when he began to develop his interest in playwriting.

Although interested in writing for much of his life, Jones did not emerge as a serious playwright until 1973, with the premiere of *The Last Meeting of the Knights of the White Magnolia.* The previous year, Jones had been appointed producer of the Dallas Theater Center's small, experimental theater. Dissatisfied with the scripts available, particularly with the lack of good regional drama, Jones decided to write something himself, drawing on his knowledge of the Southwest and especially on his experiences in Colorado City. He completed *Lu Ann Hampton Laverty Oberlander* first, following quickly with *The Last Meeting of the Knights of the White Magnolia* and *The Oldest Living Graduate.* In 1974, the three plays were performed in repertory at the Dallas Theater Center. *The Last Meeting of the Knights of the White Magnolia* was selected as the offering of the American Playwright's Theater the following year, and in 1976, the three plays broke all box-office records at the Kennedy Center in Washington and opened on Broadway. Although the reviews of the New York production were mixed, the popular and critical success of the plays across the United States established Jones as a major new American playwright.

Following *A Texas Trilogy,* Jones wrote three more full-length plays and a short one-act. All but one of the works premiered at the Dallas Theater Center, where Jones continued to work as an actor and director as well as resident playwright. While the later plays have not received the widespread production and recognition of the first three plays, they show Jones's growing maturity as a writer as well as his continuing interest in the major themes of the trilogy. Unfortunately, Jones's career was cut short when he died unexpectedly on September 19, 1979, following surgery for a bleeding ulcer. The seven plays which he finished, a remarkable feat for the relatively brief span of his writing career, represent an important contribution to American dramatic literature.

ANALYSIS

The plays of Preston Jones are remarkably consistent in their concentration on character over plot, in their exploration of the poetry inherent in ordinary speech, and in their emphasis on certain prominent themes. From the beginning of his literary career, Jones's central theme was time. He explored—sometimes seriously, sometimes humorously, but always sympathetically—the effects of the inexorable march of time on people never quite prepared for the changes it will bring. His characters are usually lonely, isolated, cut off from the mainstream of the world by social changes, by geography, by ghosts from their past. They are often people who would be considered failures by normal standards but in whom Jones finds strength and emotional depth that mitigate their lack of the usual hallmarks of success.

Jones's concerns with the fear of failure, the pain of loneliness, and the effects of time are presented principally through character. Jones's great strength as a dramatist lies in his depiction of original and distinct characters who are able to engage the audience's emotions in a profound way. Like the plays of Anton Chekhov, Jones's theater is often singularly undramatic. If his plotting is sometimes weak or contrived, however, his language never is, and it is primarily through dialogue that his characters are rendered. Jones possessed a sure ear for dialogue, an ability to capture the idiosyncratic phrases, the natural rhythms, the inherent poetry of everyday language. If that language is often rough and profane, it is just as often lyrically beautiful, reverberating with a poetry that transcends its common origins.

Jones represented a new and important force in American theater. As a successful playwright who lived and worked entirely outside New York, he helped establish a new acceptance of the work of regional theaters and writers around the country. The weaknesses of his plays, his often thin or contrived plots and an overreliance on the Southwestern setting, are more than balanced by the strength and originality of his characters, the realistic density of his imaginative world, and the natural poetry of his dialogue. His plays grew out of the life of the American Southwest, but they deal with more universal and immediate human problems. In a very short span of time, he created a body of work that should secure his place among the best American playwrights.

A TEXAS TRILOGY

Jones is best known for the three plays that make up *A Texas Trilogy*: *The Last Meeting of the Knights of the White Magnolia*, *Lu Ann Hampton Laverty Oberlander*, and *The Oldest Living Graduate*. These plays are not unified by consecutive events, as is typical in dramatic trilogies, but by a single setting, shared characters, and common themes. The action of each play is separate and independent of the others, but each deals in its own way with Jones's themes of failure, isolation, and time. The town of Bradleyville, of which Jones created a map with the locations of various characters' homes and other important landmarks carefully noted, is isolated from the present and the future, bypassed by the new highway, and its people are isolated from one another by racial prejudices, past events, and present needs. The town is a relic of a past way of life, in which most of its characters are trapped by their own pasts: Lu Ann by her marriages, the Colonel by his war experiences, Skip Hampton by his failures and his alcoholism. In the three plays, Jones examines different aspects of the passing rural way of life that Bradleyville represents.

THE LAST MEETING OF THE KNIGHTS OF THE WHITE MAGNOLIA

The first of the plays to be produced was *The Last Meeting of the Knights of the White Magnolia*. The plot of the play is very simple: The members of a social lodge gather for their monthly meeting, expecting the usual evening of drinking and playing dominoes, only to find the last remnants of the dying fraternal order disintegrate during the evening as they attempt to initiate their first new member in more than five years. Neither the individual members nor the lodge itself, with its basic ideals of white supremacy and unquestioning patriotism, has been able to adjust to the social changes of the late 1950's and early 1960's.

Although Jones ridicules the ludicrous aspects of such fraternal orders—the mystical ceremonies, the pointless rules and regulations—and while he never excuses his characters' basic ignorance and bigotry, he presents sympathetically their need for companionship and sense of community and their fears and confusions at the potential loss of these values. The play is uproariously funny, but it never loses sight of the basic humanity of the characters, each of which is etched with depth and precision. The most memorable figure is that of Colonel J. C. Kinkaid, a shell-shocked veteran of World War I whose physical and mental deterioration during the course of the evening graphically parallels the dissolution of the group and, in a broader sense, of the Bradleyville way of life.

LU ANN HAMPTON LAVERTY OBERLANDER

While *The Last Meeting of the Knights of the White Magnolia* presents a general view of Bradleyville, Jones's second play concentrates more closely on a single character. *Lu Ann Hampton Laverty Oberlander* begins in 1953, when its title character is a bubbly but dissatisfied eighteen-year-old cheerleader, and traces her life over a twenty-year period. Eager to leave her hometown and see the world, Lu Ann never gets any farther than a trailer park in a nearby town, but she survives a divorce, her second husband's death, her brother's alcoholism, and her mother's debilitating illness, and she achieves a kind of quiet dignity through her acceptance of her fate. A failure by most standards, Lu Ann is seen by Jones as a survivor, worthy of sympathy and praise. *Lu Ann Hampton Laverty Oberlander* also traces the life of Skip Hampton, a character introduced in *The Last Meeting of the Knights of the White Magnolia*. As Lu Ann grows in strength and dignity, her brother degenerates from an optimistic but ineffectual schemer to a

painfully dependent alcoholic. The plot of *Lu Ann Hampton Laverty Oberlander*, with its careful symmetry, is perhaps too contrived, but the characters are memorable and the dialogue compares well with that of Jones's other plays. In a typically realistic and poignant sample of Jones's language, Skip notes how ironic it is "when all that stands between a man and the by-God loony bin is his sister's tab down to the Dixie Dinette."

THE OLDEST LIVING GRADUATE

The last play of the trilogy, *The Oldest Living Graduate*, focuses on Colonel Kinkaid, who, as he did in *The Last Meeting of the Knights of the White Magnolia*, reflects the values and attitudes of the past. His distrust of business, his love for the land, and his insistence on salvaging a small part of his past from the ravages of time place him in conflict with his son Floyd, the forward-looking local entrepreneur. The play looks with humor at the foibles and prejudices of Bradleyville's country-club set and its small-town morality, at academic and military folderol, at the values of a lost way of life, at the conflicts between generations, and at death itself. *The Oldest Living Graduate* is the most sophisticated and finely crafted of the three plays that make up the trilogy. In it, Jones combines his skill at characterization with a more complex plot and achieves a level of poetry, particularly in the Colonel's dialogue, that is unmatched in any of the earlier plays. The character of the Colonel is perhaps Jones's finest achievement; it is a portrait that evokes sentiment without being sentimental, a feat achieved principally through the clarity and complexity of the Colonel's language.

Although each of the plays of *A Texas Trilogy* stands as a completely independent unit, the three plays have been produced as a single work. In such a production, the events in the three stories are arranged chronologically, beginning with the first act of *Lu Ann Hampton Laverty Oberlander*. *The Last Meeting of the Knights of the White Magnolia* is played after the first half of *The Oldest Living Graduate*. The performance concludes with the rest of the Colonel's story and the last two acts of *Lu Ann Hampton Laverty Oberlander*. Combining the plays in this way makes clear the intimate connection between the three works, which runs much deeper than the shared locale and characters, and reveals the novelistic aspect of Jones's vision. The details of place and characters give the plays a solid basis in realism that becomes even clearer when the plays are seen together. The town of Bradleyville takes on a level of dense reality akin to that of William Faulkner's Yoknapatawpha County: The lives of the characters interweave with and reflect one another, as they often do in Faulkner's fiction. Lu Ann and Colonel Kinkaid, in particular, take on new nuances as their stories are told together; the Colonel, who left Bradleyville and was destroyed by a war he never fully understood, is paralleled by Lu Ann, who remained at home and grew strong and forgiving by facing her troubles there. *A Texas Trilogy*, as a whole, has an import beyond the significance of any of the plays individually.

A PLACE ON THE MAGDALENA FLATS

Jones's later plays have not achieved the success of *A Texas Trilogy*. They share, however, the qualities that characterize that work. *A Place on the Magdalena Flats* was first produced in Dallas in 1976. It underwent substantial revision during later productions in New Mexico and Wisconsin in 1976 and 1979, respectively. The principal changes in the script were alterations in the plot that focused the play more clearly on the older brother, Carl. While improved, the final version is not completely satisfactory, because of the lack of resolution of the younger brother's story. Although it contains rich humor, *A Place on the Magdalena Flats* is more restrained in mood than any of the trilogy plays. Again, characters deal in isolation with ghosts from their past, this time in the drought-stricken cattle country of New Mexico. The language of the play is particularly rich in poetic imagery and metaphor, marking a growing maturity in Jones's writing.

SANTA FE SUNSHINE

With *Santa Fe Sunshine* and *Juneteenth*, the latter commissioned by the Actors' Theatre of Louisville as one of a series of one-act plays on American holidays, Jones turned to pure comedy. *Juneteenth* is a rather thin play; the plot is weak, and the one-act form does not allow Jones time to develop his characters fully. *Santa Fe Sunshine* is actually an earlier work to which Jones returned after the success of *A Texas Trilogy*. It lacks the depth of Jones's other plays, but it contains some delightfully eccentric characters and very witty dialogue. Set in Santa Fe, New Mexico, during the 1950's when the city was a growing artist colony, the play gently ridicules the local beatniks, the patrons who know little about art, and the artists themselves, who are all in the business of making art for money's sake, although they like to pretend otherwise.

REMEMBER

Although Jones drew on his own experiences for all of his plays, his last play, *Remember*, contains the most obviously autobiographical material. Jones, like his leading character Adrian Blair, was graduated from high school in 1954, after spending some time at a Catholic boarding school. Also like Adrian, he began to reexamine his religious roots as he reached middle age. Adrian is a second-rate actor who finds himself playing a dinner theater in his hometown on his fortieth birthday. He has avoided the town, and his past, for twenty years. Now he finds that little of what he remembers is left: His old home is gone, his friends have changed, his former teacher, Brother Anthony, has left the order and become a real-estate salesman. As Adrian tries to go back in time and rediscover values he has lost—religion, friendship, love—he finds that the world he once knew exists, in fact, only in his memory. When his former sweetheart offers the possibility of renewing their love, he rejects her, preferring the past to the present with its shifting values and lack of continuity.

Although *Remember* clearly deals with the themes that preoccupied Jones in all of his plays, it also represents a new direction in Jones's writing. Although the geographical location of the play remains the Southwest, the characters are better educated and more self-aware than the inhabitants of Bradleyville. This shift allows Jones a use of literary allusion and metaphor that the more limited experience of his earlier characters prohibited, and his dialogue becomes even richer and more lyric with this addition. This enhanced language, combined with Jones's usual depth of character and his engaging wit, places *Remember* among his finest achievements.

BIBLIOGRAPHY

Busby, Mark. *Preston Jones*. Boise, Idaho: Boise State University Press, 1983. Although many theses and dissertations have been written providing background on, and analysis of, Jones's plays, this slim volume (fifty-two pages) is one of very few books published on the playwright and his works. Busby's book, part of the Western Writers series of Boise State University, offers readers valuable criticism and interpretation of the playwright's drama.

Clurman, Harold. Review of *A Texas Trilogy*, by Preston Jones. *The Nation*, October 9, 1976, 348-350. Compares Jones's *A Texas Trilogy* to a farce of Eugene O'Neill's projected cycle, *A Tale of Possessors, Self-Dispossessed*, based on O'Neill's belief that "the greatest failure in history" was the United States, which, in its race for materialism, "lost all valid faith." Clurman points out that Jones's Bradleyville is a "microcosm" representing "domains beyond Texas or the South."

Cook, Bruce. "Preston Jones: Playwright on the Range." *Saturday Review* 3 (May 15, 1976): 40-42. Written three years before the playwright's death, this article provides an informative look at the man, the artist, and the intellectual. Cook calls Jones "an original, a walking bundle of contradictions," and the "most promising American playwright to come along in two or three decades." Includes brief comments by critic Audrey Wood. Contains a photograph of Jones and another of a scene from *A Place on the Magdalena Flats*.

Kroll, Jack. "Branch Water." Review of *A Texas Trilogy*, by Preston Jones. *Newsweek*, October 4, 1976, 97. Kroll includes a brief discussion of the reasons for the mixed reviews and ambiguity that followed the trilogy's Broadway opening. His comments on the three plays that form the trilogy help show the playwright's depiction of the "emptiness, despair and absurdity of small-town life." Contains a photograph of actress Diane Ladd in *Lu Ann Hampton Laverty Oberlander*.

_____. "Texas Marksmanship." Review of *A Texas Trilogy*, by Preston Jones. *Newsweek*, May 17, 1976, 95-96. Although the word "regionalism" has become outmoded in American culture, Kroll explains that regionalism, which is found in Jones's drama, may be coming back, as "more and more Americans seek their identity close to home." Kroll says that region extends beyond a physical area to become a "psychic and spiritual locale." Photographs.

Prideaux, Tom. "The Classic Family Drama Is Revived in *A Texas Trilogy*." *Smithsonian* 7 (October, 1976): 49-54. This six-page essay, strewn with photographs, contains brief biographical information, traces the playwright's career, and provides summaries of the three plays in *A Texas Trilogy*. Includes quotations from a conversation with Jones, in which the author reminisces about his youth, his high school days, and his college friends.

Kathleen Latimer

BEN JONSON

Born: London, England; June 11, 1573
Died: London, England; August 6, 1637

PRINCIPAL DRAMA

The Isle of Dogs, pr. 1597 (with Thomas Nashe; no longer extant)

The Case Is Altered, pr. 1597, pb. 1609
Every Man in His Humour, pr. 1598 (revised 1605), pb. 1601 (revised 1616)
Hot Anger Soon Cold, pr. 1598 (with Henry Chettle and Henry Porter; no longer extant)
Every Man out of His Humour, pr. 1599, pb. 1600

The Page of Plymouth, pr. 1599 (with Thomas
    Dekker; no longer extant)
Robert the Second, King of Scots, pr. 1599 (with
    Henry Chettle and Thomas Dekker; no longer
    extant)
Cynthia's Revels: Or, The Fountain of Self-Love,
    pr. c. 1600-1601, pb. 1601
Poetaster: Or, His Arraignment, pr. 1601, pb. 1602
Sejanus His Fall, pr. 1603, pb. 1605 (commonly
    known as *Sejanus*)
Eastward Ho!, pr., pb. 1605 (with George
    Chapman and John Marston)
Volpone: Or, The Fox, pr. 1605, pb. 1607
Epicœne: Or, The Silent Woman, pr. 1609, pb. 1616
The Alchemist, pr. 1610, pb. 1612
Catiline His Conspiracy, pr., pb. 1611 (commonly
    known as *Catiline*)
Bartholomew Fair, pr. 1614, pb. 1631
The Devil Is an Ass, pr. 1616, pb. 1631
The Staple of News, pr. 1626, pb. 1631
The New Inn: Or, The Light Heart, pr. 1629, pb.
    1631
The Magnetic Lady: Or, Humours Reconciled, pr.
    1632, pb. 1640
A Tale of a Tub, pr. 1633, pb. 1640
The Sad Shepherd: Or, A Tale of Robin Hood, pb.
    1640 (fragment)

OTHER LITERARY FORMS

Ben Jonson was a masterful poet as well as a dramatist. His poetry, with some justification, has the reputation of being remote from modern readers. A dedicated classicist, Jonson emphasized clarity of form and phrase over expression of emotion, and many of his poems seem to be exercises in cleverness and wit rather than attempts to express an idea or image well. Others of his poems, however, retain their power and vision: "To Celia," for example, has given the English language the phrase "Drink to me only with thine eyes."

The difficulty of Jonson's poetry originates in large part in his very mastery of poetic form. Jonson was a student of literature, and he was a man of letters with few equals in any era. He studied the poetic forms of classical Greek and Latin literature as well

as those of later European literature, and he used what he learned in his own work. The result is a body of poetry that is very diverse, including salutations and love poems, homilies and satires, epigrams and lyrics. Much of the poetry appeals primarily to academics because of its experimental qualities and its displays of technical virtuosity. Yet those who allow themselves to be put off by Jonson's prodigious intellectualism miss some of the finest verse in English.

Jonson was also a prodigious writer of masques—dramatic allegorical entertainments, usually prepared to celebrate special occasions and presented at court. Jonson's masques have in common with his poetry technical achievement and, with much of his occasional verse, a focus on the virtues, real and reputed, of nobility and royalty. Although the emphasis was on spectacle and celebration of the aristocracy, Jonson tried to make his masques legitimate works of literature, and they have enjoyed increasing critical attention in recent years.

ACHIEVEMENTS

Ben Jonson was the foremost man of letters of his time. His knowledge of literature was combined with a passionate personality and a desire to be respected; the combination resulted in his efforts to elevate authors in the estimation of society. He endeavored to demonstrate the importance of literature in the lives of people and in their culture. Although he regarded his dramatic work as merely one facet of his literary life, he was determined that the playwright should receive the esteemed title of "poet." In the Elizabethan era, plays were regarded as unimportant public amusements; satires, sonnets, and narrative verse were expected to carry the heavy freight of ideas and art. Jonson worked to establish drama as a legitimate literary form by showing that it could be a conscious art with rules of organization that were as valid as those of more esteemed literary genres.

In 1616, Jonson published *The Workes of Benjamin Jonson*, including in the volume nine of his plays in addition to other writings. Never before had any author dared to give his plays the title "Works." The term "works" was usually reserved for profound philosophical treatises. Jonson was derided by some writers for being conceited and for trying to make plays seem important; even after his death, some traditionalists found his title difficult to accept. Further, Jonson promoted the cause of drama as high art by devoting much care to the publishing of the texts of his plays, thereby establishing a higher standard for published texts of dramas than had existed before. The publication of *The Workes of Benjamin Jonson* led at least indirectly to the important First Folio edition of William Shakespeare's plays.

Jonson's reputation as a dramatist is inextricably bound with that of Shakespeare. Although Jonson was esteemed above Shakespeare by most of his contemporaries, subsequent eras have elevated Shakespeare at Jonson's expense. Thus, although Jonson's comedies are wonderful and are well received by modern audiences, they are rarely performed. Shakespeare's poetry is better than Jonson's; his tragedies are more moving; his comedies are more diverse and have superior characterizations. To acknowledge Shakespeare's superiority is not to derogate Jonson's achievement; Shakespeare is alone atop the world's authors, but Jonson is not far below. In addition, Jonson's plays are superior to Shakespeare's in consistency of plot and structure. Had there been no William Shakespeare, there might today be Jonson festivals, and *Volpone* and *The Alchemist* might be the revered standards for college drama productions.

BIOGRAPHY

Tradition has it that Benjamin Jonson was born in 1572; literary historians put his birth in 1573, probably on June 11. His father, an Anglican minister, died about a month before Jonson was born. His mother married a master bricklayer in 1574; the family lived in Westminster. While growing up, Jonson attended Westminster School and became a student of William Camden, who was perhaps the greatest classicist and antiquarian of the Elizabethan and Jacobean ages. Jonson's interest in classical literature, his care in constructing what he wrote, and his respect for learning all have their origins in the teachings of Camden. Techniques for writing that Jonson used throughout his life were first learned from Camden,

including the practice of writing out a prospective poem first in prose and then converting the prose to verse.

In about 1588, Jonson became an apprentice bricklayer. This part of his life became the subject of jokes and gibes in his later years, but he seems to have taken pride in his humble origins. His respect for achievement and general lack of respect for claims of importance based solely on heredity or accident may have had their roots in his own struggles as a lower-class laborer. He left his bricklaying work to join the army in its war against the Spanish in the Lowlands in 1591 or 1592. During his tenure in the army, he apparently served with some distinction; he claimed that he was the English champion in single combat against a Spanish champion and that he slew his opponent while the assembled armies watched. He was handy with swords and knives and was, when young, quite combative and physically intimidating.

Jonson eventually returned to England. Little is known of his activities until 1597, save that he married Anne Lewis on November 14, 1594. The mar-

Ben Jonson (Library of Congress)

riage seems to have been unhappy. Before 1597, Jonson might have been an actor with a traveling troupe, many of whose members eked out marginal livings in the towns and hamlets of England. He was imprisoned in 1597 for having finished a play begun by Thomas Nashe; *The Isle of Dogs* was declared seditious by the Privy Council of the queen. The play, like most of Jonson's collaborations, has not been preserved. After a few weeks, Jonson was released from prison.

Jonson's career as a playwright began in earnest in 1598 after the production of *The Case Is Altered*, which was performed by a troupe of boys from the Chapel Royal. In that same year, *Every Man in His Humour*, the first of Jonson's important plays, was performed by William Shakespeare's company, the Lord Chamberlain's Men. Tradition has it that Shakespeare recognized Jonson's talent and persuaded the Lord Chamberlain's Men to stage the play. Although he admired Shakespeare, Jonson never regarded himself as principally a playwright, and therefore he never became a permanent shareholder in an acting company, as did Shakespeare. This enabled Jonson to maintain his artistic freedom but prevented him from earning the good living that Shakespeare and other shareholders enjoyed.

The year 1598 was a busy one for Jonson; he was again imprisoned, this time for killing an actor, Gabriel Spencer, in a duel on September 22. Jonson's property was confiscated, he was branded on the thumb, and he was to be executed, but he saved his life by pleading benefit of clergy, which he could do under ancient English law because he could read. While in prison, he was converted to Roman Catholicism, a faith he practiced until about 1608. In 1606, he was charged with seducing young people into Roman Catholicism; the charges were dropped when he converted back to Anglicanism.

Jonson pursued an active life as an author of plays, poetry, and treatises. His comedies were successful, but his tragedies were badly received. In 1603, Queen Elizabeth died and King James assumed the English throne. Jonson's *Entertainment at Athorpe* helped to launch him on a long career as a court poet. Also that year, his son Benjamin died at the age of six. Though

Jonson was finding public acclaim and honor, his private life was miserable. He and his wife lived apart from 1602 to 1607, he lost his namesake son, and he grew obese. In 1605, he collaborated with John Marston and George Chapman on the rollicking comedy *Eastward Ho!* and was again imprisoned for a supposed slight to King James; the play made fun of Scots.

Jonson's plays *Volpone*, *Epicœne*, and *The Alchemist* enhanced his reputation among his literary peers; his court poetry and masques enhanced his status with King James. In 1616, he published *The Workes of Benjamin Jonson* and was awarded a pension by the king. The pension and Jonson's position as the leading literary figure in England in 1616 have encouraged many historians to call him an unofficial poet laureate, and he is usually honored as the first to fill that role in England. Until the death of King James in 1625, Jonson enjoyed his role as a favorite of the king and a respected author. His honors included a master of arts degree from the University of Oxford.

When Charles I assumed the throne, Jonson's status at court declined. The pension of wine and money was haphazardly delivered, and Jonson had difficulty pursuing his scholarly career because his lodgings burned down in 1623, and his books and papers were destroyed. He returned to playwriting with *The Staple of News* in 1626; the play was not as well received as his earlier comedies. In 1628, he suffered a stroke and was partially paralyzed. In 1629, his play *The New Inn* was staged by the King's Men and was a disaster. He continued to write until his death on August 6, 1637. He left unfinished the play *The Sad Shepherd*, which some critics admire. Although cranky, egotistical, and homely, Jonson retained much of his hold on the leading literary people of his time and was esteemed by younger authors even after his death. He is one of literature's most colorful figures. Combative, robust, and dedicated to his art, Jonson made major contributions to the development of English literature.

ANALYSIS

Ben Jonson's dramatic canon is large, and most of the plays in it are worthy of long and careful study.

He is best remembered for his comedies, which influenced comedy writing well into the eighteenth century and which remain entertaining. Jonson took Horace's maxim to heart—that to teach, a writer must first entertain—and he followed literary rules only so far as they enabled him to instruct and entertain his audience. By observing the neoclassical unities of time and space in his plays, Jonson gave his works a coherence often lacking in the comedies of his contemporaries: Loose ends are resolved, subplot and main plot are interwoven so that each enhances the other, and the conclusion of each play resolves the basic issues brought up during the action. Jonson's concern with entertaining makes most of his comedies delightful and attractive to modern audiences; his effort to instruct makes his plays substantial and meaningful.

From the beginning of his career as a playwright, Jonson was successful with comedy. His two attempts at tragedies are interesting as experiments but are unlikely to be successful with general audiences. His comedies are varied, ranging from the city to the countryside and including satires, comedies of manners, and farces. He was most successful when writing about city life, moralizing with good-natured humor.

Jonson's stature as a playwright is greater than current popular knowledge of him would indicate. Had Shakespeare lived at another time, Jonson would be the dramatic giant of his era. His comedies deserve to be performed more often than they are; his masterpieces play well before modern audiences, and even his minor plays have wit and ideas to recommend them. Jonson is a dramatist of the first rank.

EVERY MAN IN HIS HUMOUR

Of his early comedies, *Every Man in His Humour* is the most important. Jonson's first significant popular success, it best represents those qualities that make some of his later plays great works of literature. Typical of a Jonsonian comedy, *Every Man in His Humour* has a complex interweaving of plots that creates an atmosphere of comic frenzy. Fools are duped, husbands fear cuckolding, wives suspect their husbands of having mistresses, fathers spy on sons, a servant plays tricks on everyone, and myriad disguises

and social games confuse the characters. The audience is not left in confusion but is carefully let in on the nuances of the various plots.

The plot features Edward Knowell, who journeys to London to visit Wellbred, a wit whose devil-may-care behavior might get Edward into trouble. Old Knowell, Edward's father, follows his son to London in order to spy on him, and his servant Brainworm connives and plays tricks—as much to amuse himself as to gain anything. Subplots involve Captain Bobadill, a braggart soldier; Cob and Tib, the landlords of Bobadill; Kitely, a merchant; and Downright, Wellbred's plainspoken brother. The almost bewildering multiplicity of characters is typical of many of Jonson's plays. He borrows the plot of unwarranted suspicions from classical dramatists. Captain Bobadill is the miles gloriosus, the braggart soldier (usually a coward), a stock character in classical comedies. Brainworm is the conniving servant, another stock figure from classical comedies. Other characters also serve specific purposes: Downright is a shatterer of illusions—he points out the falseness in others. Edward Knowell is the romantic lead—a hero who retains his innocence in the middle of the turmoil of the plot. Kitely, Dame Kitely, Cob, and Tib provide much of the low comedy and serve to reflect the ridiculousness of the behavior of the main characters.

Although it shares many of the characteristics that typify Jonson's later comedies, *Every Man in His Humour* shows the dramatist still in the process of forging his mature style. He is still trying to reconcile his classical models to the traditions of English drama and to the tastes of his audience. The plot is loose, almost chaotic, and not as tightly controlled as those of *The Alchemist* and *Volpone*.

VOLPONE

"What a rare punishment/ Is avarice to itself," declares Volpone. At the heart of the complex play *Volpone* is the straightforward moral judgment that the evil one commits brings with it a suitable punishment. In *Volpone*, Jonson satirizes human nature and the baser impulses of humanity.

The play's characters pursue basely materialistic ideals, and in attaining their goals, they ensure their own downfall. Volpone begins the play with a monologue that is in itself a classic: "Good morning to the day; and next, my gold!/ Open the shrine that I may see my saint." His servant and partner in crime, Mosca, draws open a curtain and reveals piles of gold. Volpone has called the repository a "shrine" and the gold a "saint." As the rest of the monologue reveals, Volpone regards wealth with a religious fervor; gold, he asserts, is the "son of Sol"; it "giv'st all men tongues"; it "mak'st men do all things."

Volpone is not merely a clever faker, nor is his servant, Mosca. He is a devotee of an ideal, and as such he is at once more likable and more dangerous than an ordinary thief. He has the excuse that confidence men traditionally have had: that the greed of his victims is their undoing; if they were good people, he would be unable to cheat them. As long as he sticks to victimizing greedy people, he is spectacularly successful; the victims eagerly give him gold and jewels in the hope of gaining his fortune by having it left to them when he dies. When he seeks to "bed" innocent Celia, however, his empire of gold and deceit begins to crumble into its component parts of venality, lust, and spiritual morbidity.

Volpone is a captivating character. He is capable of wonderful flights of language and of clever intrigue, and he is a consummate actor; his strength is his knowledge of how much he can manipulate people into doing what he wants done; his weakness is his overweening pride—he revels too much in his ability to dupe his victims. By pretending to be an old, dying man, he helps convince his victims of his imminent death and of the possibility that one of them will inherit his wealth. They give him expensive gifts to ingratiate themselves with him. His accomplice, Mosca, is also a skilled actor, who can be obsequious one moment, gallant the next—all things to all people. Mosca convinces each victim that he is favored above all others in Volpone's will. The scheme is very successful, and there is much hilarity in the gulling of the lawyer Voltore (the vulture), the elderly Corbaccio (the crow), and the merchant and husband of Celia, Corvino (the raven). The actors should resemble their roles: Voltore is craven and menacing; Corbaccio is thin and leggy; and Corvino is quick-

eyed and aggressive. There is exuberance in Volpone's shifts from boisterous and athletic man to bedridden old cripple, in Mosca's cheerful conniving, and in the duping of three socially prominent and nasty men. The subplot of Lord and Lady Politic Would-be heightens the comedy as Volpone, in his guise as cripple, endures Lady Would-be's endless talking and her willingness to surrender her virtue for his favor. Volpone's gold-centered world would be thoroughly jolly if he were not right about gold's ability to influence people. His victims include innocents, such as Bonario, who is disinherited by his father, Corbaccio, so that Corbaccio can leave his wealth to Volpone in the hope that Volpone will reciprocate. Corvino values wealth above all else; he is a fitting worshiper at the shrine of gold, and he would sacrifice anything to the high priest Volpone in exchange for the promise of acquiring more wealth: Corvino even gives his jealously guarded and naïve wife, Celia, to the supposedly impotent Volpone; she is expected to sleep with him.

Underlying the gold-centered world is ugliness; under Volpone's dashing personality is bestiality; under Mosca's wit is spiritual paucity. Jonson shows this graphically. Volpone must pretend to be physically degenerated, yet the pretense mirrors the spiritual reality. As the play progresses, his performance becomes more extreme; eventually, he pretends to be nearly a corpse. The more complex his scheming becomes, the more wretched he must show himself to be. He is trapped in his world of gold; when he wants to leave his home to see what Celia looks like, he must disguise himself as a lowly mountebank. The physically vibrant Volpone is restricted to his gold and Mosca. When he reveals himself as ardent lover to the trapped Celia, his feigned physical degeneration emerges in his spiritual self, and he is doomed.

Volpone is a great play because it is a nearly perfect meshing of comedy, symbolism, suspense, and moralizing. Each change in any of its aspects is matched by changes in all. Its satiric targets are universals, including greed, moral idiocy, and the replacement of spiritual ideals with materialistic ones. Greed brings down most of the principal characters, including Mosca. Pride brings down Volpone; he cannot resist one more chance to display his brilliance. He pretends to be dead and to have left his fortune to Mosca, simply for the sake of seeing how his victims respond when they learn that he has left them nothing. Mosca, loyal only to the money, wants to keep all for himself. Gold turns the world upside down when made the focus of human endeavor: A husband gives his wife to another man; a father displaces his son; the just are made to look false; and a servant becomes master. Gold should serve its owner, and when Volpone enshrines it, he upsets the proper order of society.

The carnality of Volpone is discovered by Bonario, who was accidentally present during Volpone's near-rape of Celia because of one of Mosca's plots involving Corbaccio. In the ensuing trial, Volpone is presented to the court as a nearly dead old man who is incapable of molesting anyone. Voltore puts on his public mask of respectability and argues to the court that Bonario and Celia are liars and worse, and that those accused by them are honest and innocent. An important theme in the play is that of performance versus reality. Corbaccio properly *acts* the part of the kindly old gentleman. Corvino *plays* the honest merchant. Both are respected members of society. Yet just as the exuberant exterior of Volpone covers a decayed spirit, so, too, do the public personalities of Corbaccio, Corvino, and Voltore belie their evil. In a world in which gold is of paramount importance, such people can seem good; likewise, the truly honest and chaste Bonario and Celia can be made to seem conniving, greedy, and concupiscent.

Mosca almost gets the money. Corbaccio and Corvino almost escape with their reputations intact. Voltore almost wins a false case with his skillful arguments. Volpone cannot stand to lose his gold and cannot stand to see his victims succeed where he has failed. He reveals all to the court. The conclusion seems contrived—after all, the clever Volpone could start over and find new victims to gull—but it is thematically apt. No matter how often Volpone were to start over, his plotting would end the same way, because he worships a base and false god that cannot enrich his soul. The ending reveals the falseness in the principal characters and lays bare the emptiness of Volpone's world.

The use of the villain as protagonist can be found in the tragedies of Jonson's contemporaries. Shakespeare's Macbeth, for example, remains one of literature's most interesting villainous heroes. The use of a villain as protagonist in a comedy was more rare and may have come from classical comedies, in which conniving servants were often the most entertaining characters. Jonson created for himself a distinctive literary voice by using villains such as Volpone to carry his moral ideas; in *The Alchemist*, he exploited the same tension with equal success.

THE ALCHEMIST

Samuel Taylor Coleridge ranked the plot of *The Alchemist* among the three best in literature, along with those of Sophocles' *Oidipous Tyrannos* (c. 429 B.C.E.; *Oedipus Tyrannus*, 1715) and Henry Fielding's *Tom Jones* (1749). Like *Volpone*, the play is about people pretending to be what they are not. *The Alchemist*, however, goes a step further: Its characters seek to be transformed, to be made over into new people. The three characters who gull the others operate out of a house, and as in *Volpone*, the victims are brought to the house for fleecing. In contrast to the action of *Volpone*, however, the action of *The Alchemist* remains tightly focused on the house; society at large comes to the Blackfriars' house to be duped and cheated. Jeremy, the butler, goes by various names—usually Face, the conspirator. When his master leaves on a trip, he takes in Subtle, a down-on-his-luck swindler, and Doll Common, a prostitute. There is little pretense of a noble alliance, as in *Volpone*; these are criminals whose ignoble characters are never in doubt, although they, like their victims, aspire to become what they are not.

Part of the genius of the play is the fooling of the victimizers even as they prey on their victims. Doll Common plays the Queen of Faery for the stupid Dapper and a noblewoman for Sir Epicure Mammon. She throws herself into her roles with the hope that she will become—not simply pretend to be—a lady of noble character. Subtle forgets his recent destitution and begins to believe in his ability to transmute human character, even if his alchemical tricks cannot change matter. Face retains some sense of proportion as he shifts from one role to another, but even he hopes to become the important man in society that he cannot be while he remains a butler. These three quarrelsome rogues are laughable, but they also carry Jonson's moral freight: One must know oneself before a change in character is possible. All except the house's master, Lovewit, hope to be what they are not yet cannot change because they do not know themselves.

Dapper is a clerk who hopes to be a successful gambler; he hopes that Subtle, who poses as an alchemist, will be able to guarantee him good luck. Drugger is a silly shopkeeper who wants a guarantee of good business. Kastril is a country squire who wishes to become an urban wit. His sister, Dame Pliant, is an empty-headed, wealthy widow whose beautiful body hides an almost nonexistent personality. Tribulation, Wholesome, and Ananias are hypocritical Puritans who hope that Subtle will give them the philosophers' stone—which is reputed to have great alchemical powers to transmute—so that they will be able to rule the world. Sir Epicure Mammon (regarded by many critics as one of Jonson's greatest dramatic creations), egotistical and blind to his own weaknesses, wants the philosophers' stone so that he can become a kind of Volpone, ruling a materialistic realm in which he would be wonderful in his generosity and terrible in his appetites. Mammon is already living a fantasy, and he needs little encouragement from Subtle, Face, and Doll Common. The victims are motivated by greed and lust; their desires dictate the nature of their cozening.

The fun is in the increasingly complex machinations of the resourceful schemers. The satire is in the social roles of the victims, who range from clerk and shopkeeper to religious leader and gentleman. By the play's end, Surly, the friend of Mammon, has tried to reveal the schemers for what they are, but only Pliant believes him, and she believes whatever she is told. Mammon is in ardent pursuit of a prostitute in whom he sees noble ancestry; Wholesome and his aide Ananias are fearful of losing their chance to transform the world; Dapper is bound, gagged, and locked in a closet; and Subtle and Face are hopping from one deceit to another in order to keep their schemes balanced. Their small world is based on false understandings of self; no one understands who he really is. The hilarious confusion ends when Lovewit returns home and refuses to be fooled by Face's explanations.

Some critics argue that Lovewit is every bit as deluded as the other characters. They argue that the world of *The Alchemist* remains disordered at the play's finish. Yet Lovewit seems to see through Face's lies and games; he seems to know perfectly well what he is doing when he takes Pliant and her fortune for himself. While his remark to Face, "I will be rul'd by thee in any thing," can be taken to mean that master has yielded to servant, which would be a representation of disorder, it is more likely that Lovewit is expressing gratitude for the deliverance to him of Pliant, as his subsequent remarks suggest. He puts Face back in his place as servant; he puts Kastril in his proper place as his brother-in-law; and he handles the officers of the law and Tribulation and Mammon with confidence. He is in command of the problems created by Face, Subtle, and Doll Common almost from the moment he enters his home. Given the moral themes of the play, Lovewit's commanding presence provides a satisfying conclusion by showing a character who knows himself bringing order to the chaos brought on by fools.

EPICŒNE

Between *Volpone* and *The Alchemist*, Jonson wrote *Epicœne*, and after *The Alchemist* he wrote *Bartholomew Fair* and *The Devil Is an Ass*. The last-named work is an amusing play but not one of Jonson's best. The other two, however, rank among his most successful comedies. Unlike *Volpone* and *The Alchemist*, they involve broad social milieus. *Volpone* and *The Alchemist* present tight little worlds that parody reality; Volpone and Mosca rule theirs at the shrine of gold; Subtle, Face, and Doll Common are minor deities in the world encompassed by their house. In both plays, the outer world intrudes only to resolve their plots. In *Epicœne* and *Bartholomew Fair*, the larger world of Jacobean society appears on the stage.

Epicœne was written for a theatrical company made up entirely of boys, and the central conceit of the play turns on that aspect of its first performance, much as Shakespeare's *As You Like It* (pr. c. 1599-1600) has the young man playing Rosalind, a woman, pretend to be a woman pretending to be a man pretending to be a woman. Jonson's trick is to have Epicœne, played by a boy, turn out at play's end to be a boy. As in his other great comedies, false pretenses form one of the play's major themes. The duping of Morose, who loathes noise, draws in braggarts, pretentious women, and urbane wits. Coarse language, persistent lying, and brutality are revealed as the underlying traits of the supposedly refined and sophisticated members of polite society. In addition, Jonson calls into question the validity of sexual roles; Epicœne is called everything from the ideal woman to an Amazon—the boy who plays her fits easily into the society of women and is readily accepted by women until revealed as a boy.

BARTHOLOMEW FAIR

Bartholomew Fair also deals in disguises and confused identities but is more cheerful than Jonson's other great comedies. The setting of a fair encourages varied action and characters, and Jonson evokes the robust nature of the fair by providing vigorous action and scenes that would be typical of the fairs of his day. The character Ursula is representative of the fair: She is the pig-woman, the operator of a stall that sells roast pig. Big, loud, and sweaty, she embodies the earthiness of the fair, which is noisy and hot with crowding people. The language of the characters is coarse, and they often use vulgarities. The effect is one of down-to-earth good humor and the happy-ending plot. This effect contrasts with *Epicœne*, which also features grossly vulgar language; its characters are supposedly refined, but they reflect their gutter minds in gutter language. Instead of being down-to-earth, much of the humor seems dirty.

OTHER MAJOR WORKS

POETRY: *Poems*, 1601; *Epigrams*, 1616; *The Forest*, 1616; *Underwoods*, 1640.

NONFICTION: *The English Grammar*, 1640; *Timber: Or, Discoveries Made upon Men and Matter*, 1641.

TRANSLATION: *Horace His Art of Poetry*, 1640.

MISCELLANEOUS: *The Workes of Benjamin Jonson*, 1616; *The Works of Benjamin Jonson*, 1640-1641 (2 volumes).

BIBLIOGRAPHY

Butler, Martin, ed. *Re-presenting Ben Jonson: Text, History, Performance*. New York: St. Martin's Press, 1999. An examination of the theater in the time of Jonson as well as of his works. Bibliography and index.

Cave, Richard, Elizabeth Schafer, and Brian Woolland, eds. *Ben Jonson and Theatre: Performance, Practice, and Theory*. New York: Routledge, 1999. A collection of essays dealing with the dramatic works of Jonson and the English theater of his time. Bibliography and index.

Dutton, Richard, ed. *Ben Jonson*. Longman Critical Readers. Harlow, England: Pearson Education, 2000. This study presents critical analysis and interpretation of Jonson's literary works. Bibliography and index.

Evans, Robert C., ed. *Ben Jonson's Major Plays: Summaries of Modern Monographs*. West Cornwall, Conn.: Locust Hill Press, 2000. A reference work containing abstracts and bibliographies of materials by and concerning Jonson. Bibliography and index.

Harp, Richard, and Stanley Stewart, eds. *The Cambridge Companion to Ben Jonson*. New York: Cambridge University Press, 2000. A companion to the playwright and his works.

Haynes, Jonathan. *The Social Relations of Jonson's Theatre*. New York: Cambridge University Press, 1992. A look at Jonson's dramatic works with emphasis on his political and social views. Bibliography and index.

Loxley, James. *The Complete Critical Guide to Ben Jonson*. New York: Routledge, 2002. A handbook designed to provide readers with critical analysis of Jonson's works. Bibliography and index.

Martin, Mathew R. *Between Theater and Philosophy: Skepticism in the Major City Comedies of Ben Jonson and Thomas Middleton*. Newark: University of Delaware Press, 2001. An examination of the dramatic works of Jonson and Thomas Middleton, with regard to their use of comedy. Bibliography and index.

Sanders, Julie. *Ben Jonson's Theatrical Republics*. New York: St. Martin's Press, 1998. An analysis of the political and social views of Jonson as they were manifested in his dramatic works. Bibliography and index.

Summers, Claude J., and Ted-Larry Pebworth. *Ben Jonson Revisited*. Rev. ed. Boston: Twayne, 1999.

Though this book covers Jonson's nondramatic writings as well as his plays, it is an excellent starting point for understanding his drama. Each major play receives a full analysis, and Jonson's entire canon is placed in the context of its time. Bibliography and index.

Kirk H. Beetz,
updated by John R. Holmes

K

GEORG KAISER

Born: Magdeburg, Germany; November 25, 1878
Died: Ascona, Switzerland; June 4, 1945

PRINCIPAL DRAMA

Die jüdische Witwe, pb. 1911, pr. 1921
Die Bürger von Calais, pb. 1914, pr. 1917 (*The Citizens of Calais*, 1946)
Europa, pb. 1915, pr. 1920
Von morgens bis mitternachts, pb. 1916, pr. 1917 (*From Morn to Midnight*, 1920)
Die Koralle, pr., pb. 1917 (*The Coral*, 1929)
Gas, pr., pb. 1918 (English translation, 1924)
Hölle Weg Erde, pr., pb. 1919
Gas: Zweiter Teil, pr., pb. 1920 (*Gas II*, 1924)
Der gerettete Alkibiades, pr., pb. 1920 (*Alkibiades Saved*, 1963)
Noli me tangere, pb. 1922
Kanzlist Krehler, pr., pb. 1922
Gats, pr., pb. 1925
Oktobertag, pr., pb. 1928 (*The Phantom Lover*, 1928)
Die Lederköpfe, pr., pb. 1928
Rosamunde Floris, pb. 1940, pr. 1953
Der Soldat Tanaka, pr., pb. 1940
Zweimal Amphitryon, pr. 1944, pb. 1948
Das Floss der Medusa, pr. 1945, pb. 1948 (*The Raft of the Medusa*, 1951)
Plays, pb. 1980-1981

OTHER LITERARY FORMS

Georg Kaiser published film scripts, essays, and two novels: *Es ist genug* (1932; it is enough), an autobiographical work whose plot unfolds in an imaginary setting, and *Villa Aurea* (1940; *Vera*, 1939), which is—like many of Kaiser's plays—based on an abstract thought or thesis: Humankind is afraid of nothingness; it knows that nothingness is the only truth, but it does not want to acknowledge it.

During his exile in Switzerland, Kaiser wrote several short stories. Many of them draw their inspiration from political events, such as the occupation of Czechoslovakia by German troops ("Lieutenant Welzeck") or the rise of Adolf Hitler and his hypnotic power over the German masses ("Nach einem verlorenen Krieg"). Like many (former) expressionists (such as Ernst Barlach, Reinhard J. Sorge, and Alfred Döblin), Kaiser used the fairy-tale genre to express his philosophical and theological views (humanity as the devil's creation in "Die Ausgeburt"; love as a purifying force in "Das Märchen des Konigs"). Kaiser's poetry, especially the poems written during his exile, shows the strong influence of Rainer Maria Rilke. The film scripts, essays, novels, stories, and poems have been collected in the fourth volume of the 1971 edition of Kaiser's collected works, edited by Walther Huder.

ACHIEVEMENTS

Georg Kaiser was one of the most prolific playwrights in the history of German drama. He wrote approximately seventy plays, many of which were performed throughout Germany in the 1920's. Among all the expressionist dramatists, he developed the most progressive antinaturalistic dramaturgy. His influence on younger playwrights both inside and outside Germany was considerable. Bertolt Brecht, a major and influential dramatist himself, has acknowledged that he learned much from Kaiser's dramatic techniques, particularly from Kaiser's views about the role of the audience. Kaiser did not want his audience to adopt an attitude of passive empathy. Spectators were not supposed to forget themselves by means of uncritically identifying with the protagonist onstage. Kaiser's abstract style was devised to counteract such an attitude and foster an alert and critical mental disposition on the part of spectators. The fact that many of Kaiser's plays have been translated into English and other languages attests his international reputation.

BIOGRAPHY

Georg Kaiser was born on November 25, 1878, in Magdeburg, Germany. He attended elementary school in Magdeburg from 1885 to 1888 and then entered a Lutheran monastery school, which he left in 1895. During his years in the monastery school, he frequently attended concerts, operas, and plays. In 1895, he worked as an apprentice in a Magdeburg bookstore but gave up after a few weeks because his lofty ideas about literature and books were shattered by his experience of the commercial aspects of the book trade. In 1896, Kaiser worked for a commercial firm and began to study foreign languages. Three years later, he traveled to Buenos Aires, where he found employment as a clerk in the branch office of the General Electric Company (AEG) of Berlin. During

Georg Kaiser (AP/Wide World Photos)

that time, he contracted malaria. He returned to his parents in 1901. After having suffered a nervous breakdown, he was treated for half a year in a Berlin sanatorium.

During the years from 1903 to 1907, Kaiser wrote several plays. In 1908, he married Margarethe Habenicht, the daughter of a wholesale merchant. Kaiser was not drafted during World War I because of a nervous disorder. He volunteered, however, to work for the Red Cross in Weimar. The years from 1916 to 1918 brought Kaiser fame as a playwright; many of his plays were performed in German cities such as Frankfurt, Munich, Hamburg, and Berlin.

In November, 1918, Kaiser moved to Munich, where he befriended the expressionist writer Ernst Toller, who was one of the leaders of the short-lived Soviet Republic in Bavaria. Because of financial problems, Kaiser pawned and sold some furniture and art objects belonging to the owner of a house he had rented in Tutzing, Bavaria. This led, in October, 1920, to Kaiser's arrest in Berlin. Kaiser was charged with embezzlement. In February, 1921, he was sentenced to one year in prison but was released in April of the same year and placed on probation for six months. In the following years, Kaiser's plays were staged in major cities all over the world. In 1926, Kaiser became an elected member of the Prussian Academy of Arts and Letters.

The rise of National Socialism meant the end of Kaiser's career as a playwright in Germany. Publication and performances of his plays were forbidden by the new regime, and his books were burned along with those of Sigmund Freud, Karl Marx, Lion Feuchtwanger, and others in May, 1933. For a while, his plays could still be performed in Austria (before the "Anschluss" in 1938) and other countries.

In 1938, Kaiser fled to Switzerland via the Netherlands after a search warrant for his home near Berlin had been issued. Until his death in 1945, Kaiser lived in Switzerland, where he continued to write plays, novels, poetry, and film scripts. He wished to emigrate to the United States, but Albert Einstein and Thomas Mann failed in their efforts to obtain a visa for him. On June 4, 1945, Kaiser died in Ascona, Switzerland. Most of the plays that he had written after he left Germany were performed on German stages after the end of World War II.

ANALYSIS

Many of Georg Kaiser's plays are, in both form and content, part of literary expressionism, a movement in central European countries that can be regarded as an integral part of the revolutionary trends stirring literature and art in Europe around 1900. This movement, supported by the young generation of artists and writers, was a reaction against the passive reproduction of reality by the artists and authors of impressionism and naturalism. To be sure, the expressionists also intended to show certain aspects of a society shaped by industrialism and technology, but they also wished to conjure up a vision of a better world and of a "new man." This vision necessitated a new style disregarding the rules of mimesis and realism, a style that abstracted from observable actions and events what was taken to be their "essence" underneath an often misleading "appearance." Expressionist aesthetics prescribe that the primary impulse of the creative act should originate in the author's or artist's subjective creative intuition. The observable real world serves as material to be shaped according to the creator's "vision."

This is why in Kaiser's plays, as well as in those of his fellow expressionists, the characters have been reduced to "types" representing an idea or a typical social function. They no longer speak and act according to psychological role models. Indeed, they are highly artificial creatures whom one would presumably never meet in real life. Nevertheless, they embody the flaws of society or the Utopian hopes of the author for a new society. Kaiser's plays also reduce naturalistic detail to a minimum of essential props. Light and color frequently assume a symbolic function. Most of Kaiser's plays have a highly intellectual quality. Their antithetical and dialectical structure is based on an idea or a thought that is carried to its conclusion, even though in the process, the plot may take a turn toward the absurd and paradoxical. Just as Kaiser's plots often assume an utterly unrealistic quality, the characters in his expressionistic plays speak a language that is as artificial and ab-

stract as they themselves are. This is no longer the language of the naturalists, who strove to copy as faithfully as possible the way certain human beings talk in real life, right down to the shades of local dialects. Kaiser's language is one of typification and condensation. Its function is, once again, to reveal the essence behind the mask of appearance. Adjectives are used sparingly, and verbs and articles are frequently omitted.

If there is one common thematic denominator in most of Kaiser's plays, it is his deep concern about the quality and dignity of human life in a changed socioeconomic environment. Kaiser exposes the shortcomings of his characters (and of the societies in which they live) when he depicts individuals as well as entire groups of humans as victims of war, selfishness, hatred, greed, or technological "progress." These are the forces that militate against a better form of life that has not yet advanced beyond the stage of a Utopian dream. Yet Kaiser offers a glimpse of this better world, of a nonrepressive and just society ruled by the "new man" who achieves (often through personal sacrifice) a morally superior form of existence. This new life will not be the result of revolutions or political maneuvers but will—such was Kaiser's hope—eventually spring from an inner metamorphosis of the individual.

THE CITIZENS OF CALAIS

One of Kaiser's best-known expressionistic plays is *The Citizens of Calais*. Kaiser based the plot of the play on the historical siege of the French city of Calais by English troops under Edward III in 1346. The king promises to spare the city and its recently completed harbor if six citizens present the city's key to him and are willing to be executed. The elder citizen Eustache de Saint-Pierre offers himself and asks for other volunteers. When six others volunteer, Eustache first proposes to draw lots in order to eliminate one of the seven volunteers. Having second thoughts about this procedure, however, he changes his mind and makes all seven lots equal. Then he declares that he who appears last on the market square the next morning will go free. The next morning, all the others appear except Eustache. They accuse him of deception. Moments later, his corpse is brought to the square on a stretcher. It is revealed that Eustache killed himself in order to spare any of the other six the embarrassment and shame of arriving last. Presently, a messenger from the English king appears, announcing that the king will not demand the sacrifice of the six, since that night a son was born to him. Eustache's father praises his son as the "new man" who leads the way toward a new ethic. Like Christ's death on the cross, Eustache's supreme sacrifice has set a noble example that inspires those who survive him.

The seventh volunteer and the construction of the harbor are Kaiser's inventions. They are not found in the well-known chronicle by Jean Froissart (1337-1410) that tells of the historical siege of Calais and of the king's stipulation. It is likely that Kaiser consulted Froissart's work.

The play can also be read as an antiwar text. There are those who urge the defenders of Calais to continue the hopeless fight against the English troops to the bitter end, but they do not prevail. The new harbor takes on a symbolic significance as an achievement of humanity, which has conquered the irrational— symbolized by the ocean—in itself. The old values of martial heroism, honor, and power will be replaced by love and humility.

HÖLLE WEG ERDE

In 1919, Kaiser published the play *Hölle Weg Erde*, in which the expressionistic call for a new, morally superior human being and a new society cleansed of all the inequities and injustices of capitalist society is heard in a contemporary setting. In typical expressionistic fashion, the play blends a relatively realistic portrayal of society with a presentation of a Utopian world of love in which greed, crime, and egotism are superseded by brotherhood.

The artist Spazierer tries to raise money for a friend in need who threatens suicide. He approaches Lili, a rich lady who is about to purchase some costly earrings from a jeweler. Spazierer wants to sell his drawings to her, but she refuses. Enraged, he stabs the jeweler, whom he holds responsible for a society in which a man in need does not get help. Spazierer also plans to sue Lili for the "murder" of his needy friend. The attorney whom he approaches declines to take

the case. Spazierer then agrees to go to prison for the stabbing. His fellow inmates claim that they—as human beings, disconnected from the socioeconomic structures imposed on them—are not guilty: It is the social structure that breeds crime. At this point in the play, a miraculous change in the entire society takes place. This is where the Utopian vision begins to replace the relatively realistic mode of presentation. As a reflection of humanity's predicament in modern industrial society, all confess their "guilt" and at the same time plead innocent. Lili, the attorney, and the jeweler now recognize that they wronged Spazierer. The gates of the prison are opened, never to be closed again. The prison guards refuse to work and join the inmates in a proclamation of the new humanity and a new society. This proclamation condemns the notion of "achievement" calling it an enslaving social norm. A sense of purification pervades all classes of society, coupled with a belief in a new beginning ("Aufbruch") that characterizes many of Kaiser's works. In the last scene of the play, there emerge the vague outlines of a new social order in which all are equal. Spazierer is asked to accept the position of a leader but refuses, since he wants to be nothing more than an anonymous member of the crowd.

The play demonstrates Kaiser's belief that modern industrial society perverts the basic goodness of humanity. It fails, however, to provide a blueprint for a new society. The change that takes place in society happens abruptly and without any apparent motivation. If there is a general weakness or flaw in expressionist literature, it lies in its attempt to give artistic shape to a vision that—in spite of its sincerity—lacks the expertise and factual knowledge of the politically inspired social reformer. Nevertheless, Kaiser's Utopia remains a moving document of the social plight of his time and of his yearning for a better world.

FROM MORN TO MIDNIGHT

Kaiser's play *From Morn to Midnight* uses a dramaturgical structure typical of many expressionistic dramas: a mode of presentation that shows the protagonist in a sequence of selected stages or exemplary situations in his life (the German term for this mode is *Stationendrama*). A scene or an act of the play no longer follows logically or psychologically from the preceding one. Instead, their nexus is based on an underlying idea common to all the scenes, which thus become variations of a theme. The scenes and acts still constitute an ordered string of events, but there is no stringent adherence to sequentiality.

The protagonist of the play is a petit bourgeois cashier who feels stifled by the monotony of his uneventful life. He embezzles a large sum of money in order to buy for himself the excitement and the deep inner satisfaction that life has withheld from him. He quickly learns, however, that money cannot buy true love. At a bicycle race, he attempts to stir up the passions of the racers and of the spectators by offering exorbitant sums for the winners. The appearance of the emperor, however, drowns the aroused passion of the spectators in sudden silence and in an attitude of devout subservience. Deeply irritated and disillusioned, the cashier leaves the arena. He ends up at the Salvation Army, where he hopes that a complete confession of his sins, the radical gesture of laying bare his soul and its most intimate desires, will bring him a long sought for and yet elusive sense of fulfillment. He is disappointed again when a girl denounces him to the police. When he throws the remainder of his money on the floor, pandemonium breaks loose. Everybody greedily rushes forth to pick up the bills and coins. Religious feelings succumb to primitive instincts and drives. Acknowledging his fiasco, the cashier shoots himself. His body slumps into a curtain onto which a cross has been sewn. "Ecce homo" are the last words he utters. The Christ symbol is—as so often in the writings of the expressionists—secularized and stands for the sufferings endured by humanity.

THE CORAL, GAS, AND GAS II

Kaiser develops an equally pessimistic view in his trilogy *The Coral*, *Gas*, and *Gas II*. This time, he focuses on the working class and its struggle, not only against capitalists and their allies the politicians, but also against the anonymous powers of technology and industrialization. In *The Coral*, the protagonist, a billionaire, owes his riches to the horror with which he remembers his poverty-stricken youth. He has worked his way up in order to forget his past. The

memories of his working-class background still haunt him so much that he kills a man who looks exactly like him in order to assume this man's identity (he had a happy, sheltered childhood). The billionaire's son decides to become a worker in his own plant, although he still maintains a position of spiritual leadership. The plant produces gas. Its profits are shared among the workers according to a scheme based on seniority and age. Once again, Kaiser projects a Utopian image, this time of a socialist system that allows for equal distribution of wealth (without truly enhancing the quality of life of the workers). A giant explosion caused by a mistake in the production formula (a mistake that is beyond detection) forces the workers to interrupt their relentless work for seventeen days. This break gives the billionaire's son a chance to persuade his workers to start a new life, to leave the plant in shambles and to become farmers. This move "back to nature" is supposed to generate a spiritual renewal. Technology and industrialization are rejected by the humanist and idealist as a misguided effort in humanity's struggle with nature.

The workers, however, reject the billionaire's son's proposal. They know no life other than work in the factory. Besides, the leading industrialists of the country urge the billionaire's son to rebuild the plant. In the meantime, the workers begin to realize to what extent they have become merely an extension of their machines. Their lives have been reduced to the function of a hand that pulls a lever, eyes that watch a sight-tube, or a foot that presses down a pedal. Their existence is indeed a fragmented one. Technology deprives them of the wholeness and the potential richness of human life. For a brief moment, they decide to abandon the plant. Their chief engineer, however, talks them into returning to work by conjuring up a heroic and glorious image of technology and by downgrading the life of a "peasant" proposed by the billionaire's son. Furthermore, the military high command and the government of the country simply order the reconstruction of the plant because a war seems imminent.

The last play of the trilogy is set in the plant, where the production of gas has resumed while war has indeed broken out. Once more, the workers have the opportunity to evaluate their lives critically when a mechanical failure in the system causes a brief interruption of production. For the second time, the workers realize that they are slaves, and they begin to envisage a better life that would allow them to control their own destiny as free men. These dreams come to an abrupt end, however, when the enemy takes over the plant. While the workers continue to slave in their plant (profits are no longer shared), their chief engineer reveals that he has invented a deadly poisonous gas that he wants to use against the enemy. When the workers enthusiastically embrace the idea of revenge, the billionaire worker exhorts them to refrain from any act of violence. They should, so he argues, willingly accept the rule of the enemy and yet be free in spirit. This new inner sense of freedom is the freedom of the martyr based on the Christian virtue of humility. Once again, the workers reject the lofty proposal of their idealistic leader. At this point, the billionaire worker feels entitled to take fate into his own hands. He snatches the capsule with the poisonous gas from the engineer's hands and smashes it to the ground, destroying himself and all his fellow workers. Even the enemy is drawn into total annihilation. Technology and war have brought about the self-destruction of a humankind lacking the desire and the maturity to break out of its self-imposed prison (industrialized society). The "new man" remains a noble specter whose realization seems remote if not impossible.

This trilogy shows Kaiser at the height of his expressionistic skill. Its characters are types, not individuals ("The Daughter," "The Officer," "The Engineer," "First Workman," "Second Workman," and so on). The two parties at war are distinguished by color ("Figures in Blue" versus "Figures in Yellow"). Kaiser's language is abstract and highly metaphorical. Furthermore, he revives and refines the ancient tradition of the chorus. Groups differentiated by profession, age, or sex ("The Workmen," "The Girls," "The Women," or simply "Voices") speak in alternate order to individuals who in turn represent a collective or group. In some scenes, the dramatic dialogue approaches the form of the liturgy. Certain lines are repeated over and over again, as in a responsory or an oratorio. Such collective speeches conform with the antimimetic aesthetics of expressionism. The characters speak according to preestablished patterns and not in a quasi-spontaneous fashion because they represent ideas or typical social positions and are therefore stripped of individualistic psychological features.

Kaiser's trilogy can also be interpreted as a portrayal of the antagonism between the masses and the leader. It is one of the ironies of German cultural history that many expressionists struggled with this problematic theme long before National Socialism provided its own answer to the question: How do the leader and the masses relate to one another? In the Gas trilogy, the masses repeatedly refuse to follow their leader, who seeks no elevated social status but merely stands apart intellectually from his fellow workers. In the end, the leader annihilates himself as well as those who would not be led.

In a brief sketch entitled "Die Erneuerung: Skizze für ein Drama" (the renewal), written in 1919 for a planned (but never completed) play, Kaiser deals once more with the problematic relationship between the leader and the masses. On one hand, the leader figure of this sketch wishes to abandon his role. His aim is to become totally absorbed into the anonymous collective. On the other hand, the masses need the leader. They insist on giving a "name" to the one they have chosen for this elevated social position. The designated leader argues that the individual, once he emerges from the collective, becomes utterly self-centered and egotistical and loses all instincts of brotherly love. Man can be good only if he fuses with the masses. Because the collective insists on giving the leader a "name" and thus sets him apart from all the others, the only way out of the dilemma for the individual is to commit suicide and thus initiate the spiritual "renewal" of the collective. The most striking issue in Kaiser's abstract dialectical sketch is his positive image of the masses, in stark contrast to the views of Friedrich Nietzsche or Gustave Le Bon, who described the masses as dangerous plebeians who lack a sense of responsibility, as a herd with the potential for destruction (although Le Bon also counted dedication and self-sacrifice among the virtues of the masses). Kaiser, like many of his fellow expressionists, interpreted the masses as ethically superior to the individual. The Protestant theologian Paul Tillich expressed similar views in some of his writings of the early 1920's.

As far as the fate of the masses is concerned, the contrast within Kaiser's own work between the Gas trilogy and "Die Erneuerung" is quite obvious. The workers in the trilogy intermittently glimpse a more dignified and humane life, but they fall prey to the instincts of greed and violence. Their leader, the billionaire worker, who does not attempt to relinquish his role as a leader, finally destroys the masses as well as himself in an act of both supreme despair and punishment. He fails to bring about a "renewal," and the workers fail to understand his vision of a better life (regardless of its practicality and validity). In "Die Erneuerung," however, the designated leader sacrifices himself, thus bringing about a positive ethical transformation of the collective.

NOLI ME TANGERE

Kaiser takes up the theme of renewal once more in his play *Noli me tangere*. The play has two protagonists, both prisoners, identified by numbers only. Prisoner "16" has been imprisoned by mistake. As soon as his innocence is established, he is told that he can leave, yet he decides to help his fellow inmate "15" escape by giving him his coat so that "15" (whom the prison guards now take to be "16") is able to regain his freedom while "16" stays behind. Before the escape takes place, however, "16" and "15" have a highly significant conversation. Prisoner "15" declares that he is the prophet and forerunner of a new humankind. Like Spazierer and the billionaire worker, he proclaims the dawn of a new (yet undefined) social order and a "new man." Prisoner "16," however, criticizes the flaming rhetoric and the revolutionary impetus of "15" by telling him that he wants too much too fast. History, so "15" is told, moves at a much slower pace than he anticipates. It will not be accelerated by untimely prophets but advances at a slow pace, controlled by God. Thus, a Christian philosophy of history takes the place of a pseudoreligious revolutionary concept of historical

change. Indeed, prisoner "16" turns out to be Christ himself, who shows "15" the wounds on his hands while speaking the words: "Noli me tangere." It seems as though Kaiser, in this play, found fault with the all-too-stormy prophetic thrust of the social philosophy of expressionism and created in the character of prisoner "15" almost a caricature of the expressionistic leader-prophet. Far from abandoning the ideal of a social and moral renewal, Kaiser's message in *Noli me tangere* is that no revolutionary fervor (least of all one inspired by Marxism) will force into existence the new order. God as the supreme social engineer will—in the course of history—bring about the desired change. Kaiser's play is one of the few texts within German expressionism that presents Christ as a truly divine being—as the Son of God. In most expressionist texts, Christ (or a Christ-figure) is a secular symbol for the sufferings of man, as in the last scene of *From Morn to Midnight*.

DIE LEDERKÖPFE

In some of his postexpressionist plays, Kaiser takes up once more the theme of war. Plays such as *The Citizens of Calais* and the Gas trilogy had already denounced war as a cruel, inhuman, and meaningless endeavor. World War I demonstrated to the young generation of artists and writers in Germany that war was the ultimate expression of a social and economic system that cultivated greed, national megalomania, and brutality.

In *Die Lederköpfe*, Kaiser launched his strongest attack against the ruthlessness of the military authorities and the degrading impact of war on human beings. The city commander is supposed to recruit a new army for his general, The Basilius, but the mutinous soldiers threaten to kill the commander, who evades death only by offering them The Basilius's daughter. At that moment, The Basilius himself returns after having taken a city that belonged to the enemy. He owes this victory to a spectacular ruse. One of his soldiers mutilates his face, slips into the enemy's camp, and pretends that The Basilius disfigured him and that he is therefore offering his services to them in order to avenge the cruel treatment he received at the hands of his general. His plight seems to vouch for his honesty, and the enemy believes him.

At night, this soldier opens the city gates so that The Basilius can take the city. The general rewards his soldier by appointing him field commander and giving him his daughter. The new field commander has to wear a leather hood over his head to hide his disfigured face. When The Basilius learns of the mutiny, he decides to punish the mutineers by having their faces disfigured in the same manner in which the field commander mutilated himself. He wants to build an entire army of faceless human beings wearing leather hoods. The field commander (who is deeply shocked by his general's preposterous hubris and by his extreme brutality) offers to execute the proposed punishment himself. His true intention, however, is to incite his troops to kill The Basilius. Before the general is whipped to death by his outraged troops, he kills the field commander who has refused to mutilate his soldiers. The play ends, though, on a hopeful note: The destroyed city taken earlier by The Basilius will be rebuilt.

A grim picture of war is painted by the characters who are involved in it. The city commander calls war an all-devouring monster with "the mouth of a crocodile." The sole purpose of war is the expansion of power of those who are already in power. Humankind becomes a faceless animal in war—this is the meaning of the symbolism of disfigurement and of the leather hood. Once a human being wears the hood, he is "everybody and nobody"; he loses his individuality and with it his human dignity. Even The Basilius seems to realize that war brings out in him only the faceless destroyer and the raging animal. He knows that there are "voices" in the depth of his soul to which he must not listen if he wants to be an effective general. He must look on his soldiers as if they were a swarm of ants.

The Raft of the Medusa

One of Kaiser's last plays, *The Raft of the Medusa*, also known as *Medusa's Raft*, focuses once again on the theme of war. The setting is a lifeboat on the ocean. During World War II, a passenger boat has been sunk by enemy torpedoes, and thirteen children, ranging in age from ten to twelve years, are crammed into the lifeboat. The youngest and weakest child of the group is a red-haired boy whom the others name

"little fox." Out of superstition, many of the children think that one of them must be sacrificed because the number thirteen spells doom. The leader of the group, Allan, finally agrees that they all draw lots in order to determine who will have to leave the boat. When Allan realizes that the girl Ann, whom he loves, will draw the lot that calls for her death, he quickly snatches up all the lots and throws them into the water. There is a happy interlude during the grim voyage of the shipwrecked children: Allan and Ann celebrate their "wedding" with imaginary pomp and circumstance. They place a report about the wedding in a bottle that is then committed to the waves. While Allan is asleep, the others throw the "little fox" (who has been protected by Allan) into the water just before a rescue seaplane arrives (a patrol boat found the bottle). Outraged because of the fate of the "little fox," Allan refuses to board the plane. He stays in the lifeboat and is later killed by an enemy airplane that makes a strafing attack on the boat. As so often occurs in Kaiser's plays, the figure of Christ is evoked to demonstrate the ideal of the supreme sacrifice. Allan's death in this case atones for the sin of the other children, just as Christ atoned on the Cross for all the sins of humankind.

Other major works

LONG FICTION: *Es ist genug*, 1932; *Villa Aurea*, 1940 (*Vera*, 1939).

MISCELLANEOUS: *Stücke, Erzählungen, Aufsätze, Gedichte*, 1966; *Werke*, 1971 (6 volumes).

Bibliography

Benson, Renate. *German Expressionist Drama: Ernst Toller and Georg Kaiser*. New York: Grove Press, 1984. A study of German expressionist drama, focusing on the works of Kaiser and Ernst Toller. Bibliography and index.

Henn, Marianne, ed. *Bibliography of the Georg Kaiser Collection at the University of Alberta*. Edmonton: University of Alberta, 1998. A bibliography of the Kaiser collection at the University of Alberta, Canada. Index.

Lambert, Carole J. *The Empty Cross: Medieval Hopes, Modern Futility in the Theater of Maurice*

Maeterlinck, Paul Claudel, August Strindberg, and Georg Kaiser. New York: Garland, 1990. A scholarly study of the influence of medieval thought, particularly the concepts of futility and frustration, on the works of Kaiser, Maurice Maeterlinck, Paul Claudel, and August Strindberg.

Christoph Eykman

KĀLIDĀSA

Born: India(?); c. 100 B.C.E. or c. 340 C.E.
Died: India(?); c. 40 B.C.E. or c. 400 C.E.

PRINCIPAL DRAMA

Mālavikāgnimitra, c. 70 B.C.E. or c. 370 C.E.
   (English translation, 1875)
Vikramorvaśīya, c. 56 B.C.E. or c. 384 C.E.
   (*Vikrama and Urvaśī*, 1851)
Abhijñānaśākuntala, c. 45 B.C.E. or c. 395 C.E.
   (*Śakuntalā: Or, The Lost Ring*, 1789)
The Dramas of Kālidāsa, pb. 1946

OTHER LITERARY FORMS

Apart from the three plays, two epic poems and two lyric poems are commonly ascribed to Kālidāsa. Most critics agree that the lyrics—*Ṛtusaṃhāra* (c. 75 B.C.E. or c. 365 C.E.; English translation, 1867) and *Meghadūta* (c. 65 B.C.E. or c. 375 C.E.; *The Cloud Messenger*, 1813)—are earlier compositions, and the epics—*Kumārasambhava* (c. 60 B.C.E. or c. 380 C.E.; *The Birth of the War-God*, 1879) and *Raghuvaṃśa* (c. 50 B.C.E. or c. 390 C.E.; *The Dynasty of Raghu*, 1872-1895)—appear to be contemporaneous with the plays, among Kālidāsa's later work. In addition, many scholars over the years have attributed numerous pieces of doubtful authenticity to Kālidāsa. These apocrypha span the literary gamut from religious hymns to astrological treatises to erotic verses, but their authorship remains questionable on stylistic grounds.

As in the plays, love is the unifying passion in the lyric poems of Kālidāsa. *Ṛtusaṃhāra* paints in its six cantos the six Indian seasons as perceived through the eyes of one in love. The depiction of lovers in union in that poem is countered by the theme of lovers sepa-

rated in *The Cloud Messenger*, which has as its central metaphor one of the most charming romantic conceits of all literature: a cloud personified as the go-between carrying a message from lover to beloved, who pine away for each other, parted by vast distances. The epics, however, are of a somewhat different temper. *The Birth of the War-God* treats the mythological union of Śiva, the Hindu god of destruction, and Pārvatī, his consort, representing the principles of Good and Beauty respectively. Their son Kumāra, the god of war, symbolizes the power born to crush evil in the world. The elaborate, quasihistorical *The Dynasty of Raghu* presents the ideal virtues of legendary Indian kings and heroes, perhaps as an implicit guide to rulers of Kālidāsa's own time. Despite their more conventional elevated approach, both epics are infused with Kālidāsa's characteristic poetic style.

ACHIEVEMENTS

Kālidāsa is unanimously recognized as India's national poet, the foremost literary exponent of the Indian consciousness. Since his own lifetime, his works have signified the zenith of literary accomplishment in India, unrivaled in every genre that he attempted. His life also conveniently marks a turning point dividing old and new, serving as a watershed between the classical and romantic periods in Sanskrit literature. Most important, perhaps, by distilling abstract virtues into human form he converted Vedantic philosophy into easily comprehensible literature with more success than most of his predecessors and virtually all of his successors. Consequently, many of his couplets or quatrains have passed into the popular vocabulary as proverbs and maxims, and he has attained cult stature among average Indians, arguably as much as his precursors, the epic poets Vyāsa and Vālmīki, becoming, like them, the much-beloved subject of several folktales.

According to tradition, "Of literary forms drama is the most pleasing; and of dramas *Śakuntalā*; and in *Śakuntalā* the fourth act; and in that act four verses"—alluding to Kanva's valedictory remarks to the heroine before she leaves his hermitage. Kālidāsa made significant changes in Sanskrit drama, especially introducing the note of the delicate and often heartrending lyricism that has enchanted commentators ever since. The strict norms of Sanskrit dramaturgy in no way inhibited him. Working for the most part within their boundaries, he did not discard the prevailingly austere tone but raised it to a level of dignity. He did not ignore conventions but rather crystallized each into diamonds. He developed the art of characterization and simultaneously introduced a heightened intensity as well as a relative realism. Above all, he explored in depth the *śṛṅgāra* (erotic) *rasa* as no one had before him, exhausting its possibilities. His poetry won for him as much fame as did his drama. Although both of his epics are incomplete, critics acknowledge them as models in their genre (the courtly, or "art," epic), conforming to all rules of construction. Kālidāsa also invented the long lyric poem in Sanskrit, and his two compositions in this mode remain among his most popular works. They pioneered the move toward romanticism and individuality in Sanskrit poetry.

Kālidāsa's style attracts the highest encomiums. Even the severest Sanskrit purists maintain that his defects are more poetic than other poets' successes. Kālidāsa presented Sanskrit, one of the most precise of languages, in its mature perfection. His creativity manifested itself in his uncanny choice of the correct word and his innovative construction of compounds, yet his writing epitomized economy. He was the uncontested master of similes, his nature imagery exemplifying his originality and minute observation. Kālidāsa's descriptions of nature are a byword in Sanskrit scholarship, regularly cited in discussions of poetics. He displayed consummate artistry in the powers of subtle suggestion and internal assonance, the hallmarks of excellent poetry according to Sanskrit theoreticians. His use of rhetoric showed little trace of cliché, artifice, or hyperbole. The harmony of his writing—technique perfectly allied with meaning—was always evident.

BIOGRAPHY

Unfortunately, nothing is known concerning Kālidāsa's life. The folk stories about him that have survived are almost certainly fictitious, and recorded Indian history does not offer any verifiable accounts. Therefore, scholars turn to internal evidence and scattered references to Kālidāsa for clues to date him, but these, too, are often nebulous or ambiguous. Critical opinion has narrowed the plausible time frames for Kālidāsa to either the first century B.C.E. (the traditional view) or the fourth century C.E. (the modern hypothesis). The dates indicated in this essay come from K. Krishnamoorthy's conjectural chronology, based on these two commonly held theories.

Reconstructions of Kālidāsa's life are generally founded on the ancient legend that he was the court poet of King Vikramāditya, a patron of the arts whose capital was Ujjain, in west-central India. The existence of such a king in the first century B.C.E. has never been confirmed historically, whereas it is known that the Gupta emperor Chandragupta II of the fourth century C.E. assumed the title Vikramāditya (admittedly a common honorific) and cultivated artists at court. Whatever Kālidāsa's period, it seems obvious that he served as a court poet. Moreover, his writing reveals a rigorous education in every conceivable field of study and a thorough knowledge of Indian geography that points to extensive travels, perhaps in royal service. He definitely lived at some time in Ujjain, because he describes the city in loving detail. Scholars of Kālidāsa have also inferred from the tone of his works that he lived in comparatively peaceful and prosperous times, possibly during what is now considered to be the golden age of the Gupta empire.

Krishnamoorthy reconstructs Kālidāsa's literary career as follows: The poet wrote the relatively immature *Ṛtusaṃhāra* at the age of twenty-five, then attracted notice with *Mālavikāgnimitra* at court. Possibly *The Cloud Messenger* alludes to a separation from his wife while he was away in southern India on royal business. Afterward, *The Birth of the War-God* may have celebrated the nativity of his patron's heir (Chandragupta II had a son named Kumāragupta, who eventually succeeded him); in its title, *Vikrama and Urvaśī*, may have been intended to honor the king himself, identifying him with its hero. In full maturity, when he was fifty years old, Kālidāsa began *The Dynasty of Raghu*, but he stopped abruptly after nineteen cantos, his last portrait that of a ruler who was effete, dissolute, and corrupt. Kālidāsa recovered from this vision of steady degeneration to attain the serenity that enabled him to compose *Śakuntalā*, and died soon after.

ANALYSIS

If any writer deserves the title of "poet's poet," it is Kālidāsa. The pure beauty of his language has prompted many poets over the centuries—both Indian and Western—to compose tributes to him. Notable among Western devotees is Johann Wolfgang von Goethe, who saw in Kālidāsa the poet's "highest function as the representative of the most natural condition, of the most beautiful way of life, of the purest moral effort, of the worthiest majesty, of the most sincere contemplation." In the West, critics have consistently placed Kālidāsa among the ranks of Sophocles, Vergil, Dante, and William Shakespeare, giving proof of his universal appeal.

SANSKRIT DRAMA

To appreciate Kālidāsa's plays, one must first understand the fundamental concepts that underlie Sanskrit drama. The essence of Western dramaturgy has always been conflict; a play usually traces the development and resolution of a particular set of opposing forces. To Indian dramatists, however, conflict is only a secondary consideration; their actual aim is the opposite, to depict harmony in their plays. They do this by evoking *rasa* in the audience, presenting the nine basic emotions (desire, laughter, anger, sorrow, pride, fear, disgust, wonder, and peace) in perfect balance during the play so as to produce at the end an illuminating revelation of oneness, in which for the

moment the spectator is vouchsafed a dispassionate insight into the life of things. Ideally the drama therefore functions as an art that enlightens the spirit, instructing while entertaining.

Therefore, by Western standards, an Indian play is bound to be more or less deficient in action (etymologically, too, the Greek root of "drama" meant "action"). Onstage, the Sanskrit drama revealed other distinguishing features. It was a courtly entertainment, more often than not produced on special occasions in the presence of the king. It was metatheatrical by convention—at the beginning of each performance, a benedictory hymn would invoke the gods for their blessings, and the director (often with an actor) would introduce the play to the audience. There was no attempt at creating an illusion, picture-frame or otherwise. Although commentators emphasize the equal importance of the visual and audible portions, the visual spectacle did not depend on sets or scenery, but on costumes, makeup, and the art of acting, which relied on a codified system of stylized gestures and movements to represent everything: gods and goddesses, natural objects, human actions, abstract ideas, and subtle feelings. Not the least important among the audible elements was the poetry, which amply sufficed to suggest the settings of the various scenes. The Sanskrit drama was also a *Gesamtkunstwerk* synthesizing all the performing arts—music and dance commonly accompanied the play, act 2 of *Mālavikāgnimitra* and act 4 of *Vikrama and Urvaśī* providing typical examples.

Kālidāsa's plays deal with the *rasa* of erotic desire. On a superficial level, they appear to center on similar, if not identical, circumstances: A heroic king falls in love with a beautiful girl who reciprocates the passion, external forces oppose or thwart their permanent union, and they are reunited after a period of suffering. Yet critics recognize each of the three plays as a prototype in its own fashion, each of them being much imitated by Kālidāsa's successors. The five-act *Mālavikāgnimitra*, its characters historical, is a light courtly piece that introduced the spirit of happy comedy to Sanskrit drama. Also in five acts, *Vikrama and Urvaśī* is based on mythology, a romantic comedy with a supernatural flavor that examined the consuming passions of love in a quite unprecedented manner. The poet's tour de force in seven acts, *Śakuntalā*, also derived from mythological sources, transcended the form of a romantic play to become a sublime drama against a cosmic backdrop, offering a unique vision of the spiritual bliss and fullness attained by ideal love.

THE PLOTS

Given the close similarities among the plays, the best approach to Kālidāsa's dramatic œuvre might be to follow the development of his treatment of the same theme. Take, for example, the three plots. *Mālavikāgnimitra* has a fairly complicated plot that unravels quite swiftly, befitting a love intrigue, but the plot seems to be imposed on the characters—character by no means makes destiny. Two devices appear, though, which Kālidāsa would use to greater effect later: Mālavikā's incognito stay at King Agnimitra's court and Queen Dhāriṇī's signet ring. The plot of *Vikrama and Urvaśī* is transitional: As in the preceding play, the king's affair with the heroine is hindered by his jealous queen, but as in *Śakuntalā*, the lovers are separated for a long period and are ultimately reconciled, the king seeing his son for the first time in the last act. Meanwhile, Urvaśī has fallen prey to a curse, and a magic gem has been given a significant part in assuring her reunion with the king. The curse of Durvāsas gets prime importance in *Śakuntalā*, becoming the crux of the plot (in *Mālavikāgnimitra* there was no malignant curse, only a neutral prophecy) together with King Dushyanta's ring, so crucial to the plot that it finds a place in the title of the play. Added irony attaches to the curse because Śakuntalā has no knowledge of it. What is significant, however, is that the curse and the ring are no longer mere devices, as in the other plots. Their seeds lie in the characters of the protagonists: Śakuntalā was so engrossed in love thoughts that she neglected her duty and virtually courted the curse. *Śakuntalā* shows otherwise a relatively simple plot developed without any hurry. Kālidāsa's priorities have clearly changed.

HEROES AND HEROINES

The heroes and heroines provide another basis for comparison. Agnimitra's virtue is debatable. With a son old enough to be a victorious general, he himself would probably be middle-aged, and his fascination for a teenaged maidservant unbecoming, if not ludicrous. Physical attraction draws him to Mālavikā, or at best a sensuous appreciation of external beauty. He commits no heroic deeds and cannot even further his own love-cause; the portrayal suggests an indolent aesthete rather than a valiant king. Purūravas, of *Vikrama and Urvaśī*, reveals much greater depth of character. He is courageous in rescuing Urvaśī, passionately in love with her, and dignified in his dealings with other people. Like all ancient kings, he has many wives, but he displays deep respect for his chief queen, Auśīnarī, and seems a chivalrous husband. For a hero, however, he is perhaps too emotional. His poetic imagination unsettles his equilibrium when Urvaśī leaves him out of jealousy. In Dushyanta, of *Śakuntalā*, Kālidāsa pictures his ideal hero, not merely possessed of conventionalized kingly traits but an ideal man as well. Handsome, brave, and virtuous, he is also sensitive, cultured, a romantic. Neither vain nor despotic, he is humble and religious. He respects the opinions of others and appears to be a stable, thoughtful person who places duty and righteousness above all else. Kālidāsa needed a flawless monarch for his magnum opus; therefore, Dushyanta does not possess the slightest blemish, unlike the dramatist's previous heroes.

If the heroes develop toward an image of the perfect king, the heroines grow away from sophistication and artificial refinement and toward natural goodness and simplicity. Although Mālavikā is timid, fearful, and submissive, she is still a well-bred princess, an accomplished singer and dancer. Critics argue that she rarely displays her royal upbringing, but they forget that she must suppress these qualities so that her disguise as maid may succeed. In fact, she almost betrays herself on one occasion, questioning the steadfastness of Agnimitra's love. In contrast, Urvaśī is a much stronger and more active figure, more mature, bolder, and more sensual. She takes the initiative in the plot more readily than does Purūravas, returning from Heaven of her own accord to see him again. A possessive woman, she is also unnaturally selfish in her love, deliberately keeping their son away from

Purūravas's sight so that she does not have to leave him, as decreed by Indra. On the other hand, Śakuntalā has neither the urban polish of a princess nor the sophistication of a celestial nymph. Brought up in a hermitage, she is relatively innocent of life but is naturally graceful. She embodies the idyllic natural surroundings of the ashram. Love awakens her dormant beauty, and her passion obscures her sense of duty. In the second half of the play, the audience observes her devotion and nobility, too. Kanva's message to Dushyanta reads, "Śakuntalā is womanly virtue incarnate"; no doubt the message speaks for Kālidāsa as well.

SECONDARY CHARACTERS

Kālidāsa's deployment of secondary characters also indicates the development of his dramatic art. In *Mālavikāgnimitra* he depicts two of Agnimitra's queens, Dhārinī and Irāvatī, both of whom occupy important roles in the play. Both are incensed by their husband's infatuation with Mālavikā, but the head queen Dhārinī typifies wifely devotion after some initial resentment of her newest rival, resigning herself to the idea that a king, after all, will remain like a bee, ever seeking fresh honey. Irāvatī, vehemently against Agnimitra's newfound affection, indirectly presents a problem to the discerning spectator. She is Agnimitra's erstwhile favorite, as beautiful and as talented as Mālavikā, but nothing in the play suggests that Mālavikā, in her turn, will not be replaced by a newer object of the king's transitory emotions. The self-sacrificing older queen is a stereotyped figure, recurring in *Vikrama and Urvaśī* as Auśīnarī, who, like Dhārinī, plays a significant part but is much more dignified. She, too, eventually succumbs, exemplifying the self-surrender of the all-suffering wife in order to indulge the husband's latest fancy. By including the king's wives in the earlier plays, Kālidāsa inevitably diverted sympathy toward them, which unhappily leads to some polarization of interest, especially since neither of the two pairs of lovers is totally attractive. In *Śakuntalā* he removed this difficulty. Dushyanta, too, has a harem; Vasumatī is referred to and Hamsavatī is heard singing offstage, but none of the queens actually appears, purposely leaving that aspect of Dushyanta's life almost unnoticed.

In every way, Kālidāsa tried to dispense with stock characters as he matured. The best example is that of the Brahman court jester, a familiar figure in Sanskrit drama: gourmand, confidant to the king, and source of general merriment. Gautama is present in every act of *Mālavikāgnimitra*, and on his machinations pivots the entire plot. He is perhaps the most important Sanskrit jester as regards dramatic construction, a troubleshooting Machiavelli or Chānakya, to use an Indian analogy. Mānavaka in *Vikrama and Urvaśī* is as gluttonous as Gautama but less shrewd. He gives away Purūravas's secret affair the minute he is first asked about it and loses Urvaśī's love letter, which predictably reaches the queen. Even in his bungling, therefore, he furthers the action of the play. Significantly, however, he figures in only three acts. In *Śakuntalā*, Dushyanta himself calls his friend Mādhavya a "blockhead." This jester is of no help whatsoever to either the king or the plot. He, too, appears in only three acts; moreover, he does not even get to meet Śakuntalā, and Dushyanta does not trust him to keep his mouth shut. Kālidāsa has successfully relegated the role of the jester to incidental comic relief, thereby focusing the undistracted attention of the audience on the predicament of the two lovers.

Similarly, he disposes of other secondary agents engaged in helping the plot along, or at least individualizes their portraits. In *Mālavikāgnimitra*, the heroine's companion, Bakulāvalikā, works almost as hard as Gautama to advance the cause of love, as does (more surreptitiously) the nun Kauśikī, who knows Mālavikā's actual identity. Chitralekhā, Urvaśī's friend in the second play, has hardly any such function, while Priyamvadā and Anasūyā, Śakuntalā's helpmates, also do not directly affect the plot. Instead, Kālidāsa gradually individualizes his characters. Thus the garrulous and playful Priyamvadā and the correct and practical Anasūyā are not merely stereotypical confidantes but distinct individuals with their own personalities. In like fashion, Kālidāsa differentiates the three sages—the wise Kanva, the irascible Durvāsas, the majestic Kaśyapa—and juxtaposes the natures of the two disciples who escort Śakuntalā to the court. Every character in *Śakuntalā* exists not on account of convention but as a portrait from life. The episode of the fisherman who discovers the ring and the policemen who apprehend him best illustrates this point.

Besides the intensified concentration on the lovers, there is one other role in Kālidāsa's drama that receives greater attention in the process of the playwright's development. Mālavikā and Agnimitra do not have a child during the course of the play, and the crown prince Vasumitra, son of Dhārinī, is mentioned but remains unseen. Urvaśī does bear Purūravas a son, Āyus, who appears in the last act. He is much younger than Vasumitra, but what is most striking is that this last scene resembles its counterpart in *Śakuntalā* so much that it might even have served as a rough draft. Younger still is Bharata, the son of Śakuntalā and Dushyanta, crucial to the conclusion of the play because Dushyanta, like Purūravas, was childless. The birth of Bharata continues the dynastic line. Bharata also has a special significance for Indians, as the eponymous figure in the national epic the *Mahābhārata*, after whom the country was and still is named "Bhārata."

ŚAKUNTALĀ

Śakuntalā demands separate consideration on two other counts: its structure in the light of Indian aesthetics, and its expression of Kālidāsa's view of love. While the entire play is an exercise in the erotic *rasa*, to achieve comprehensive harmony, the Sanskrit drama must also evoke the other eight emotions in the course of enactment. *Śakuntalā* resembles an extended symphony, with each act one movement, and many variations within each act. Thus, the overall *rasa* of the first three acts is the erotic, and that of the next three acts is the pathetic. Tranquility is the *rasa* of the last act. These major sentiments must be compatible; of the nine emotions, desire, sorrow, and peace are obviously most attuned to the theme of love. Within each act there are suggestions of a secondary *rasa*—for example, the fear in the hunted deer of act 1, the laughter produced by the jester in act 2, the anger of Śakuntalā at Dushyanta in act 5, the disgust shown by Śakuntalā's escort in act 5, and the wonder at the supernatural effects of act 7. Commentators always single out

the fourth act for unstinted praise because of its evocation of the acute sadness when a daughter leaves the home in which she has grown up, in order to get married. The sentiment is not peculiar to Indian hearts, but one must empathize with it in order to appreciate the play fully. It also points out that Kālidāsa's concern was not solely with erotic love. Fatherly and sisterly love, and love of Śakuntalā for animals and plants—all receive full and touching treatment in this act.

The clue to Kālidāsa's conception of ideal love lies in the two visions that Dushyanta has of Śakuntalā. In the first act, he is overcome by Śakuntalā's physical beauty: "Her lips glisten like new leaves,/ Her arms are shoots,/ and her youth sprouts a glory of glittering flowers." When his eyes see clearly in the last act, he observes "the pure-minded one,/ Wearing saffron, her face thin with penance,/ Forced to separate from a heartless husband." He sees at last what had eluded him all along: that internal beauty must be cherished above external beauty. Dushyanta may have been blinded by the curse on Śakuntalā, but the curse also expresses metaphorically his own blindness to the true nature of love. Rabindranath Tagore wrote of two unions in *Śakuntalā*, the physical first and the spiritual at the end, although he was incorrect in attributing Śakuntalā's suffering to his belief that she had sinned. Physical and spiritual love are not incompatible in Indian thought; on the contrary, both are essential in fulfilling the human experience of love. Neither would be complete without the other. Kālidāsa implies that the lovers' suffering makes them arrive at a full understanding of the sacred bond between husband and wife; he may also be implying that reunion after a period of separation strengthens the ties of love.

An optimist, Kālidāsa had complete faith that the powers of good will triumph in the end, but he was also aware that happiness and sadness share equal portions in the lives of men. *Śakuntalā* is Kālidāsa's mature vision of life: Humankind will celebrate, it will suffer, and it will comprehend. The play presents a panoramic span covering heaven and earth and, as Goethe put it in his poem, "the flowers of early years/and the fruits of age advanced." In the end, however, if one has to choose between them, it would seem that the ascetic ideal holds sway over Kālidāsa's mind. He shows a clear preference for life in the country as against life at court. It is no coincidence that two hermitages figure prominently in this play. Their atmosphere seeps into the consciousness of the audience. Kanva predicts that the lovers will return to his ashram in their old age, and the final lines of the play, spoken by Dushyanta, also appear deliberate: "May I be released from further lives."

OTHER MAJOR WORKS

POETRY: *Ṛtusaṃhāra*, c. 75 B.C.E. or c. 365 C.E. (English translation, 1867); *Meghadūta*, c. 65 B.C.E. or c. 375 C.E. (*The Cloud Messenger*, 1813); *Kumārasambhava*, c. 60 B.C.E. or c. 380 C.E. (*The Birth of the War-God*, 1879); *Raghuvaṃśa*, c. 50 B.C.E. or c. 390 C.E. (*The Dynasty of Raghu*, 1872-1895).

BIBLIOGRAPHY

Aggarwal, Vinod. *The Imagery of Kālidāsa*. Delhi, India: Eastern Book Linkers, 1985. An examination of the literary style of Kālidāsa. Bibliography and index.

Kalla, Lachmi Dhar. *The Birth-place of Kālidāsa: With Notes, References, and Appendices*. Delhi, India: Publication Division, University of Delhi, 2000. An examination of Kālidāsa's birthplace that sheds light on his works. Bibliography.

Kawthekar, P. N. *Kālidāsa, the Man and the Mind*. New Delhi, India: Rashtriya Sanskrit Sansthan, 1999. An examination of Kālidāsa's life and works. Bibliography.

Krishnamoorthy, K. *Kālidāsa*. New Delhi, India: Sahitya Akademi, 1994. A critical analysis and interpretation of the works of Kālidāsa. Bibliography.

Mandal, Paresh Chandra. *Kālidāsa as a Dramatist: A Study*. Dhaka, Bangladesh: University of Dhaka, 1986. Mandal provides a critical examination of Kālidāsa's dramatic works. Bibliography and index.

Panda, Gangadhar. *Dramas of Kālidāsa: The Treatment of the Supernatural*. Puri, Orissa, India: Shree Sadashiva Kendriya Sanskrit Vidyapeetha, 1983. An analysis of the plays of Kālidāsa, with emphasis on his treatment of the supernatural. Bibliography and index.

Ananda Lal

SARAH KANE

Born: Essex, England; February 3, 1971
Died: London, England; February 20, 1999

PRINCIPAL DRAMA

Blasted, pr. 1995, pb. 1996
Sick, pr. 1996
Phaedra's Love, pr., pb. 1996
Cleansed, pr., pb. 1998
Crave, pr., pb. 1998
4.48 Psychosis, pr., pb. 2000
Complete Plays, pb. 2001

OTHER LITERARY FORMS

Sarah Kane wrote exclusively for the theater, with the exception of *Skin*, an eleven-minute film first broadcast in June, 1997, for England's Channel 4, for which she wrote the teleplay.

ACHIEVEMENTS

Sarah Kane received no major literary awards during her brief lifetime. Critics in England were divided about her work, many deriding it as shocking and disgusting, others defending her as a poet and an important new dramatic voice. After her arrival on the professional London theater scene with the opening of *Blasted* in 1995, her plays have been widely performed and acclaimed in Europe, and all of her major plays—*Blasted*, *Phaedra's Love*, *Cleansed*, *Crave*, and *4.48 Psychosis*—have been published both separately and in collections in English, French, German, and Italian. In 1996, she served as playwright-in-residence for Paines Plough, a prestigious London theater company dedicated exclusively to the presentation of new work.

Biography

Sarah Kane was the daughter of Peter and Janine Kane, both of whom were English journalists. Peter was a reporter for London's *Daily Mirror*, and the family members, for a short time during Kane's teenage years, became fervent born-again Christians. Kane renounced her Christianity in her early twenties but admitted that the violent imagery she found in the Bible inspired her work as a playwright. Kane joined local drama groups as a teenager and directed plays by William Shakespeare and Anton Chekhov. For a time, she skipped school altogether to work as an assistant director for a production at a school in London's Soho district.

Kane attended the University of Bristol, acting in school plays and directing a number of student productions, including Shakespeare's *Macbeth* (pr. 1606) and Caryl Churchill's *Top Girls* (pr., pb. 1982). After graduating with top honors in drama, she enrolled at the University of Birmingham, where she received her M.A. degree. While at school, Kane gained a reputation for nightclubbing and having affairs with women, though her work does not contain noticeable lesbian themes.

In 1996, her first full-length play, *Sick*, composed of three monologues (*Comic Monologue*, *Starved*, and *What She Said*) was performed at the Edinburgh Festival Theatre in Edinburgh, Scotland. However, it was her play, *Blasted*, which she had written in 1994 while at Birmingham University and which was presented at the students' end-of-year show, that brought Kane to the forefront of the New Wave theater scene.

The first professional production of *Blasted* opened at London's Royal Court Theatre in January,

1995, in a secondary theater that held sixty-two seats, forty-five of which were occupied by critics. No more than a thousand people saw *Blasted* during its short run, but the virulent critical response to Kane's violent imagery and language splashed her name not only across newspaper arts sections but also across the pages of the British tabloids and made her the topics of television gossip shows as well. The play did have its share of admirers—among them, playwright Harold Pinter, whose hand-delivered fan letter to Kane shortly after seeing *Blasted* was among her most cherished possessions. Before Kane's death, *Blasted* had already been produced in Germany, Austria, France, Australia, Serbia, Belgium, and Italy.

In 1995, Kane also wrote the teleplay for *Skin*, a short film about a black woman who comes into contact with a skinhead and the unexpected twist as to who will be the victim. During her season at Paines Plough, Kane wrote *Crave*. Because of the critical outrage over *Blasted* and because Kane wanted theatergoers to judge the play on its own merits, *Crave* was first presented under the pseudonym Marie Kelvedon.

Critical outrage and accusations of what was perceived as a childish attempt to shock depressed Kane but did not deter her from continuing her work, and actors, directors, and producers with whom she worked—as well as fellow playwrights Pinter, Caryl Churchill, and Steven Berkoff—continued to defend her as a thoughtful, brave, and angry poet.

Kane battled mental illness and depression throughout most of her adult life, each new bout of depression affecting her more seriously than the last. In the two years before her death, she checked herself into mental hospitals several times and was treated with a number of antidepressant drugs. After her death, Tom Fahy, a psychiatrist who treated Kane in 1997 at Maudsley Hospital in London, told British reporters that Kane had told him she expected to be dead by the time she was twenty-seven.

On February 18, 1999, at the age of twenty-eight, Kane left a short note on her kitchen table ("I have killed myself") and took an overdose of antidepressants and sleeping pills. She was discovered and taken to King's College Hospital in south London, where she was resuscitated. Kane had been scheduled to be moved to a psychiatric ward at Maudsley Hospital, but on February 20, before she could be transferred from King's College, she committed suicide by hanging herself on the back of a lavatory door.

Her final play, *4.48 Psychosis*—so titled, Kane said, because she awoke many mornings at that time filled with extreme clarity alongside thoughts of suicide—was produced posthumously at the Royal Court Theatre, where *Blasted* had made such an impact just five years earlier. Shortly before her death, she had been working on an adaptation of Johann Wolfgang von Goethe's *Die Leiden des jungen Werthers* (1774; *The Sorrows of Young Werther*, 1779), in which the love-stricken hero kills himself after failing to gain what he desires.

ANALYSIS

Like the deaths of playwright Joe Orton and novelist Sylvia Plath before her, Sarah Kane's early death forced many critics to reexamine her work. Some felt that her plays, especially her final play, *4.48 Psychosis*, were merely reflections of her own suicidal depression. Critic Charles Spencer of the London *Telegraph* suggested that Kane's work owed more to clinical depression than to artistic vision. Admirers such as Pinter and Kane's brother, Simon, however, have refuted these statements, insisting that to treat Kane's plays as suicide notes is to do an injustice to the playwright's talent and motives. British drama anthologist David Tushingham agreed, insisting that as a mental patient, Kane was far less exceptional than as a writer and that the most extraordinary thing about her was not her illness but her talent.

Kane's plays relied more on classical than contemporary structure and technique. She was more influenced by the scope of Shakespeare's large dramatic conflicts than by the work of her peers in the London theater scene. The body of her work tackled human and political issues by placing those issues onstage in violent, distorted, and extremely personal situations. Her raw language and graphic visual images were particularly disturbing to theatergoers because she left conflicts unresolved and perpetrators unpunished, although, as in the works of Samuel Beckett, she continually showed the basic human impulse to connect with another even in the most hopeless of circumstances.

Kane was certainly one of the most controversial voices in a decade that was filled with controversy. The self-titled "in-yer-face" theater in Britain began in 1991 with Philip Ridley's *The Pitchfork Disney*, shocking audiences with its scenes of cockroach eating, and continued in 1994 in Glasgow, Scotland, with *Trainspotting*, playwright Harry Gibson's adaptation of the novel by Irvine Welsh, which in 1995 became a critically acclaimed film.

The "in-yer-face" movement of 1990's theater reached its zenith with Kane's *Blasted* in 1995 and continued in 1998 with *Cleansed*, which Kane had originally conceived, along with *Blasted*, as part of a trilogy. After *Cleansed* was produced, however, Kane stopped work on the trilogy and turned instead to *Crave*, a play for four voices. Not until *Crave* premiered at Edinburgh's Traverse Theatre in 1998 did Kane overcome the vitriolic early critical response to *Blasted*.

Kane's work is an ongoing influence in British theater and continues to be acclaimed by an ever-increasing number of British dramatists and by critics and audiences in continental Europe. Her body of work follows an ever-narrowing path, from the gory conflicts of civil war in *Blasted* to the destruction of the family in *Phaedra's Love*, into the fragmentation of the self in *Crave* and further into a singular mind in *4.48 Psychosis*, always chipping away at the naturalistic boundaries of modern theater and charting a lonely internal world of darkness, violation, misuse of power, and frequently, a reaching out for love.

BLASTED

Kane's first professional production was both the most maligned and acclaimed of her short career. *Blasted*, which was the playwright's response to the war and human atrocities taking place in Bosnia in the early 1990's, opens with the young, mentally handicapped Cate and middle-age tabloid journalist Ian, who enter a hotel room in Leeds, England. The setting immediately suggests the type of relationship piece with which audiences are comfortable, but from the opening bit of dialogue, it becomes clear that this is no ordinary bedroom drama. Ian is obnoxious and perhaps amoral, but Kane does not provide a moral framework to comfort either Cate or the audience, and the rape of Cate by Ian, coupled with the later appearance of a soldier who joins them from a world fraught with its own terrors, only adds to the disturbing and violent world in which the characters find themselves trapped.

The play's structure also fueled the audience's discomfort. Although the first half of *Blasted* provides a naturalistic setting, the second half flouts theatrical convention with its eerie, nightmarish qualities and symbolism, ending with the destruction of all Ian holds dear, with the character reduced to a base shadow of what he once had been. The symbolism is more evocative of King Lear as he roams the heath facing his own self-imposed destruction than of the confines of most contemporary drama.

PHAEDRA'S LOVE

Kane was commissioned by London's Gate Theatre to write her next play and chose *Phaedra's Love*, a contemporary retelling of the Greek myth of Phaedra and her fatal love for Hippolytus, her spoiled stepson. Kane also directed the piece, which was the first of her plays to deal explicitly with the desire for love—a theme that runs throughout the remainder of her work. *Phaedra's Love* contains some of Kane's wittiest dialogue, set against the bleak backdrop of a situation fraught with taboos and impossible desires.

Phaedra, wife of Theseus, has fallen in love with her stepson, the prince Hippolytus, who is threatened by the ideas of real love and emotion. His sex drive, which would normally draw him into relationships with others, is abhorrent to him, and the desire of his stepmother to submit herself sexually to him is therefore an unbearable threat, leading to the violent destruction of the royal family.

CLEANSED

Dealing with drug abuse, amputation, and sex changes, *Cleansed* is considered the bleakest of Kane's plays—and the most difficult to stage, due in part to the inclusion in the cast of a family of rats. Set in a bizarre university/concentration camp under the rule of brutal Tinker, a drug dealer and doctor, the

play reveals an ongoing attempt by Kane to find new structures to fit the context of her writing and offers stripped-down narrative and dialogue in an attempt to discover the limits of love. When the lead actress was injured, Kane herself took on the role for the final performances.

CRAVE

Expanding a technique she had used less successfully in her first play, *Sick*, which she wrote as a student and which debuted after *Blasted*, Kane's characters in *Crave* are four voices, known only as A, B, M, and C. As in *Sick*, each character's part in the play is essentially a monologue, but here the monologues are combined so the voices speak together, four bodies making up one life. These voices speak seemingly without a defined narrative, describing their loves and losses as each character moves emotionally into the boundaries of the next.

Influenced by music throughout her life, Kane uses the characters almost as a symphony, with each monologue rendered meaningless without the concurrent monologues of the others, as the individual voices move into a combined but fragmented whole.

4.48 PSYCHOSIS

Kane awoke at 4:48 on many mornings during her periods of depression and felt she found clarity in the predawn hours, paradoxically at a time when, according to her research for the play, the psychotic delusion is strongest. Here Kane wrote with dry humor and a bleak outlook, still churning out lines of poetry about the fragmentation and final despair of the self, a prisoner by now of her own mental illness but determined to share her last weeks and months with an audience. In attempting to give voice to a mostly silent condition, Kane explores the depths of her own despair and emerges with a witty and eerie artistic success, though early audiences and critics understandably found it difficult to separate the finished product from the recent death of its author.

BIBLIOGRAPHY

Dromgoole, Dominic. *The Full Room*. London: Methuen, 2001. A broad overview of how the dramatic playwrights of the 1990's have shaped the New British Theatre movement. Along with Kane, playwrights discussed include Conor MacPherson, Jonathan Harvey, Philip Ridley, Sebastian Barry, and Naomi Wallace.

Greig, David. Introduction to *Sarah Kane: The Complete Plays*, by Sarah Kane. London: Methuen Press, 2001. Scottish playwright and editor David Greig provides an excellent introduction to Kane's body of work, including an insightful assessment on the difficulties in staging a Kane play.

Saunders, Graham. *Love Me or Kill Me: Sarah Kane and the Theatre of Extremes*. Manchester, England: Manchester University Press, 2002. The first volume devoted to Kane's life and works. Contains analyses of her various works, interviews with producers and directors who worked

with Kane, and a thoughtful preface by prolific British playwright Edward Bond.

Sierz, Aleks. *In-Yer-Face Theatre: British Drama Today*. London: Faber & Faber, 2001. This overview of young British playwrights has thirty-two pages on Kane, including a biography and a critical breakdown of her plays.

Tushingham, David. *Live 3: Critical Mass*. London: Methuen Press, 2001. An introduction to playwrights who are reshaping the British theater. Kane is represented by *Blasted*; other playwrights represented are Patrick Marber, Philip Ridley, and Jonathan Harvey.

Jarre Fees

TADEUSZ KANTOR

Born: Wielopole, Poland; April 6, 1915
Died: Warsaw, Poland; December 8, 1990

PRINCIPAL DRAMA

Umarła klasa, pr. 1975 (*The Dead Class*, 1979)
Wielopole, Wielopole, pr. 1980, pb. 1984 (*Wielopole/ Wielopole: An Exercise in Theatre*, 1990)
Niech sczeną artyści, pr. 1985 (*Let the Artists Die*, 1985)
Nigdy tu już nie powrócę, pr. 1988 (*I Shall Never Return*, 1988)
Today Is My Birthday, pr. 1991

OTHER LITERARY FORMS

Tadeusz Kantor was best known in the West as a theater director because of his avant-garde, highly unusual and individualized productions. His career, however, touched on many other aspects of the arts. He originally studied painting and achieved a reputation as a painter; he then gained extensive recognition as a creator/director of "happenings" in the 1960's and 1970's and wrote several free-verse tracts or "manifestos" on his theories of the theater. In addi-

tion to the areas of expertise already listed, Kantor's work in graphics, stage design, and costume design was internationally recognized.

ACHIEVEMENTS

Throughout his long career, Tadeusz Kantor remained an uncompromised force in the postwar avant-garde in the theater and in other creative fields, such as painting. As a disciple of the ideas of Edward Gordon Craig, he achieved an extraordinary integration of all the different art forms that compose the theater's *mise en scène*, from innovative notions of acting and the treatment of dramatic literature to the imaginative redefinition and selective reduction of the theater's auditory and visual elements.

Kantor was twice appointed to the faculty of the Academy of Fine Arts in Krakow, in 1948 and in 1968. On both occasions, the professorship was revoked within one year because of his unwillingness to follow government orthodoxy concerning the arts. He was, however, awarded a Polish State Prize for his work in 1962. Kantor received two Obie Awards for Best Play, the first for *The Dead Class* in 1979 and the second for *Wielopole/Wielopole* in 1982.

Significantly, Kantor's theater company, Cricot 2, never received support from the Polish government, despite its enormous international success. That success is a mark of the high regard in which Kantor's work was held among both theater artists and the theatergoing public in Poland and elsewhere. Perhaps the most remarkable achievement of his theatrical career is the visceral and intellectual impact of his later, intensely personal productions, such as *Wielopole/ Wielopole*.

BIOGRAPHY

Tadeusz Kantor was born in 1915 in Wielopole, a small town in southern Poland. His father, a teacher, was killed in World War I, and therefore, Kantor grew up in the house of his great-uncle, a priest. He took an early interest in the theater but decided instead to become a painter, learning drawing and painting under the influence of the Polish Symbolists: Stanisław Wyspiański, Witold Wojtkiewicz, and Jacek Malczewski. From 1934 to 1939, he attended the Academy of Fine Arts in Krakow, where he studied scene design with Karol Frycz, who was himself a highly innovative stage designer as well as a painter, theatrical director, theater manager, and follower of the ideas of Gordon Craig and Wyspiański. Frycz's and Kantor's careers are in keeping with the twentieth century traditions of Krakow, a Polish center for the avant-garde both in the visual arts and in stage design, where visual artists often became theater directors and managers.

In 1942, Kantor and a group of young painters formed the underground, experimental Independent Theatre during the German occupation. In 1946, Kantor began his career as a scene designer, creating sets and costumes for theaters throughout Poland until he went to study in France in 1947. He returned in 1948 to organize the first postwar exhibition of modern Polish art in Krakow and was appointed to the faculty of the Krakow Academy of Fine Arts.

Poland fell under the control of Joseph Stalin in 1949, and the authorities officially imposed Socialist Realism on the arts and artists. Kantor's professor-

ship was revoked, and he began to collaborate with Maria Jarema, a widely recognized painter and sculptor who had done scene design for Cricot 1, an important Krakow avant-garde theater between the world wars. Kantor continued designing in this manner until the collapse of Stalinism under Nikita Khrushchev in

Tadeusz Kantor on stage during a performance of Let the Artists Die *in Warsaw, Poland, in 1986.* (AP/Wide World Photos)

1956. With the increased independence of Poland, at least in areas of culture, Polish theater began to flourish. During this time, Kantor's style began to intensify and vary. It was also in 1956 that Kantor opened Cricot 2, which would eventually be housed in the basement of the Gallery Krysztofory in the old city of Krakow. Cricot 2 became Kantor's base of operations and a homing point for actors, painters, and poets who sought to explore new dimensions in the arts.

During the late 1950's, Kantor mounted productions at Cricot 2 while traveling and exhibiting his painting in various parts of Western Europe. In 1961, he published the first of his theoretical works on theater, *Teatr Informel* (1961; *The Manifesto of the Informel Theatre*, 1982), which dealt with the concept of a fluid theater composed of "shapeless matter" in which the substance of the performance lay in the artist's struggle with the material, not in the aggregate result of the performance. Kantor was, in the early 1960's, a professor at the Akademie Kunste in Hamburg, where in 1961 he published "Ob die Ruckkehr von Orpheus moglich ist?" (is Orpheus's comeback possible?).

In 1962, Kantor wrote his *Emballage Manifesto*, which propounded the creation of art objects from the lowliest of wrappings, such as discarded sacks, bags, and envelopes, which, from their despised position as disposable receptacles, acquired an autonomous but utterly empty existence. The *Teatr Zerowy* (1963; *Theatre Zero Manifesto*, 1982) followed, and it argued that a play ought not to be enacted but commented on by the performers; its text was to be destroyed and replaced by a theatrical universe of humdrum, discarded objects that are transformed in performance and interact with the actors in a struggle with them for presence on the stage.

From this point on, Kantor continued to create productions in which the text—in many cases the plays of Stanisław Ignacy Witkiewicz—had been radically altered. He also continued to mount happenings, to paint, to design, and to write. By the mid-1970's, Kantor was working away from the texts of others by combining parts of other works and adapting them to his special theatrical form, as in the case of *The Dead Class*, until he began on his two major

autobiographical pieces, *Wielopole/Wielopole* and *Let the Artists Die*. Also during this time, he published his *The Theatre of Death Manifesto* (1975), in which he argues that life can only be expressed in the theater through reference to death.

Throughout his career, Kantor traveled extensively to the major international theater festivals with his productions. Long recognized in Eastern and Western Europe, he first gained attention in North America when he presented *The Dead Class* in Mexico and in the United States at La Mama in 1979. His subsequent tours of *Wielopole/Wielopole* and *Let the Artists Die* secured Kantor's position as a world-class director and one of the creative forces in the twentieth century avant-garde theater.

ANALYSIS

Tadeusz Kantor's theater could be characterized to a large extent as a theater of objects, a description that applies to both his actors and himself. In his later productions, Kantor was sometimes the subject of his own work, and he appeared onstage as a visual element of his own productions—giving directions to the actors and technicians, musing over the action, and playing the role of Tadeusz Kantor in his black jacket and trousers and tieless, plain white shirt. His stage presence was greatly enhanced by his long, gaunt face, which he set in a mask of haunted contemplation briefly interrupted with small bursts of irritation or humor.

Kantor's work reflected such an imaginative and insightful ability to transform objects and people into complex, unique performances in large part because of his background in the visual arts. He clearly subscribed to Craig's notion of the total theater artist and, as such, personally designed and shaped every aspect of his productions. His dramatic works employed virtually none of the conventions of traditional theatrical staging, and his scenography was completely composed of discarded, worn-looking objects and clothing, which he altered to bring them into his special theatrical universe and put to ingenious, surprising use. The colors in his productions were predominantly flat, pale grays, bone, and black, with accents of purple and red.

The other cause of his theatrical inventiveness has been necessity. His early productions with the Independent Theatre had to be staged in secret because artistic activity of any sort was prohibited by the Germans under penalty of death. In the case of Wyspiański's *Powrót Odysa* (pb. 1907, pr. 1917; *The Return of Odysseus*, 1966), Kantor staged this brooding and sinister play as a modern story of a soldier returning home from the front. Performed in a room of an apartment that had been partially destroyed by the war, without benefit of a stage or set, Kantor transformed the space through the use of objects into the metaphoric waiting room of a train station. Odysseus returns to find his homeland under Nazi domination. Partly as a reaction against the then fashionable school of constructivism, Kantor employed objects such as a decayed wooden board, a muddy broken cartwheel, a mastlike object, an object that looked like the barrel of an old rifle, large, anonymous parcels covered with dust, and a soldier's uniform to create a total environment. In this way, he meant to overwhelm the text with the historical circumstances and the style of performance into which it had been thrust.

After the war, Kantor went to Paris, where he became familiar with Surrealism and abstract expressionism, both hitherto unknown in Poland. He was appointed to the faculty of the Krakow Academy of Fine Arts but subsequently lost his professorship after he refused to participate in official cultural life after the imposition of Socialist Realism. His paintings continued to be exhibited underground, and he made his living as a scene designer. With the collapse of Socialist Realism and the onset of the "thaw" in government cultural repression in the late 1950's, Kantor tried again to insinuate his theatrical aesthetic into the official theaters.

When this proved impossible, he limited his work to the Cricot 2 Theatre, which had been in the planning stages for several years. In 1960, Kantor staged the first postwar performance of Witkiewicz's *Matwa: Czyli, Hyrkaniczny światopogląd* (pb. 1923, pr. 1933; *The Cuttlefish: Or, The Hyrcanian Worldview*, 1970), which had previously been banned. This production, which was staged as a happening, illus-

trated Kantor's concept as described in *Teatr autonomiczny* (1963; *The Autonomous Theatre*, 1986) in the following manner: "The theatre which I call autonomous/ is the theatre which is not/ a reproductive mechanism,/ i.e., a mechanism whose aim is to/ present an interpretation of a piece of literature/ on stage,/ but a mechanism which/ has its own independent/ existence."

Kantor's ideas continued to evolve throughout his complex career. Although these shifts often ran parallel to current trends in the arts, Kantor was not a follower of movements. For example, when he visited the United States in 1965, he met people who also made happenings. He would later remark that he had been staging happenings since the end of World War II, lacking only the popular name given these events. He would eventually reject happenings because of their necessary physicality, preferring an increasingly reduced theater of essential images. His production of Witkiewicz's *Nadobnisie i koczkodany: Czyli, Zielon pigułka* (wr. 1922, pb. 1962, pr. 1967; *Dainty Shapes and Hairy Apes: Or, The Green Pill*, 1980) in 1973 paralleled his new theory espoused in *Le Théâtre impossible* (1972; *The Impossible Theatre*, 1973). Audience participation, used in the happenings, was abandoned, and the actors performed the play in a cloakroom in which, bereft of their humanity, they hung like lifeless objects. Through these methods, Kantor hoped to work beyond the borders of art into an aesthetic space so rarefied and charged with an extraordinary theatrical reality that art would be impossible.

THE DEAD CLASS

Kantor's work as a director also was a struggle against illusion in the theater in the service of reality. Thus, for example, he often used dummies in his productions, as in *The Dead Class*. In this play, dead schoolboys wander between This Side and That Side, sitting again in the benches they had filled during their school days. The principal character, an old man, has decided to return to school at the end of his life. He carries a wax dummy that mirrors his appearance but in a cheap, debased form, a problem that Kantor finds with all imitation in the arts.

WIELOPOLE/WIELOPOLE

His autobiographical works—*Wielopole/Wielopole* and *Let the Artists Die*—are representative of the essence of Kantor's theatrical structure. It has been said of his work that it is as much musical as it is theatrical. Images and themes are presented not through narrative chains of causation, as in most conventional drama, but rather through varied repetitions and recapitulations.

Wielopole/Wielopole deals with Kantor's memories of his early life between the wars. In this play, Kantor rebuilds a village from before the war and peoples it with nothing but the ghosts of his memories. These ghosts move with a mechanical, repetitive, constant motion. The play begins with Kantor entering and moving the onstage objects, including a bed, wardrobe, chair, and table. After the actors enter, Kantor takes the audience through the historical events that held importance for him.

LET THE ARTISTS DIE

In *Let the Artists Die*, Kantor depicts the interaction of the worlds of death and life in the "Poor Room of the Imagination." In this play, the cast appeared again and again repeating a pattern of movement or series of actions that had already been performed with minor variations. These become reexplorations of these themes and images for the audience and for Kantor, who both watches and participates in the production. The effect is not so much one of the musicality of harmonics as one of juxtaposition through contrasts. For example, several times in the production a general, reminiscent of Józef Piłsudski, is wheeled onstage riding a comic-grotesque skeleton of a horse. With each turn, depending on the actions surrounding each circuit, the feeling the general evokes is enriched and slightly transformed.

OTHER MAJOR WORKS

NONFICTION: *Teatr Informel*, 1961 (*The Manifesto of the Informel Theatre*, 1982); *Emballage Manifesto*, 1962; *Teatr Zerowy*, 1963 (*Theatre Zero Manifesto*, 1982); *Teatr autonomiczny*, 1963 (*The Autonomous Theatre*, 1986); *Le Théâtre impossible*, 1972 (*The Impossible Theatre*, 1973); *The Theatre of Death Manifesto*, 1975; *A Journey Through Other Spaces: Essays and Manifestos, 1944-1990*, 1993.

BIBLIOGRAPHY

Elsom, John. "Polish Madness: Tadeusz Kantor's Eccentric Genius." *The World and I* 16, no. 7 (July, 2001): 76-83. Elsom sees Kantor's work as capturing the disintegration of twentieth century Poland. Provides analysis of his dramatic works and a concise biography.

Kantor, Tadeusz. *A Journey Through Other Spaces: Essays and Manifestos, 1944-1990*. Berkeley: University of California Press, 1993. This translation of Kantor's work contains a critical study of his theater by Michal Kobialka. Bibliography and index.

Kobialka, Michal. "Tadeusz Kantor's Happenings: Reality, Mediality, and History." *Theatre Survey* 43, no. 1 (May, 2002): 58-79. Kobialka examines Kantor's "happenings," produced during the 1960's in socialist Poland.

Margolies, Eleanor. "Ventriloquism: Kantor, Templeton, and the Voices of the Dead." *New Theatre Quarterly* 16, no. 63 (August, 2000): 203-210. Margolies examines how the spirits of the dead "speak" through the works of Kantor and Fiona Templeton, a performance artist.

Miklaszewski, Krzysztof. *Encounters with Tadeusz Kantor*. Routledge Harwood Polish and East European Theatre Archive 8. New York: Routledge, 2002. Contains criticism and interpretation of Kantor's dramatic works. Includes an extensive bibliography and index.

Steven Hart

GEORGE S. KAUFMAN

Born: Pittsburgh, Pennsylvania; November 16, 1889
Died: New York, New York; June 2, 1961

PRINCIPAL DRAMA

Someone in the House, pr. 1918 (with Larry Evans and Walter Percival; originally as *Among Those Present*, pr. 1917)

Dulcy, pr., pb. 1921 (with Marc Connelly)

To the Ladies, pr. 1922, pb. 1923 (with Connelly)

Merton of the Movies, pr. 1922, pb. 1925 (with Connelly; based on Harry Leon Wilson's novel)

Helen of Troy, N.Y., pr. 1923 (musical comedy with Connelly; music and lyrics by Bert Kalmar and Harry Ruby)

The Deep Tangled Wildwood, pr. 1923 (with Connelly)

Beggar on Horseback, pr. 1924, pb. 1925 (with Connelly)

Be Yourself, pr. 1924 (musical comedy with Connelly; music by Lewis Gensler and Milton Schwartzwald)

Minick, pr., pb. 1924 (with Edna Ferber)

The Butter and Egg Man, pr., pb. 1925

The Cocoanuts, pr. 1925 (musical comedy; music and lyrics by Irving Berlin)

The Good Fellow, pr. 1926, pb. 1931 (with Herman J. Mankiewicz)

If Men Played Cards as Women Do, pr., pb. 1926

The Royal Family, pr. 1927, pb. 1928 (with Ferber)

Animal Crackers, pr. 1928 (musical comedy with Morrie Ryskind; music and lyrics by Kalmar and Ruby)

June Moon, pr. 1929, pb. 1931 (with Ring Lardner)

The Channel Road, pr. 1929 (with Alexander Woollcott)

Strike Up the Band, pr. 1930 (musical comedy with Ryskind; music by George Gershwin and lyrics by Ira Gershwin)

Once in a Lifetime, pr., pb. 1930 (with Moss Hart)

The Band Wagon, pr. 1931 (musical revue with Howard Dietz; music by Arthur Schwartz and lyrics by Dietz)

Of Thee I Sing, pr. 1931, pb. 1932 (musical comedy with Ryskind; music by George Gershwin and lyrics by Ira Gershwin)

Dinner at Eight, pr., pb. 1932 (with Ferber)

Let 'em Eat Cake, pr., pb. 1933 (musical comedy with Ryskind; music by George Gershwin and lyrics by Ira Gershwin)

The Dark Tower, pr. 1933, pb. 1934 (with Woollcott; based on Guy de Maupassant's story "Boule de suif")

Merrily We Roll Along, pr., pb. 1934 (with Moss Hart)

First Lady, pr. 1935, pb. 1936 (with Katherine Dayton)

Stage Door, pr., pb. 1936 (with Ferber)

You Can't Take It with You, pr. 1936, pb. 1937 (with Moss Hart)

I'd Rather Be Right, pr., pb. 1937 (musical revue with Moss Hart; music by Richard Rodgers and lyrics by Lorenz Hart)

The Fabulous Invalid, pr., pb. 1938 (with Moss Hart)

The American Way, pr., pb. 1939 (with Moss Hart)

The Man Who Came to Dinner, pr., pb. 1939 (with Moss Hart)

George Washington Slept Here, pr., pb. 1940 (with Moss Hart)

The Land Is Bright, pr., pb. 1941 (with Ferber)

The Late George Apley, pr. 1944, pb. 1946 (with John P. Marquand; based on Marquand's novel)

Park Avenue, pr. 1946 (musical comedy with Nunnally Johnson; music by Arthur Schwartz and lyrics by Ira Gershwin)

Bravo!, pr. 1948, pb. 1949 (with Ferber)

The Small Hours, pr., pb. 1951 (with Leueen MacGrath)

The Solid Gold Cadillac, pb. 1951, pr. 1953 (with Howard Teichmann)

Fancy Meeting You Again, pr., pb. 1952 (with MacGrath)

Silk Stockings, pr. 1955 (musical comedy with MacGrath and Abe Burrows; music and lyrics by Cole Porter; based on Menyhért Lengyel's film *Ninotchka*)

OTHER LITERARY FORMS

George S. Kaufman began his literary career by voluntarily writing humorous verse and prose for Franklin P. Adams's column in the New York *Evening Mail*. Later, he was hired to write his own column in the *Washington Times*. Kaufman then replaced Adams at the *Evening Mail* for a short time, was fired, and took a job as a reporter on the New York *Tribune*. Shortly thereafter, he was made drama editor, only to leave the *Tribune* in 1917 for the same position at *The New York Times*. He held on to his relationship with *The New York Times*, despite his success as a playwright, until 1930, when he was asked to resign because his career as a playwright was taking too much of his time. Throughout his life he contributed short sketches, prose humor, and light verse to such magazines as *Saturday Review*, *The Nation*, *Life, Theatre* magazine, *Playbill*, and *The New Yorker* (founded by his friend Harold Ross), as well as various newspapers.

Kaufman also wrote several screenplays, although he disliked Hollywood and, as a rule, avoided long-term relationships with the film industry. The Marx Brothers' films *The Cocoanuts* (1929) and *Animal Crackers* (1931), which Kaufman wrote in collaboration with Morrie Ryskind, were adapted from their plays and filmed in New York. Later, Samuel Goldwyn hired Kaufman and Robert E. Sherwood to write the screenplay for *Roman Scandals* (1933); a disagreement with star Eddie Cantor caused Kaufman to invoke the clause of his contract that stipulated that he would not have to work with Cantor. In 1935, Irving Thalberg of Metro-Goldwyn-Mayer guaranteed Kaufman $100,000 to write (with Ryskind) the Marx Brothers' classic *A Night at the Opera* (1935). By 1936, his distaste for Hollywood was such that he refused to adapt his and Moss Hart's Pulitzer Prize-winning play *You Can't Take It with*

You for the screen. Ironically, the film later won the 1938 Academy Award for Best Picture.

ACHIEVEMENTS

Although George S. Kaufman is generally considered to be one of the greatest geniuses of the Broadway theater, it is difficult to assess his individual talents because he wrote nearly all his plays in collaboration. *The Butter and Egg Man*, his only full-length comedy written solo, was composed early in his career and shows his talent; nevertheless, apparently never fully confident of his talent even after dozens of successful plays, he continued, until his death, to work with collaborators, some of whom were among the major literary figures of his period. From 1918 to 1955, Kaufman's name appeared as author or coauthor on more than forty productions, some of which were unsuccessful and many of which were successful. Forty-eight full-length motion pictures from 1920 to 1961 were based on plays Kaufman had either written or directed. He directed some forty-five plays, many by notable authors other than himself. As a result, perhaps no one had more influence on the shape and direction of popular drama from the 1920's through the 1950's than Kaufman. He was considered a master of stage technique, an incomparable wit, and an extraordinary satirist. His record of success on the Broadway stage is without equal.

BIOGRAPHY

George Kaufman was born to Joseph S. Kaufman and Henrietta Myers, both members of the German-Jewish community of Pittsburgh. Joseph Kaufman had once worked as a deputy sheriff in Leadville, Colorado, and participated in one of the Ute Indian wars, but he returned to Pittsburgh poorer than when he had left. Marrying the wealthiest woman in his social circle was no help, as he soon brought his family to the brink of poverty. Mrs. Kaufman was a hypochondriac, and young George, who had been overprotected because of the infant death of his older brother, became an introverted, skinny adolescent who read adventure stories in *Argosy* magazine. (He even attempted to write for *Argosy* but had nothing accepted.) His father determined to toughen him up by

George S. Kaufman (AP/Wide World Photos)

sending him to an old family friend's ranch in Idaho, but the boy was only confirmed in his reclusive tendencies.

In his teens, Kaufman became interested in theater. Encouraged by a rabbi, he first acted the part of a Scotsman in a religious production, and thereafter he was hooked for life. He collaborated on a play in 1903 with another boy, Irving Pichel, who would later become a Hollywood actor-director. The play was entitled *The Failure*, and both boys acted in it.

Kaufman studied law for three months, then gave it up, and on the advice of a physician took a job on a surveying team in West Virginia. That job did not last either, and other jobs followed. He went to secretarial school and became a stenographer for the Pittsburgh Coal Company. He became a window clerk for the Allegheny County tax office. In 1909, Joseph Kaufman got a job with the Columbia Ribbon Manufacturing Company in Paterson, New Jersey, and George became a traveling salesperson for the company. It was in Paterson and on his trips into New

York City selling ribbons that Kaufman began reading Franklin P. Adams's column "Always in Good Humor" in the New York *Evening Mail*. The column consisted of humorous contributions from throughout the area, as well as Adams's witticisms, and Kaufman began submitting pieces under the initials "G.S.K." to mimic Adams's use of "F.P.A." (only later in his life did Kaufman, who did not have a middle name, decide that the "S" represented "Simon," his grandfather's name.)

Adams recognized Kaufman's talent and urged him to take acting lessons at the Alveine School of Dramatic Art as well as a playwriting course at Columbia University. In 1912, Adams maneuvered Kaufman into a position on the *Washington Times*, where he wrote a column entitled "This and That," similar to Adams's. He became familiar with the works of Mark Twain while there and honed his staccato writing style and ability to play poker. Within a year, however, the owner of the paper, who had never seen Kaufman face-to-face, noticed him in the office and remarked, "What is that Jew doing in my city room?" After several words were exchanged, Kaufman was fired and returned to New York, where he succeeded Adams at the *Evening Mail*, only to be dismissed. Adams then got him a job on the *Tribune*, where he covered local news. While reporting on incoming ships and other insignificant events, he began cadging free admission into the theaters, and eventually got himself assigned to the drama desk. In 1914, he became the drama editor. Three years later, after losing out to Heywood Broun for the position of top drama critic, he became drama editor of *The New York Times*.

In March of 1917, Kaufman married Beatrice Bakrow, whose ambitions and contacts helped thrust him into the theatrical world. She provided emotional support and critical and social guidance for the always uncertain Kaufman for most of his long career, despite the deterioration of their marital relationship after the stillbirth of a deformed child. They later adopted a daughter, Anne, but, as part of their "arrangement," sought sexual relationships outside the marriage. They remained married until Beatrice's death in 1945.

In 1917, John Peter Toohey noticed a play submitted by Kaufman to the Joseph W. Stern Music Company. The play was never produced, but Toohey introduced Kaufman to impresario George C. Tyler, who offered Kaufman the task of revising a play by Larry Evans and Walter Percival. Though produced, *Among Those Present*, which finally reached Broadway after still more revisions as *Someone in the House*, was never a success. Kaufman next tried to adapt Hans Miller's *Jacques Duval*, a European hit. Although George Arliss played the lead, it, too, failed. Tyler, however, continued to have faith in Kaufman, and put him to work on *Dulcy* with Marc Connelly. Based on a character, Dulcinea, created by Kaufman's friend Adams, the play opened in New York on August 13, 1921, and became an immediate hit.

Connelly and Kaufman worked together until 1924, when each decided to write a play on his own. Connelly became successful on his own and would eventually write the remarkable *The Green Pastures: A Fable* (pb. 1929, pr. 1930). After the breakup, Kaufman did write *The Butter and Egg Man*, a rare solo effort, but working alone was not to his liking, and he spent most of the rest of his life collaborating. Through the rest of his career, his collaborators included some of the most successful writers of the time: Edna Ferber, Alexander Woollcott, Herman J. Mankiewicz, Ring Lardner, John P. Marquand, Moss Hart, and Abe Burrows. He also collaborated with Morrie Ryskind; Howard Dietz; Katherine Dayton; Nunnally Johnson; his second wife, Leueen MacGrath; and his biographer, Howard Teichmann. Although he was never much interested in music, Kaufman was associated with George and Ira Gershwin and Cole Porter, and he rewrote W. S. Gilbert and Arthur Sullivan's *H.M.S. Pinafore: Or, The Lass That Loved a Sailor* (pr., pb. 1878). He served as a "play doctor" for an unknown number of plays for which he got no credit, and he advised John Steinbeck on adapting *Of Mice and Men* (1937) for the stage.

After having codirected *The Good Fellow* with Howard Lindsay in 1926, Kaufman was persuaded by producer Jed Harris in 1928 to direct *The Front Page* by Ben Hecht and Charles MacArthur. After he had overcome his shy way of sending notes to the stage,

Kaufman also had a remarkable career as a director. Besides his own plays, which he felt might be botched by another director, Kaufman directed *Joseph* (pr. 1930) by Bertram Bloch, *Here Today* (pr. 1932) by George Oppenheimer, *Of Mice and Men* (pr. 1937) by John Steinbeck, *My Sister Eileen* (pr. 1940) by Jerome Chodorov and Joseph Fields, *Mr. Big* (pr. 1941) by Arthur Sheekman and Margaret Shane, *The Naked Genius* (1943) by Gypsy Rose Lee, *Over Twenty-One* (1944) by Ruth Gordon, *While the Sun Shines* (pr. 1943) by Terence Rattigan, *The Next Half Hour* (pr. 1945) by Mary Chase, *Town House* (pr. 1948) by Gertrude Tonkonogy (based on short stories by John Cheever), *Metropole* (pr. 1949) by William Walden, *The Enchanted* (pr. 1950) by Jean Giraudoux, *Guys and Dolls* (pr. 1950) by Abe Burrows and Jo Swerling, and *Romanoff and Juliet* (pr. 1957) by Peter Ustinov. This extraordinary list ought to have been more than enough for one man's lifetime, but when one includes the list of plays he wrote, one sees exactly how inexhaustible Kaufman was.

Yet the anxieties of Kaufman's childhood drove him to do even more. He adapted two of his plays (with Ryskind) for the Marx Brothers for the screen and then (also with Ryskind) wrote *A Night at the Opera* for them. He directed the movie *The Senator Was Indiscreet* with William Powell and Ella Raines in 1947, but—basically uninterested in the mechanics of filmmaking and disappointed with the way Hollywood was handling McCarthyism—he returned to the theater. He also acted in productions of *Once in a Lifetime* and *The Man Who Came to Dinner* and served as a panelist on an early television show, *This Is Show Business*. Given his extraordinarily productive working life, the legends portraying Kaufman as an incessant womanizer, a skilled poker player, and a regular member of the Algonquin Round Table may seem exaggerated, but the sheer number of these stories testifies to their probable basis in fact, to his incredible capacity for unceasing activity, and perhaps to a neurotic inability to relax.

The least productive period of Kaufman's life followed the death of Beatrice in October, 1945, and lasted until he married actress Leueen Emily MacGrath in May, 1949. The disparity in their ages led to an eventual separation in 1957, but even after their divorce, Leueen spent much time helping him in various ways as his health declined. Small strokes hindered his ability to work, so much so that he was a mere shadow of himself when directing *Romanoff and Juliet*. In the last few years of his life, his mind deteriorated, and, among other things, he would wander onto Park and Madison Avenues in his nightshirt. After he fell against a radiator in 1961 and was badly burned, he rarely left his bed, and he died peacefully in June, 1961.

ANALYSIS

As a practical man of the theater, George S. Kaufman concerned himself with the meticulous details of whatever project he was working on and gave little consideration to his place in the literary world or posterity. If he was writing, he would badger his collaborators to write better exit lines, to add more humor, to refine every sentence. When directing, he acidly chastised the slightest carelessness of an actor. As a literary figure, though, he was peculiarly unconcerned with plays or productions he had done in the past, eschewing the role of an author of drama, ignoring the possibility that what he had written with his collaborators had literary merit. Only once was he active in the revival of one of his plays, *Of Thee I Sing*. Indeed, his own attitude toward his art has contributed to the critical neglect of his work.

Primary among Kaufman's talents was his wit. The only weapon of a slim, shy boy and honed by his association with Adams, Woollcott, Dorothy Parker, Groucho Marx, and others of the Algonquin Round Table, "wisecracks" became characteristic of a Kaufman play and are obvious in every play on which he worked, from *Dulcy*, his first success, to *The Solid Gold Cadillac*. After three failures on Broadway, the success of *Dulcy*, with Lynn Fontanne in the title role, surprised Kaufman as much as anyone else (he always seemed to see his success as undeserved and always expected a disaster). As Malcolm Goldstein observes, *Dulcy* was basically a rehash of materials used by dozens of writers; what made it different from other plays was its flow of wit.

Although Kaufman would use any form of humor or stage technique to achieve his desired effect—in his plays there are many examples of slapstick, parody, nonsense, and various levels of verbal humor—satire is a recurring element. Ironically, one of the most famous quotations of Kaufman is "Satire is what closes Saturday night," as if he wished to ignore his own use of it. His wit could be quite vicious, particularly toward those who he felt had crossed him in some way. Even Dorothy Parker, the master of the acid quip, was severely wounded by Kaufman's barbs on more than one occasion. Earl Wilson once commented that Kaufman had been "blasting away at somebody or something all his life." It was only natural that such wit would be turned to satiric purpose against the pompous, the pretentious, the rich, and the powerful.

Little in society escaped his satire. *Beggar on Horseback* (written with Marc Connelly), the only commercially successful American expressionist play, satirized the American obsession with success, as if Kaufman were trying to exorcise the ghosts of failure from his own childhood. *Merton of the Movies* (also with Connelly) and *Once in a Lifetime* (with Moss Hart) mocked Hollywood. *June Moon* (with Ring Lardner) satirized Tin Pan Alley. *I'd Rather Be Right* (with Moss Hart) satirized Franklin D. Roosevelt, while *Of Thee I Sing* (with Ryskind) took on the presidential election process and vice presidency. *The Solid Gold Cadillac* (with Teichmann) poked fun at big business. One of his more curious satiric vehicles is *The Man Who Came to Dinner* (with Moss Hart), in which the major character was based on Kaufman's pompous friend Alexander Woollcott, who even good-humoredly agreed to play the title role in one production. It was perhaps convenient, even wise, for Kaufman to deny that he had satiric intent, particularly when he was more concerned with giving an audience a pleasant evening, but the moral outrage, sarcasm, and derision that is characteristic of satire is present to an extraordinary degree in his work.

Yet another element that can be observed in many of Kaufman's plays is the struggle and eventual triumph of the "little man" against the forces that oppress him, particularly big government and big business. In play after play, regardless of his collaborators, people in low social positions turn the tables on their social superiors. In his early plays, there is usually a relatively innocent young man who is ambitious but not intelligent enough to carry out his plans for advancement without the help of a more intelligent, maternal young woman in love with him. In Kaufman's play *The Solid Gold Cadillac*, an old woman triumphs over the executives of General Motors. It is a pattern observed in many of the plays and films of the 1920's and 1930's. Such plays, particularly in the Depression, seemed to draw much of their appeal from the general feeling that the titans of business and their governmental allies had let down or betrayed the common person.

OF THEE I SING

Despite the popularity of Kaufman's plays and their nearly predictable success, only two of his works were taken seriously enough to win the Pulitzer Prize. The first play to win was *Of Thee I Sing*, written with Morrie Ryskind, with music and lyrics by George and Ira Gershwin. Although Kaufman had been forced to soften the satire of *Strike Up the Band* only a few years previously, he believed that the country was weary of the Depression and the Republican platitudes of prosperity being "just around the corner," and might just be serious-minded enough to accept a play that satirized American politics, especially presidential elections. He invited Ryskind to join him on the project. Ryskind, who never believed such a scathing play would ever be produced, thought it might be fun to write. They began with the working title "Tweedledee" to refer to two virtually indistinguishable parties, and the plot of a presidential election hinging on the selection of a national anthem ("The Star-Spangled Banner" was not made the official national anthem until March 3, 1931). The Gershwins, who were attracted by the musical possibilities, were immediately interested and quickly began composing.

Ryskind and Kaufman soon realized the abstractness of their plot and decided to put a romantic interest into it, even though Kaufman maintained an absolute abhorrence of romantic scenes and generally refused to write them, leaving them to his collabora-

tors. In the play, presidential candidate John P. Wintergreen uses the notion of marriage to a "typical American girl" as a device to win votes: He agrees to marry the winner of an Atlantic City beauty contest arranged by his managers. Once elected, however, he rejects the winner, marries his secretary, and causes international turmoil (she is of French descent). Facing impeachment, he is finally saved by his wife's delivery of twins and by a curious interpretation of the Constitution that forces the vice president to marry the contest winner.

In August, 1931, over a period of seventeen days, the collaborators completed the book, turning the harmless fluff of their plot into withering satire. It opened to rave reviews in Boston and became an extraordinary hit on its opening in New York, when George Gershwin conducted the orchestra and the audience was filled with such luminaries as Mayor Jimmy Walker, former presidential candidate Al Smith, Florenz Ziegfeld, Beatrice Lillie, Ethel Barrymore, Condé Nast, and Samuel Goldwyn. The play was praised in every way possible, although critic Robert Benchley dissented. It was compared to Gilbert and Sullivan's *Iolanthe: Or, The Peer and the Peri* (pr., pb. 1882) and called a new departure from the musical comedy style. The songs were considered so well integrated that some critics went to the extreme of calling *Of Thee I Sing* more an "operetta" than a "musical," particularly ironic praise because Kaufman would later do an unsuccessful updating of *H.M.S. Pinafore* called *Hollywood Pinafore* (pr. 1945). He was not much interested in music and often resented the intrusions of songs into his comic plots. In 1932, when the Pulitzer Prize committee astounded the theater world by awarding the prize to a musical for the first time in its history, it caused much controversy, because such plays as *Mourning Becomes Electra* (pr., pb. 1931) by Eugene O'Neill and Robert E. Sherwood's *Reunion in Vienna* (pr. 1931) were passed over. The critic of *Commonweal* defended the decision, however, when he wrote that "*Of Thee I Sing* . . . is much closer to Aristophanes than O'Neill ever came to Euripides."

The remark was particularly well-founded. A. Cleveland Harrison has commented extensively on what he perceives as the revival of Aristophanic Old Comedy in the Kaufman-Ryskind play, noting how the episodes of the plot are linked less by a cause-effect relationship than by the development of aspects of the central topic. Extreme characters and situations are used to put ideals into conflict. The ideal of democracy, for example, is in conflict with the reality of it, where politicians use side issues to get themselves elected. The stereotyped characters themselves are less important than the allegorical concepts they represent. Furthermore, a wide range of societal types is represented, from Irish and Jewish power brokers, to newspapermen and Southern pork-barrel senators, each using their particular slang, with many of society's institutions, such as the beauty contest and the vice presidency, subjected to ridicule. The satire was sufficiently irreverent to lead Victor Moore, who played Vice President Throttlebottom, to wonder if he would be arrested on opening night. Today, however, *Of Thee I Sing*, like many of Kaufman's works, seems somewhat dated. The Aristophanic nature of most of his comedies may indeed contribute to the general current impression of them as extremely amusing, cleverly written, brilliantly constructed period pieces.

OTHER MAJOR WORKS

SCREENPLAYS: *Business Is Business*, 1925 (with Dorothy Parker); *The Cocoanuts*, 1929 (with Morrie Ryskind); *Animal Crackers*, 1931 (with Ryskind); *Roman Scandals*, 1933 (with Robert E. Sherwood, George Oppenheimer, Arthur Sheekman, Nat Perrin, and W. A. McGuire); *A Night at the Opera*, 1935 (with Ryskind); *Star-Spangled Rhythm*, 1943.

BIBLIOGRAPHY

Goldstein, Malcolm. *George S. Kaufman: His Life, His Theater.* New York: Oxford University Press, 1979. This volume is considered the standard biography of the prolific man who wrote or collaborated on more than forty Broadway plays.

Mason, Jeffrey. *Wisecracks: The Farces of George S. Kaufman.* Ann Arbor, Mich.: UMI Research Press, 1988. A scholarly study of the comedic dramas of Kaufman. Index.

Meredith, Scott. *George S. Kaufman and His Friends.* Garden City, N.Y.: Doubleday, 1974. This useful biography offers much Broadway local color and theater lore. It is also available in abridged form under the title *George S. Kaufman and the Algonquin Round Table.*

Pollack, Rhoda-Gale. *George S. Kaufman.* Boston: Twayne, 1988. Pollack has written a concise but useful biography on the playwright. Supplemented by a short bibliography.

Teichmann, Howard. *George S. Kaufman: An Intimate Portrait.* New York: Atheneum, 1982. Although dated, this volume is still useful, especially in its discussion of Kaufman's origins in Pittsburgh and his early career. It is exhaustive and carefully illustrated.

J. Madison Davis,
updated by Peter C. Holloran

ADRIENNE KENNEDY

Born: Pittsburgh, Pennsylvania; September 13, 1931

PRINCIPAL DRAMA
Funnyhouse of a Negro, pr. 1962, pb. 1969
The Owl Answers, pr. 1963, pb. 1969
A Rat's Mass, pr. 1966, pb. 1968
The Lennon Play: In His Own Write, pr. 1967, pb. 1968 (with John Lennon and Victor Spinetti)
A Lesson in Dead Language, pr., pb. 1968
Sun: A Poem for Malcolm X Inspired by His Murder, pr. 1968, pb. 1971
A Beast's Story, pr., pb. 1969

Boats, pr. 1969

Cities in Bezique: Two One Act Plays, pb. 1969

An Evening with Dead Essex, pr. 1973

A Movie Star Has to Star in Black and White, pr. 1976, pb. 1984

A Lancashire Lad, pr. 1980

Orestes and Electra, pr. 1980

Black Children's Day, pr. 1980

Adrienne Kennedy in One Act, pb. 1988

The Alexander Plays, pb. 1992

The Ohio State Murders, pr., pb. 1992

June and Jean in Concert, pr. 1995

Sleep Deprivation Chamber, pb. 1996 (with Adam Patrice Kennedy)

OTHER LITERARY FORMS

In addition to her plays, Adrienne Kennedy has published a wide-ranging memoir, *People Who Led to My Plays* (1986). In 1990, she published *Deadly Triplets: A Theatre Mystery and Journal*. In 2001, the University of Minnesota Press published Kennedy's *The Adrienne Kennedy Reader*. A collection of some of her best plays, the book also includes short stories and other prose works, including both published and previously nonpublished material.

ACHIEVEMENTS

Adrienne Kennedy departs from the theatrical naturalism used by other African American playwrights in favor of a surrealistic and expressionistic form. Her plays capture the irrational quality of dreams while offering insight into the nature of the self and being. Most of her works are complex character studies in which a given figure may have several selves or roles. In this multidimensional presentation lies Kennedy's forte—the unraveling of the individual consciousness.

The playwright received an Obie Award in 1964 for *Funnyhouse of a Negro*, her best-known play, and two Obies in 1996 for *June and Jean in Concert* and *Sleep Deprivation Chamber*. She held a Guggenheim Fellowship in 1967 and was given grants from the Rockefeller Foundation, the New England Theatre Conference, the National Endowment for the Arts, and the Creative Artists Public Service. She also received the Third Manhattan Borough President's

Award for Excellence, an Award in Literature from the American Academy of Arts and Letters, a Lila Wallace-Reader's Digest Fund Writer's Award, the Pierre LeComte duNoy Foundation award, and the American Book Award in 1990 for *People Who Led to My Plays*. Kennedy is included in *The Norton Anthology of African American Literature* and is one of a select few playwrights in the third edition of *The Norton Anthology of American Literature*. The Signature Theatre Company in New York dedicated its 1995-1996 season to Kennedy, offering audiences a retrospective of her dramatic works.

She was a lecturer at Yale University from 1972 to 1974 and a Yale Fellow from 1974 to 1975. In addition to lecturing at Yale, Kennedy has taught playwriting at Princeton and Brown universities.

BIOGRAPHY

Adrienne (Lita Hawkins) Kennedy was born on September 13, 1931, in Pittsburgh, Pennsylvania, the daughter of Cornell Wallace Hawkins, a social worker, and the former Etta Haugabook, a teacher. She grew up in Cleveland, Ohio, and attended Ohio State University, where she received a bachelor's degree in education in 1953. A few years later, she moved to New York and enrolled in creative writing classes at Columbia University and the New School for Social Research. In 1962, she joined Edward Albee's Playwrights' Workshop in New York City's Circle in the Square. She wrote *Funnyhouse of a Negro* for Albee's workshop. A decade later, she became a founder of the Women's Theater Council. In 1953, the playwright married Joseph C. Kennedy, whom she divorced in 1966. She has two sons.

Kennedy settled in New York, where she divided her time between writing and teaching. She continued to receive awards and recognition for her writing. On March 7, 1992, the opening date of her play *The Ohio State Murders*, the mayor of Cleveland proclaimed the day Adrienne Kennedy Day in Cleveland.

ANALYSIS

Adrienne Kennedy dares to be innovative both in her subject matter and in theatrical form. She writes difficult plays that raise questions rather than providing answers. From *Funnyhouse of a Negro* onward, Kennedy chose a subjective form that she has retained throughout her literary career. Her plays grow out of her own experiences as a sensitive and gifted black American who grew up in the Midwest. There may be little plot in Kennedy's plays, but there is, to be sure, a wealth of symbolism concerning the inherent tensions of the African American experience. Kennedy's daring break from a realistic style in theatrical writing, as well as her bold exploration of her own family history, cultural experience, and identity, provides a foundation for contemporary writers such as Suzan-Lori Parks, Ntozake Shange, and Anna Deveare Smith. These writers join Kennedy in expanding theatrical boundaries, creating theater that offers unforgettable images in culturally resonant, historically significant, and deeply personal plays.

Kennedy's plays are consistent in their exploration of the double consciousness of biracial African Americans who are inheritors of both African and European American culture and tradition. Symbolically represented by the split in the head of Patrice Lumumba, one of the selves in *Funnyhouse of a Negro*, this double identity frequently results in a schizophrenic division in which a character's selves or roles are at odds with one another. Typically it is the African identity with which the protagonist—who is often a sensitive, well-read young woman—is unable to come to grips. By using a surrealistic form to treat such a complex subject, Kennedy is able to suggest that truth can be arrived at only through the unraveling of distortion. Indeed, what Kennedy's protagonist knows of Africa and of blacks has come to her filtered through the consciousness of others who are eager to label Africans and their descendants "bestial" or "deranged." This seems to be what theater critic Clive Barnes meant when he said that Kennedy "thinks black, but she remembers white." For this reason, animal imagery, as well as black and white color contrasts, dominates Kennedy's plays.

Kennedy's concerns with isolationism, identity conflict, and consciousness are presented primarily through character. She has called her plays "states of mind," in which she attempts to bring the subcon-

Adrienne Kennedy

scious to the level of consciousness. She achieves this essentially by decoding her dreams. Indeed, many of the plays were actually dreams that she later translated into theatrical form. This surrealistic or dreamlike quality of her work has been compared to August Strindberg's dream plays, in that both dramatists render reality through the presentation of distortion. Extracting what is real from what is a distortion as one would with a dream is the puzzle Kennedy establishes for her characters, as well as for her audience, to unravel in each of her major plays: *Funnyhouse of a Negro*, *The Owl Answers*, *A Rat's Mass*, and *A Movie Star Has to Star in Black and White*.

FUNNYHOUSE OF A NEGRO

As in life, truth in Kennedy's plays is frequently a matter of subjectivity, and one character's version of it is often brought into question by another's. This is the case in *Funnyhouse of a Negro*, Kennedy's most critically acclaimed play. From the moment a somnambulist woman walks across the stage "as if in a dream" at the beginning of the play, the audience is aware that it is not viewing a realistic performance.

Such figures onstage as the woman sleepwalker, women with "wild, straight black hair," a "hunchbacked yellow-skinned dwarf," and objects such as the monumental ebony bed, which resembles a tomb, suggest a nightmarish setting. The action of the play takes place in four settings: Queen Victoria's chamber, the Duchess of Hapsburg's chamber, a Harlem hotel room, and the jungle. Nevertheless, it is not implausible to suggest that the real setting of *Funnyhouse of a Negro* is inside the head of Sarah, Kennedy's protagonist. As Sarah tells the theater audience in her opening speech, the four rooms onstage are "[her] rooms."

As with the four sets that are really one room, Sarah has four "selves" who help to reveal the complexity of her character. At first, Sarah appears to be a version of the kindhearted prostitute, or perhaps a reverse Electra who hates rather than loves her father. Kennedy builds on these types to show Sarah's preoccupation with imagination and dreams, as well as her divided consciousness as a partaker of two cultures. Queen Victoria and the Duchess of Hapsburg are identified with Sarah's mother, or with her white European identity. The other two personalities, Jesus and Patrice Lumumba, the Congolese leader and martyr, on the other hand, are identified with Sarah's father, or with her black African heritage. Significantly, Sarah's four personalities tell the story of the parents' marriage and subsequent trip to Africa and the rape of the mother, which results in the conception of Sarah, each of which events can be called into question by the dreamlike atmosphere of the play and by the mother's insanity. One by one, the four alter egos add details to the story that allow the picture of Sarah's family to build through accretion. Even so, this story is undermined by the final conversation between the landlady and Sarah's boyfriend, Raymond. Doubling as "the Funnyman" to the landlady's "Funnylady," Raymond comes onstage after Sarah's suicide to tell the audience the truth about Sarah's father in the epilogue to the play. Although Sarah claimed to have killed her father, Raymond tells the audience that the father is not dead but rather "liv[ing] in the city in a room with European antiques, photographs of Roman ruins, walls of books and oriental carpets."

THE OWL ANSWERS

The same eschewal of linear progression in *Funnyhouse of a Negro* occurs in *The Owl Answers*, the first of two one-act plays appearing with *A Beast's Story* in the collection titled *Cities in Bezique*. Clara Passmore, the protagonist in *The Owl Answers*, like Sarah in *Funnyhouse of a Negro*, is a sensitive, educated young woman torn between the two cultures of which she is a part. Riveted by her fascination for a culture that seems to want no part of her, Clara, a mulatto English teacher from Savannah, Georgia, learns from her mother that her father, "the richest white man in town," is of English ancestry. She comes to London to give him a fitting burial at Saint Paul's Cathedral, among the "lovely English." Once there, she has a breakdown and is imprisoned in the Tower of London by William Shakespeare, Geoffrey Chaucer, and William the Conquerer, who taunt her by denying her English heritage. Clara, who is the daughter of both the deceased William Mattheson and the Reverend Mr. Passmore (who, with his wife, adopted Clara when she was a child), is as firm in her claim to English ancestry as she is in her plans to bury her father in London. Like Sarah in *Funnyhouse of a Negro*, Clara's true prison exists in her mind. Ironically, Clara Passmore, whose name suggests racial passing, passes only from human into animal form. In a final, violent scene in which the third movement of Haydn's Concerto for Horn in D accentuates the mental anguish of Clara and her mother, Clara's mother stabs herself on an altar of owl feathers. Clara, in the meantime, fends off an attack from a man whom she calls "God," who has assumed that the love she seeks from him is merely sexual. Clara, who has grown increasingly more owl-like as the play has progressed, utters a final "Ow . . . oww." In this play, as in *Funnyhouse of a Negro*, Kennedy leaves the audience with questions about the nature of spiritual faith in a world in which one calls on God, yet in which the only answer heard comes from the owl.

A RAT'S MASS

Similar preoccupations with the clash of African and European culture in *Funnyhouse of a Negro* and *The Owl Answers* can be seen in *A Rat's Mass*, a one-act play set in the time of the marching of the Nazi armies. Brother and Sister Rat, who have a rat's head and a rat's belly, respectively, are both in love with Rosemary, a descendant of "the Pope, Julius Caesar, and the Virgin Mary." The two rat siblings struggle to atone for the dark, secret sin they committed when they "went on the slide together," which has forced them into hiding in the attic of their home. Alone together in their misery, Kay and Blake, the sister and brother, remember a time when they "lived in a Holy Chapel with parents and Jesus, Joseph, and Mary, our wise men and our shepherd." Now they can only hear the gnawing of rats in the attic. In desperation, they turn to Rosemary to help them atone for their sins. Rosemary refuses, stating that only through their deaths will there be a way of atonement. The way comes when Jesus, Joseph, Mary, two wise men, and the shepherd return as the Nazi army to open fire on the rats, leaving only Rosemary, like the evergreen shrub for which she is named, to remain standing.

A MOVIE STAR HAS TO STAR IN BLACK AND WHITE

The animal motif employed in *The Owl Answers* and *A Rat's Mass* is less apparent in *A Movie Star Has to Star in Black and White*. Clara Passmore of *The Owl Answers* returns for a "bit role" in which she reads from several of Kennedy's plays. The English literary tradition highly esteemed by the protagonist in *Funnyhouse of a Negro* and *The Owl Answers* is replaced by the American film tradition. Reinforcing the theme of illusion versus reality begun in *Funnyhouse of a Negro*, *A Movie Star Has to Star in Black and White* is actually a series of plays-within-a-play in which scenes from the films *Now, Voyager* (1942), *Viva Zapata* (1952), and *A Place in the Sun* (1961) take place in a hospital lobby, Clara's brother's room, and Clara's old room, respectively. As the title of the play indicates—as well as a stage note directing that all the colors be shades of black and white—Kennedy continues her experimentation with black and white color contrasts onstage. As in other plays by Kennedy, linear progression is eschewed and the illusion of cinema merges with the reality of the life of Clara, a writer and daughter to

the Mother and Father, the wife of Eddie, the mother of Eddie, Jr., and the alter ego of the film actresses.

Through lines spoken in the first scene by Bette Davis to Paul Henreid, the audience learns of Clara's parents' dream of success in the North, which ends in disappointment when they learn that racial oppression is not confined to the South. The scene takes place simultaneously in an ocean liner from *Now, Voyager* and a hospital lobby in which Clara and her mother have come to ascertain the condition of Wally, Clara's brother, who lies in a coma.

Scene 2 moves to Wally's room, while Jean Peters and Marlon Brando enact lines from *Viva Zapata*. History repeats itself when it is revealed that Clara, like her mother before her, is having marital problems with her husband, Eddie. In the meantime, Marlon Brando's character changes the bed sheets onto which Jean Peters's character has bled, reminding the audience of Clara's miscarriage while Eddie was away in the armed services.

In the following scene, Shelley Winters and Montgomery Clift appear onstage in a small rowboat from the film *A Place in the Sun*. In this scene, Clara reveals her frustration as a writer who is black and a woman. She says that her husband thinks that her life is "one of my black and white movies that I love so . . . with me playing a bit part." The play ends with the news that Wally will live, but with brain damage. In the interim, Shelley Winters's character drowns as Montgomery Clift's character looks on, suggesting a connection between Clara's fantasy life in motion pictures and the real world, from which she struggles to escape.

OTHER PLAYS

Kennedy's other plays deal with themes similar to those in the works discussed. The animal motif, coupled with the theme of sexuality, is continued in *A Beast's Story* and *A Lesson in Dead Language*. In *A Beast's Story*, Beast Girl kills her child with quinine and whiskey and then kills her husband with an ax after he attempts to make love to her. Her parents, Beast Man and Beast Woman, preside over the dark course of events as shamans eager for their daughter to rid the household of the "intruder" whose presence has caused a black sun to hover above them. Animal imagery is paired with the rite-of-passage motif in *A Lesson in Dead Language*. In this play, a schoolteacher who is a white dog "from the waist up" instructs seven young girls about menstruation. Similarly, the dreamlike quality of earlier plays continues in *Sun*, a play-poem written about the death of Malcolm X, and in *An Evening with Dead Essex*, based on the assassination of black sniper Mark James Essex.

With the 1980's, Kennedy branched out into the writing of children's plays on commission. Among these plays are *A Lancashire Lad*, *Orestes and Electra*, and *Black Children's Day*. Kennedy was a prolific writer in the late 1980's and early 1990's, with her esteemed "scrapbook of memories" *People Who Led to My Plays*, *Deadly Triplets: A Theatre Mystery and Journal*, and *The Alexander Plays*, the latter centering on the protagonist Suzanne Alexander and including such pieces as *The Ohio State Murders*, *She Talks to Beethoven*, *The Dramatic Circle*, and *The Film Club*.

Notable among her later works is her play *The Ohio State Murders*, the source of which was Kennedy's emotionally scarring experience as an undergraduate at Ohio State University. According to dramaturge Scott T. Cummings, "the play reflects [Kennedy's] abiding feeling that 'nothing has changed for American blacks,' that 'American blacks would have been better off leaving this country.'"

OTHER MAJOR WORKS

NONFICTION: *People Who Led to My Plays*, 1986.

MISCELLANEOUS: *Deadly Triplets: A Theatre Mystery and Journal*, 1990 (novella and journal); *The Adrienne Kennedy Reader*, 2001.

BIBLIOGRAPHY

Benston, Kimberly W. "Cities in Bezique: Adrienne Kennedy's Expressionistic Vision." *College Language Association Journal* 20 (1976): 235-244. In this essay on *The Owl Answers* and *A Beast's Story*, Benston delineates Kennedy's skillful use of expressionism. Sees part of Kennedy's richly symbolic form as having been borrowed from both the folktale and August Strindberg's dream plays.

Blau, Herbert. "The American Dream in American Gothic: The Plays of Sam Shepard and Adrienne Kennedy." *Modern Drama* 27 (1984): 520-539. Blau examines three plays by Shepard and three by Kennedy. Combines personal reflections on his work with Kennedy with sociological, psychological, and thematic approaches to her plays. Sees her as having been "out of place in the emergence of Black Power" and views powerlessness and death as obsessions in her œuvre.

Bryant-Jackson, Paul, and Lois More Overbeck, eds. *Intersecting Boundaries*. Minneapolis: University of Minnesota Press, 1992. An anthology of essays on Kennedy's work, this volume consists of four parts, including interviews and critical analyses of her work by various scholars. The first of its sort on Kennedy's plays, it makes a substantial contribution to Kennedy scholarship.

Curb, Rosemary. "Fragmented Selves in Adrienne Kennedy's *Funnyhouse of a Negro* and *The Owl Answers*." *Theater Journal* 32 (1980): 180-195. Curb argues that Kennedy eschews linear narrative progression to portray "the fragmented mental states of her characters," with the central conflict occurring inside the main character's mind. Suggests that Kennedy is a "poet-playwright," examines Kennedy's central images alongside her theme of death, and compares her work to that of Ntozake Shange.

Kennedy, Adrienne. "A Growth of Images." *Tulane Drama Review* 21 (1977): 41-47. Kennedy discusses her reasons for selecting autobiographical materials for her plays and states that most of them grow out of her dreams. Provides sources for Clara Passmore in *The Owl Answers*.

McDonough, Carla J. "*God and the Owls: The Sacred and the Profane in Adrienne Kennedy's 'The Owl Answers.'*" In *Modern Drama* 40 (1997): 385-402. McDonough explores the recurring motifs, dialogue, and theatrical images in both *The Owl Answers* and Kennedy's other plays, with particular attention to the blending of religious idolatry, colonialism, mixed-race heritage, family history, and female sexuality that *Owl* examines.

Meigs, Susan. "No Place but the Funnyhouse: The Struggle for Identity in Three Adrienne Kennedy Plays." In *Modern Drama: The Female Canon*, edited by June Schlueter. Rutherford, N.J.: Fairleigh Dickinson University Press, 1990. Meigs begins her discussion of *Funnyhouse of a Negro, The Owl Answers*, and *A Movie Star Has to Star in Black and White* by noting the significance of Kennedy's trip to Africa in 1960, which had a substantial impact on her worldview. Believes that the conflict between Western and African tradition and culture undergirds the major theme of Kennedy's "complex, surrealistic psychodramas."

Sollors, Werner. "Owls and Rats in the American Funnyhouse: Adrienne Kennedy's Drama." *American Literature: A Journal of Literary History, Criticism, and Bibliography* 63 (1991): 507-532.

States that Kennedy's œuvre is best seen as "a full-fledged modern American attempt at rewriting family tragedy." Examines seven plays against the background of her autobiography, *People Who Led to My Plays*.

Zinman, Toby Silverman. "'In the Presence of Mine Enemies': Adrienne Kennedy's *An Evening with Dead Essex*." *Studies in American Drama, 1945-Present* 6 (1991): 3-13. Notes that unlike most of Kennedy's plays, this one "is based on a newspaper account, and is mostly male, apparently realistic, and raggedly structured." Concludes that Kennedy has enormous enemies in mind, including the American government and American society.

P. Jane Splawn,
updated by Sheila McKenna

SIDNEY KINGSLEY
Sidney Kirshner

Born: New York, New York; October 22, 1906
Died: Oakland, New Jersey; March 20, 1995

PRINCIPAL DRAMA

Men in White, pr., pb. 1933
Dead End, pr. 1935, pb. 1936
Ten Million Ghosts, pr. 1936
The World We Make, pr., pb. 1939 (adaptation of Millen Brand's novel *The Outward Room*)
The Patriots, pr., pb. 1943
Detective Story, pr., pb. 1949
Darkness at Noon, pr., pb. 1951 (adaptation of Arthur Koestler's novel)
Lunatics and Lovers, pr. 1954
Night Life, pr. 1962, pb. 1964
Sidney Kingsley: Five Prizewinning Plays, pb. 1995

OTHER LITERARY FORMS

Sidney Kingsley is known exclusively for his plays.

ACHIEVEMENTS

Sidney Kingsley is generally regarded as a social dramatist, one who made the social and political problems of his age the subject matter of his plays. Because his early work was done in the 1930's, a time of economic depression and of a crisis for capitalism, there are strong liberal (at times leftist) perspectives in his dramas. Invariably his characters struggle with a fate not simply personal but, in a very explicit sense, social as well. George Ferguson in *Men in White*, Thomas Jefferson in *The Patriots*, Nicolai Rubashov in *Darkness at Noon*, and Will Kazar in *Night Life* are very different as characters, yet all of them, in Kingsley's plays, must weigh their personal desires and private dreams against their social responsibilities and public ambitions.

Kingsley's plays demonstrate his interaction with the world of his day: its politics, its institutions, its social issues, and its technologies. The movies inspired by three of his plays—*Men in White* (1934), *Dead*

Sidney Kingsley in 1951. (AP/Wide World Photos)

End (1937), and *Detective Story* (1951)—expanded his already strong influence on the popular culture of his day.

By concentrating on the interaction between the idealist and the community in which he functions, Kingsley was able to project the tensions and dynamics of society in the midst of industrial transformation. Although the actions in Kingsley's plays are often melodramatic, they serve to illuminate the struggle between materialism and idealism, between the structures of a society and the people trying to adjust to their social institutions. Few twentieth century writers were more thorough in examining the dedicated professional and the meaning of work to those whose work is the property of others.

Kingsley is also significant because he interacted with many of the major talents of his age. The varied list of prominent theatrical people associated with his productions is impressive in itself: Luther Adler, Morris Carnovsky, Elia Kazan, Clifford Odets, Lee Strasberg, Norman Bel Geddes, the Dead End Kids,

Lee Grant, Ralph Bellamy, Orson Welles, Howard Lindsay, Russel Crouse, Claude Rains, Jack Palance, Kim Hunter, Buddy Hackett, and Kingsley's wife, Madge Evans. In addition to pursuing his own active career as a creative artist, Kingsley has attempted to encourage the creativity of others, particularly in his work with the Dramatists Guild. Playing many different roles, Kingsley has been a major figure in American theatrical history.

Kingsley has received extensive recognition for his accomplishments. He received a Pulitzer Prize for *Men in White* as well as New York Theatre Club Medals for it, for *Dead End*, and for *The Patriots*. Kingsley also received New York Drama Critics Circle Awards for *The Patriots* and for *Darkness at Noon*. *The Patriots* also earned for him the New York Newspaper Guild Front Page Award, and for *Detective Story*, he earned a Newspaper Guild Page One Citation and an Edgar Allan Poe Award. *Darkness at Noon* also won a Donaldson Award for Outstanding Achievement and an American Academy of Arts and Letters Award of Merit Medal. Finally, Kingsley has received a Yeshiva University Award for Achievement in the Theatre (1965), a doctor of letters degree from Monmouth College (1978), and an induction into the Theatre Hall of Fame (1983).

BIOGRAPHY

Sidney Kingsley was born Sidney Kirshner on October 22, 1906, in New York City. He spent most of his life in the New York area. Involved in the theater from an early age, he was already writing, directing, and acting in one-act plays at Townsend Harris Hall in New York City while a teenager. After he was graduated from high school in 1924, Kingsley attended Cornell University, where he was a member of the Dramatic Club and acted with Franchot Tone. At Cornell, he continued to write plays: His play "Wonder-Dark Epilogue" won a prize for the best one-act play written by a student. After receiving his bachelor of arts degree in 1928, Kingsley did some acting with the Tremont Stock Company in the Bronx. Although he had a role in the 1929 Broadway production *Subway Express*, he decided at that time that acting was not the career for him.

That year, Kingsley went to California, where he worked for Columbia Pictures as a play reader and scenario writer, but he soon returned to New York. At this time, he was working on his own play, originally entitled *Crisis*, later to be *Men in White*. During the writing he began to research the subject matter systematically, a procedure he would employ during the composition of several other plays. Because his play was to be about doctors, he visited various hospitals in the New York City area—Bellevue, Beth Israel, and Lebanon—to gather material and to render as accurate a social picture as he could. (One story has it that he once masqueraded as an intern.) Although several would-be producers had options on the play, it was finally presented by the soon-to-be-famous Group Theatre. It was their first major success, and the play established Kingsley as a prominent American playwright, winning for him the Pulitzer Prize (in a controversial decision) and the Theatre Club Award. It was also a financial success; Kingsley reportedly received forty-six thousand dollars for the motion-picture rights. Kingsley had become a principal figure in the theatrical community of New York.

Kingsley directed all of his plays except *The Patriots*. Perhaps because he himself was an amateur painter and sculptor, he showed great concern throughout his career for the physical appearance of his plays onstage. His second drama, *Dead End*, owed its immediate impact in no small part to a spectacular New York setting created by Bel Geddes. Animated by the energetic argot of his New York boys, the Dead End Kids, Kingsley's second play was even more popular and critically acclaimed than his first effort. Although the next two plays, *Ten Million Ghosts* and *The World We Make*, were not the popular hits his first two had been, they also featured memorable visual effects. By this time, Kingsley was regarded as a dramatist of social realism and spectacular staging effects, one whose plots inclined to melodrama and whose sympathies were clearly with the less fortunate.

In July, 1939, Kingsley married actress Madge Evans, a marriage that would last until her death in 1981. She retired from her film career soon after the marriage and assisted Kingsley in the historical research for his new play, tentatively entitled *Thomas Jefferson*. She later appeared in the 1943 production version, *The Patriots*. Kingsley found himself inducted into the United States Army in March, 1941, about the time he finished the first version. He spent his free time polishing the play and was rewarded by largely favorable notices, most of which found Sergeant Kingsley's dramatization of the precarious nature of freedom in the early republic pertinent to the contemporary struggle of the United States in World War II. Later in 1943, Kingsley was promoted to lieutenant.

After his discharge from the army, Kingsley spent some time working for Metro-Goldwyn-Mayer on the movie scripts for *Cass Timberlane* (1947) and *Homecoming* (1946). Much of the time in the late 1940's, however, he was back in New York, haunting detective squad rooms to gather material for his new production, *Detective Story*. Even though it did not win the great awards some of his earlier efforts received, *Detective Story*, with its harsh, intense drama and convincing factual setting, is considered by many critics to be Kingsley's best play. Like *Men in White* and *Dead End*, it was made into a successful motion picture.

Kingsley's next drama, *Darkness at Noon*, was based on Arthur Koestler's 1941 novel of the same title. The production, featuring Claude Rains, Jack Palance, and Kim Hunter, was successful enough to win for Kingsley the Donaldson Award and the New York Drama Critics Circle Award. Kingsley and Koestler, however, quarreled publicly about the play; indeed, Koestler threatened to take Kingsley to court for what he thought were distortions of his text. In addition, Brooks Atkinson, the reviewer for *The New York Times*, raised similar unfavorable comparisons between the novel and the play. Produced in 1951, a time of strong anticommunist feeling (and of reaction against that feeling), the play may have been a victim of its era. In spite of inspiring some harsh criticism, the play ran for almost two hundred performances.

For his next effort, *Lunatics and Lovers*, Kingsley shifted to totally different dramatic material, presenting the mid-1950's in a farce complete with lots of noise, various con games, and a plethora of sexual comedy. Although most critics were not fond of the play, it had a respectable run of more than three hundred performances. *Night Life*, presented in 1962, focuses on a labor racketeer, but in its frenzied surreal quality, it reflects an era's growing emphasis on style rather than on social or political issues, an emphasis not suited to Kingsley's talents.

After *Night Life*, much of Kingsley's creative energy went into the writing of a dramatic trilogy, *The Art Scene*, which was to examine the phenomenon of radical change in the contemporary world as reflected in graphic arts, modern dance, and the theater. Kingsley finished the first part, *Man with a Corpse on His Back*, in the early 1970's, but it was never published or produced.

When not involved with his own work, Kingsley was concerned with encouraging and improving the artistic endeavors of others. Convinced that television was going to set the intellectual and spiritual climate of the age, he was briefly in the 1950's a television consultant to the Columbia Broadcasting System. As president of the Dramatists Guild from 1961 to 1969, he was active in efforts to help young playwrights and to preserve Off-Broadway theater. In the late 1970's, as chairman of New Jersey's Motion Picture and TV Authority, he was able to encourage film companies to shoot movies in the New Jersey area.

In recognition of his many contributions to the cultural scene, Kingsley was inducted into the Theatre Hall of Fame in May, 1983. He was awarded the Gold Medal for Drama by the American Academy of Arts and Letters in 1986 and won the William Inge Award for Lifetime Achievement in 1988. Kingsley died in 1995, in Oakland, New Jersey.

ANALYSIS

As a dramatist, Sidney Kingsley is noted for being a theater technician—not a surprising reputation, since he spent all of his life in the theater and directed all of his plays except *The Patriots*. Typically, the characters in his plays represent a social spectrum and dramatize sharp, overt ideological differences. Within this pattern, there are also more subtly contrasting pairs of individuals: Gimpty and "Baby-Face," former members of the same youth gang in

Dead End; the two proletarian brothers in *The World We Make*; the two women who love George Ferguson in *Men in White*; and Rubashov and his inquisitor in *Darkness at Noon*.

Few dramatists have more consistently articulated in their works the liberal political philosophy than has Kingsley. Keenly attentive to the social and political events of his day, Kingsley's plays demonstrate his faith in the essential goodness of people, his suspicion of authority and power, his belief in progress, and his admiration for the life of reason. Jefferson, the hero of *The Patriots*, is Kingsley's ideal intellectual. Those people who work with dedication and integrity are the cornerstones of his hope for the future. At times, Kingsley tended to be sentimental about the working class, and frequently his idealism and his belief in the value of work for its own sake led him into melodramatic conflicts and facile resolutions. At his best, however, he powerfully embodied the virtues of liberal humanism.

Kingsley's plays have invariably displayed his fondness for spectacle. His settings are obviously the result of studied decisions, and they appear in virtually every production to be an indispensable element in the play. Bel Geddes's stunning set for *Dead End* articulated the social contrasts at the heart of the play as much as did its plot. The prison set in *Darkness at Noon*, with its spectacular tapping out of communication from one cell to another, starkly defined Soviet Russia for Kingsley's audience. The operating room in *Men in White* and the squad room of *Detective Story* anticipated in their powerful immediacy the television series of a later era. Indeed, Kingsley's sets have sometimes been disproportionately powerful: The expressionistic set of *Ten Million Ghosts* may in fact have been too heavy for the play, and the first two settings in *The World We Make* convey such a sharp, deterministic insistence that the rest of the play, set in John's room, seems too sequestered.

THE WORLD WE MAKE

Dr. Schiller's statement in *The World We Make*, that no normal human being lives alone in the world, is a basic truth for Kingsley's plays, which stress the working out of the necessary difficulties in social existence. His characters tend to be types, figures who seem vibrantly alive only when struggling with the idea of their social duties. In this respect, it is society that animates them. Like other social realists, Kingsley has the gift of evoking a sense of community, the feeling that his characters are bound, for better or worse, by a system of deeply felt values. When this system breaks down, as it does in Kingsley's later work, the basic unity of the plays begins to fragment.

MEN IN WHITE

The title of Kingsley's first play, *Men in White*, indicates the play's focus on the profession of medicine itself. Throughout, Kingsley is concerned with what a doctor's life is and what it should be, examining the ethics, economics, and dedication of the medical community. The entire play is confined to various parts of St. George's Hospital, and in one of the most crucial scenes, Kingsley takes the audience into the operating room, where the real and the melodramatic mingle. As Laura prepares to witness her fiancé operating, she suddenly discovers that the case, a botched abortion, is the result of her fiancé's affair. As this is happening, the visual dimension of the play emphasizes the ritual, the impersonal element, of medicine, so much so that the scene becomes an ironic comment on the plot and the action, a measure of the personal frustrations of the characters. The efficiency and sterility of the operating room convey an atmosphere of professional mystery: The putting on of the gloves, the scrubbing, and the masks all blend to suggest the distinct, new nature of this community and the people in it, and the scientific impersonality of its activities.

Two doctors, one mature and one at the beginning of his career, are at the center of the action. The older man, Dr. Hochberg, is a model for those around him. Although he seems casual in his initial appearance, it is soon apparent that he is a very disciplined, confident practitioner, the expert to whom everyone turns for advice and direction. He is a man of principle, informing the rich Mr. Hudson that doctors are more interested in working and learning than in making money, yet he is practical enough at board meetings to realize that the hospital's economy requires wealthy friends. In explaining his profession, he states that

success in medicine is essentially a kind of glory, that one lifetime is not long enough to get at all the problems that confront medicine.

The younger man, Dr. George Ferguson, is more dynamically involved in the plot. At a position in life where he must make many crucial career decisions, George finds himself torn between Hochberg's demand for dedication—ten more years of hard work—and the insistence of Laura that he devote more time to her and to his personal life. Despite George's genuine respect for the master professional, Hochberg, his fiancé's request does not seem unreasonable. The conflict here defined, between the responsibilities and ambitions inherent in public life and the demands of private life, is a recurrent situation in Kingsley's drama.

George seems to acquiesce to Laura's wishes, though he wants to compromise with Hochberg rather than reject him. At this point, the plot is complicated by the botched abortion, a problem, the play suggests, resulting from a thoughtless moment between George and a sympathetic nurse. When Laura discovers the situation, she rejects George, saying that there is no excuse for what he did. Hochberg is much more tolerant and objective, noting that human bodies are human bodies and that the pregnancy was an accident. George seems about to marry the nurse, but she conveniently dies. In the conclusion, George explains to a more forgiving Laura that the hospital is where he belongs and where she ought to leave him. In terms of what the play has presented, he seems to be right.

DEAD END

Kingsley's most popular play, *Dead End*, owed its success to its theatrical boldness and to its projection of the mood of the 1930's. The spectacular set by Bel Geddes emphasized the contrasts of a New York neighborhood by placing a tenement house opposite the exclusive East River Terrace Apartment. For the river, a play area for the boys of the neighborhood, Bel Geddes flooded the orchestra pit. To give the flavor of the working city, a huge, red sand hopper stood prominently in the right center of the stage and a Caterpillar steam shovel stood farther back, up the street.

The boys of the neighborhood—later to be known in motion pictures as the Dead End Kids—carry much of the action of the play. Eager and energetic, they project vividly the communal intimacy of the neighborhood and define the kind of life that is nurtured by such surroundings. Kingsley's transcription of the lower-class New York dialect ("Howza wawda?"—"How's the water?") and his ethnic mixing add local color to his cultural portrait.

Insistent in its emphasis on economic desperation, *Dead End* is one of the representative literary documents of the 1930's. Like other literary works that examine the social problems of the era, it romanticizes the inner goodness of the poor and treats the rich with contempt. The play is a grim speculation about the power of social conditions to define the fate of the individual.

Two former residents of the neighborhood, Gimpty and "Baby-Face" Martin, have been marked by growing up in this environment, each in his own way. Gimpty, a lame but resourceful slum boy who has become an architect but cannot find work in the barren economy of the day, suggests the inability of his generation to build a new world, having been deprived of the chance to make its own future. His physical disability symbolizes his socially disadvantaged state. Gimpty is in love with Kay, who has overcome poverty by becoming a rich man's mistress.

Martin, a criminal on the run, serves to trace a more disastrous path for a tenement boy, from the ranks of the underprivileged to the criminal class. He advises the kids to become more violent in their gang wars, to forget about fighting fair. His corruption is certified when even his mother rejects him. Gimpty turns Martin in just when he seems on the verge of hatching a kidnapping scheme, and the G-men kill Martin. In one sense, Gimpty's action is a betrayal of a neighborhood code—indeed, he is filled with anguish over his part in Martin's death, but by this time Martin can be seen as one who has gone too far to be saved. In the end, Kay declares her love for Gimpty but will not give up her luxurious life for him.

In the subplot, a Dead End Kid, Tommy, gets into trouble when he plays a trick on a rich boy and then stabs the boy's father in a struggle. This situation opens the possibility that he will go Martin's way. The boys enthusiastically point out that he can pick up all kinds of criminal know-how in reform school. In contrast, his sister Drina is horrified by what seems an inevitable direction for his life. Her plea for the forgiveness of Tommy proves not a strong argument with the rich, but because Gimpty now has the reward money he got from turning in Baby-Face, the two can hire a good lawyer and work to make the social system operate for their benefit.

The conclusion of the play moves back, appropriately, to focus on the rest of the Dead End Kids and their innocent (and ignorant) energy. As they play around with the song "If I Had the Wings of an Angel," the audience is reminded that the boys must fly over the walls of a social prison if they are to have a chance in life.

THE PATRIOTS

As a play, *The Patriots* is a skillfully crafted historical drama centered on the conflict in early American history between Jeffersonian democracy and Hamiltonian conservatism. It is also Kingsley's warning about the precarious nature of freedom, a warning that prompted many reviewers to call attention to the play's relevance to World War II and the struggle to preserve democratic institutions. The action begins with Thomas Jefferson's return from France to accept, albeit reluctantly, President George Washington's offer to make him his secretary of state and concludes with Jefferson's election as president. Throughout the play, three historical giants—Washington, Jefferson, and Alexander Hamilton—dominate the stage. Kingsley did extensive research for the play, and he succeeded in introducing much material from original documents, but the strength of *The Patriots* lies in Kingsley's talent for endowing these historical characters with believable personalities.

Throughout the conflict between Jefferson and Hamilton, Washington represents a middle ground, the understanding of two American political extremes. In his concise portrait of the first president, Kingsley brings out a struggle between Washington's weariness with politics and his sense of public responsibility. It is this conflict treated on a larger dramatic scale that animates, as well, the character of Jefferson. Kingsley's Jefferson is a private doer, an inventor and architect who would rather retire to the comforts of private life than deal with Hamilton's petty political intrigues.

Hamilton is more completely the politician, one who will connive but who is also statesman enough to compromise for the better candidate when his side cannot win. The play treats neither Hamilton's ambitions nor his ideas kindly. In fact, Kingsley seems to have gone out of his way to bring in a nasty case involving Hamilton's philandering, perhaps to contrast Hamilton's sense of private pleasures with Jefferson's pastoralism. Although Hamilton is not simply a villain in this version of American history, there is no question that Kingsley's sympathies are with Jefferson, the man who trusts the people. At the end, it is Jefferson who has come to be in the middle, standing between the extremes of anarchy (the excesses of the French Revolution) and monarchy (Hamilton's desire for an aristocratic America). The conclusion places Jefferson's election in the context of progressive history. Hamilton laments that he lacks Jefferson's faith in the people, and both he and Jefferson conclude finally that their particular portion of American history has been fashioned by an irresistible destiny, the people's need for freedom.

DETECTIVE STORY

In preparation for the writing of *Detective Story*, Kingsley spent two years haunting detective squad rooms in Manhattan, gathering the naturalistic details that would give his dramatization of New York police work a searing authenticity. The resulting production featured a combination of the contemporary and the timeless, a blending of the texture of realism with a structure drawn from dramatic tradition.

The opening of the play features a symphonic blending of the varied characters of the police world and suggests immediately the richness and flexibility of the social interaction in this place of emerging good and evil. The initial dialogue presents the quotidian nature of police work—even its monotony. More idiosyncratic elements appear with Keogh, the singing policeman, and the paranoid Mrs. Farragut. These elements help to sketch out the varied nature of humanity's furtive desperation, an idea basic to Kingsley's vision.

The play focuses on the character of Detective James McLeod and the series of events that combine to destroy him. Although he seems a good man, committed to justice and integrity, his cruelty and his tendency to make absolute judgments are his tragic flaws. His understandable impatience with the criminal justice system lures him into a false confidence in his own instinctive sense of the evil in people. Although his superior tells him that he has a messianic complex, McLeod sees himself as a man of principle fighting both criminals, whom he believes are a separate species, and the justice system, which he sees as hopelessly flawed by loopholes for criminals. The plot centers on his search for evidence to convict an abortionist, the notorious Dr. Schneider. McLeod is also interrogating a shoplifter and a burglar, Arthur, who is a young first offender. Even though the complainant is willing to drop the charges against Arthur, McLeod refuses to release him, and he also beats Dr. Schneider severely during questioning, seriously injuring him. Ironically, McLeod's relentless quest for truth leads to the discovery that his own wife, Mary, whom he has idealized, has had an abortion performed by Dr. Schneider.

Kingsley's stage directions refer to the squad room as "ghost-ridden," and the play reveals McLeod as a prisoner of an unexamined past. His wife's accusation that he is cruel and vengeful, like the father he has despised, rings true: Though torn by his love for Mary, McLeod cannot help but condemn her. For him, forgiveness is too great a price to pay to a flawed world. His whole existence is at stake, yet he is unable to take the action—the act of forgiveness—that would save him. Indeed, his inflexibility is so inherent in his character that when, dying from wounds he received when the burglar tried to escape, he relents—letting young Arthur go and forgiving his wife—this final insistence on the possibility of change seems implausible and melodramatic.

Because McLeod's attitudes are tied to the social system, tragic form and cultural realism blend rather smoothly. The other characters contribute to the tragic dimension as well. The uncooperative attitude of the suborned witness, Miss Hatch, gives credence to McLeod's view that his instincts are more reliable than the system of courts and juries. Both Dr. Schneider's lawyer and McLeod's own lieutenant warn him not to act as judge and jury, and Joe Feinson, a journalist, advises him to humble himself before he digs his own grave. Arthur represents the essential goodness McLeod would deny, and the complainant's willingness to forgive Arthur stands out as one alternative for the detective-accuser. Detective Brody, who has been humanized by the death of his son, makes the strongest case for a belief in the fundamental goodness of human beings.

BIBLIOGRAPHY

Atkinson, Brooks. "Darkness at Noon." Review of *Darkness at Noon*, by Sidney Kingsley. *The New York Times*, January 15, 1951, p. 13. Finds the acting of Claude Rains, as Rubashov, to be effective but believes that Kingsley, "less a writer than a showman in this theatre piece," does not do justice to Arthur Koestler's novel: "His melodrama comes with elements of the glib propaganda play that we find so distasteful when it is on the other side." Also finds fault with Kingsley's "cumbersome and diffuse" scenes. Kingsley directed this play, as he did all of his Broadway plays except *The Patriots*.

_____. "Detective Story." Review of *Detective Story*, by Sidney Kingsley. *The New York Times*, March 24, 1949, p. 34. This review of Kingsley's "vivid drama with a disturbing idea" cites Kingsley's reputation as a responsible playwright, finding this play of intolerance in "the day's grist of crime in a New York precinct police station . . .

often pithy and graphic," especially in the minor characters. Kingsley "has the saving grace of being thorough and sincere; and he makes quite a play of it in the end." The play marked the beginning of Kingsley's reputation as an artist and a technician, rather than a visionary.

Gassner, John. *Theatre at the Crossroads: Plays and Playwrights of the Mid-Century American Stage*. New York: Holt, Rinehart and Winston, 1960. An overview of Kingsley's work from the Group Theatre days to *Darkness at Noon*, of which Gassner opines: "more workmanlike than inspired, more melodramatic than tragic, more denunciatory than psychologically and intellectually explorative."

Morphos, Evangeline. "Sidney Kingsley's *Men in White*." Review of *Men in White*, by Sidney Kingsley. *Tisch Drama Review* 28 (Winter, 1984): 13-22. A full and thorough study of the Group Theatre's production of *Men in White*, offering several insights into the selection, rehearsal, and performance processes. Particularly valuable is the discussion of the Lee Strasberg/Sidney Kingsley partnership. Includes many comments by Kingsley about the process, production history, and actors' methods. This issue is devoted entirely to Group Theatre productions.

"Sidney Kingsley: Playwright Won Pulitzer Prize." *Los Angeles Times*, March 22, 1995, p. 10. The life and works of Kingsley are summed up in this obituary.

Walter Shear,
updated by Thomas J. Taylor

HEINAR KIPPHARDT

Born: Heidersdorf, Germany; March 8, 1922
Died: Munich, West Germany; November 18, 1982

PRINCIPAL DRAMA

Shakespeare dringend gesucht, pr. 1953, pr. 1954
Der Aufstieg des Alois Piontek: Eine tragikomische Farce, pr., pb. 1956

Esel schreien im Dunkeln, pb. 1958
Die Stühle des Herrn Szmil, pr., pb. 1961 (adaptation of Ilya Ilf and Evgeni Petrov's *The Twelve Chairs*)
Der Hund des Generals, pr. 1962 (staged and televised), pb. 1963
In der Sache J. Robert Oppenheimer, pr. 1964

(staged and televised), pb. 1966 (*In the Matter of J. Robert Oppenheimer*, 1967)
Die Nacht in der Chef geschlachtet wurde, pr. 1967, pb. 1974
Die Soldaten, pr., pb. 1968 (adaptation of Jakob Michael Reinhold Lenz's play)
Sedanfeier, pr. 1970, pb. 1974
März, ein Künstlerleben, pb. 1979, pr. 1980 (adaptation of his novel *März*)
Bruder Eichmann, pr., pb. 1983 (*Brother Eichmann*, 1989)

OTHER LITERARY FORMS

Heinar Kipphardt's popularity as a playwright is equally matched by his reputation as a director and as a freelance writer of principally prose works. His only novel, *März* (1976), and most of his short stories are characteristically in the documentary vein, as are a large majority of his plays. The adaptation, in prose, of his previously produced play *Der Hund des Generals* and the dramatic adaptation, *März, ein Künstlerleben*, of his earlier novel, *März*, attest the ability of Kipphardt as a narrator.

Kipphardt wrote one volume of poetry, *Angelsbrucker Notizen* (1977), and edited several volumes of preponderantly historical-documentary and critical essays. Kipphardt's adaptation of Jakob Michael Reinhold Lenz's *Die Soldaten* (1776; *The Soldiers*, 1972) not only proves Kipphardt's unique skill in dealing with legal and military subject matter but also shows Kipphardt, the psychiatrist, as a master of the psychological study.

ACHIEVEMENTS

Heinar Kipphardt's reputation rests on his contributions to the so-called documentary theater. This new genre, still within the perimeters of conventional modern drama, constituted yet another new development in the series of *renouvellements* that German literature, in general, and German theater, in particular, experienced in the 1950's and 1960's, in the aftermath of World War II and the Nazi era.

A proponent of Marxist philosophy, Kipphardt constructed his works to meet the demands of political theater. His plays are based on historical materials, combining a documentary texture with a psychological probing of figures such as J. Robert Oppenheimer and Adolf Eichmann. Kipphardt's extensive psychiatric training provided him with the necessary insight to develop his characters fully.

Kipphardt began his career as a playwright in East Berlin with *Shakespeare dringend gesucht*, a mildly satiric play about the problems of a play reader in an East German theater. Although the play was a critique of narrow-minded Communist attitudes, lampooning the East German taste for socialist realist theater of the worst kind, it won for him, in 1953, the National Prize of the German Democratic Republic. Kipphardt was, at that time, the chief dramatist and director at the Deutsches Theater, where he remained until 1959. His play *Die Stühle des Herrn Szmil* created such an uproar among East German censors (who subsequently banned it) that Kipphardt was forced to leave East Germany, in 1960, for Munich, where he became a freelance writer. As it turned out, he remained in West Germany for the remainder of his career.

In 1962, Kipphardt was awarded the Schiller Memorial Prize, and *In the Matter of J. Robert Oppenheimer* won for him the Gerhart Hauptmann Prize in 1964. It was first staged at Erwin Piscator's Free People's Theater in West Berlin in 1964 and played throughout West Germany before its arrival in New York in 1968, where it became one of the successes of the season. It was eventually performed as well in London, Paris, Los Angeles, and East Berlin. Kipphardt received the Adolf Grimme Prize in 1965, the Television Prize from the German Academy of Representational Arts in 1975, the Film Prize of the Society of German Doctors and the Prix Italia in 1976, and the Bremer Literature Prize in 1977.

Kipphardt's greatest contribution to world drama is perhaps his true-to-life portrayal of soldiers, criminals, scientists, and businessmen, who reappear after World War II, recalling their experiences with stenographic precision in the form of trials, interrogations, and reminiscences. The documentary, quasi-political character of Kipphardt's dramatic œuvre in no way diminishes the audience's unabashed reaction of horror, consternation, and, frequently, pity.

BIOGRAPHY

Heinar Kipphardt was born in Upper Silesia. His father, a dentist, was an opponent of the Nazis and spent five years in a concentration camp at Buchenwald. In 1942, Kipphardt was drafted out of medical school to serve on the Russian front in the Wehrmacht panzer division, from which he is said to have deserted. He finally earned his medical degree at Düsseldorf in 1950 and became a staff psychiatrist at the Charité Neurological Clinic in East Berlin, also joining the Deutsches Theater as literary adviser.

Throughout the 1950's, Kipphardt alternated between treating mentally ill individuals at the clinic and satirizing a morally ill society onstage. When his play *Die Stühle des Herrn Szmil*, an adaptation of the novel *Dvenadtsat stuliev* (1928; *The Twelve Chairs*, 1961) by the Russian comic writers Ilya Ilf and Evgeni Petrov, was banned by the state censor in 1959, he departed for West Germany, eventually settling in Munich, where he began writing the kind of hard-hitting documentary theater practiced by Rolf Hochhuth in *Der Stellvertreter* (1963; *The Deputy*, 1963). Kipphardt wrote *Der Hund des Generals*, about the inability of Germans to acknowledge the shameful past, in this style before writing *In the Matter of J. Robert Oppenheimer*. Whatever emotions the play evoked in German audiences, in the United States it was recognized as having a direct bearing on the Vietnam War, organized opposition to which was then beginning. *In the Matter of J. Robert Oppenheimer*, wrote Catharine Hughes in her book *Plays, Politics, and Polemics* (1973), "was easily one of the most significant American theatrical events of the sixties, even if it did require a European to confront us with ourselves."

Kipphardt's next drama, the teleplay *Joel Brand: Die Geschichte eines Geschäfts* (1964), was a documentary drama about the Hungarian Jew who was forced by the Nazis to negotiate a business deal involving the exchange of one million Hungarian Jewish lives for ten thousand British trucks. The British refused, and the Jews were killed.

While he was the chief dramatist at the Munich Kammerspiele, Kipphardt wrote *Die Nacht in der Chef geschlachtet wurde*, a satire about bourgeois West Germans; *Die Soldaten*, an adaptation of a play

by the late eighteenth century Sturm und Drang dramatist Jakob Michael Reinhold Lenz; and a novel, teleplay, and stage play about a schizophrenic poet named Alexander März.

Kipphardt owed much to Piscator's example and influence, as he himself admitted. He refused to accept the label of "documentary theater," claiming that, though a digest of the three thousand pages of the Oppenheimer hearings in the United States, *In the Matter of J. Robert Oppenheimer* is a true drama in its own right about the loyalties and individual responsibilities of the scientist in the nuclear age.

Kipphardt died in Munich at the age of sixty, during preparations for the production of his last play, *Brother Eichmann*, which was produced in 1983.

ANALYSIS

Heinar Kipphardt was one of the foremost practitioners of the documentary drama, a style of playwriting popular in the 1960's in which pieces of recorded history (transcripts, tapes, and publications) are adapted creatively to illuminate issues of social and moral concern. The author's aim by dramatizing an event is clearly not to eradicate every social evil but rather to present it in minute detail, thereby provoking and challenging the audience to judge, deplore, and commiserate, whichever would come first as a natural reaction. Bertolt Brecht's epic and moralizing theater without any doubt left its indelible mark on Kipphardt's dramas, not so much influencing their structure or subject matter as perhaps shaping them in a uniquely Brechtian atmosphere of alienation (*Verfremdung*). Kipphardt's *Die Stühle des Herrn Szmil* or *Die Nacht in der Chef geschlachtet wurde* could in no way affect the audience as, for example, the French *comédie larmoyante* did. In the face of these dramas, the audience remains dumbfounded but at the same time works itself into a rage that goes far beyond disbelief or amusement. Again, it is not only the sociopolitical content in Kipphardt's plays that strikes the audience as unconventional, but also, and more important, the deceptively bland manner in which his issues are presented.

Kipphardt's rather early confrontation with the theater of Socialist Realism (so aptly ridiculed in

Shakespeare dringend gesucht) could very well have marked him for the remainder of his career. The sheer colorless atmosphere omnipresent in Socialist Realist theater and its influence on Kipphardt could in part account for the development of his dry, oftentimes flat style. This early development of an individual Kipphardtian style also included the element of psychoanalysis. A psychiatrist by profession, Kipphardt, as noted above, exercised the art of healing at the Charité Clinic in East Berlin, as well as the art of moralizing onstage. He was chief dramatist and director of the Deutsches Theater for nine years (1950-1959), a period that finally ended in disillusionment and defection to the West.

IN THE MATTER OF J. ROBERT OPPENHEIMER

Artistically, though, this period was a turning point for Kipphardt, who shortly thereafter created *In the Matter of J. Robert Oppenheimer*, his most significant documentary drama. Originally planned as a radio play but revised by Kipphardt for stage production, it soon appeared, with spectacular success, in theaters in Berlin (produced by Piscator) and Munich and throughout West Germany. Other European capitals soon saw productions of the play, whose true-life hero, J. Robert Oppenheimer, threatened to sue the playwright.

The play is based on the 1954 hearings of the Atomic Energy Commission, after which Oppenheimer was branded as a security risk. Kipphardt's dramatization is clearly critical of American policies; at one point in the play, Oppenheimer, not eager to develop the hydrogen bomb, dramatically explains that the Soviet Union has only two targets of value, Moscow and Leningrad, while the United States has fifty.

In the course of the play, the commission's counsel and several hostile witnesses fight fiercely against Oppenheimer. Edward Teller appears as a somewhat friendly, if occasionally grouchy, mediator between the extremes. Senator Joseph McCarthy broods demoniacally over the play, prompting the thought that no dramatist as yet has presented a full and convincing picture of McCarthy in all his evil aspects.

In relation to Kipphardt's play, the actual Oppenheimer objected to what he described as "improvisa-

tions which were contrary to history and to the nature of the people involved," particularly referring to Kipphardt's representation of Niels Bohr, who had died two years before the play's premiere, as being opposed to the creation of the bomb at Los Alamos. Oppenheimer (who himself died not long after the controversy, in 1967) also stated that, contrary to the play, he was not opposed to the making of the original bomb. In a letter to Kipphardt, he recalled the atmosphere of the time: "You may have forgotten Guernica, Dachau, Coventry, Belsen, Warsaw, Dresden, and Tokyo. I have not."

The truth is that Kipphardt, while preserving the original trial structure in *In the Matter of J. Robert Oppenheimer*, condensed the three-thousand-page report on the proceedings of the Security Committee of the United States Atomic Energy Commission, recorded in 1954, while reducing the number of witnesses from forty to six. He rewrote the dialogue here and there, added Oppenheimer's monologue at the end, and polished some of the courtroom skirmishes to make them more theatrically effective. His most substantial departure from the documentary record—and it is admittedly a significant distortion—occurs in his presentation of Oppenheimer's views, fully justifying the scientist's rebuke.

In general, however, the play simply follows the historical record. Oppenheimer is accused of having been a Communist sympathizer, of endangering the security of the atom bomb project through his private and professional connections with communists and former communists, and of exposing the United States to the machinations of its enemies by deliberately slowing up work on the hydrogen bomb. He is found guilty on the latter count and forfeits his right of access to top-security scientific work.

Despite some stirring dramatic moments, *In the Matter of J. Robert Oppenheimer* is rather flat and dull. The author is hamstrung by the anonymity to which his factual material condemns him. Kipphardt's play laboriously rehearses a debate in terms that are invalid by virtue of the existence of Brecht's *Leben des Galilei* (pr. 1943; *Life of Galileo*, 1947). Kipphardt's play does not attack the crucial issue of the moral responsibility of the scientist until the very end. Indeed, how could it, when Oppenheimer's task is not to define the position of the scientist but to defend himself against the charge that his qualms about the hydrogen bomb jeopardized the security of the state? Indeed, the play reveals more about the paranoid nature of American politics of the 1950's than about science.

Brecht's argument is obviously important to Kipphardt, but Kipphardt can turn to it only after Oppenheimer has been condemned and has seen the pernicious side of the scientist's collusion with the state military apparatus. Even in his final monologue, Oppenheimer's self-criticism lacks the forcefulness of Galileo's. Where Brecht's Galileo judges himself first and foremost as a human being—"A man who does what I have done cannot be tolerated in the company of scientists"—Oppenheimer wonders rather vaguely whether he has betrayed the "spirit of science": "I begin to wonder whether we were not perhaps traitors to the spirit of science when we handed over the results of our research to the military, without considering the consequences." To atone for his error, he decides to keep away from military work and take up "pure" research. For Galileo, the retreat of the scientist into the anonymity of research is but another form of betrayal.

DER HUND DES GENERALS

An earlier play, *Der Hund des Generals*, although not based on a historical incident, is presented in documentary style. The action takes place in a courtroom. General Rampf has been brought before a commission for the investigation of war crimes and accused of sending three tanks into a hopeless battle during the Russian campaign merely because one of his men, Corporal Pfeiffer, shot his dog. The general is able to refute the charge by proving that what might have appeared to the soldiers as a brutal act of revenge did, in fact, coincide with a senseless order from General Headquarters to send them into combat. Although crazy, the general's order was not motivated by the shooting of his dog. As far as the law is concerned, the general is innocent of the deaths of his men, though one of the judges argues that legal innocence does not exclude moral guilt. Whatever the truth of the matter, the general's behavior at a particu-

lar point in time is uncannily symbolic of the frightful caprice and indifference to human life in war. The theme of Kipphardt's play is the inhumanity of war, but toward the end, this theme is abandoned for the sake of theatrical effect. Kipphardt is determined that the general's head shall roll. The tape recording of a Gestapo interrogation after the July, 1944, plot against Adolf Hitler is played. On it the general is heard denouncing the conspiracy, though in the trial he had insisted that he sympathized with it. If he lied on this point, then it must be assumed that his version of the affair with the dog is also false. The general is discredited, but the main theme of the play tends to get lost in the process.

BROTHER EICHMANN

Kipphardt's last play, *Brother Eichmann*, is similar in many respects to *Der Hund des Generals*. It too is presented in the form of a war-crimes trial, and the play consists for the most part of the testimony of the accused. *Brother Eichmann*'s central figure is Adolf Eichmann, whose trial in 1961 received a large amount of publicity despite the efforts of the Israeli government to keep the kidnaping and subsequent imprisonment of Eichmann a secret. Kipphardt's *Brother Eichmann* succeeds in bringing Eichmann, the war criminal, as well as the private citizen before the audience in an atmosphere of authentic historical immediacy. Based on documents about the Third Reich obtained from a variety of sources, the play portrays Eichmann as the leader of an organization whose task it was to annihilate Jewry in Europe. Here is a man who had been elevated by the Third Reich to the dizzying heights of Olympus, where gods and criminals alike came to share a responsibility unparalleled in history. It is not at all surprising that Kipphardt chose as his motto for the play Blaise Pascal's words: "Never does one commit a crime so perfectly and so well, as when one does it with a clear conscience."

The singling out of Eichmann for the role of a leader can itself be viewed as a stroke of fate. He was a man whose character allowed his diabolical motivation to erase the last few vestiges of reason, just, as at his trial, the so-called scapegoat philosophy could leave no room for historical or psychological considerations. The trial of Eichmann in Jerusalem and its dramatization also contributed, in an adverse manner, to world publicity that enhanced his demoniac image. Via an intricate security mechanism, the mass-murderer Eichmann was cut off from the rest of the world, including his witnesses and spectators: He was placed in a bulletproof glass cage equipped with a separate air supply system. No one was allowed to breathe the same air as the accused.

The enormity of Eichmann's guilt cannot be explained or diminished by any argument. On the contrary, the more objectively this guilt is viewed in historical and chronological perspective, the more punishing and crushing its effect on the audience. The audience would like to stand in judgment over Eichmann, who embodies the "banality of evil," in Hannah Arendt's celebrated formulation. The audience, however, cannot enlighten itself, as would be customary in conventional theater, through the feeling of either contempt or humor.

This unusual reaction on the part of the audience stems from its inability to identify with what Eichmann did or the way he did it. His blind, insensitive functionalism has totally replaced his conscience. Whoever is able to "function" without asking about the consequences or the meaning of his or her actions will be spared the questions, "Who are you, what do you feel, what is your personal opinion?" Indeed, one of the reasons for his two-year incarceration and interrogation in Israel had to be the fact that Eichmann himself finally felt a great need to be asked about things about which he had never been asked before.

Brother Eichmann reminds the audience not only of its responsibility to relate past crimes with the crimes of the present, but also of its solemn duty to view personal questions on a morally sound basis learned from the lessons of history. Thus a small theater can become a large arena, a world tribunal, from which each spectator can pronounce the verdict and feel entirely justified in doing so. Eichmann's life or death will not matter any more to those who have found peace within themselves.

OTHER MAJOR WORKS

LONG FICTION: *März*, 1976.

SHORT FICTION: *Die Ganovenfresse*, 1964; *Der Mann des Tages und andere Erzaehlungen*, 1977.

POETRY: *Angelsbrucker Notizen*, 1977.

SCREENPLAY: *Die Soldaten*, 1977.

TELEPLAYS: *Bartleby*, 1962; *Joel Brand: Die Geschichte eines Geschäfts*, 1964; *Leben des schizophrenen Dichters, Alexander März*, 1975.

MISCELLANEOUS: *Der Engel der Geschichte*, 1976; *Aus Liebe zu Deutschland*, 1980; *Traumprotokolle*, 1981; *Vom deutschen Herbst zum bleichen deutschen Winter*, 1981.

BIBLIOGRAPHY

Cuomo, Glenn R. "Vergangenheitsbewaltigung Through Analogy: Heinar Kipphardt's Last Play *Bruder Eichmann*." *The Germanic Review* 64, no. 2 (Spring, 1989): 58. An analysis of the character of Adolf Eichmann as portrayed by Kipphardt.

Freinberg, Anat. "The Appeal of the Executive: Adolf Eichmann on the Stage." *Monatshefte* 78 (1986): 203-214. A look at Kipphardt's *Brother Eichmann*.

Hofacker, Erich P., Jr. "Heinar Kipphardt." In *Twentieth Century German Dramatists, 1919-1992*. Vol. 124 in *Dictionary of Literary Biography*, edited by Wolfgang D. Elfe and James Hardin. Detroit, Mich.: The Gale Group, 1992. A concise overview of the life and works of Kipphardt.

Schumacher, Claude, ed. *Staging the Holocaust: The Shoah in Drama and Performance*. Cambridge, England: Cambridge University Press, 1998. A collection of essays on dramatic works that deal with the Holocaust. Contains an analysis of Kipphardt's plays on the subject.

Thomas, R. Hinton, and Keith Bullivant. *Literature in Upheaval: West German Writers and the Challenge of the 1960's*. New York: Barnes & Noble, 1974. An examination of the time in which Kipphardt lived and worked, along with some discussion of his role. Bibliography and index.

Paul A. Jagasich

JACK KIRKLAND

Born: St. Louis, Missouri; July 25, 1901(?)
Died: New York, New York; February 22, 1969

PRINCIPAL DRAMA

Frankie and Johnnie, pr. 1928
Tobacco Road, pr. 1933, pb. 1934 (adaptation of
    Erskine Caldwell's novel)
Tortilla Flat, pr. 1938 (adaptation of John
    Steinbeck's novel)
I Must Love Somebody, pr. 1939 (with Leyla
    George)
Suds in Your Eye, pr., pb. 1944 (adaptation of Mary
    Lasswell's novel)
Georgia Boy, pr. 1945 (with Haila Stoddard;
    adaptation of Caldwell's novel)
Mr. Adam, pr. 1949 (adaptation of Pat Frank's
    novel)
The Man with the Golden Arm, pr. 1956
    (adaptation of Nelson Algren's novel)
Mandingo, pr. 1961 (adaptation of Kyle Onstott's
    novel)

OTHER LITERARY FORMS

Although Jack Kirkland wrote or worked on a
number of screenplays, he is best known for his stage
plays.

ACHIEVEMENTS

Jack Kirkland is remembered less for the literary
or dramatic quality of his plays than for their social
impact. From his first play, *Frankie and Johnnie*, to
his last, *Mandingo*, he challenged the accepted standards of the American stage. His plays never won
awards and were often castigated by critics for their
perceived crudeness, artlessness, and obscenity.
Kirkland, in fact, consistently received some of the
worst reviews accorded to any major playwright.
Nevertheless, his dramatization of Erskine Caldwell's
Tobacco Road, which premiered on December 4,
1933, became at the time the longest-running play in
the history of the Broadway stage, a veritable institution for seven and a half years in the New York the-

aters. Deplored by most first-night critics, it won influential fans and supporters, who rallied to it as
something more than a shocking, brutal (though often
humorous) portrait of poor Georgian sharecroppers.
Over the years, the play earned a grudging admiration
for its frankness, vitality, and dramatic power. From a
social standpoint, it led the battle against outdated,
unfair, often arbitrary, and conflicting censorship laws
across the country. None of Kirkland's other works
achieved such success (nor did they deserve it), although they did provoke similar indignation and outrage (often justified). Thus, Kirkland's fame rests primarily on the reputation of *Tobacco Road*, which
forever changed the state of modern drama.

BIOGRAPHY

Jack Kirkland was a member of the hard-living,
no-nonsense school of professional writers (as opposed to artists) epitomized by such figures as Ben
Hecht and Charles MacArthur. Like them, he began
his career as a reporter, working for such papers as
The Detroit News, the *St. Louis Times*, and the *New
York Daily News*; and like them, he turned his talents
to both film and stage. From this background, he
brought to his drama a scorn for sentimentality, a tendency toward sensationalism, and a penchant for a
kind of vulgar, black comedy that seems to have characterized his view of the world. He was not so much
interested in art as in effect, and the subjects he chose
often came from the demimonde familiar to any
streetwise reporter.

Kirkland was born in St. Louis, Missouri, on July
25, 1901 (or possibly 1902, since there was no official
birth record and other sources conflict on these dates);
he was the son of William Thomas and Julia Wood-
ward Kirkland. In his teens, he roamed about the country, working from state to state at odd jobs and often
living with and observing the kind of people about
whom he would later write. He claimed to have developed a kinship with the poor and homeless that enabled him to understand and sympathize with them in
such works as *Tobacco Road*. Soon thereafter he be-

gan his newspaper career and made his way to New York, where he attended Columbia University and worked at the *New York Daily News*. In 1924, he married Nancy Carroll, the first of his five wives. (His subsequent wives were Jayne Shadduck, Julia Laird, Haila Stoddard, and Nancy Hoadley.) Carroll was a noted Broadway chorine, and when she was called to Hollywood, Kirkland accompanied her and began to write films, among them *Fast and Loose* (1930), with Miriam Hopkins, and *Now and Forever* (1934), with Gary Cooper, Shirley Temple, and Carole Lombard. Nancy Carroll became one of the most popular stars of the 1930's and was nominated for an Academy Award for her performance in *The Devil's Holiday* in 1930. She and Kirkland were divorced in 1935.

Kirkland's main interest, however, lay in the theater. His first play was *Frankie and Johnnie*, which he wrote in 1928. In 1929, during its Chicago performance, it was attacked as obscene and was closed. Kirkland brought the play to New York in 1930 where, once again, it was closed on charges of obscenity, and Kirkland was arrested. He and the theater owners took the case to court, and in 1932, in a landmark ruling, the play was judged not to be obscene. Kirkland would be involved in many such court cases throughout his career.

In 1931, while in Hollywood, Kirkland was given a copy of Erskine Caldwell's scandalous new novel *Tobacco Road*, which dealt with the almost subhuman existence of a family of Georgian sharecroppers. In the spring of 1933, Kirkland (having spent much of his film earnings on the legal battles surrounding *Frankie and Johnnie*) retreated to the island of Majorca to write a dramatic treatment of the book. He took the play to New York, where it was turned down by every Broadway producer whom Kirkland approached. Finally, producer Harry Oshrin agreed to cosponsor the play. Kirkland put up his last six thousand dollars as investment and went into partnership with Oshrin and Sam H. Grisman, who became his lawyer and personal representative. The play, directed by Anthony Brown, opened at the Masque Theatre in New York on December 4, 1933, the day Prohibition ended. Despite praise of the acting, initial reviews were generally negative (although not as aw-

ful as theater lore has it), and the play lost thirty-eight hundred dollars in the first five weeks. To keep the play alive, ticket prices were reduced, the cast took pay cuts, and Kirkland and the others (except Caldwell) waived their royalties. "I had a hunch after that first night at the Masque that the show would click," Kirkland later remembered. "It left me all in a heap." After this shaky start, *Tobacco Road* established itself as a crowd-pleaser, and its popularity continued largely unabated during its record run of 3,180 performances. Because Kirkland held more than half ownership (approximately 66 percent) and sold the film rights to Twentieth Century-Fox for $200,000 plus a percentage of the earnings (Kirkland and Oshrin were listed as associate producers of the film, which was directed by John Ford), he became a rich man. "I hate to think how much money I made," he said shortly before his death, "because so much isn't there any more."

Kirkland never repeated the success he achieved with *Tobacco Road* but remained active on the New

Jack Kirkland (AP/Wide World Photos)

York theater scene for the next thirty years. In 1936, he coproduced two unsuccessful plays, *Forbidden Melody* and *Bright Hour*. In 1938, he adapted and coproduced John Steinbeck's short novel *Tortilla Flat* (1935) for the stage, but the play quickly failed. Kirkland, furious at the reviews, threw a punch at the New York *Herald Tribune* drama critic Dick Watts, causing *The New York Times* critic Brooks Atkinson to call him "Killer" Kirkland in his review of Kirkland's next play, *I Must Love Somebody*, which Kirkland cowrote (with Leyla George) and produced in 1939. *I Must Love Somebody* proved to be Kirkland's second hit, although its run of 191 performances did not challenge the success of *Tobacco Road*. From 1940 to 1943, Kirkland produced three other plays—*Suzanna and the Elders* (1940), *Tanyard Street* (1941), and *The Moon Vine* (1943)—but the longest run of any was only thirty performances.

In 1944, Kirkland wrote *Suds in Your Eye*, based on Mary Lasswell's popular 1942 novel about the American home front during World War II. The play was an inoffensive comedy, but it failed to equal the success of the book and closed after thirty-seven performances. The following year, Kirkland returned to the work of Erskine Caldwell with a dramatization of Caldwell's 1943 novel *Georgia Boy*, which Kirkland cowrote with his fourth wife, Haila Stoddard. He also directed and coproduced this effort, which opened and closed in Boston. In 1949, he wrote, produced, and directed *Mr. Adam*, based on a novel by Pat Frank concerning life after a nuclear explosion. It was savaged by every critic who bothered to review it, was called the worst play of the year, and quickly disappeared. *The Man with the Golden Arm*, taken from Nelson Algren's novel about drug addiction, met with more favorable reviews and ran for seventy-three performances, but Kirkland's last play, *Mandingo*, inspired by Kyle Onstott's pulp novel of slavery in the antebellum South, was howled off the stage after only eight performances.

When Kirkland died of heart trouble, he was remembered primarily for *Tobacco Road*. Indeed, he never wrote anything as good, and he returned to the material at various times in his career, through revivals (in 1950 it was revived with an all-black cast) or

revisions (at his death he had recently completed a musical version called "Jeeter").

ANALYSIS

Most of Jack Kirkland's work was derived from other sources, usually popular novels, and it would probably be pushing matters to discuss too intently the overriding themes or concerns in his plays. His works reflected not so much a personal philosophy as a desire to entertain. Kirkland did speak of the social significance of *Tobacco Road*, noting that the play realistically illustrated the plight of poor Southern sharecroppers caught in an economic and cultural dead end. He also spoke of Jeeter Lester, his most enduring character, in terms of his universal qualities, stating that his "tolerance for the sins and beliefs of others makes him a man apart, a man whose one great virtue is more important than his lack of lesser ones." In his other plays, Kirkland dealt with such problems as nuclear war, slavery, and drug addiction, but rarely did he aim for more than a superficial treatment of complex issues. In *Mr. Adam*, for example, the bomb is nothing more than a pretext for a series of dirty jokes, and *Mandingo* uses its historical setting as an excuse to indulge in sexual titillation and sadistic violence. Kirkland was a competent playwright who, with *Tobacco Road*, did achieve a dramatic power above the average, but who all too often appealed to the lowest common denominator among his audiences.

Of Kirkland's plays, only *Tobacco Road* is likely to be remembered. It is a better work than its reputation suggests, more important than is suggested by the popular hoopla and controversy that surrounded it. In its original form, before it became a parody of itself, it was a brave dramatization of a serious novel. It affected its audiences (both in the United States and abroad) because it acknowledged human beings' universal suffering and celebrated their ability to endure. In Jeeter Lester, Kirkland (although greatly indebted to Caldwell) gave the modern stage one of its classic roles. Finally, through his willingness to defend his work against censorship, Kirkland expanded the range and depth to which other and better artists could explore the human condition. For these reasons, Kirkland deserves to be remembered as an important figure of twentieth century American drama.

FRANKIE AND JOHNNIE

As a professional man of the theater, Kirkland believed strongly in the need for artistic freedom. His willingness to challenge, through lengthy and costly legal battles, the prevailing concepts of obscenity changed the standards of what could be presented on the legitimate stage. For example, Kirkland's first play, *Frankie and Johnnie*, was based on the popular and racy American folk song, which told of love, betrayal, and murder. Kirkland's drama was set in 1849, in the red-light district of St. Louis among the waterfront dens and gambling houses. Like the couple of the song, Frankie is a prostitute and Johnnie a gambler. When Johnnie has a run of luck, he is secretly stolen from Frankie by a rival prostitute, Nellie Bly, on whom he spends all his money. Meanwhile, to maintain his lifestyle, Johnnie acts as pimp for Frankie, who works for him out of love. When Frankie discovers that Johnnie has "done her wrong," she shoots and kills him.

Reviewers of the play found it to be coarse, vulgar, and clumsy. As Atkinson put it, "A gaudy lithograph, dramatizing literally the song . . . it has moments of theatrical effectiveness, split seconds of amusement. But it does not sustain itself or what it attempts in the way that Mae West did in *Diamond Lil.*" When first performed, the play was ruled obscene and closed in Chicago, only the second time the city had taken such action. When it opened Off-Broadway at the Carlton Theatre in New York in September of 1930, it was raided following the third performance by plainclothes police officers who arrested Kirkland, the cast, and others connected with the play. Found guilty of obscenity, Kirkland fought for the next two years to have the judgment overturned. In a landmark decision made in March, 1932, Judge Cuthbert W. Pound of the New York Court of Appeals wrote that although the play was "indecent" and "degrades the stage," it "does not counsel or invite to vice or voluptuousness" and, therefore, could not be considered obscene. The play itself had opened on Broadway at the Republic Theatre on September 25, 1930, where it ran for sixty-one performances. By the time of the court ruling, the play was long forgotten.

TOBACCO ROAD

The *Frankie and Johnnie* ruling, however, set the precedent for the legal maneuverings surrounding Kirkland's second play, *Tobacco Road*, which became a *cause célèbre* for the defenders of free speech and a public event that reached beyond the merits of the play itself. When the play was accepted by the Masque Theatre in New York, its acceptance was contingent on a special clause that allowed either party to break the contract at the end of the first three weeks. Rehearsals started without an actress to play Jeeter's wife Ada (Fay Bainter, Jessie Royce Landis, and Dorothy and Lillian Gish had all refused the role, which was finally taken by Margaret Wycherly). The initial reviews praised the acting of Henry Hull as Jeeter Lester, but they found the play offensive, although infused with a kind of brutal realism. As *The New York Times* review put it, "Although *Tobacco Road* reels around the stage like a drunken stranger to the theatre, it has spasmodic moments of merciless power when truth is flung into your face with all the slime that truth contains." When, after poor business, the Masque Theatre owners exercised their option, the play moved to the Forty-eighth Street Theatre, where it was nursed along with cut-rate prices until it had built an audience largely through word of mouth. In the summer, Henry Hull left the show to try his luck in films. As a result, the play was once again asked to move. The owners leased the Forrest Theatre, where, in September of 1934 (with James Barton as Jeeter), the play settled in for its record-setting run. There would be five Broadway Jeeters in all (James Bell, Eddie Garr, and Will Geer all played the role, which became known as "the American Hamlet") in addition to other Jeeters in the three road-show companies that traversed the country.

When the play opened, it was considered a serious portrayal of social dehumanization. *Theatre Arts Monthly* called it "one of the bitterest plays ever produced in New York, but one of the most compelling." Most thought it too brutal for the average audience. Like Caldwell's novel, the play deals with the Lesters, a family of impoverished sharecroppers abandoned on a worn-out farm, which had once belonged to Jeeter's people. Kirkland focused the play on Jeeter's sincere love of the land and, conversely, his basic shiftlessness and immorality. In truth, Kirkland had toned down the more outrageous and shocking episodes found in the book. For example, he had Ada tell Jeeter that Pearl (the daughter Jeeter sold in marriage to Lov Bensey for seven dollars) was not really his child, thus diluting the incestuous nature of Jeeter's desire for her. Grandmother Lester simply disappears in the woods rather than being run over and left to die while the family ignores her, as occurs in the book. Jeeter and Ada are no longer burned to death at the story's end; instead, it is Ada who is killed by Sister Bessie's car as she tries to help Pearl escape to a better life in Augusta. The play thus ends with Jeeter facing an uncertain future, alone but still alive.

Moreover, the longer the play ran, the more its tone began to shift, and soon it was staged more for its comedy than for its supposed realism. Caldwell's novel, to be sure, has many moments of dark humor throughout, but overriding them is a sense of intense outrage. When James Barton, a former vaudevillian, took over the role of Jeeter, he played the character as a reprobate and rascal; lost was the sense of despair and doom that Caldwell's characterization of Jeeter evokes. By the end of its run, the play had become a rollicking and bawdy good time, having long since lost its original seriousness.

Despite its shocking nature, *Tobacco Road* aroused little legal opposition until it began to tour the country. In October of 1935, after it had played for seven weeks without protest in Chicago, its license was suddenly revoked by Mayor Edward H. Kelly, who proclaimed the play "an insult to decent people." Kirkland immediately responded. "I am opposed to arbitrary censorship, particularly when it affects something which has been accepted nationally and possesses a definite social purpose," he said, asking for an injunction against the mayor's ban. Following Chicago's lead, other cities, such as Detroit, Boston, St. Paul, Tulsa, Albany, and even New Orleans, also stopped production of the play, while still other cities allowed only expurgated versions to be per-

formed. In each case, Kirkland and his co-owners went to court. A permanent legal staff was kept busy following the road shows from place to place. By 1939, Kirkland had won thirty-two out of thirty-five court cases. Many celebrities and advocates of free speech had spoken out in favor of the work; even Eleanor Roosevelt defended it as a play of fundamental seriousness and social importance.

By the time *Tobacco Road* closed, it had permanently changed the American stage. *The New York Times* ran an article on May 31, 1941, which colorfully captured the effect of the play: "*Tobacco Road* Retires Tonight Undefeated; Champ of All Plays Beat Critics 3,180 Rounds." More important, it had altered the acceptable moral standards of the stage throughout the country. Cities that had originally banned the play during its first tour accepted it without protest in following years. The play itself was re-evaluated as well. As George R. Kernodle observed in a 1947 retrospective article, "The Audience Was Right," in *Theatre Arts Monthly*, the play illustrated people's ability to endure and thus offered reassurance during the Depression years of its run. Kirkland himself believed that the play was an "American classic," as, in fact, it has proved to be.

TORTILLA FLAT

In his next play, *Tortilla Flat*, Kirkland tried once again to adapt a book by a leading American writer, but John Steinbeck's short episodic novel of Danny and the other *paisanos* living on the outskirts of Monterey, California, had less substance than Caldwell's work, and none of the characters was as original or fascinating as Jeeter Lester. Moreover, whereas *Tobacco Road* had starkly portrayed the grinding effects of poverty on the human will, *Tortilla Flat* tried to make its impoverished inhabitants seem comic and charming free spirits in rebellion against the soul-killing inducements of the materialistic world. As long as Danny and his companions are poor, they are happy, but when Danny inherits two shacks, the responsibility of ownership comes between him and the others. Only by burning down the shacks in an act of deliberate repudiation can Danny recapture the good and easy life. Compared to *Tobacco Road* (however burlesque the play had become), *Tortilla Flat* seemed an abrupt turnabout for Kirkland, and the play lasted only five performances after its premiere on January 12, 1938.

I MUST LOVE SOMEBODY

With his next play, *I Must Love Somebody*, Kirkland returned to sexually suggestive material and to the legal arena. He coauthored the play with Leyla George, a former actress who had originated the role of Charmaine in Maxwell Anderson's *What Price Glory?* (pr. 1924). *I Must Love Somebody* is a fictionalized account of the Florodora Girls, six chorines who had appeared in the play *Florodora*, a musical imported in 1900 from London to the Broadway stage, where it ran for 505 performances (only the second musical to break the five-hundred-performances mark). The girls, according to legend, all married millionaires. Kirkland and George's version concentrates on the backstage affairs of these high-living women and their top-hatted stagedoor Johnnies, with scenes in the dressing rooms of the Casino Theatre, in private rooms of Canfield's gambling establishment, and in the girls' apartments. Like *Frankie and Johnnie*, the play emphasizes atmosphere more than story. One of the girls, Birdie Carr, falls in love and decides to give up the fast life. Another of the girls, Ann Gibson, discovers that her "protector" has infected her with a venereal disease and kills him. While Birdie and her friends try to keep Ann out of jail, Birdie learns that her lover, Bob Goesling, has no intention of marrying her as he has promised but plans only to set her up as his mistress. The play was judged poorly written and poorly acted when it opened on February 7, 1939, at the Longacre Theatre in New York. It moved, on April 24, from the Longacre to the Vanderbilt Theatre. There, the owners claimed that Kirkland had added salacious material to the show and demanded that it vacate by May 6. Kirkland asked for an injunction against the owners but lost. Nevertheless, the play ran for 191 performances, making it Kirkland's second most successful show.

SUDS IN YOUR EYE

Kirkland's next work (which he both wrote and directed) was *Suds in Your Eye*, an inoffensive and rather frothy comedy based on a popular novel by Mary Lasswell. When Kirkland adapted it to the stage, the book had sold more than seventy thousand copies since its publication in 1942. Like the book, the play relies heavily on the Irish charm of the main character, Mrs. Nora Feeley (portrayed by Jane Darwell). Mrs. Feeley, a type of Tugboat Annie in drydock, owns a junkyard in San Diego, California, during World War II. Living with her is a small Oriental boy named Chinatown, who actually runs the business; Miss Tinkham, a refined, retired music teacher; and Mrs. Rasmussen, a neighbor who can no longer abide to stay with her daughter and her daughter's crass husband. What plot there is revolves around the efforts of this unusual group to save the junkyard from the tax collector and to fix up Mrs. Feeley's nephew, a sailor home from the war, with a local teacher. The play is pure escapism, sweet, sentimental, and silly enough to make it an anomaly among Kirkland's works. It closed on February 12, 1944, after thirty-seven performances.

MR. ADAM

With *Mr. Adam*, which Kirkland wrote and directed in 1949, he reached the nadir of his career. The play was inspired by a novel by Pat Frank concerning the last sexually competent male on earth after an atomic explosion has left all other men sterile. Homer Adam (who was in a lead mine at the time of the accident) is called on by the National Refertilization Program to perpetuate the race with a number of desperately willing women. The play was set to premiere at the Lobero Theatre in Santa Barbara, California, on March 12, 1949, but was banned by the city council. After playing in San Francisco, Chicago, and Detroit, *Mr. Adam* opened at the Royale Theatre in New York on May 25, 1949, to the most devastating reviews received by any of Kirkland's works. Both *The New York Times* and *Theatre Arts Monthly* deemed it the worst play of the year. Words such as "gruesome," "loathsome," "tasteless," and "stupid" were used to describe it, and *Mr. Adam* closed after five performances, much to Kirkland's anger and bafflement.

THE MAN WITH THE GOLDEN ARM

Kirkland's next play was a redemption of sorts and remains one of his most interesting works. *The Man with the Golden Arm*, based on the novel by Nelson Algren, opened at the Cherry Lane Theatre on

May 21, 1956. The book had been made into a hit film by Otto Preminger during the previous year, and the film had provided Frank Sinatra with one of his best dramatic roles as Frankie, the small-time Chicago gambler who becomes addicted to drugs. In the opening run of Kirkland's play, Frankie was compellingly portrayed by Robert Loggia. His downfall, leading to murder and suicide, is dispassionately shown through a series of short episodes, chronologically arranged, making the play more impressionistic than realistic. In one sense, the play was a return to the underworld that Kirkland had romantically portrayed in *Frankie and Johnnie*, but in *The Man with the Golden Arm*, the tone is stark and darkly shaded. The dialogue is rough and accurate, and Frankie's doom is inevitable. It is a hard play to like, one that challenges an audience, but it enjoyed a first run of seventy-three performances.

MANDINGO

Kirkland's last play was *Mandingo*, a ludicrous and sensationalized reworking of a ludicrous and sensationalized novel by Kyle Onstott. Ostensibly a study of the evils of slavery in antebellum Alabama, the play (like the book and the later film) revels in violence, racism, and sexual perversity. *Mandingo* opened at the Lyceum Theatre on May 22, 1961, with Franchot Tone as the vile plantation owner Warren Maxwell, Dennis Hopper as his crippled son Hammond, Brooke Hayward as Hammond's wife Blanche, and Rockne Tarkington as the Mandingo slave Mede. The play uses every racial and sexual stereotype imaginable: The alcoholic Warren Maxwell beats his slaves, breeds them to sell, and keeps a special one as his mistress. His son, who believes in more humane treatment of slaves, marries a Southern belle who has been her brother's lover and who develops an insatiable craving for the proud slave Mede. Disgusted by his wife, Hammond Maxwell falls in love with a beautiful octoroon, much to his father's outrage. The play ends with Blanche flogging the pregnant octoroon to death and the elder Maxwell shooting his son and the Mandingo in order to preserve the old Southern way of life. A critic in the

July, 1961, issue of *Theatre Arts* aptly put it, "The play is so offensively ill-written, wantonly violent, pointless and immoral that everyone connected with it should be ashamed." It closed after eight performances.

OTHER MAJOR WORKS

SCREENPLAYS: *Fast and Loose*, 1930; *Zoo in Budapest*, 1933; *Now and Forever*, 1934; *Adventures in Manhattan*, 1936; *Sutter's Gold*, 1936.

NONFICTION: "How Long *Tobacco Road*," 1939 (in *The New York Times*).

BIBLIOGRAPHY

Fearnow, Mark. *The American Stage and the Great Depression: A Cultural History of the Grotesque.* New York: Cambridge University Press, 1997. Contains a discussion of how Kirkland's *Tobacco Road* combined sex and poverty to create what the author called a "burlesque of anxiety." Details audience reaction and changes in the subsequent film version.

Howard, William L. "Caldwell on Stage and Screen." In *Erskine Caldwell Reconsidered*, edited by Edwin T. Arnold. Jackson: University Press of Mississippi, 1990. In this chapter about adaptations made of Caldwell's novels, Kirkland's interpretation of *Tobacco Road* is compared unfavorably to the original novel. Howard believes that the play distorted Caldwell's intentions, turning sympathetic understanding and a respect for the social realities of poor whites into slapstick comedy and sentimentality.

"Jack Kirkland Is Dead at Sixty-six; Was *Tobacco Road* Adapter." *The New York Times*, February 23, 1969, p. A73. This obituary is a good source of biographical facts and includes a list of the most notable writings. Kirkland was predisposed to *Tobacco Road* because his family's roots extended to a part of South Carolina very near tobacco-road country.

Edwin T. Arnold,
updated by William L. Howard

ALEKSIS KIVI
Aleksis Stenvall

Born: Palojoki, Finland; October 10, 1834
Died: Tuusula, Finland; December 31, 1872

PRINCIPAL DRAMA

Kullervo, wr. 1859-1860, revised pb. 1864, pr.
  1885
Nummisuutarit, pb. 1864, pr. 1875
Kihlaus, pb. 1866, pr. 1872 (*Eva*, 1980)
Olviretki Schleusingenissä, wr. 1866, pb. 1916
Karkurit, pb. 1867, pr. in Swedish 1872, pr. 1877
Yö ja päivä, pb. 1867, pr. 1875
Leo ja Liina, wr. 1867-1869, pb. 1878
Canzio, wr. 1867-1869, pr., pb. 1897 (fourth act),
  pr. 1901, pb. 1916
Selman juonet, wr. 1868-1869, pb. 1916 (fragment)
Alma, wr. 1868-1869, pb. 1916 (fragment)
Lea, pr., pb. 1869
Margareta, pb. 1871, pr. 1872

OTHER LITERARY FORMS

Aleksis Kivi's only novel, *Seitsemän veljestä*
(1870; *Seven Brothers*, 1929, revised 1973), is a cor-
nerstone of literature in Finnish; his lyric production,
although small and long regarded as subsidiary to his
novel and his dramas, also forms part of the classical
corpus of Finland's letters.

ACHIEVEMENTS

When Finland, since the twelfth century a part of
Sweden's Baltic empire, passed into Russian hands in
1808-1809, its theatrical history consisted essentially
of a few student plays, based partly on neo-Latin
originals, performed in Swedish at Abo Academy (in
Turku) in the middle of the seventeenth century, and,
subsequently, the sporadic appearances of strolling
players from Sweden and Germany. The opening of
theaters in Helsinki (1827), Viipuri (1832), and Turku
(1838) gave evidence of a stronger dramatic consciousness, but it was not until mid-century that texts
by native playwrights were produced. These plays
were still in Swedish, however, the language of edu-

cation, culture, and commerce in Finland at the time,
and it was not until May 10, 1869, when Aleksis
Kivi's *Lea* premiered at Helsinki's New Theater, that
the modern Finnish drama was born. The main role
had been memorized by an actress who knew no
Finnish, Hedvig Charlotte Raa; like other members of
the professional company at the New Theater, she
had been imported from Sweden.

Unhappily, Kivi's own increasing emotional difficulties kept him from attending the first performance
of *Lea*; indeed, it is doubtful that he ever saw any of
his plays performed. By the time Kivi's friend Kaarlo
Bergbom, a member of the Helsinki upper class and a
sometime playwright, had organized his Finnish Theater, Kivi was far gone in madness. The first appearance of Bergbom's troupe took place at a hotel in the
small coastal town of Pori on October 23, 1872, with
Kivi's *Margareta*; the repertoire of the ensemble,
which made its debut in Helsinki the following
March, also included Kivi's *Eva*. A staging of Kivi's
tragedy *Karkurit* (the fugitives) took place, in Swedish translation, at the New Theater on December 13
and 15, 1872; the proceeds from these performances
were used to pay for his funeral.

Thus Kivi has come to be regarded as the brilliant
and unfortunate pioneer, or martyr, of drama in Finnish; his statue—depicting Kivi seated, his head
bowed in melancholy—was unveiled, on his birthday,
in 1939, before Finland's National Theater in Helsinki. Only two of Kivi's comedies (and dramatiza-
tions of his novel, *Seven Brothers*), however, hold the
stage today: *Nummisuutarit* (the heath cobblers),
which has attained the status of a national play, and
the one-act *Eva*. In these works, his peculiar strengths
are best seen: his sympathy with weak and even silly
characters, his remarkable verbal inventiveness, and
his sense that ludicrous events contain their element
of sadness. In 1866, Kivi had planned to join a traveling theatrical company that another of his idealistic
patrician friends, Emil Nervander, intended to organize; the project, never carried out, is assumed to

have encouraged Kivi in his feverish dramatic production of the later 1860's. The modern novelist and dramatist Veijo Meri has conjectured that, if Nervander's plan had been realized, Kivi, "as playwright, dramaturg, director, and actor, would have been able to play as many-sided a role as . . . Shakespeare . . . in his time." Whether Kivi would have been able to expand his effective dramatic range, had he lived longer and regained his sanity, is a moot question. Probably, Kivi himself had ambitions of becoming a Finnish Shakespeare; instead, he became Finland's Ludvig Holberg—but a Holberg drunk on the rich possibilities of a language hitherto unused for dramatic literature.

BIOGRAPHY

Born Aleksis Stenvall on October 10, 1834, Aleksis Kivi (he later took this as his nom de plume) came from the northern reaches of Uusimaa, the province in which Helsinki lies, a region still known, at the time of his birth, for its lawlessness. Indeed, Kivi's paternal great-uncle, Matti Stenvall, was sentenced to life imprisonment for banditry in 1829, spending the rest of his days incarcerated at Suomenlinna, the fortress-complex in Helsinki harbor. Matti's brother, Kivi's grandfather, was a sailor who returned to the countryside only late in life, and Kivi's father, the village tailor, had briefly attended school in the capital and, at the time of his confirmation, was described in Nurmijärvi's records as a "Swedish-speaker." The Stenvalls were certainly well known in their home community; the command of Swedish gave Kivi's father considerable authority (especially on legal matters) in his village. He was, as well, ambitious for his offspring: His oldest son, Juhani, nine years Aleksis's senior, had been sent to a private school to learn Swedish, the key to business and social success, and when the gifted Aleksis, the youngest of the four sons, was dispatched to Helsinki at the age of twelve for schooling, Juhani, then employed as a clerk in the capital, was expected to help with the boy's expenses, which he did grudgingly.

Kivi's schooldays were made difficult not only by his poverty but also by the disparity in age between him and his fellow pupils, who as a rule were between three and four years younger. His education took place entirely in Swedish, which he mastered so completely that he at first thought of following a literary career in the language. His knowledge of Swedish also gave him access to the authors who perhaps meant the most to him in his own literary creation: Ludvig Holberg, whose Danish was easy to grasp, and Miguel de Cervantes, Homer, and William Shakespeare, all of whom he devoured in Swedish, learning whole passages of Karl August Hagberg's translation of Shakespeare by heart, including the entire role of Cordelia in *King Lear* (pr. c. 1605-1606). Each summer, the boy returned to the Finnish-speaking milieu of Nurmijärvi; Helsinki itself, and much of its adjacent territory, was still overwhelmingly Swedish in language.

After many vicissitudes, Kivi, at the age of eighteen, completed his preparatory training at Helsinki's "advanced elementary school," He then decided to prepare privately for the university and spent some time at cramming schools very much like the school Henrik Ibsen had attended in Norway a few years earlier, taking the university entrance examinations in December, 1857. Again, with characteristic dilatoriness, he delayed his formal entrance to the university until 1859 and pursued his studies in a desultory fashion, staying on the enrollment books until 1865 but never attaining an academic degree.

The advantages he drew from these apparently aimless years lay, on one hand, in the acquisition of supportive and sometimes affluent friends (such as Bergbom, Nervander, and the German-born poet Julius Krohn), who admired the genius from the countryside, and, on the other, in the inspiration he drew from two of his teachers: Elias Lönnrot, the compiler of the Finnish national epic, the *Kalevala*, and the aesthetician and critic Fredrik Cygnaeus, who lectured on drama (and who, in 1853, had published an essay, "The Tragic Element," on the newly restored national epic). Lönnrot and Cygnaeus may fairly be regarded as the godfathers of Kivi's first play, the tragedy *Kullervo*, based on cantos 31-36 of the *Kalevala*. The first version of the play, still in manuscript, got Kivi a prize, in March, 1860, from the Finnish Literary Society, for "the best theatrical work in Finnish"; Kivi suddenly became the great hope of a literature still *in statu nascendi*. Dissatisfied with what he had written, Kivi continued to work at the play until, entirely revised, it was published by the Finnish Literary Society in 1864. The same year, he issued another play, *Nummisuutarit*, a peasant comedy. (The cost of printing was paid by his generous friend, Bergbom.) Many years before, at the time of his qualifying examination, Kivi had written a sketch in Swedish (now lost) called "The Bridal Dance"; he developed his major theatrical work from this modest source. (Kivi had shown the manuscript as a proof of his talent to Topelius, Cygnaeus, and Johan Vilhelm Snellman—the last-named a brilliant polemical stylist in Swedish who, paradoxically, was the leading advocate of Finland as a monolingual, Finnish-speaking entity.)

Work on these two projects, the tragedy and the comedy, had been carried out in part at a farm leased by Juhani, Myllymaa, in Nurmijärvi (whose Finnish dialect Kivi employed in the play about the cobblers on the heath). He stayed there from the winter of 1862 until the spring of the following year. He was thrown out, he told Bergbom later on, by the niggardly Juhani. In considering Kivi's unhappy relations with his brothers, one should make some effort to imagine their side of the story. Kivi had not yet found, and never would find, a means of supporting himself. He was already a heavy drinker, and as such could embarrass his siblings, who in particular needed the goodwill of the noble Adlercreutz family, on whose estates they found employment, and he was not above contrasting his fine city friends with his intellectually limited brothers.

After his departure from the farm, Kivi moved to the nearby district of Siuntio, where he found refuge with Charlotta Lönnqvist, a successful countryside cateress some nineteen years his senior, who sheltered him at her farm, Fanjunkars, for the next half-decade and more. The relationship between Kivi and Lönnqvist, whom he simply called "the woman" in his letters, has given rise to much comment among Kivi scholars: It has been argued that she was a replacement for Kivi's beloved mother (who was forty-one when Aleksis was born and died in the very year

of his removal to Fanjunkars). In earlier, hagiographic Kivi research, the possibility of a love relationship was violently denied; but less prudish scholarship, somewhat encouraged by *Leo ja Liina*, Kivi's semiautobiographical little play about the attraction between a twenty-year-old youth and a rather mannish twenty-eight-year-old woman, has concluded that the two became lovers and were regarded as such by their neighbors. Whatever the physical case may have been, the sojourn at Fanjunkars was the most productive period in Kivi's life, although he often complained about his linguistic isolation. Siuntio was a Swedish-speaking district, and Lönnqvist herself could not read what Kivi wrote.

While at Fanjunkars, Kivi's fortunes seemed to take a marked turn for the better. In 1865, *Nummisuutarit* got a prize of twenty-five hundred marks announced by the government as an "encouragement to awaken and further literary activity within the country." Kivi's cause was aided in particular by his former teacher, Cygnaeus, who wrote an enthusiastic review of the comedy for Zacharias Topelius's newspaper, *Helsingfors tidningar*. The selection of Kivi annoyed Johan Ludvig Runeberg's wife, Fredrika, who thought her husband deserved it for his Greek tragedy, *Kungarne på Salamis* (1863; the kings on Salamis). She suspected that Kivi had been chosen because, alone among the candidates, he had written in Finnish. Yet she went on to confess that her knowledge of Finnish was insufficient for her to judge the quality of Kivi's work.

Grown somewhat more self-confident, Kivi brought out his lyric collection *Kanervala* (the heather dweller) in 1866, continued to write play after play for a Finnish stage that, thus far, existed only in his imagination and those of his admiring friends, and worked at his novel, *Seven Brothers*, which he submitted to the Finnish Literary Society in the spring of 1869, at the same time that his play *Lea* was produced at the New Theater. The novel was published in four installments by the Society; as soon as the last of these had appeared, August Ahlqvist, Lönnrot's successor as professor of Finnish language and literature at the university, wrote a savage review (in Swedish) of the book for a conservative newspaper, in which he described Kivi's picture of the undisciplined seven brothers, who flee civilization for a time, as an insult to the "quiet and earnest" Finnish people.

Frightened, the Finnish Literary Society was very slow to come to its former favorite's defense; a statement by Kivi's champion, the generous Cygnaeus, was delayed by the latter's long illness; and the promised book edition of the novel was postponed until 1873. The blow was too much for the labile Kivi. In the spring of 1870, he made one of his many trips, away from Lönnqvist's guardian eyes, to Helsinki and, after a drinking bout that lasted several days, fell victim to delirium tremens. His drunkenness led to painful scenes at his refuge in the countryside. In the autumn of the same year, left alone at Fanjunkars while Lönnqvist arranged a wedding reception, he was assailed by severe anxiety and followed her to the celebration, causing a general scandal by his behavior. For nine months, from May, 1871, to February, 1872, he was confined at Lapinlahti Asylum in Helsinki (the exact nature of his illness, never fully diagnosed, later became the object of fascinating research by a psychiatrist at that institution); then he was released in the care of his brother Alpertti. Accounts of his last months make painful reading, especially the stories of his begging for food at nearby farms. Alpertti, who, after his late brother's fame was secure, played guide for pilgrims to the site of Kivi's death, seems to have kept the deranged man on short rations. Kivi died of an inflammation of the lungs on New Year's Eve, 1872; his last words, like those of Johann Wolfgang von Goethe and Henrik Ibsen, have given rise to much speculation. They were: "I live, I live."

ANALYSIS

Three chief impulses are at work in the dramas of Aleksis Kivi. The first is his desire to create classics that, by their very presence, would make literature in Finnish a worthy part of European letters. The second is the infinitely more modest wish to write short plays readily accessible to amateur actors. Kivi could only hope that, sooner or later, professional theater in Finnish would come into being. The third is his own

urge toward self-expression. Scholarship has detected self-portraits, or at least self-comments, in his plays on the stage of his imagination and of aspects of his own life.

KULLERVO

The publication of the national epic, the *Kalevala* (in 1835, and, revised and expanded, in 1849), had been a source of intense national pride. Kivi was one of the first authors to use its themes for drama in his *Kullervo*; Topelius's curious mix of Greek and Finnish material in *Prinsessan of Cypern* (1860; the Princess of Cyprus) is another example. Even if Cygnaeus had not suggested that the Kullervo story in the *Kalevala* was an apt subject for treatment in a tragedy, Kivi might well have been drawn to it; it provided expression for his own sense of isolation and his awareness of his great-uncle's fate. When Kullervo, in the play's most famous monologue, laments that he has been "locked into a mountain of steel," into a "cell so small that he can only sit curled up within it," Kivi must have thought of Matti Stenvall, chained for life to a wall inside Suomenlinna. In Lönnrot's *Kalevala*, Kullervo's family has been wiped out (or so he believes), by his evil uncle Untamo. Brutally brought up by Untamo and sold as a slave to the smith, Ilmarinen, Kullervo takes revenge on Ilmarinen's malicious wife, who has given him a stone instead of bread as he goes out to tend the family's cattle. He drives the livestock into a bog, where they drown. By magic, he then gives cattle's shape to bears and wolves, and brings them home, where they devour his tormentor. Learning that his parents are still alive, Kullervo finds them on the frontier of Lapland, but discovers that one of his sisters has vanished while berrying. Incapable of carrying out even the simplest of tasks at his father's farm (a trait left over from his unhappy childhood and youth), he is sent to deliver the taxes, and as he returns, he meets and swiftly seduces a young girl. Realizing, after their night of love, that they are siblings, she kills herself. Kullervo tells his mother what has happened, and she persuades him not to take his own life. Cursed by his father, his brother, and his surviving sister, he sets out to take bloody vengeance on Untamo; going home again, he finds that his family has been slaughtered, as the feud continues. Accompanied only by the family dog, Musti, he roams the woods until he comes to the place of the encounter with his sister; there, "the luckless one" throws himself on his sword.

Kivi makes several important changes in the tale: Forever lonely in the original, the drama's Kullervo is given both a devoted companion, Kimmo, and a boastful and cowardly one, Nyyrikki—Shakespeare's Pistol transferred to the Finnish wilderness. In the second act, Kullervo, pondering revenge, is confronted by two spirits of the woods, the evil Ajatar, who urges him to follow his murderous urge, and the good Sinipiika, who counsels self-control. (A resemblance to the myth of Hercules at the crossroads, the subject of the most important piece of Swedish literature from the seventeenth century, a hexameter poem by Georg Stiernhielm, has been noted in the scene.) Though far more introspective than the impulsive Kullervo of the epic, Kivi's hero, not heeding the wiser voice, slays Ilmarinen's wife. Aware of nineteenth century sensibilities and stage practicalities, however, Kivi does not employ the original's magnificently grotesque transmogrification of the cattle; rather, he simply has Kullervo slay the woman after she calls him a slave. Similarly, the third act deals in a very gingerly fashion with the seduction of the sister, here given the name of Ainikki. While Kullervo is in pursuit of Untamo, Kivi causes him to fall in with a company of bear hunters, crude and almost comical lovers of violence for its own sake, who show more than a passing resemblance to the members of Karl Moor's band in Friedrich Schiller's *Die Räuber* (pb. 1781; *The Robbers*, 1792). At the end, Kimmo goes mad on learning that Kullervo's parents have been slain in the feud; obeying the voice of his mother's ghost, Kullervo withdraws to the forest, where he kills himself. His mother's spirit has asked the forest nymph Sinipiika to forgive his deeds, and his death is witnessed by the three great heroes of the *Kalevala*, Väinämöinen, Lemminkäinen, and Kullervo's sometime master, Ilmarinen, who, though he still mourns his wife, prays that the youth will be granted peace in death.

Readers, or viewers of the play's occasional revivals, may smile at the apparently old-fashioned device of the evil nymphs and good nymphs and the mother's ghost; the exchanges between the mother's spirit and Sinipiika in the final act are particularly trying. It must be remembered, however, that the young Ibsen, almost simultaneously, used similar melodramatic effects: for example, the struggles between Aurelia and Furia in his *Catalina* (pb. 1850, rev. pb. 1875; *Catiline*, 1921) and the appearance of the vengeful spirit of Bishop Nicholas in *Kongsemnerne* (pb. 1863; *The Pretenders*, 1890). Also, choosing prose instead of blank verse, Kivi broke free of the standard linguistic dress of high tragedy in his age—just as Ibsen did in *Hærmænde paa Helgeland* (pr., pb. 1858; *The Vikings at Helgeland*, 1890), *Fru Inger til Østraat* (pr. 1855; *Lady Inger of Østraat*, 1906), and, again, *The Pretenders*. Although the play does not expressly address the topic, *Kullervo* is one of those several idea dramas of the mid-century (such as Friedrich Hebbel's trilogy *Die Nibelungen* of 1861) in which pagan and Christian codes of conduct are contrasted. Most important, in the depiction of the violent yet intelligent Kullervo, the gifted man who cannot rise above his misfortunes but rather is twisted by them, Kivi made a first effort to plumb his own nature. Kullervo, it is hinted, realizes that, whatever effort he may make to escape, he is trapped, as much by personality as by circumstance.

NUMMISUUTARIT

Kullervo has a single complex character, the eponymous hero; the main strength of *Nummisuutarit* lies in its large gallery of memorable portraits. Writers on Kivi have repeatedly said that the debt to Holberg is obvious: The dictatorial mother of the play's main family, Martta, is kin to the shrewish Rille in *Jeppe paa Bjerget* (pr. 1722, pb. 1723; *Jeppe of the Hill*, 1906), and Sepeteus, the half-educated parish clerk, resembles Per Degn in *Erasmus Montanus* (wr. 1723, pb. 1731; English translation, 1885). Nevertheless, in both cases, Kivi has expanded the pattern; he lets his audience know that a weak husband and silly sons have turned Martta into a bossy and scheming woman, and he gives Sepeteus a voice of reason amid the complications of *Nummisuutarit*'s final act, where the play's several strands, in the best comic tradition, are brought together. The male members of Martta's family are prone to an extraordinary credulity: Believing that he has arranged a marriage between his older son, Esko, and Kreeta, the foster daughter of a prosperous farmer, the cobbler Topias sends the trusting Esko off to fetch his bride. (Both Martta and Topias want to get Esko married as quickly as possible, lest a mysterious inheritance, left behind by a whimsical old corporal, fall to Jaana, who has been reared as a ward of the cobbler's household. The first of the children to marry, Esko or Jaana, will get the money. The high-minded Jaana *does* want to get married, to the honest smith Kristo; but she is moved by true love, not the thought of the five hundred rixdollars.) Accompanied by the quick-witted Mikko, Esko proceeds to the nearby farm; it takes him some time to realize that the wedding preparations there are intended not for him but for Kreeta's union with Jaakko, a maker of wooden shoes who wants to be a farmer, like his father-in-law-to-be. Baffled, then foolishly aggressive, and egged on by Mikko, Esko is twice bested in fights, first with the hot-tempered Teemu, a fiddler, and then with Teemu and the fiddler's father. Unable to bear so much humiliation, Esko goes berserk and wrecks the bridal hall. The angry guests at their heels, Esko and Mikko run away. The scene is not unlike the conclusion of the second act of Ibsen's *Peer Gynt* (pb. 1867, English translation, 1892): There, to be sure, the outsider Peer abducts the willing bride.

Meanwhile, Iivari, Esko's younger brother, has been sent to the city to buy provisions for the coming nuptials of Esko and Kreeta at Topias's house; already as assiduous a toper as his father, Iivari has fallen in with his maternal uncle, Sakeri (a shiftless former policeman whom his sister, Martta, thoroughly despises) and has drunk up all the money entrusted to him. Terrified of Martta, nephew and uncle decide that they must track down a criminal who has robbed a foreign nobleman, and then use the reward money to save the day. Their plan is overheard by Niko, Jaana's long-lost seaman father, who disguises himself as the robber described in the warrant, thinking in this way to get a free ride home. His plan succeeds; he lets himself be "captured." As afraid of confronting his mother as Iivari has been, Esko, in the

fourth act, is persuaded by Mikko to take his first drink. Similarly fearful of what the hard-handed Martta will do to him, Mikko wants to escape Esko's company. He flees, leaving the hopelessly intoxicated Esko alone—but only briefly, for Esko meets the clarinetist Antres, who is on his way to the festivities at Topias's place, and, in another fit of rage, throttles him.

At the finale, the situation of the several culprits grows darker still. Iivari and Sakeri learn that they have been tricked by the clever Niko. Esko has to confess that his expedition has come to a catastrophic end. Mikko, who has sprained his foot, is hauled before the terrible-tempered Martta. Yet all's well that ends well. Niko gives his blessing to the immediate marriage of Jaana, his daughter, and Kristo. Generously, Jaana proposes that the inheritance be divided between Esko and herself. At the same time, with remarkable forgiveness, she thanks Martta for the stern upbringing the tyrannical woman has given her. Encouraged by Niko, Iivari decides to go to sea. Esko resolves to stay at home forever, and Martta, mollified by the turn of events, invites the company to Esko's wedding board, which will now serve as an engagement banquet for Jaana and Kristo. The play ends with a procession to the sound of Antres's clarinet; he has nicely recovered—the impulsive Esko is not a murderer after all. Plainly, the intrigue is a little artificial; yet *Nummisuutarit* is full of the same good humor and understanding that characterize great epithalamic comedies from more elegant milieus, Pierre-Augustin Caron de Beaumarchais's *La Folle Journée: Ou, Le Mariage de Figaro* (wr. 1775-1778, pr. 1784, pb. 1785; *The Marriage of Figaro*, 1784), for example, or Oscar Wilde's *The Importance of Being Earnest: A Trivial Comedy for Serious People* (pr. 1895).

What makes the play a fascinating and satisfying stage work is Kivi's ability to turn comic types into full human beings: Martta; Sepeteus; the boastful but timid Topias; the loudmouthed Iivari; the irascible Teemu (who is deathly afraid of *his* father); Mikko, the troublemaker not nearly as clever as he thinks; the genuinely bright but irresponsible Niko; the baffled and then terrified Antres; and above all, Esko. Suppressed and gullible, strong of limb and weak of mind, he will never escape (nor does he want to) from the family cocoon. Casual theatergoers may laugh at Esko's outbursts of violence; they are the expressions, though, of a permanently stunted—and quite lovable—personality.

EVA

The same leavening of the burlesque with a hint of melancholy is to be found in *Eva*, in which, again, an inescapable fate is described in comic terms. Two tailors, Aapeli and Eenokki, well along in years, have spent their lives as bachelors; Aapeli has decided to take a wife, choosing Eeva, the experienced housekeeper of some "young gentlemen" in the neighborhood. Eeva, though, is too sophisticated to endure more than a small taste of Aapeli's life and abruptly leaves the engagement dinner at his cottage; Aapeli and Eenokki dance a little bridal waltz together, accompanied by the song of Jooseppi, Aapeli's apprentice. After some wondering about what has gone wrong, Aapeli is happy to sink back into his old life, and Eenokki is happy that the danger has past. Eeva, with her citified airs, is well out of the marital trap, too. Modern audiences may spy elements in the little comedy of which their forebears, laughing heartily, were unaware: Eenokki, it is plain, is a better bride for Aapeli than Eeva (or any other woman) could have been.

OLVIRETKI SCHLEUSINGENISSÄ

Eva has often and rightly been called a by-blow of *Nummisuutarit*; Aapeli and Eenokki come, as it were, from Topias's and Esko's good-natured village. Unfortunately, Kivi could be lured away from this beloved place into other realms. In *Olviretki Schleusingenissä* (the beer campaign at Schleusingen), Kivi at least stayed close to a theme, drunkenness, that he knew very well, even if the setting was foreign to him. He had read a newspaper item about an episode in the Austro-Prussian War of 1866 in which a small band of Prussians bloodlessly conquered a much larger force of Bavarians, addled by excessive consumption of beer. (Once again, Kivi's attitude toward alcohol is ambiguous; it can save lives and liberate imaginations, as it does here.) Nevertheless, unable to use the local color of Nurmijärvi, Kivi turns to the

time-honored figure of the boastful soldier and essays the mock-heroic mode: The Prussians manage to persuade the intoxicated Bavarians that they have entered the realm of the dead and are among the heroes of antiquity. (Kivi evidently meant to emulate Holberg's Homeric parody *Ulysses von Ithacia*, pr. 1724, pb. 1725, but his hand is much heavier than Holberg's.) The play, it must be added, was among Kivi's manuscripts, and he perhaps intended to give it a final tightening; it could have gained, surely, by a reduction of its large cast of semi-amusing military men.

KARKURIT

In the play *Karkurit*, Kivi demonstrated much loftier literary ambitions. The weakness that besets *Olviretki Schleusingenissä*, the stultifying effect of an unfamiliar milieu, is magnified, even though the setting is in Finland. Kivi attempted to move the story of Romeo and Juliet to a Finnish manor house, a social world to which he seldom had admittance. The son of Baron Markus, Tyko, has been a prisoner of war; returning to the family estate, he learns the Niilo, his foster brother and an imitation of the villainous Franz Moor in *The Robbers*, has deprived him of his beloved Elma, the daughter of Baron Mauno. She has been led to believe that her marriage to Niilo will free her father from the burden of debts owed to Markus. When the play is over, Tyko, Elma, and Niilo are all dead, and the survivors of the two families are reconciled. Admirers of Kivi have attempted to find poetic virtues in the several descriptions of Finnish nature *Karkurit* contains. Its best passages, perhaps, are those in which Kivi—here having learned from Runeberg's little verse epic, *Julkvällen* (1841; Christmas Eve)—portrays the tender relationship between the much-tried Elma and her foster sister, Hanna.

CANZIO

Kivi's *Canzio* was described by him in January, 1868, as "a five-act tragedy, which takes place on the banks of the Arno." For explorers of Kivi's personality, the play's interest lies in its attempts to fathom the evil that has taken possession of the inherently noble hero. (Thus it bears traces of the familiar, Byronic pattern continued by Alfred de Musset in another play with a Florentine setting, his *Lorenzaccio*, pb. 1834; English translation, 1905.) Canzio is a proclaimed atheist, a richly gifted but unhappy youth torn, like many other figures in nineteenth century stage works, between women, evil and good—between the wildly passionate Marcia, the widow of a robber chieftain, and the saintly Mariamne, Canzio's fiancée. Mariamne's goodness is reinforced by the figure of Rachel, Canzio's devoted sister, who has looked after him since childhood. Like so many of his contemporaries, Kivi believed firmly in the corpse-strewn stage: Claudio, Canzio's dearest friend, insults Marcia and is challenged to a duel by Canzio. Marcia gives Claudio's servant a cup of poison for his master, and Claudio falls easily beneath Canzio's sword, but, before he dies, he tells Canzio the truth about Marcia: that she is in fact Flaminia, the murderer of Canzio's father. As the police lead the femme fatale away, she momentarily slips free and stabs the unhappy Rachel with Canzio's sword. (Just prior to the curtain's final fall, a policeman reports that Marcia has escaped a second time and, "strong and lithe as a lion," has thrown herself into a ravine.) Once more, Kivi is derivative. Rachel's madness after Canzio's death suggests Ophelia, and the cynical joviality of Varro, Canzio's uncle, suggests Sir John Falstaff; in fact, the play is often described as a tardy imitation of Shakespeare, Kivi's last effort to make a great tragedy for the Finnish stage.

Yö ja päivä and Lea

In contrast to the ponderous *Karkurit* and *Canzio* (which was left unfinished by Kivi, in two versions), the short plays from the latter years of Kivi's brief creative career were of great value to Bergbom in filling out his repertoire with material at once actable and edifying. *Yö ja päivä* (night and day) shows how, in a single summer night, Liisa, blind since childhood, miraculously recovers her sight and then reconciles her family with that of her beloved, Tapani. The little play is based on a popular Danish Romantic work of 1845, *Kong Renés Datter*, by Henrik Hertz. In *Lea*, the heroine succeeds in leading her father, Saakeus, and the man she loves, Aram, to a belief in Jesus as he passes through Jericho. (Of course, Jesus does not appear onstage in this expansion of the story of Zacchaeus, the rich publican, from Luke 19:2-9.) Even the Pharisee Joas, to whom Lea has become engaged, in compliance with her father's wishes, is touched; he leaves Zacchaeus's home without complaint, as the tax gatherer embraces his daughter and Aram.

Margareta

Finns liked to think of their new theater as a place of uplift and instruction, in contrast to what they argued was the worldly and frivolous theater of the country's Swedish speakers, and such plays as *Yö ja päivä* and *Lea* were perfect instruments for this earnest concept, as was Kivi's final play, *Margareta*. Runeberg's narrative poems about Finnish bravery in the war of 1808-1809, *Fänrik Ståls sägner* (1848-1860; *The Tales of Ensign Stål*, 1925), had become enormously popular; Kivi's friend Nervander had sketched a drama from the same conflict, about the capitulation of the Helsinki fortress, Suomenlinna, to the Russians. Bergbom had taken up Nervander's plan and then passed it along to Kivi for completion. A young officer, Anian, has been present at the surrender of the fortress; his fiancée, Margareta, is filled with shame, only to grow ecstatic on learning, from Anian, that he plans to join the Swedish-Finnish army in the north, there to seek glorious death on the battlefield. The play's early popularity no doubt came from the fact that it so strongly reminded audiences of Runeberg's patriotic rhetoric; what actually belongs to Kivi in the play is its affection for Finland's nature and not its salute to blind Finnish valor.

Later works

Among the manuscripts Kivi left behind are *Leo ja Liina* (Leo and Liina) and the fragmentary *Alma* and *Selman juonet* (Selma's dodges). In the completed play, Kivi looked bravely at his own dependence on Charlotta Lönnqvist: Leo is inspired by the presence of a new railroad line to think about migration to America but realizes that he is in fact deeply in love with the brusque Liina. The two fragments have nothing of the confession about them, but are meant to be, above all else, effective works for the stage; in a letter, Kivi called them the best things he had written. *Alma*, in which the spirit of a young woman is tested by reports of a series of misfortunes, was fashioned as a new starring role for Hedwig Charlotte Raa, the actress who had created Lea's part.

Selman juonet is a comedy in the Holbergian vein. A tyrannical father, Herman, wants his daughter, Selma, to marry the miser Fokas, but her brother Konrad, disguising himself as a magician from Lapland, persuades Fokas that he should reject Selma and take Thekla, who is in fact Konrad's fiancée. The text breaks off here, but it is clear what will happen. Herman has observed the foolish superstitions of Fokas and will no longer place any barrier in the way of Selma and her young man, Kilian, while Konrad will marry Thekla.

Kivi attempted too much in the years leading up to his mental collapse. The disappointment even his admirers feel at the large dramatic production after *Kullervo*, *Nummisuutarit*, and *Eva* must be tempered by the thought that, almost single-handedly, he was attempting to create representative works for a new literature, in a language hitherto little used for literary purposes, and that he was at work on his novelistic masterpiece, *Seven Brothers*, while he struggled to provide a whole theatrical repertoire.

OTHER MAJOR WORKS

LONG FICTION: *Seitsemän veljestä*, 1870 (*Seven Brothers*, 1929, revised 1973).

POETRY: *Kanervala*, 1866; *Odes*, 1994.

BIBLIOGRAPHY

Ahokas, Jaakko. *A History of Finnish Literature*. Bloomington: Indiana University Press, 1973. Presents a broad overview of Finnish literature, touching on Kivi's fiction and drama. Bibliography.

James, Anthony. *Introducing Kivi: Poems and Translations*. Swansea, England: Karhu, 1994. Although this work focuses on Kivi's poems, it includes an introduction that looks at the life and works of the Finnish author.

Vähämäki, Börje. "Aleksis Kivi's *Kullervo*: A Historical Drama of Ideas." *Scandinavian Studies* 50 (1978): 269-291. This essay examines Kivi's best-known play, *Kullervo*, from a historical perspective.

George C. Schoolfield

HEINRICH VON KLEIST

Born: Frankfurt an der Oder, Prussia (now in Germany); October 18, 1777
Died: Wannsee bei Potsdam, Prussia (now in Germany); November 21, 1811

PRINCIPAL DRAMA

Die Familie Schroffenstein, pb. 1803, pr. 1804 (*The Feud of the Schroffensteins*, 1916)
Amphitryon, pb. 1807, pr. 1899 (English translation, 1962)
Penthesilea, pb. 1808, pr. 1876 (English translation, 1959)
Der zerbrochene Krug, pr. 1808, pb. 1811 (*The Broken Jug*, 1930)
Robert Guiskard, pb. 1808, pr. 1901 (English translation, 1962)
Das Käthchen von Heilbronn: Oder, Die Feuerprobe, pr., pb. 1810 (*Cathy of Heilbronn: Or, The Trial by Fire*, 1927)
Die Hermannsschlacht, pb. 1821, pr. 1839
Prinz Friedrich von Homburg, pr., pb. 1821 (*The Prince of Homburg*, 1875)

OTHER LITERARY FORMS

Heinrich von Kleist's fame as the author of short stories and novellas almost matches his fame as a playwright. The novella *Michael Kohlhaas* (1810; English translation, 1844), perhaps Kleist's best-known narrative work, tells the story of a Reformation-era merchant whose thirst for justice becomes an obsession, overturning the social order but never achieving satisfaction. *Die Marquise von O——* (1808; *The Marquise of O——*, 1960), incorporating themes of objective versus subjective reality often found in

Heinrich von Kleist (Hulton Archive by Getty Images)

Kleist's plays, presents the predicament of a young unmarried woman impregnated while unconscious. She knows herself to be virtuous, yet she is spurned by society. Other stories include "Das Erdbeben in Chile" (1807; "The Earthquake in Chile," 1946), "Die Verlobung in St. Domingo" (1811; "The Betrothal in St. Domingo," 1960), "Das Bettelweib von Locarno" (1811; "The Foundling," 1960), and "Die heilige Cäcilie: Oder, Die Gewalt der Musik" (1811; "The Duel," 1960). Much of Kleist's fiction can be found in the two-volume *Erzählungen* (1810-1811; *"The Marquise of O" and Other Stories*, 1960).

ACHIEVEMENTS

Perhaps the most misunderstood of German literary figures, Heinrich von Kleist was long considered a cheerleader of Prussian militarism. Critics misread the profound criticism of the military establishment in the play *The Prince of Homburg*, seeing only the highly emotional patriotism. There is still disagree-

ment between those critics who consider Kleist an early Romantic with Ludwig Tieck and Clemens Brentano and those who emphasize his kinship with Friedrich Schiller and Johann Wolfgang von Goethe, the giants of German classicism.

Kleist's appeal to modern readers is attested by the many adaptations of his works. The best-selling novel *Ragtime* (1975), by E. L. Doctorow, follows closely the plot of *Michael Kohlhaas*, and director Eric Rohmer's film *Die Marquise von O* (1976) received great critical acclaim. The French playwright Jean Giraudoux added his touch to the Amphitryon material in 1929 with *Amphitryon 38*. Georg Kaiser's *Zweimal Amphitryon* (1944; twice Amphitryon) and the 1968 play *Amphitryon* by Peter Hacks (English translation, 1970) show the further adaptation of the mythological material Kleist himself had adapted from Plautus and Molière. Finally, poets from the early Romantics to the expressionists and existentialists have acknowledged their debt to Kleist.

BIOGRAPHY

The tragedy of Bernd Heinrich Wilhelm von Kleist's brief life was determined by the extremely limited role of the minor aristocracy in eighteenth and nineteenth century Prussia. Originally semi-independent rulers in a feudal sense, the landed aristocracy moved up into a small court nobility supported by investments—or down, as with Kleist's family, into a military caste. A Junker was not permitted to practice law or medicine, to engage in trade, or to join the middle class in any manner. Kleist, sickened with military brutality, resigned his commission after seven lost years. Kleist wrote that he had been constantly troubled by the inevitable conflict between his duty as an officer and his duty as a human being. The soldiers seemed little more than slaves to Kleist, the famed Prussian discipline a living monument to tyranny. Giving up a military career was synonymous with giving up membership in the Junker class, at least for the landless Kleist. Therefore, when at the age of twenty-two he became a student of government and philosophy at Frankfurt an der Oder, he began writing his name without the aristocratic "von." In giving up his military career, Kleist was giving up his heritage, his pride, his class, his future security, and even a portion of his name.

The career for which Kleist was preparing himself during his student years was that of a government trade administrator. The closing of two doors ended Kleist's hopes for such a career. Kleist discovered in 1800 that Immanuel Kant, by detailing the limits of human perception, threw all human knowledge into doubt. The second door closed the same year. Kleist went on a secret mission for the Prussian government, discovering in the process that his future employment would consist almost totally of industrial espionage. Thereafter Kleist wrote plays and short stories, traveled feverishly, flirted with the notion of becoming a Swiss peasant farmer, made unsuccessful stabs at joining the French army or the Austrian army, suffered a nervous breakdown, and was imprisoned for six months by the French as a spy. During a brief time in Dresden (1807-1809), Kleist interacted with a literary circle. In collaboration with the political philosopher Adam Müller, Kleist published the journal *Phöbus*. In 1811, Kleist successfully published a daily newspaper, the *Berliner Abendblätter*. When the newspaper succumbed to vindictive censorship, Kleist was left without money and without alternatives.

Probably the bitterest blow Kleist suffered was Goethe's condemnation of his work—an ironic twist because it was the very qualities that Kleist shared with the young Goethe that were so intolerable to the old Goethe. An incurably ill woman of Kleist's acquaintance, Henriette Vogel, implored him to end her life. Kleist shot her, then himself, in the Potsdam countryside near the Wannsee. Kleist was thirty-four years old. The government-controlled newspapers and journals of the day exploited his suicide as evidence of the sickness and immorality of the new literature.

ANALYSIS

In Heinrich von Kleist's works, extremes of emotion, often combined with natural catastrophes or war, illuminate the contradictions inherent in the human condition. Kleist was especially concerned with the limits of human knowledge and its interplay with

other modes of perception, such as intuition, instinct, and the operations of the unconscious mind.

THE FEUD OF THE SCHROFFENSTEINS

The great stress laid on family relationships in Kleist's novellas, as well as in his play *The Feud of the Schroffensteins*, suggests that family motifs in the other plays emanate from a single family theme. Rupert Schroffenstein, for example, seems to return in the dark excesses and desperation of Amphitryon, Piachi ("The Foundling"), and to some extent Michael Kohlhaas. The innocence and inner serenity of Kathy, Agnes, Alkmene, and the Marquise of O seem similar or identical.

Much has been written about the unsolved mystery of Kleist, especially his penchant for constructing metaphysical analogies without revealing the key. Family relationships connect people without their volition, sometimes without their knowledge. To examine the often mysterious workings of the family in Kleist's works may serve to clarify some other Kleistian mysteries, such as the interplay of truth, human knowledge, perception, intuition, and the unconscious. An investigation of the role of the family in Kleist's works must necessarily start with *The Feud of the Schroffensteins*, a five-act play in blank verse. Kleist wrote the play as a spoof of contemporary knight-in-armor potboilers—hence the one-sided extremism of the characters. In the course of this play, every turn of the plot leads to the most horrible consequences imaginable. Characters jump to conclusions and threaten terrible acts of revenge for supposed crimes. Kleist, who wrote the play with tongue firmly in cheek and who could hardly speak for laughing when reading his play aloud, saw it taken very seriously. Indeed, it enjoyed more popularity than many of the knight-in-armor plays that it was meant to satirize. Originally titled *Die Familie Ghonorez*, then *Die Familie Thierez*, the play was moved to a German setting in its final version. Totally misunderstood by the public, it was Kleist's most successful play during his lifetime.

The religious ceremony in the opening scene of *The Feud of the Schroffensteins* is revealed to be a blasphemous one dedicated solely to revenge. A transformation of human beings into vicious beasts occurs during this scene. The participants in the ceremony are not even called people but, rather, wild ones. It is a logical continuation of this development, in which Rupert claims—in a long, sermonlike harangue—that the mercy of ravenous wolves and other carnivores would be preferable to Sylvester's mercy. Rupert announces his conviction that the child's fable of Nature has been exploded by the murder of his son. Qualities such as love, innocence, and purity are as believable as talking animals. Rupert says that the last vestige of human feeling has been extinguished. The other house of Schroffenstein has become a brood of poisonous snakes to be exterminated relentlessly. The final message Rupert sends to Sylvester clearly has neither human nor natural origin; by the testimony of his own words, Rupert has deserted humanity and Nature to become a demon thirsting for Sylvester's blood and that of his child.

The song with which the play begins sets up a non-Christian cosmology just before and during Holy Communion, which becomes in itself a vehicle of vengeance. The choir of maidens tells a continuous story that describes how Rupert sees his son's (unwitnessed) murder. The response to love from the child is steel from the murderer, a sequence that anticipates Rupert's metamorphosis in the harangue described previously. This sequence provides the human-to-demon transformation with more motivation than is present in the speech itself. The adoration of the dead child, particularly as described in the last stanza of the song, verges on idolatry. Considering that this song functions as a hymn during a supposedly Christian mass, it contains very few Christian ideas. The central theme is vengeance. The mass is actually a Black Mass, as revealed in the litany sung repeatedly by the choir of youths. The unnamed deity whom they invoke has an empire limited by the stars and a throne covered by the open spaces. This is clearly not the Christian God; it is the devil.

It has often been said of Kleist that what his characters say to one another usually creates misunderstanding, that words constitute barriers rather than communication and that often a character says just the opposite of what he intends to say. This is of interest in regard to the changing configurations of the family. The Schroffenstein family at Rossitz self-righteously considers itself far above the Schroffensteins of Warwand, whom it proposes to exterminate like a nest of vermin. Yet in the process of swearing vengeance, the Rossitz house identifies itself first with wild animals, then with supernatural forces of evil. It is as if the Rossitz house, in its efforts to vanquish the rival house, must become more evil than it accused Warwand of being. In Rupert's harangue, it is as if two polar forces approach each other, then quickly exchange places, retaining only their polarity. The forces behind Rupert are unmasked in the course of the scene. They are not divine but infernal, just as in Kleist's plays words are often unmasked as the exact opposite of the pure expression of truth they are assumed to be.

This double level of meaning is already present in the opening hymn, unmasked as a devil's litany. It is present in the one utterance of the accused accomplice under torture. "Sylvester," his dying shriek, could be interpreted as an appeal for help rather than an accusation, yet the Rossitz house seizes on it as proof of the Warwand house's guilt. The later discovery of the real cause of death witnesses to the fact that this "word" was inadequate to its speaker's intention. The lack of understanding and of communication is particularly evident between Rupert and Sylvester, heads of the two enemy camps whose only connection is an ancient contract allowing the lands and chattels of an extinct house to all into the hands of the other. A bitter feud results, whose beginning is forgotten and whose end is not in sight. It is the classic Montague-Capulet situation made more poignant by the inclusion of both houses in the same family.

Overwhelming circumstantial evidence convinces each of the two warring parties of the other's guilt in the death of a child. Unfortunate accidents, mistrust, and misunderstanding form a terrifying chain reaction that leads to the final catastrophe. Yet for all their enmity, the houses are strikingly similar. If it is true that Kleist set up Rupert and Sylvester in crassest opposition—Rupert the impulsive, deluded mystic, Sylvester the cautious, yet trusting realist—then it is also true that he set up the wives in opposition to these men. The children Ottokar and Agnes are basically innocent and trusting, but they are prejudiced by their upbringing. The vassals of each house, strange to note, remain on the side of the mistrusting parent—in Warwand, Gertrude; in Rossitz, the fierce Rupert. Sylvester is the only character in the play with a clear view of what is about to happen: He sees that, to the diseased mind, innocence will always seem like guilt.

The first scene of the fifth act, in which the audience sees the perfect understanding and mutual trust of Agnes and Ottokar, reveals the ideal condition of human beings. Their secret betrothal takes place when they are both in great danger. Even in this relationship, however, there is an element of deception. Ottokar lies to induce Agnes to exchange clothes with him so that she might escape the pursuing Rupert. She believes him and complies. Their state of perfect trust, in spite of the minor deception, stands in direct contrast to Rupert's blind mistrust. Ottokar describes a magic wedding night; the fateful change of clothes unites him with Agnes. This takes place in defiance of the whole framework of false reality built up in the play. The lovers unite, not only in spite of language and appearances but also in spite of the whole world as it appears to them. Their inner equilibrium guides them in opposition to everyone and everything else in the world except each other. It is not in vain that this happens, for they are finally vouchsafed access to the truth about the child's death, Sylvester's innocence, and all the subsequent wrongs on both sides. With their perfect trust has come truth. Ottokar says that everything is solved, the whole mystery clear; he is speaking not only of the riddle of the child's death but also of the riddle of reality itself.

As Rupert is ruined by suspicion, Sylvester is ruined by faith. Despite his innate feeling for justice, he eventually begins to give credence to the horrible suspicions of his companions and to the undeniably strong circumstantial evidence. Sylvester becomes guilty when he denies his inner certainty in the face of apparent facts. He and Rupert finally find reality, but it appears in the form of the witch Ursula. She found the child's body drowned, not murdered. A reality dependent on a witch's testimony and Rupert's dark delusions—is there any difference? Kleist's answer is not nihilistic, for the inner balance of Ottokar and Agnes preserves them free from guilt.

The vendetta, or feud, is an old and beloved vehicle in literature for expressing the need for harmony and trust between people. The innocent lovers who are usually the victims of such tragedies remain true to each other and prove to the world that love conquers all, even in death; the prototypical example is Romeo and Juliet. In traditional treatments of this theme, the family is little more than a framework used to assign characters to opposing parties, while Kleist's enemy houses are both part of the same family—a refinement that renders the disastrous events even more disastrous, if possible. Unlike the Montagues and Capulets, neither house of Schroffenstein is united in opposition to the other; each set of parents contains one more reasonable and one more impulsive member. Within these couples, the balance of power is always on the side of the irrational. Even Sylvester eventually succumbs to the pressures of wife, vassals, and environment, which lead him away from his inner certainty. Kleist emphasizes the innate closeness of human beings, compromised by their artificial alienation from one another and from their environment. Ties of blood are bridges between people that cannot be overlooked. The isolation of individuals from one another and Nature is increased by the world's bloodthirsty Ruperts and Gertrudes. There is no doubt about the guilt of individuals such as these, but the real villain is whatever force creates the illusions, the accidents, and the circumstantial evidence. It is the force that causes the old witch to skulk away from human society. Kleist's family is a configuration, not only of individuals but also of forces behind them.

AMPHITRYON

Kleist's drama *Amphitryon* contains no complex family structure with a full complement of children, as is found in *The Feud of the Schroffensteins*, yet although *Amphitryon* is basically a marital drama, essentially similar problems of estrangement and reconciliation occur. Molière's *Amphitryon* (pr., pb. 1668; English translation, 1775) is a witty comment on the social customs and sexual mores of the French court; Kleist's *Amphitryon*, nominally a comedy, is much more than an individualized and internalized variation on the same theme. Kleist shifts Molière's biting satire into a metaphysical frame of reference.

According to legend, Jupiter was forced to take on the appearance of Amphitryon to facilitate spending a night with the beautiful Alkmene, the implication being that she loved her husband too much to share her bed with anyone else, even the ruler of the gods. Such a marriage would seem to be as idyllic as the pure love of Ottokar and Agnes in *The Feud of the Schroffensteins*. Yet conversations between husband and wife are charged with misunderstanding, mistrust, and reproach, from act 2—where the shadow of Jupiter separates them for the first time—to the last scene of the play—where Jupiter reveals his true identity, announces the impending birth of Hercules, and departs.

Alkmene can easily accept Jupiter's idealized portrayal of Amphitryon because it confirms her own previous idealization of her husband. (It is ironic that even when she prays to Jupiter she imagines him in the form of Amphitryon.) Alkmene reacts with protest and shock on discovering the true identity of her nocturnal visitor. Jupiter in the guise of Amphitryon commands Alkmene to pray to Jupiter as himself rather than as a sort of super-Amphitryon; she replies that she will forget Amphitryon when she prays but forget Jupiter the rest of the time.

Amphitryon's main failing with regard to Alkmene is mistrust, for he accuses her of unfaithfulness, knowing full well that she believed the visitor to be her husband. In a speech reminiscent of Rupert Schroffenstein's harangue, he reveals the depth of his injury in the strength of his alienation from his former existence. He rages both at the gods and at the shameless rascal disguised as himself, without knowing that these objects of his wrath are identical.

As in *The Feud of the Schroffensteins*, the real culprit is not the suspected family member but the old witch, deceptive reality. The unheard of and unimaginable happens, propelling Amphitryon onto a path of rage that renders him inaccessible to reason. The supposed crime against the family—murder or adultery—seems almost harmless compared with the devastation caused by pursuing vengeance for the sake of honor.

No Greco-Roman god fits the description Jupiter gives of himself in the fifth scene of the second act. The words omnipotent, omniscient, and omnipresent—listed as attributes of God the Father in the Christian catechism—point to the incorporation of aspects of the Christian God in the figure of Jupiter. The intrusion of Jupiter is more than the intrusion of the supernatural—it is the intrusion of an entity composed of elements of two conflicting religions. It is clear that the estrangement of Alkmene and Amphitryon is accompanied by a mixed cosmology comparable to that of *The Feud of the Schroffensteins*. The mixture of Christianity with something quite alien to it is associated with family strife.

Throughout the play, Amphitryon is motivated only by a desire to return to his family and his identity, both of which are inextricably entwined in the person of Alkmene. It is precisely Amphitryon's outrage at the estrangement brought about by Jupiter that alienates him from her all the more. Having been exorcized from his own identity, Amphitryon's struggle to return to his former state, ironically enough, effects real changes in his personality, thereby removing him another step from Alkmene. Jupiter's final pronouncement cannot patch up the marriage but merely emphasizes that their alienation has come about through no fault of theirs. Alkmene, who has borne all the rest with comparative equanimity, retreats to a faint that is first cousin to death. Her tortured "ach," which is the final word of the play, expresses her shock at the fate that has been visited on her.

PENTHESILEA

The destructive force of love is also central to Kleist's *Penthesilea*, an eccentrically structured one-act tragedy in blank verse, the twenty-four scenes of which comprise some three thousand lines. The play is based on the post-Homeric legend of the slaying of the Amazon Penthesilea by Achilles during the Trojan War. Kleist, however, departs radically from his source: In his version, Penthesilea kills Achilles.

In the fifteenth scene of *Penthesilea*, the Amazon chieftain speaks of a future in which she will be able to dedicate herself entirely to Achilles, much as Alkmene is dedicated to Amphitryon. Achilles brings to mind the predicted birth of Hercules in *Amphitryon* when he declares, "You shall bear me the god of the earth." The future family envisioned in this scene indicates how the previous existence of each individual is overthrown by another's love. The duties, allegiances, and circumstances that thrust them apart are no longer capable of determining the direction of their lives, for each embodies hope, happiness, and fate for the other. This absolute dependence on one another, coupled with the complete failure of mutual understanding and communication, brings about the ultimate failure of the family to exist—the self-destruction of the lovers.

CATHY OF HEILBRONN

In *Cathy of Heilbronn*, a five-act play in blank verse, the same overwhelming sense that the lovers are destined for each other prevails, although with a happier resolution. Here it is consciously invoked by the lovers as an irrational, semireligious necessity; here, too, a lack of communication determines the sequence of events. (Kleist wrote in a letter to Henriette Hendel in 1807 that Cathy and Penthesilea belong together like the plus and minus of algebra, and in a letter to Heinrich Joseph von Collin on December 8, 1808, Kleist wrote that Cathy and Penthesilea are one and the same being under opposite circumstances.) In *Cathy of Heilbronn*, however, in contrast to *Amphitryon* and *Penthesilea*, which evoke the classical concept of fate, the mood is closer to that of a fairy tale, overlaid with the gothic trappings that were so much in vogue in the early nineteenth century.

Cathy, reared as the daughter of a Heilbronn armorer, is in fact the illegitimate daughter of the emperor, although this is not established until the end of the play. The action is set in motion when a handsome knight, Friedrich Wetter, Count vom Strahl, comes to Cathy's father's forge. When Cathy sees the count for the first time, she collapses at his feet. Convinced by a dream that she is to marry him, she follows him everywhere as if in a trance. The count, however, has been granted a revelation of his own: He is to marry an emperor's daughter. Thus, he rebuffs Cathy's attentions, gently at first, then more harshly. Eventually, however, communication and understanding do come about, and the lovers find each other. The play is a near tragedy; even in the general eupho-

ria of the happy ending, it is clear that all this happiness might never have been. The emperor might have seemed a *deus ex machina* and Cathy a comic-opera princess, but these possibilities are lost in the fairy-tale atmosphere of the play as a whole.

Cathy's inexplicable actions remove her completely from the rational material world. When she is brought before a secret court, Cathy herself has no conscious justification for her bizarre pursuit of the count. When faced with repeated evidence that Count vom Stahl does not want her company, indeed regards her doglike devotion as a curse, Cathy persists. She is serenely at one with herself in a world completely at odds with her perception of it. Forced to promise to return to her father, Cathy sees the inescapability of her predicament for the first time. Although she does not allow the demands and expectations of her father and the count to throw her into conflict with herself, she faints when confronted with an action that she knows would destroy her.

From the end of the trial to act 4, scene 2, the count has been admitting to himself ever more fervently that he loves Cathy, but for him the dream-prophecy that his future wife be a daughter of the emperor is important enough to blind him to the witchlike Lady Kunigunde, who happens to be a granddaughter of a previous emperor. Like Amphitryon, Cathy's count has difficulty disentangling himself from the lying and artifical truths—above all, Kunigunde is artificial—of the external world. As the count questions Cathy in her sleep, however, the process of understanding slowly grows, not out of the words but out of the images themselves. The lovers have shared the same dream, guided by an angel.

It is the angel who, in the play's climactic scene, rescues Cathy from a burning castle; it is the angel, whose presence attests the absolute faith and trust in God, that envelops Cathy in a mystic certainty wholly alien to the other characters in the play. Like Penthesilea and Alkmene, she is regarded as crazy by the count and others. She pursues her God-given objectives with all the zeal and unswerving valor of a saint or martyr. As in the case of Alkmene, the "Weg des Weibes . . . zur Gottheit" alienates her lover and her entire world. Her close, naïve relationship to the absolute very nearly destroys her relationship with the count. The alienation that accompanies the enmity of faith and reality in the beginning of the play is ended with the allegiance of Cathy and the count in their matching dreams. The family longed for by both lovers is happily founded in their marriage at the play's end.

THE PRINCE OF HOMBURG

The Prince of Homburg, a five-act play in blank verse, is based on a historical event: the Battle of Fehrbellin in 1675, in which Friedrich Wilhelm of Brandenberg, the Great Elector, triumphed over the Swedes. The play's titular protagonist was also a historical figure; typically, however, Kleist felt free to change the facts as he saw fit.

Kleist's Homburg, like many of his protagonists, is out of tune with his environment. In the opening scene, he is sleepwalking—a symbolic expression of his alienation. The Elector teases Homburg with promises of fame and marriage to Princess Natalie von Oranien, the Elector's niece, all wordlessly conveyed in the presentation of a laurel wreath. In his unconscious—and therefore naïve—state Homburg reaches out to them both, calling, "Natalie! Meing Mädchen! Meine Braut!" and "Friedrich! Mein Fürst! Mein Vater!" Later Homburg demonstrates his desire to win their approval through recognition as a successful militarist, which causes him to make the fatal military mistake of advancing without command. A forgotten glove of Natalie is a paradox to the prince when he awakes; it marks the entrance of the inexplicable in the play.

The dream that is not a dream is the cause of the prince's later predicament. Lost in speculation about the glove and the miraculous realm to which it belongs, Homburg ignores important demands of the material world. He does not listen to his orders when the battle plan is discussed but merely repeats mechanically what he has heard, for he is still musing over the glove. Later, when Kottwitz repeats that he is to wait for orders before advancing, Homburg purposely closes his mind to what he is being told, too intent on winning for himself the fame and glory promised him the night before. The prince's actions win the battle, but the Elector (before he has learned

the identity of his insubordinate commander) sentences him to death for his disobedience. When the Elector is told that the prince is begging for mercy, he responds: "I have the highest respect for his feeling. If he feels the judgment is unfair, I will rescind it." Feeling dominates the relationship of the prince to the Elector, whom he longs to have for a father, as is seen in the sleepwalking sequence. The dependent status of the prince is emphasized in his helpless pleas for his life in the fifth scene of the third act. Homburg appeals to the Elector's lady as "Oh, my mother!" She continually refers to him as "my son." The prince explains that the sight of his own open grave has brought him to this desperate emotional extreme. It is this great flood of feeling—fear of death—that propels the prince back to the refuge of childhood, in which the parents bear the responsibility of protecting the child. The boy-prince begs his surrogate parents to save him from death, and the Elector responds to the same feeling that has brought the prince to childhood. Feeling is now to return the prince to decisive manhood, for the Elector returns the "to be or not to be" predicament to the prince.

Here feeling turns traitor, throwing Homburg back to childlike dependence, while the Elector assumes he can function as a responsible man in resolving the predicament of the execution. Homburg expects the Elector to be a father, and the Elector expects Homburg to be a man.

THE FAMILY AS THEME

In *Penthesilea*, *Cathy of Heilbronn*, *Amphitryon*, and *The Prince of Homburg*, there is a breakdown in communication between the individuals most precious to each other. This is at least partially a result of the failure of language to communicate that which is most vital to human beings. The estrangement is so great in *Amphitryon* that only the promise of the child Hercules retrieves the play from tragedy, while Achilles' vain hope of a child from Penthesilea indicates their one fragile possibility of redemption.

Real stability belongs only to those possessed of an inner balance, a sort of "schöne Seele" awareness of oneself and one's role. Cathy, Alkmene, and Natalie are exemplary of this, as is Penthesilea in her own world; it is the completely alien world of Achilles that hurls her into despair and madness, as the strangeness of their men confuses and upsets the lives of the other three. The inner harmony of Alkmene, Cathy, and Natalie is what marks their rightful and proper course through their own worlds—which are bent on opposing them in every way.

These four plays are primarily concerned with the basic unit of the family structure—the husband-wife relationship. Predestined lovers find their way to each other for the first time, not because of intellectual or emotional communication but without any apparent empirical cause, like people in a dream. The fact that Kleist uses dream sequences to express the birth of this inexorable sense of destiny is no coincidence, for reality is the dream unmasked. Much has been said of Kleist's use of accidental circumstances to express the futility of humanity's striving. In these four prefamilial plays, true accidents are of minuscule importance, while Kleist makes fairly constant reference to a supernatural power, be it God or fate. The union of the lovers in *Cathy of Heilbronn* and *The Prince of Homburg* is just as directly a result of the influence of this higher power as is the stalemate in *Amphitryon* and the ultimate disunion in *Penthesilea*.

OTHER MAJOR WORKS

LONG FICTION: *Die Marquise von O———*, 1808 (novella; *The Marquise of O———*, 1960); *Michael Kohlhaas*, 1810 (novella; English translation, 1844).

SHORT FICTION: *Erzählungen*, 1810-1811 (2 volumes; *"The Marquise of O" and Other Stories*, 1960).

NONFICTION: *Phöbus: Ein Journal für die Kunst*, 1807-1808 (serial), 1961 (book); essays in the *Berliner Abendblätter*, 1810-1811 (collected in *An Abyss Deep Enough: Letters of Heinrich von Kleist, with a Selection of Essays and Anecdotes*, 1982).

MISCELLANEOUS: *Heinrich von Kleists gesammelte Schriften*, 1826 (Ludwig Tieck, editor).

BIBLIOGRAPHY

Allan. Seán. *The Plays of Heinrich von Kleist: Ideals and Illusions*. New York: Cambridge University Press, 1996. A critical analysis of the ideals and illusions in Kleist's drama. Bibliography and index.

_____. *The Stories of Heinrich von Kleist: Fictions of Security*. Rochester, N.H.: Camden House, 2001. Although this work focuses on the stories of Kleist, it sheds light on his plays. Bibliography and index.

Brown, H. M. *Heinrich von Kleist: The Ambiguity of Art and the Necessity of Form*. New York: Oxford University Press, 1998. A scholarly look at the works of Kleist. Bibliography and index.

Reeve, William A. *Kleist on Stage: 1804-1987*. Buffalo, N.Y.: McGill-Queen's University Press, 1993. An analysis of Kleist's major plays and details about their staging and production history. Bibliography and index.

_____. *Kleist's Aristocratic Heritage and "Das Käthchen von Heilbronn."* Buffalo, N.Y.: McGill-Queen's University Press, 1991. A closer look at Kleist's familial background and its connection with his play *Cathy of Heilbronn*. Bibliography and index.

Stephens, Anthony. *Heinrich von Kleist: The Dramas and Stories*. Providence, R.I.: Berg, 1994. Critical analyses of many of Kleist's works. Bibliography and index.

Fredericka A. Schmadel

FRIEDRICH GOTTLIEB KLOPSTOCK

Born: Quedlinburg, Saxony (now in Germany); July 2, 1724
Died: Hamburg (now in Germany); March 14, 1803

PRINCIPAL DRAMA

Der Tod Adams, pb. 1757 (*The Death of Adam*, 1763)

Salomo, pb. 1764 (*Solomon: A Sacred Drama*, 1809)

Hermanns Schlacht, pb. 1769

David, pb. 1772

Hermann und die Fürsten, pb. 1784

Hermanns Tod, pb. 1787

OTHER LITERARY FORMS

Friedrich Gottlieb Klopstock is known primarily as a lyrical poet. His masterpiece is the monumental epic poem *Der Messias* (*The Messiah*, 1776), begun in 1748 and completed in 1773, but he was also famous as a writer of odes and elegies. A number of his influential critical writings deal with theoretical and critical aspects of poetry, language reform, and the establishment of a utopian German society of intellectuals.

ACHIEVEMENTS

Friedrich Gottlieb Klopstock's creative life fell between the period of the German Enlightenment, dominated by the influence of French neoclassicism, and the emergence of the youthful, German nationalist writers of the Sturm und Drang and the early Romantic period, dominated by the young Johann Wolfgang von Goethe. This transitional position has led to Klopstock's being praised as the godfather of a self-confident new generation of German writers while being criticized as long-winded, excessively ornate, and obtuse. Therefore, the author of *The Messiah* paradoxically is praised more for his literary influence than for his literary output. This is particularly true for his plays, which were seldom performed onstage—indeed, his biblical plays were more popular in Italy and France than in Germany. Klopstock's enthusiastic endorsement of the French Revolution led to his being made an honorary citizen of France by the National Assembly in 1792, a title he retained even after he was deeply disappointed by the subsequent reign of terror. His funeral in Hamburg was attended by a large number of dignitaries and thousands of mourners—further proof of the accuracy of Gotthold Ephraim Lessing's prediction in 1753 that Klopstock would be honored by many but read by only a few.

BIOGRAPHY

Friedrich Gottlieb Klopstock was born on July 2, 1724, to an a middle-class northern German family. At the age of fifteen, he was admitted to Schulpforta, a prestigious school maintained by the ruler of the region, which emphasized instruction in classical languages and literatures. At the same time, Klopstock became acquainted with English authors, particularly Joseph Addison and John Milton, and at the occasion of his graduation speech in 1745, he not only expressed the wish that German poets should produce works rivaling Homer, Vergil, and Milton but also confessed that he himself felt called on to become their German successor.

While studying theology first at the University of Jena, then later in Leipzig, Klopstock began to work on *The Messiah*, publishing the first three cantos in 1748. His growing reputation, bolstered by strong support from the famous Swiss literary theoreticians Johann Jakob Bodmer and Johann Jakob Breitinger, led King Frederick V of Denmark to invite Klopstock in 1751 to come to Copenhagen and to complete the work on *The Messiah* with the support of a lifelong annuity. On his trip to Denmark, he met his future wife, Meta Moller, with whom he spent the happiest time of his life at the court in Copenhagen, until she died in childbirth in 1758.

After the death of King Frederick in 1766, Klopstock's friend and patron Count Bernstorff had to go into exile, and Klopstock followed him to Hamburg. This change led to a renewed outburst of creativity. He finished a large collection of odes in 1771, and in 1773 *The Messiah* was finally completed. With his literary reputation at its zenith, he was able to sell his literary utopia *Die deutsche Gelehrtenrepublik* (the German republic of scholars, 1774) on a subscription basis and was consequently invited to the court of Karl Friedrich of Baden to oversee the founding of a "German Society" based on the principles he had articulated in this work.

Klopstock's inability to cope with the intrigues at Karl Friedrich's court and his return to Hamburg after only a few months in Karlsruhe effectively ended his literary career. Overtaken by the youthful movements whose beginnings he himself had inspired, he became more of a point of reference than a writer, a judge and a critic more than a poet. A strong advocate of the American and French revolutions, he became disillusioned by the subsequent political chaos in Europe, and his poetry became nostalgic and bitterly critical. There can be no doubt, however, that it is largely because of his efforts that the German language was no longer considered too coarse for the production of sublime epic and dramatic poetry: *The Messiah* had become Germany's answer to Milton's *Paradise Lost* (1667, 1674). His conviction that literature should strive to reveal the sublime through the use of the imagination rather than through reason and probability opened the door for the English early Romantic writers to displace the influence of French neoclassicism in Germany and to set the stage for an autonomous modern German literature. Even though many of his early admirers and imitators, like Goethe and Friedrich Schiller, had become detractors by the time Klopstock died, his place in the history of German literature had become secure.

Friedrich Gottlieb Klopstock (Hulton Archive by Getty Images)

ANALYSIS

After *The Messiah*, Friedrich Gottlieb Klopstock's name was almost exclusively associated with lyric and epic poetry. His often stated intention was to demonstrate that German poets were capable of producing poetry that could equal the works of the ancient masters. *The Messiah* was to rival the epic poems of Homer, Vergil, and Milton; his odes attempted to reach the grandeur of the works of Pindar and Horace. It was therefore logical for him to extend his ambitions to dramatic poetry and to show that an original German tragedy could be created from a synthesis of classical tragedy and German-Christian cultural material. In pursuit of this ambition, Klopstock wrote six plays that are evenly divided between religious and patriotic subjects. In his biblical tragedies (*The Death of Adam*, *Solomon*, and *David*), Klopstock attempted to preserve the main precepts of Aristotelian dramatic theory while replacing Greek with Christian mythology; in his Hermann trilogy (*Hermanns Schlacht* [Hermann's battle], *Hermann und die Fürsten* [Hermann and the princes], and *Hermanns Tod* [Hermann's death]), he goes one step further by claiming to create a new, typically Germanic dramatic genre, the Bardiet, to deal with a heroic subject from Germanic mythology.

THE DEATH OF ADAM

Klopstock's contemporaries were taken aback by his first attempt at drama because it defied all expectations and conventions of the theater of his time. *The Death of Adam* has only three very short acts instead of the conventional five; it deals neither with the heroic subject matter of neoclassical tragedy with its elegant Alexandrine verses, nor with the middle-class subjects of the bourgeois tragedy in the fashion of Gotthold Ephraim Lessing's *Miss Sara Sampson* (pr., pb. 1755; English translation, 1933). Instead it is a static, very simple play, in elegant prose, without much of a plot, vaguely related to the French "lyrical tragedy" of the early part of the eighteenth century.

The tragedy of Adam lies in the fact that, after having lived for nearly nine hundred years, he must now face death, keenly aware that his original sin has led to the introduction of death into the world and made him responsible for the death of all future generations. Adam's apprehensions about his impending death alternate with highly poetic praises of the beauty of earthly life. There are only two truly dramatic episodes in the play to keep the audience in suspense: the disappearance of a child who is eventually found unharmed and the return of Cain, who has come to curse his dying father but is later overcome by filial devotion and runs away.

Eve does not appear until the very end, and the obvious devotion the couple have for each other introduces a sentimental element to mitigate the harshness of Adam's impending death. Finally, as has been prophesied, the rocks of the surrounding hills come crashing down to bury Adam.

The Death of Adam strictly observes the unities of time, place, and action of neoclassical drama: Adam's death is foretold in the morning, and he dies in the evening. The cycle of nature reflects the cycle of human life: On the day Adam dies, his son Seth marries Selima, and the child Sunim, believed to have died in the wilderness, is found unharmed. Adam's (and all humans') mortality is God's punishment for the Original Sin, but it is at the same time also the means for gaining access to heaven.

Contemporary German critics, most of them strong proponents of neoclassical Alexandrine tragedy, did not respond kindly to Klopstock's first attempt as a playwright and urged him to concentrate his efforts on the completion of *The Messiah*.

Except for an amateur performance in 1766, there are no records of any German stage productions of the play; however, a number of translations and stage adaptations are recorded in France and Italy, and Napoleon Bonaparte is said to have had the play read to him on the eve of the Battle of Acre in 1799.

HERMANNS SCHLACHT

According to an account in *Ab excessu divi Augusti* (c. 116, also known as *Annales*; *Annals*, 1598) by Tacitus, in 9 C.E. a young Cheruscan prince, leading an irregular force of Germanic tribes, annihilated three Roman legions commanded by Publius Quinctilius Varus after having led them into an ambush in the dense Teutoburg forest, near the present city of Detmold in northern Germany. This victory effectively kept Germany free of Roman rule and elevated the young chief, called Arminius by Tacitus and Hermann by the Germans, to the status of national hero. The Battle of Teutoburg Forest is therefore commonly known as "Hermann's Battle" in German history and literature.

It should not be surprising that Klopstock chose Hermann as the subject of his patriotic trilogy; he had strongly German nationalist feelings and was engaged in discussions about a future, unified Germany under enlightened leadership and the elimination of foreign political and cultural influences. The legendary Hermann thus became for him and many of his contemporaries the symbol for the possibility of German political and cultural autonomy, and he returned frequently to the Hermann theme during his career, for instance, in his odes "Hermann und Thusnelda" (1752) and "Hermann aus Walhalla" (1794).

The theme of German unity and autonomy and of the rejection of foreign dominance that form the nucleus of the Hermann theme demanded an equally autonomous dramatic form, and Klopstock thus invented a new dramatic genre, the Bardiet. Paradoxically, this term is based on a confusion of the Latin word *barritus*, used by Tacitus to describe a Germanic battle cry accompanied by the pounding of weapons on shields, with the word *barditus*, wrongly derived by Klopstock from the Celtic *barde* (poet). Therefore, the term Bardiet was supposed to be Germanic for "Bardic Song."

Despite Klopstock's claim of having created a new dramatic subgenre, *Hermanns Schlacht* is closely modeled on the classical Greek tragedy. There are no act divisions, but fourteen prose episodes alternate with bardic hymns and patriotic incantations that essentially serve the same purpose as the choral odes in Greek tragedy: They comment on the action, provide mythological background, and invoke the favor of the gods. The action is relatively static: All the fluctuations of the battle are narrated from a vantage point above the battlefield so that no violent acts are, in fact, shown onstage. The events are less important than the effect they create on the observers, and suspense is created by the alternating good and bad news from the field. The dramatic unities are strictly observed.

The play takes place during the third day of the battle, whose outcome is still in the balance. At a crucial point, when the Romans appear to gain the upper hand, Hermann's father, Siegmar, decides to join the fray despite his advanced age. He is promptly wounded but lives long enough to see Hermann turn the tide of the battle. When Hermann's mother, Bercennis, hears of her husband's death, she wants all Roman prisoners, including Hermann's brother Flavius, put to the sword, but the young warrior shows his statesmanship by showing mercy and by cleverly settling some disputes among his own followers. However, he vows bloody vengeance on any further Roman invaders daring enough to follow their defeated compatriots. A hymn to Wodan ends the action.

Hermanns Schlacht has been performed more frequently than the other two parts of the trilogy, probably because of its optimistic and triumphant mood, although it is clearly the least dramatic play of the three. In the second play, *Hermann und die Fürsten*, the Germanic unity is already dissolving into intertribal squabbles and petty jealousies, which lead to a disastrous defeat at the hands of the Romans. Eventually, this discord results in Hermann's murder by his own people in the final play, *Hermanns Tod*. This development indicates that by the end of the century, Klopstock's youthful belief in the creation of a unified Germany had turned sour and that his bitterness over having become a literary relic, albeit a publicly revered one, extended to his view of the political future of Germany. Instead of a proud "republic of scholars," he predicted prolonged feuds between regional feudal rulers and a continued threat from foreign invaders. The emergence of Napoleon Bonaparte during the last years of Klopstock's life must have confirmed him in this pessimistic view.

OTHER MAJOR WORKS
POETRY: *Der Messias*, 1748-1773 (*The Messiah*, 1776); *Oden*, 1771; *Geistliche Lieder*, 1758-1769 (2 volumes; *Odes of Klopstock*, 1848).

NONFICTION: *Die deutsche Gelehrtenrepublik*, 1774; *Grammatische Gespräche*, 1794.

MISCELLANEOUS: *Klopstocks sämmtiliche Werke*, 182301830 (18 volumes).

BIBLIOGRAPHY
Heitner, Robert H. *German Tragedy in the Age of Enlightenment*. Berkeley: University of California Press, 1963. Contains a discussion of Klopstock's biblical plays, with a particularly detailed discussion of *The Death of Adam*.

Hilliard, Kevin. *Philosophy, Letters, and the Fine Arts in Klopstock's Thought*. London: Institute of Germanic Studies, University of London, 1987. An examination of Klopstock's philosophy and aesthetics as they presented themselves in his works. Bibliography and index.

Lee, Meredith. *Displacing Authority: Goethe's Poetic Reception of Klopstock*. Heidelberg, Germany: Universitätsverlag C. Winter, 1999. Lee examines Klopstock's influence on Goethe. Bibliography and index.

Peucker, Brigitte. "Friedrich Gottlieb Klopstock." In *European Writers, Vol. 4*, edited by George Stade. New York: Scribner's, 1984. A brief but thorough critical resume of Klopstock's life and work, with a fine section on his biblical and patriotic plays. Includes a comprehensive bibliography and a list of translations of Klopstock's works into English.

Franz G. Blaha

JAMES SHERIDAN KNOWLES

Born: Cork, Ireland; May 12, 1784
Died: Torquay, England; November 30, 1862

PRINCIPAL DRAMA
Leo: Or, The Gypsy, pr. 1810, pb. 1873

Caius Gracchus, pr. 1815, pb. 1823

Virginius: Or, The Liberation of Rome, pr., pb.
    1820

William Tell, pr., pb. 1825 (based on Friedrich
    Schiller's play)

The Beggar's Daughter of Bethnel Green, pr., pb.
    1828, revised pr., pb. 1834 (as *The Beggar of
    Bethnel Green*)

Alfred the Great: Or, The Patriot King, pr., pb.
    1831

The Hunchback, pr., pb. 1832

The Vision of the Bard, pr., pb. 1832

The Wife: A Tale of Mantua, pr., pb. 1833

The Daughter, pr. 1836, pb. 1837

The Love Chase, pr., pb. 1837

Woman's Wit: Or, Love's Disguises, pr., pb. 1838

Love, pr. 1839, pb. 1840

John of Procida: Or, The Bridals of Messina, pr.,
    pb. 1840

Old Maids, pr., pb. 1841

The Secretary, pr., pb. 1843

OTHER LITERARY FORMS

Though James Sheridan Knowles is now remembered almost exclusively for his drama, he wrote several other works that were highly regarded in his own time. At the beginning of his literary career, he wrote a popular ballad, *The Welch Harper* (1796), which the critic William Hazlitt praised in his critical volume *The Spirit of the Age* (1825). In 1810, Knowles published (by subscription) a collection of his best early verses entitled *Fugitive Pieces*; this work received little acclaim, and Knowles subsequently wrote little nondramatic poetry.

Knowles's most significant nondramatic writings concerned oratory and theater. The most famous and influential of these was *The Elocutionist* (1823), a textbook on debate that he wrote for his students while teaching at Belfast. This book expresses Knowles's view that the effective speaker must avoid artificiality and be in earnest, and it contains one of his most popular model debates, "Was Julius Caesar a Great Man?" *The Elocutionist* became a very popular textbook in both English and American schools and went through many editions dur-

ing Knowles's lifetime. His writings and lectures on poetry were also well received by his contemporaries, and his *Lectures on Oratory, Gesture, and Poetry*, published posthumously in 1873, considered the adaptability of poetry for elocutionary purposes. Though these discourses often concerned poetry by important writers, such as Sir Walter Scott and Lord Byron, they were neither profound nor influential as literary criticism.

Knowles's *Lectures on Dramatic Literature*, also posthumously published in 1873, reveals the depth of his practical knowledge of stagecraft. These discourses consider important dramatic subjects, such as Greek drama and William Shakespeare's plays, and address significant technical questions of unity, plot, and characterization. Typically, Knowles concentrated more on issues relating to acting than to literary criticism, but his critical judgments were often sound. For example, his view that the unity of action is more essential to successful drama than are the unities of time and place reflects a significant departure from neoclassical dramatic theories. Knowles realized how much his audience valued carefully developed climactic action and powerful characterizations.

Knowles was not a sophisticated theologian, and the religious writings he produced after 1843 were zealous but unsophisticated. These tracts, such as *The Rock of Rome: Or, The Arch Heresy* (1849), were published during a period of great religious controversy in England involving the Oxford Movement, which sought to ally the Anglican Church with Roman Catholicism. In an age during which religious inquiry occupied some of England's greatest minds, Knowles's contribution was negligible. As a preacher, his elocutionary training served him well, but, though he could keep his congregation's attention, his published sermons were undistinguished.

In his youth, Knowles wrote several operas and adaptations of plays written by others, but these are of little significance. His two novels, *Fortesque* (1846) and *George Lovell* (1847), though somewhat more successful in the United States than in England, have now been largely forgotten. Knowles's fame rests primarily on his plays.

ACHIEVEMENTS

During the course of the nineteenth century, England's population quadrupled, and the nation became increasingly democratic. The rapidly growing theater audience of the time was largely uneducated. They had little use for either the poetry of Shakespeare or the numerous imitations of Jacobean drama that writers such as Samuel Taylor Coleridge—and a host of lesser talents—inflicted on them. Instead, they favored the melodrama, with its sentimentalized faith in justice and moral purity and its thrilling, often spectacularly staged, plots.

Though James Sheridan Knowles followed the traditional Aristotelian model in writing his tragedies, he consciously tried to write a less ornate poetic language that would be more appealing to his audience. The critic Hazlitt praised Knowles's avoidance of artificial poetic language, and a reviewer in *The London Magazine* wrote in June, 1820, that the diction of his play *Virginius* was "colloquial and highspirited; in short it is the true language of life." Though Knowles's attempt to write tragedy in a more realistic style was not always so well received by more conservative critics, his prosaic blank verse was the product of a conscious attempt to reconceive drama in the realistic terms required by his audience. Furthermore, Knowles's concern for English domestic, patriarchal values, a theme that recurs frequently in his plays, touched the lives of his audience and contributed significantly to the success of *Virginius* and that of many of his later dramas. Though critics have complained that Knowles's anachronisms and stilted verse result in inferior tragedy, his attempt to make his drama more realistic and contemporary suited the tastes of his audience. It also can be seen as a significant transition between the obsolete pseudo-Elizabethan style of the late eighteenth and early nineteenth century tragedies and gothic dramas and the more carefully crafted, satiric, and socially conscious dramas of W. S. Gilbert, Arthur Wing Pinero, and Henry Arthur Jones.

A further ground of Knowles's achievement lay in his collaborations with the greatest actor of his day, William Charles Macready, who played the title role in Knowles's *Virginius*. The great success of *Virginius* launched Knowles's career as a playwright; at the same time, the success of *Virginius* also helped establish Macready as, in Harry M. Ritchie's words, "the leading actor in England, confirming the supremacy of a new [acting] style based on 'domesticity' and 'humanity.'" Until this time, Edmund Kean, another of Knowles's acquaintances, had been the most celebrated actor in England, largely praised for his declamatory—some would say ranting—portrayals of Shakespeare's tragic heroes. When Kean opened in his own version of the Virginius story a few days after the first performance of Knowles's play, he failed completely.

This was Kean's first London defeat, and as such it can be considered the beginning of the decline of the exaggerated, romantic acting style for which he was so famous. From this point on, Kean's acting career declined, while Macready's flourished. *Virginius* not only established Macready as a powerful figure in the London theater but also marked his debut as the leading practitioner of a more natural style of tragic acting. More than one-third of Knowles's subsequent plays were written for Macready or at his suggestion, and their symbiotic relationship enabled both to achieve considerable success and to influence the development of nineteenth century English drama.

Though Knowles was an actor as well as a playwright, his own performances were generally not very successful in England. He lacked the physical stature and intensity required of a great performer, and he had an Irish brogue that many English critics found objectionable. Nevertheless, in September, 1833, he was elected an honorary member of the Cambridge Garrick Club. Knowles's English audience recognized him primarily for his playwriting, but when he toured America in 1834, he was phenomenally successful as an actor and as a lecturer with the less sophisticated American audiences.

Perhaps the most eloquent testimony to the English public's esteem of Knowles as a playwright is the fact that, in 1850, he was one of four writers nominated to succeed William Wordsworth as poet laureate of England. The other nominees were John Wilson, Sir Henry Taylor, and Alfred, Lord Tennyson; the latter was finally chosen by Queen Victoria, largely because of Prince Albert's liking for Tennyson's great elegy *In Memoriam* (1850). The fact that a writer of Knowles's limited poetic talents could be seriously considered for such an honor might now seem peculiar—even ludicrous—but it shows how highly Knowles's contemporaries regarded his dramas.

BIOGRAPHY

James Sheridan Knowles was born on May 12, 1784, in the city of Cork, Ireland. His father, James Knowles, a somewhat well-known Protestant schoolmaster and lexicographer, was also a first cousin of the great playwright Richard Brinsley Sheridan, for whom he named his son. Knowles was such a frail child that his parents frequently feared for his life, until he finally recovered his health at about the age of six. When he was twelve years old, he made his first visit to the theater; it was at that point that he resolved to be a dramatist.

Knowles's parents had originally intended that he study medicine, but, when his mother died in 1800, his father remarried, and young James, who disliked his stepmother, left home. When he finally did begin to study medicine in 1806, his heart was not in it. Instead, he became interested in the ministry and spent considerable time listening to sermons and yearning to preach to vagrants in the streets of London. Knowles still longed to be a dramatist, and the moral and didactic fervor that he had inherited from his father found expression in the plays that he soon began to write. After receiving his medical degree and practicing for three years, Knowles abandoned his medical career and joined a professional acting company in 1808.

Knowles's acting debut, in which he ill-advisedly attempted the demanding role of Hamlet, was a total failure, and he soon joined another company at Wexford. There, in July of 1809, he met Catherine Charteris, a young Edinburgh actress, whom he married, after a rather tempestuous courtship, on October 15 of the same year. The newlyweds moved to Waterford and joined Cherry's acting company. At Waterford, Knowles first met the as yet unknown actor Edmund Kean, who encouraged him to complete a play entitled *Leo: Or, The Gypsy*, which became a

minor hit. Knowles was also improving as an actor, and by the time he and his wife moved to Swansea in 1811, he had acted successfully in operas, comedies, and tragedies. His first child, James, was born the same year, and the young family moved to Belfast.

At this point, Knowles's budding stage career was temporarily halted when his depleted finances forced him to accept a teaching position. Knowles enjoyed teaching, and his love of oratory made him so successful at it that he opened his own school in Belfast. A short time later he joined his father, who was then headmaster at the Belfast Academical Institution, as his assistant. When the two quarreled violently over the son's theory of elocution, the father was fired and the son resigned his post. Then, in 1815, the success of Knowles's first mature play, the tragedy *Caius Gracchus*, rekindled his theatrical ambitions, and the family moved to Glasgow, where Knowles was teaching in 1820 when the success of *Virginius* made him famous.

Following the triumph of *Virginius*, Knowles established a Whig newspaper, *The Free Press*, in Glasgow, but the enterprise collapsed after three years. In 1825, Knowles was rescued from financial problems by the success of his historical drama *William Tell*, but his first comedy, *The Beggar's Daughter of Bethnel Green*, performed in 1828, failed miserably. Beset again by financial problems, Knowles lectured publicly to supplement his income. His lectures on poetry, elocution, and drama were generally admired, and his financial situation improved accordingly.

In 1832, Knowles presented a petition to Parliament seeking greater protection for authors' rights through a copyright bill. In 1833, he supported an actors' movement that opposed the monopoly theaters. Neither enterprise produced results, and Knowles continued to increase his acting roles both in his own dramas and in productions of Shakespeare's plays. Because his stage activities had become full-time, the Knowles family had settled in London, but by that time Knowles had ten children, and, when an acting tour of Ireland in April and May of 1834 was unsuccessful, he resolved to travel to the United States, where his dramas had been much more widely acclaimed than in England.

When Knowles arrived in New York on September 6, 1834, he was hailed as the greatest living English playwright. The tour was a resounding success; Knowles himself was thoroughly surprised by the warmth and praise of the American audiences. He captivated them with dramatic performances in his own plays, lectures, and readings from his poems; indeed, so great was his American success that he formed a lasting friendship with President Andrew Jackson, and, as a farewell gesture, a huge dramatic festival was held in his honor on April 8, 1835. Knowles understandably retained a warm regard for the United States until his death and continued to correspond with his many American friends.

During the eight years following his return to England in 1835, Knowles continued to act in his own plays and wrote several more dramas. He toured Dublin and Edinburgh in 1836 and acted in *William Tell*, *The Hunchback*, *The Wife*, *Virginius*, *The Beggar of Bethnel Green* (his revised version of the earlier, failed effort), and *Alfred the Great*; later that year, he performed in several plays by Shakespeare. Though he announced in November, 1837, that he would retire from acting, he continued to perform from time to time and to manage his own plays until as late as 1849. *The Secretary* was produced in 1843, but he continued to write plays until 1846. Nevertheless, by 1843, Knowles, for all practical purposes, was no longer actively involved with the stage.

Knowles's retirement from the stage and his subsequent ordination as a Baptist minister can be at least partly explained by certain character traits that he had always possessed. Throughout his life, he had been a man of strong moral principles, and his plays often reflected his convictions. His love of oratory and elocution, combined with his concern with matters of conscience, had almost turned him to preaching in the streets earlier in his life, so Knowles's conversion from the boards to the pulpit was not so radical a change as it might at first appear. Knowles himself was not comfortable preaching against acting and drama, as his new calling required him to do; in fact, he wrote two novels after being ordained and continued to present friends with copies of his plays.

Though his American tour had made him wealthy, Knowles was both generous and careless with his earnings. He continued to realize some income from his popular plays, but not nearly what he would have received if copyright laws had been more stringent. His financial state, therefore, became so critical that in 1846 a group of his friends tried to obtain a pension for him, finally succeeding in establishing a fund for his benefit in 1848. Knowles himself succeeded in securing a pension of two hundred pounds a year. This, with his earnings as curator of Shakespeare's house at Stratford—a post he was awarded in 1848—enabled him to support himself until his death on November 30, 1862.

ANALYSIS

As a dramatist, James Sheridan Knowles was trying to achieve two conflicting goals. He wanted to reach his audience by banishing artificiality from dramatic poetry and by using more natural cadences of speech, yet he could not help but aspire to the traditional poetic standards of the greatest Renaissance writers. Both Knowles's tragedies and his comedies reflected the taste of his time as well as the limitations of his creative abilities. Nevertheless, they are often superior to the dramas of his contemporaries, many of whom gave themselves up to writing facile and sensationalized melodramas. Knowles's drama has its share of such elements, but their presence is always counterbalanced by the playwright's attempt to restore the grandeur of the Renaissance tradition to the nineteenth century stage.

CAIUS GRACCHUS

Though critics have maintained that Knowles's tragedy *Virginius* is his greatest play, many of Knowles's most characteristic themes find their earliest expression in his first mature and original play, the tragedy *Caius Gracchus*. *Caius Gracchus* is not a great play, but in spite of its flaws, it is in some respects both intense and compelling. Knowles's radical political attitudes were crudely but vividly presented in some of the title character's speeches, and the prosaic quality of the blank verse reflects Knowles's intention of writing dialogue in a language that would be more accessible to his audience. The play also seeks to combine elements of the popular melodrama with the more traditional themes of political intrigue and ambition that characterize Shakespearean and Jacobean tragedy. *Caius Gracchus* is, in fact, modeled on Shakespeare's *Coriolanus*, and Knowles's title character closely resembles Shakespeare's protagonist, particularly in his self-destructive devotion to the state. *Caius Gracchus* was Knowles's first attempt to synthesize different dramatic influences into a popular form, the domestic tragedy. The later success of *Virginius* can largely be attributed to the fact that in that play Knowles achieved a more natural synthesis of these disparate influences than he did in *Caius Gracchus*. Therefore, the earlier play is interesting as a precursor of the values and techniques that Knowles tried to refine in his later tragedies.

VIRGINIUS

Part of the problem with *Caius Gracchus* was that Knowles had selected an inappropriate story on which to graft his rather mundane and sentimental values. His choice of the traditional and popular story of Virginius, the noble Roman who kills his own daughter, Virginia, rather than allow her to be defiled by the tyrant Appius, was a much more appropriate vehicle to express his ideals of virtue, honor, and liberty. Knowles probably based his tragedy on the version of the story told by Livy, the Roman historian, though he often departed significantly from that model. In *Virginius*, as in his other tragedies, Knowles used the classical five-act structure and emphasized many of the themes he had developed in *Caius Gracchus*: oppression of the common people, the purity of familial (domestic) love, and the importance of justice and liberty.

The villain, Appius, is a deceitful Roman senator who has turned against the citizens who elected him, and Knowles's characterization of him is effective. Appius's evil machinations, though somewhat improbable, are cleverly conceived, and the audience certainly appreciated the malice, if not the psychological subtlety, of his character. Appius is reminiscent of Shakespeare's Richard III, and, though he lacks Richard's complexity, his absolute depravity generates an exciting plot. Appius's character was clearly conceived in the tradition of the "fall of

princes" tragedy, and Knowles obviously intended his audience to rejoice loudly at his demise. In fact, the playwright seems consciously to have sacrificed psychological complexity for moral effect.

Virginius, on the other hand, is as noble as Appius is evil. In act 4, Virginius reviles Appius for his treachery and incites the crowd to attack him. After leading the charge, Virginius is deserted by the cowardly citizens. Realizing that he can no longer save his daughter from Appius, Virginius stabs her to death and races, mad with grief, from the Forum. Knowles conceived the daughter's character along typically sentimental Victorian lines. She is beautiful and pathetic in her innocence and vulnerability, but she lacks any deeper qualities. Thus, her death has no real tragic impact. Though it is Virginia who dies, Knowles directs the audience's real pity toward her father, forced by circumstances to kill his only child.

WILLIAM TELL

Like *Caius Gracchus* and *Virginius*, Knowles's next tragedy, *William Tell*, has civic liberty as its main theme. *William Tell* is based on a play by the great German playwright Friedrich Schiller, but it lacks the philosophical depth of its model. By modern standards it also suffers considerably from the excessive ranting of the protagonist. Knowles was probably influenced by the work of Lord Byron in this regard, but while the Byronic hero is driven by some mysterious obsession, the emotions of Knowles's hero are superficial. The addition of humorous episodes and lyrics also tends to detract from the play's unity, and it was later revised from five to three acts, which improved it greatly. Next to *Virginius*, *William Tell* was Knowles's most popular tragedy. Its romantic excesses and volatile speeches were well suited to Macready's acting style and thus made it successful onstage.

COMEDIES

Knowles's comedies are somewhat less competent than are his tragedies. Though his tragedies frequently suffered from shallow characterizations and unimpressive poetry, they often succeeded in terms of presenting an exciting plot that could keep an audience involved. Furthermore, both *Caius Gracchus* and *Virginius* combine contemporary, Renaissance, and classical dramatic influences into a compelling whole. In his comedies, however, Knowles's characters are often poorly conceived, while the complex plots and subplots, inspired by Elizabethan comedies, are poorly integrated. Knowles's penchant for the five-act structure caused him to include considerable extraneous material in his comedies. In fact, one of his best comedies, *The Beggar of Bethnel Green*, is a three-act revision of the earlier, unsuccessful five-act play *The Beggar's Daughter of Bethnel Green*. Knowles's most popular comedy, *The Hunchback*, was also much improved by revision from five to three acts. None of his comedies, however, showed the artistic consistency of *Virginius*.

OTHER MAJOR WORKS

LONG FICTION: *Fortesque*, 1846; *George Lovell*, 1847 (3 volumes).

SHORT FICTION: *The Magdalen and Other Tales*, 1832; *The Letter-de-Cachet*, 1835; *Tales and Novelettes*, 1874.

POETRY: *The Welch Harper*, 1796; *Fugitive Pieces*, 1810.

NONFICTION: *The Senate: Or, Social Villagers of a Kentish Town*, 1817; *The Elocutionist*, 1823; *The Rock of Rome: Or, The Arch Heresy*, 1849; *The Idol Demolished by Its Own Priest*, 1851; *The Gospel Attributed to Matthew Is the Record of the Whole Original Apostlehood*, 1855; *A Debate upon the Character of Julius Caesar*, 1856; *Lectures on Dramatic Literature*, 1873; *Lectures on Oratory, Gesture, and Poetry*, 1873; *Lectures on Dramatic Literature: Macbeth* 1875; *Sheridan Knowles's Conception and Mrs. Irving's Performance of Macbeth*, 1876.

BIBLIOGRAPHY

Davies, Robertson. "Playwrights and Plays." In *The Revels History of Drama in English, 1750-1880*. Vol. 6. London: Methuen, 1975. Davies describes and evaluates each of Knowles's plays in chronological order. He draws attention to the recurring theme of "fatherhood" and focuses on Knowles's artistic development.

Fletcher, Richard M. *English Romantic Drama: 1795-1843*. New York: Exposition Press, 1966. Basing his work on previously unavailable materials, Fletcher seeks to correct evaluations previously made about English Romantic drama. He concludes that it is more vibrant, vital, and artistic than has been generally acknowledged. He recognizes Knowles's success and original approach but laments his lack of savoir faire. Extensive bibliography.

Meeks, Leslie Howard. *Sheridan Knowles and the Theatre of His Time*. Bloomington, Ind.: The Principia Press, 1933. This classic introduction to Knowles's plays is based mainly on primary sources. Meeks places the works into historical and literary context and provides a thorough analysis of *Virginius*, *The Hunchback*, and *William Tell*. The other plays are examined only briefly. Bibliography and index.

Parker, Gerald D. "'I Am Going to America': James Sheridan Knowles's *Virginius* and the Politics of 'Liberty.'" *Theatre Research International* 17, no. 1 (Spring, 1992): 15. Contains a profile of Knowles and an examination of the political and moral contents of his work, particularly *Virginius*.

Michael McCully,
updated by Gerald S. Argetsinger

PAVEL KOHOUT

Born: Prague, Czechoslovakia; July 20, 1928

PRINCIPAL DRAMA

Dobrá píseó, pr., pb. 1952

Zářijové noci, pr. 1955, pb. 1956
Sbohem smutku!, pr. 1957, pb. 1958
Taková láska, pr. 1957, pb. 1958
Třetí sestra, pr., pb. 1960

Ríkali mi soudruhu, pr. 1961

Cesta kolem světa za 80 dní, pr., pb. 1962 (adaptation of Jules Verne's novel *Around the World in Eighty Days*)

Válka s mloky, pr., pb. 1963 (adaptation of Karel Čapek's novel)

Dvanáct, pr., pb. 1963

Josef Švejk, pr. 1963, pb. 1966 (adaptation of Jaroslav Hašek's novel *Osudy dobrého vojáka Švejka ve světove války*)

August, August, August, pr. 1967, pb. 1968

Aksál, pb. in German as *Evol*, 1969, pr. 1970?

Válka ve třetím poschodé, pr., pb. in German as *Krieg im dritten Stock*, 1971 (*War on the Third Floor*, 1984)

Ubohý vrah, pb. in German as *Armer Mörder*, 1972, pr. 1974 (*Poor Murderer*, 1975)

Život v tichém domě, pr. 1974

Pech pod střechou, pr., pb. in German as *Pech unterm den Dach*, 1974

Požár v suterénu, pr., pb. in German as *Brand im Souterrain*, 1974 (*Fire in the Basement*, 1984?)

Ruleta, pr., pb. in German as *Roullette*, 1975

Atest, pr. in German as *Attest*, 1979 (*Permit*, 1984?)

OTHER LITERARY FORMS

Apart from his dramatic works, Pavel Kohout has written several successful novels: *Bílá kniha* (first published in German, as *Weissbuch*, in 1970; *White Book*, 1977), *Katyně* (1978; *The Hangwoman*, 1981), *Nápady svaté Kláry* (1982; the ideas of Saint Claire), *Snezím* (1993; *I Am Snowing*, 1994), and *Hvezdná hodina vrahů* (1995; *The Widow Killer*, 1998). He has also written poetry, literature for children, screenplays, essays, translations, and lyrics.

ACHIEVEMENTS

Pavel Kohout belongs to the group of outstanding Czech authors that includes Milan Kundera, Josef Škvorecký, and Václav Havel, who—with the exception of Havel—following a brilliant career in Czechoslovakia left their homeland some time after the Soviet occupation in 1968. At their most essential, Kohout's dramas, as well as his novels, have a common theme: disillusionment with the product of mod-

ern rationalism and with rationalism itself. His work challenges official explanations of reality, whether of political, philosophical, or even scientific origin. Kohout achieves this in a number of ways: by recasting, through creative adaptation, an established literary or dramatic work; through his original dramatic works; and finally, by joining other playwrights in a cooperative venture that documents the evils of his age and then exorcises them through comedy. His plays have enjoyed tremendous success not only in Czechoslovakia but also in the Soviet Union, Western Europe, and even the United States and Canada. In 1978, he was awarded the Austrian State Prize for his work.

BIOGRAPHY

Pavel Kohout is one of the most controversial figures in postwar Czech cultural and political history. A poet, author, and playwright, Kohout has been influential as a devoted Stalinist, a communist reformer, a dissident involved in the underground, and finally as a *persona non grata* in his homeland. He remains a highly regarded and successful European author.

Born in 1928 to a middle-class family in Prague, Czechoslovakia, Kohout was graduated from high school in 1947 and then studied arts at the Charles University in Prague, from which he was graduated in 1952. He simultaneously embarked on his literary career by publishing, in 1945, his first verses. Between 1947 and 1949, Kohout worked for the Czechoslovak Radio and, after the communist coup in 1948, experienced a meteoric rise in his career as he became cultural attaché in Moscow (1949-1950), the editor in chief of the satiric weekly *Dikobraz* (*Porcupine*, 1950-1952), and then the editor of the *Czechoslovak Soldier* (1953-1955). Finally, after the inauguration of television broadcasting, he worked as an editor for Czechoslovak Television (1955-1957).

Disillusioned with the West, which had ceded Czechoslovakia to the Nazis and their atrocities as part of the "Appeasement Policy" of 1938, Kohout, like many of his countrymen (including author Kundera), became infatuated with Stalinist communism. A popular figure in Prague in the 1950's, Kohout grandstanded publicly in favor of communists, certainly aware and even approving of the terri-

Pavel Kohout in Vienna, Austria, outside the Czechoslovakian embassy where officials informed him that his Czech citizenship had been revoked.
(AP/Wide World Photos)

ble crimes perpetrated by communist leaders in Czechoslovakia (thousands of dissidents, including poets, were imprisoned in mining camps or executed). Kohout supported the communists by writing satirical poems and plays lambasting the enemies of "our socialist state," even to the point of accusing his personal enemies of anticommunism and applying to join the secret police (he was declined).

During the Nikita Khrushchev years, it gradually became clear to Kohout and other Czech cultural figures that they had allowed their country to become a subjugated province of the Soviet Union and would never achieve the utopia they had hoped communism would provide. The 1960's marked a rise in a reformist communist movement in Czechoslovakia for which Kohout became as visible and as aggressive an advocate as he had been for Stalinism in the 1950's. This was for him a far riskier prospect because now he opposed the dangerous and murderous political regime he had helped to create.

Kohout's first stage triumph was his play *Taková láska* (such a love), which became the most performed play in Czechoslovakia, with 770 performances within four years of its appearance. It ran for more than five hundred performances in neighboring East Germany and was performed abroad—in the Soviet Union, Israel, South America, and South Africa. Kohout's surprising success has to be considered in the light of the stilted, sterile dramatic productions of dogmatic Socialist Realism, which inhibited not only theater but also all the arts in the countries that subscribed to it. In *Taková láska*, Kohout rejected Socialist Realism in a play that, although by no means revolutionary or highly original by today's standards, was nevertheless a courageous application of techniques that had been pioneered by such playwrights as Luigi Pirandello and Bertolt Brecht. This was enough to win for him the fame that he continues to enjoy.

Kohout engaged in a dialogue with Günter Grass in 1967, during the highly politically charged atmosphere on the eve of the heady experience that resulted in the Prague Spring, an ill-fated democratic revolution that was the culmination of reforms instigated by Kohout and others to achieve what they called "communism with a human face." The revolution incited the Warsaw Pact in August of 1968: a check on the reformers that ended with Soviet tanks rolling into Prague to establish a vicious neo-Stalinist regime that persisted through the 1980's. The damage inflicted by the hardline communists resulted in a general demoralization and arrested the social development of the Czech people. Kohout's correspondences with Grass were published in the aftermath of this crackdown, elevating Kohout to a level of international celebrity almost equal to that of Grass. During this time Kohout also enjoyed his one and only Broadway production: *Poor Murderer*, a play based on the short story "Msyl" by Leonid N. Andreev, appeared at the Ethel Barrymore Theatre, running from October of 1976 to January of 1977 for a total of eighty-seven performances. Directed by Herbert Berghof, the production starred Laurence Luckinbill: Both men also worked on the English translation.

In 1967 and 1968, Kohout was among the most politically active writers during the remarkable congress of the Czechoslovak Writers' Union (1967) and during the process of liberal reforms (1968). He stood in the forefront of those who pressured the Communist government to undertake such reforms as would turn the country away from the inhumanity inherent in the communist system and make it respectful of the democratic and humanistic values befitting a central European country. For his collaboration with the communist reformers of the Prague Spring, he was later, following the Soviet military invasion of Czechoslovakia in 1968, branded a "counterrevolutionary." Kohout's characteristic and courageous reply to the regime that successfully managed to turn the clock back was to accept the challenge expressed in the label "counterrevolutionary" and to publish abroad his *Aus dem Tagebuch eines Konterrevolutionaers* (1969; *From the Diary of a Counterrevolutionary*, 1972). Indeed, many of Kohout's works written in the late 1960's and throughout the 1970's were first published in German, although written in Czech.

During the crackdown, Kohout quite courageously joined the dissident underground with his characteristic aggressive approach. He became a close collaborator with Václav Havel and actively assisted in the drafting of an important human rights manifesto called Charter 77 in 1977. Kohout's production of underground theater despite the Soviet prohibitions attracted the attention of Czech-born playwright Tom Stoppard, whose *Dogg's Hamlet, Cahoot's Macbeth* (pr. 1979, pb. 1980) was inspired by a 1977 visit with Kohout. This document attempted to hold the government to its previous agreements, such as its signing of the Helsinki Accord, which committed Czechoslovakia to a far-reaching acceptance of international norms of behavior that respected human rights. Havel was jailed and persecuted for his dissidence, Kohout was not, although he was perhaps more hated than Havel. The secret police attempted to assassinate Kohout, but the two policemen sent refused to carry out the murder: This scenario is eerily echoed by the events of Havel's play *Largo Desolato* (pb. 1985; English translation, 1987), in which a dissident awaits assassination only to be told he is no longer important enough to warrant a bullet. Kohout was allowed, in 1978, to go to Vienna, Austria, to direct Nikolai Gogol's *Revizor* (pr., pb. 1836; *The Inspector General*, 1890) in Vienna's Burgtheater. Mercifully, Kohout was happy to find in Austria many loyal supporters among the theatergoers as well as among the influential personalities, a fact reflected in his winning the prestigious Austrian State Prize.

Being realistic about the true motivation behind the Czechoslovak authorities' permission that allowed him to stay in Austria, Kohout brought along an Austrian television crew as he returned to the border crossing, sensing that he might not be allowed back. In 1982 Kohout dramatically landed at the Prague airport and demanded to see his daughter, further vexing the secret police. In 1989, the Soviets were removed from Czechoslovakia in a successful democratic revolution, and Havel was made president of the new Czech Republic, but his friend Kohout would never be allowed to return to Prague or reclaim his Czech citizenship. Kohout continues to write novels appreciated by German- and English-speaking countries, including his *The Widow Killer*, a 1940's murder mystery featuring a Gestapo officer questioning his devotion to the Nazis, perhaps just as Kohout once questioned his devotion to hardline Stalinists.

ANALYSIS

If an entity called "Central European literature" truly exists, as some believe (and their most persuasive spokesperson is Milan Kundera, a novelist, playwright, and Pavel Kohout's countryman), then it would exhibit features that could define the work of Kohout as well. It would be literature (and drama) concerned with the nature of reality. It would have an obsessive urge to unmask, to demythologize, and to tear off the disguises. It would try to approach the truth mindful of the fact that the ultimate truth remains hidden.

TAKOVÁ LÁSKA

Rationalism, the belief underpinning the modern doctrine of progress, is itself challenged when the results of the application of the most progressive thought are as disappointing as the Central European experience suggests. Furthermore, there are areas in human life that resist cool, rational analysis, in which the inquisitor is helpless. Kohout dramatizes this belief in his triumphantly successful early play *Taková láska* through the ostensibly trivial but eternal love triangle, in which A loves B, but B loves C (who is unfortunately already married). The twist is that the love of two men and one woman leads to a tragedy, the suicide of the woman, Lida, and that this suicide is treated as a social case, like a murder, for which a judge—in the play identified only as "The Man in a Legal Robe"—attempts to find a cause, that is, a guilty party.

Formally, the interesting premise of the play is fortified by a judicious use of elements borrowed from avant-garde dramatists such as Pirandello and Brecht. Although the play has about it an air of absurdity, in the light of far more absurd stage trials (in which obviously innocent victims perished) such an air of absurdity paradoxically brings to the stage a semblance of normality rather than contrived absurdity. Compared with the lifeless propaganda plays of Socialist Realism, the viewers in Czechoslovakia and

elsewhere in the Eastern Bloc viewed the play as refreshingly authentic: It dealt with human problems that are impervious to neat solutions and that are offered wholesale in a world in which ideology attempts to eliminate uncertainty and present the world as monochromatic. The very fact that the play's topic has absolutely nothing to do with politics or ideology of any kind (because the tragedy is derived from the timeless theme of love) itself makes the play political: It proves there are limits to politics, as well as to reason.

In a Brechtian move, the audience is asked to make its own judgment, to become the judges establishing the guilt of those responsible for the death of Lida. It turns out that it is impossible to make a clear-cut judgment, that life is too complex even in the case about which one knows the details. There is a Pirandello-like minimalism about the staging that underlines the philosophical implications of the play. A courtroom set is transformed into a variety of locations, without elaborate stage sets, by the use of light. The play progresses through carefully administered doses of "illuminations," gradually stripping the certainty from the heretofore rather predictable plot. While the series of flashbacks does illuminate the past, it also paradoxically relativizes it: The audience moves closer to the truth, only to see it (the truth) become more elusive.

DRAMATIC ADAPTATIONS

After this success, Kohout embarked on a series of dramatic adaptations of novels and short stories from a variety of sources. Not all of them merit much critical interest, but some are definitely masterpieces. Perhaps it is unfortunate that the modern age puts such a stress on originality. Kohout would have found a more sympathetic audience in the age of William Shakespeare. It is refreshing, however, that Kohout himself lacks any embarrassment on this score, regarding his dramatic adaptations as a challenge, whether he is adapting Jules Verne's *Le Tour du monde en quatre-vingts jours* (1873; *Around the World in Eighty Days*, 1873), Karel Čapek's *Válka s mloky* (1936; *War with the Newts*, 1939), or Jaroslav Hašek's *Osudy dobrého vojáka Švejka ve světove války* (1921-1923; *The Good Soldier Švejk*, 1930).

Each of these projects posed a truly formidable challenge, and in each case, Kohout surmounted the difficulties imaginatively. Verne's novel, with its huge cast of characters and locations, is staged with half a dozen characters playing ten roles each, with a twentieth century commentator/*raisonneur* supplying an additional dimension as well as a bridging device. *Válka s mloky* was staged as a television broadcast featuring the apocalyptic destruction of the world. Yet it was Hašek's *The Good Soldier Švejk* that presented Kohout with the biggest challenge. No fewer than thirty dramatists had tried to stage the novel, from Erwin Piscator to Bertolt Brecht. Brecht's adaptation was particularly unsuccessful, but it taught Kohout a lesson. Where Brecht put Švejk in a German uniform and sent him to fight in World War II, Kohout decided to let Švejk be Švejk. He did it by concentrating on the first of four books of the novel and on a single theme: little Josef Švejk against the entire Austro-Hungarian Empire. Kohout further preserved the original flavor of Hašek's work by incorporating quotations with minimal changes and transforming the play into a multimedia extravaganza with the use of music and projection techniques.

Each of the three plays is much more than an adaptation of an entertaining novel with comical and satirical possibilities. *Cesta kolem světa za 80 dni* contrasts the travel and technology of the nineteenth century with the technology of the twentieth century, with its space travel. Yet the audience in Prague could not even travel to Vienna, because it was "in the West," though only in the political sense (geographically, Vienna is east of Prague). The freedom to move freely where one wants was among the most desired in the liberal 1960's and remains the dream of intellectuals and ordinary people alike. Technological advances did nothing to enable one to travel to neighboring Vienna, hence the disappointment. Furthermore, the rational application of technology, which harnessed the labor of the newts, results in an apocalyptic war instead of a millennium. Švejk is an example of a man who turns the very thought of rational organization of society (best exemplified in the military) into a joke.

Švejk is a clown who knows that he is clowning in order to survive. His wits are all that keep him from ending up as common cannon fodder, as did his comrades. What makes him special is his analysis of reality and his strategy to deal with it, both of which escape a common soldier. Švejk is not only amusing but also cynical and cruel. He is the opposite of the dreamer. In fact, he is the bane of all dreamers, as becomes abundantly clear in Švejk's clashes with many-hued dreamers in Hašek's novel. It is perhaps because of Kohout's deep involvement with the character of Švejk that he turned, in his next play, to an original creation of an anti-Švejk: the clown-dreamer hero of his *August, August, August* (August, August, the clown).

AUGUST, AUGUST, AUGUST

August is a clown-dreamer, as opposed to the clown-cynic of the Švejk type. Instead of cynicism, one finds lyricism; instead of the war, there is circus; instead of the Austro-Hungarian monarchy, a circus manager. The play deals very artfully with the timeless problems through allegories that are purposefully transparent but nevertheless effective. It was also the last major play that Kohout saw staged in his own country.

ŽIVOT V TICHÉM DOMĚ

Three one-act plays—*Pech pod střechou* (bad luck under the roof), *Fire in the Basement*, and *War on the Third Floor*—were staged in Ingolstadt, Bavaria, in 1974 as a trilogy under the common title *Život v tichém domě* (life in a quiet house). These are plays that could not be shown in Czechoslovakia and that one could define as dissident plays, if only because their common theme is the powerlessness of ordinary people confronting an all-pervasive totalitarian machinery that invades the "quiet" private space of an individual like a Kafkaesque nightmare.

POOR MURDERER

Without any doubt, the most powerful of Kohout's plays is his creative adaptation of a short story by Leonid Andreyev, "Mysl" ("Thought"), entitled *Poor Murderer*. This work, more than other Kohout adaptation, provides an ample justification for adaptations in general. It is also a borderline case in the sense that Kohout has taken liberties with the story, making some important changes that invest the original with possibilities that it did not have as a short story. In the original story, a physician, Kerzhentsev, is interrogated by a board of psychiatrists to determine whether he is sane as he is to be tried for murder. As Kerzhentsev reconstructs the murder, it becomes clear that some time before he attempted the murder, he had decided to pretend to be insane to evade legal responsibility for the crime. Kerzhentsev's tragedy follows his realization that his pretense was so thorough that even he no longer knows for sure whether he is normal.

In Kohout's play, Kerzhentsev is turned into an actor and allowed to reenact his crime with the help of his fellow inmates in a mental hospital, under the watchful eye of the chief psychiatrist, who attempts to understand Kerzhentsev's problem through the reenactment of a "play" written by Kerzhentsev. The wealth of meanings and different levels of interpretation enter through the device of the play-within-a-play.

Kerzhentsev was in love with a woman (who did not reciprocate his love) married to an unworthy has-been of an actor, a philanderer, a drinker, and a man of very little talent. Kerzhentsev believed that he was a much better man and feigned madness to kill his actor/rival. When he reenacts the murder in the play-within-a-play, he is stopped, and it is revealed to him that he never murdered his rival. Crushed, Kerzhentsev is seen smiling dementedly as his beloved actress finally realizes the depth of Kerzhentsev's passion and, blaming herself for his insanity, decides to dedicate her life to nursing Kerzhentsev. At this point, the rival admits defeat and congratulates Kerzhentsev for his successful "killing." The ambiguity inherent in this ending is not resolved. It is impossible to know what Kerzhentsev is truly thinking or whether he is in fact insane. One thing is clear: Kerzhentsev planned to get rid of his rival and planned a revenge and a "killing." Although not a drop of blood was spilled, Kerzhentsev carried out his threat of revenge and even succeeded in getting the attention of his beloved.

The play is a masterpiece of tense, concentrated, highly choreographed *danse macabre*, in which meaning suddenly shifts and the focus moves among several

levels of reality. One message is relentlessly driven home: Rationality has its limits. If Kerzhentsev's plan truly did work, did it not work perhaps too well? There are serious doubts about Kerzhentsev's sanity no matter what the outcome. Perhaps even more relevant, bearing in mind the general direction of Kohout's long-standing preoccupation with rationalism, the play provides yet another example of rationality in the service of evil.

As an outstanding example of Kohout's disillusionment with rationalism, the play has no rivals in his dramatic repertoire. The theme has ample support, however, in Kohout's novels. In *White Book*, a high school teacher challenges the traditional understanding of physics symbolized by the law of gravity when he levitates at will (to the distress of the local scientific and political authorities). In *The Hangwoman*, modern education produces an executrix versed in the art of execution and torture after being systematically trained by several knowledgeable, even scholarly, executioners. In *Nápady svaté Kláry*, a high school girl causes consternation by her accurate fortune-telling.

The irrationality of the three novels clashes with an only apparent rationality of the authorities, be they political or scientific. The outcome of such clashes is the underlying doubt about the rationality of a wide variety of beliefs. In this, Kohout joins the chorus of other Eastern European dramatists and novelists, whose experience motivates them to regard the nature of belief in all of its guises with suspicion. It is a suspicion well-founded, as Kohout convincingly demonstrated in his first truly internationally successful play, *Taková láska*. It was perhaps his desire to convey this conclusion clearly that motivated him to turn to adaptations and rely on transparent allegories. The effect of such cautionary tales as he provides in his plays and novels is often liberating. Far from encouraging a pessimism, disdain, or contempt, they promote understanding, sympathy, and compassion, even toward those authorities who so richly deserve his censure.

OTHER MAJOR WORKS

LONG FICTION: *Bílá kniha*, 1970 (in German as *Weissbuch*; *White Book*, 1977); *Katyně*, 1978 (*The*

Hangwoman, 1981); *Nápady svaté Kláry*, 1982; *Snezím*, 1993 (*I Am Snowing*, 1994); *Hvezdná hodina vrahů*, 1995 (*The Widow Killer*, 1998); *Konec velkých prázdnin*, 1996.

NONFICTION: *Briefe über die Grenze: Versuch eines Ost-West-Dialogs*, 1968 (with Günter Grass); *Aus dem Tagebuch eines Konterrevolutionaers*, 1969 (*From the Diary of a Counterrevolutionary*, 1972).

CHILDREN'S LITERATURE: *Jolana a Kouselnik*, 1980 (in German as *Jolana und der Zauberer*).

MISCELLANEOUS: *Verśe a pisné z let, 1945-1952*, 1952.

BIBLIOGRAPHY

Ambros, Veronika. *Pavel Kohout und die Metamorphosen des sozialistichen Realismus*. New York: Peter Lang, 1993. This English-language work, the revision of the author's thesis, provides a look at the relationship between Kohout and Socialist Realism.

Goetz-Stankiewicz, Marketa. *The Silenced Theatre: Czech Playwrights Without a Stage*. Toronto: University of Toronto Press, 1979. Goetz-Stankiewicz provides a look at various dissident playwrights, including Kohout, under the Czechoslovakian communist regime.

McCulloh, T. H. "*Poor Murderer*: An Engrossing Labyrinth." Review of *Poor Murderer*, by Pavel Kohout. *Los Angeles Times*, October 14, 1992, p. 4. This review of Kohout's *Poor Murderer*, at the Open Fist Theater in Hollywood, California, examines its theme and finds its plot intriguing.

Peter Petro,
updated by Michael M. Chemers

ARTHUR KOPIT

Born: New York, New York; May 10, 1937

PRINCIPAL DRAMA

The Questioning of Nick, pr. 1957 (staged), pr. 1959 (televised), pb. 1965 (one act)

Gemini, pr. 1957

Don Juan in Texas, pr. 1957 (with Wally Lawrence)

On the Runway of Life, You Never Know What's Coming Off Next, pr. 1957

Across the River and into the Jungle, pr. 1958

Aubade, pr. 1959

Sing to Me Through Open Windows, pr. 1959, revised pr. 1965, pb. 1965

To Dwell in a Palace of Strangers, pb. 1959

Oh Dad, Poor Dad, Mamma's Hung You in the Closet and I'm Feelin' So Sad: A Pseudoclassical Tragifarce in a Bastard French Tradition, pr., pb. 1960

Mhil'daiim, pr. 1963 (one act)

Asylum: Or, What the Gentlemen Are Up To, Not to Mention the Ladies, pr. 1963 (also as *Chamber Music*, pb. 1965, pr. 1971)

The Conquest of Everest, pr. 1964, pb. 1965

The Hero, pr. 1964, pb. 1965

The Day the Whores Came Out to Play Tennis, pr., pb. 1965 (one act)

The Day the Whores Came Out to Play Tennis and Other Plays, pb. 1965 (includes *Sing to Me Through Open Windows*, *Chamber Music*, *The Conquest of Everest*, *The Hero*, *The Questioning of Nick*; reissued as *Chamber Music and Other Plays*, pb. 1969)

An Incident in the Park, pb. 1967

Indians, pr. 1968, pb. 1969

What Happened to the Thorne's House, pr. 1972

Louisiana Territory, pr. 1975

Secrets of the Rich, pr. 1976, pb. 1978

Wings, pr. 1977 (radio play), pr., pb. 1978 (staged), pr. 1983 (televised)

Good Help Is Hard to Find, pb. 1982 (one act)

Nine, pr. 1982, pb. 1983 (music, libretto, and lyrics by Maury Yeston; adaptation of Federico Fellini's film 8½)

End of the World with Symposium to Follow, pr.,
  pb. 1984
Bone-the-Fish, pr. 1989 (also as *Road to Nirvana*,
  pr. 1990, pb. 1991)
Phantom of the Opera, pr. 1991, pb. 1992 (music
  and lyrics by Yeston; adaptation of Gaston
  Leroux's *Phantom of the Opera*)
Success, pr. 1991, pb. 1992
Discovery of America, pr. 1992
Three Plays, pb. 1997
Y2K, pr., pb. 1999 (later retitled *BecauseHeCan*)
Chad Curtiss, Lost Again, pr. 2000

OTHER LITERARY FORMS

Arthur Kopit has written *The Conquest of Television* (1966) and *Promontory Point Revisited* (1969) for television. In addition, an article by Kopit entitled "The Vital Matter of Environment" was published in *Theatre Arts* in April, 1961. His television miniseries, *Phantom of the Opera*, based on Gaston Leroux's novel, was aired in 1990. He has also written two screenplays, *Treasure Island* (1994) and *Stealing Father* (n.d.), and he has translated Henrik Ibsen's *Gengangere* (pb. 1881) as *Ghosts* (1984).

ACHIEVEMENTS

Critics have applied labels to Arthur Kopit based on his first successful work, *Oh Dad, Poor Dad, Mamma's Hung You in the Closet and I'm Feelin' So Sad*, and although his work has continued to evolve, the labels have stuck. Reviewers called the play an unsuccessful example of the Theater of the Absurd and Kopit an absurdist whose extraordinary titles have been far more enticing than his plays. In spite of these charges, *Oh Dad, Poor Dad, Mamma's Hung You in the Closet and I'm Feelin' So Sad* won the Vernon Rice Award and the Outer Circle Award in 1962 and was popular enough to be made into a motion picture (directed by Richard Quine and Alexander Mackendrick) in 1967.

Although Kopit's titles certainly attract attention, he is more than a clever deviser of titles. *Indians*, for example, must be considered one of the major American plays written in the 1960's, and *Wings* was one of the major dramas of the 1970's. *Nine* was awarded an Antoinette Perry (Tony) Award. Furthermore, he has displayed a diversity of style and a range of theme uncommon among his contemporaries. Kopit has publicly criticized the American theatrical tradition, especially as embodied by Broadway—a stance that may in part account for his lack of critical recognition. Subsidized by a Harvard University Shaw Traveling Fellowship, Kopit toured Europe and studied continental theater in 1959, and his essay "The Vital Matter of Environment" summed up his feelings about the mediocrity and lack of vitality of the American theater in comparison to European drama. "One can never wholly dissociate a work of art from its creative environment," he wrote, "Tradition has always been the basis of all innovation. . . . Style is related to tradition to the extent that it is representative of a cultural or social characteristic of its creative environment, and is itself characteristic to the extent that it has evolved from or rebelled against any of these." Consequently, Kopit charged, the lack of tradition in the U.S. theater forces American playwrights to rely on European dramatic innovations. Clearly, Kopit has used his knowledge of European traditions to bring innovations to the American stage. Although some of his work is obviously and even consciously derivative, he has gone beyond his models to produce distinctive plays of great strength.

In 1964, Tyrone Guthrie, with the help of a Rockefeller Foundation grant of seventy thousand dollars, offered to mount Kopit's one-act plays *The Day the Whores Came Out to Play Tennis* and *Mhil'daiim* in connection with the University of Minnesota, but a problem arose with university officials. The university's position was that the intent of the grant was to provide playwrights with an opportunity to revise scripts under experimental conditions and that the plays were not meant to be performed publicly, in spite of Kopit's assumption to the contrary. Kopit withdrew his plays from rehearsal, and in a scathing interview in the January 13, 1964, issue of *The New York Times*, he accused the university of "deceit" and "censorship in its most insidious form" in denying him the benefit of an audience.

Like all successful playwrights, Kopit roots his plays in performance. His recognition of the importance of producing an effect on his audience is central to his writing, yet his intellectual approach to his themes keeps his dramas from degenerating into melodramas. The combination of powerfully emotional theatrical moments and significant subject matter is a staple in Kopit's drama.

Kopit is sensitive both to the dignity of humankind and to the absurdity of the human condition. To explore this tension between dignity and absurdity, he has used a number of different formats and techniques; *The Questioning of Nick* is realistic, *Oh Dad, Poor Dad, Mamma's Hung You in the Closet and I'm Feelin' So Sad* contains absurdist elements, *Indians* owes some of its structure to Bertolt Brecht's concept of epic theater, and *Wings* is surreal, impressionistic, psychological realism. Kopit's musical books for *Nine* and *Phantom of the Opera* have demonstrated his flexibility in form. The combination of mythic elements with almost hyper-realistic dialogue in *Bone-the-Fish* (its working title, which parodies David Mamet's 1988 *Speed-the-Plow*, also about Hollywood, was changed to *Road to Nirvana* when the play reached New York) points up Kopit's humor and seriousness at the same time. With *Discovery of America*, the dramatist continued to fulfill the promise of his earlier experimental work.

BIOGRAPHY

Arthur Lee Kopit was born in New York City, New York, on May 10, 1937, the son of George Kopit, a jeweler, and Maxine (née Dubkin) Kopit. He married Leslie Ann Garis, a concert pianist and writer from Amherst, Massachusetts, on March 14, 1968; they have three children: Alex, Ben, and Kathleen.

During an "uneventful" childhood, living in a prosperous suburb in which he found himself to be the "victim of a healthy family life," Kopit demonstrated an interest in dramatics by entertaining his friends with puppet shows. Radio was an important element in his development; he says, "It's a much more exciting medium than TV because it involves your creative faculties." Although he wrote for the school newspaper while attending Lawrence (Long Island) High School, Kopit showed little inclination toward a career in the arts when he was graduated in 1955, and he entered Harvard University with a scholarship to study electrical engineering. After taking some creative writing courses, however, he decided that he wanted to become a playwright, and he was graduated cum laude and Phi Beta Kappa with a bachelor of arts degree in June, 1959.

Kopit's first theatrical experiences at Harvard took place during his sophomore year; as he reports in the introduction to *The Day the Whores Came Out to Play Tennis and Other Plays*, "My career was determined." His class work with Robert Chapman and his success under the tutelage of Gaynor Bradish, a tutor in Dunster House who was in charge of its Drama Workshop, stimulated Kopit's interest in the stage and introduced him to the fundamentals of play-

Arthur Kopit in 1982. (AP/Wide World Photos)

writing. Over a period of three or four days during his spring vacation, the aspiring dramatist wrote *The Questioning of Nick*, a one-act play that won a college-wide playwriting contest the following fall; it was subsequently performed on television in New Haven, Connecticut, in June, 1959. The seven other dramas that Kopit wrote while studying at Harvard include *Don Juan in Texas*, written in collaboration with Wally Lawrence; *On the Runway of Life, You Never Know What's Coming Off Next*; *Across the River and into the Jungle*; "Through a Labyrinth"; and the productions of his senior year, *Aubade*, *Sing to Me Through Open Windows*, and *To Dwell in a Palace of Strangers*, the first act of a projected three-act drama that was published in the *Harvard Advocate* in May, 1959. A revised version of *Sing to Me Through Open Windows* was produced Off-Broadway in New York in 1965 and in London in 1976.

During a tour of Western Europe in 1959, Kopit wrote *Oh Dad, Poor Dad, Mamma's Hung You in the Closet and I'm Feelin' So Sad* "to enter [in another] playwriting contest at Harvard," this time in the Adams House competition. Again Kopit's work won a prize, and the reaction when the play was mounted as a major undergraduate production was so overwhelming that, with the aid of a Ford Foundation grant, it was moved to the Agassiz Theatre in Cambridge, Massachusetts, in January, 1960. Kopit had cast a young woman from Radcliffe College in one of his Harvard productions, and through his friendship with her, he was introduced to the Broadway producer Roger L. Stevens. *Oh Dad, Poor Dad, Mamma's Hung You in the Closet and I'm Feelin' So Sad* opened at the Phoenix Theatre in New York City on February 26, 1962, as part of their repertory offerings, produced by Stevens and directed by famed choreographer Jerome Robbins. The play ran for 454 performances before it closed on March 31, 1963, and it then toured for eleven weeks. On August 27, 1963, it returned to the Morosco Theatre in New York for a brief revival (forty-seven performances). *Oh Dad, Poor Dad, Mamma's Hung You in the Closet and I'm Feelin' So Sad* was the first of Kopit's plays to be published by a major house, Hill and Wang, and it has been performed in London, Paris, Australia,

Belgium, Canada, Italy, Mexico, the Scandinavian countries, Turkey, and West Berlin.

Asylum: Or, What the Gentlemen Are Up To, Not to Mention the Ladies, was scheduled to open at the Off-Broadway Theatre de Lys in March, 1963, but after five preview performances, Kopit decided to cancel the production. The dramatist reports that the bill was actually composed of two one-act plays, *Chamber Music* and a companion piece that he intended to expand into a three-act play later. The concept for *Chamber Music* occurred to Kopit sometime in 1959, though he did not begin writing the play until late in the spring of 1962, finishing it that summer. The author withdrew the plays because he "wanted to do more work on them." *Chamber Music* was revised and rewritten during the summer of 1964 and staged in London in 1971. With *The Day the Whores Came Out to Play Tennis*, *Sing to Me Through Open Windows*, *The Hero*, *The Conquest of Everest*, and *The Questioning of Nick*, it was collected in *The Day the Whores Came Out to Play Tennis and Other Plays*, the second of Kopit's five volumes to be published by Hill and Wang. The collection was published under the title *Chamber Music and Other Plays* in England four years later.

The Hero and *The Conquest of Everest* were both written in March, 1964. Kopit explains that *The Hero* contains no dialogue because he was "struck dumb by the prospect of writing two plays in a single day." *The Conquest of Everest* was produced in New York in 1964 and in London in 1980; *The Hero* was produced in New York in 1964 and in London in 1972.

As part of a Rockefeller Foundation grant, two other one-act plays, *The Day the Whores Came Out to Play Tennis* and *Mhil'daiim*, were to be staged at the Tyrone Guthrie Theatre in Minneapolis, Minnesota, in February, 1964, but, as mentioned above, Kopit withdrew the plays because of a disagreement with the University of Minnesota. On March 15, 1965, director Gerald Freeman opened *The Day the Whores Came Out to Play Tennis* on a double bill with *Sing to Me Through Open Windows* (directed by Joseph Chaikin) at the Player's Theatre in Greenwich Village. *Sing to Me Through Open Windows*, written while Kopit was at Harvard, had actually served as a curtain raiser for *Oh Dad, Poor Dad, Mamma's Hung You in the Closet and I'm Feelin' So Sad* in the New York previews in 1962, but because of production difficulties, it, too, had been canceled before opening night. The revised version also played in London in 1976. Next came *An Incident in the Park*, published in Bob Booker and George Foster's *Pardon Me, Sir, but Is My Eye Hurting Your Elbow?* in 1968; in 1969, one of his television plays, *Promontory Point Revisited*, a segment of the series *Foul* on the New York Television Theatre, followed.

Kopit's next major play, *Indians*, was written with the aid of a Rockefeller Foundation grant. It premiered as part of the Royal Shakespeare Company's repertory at the Aldwych Theatre in London under Jack Gelber's direction on July 4, 1968, a symbolically appropriate date for this play. On May 6, 1969, the play was transferred to the Arena Stage in Washington, D.C., and on October 13 of the same year, it was moved again to the Brooks Atkinson Theatre in New York under the direction of Gene Frankel (ninety-six performances). High production costs were blamed when the play, cited by Otis L. Guernsey, Jr., as one of the "best plays of 1969-1970," closed on January 3, 1970. *Indians* was met with critical acclaim and has been performed in France, Germany, Japan, and the Scandinavian countries. In 1976, Robert Altman, working from a script suggested by Kopit's play, directed a film entitled *Buffalo Bill and the Indians: Or, Sitting Bull's History Lesson*. Kopit received $500,000 for the screen rights to *Indians*.

Between 1969 and 1977, Kopit's output diminished, and he wrote nothing of great significance for the stage. The Impossible Time Theatre held a Kopit Festival in 1977; in the same year, Kopit wrote *Wings*, which had been commissioned in the fall of 1976 by Earplay, the drama project of National Public Radio. John Madden directed the version of *Wings* broadcast on National Public Radio in 1977, and when Kopit, at the urging of Robert Brustein, then dean of the Yale School of Drama, rewrote the work for a stage presentation during the Yale Repertory Theatre's 1978 season, Madden again served as director. *Wings* was produced at the New York Shakespeare Festival in 1978 (sixteen performances at the Public/Newman

Theatre), at the Lyceum Theatre in 1979 (113 performances), and in London in 1979; it was published simultaneously in the United States and Canada in 1978, with British publication coming the following year. *Wings* was televised on the Public Broadcasting Service in 1983. *Wings* marked the return to productivity for Kopit, with his musical books for the Tony Award-winning *Nine* (based on the Federico Fellini film *8½*, with music and lyrics by Maury Yeston) and *Phantom of the Opera* (the libretto for which he wrote as early as 1984, a project temporarily shelved when Andrew Lloyd Webber produced his version in 1985 but subsequently produced with music and lyrics again by Yeston and rated more highly by many critics than the Lloyd Webber version) and his full-length works, developed in regional theaters such as the Actors Theatre of Louisville, the Circle Repertory Theatre, the Actors Repertory Theatre, and the Mark Taper Forum. Over the years Kopit has continued to show an interest in musicals, having penned *Tom Swift and the Secrets of the Universe* (music and lyrics by Yeston), *Zhivago* (music by Lucy Simon, lyrics by Susan Birkenhead), and *High Society*, an adaptation of the Cole Porter film.

Like many modern American playwrights, Kopit has subsisted at least in part through the support of foundation grants, supplemented by academic positions. He was awarded a Guggenheim Fellowship in 1967 and a Rockefeller grant in 1968; he was a National Endowment for the Arts grantee and a Fellow at the Center for the Humanities at Wesleyan University from 1974 to 1975; he served as playwright-in-residence at Wesleyan from 1975 to 1976; he was a Columbia Broadcasting System (CBS) fellow at Yale University from 1976 to 1977; and in 1979 he became an adjunct professor of playwriting at the Yale School of Drama.

In addition to the awards already noted, Kopit was the recipient of a National Institute of Arts and Letters Award and was elected to the American Academy of Arts and Letters in 1971; in 1979, he won both the Italia Prize for his radio version of *Wings* and the Pulitzer Prize for the stage version.

Kopit, who settled in Connecticut, prefers to live and work away from people ("any holiday resort in the off-season . . . Majorca . . . [in] a huge hotel almost empty"). A man of the theater, he has also directed some of his own works, including the 1959 television production of *The Questioning of Nick*, and the stage productions of *Oh Dad, Poor Dad, Mamma's Hung You in the Closet and I'm Feelin' So Sad* in Paris, in 1963, and of *Louisiana Territory* in Middletown, Connecticut, in 1975.

ANALYSIS

There has been relatively little scholarly attention paid to the works of playwright Arthur Kopit, with almost nothing written about his entire canon, and most of the criticism that has been published is not very impressive. Furthermore, those critics who attempt an overview of the plays usually devote a fair amount of time to discussing the plays that he wrote as an undergraduate at Harvard. While Sherwood Anderson, Robert E. Sherwood, Eugene O'Neill, and other playwrights have moved from Harvard to Broadway in the past, critical studies of their works have focused on what they wrote as professional playwrights. There are three related reasons that have been used to justify a different approach to Kopit. First, the Harvard plays represent a goodly portion of the author's output; second, the majority of his later plays have been short and relatively insignificant; and third, as a result of these first two points combined with the reputation established by his major plays, several of the Harvard pieces have been published and are thus easily accessible. Still, his major works are impressive and deserving of critical examination.

Despite the continued popularity among college students of *Oh Dad, Poor Dad, Mamma's Hung You in the Closet and I'm Feelin' So Sad*, Kopit's reputation no longer rests solely on this work. With *Indians* and *Wings*, he proved his early promise; with his later work, such as *Discovery of America* and *Y2K*, his technical skills (in several genres) have served his personal voice to present strong dramatic statements on significant topics. He continues to have fun in the theater, too, experimenting to see whether he can stretch the medium's dimensions, as was the case with *Chad Curtiss*, *Lost Again*, a collection of three ten-minute plays in serial form fashioned after the motion picture serials of the 1910's through the 1940's. After David Mamet, Sam Shepard, and Edward Albee, Kopit belongs among the major American playwrights of the late twentieth century.

SING TO ME THROUGH OPEN WINDOWS

The best of Kopit's early plays is *Sing to Me Through Open Windows*. Clearly not meant to be realistic (the set is a bare stage hung with black curtains), the drama is in the tradition of Theater of the Absurd and shows the influence of Samuel Beckett in its setting, language, pauses, minimal plot, and mysterious characters. In spite of Kopit's statement that Beckett "has had no influence on me as far as I know," critics have pointed out structural and linguistic resemblances between this play and Beckett's *Fin de partie: Suivi de Acte sans paroles* (pr., pb. 1957; *Endgame*, 1958).

The protagonist of the play is a boy, Andrew Linden, who visits the home of a magician, Ottoman Jud, and his helper, Loveless the Clown, in the middle of a dark forest. Ottoman and the Clown have entertained Andrew on the first day of spring every year for five years. This year, however, Ottoman's illusions fail, and Andrew is exposed to the games that Ottoman and the Clown play, mysterious games that also prove unsuccessful. This year, too, Andrew announces that he wants to stay with Ottoman, but the announcement is made in the third person, answering a "Distant Voice of Ottoman," as though the event is being recalled even while the present action continues: "And although I say them, some time later I will ask myself, Now what was it again that you said to him . . . back there? . . . And the boy said yes, he wanted to stay there. . . . I love you, Mr. Jud." The play ends with Ottoman apparently dead and Andrew gone.

The format of the work combines with its symbolism to depict a transitional moment in life. Memory and the present intermix as Andrew must leave the unworried, love-filled, exciting, circuslike atmosphere of his childhood and move into manhood. Ottoman, a symbolic father figure, is failing, certainly growing old and perhaps even dying (another transition), and while he can put his arm around the boy's shoulder to encourage him, the youngster must continue his journey through life alone. Symbolically, the time of year during which the action takes place represents hope, birth, and renewal, but it is cold, and snow is falling as the play ends, negating the positive aspects of spring and suggesting the fear that both old man and young man feel as they approach the unknown. Kopit has said that *Sing to Me Through Open Windows* is "about the necessity of certain things dying to enable certain things to live. It deals with memory and time. . . ."

OH DAD, POOR DAD, MAMMA'S HUNG YOU IN THE CLOSET AND I'M FEELIN' SO SAD

Oh Dad, Poor Dad, Mamma's Hung You in the Closet and I'm Feelin' So Sad caught theatergoing audiences in the United States by surprise, and a summary of the action provides a clue as to why this happened. The three-scene production, subtitled *A Pseudoclassical Tragifarce in a Bastard French Tradition*, is set in a Caribbean island hotel where Madame Rosepettle, her son Jonathan, two large Venus flytraps, and a cat-eating, talking piranha fish named Rosalinda (after Rosepettle's husband's former secretary) are in transit. Also traveling with the family is the stuffed body of Rosepettle's husband, which is kept in a coffin when traveling and hangs from a hook in Rosepettle's bedroom closet the rest of the time: "He's my favorite trophy. I take him with me wherever I go," she chortles. In scene 1, Rosepettle harangues the bellboys and dominates her son. Scene 2, set two weeks later, brings Jonathan together with a young governess, Rosalie, who tries to seduce him, but who is run off by his mother. One week later, in scene 3, Rosepettle is courted by elderly Commodore Roseabove, but her story of how she brought about her husband's death (a description that paints men as bestial and women as virginal) unnerves him. She proclaims that her goal in life is to protect her son (he was delivered after a twelve-month term, so she obviously began her campaign early): "My son shall have only Light!" Later, while Rosepettle is out on her habitual round, searching for couples making love on the beach so she can kick sand in their faces, Rosalie returns to try to persuade Jonathan to run off with her, but she is so self-centered and insensitive that her sexual desire arouses only terror in Jonathan. When his father's corpse falls on them, Rosalie commands,

"Forget about your father. Drop your pants on top of him, then you won't see his face." The play concludes when Rosepettle returns to find that Jonathan has killed the girl by smothering her.

There are many Freudian and Oedipal overtones to *Oh Dad, Poor Dad, Mamma's Hung You in the Closet and I'm Feelin' So Sad*, with its theme of a domineering mother and Milquetoast son. The theme is not a new one, having been dealt with in Sidney Howard's *The Silver Cord* (pr. 1926, prb. 1927) and later in Harold Pinter's *A Night Out* (pr. 1960) and Philip Roth's *Portnoy's Complaint* (1969), yet Kopit's embroidering of the theme with man-eating plants (symbolic of the emasculating wife/mother), maniacal cuckoo clocks, uncontrollable tape recorders (as in Arthur Miller's *Death of a Salesman*, pr., pb. 1949), and self-propelled chairs, spiced with a loved one's body (as in Joe Orton's *Loot*, pr. 1965), results in a unique creation.

Some critics claim that Kopit is metaphorically portraying the neurosis brought about by the tensions of the nuclear age. This reading is certainly reinforced by the dramatist's use of absurdist techniques, though this interpretation is not completely convincing. The play is not really an absurdist play, in spite of Kopit's use of absurdist techniques—a careful examination of Rosepettle's dialogue, for example, reveals the psychological realism that underlies the bizarre surface of the action. There are flashes of brilliance in the grotesque humor, but they are not sustained throughout the play. Some critics called the work a satire that mimics avant-garde conventions, while others dismissed it as an unsuccessful example of the Theater of the Absurd. In any case, the play conclusively established Kopit's theatrical talent.

INDIANS

After a series of lesser works, Kopit surprised audiences again with *Indians*, his second major play. *Indians* fuses the principal themes and techniques of Kopit's previous works. The conception of the play dates to March, 1966, when Kopit read a statement made by General William Westmoreland, the commander in chief of U.S. forces in Vietnam, regarding incidents in which U.S. soldiers had killed Vietnamese civilians: "Of course innocent people have been killed.

In war they always are. And of course our hearts go out to the innocent victims of this." Realizing that this sentiment could be traced throughout U.S. history, Kopit put Westmoreland's exact words in the mouth of a character in *Indians*, Colonel Forsythe, who speaks them while looking over the site on which a group of Indians have been massacred the day before. The casual dismissal of the action is overwhelming. At the moment that he read Westmoreland's quote, Kopit has recalled, he "was listening to Charles Ives's Fourth Symphony. There are two orchestras playing counterpoint. The orchestras play completely opposing pieces of music based on American Folk songs— 'Shenendoah,' 'Columbia the Gem of the Ocean.' . . . You have this serene, seraphic music based on these folk songs, and then the violent opposition of a marching band drowning it out." The dramatist admits that when the Westmoreland quote was juxtaposed to the music, "I just sort of went berserk."

Another ingredient that contributed to the play's success was the tempering influence of Kopit's intellectual approach to his material. In both *Don Juan in Texas* and *Across the River and into the Jungle*, he had touched on the source of mythic heroes. In *Indians*, he complemented this interest with research. The emotional content and the research came together in the composition process to create interwoven subtexts: "Most of the scenes in the play are based on real incidents that were then distorted." For example, Kopit notes, "The scene on the Plains is based upon a famous expedition of the Grand Duke Alexis. Spotted Tail was not killed then, but he could have been." He goes on to observe that "in a way he was killed; he was made to play the stage Indian for the Grand Duke."

The play is composed of thirteen scenes, alternating between Buffalo Bill's Wild West Show and an 1886 Indian Commission hearing. The extravagant Wild West Show segments illustrate American prejudices, reveal Buffalo Bill's character, comment on historical events, and develop Kopit's theme that Americans create heroes through a mythmaking process that lets their society justify the destruction of other less powerful societies. The commission scenes demonstrate how alien the white and Indian societies appear to each other. The whites do not understand why Indians will neither abide by their treaties nor recognize the innate inferiority of their race. The Indians do not understand how the treaties can be valid, since land cannot be owned, and also why, if there are treaties, the whites do not abide by the agreed-upon terms. Neither side understands, respects, or grants dignity to the opposing side.

The conflict between basic cultural instincts is emphasized by the tension between the alternating scenes and epitomized by the contrast between Westmoreland's words and the noble, moving surrender speech given by Chief Joseph in 1877, which Kopit incorporates into the play twice, the second time as the concluding speech in the play:

> I am tired of fighting. Our chiefs have been killed. . . . The old men are all dead. It is cold and we have no blankets. The children are freezing. My people, some of them, have fled to the hills and have no food. . . . No one knows where they are—perhaps frozen. I want to have time to look for my children and see how many of them I can find. Maybe I shall find them among the dead. Hear me, my chiefs. I am tired. My heart is sick and sad! From where the sun now stands, I will fight no more, forever.

For his part, Buffalo Bill is trapped by his own nature, by historical events, and by America's need to create heroes. He is instrumental in destroying a people and a way of life he admires.

Kopit does not intend his play to be understood on a literal level. The chronology (referred to as a "Chronology for a Dreamer") that is supplied in the printed version of the play is not the chronology followed in the drama. Spotted Tail rises after his death to make a speech. The opening, in which the figures of Buffalo Bill and Sitting Bull are seen as though they are in museum cases, is intended to alert the viewer immediately that the play is not to be taken realistically. Instead, Kopit offers an emotional gestalt, an impressionistic, surreal representation of his theme. By means of a deliberately confusing Brechtian production through which the spectators are made aware of historical processes, the playwright forces them to realize that those processes are human-made, not natural elements, and that they are alterable. The play gets off to a weak start, but after the first three or four scenes, the cumulative effect of Kopit's dramatic structure begins to build, and the play gathers power as it progresses, each scene taking its strength from the scenes that precede it while simultaneously adding to their impact.

WINGS

As impressive as *Indians* was, *Wings* was the product of an even more mature dramatist and is probably Kopit's finest work. Again he combined a strong emotional expression with an intellectual context, and again he relied on the themes and techniques that had served him well in the past, but he explored new material as well. Stylistically there is an impressive distance between the realism of *The Questioning of Nick* and the impressionism of *Wings*; there is also an interesting thematic progression from the commonplace subject matter of the early plays to the public, social impulse behind *Indians* and then to the personal, individual content of *Wings*.

In the spring of 1976, Kopit's father suffered a massive stroke that rendered him incapable of speech. This event became the source of *Wings*'s emotional content. During his visits to the Burke Rehabilitation Center in White Plains, New York, as he explains in a Shavian preface to the published script, Kopit formulated what became the operative or controlling questions for the play, going beyond a mere exploration of the problems of communication and of the nature of language: "To what extent was [his father] still intact? To what extent was he aware of what had befallen him? *What was it like inside?*" In addition to his father, the dramatist observed several other patients, on whom the protagonist, Emily Stilson, was to be modeled. Kopit not only became involved in trying to convey what it would be like to undergo the personal and terrifying catastrophe of a stroke but also began examining the nature of identity and of reality itself, for to the disoriented victim, reality is confused and unverifiable, and the resultant terror must be faced in virtual isolation.

To supplement his own observations, Kopit once more turned to exhaustive research. The published text of the play has an epigraph from Charles Lindbergh's *The Spirit of St. Louis* (1953), which describes the pilot's feeling of being cut off and unsure of what is real; ironically, the feeling is similar to that experienced by a stroke victim, and Lindbergh's words are later echoed in Emily's dialogue. Kopit also drew on two books concerning brain damage, Howard Gardner's *The Shattered Mind* (1975) and A. R. Luria's *The Man with a Shattered World* (1972), and on the experience of the center's therapist, Jacqueline Doolittle, herself a former stroke victim.

The effective representation of the mind of the victim is what sets this drama apart from most of its contemporaries and supplies a strength that would be missing if the playwright had adopted a documentary approach. The ninety-minute play moves from fragmentation to integration, a movement synchronized with stage effects—live and recorded sound, colored and flashing lights, shifting points of view, a minimal set conveying a sense of limbo, overlapping dialogue, loudspeakers situated throughout the theater, and other such devices, which exercise the potential of the theater to the maximum.

The play is open-ended in that it comes to no climax or conclusion. Performed without intermission, it is composed of four segments. In "Prelude," Emily suffers her stroke. In "Catastrophe," she realizes that something has happened, but she cannot determine what or identify her status. "Awakening" traces Emily's transition from a total lack of understanding to the dawning of understanding. In "Explorations," the final segment, she begins to sort out her identity and starts to appreciate the significance of her condition. Although these states of being are distinct, the person progressively experiencing them cannot perceive either edge of the transition, a condition that Kopit reproduces nicely while still managing to maintain a sense of Emily's gradual reconstruction of her personality and of reality itself.

The dramatist's careful combination of logic and nonsense, of articulate speech and babble, parallels his stage effects to depict an extraordinary, nonverbal sequence of events. There is not much action in *Wings*, and what there is seems confusing and unstructured. The audience, however, soon becomes deeply involved with Emily; tension is created not by dramatic action, but by the audience's effort to decipher what is happening in the play and what is real, and by their concern for Emily. The charge that *Wings* is not interesting because it lacks sufficient rising action is similar to the criticism leveled against Eugene O'Neill's *Long Day's Journey into Night* (pr., pb. 1956) and is equally invalid. *Wings* is not meant to entertain superficially in the way that Lanford Wilson's *Talley's Folly* (pr., pb. 1979) or Neil Simon's plays do; like *Long Day's Journey into Night*, it sheds light on the perennial human condition.

BONE-THE-FISH

Road to Nirvana (1990) was originally titled *Bone-the-Fish* and was in part a spoof of David Mamet's *Speed-the-Plow*. The play premiered at the 1989 Humana Festival of New American Plays at the Actors Theatre of Louisville, where it created quite a stir. A harshly satirical look at Hollywood and the motion picture industry (and the world of business in general, as well as religion and other topics ripe for the picking), the drama was filled with humor and spectacle—a starlet is carried onstage on a litter, much as Cleopatra was. Still, the work was so offensive to some (a Hollywood wannabe is forced to eat "nunshit" in a test to see if he qualifies to join the ranks of the industry's depraved arbiters of artistic taste) that it was deemed over the top. Like Henry Moore's readers of an earlier generation, the audience was so put off by the excesses in form that they were unable to appreciate the substance (the nature of art and the artists and the relationship between art and commerce, for instance).

Y2K

Y2K (later retitled *BecauseHeCan*), like *Road to Nirvana*, was first staged at the Humana Festival. Theater critics from around the world voted the drama the best play at the 1999 festival. The title plays off the fear of universal chaos and the crashing of computers that is predicted to arrive with the new millennium because not all computer programs were designed to recognize the change from 1999 to 2000 (potentially reacting instead as though the new year was 1900, thus invalidating critical operations).

Compared to John Guare's *Six Degrees of Separation* (pr., pb. 1990) and Craig Lucas's *Dying Gaul* (pr. 1999), with a plot out of Franz Kafka or George Or-

well, the theme of this thriller, however, is the erosion of personal privacy. Joseph Elliott, a Random House art books editor, and his wife, Joanne, an appraiser at Sotheby's, are enjoying their upscale life in a Manhattan apartment when they experience a phenomenon that is becoming a national crisis—the invasion of their private lives by a computer stalker, Costa Astrakhan. The comfort of their modernistic Park Avenue home, which is dominated by a huge Hanz Klein painting, is destroyed by a man who boasts that he can reach into their lives at anytime because he is "everywhere": "On the outskirts of your mind, in the ether, in the darkness."

Stylistically, the use of hacker jargon helps keep the audience slightly off balance, as does the awareness that the issue of deteriorating privacy applies not just to this nice couple but to the audience as well. The Elliotts learn that computers can control their lives and that their computer illiteracy makes them vulnerable to cyber geeks who can take over their bank accounts—and their lives. *Y2K* is a thriller that insists that paranoia can be based on reality. The chilling fact that the drama ends without a resolution leaves the audience as entrapped and vulnerable as the play's protagonists.

OTHER MAJOR WORKS

SCREENPLAY: *Treasure Island*, 1994.

TELEPLAYS: *The Conquest of Television*, 1966; *Promontory Point Revisited*, 1969; *Hands of a Stranger*, 1987; *Phantom of the Opera*, 1990 (based on Gaston Leroux's novel); *Roswell*, 1995.

NONFICTION: "The Vital Matter of Environment," 1961 (in *Theatre Arts*).

TRANSLATION: *Ghosts*, 1984 (of Henrik Ibsen's play *Gengangere*).

BIBLIOGRAPHY

Dieckman, Suzanne Burgoyne, and Richard Brayshaw. "Wings, Watchers, and Windows: Imprisonment in the Plays of Arthur Kopit." *Theatre Journal* 35 (May, 1983): 195-212. Concentrates on *Wings* and earlier short plays but speaks intelligently of *Indians* and *Nine* as well. The authors find that Kopit's later work "explores the process of transformation, a process which involves the interplay between freedom and limitations." Imprisonments are mental and political, and Kopit dramatizes "the process of transcending those limitations."

Kauffmann, Stanley. *Persons of the Drama: Theater Criticism and Comment*. New York: Harper and Row, 1976. A collection of reviews that includes a long look at *Indians*, in which Kauffmann sees more intention than fulfillment. Pointing to some awkward moments in the work, he comments that "the playwright who could sink to such depths has a foggy conception of the heights."

Kelley, Margot Anne. "Order Within Fragmentation: Postmodernism and the Stroke Victim's World." *Modern Drama* 34 (September, 1991): 383-391. A study of *Wings*, written for radio in 1976 and revised for the stage in 1978. Kopit, in addition to examining the character possibilities, also "manipulates contemporary cultural ideas from the sciences and literature through his disability metaphor," a change from earlier treatments of this disorder.

Rich, Frank. "Art Imitates Art (and Artists)." Review of *Bone-the-Fish* by Arthur Kopit. *The New York Times*, March 8, 1991, p. C1. This review demonstrates what is wrong with the New York theater criticism system: Rich did not like the play but in the act of damning it points out its strengths. The fullness and insight of Kopit's parody of David Mamet is not the weakness but the strength of this play. The review analyzes Kopit's comic voice but without appreciating its subtleties.

Szilassy, Zoltan. *American Theater of the 1960's*. Carbondale: Southern Illinois University Press, 1986. Discusses Kopit's works throughout, especially *Indians*, but also covers the one-act plays surrounding *The Day the Whores Came Out to Play Tennis*. Szilassy speaks well of these "one-acters, improvisations, and trifles" and discusses *Chamber Music* at some length. Index.

Watt, Stephen. "Arthur Kopit: British Stage Design." *Theatre Journal* 35, no. 2 (May, 1983). Discusses Kopit's work from a production point of view.

_____. *Postmodern/Drama: Reading the Contemporary Stage*. Ann Arbor: University of Michigan Press, 1998. Watt resists the critical tendency to label texts and writers as "postmodern." Kopit is among those whose work is analyzed to determine what in his plays is open to being termed postmodern in emphasis.

Westarp, Karl-Heinz. "Myth in Peter Shaffer's *The Royal Hunt of the Sun* and in Arthur Kopit's *Indians*." *English Studies: A Journal of English Language and Literature* 65 (April, 1984): 120-128. A good introduction to the vocabulary of myth criticism, and a strong source of comparison between *Indians* and Shaffer's own examination of the fall of the Incas at the hands of the Spanish. Kopit is seen here as a "demystifier" rather than a mythmaker, an important distinction for understanding his later work, especially *Road to Nirvana*.

Steven H. Gale,
updated by Thomas J. Taylor and Steven H. Gale

BERNARD KOPS

Born: London, England; November 28, 1926

PRINCIPAL DRAMA

The Hamlet of Stepney Green, pr. 1958, pb. 1959
Good-Bye World, pr. 1959
Change for the Angel, pr. 1960
The Dream of Peter Mann, pr., pb. 1960
Enter Solly Gold, pb. 1961, pr. 1962 (music by Stanley Myers)
Stray Cats and Empty Bottles, pr. 1964 (televised), pr. 1967 (staged)
The Boy Who Wouldn't Play Jesus, pr., pb. 1965

David, It Is Getting Dark, pr. 1966

It's a Lovely Day Tomorrow, pr. 1975 (televised),
    pr. 1976 (staged; with John Goldschmidt)

More Out than In, pr. 1980

Ezra, pb. 1980, pr. 1981

Simon at Midnight, pr. 1982 (radio play), pr. 1985
    (staged)

Sophie (The Last of the Red Hot Mamas), pr. 1990

Playing Sinatra, pr. 1991, pb. 1992

Dreams of Anne Frank, pr. 1992, pb. 1993

Call in the Night, pr. 1995, pb. 2000

Plays: One, pb. 1999

Plays: Two, pb. 2000

Plays: Three, pb. 2002

OTHER LITERARY FORMS

Bernard Kops is a prolific writer. He has published numerous novels, including *Awake for Mourning* (1958), *Motorbike* (1962), *Yes from No-Man's Land* (1965), *The Dissent of Dominick Shapiro* (1966), *By the Waters of Whitechapel* (1969), *The Passionate Past of Gloria Gaye* (1971), *Settle Down Simon Katz* (1973), *Partners* (1975), and *On Margate Sands* (1978). His books of poetry include *Poems* (1955), *Poems and Songs* (1958), *An Anemone for Antigone* (1959), *For the Record* (1971), and *Grandchildren and Other Poems* (2000). Kops's powerful autobiography, *The World Is a Wedding*, was published in 1963. His dramatic writing includes work for television and radio as well as for the stage.

ACHIEVEMENTS

The relative critical neglect of Kops may result in part from his extensive work in nontheatrical dramatic forms such as radio and television; his prolific activity as a novelist may have further distracted attention from his dramatic achievements. Nevertheless, following the widespread publicity given to his brilliant evocation of Ezra Pound's insanity in *Ezra*, Kops began to be recognized in England as a supreme master of dramatic dream poetry. Kops was the first person to be awarded the C. Day Lewis fellowship (1980), was the recipient of several Arts Council bursaries, and has been writer-in-residence in Bristol and the London Borough of Hounslow.

BIOGRAPHY

Bernard Kops's work is intensely autobiographical. Details of his early life may be found in *The World Is a Wedding*. He was born in Stepney in the East End of London in 1926. His father was a Dutch Jewish immigrant cobbler who came to London's East End in 1904, and his mother was born in London of Dutch Jewish parents. Kops was the youngest of a family of four sisters and two brothers. Although his family was very poor, Kops grew up in an intense, colorful, and cosmopolitan environment. The English fascist demonstrations and counter-demonstrations of the late 1930's in the East End of London provided a personal background for the awareness of anti-Semitism that pervades Kops's work.

Kops left school when he was only thirteen to earn a living as best he could—as a docker, chef, salesman, waiter, liftman, and barrow boy, selling books in street markets. Already writing and reading intensely, he was particularly moved by Eugene O'Neill's *Mourning Becomes Electra* (pr., pb. 1931) and its depiction of family conflicts and fantasy states. T. S. Eliot was another early literary influence, from whom Kops gained insight into the theatrical use of popular songs. The foundations for Kops's dramatic methodology were formed at the evening drama classes he attended at Toynbee Hall in London's East End.

During World War II, Kops's family moved around England in frequent evacuations and return trips to the badly blitzed East End. The postwar years saw Kops acting in repertory theater; traveling through France, Spain, and Tangier; living in a caravan in Camden Town, North London; and taking drugs. Following the death of his mother in 1951, Kops was committed to a psychiatric hospital. Kops has twice been institutionalized; the concern with extreme mental states in his work clearly has a personal genesis. Kops's meeting with and marriage in 1956 to Erica Gordon, a doctor's daughter, eased his bereavement and transformed his life, giving him the support he so desperately needed. They had four children, and, beginning in the late 1950's, he earned his living as a professional writer.

Kops's first play, *The Hamlet of Stepney Green*, was produced by Frank Hauser at the Oxford Playhouse in 1957, subsequently moving to London's Lyric Theatre and then to New York. With the success of this play, Kops arrived on the theatrical scene. Kops settled in London, where he continued to write frequently on the artistic life, especially in retrospect from his earlier days in SoHo. His play *Ezra*, based on the life of Ezra Pound, is often performed in colleges; *Simon at Midnight* was broadcast on radio in 1982 and was made into a stage play in 1985.

ANALYSIS

First and foremost, Bernard Kops is a lyric poet who uses the theater, television, and radio as vehicles for poetry. Theatrically, he is an innovator in his use of music and songs and in his often successful attempts to restore vitality to hackneyed themes. Kops's exploration of fantasy, of inner states of being, and of schizophrenia is juxtaposed to the presentation of realistic, sordid surroundings. His handling of dream logic is superb and explains why he is so attracted to the radio as a dramatic form. Radio drama depends on pauses, sounds, words, silences, and the intimate relationship between the listeners (the unseen audience) and the unseen performers in the studio. Such a form is ideally suited to Kops's synthesis of past and present, actuality and fantasy.

Kops's plays have been hailed as triumphs of sordid realism much in the kitchen-sink mold, as imaginative explorations of psychic worlds, and as politically charged allegories. Kops was at first bracketed with Harold Pinter and Arnold Wesker, two other East End Jewish dramatists who emerged in the new wave of British drama heralded by the 1956 Royal Court Theatre performance of John Osborne's *Look Back in Anger*. Each subsequently went his own way, the differences being greater than the similarities. Unlike Pinter's work, Kops's theater is frequently overtly Jewish. While hostility in Pinter is characterized by innuendo and body movement, sometimes erupting into violence, hostility in Kops is overt; it does not simmer. Unlike Wesker, Kops does not preach. Most of Kops's drama, even when focusing on old age and death, has a vitality, an instinctive sense of life, and often a coarse humor that are lacking in Wesker.

Much of Kops's work revolves around family situations, the basic conflict he sees in such situations, and the individual's doomed attempt to free himself from the family and its nets. He is obsessed with family themes, with people tied together in intense love-hate relationships. Like O'Neill, Kops uses the theater to express the inner life of human beings. All of his plays are shadowed by the streets and sounds of the London of his childhood, by his Jewishness, by his family, and by his wild, anarchic, surrealistic inner life.

THE HAMLET OF STEPNEY GREEN

The plot of *The Hamlet of Stepney Green* provides a good illustration of the nature of Kops's drama. Kops transforms William Shakespeare's *Hamlet* into an East End London Jewish lyric fantasy. Hamlet becomes David Levy, twenty-two years old, tall, and intelligent, who wants to be a singer like Frank Sinatra. He refuses to see his future in terms of inheriting his aging father's small pickled-herring street stall. Kops describes two ways in which David Levy can be played—as someone who can sing, or as someone who cannot: "The crucial thing about David is that although he is bored with the life around him he is waiting for something to happen." Hava Segal, the daughter of Solly Segal, David's father's best friend, becomes Ophelia and dotes on David. Throughout the first act, Sam, David's father, is dying; the curtain to the first act falls as he dies. At the moment of death, father and son are united. Like so many of Kops's subsequent creations, the old man is unwilling to relinquish his hold on life. He is sad because there is a gulf between him and his son and because there is no love in his relationship with Bessy, his young and still quite attractive wife.

In the second act, Sam returns to the stage as a ghostly figment of his son's imagination, calling on David to avenge his death. In David's heightened imagination, his mother has poisoned his father. Bessy is going to marry Solly Segal. David, imitating Hamlet, dresses in black and is treated as though he were insane by relatives and a chorus of salesmen. Meanwhile the ghost attempts to dampen David's vengeful desires. Sam, aware that only good can come through Bessy's marriage to Solly, arranges, through a séance, for the marriage to take place.

In the final act, the ghost persuades David to mix a seemingly deadly potion to be used on the wedding day, but the potion is actually life-giving. The drama concludes on a frenzied note of love and reconciliation, and the ghosts haunting David's mind are liberated and disappear into nothingness.

Throughout *The Hamlet of Stepney Green*, realism and fantasy interweave. The play, like much of Kops's work, is rooted in the East End of London (the equivalent of New York's Lower East Side)—its characters, noise, bustle, rhythms, and songs. Music is used to great effect by Kops, to re-create the East End ambience, to evoke nostalgia, and to provide a sad, ironic commentary on the action. During the mourning period at the end of the first scene of the second act, for example, Sam's family and friends gather around the home in the traditional Jewish way to remember him. David, in black, disrupts tradition by singing "My Yiddisher Father" to the tune of Sophie Tucker's famous "My Yiddishe Mamma." The "shiva" rituals (for mourning the dead) are parodied by transforming the gender of popular song lyrics. Reviewers noted that the play was far too long, especially when it indulged in lyric fantasies concerning the past—a reflection of Kops's lack of discipline. Kops often forgets his plot, forgets the limitations of the stage, and even forgets the patience of an audience; Sam takes a long time to die. In spite of these defects, the play generates a tremendous sense of life and bustle, brilliantly rendering ordinary London Jewish existence with its hopes, fears, music, and tears.

Good-Bye World

Good-Bye World, performed in Guildford Surrey in 1959, has long, rambling dream sequences that make it theatrically unsatisfactory. Kops enjoys conveying the details of low-life London. His setting is a Paddington boardinghouse, and the protagonist is a thuggish, obsessive dreamer, a hardened criminal of twenty-two who breaks out of prison because his mother has committed suicide. The play contains three of Kops's basic dramatic ingredients: London rhythms and atmosphere, dreams and fantasies, and mothers and their influence on their sons. The protagonist, John, has two objectives: to find out whether

his mother has left him a message, and to give her a decent burial. In his room, the characters who knew his mother—a landlady, a drunken Irishman, and a blind circus clown—come and talk to him. While John listens, the police wait outside to recapture him. The long personal monologues of each character reveal Kops's fascination with the poetry of the inner mind, his handling of dream logic, his sudden switches of mood and tone, and his exploration of schizophrenia. These dramatic elements achieve their summit in his mature drama, *Ezra*.

Change for the Angel

Kops's next play, *Change for the Angel*, which had a limited run at the Arts Theatre in London in March, 1960, develops many of the ideas introduced in *The Hamlet of Stepney Green* and *Good-Bye World*. Paul Jones is a teenager in search of a meaningful life; his sister, Helen, is a machinist; and his brother, Martin, is the leader of a local gang of fascist youths. Paul's father, Joe, is a baker whose business has been adversely affected by a supermarket. He takes to drinking in the pub to escape from work and the family. Paul wants to be a writer and resists his father's efforts to turn him into an engineer. By the end of the first act, Paul is praying for his father's death, and Helen has been seduced by an American serviceman.

The second act introduces the first of a long line of Kopsian characters, just released from mental institutions, who have to face a hostile world. In this instance, the former mental patient is the victim of Joe's attempted rape.

In the third act, Paul hates his father so much that he invokes the Angel of Death, who takes the wrong life—his mother's instead of his father's. The audience is treated to a very lengthy deathbed scene and to frenetic, hysterical reactions. Paul leaves home and, in a manner reminiscent of the ending of D. H. Lawrence's *Sons and Lovers* (1913), goes into a hostile world after his beloved mother, rather than the detested father, dies.

The name of the family in *Change for the Angel* may be Jenkins, but the cadences are those of East End Jewish family life. The play contains Kops's recurrent ingredients, but there is also an overt political conviction not so evident in his earlier plays. The threat of nuclear disaster dominates the play, as does the continual fear of anti-Semitism.

THE DREAM OF PETER MANN

Oedipal elements, the bomb, and lyric fantasy are the essential ingredients of *The Dream of Peter Mann*, which suffered the insult, on its Edinburgh Festival premiere early in September, 1960, of having half the first-night audience walk out. The play proved to be too expensive to perform satisfactorily and too much goes on in it; nevertheless, it remains one of Kops's most interesting works. The author reflected in a personal communication that he "wanted to write a play about a man who was up with progress but got mixed up in power and in so doing helped to create the destruction of the world." The protagonist, Peter Mann, dominated by his strong Jewish mother, has grown up in a London street of run-down small shops. A small, cunning tramp named Alex persuades Peter to travel the world to make his fortune. After he robs his mother's safe, Peter's fantasies take over most of the remainder of the play. The people in the street become robots compulsively digging for uranium, then change into savages prepared to lynch Peter on his return from his travels, into slaves working twenty-four hours a day preparing shrouds for the next war, into rebels, and finally back into themselves. During the action of the play, Peter is defeated, victorious, penniless, and enormously wealthy. Clearly, Peter Mann is Everyman, a leader and a victim, hopeful and despairing, generous and selfish, shrewd and simple. The fantasy is an enlargement of reality, another dimension of the everyday. Kops keeps the play in control by grounding its frenetic fantasy in the sounds of London Jewish life, conveyed through colloquial dialogue, Cockney backchat, dance-hall rhythms, catchy songs, and contemporary political references.

ENTER SOLLY GOLD

Superficially, *Enter Solly Gold* may appear to be different from Kops's earlier working-class-oriented plays; nevertheless, it has much in common with them. It won a competition organized by Centre 42, an early 1960's movement designed to bring the theater to people outside London and to factory districts where little if any theater had been performed. The hero of the drama is a carpetbagger, Solly Gold, who informs the audience within the first few minutes that "work is all right for workers . . . but for Solly Gold?" Solly is scavenging in London's East End, trying to get enough money to emigrate to America, his "spiritual home," where he believes "dog eats dog and . . . that's the way [he] like[s] it."

The opening scene is Rabelaisian. Solly fiddles money out of a tailor, carries on with the tailor's wife, sleeps with a hard-bitten prostitute, and dons the clothes of a widow's deceased husband, a rabbi, in order to cheat her out of a bunch of large chickens.

In the second scene, Solly, still disguised as a rabbi, has gate-crashed a wealthy home where a wedding is taking place. Solly announces the start of "Rabbinical Chicken Sunday" and gradually takes over the household, making himself indispensable to Morry Swartz, head of the house and king of a shoe business, a melancholy millionaire. Solly sets about making Morry the Messiah so that Morry will find the peace of mind he lacks and Solly will get the cash he needs.

In the course of the drama, Kops lashes out at Bar Mitzvahs, weddings, and big business, writing some of his most sustained and brilliant comic lines. Many of these reflect the love-hate attitude he has toward his own Anglo-Jewish background. The play's warm reception in non-Jewish communities is evidence, however, of its universality: Carpetbaggers exist everywhere, and Kops's depiction of greed and hypocrisy speaks to audiences of all kinds, as does his blend of slapstick comedy and exuberant verbal wit.

DAVID, IT IS GETTING DARK

David, It Is Getting Dark, produced and performed in France in 1970 by the distinguished French actor Laurent Terzieff, depicts the conflict between a right-wing English writer and a socialist English Jewish writer. In this play, Kops tackles an issue that has continued to absorb him: how to reconcile great writing with inhuman political theories. The play also examines the relationship between victim and victor. While *David, It Is Getting Dark* can be viewed as a trial run for *Ezra*, it is a valuable work in its own right. Success and failure, the need to love and be loved, loneliness and the need to communicate, Jewishness and anti-Semitism, the need for God, the way human beings use and are used in turn by one another, sterility, and creativity, the dark forces within the self transcending political conviction—all these themes swirl together in the play. The long final scene, which depicts David, the Jewish poet, returning to his room and dancing with his mistress, Bella, while Edward, the reactionary artist, pleads with him to look at his manuscript, is made unforgettable by Kops's powerful, haunting, and evocative poetry.

David, It Is Getting Dark is intensely autobiographical: David's sense of failure is Kops's. There is superb irony in the fact that nearly a decade after its composition, Kops decided to restore Ezra Pound to life. A seemingly failed English Jewish writer uses a great anti-Semitic writer's last, sad years to show how human that writer was and, in the process, achieves fame for himself. In *David, It Is Getting Dark*, Edward Nichols appropriates David's autobiography; Kops transforms Pound's last years in *Ezra*.

EZRA

Ezra explores the relationship between insanity, political extremism, and poetic power. Kops has long been obsessed with the question of how great poetry can be written by a man holding vicious political opinions and insidious economic ideas. At the same time, *Ezra* continues his exploration of extreme mental states. Kops gets inside Pound's mind by creating a world in which all things coexist at the same time: the past and the present, the living and the dead, fact and fantasy, truth and illusion. Once again, Kops's drama inhabits the territory of fantastic juxtapositions. Benito Mussolini and Antonio Vivaldi are as real for Pound as his wife, his mistress, and the officials who put him into a cage and then into a Washington, D.C., asylum. Kops's Pound is sensitive, learned, egotistical, and eccentric. Onstage he is exhibited as a gorilla in a large cage, all the while producing poetry for his seminal work, *The Cantos*. Kops intertwines snatches of poetry, dialogue, ranting, animal sounds, contemporary popular songs, and fragments of great lyric insight. The effect is profoundly moving—the summit of Kops's theatrical achievement. Using stream-of-consciousness techniques, Kops enters Pound's mind, developing surreal scenic juxtapositions to structure the text and convey the howling sounds of genius at bay. *Ezra* encapsulates all of Kops's recurring themes and techniques: his social and political awareness, his obsession with down-and-outs, with the antisocial and the insane, with the victim-predator relationship, and with the family. Pound is caught in a love-hate relationship with his wife, his mistress, his country—and himself. Theatrically, the power of the play lies in the visual presentation of entrapment. Kops uses a wooden set with protruding nails. The prison and the cage are projections of the entangled web of Pound's mind. Ian McDiarmid played Pound in the London performance. His long white hair hung from his head like that of an Old Testament prophet. Accompanied by the music of Antonio Vivaldi and Richard Wagner in the background, McDiarmid switched in mood from King Lear to his Fool in less than a second.

Kops is a supreme dramatist of frenetic states. The distinguished English theater critic Irving Wardle, in a 1980 review in *The Times* (London), wrote that "no other living playwright matches" Kops "in the virtuoso handling of dream logic." Kops has progressed from the often undisciplined rendering of Oedipal fantasies and dreamy young poetic rebels and confidence tricksters to the exploration of the subconscious mind, where reality and illusion intertwine and provide the vehicle for richly resonant dramatic poetry. Kops is a writer aware of the drama inherent in the sudden shifts in perception and changes of mood he has always found so natural. In *Ezra*, the London working-class Jewish poet has found his métier: *Ezra* places Kops in stature and achievement with the best dramatists of his generation.

OTHER MAJOR WORKS

LONG FICTION: *Awake for Mourning*, 1958; *Motorbike*, 1962; *Yes from No-Man's Land*, 1965; *The Dissent of Dominick Shapiro*, 1966; *By the Waters of Whitechapel*, 1969; *The Passionate Past of Gloria Gaye*, 1971; *Settle Down Simon Katz*, 1973; *Partners*, 1975; *On Margate Sands*, 1978.

POETRY: *Poems*, 1955; *Poems and Songs*, 1958; *An Anemone for Antigone*, 1959; *Erica, I Want to*

Read You Something, 1967; *For the Record*, 1971; *Barricades in West Hampstead*, 1988; *Grandchildren and Other Poems*, 2000.

TELEPLAYS: *I Want to Go Home*, 1963; *The Last Years of Brian Hooper*, 1967; *Alexander the Great*, 1971; *Just One Kid*, 1974; *Moss*, 1975; *Rocky Marciano Is Dead*, 1976; *Night Kids*, 1983.

RADIO PLAYS: *Home Sweet Honeycomb*, 1962; *The Lemmings*, 1963; *The Dark Ages*, 1964; *Bournemouth Nights*, 1979; *Over the Rainbow*, 1980; *Trotsky Was My Father*, 1984.

NONFICTION: *The World Is a Wedding*, 1963 (autobiography); *Neither Your Honey nor Your Sting: An Offbeat History of the Jews*, 1984; *Shalom Bomb: Scenes from My Life*, 2000.

BIBLIOGRAPHY

Cohn, Ruby. *Modern Shakespeare Offshoots*. Princeton, N.J.: Princeton University Press, 1976. Kops wrote *The Hamlet of Stepney Green* in 1957, here discussed in the context of modern interpretations of the universal Hamlet character in "the life of Jewish immigrants in London's East End—[Kops's] own background." Cohn sees Kops's work as essentially a melodrama in which "everyone else [but Hamlet] lives happily ever after."

Glanville, Brian. "The Anglo-Jewish Writer." *Encounter* 14 (January, 1960): 62-64. Glanville, in this overview of the Anglo-Jewish writer, refers to Kops as "a young playwright [who] has written plays in the . . . romantic genre." He discusses the scarcity of important Anglo-Jewish writers and their avoidance of Jewish life as a topic. Mentions Peter Shaffer's *Five Finger Exercise* (pr., pb. 1958) and several novelists as well.

Klass, Philip. "Bernard Kops." In *British Dramatists Since World War II*, edited by Stanley Weintraub. Vol. 13 in *Dictionary of Literary Biography*. Detroit, Mich.: The Gale Group, 1982. Traces the life of Kops, focusing on the development of his stage craft.

Kops, Bernard. "The Modest Muse." Interview by Sue Limb. *Listener* 107 (April 29, 1982): 32. An interview with Kops on the occasion of the radio broadcast of *Simon at Midnight*. Kops's life "pours through" the play, in "the surges of emotion; the all-powerful mother still laying down the law long after her death. . . ." Kops views radio as "a close-up medium . . . intensely personal." He mentions his large family, his writer-in-residence post at Hounslow, and his commissions for television and film scripts. Includes a photograph of the playwright.

_____. "Oasis for Misfits." *New Statesman Society* 3 (June 1, 1990): 40-41. Kops remembers the SoHo lifestyle from the late 1940's to the mid-1950's, when he was living on Arts Council awards and finding his creative voice, "talking, taking drugs, women, reading *Finnegan's Wake* at 3 A.M." A good self-sketch.

Taylor, John Russell. *The Angry Theatre: New British Drama*. Rev. ed. New York: Hill and Wang, 1969. A fairly long description of Kops's start at the Oxford Playhouse and Centre 42, and his contribution to British theater, especially *The Hamlet of Stepney Green*, *The Dream of Peter Mann*, and *Enter Solly Gold*.

Wellwarth, George E. *The Theater of Protest and Paradox*. Rev. ed. New York: New York University Press, 1972. A chapter on Kops titled "The Jew as 'Everyman'" deals with *The Hamlet of Stepney Green*, *The Dream of Peter Mann*, and *Enter Solly Gold*, all set in London but "modeled on the type of Jewish folk literature written by Sholom Aleichem or Isaac Babel." The first two plays, says Wellwarth, are "sophomoric philosophy," but *Enter Solly Gold* is "gay and witty," and thus will not be taken seriously by "English critics who are fostering the new movement."

William Baker,
updated by Thomas J. Taylor

AUGUST VON KOTZEBUE

Born: Weimar, Saxony (now in Germany); May 3, 1761

Died: Mannheim, Baden (now in Germany); March 23, 1819

PRINCIPAL DRAMA

Menschenhass und Reue, pr. 1789, pb. 1790 (*The Stranger: Or, Misanthropy and Repentance*, 1798)

Die Indianer in England, pr. 1789, pb. 1790 (*The Indians in England*, 1796)

Die Sonnenjungfrau, pr. 1789, pb. 1791 (*The Virgin of the Sun*, 1799)

Doktor Bahrdt mit der eiserner Stirn: Oder, Die deutsche Union gegen Zimmermann, pb. 1790

Das Kind der Liebe, pr., pb. 1790 (*Love's Vows: Or, The Natural Son*, 1798)

Die Spanier in Peru: Oder, Rollas Tod, pr. 1794, pb. 1795 (*The Spaniards in Peru: Or, Rolla's Death*, 1799)

Der Wildfang, pr. 1795, pb. 1798 (*The Wild Goosechase*, 1798)

La Peyrouse, pr. 1796, pb. 1797 (English translation, 1799)

Die Versöhnung, pr. 1797, pb. 1798 (*The Reconciliation*, 1799)

Der Graf von Burgund, pr., pb. 1798 (*The Count of Burgundy*, 1798)

Der Schreibepult: Oder, Die Gefahren de Jugend, pr. 1798, pb. 1800 (*The Writing Desk: Or, Youth in Danger*, 1799)

Johannes von Montfaucon, pr. 1799, pb. 1800 (*Johanna of Montfaucon*, 1800)

Die beiden Klingsberg, pr. 1799, pb. 1801 (*Father and Son: Or, Family Frailties*, 1814)

Die deutschen Kleinstädter, pr. 1802, pb. 1803 (*The Good Citizens of Piffelheim*, 1990)

Die Hussiten vor Naumburg im Jahr 1432, pr. 1802, pb. 1803 (*The Patriot Father*, 1819)

Pagenstreiche, pr. 1803, pb. 1804

Heinrich Reuss von Plauen, pr., pb. 1805

Rudolf von Hapsburg und König Ottokar von Böhmen, pr. 1813, pb. 1815

Theater, pb. 1840-1841 (40 volumes)

OTHER LITERARY FORMS

August von Kotzebue also wrote poems, novels, reviews, historical treatises, travel descriptions, autobiographical works, essays, opera librettos, anecdotes, and apologies and retractions. He edited several journals, such as *Der Freimüthige* (1803-1807), *Die Biene* (1808-1810), and *Die Grille* (1811-1812). Editions of his letters to his mother and to his publisher also exist, as well as letters and papers published from his estate. The most important collections of these works are *Ausgewählte prosaische Schriften* (1842-1843), *Kleine gesammelte Schriften* (1787-1791), *Vom Adel* (1792), and *Unparteiische Untersuchung über die Folgen der französischen Revolution auf das übrige Europa* (1795). Among the English collections and translations is *Historical, Literary, and Political Anecdotes and Miscellanies* (1807).

ACHIEVEMENTS

It is no exaggeration to say that few German writers influenced European literature as much as did August von Kotzebue. His tremendous success with the theatergoing public in Germany, England, France, Russia, and other European nations engendered a multitude of translations, adaptations, and emulations of his dramatic style; his popularity also caused literary feuds in the artistic community and generated suspicion about Kotzebue's political loyalties in his dealings with foreign powers and governments. The perceived inconsistencies in his views, for example, the depiction of a degenerate nobility in his plays and the apology for hereditary nobility in his treatise *Vom Adel*, or his apparent support of the French Revolution, his polemics against Napoleon, and his lifelong fascination with Russia and its czars, led to misunderstandings and finally to his assassination. Literary historians, far from celebrating the king of dramatists in his time, viewed with disdain his admitted goal to please the public and did not forgive him his quarrels with (and frequently his verbal victory over) the giants of German literature such as Johann Wolfgang von Goethe and the brothers August William von Schlegel and Friedrich von Schlegel. The playwright, whose productivity was so immense that he himself lost count of the number of tragedies, comedies, librettos, and farces that he had written (he thought them to number 211, but he actually wrote at least 230), was accused of lacking morality and of encouraging frivolity in his works. Kotzebue refused to see an educational function in the theater and perceived it instead as an entertaining institution; this attitude was unforgivable in the judgment of later literary historians. Critical works either ignore Kotzebue's contribution to the theater entirely or are generally hostile. From the nineteenth century onward, literary historians have set the evaluative trends by calling Kotzebue a "procurer" for the brothel he made of literature (Wolfgang Menzel, Die deutsche Literatur, 1827, 1836); by claiming that he was guided by the "pernicious principle" (Julian Schmidt, Geschichte der deutschen Literatur im 19. Jahrhundert, 1886-1896); by announcing that although he is not dispensable, "we can despise him" (Georg Gottfried Gervinus, Geschichte der deutschen Dichtung, 1871-1874); by calling him a "characterless destroyer of our culture" (Max Martersteig, Das deutsche Theater im 19. Jahrhundert, 1904); or by scolding him as a "thorough scamp" (Adolph Bartels, Geschichte der deutschen Literatur, 1901-1902) while acknowledging his theatrical talents. Although Kotzebue's work tends to be light in spirit and very frequently also in thought or content, it has highly entertaining qualities and is far from "immoral," though negating dogmatism of all types. Above all, it possesses a sure sense of dramatic structure, scenic possibilities, dialogue, and satiric and comic elements. His literary influence in Germany and abroad offers evidence that he scarcely merits the treatment that he has received from critics and historians in his own country.

BIOGRAPHY

August Friedrich Ferdinand von Kotzebue was born on May 3, 1761, in Weimar, Saxony, the son of a well-to-do, middle-class bureaucrat who died while Kotzebue was still young. Under the doting care of his mother, he spent his childhood and youth in Weimar, going to school at the local gymnasium until he was sixteen and acting with his sister Amalie in one of Goethe's plays. After spending a year at Jena, he matriculated at the University of Duisburg in 1778, returned to Jena in 1779, and finished his studies of law there in 1780. In Weimar he opened a law practice but showed little enthusiasm for his chosen profession and became involved in legal difficulties as a result of his sharp tongue. He left for St. Petersburg, Russia, in 1781.

There his career took a decidedly favorable turn. Originally the private secretary of a well-to-do German, he later became assistant director of the German theater at St. Petersburg. Before his employer died in 1783, he recommended Kotzebue to Catherine the Great, who made him assessor to the high court of appeal in Reval (now Tallinn). There he founded a private theater in 1784, wrote several stories and plays, and edited a journal. In the same year, he fell passionately in love with Friederike von Essen, to whom he was married despite the objections of her parents. In 1787, he was promoted to president of the magistracy in the province of Estonia and was ennobled by Catherine the Great. For reasons of health, he went to Pyrmont on the advice of Dr. Johann Georg Zimmermann, who soon became his friend. Shortly thereafter, two of his plays, The Stranger and The Indians in England, made him world-famous—the former competing favorably with Goethe's novel Die Leiden des jungen Werthers (1774; The Sorrows of Young Werther, 1779) for public success. Other plays followed in quick succession, including The Virgin of the Sun, and Kotzebue boasted that he could write a play in three days. His biting wit and a satiric pen, along with his success, brought forth the envious as well as the admiring. Two occurrences of 1790 hurt his reputation for some time to come: His wife died in childbirth, and Kotzebue, not awaiting her final moments, left for Paris to console himself, writing an autobiographical account, Meine Flucht nact Paris im Winter 1790 (1791; flight to Paris), which was received as the epitome of tastelessness. In 1790, he also wrote a defense of his friend Dr. Zimmermann in a play entitled *Doctor Bahrdt mit der eiserner Stirn*, which contains numerous highly objectionable portrayals of well-known personages. Kotzebue publicly apologized for this piece of slander in 1792. In the same year, he returned to Russia and married Christel von Krusentjern.

Apparently to satisfy the doubts of his benefactress Catherine the Great concerning his political loyalties, he wrote a very conservative historical work on nobility (*Vom Adel*) but then left the Russian civil service in 1795 to write and live on his estate, Friedenthal. In 1798, he briefly went to Vienna, accepting the directorship at the Viennese royal theater, but he disliked the intrigues there and did not stay. In 1799, he was in Weimar for a short time. Early in 1800, Kotzebue returned to Russia with his family but was taken prisoner at the border and sent to Siberia on suspicion of political infidelities. He wrote a piece that excessively praised a charitable action of the emperor, delighting Czar Paul I so greatly that he immediately pardoned Kotzebue, presented him with an estate, and made him director of the St. Petersburg theater. Between 1798 and 1801, Kotzebue wrote some of his most successful plays, among them *The Count of Burgundy* and *Johanna of Montfaucon*. About his Siberian adventure he wrote the novel-length report *Das merkwürdigste Jahr meines Lebens* (1801; *The Most Remarkable Year in the Life of August von Kotzebue*, 1802).

In 1801, he returned to Germany, living in Weimar, Jena, and from 1803 on in Berlin. His residency in Weimar was marked by conflicts with Goethe, who viewed Kotzebue with scorn and disdain yet envied his successes with the public. Kotzebue's second wife died in 1803, prompting another trip of refuge to Paris, where he was presented to Napoleon. The following year he married for the third time, choosing a cousin of his second wife. Beginning in 1803, Kotzebue edited the journal *Der Freimüthige*, which gave him ample opportunity to carry on his feud with the Romantic school of Goethe and the Schlegel brothers, and which appeared under his direction until 1807. Between 1807 and 1813, he wrote numerous plays on his estate in Estonia, where he

had fled with his family from the French. In his journals *Die Biene* and *Die Grille*, he fought Napoleon with political articles. After Napoleon's defeat, Emperor Alexander named Kotzebue General Consul of Prussia; Kotzebue also took over the directorship of the theater in Königsberg (now Kaliningrad).

In the aftermath of the wars of liberation, many German students became politically active, and their activities met with stringent government control and persecution. Meanwhile Kotzebue had undertaken the task of writing reviews about German and French literature and science and forwarding them to Russia. On July 17, 1817, he sent off the first of these surveys, discussing more than one hundred works. He thereby came under suspicion by the student groups of being a spy for reactionary Russia. Among the books burned at the Wartburg Festival of 1817, which brought the student groups into public political focus, was Kotzebue's historical work *Geschichte des deutschen Reichs, von dessen Ursprunge bis zu dessen Untergange* (1814-1832). Critical of the German democratic movement, Kotzebue reacted with mockery and thereby encouraged suspicion and rage among the various student organizations. One of the more fanatic of their number, a theology student named Karl Ludwig Sand, from Jena, assassinated Kotzebue on March 23, 1819, in Mannheim, Kotzebue's place of residence since 1818. As a consequence of this killing, the government further suppressed university student groups with stricter surveillance and supervision.

ANALYSIS

August von Kotzebue's position in literary history is unique. Although his 230 plays were immensely popular in Germany during his lifetime and scarcely a theater director could afford to ignore the public's favorite playwright, he was ostracized not only by his contemporaries of the literary schools (classicism, Romanticism and its major representatives) but also by later generations of critics. Kotzebue's cosmopolitanism and his recalcitrant spirit, combined with his enormous success as a dramatist, created for him at once a favorable climate outside Germany and an envious and hostile atmosphere within. His major influence as a writer therefore was exerted chiefly outside his homeland, notwithstanding his box-office success within Germany.

In England, German authors were fashionable and popular at the turn of the eighteenth century; more than fifty German writers in all genres had their works translated between 1790 and 1810. Of these, Kotzebue, with 170 editions (plays, novels, and biographies) of his works appearing in the English language, by far outnumbered all others in popularity. Between 1796 and 1842, thirty-six of his plays were translated into English—many of them several times—and twenty-two were produced onstage. In many instances, the plays were severely altered in the process of making them palatable to English audiences. Characters were added or deleted, plots were changed and various other adulterations were committed in order to present in Kotzebue's name plays that would be congenial to English tastes.

Kotzebue wrote his first successful play, *The Stranger*, between October and November of 1788, while he was very ill. By 1860, it had been translated eighty times. After it was given in London for the first time on March 24, 1798, it was staged more frequently than were the plays of William Shakespeare. Undoubtedly Kotzebue's popularity resulted in large part from the liberties that the translators took in adapting his plays for English audiences, which ensured their lasting success, for the critical reviews praise exactly that element that the German critics perceived as lacking: the morality. Although one of the main critical objections to Kotzebue in Germany was that he so freely depicted vice and immorality, thus undermining public virtue, the London *Times* of March 25, 1798, declared: "The heart is improved, and the fancy entertained, while a confirmed detestation of conjugal infidelity, which forms the chief moral of the play is irresistibly impressed." While the *Times* critic noted that the characterization lacked originality, he also pointed out that "there is novelty of sentiment, passion, diction, and above all, there is that which we but rarely meet with in our modern dramas, novelty of virtuous principle and edifying morality." English audiences, like their German counterparts, wanted to be entertained and not confronted

with conflicts that required profound intellectual involvement. They wanted to be moved to tears, to see repentance and forgiveness, misunderstandings and happy endings. They perceived the complicated plots with separated lovers and families, fantastic familial interrelationships, and the all-pervasive, all-powerful manipulative factor of chance as a pleasant escalation of dramatic tension. In Kotzebue's work, they saw their own social views vindicated and their expectations met while being pleasantly entertained.

Kotzebue's box-office success in England prompted imitation by native playwrights. L. F. Thompson, in *Kotzebue* (1928), lists a substantial number of English plays that borrowed from Kotzebue's plots, characters, and scenes. For example, Richard Cumberland's *The Wheel of Fortune* (pr., pb. 1795) borrows the character Penruddock from Kotzebue's *The Stranger*; a play by George Colman, the younger, contains the attempted seduction of a poor officer's daughter—a parallel to Kotzebue's play *The Writing Desk*. In addition to serving as a model for similar native productions, Kotzebue added some new perspectives to English theater, including scenes from low-life alternating between the farcical and the tragic. He liberated English dramatists from an excessively moralistic perspective and thereby furthered a more realistic depiction of life onstage, and while he did not initiate it, he certainly contributed greatly to the development of the melodrama.

FRANCE AND THE PLAYWRIGHT

In France, the situation was somewhat different. Rather than being imitated, Kotzebue was to a great extent an imitator. He was, for example, greatly indebted to Molière, but many of the characters and situations that Kotzebue adopted can be found in prerevolutionary French plays in general. Although he probably also borrowed from Louis-Sébastien Mercier and Pierre-Augustin Caron de Beaumarchais, he apparently also exchanged ideas with contemporary writers such as Louis-Benoît and Alexandre Duval. As in England, *The Stranger* initiated Kotzebue's success in France. It was first staged on December 28, 1798, at the Odéon, and was performed sixty times in its initial season. Its immediate impact was felt in the parodies that it engendered. Among them are Hyacinthe Dorvo's *La veille de Noces: Ou, L'Après-souper de Misanthropie et Repentir* (1799), which was performed at the Théâtre Molière; Marc Antoine Desaugiers's *Cadet Rousselle misanthrope et Manon repentante* (1800); and Paul Aimé Chapelle Laurencin's *Édouard et Clémentine, une comédie en trois actes mêlée de couplets* (1842). For the French stage, the novelty of this play consisted chiefly of the weight and color that Kotzebue gave to supporting characters. More than forty of Kotzebue's stage works were translated into French between 1790 and 1840, of which *The Reconciliation* rivaled *The Stranger* with some three hundred performances at the Comédie-Française between 1797 and 1845. Even between 1840 and 1902, Kotzebue's *The Good Citizens of Piffelheim* saw more than twenty editions in print.

To a much greater extent than in England, Kotzebue shared the faults and merits of contemporary dramatists in France, although he was more versatile and considerably more successful than many of his French colleagues. French critical opinion, too, was divided. In his *Erinnerungen aus Paris im Jahre 1804* (1804; *Travels from Berlin Through Switzerland to Paris in the Year 1804*, 1804), Kotzebue recalls the conflicting statements about his work and concludes that his plays endured despite their faults because of their true depiction of feeling and sentiment. Part of his success can probably be attributed to the fact that his work was not considered particularly innovative in France but was indebted to cross-fertilization: More than thirty of his plays can be considered adaptations of (mostly contemporary) French originals. Kotzebue revitalized these plays by providing a greater realism in characterization, departing from existing rules governing the French theater. What Kotzebue called realism in characterization, the French often called grotesqueness, yet they adapted enthusiastically to the liberation of theatrical customs and tastes both in the depiction of individuals onstage and in the new situations that Kotzebue provided. Often tapping existing resources, he expanded the possibilities for the theatrical treatment of the borrowed material and in turn opened vistas for native French writers concerning plot and figuration. Such a cul-

tural interchange is the basis for Kotzebue's influence on French theater.

RUSSIA AND KOTZEBUE

In Russia, the theater lacked any strong identification with nationalistic concerns and was influenced to a very large degree by French classicism. For some time before Kotzebue entered the scene, German literature had begun to assume a position of importance; yet Kotzebue is the first German dramatist whose work influenced Russian literature extensively and consistently by the number of his translations and the persistence of his popularity. By 1800, more than forty of his dramatic works had been printed in German, and approximately 80 percent of these appeared in translation—very frequently in more than one version, with different titles, and by various translators. Kotzebue's reception in Russia varies in relation to locality. *The Stranger*, in translation by A. F. Malinovsky, was a staple on the repertoire of Moscow's Medoks theater from 1791 on and was staged at least eighteen times between 1791 and 1800. The reason for this open reception can be traced in part to the cultural enlightenment of Moscow's audiences, in part to the support of N. M. Karamzin, who had seen the play in Berlin and praised it highly in his journal, and also to the encouragement of the theater's owner, M. Maddox. The situation was entirely different in St. Petersburg, where the German theater group, which had staged the play six times between October 30, 1790, and February 13, 1791, was disbanded on May 1, 1791. The conservative attitude of the court toward theatrical productions resulted in an almost exclusive continuance of French classical plays, and this in turn greatly influenced the repertoire of the two public theaters in St. Petersburg. Toward the end of the decade, however, the situation changed. Kotzebue's mounting influence can be measured by three occurrences: the adoption of his plays in the repertoire of the French theater in St. Petersburg; the publication of plays under Kotzebue's name that were not of his pen; and the first adaptations of his work by other writers. Kotzebue's plays *Johanna of Montfaucon* and *The Stranger* were staged at the end of 1800 and in January, 1801, respectively, by the St. Petersburg ensemble in the French translation—an event that marks a high point in esteem accorded to him in that city. In Moscow, meanwhile, the plays of other German playwrights were staged under the fictitious authorship of Kotzebue. In the early years of the nineteenth century, Russian writers imitated Kotzebue by incorporating scenes, plots, and characters reminiscent of his plays and style into their own works. Frequently some reference to a Kotzebue drama was included in the title.

For the most part, Russian actors and playwrights perceived Kotzebue's style as a liberation from the stringent limitations that French classical theater had placed on their initiative. The artificial language and the adherence to the unifying factors of time, place, and action within the classical tragedy were discarded in favor of a more freely developed plot and a greater display of feeling. In addition, plays such as *The Stranger* were based on social and personal conflicts with which the Russians could identify. Indeed, the very acceptability of and identification with the situations Kotzebue depicted in the European cultural community regardless of nationality were largely responsible for his international acceptance and success. Further, with his universal appeal, Kotzebue united actors, theoreticians, playwrights, translators, and the public in their effort to establish an independent national theater in Russia; in the interim between excessive dependence on foreign literary models and the development of a strictly Russian style, Kotzebue fused the German and French traditions already extant in the Russian repertoire with the emergence of a national literary spirit in that country.

Shortly after Kotzebue resigned as director of the St. Petersburg German theater in 1801, some criticism of his sentimental *Rührstücke* began to be heard. By 1803, Russian criticism of Kotzebue was colored by the realization that a Russian national theater could be achieved only be severing emotional ties to the German playwright. Literary discussions portrayed him negatively by associating his work with the achievements of other European literatures and finding his contribution lacking in substance: Kotzebue was inferior to Voltaire's brilliant wit, to the tender spirit of Laurence Sterne, and to Jean-François

Marmontel's exquisite style. Despite vocal criticism, however, Kotzebue remained a considerable influence in the Russian theater until his death: Not until the second decade of the nineteenth century was there a decline in the popularity of the *Rührstücke*.

The discrepancy between public taste and critical opinion was as apparent in Russia as it was in Germany. A wealth of translations and the immense popularity that Kotzebue enjoyed with the theatergoing public necessitated in Russia as well as in Germany an intensive dialogue between playwrights and critics that continued far into the nineteenth century. Imitations of his style and plots flourished even as a distinctly Russian literature began to emerge. The extent of the division in Russia between detractors of Kotzebue and those who favored his approach may perhaps be discerned by the fact that Kotzebue's influence is apparent in the work of a writer of the stature of Nikolai Gogol, whose comedy *Revizor* (1836; *The Inspector General*, 1890) shows many similarities to Kotzebue's *The Good Citizens of Piffelheim*. Kotzebue was a European phenomenon and could not and cannot be disposed of as a marginal literary figure.

Most of Kotzebue's plays can be divided among four categories: sentimental or family-centered plays (*Rührstücke*); farces or carnival sketches; comedies; and historical plays. Similar to the modern situation comedy, many of Kotzebue's farces and comedies depended less on a coherent plot for their effect than on their witticisms, wordplay, and humorous set pieces. A plot summary for each category may suffice to illustrate the variables.

THE STRANGER

The Stranger was an early and immensely successful *Rührstücke*. The plot evolves around the Baroness von Meinau, who after two years of marriage has permitted herself to be seduced by her husband's "friend." Full of remorse, she has fled her home and now earns a meager living as a humble housekeeper at the castle of a countess. Her husband, deeply wounded but still in love with her, has also left his home and is eventually revealed to be the stranger living in the countess's cottage. Although they do not know of each other's close proximity, the estranged husband and wife each earn a reputation as an honorable and humanitarian individual through numerous noble deeds. When at last they are confronted with each other, they renounce each other in self-abnegation to spare each other's feelings, hoping for a reunion in the hereafter. It is only when, through the intervention of the countess, their children are brought before them, that the Baron and Baroness von Meinau fall into each other's arms. Kotzebue retains the spectator's interest by keeping the identity of the two strangers a secret. Little by little, the reason for the housekeeper's depression is revealed. When the couple are finally identified, the tension remains until the end, because their reunion in marriage is delayed.

PAGENSTREICHE

The farce *Pagenstreiche* (pageboy tricks) depends on stereotyped comedy characters for the delivery of witticisms. The plot is of the utmost simplicity: The three daughters of Baron Stuhlbein, entirely undifferentiated in their womanhood, fall in love with their cousin and refuse to marry the three young lieutenants who are wooing them (the young men are equally stereotyped). Only when the baron threatens to give his daughters in marriage to three elderly country squires do the young women agree to return to their erstwhile lovers. The various escapades of the irresistible pageboy (the cousin) are the foil to the quick-witted dialogue and to the antics of the elderly characters.

FATHER AND SON

Comedy on a somewhat less undifferentiated and stereotypical plane is the substance of *Father and Son*. The erotic escapades of the Klingsbergs, father and son, who court the same women and are foiled by the clever sister of the elder Klingsberg, shape a plot of intrigue, love, estrangement, tempted virtue, and impoverished nobility. Young Klingsberg finds his true love, and the husband of Baroness von Stein is offered employment (reuniting this estranged couple), whereas the old Klingsberg is punished for his lecherous behavior (he must stay with his sister).

THE SPANIARDS IN PERU

If the line between farce and comedy is fluid in Kotzebue's plays, the same can be said of his *Rührstücke* and historical dramas. The latter employ comic characters sparingly or not at all, but the historical figures are little more than homely philistines beneath the disguise of their exotic names. The tragedy *The Spaniards in Peru* takes its historical background from the invasion of Mexico by Francisco Pizarro's troops. It is the sequel to *The Virgin of the Sun* and casts Pizarro as the cruel invader from whose grasp Rolla, the hero, snatches the child of Cora (the Virgin of the Sun). While saving the boy, Rolla is mortally wounded, and the tragedy concludes with his death. Kotzebue again exploits the emotions, this time to the accompaniment of scenes of war and atrocities. Pizarro is depicted entirely negatively, Cora as the insanely desperate mother, Rolla as the brave and righteous hero. Although the setting is exotic, the spectators can easily identify with the depicted emotions, which do not deviate from those customarily encountered at the hearth and in the home.

OTHER MAJOR WORKS

LONG FICTION: *Iche, ein Geschiche in Fragmenten*, 1781; *Die Geschichte meines Vaters*, 1785 (*The History of My Father*, 1898); *Die Leiden der Ortenbergischen Familie*, 1787 (2 volumes; *The Sufferings of the Family of Ortenberg*, 1799); *Die gefährliche Wette*, 1790.

NONFICTION: *Meine Flucht nact Paris im Winter 1790*, 1791; *Vom Adel*, 1792; *Unparteiische Untersuchung über die Folgen der französischen Revolution auf das übrige Europa*, 1795; *Das merkwürdigste Jahr meines Lebens*, 1801 (*The Most Remarkable Year in the Life of August von Kotzebue*, 1802); *Erinnerungen aus Paris im Jahre 1804*, 1804 (*Travels from Berlin Through Switzerland to Paris in the Year 1804*, 1804); *Erinnerungen von einer Reise aus Liefland nach Rom und Neapel*, 1805 (*Travels Through Italy in the Years 1804 and 1805*, 1806); *Selbstbiographie*, 1811; *Geschichte des deutschen Reichs, von dessen Ursprunge bis zu dessen Untergange*, 1814-1832 (4 volumes); *Sketch of the Life and Literary Career of August von Kotzebue with the Journal of His Exile to Siberia Written by Himself*, 1830.

MISCELLANEOUS: *Kleine gesammelte Schriften,*

1787-1791 (4 volumes); *Historical, Literary, and Political Anecdotes and Miscellanies*, 1807; *Ausgewählte prosaische Schriften*, 1842-1843 (45 volumes).

BIBLIOGRAPHY

Mandel, Oscar. *August von Kotzebue: The Comedy, the Man*. University Park: Pennsylvania State University Press, 1990. A basic biography of Kotzebue that covers his life and works. Bibliography and index.

Taylor, Harley U., Jr. "The Dramas of August von Kotzebue on the New York and Philadelphia Stages from 1798 to 1805." *West Virginia University Philological Papers* 23 (1977) 47-58. A look at Kotzebue's plays as they were presented on the early American stage.

Williamson, George S. "What Killed August von Kotzebue? The Temptations of Virtue and the Political Theology of German Nationalism, 1789-1819." *The Journal of Modern History* 72, no. 4 (December, 2000): 890-943. An examination of how Kotzebue's reputation as a "seducer of virtue" helped lead to his assassination by a German nationalist. He also describes the state of nationalism in Germany at the time of the killing.

Helene M. Kastinger Riley

LARRY KRAMER

Born: Bridgeport, Connecticut; June 25, 1935

PRINCIPAL DRAMA

Sissie's Scrapbook, pr. 1973, revised pr. 1974 (as *Four Friends*)
The Normal Heart, pr., pb. 1985
Just Say No: A Play About a Farce, pr., pb. 1988
The Destiny of Me, pr. 1992, pb. 1993

OTHER LITERARY FORMS

Larry Kramer's career began as a screenwriter for Hollywood studios, with *Here We Go Round the Mulberry Bush* (1966), *Women in Love* (1969, an adaptation of D. H. Lawrence's novel), *Lost Horizon* (1973, an adaptation of James Hilton's novel), and several unproduced screenplays. His novel, *Faggots* (1978) first gained him national recognition, although Kramer will probably be best remembered for his gay activism as reflected in his nonfiction work, *Reports from the Holocaust: The Making of an AIDS Activist* (1989, revised in 1994 as *Reports from the Holocaust: The Story of an AIDS Activist*). He has also published a short story, "Mrs. Tefillin," an excerpt from his unfinished novel *The American People*, which he began in 1978. This story appears in *The Penguin Book of Gay Short Stories* (1994), edited by David Leavitt and Mark Mitchell.

ACHIEVEMENTS

In 1970, Larry Kramer's screenplay *Women in Love* received an Academy Award nomination and a British Film Academy nomination for the best screenplay of the year. His drama *The Normal Heart* was awarded the Dramatists Guild Marton Award, the City Lights Award, and the Sarah Siddons Award for the best play of 1986 and was also nominated for the Olivier Award. In the same year, Kramer was named Man of the Year by Aid for AIDS of Los Angeles. The following year, the Human Rights Campaign Fund honored him with its Arts and Communication Award.

No voice in the gay community has been more strident and effective than Kramer's in drawing attention to the plight of acquired immunodeficiency syndrome (AIDS) victims and to governmental indifference regarding their problems in the early years of the epidemic, the late 1970's and early 1980's. Drug companies were not forthcoming with medications to treat the disease, and the Ronald Reagan administration cast a blind eye on what was fast becoming a national health crisis.

In 1981, Kramer cofounded the Gay Men's Health Crisis, and six years later, in 1987, established the AIDS Coalition to Unleash Power (ACT UP). The following year, he tested positive for human immuno-deficiency virus (HIV), the precursor of AIDS and has been battling that condition ever since.

As an activist in gay organizations, Kramer was among those who "outed" New York City mayor Ed Koch and others activists deemed hypocritical. Some of these activities offended mainstream Americans, but Kramer's writing, particularly his two most effective plays, *The Normal Heart* and its sequel, *The Destiny of Me*, reached broad heterosexual audiences. The former holds the record for the longest run at the Public Theatre of New York City's Shakespeare Festival and has been produced more than six hundred times in the United States and abroad.

BIOGRAPHY

Larry Kramer grappled with his sexual identity from childhood but did not acknowledge to himself that he was gay until the spring of his freshman year at Yale University, when one of his professors seduced him. This seduction made the young Kramer aware for the first time of his true sexual nature.

The son of a Bridgeport attorney, George L. Kramer, and his wife, Rea Wishengrad Kramer, a social worker, Larry entered Yale in 1953 and was plagued by health problems including a persistent cough that soon landed him in the infirmary. Before his first semester ended, Kramer had attempted suicide, perhaps gleaning what his sexual orientation was and being terrified by the prospect. When one of his professors seduced him, a new world opened to the unhappy youth, who then was able to settle into his studies and complete his undergraduate degree at Yale.

Upon graduation, Kramer entered the United States Army for one year, after which he joined a training program with the William Morris Agency, often a step that led talented young people into pursuits in film or theater. This program helped land Kramer at Columbia Pictures in 1958. By 1960, he had become an assistant story editor in New York City for that corporation. He was promoted and trans-

ferred to London as a production executive, where he served from 1961 until 1965. In 1965, he became an assistant to the president of the United Artists Film Company.

His career as screenwriter and producer proceeded with his production of *Here We Go Round the Mulberry Bush* in 1967 and his celebrated screenplay of D. H. Lawrence's *Women in Love*, a controversial film that received considerable attention and several awards. Kramer's screenwriting continued until the publication of his novel *Faggots* in 1978 brought him to the attention of the homosexual community nationally. He then devoted himself to working with the problems of gays and lesbians in contemporary American society.

This concern broadened and deepened in the years following 1981, when AIDS began to cast its long and intimidating shadow over gay enclaves across the nation. With AIDS emerging as a national threat, Kramer was outraged at public and governmental indifference to the illness, which was at that time viewed as a gay disease unworthy of much public support. Kramer was strident, indeed often shrill, in trying to arouse a lethargic public.

In 1981, he became a cofounder of the Gay Men's Health Crisis and was actively involved in its daily operation until 1983, when he came under fire from the organization after his article, "1,112 and Counting," appeared in the March 14-17, 1983, issue of *New York Native* and was widely disseminated in gay publications throughout the country. This piece authenticated 1,112 cases of AIDS and 418 deaths. Some in the gay community, still apathetic toward the disease, accused Kramer of overstating its dangers and of running the risk of creating a panic.

Relieved of his daily involvement with the Gay Men's Health Crisis, Kramer had more time to write, turning his attention to writing one of the earliest plays about AIDS, *The Normal Heart*, which was well received by audiences and critics alike. It ran for more than a year on Broadway.

On March 10, 1987, purely by chance, Kramer was asked to replace Nora Ephron as the speaker at a meeting of gays at the New York City Gay and Lesbian Community Center. This speech was possibly the most effective in Kramer's career as a gay activist. He called on gays to demand that government give increased attention to the AIDS plague. He outlined how difficult it was for physicians to obtain new drugs for treating the disease and urged his audience to force the Food and Drug Administration to accelerate the testing procedures for AIDS medications and to pressure the pharmaceutical industry to intensify its research to create drugs to treat and possibly eliminate the disease.

It was this speech that convinced an inflamed audience to join Kramer in establishing ACT UP, a radical organization that demanded that the public focus on the AIDS problem. The organization used unconventional tactics—including the outing of public officials—that threatened many people. In the end, however, these tactics succeeded. *The Normal Heart* had given Kramer increased credibility within both mainstream and gay communities, and its sequel, *The Destiny of Me*, produced in 1992, increased this credibility. His farce, *Just Say No*, which played Off-Broadway in 1988, was neither a critical nor a popular success.

Faggots condemned the sort of gay life Kramer found in New York, which centered around gay bars, bath houses, and Fire Island weekends. Kramer had long considered stability more important than sex in gay relationships but had been unable to find a compatible partner who shared his views. This situation changed, however, in 1993 when he met and fell in love with David Webster, an architect, with whom he shares a vintage Connecticut house.

Fully dedicated to the gay causes to which he devoted his life, Kramer in 1997 offered Yale University, his alma mater, several million dollars to establish a tenured professorship in gay and lesbian studies. This offer was rejected as too narrow a specialty to justify an endowed, tenured professorship. Kramer's papers, however, have been bequeathed to Yale.

Despite the domestic tranquillity he has achieved, Kramer's later years have been plagued by illness. He has had to cope with HIV, and as *Newsweek* reported in its June 11, 2001, issue, he suffers from cirrhosis of the liver. He was initially denied a place on the waiting list for a badly needed liver transplant but was later placed on that list. His physician at the time of the *Newsweek* report estimated that Kramer had no more than eighteen months to live.

ANALYSIS

Throughout his writing career, even as a screenwriter, Larry Kramer focused on matters relating to homosexuality. His screenplay of Lawrence's *Women in Love* emphasized Lawrence's thinly veiled dealings with homosexuality in that novel. Kramer emphasized this in his film version. His gay novel, *Faggots*, although it cannot legitimately be called a critical or artistic success, has stayed in print almost continuously since its publication in 1978 and is said to have sold close to half a million copies. In it, as in his unhappy experience with the bureaucracy of the Gay Men's Health Crisis, are found intimations of themes explored in his two most strident plays, *The Normal Heart*, which has evoked comparisons to Henrik Ibsen's *En folkefiende* (pb. 1882; *An Enemy of the People*, 1890), and *The Destiny of Me*. Kramer's nonfiction also emphasizes the inroads that AIDS has made on the lives of all Americans.

THE NORMAL HEART

The Normal Heart is transparently autobiographical. Ned Weeks, the protagonist, devotes himself to arousing the public about the dangers of AIDS. As the play progresses, Kramer, as playwright, becomes increasingly angry, finally erupting into an unequivocal rage against the government, the medical profession, the press, and the gay community for their reluctance to deal with the crisis and to work toward eliminating it.

The play takes place in the early years of AIDS, the years in which Kramer was deeply involved in the Gay Men's Health Crisis. He wrote the play shortly after his unhappy departure from that organization. He attacks gay leaders who lack the courage to deal effectively with the situation, focusing on the feeling of many of them that they cannot condemn promiscuous sex, as Kramer did in *Faggots*, because they have been chanting the mantra of sexual liberation for so long.

Ned Weeks joins an organization that seeks to assist people with AIDS but—more important—to promote safe sex among gays. Ned becomes so abrasive in his fanatical demands that promiscuity cease that he is expelled from the organization, as Kramer was from the Gay Men's Health Crisis. Ned's lover subsequently dies of AIDS, which intensifies Ned's zeal. He castigates *The New York Times* for not using its clout to draw attention to the crisis. He blames New York City mayor Ed Koch for not caring about the plight of AIDS patients, and he accuses the gay community of failing to deal realistically with the disease through the practice of safe sex.

The Normal Heart had a highly successful and prolonged run in New York. It garnered several prizes for its author, but its chief contribution was that it exposed a seemingly complacent public to a situation it could not ignore for much longer.

JUST SAY NO

Just Say No is a farce that attacks the hypocrisy of those who control society, those who determine what is right and attempt to impose this determination on everyone else. The play is set in Georgetown in the fictional nation of New Columbia. The leading characters are Mrs. Potentate, the wife of the Potentate-in-Chief; Junior, their gay son; and the gay mayor of Appleberg, the country's largest northeastern city. Kramer admitted that the play was very controversial and did not hold great hope for its success. It was produced Off-Broadway by the WPA Theater for a limited run. It was generally considered a failure.

THE DESTINY OF ME

This sequel to *The Normal Heart* again has Ned Weeks as its protagonist, but in this play, Ned is dying of AIDS. The action takes place in his hospital room. Ned has developed full-blown AIDS and is seeking experimental treatment that could save his life. Flashbacks transport audiences to scenes from Ned's early childhood and adolescence. They reflect his difficulties, reminiscent of those Kramer experienced, in realizing he was homosexual and in trying to come to grips with this realization. Because he is coping with a condition that the society of his day

neither accepted nor understood, Ned's relationships with his parents are strained as are those with his brothers and sisters.

This play did not enjoy the popular success that *The Normal Heart* did, probably because it was less polemic, less angry, and more reflective. It, nevertheless, offers a penetrating insight into what it is to grow up gay in an environment that is hostile toward homosexuality.

OTHER MAJOR WORKS

LONG FICTION: *Faggots*, 1978.

SCREENPLAYS: *Here We Go Round the Mulberry Bush*, 1966; *Women in Love*, 1969 (adaptation of D. H. Lawrence's novel); *Lost Horizon*, 1973 (adaptation of James Hilton's novel).

NONFICTION: *Reports from the Holocaust: The Making of an AIDS Activist*, 1989, revised 1994 (as *Reports from the Holocaust: The Story of an AIDS Activist*).

BIBLIOGRAPHY

Clum, John M. *Acting Gay: Male Homosexuality in Modern Drama*. New York: Columbia University Press, 1992. This comprehensive study of gay drama gives considerable attention to Larry Kramer and his activism as reflected in his major plays. Strong, insightful analysis.

_____. *Still Acting Gay: Male Homosexuality in Modern Drama*. New York: St. Martin's Press, 2000. This updated version of *Acting Gay* includes useful analysis of *The Destiny of Me*, which had not been produced when the earlier volume was published.

Mass, Lawrence D., ed. *We Must Love One Another or Die: The Life and Legacies of Larry Kramer*. New York: St. Martin's Press, 1997. This collection of twenty essays written by experts in the field treat most aspects of Kramer's life and writing. The collection ends with a revealing interview between the editor and Kramer.

R. Baird Shuman

ZYGMUNT KRASIŃSKI

Born: Paris, France; February 19, 1812
Died: Paris, France; February 23, 1859

PRINCIPAL DRAMA

Nie-Boska komedia, pb. 1835, pr. 1902 (*The Undivine Comedy*, 1846)
Irydion, pb. 1836, pr. 1908 (*Iridion*, 1875)

OTHER LITERARY FORMS

The earliest literary activity of Zygmunt Krasiński was devoted to the composition of historical novels, in which he imitated the narrative techniques of Sir Walter Scott. The finest of these youthful endeavors is the novel *Agaj-Han* (1833). The eponymous hero of this tragic romance—set in the early seventeenth century, when Poland temporarily held military superiority over the Muscovites and its forces actually occupied the Kremlin for a brief period—is a Tartar chieftain who is in love with the Polish wife of one of the Russian czars. Immediately after the publication of this novel, Krasiński proceeded to write two plays in quick succession. Despite the critical acclaim for both these works, Krasiński abandoned the dramatic genre in favor of composing discourses in prose and works of poetry. The patriotic and religious themes that he set forth in prose are, for the most part, reiterated to greater effect in his poetry. Among the most important poems are *Trzy myśli pozostale po ś.p. Henryku Ligenzie* (1841; three thoughts left behind by the late Henry Ligenza), *Przedświt* (1843; dawn), *Psalmy przyszłości* (1845; psalms of the future), *Ostatni* (1847; the last), and *Niedokończony poemat* (1852; the unfinished poem). Some of the best prose that Krasiński ever wrote is, moreover, to be found in his extensive correspondence, especially in those letters written to his father and to Delfina Potocka. Also noteworthy is the correspondence that he conducted in French with his English friend Henry Reeve between the years 1830 and 1838.

ACHIEVEMENTS

There is little doubt at present that Zygmunt Krasiński's true merit as a writer rests on the two dramas he composed while still in his early twenties. Nevertheless, during the nineteenth century he was also highly esteemed as a poet and generally ranked alongside Adam Mickiewicz and Juliusz Słowacki. Once the messianic view of Polish history had lost credence in his homeland, the aesthetic limitations of his poetry soon became painfully obvious to the reading public. Those literary historians who were still inclined to preserve a trinity of Romantic poets in Polish literature were quick to elevate Cyprian Kamil Norwid to its number in place of Krasiński. On the other hand, his two plays, *The Undivine Comedy* and *Iridion*, have retained the status of literary classics.

BIOGRAPHY

The life and work of Count Zygmunt Krasiński are inextricably linked to the political and social unrest that prevailed in Poland as a consequence of its loss of independence at the close of the eighteenth century. With their territory partitioned among Russia, Prussia, and Austria, the Poles decided that the best way to regain their national sovereignty lay in making common cause with the military forces of revolutionary France. The first Polish legion to fight alongside French troops under the command of Napoleon Bonaparte was formed in 1797, and two similar units were subsequently organized in 1798 and 1800. In all, some twenty-five thousand Poles were to serve in these three legions. In gratitude for the contributions made by these volunteers to his military victories, Napoleon decided to grant the Poles a small measure of national independence by creating a political entity known as the Duchy of Warsaw in 1807 out of Polish territories that had been under Prussian occupation since the time of the partitions. The Poles, however, had far grander political aspirations than those embodied by the tiny duchy and eagerly looked forward to a military conflict between the forces of Napoleon and those of Czar Alexander I in the hope that a French victory would enable them to redeem their eastern provinces from Russian annexation.

Their hopes appeared to have materialized when Napoleon invaded Russia in the spring of 1812 with a multinational coalition numbering more than 600,000 men. The euphoria of the Polish gentry on the eve of the invasion is vividly depicted within the pages of Mickiewicz's epic poem entitled *Pan Tadeusz* (1834; English translation, 1917). Of the 100,000 Poles who accompanied Napoleon on this ill-fated campaign, only a small fraction were destined to return unscathed from the steppes of Russia.

Among Napoleon's devoted Polish adherents, none was more steadfast than Zygmunt Krasiński's father, Count Wincenty Krasiński (1782-1858). The count's family was one of the oldest aristocratic houses in Poland, and its vast wealth entitled him to be ranked with the nation's magnates. Above all else, however, Wincenty Krasiński considered himself a professional soldier, and he entered French service as colonel of a cavalry unit in 1806. Having become a personal favorite of Napoleon, he was soon made a general in the elite Imperial Guard and fought with great valor in the battles of Elyau and Wagram as well as in the Peninsular War in Spain. General Krasiński also served the emperor with great fidelity in Russia, remaining with him throughout the entire retreat from Moscow up to his defeat at the Battle of Nations near Leipzig and his subsequent abdication at Fontainbleau. With Napoleon in exile on the island of Elba, General Krasiński accepted the magnanimous grant of amnesty offered by Czar Alexander and, in 1814, led the remnants of the Polish forces who had fought on behalf of the emperor back to their homeland.

Accompanying General Krasiński on the occasion of this departure from France were his wife and son. His wife was the former Princess Maria Radziwill, a somewhat older woman whom he had married primarily for her preeminent aristocratic status. After being childless for nine years, save for an infant daughter who died during childbirth, the couple was overjoyed at the birth of a son in Paris on February 19, 1812, while final preparations for the invasion of Russia were underway. The boy was christened Napoleon Stanisław Adam Feliks Zygmunt, a series of names from which the bearer eventually selected the last as his preferred designation. Both mother and child remained in Paris for the next two years while General Krasiński was entangled in Napoleon's ill-starred military ventures. Once back in Poland, General Krasiński and his forces were integrated into a reconstituted national army under the command of Czar Alexander's brother. The plan being entertained by Alexander was to set up a hereditary monarchy to be called the Kingdom of Poland in which the office of king would be filled by the Russian czar himself. The establishment of this semiautonomous state was duly ratified by the representatives of the victorious coalition at the Congress of Vienna in 1815. Paradoxically, it was General Krasiński, the erstwhile adversary of Czar Alexander, who became one of the staunchest defenders of the Kingdom of Poland's legitimacy. As its trusted servant, he succeeded to the occupancy of several increasingly important governmental posts and was eventually appointed acting viceroy in Warsaw.

Young Zygmunt received his entire early education from distinguished tutors within the confines of the family palace in Warsaw, and because of his father's ambitions for him, he was kept at his lessons for the greater part of the day. From the very outset, the boy was somewhat of a prodigy. At age four, he was priviledged to display his talents in the presence of Czar Alexander himself by reciting the defense of democracy that is delivered by the protagonist of Voltaire's play *Brutus* (1730; English translation, 1761). In 1822, when the boy was but ten years old, his mother died of a hereditary lung disease. In the hope of filling the void in his son's life, General Krasiński redoubled his commitment toward fostering Zygmunt's emotional welfare. As a consequence of this inordinate display of affection on the part of his father, Zygmunt developed a deep psychological need for paternal approbation that was to stay with him for the rest of his life. His intellectual development benefited greatly from this close association with his father, for General Krasiński was a man of broad cultural interests who regularly played host to the literary and political elite of Warsaw. By age fourteen, the boy had made such progress in his education that he was sent to the Warsaw Lyceum to prepare for the university and completed the prescribed studies in a single year. After this, the fifteen-year-old boy matriculated in the faculty of law at the Alexander University of Warsaw, an institution that had been founded in 1816.

Two years before Krasiński entered the university, Czar Alexander had been succeeded by his brother Nicholas I. In addition to being an inveterate enemy of constitutional government, the new czar immediately instituted a policy aimed at rooting out all seditious activity among his Polish subjects. When a tribunal of senators from the Polish parliament was convened to preside over a treason inquiry involving a secret patriotic society in 1828, the sole member of the commission to vote in favor of convicting its ringleaders on this capital offense was Krasiński's father. This action on the part of the elder Krasiński mortified his son and alienated him from most other students at the university. In the early part of 1829, this situation was exacerbated when the general ordered his son to show up for lectures on the day that the rest of the student body had decided to attend the funeral of the president of the parliamentary commission, who, in defiance of the Russian authorities, had directed a verdict of acquittal against the secret society's ringleaders. On the following day, Krasiński's fellow students mobbed him and tore the university insignia from his uniform. The rector of the university, moreover, advised Wincenty Krasiński to remove his son from the institution for a period of a year so as to permit passions to cool. The general decided thereupon that it would be best for Zygmunt to complete his education in Geneva. During the months before he left for Switzerland in the fall of 1829, the youth distracted himself from the recent unpleasantness at the university by writing a number of tales and romances, which were duly published the following year.

Despite his intense homesickness, Krasiński found a number of compensations in Geneva. At the university, he was free to study whatever subjects appealed to him. He also formed a close friendship with a student from England named Henry Reeve, whose subsequent career in journalism included service as editor of the *Edinburgh Review* as well as political

analyst for *The Times*. Henrietta Willam, also a native of England, became his first lover. Knowing that his father would never allow him to marry an Englishwoman without any claim to aristocratic lineage, Krasiński experienced profound emotional distress over the hopeless nature of his passion. Henrietta was obliged to return to England with her family in the spring of 1830, and their physical separation enabled Krasiński to terminate their relationship through correspondence. In the following summer, Krasiński himself left Switzerland to take up residence in Rome at the request of his father after the outbreak of the so-called July Revolution in neighboring France. These disorders soon spread to other countries and eventually led to an insurrection in Poland on the night of November 29, 1830. Upon learning of the uprising, Krasiński wrote a letter to his father requesting permission to return to Poland for the purpose of joining his compatriots in their struggle to win national independence. His father, however, was totally opposed to the insurrection and had even fled to St. Petersburg to be at the side of Czar Nicholas in this hour of crisis. It was not until May, 1831, that Krasiński received a response from his father, in which he was instructed to remain in Italy for the duration of the insurrection. Although his first impulse was to disregard these instructions, he eventually decided to yield to parental authority. Reeve and other friends of his reproached him bitterly for placing filial subservience above patriotic duty. The hostilities were to continue until the latter half of October, at which time the last Polish units capitulated to the Russians. Because of the unsettled conditions prevailing in Poland, Krasiński decided to wait awhile before going back to his homeland and returned to Geneva instead. There, in addition to writing the patriotic novel *Agaj-Han*, he read so intensely that his eyesight became severely impaired. Krasiński then went to Vienna for medical treatment from physicians specializing in eye disorders.

When Krasiński finally went home to Poland in August, 1832, he spent the next few months on the family estate, located approximately fifty miles due north of Warsaw at Opinogóra. In October, he accompanied his father to St. Petersburg on a visit that lasted five months. He was presented at the Imperial Court there, and Czar Nicholas was sufficiently impressed with the young man's demeanor and family background to offer him a post at court or in the diplomatic service, an invitation that Krasiński declined on grounds of ill health. He did, however, receive the coveted privilege to travel abroad and was henceforth to spend most of his time residing in France, Switzerland, and Italy rather than in his subjugated homeland. Krasiński commenced work on *The Undivine Comedy* in the early part of 1833 while still in St. Petersburg and completed it in Vienna and Venice within the same year. The writing of *Iridion* was also begun in St. Petersburg. Krasiński continued to work on the play in Rome and other Italian cities until 1836. After this, he was to restrict his literary enterprises to the publication of discourses in prose and works of poetry. One of the main reasons why Krasiński decided to try his hand at poetry must surely have been the encouragement to do so that he received from Słowacki when he made his acquaintance in Rome during the spring of 1836.

While still at work on *Iridion*, Krasiński fell passionately in love with a Polish woman, Joanna Bobrowa, whom he met in Rome. Five years his senior, she was the wife of a wealthy landowner and the mother of two small children. Krasiński was so taken by her that both *The Undivine Comedy* and *Iridion* were dedicated to her when these plays were published. The elder Krasiński was distraught over this illicit affair and managed to pressure each of the parties into terminating the relationship in the summer of 1838. Shortly thereafter, Krasiński met a beautiful Polish woman, Delfina Potocka, and fell deeply in love once again. Although married, Countess Potocka was estranged from her husband and lived abroad. She had been a pupil of Frédéric Chopin and was even rumored to have been his mistress. (It is interesting to note that one of the nineteen Polish songs that Chopin composed is a musical setting of Krasiński's poem entitled "Melodia.") Krasiński's affair with Delfina Potocka continued up to the summer of 1843, at which time he consented to marry the Countess Elżbieta Branicka at his father's insistence, despite the fact that she was virtually a stranger to him. Feeling little

affection for his wife, Krasiński continued to correspond with his beloved Delfina for several years after his marriage to Elżbieta. With the passage of time, however, he came to appreciate the fine qualities of his wife and to view his marriage in a positive light. When Krasiński died of tuberculosis in Paris on February 23, 1859, scarcely three months after the death of his father in Poland, he was survived by his wife and three children. His body was returned to Poland and interred at the family estate of Opinogóra, where the Polish government currently maintains a museum devoted to the accomplishments of the Romantic movement.

ANALYSIS

Long regarded as closet dramas, Zygmunt Krasiński's two plays *The Undivine Comedy* and *Iridion* have been staged with great success in the twentieth century by a number of technically innovative directors. One of the chief attractions of *The Undivine Comedy* for the contemporary reader stems from its acute analysis of the role of class conflict in the process of historical change. In contrast, most of the political content of *Iridion* has lost its relevance. For this and other reasons, *Iridion* is a far less important work than its predecessor.

THE UNDIVINE COMEDY

The Undivine Comedy, however, suffices to ensure Krasiński's position as a dramatist of international stature. *The Undivine Comedy*, a work already completed by Zygmunt Krasiński at age twenty-two, consists of four parts, each of which is preceded by a prose poem by way of introduction. The first two parts are devoted to domestic concerns, and the last two parts deal with social revolution. The domestic and social dramas, however, are linked through the person of Count Henryk and the problems arising from his dedication to the muse of poetry.

In the opening scene of part 1, Henryk is depicted as about to enter into an earthly marriage in the belief that he has at long last found someone who corresponds fully to his poetic fancies of the ideal woman. A guardian angel flying over the house on the eve of the wedding proclaims that Henryk may yet be worthy of redemption if he should prove himself capable of fulfilling his duties in the mundane sphere of marriage. At this point, a chorus of evil spirits makes a response of its own. These demons announce that they intend to redouble their efforts to capture Henryk's soul by operating under the guise of poetic fantasy and personal ambition. The wedding takes place as planned, and the couple live together contentedly until an evil spirit in the image of the ideal woman appears to Henryk in a dream. Upon awakening, he realizes that his wife, though otherwise exemplary, is devoid of the poetic spirit. Even the birth of a son fails to dispel the mood of boredom that has now descended on him. Henryk's absence from the christening ceremony for his son scandalizes his wife as well as the guests who have assembled to witness the event. The rite, nevertheless, takes place without him, and his wife uses the occasion to make a formal supplication in which she urges the boy to develop the soul of a poet so as to ensure his father's affection for him. In the meantime, Henryk has been lured into the wilds of nature in pursuit of the phantom maiden who symbolizes the spirit of poetry. Standing atop a mountain ridge, she urges the poet to soar above the abyss that separates them by means of the wings of poetry. Before he has time to respond to her bidding, her form suddenly turns into an apparition of utter deformity when a violent wind blows the garland of flowers from her head and tears her ornate dress to shreds. Recoiling from this hideous sight, Henryk hastens home to his family, only to find that his wife has gone mad and has been sent to an asylum. At the asylum, she informs him that in his absence she had beseeched God to transform her into a poet and that after three days of prayer her request had been granted. She then delivers a number of sibylline utterances, including the prediction that their son will also become a poet, and dies happily in Henryk's arms.

The attack that Krasiński directs at the Romantic poet in part 1 is obviously intended to serve as an exercise in self-criticism. The theme involving the incapacity of the poet to function in real life is further developed in part 2. Here, however, the dramatic action revolves around Henryk's son, Orcis. The boy not only is mentally abnormal but also is gradually losing his eyesight. The opening scene takes place in a cemetery, where the father has taken the nearly blind child on the tenth anniversary of his mother's death. (It is by no means incidental that Krasiński himself was ten years old when his own mother died and was almost sightless while composing *The Undivine Comedy*.) Standing beside her tomb, Orcis is intermittently seized by a compulsion to recite verses in praise of poetry—verses he claims to have learned from an apparition resembling his mother, who comes to him in his dreams. When his son goes on to assert that these nocturnal visitations occur with frequency, Henryk becomes genuinely concerned for the boy's sanity. In a subsequent scene that takes place four years later, a doctor who examines Orcis finds him to be totally blind and states that the boy is threatened with catalepsy. Mind has utterly triumphed over body. Although the despondent father would like to be on hand to minister to the needs of his son, he is obliged to depart in response to a call to arms previously delivered to him at a mountain pass by an eagle. The appearance of the eagle with its summons to battle serves to mark the transition from the domestic drama of the first half of the play to the social drama of the second half. Because Krasiński originally planned to publish the play under the title of "Maz" (the husband), there is good reason to believe that the decision to incorporate the question of class conflict within the framework of the plot occurred to him only after the work was already in progress.

In parts 3 and 4 of *The Undivine Comedy*, Krasiński voices the conviction that members of his social class are living on borrowed time. Here, the masses of humanity are depicted as being embroiled in a general rebellion against the ranks of the aristocracy, a revolt that has already succeeded to the point where but a single outpost of the *ancien régime* still remains to be subdued. For reasons that are never made clear, Count Henryk has been chosen to conduct the defense of the Holy Trinity Castle. It is at this castle that the remnants of European aristocracy have taken refuge and are now awaiting the final onslaught of the masses. The leader of the revolt is named Pankracy, a man whose desiccated, bloodless face fully reflects the spiritual void within him. For all his fanatical hatred of aristocracy, Pankracy has come to admire Count Henryk and would be willing to spare both him and his son on the condition that the count concede the historical necessity of the revolution and cease his opposition to it. It is Pankracy's view that Count Henryk best embodies the traditional virtues of the old nobility. Hence, by convincing him, Pankracy would be able to vindicate the cause of revolution beyond doubt. The survival of a single pair of aristocrats would, moreover, be of little consequence.

The two men agree to meet at the Holy Trinity Castle. On the eve of the meeting, Count Henryk decides to disguise himself as a revolutionary so he can observe his adversaries at first hand within their own encampment. There, he wanders about apprehensively among various groups of rebels, all of whom he finds to be obsessed by a desire to inflict savage retribution on their former oppressors. Within the camp, moreover, are many "liberated" women who, having escaped from the bonds of matrimony, now freely bestow their sexual favors among the rank and file. Another prominent element inside the camp consists of a group of baptized Jews who seek to ally themselves with the revolt against the old order. From a number of remarks that these converts make to one another and to the audience, it is clear from the outset that their apostasy from Judaism is but feigned and that they intend to transform the revolution into a vehicle that will advance the narrow interests of their own race. More than one critic has remarked on the similarity between this conspiracy and the one set forth in the *Protocols of the Learned Elders of Zion* that mysteriously surfaced in czarist Russia shortly after 1900. Krasiński's suspicion of the Jews, it should be noted, stands in stark contrast to the sympathy for this race displayed by both Mickiewicz and Słowacki.

As day draws near, Count Henryk departs from the camp and returns to the Holy Trinity Castle. That same evening, Pankracy comes to the castle for the purpose of persuading the count to surrender. During their ensuing debate, Pankracy expounds a view of social evolution that bears a strong affinity to the philosophy of historical materialism that was to be promulgated as official Communist doctrine by Karl Marx and Friedrich Engels during the next few decades. Henryk, moreover, is surprised to hear Pankracy proceed to disparage the untutored masses who make up the bulk of his forces, asserting that their cause would be without any prospect of success were it not for the leadership provided by professional revolutionaries such as himself. (Here, Pankracy's point of view closely approximates the theory and practice of party organization that enabled Vladimir Ilich Lenin to engineer the October Revolution.) Despite the inexorable logic of Pankracy's contention that the fossilized institutions of the Middle Ages must be swept away for the sake of humankind's progress, Henryk's deep attachment to the chivalric values of his ancestors and to the picturesque rituals of Christianity precludes the possibility of surrender. The issue must, therefore, be resolved in mortal combat on the ramparts of the Holy Trinity Castle. Count Henryk's failure to come to terms with Pankracy is a great disappointment to the other aristocrats who are trapped in the castle, and he needs to employ all of his rhetorical skills to prevent a mass defection from his ranks. His followers are obviously a thoroughly effete assemblage of noblemen who are willing to sell their birthright so long as they can save their own skins. Henryk, for his part, wishes to defend the castle to the bitter end so as to keep faith with his ancestral heritage. In short, he prefers a romantic death to life in a prosaic world dominated by the ideologies of populism and scientific atheism.

The fateful battle begins a few days later, and the count's forces actually succeed in holding the enemy at bay for a while. During a lull in the fighting, Henryk is confronted with the sins of his forefathers, as well as his own sins, when Orcis lures him into visiting the underground dungeon that is located in the castle. There, his blind son is able to conjure up the voices of those who had died in torment within these vaults. Unlike his sighted father, he can also see the forms of these victims in his mind's eye by virtue of his vatic powers. The vision that Orcis subsequently describes to his father is that of a man being tortured as punishment for his indifference toward the welfare of others. Presiding over the imposition of these penalties is Satan himself. Orcis goes on to reveal that it is Henryk himself who is fated to suffer these torments. The boy further claims that it was his dead mother who summoned him to persuade his father to visit the dungeon. Utterly dismayed by the experience, Count Henryk hastens back to his feckless followers and exhorts them to muster the courage to meet the final assault of the masses. When the fighting resumes, Orcis is struck by a random bullet and dies on the spot. The castle is finally overrun by Pankracy's troops, and the count retreats to a remote bastion situated along a precipice. Seeing that his capture is imminent, he utters a curse against the spirit of poetry and leaps into the gorge below. By taking his own life, Henryk has violated one of the cardinal prohibitions of Christianity and thereby demonstrated the emptiness of his claim to be the defender of the faith.

Pankracy learns of the count's suicide as he is dispensing summary justice to the last remaining members of the aristocracy. On hearing the news, he decides to take a stroll along the ramparts of the Holy Trinity Castle in the company of one of his closest confederates. Just as Pankracy is disclosing his plans for transforming society, he sees an awesome vision in the sky. It is nothing less than the figure of Jesus Christ leaning against a cross. Completely overwhelmed by this apocalyptic vision, Pankracy falls into the arms of his befuddled companion and promptly expires. He does, however, have time to reiterate the last words allegedly spoken by the anti-Christian Roman emperor known as Julian the Apostate (331-363 C.E.): "Galillee vicisti!" ("Galilean, thou hast conquered!"). This utterance on the part of Pankracy should not be interpreted as an indication that he has finally come to recognize the moral superiority of his adversaries. If the situation is viewed in terms of the dialectical principles espoused by Georg Wilhelm Friedrich Hegel, a philosopher whose writings exerted a profound influence on Krasiński, it is clear that the meaning of the final scene is far more complex. In keeping with the nature of the Hegelian triad, the struggle between the aristocracy and the masses depicted in Krasiński's play is similar to the dialectical relationship of thesis and antithesis. Out of this opposition, a synthesis is to emerge. It was Krasiński's belief that humankind's progress toward a higher form of civilization required an amalgamation of the competing ideologies respectively embodied by Count Henryk and Pankracy. Pankracy's attraction to Count Henryk is, in fact, based on a subliminal need to transcend his differences with the aristocracy. It is also the reason why Krasiński chooses to grant Pankracy, rather than Count Henryk, the privilege of perceiving the image of the Savior that emerges from behind the rays of the setting sun.

IRIDION

Iridion differs from *The Undivine Comedy* in many important ways. First, its length is more than three times that of *The Undivine Comedy*, and its prolix style contrasts sharply with the economy of language employed in the earlier play. Whereas the setting of *The Undivine Comedy* is left indeterminate, *Iridion* has a precise locale. In *Iridion*, the plot unfolds against the background of ancient Rome, during the reign of the emperor Elagabalus (218-222 C.E.; Heliogabalus in the drama). The protagonist is a young Greek named Iridion who is bent on destroying the despotic power of Rome that has kept his homeland in bondage for so many centuries. The destruction of Rome had also been the ruling passion of Iridion's father, Amphilochus Hermes. The extensive prologue to the play relates how Amphilochus migrated temporarily to a region in Scandinavia and married a woman named Grimhilda. By entering into wedlock with a priestess of the Norse god Odin, he hoped to be able to sire offspring that would combine Hellenic intellect with Germanic vitality. Back in Greece, his wife bore him a son and a daughter, Iridion and Elsinoe. Both children were reared to be implacable enemies of imperial Rome and were sworn to dedicate their lives to its destruction. Assisting Amphilochus in indoctrinating his offspring was a mysterious tutor of advanced age who called himself Masinissa. After the death of Grimhilda, Amphilochus departed from Greece together with his children and their tutor, as well as with an urn containing his wife's ashes, and took up residence in a palace situated in the heart of Rome.

As the play formally opens, Amphilochus has already expired. To fulfill his oath to destroy Rome, Iridion has now devised a plan to undermine the empire from within, one that requires him to ingratiate himself with Emperor Heliogabalus (Elagabalus). To this end, Iridion deems it best to induce his own sister to become one of the emperor's concubines. With great reluctance, Elsinoe agrees to the scheme and is thereupon taken to the emperor's palace. Heliogabalus is duly grateful for this favor, and Iridion actually assumes command of the Praetorian Guard before long. The emperor is a degenerate youth who is in imminent danger of being deposed by a group of high-minded patricians led by his cousin Alexander Severus. Iridion is thus faced with two sets of enemies. In many respects, the patrician party poses a far greater obstacle to Iridion's plans than does the effete emperor himself. The Roman state would surely be rejuvenated and its decline halted in the event that Alexander Severus and his followers were ever to come to power.

To augment his own forces, Iridion solicits support from various disgruntled segments of Roman society such as the plebeians, slaves, gladiators, and barbarians. Masinissa, however, informs him that the combined strength of all these groups is insufficient for the task at hand. He therefore urges Iridion to seek recruits among the Christians. These followers of Jesus would, however, need to be persuaded to abandon their commitment to nonviolence if they were to be of any use in the struggle. For the sake of making inroads among them, Iridion pays court to a Christian maiden named Cornelia Metella; he also permits himself to be baptized into the faith under the name of Hieronimus. Many Christians do, in fact, prove receptive to Iridion's exhortations to take up arms against their mutual foe. At the moment of crisis, however, they are dissuaded from coming to his aid by their bishop. Cornelia herself dies when the bishop subjects her to a rite of exorcism aimed at restoring her Christian orthodoxy. All of Iridion's machinations, consequently, end in failure. Heliogabalus is deposed by Alexander Severus, who then becomes emperor; Elsinoe, although in love with Alexander, commits suicide because she cannot reconcile herself to betraying her brother's cause.

Iridion, whose troops have abandoned him in favor of Alexander, now attempts to summon death by throwing himself on his sister's funeral pyre. Masinissa, however, restrains him. At this point, Iridion learns that his former tutor is actually the Devil himself. On top of a mountain overlooking Rome, Masinissa offers to grant him the privilege of seeing the ancient city reduced to ruins in exchange for his soul. Iridion's thirst for vengeance is still unquenched, and he eagerly accepts Masinissa's offer. Because that fateful day is far off, Iridion must spend the intervening period in a comatose state within a mountain cavern. Masinissa awakens Iridion in 1835 and takes him on a tour of the landmarks of ancient Rome, all of which now lie in ruins. When Iridion enters the Colosseum and sees a giant crucifix standing in isolated splendor within its walls, he is overwhelmed by emotion. Having fulfilled his part of the bargain, Masinissa wishes to lay claim to Iridion's soul. At this moment, the spirit of Cornelia Metella appears and argues for her former suitor's redemption. She asserts that while Iridion hated Rome, he loved Greece. The competing claims of Cornelia and Masinissa are finally resolved when God condescends to grant Iridion an opportunity to atone for his former obsessive hatred of imperial Rome. He is instructed to go northward in the name of Christ until he reaches "the land of graves and crosses" and to work for its national liberation through the spirit of love. Krasiński, thus, repudiates the doctrine that the end justifies the means, a principle that appears to have been embodied in the person of Masinissa.

OTHER MAJOR WORKS

LONG FICTION: *Grób rodziny Reichstalów*, 1830; *Władysław Herman i dwór jego*, 1830; *Agaj-Han*, 1833.

POETRY: *Trzy myśli pozostałe po ś.p. Henryku Ligenzie*, 1841; *Przedświt*, 1843; *Psalmy przyszłości*, 1845, enlarged 1848; *Ostatni*, 1847; *Niedokończony poemat*, 1852.

NONFICTION: *Correspondance de Sigismond Krasiński et de Henry Reeve*, 1902 (2 volumes); *Listy Zygmunta Krasińskiego do Delfiny Potockiej*, 1930-1939; *Listy do ojca*, 1963.

BIBLIOGRAPHY

Eile, Stanislaw. *Literature and Nationalism in Partitioned Poland, 1795-1918*. New York: St. Martin's Press, in association with School of Slavonic and East European Studies, University of London, 2000. An examination of Polish literature during the time in which Krasiński wrote. Bibliography and index.

Gardiner, Monica M. *The Anonymous Poet of Poland: Zygmunt Krasiński*. Cambridge, England: Cambridge University Press, 1919. A classic work describing the life and works of Krasiński.

Krzyżanowski, Julian. *Polish Romantic Literature*. 1931. Reprint. Freeport, New York: Books for Libraries, 1968. A study of the Romantic literature of Poland, including that of Krasiński.

Lednicki, Wacław, ed. *Zygmunt Krasiński, Romantic Universalist: An International Tribute*. New York: Polish Institute of Arts and Science in America, 1964. A group of essays on Krasiński and his works, collected at a gathering of scholars.

Victor Anthony Rudowski

KARL KRAUS

Born: Gitschin, Bohemia (now Jičin, Czech Republic); April 28, 1874
Died: Vienna, Austria; June 12, 1936

PRINCIPAL DRAMA

Literatur: Oder, Man wird doch da sehn, pr., pb. 1921
Die letzen Tage der Menschheit, pb. 1922, pr. 1930 (*The Last Days of Mankind*, 1974)
Traumstück, pb. 1923, pr. 1925 (verse play)
Wolkenkuckucksheim, pb. 1923 (verse play)
Traumtheater, pb. 1924, pr. 1925
Die Unüberwindlichen, pb. 1928, pr. 1929
Dramen, pb. 1967

OTHER LITERARY FORMS

Karl Kraus, widely regarded as one of the greatest satirists of the twentieth century, was primarily a prose writer, producing thousands of essays and aphorisms. He also wrote much poetry, which was collected in nine volumes entitled *Worte in Versen* (1916-1930; words in verse). Most of Kraus's writings first appeared in his own journal, *Die Fackel* (the torch).

ACHIEVEMENTS

Karl Kraus, a man who forced the powerful and the pitiful alike to stand before his tribunal of satire, was a legend in his lifetime, both adored and vilified by his contemporaries. Following a decade of neglect, his work was rediscovered and reissued in Germany, Austria, and other countries after World War II. Numerous editions, studies, and translations have focused critical and popular attention on this satirist, whose dictum that "I have to wait until my writings are obsolete; then they may acquire timeliness," seems to be coming true.

The key to Kraus's life and work is his relationship to language. As Erich Heller put it, "Karl Kraus did not write 'in a language,' but through him the beauty, profundity, and accumulated moral experience of the German language assumed personal shape and became the crucial witness in the case this inspired prosecutor brought against his time." The man who once said "Word and substance—that is the only combination I have striven for in my life," saw an absolute congruity between word and world, language and life; the unworthiness of his "language-forsaken" age was for him defined by its treatment of language. Kraus continually emphasized the connection between language and morality; for him, language was the moral criterion and accreditation for a writer or speaker. J. P. Stern has termed this equation of linguistic incompetence, obtuseness, or dishonesty with moral torpor or degeneracy Kraus's "moral-linguistic imperative." To Kraus, language is the mother of thought, not its handmaiden.

Despite the fact that Kraus raised language to an almost apocalyptic significance, he never developed a theory or philosophy of language, being essentially an unsystematic and antiphilosophical thinker. The Vienna Circle of logical positivists and the thinkers around Ludwig von Ficker's periodical *Der Brenner* (Innsbruck), however, were greatly interested in Kraus's relationship to language, and there are certain parallels between Kraus and Ludwig Wittgenstein—for example, their insight into the fundamental connection between, or even identity of, aesthetics and ethics.

Quotation is the hallmark of Kraus's satire, and in keeping with his conviction that what was most unspeakable about his age could be spoken only by the age itself, he set out to fashion the imperishable profile of his time from such perishable materials as newspaper reports. The thirty-seven volumes of Kraus's periodical *Die Fackel* constitute an enormous pillory, a running autobiography, and a uniquely personal history of Austria-Hungary (the empire that Kraus regarded as a "proving ground for the end of the world"). His apocalyptic stance as a "late" warner derives from his epoch's *Zeitgeist*: transitoriness, disintegration, and inner insecurity. Kraus's unremitting satiric warfare against the press (and in particular the influential *Neue freie Presse* of Vienna) was motivated by his view of journalism as a vast switchboard that concentrated and activated the forces of corruption, dissolution, and decay. Recognizing a disturbing identity of *Zeit* and *Zeitung*, the age and the kind of newspapers it spawned, with *Worte* (words) usurping and destroying *Werte* (values), he had apocalyptic visions of the world being obliterated by the black magic of printer's ink. Decades before Hermann Hesse coined the phrase "*das feuilletonistische Zeitalter*" in his Utopian novel *Das Glasperlenspiel* (1943; *Magister Ludi*, 1949), Kraus recognized his age as "the age of the feuilleton," in which newspaper reports took precedence over events, form eclipsed substance, and the style, the atmosphere, the "package" were all-important. Excoriating the press, that "goiter of the world," for its pollution of language and its poisoning of the human spirit, Kraus anticipated the judgments of contemporary critics of the media, and his diagnosis still has relevance.

BIOGRAPHY

Karl Kraus was the fifth son of Jakob Kraus, a well-to-do manufacturer of paper bags, and Ernestine Kantor Kraus. In 1877, the family moved to Vienna, and Kraus was to spend the rest of his life in the city with which he, like Sigmund Freud, had a love-hate relationship ("My hatred of Vienna is not love gone astray. It's just that I've discovered an entirely new way of finding it unbearable"). From 1884 to 1892, Kraus attended the Franz-Josefs-Gymnasium, where he was a mediocre student. Following the death of his mother in 1891, Kraus studied law, philosophy, and German literature at the University of Vienna, but he attended few lectures and did not take a degree. In 1893, he made an unsuccessful debut as an actor at a theater in suburban Vienna. His failure on the stage irrevocably turned him to journalism and literature, though his talent for mimicry and parody as well as his penchant for verbal play found ample expression in his later public readings and his writings.

During the next several years, Kraus contributed book reviews, drama criticism, and satiric sketches to

Karl Kraus

many Austrian and German newspapers and periodicals. His satiric impulse soon became too strong for any kind of accommodation, however, and Kraus rejected the prospect of becoming a sort of culture clown absorbed by a deceptively slack and effete environment and accorded, as he put it, "the accursed popularity which a grinning Vienna bestows." Because work within the establishment seemed to be hedged in with multifarious taboos and considerations of a commercial and personal nature, Kraus turned down a job offer from the *Neue freie Presse* and founded his own journal, *Die Fackel*, the first issue of which appeared on April 1, 1899, and which from the beginning had an incomparable satiric *genius loci*. After 1911, the irregularly issued periodical contained Kraus's writings exclusively ("I no longer have contributors. I used to be envious of them. They repel those readers whom I want to lose myself"). *Die Fackel* did continue to have numerous "contributors," albeit unwitting and unwilling ones: the people who were copiously quoted in its pages and allowed to hang themselves with the nooses of their own attitudes, actions, and statements.

Kraus's first major work, *Die demolirte Literatur* (1897; a literature demolished), appeared in the form of a witty obituary of the Café Griensteidl, the headquarters of Austria's men of letters, particularly the "Young Vienna" circle. The work lampoons such literary contemporaries as Hermann Bahr, Hugo von Hofmannsthal, Richard Beer-Hofmann, and Arthur Schnitzler. Kraus's pamphlet *Eine Krone für Zion* (1898; a crown for Zion) attacks political Zionism and its leader Theodor Herzl, who was also serving as the cultural editor of the *Neue freie Presse*, from the standpoint of an assimilated European Jew in sympathy with Socialism. (Kraus left the Jewish fold as early as 1899 and was secretly baptized in 1911, but he broke with the Catholic Church eleven years later and then remained religiously unaffiliated. He has, with some justification, been called everything from "an arch-Jew" and "an Old Testament prophet who pours cataracts of wrath over his own people" to "a shining example of Jewish self-hatred.") After the death of his father in 1900, Kraus detached himself from his family fortune, and went to live in a bachelor apartment.

If Kraus's early writings were directed largely against standard aspects of corruption, the second period of his creativity may be dated from the appearance, in 1902, of his essay *Sittlichkeit und Kriminalität* (morality and criminal justice; it was reissued in book form in 1908), which focused on the glaring contrast between private and public morality and exposed the hypocrisy inherent in the administration of justice in Austria. The book edition of that essay contains forty related essays on subjects and attitudes that are also germane to present-day problems: education, child abuse, sexual mores, women's rights. The gloomy, bitter wit of these essays gave way to lighter humor in Kraus's next collection, *Die chinesische Mauer* (1910; the great wall of China). Having published his first collection of aphorisms, *Sprüche und Widersprüche* (dicta and contradictions, or sayings and gainsayings), in 1909, Kraus issued during the following year his pamphlet *Heine und die Folgen* (Heine and the consequences), in which he attacks the German-Jewish writer for establishing the meretricious tradition of feuilletonistic journalism, deemed a dangerous intermediary between art and life and a parasite on both. With his address (and pamphlet) *Nestroy und die Nachwelt* (1912; Nestroy and posterity), Kraus revived interest in the nineteenth century Viennese comic playwright and actor, whom he presented in his full stature as a great German dramatist and social satirist who, like Kraus himself, achieved his critical and satiric effects through an inspired use of language.

In 1913, Kraus met Baroness Sidonie Nádherný, a Czech aristocrat to whom he unsuccessfully proposed marriage on several occasions. Despite her engagement to an Italian and her brief marriage to an Austrian doctor in 1920, Kraus's affectionate (and sometimes subservient) relationship with her continued for the remainder of his life, though with some periods of estrangement ("To love, to be deceived, to be jealous—that's easy enough. The other way is less comfortable: To be jealous, to be deceived, and to love!"). For many years Kraus found relaxation and inspiration at Sidonie's family estate at Janowitz and on trips taken with her. Much of his poetry refers to their relationship or is dedicated to her.

The outbreak of World War I inspired the outraged and anguished pacifist and humanitarian to produce his most powerful and characteristic work, beginning with the address "In dieser grossen Zeit" (in these great times), which was delivered in Vienna on November 19, 1914, and may be regarded as the germ of his extensive wartime output. The following year, Kraus began work on his mammoth drama *The Last Days of Mankind*, reading parts of it at recitals and publishing the text in several issues of *Die Fackel*. The year 1918 marked the appearance of *Nachts* (at night), Kraus's third and last collection of aphorisms, and, the next year, a two-volume compilation of *Die Fackel* articles was issued under the title *Weltgericht* (last judgment).

The story of Kraus's postwar writings and polemics is basically the history of his disillusionment as his "homeland's loyal hater." The best that Kraus could say about the Austrian Republic, a truncated and scarcely viable country still bedeviled by "the parasites remaining from the imperial age and the blackheads of the revolution," was that it had replaced the monarchy and relieved the satirist of "that burdensome companion, the other K.K." (The reference is to the abbreviation of *kaiserlich-königlich*, royal-imperial, the designation of many Austro-Hungarian institutions.) The 1920's were a fertile period for Kraus the dramatist; during this time he wrote, recited, and published five plays: *Literatur: Oder, Man wird doch da sehn*, *Traumstück*, *Traumtheater*, *Wolkenkuckucksheim*, and *Die Unüberwindlichen*. In 1929, Kraus's collection *Literatur und Lüge* (literature and lies) appeared, and between 1930 and 1932, his adaptations of Jacques Offenbach and William Shakespeare were broadcast by the Berlin and Vienna radio.

"*Mir fällt zu Hitler nichts ein*" (I can't think of anything to say about Hitler): This is the striking first sentence of Kraus's prose work *Die dritte Walpurgisnacht* (1952; the third Walpurgis Night)— the title refers to both parts of Johann Wolfgang von Goethe's *Faust: Eine Tragödie* (pb. 1808, pb. 1833; *The Tragedy of Faust*, 1823, 1828) as well as to the Third Reich—written in 1933 but not published in its entirety during Kraus's lifetime. That sentence,

which gave rise to misunderstandings and conflicts that were the bane of Kraus's existence in his last years, may be indicative of resignation, but it is also a hyperbolic, heuristic device for depicting the circumstances of the time. The satirist sadly realized the incommensurability of the human spirit with the unspeakably brutal and mindless power structure across the German border. Once again, language was in mortal danger, and the perpetrators of the new horrors were not characters from an operetta (as Kraus had perceived the "cast" of World War I).

In voicing genuine concern over Germany's pressure on his homeland, Kraus assumed the unaccustomed mantle of an Austrian patriot. Paradoxically, this stance led him to side with the clerico-Fascist regime of Chancellor Engelbert Dollfuss, whose assassination, in 1934, was a severe shock to Kraus. Many of the satirist's erstwhile adherents expected him to join them in their struggle, perhaps hoping that he could stop Fascism with a special issue of *Die Fackel*, but they were disappointed at what they regarded as the equivocation of the essentially apolitical satirist. *Die Fackel* now appeared at even more irregular intervals than before, and Kraus was content to reduce his readership to those who not only heard "the trumpets of the day" but also cared about Shakespeare, Nestroy, Offenbach, and German style, including Kraus's unique "comma problems." Preparing to "live in the safe sentence structure," Kraus pathetically and futilely strove to pit the word against the sword. His death, of heart failure, at the end of a long period of physical and spiritual exhaustion, four months after the appearance of number 922 of *Die Fackel*, mercifully saved Kraus from witnessing the Nazi takeover of Austria to the cheers of most of its population, the destruction of his belongings, the deaths of close friends in concentration camps, and untold other horrors.

ANALYSIS

The life and work of Karl Kraus were eminently theatrical, and he also served the theater in a variety of capacities: as a critic, translator, adapter, playwright, reciter, and a sometime actor. Kraus thought of himself as possibly the first writer who experienced his writings theatrically, the way a performer does: "When I give a public reading, it is not acted literature; but what I write is written acting." Kraus's mode of thinking and writing was essentially theatrical, and *Die Fackel* may in itself be regarded as a theater, an enormous world stage on which Kraus dramatized himself and his ethical, didactic, aesthetic, and, above all, satiric mission. His celebrated prose style and his poetry are replete with expressive, rhetorical, theatrical elements. In his life and work, criticism and showmanship, ethics and aesthetics were invariably linked.

Many of Kraus's feuds were carried on with theater people (Bahr, Wolfgang Bauer, Bernhard Buchbinder, and Emmerich Bukovics), and he came to take a highly personal and polemical view of such celebrated actors as Otto Tressler, Josef Kainz, Helene Odilon, and Alexander Moissi (all negative), Alexander Girardi, Adolf Sonnenthal, and Charlotte Wolter (all positive). All his life, he championed and yearned for the old Burgtheater with its dignity, integrity, artistry, and congruence of ethical and aesthetic purpose. Later in life, he evoked that theater's traditional style in programmatic opposition to what he regarded as the corruption, commercialism, politicization, charlatanry, sensationalism, and "feuilletonism" of the super-productions of directors such as Leopold Jessner, Erwin Piscator, and Max Reinhardt. (Kraus attacked the last named, one of the founding fathers of the Salzburg Festival, for the commercialization and vulgarization of culture in unholy alliance with the Catholic Church.) Kraus drew a distinction between *Buchdrama* (literary drama) and *Bühnendrama* (stage drama), and he increasingly came to take a reader-centered view, regarding drama as literature in which language and ideas were paramount and the reader's imagination was enlisted. (His all but unperformable play, *The Last Days of Mankind*, may be viewed as an extreme form of *Buchdrama*.) Between 1916 and 1925, three out of four of Kraus's readings were devoted to plays by other authors, and these included *Bühnendramen*, or actors' vehicles, though Kraus was aware that he could not have acted the roles he read in such austere fashion.

THE LAST DAYS OF MANKIND

Kraus's *magnum opus* as a dramatist (and satirist) is his powerful pacifistic play *The Last Days of Mankind*, a monumental dramatic repository of most of his satiric themes and techniques. Most of the 209 scenes of its five acts were first sketched during the summers of 1915, 1916, and 1917; the rhymed prologue dates from July, 1915, and the epilogue, from July, 1917. In his preface to this early example of a documentary drama, Kraus wrote:

> The performance of this drama, which would, in earthly terms, require about ten evenings, is intended for a theater on Mars. Theatergoers of this world would not be able to bear it. For it is blood of their blood, and its contents are those real, unthinkable years, out of reach for the wakefulness of the mind, inaccessible to any memory and preserved only in gory dreams, when characters from an operetta enacted the tragedy of mankind.

Having refused offers by Reinhardt and Piscator to stage this play, which covers more than eight hundred printed pages, Kraus permitted only performances of the epilogue in Vienna (1923, 1924) and Berlin (1930), in addition to reading his own "stage version" in 1930. After World War II, however, an abridgment for the stage and television by Heinrich Fischer and Leopold Lindtberg paved the way for highly controversial performances of the complete work in Basel, Vienna, and elsewhere.

The Last Days of Mankind begins with the voice of a newspaper vendor and ends with the voice of God. It is set in public rather than private places—in the streets of Vienna and Berlin, in offices and barracks, churches and cafés, amusement places and military hospitals, railroad stations and army posts, "in a hundred scenes and hells." The play's five hundred characters include pastors and prostitutes, chauvinists and showmen, professors and politicians, teachers and tradesmen, soldiers and sycophants, children and churchmen, inspectors and innkeepers, journalists and jesters, profiteers and policemen, editors and emperors. There are actual persons as well as fictitious ones, and all of them reveal (and often judge) themselves by their authentic speech patterns.

The play is a striking amalgam of naturalistic and symbolic elements. The scenes are, by turns, lyric and prosaic, comic and tragic; but even what seems to be purely humorous acquires a certain grimness in the context and usually appears as gallows humor. The play has no hero or plot in the conventional Aristotelian sense; it is episodic, with scenes recurring in cyclical patterns and inexorably grinding on to a cataclysmic conclusion. The scenes range in length from one-line "black-outs" in the tradition of the cabaret (more often than not, what is blacked out is the human spirit) to lengthy dialogues, monologues, dramatized editorials, and phantasmagoric tableaux. About half of this dramatic typology of humanity's inhumanity to humanity consists of authentic (though artistically presented) newspaper articles, war communiqués, court judgments, advertisements, letters, and other documents. Even the scenes and events invented by Kraus reproduce with uncanny accuracy the language of the "great times," which becomes the index of the Nietzschean vision of the disintegration of European culture and of a dying way of life.

"A sorcerer's apprentice seems to have utilized the absence of his master," wrote Kraus in reference to Goethe's poem, "but now there is blood instead of water." Kraus's wartime waxworks of "Goethe's people" and his fellow Austrians includes such characters as two fatuous privy councilors who vie with each other in mangling one of the glories of German poetry, Goethe's "Wanderer's Night Song"; the Bavarian storyteller Ludwig Ganghofer, who yodels his way along the front, writes war reports for the *Neue freie Presse*, and swaps jokes with an appreciative kaiser; "patriotic" pastors of the "praise-the-Lord-and-pass-the-ammunition" variety, to whom Kraus gives the names of birds of prey; a judge who celebrates his hundredth death sentence; two fat Berlin profiteers who disport themselves in the snows of the Swiss Alps; Alice Schalek, the first woman accredited to the Austrian army as a correspondent, whose gushy effusions about the emotions of the common man, "liberated humanity," and "the fever of the adventure" and whose search for "human-interest" material amid destruction, degradation, and death made her a macabre joke and a frequent Krausian target;

the grocer Chramosta, whom followers of the contemporary Austrian cultural scene will recognize as an ancestor of the cabaret character "Herr Karl"; and the "happy hangman," another all-too-familiar type, who appears on a picture postcard (used by Kraus as an illustration), holding his paws over the head of an executed man while the grinning or smug bystanders gather around the lifeless, dangling body. Another prime target of Kraus's satire was Moriz Benedikt ("Maledikt"), the editor of the *Neue freie Presse*, whom Kraus depicts as the "Lord of the Hyenas" and the "Antichrist." Old Man Biach, one of Kraus's fictitious characters and an assiduous mouther of Benedikt's editorials, dies, as it were, of linguistic convolution and spiritual poisoning when even he can no longer reconcile the harsh reality with all the journalistic double-talk and governmental double-think. The twenty-three conversations between the Grumbler, a Kraus figure, and the Optimist function as the choruses of a tragedy; they represent oases of relative repose and reflection. In his running commentary, the Grumbler constitutes the ever-present, anguished conscience of the times and the voice of reason, presenting eschatological views rather than espousing *Realpolitik*, and displaying the kind of conscience, compassion, and consistency that might have saved European civilization.

Although the prologue—ranging from June 28, 1914, the day on which the successor to the Austrian throne, Archduke Franz Ferdinand, and his wife were assassinated, to their third-class funeral—shows with grim realism what lies underneath the veneer of the vaunted Austrian *Gemütlichkeit*, or easy geniality; Surrealistic touches are introduced as the tragedy (and the war) rush toward their cataclysmic conclusion. "Corybants and Maenads" spew forth word fragments, and there are choruses of Gas Masks, Frozen Soldiers, twelve hundred Drowned Horses, and the Dead Children of the Lusitania. The rhymed epilogue is a harrowing poetic satire raised to a supernatural plane in which many motifs of the play are recapitulated in cinematographic or operatic form. After the silence that follows utter destruction, God's voice is heard speaking the words of Kaiser Wilhelm II at the beginning of the war: "*Ich habe es nicht gewollt*" (I did not will it so)—possibly a final glimmer of hope that humankind can yet redeem itself and work toward a better destiny.

LITERATUR

In 1921, Kraus published *Literatur: Oder, Man wird doch da sehn* (literature or we'll see about that), a "magical operetta" satirizing a literary movement in general and Franz Werfel, a Kraus apostle turned apostate, in particular. For the second time, Kraus has occasion to demolish a literature (expressionism rather than Young Vienna)—this time not with witty glosses and *aperçus* but by letting it manifest its unworthiness and speak its death warrant directly. Again the scene is a Vienna café—not the Griensteidl but the Central, a place that Kraus peoples with bourgeois bacchantes and meandering maenads. The Werfel figure is named Johann Wolfgang, and the pretentious, pompous son rebels against his business-minded father in true expressionistic fashion. Kraus satirizes, among other things, the effect that expressionist poets and playwrights, fashionable pseudo-philosophical essayists, psychoanalysts, and other "redeemers" have had on the impressionable *hoi polloi*. The parodistic play includes one of Kraus's best-remembered chansons, the "Song of the Press," a concentrated account of Creation sung by a character named Schwarz-Drucker (Ink-Printer), an operetta version of Benedikt.

TRAUMSTÜCK

In *Traumstück* (dream play), a one-act verse drama written during the Christmas season of 1922, lyric and grotesque elements intermingle. Kraus himself described this Surrealistic fantasy as "a series of visions of dozing and dreaming, born of the experiences of the war, the horrors of the postwar period, bad life and bad knowledge, newspapers, psychoanalysis, love, language, and dreams themselves." A pessimistic monologue of the Poet is succeeded by the dream world in which "The Psychoanals" identify themselves as killers of dreams, blackeners of beauty, compilers of complexes, and exhibitors of inhibitions—people to whom even Goethe's poems are nothing but badly repressed material. After several other visions and encounters, the Poet awakens to the insight that the dream has really clarified for him his

mission in life: to serve the Word and thus give permanence to his life.

TRAUMTHEATER

The legacy of Annie Kalmar, an actress whom Kraus admired and loved at the turn of the century and who died tragically young, also shaped the one-act play *Traumtheater* (dream theater), dedicated to her memory and published in 1924. Kraus has the beloved actress "play love" for him so that his love might be purged of jealousy. This improvisatorial philosophical-dramatic vignette consists of very brief scenes in both prose and verse that, in reality and in dreams, explore and illuminate the interpersonal relationships between the Actress, the Poet, the Director, the Old Ass (a member of the audience and a father symbol), and Walter, a high school student.

WOLKENKUCKUCKSHEIM

Kraus regarded his reading of *Wolkenkuckucksheim* (cloud-cuckooland) before an audience of workers as a most beautiful and fitting celebration of the Austrian Republic. Based on a German translation of Aristophanes' *Ornithes* (414 B.C.E.; *The Birds*, 1824), this "apotheosis of the republican idea" reflects an old tradition of the Viennese popular theater, the travesty of classical motifs. Two Athenians, who find conditions in their native city (a barely disguised Vienna) unbearable, emigrate and become birds in a Bird City. Soon enough, however, the coffeehouse culture, complete with prying journalists, avant-garde poets, psychoanalysts, and warmongers, catches up with them and sets the stage for The Last Days of Birdkind. The play does have a happy ending, however, and the Lark ends it with a Shakespearean solo: All have been dreaming; the confusion of purpose and function is now ended; the birds do not wish to be worshiped by men as gods; there will be no more violence or wars. "We dreamt of power, we live as republicans. . . . *Nie wieder Krieg!*"

DIE UNÜBERWINDLICHEN

With his last play, *Die Unüberwindlichen* (the unconquerables), printed in 1928, Kraus returned to the form of the documentary drama. This play memorializes two of the satirist's feuds: with Imre Békessy, a corrupt Hungarian-born press czar, and Johannes Schober, Vienna's chief of police (and Austria's sometime chancellor). Kraus not only accused Schober of collusion with Békessy but also held him responsible for the police riot of July, 1927, following the burning of the Ministry of Justice by people enraged by the recent acquittal of killers. "Once again, as in the last days of a mankind whose mysterious continued existence has now given us these scenes," wrote Kraus in his preface, "documents have become figures, reports have materialized as forms, and clichés stand on two legs." In this *pièce à clef*, which combines a Bekessiad with a Schoberiad, Kraus appears as Arkus and Békessy as Barkassy (*Barkasse* means "cash money"). Schober is made to sing the mordantly self-revealing "Schoberlied" to a tune of the satirist's own devising. By the time that this play was written, Kraus had managed almost single-handedly to "kick the crook out of Vienna," as the slogan of his campaign against Békessy read. Yet, despite the fact that such eminent actors as Peter Lorre, Ernst Ginsberg, Leonhard Steckel, and Kurt Gerron starred in the Berlin premiere of Kraus's witty and hard-hitting documentary play in October of 1929, it was evident that plays of standard length were not Kraus's forte. Further performances were canceled at the insistence of the Austrian embassy, but there was a revival in Leipzig two years later. Kraus continued to be painfully aware that his admirers-turned-detractors and the combined forces of the press, the financiers, and the police force in the first Austrian Republic were truly unconquerable.

ADAPTATIONS

Shakespeare was a living force throughout Kraus's life. Between 1916 and 1936, Kraus recited his adaptations of thirteen plays of the Bard; seven of these as well as Kraus's versions of his sonnets were published in book form between 1930 and 1935. Because Kraus knew little or no English, he was dependent on existing translations; he used these as a basis for renditions that reflect his unerring dramatic, poetic, and, above all, linguistic sense. One hundred twenty-three of his recitals were devoted to Jacques Offenbach. Having attended performances of Offenbach operettas at a summer theater as a child, Kraus developed a lifelong affinity with "the greatest musical dramatist of all times" and championed him in programmatic

opposition to the Austrian operetta in its "silver age," which he regarded as inane. Kraus presented fourteen of Offenbach's operettas, several in his adaptation, with only piano accompaniment, and although he could not read music, he sang all the roles. The couplets he sang in Offenbach's and Nestroy's works often included Kraus's own *Zusatzstrophen*, or topical stanzas. Kraus regularly performed dramas of Gerhart Hauptmann, Bertolt Brecht, Goethe, Nikolai Gogol, Ferdinand Raimund, and Frank Wedekind. In 1905, Kraus arranged the first Viennese performances of Wedekind's controversial Lulu play *Die Büchse der Pandora* (1904; *Pandora's Box*, 1918).

OTHER MAJOR WORKS

POETRY: *Worte in Versen*, 1916-1930 (9 volumes); *Poems*, 1930.

NONFICTION: *Die demolirte Literatur*, 1897; *Eine Krone für Zion*, 1898; *Sittlichkeit und Kriminalität*, 1902 (serial), 1908 (book); *Sprüche und Widersprüche*, 1909; *Heine und die Folgen*, 1910; *Die chinesische Mauer*, 1910; *Nestroy und die Nachwelt*, 1912; *Pro domo et mundo*, 1912; *Nachts*, 1918; *Weltgericht*, 1919, 1965 (2 volumes); *Untergang der Weltdurch schwarze Magie*, 1922, 1960; *Epigramme*, 1927; *Literatur und Lüge*, 1929, 1958; *Zeitstrophen*, 1931; *Die dritte Walpurgisnacht*, wr. 1933, pb. 1952; *Die Sprache*, 1937, 1954; *Widerschein der Fackel*, 1956; *Half-Truths and One-and-a-Half Truths: Selected Aphorisms*, 1976.

MISCELLANEOUS: *In These Great Times: A Karl Kraus Reader*, 1976; *No Compromise: Selected Writings of Karl Kraus*, 1977.

BIBLIOGRAPHY

Grimstad, Kari. *Masks of the Prophet: The Theatrical World of Karl Kraus*. Buffalo, N.Y.: University of Toronto Press, 1982. Presents critical analysis and interpretation of the plays of Kraus. Bibliography and index.

Halliday, John D. *Karl Kraus, Franz Pfemfert, and the First World War: A Comparative Study of "Die Fackel" and "Die Aktion" Between 1911 and 1928*. Passau, Germany: Andreas-Haller-Verlag, 1986. An examination of the political viewpoints of Kraus and Pfemfert as they were expressed in their periodical writings. Bibliography.

Theobald, John. *The Paper Ghetto: Karl Kraus and Anti-Semitism.* New York: Peter Lang, 1996. An examination of Kraus's views on Jews and the intellectual life of Jews during his lifetime. Bibliography and index.

Timms, Edward. *Karl Kraus, Apocalyptic Satirist: Culture and Catastrophe in Habsburg, Vienna.* New Haven, Conn.: Yale University Press, 1986. An examination of the writings of Kraus and the intellectual life in Vienna in the early twentieth century. Bibliography and indexes.

Zohn, Harry. *Karl Kraus.* New York: Twayne, 1971. A basic biography of Kraus that covers his life and works. Bibliography.

_____. *Karl Kraus and the Critics.* Literary Criticism in Perspective. Columbia, S.C.: Camden House, 1997. A study of the critical response to Kraus's works over the years. Bibliography and index.

Harry Zohn

FRANZ XAVER KROETZ

Born: Munich, West Germany; February 25, 1946

PRINCIPAL DRAMA

Als Zeus zum letzten Mal kam: Oder, Die Nacht der weissen Segel, wr. 1966, pb. 1983

Hilfe, ich werde geheiratet!, pr. 1969, pb. 1976

Hartnäckig, pb. 1970, pr. 1971

Männersache, pb. 1970, pr. 1972 (*Men's Business,* 1976)

Wildwechsel, pr. 1971, pb. 1973

Heimarbeit, pr., pb. 1971 (*Homeworker,* 1974)

Michis Blut, pr., pb. 1971 (*Michi's Blood,* 1976)

Stallerhof, pb. 1971, pr. 1972 (*Farmyard,* 1976)

Gute Besserung, pr. 1972 (radio play), pb. 1976, pr. 1982 (staged)

Geisterbahn, pb. 1972, pr. 1975

Leiber Fritz, pb. 1972, pr. 1975

Wunschkonzert, pb. 1972, pr. 1973 (*Request Concert,* 1976)

Dolomitenstadt Lienz, pr. 1972, pb. 1974

Herzliche Grüsse aus Grado, pr. 1972 (televised), pr. 1976 (staged), pb. 1976

Globales Interesse, pr. 1972

Oberösterreich, pr. 1972, pb. 1973 (*Morecambe,* 1975)

Bilanz, pr. 1972 (radio play), pb. 1976, pr. 1980 (staged)

Ein Mann ein Worterbuch, pb. 1973, pr. 1977 (*A Man, a Dictionary,* 1976)

Maria Magdalena, pr., pb. 1973 (staged), pb. 1974 (televised; based on Friedrich Hebbel's play *Maria Magdalena*)

Münchner Kindl, pr. 1973, pb. 1974

Die Wahl fürs Leben, pr. 1973 (radio play), pb. 1976, pr. 1980 (staged)

Sterntaler, pb. 1974, pr. 1977

Weitere Aussichten pr. 1974 (televised), pr. 1975 (staged), pb. 1976

Das Nest, pr. 1975 (staged), pb. 1975, pr. 1979 (televised; *The Nest,* 1984)

Reise ins Glück, pr. 1975 (radio play), pr. 1976 (staged), pb. 1976

Agnes Bernauer, pb. 1976, pr. 1977 (based on Friedrich Hebbel's play *Agnes Bernauer*)

Farmyard and Four Other Plays, 1976

Verfassungsfeinde, pr. 1977, pb. 1981

Mensch Meier, pr. 1978 (staged), pb. 1978, pr. 1982 (televised; English translation, 1983)

Der stramme Max, pb. 1979, pr. 1980

Wer durchs Laub geht . . . , pb. 1979, pr. 1981 (*Through the Leaves,* 1983)

Jumbo-track, pb. 1981, pr. 1983

Nicht Fisch nicht Fleisch, pr., pb. 1981

Der Weihnachtstod, pr. 1983, pb. 1984

Der Soldat, pb. 1983

Furcht und Hoffnung der BRD, pr., pb. 1984

Bauern Sterben, pr. 1985, pb. 1987

Der Nusser, pr. 1985 (adaptation of Ernst Toller's play *Hinkemann*)

Stücke, pb. 1989 (4 volumes)

Bauerntheater, pr. 1990, pb. 1991

Das Schaf im Wolfspelz, pr. 1990, pb. 1996

Through the Leaves and Other Plays, pb. 1992

Der Drang, pr. 1994, pb. 1996

Ich bin das Volk, pr., pb. 1994

Woyzeck pb. 1996 (adaptation of Georg Büchner's play *Woyzeck*)

Die Eingeborene, pr. 1999, pb. 2002

Das Ende der Paarung, pr. 2000, pb. 2002

Die Trauerwütigen, pr. 2001, pb. 2002

OTHER LITERARY FORMS

Even though Franz Xaver Kroetz is known primarily as a playwright, he has been productive in other genres as well. He has written numerous poems, novels, short stories, and diaries, and he has been a frequent contributor to newspapers, magazines, and journals.

ACHIEVEMENTS

In the late 1960's, a group of West German writers chose to write in a form that seemed out-of-date; the genre they selected became known as the "critical folk play." Its subject was no longer the dramatization of the traditional virtues of the simple folk, but the naked portrayal of the life of the common man in the country, the villages, and the small towns. The most important writers who engaged in this type of literature were Martin Sperr, Rainer Werner Fassbinder, Wolfgang Bauer, Harald Mueller, Wolfgang Deichsel, Heinrich Henkel, and Franz Xaver Kroetz. They chose as their most influential precursors Bertolt Brecht, Ödön von Horváth, and Marieluise Fleisser, writers who had dealt with sociopolitical problems of the Weimar Republic that seemed acute again during the period of the Grand Coalition (1966-1969), when the fledgling democracy of the Federal Republic—for lack of a real parliamentary opposition—appeared to be in danger. Sperr and Fassbinder had already made their mark when Kroetz, a relative latecomer among the playwrights of the "critical folk play," skyrocketed to fame in 1971. Although the others were soon forgotten, Kroetz's plays continued to enjoy public and the critics' attention and acclaim during the 1970's and the early 1980's. He has been by far the most frequently performed German playwright during this period and has been dubbed by his admirers as the "Wunderkind" of contemporary German theater.

Kroetz's initial reception was in part based on a misperception: His work was seen as scandalous, pornographic, and exotic, and as such it was categorized as sensational and salacious material not of interest to the general public. The emphasis placed on sex and violence at first deflected attention from Kroetz's attack on German society, in particular on the German middle class that was enjoying the fruits of the Economic Miracle and seemed blind to the misery of the less fortunate, who were being crushed by the same economic forces that had produced the boom days of postwar Germany. Kroetz's criticism is specifically leveled at the inhuman aspects of the free market system—its competitiveness and disregard for human values and institutions—and at the hypocrisy of the middle-class value system, which preaches order, obedience, and hope of success for everyone when in fact these values are but a camouflage for the ruthless struggle for power and selfish material interests as well as for the obstruction of the self-realization of a large segment of the population by a language that is borrowed and no longer functions as a medium of communication.

Kroetz's joining of the Communist Party (DKP) in 1972 introduced another factor that, at least temporarily, detracted from the legitimacy of his criticism. It did not, however, seriously affect his popularity. By 1982, ten of his plays that had been adapted to television reached a mass audience with great success; the television ratings of his plays were unusually high. It can be argued that the economic slowdown following the 1973 oil crisis, the threat to the environment, and the nuclear menace made the German public more receptive to Kroetz's criticism, and his withdrawal from the Communist Party in 1980 freed him from the charge of ideological partisanship. He has chronicled the shortcomings of West German society in more than thirty plays (not counting numerous adaptations for radio and television). The public responds to his productions with vociferous approval or emotional protest but never with indifference.

State institutions, cities, and publishing houses have awarded numerous honors and prizes to Kroetz, of which only the most prestigious will be mentioned here: a dramatist stipend from the Suhrkamp publishing house in 1970, the Ludwig Thoma medal from the city of Munich in 1971, a literary stipend from the Kunstpreis Berlin (West) in 1972, the prize of the West Berlin critics in 1973, the dramatist prize of Hannover for the play *Sterntaler* in 1974, the Wilhelmine-Lübke prize for *Weitere Aussichten* in 1975, and the dramatist prize of the city of Mühlheim for *The Nest* in 1976.

BIOGRAPHY

The publication in 1983 of a collection of works by Franz Xaver Kroetz, *Frühe Prosa, frühe Stücke*, revealed an artist much more complex than the rather naïve figure who had been created in the mind of the public. The legend, fostered in part by Kroetz himself, of the rise of this rough-hewn youth from the Bavarian countryside who struggled through acting school, gained experience in the theater by acting in traditional folk plays and producing one himself at the Ludwig-Thoma-Bühne in Rottach-Egern, and then burst on the German stage as the master of the "critical folk play," clearly needed revision.

Kroetz was born in Munich on February 25, 1946, into a traditional middle-class family. His father, a very conservative and authoritarian figure, wanted his son to become an independent tax consultant. The young boy was placed in the Wirtschaftsoberrealschule, a new school that specialized in subjects related to business. Kroetz hated the school and all of his teachers, with the exception of one who encouraged Kroetz's burgeoning interest in literature and the theater. When the young Kroetz failed in his fifth year, his dying father gave up his opposition to his son's

desire to take up acting. Kroetz attended the Neue Münchner Schauspielschule for about two years, but in 1963 he switched to the prestigious Max Reinhardt Seminar in Vienna. Independent and somewhat rebellious, he did not submit to the traditional approach that prevailed at both schools; as a result, he did not complete his course at the former and failed the acting test at the latter. He returned to Munich, passed that actors' guild examination, and became a professional actor.

In 1965, he joined a group of young actors who performed in the Kellertheater, a small, avant-garde theater in Munich. It was at this time that he read Mauricio Kagel, John Cage, James Joyce, and Samuel Beckett and experimented with forms of the absurd and expressionistic theater. Because he could not support himself as an actor, he took on a great variety of odd jobs, working for a living during the day and writing at night. One important experience in his development as a playwright was his appearance in the role of a lieutenant in Fassbinder's 1968 production of Fleisser's *Pioniere in Ingolstadt* (pr. 1928); Kroetz later openly admitted his indebtedness to Fleisser's analysis of the prefascist consciousness of the lower-middle class and especially to her use of language. In the fall of 1968, he joined the cast of the Ludwig-Thoma-Bühne in Rottach-Egern, where he took on traditional roles and produced his own folk comedy *Hilfe, ich werde geheiratet!* with great success. Yet this type of theater was not to his taste. The traditional folk theater was interested only in entertainment, not in social criticism.

Kroetz's breakthrough came in August, 1970, when the Suhrkamp publishing house awarded him a stipend that enabled him to devote all of his time and efforts to writing. One year later, *Wildwechsel* was produced in Vienna, and that same year, the Münchner Kammerspiele accepted *Homeworker* and *Hartnäckig* for its season's schedule. Beginning with 1971, a whole series of his plays appeared in print and on many stages; his plays could be heard on radio and seen on television. In 1972, he joined the Communist Party (DKP), a step that cost him the sympathy of many spectators and especially of conservative critics, yet it hardly deflated the success of his plays onstage and on television. After 1972, his work assumed a decidedly didactic and at times openly political note, attacking specific social problems and advocating reform and change.

In the early 1980's, however, the optimism and activism gave way to a tone of somber resignation and cautious reflection. The political as well as the cultural landscape in the Federal Republic changed drastically in 1982 when a coalition under the chancellorship of Kohl took over the government and reigned in an era of conservatism that lasted until 1998. Kroetz's popularity sank, his critical anticapitalist stance seemed out of fashion, his dialectical method appeared worn and less effective. He experienced a personal crisis that he tried to overcome by flying to Nicaragua to recover his failing creativity and assist the disintegrating revolution in any way possible. He returned home disillusioned; he had misjudged Nicaragua's revolution, which was not really a socialist-inspired movement but rather more of struggle of liberation from a dictatorial yoke. A similar trip to South America, to Brazil and Peru recorded more or less the same disappointing impressions. Kroetz's productivity slowed down in the 1980's and 1990's even though he had a successful premiere in 1985 with *Bauern Sterben*. He continued to produce plays and adapt dramas by other German playwrights, but his productions became fewer in number and less successful than in the past. His house in Kirchheim, a small hamlet in Southern Bavaria, became his favorite retreat.

ANALYSIS

The more than forty plays of Franz Xaver Kroetz can be grouped according to four developmental phases: first, an experimental phase, from 1965 to 1968; second, a phase labeled by Kroetz himself as "descriptive realism," from 1968 to 1972; third, a phase with the provisional title "didactic realism," from 1972 to 1979-1980; an extension of this phase, a subphase so to speak, called "dialectical realism" (dialectical because the contradictions are laid bare, and it is up to the spectator to take the next step); and fourth, a phase after 1982 for which the label "Kroetz revisited" will have to serve as a collective term. Af-

ter 1982 Kroetz—with one exception—keeps coming back to former themes and dramaturgical practices of his œuvre.

The division into developmental phases presupposes certain changes in Kroetz's dramaturgical practice as well. Leaving aside the experimental period during which he was still exploring various styles, Kroetz's own theoretical pronouncements leave no doubt that in his second phase he was on the whole indebted to the dramaturgy of identification as it had been practiced by the German naturalists and later by Horváth and Fleisser. The phenomenon of identification of Kroetz is, however, different from the concept of the naturalists and closer to that of Horváth and Fleisser. Kroetz deviates from the naturalistic dictum of the faithful reproduction of the minutest details of social reality; he makes use of stylization and reduction—in language, composition, and scenery—to introduce a limited kind of alienation effect. In his third phase, Kroetz turned to Brecht and was guided by Brecht's concept of "didactic persuasion" as it had been illustrated in his *Lehrstücke* (didactic plays). The emotional appeal, the result of identification, is alienated, that is, broken, in Kroetz's plays of this period through the didactic orientation and specific alienating devices largely borrowed from Brecht. What saves Kroetz from producing theoretical tracts or moralizing sermons is his fundamental approach to writing: He invariably starts with concrete experience, not with a theoretical, abstract conception. He has been the first to admit that his failures have been the result of not adhering to this practice. The spectator is to be persuaded, not by a series of theoretical arguments, but by authentic situations from life. In the subphase "dialectical realism," Kroetz returned to his former practice of distant and limited identification, while introducing ambiguous images of compelling complexity. For most of the 1980's and 1990's, Kroetz revisits his prior work and produces plays that tend to be more somber and more strident in their criticism of contemporary capitalist society. Thus, Kroetz seems to have come full circle, from a dramaturgy of limited identification, to one of didactic persuasion via examples of concrete experience, to a dialectical process in which contradictions are exposed and left unresolved, and back to his interest in the Theater of the Absurd.

Kroetz has created a style of language that distinguishes him from everyone else. The speech of his characters is not a naturalistic imitation of a sociolinguistic stratum but rather an artificial, supraregional quasi dialect that is not authentic or specific to one class alone—it can be understood by almost any speaker in Germany. The success of Kroetz's plays in Northern Germany is proof of that. The language possesses great revelatory and unmasking powers (the word used by critics in Germany is *Ausstellungscharakter*) that expose the conditions of oppression and dependency to the spectators, while at the same time keeping the speakers ignorant of their problems. This places the spectators in a position of superiority, but the authenticity of tone and the reduction in plot and action to very fundamental human situations force them to realize that the characters onstage are not that far removed from them.

The compelling force of these formal elements is heightened by the topicality of Kroetz's themes. He protests against the dehumanizing effects of economic exploitation, modernization and so-called technological progress, and bureaucratization. Kroetz, who was never a member of the revolutionary student movement of the late 1960's, has called himself a "communist conservative"; on one hand, he takes a cautiously progressive attitude toward the institution of the family, gender roles, and children—he advocates individual self-realization and liberation from traditional bonds—but, on the other hand, he wants to protect these traditional patterns from the onslaught of modernization and technology, which he fears will depersonalize social relations and impose a fragmentary existence on man without offering anything in return.

THE FIRST PHASE

During the experimental phase (1965-1968), Kroetz explored various styles, from the avant-garde theater to the traditional folk theater. Only two examples of that early period, *Als Zeus zum letzten Mal kam* and *Hilfe, ich werde geheiratet!*, have survived; the others were destroyed by Kroetz as soon as he had found the realistic style of his next phase. The

first of these plays is clearly a takeoff on Beckett's *Fin de partie: Suivi de Acte sans paroles* (pr., pb. 1957; *Endgame: A Play in One Act, Followed by Act Without Words: A Mime for One Player*, 1958). Two partially paralyzed cripples, stranded on a garbage heap in a sea of wasteland, are periodically faced by a Sisyphean task: They must rebuild their shack, which is destroyed by recurrent floods. Survival seems to be the only meaning to life; language and literature provide entertainment, helping the characters endure a life of utter boredom and monotony. The second play of this period represents a complete turnabout in subject matter as well as in technique; it is a situation comedy with all the necessary requisites of the traditional folk theater. A farmer's wife successfully contrives to overcome her son's misogyny by disguising his future bride as a man and hiring her as a house servant.

THE SECOND PHASE

The second phase of Kroetz's drama centers on the struggles of lower-class people—homeworkers, factory workers, unskilled laborers, small farmers and their servants—against societal injustice. The characters are victims, oppressed by a system the values of which they have internalized and by a language that does not permit comprehension of themselves or the forces that imprison them. The term "descriptive realism" not only encompasses social reality but also defines Kroetz's skeptical stance; he refrains from commenting, allowing the characters to exhibit emotional debilities through characteristic speech patterns and silent actions. Although the characters themselves see no end or solution to their problems, the spectator is implicitly urged to reflect on the determining circumstances.

Among the plays of this phase, *Farmyard* and its continuation, *Geisterbahn*, are probably the most representative. In *Farmyard*, Beppi, the somewhat retarded daughter of the Staller farm, and Sepp, an older and sickly servant, develop a relationship that is based on blunt, unmitigated gestures and actions of affection rather than on verbal forms of communication; the two are unable to articulate clearly what they feel and think. When Beppi becomes pregnant, Sepp has to leave the farm and move to the city. The

Stallers want to force their daughter to have an abortion, but Beppi threatens to kill herself in that case. An antiquated code of honor rules the consciousness of the parents; the illegitimate child is an unbearable embarrassment to them, and they insist that it be placed in a home. Beppi vehemently refuses, packs up her belongings, and moves into a tiny one-room apartment with Sepp. Because Sepp is sick and no longer able to work, Beppi keeps the family alive by working at home. The two experience moments of happiness that stand in stark contrast to the nervous irritability and the carefully structured but joyless daily routine of Beppi's parents. When the Stallers persist in their efforts to have the boy institutionalized, Beppi suffocates the child, puts him in a box, and deposits the box in the "ghost-train" in which she and Sepp had met.

Farmyard and *Geisterbahn* contain the major elements of Kroetz's second phase: the damaged speech that prevents understanding of one's problems and their causes and that is relieved in sometimes brutal actions, and the bourgeois value system that, as in these two plays, oppresses the outcast and downtrodden. It is Kroetz's paradoxical message that the emotionally crippled and retarded show, despite their inarticulateness and violent explosions, more humanity than the so-called normal, who are barricaded behind a wall of suppressed violence. The parents are actually the more pitiful creatures: They cannot break through the disingenuously upheld code of honor and propriety; appearances must be kept up even at the loss of their own child. Other important plays of this phase are *Homeworker*, *Hartnäckig*, *Michi's Blood*, *Wildwechsel*, *Men's Business*, and *Dolomitenstadt Lienz*.

THE THIRD PHASE

Kroetz's declaration of solidarity with the Communist Party marked a definite change in his writing. No longer satisfied with the descriptive exposition of problems and the stirring up of the spectator's conscience, he wanted to effect change through political agitation, activism, and open argumentation. His characters began to resist oppression, striving to emancipate themselves, some with more, some with less, success. The plays tackle specific social and individual problems and advocate a wide range of responses. *Morecambe* describes the decision of a couple not to sacrifice their child merely to preserve a comfortable standard of living; *Münchner Kindl* calls for political action against modernization plans for the city of Munich that would evict the elderly and the poor; *The Nest* depicts the fight of a politically awakened worker against the illegal dumping of toxic wastes; *Lieber Fritz*, the liberation of an erstwhile sexual deviant; *Verfassungsfeinde*, opposition to the "radicals' decree"; *Mensch Meier*, the emancipation from traditional dependencies in the patriarchal family structure; and *Through the Leaves*, the self-assertion of a woman. Not all Kroetz's plays of this period call for political and social action; a number of them—among them *Maria Magdalena*, *Weitere Aussichten*, *Reise ins Glück*, and *Der stramme Max*—still represent unopposed oppression but not in the manner of the plays of the second phase. The characters are not as deficient in their speech as before. While they may not be able to escape their circumstances, they are capable of insight and therefore offer the spectator less emotional identification with their lot.

THE NEST

A discussion of *The Nest* will illustrate the didactic realism of the third phase. Kurt, an obedient and loyal truck driver, is told by his boss to dump a few barrels of supposedly harmless liquid. He pours it into his family's favorite lake, which, soon thereafter, is visited by his wife and son. The child becomes deathly ill, and Kurt, blaming himself, thinks of committing suicide, but in his despair and agony he undergoes a radical change of conscience: He realizes the escapist nature of his attempt on his life and decides to oppose his boss publicly in court. The "trained monkey," as his wife called him before, now acts responsibly, regaining his self-respect and the admiration of his wife. The radical change in Kurt's political stance also manifests itself in his language; his speech loses many of the stereotypical clichés and the sanctimonious hollow phrases that had characterized it before his conversion. Even though the play focuses on a particular problem, its scope is general enough in its portrayal of an individual's development toward personal and public maturity and independence to escape the charge of espousing only narrow ideological goals. Except for *Münchner Kindl*, written for a specific political occasion, Kroetz's didactic plays of this period cannot be accused of partisan prejudice; they stand for liberal humanistic values of universal significance.

DIALECTICAL REALISM

In 1980, Kroetz withdrew from the Communist Party, a step that was immediately reflected in his work. It is not certain which came first, resignation from the party or a change in his writing. Whatever the truth may be, the two were intricately linked. The perspective of optimism and hope for change of the 1970's gave way to a more sober assessment and a mood of stoic resignation. To render the perplexity of the contemporary German condition of the early 1980's, Kroetz began to employ surrealistic images of the absurd that remind one of his early experimental phase. In the plays of this phase, social and economic problems are still critically presented for inspection and public discussion, but without answers or hints at resolution.

NICHT FISCH NICHT FLEISCH

Of the few plays of this subphase, called "dialectical realism," the play *Nicht Fisch nicht Fleisch* combines the descriptive realism of the second phase and the practices of the early experimental period, whereas *Furcht und Hoffnung der BRD* relies more on the realistic method of the second phase. Because Kroetz himself has described the latter as a rather limited and subjective picture of his frame of mind during the year 1983, *Nicht Fisch nicht Fleisch* will be examined here as the more representative piece of this period.

The play provides a juxtaposition of two types of workers and two types of women. Edgar, the traditional, politically accommodating type, wants peace, order, and a secure job. Modernization measures that are being implemented in his firm require retraining in computerized methods. Edgar feels inept and inadequate; he cannot adapt, so he quits his job. He is married to Emmi, a very enterprising woman whose success in a small business venture threatens his male ego. The loss of his job and the reversal of roles in his

marriage shatter his notion of what a man is supposed to be; in his despair, he is contemplating suicide. Hermann, on the other hand, represents the progressive reformer who is convinced that technology can be advantageous to the workers in their struggle for more economic power and political independence. Hermann is married to Helga, a woman who is totally fulfilled in her role as mother and wife. The men are obviously married to the wrong women, or vice versa. Toward the end of the play, the two men meet in a surreal, Hades-like, watery setting, each one in utter misery. Hermann's militancy has earned for him the wrath of the more conservative and security-minded work force: They blow him up with a bicycle pump. While he writhes in agony, Edgar raves about swimming to another shore where he will be free. The last scene shows both couples around a table, eating in silence—all questions left hanging in the air, nothing resolved.

Nicht Fisch nicht Fleisch treats some of Kroetz's major themes—the breakup of traditional gender roles and its consequences, the choice between children or a comfortable standard of living, the meaning of work and the destructive influence of unemployment—but the ambivalent impact of technology is at the center of the play. Hermann and Edgar represent two major trends in the work force, the progressive faction that sees in technology the means to a brighter future, and the traditionalists who stand for stable conditions and thus fear technology for its disruptive influence. The conflict between the two positions is not resolved but rather embodied in a surrealistic setting that tries to capture the unmanageable nature of the problem. Traces of a symbolic, more indirect mode of representation that is not readily accessible to interpretation, as had been the case with symbolic, silent gestures, actions, and situations throughout Kroetz's work, can also be found in the language. Several statements toward the end of the play are simply suggestive and ambivalent. The title is the epitome of this evocative and ambiguous use of images: Does it imply that humankind has lost its freedom, leaving only the choice of either living like a fish in a tank, always in fear of being eaten by a bigger fish, or of returning to the past, to a simpler lifestyle (which seems to be Edgar's regressive dream of freedom)? The spectators are left to ponder the question for themselves.

THE FOURTH PHASE

Although Kroetz kept experimenting in the early 1980's, on the whole, his productions—with one exception—do not represent a novel orientation in dramaturgy, but rather connect with earlier approaches, however extreme he may have taken them in their execution. Thus, one could label the phase after 1982 as "Kroetz revisited." He, for example, picks up previously used themes such as unemployment and xenophobia, in *Der Weihnachtstod*, and he readapts a former play, *Lieber Fritz*, in *Der Drang*. *Bauern Sterben* uses surrealistic images of the first and third phases, *Bauerntheater* reminds one very much of Kroetz's experimental phase in the Theater of the Absurd, and *Ich bin das Volk* combines practices from all phases. Kroetz also adapts Ernst Toller's *Hinkemann* (pr., pb. 1923; English translation, 1926), which he renames *Der Nusser*, and Georg Büchner's *Woyzeck* (wr. 1836, pb. 1879; English translation, 1927). The only novel dramaturgical technique can be found in *Bauern sterben* in which Kroetz returns to the traditional form of the station play, a structure that dates back to the religious passion plays. A discussion of the three major plays written during the 1980's and 1990's will reveal Kroetz's indebtedness to his previous productions, and point out minor innovations and his tendency toward extremism.

BAUERN STERBEN

Bauern Sterben is a station play about the flight of siblings, a brother and his sister, from their farm in the country to the city, where they hope to enjoy the comfortable life promised by consumer advertising. The senile and stigmatically bleeding patriarch of the family resists all efforts of his son at modernization. The farm can no longer sustain the independent livelihood farmers supposedly enjoyed in the past; the same economic forces that dominate the city have also invaded the lives of peasants in the country. Industrial, technological modernization dominates the country as well as the city, and because Kroetz sees above all else the negative aspects of capitalism, this

means that unemployment, the destruction of the environment, and homelessness will devastate the lives of all people. Despite explicit and symbolic warnings on their journey of what lies in store for them, the siblings sell their tractor and settle down in an unfinished flat. They soon succumb to the lures of consumerism, run out of money, and are reduced to eating dog food. In extreme anguish they turn to an animistic and superstitious kind of adoration of a crucifix they had brought with them. When the brother can see no other way to survive, he forces his sister into prostitution and even rapes her. At their wits' end, they finally return home to find that their farm has been cemented over. Sitting on the grave of their parents, they await the end.

To expose the dehumanization of humankind brought on by the bewildering changes of rapid modernization, Kroetz uses surrealistic images and scenes of extreme cruelty and anguish: The father bleeds stigmatically over the only product they still have to sell, namely milk; the sister hides her aborted foetus in the worm-eaten belly of her grandmother; a figure of Christ is disemboweled while nobody pays attention, and the brother carries home the idol of the crucifix on his back. Although Kroetz employs the station play form, he departs dramatically from the ethos of the traditional passion play. *Bauern Sterben* has none of the redemptive implications of the traditional passion plays; God is dead, humankind has to carry its own cross. The play is a dark condemnation of the consequences of rapacious capitalism.

BAUERNTHEATER

In the comedy *Bauerntheater*, Kroetz returns to his early experiments in the Theater of the Absurd. In fact, all of the characters in this play could very well have come right out of Beckett's *Endgame*. It is also important to note that Kroetz had written comedies for the folk or peasant theater during his first experimental phase. Despite the protagonist's assertion that it is impossible to bring these two strands of theater together, that is, to imbue the peasant comedy with the spirit of modern life, Kroetz, the author, does just that. The result is a grotesque, nihilistic farce in the tradition of his earliest absurd experiments.

A frustrated writer of peasant farces—through the writing of which he earns his living—disingenuously engages in aesthetic and social questions regarding his own work; his reflections are deflated by the vulgar behavior of his mother. The spectator is confronted by a totally dysfunctional family, every member of which is a selfish, amoral egoist solely intent on satisfying his or her desires. This cast of social misfits rehearses one of the writer's peasant comedies in which an elderly possessive peasant widow is duped by her daughter and her lover. Dissatisfied with his own work, the writer interrupts the performance. His homosexual son, Garfunkel, storms into the house suicidally depressed because one of his pickups rubbed Vicks Vaporub into his anus. The father berates his son for being an effeminate homosexual—even though he admits that he had had a temporary lapse of this kind as well—and demands of his son that he own up to his manhood. In despair, Garfunkel locks himself into the bathroom; his father's former wife and a neighbor beg the father to show affection for his son, but his reluctant display of love comes too late. By the time they break the door open, Garfunkel has committed suicide. While the father holds his dead son in his lap, he asks for a typewriter; he intends to write one good sentence. He then carries Garfunkel into the bathroom, and we are told by his youngest son peeping through the key hole that the father is making love to his son.

The attempt to bring "real life" into the peasant or folk theater turns the rehearsed peasant comedy as well as the entire play into a grotesque farce, which is what the writer within the play seemed to predict. Because "real life," at least the way Kroetz represents it in the play, is totally corrupt and devoid of any meaning, it cannot infuse "new life" into the peasant comedy. The opposite is true; the introduction of contemporary reality robs the peasant comedy of all humor.

Kroetz published the peasant comedy under the title *Das Schaf im Wolfspelz* (the sheep in wolf's skin) in 1990 as a separate play in its traditional mode. Although the plot remains the same as the play-within-a-play in *Bauerntheater*, the stock characters' foibles

and shortcomings evoke the kind of humorous responses associated with the traditional peasant or folk comedy.

ICH BIN DAS VOLK

The play *Ich bin das Volk* (I am the people) consists of a loose collection of mainly short scenes, the number of which was reduced from forty to twenty-four for its premiere in 1994. In an introductory note, Kroetz makes it very clear that the play was written against an extremely worrisome background, namely the rise of xenophobia, the resurgence of Nazism, the continued existence of poverty, and the cowardice of most Germans facing these problems.

Kroetz employs the entire repertoire of his dramaturgical approaches from all phases. In the majority of cases he uses the dialectical method of unmasking the false consciousness, the concealed deeper motives of the characters he presents onstage. A discussion of several exemplary scenes will describe the various techniques he resorts to in order to reveal—as he perceives it—a still persistent deepseated layer of xenophobia and neofascism in certain segments of the German population.

In "Gedenktag," a conservative politician prepares a speech commemorating an amendment to the German constitution restricting asylum. His basic point is that the German constitution, the result of the capitulation in 1945, is outdated and needs to be adjusted to the realities of today, notwithstanding the fact that the rights he would like to change are basic human rights. In his speech, he frequently switches from High German to the Bavarian dialect. Whereas his loquaciousness in High German has a quasi-rational tone to it—he would like to convince his listeners—his lapses into Bavarian are clearly defamatory and extremely vulgar. The application of dialect has a purely tactical function; it is no longer a naturalistic device to reproduce the speech of a particular class.

The best example of the tactical use of dialect can be found in a very short scene called "Ziel" (goal). A German tourist who has just returned from a visit to Israel expresses his disappointment over the stubborn unwillingness of Israelis to come to some sort of reconciliation with Germans. At the end of his short monologue, he lapses into Bavarian, "*Nur weis amoi vahoazt worn san, hams a ned oiwei recht*" ("Just because they have been cremated once, doesn't mean they are always right")—speaks for itself. The utterance in dialect leaves no doubt about the true convictions of the speaker.

In "Ritter der Ausgewogenheit" (knights of balanced reporting), Kroetz makes use of a method one can observe in many of the twenty-four scenes: He lets his characters ramble on in seemingly spontaneous speech—the written text is entirely without punctuation marks—until they contradict themselves or utter thoughts that betray their real intentions. In this particular scene, an executive addresses his colleagues in the conference room of a radio station in order to convince them that they should be more balanced in their reporting of arson attacks against Turks. By suggesting to them that they place these attacks into the broader contexts of fire hazards, he achieves exactly the opposite of what he tried to avoid, namely a gross trivialization of racist crimes.

In "Versöhnen durch erinnern," a gymnasium teacher has her class perform a scene from the Eichmann trial to illustrate the Abitur topic "reconciliation through remembrance." The rector of the school and a political representative of the government are shocked at first, but tolerate the performance because in the scene, which takes place in a concentration camp, gypsies refuse to be treated by a Jewish doctor. Thus, they conclude that racism was not only a German problem. The stark realism of the excerpt from the Eichmann trial—Kroetz wanted the scene to be played by very young actors, preferably by children—unmasks the false consciousness of the characters in the outer frame and exposes their latent fascist tendencies.

In the last exemplary scene, "Dachau Fantasie," Kroetz not only uses the theatrical device of juxtaposing conflicting and contradictory events but also resorts to shocking surrealistic images. A reconciliation church in a former concentration camp is overrun by asylum seekers desperately looking for shelter. The authorities, who regard the actions of the refugees as a sacrilege dishonoring the memory of those who died in the camp, try to clear out the church. One asylum seeker is discovered draped around a cross and is forcibly removed. A Catholic prelate kneeling before the cross is startled by an apparition of Christ who spits in his face and disappears. This surrealistic incident dramatically uncovers the contradiction between the church's religious pretensions and its actions.

Taken together, the twenty-four scenes present a panoramic exposé of xenophobia and, at least in Kroetz's opinion, deep-seated fascist tendencies. The dramaturgical means Kroetz uses are not new, but they are utilized very effectively and are intended to have a shocking impact. The spectators are not told what to do, but Kroetz would like to open their eyes to the realities as he sees them.

A critical evaluation of the playwright Franz Xaver Kroetz must assess his position within the sociopolitical context of his time and investigate the reasons for his success. The effect of Kroetz's plays can be attributed to two major sources: One is related to the formal character of his plays—his peculiar use of language and speech patterns and the reduction in characters, plot, action, and scenery—the other to the topicality of his themes.

OTHER MAJOR WORKS

LONG FICTION: *Tiroler Elegien*, 1983 (written in 1967); *Der Mondscheinknecht*, 1981, 1983 (2 volumes); *Nicaragua Tagebuch*, 1985.

SHORT FICTION: *Koreanischer Frühling*, 1983 (written in 1969).

SCREENPLAY: *Wildwechsel*, 1973.

TELEPLAYS: *Herzliche Grüsse aus Grado*, 1973; *Der Mensch Adam Deigl und die Obrigkeit*, 1974; *Muttertag*, 1975; *Mitgift*, 1976; *Heimat*, 1980.

NONFICTION: *Tagebuch 1983*, 1983; *Braslien-Peru-Aufzeichnungen*, 1991.

MISCELLANEOUS: *Chiemgauer Geschichten*, 1977; *Frühe Prosa, frühe Stücke*, 1983; *Heimat Welt: Gedichte eines Lebendigen*, 1996.

BIBLIOGRAPHY

Blevins, Richard W. *Franz Xaver Kroetz: The Emergence of a Political Playwright*. New York: Peter Lang, 1983. Examination of Kroetz's political agenda during the 1970's.

McGowan, Moray. "'Die Stadt ist der Metzger': The Crisis of Bavarian Peasant Identity in Franz Xaver Kroetz's *Bauern sterben.*" *German Studies Review* 19, no. 1 (February, 1996): 29-40. Detailed discussion of Kroetz's social conservatism.

Mattson, Michelle. *Franz Xaver Kroetz: The Construction of a Political Aesthetic.* Washington, D.C.: Berg, 1996. Precise study of the peculiar relationship between politics and aesthetics in Kroetz's work.

Walther, Ingeborg. *The Theater of Franz Xaver Kroetz.* New York: Peter Lang, 1990. Thorough analysis of Kroetz's communicative use of dialogue.

Hans Ternes

TONY KUSHNER

Born: New York, New York; July 16, 1956

PRINCIPAL DRAMA

Yes Yes No No, pr. 1985, pb. 1987 (children's play)

A Bright Room Called Day, pr., pb. 1987

Hydriotaphia: Or, The Death of Dr. Brown, pr. 1987, pb. 2000

Stella, pr. 1987 (adaptation of Johann Wolfgang von Goethe's play)

The Illusion, pr. 1988, pb. 1992 (adaptation of Pierre Corneille's play *L'Illusion comique*)

Widows, pr. 1991 (with Ariel Dorfman; adaptation of Dorfman's novel)

Angels in America: A Gay Fantasia on National Themes (*Part One: Millennium Approaches*), pr. 1991, pb. 1992

Angels in America: A Gay Fantasia on National Themes (*Part Two: Perestroika*), pr. 1992, pb. 1993, revised pb. 1996

The Good Person of Setzuan, pr. 1994 (adaptation of Bertolt Brecht's play)

Slavs! (Thinking About the Longstanding Problems of Virtue and Happiness), pr. 1994, pb. 1995

A Dybbuk: Or, Between Two Worlds, pr. 1997, pb. 1998 (adaptation of S. Ansky's play *The Dybbuk*)

Terminating: Or, Lass Meine schmerzen nicht verloren sein, Or, Ambivalence, pr., pb. 1998 (adaptation of William Shakespeare's sonnet 75)

Death and Taxes: Hydriotaphia and Other Plays, pb. 2000 (includes *Reverse Transcription*, *Hydriotaphia*, *G. David Schine in Hell*, *Notes on Akiba*, *Terminating*, and *East Coast Ode to Howard Jarvis*)

Homebody/Kabul, pr. 2001, pb. 2002

OTHER LITERARY FORMS

Tony Kushner is primarily known for his plays, although he has written a children's book, *Brundibar* (2002), and his thoughts are collected in *Tony Kushner in Conversation* (1998), edited by Robert Vorlicky.

ACHIEVEMENTS

Tony Kushner won directing fellowships from the National Endowment of the Arts in 1985, 1987, and 1993. He received a playwriting fellowship from the New York State Council for the Arts in 1987. Kushner won the John Whiting Award from the Arts Council of Great Britain in 1990. Kushner's other awards include the Kennedy Center/ American Express New American Play Award in 1992 and the Will Glickham playwriting prize in 1992. *Angels in America* earned Kushner a Pulitzer Prize, two Tony Awards, two Drama Desk Awards, the *Evening Standard* Award, two Laurence Olivier Award Nominations, the New York Critics Circle Award, the Los Angeles Drama Critics Circle Award, and the Lambda Liberty Award for Drama. In 1998, London's National Theatre selected *Angels in America* as one of the ten best plays of the twentieth century. Kushner's plays have been produced in more than thirty countries around the world and at the Mark Taper Forum, the New York Shakespeare Festival, New York Theatre Workshop, Hartford Stage Company, Berkeley Repertory Theatre, and the Los Angeles Theatre Center.

BIOGRAPHY

Tony Kushner was born in New York City in 1956, but the family soon moved to Lake Charles, Louisiana, so his parents, classical musicians, could pursue professional opportunities there. From an early age, Kushner's parents encouraged him to participate in music, literature, and the performing arts. Kushner's mother was also an actress, and he vividly recalls seeing his mother perform when he was only four or five years old, which made a powerful impression on him and probably inspired him to pursue a life in theater. His artistic and literary interests, his Jewish background, and his homosexuality set him apart from other children. In an interview with Richard Stayton of the *Los Angeles Times*, Kushner said that he has distinct memories of being gay since he was six. Kushner knew that he felt slightly different from most other boys. By the time he was eleven, Kushner had no doubts about his homosexuality.

However, Kushner kept his sexuality a secret throughout his college education at Columbia University in New York, even undergoing psychotherapy designed to make him heterosexual. Kushner eventually came out, or revealed his sexual orientation, to his family and friends. Coming out as a homosexual became a prominent theme in his writing, and many of his plays depict characters struggling with their sexuality. Kushner received his B.A. from Columbia in 1978, where he studied medieval literature, and he pursued an M.F.A. at New York University, where he studied directing. Kushner began working as a switchboard operator before his professional theater career took off with the production of *A Bright Room Called Day* in 1987 and the momentous hit, *Angels in America* in 1991. Kushner has served as an artist-in-residence and director at New York University, Yale,

Princeton, the Julliard School of Drama, and at the St. Louis Repertory Theater.

ANALYSIS

Tony Kushner has forged a new reputation as a spokesperson for change and progress during politically conservative times. In the early 1990's, his seven-hour, two-part Broadway production of *Angels in America* transformed him from an unknown gay Jewish activist into the most promising, highly acclaimed playwright of his generation, who insisted on the power of theater to convey important truths. In this work, Kushner is concerned with the moral responsibilities of people during war and politically repressive times. He insists on political messages in all of his plays, opposing the popular notions that Americans do not like politics and that entertainment cannot be political. Although socialist politics and gay rights are not always mainstream topics, Kushner feels that artists need to be willing to take an issue that they feel passionately about and to address themselves to it extensively to build a consensus among groups. Kushner wants his plays to be part of a large political movement that teaches responsibility, honesty, social justice, and altruism. Kushner's plays are dark and speak about death, but they are full of hope for future change. He does not back away from difficult and unpopular social issues.

A BRIGHT ROOM CALLED DAY

Kushner's first important play was conceived during President Ronald Reagan's re-election in 1984, but its historical setting is 1932-1933 in the Weimar Republic of Germany before World War II. A close group of friends lose track of each other as they are forced into hiding during Adolf Hitler's rise to power. Kushner attempted to link the politics of Nazi Germany with the conservative Republican administration of Reagan, which caused many critics to complain about Kushner's implicit comparison of Reagan to Hitler, the Nazi totalitarian. In one version of the play, a contemporary American character, Zillah Katz, moves to Berlin in the recently reunified Germany, where she lives in the apartment of Agnes Eggling, one of the original members of the German friends during World War II. Zillah and Agnes com-

Tony Kushner in 1993. (AP/Wide World Photos)

municate to each other through dreams, though separated by forty years in time, and Zillah is inspired to political activism. Kushner raises the idea that all human actions are political.

ANGELS IN AMERICA, PART ONE

This play initially came to life in a poem that Kushner wrote after finishing graduate studies at New York University. The poem was about gay men, Mormons, and the famous lawyer Roy Cohn. Originally conceived as a ninety-minute comedy, the play blossomed into two parts about the state of the United States and its struggles with sexual, racial, religious, and social issues such as the AIDS (acquired immunodeficiency syndrome) epidemic. *Angels in America* mixes reality and fantasy. Though it is filled with many different characters, Kushner designed *Angels in America* to be performed by eight actors each of whom plays several roles. This groundbreaking play focuses on three households in turmoil: a gay couple, Louis Ironson and Prior Walter, struggling with AIDS; another couple Harper Pitt and Joe

Pitt, who is a Morman man coming to terms with his own sexuality; and the high-profile lawyer Roy Cohn, a historical person who died of AIDS in 1986. Cohn denied his homosexuality his whole life and persecuted gays. Cohn also helped Senator Joseph McCarthy persecute suspected members of the Communist Party in the 1950's. The subtitle *Millennium Approaches* describes the impending doom that the character Prior feels when dealing with the deadly disease AIDS. Prior's illness heightens his sense of a coming apocalypse. Toward the conclusion of the play, a gloriously triumphant angel descends on Prior, rescuing him from death. Prior's lover Louis has abandoned him in cowardly fear of the illness. The angel tells Prior he has been selected to be a prophet: "Greetings, Prophet;/ The Great Work begins:/ The Messenger has arrived." The play's main statement is that the United States' response to the AIDS epidemic has been politicized and ineffective.

ANGELS IN AMERICA, PART TWO

This play continues the themes of Part One, but it is a more somber play, getting its subtitle, *perestroika*, from Soviet president Mikhail Gorbachev's Russian word for the attempt at "restructuring" the nation's economic and social policies. The story of Prior's encounter with the angel continues. The angel tells Prior that God has abandoned his creation and that Prior has been anointed to resist modernity and return the world to the "good old days." Rejecting the authority granted him, Prior tells the angel that he is not a prophet and wants to be left alone to die in peace. Prior journeys to heaven to talk with God. The wondrous being that visited Prior at the end of Part One turns out to personify stagnancy or death, causing Prior to reject his commission. The lawyer Roy Cohn dies, but his spirit makes appearances later in the play, taking on the role of a lawyer for God. Even as he is dying, Roy Cohn tries to manipulate the system and get special medical attention and trick the ghost of Ethel Rosenberg into singing him a lullaby. At the play's conclusion, the major characters are gathered around the statue of the Bethesda angel in Central Park, where no water runs in the winter. Prior has been living with AIDS for five years, and he and his friends tell the story of the original fountain of

Bethesda: When the millennium comes, everyone suffering in body or spirit who walks through the waters of the fountain will be healed and washed clean of pain. Prior and his friends represent a variety of religious and racial backgrounds and various sexual orientations. Even though the real angels seem incompetent and careless, the friends gathered at the Bethesda fountain represent a positive coalition working together to cure the ills of society. The *perestroika* of the subtitle speaks about the fundamental restructuring necessary in order to confront grave medical, social, and economic issues of the late twentieth century.

SLAVS!

This play uses materials from the two-part *Angels* play, and it resembles the earlier play because of its interest in the matrix of social, economic, and political change resulting from the collapse of the Soviet Union. The play portrays the negative effects on people resulting from a lack of coherent leadership. The play begins on a frozen Moscow street in 1985, where two women discuss the failures of Soviet socialism. The character Aleksii Prelapsarianov, borrowed from the second part of *Angels in America*, is called "the world's oldest living Bolshevik" in *Slavs!* Prelapsarianov is concerned that the modern reformers do not have sufficient intellectual principles to guide them: "How are we to proceed without theory? Is it enough to reject the past, is it wise to move forward in this blind fashion, without the cold brilliant light of theory to guide the way?" Kushner makes a statement about the lack of direction in modern times. Socialism looks to the past in order to get the structure of the future, but modern restructuring does not have coherent theory to direct it. The very last line of the play, "What is to be done?" is asked throughout the play. Despite the failure of communism and the discrediting of socialist theory, the capitalism of the West has failed to find an answer to social and economic injustice. The most emotional statement of this conundrum comes from the lips of Vodya Domik, an eight-year-old mute girl who died as a result of the Chernobyl nuclear reactor meltdown. She regains her voice along with a disheartened vision of the bitter reality of history: "Perhaps it is true that social justice, economic justice, equality, community, an end to master and slave, the withering away of the state: these are desirable but not realizable on the Earth."

A DYBBUK

The play is an adaptation of Sy Ansky's 1920 Yiddish play concerning the marriage of Leah, the daughter of a wealthy man who has pledged her to the son of another wealthy family. Leah experiences anguish and frustration because her true love is a penniless Yeshiva student named Khonen. Leah secretly returns Khonen's passion. When the father formally proclaims the appropriate husband for Leah, Khonen gets revenge by entering Leah's body as a "dybbuk," a Yiddish word meaning "a disturbed spirit" who takes possession of another's body. The father turns in frustration to the revered Rabbi of Miropol for an exorcism. However, the father finds himself under judgment by the rabbinical court. Long ago, the father had promised Leah to Khonen, but his greed blinded him to Leah's true desires when he tried to marry her to a rich young man. In the end, he pays for his vices by giving half of his wealth to the poor. Even the most unintended immoral act can have profound social consequences. The play tries to foreshadow the forthcoming evils of the Holocaust in the closing epitaph.

OTHER MAJOR WORKS

NONFICTION: *Tony Kushner in Conversation*, 1998 (Robert Vorlicky, editor).

CHILDREN'S LITERATURE: *Brundibar*, 2002 (illustrated by Maruice Sendak).

MISCELLANEOUS: *Thinking About the Longstanding Problems of Virtue and Happiness: Essays, a Play, Two Poems, and a Prayer*, 1995.

BIBLIOGRAPHY

Bras, Per K. *Essays on Kushner's Angels*. Winnipeg, Canada: Blizzard Publishing, 1996. This collection of essays and an interview with the playwright discuss the impact of productions of *Angels in America* in regions and nations outside the United States, including Scandinavia, England, and Australia.

Fisher, James. *The Theater of Tony Kushner: Living Past Hope*. London: Routledge, 2001. A complete study of Kushner's work, Fisher's work covers all full-length, one-act, and adapted works by this Pulitzer Prize-winning dramatist. Fisher argues that Kushner is unusual among American playwrights because he believes that all theater is political. His plays explore the moral, social, religious, and political questions that shape the future of the United States in the world community.

Geis, Deborah R., and Steven F. Kruger. *Approaching the Millennium: Essays on Angels in America*. Ann Arbor: University of Michigan Press, 1997.

The book is divided into sections on Ronald Reagan's America and politics, identities in *Angels*, Kushner's theater, and *Angels* in performance contexts.

Osborn, M. Elizabeth, Terrence McNally, and Lanford Wilson. *The Way We Live Now: American Plays and the AIDS Crisis*. New York: Theatre Communications Group, 1990. Plays by a variety of contemporary playwrights including Susan Sontag, Harvey Fierstein, and Kushner demonstrate how the performing arts community has been devastated by the AIDS crisis.

Jonathan L. Thorndike

THOMAS KYD

Born: London, England; November 6, 1558 (baptized)
Died: London, England; August, 1594

PRINCIPAL DRAMA

The Spanish Tragedy, pr. c. 1585-1589, pb. 1594(?)
Soliman and Perseda, pr. c. 1588-1592, pb. 1599
Cornelia, pr. c. 1593, pb. 1594 (translation of Robert Garnier's *Cornélie*; also known as *Pompey the Great: His Fair Cornelia's Tragedy*, pb. 1595)

OTHER LITERARY FORMS

Although Thomas Kyd was cited by Francis Meres for commendation not only for tragedy but also for poetry, no verse remains that can with certainty be ascribed to him. The translation of Torquato Tasso's *Il padre di famiglia* (pr. 1583), published in English in 1588 as *The Householder's Philosophy*, is the only nondramatic work now generally attributed to Kyd.

ACHIEVEMENTS

Probably no one questions Thomas Kyd's historical importance in the development of Elizabethan English drama, and few who read *The Spanish Tragedy* doubt his power to move audiences even today. Though he has, inevitably, been damned for his failure to be William Shakespeare, modern critics and historians have generally regarded Kyd, along with Christopher Marlowe, as one of Shakespeare's most important forerunners. Kyd entered the theatrical world of Elizabethan London at a time when medieval popular drama had run its course and classical drama, though influencing such plays as Thomas Norton and Thomas Sackville's *Gorboduc* (pr. 1562), had not effected a reshaping of contemporary English drama. Kyd brought the traditions together in *The Spanish Tragedy*, probably the most famous play of the sixteenth century. He combined an intrigue plot worthy of the comic machinations of Plautus or Terence with the revenge motif and violence suggested by Seneca's closet dramas and presented it all with spectacular theatricality. He rescued blank verse from the boredom of discourse and used it to create the excitement of psychological realism. He exploited the possibilities of the theater by employing imaginative staging techniques. Although his reputation rests safely on *The Spanish Tragedy* alone, the fact that scholars have so easily believed through the years that Kyd may be responsible for a pre-Shakespearean version of *Hamlet* suggests the imaginative power most readers attribute to him.

BIOGRAPHY

What is known of Thomas Kyd is based on a very few public documents and a handful of allusions and references to him, most of them occurring after his death. Contemporary biographical accounts of Kyd are indebted to Arthur Freeman's careful investigation of Kyd's life in *Thomas Kyd: Facts and Problems* (1967). Records show that Kyd was baptized in London on November 6, 1558. Though there is no documentary identification of his parentage, scholars generally believe that his father was Francis Kyd the scrivener. If one may judge by other scriveners (John Milton's father was a scrivener), Francis Kyd would have been educated and reasonably well-to-do. Records also show that Kyd was enrolled at the Merchant Taylors' School in October, 1565. There—like Edmund Spenser, who was an older pupil in the school when Kyd entered—Kyd came under the influence of the school's well-known headmaster, the Humanist Richard Mulcaster. The date of Kyd's leaving the Merchant Taylors' School is not recorded; indeed, nothing is known with any certainty about Kyd for the decade after he should have left school. Although some have conjectured that Kyd may have entered a university or traveled abroad, there is no evidence for either. The curriculum of the Merchant Taylors' School was sufficient to have taught him the Latin he used in *The Spanish Tragedy* and in the translations he made.

In a tantalizing allusion that most scholars have interpreted as a reference to Kyd, Thomas Nashe, in his preface to Robert Greene's *Menaphon* (1589), complains of someone who has left the trade of scrivener, to which he was born, and is busying himself with the "indevors of Art," apparently writing imitations of Senecan tragedy and dabbling in translations. Though much has been made of this passage, especially in an effort to link Kyd with an early version of *Hamlet* (also mentioned in the passage), the allusion, if it does in fact refer to Kyd, yields very little biographical information other than that Kyd was active

in the theater by, and probably before, 1589. T. W. Baldwin has shown in "Thomas Kyd's Early Company Connections" (1927) that a reference by Thomas Dekker in a 1607 pamphlet to "industrious Kyd" and his associates at that time indicates clearly that Kyd was writing for the theater as early as 1585. It was probably during these years, 1583 to 1589, that he wrote *The Spanish Tragedy* as well as *Soliman and Perseda* and translated a dialogue by Tasso, *Il padre di famiglia*, as *The Householder's Philosophy*. If he was truly "industrious Kyd," as Dekker labeled him, and if he was of real concern to Nashe, it must be assumed that he wrote, or had a hand in, many other plays.

Kyd's career came to an inglorious end. He died, apparently abject and desolate, in 1594 after a period of imprisonment and a seemingly unsuccessful effort to stage a comeback. In a letter to Sir John Puckering, an important member of the Privy Council, Kyd recounts some of the circumstances surrounding his arrest, defends himself against the charges, and pleads for assistance in regaining the favor of his former patron. Because the letter was written shortly after Kyd's release from prison and refers to Marlowe as already dead, it was probably written in the summer of 1593. Kyd was arrested earlier that year under suspicion of having written some libelous attacks on foreign residents of London. A search of his quarters revealed even more incriminating papers, containing "vile heretically Conceiptes." Kyd was jailed and tortured, although the papers were not written by him and belonged, he said, to Marlowe, having by mistake been mixed with some of his own when they were "wrytinge in one chambere twoe yeares synce."

After his release, Kyd apparently hoped to regain favor with his former lord. When he was not reinstated to that service, he wrote to Puckering asking for help. From the letter, it is clear that Kyd had been for some years in the service of a patron, that he at one time had shared quarters—or at least had written in the same chamber—with Marlowe, that he had been arrested, imprisoned, and released, and that he found life after imprisonment difficult without assistance from his patron. A reference to "bitter times and privie broken passions" in the dedication to *Cornelia*, published early the next year, suggests that his suit was unsuccessful and that he had resumed his writing in an effort to regain favor. In only a few months, however, Kyd was dead. The parish register of St. Mary Colchurch, London, records his burial on August 15, 1594. The final public document relating to Kyd is a formal renunciation by Anna and Francis Kyd of the administration of their son's estate, a legal means of dissociating themselves not from their son but from his debts.

ANALYSIS

Whatever is said of Thomas Kyd's other works, *The Spanish Tragedy* is an enduring achievement. Kyd adapted to his own purposes the horrors, the theme of revenge, the trappings of ghosts and chorus, the long speeches, and the rhetoric of Senecan drama. He pointed the way to a new form merging the impulses of the popular drama with the structure and methods of classical drama—both tragedy and comedy. He demonstrated that what gives life to a play is not argument or idea so much as psychological reality—characters that develop naturally out of the action of the play. He brought together in one play, perhaps not with perfect success, a variety of styles ranging from the sententiousness of his Senecan models to the lyric love combat between Bel-imperia and Horatio and the anguished cries of a distraught father. The extravagance Kyd permitted himself in Hieronimo's raving ("O eyes! no eyes, but fountains fraught with tears. . . .") made the play a byword in Ben Jonson's day, but Kyd's sense of dramatic propriety helped rescue blank verse from monotony for use in genuine dramatic expression. Kyd's flair for the theatrical allowed him to pave the way for an exciting and meaningful use of the stage; later developments in stagecraft may have proved more subtle, but few have surpassed the power of the final scene of *The Spanish Tragedy*. If the play could be dated with exactness, *The Spanish Tragedy* might well prove to be historically the most important play written before those of Shakespeare. Even without exact dating, however, the play makes Kyd, with Marlowe, one of the two most significant predecessors of Shake-

speare. Whatever its historical importance, the play retains, even today, its own intrinsic power.

THE SPANISH TRAGEDY

Although the early editions of *The Spanish Tragedy* are anonymous, few readers have seriously disputed Kyd's authorship, since the play was first attributed to him by Thomas Heywood (in his *An Apology for Actors*) in 1612. Most readers of *Cornelia*, ascribed to Kyd in the original edition, and of *Soliman and Perseda*, presumed by most to be by Kyd, point to similarities that suggest common authorship with *The Spanish Tragedy*. The play has traditionally been dated between 1582 (when a work by Thomas Watson, which it seems to echo, was published) and 1592, the date the play was first entered in the Stationers' Register. Modern biographers do not agree when they attempt to narrow the limits, but the lack of any reference in the play to the famous English victory over the Spanish Armada and the suggestion in Ben Jonson's *Bartholomew Fair* (pr. 1614) that the play had been around for twenty-five or thirty years make the period from 1585 to 1589 more likely. Kyd's influence on the development of Elizabethan drama could be more surely assessed if the date of *The Spanish Tragedy* were certain, but, whether it or Marlowe's *Tamburlaine the Great* (pr. c. 1587) came first, *The Spanish Tragedy* holds a place of high importance in English dramatic history.

Critical assessment of *The Spanish Tragedy* has been made difficult by a perplexing textual problem. Scholars who have sorted out the extant texts from the 1590's are able to agree that the authoritative text is the unique copy of the undated octavo printed by Edward Allde for Edward White. What has baffled researchers, however, is the presence of about 320 lines of additions deriving from a quarto of 1602. Most editors, though they assume that the lines are by a later hand, include them nevertheless, set in a different typeface, within the text of the play, so that the additions have, in effect, become a part of most modern readers' experience of the play. It is possible, as Andrew S. Cairncross notes in his Regents edition of the play (1967), that the so-called additions were originally written by Kyd, later cut, and still later restored as "additions." Much scholarly effort has gone into trying to identify the author of the additions. *Henslowe's Diary* records payment in 1601 and 1602 to Ben Jonson for "adicyons" to "Jeronymo." If the reference is to *The Spanish Tragedy*, Jonson was employed to rework to some degree a play that he ridiculed in other places. Without further evidence, modern readers have no way of knowing who wrote the additions. It is probably safest to believe that they were not written by Kyd and to attempt to see the play whole without them, in spite of the fact that some of them, especially the "Painter Scene," are interesting both in their own right and as they are integrated into the play.

Coming at the outset of Elizabethan drama, *The Spanish Tragedy* is inevitably seen in historical perspective, but what is remarkable about the play is its own interest apart from historical considerations. Although it is clear that Kyd is doing some things either for the first time or quite crudely in comparison to later dramas, it is possible to understand how *The Spanish Tragedy* enthralled audiences in Kyd's day and to read it with pleasure even today.

The play opens with a long speech by the Ghost of Andrea, but if there is little that is dramatic in that technique, the vividly descriptive speech illustrates the theatricality that characterizes this play from start to finish. From "dreadful shades of ever-glooming night," Revenge and the Ghost of Andrea have come to witness the working out of vengeance for Andrea's death at the hand of Balthazar on the battlefield. They remain to "serve for Chorus in this tragedy" and return after each act to reestablish this infernal atmosphere and to comment on the progress—or the apparent lack of progress—toward the goal of revenge.

Kyd plants the seeds of a psychological conflict between Andrea's friend Horatio and Lorenzo, son of the Duke of Castile and brother of Horatio's beloved Bel-imperia, in scene 1, when Lorenzo claims credit for capturing Balthazar and when the King of Spain, Lorenzo's uncle, rewards him with the captive prince's horse and weapons. Because Horatio had bested Balthazar in single combat, he feels cheated of spoils and honor that should have been his. When he submits to the king's decision, a spectator might wonder how the conflict, here seemingly prepared for, is

going to effect Andrea's revenge. In truth, the play shifts even more radically in the next act to reveal not Horatio but his father, Hieronimo, as the inheritor of his son's conflict and as the chief character in the developing tragedy. Though Kyd does not fully develop the psychological conflict he sets up here, it is characteristic of *The Spanish Tragedy* to get beneath the surface of events to that psychological level, and it is this tendency to get at the heart of human action that sets Kyd's work apart from the plays of the previous two decades that he might have chosen as models to follow.

The following scene has proved a problem for critics. The action shifts abruptly to the Portuguese court, where the nobleman Villuppo forges a tale about how his enemy Alexandro (another nobleman) shot Balthazar in the back and caused Portugal to lose the battle. Some readers believe that Kyd introduces essentially extraneous material in this second plot line. The similarity of the situations, however—each turning on a vicious man's deception of his ruler to the hurt of another—suggests that Kyd may have intended that the subplot amplify and comment on the main plot. If so, the Portuguese viceroy's decision to investigate before taking action against Villuppo may suggest to the audience that Hieronimo, who will soon have cause to act, must also be sure before he moves.

At this point, there is still no hint of how Andrea's revenge is to be effected. To make Horatio, and ultimately Hieronimo, the instruments of Andrea's revenge, Kyd must provide a greater reason for the involvement of Horatio with Bel-imperia. In the next scene, without very much regard for consistency in Bel-imperia's character, Kyd reveals that she has chosen Horatio not only as the agent of her revenge but also as her "second love." The action has come back to the subject announced by the Ghost and Revenge, but the real subject of the play has not yet been broached. Though spectators are reminded at the end of each act that Andrea's revenge is the true concern of the tragedy, the play takes a turn in the next act that puts Hieronimo at the center. As yet, this central figure has appeared in only a minor role. His next appearance is in scene 5, where—again with no suggestion of his later importance—he presents at court a dumb show depicting England's conquest of Portugal and Spain. Remarkably, this spectacle pleases both the Spanish king and the Portuguese ambassador (and doubtless appealed to the patriotism of Kyd's English audience as well). The first act ends with the Ghost of Andrea complaining bitterly about this "league, love, and banqueting" between the Spanish and the Portuguese. He wants vengeance. Revenge promises to turn it all sour in due time. Essentially that is what happens: It all turns sour, and Andrea is revenged after a fashion, but Andrea is never the focus of the play. In the second act, Hieronimo assumes that position.

A new cry of revenge is heard as act 2 begins. On learning that Bel-imperia loves Horatio, Balthazar vows to take revenge against this man who first took his body captive and now would "captivate" his soul. He is encouraged by Lorenzo, who—without an apparent motive for his evil deeds—manipulates much of the action in the second act. Kyd's early development of a character reflecting the popular notion of a Machiavellian villain suggests once again his importance as a forerunner of the creator of Iago. As manipulator of the action, Lorenzo arranges for Balthazar to spy on Horatio and Bel-imperia as they make an assignation to meet in her father's "pleasant bower." The staging of this scene reveals Kyd's skill in using several levels of the stage at once. Balthazar and Lorenzo observe the conversation between Horatio and Bel-imperia from "above," while the Ghost of Andrea and Revenge, from their vantage point, watch the couple being watched.

When in the third scene a state marriage is arranged for Balthazar and Bel-imperia (the Spanish king's niece), it seems certain that the direction of the play is fixed: Bel-imperia has succeeded in involving Horatio so intimately in her life that this announced marriage will be the spark that triggers Horatio's anger toward Balthazar, and Andrea, through that anger, will be revenged. The play, however, here moves structurally, as a Roman comedy might, and introduces a significant bit of action that will provide a basis for the intrigue worked out in the double-length third act. When Horatio and Bel-imperia meet and

wage a poetic "war" of love, they are surprised by Lorenzo, Balthazar, and his servant Serberine. Horatio is hanged and stabbed, and Bel-imperia is taken away as their captive. Hieronimo hears Bel-imperia's cry and finds Horatio's body; the play now becomes the story of Hieronimo's revenge. In what surely must have been both visually and aurally a spectacular moment, Hieronimo, in fourteen lines of Latin and with a dramatic sword-to-breast gesture, vows revenge. Modern critics recognize the significance of Kyd's innovation in this development of tragic materials with comic methods and within a comic structure.

Not surprisingly, the Ghost of Andrea renews his complaint that events are not moving very directly toward his revenge: His friend, not his enemy, has been slain. Telling him that he must not expect harvest "when the corn is green" and promising to please him, Revenge allows act 3 to begin. The sudden reappearance, after seven scenes, of the matter of Alexandro and Villuppo is doubtless the reason some critics regard this "subplot" as an intrusion. Others, calling attention to the parallel between the Portuguese viceroy and Hieronimo, see this scene as a warning to Hieronimo not to be too hasty in reacting to his son's murder. The intrigue plot that feeds Hieronimo's delay is set in motion when a letter written in blood (the stage direction specifies "red ink") falls into Hieronimo's hands. It is a message from Bel-imperia revealing that Lorenzo and Balthazar are Horatio's murderers. Lorenzo suspects that Serberine has talked. One intrigue leads to another: He hires Pedringano to kill Serberine and then sets up a time for them to meet when the watch, whom he has alerted, will be able to catch Pedringano in the act of murder. Serberine will be murdered, Pedringano will be executed, and Lorenzo will be rid of them both. When, after Pedringano is arrested, he sends to Lorenzo for help, the action—in keeping with the structure—becomes darkly comic. Lorenzo plays a cruel joke on Pedringano. He sends him word that he will save him and then sends a page to him bearing a box that supposedly contains a pardon. Despite instructions to the contrary, the page opens the box and sees that it is empty, but he decides to go along with the deception. The comedy with the cloud of death looming over it continues as Pedringano, certain that he will be saved, confesses recklessly in Hieronimo's court of justice and jests with the hangman even as he is turned off the scaffold.

With this third death onstage, spectators may begin to suspect that Kyd is exploiting in action the horrors only reported in Seneca. Neither the horror nor the comedy of the situation can obscure the painful irony of Hieronimo's position as minister of justice, himself crying out for justice. This theme, introduced near the midpoint of the long third act, grows to major significance in the second half. When in scene 7 the hangman brings to Hieronimo Pedringano's letter, written to reveal all in death if Lorenzo has failed to deliver him, Hieronimo has the evidence he needs to confirm Bel-imperia's identification of Horatio's murderers. Still able to believe that justice exists, he resolves to "go plain me to my lord the king,/ And cry aloud for justice, through the court. . . ."

This theme of justice, placed for development in close juxtaposition to the darkly comic, promises to shift the play from a mere revenge intrigue to an exploration of a genuinely tragic experience. Not all critics agree that Kyd is successful in bringing the play from mere sensational display of horror and intrigue into the realm of tragedy, but most readers will agree that the play takes on that potential at this point. The revenge theme that has informed the play up to this point will inevitably clash with the theme of justice. Hieronimo will cry out for both. Critics lament that Kyd's control of this conflict is uncertain. It is not clear exactly what Kyd intends when he has a minister of justice desert his own quest for justice and resort to private revenge, as Hieronimo does in the final act. Perhaps Kyd—among the first to attempt to reconcile this pagan theme of revenge, which he and his contemporaries found so attractive in Seneca, with the Christian conscience of his audience—was not careful enough with the consistent development of his central character. Modern readers, at least, are left unsure of his intent. Perhaps Kyd was also.

The remainder of this long third act is given over to two things: taking care of plot necessities in order to set up Hieronimo's revenge in act 4 and exhibiting

Hieronimo in various states of calm or distraction, always searching for justice. The plans for the marriage of Balthazar and Bel-imperia proceed; the Portuguese viceroy arrives and announces that he intends to give his son Balthazar his crown upon Balthazar's marriage to Bel-imperia. It is this royal wedding that later provides the occasion, in act 4, for Hieronimo's revenge. Hieronimo, meanwhile, confronts the Spanish king and demands justice, but his wild manner of doing so makes it easy for Lorenzo to persuade the king that he is "helplessly distract." An entire scene is given to exhibiting Hieronimo distraught and to underscoring the reason: his failure to find justice in his own cause. The man who had been the best advocate in Spain is now so distracted by his own frustrated efforts to find justice for himself that he is incapable of doing his duty. In the final scene of act 3, Kyd—his eye always on the theatrical—has Lorenzo's father demand to know why the relationship between Lorenzo and Hieronimo is so strained. The Duke of Castile accepts his son's explanation and requires the two to embrace. Hieronimo, on the verge of executing his revenge, accedes, and the Ghost of Andrea labors the irony by his furious reaction to seeing "Hieronimo with Lorenzo . . . joined in league." To calm Andrea down, Revenge shows him an ominous dumb show—another Kyd spectacular—revealing two bearing nuptial torches burning brightly, followed by a sable-clad Hymen, who puts them out.

In act 4, Hieronimo moves swiftly to act on his plan for revenge. He confides his plan to Bel-imperia and asks her to cooperate in whatever way he asks. When Hieronimo is asked for an entertainment for the court on the first night of the wedding feast, he agrees, provided the courtiers themselves consent to act in his tragedy of Soliman and Perseda. They agree also to the strange request that they speak their lines in different languages. Hieronimo promises to explain all in a final speech and "wondrous show" which he will have concealed behind the curtain. Before the entertainment can begin, Isabella cuts down the arbor in which Horatio was hanged and stabs herself. Her death, the fourth in this tragedy, is only the beginning. With all locked in the room and with the keys securely in Hieronimo's possession, the play begins. What seems to be a play-within-a-play, which is itself being watched by two who have been an onstage audience throughout, turns out to be all too real for those who think they are acting. The Bashaw (Hieronimo) stabs Erasto (Lorenzo); Perseda (Belimperia) stabs Soliman (Balthazar) and herself. Hieronimo reveals the "wondrous show" behind the curtain (his dead son) and explains his "play" as revenge for Horatio. He then runs off to hang himself but is stopped. Though it is not perfectly clear what more they want to know, the king and Castile try to force Hieronimo to give further explanation. Kyd's taste for the spectacular is not yet satiated: Hieronimo bites out his tongue rather than talk. Then, calling for a knife to mend his pen in order to write an answer, he stabs Castile and finally himself.

A dead march ends the action except for the chorus. Finally, the Ghost of Andrea is happy, though his own death is avenged only in the fact that Balthazar has died in Hieronimo's revenge for Horatio. The final chorus, like all the others, recalls the ostensible subject of the play, but even more it points up the fact that Andrea's primary function has been to provide atmosphere. If spectators have come to accept him and Revenge as a touch of atmosphere, they are not shocked to hear him say that "these were spectacles to please my soul." To be pleased by these "spectacles," which include the deaths of his lover, his best friend, and his friend's father and mother, is certainly to go beyond his function as a real character. As a bit of spectacle, however, and as a means of providing both atmosphere and obvious structural links for the various revenges in the play, the chorus serves well.

The ambiguity of Hieronimo's portrayal precludes the possibility of a confident assessment of the meaning of the play. A more certain hand might have drawn Hieronimo clearly as one who tragically fails to wait for God's justice and destroys himself in the process or, alternatively, as one who seeks diligently and finds the world void of justice and in despair seeks his own redress. Hieronimo is probably best understood as a person destroyed by the tragic dilemma of being a minister of justice who is forced—or feels that he is forced—to take justice into his own

hands. On reflection, this looks very much like private revenge, but there is little doubt that even Kyd's first audience, constantly reminded from the pulpit that God claims vengeance for his own, would fail to make allowances for a man so sorely abused and so faithful in his own administration of justice to others. The tragedy is that he destroys himself and his own faith in justice in the process.

CORNELIA

Kyd's other works are of lesser interest. The only play ascribed to Kyd in the first edition is *Cornelia*, his translation of Robert Garnier's *Cornélie* (pb. 1574), which had appeared in a collected edition of Garnier's works in 1585. Kyd was trying to recover from the disgrace of imprisonment by offering to a potential patron this translation, done under the influence of an earlier translation by the Countess of Pembroke (*Antonius*, 1592) of Garnier's *Marc Antoine* (pr. 1578). He excuses the flaws in his translation by reference to "those bitter times and privie broken passions that I endured in the writing of it." To read *Cornelia* after reading *The Spanish Tragedy* is to understand the originality of the latter. One coming to *Cornelia* from *The Spanish Tragedy* would be surprised to find a play filled with talk rather than action—talk voiced in rather uninspired blank verse. *Cornelia* preserves Garnier's brand of French Senecanism in its quiet, reflective, and very long speeches. Act 1, for example, consists of one long speech by Cicero, lamenting Rome's war-torn state, followed by further lamentation and reflection by the chorus. In act 2, Cornelia debates with Cicero whether she should take her own life. Having lost two husbands, she believes that she is a plague on any who love her. Much of the middle part of the play is about Caesar's tyranny. The focus returns to Cornelia in act 5 when a messenger, in a speech of nearly three hundred lines, provides a detailed account of the defeat of her father, Scipio, and his decision to take his own life rather than submit to captivity. Lamenting, Cornelia, who has longed for death throughout the play, wonders if the time has now come for her to die. She decides against suicide, however, because no one would be left to provide proper burial and tombs for Scipio and her husband, Pompey. The play ends with her quiet resolve to live. For all of its quiet manner, however, *Cornelia* was, as Freeman notes, Kyd's "most celebrated work for nearly two centuries."

SOLIMAN AND PERSEDA

Soliman and Perseda, published anonymously in 1599 by the same publisher who issued *The Spanish Tragedy*, is ascribed to Kyd by most literary historians because of the plot relationship to Hieronimo's final "entertainment" in *The Spanish Tragedy* as well as other parallels, echoes, and stylistic considerations. If it is indeed Kyd's, he probably wrote it during the same period when he was writing *The Spanish Tragedy* and Marlowe was writing *Tamburlaine the Great*, another play of death and destruction set in the Near East. Critics have paid little attention to *Soliman and Perseda*, but Kyd's mingling of the comic and tragic, evident in *The Spanish Tragedy*, is given such full development here that *Soliman and Perseda* should surely be seen as a forerunner of a long line of Elizabethan plays that integrate the two modes. Freeman believes that Kyd may have been the first to effect a "true confrontation of comic and tragic themes within mixed scenes," a confrontation that goes beyond the mere mixing of tragic matter with unrelated buffoonery. Like *The Spanish Tragedy*, *Soliman and Perseda* employs a chorus to preside over a bloody story. Love, Fortune, and Death vie for position as chorus, each claiming a major role in causing the story. In the end, Death lists twelve dead, brutally murdered onstage, as evidence of his power. (At that, Death must have lost count, for the toll is even larger.) The play also offers the beautiful love of Erastus and Perseda, the comic pursuit of Perseda by the boastful but cowardly Basilisco, and the murderous obsession of Soliman for Perseda—a desire so strong that he is persuaded to kill Erastus, whom he loves and admires, for her. In the final scene, Soliman kills Perseda herself. Having disguised herself as a man and vowed to defend Rhodes against Soliman's attack, Perseda challenges Soliman to single combat, promising to yield Perseda to him if he wins the duel. When she is mortally wounded, she reveals herself, and Soliman asks for a kiss before she dies. Perseda, having earlier poisoned her lips, grants his request, and Soliman dies giving orders that his soldiers take

Rhodes ("Spoil all, kill all. . . .") but that he and Perseda be buried with his friend and her husband, Erastus.

OTHER WORKS

Of several other plays that have been attributed to Kyd, the most difficult attribution to prove or refute is that of the *Ur-Hamlet*. Assuming that Nashe was referring to Kyd as the "English Seneca" who would, "if you intreate him faire in a frostie morning, . . . afford you whole *Hamlets*," many scholars have concluded that there was some pre-Shakespearean dramatic version of *Hamlet* and that Kyd was probably the author of it. Kyd's obvious interest in the revenge theme has fed this suspicion. No such play is extant, however, and it seems fruitless to try to reconstruct the lost play—if one ever existed—unless further evidence comes to light. *The First Part of Jeronimo* (pb. 1605), though it has been advanced as a first part of *The Spanish Tragedy*, was probably not by Kyd but, like the *Spanish Comedy* (mentioned in *Henslowe's Diary*), a spin-off from Kyd's extremely popular play.

OTHER MAJOR WORKS

TRANSLATION: *The Householder's Philosophy*, 1588 (of Torquato Tasso's *Il padre di famiglia*).

MISCELLANEOUS: *The Works of Thomas Kyd*, 1901 (Frederick S. Boas, editor).

BIBLIOGRAPHY

Ardolino, Frank R. *Apocalypse and Armada in Kyd's "Spanish Tragedy."* Kirksville, Mo.: Sixteenth Century Journal Publishers, 1995. Ardolino looks at Kyd's major work, finding it to be a Reformation play, complete with apocalyptic symbolism. Contains bibliography and index.

_____. *Thomas Kyd's Mystery Play: Myth and Ritual in "The Spanish Tragedy."* New York: Peter Lang, 1985. Though somewhat specialized in focusing on a specific aspect of a particular play, this book places Kyd's best-known tragedy in the context of previous, not subsequent, plays, looking at allegorical and mystery-play elements in *The Spanish Tragedy*. Includes index.

Barber, C. L. *Creating Elizabethan Tragedy: The Theater of Marlowe and Kyd*. Chicago: University of Chicago Press, 1988. Barber analyzes the works of early Elizabethan dramatists Kyd and Christopher Marlowe. Includes bibliography and index.

Erne, Lukas. *Beyond "The Spanish Tragedy": A Study of the Works of Thomas Kyd*. Manchester, England: Manchester University Press, 2001. Erne examines Kyd's best-known play, revealing how the drama of William Shakespeare and his contemporaries developed. He discusses the additions and adaptations.

Freeman, Arthur. *Thomas Kyd: Facts and Problems*. Oxford, England: Clarendon Press, 1967. As its title suggests, this book concerns itself mostly with the factual matters of dating, biography, and authorship, yet it contains some limited analysis of structure, style, and performance history of Kyd's plays. Though there are more problems than facts in determining what Kyd wrote, Freeman never presents scholarly guesses as fact.

E. Bryan Gillespie,
updated by John R. Holmes

L

EUGÈNE LABICHE

Born: Paris, France; May 5, 1815
Died: Paris, France; January 23, 1888

PRINCIPAL DRAMA

Un Chapeau de paille d'Italie, pr., pb. 1851 (*The
   Italian Straw Hat*, 1873)
Le Misanthrope et l'Auvergnat, pr., pb. 1852 (with
   P.-M. Lubize Siraudin and Paul Siraudin)
L'Affaire de la rue de Lourcine, pr., pb. 1857 (with
   Édouard Martin and Albert Monnier)
Le Voyage de M. Perrichon, pr., pb. 1860 (with
   Martin; *The Journey of Mr. Perrichon*, 1924)
La Poudre aux yeux, pr., pb. 1861 (with Martin;
   Throwing Dust in People's Eyes, 1930)
Célimare le bien-aimé, pr., pb. 1863 (with Alfred
   Delacour; *Celimare*, 1959)h
La Cagnotte, pr., pb. 1864 (with Delacour; *Three
   Cheers for Paris*, 1971)
Le Plus Heureux des trois, pr., pb. 1870 (with
   Edmond Gondinet; *The Happiest of the Three*,
   1973)
29 degrés à l'ombre, pr. 1873, pb. 1886 (*90
   Degrees in the Shade*, 1962)
Théâtre complet, pb. 1878-1879 (10 volumes)

OTHER LITERARY FORMS

Eugène Labiche is known only for his plays.

ACHIEVEMENTS

Eugène Labiche's 175 works, a moderate total for
the period, encompass many varieties of comic theater and include operettas. The quality of these works
varies. At worst, the single-act vaudeville pieces are
amusing, with their exuberant humor and caricatures;
at best, the more substantial comedies of character
and manners contain portraits in the moralistic tradition of Jean de La Bruyère and Molière. The comic

elements of Labiche's plays are not of the witty type;
they tend instead to be of the kind Henri Bergson described in his essay *Le Rire* (1900; *Laughter*, 1911).
Actions more than words form their basis. The most
influential theater critics of his period credited Labiche with having revolutionized the vaudeville comedy form in France by enlarging its traditional scope
and format to include realistic observation. Thoroughly bourgeois in status and formation himself,
Labiche wrote plays primarily for and about his own
social class. It is for his double portrait of middle-
class French society, astutely observed from an interior vantage point, and of human vanities in general,
that he is justly acclaimed.

Only six of his plays were written without collaborators. Nevertheless, all the works possess a continuity of style and tone that seems attributable to
Labiche himself. Several of his collaborators asserted
that their role in the creative process was to act primarily as a sounding board for ideas that Labiche had
already elaborated. The best of Labiche's plays have
entered the classic repertory of French theater and are
still performed regularly. Outside France, the popularity of Labiche's comedies rests largely on what is
perceived as their Gallic humor and on the playwright's skillful handling of movement and rhythm.

BIOGRAPHY

Eugène-Marin Labiche, the son of Jacques Philippe
Marin Labiche, owner of a glucose factory at Reuil,
was born into a comfortable bourgeois household.
Only a mediocre student at the Collège Bourbon, the
future playwright passed his baccalaureate examinations, achieving high honors because, according to his
own admission, he had memorized the study manual.
With three classmates, he then toured Switzerland, Italy, and Sicily before entering law school in 1834.

Labiche eventually received a law degree, but he became increasingly interested in writing and the theater. He published travel pieces, short stories, drama reviews, and miscellaneous literary pieces in journals such as *Essor, Chérubin*, and the *Revue du théâtre*. Frequenting the popular cafés and the theater wings, he established a reputation as a reasonable, well-behaved young man-about-town. Although in later years Labiche placed his theatrical debut in 1838 with *M. de Coyllin: Ou, L'Homme infiniment poli* (the infinitely polite man), he had in fact collaborated on a comedy the year before with Auguste Lefranc and Marc-Antoine-Amédée Michel. This play, *La Cuvette d'eau* (the bucket of water), and another one from the same year were never published and so have left no visible traces. Two additional comedies and a drama were only moderately successful. Labiche did not take his efforts at playwriting seriously but continued because he enjoyed it and wrote easily.

The year 1839 marked two important turning points in Labiche's career. He saw his aspirations for becoming a novelist dashed by the unsuccessful reception accorded *La Clef des champs* (the key of the fields); only three hundred copies were printed, and Labiche had them withdrawn almost immediately. At the same time, he had written a vaudeville piece with Lefranc and Michel that they signed under the collective pseudonym Paul Dandré. Its popular success convinced Labiche that he had found his place as a writer.

In 1840, Labiche moved from the family home into his own apartment. Two years later, he married Adèle Hubert, a young woman whose bourgeois background matched his own. A popular story recounts how his future father-in-law demanded that Labiche renounce playwriting and how, after a year of marriage, his wife released him from that restriction when she saw how unhappy he was. Regardless of whether this story is true, the fact remains that from 1843 until his retirement from writing in 1877, Labiche produced a constant stream of plays. His prolific pen reached a high point of eleven plays for the year 1852. Twice he dabbled in politics: He ran unsuccessfully for a seat in the legislature in 1848, and he served as mayor of Sologne in the early 1870's.

Labiche's first unqualified success came in 1851 with *The Italian Straw Hat*. The play tallied three hundred consecutive performances, a rare accomplishment for the period. He established himself as the favorite playwright of the Palais-Royale Theatre, while continuing to contribute regularly to the Variétés and the Gymnase. By 1853 his royalty income made it possible for him to purchase the Launoy château in Sologne. From that time on, and especially after 1864, Labiche became ever more a gentleman farmer, spending progressively less of each passing year in Paris.

The nine-year period between *The Italian Straw Hat* and his next great triumph with *The Journey of Mr. Perrichon* saw Labiche attain a reputation as France's foremost author of vaudeville comedies. Several times he attempted to break away from the type of play for which the public knew him in order to write works of a more serious and satiric nature. The theatergoing public, however, refused to accept Labiche when it seemed that the playwright was laughing at them and not with them. Among his more somber plays that were either outright failures or only partial successes were *La Chasse aux corbeaux* (1853; crow hunt), which depicted the financial establishment, and *L'Avare en gants jaunes* (1858; the miser in yellow gloves). Another such play, written especially for the Comédie-Française, was *Moi* (1864; me); it met with only polite applause, although Gustave Flaubert proclaimed it a comedy worthy of Molière.

Following the Franco-Prussian War of 1870-1871, the temper of the French public changed and, at the same time, Labiche's humor became less exuberant. When three of his plays met successively with very short runs in 1876, Labiche decided to retire gracefully. His last play, *La Clé* (the key), was staged in 1877. There were successful revivals of his works, but he resisted all offers to write new plays, preferring to manage his country estate instead. At the insistence of Émile Augier, his friend and fellow playwright, Labiche selected fifty-seven of his favorite plays to be published as his "complete" works. The resulting tomes began appearing in 1878, and the set of ten volumes rapidly became a best-seller. Labiche's reputation soared once again. This new popularity succeeded in vanquishing the objections of many to admitting a mere writer of vaudeville comedies to the French Academy, and Labiche was elected to this august body in 1880.

ANALYSIS

Movement and timing are fundamental to the success of Eugène Labiche's comedies. The fast-paced rhythm of a performance distracts an audience from any prolonged consideration of situations that would not be so amusing if removed from their comic vehicle. It is only when Labiche's plays can be examined at leisure in their written form and the visual comic elements recede that a critical view of bourgeois society and men's egotism emerges. Some critics have concluded that the laughter of these plays conceals what is actually a very harsh and cruel attitude. Certainly Labiche's characters and the society they inhabit embody many negative qualities. One cannot fail to observe, however, that although the stupidity of these characters may be great—since they rarely provide the solution to their problems by themselves and only occasionally seem to have learned anything constructive or helpful from their experiences—their creator consistently treats them in a good-humored manner, never overtly judging them. As much as the audience may believe that these creatures deserve chastisement for their foolish actions and attitudes, the playwright himself always extricates them from their predicaments in the end. It is left to the audience to decide if any moral conclusion is to be drawn. Seen on the stage, Labiche's plays continue to offer diverting comedy; perused at home in the armchair, their overtones of social criticism add an appealing intellectual depth to situations still pertinent to today's society.

THE ITALIAN STRAW HAT

The Italian Straw Hat was the first example of Labiche's new kind of vaudeville. The manager of the Palais-Royal Theatre, where this play premiered, judged it to be so stupid that he left Paris to avoid the opening-night reviews. Audiences, however, were delighted. (In 1927, René Clair transformed Labiche's script into an equally successful silent film.) The play's appeal rests on a combination of elements: the comic devices, the incongruous situations, and Labiche's choice of a popular target for his humor.

The comic procedures and devices employed do not differ notably from those that can be found in almost any comedy. Bergson's *Laughter* discusses most of them. The characters of *The Italian Straw Hat* are perfect examples of the mechanical inelasticity that Bergson asserted was basic to provoking laughter. They go charging blindly and unthinkingly after the hero. A pair of tight shoes or a pin stuck in a dress causes the victim to jerk like a marionette. The characters repeat words and actions to the point that the audience anticipates them; laughter begins to swell with the anticipation. Nonancourt's myrtle tree, which he insists on carrying everywhere, and his now proverbial exclamation that echoes throughout the play—"*Mon gendre, tout est rompu!*" ("Son-in-law, it's all off!")—are two memorable instances of such repetition. Labiche's talent for comedy lies not in the fact that he employed these devices but rather in the appropriateness of his selection and in his sense of timing when applying them to particular situations.

Essentially a comedy of complications, *The Italian Straw Hat* depicts the escapades of Fadinard, a man who is pursued around Paris by his own wedding party as he attempts to replace a lady's straw hat, which was ruined by his horse. This situation is delightfully incongruous and is exploited in each act in a similar manner. The scene is set, and Fadinard, the impatient groom, enters and attempts to explain his unusual quest. The wedding party inevitably arrives in pursuit, convinced that they are somewhere that they are not. They mistake a milliner's salon for the mayor's office, a baroness's dining room for the restaurant where the wedding feast is to be held, and someone else's apartment for Fadinard's. The confusion they perpetrate in one scene adds to the expectation of what they will do in the next one. One hilarious episode follows another before Fadinard is able to replace the hat with one he accidentally discovers among his own wedding gifts.

A salient characteristic of Labiche's comedy is the sense of movement it carries. The comic motifs accumulate with dizzying rapidity, and even the situations themselves can contribute to the impression of movement. An important factor here are the four or five doors commonly found in a Labiche stage setting. These multiple doors can create an accumulation of characters onstage (such as the wedding party) or they can control the speed with which characters appear or disappear (multiple entries or exits). They can conceal characters (the wedding party in the bedroom of the wrong apartment) as well as produce unexpected and compromising encounters when the wrong character opens the right door at the right moment (Fadinard meets an old girlfriend, and the adulteress Madame Beauperthuis, her maid). The viewer is whisked along from one situation to the next by the opening and shutting of the doors and by the characters who enter or exit through them.

The target of Labiche's humor is the lower middle class—their material concerns and their basic inability to function outside their own limited circles without creating embarrassing situations. The details by which he creates his characters and their situations are astutely chosen. The unaccustomed and uncomfortable clothes that characters wear in order to appear properly dressed for a special occasion, for example, bring a smile of recognition to the viewer. Labiche was not alone in his generation to single out the bourgeoisie as a humorous target; Flaubert did so as well. Unlike Flaubert, however, Labiche does not assume any obvious attitude of superiority, although the occasions to do so are frequent. Middle-class social idiosyncrasies are dismissed with a bemused shrug.

All the playwright's favorite themes—marriage, adultery, family, and middle-class dull-mindedness—are to be found in *The Italian Straw Hat*. Marriage represents a highly desirable status. Not least among its attractions is the financial well-being it may bring. Suitors and prospective fiancées are initially judged acceptable or not on the basis of their monetary worth. Perhaps not surprisingly, the outcome of such unions is not always happy, as the adultery of Madame Beauperthuis proves. In this exuberant comedy, however, adultery and unfaithfulness are treated lightly: The cuckolded husband acts in such a grotesquely comical manner that his blustering attempts to catch up with his wife gain no sympathy, and the

discomfort and embarrassment that she must endure in the course of the play seem sufficient punishment for her transgression. For the most part in Labiche's plays, adultery constitutes an unimportant event in a marriage, an incident best taken in a philosophical manner should it be discovered.

The family that Fadinard will join by his marriage merits close observation. Certainly the mechanical inelasticity its members exhibit in all situations provokes laughter, but this same inability to bend can be seen in another light as well. Nonancourt is amusing, but he is also a domineering and authoritarian patriarch. He is even the ultimate obstacle that Fadinard must conquer—it is the father, not the daughter, who in reality must be courted. This family knows little of the world beyond the nursery and seed business they operate, and some of them cannot even pronounce the name of their profession correctly. With such a limited frame of reference, their social behavior and manners are woefully inadequate for attending a wedding in the sophisticated big city. Dim-witted Bobinard's amorous attentions to his cousin the bride even hint at an unhealthy degree of inbreeding. When the laughter is stilled for a moment, a claustrophobic milieu can be glimpsed beneath the prosperous façade of this typical bourgeois family.

THE JOURNEY OF MR. PERRICHON

The Journey of Mr. Perrichon is both a comedy of character and a comedy of manners. In this play, another typical Labiche family—a wealthy, retired carriage maker and his wife and daughter—embarks on a trip to the Alps. They are followed by two suitors. One of these young men, Armand, saves Mr. Perrichon from falling into a crevasse. Once recovered from the fright, however, Perrichon quickly discredits the importance of Armand's action. Daniel, the other suitor, surmises correctly that Perrichon dislikes being indebted to anyone, so he determines to win favor by allowing Perrichon to be of use to him. Accordingly, he pretends to fall into another crevasse so that the carriage maker may "rescue" him. The ruse succeeds admirably, and Daniel rises in Perrichon's esteem.

Back in Paris, Armand again finds himself in a position to do Perrichon a favor, but his well-intentioned efforts succeed only in creating an embarrassing situation and in intensifying Perrichon's struggle with his conflicting feelings of gratitude and ingratitude. Faced with a duel, Perrichon backs down and apologizes to his adversary in Armand's presence. The young man thus becomes even less attractive to Perrichon, for he has witnessed the carriage maker's weakness and embarrassment. The play ends happily, nevertheless, because Perrichon overhears Daniel boasting of his schemes. Possibly more because he is disgruntled at having been manipulated than as recognition of his gratitude, Perrichon finally grants his daughter's hand to Armand.

The comic element of this play derives from different sources and is of a different tenor from those Labiche employed in *The Italian Straw Hat*. Here the comedy results from the ludicrous discrepancy between Perrichon's restricted personal sphere and the wider world beyond, and to an even greater extent from the discrepancy between Perrichon's inflated self-image and his all-too-human weaknesses. One laughs at his bourgeois inability to cope with the complexities of checking baggage at a train station, at his choice of an inoffensive picture book as appropriate reading material for his daughter, at his spelling error that transforms *mer* (sea) into *mère* (mother), and at his inability to understand others correctly. As long as Perrichon's foibles and vanity reflect only on himself, they are quite amusing. When his myopic attitude and hypocrisy begin to interfere with others' lives, the humor becomes more tenuous and would disappear altogether without the chance discovery that leads to a happy, albeit ambiguous, ending.

THROWING DUST IN PEOPLE'S EYES

Throwing Dust in People's Eyes, a comedy of manners, is another of Labiche's plays written in an ambiguous tone. Two families are shown, each in turn, in their typically bourgeois salons; once again, an impending marriage provides a framework for the plot. The young couple in question love each other in a straightforward, honest manner. Once the formal visits and negotiations between the parents begin, each family increasingly attempts to create the illusion of greater riches than it possesses. Carriages, clothes, important clients, servants, boxes at the theater—their vanity piles pretension on pretension in a comic snowball effect. When the parents can proceed no further without financial disaster and are on the verge of calling off the marriage desired by their children, an outside catalyst arrives in the person of an uncle. This relative is a rich entrepreneur, but he has never let his wealth go to his head. He breaks the deadlock and restores common sense to the proceedings. The children will marry, and the parents good-naturedly admit the folly of their vanity; they have allowed themselves to be carried away by the customs of the times. Chastened, they sit down to dinner—six courses, all with truffles, will be their punishment.

The mothers instead of the fathers dominate the families of *Throwing Dust in People's Eyes*. This topsy-turvy state of affairs nearly leads to disaster before the men can assert themselves and correct it. Most female characters in a Labiche comedy tend to fade into the background as demure daughters or nondescript wives. Those who do occasionally stand out are presented in an unflattering manner—as vengeful shrews pursuing unfaithful husbands (*Si Jamais je te pince*, 1856, if I ever catch you); *J'invite le colonel!*, 1860, I'll invite the colonel), or as broad caricatures (*Three Cheers for Paris*). Reproached for never having written any good roles for women, Labiche reportedly replied that it was because women were basically not funny.

THREE CHEERS FOR PARIS

Three Cheers for Paris (the piggy bank), a midcareer work, represents Labiche at his most typical and best. A comedy of both complications and manners, *Three Cheers for Paris* depicts the misadventures of a provincial family and two of their close friends who journey to Paris to spend the sum accumulated in their collective piggy bank. The comic elements of the play oscillate, beginning in comedy and often slipping into moments of farce. There are unexpected encounters. Repeated motifs—such as buttons in the piggy bank, mention of manure during a dinner conversation, and a smoking lamp whose wick requires adjustment every few minutes—become more amusing with each repetition. During a serious situation, Labiche turns his characters into Bergsonian marionettes by having them pop up and down from their seats side by side on a bench.

The first act is a masterful creation of tone and atmosphere. The family is set snugly in its comfortable salon: father, daughter, and son-in-law-to-be. The mother is replaced in this instance by a maiden aunt. Among the father's friends who complete the family circle, there is one who could be the aunt's suitor. The interplay of contrasting identities and personalities is rich: A young girl and an aging spinster are both set on marriage; there is constant bickering between siblings and much animosity between sexes; comfortable retirees are faced with young people who are just beginning a career; and there are conflicts between individual egos and interests. The likes, dislikes, phobias, complaints, and illusions the characters voice are so many deft touches with which Labiche creates scenes of marvelous human veracity. The individual personalities emerge, as does a collective portrait of the society they represent. As in the other plays, a not too flattering impression is submerged beneath the comic one. The characters in *Three Cheers for Paris* may be sympathetic, but they are also selfish, hypocritical, and dishonest in small matters. Beneath the easy familiarity that reigns in this drawing room is the same claustrophobic atmosphere that characterizes Labiche's other bourgeois families.

When these country folk arrive in Paris in act 2, the playwright's acute sense of observation accompanies them, highlighting the incongruous results of the conflict between middle-class values and assumptions and those of a more cosmopolitan reality. The group's activities are typically those of tourists: They shop for friends at home, dash to visit the famous monuments, and dine at a good restaurant. The situations they encounter, however, become comically exaggerated when the group reacts according to their bourgeois attitudes. Through these situations, Labiche presents his basic themes: a middle-class family coming to grips with problems of money, marriage, their own egos, and the narrowness of their world. The meal costs much more than the sum they had calculated, because the frame of the menu hides the final zeros of all the prices. They refuse to pay and are arrested. At the police station, they are mistaken for a ring of pickpockets. They manage to escape, but without their money. After they are recognized at a marriage broker's ball, they are obliged to spend the night hiding in a construction area. When morning comes they are faced with the problem of returning to home and safety on only ten sous. They are rescued by the appearance of the young suitor who was to have come with them but who had missed the train.

Money, the cause of all their troubles to begin with, also releases the family from their predicament. They do not pause to reflect on their experiences. Anxious only to satiate the hunger they feel from not having eaten since the grand meal of the previous day, they troop off merrily to another good meal, planning to return to the police station afterward to claim their belongings and money, since the real pickpocket has now been arrested. They merely remark that in the future they will stay home to spend their money. At that point, the argument over precisely how they should spend it breaks out again. The play thus ends on a bittersweet note: The repetition of their previous squabbling is amusing, but the sad certainty is that they will return to their claustrophobic life exactly as they left it to continue their same petty ways.

In *Three Cheers for Paris*, as in all of his best works, Labiche succeeded in creating and maintaining a delicate tension between comedy and pathos. His treatment of the aging spinster Leonida Chambourcy illustrates a technique he often used to accomplish this feat. Leonida has finally received a response to her newspaper advertisement for a husband. This situation is presented in a humorous but not exaggerated tone. When the naïve woman appears from the wardrobe at the Parisian marriage broker's, dressed unaccustomedly in a ball gown, what was amusing veers toward the ludicrous. When it turns out that one of her would-be suitors is Cordenbois, the hometown pharmacist with whom she has been playing cards for twenty years, the ludicrous becomes pathetic. The pathos is both intensified and moderated by Cordenbois's preening. He has purchased a waist-cincher that comically rearranges his middle-age girth. He has also rented elegant evening attire that unfortunately still carries a strong odor of cleaning fluid.

Labiche does not allow the pathetic note to remain for more than a few moments. The set's multiple doors enter the action: Leonida and the pharmacist, not understanding that they are the intended match, try to lose each other as each of them seeks the attractive young person whom the broker has described. They exit together and reenter separately but simultaneously, their movements punctuated by those of the broker, who pops in and out of the room looking for them. When Leonida's second suitor appears, he turns out to be the police commissioner who had earlier incarcerated the group; the exits and entrances increase wildly as the situation careens into farce and another act.

BIBLIOGRAPHY

Pao, Angela C. *The Orient of the Boulevards: Exoticism, Empire, and Nineteenth Century French Theater.* Philadelphia: University of Pennsylvania Press, 1998. A look at nineteenth century French theater that focuses on Orientalism. Bibliography and index.

Pronko, Leonard C. *Eugène Labiche and Georges Feydeau.* New York: Grove 1982. This study examines the lives and works of Labiche and Georges Feydeau. Bibliography and index.

Joan M. West

PIERRE-CLAUDE NIVELLE DE LA CHAUSSÉE

Born: Paris, France; 1692
Died: Paris, France; March 14, 1754

PRINCIPAL DRAMA

La Fausse Antipathie, pr. 1733, pb. 1734
Le Préjugé à la mode, pr., pb. 1735 (*Fashionable Prejudice,* 1927)
L'École des amis, pr., pb. 1737
Mélanide, pr., pb. 1741 (English translation, 1973)
Paméla, pr. 1743, pb. 1762 (adaptation of Samuel Richardson's novel *Pamela*)
L'École des mères, pr. 1744, pb. 1745
La Gouvernante, pr., pb. 1747
L'École de la jeunesse: Ou, Le Retour sur soi-même, pr. 1749, pb. 1762
L'Homme de fortune, pr. 1751, pb. 1762

OTHER LITERARY FORMS

Although Pierre-Claude Nivelle de La Chaussée's fame rests solely on the so-called *comédies larmoyantes* (tearful comedies) listed above, his first publication of note was a nondramatic work, *Épître de Clio, à Monsieur B . . .* (epistle of Clio to Monsieur B . . .), published in 1731. In this verse polemic of approximately nine hundred lines, La Chaussée defends tradition and classical principles, including the use of verse in tragedy, against their detractor Antoine Houdar de La Motte. During the 1720's, La Chaussée composed a series of *Contes* (tales in verse). His first dramatic efforts were a number of *parades*, rather obscene, satiric farces that were very popular in his time. One such *parade*, entitled *Le Repatriage*, was published posthumously in 1762.

ACHIEVEMENTS

Critics generally credit Pierre-Claude Nivelle de La Chaussée for popularizing a new genre in French drama: the *comédie larmoyante*. Gustave Lanson, the influential nineteenth century French critic, defines the genre:

> The *comédie larmoyante* is an intermediary genre between comedy and tragedy, which presents ordinary people, virtuous or nearly so, in a serious action, occasionally arousing pathos, and which excites us to virtue, moves us by virtue's misfortunes, and makes us applaud at its triumph.

The "tearful comedy" of La Chaussée deviates from the strict separation of genres, a cardinal principle of French seventeenth century dramaturgy. Although dramatists of the classical period occasionally created generically hybrid plays (the *comédies héroïques* or the more numerous *tragi-comédies*, for example), purist critics attacked La Chaussée's highly popular work as a "bastard genre," saying "Thalia must laugh; a comedy which provokes tears is against reason." Despite this opposition from influential writers such as Voltaire, the *comédie larmoyante* marks a turning point in the evolution of French theater. Its popularity paved the way for the *drame bourgeois* of Denis Diderot and Michel-Jean Sedaine later in the century. Portraying the domestic problems of middle-class families, the sentimental *drame bourgeois* preached social reform with a moral basis and led in turn to the romantic social plays of such writers as Alexandre Dumas, *fils*, in the nineteenth century.

The *comédie larmoyante* also represents a deviation from the comic norm in France since the death of Molière in 1673: Substituting emotion for laughter, La Chaussée's comedy stresses a moral appeal to the audience based on sentiment, or *sensibilité*. The notion of *sensibilité* characterizes many aspects of eighteenth century literature; it is a kind of self-conscious exercise in emotional display, and La Chaussée's *comédie larmoyante* was written particularly to elicit a sentimental response from its audience. La Chaussée's characters are above all *sensible* (sensitive), and this *sensibilité* manifests their innate goodness and virtue. Although it was the mainspring of his art, La Chaussée did not create the concept; he merely exploited a shift in taste. Whereas Molièresque comedy elicited laughter at the expense of vice, La Chaussée's moralistic theater provoked tears on behalf of virtue.

BIOGRAPHY

Born to a well-established and rich family in Paris, Pierre-Claude Nivelle de La Chaussée attended the Jesuit Collége Louis-le-Grand and received his training in rhetoric and philosophy at Plessis. His family's fortune and connections apparently aided his entrée into Parisian society. A letter written in 1711 suggests ties with Voltaire. Letters full of obscenities

and jokes to his friends during a stay in Amsterdam in 1720 offer insights into La Chaussée's personality: Bored by Holland and the business matters that kept him there, La Chaussée reveals a deep interest in the stage and speaks of his love for writing poetry. Although he had lost most of his fortune in 1720 as a result of the collapse of the Law Bank, La Chaussée continued in the 1720's to associate with the literate and libertine *gens du monde* of the Regency period. Long an amateur of letters, La Chaussée composed, mainly for his large circle of friends, obscene *parades* and short narrative poems (the *Contes*). It is ironic that the "moralistic" La Chaussée, who was praised later as "this zealous dramatic preacher, who has converted so many souls by his homelies, this pious orator of Parnassus who always put virtue in his plays," created early works remarkable for their lack of morals. Elected to the French Academy in 1736, La Chaussée was forty-one years old when his first play, *La Fausse Antipathie*, appeared three years earlier: His work was immediately and consistently popular until the failure of *Paméla* in 1743.

La Chaussée died in March, 1754, apparently from a chill he had caught after working in the garden of his house on the outskirts of Paris.

ANALYSIS

Pierre-Claude Nivelle de La Chaussée's drama, which set the scene for later generations of bourgeois drama, is significant for its place in the development of comedy; it also affords insights into the cultural interests of his day. His numerous dramatic devices weave around his appealing plots, in accordance with the audience-pleasing philosophy of his first play, *La Fausse Antipathie*. Amusing the middle class and flattering their pretensions and aspirations, he enjoyed a full decade of success in the theater.

Critics, however, have judged La Chaussée's work mediocre at best. Usually considered an inspired follower of public taste rather than a true innovator, La Chaussée has been criticized for improbable plots, vague, pretentious style, and dull poetry. His comedy does not focus on character analysis in the fashion of Molière; it is predicated rather on a comedy of situation. His characters are distinguished mainly by their high degree of *sensibilité* and virtue, which are brought to the fore through circumstances of the plot. Despite a plot structure complicated by numerous peripeteia, characters incognito, fortuitous scenes of recognition, superfluous scenes of *dépit amoureux* (loving spite), the denouement typically involves the revelation of a secret that quickly resolves the main conflict; the other plot elements merely serve to delay this resolution. La Chaussée's character development and subtlety bow to the studied exposé of a moral lesson. This tendency results in long speeches full of moral sentences that, general in tone, apply only obliquely to the particular situation: The character's voice becomes that of the preaching, ever-present author.

FASHIONABLE PREJUDICE

La Chaussée's best-known play is doubtless *Fashionable Prejudice*, presented in 1735. Its great success lasted throughout the author's lifetime, both in France and abroad. The "prejudice" on which the action of the play is based appears incredible to a modern audience: Durval loves his wife, Constance, yet dares not declare his love for fear that society will consider him ridiculous—such is the prejudice against conjugal love. Literary historians have debated whether the penchant for affairs outside marriage among the nobility actually created such disdain for fidelity in marriage. Given the moralistic resonance of La Chaussée's work, it would appear that he was assailing a fashionable prejudice that actually existed.

Durval's fear is such that he feigns indifference and scorn toward the virtuous, sensitive, and loving Constance. For her part, she refuses to reveal her despair to Durval. Durval has sent magnificent presents to her without daring to disclose their origin; this merely exacerbates Constance's suffering, for she attributes the presents to two foppish admirers, Clitandre and Damis. She believes that her husband is pursuing other women, which he in fact has done to conform to society's expectations. Durval's friend and confidant Damon urges him to admit his love, but Durval continues to prevaricate. He is about to declare himself to his wife when the two fops enter, poking fun at another husband, who has abandoned

society to live alone with his wife in the country. Durval, ever the fearful conformist, joins in this merriment and even agrees to play the role of the faithful husband in a satiric farce called "The Husband in Love with his Wife." Contemptuous of this project, Damon urges Durval ever more strongly to end his wife's suffering by avowing his love. Durval finally decides to send a letter, accompanied by a gift, to Constance. At the last moment, however, he withdraws the letter and sends only the gift. On receiving the gift, which she believes to be from an unknown lover, Constance is doubly wounded, for she has just received a packet of love letters that Durval had sent to a certain duchesse; it is obvious to her that her marriage is a sham.

At this point in the play, the action rebounds: Durval participates in a conversation with Damis and Clitandre in which each one boasts that Constance loves him. Damis reveals a miniature of Constance, thus "proving" that Constance prefers him. Although Damis has in reality stolen the portrait, Durval suspects the ever-faithful Constance of infidelity and, furious, confronts her with his suspicions. She, in a near faint, drops the packet of letters incriminating Durval, on which he immediately seizes as further proof of Constance's inconstance. The entire household, including Constance's father Argent, his niece Sophie, and Damon (who loves Sophie), gathers to discover why Durval is shouting. Durval triumphantly opens the letters only to discover that he, not Constance, is proven to be a cheat.

Contrite and confused, Durval finally determines to ask his wife's forgiveness and to declare his love. That evening, disguised, Durval speaks to Constance at a ball. Mistaking her husband for Damon, the *sensible* Constance confides her sadness and her profound affection for her husband. Durval, overcome with emotion, remorse, and above all tears, unmasks himself and falls to his knees, begging his wife's forgiveness; she tearfully accepts his love. In the last scene, Durval declares to the assembled characters (and audience) the play's moral lesson: "Perhaps my example will have more authority:/ Others may imitate me. No, it is not possible/ That such a false prejudice will forever prevail."

As this résumé clearly demonstrates, the complexities of the play's action serve simply to delay Durval's ultimate avowal of love. The plot revolves around one question: Will he or will he not do the proper, obvious thing? The answer to the question is evident from the beginning. The characters possess little psychological depth. Constance, a favorite among La Chaussée's contemporaries, is virtue personified; Durval, timidity incarnate. The morality instilled in the play is clear and absolutely irrefutable: Conjugal love must triumph over illicit affairs, and he who loves his wife must not be ashamed.

MÉLANIDE

Although *Fashionable Prejudice* is La Chaussée's most celebrated play, critics regard *Mélanide* as the most accessible and illustrative of his *comédies larmoyantes*. A huge success from its first presentation in 1741, *Mélanide* provoked buckets of tears among its first audiences. Even La Chaussée's enemies reacted favorably to the play; the Abbé Desfontaines opined that it was "worth one hundred sermons." The same critic in effect legitimized the new genre by groping for a name to call it: *drame romanesque? romanédie*? The play's title—simply the name of a major character—marks the author's attempt to make the tearful comedy a more independent and original genre. Heretofore only tragedies carried the name of a major character, already known by the public, whereas the title of a comedy generally suggested the play's main themes. The choice of an unknown character's name as title of a new "comedy" surprised La Chaussée's contemporaries and no doubt contributed substantially to the play's renown.

After many years of painful, self-imposed, and mysterious isolation in Brittany, Mélanide has come to Paris to visit her friend Dorisée. The widowed and financially distressed Dorisée intends to select as husband for her daughter Rosalie the Marquis d'Orvigny, an old but honorable and rich man who loves Rosalie. Dorisée asks her old friend Mélanide to tell the young man she has reared, Darviane, to leave Paris immediately, in order to put an end to the love between Darviane and Rosalie. Mélanide confides her past to Dorisée's brother-in-law Théodon: Many years before she fell in love and intended to marry the Comte

d'Ormancé. His family, however, disapproved of the marriage and broke off the engagement. Mélanide, pregnant, was disinherited by her parents and forced to live in shame far from Paris. This story astonishes Théodon, for it bears an incredible similarity to his friend d'Orvigny's past. Théodon tells Mélanide that d'Orvigny may be her long-lost love, but the difference in names stymies them. Mélanide manages to catch sight of d'Orvigny: He, of course, is the Comte d'Ormancé, Mélanide's former love.

The sensitive and admirable Théodon informs d'Orvigny that the woman he loved so long ago is not dead, as he thinks, but alive and available. Although Théodon had hoped that d'Orvigny would forget about Rosalie and fly back to Mélanide at this news, he finds that d'Orvigny's heart now belongs to Rosalie. After Théodon's arguments, d'Orvigny agrees to attempt to master his emotions and return to his former love. In a conversation with Darviane in which Mélanide reprimands him for insulting the honor of d'Orvigny, she reveals that she is his mother. After this tearful scene, Darviane begins to suspect more, for his mother has told him henceforth to show only the greatest respect for d'Orvigny. Might this man be his father? Another scene full of *sensibilité* follows: Darviane apologizes to d'Orvigny, who accepts gladly, since Théodon has disclosed to him that Darviane is his son. The suspicious Darviane pushes the older man to admit finally that he is his father. The sudden arrival of Mélanide reignites d'Orvigny's not yet extinguished passion for her; Dorisée accepts Darviane as her future son-in-law. Thus d'Orvigny remains faithful to his first love; awash in tears, he has the play's last words: "From now on let us be a single family./ Oh heaven, you have shown me, by satisfying all my wishes,/ That duty exists only to make us happy." Virtue is above all a source of pleasure in La Chaussée.

This extremely romanesque plot—in which a father and son become amorous rivals—exploits fully the sentimentality of the situation. Whereas La Chaussée injected comedy in *Fashionable Prejudice* through the time-honored device of amusing valets and maids, comedy in this play derives mainly from rather incongruous scenes of amorous spite (*dépit amoureux*) between Darviane and Rosalie. In neither play does La Chaussée weave the comic episodes into the fabric of the action. Far from being humorous or objects of humor, the characters are above all virtuous. D'Orvigny emerges as the most vibrant—and virtuous—character in *Mélanide*. After years of searching and weeping for his lost first love, d'Orvigny attempts to rediscover happiness by falling in love with the young and charming Rosalie. His initial, adverse reaction to the revelation that Mélanide still lives is human yet marks his inherent goodness: "Whatever this fatal love may be [his new love for Rosalie],/ I will struggle against it with all of my virtue." The energetic efforts of his son and, above all, the sight of Mélanide (whom he sees, after seventeen years, only in the last scene) awaken his natural integrity and moral nobility. D'Orvigny exemplifies a basic principle of La Chaussée's psychology, which parallels a basic tenet of eighteenth century ethical thought: that natural instinct is good, that knowledge and will, therefore, are not essential to ethical behavior. It follows that the sensitive, emotional individual is most in tune with his or her natural instincts, and that this person will naturally incline to virtue. In this system, *sensibilité* becomes an outward proof of natural morality. Given this belief, it is not difficult, perhaps, to comprehend the rage for tears in the eighteenth century theater.

After all, were not the audiences at least as virtuous as the characters for whom they wept?

OTHER MAJOR WORKS

POETRY: *Épître de Clio, à Monsieur B . . .* , 1731.
MISCELLANEOUS: *Œuvres de Monsieur Nivelle de La Chaussée*, 1762 (5 volumes).

BIBLIOGRAPHY

Brereton, Geoffrey. *French Comic Drama from the Sixteenth to the Eighteenth Century*. London: Metheun, 1977. Brereton examines the comedic drama of France from the sixteenth to the eighteenth century, touching on La Chaussée.

Connon, Derek, and George Evans, eds. *Essays on French Comic Drama from the 1640s to the 1780s*. New York: Peter Lang, 2000. These essays focus on French comedic drama during the seventeenth and eighteenth centuries. La Chaussée made a significant contribution to French comedic drama with his *comédie larmoyante*.

Weber, Caroline. "Overcoming Excess: Jouissance and Justice in Nivelle de la Chaussée's *L'École des mères*." Weber challenges the view of La Chaussée as overly and uncritically emotional in her analysis of *L'École des mères*.

Robert T. Corum, Jr.

PÄR LAGERKVIST

Born: Växjö, Sweden; May 23, 1891
Died: Lidingö, Sweden; July 11, 1974

PRINCIPAL DRAMA

Sista mänskan, pb. 1917
Den svåra stunden, pr., pb. 1918 (*The Difficult Hour, I-III*, 1966)
Himlens hemlighet, pb. 1919, pr. 1921 (*The Secret of Heaven*, 1966)
Den osynlige, pb. 1923, pr. 1924
Han som fick leva om sitt liv, pr., pb. 1928 (*The Man Who Lived His Life Over*, 1971)

Man Who Lived His Life Over, 1971)
Konungen, pb. 1932, pr. 1950 (*The King*, 1966)
Bödeln, pb. 1933, pr. 1934 (adaptation of his novella; *The Hangman*, 1966)
Mannen utan själ, pb. 1936, pr. 1938 (*The Man Without a Soul*, 1944)
Seger i mörker, pb. 1939, pr. 1940
Midsommardröm i fattighuset, pr., pb. 1941 (*Midsummer Dream in the Workhouse*, 1953)
De vises sten, pb. 1947, pr. 1948 (*The Philosopher's Stone*, 1966)

Låt människan leva, pr., pb. 1949 (*Let Man Live*, 1951)

Barabbas, pr., pb. 1953 (adaptation of his novel)

Dramatik, pb. 1956 (3 volumes)

OTHER LITERARY FORMS

Pär Lagerkvist is, outside Sweden, best known as a novelist. In his own country, he is highly esteemed both as a poet and as a novelist and is ranked second only to August Strindberg in Swedish drama (excluding the cinema). He is also the author of essays on drama, literature, and painting; prose poems; sketches; travel essays; and many short stories.

ACHIEVEMENTS

As a Scandinavian playwright, Pär Lagerkvist now belongs to a triumvirate that includes Henrik Ibsen and August Strindberg. Thomas Buckman, the translator of seven of Lagerkvist's plays and of his essay on modern theater, recognizes him as having introduced "a new spirit of modernism" into drama. The scholar Alrik Gustafson, who was a friend and frequent guest of Lagerkvist, observed in 1951 that "Lagerkvist has placed his stamp so firmly on Swedish literary culture that a recent Scandinavian writes: 'If Swedish literature after 1914 may be expressed by a single name, that name must without question be Pär Lagerkvist.'" One may perhaps expect high praise from Scandinavians and from professors of Scandinavian studies, and indeed Martin Seymour-Smith, insisting that "Scandinavians overvalue their literature," says that "no better example of this habit could be found than in the vastly inflated reputation of Lagerkvist" and adds that in expressionist drama "his example has been disastrous." This somewhat peevish appraisal is at least explicit on the magnitude of Lagerkvist's influence. For better or worse, Lagerkvist has been a real force in modern Swedish drama and literature. Richard B. Vowles, a critic of Lagerkvist's fiction, has written, fairly and noncommittally, "Between 1912 and 1918 he largely established the expressionist direction of Swedish modernism." It would be difficult to deny that Sweden's renowned film director Ingmar Bergman followed this direction. "Lagerkvist," according to Peter Cowie in his 1982 biography of Bergman, "is the only twentieth century Swedish artist whose religious preoccupations are on a par with Bergman's." Lagerkvist's theme of the need for faith in a world unable to make proper provision for it is, again according to Cowie, "crucial to Bergman's films of the fifties, and in particular *The Seventh Seal* and *The Virgin Spring*." In his much-quoted praise of the novel *Barabbas* (1950; English translation, 1951), which was subsequently dramatized, André Gide wrote, "It is the measure of Lagerkvist's success that he has managed so admirably to maintain his balance on a tightrope which stretches across the dark abyss that lies between the world of reality and the world of faith." Gide's statement may serve as a summary of the tension that informs Lagerkvist's drama; it is also evidence that appreciation of Lagerkvist is not limited to Scandinavia or to academe.

Pär Lagerkvist (© The Nobel Foundation)

In the Scandinavian triumvirate there is, generally, in Ibsen a movement from psychological realism to symbolic naturalism, in Strindberg a movement from psychological naturalism to symbolic expressionism, and in Lagerkvist a movement from Strindbergian expressionism to metaphysical cubism. "Metaphysical" and "cubist" are terms that have become commonplace in Lagerkvist criticism. Others are visionary, anguished, spiritual, uncompromising, and honest. The term "moral" also appears in such criticism. Lagerkvist's morality proved to be as unconventional as his religion (he identified himself as a religious atheist). In his work, simplistic notions of good and evil give way to the moral tension between love and evil, with "good" and "bad" being understood as functional opposites: Subject to moral tension, the individual becomes good *at*, or bad *at*, being a human (*människa*). The Lagerkvistian individual determines his own character, or ethical identity, by resolving this tension from within, by finding the kingdom of God, not in an external heaven or a prescriptive tradition but within the self. Existentialists would call this anguished search a quest for authenticity and an ethical imperative. In his book *On Moral Fiction* (1978), John Gardner, attesting Lagerkvist's achievements as novelist and poet (to which must be added playwright), declared: "We have seen in recent years a few great novelists and poets like Pär Lagerkvist, who have interested themselves not only in the anguish of the social moment but also in a larger or at least more enduring problem: metaphysical anguish."

BIOGRAPHY

Pär Fabian Lagerkvist displayed his predisposition to independence in his very first appearance in print, a letter to the local newspaper in October, 1905, written when he was fourteen:

Every schoolboy is surely aware of the hostility that exists, not only in Växiö but in other cities as well, between elementary- and secondary-school pupils. This hostility may appear to be insignificant, but it certainly is not; it is nothing other than the beginning of a pernicious class hatred in Sweden. For how easily does a boy from elementary school, who during his entire schooling grows accustomed to harboring the same

hostility toward a secondary-school pupil that the socialists harbor toward the upper social classes, how easily does such a boy fall victim to pernicious socialism. Conversely, a secondary-school pupil can easily begin to hate not only the elementary-school students but also, when he is older and more mature, all members of the working class. Therefore, comrades, let's begin to lay aside this bad habit and rather try, in harmony, to further the best interests of our country. [*signed*] *A schoolboy.*

In five to seven years' time, Lagerkvist would become sufficiently amenable to socialism to lend his creative talents to the Social Democratic journals *Fram*, *Stormklockan*, and *Norskensflamman*.

Thirteen months after his debut in the local newspaper, he published a prose sketch entitled "Moderskärlek" and signed "Jagibus." It is a sentimental piece with a trace of bitterness over the emigration to the United States of which Småland had seen much during the last half of the nineteenth century.

The burgeoning of Lagerkvist's literary career coincides with the development of cubism from 1907 to 1914. In 1909 and 1910 he published thirteen poems under the pen name "Stig Stigson." The first work published in his own name was the poem "Kväll" ("Evening"), written in February, 1911, in honor of the poet Gustaf Fröding, who had recently died. In 1912, he published seven new poems, a copy of two hitherto unpublished Strindberg letters that he had discovered, a prose fantasy entitled "Gudstanken" ("God's Thought"), and his first novel, *Människor* (people). Many of Lagerkvist's early works, particularly his poems, have a militant socialist focus that would give way by 1916 to his broader humanistic expressions of *längtan* (longing), *ångest* (anguish), and *kärlek* (love). Adumbrations of his plays and later novels are evident in "God's Thought," in which a Diana figure (to reappear in a 1960 novel), as a vestige of a dead religion, serves to turn a man toward the experience of his own being and, consequently, away from preoccupation with the supernatural, and in a 1912 poem, "Min Gud" ("My God"), which begins, "My god is a proud, defiant man/ — —my god is a child gone astray," asserts midway, "My god is what life has given me/ to mold into worship and belief," and concludes, "my god—my god—: he is I!—he is I!— — —." Lagerkvist's maternal grandparents had been farm people, severely uncompromising in their fundamentalist religion. In their presence, Lagerkvist learned the cold terror of a religion of judgment. His father, Anders Johan Lagerkvist, a foreman at a railroad yard, and his mother, née Johanna Blad, were devout Christians, but their persuasion was marked more by the solace of the Gospel than by the rigidity of the Law. Ultimately, Lagerkvist abandoned the faith of both his grandparents and his parents.

In 1913, Lagerkvist published three poems and two prose sketches in *Stormklockan*, to which he also contributed twelve reviews, including his review of Fyodor Dostoevski's *Unizhennye i oskorblyonnye* (1861; *The Insulted and Injured*, 1887). His review article on Guillaume Apollinaire's *Les Peintres cubistes: Méditations esthétiques* (1913; *The Cubist Painters: Esthetic Meditations*, 1944) appeared in *Svenska dagbladet*. He also published that year *Två sagor om livet* (two tales of life, a pair of short stories) and his very important essay *Ordkonst och bildkonst* (*Literary Art and Pictorial Art*, 1982), which established his championship of cubism and helped to change the literary climate in Sweden. He saw cubism as greatly superior to impressionism and naturalism and developed the suggestion that the literary artist would do well to adhere to the mathematical technique and the structural principles of the cubist painter.

Lagerkvist passed his student-examination in Växjö at the age of nineteen, entitling him to wear the white *studentmössa* (student-cap), indicative of his eligibility for university study. He entered Uppsala University in 1911 but gave it up after a single term. *Människor* includes passages expressive of his dissatisfaction with student life. He carried on his studies independently. During the first half of 1913, he was in Paris, carefully appraising the theories and methods of French painting, particularly expressionism, Fauvism, and, as noted, cubism.

He lived in Denmark during World War I and recorded his bitter but lyric lament over the waste and inhumanity of war in *Järn och människor* (iron and men), a collection of five short stories published in 1915. In the next year, his first collection of poems appeared under the title of the poem that opens the collection, *Ångest*. The title, translated as "anguish," denotes a painfully intellectual emotion. Lagerkvist's first major renditions of the theme coincided with his residence in the country of Søren Kierkegaard, who had defined the existentialist concept of *ångest* as "a sympathetic antipathy and an antipathetic sympathy."

Lagerkvist developed a presentation of *ångest* as an intensified consciousness of *längtan* (longing). *Längtan* is common to both innocence (ignorance) and loss of innocence (awareness); it is in the loss of innocence that *längtan* becomes *ångest*. Both Lagerkvist and Kierkegaard see spirit as an intellectual emotion, as the imaginative awareness that is at once the source, the sustenance, and the identity of "anguish"; both see it as a synthesis of body and soul, a synthesis that spirit itself effects when it awakens from its own dream. Lagerkvist's *längtan* is Kierkegaard's *Aand . . . drømmende* (spirit . . . dreaming).

It was during this period in Denmark that Lagerkvist added to his independent curriculum a thoroughgoing study of drama. He concluded that modern theater, like modern literature, was seriously oppressed by naturalism; in "Modern teater: Synpunkter och angrepp" (1918; "Modern Theatre: Points of View and Attack," 1966), he criticized contemporary drama as vigorously as he had criticized contemporary literature in *Literary Art and Pictorial Art*, and his suggestion for its rejuvenation was much the same as the one he had made for literature—chiefly, mathematical construction and an application of the principles of cubist painting. He berated the naturalistic theater for its failure to express the time in which people were currently living, a time greatly in need of giving adequate expression to its *ångest*.

His first play, *Sista mänskan* (the last man), was published in 1917. Like his first novel, it was patently expressionistic, depressingly informed by the imagery of darkness, and presumably a failure. Lagerkvist never permitted any reprinting of *Människor*; and while he did not object to reprintings of *Sista mänskan*, he seems never to have sought or encouraged its production once he had achieved success with his subsequent plays. The number of plays he wrote is relatively small, thirteen in the thirty-six years from 1917 through 1953, with two of these being adaptations from his prose fiction. He published no dramatic works during the last twenty-one years of his life. The film production of his *Barabbas* in 1962 was essentially the work of others. Ibsen, having written twice that many plays in fifty-one years, remained active as a playwright until only seven years before his death. Strindberg, who wrote his last play only three years before his death, had completed forty-six plays in, at most, thirty-seven years.

By the time Lagerkvist had written his second and third plays, his second comprising three one-act plays and his third being a one-act play, he had succeeded August Brunius, his good friend and the author of the foreword to *Literary Art and Pictorial Art*, as art and drama critic for *Svenska dagbladet*. During 1918-1919, he wrote forty-six reviews for the newspaper. In 1922 he collected his thoughts on innocence, awareness, and spirit and wrote them down in "Myten om människorna" (the myth of humankind). This work deals with the beginning, as *Sista mänskan* deals with the end, of humankind. Only a fragment of it has been published. By 1925, Lagerkvist was well established as a significant figure in Swedish literature. In 1928, having successfully worked in all the literary genres that mark his canon, he received the prestigious literary prize awarded by Samfundet De Nio (The Committee of Nine).

Lagerkvist's most challenging works during the next decade were *Bödeln* (1933; *The Hangman*, 1936) and *Den knutna näven* (1934; *The Clenched Fist*, 1982), the latter written in conjuction with his travels to Greece and Palestine. In these works, he measures *ångest* against the problem of evil with which he had struggled in *Sista mänskan* and which he had elucidated in his collection of short stories *Onda sagor* (1924; evil tales). *The Hangman* is a lyric comment on the brutalism of fascist sovereignty; more important, it develops in sympathetic antipathy the theme of the necessity and persistence of evil. The subject is expanded in lyric essays in *The Clenched Fist* as Lagerkvist elaborates his version of Friedrich Nietzsche's Apollonian and Dionysian duality. Unlike Nietzsche, he limits these motifs almost exclusively to morality, yet, like Nietzsche, he recog-

nizes the positive and negative forces in each and the great dangers resulting from the ascendance of either one over the other. These themes receive masterful treatment in the novel *Dvärgen* (1944; *The Dwarf*, 1945) with its Apollonian artist-scientist Messer Bernardo, its Dionysian dwarf Piccoline, and its theme of inherent human evil.

Four years before publication of *The Dwarf*, Lagerkvist had succeeded to the chair of the deceased Verner von Heidenstam as a duly elected member of the Swedish Academy of Literature, that body of "immortals" that selects the winners of the Nobel Prize in Literature. Lagerkvist was himself nominated for the Nobel Prize in 1950, the year in which he published his novel *Barabbas*. André Gide had won the prize in 1947, T. S. Eliot in 1948. The 1949 prize was held over to 1950, the year of Lagerkvist's nomination; it was won by William Faulkner, for whom it is said Lagerkvist had cast his ballot, and the 1950 prize was awarded to Bertrand Russell. The 1951 prize was awarded to Pär Lagerkvist, the Uppsala University dropout who had received an honorary Ph.D. from the University of Gothenburg in 1941 and whose works became the subject of study at Uppsala. Lagerkvist's speech at the Nobel Prize ceremonies consisted of the aforementioned fragment from his 1922 composition "Myten om människorna."

From 1951 until his death in 1974, Lagerkvist published only six works—his ninth and last volume of poetry and five short novels. In 1977, his daughter Elin Lagerkvist published *Antecknat*, a collection of his notes, jottings, and diary entries, dating from 1906, and seven previously unpublished poems.

ANALYSIS

Ångest is a subject that does not lend itself to comedy readily. Even the comedian Woody Allen had to move from farce to the seriocomic and serious in order to accommodate his attention to his Manhattan-esque angst. Pär Lagerkvist's brooding seriousness—the Swedish word for it is *grubbel*—is rarely relieved in his work by a light touch or a comic lift. None of his plays is a comedy. Those that are not tragedies, or tragic, are, at their most positive level, hauntingly melancholy.

SISTA MÄNSKAN

A good approach to his first play, *Sista mänskan*, is to see its world as the terminus of the world brought into being in "Myten om människorna," which begins, "Once upon a time there was a world." In "Myten om människorna," a man and a woman come to this world for a short visit. They make a home. The husband hunts and tills the soil. The wife bears three sons. One evening she tells her children about the other worlds she knows. When the youngest son dies, it is understood that he has gone to another world. The man and his wife grow old. After they die, their surviving sons feel great relief. Unbothered by further contemplation of other worlds, the two young men joyously go out to take possession of the earth, on which human life is burgeoning. From this paradisiacal setting, Lagerkvist has excluded a creator and for the visit of Lucifer has substituted the event of death. The Adam and Eve of this myth have come from a heavenly realm where all was clear, bright, and glorious and where their love for each other was taken for granted. On earth, their love could not be taken for granted. It was a miracle, infinitely precious because it could not last. In their love and in their life on earth, they lost their knowledge of Heaven; it became a mystery. When the woman told her sons about the other world, she could not remember enough to satisfy her youngest, who, quite unlike his brothers, yearned for Heaven. In his yearning, he withers and dies, while his brothers revel in life on Earth. There are two ideas expressed here. The first is that the price of earthly life is ignorance of Heaven; its corollary is that in the human presumption to know a no longer knowable Heaven, earthly life is wasted. The divinity of the other world separates the individual from the divinity within the self in proportion as the self yearns for the other world. The second idea is that loss of innocence is the price of human love and of the awakening of spirit in the physical consummation of that love.

The two ideas constitute the lesson that has not been learned in *Sista mänskan*, in which Earth's last humans struggle for survival in the cold and the encroaching darkness of a world whose sun is dying. Adam and Eve have become Gama, a blind man, and

Vyr, mother of a young boy named Ilja. Present also are a paralytic, a cripple, a leper, a redhead, old women, the last humans, the dead, and a chorus of suppliants. In the past, which is to say in the course of human history, Gama had raped Vyr, who in turn blinded him while he slept and then went off to live alone and bear and rear the son she had conceived. Blind Gama returns and attempts to love Vyr and her son without at first knowing that Vyr is the former victim of his lust and that Ilja is his son. Vyr desperately needs Gama's love, and Ilja hungers for the knowledge of what love is. Gama and Vyr fall in love, but when Gama learns who Vyr is and that she was the one who blinded him, he strangles her. Ilja loses his desire to live and sinks to the ground. Gama, losing his sanity, calls out his son's name and sinks to the ground. In this short three-act play, Lagerkvist's pessimism is at its peak: He offers no hope that humankind will learn, not the meaning, but the lesson of life—namely, the need to stabilize evil by means of love. The meaning of life is something for each individual to determine through apprehending the divinity within the self.

Sista mänskan is Lagerkvist's expressionistic attempt to sustain what he considers to be Strindberg's rebellious renaissance in theatrical art. In "Modern Theatre," the 1918 essay in which he extols Strindberg's dramaturgy and condemns what he sees as Ibsen's tediously formalistic naturalism, Lagerkvist insists that modern theater should be true to its time, and he makes a statement that could pass for a description of the *mise en scène* of *The Last Man*: "At this time everything is torn apart, at loose ends, harsh, contradictory, with light and darkness irreconcilably opposed. And we must live within what encompasses us, in the time that is our own, feeling our way about in it and trying to understand."

THE DIFFICULT HOUR, I-III

The expressionistic chiaroscuro of *Sista mänskan* is retained in *The Difficult Hour, I-III*, a more successful theatrical encounter with the lesson of life. The "difficult hour" is that critical moment at which life passes into death. Each of the one-act plays in this trilogy of death shows an individual—respectively, a young man, an old man, and a boy—learning the lesson of life during the moment in which he learns that he is dead. Although *The Difficult Hour, I-III* comprises three plays, it is a dramatic unit with a progressive lessening of the difficulty of the critical moment: The young man dies screaming in remorseful confusion; the old man dies in resignation; and the boy dies with full acceptance of his fate. Lagerkvist uses the image of physical deformity to symbolize human imperfection and limitation: a blind man, a paralytic, a cripple, and a leper in *Sista mänskan*; a hunchback and a dwarf in *The Difficult Hour, I-III*.

THE SECRET OF HEAVEN

In the one-act play *The Secret of Heaven*, there is a blind man, a cripple, and a dwarf. Fate is represented by a man in tights who pulls the heads off dolls as indiscriminately as the spinning Parcae broke the threads of human lives. Religion takes the form of a man wearing a yarmulke who claims to understand everything except God. God appears, as he appears in the novella *Det eviga leendet* (1920; *The Eternal Smile*, 1934), in the person of an old man sawing wood. A young man asks the old woodsman for the meaning of everything and is told that meaning consists in the fact that everything whirls around (*Allting snurrar runt*). Later, when the young man receives the same answer from the man in the yarmulke, who adds a note of determinism by saying that everything must whirl around (*allting ska snurra runt*), he leaps into the void, screaming in frustration. The play's setting, which also reappears in *The Eternal Smile*, is Heaven, or eternity, wherein only God, darkness, and the dead are to be found.

DEN OSYNLIGE

Sista mänskan and *The Difficult Hour, I-III* both exhibit what Wylie Sypher has called "cubist simultaneous perspective" in that both view human existence from the coextensive and intersecting planes of life and death and against the irreconcilable forces of light and darkness. In the three acts of his fourth play, *Den osynlige* (the invisible one), light and darkness are reconciled as the complements of a dualism. Like Aeschylus's *Oresteia* (458 B.C.E.; English translation, 1777), which discloses the mean between light and darkness and not the elimination of darkness in favor of light to be the proper object of human seeking, the

play begins in darkness, wherein the voice of the Invisible One is heard, and ends in light, with the Invisible One identifying himself as *människoanden* (the human spirit), predicting his victory over and survival of Death, and dismissing Death.

The refrain of the play's third act is "God is dead." When Death asks the Invisible One if he is God, he says, "No, God is dead," and asserts that he, the human spirit, is alive. Two limited forces, tyranny and rebellion, personified respectively as the Administrator and the Hero, both come to an end: The Administrator is struck down by the Invisible One, and the Hero is mortally wounded in fighting for his beliefs. Death and the human spirit remain as the forces of opposition, which, in a type of Zoroastrian dualism, make the world go round, or ensure that everything whirls around. The Invisible One does emerge as God, not the eternal and external woodcutter, but the divinity resident in the heart of each human being.

THE MAN WHO LIVED HIS LIFE OVER

The Man Who Lived His Life Over begins with a voice in darkness telling a dead man named Daniel that he may live again. Daniel is restored to his youth and his shoemaker's trade and determines that his second life will be the right one. It proves to be quite as bad as the first because again Daniel expects life, or God, to conform to his own true and unique identity. Daniel cannot really live, he can only exist because, looking for life to live him, he fails to make his life his own. The voice from the darkness proves to have been Death. God, as the human spirit, appears at the beginning of Daniel's second life in the form of an alcoholic man with a wooden leg who sells shoelaces. His name is Boman (Home-man or Living-man). He teaches Daniel how to make one's life one's own, but Daniel does not learn the lesson.

In his first life, Daniel had followed the dictates of passion—a course that led him to prison, convicted of the murder of a disreputable woman who flouted his desire. In his second life, he becomes a slave to conventional morality and drives his youngest son to suicide by refusing to let him carry on with the woman he loves, a woman of loose morals. The two lives are presented in simultaneity and from the simultaneous perspectives of a fantastic premise and a realistic setting, as Lagerkvist's cubism here supersedes his expressionism.

All three acts of *The Man Who Lived His Life Over* reverberate with the call for existentialist authenticity. In the first act, for example, Daniel tells Boman that "we live out something that has been thrown to us"; Boman quite agrees and is pleased with Daniel's insight into what Martin Heidegger had termed *Geworfenheit* (throwness) and adds that this thrown life "somehow becomes our own," that "we get used to it, and it becomes, so to speak, our self."

THE KING

Lagerkvist's sixth play, *The King*, in three acts, is a mythic drama concerning the ritual of a king's being reduced to beggary for one day, during which a member of the lowest class, in this case a criminal, rules as king. The criminal-king instigates a rebellion of his class against the upper classes and with its success assumes permanent power. The real king, as a member of the rebel horde, has been killed. Apart from its mythic information, the play is entirely conventional in structure and development. The image of deformity is retained, this time in a king's fool who is hunchbacked and a dwarf. The theme of authenticity is worked out as both the real king and the criminal-king realize their true selves in their changed roles. Historically, the play reflects the proletarian and God-is-dead movements: The new king commends a young man, whose life he has spared, for vowing to serve humankind after he, the king, has declared, "There are no divine laws any more." Stylistically, the play shares the simplicity and spareness of Lagerkvist's later narrative fiction.

THE HANGMAN

A long one-act play adapted from his novella of the same title, *The Hangman* (also known as *The Executioner*), shows Lagerkvist at the peak of his talent as a dramatist. The play begins in a medieval tavern that later becomes a modern nightclub and the scene of a race riot with Nazi-like whites shooting and killing members of a black jazz band. There are three separate tableaux, each implicating the executioner, as a figure of evil, in an act of love. In the first, he lets a boy drink from his hand and thereby frees the boy from a curse. In the second, he saves the life of a

woman whom he is to behead by marrying her and loving her. In the last, he presides over the Crucifixion of Christ, who calls him brother; the executioner then calls out that God is dead and that he himself is the living Christ whose task it has always been and always will be to shed blood as the means of relieving humankind of its burden of guilt.

The image of deformity is limited to blindness in *The Hangman* and, except for Deaf Anna in *Midsummer Dream in the Workhouse*, in Lagerkvist's last six plays. In two of those last six plays, *Seger i mörker* (victory in the dark) and *Barabbas*, there is not even a blind person, but both plays sustain and intensify Lagerkvist's expression of anguish at human blindness to human values.

THE MAN WITHOUT A SOUL

The Man Without a Soul and *Seger i mörker*, in, respectively, five acts and four acts, are political dramas reminiscent of the Spanish civil war and other European events of the late 1930's. The man without a soul is the unfeeling murderer of a member of the political opposition. He enters into a relationship with a woman whom he learns is the mistress of the man he has killed. The knowledge of his evil coupled with his experience of love for the woman gives birth to his soul, or his authenticity, as the woman gives birth to her former lover's son. The woman dies in childbirth. The man, sentenced to death for deserting his comrades, dies in soul-birth as he goes to his execution in a flood of light with head uplifted.

SEGER I MÖRKER

Seger i mörker follows the mythic device of rival brothers. Robert Grant, stepbrother to Gabriel Fontan, the premier of a democratic government, conspires to overthrow the government and install a military dictatorship. He succeeds, but Gabriel gains a victory of the spirit as he, having been unfaithful to his wife, Stella, is reconciled with her before both are to be executed. They reaffirm their love and their faith in the political ideals they have shared. Robert, distraught over Stella's refusal to be spared, remains alone in the cell from which the husband and wife have been led to the firing squad, collapses on hearing the salvo, and crawls about like an animal as the sounds of airplanes and bombs draw ominously nearer and nearer. The darkness enshrouding Robert's victory is the darkness of the jungle.

Both these political dramas are as dramaturgically conventional and as formal as any of Ibsen's plays. The same is true of *The Philosopher's Stone*. At the same time, all three maintain and intensify Lagerkvist's constant themes of light and darkness, love and evil, individual authenticity, and the divinity of the human spirit. He reverts to Strindbergian expressionism in *Midsummer Dream in the Workhouse* and *Let Man Live*, but only as he nears the end of working his vein of drama.

MIDSUMMER DREAM IN THE WORKHOUSE

Midsummer Dream in the Workhouse, with *The Difficult Hour, I-III*, *The Man Who Lived His Life Over*, and *The Hangman*, is the most successful of Lagerkvist's plays. *Midsummer Dream in the Workhouse* is a dream play in which Blind Jonas creates an imaginary world for a young Cecilia and manages to inhabit that world himself. If this play were to have an epigraph, it would be the words of Boman in *The Man Who Lived His Life Over*:

> Yes, we live as well as we can . . . this hard, hard life . . . we endure it . . . drag ourselves through it . . . day by day, year after year . . . as well as we are able to. . . . And we have our dreams, we have our dreams! Have you thought about that? Oh, there is generosity, there is generosity. . . . And we have our dreams.

Gustafson has written that in this play "Lagerkvist experiments with a strange blend of delicate dream elements and a coarse realism of situation and dialogue to produce a dramatic fantasy of haunting beauty."

THE PHILOSOPHER'S STONE

The Philosopher's Stone (literally, "the wise men's stone"; the pun on alchemy and the Magi of the New Testament is lost in translation) is Lagerkvist's longest play. Its four acts are somewhat marred by passages of awkward exposition and unengaging, lengthy dialogue. Albertus is an alchemist with faith in science but without religious faith. His wife, Maria, is a devout Christian. His friend Simonides is a dedicated rabbi, whose son Jacob wants to marry Albertus's daughter Catherine. Neither father approves

of the marriage, which does not take place. Instead, Jacob is executed for killing a constable from whose hands he sought to rescue Catherine. Simonides and his followers are expelled from their ghetto. Catherine, to her mother's joy, decides to become a nun. Albertus lets the fire in his laboratory oven go out. Neither Albertus, obsessed with his chemical search for gold, nor Maria and Simonides, obsessed with their respective gods, fosters the human love that Catherine and Jacob wished to consummate. Science and religion are not at odds in this play, although initially they seem to be. Actually, they prove to be unwitting coconspirators against the human spirit.

LET MAN LIVE

From the conventional format of *The Philosopher's Stone*, Lagerkvist turns to a one-act recitative in *Let Man Live*. There are fourteen speakers: Judas Iscariot, who committed suicide, and thirteen who were executed: Richard, a seventeen-year-old radio operator killed while working for the underground; Joe, a black man who wanted to be a jazz saxophonist and who was lynched on suspicion of having danced with a white woman; Comtesse de la Roche-Montfaucon; a serf caught stealing meat; a witch who had had sexual intercourse with Satan; Giordano Bruno; an Inca chief killed by Christians; Jeanne d'Arc; Paolo and Francesca; a Christian martyr; Jesus; and Socrates. Each of the speakers addresses the audience directly and attests fidelity to his or her true self: Each has died as the price of having lived authentically. The plotless recitative ends with Paolo and Francesca calling on the audience to let man live. The work has been called an oratorio; it is also something of an oral chaconne.

BARABBAS

Lagerkvist's dramatization of his novel *Barabbas* is cast in two acts, each divided into five scenes. The play opens and closes with a prospect of the three crosses on Golgotha. *Barabbas* is the story of an evil man redeemed by his authentic desire for a faith that he cannot achieve or understand and for a love that he cannot experience. At the end of both the novel and the play, Barabbas goes to his death physically with, but psychologically apart from, the Christians, whose Lord is love. Of the filmed *Barabbas*, it may be said that many of the scenes—the crucifixions, the eclipse of the sun, the copper-mine episode—and the character of Sahak are evocative of effects of Lagerkvist's novel and play, but such excesses as the needlessly complex scenario and the transformation of Barabbas into a gladiator are inconsistent with Lagerkvist's dark simplicity.

In the play *Barabbas*, the physical and psychological chiaroscuro and the titular character's groping for love do much to evoke the effects of *Sista mänskan*, but with *Barabbas*, Lagerkvist seems to have realized his intention with regard to those effects and seems also to have satisfied himself that he has done what he set out as a playwright to do. In *Sista mänskan*, there is this note on *Seger i mörker*: "Love is the one essential thing. All the other things are side effects. They have their importance as props—but love is the play itself." This note may be equivalent to a summary of Lagerkvist's intention as a playwright.

OTHER MAJOR WORKS

LONG FICTION: *Människor*, 1912 (novella); *Det eviga leendet*, 1920 (novella; *The Eternal Smile*, 1934); *Gäst hos verkligheten*, 1925 (novella; *Guest of Reality*, 1936); *Bödeln*, 1933 (novella; *The Hangman*, 1936); *Dvärgen*, 1944 (*The Dwarf*, 1945); *Barabbas*, 1950 (English translation, 1951); *Sibyllan*, 1956 (*The Sibyl*, 1958); *Ahasverus död*, 1960 (*The Death of Ahasuerus*, 1962); *Pilgrim på havet*, 1962 (*Pilgrim at Sea*, 1964); *Det heliga landet*, 1964 (*The Holy Land*, 1966); *Pilgrimen*, 1966 (collective title for previous 3 novels); *Mariamne*, 1967 (*Herod and Mariamne*, 1968).

SHORT FICTION: *Två sagor om livet*, 1913; *Järn och människor*, 1915; *Onda sagor*, 1924; *Kämpande ande*, 1930; *I den tiden*, 1935; *The Eternal Smile and Other Stories*, 1954; *The Marriage Feast and Other Stories*, 1955; *Prosa I-V*, 1956; *The Eternal Smile: Three Stories*, 1971.

POETRY: *Ångest*, 1916; *Den lyckliges väg*, 1921; *Hjärtats sånger*, 1926; *Vid lägereld*, 1932; *Genius*, 1937; *Sång och strid*, 1940; *Dikter*, 1941; *Hemmet och stjärnan*, 1942; *Aftonland*, 1953 (*Evening Land*, 1975).

NONFICTION: *Ordkonst och bildkonst*, 1913 (*Literary Art and Pictorial Art*, 1982); *Teater*, 1918; "Modern teater: Synpunkter och angrepp," 1918 ("Modern Theatre: Points of View and Attack," 1966); *Det besegrade livet*, 1927; *Den knutna näven*, 1934 (*The Clenched Fist*, 1982); *Den befriade människan*, 1939; *Antecknat*, 1977.

MISCELLANEOUS: *Motiv*, 1914 (poetry, essays, and prose sketches); *Kaos*, 1919 (poetry and the play *The Secret of Heaven*); *Modern Theatre: Seven Plays and an Essay*, 1966; *Five Early Works*, 1989.

BIBLIOGRAPHY

Scobbie, Irene. *Pär Lagerkvist: Gäst hos verkligheten*. 2d ed. Hull: Orton and Holmes, 1976. A study of Lagerkvist that focuses on his novel, *Guest of Reality*. Provides insights into the drama. Bibliography.

_____, ed. *Aspects of Modern Swedish Literature*. Rev. ed. Chester Springs, Pa.: Dufour Editions, 1999. Contains an in-depth study of Lagerkvist, among other writers.

Sjöberg, Leif. *Pär Lagerkvist*. New York: Columbia University Press, 1976. A study that combines biographical information on Lagerkvist with criticism of his works. Bibliography and index.

Spector, Robert Donald. *Pär Lagerkvist*. New York: Twayne, 1973. A basic biography of Lagerkvist that covers his life and works. Bibliography.

Warme, Lars G. *A History of Swedish Literature*. Lincoln: University of Nebraska Press, 1996. A scholarly study of Swedish literature that covers significant writers such as Lagerkvist.

White, Ray Lewis. *Pär Lagerkvist in America*. Atlantic Highlands, N.J.: Humanities Press, 1979. A look at the appreciation for Lagerkvist in the United States. Bibliography.

Roy Arthur Swanson

ARTHUR LAURENTS

Born: Brooklyn, New York; July 14, 1918

PRINCIPAL DRAMA

Home of the Brave, pr. 1945, pb. 1946

Heartsong, pr. 1947

The Bird Cage, pr., pb. 1950

The Time of the Cuckoo, pr. 1952, pb. 1953

A Clearing in the Woods, pr., pb. 1957

West Side Story, pr. 1957, pb. 1958 (libretto; lyrics by Stephen Sondheim, music by Leonard Bernstein)

Gypsy, pr. 1959, pb. 1960 (libretto; adaptation of Gypsy Rose Lee's autobiography; lyrics by Sondheim, music by Jule Styne)

Invitation to a March, pr. 1960, pb. 1961

Anyone Can Whistle, pr. 1964, pb. 1965 (music by Sondheim)

Do I Hear a Waltz?, pr. 1965, pb. 1966 (libretto; lyrics by Sondheim, music by Richard Rodgers)

Hallelujah, Baby!, pr., pb. 1967 (libretto; lyrics and music by Styne, Betty Comden, and Adolph Green)

The Enclave, pr. 1973, pb. 1974

A Loss of Memory, pr. 1981, pb. 1983

Nick and Nora, pr. 1991 (libretto; lyrics by Richard Maltby, Jr., music by Charles Strouse)

Jolson Sings Again, pr. 1995, revised pr. 1999

The Radical Mystique, pr. 1995, pb. 1996

My Good Name, pr. 1997

Big Potato, pr. 2000

Venecia, pr. 2001 (adaptation of Jorge Accame's play)

Claudia Lazlo, pr. 2001

OTHER LITERARY FORMS

Although primarily a playwright and author of librettos for several musicals, Arthur Laurents has also written for both radio and the movies. Shortly after his first Broadway success, he began writing screenplays as well, producing eight over the next thirty years: *The Snake Pit* (1948, with Frank Partos and Millen Brand), *Rope* (1948, with Hume Cronyn), *Caught* (1949), *Anna Lucasta* (1949, with Philip Yordan), *Anastasia* (1956), *Bonjour Tristesse* (1958), *The Way We Were* (1973), and *The Turning Point* (1977). Because of their wide popularity with moviegoers, Laurents wrote novelizations of both *The Way We Were* and *The Turning Point*. His foray into work for television came in 1967, with the script for *The Light Fantastic: How to Tell Your Past, Present, and Future Through Social Dancing*. In 2000, Laurents published *Original Story By: A Memoir of Broadway and Hollywood*.

ACHIEVEMENTS

Among American dramatists of his generation, Arthur Laurents certainly stands out as one of the more versatile: He is the author of plays that have received New York productions as well as of Broadway musicals, several radio plays and one-act plays, Hollywood screenplays, novels based on screenplays, and a teleplay. Other plays or musicals have been given minor productions—all this while Laurents himself has become involved in directing, both his own works and those of others, and even in coproducing a film. A few of his radio plays, including *Western Electric Communicade* (1944) and *The Face* (1945), have been selected for inclusion in collections of "best" one-act plays. His first Broadway success, *Home of the Brave*, won for him the Sidney Howard Memorial Award in 1946; this was followed in the next decade by three additional Broadway productions: *The Bird Cage*, *The Time of the Cuckoo*, and *A Clearing in the Woods*.

In the mid-1950's, Laurents began his collaboration with Stephen Sondheim, writing the librettos for a series of musicals—an association that would last a decade and result in two of the most important works in the genre, *West Side Story* and *Gypsy*. The libretto for the latter work is so strong that it could almost stand on its own, without the songs, as a serious play, making it both the culmination and the epitome of a long line of book musicals. Little wonder that Sondheim singled out Laurents as one of the best book writers in the musical theater, or that he collaborated with him on the original *Anyone Can Whistle*. Sandwiched in between the musicals with Sondheim was Laurents's last Broadway play *Invitation to a March*, although his full-length work *The Enclave* did receive an Off-Broadway production in 1973.

Ever since the late 1940's, Laurents has lent variety to his writing career by work in film, providing screenplays for a number of well-received movies, including *Anastasia*, *Bonjour Tristesse*, *The Way We Were*, and *The Turning Point*, the last of which he coproduced and which won the Writers Guild of America Award, the Golden Globe Award, and the National Board of Review Best Picture Award. The 1960's and 1970's saw Laurents extend his expertise to yet another area of theatrical activity when he began to direct a number of his own works, including the highly successful London and New York revival

Arthur Laurents watches dance rehearsals for the film version of West Side Story *in 1960.* (Hulton Archive by Getty Images)

of *Gypsy* during the 1973-1974 season. He also directed the Broadway blockbuster *La Cage aux Folles*, which won the 1984 Tony Award for Best Musical.

BIOGRAPHY

The son of a lawyer (Irving) and a schoolteacher (Ada), Arthur Laurents was born in Brooklyn on July 14, 1918. A summer camp gave him his first theater experience when he was cast in a play, *The Crow's Nest*, for his ability to climb up a ship's mast and remember his lines at the same time. "Theatre is fantasy, and you can make it all come true," he remarked in a later interview, when asked of his love for theater. He was graduated from Erasmus Hall High School and continued his education at Cornell University, earning a B.A. degree in English in 1937. He wrote radio plays until World War II, when he enlisted in the U.S. Army and eventually worked in films that helped train the troops. *The Face*, a short radio play from that period, appeared in *The Best One-act Plays of 1945-1946*.

After a few partially successful plays (such as *Home of the Brave* in 1945) and failed dramatic efforts, Laurents found Hollywood and his flair for writing mysteries and thrillers, such as *Rope* and *The Snake Pit*. He tried Broadway once again with *The Bird Cage* in 1950, and in 1965 he collaborated on the more successful *Do I Hear a Waltz?* with Richard Rodgers and Sondheim. His play *A Clearing in the Woods* was praised by critics as "ambitious and original." Laurents visited the musical genre once more in 1957 and wrote the book for Sondheim's and Leonard Bernstein's *West Side Story*, finally experiencing all the joys of a full Broadway hit; the film version (1961) earned eleven Academy Awards. The next musical success, *Gypsy*, was a collaboration with Sondheim and Jule Styne. It has been revived several times, including in 1989, with Laurents directing and Tyne Daly in the role of Rose, a role that had been played by Ethel Merman in the original and by Angela Lansbury in the 1974 revival.

The 1970's saw Laurents's most successful film work: the screenplays for both *The Way We Were* (1973, with Barbra Streisand and Robert Redford) and *The Turning Point* (1977, with Anne Bancroft and Shirley MacLaine). In 1983, he directed *La Cage aux Folles*. Returning to writing Broadway musical theater after some years, Laurents pinned his hopes on *Nick and Nora* (a musical version of the novel and film series *The Thin Man*), which opened in December of 1991, and which he directed. *Nick and Nora* closed after one week to depressingly negative but apparently well-aimed reviews.

During the 1990's Laurents returned to writing drama; six of his new plays were produced at regional theaters and Off-Broadway. *The Radical Mystique*, also directed by Laurents, is set in a 1970's party given by well-intentioned liberals for Black Panthers. *My Good Name* explores self-hatred among successful Jews. *Jolson Sings Again*, a revised version of a play first produced in Seattle in 1995, deals with the 1950's anticommunist Hollywood witch-hunt. Laurents repudiated the 2000 production of *Big Potato*, an examination of Jewish reactions to the Holocaust. *Venecia* was adapted by Laurents from an original play in Spanish by Argentinean Jorge Accame that had been translated by Laurents's lover Tom Hatcher. *Claudia Lazlo* used a play-within-a-play to examine Jewish reactions to former Nazis after World War II.

ANALYSIS

If Arthur Laurents can be said to belong to any group of post-World War II American dramatists, his closest affinity is surely with those who might be called psychological realists and who came into maturity in the late 1940's and early 1950's, especially William Inge and Robert Anderson. Like them, Laurents is primarily a playwright who focuses on character. He often, though not always, portrays women caught up in the age of anxiety, beset by self-doubt or even self-loathing. Yet unlike either Inge or Anderson, Laurents reveals a solid measure of Thornton Wilder's influence, both in the generally optimistic philosophy as well as in the nonrealistic stylistic techniques of some of his later plays and musical books. Although he has, like Anderson, decried those playwrights, particularly of the late 1960's and 1970's, who value experiments in form and style over content, who make the manner rather than the matter count most, Laurents will depart from strict realism

and from a linear method of dramatizing his story when a legitimate reason exists for doing so, as he does in his use of narrators in *Invitation to a March* and *Anyone Can Whistle*, in his use of characters to change sets in *The Enclave*, and in his use of variations on the flashback technique in *Home of the Brave* and *A Clearing in the Woods*. As he says in the preface to *A Clearing in the Woods*, he willingly embraces greater theatricality if it brings with it a greater ability to illuminate the truth.

In that same preface, Laurents provides perhaps his clearest statement of the central insight into the human condition that pervades all of his writing for the theater: If men and women are lonely, and they are, it is because they cannot accept themselves for the flawed, imperfect creatures that they are; and until they achieve such self-acceptance, they will be unable to feel sufficiently, or to give of themselves sufficiently, to experience a sense of completion and fulfillment. When Laurents's characters are unhappy in this way, when they are hurting within themselves, they lash out and, attempting to deflect their own misery, hurt others. The pattern is as applicable to Peter Coen (*Home of the Brave*), Leona Samish (*The Time of the Cuckoo*), and Virginia (*A Clearing in the Woods*) as it is to Wally Williams (*The Bird Cage*), Mama Rose (*Gypsy*), or Ben (*The Enclave*). Wally, for example, is a sexually disturbed egomaniac who destroys others and eventually himself, while Ben has been hurting for so long from having to keep his homosexuality hidden that he finally decides to hurt his friends back by shocking them into recognition, if not acceptance, of his lover Wyman. Rose is the archetypal stage mother, seeking in her daughter's accomplishments a substitute for the success she never had. (The influence of parents in Laurents's work, it should be noted, is not invariably restrictive; for every Rose who uses a child to gain something for herself, there is a Camilla Jablonski—*Invitation to a March*—who, by example and urging, liberates the child.)

The diminished sense of self-worth exemplified by so many of Laurents's characters has an individual psychological basis, but it can also be greatly exacerbated by social forces, such as prejudicial attitudes and the drive to conform. The prejudice may be racial, as in *Home of the Brave*, *West Side Story*, and *Hallelujah, Baby!*, or sexual, as in *The Enclave*, while the conformity may be either in the area of perpetuating the success syndrome through seeking a comfortable economic status, as in *A Clearing in the Woods* and *Invitation to a March*, or in the inability to break free of repressive sexual mores and conventions, as in *The Time of the Cuckoo* and *Invitation to a March*. Finally, Laurents's characters are often plagued by an impossible dream, by a desire to find magic in their lives. Sometimes the magic is short-lived, as it is for Leona in *The Time of the Cuckoo* or for the young lovers in *West Side Story*; at other times, it endures, as it does for Camilla, Norma, and Aaron in *Invitation to a March* or for Fay Apple in *Anyone Can Whistle*. Indeed, characters such as Camilla and Fay (complicated women who need and, luckily, find heroes) come closest to embodying Laurents's ideal of being free and wholly alive, of enjoying each and every moment, an ideal that he seems to have inherited from Wilder. If Laurents's upbeat endings sometimes seem slightly forced and if his sentiment once in a while veers over into sentimentality, he remains an intelligent, sensitive, and thoroughly professional man of the theater.

No one would claim that Laurents belongs among the indisputably first-rank dramatists (with Eugene O'Neill and Tennessee Williams, for example). Still, he has produced, along with librettos for two of the best works of the musical theater—*West Side Story* and *Gypsy*—one or two memorable plays that readers will return to and little theaters will revive: *The Time of the Cuckoo* and *Invitation to a March*. The latter work, in fact, with its deft handling of tone and comfortable assimilation of Wilder's philosophical outlook and stage techniques to Laurents's own purpose, may finally be seen as his most significant play.

Because Laurents's major efforts are so varied in form and structure, he remains difficult to categorize. He resembles both Lillian Hellman and Arthur Miller in his hatred of prejudice and his compassion for those who must hide a facet of themselves, whether racial or sexual, to avoid rejection. In Laurents, however, it is not only, or even primarily, the other person or society that seeks to limit his characters' world;

rather, the central characters themselves, through their psychological inhibitions and moral or sexual repression, circumscribe their own existence. Like several other playwrights from the decade immediately following World War II, Laurents has not always escaped criticism for his "group therapy session" or "pop psychologizing" plays, which have, admittedly, sometimes ended with victories too contrived or too easily won: Simply recognizing one's own frailties does not always assure a newfound freedom and integration and maturity. Laurents's accurate reading of modern human beings' injured psyches, awash in the anxiety and self-doubt that inevitably accompany any search for an ethical system running counter to traditional social and sexual mores, remains in somewhat uneasy balance with his innately positive view that the individual can win through to a sense of personal wholeness. Yet Laurents dramatizes this tension with such honesty and in such understated terms that Coney's and Leona's and Norma's victories seem to be the audience's own; the illusion complete, they, too, at least momentarily hear a waltz. Like his spokeswoman Camilla in *Invitation to a March*, Laurents at his best can be an adroit stage manager, gently pulling the strings that have always moved audiences in the theater.

HOME OF THE BRAVE

A taut drama about prejudice during World War II, Laurents's *Home of the Brave* dramatizes how the experience of being condemned as an outsider, being made to feel different from others, affects the victim. Although not as theatrically elaborate as Peter Shaffer's *Equus* (pr. 1973) three decades later, *Home of the Brave* employs a surprisingly similar dramatic strategy: A doctor attempts to uncover the cause of a patient's symptoms by having the patient, under the influence of drugs, abreact, or therapeutically act out traumatic events from the past; what might appear to be flashbacks, then, are more accurately considered as deeply embedded memories now reenacted. Private First Class Peter Coen (nicknamed "Coney") suffers from paralysis and amnesia brought on when, of necessity, he left behind his friend Finch during a dangerous reconnaissance mission on a Japanese island. For a long time, the sensitive Finch (he retches after having to kill an enemy soldier) had been one of the few to refrain from—and even physically defend Coney against—the anti-Semitic remarks rampant among the other soldiers. Especially guilty is Colonel T. J. Everitt, a former company vice president who makes Coney the butt of his resentment over finding himself at war, not seeing any connection between his attitudes and those of the enemy.

Coney has been on the receiving end of such hatred ever since grade school, and Doctor Bitterger counsels that for his own good Coney must, to a degree, become desensitized to such unthinking prejudice. Under the pressure of their fatal wartime mission, Finch had hesitatingly called him a "lousy yellow . . . jerk," and Coney sensed then that Finch had caught himself just in time to prevent "Jew bastard" from slipping out. When Finch died and Coney's gut reaction was to be glad that it was not he who was killed, he felt shame and guilt, and he continues to imagine that there was some connection between the momentary hatred he experienced for Finch and his not staying behind and dying with him. Although Bitterger helps his patient understand intellectually that he acted in much the same way in which anyone else might have under the same circumstances, this realization does not sink into Coney's heart until another soldier, Mingo, recounts a similar experience.

Coney is not the only soldier whom Mingo tutors. Their commander, Major Robinson, though—like Mingo and Finch—essentially free of judging others in terms of racial distinctions, still experiences some difficulty in knowing how to command a group of men. Younger than some of the soldiers under him, Robinson attempts to compensate for lack of experience through an excess of enthusiasm, seeing war metaphorically as a game to be won. He cannot easily admit that his men might instinctively know more than he does—he fails, for example, to see T. J. for the bigot he is—nor does he fully understand that they deserve respect as men just as much as he does as an officer. Mingo, already overly sensitive to the fact that his poet-wife is better educated than he, has recently received a "Dear John" letter telling him she is leaving him for another man. When, as a result of

the mission on which Finch was killed, Mingo loses an arm, he feels doubly afraid to return home, since as a disabled person he will now be one of society's outsiders.

When Coney discovers that Mingo, too, despite his crippling injury, felt glad to be alive when he saw comrades die, he has a vision of his communion with all humanity: Despite differences, all men are fundamentally the same. Two frightened individuals can now go home from the war brave enough to start life again. Together Coney and Mingo will open the bar that Coney had originally planned to run with Finch. The land to which they will return is not yet free of the prejudice that wounds men like Coney and Mingo, and this helps keep Laurents's ending from being too saccharine. If the revelation that Coney receives seems perhaps too meager to effect much in the way of a permanent cure, Laurents's play is for that very reason both honest and understated.

THE TIME OF THE CUCKOO

Perhaps because of the perennially popular 1955 Katharine Hepburn movie *Summertime* that was adapted from it, *The Time of the Cuckoo* will probably remain the best remembered of Laurents's plays. This bittersweet romance concerns a clash of cultures, of lifestyles, that occurs when Leona Samish, a thirtyish American single woman, has a brief affair in Venice with the somewhat older and attractively silver-haired Renato Di Rossi. As Leona remarks, Americans abroad carry with them "more than a suitcase": They bring a whole trunk load of attitudes and values, manners and mores. New World brashness confronts Old World charm; money—in the person of the boorish Lloyd McIlhenny on a hop-skip-and-a-jump tour with his wife—meets culture; and puritan guilt and repression come up against an instinctive lust for life. Partly under the tutelage of Signora Fioria, at whose pensione the action occurs, Leona can overcome her initial qualms and experience her night of love with Di Rossi, a devoted father enduring a now loveless marriage.

Signora Fioria and Di Rossi both serve as foils to the American tourist in matters of sexual morality. Di Rossi, regarding himself as a kind of spokesperson for Mediterranean culture, believes that abstract notions of right and wrong simply do not exist; to live life fully and to make contact with others is the only good, and so he bemoans the tendency of Americans to always "feel bad" and wallow in sexual guilt. Signora Fioria, who had an affair while her husband was alive and is having another now, also deems as "impractical" any morality except discretion, urging others to live life as it is, being certain only to leave it a little "sweeter" than they found it by entering a giving relationship from which they do not necessarily get anything in return. The values of these two Italians gain added weight when Laurents shows the shortcomings of the traditional notions of sexual morality by which another American couple, the young, beautiful, blond Yaegers, live and love. Eddie Yaeger, an artist whose later work has never measured up to his first exhibit, suffers from painter's block; his wife June, earlier married to a musician, suffers from something even less tangible but equally destructive: the romantic ideal that a wife must be her husband's complete life. She attributes Eddie's infidelities with Signora Fioria to his temporary inability to create, and she reconciles with him—albeit in an uneasy truce—only after he comes around to her strict notion that love cannot be love without complete fidelity. Into this subplot, Laurents introduces as well a staple theme of the 1950's, lack of communication, through Eddie's comment that language is often a method of "excommunication" and June's observation that people without the ability to talk might feel less alone.

What finally prevents Leona and Di Rossi from achieving even a shaky truce is not so much their differing attitudes toward sexual morality and the need for love as a failure within Leona herself. A woman who prides herself on independence but who is increasingly hiding her insecurities behind drink, she underestimates her attractiveness to Di Rossi; if she at first acts insulted by his forwardness, she later thinks he must want her only for her money. What finally brings her around to Di Rossi is not, however, his and Signora Fioria's accusations that she actually insults herself by having so little self-esteem, but rather his gift of a garnet necklace, a gesture so overwhelming that she—together with the audience—hears a waltz. When it appears that he has made

money off her by exchanging her dollars for counterfeit on the black market, however, she rejects him. Emotionally bruised herself, she must hurt others by telling June about Eddie and Signora Fioria. The "wonderful mystical magical miracle," the impossibly romantic ideal she had hoped to and did fleetingly meet in Italy, evaporates quickly, yet it leaves Leona with a new awareness of her limitations: her inability to love herself; her need for someone outside herself to confirm her value and self-worth by wanting her.

Her souvenirs of Venice—two wine-red eighteenth century goblets that she buys in Di Rossi's shop and the longed-for garnet necklace that he gives her—suggest by their color her long repressed passion. That she insists on keeping the necklace, that she must take something tangible home with her, indicates her insecurity, her need for things as a proof of feelings. Leona has not yet outgrown her inability to give of herself without getting something in return, and she finds it difficult to believe that others can either: When the street urchin Mauro, who has been trying to swindle her all along, offers a souvenir for free, she still instinctively wonders why, rather than simply saying thank you. It is not clear whether she will return to America any the wiser, but at least she stays in Venice to complete her vacation rather than fleeing further experiences that might test her conventional moral code.

A CLEARING IN THE WOODS

A Clearing in the Woods concerns a woman who must confront the past in order to move into the future, thus continuing Laurents's exploration of the need for psychological wholeness. The most theatrically intricate—and, according to the playwright's own testimony, the most difficult yet satisfying of his plays to write—it does not lend itself to simple categorization. Laurents himself discounts all the formulas—flashback, dream, nightmare, hallucination, psychoanalysis, psychodrama—that might readily describe this play in which not only the woman Virginia but also her three former selves appear onstage. Even stream of consciousness does not seem an accurate enough classification; perhaps nonrealistic fantasy, with a dose of expressionism, comes closest. Each of Virginia's three earlier selves is seen mainly in the way she interacts with a man—father, teenage "lover," husband—in acted out fragments of her past experience.

Jigee, Virginia as a little girl of nine or ten, rebels against both the restraints and lack of attention of her father Barney; she feels, in fact, cut off from both her parents—distant from a mother too absorbed in her father, as well as jealous of her mother's hold over him. In a plea that he pay attention to her, she cuts off his necktie, wishing it were the tongue that had lashed out. Virginia's initiation into sexuality is seen through Nora, her seventeen-year-old self who goes off with a woodchopper, as simultaneously in the present, Virginia enters the cottage for an abortive assignation with George, a suspect homespun philosopher who counsels enjoying the pleasures of today that lead to pleasant memories tomorrow while he advocates a belief in "Nothing," for then there can be no risk of disappointment and disillusionment. Virginia's lack of success in marriage is seen through twenty-six-year-old Ginna's relationship with Pete. The big man on campus, he had married her thinking she was pregnant; he never reaches his potential, and his life seems to have peaked at twenty. No longer sexually excited by her and believing not only that she has given up on him but also that she actually feels glad when he fails, Pete is temporarily impotent, effectively emasculated by Ginna.

Like Virginia now, neither Nora nor Ginna wanted to be ordinary; each wanted a life somehow special and set apart from that of ordinary people. This same desire stands in the way of Virginia's marrying Andy. Two years before the present time of the play, she had called off their engagement on their wedding day, knowing that he would always be simply a competent researcher rather than a brilliant discoverer. Virginia now invites him to cross over the magic circle and enter the fantasy world of the clearing in the woods with her, hoping to erase that day as if it had never happened, but like Ginna with Pete, Virginia demands that Andy live up to her goals for him and will be angry if he fails, while he is happier accepting and living within his limitations. Because Virginia has never been satisfied with herself, she has placed unhealthy, destructive expectations on others. As Bit-

terger does for Coney in *Home of the Brave*, Andy acts as a kind of therapist for Virginia, helping her see that she has never really loved anyone, even herself, and that she has consequently destroyed the men in her life. Yet as each of the men returns in the present, she discovers that her impact on them has not been wholly negative: The boy in the woods, who actually thought Nora pretty and not ordinary, surreptitiously left a bouquet of flowers behind; Pete, now remarried, reveals that Ginna actually provided color and excitement in his rather ordinary existence; and Barney, now on the wagon, can be reconciled with his adult daughter by their mutual understanding that a parent sometimes needs more love than a resentful child is willing to offer. Virginia, by becoming content with herself as she is rather than seeking a false image that could never be, can finally accommodate her former selves rather than deny their existence. By accepting them for what they can teach her about herself, she can reach integration and move freely and with hope into the future.

INVITATION TO A MARCH

Invitation to a March is a charming romantic comedy about people's need to march to no drummer at all, even to break out and dance. Deedee and Tucker Grogan have come east to the Long Island coast to see their son Schuyler married to Norma Brown. Deedee and Norma's mother, Lily, the widow of a General who starts each day with a flag ceremony complete with toy bugle, are conventional, status-happy women: Deedee has wealth, Lily, social position, and both are morally proper; yet their limited lives are dull, dreary, without adventure, and it annoys them even to think that others might have something more. The bride-to-be's one peculiarity is her propensity to fall asleep for no apparent reason; this odd habit is her quiet revolt against the conformity and complacency that surround her. She sleeps because life is not worth staying awake for—that is, until Aaron Jablonski, riding on a horse in the rose-colored light, arrives to fix the plumbing and wakes her with a kiss. If Schuyler's mother, Deedee, is literary cousin to Lloyd McIlhenny from *The Time of the Cuckoo*, Aaron's mother, Camilla, is drawn in the same mold as Signora Fioria and Renato Di Rossi.

Although many of the characters in *Invitation to a March* at times face front and unselfconsciously and ingratiatingly address the audience, taking them into their confidence and interpreting for them, Camilla is the chief of these narrators—and the playwright's mouthpiece. There is more than a little of the down-to-earth philosophizing of Wilder's Stage Manager about her, and more than a bit of Wilder's point of view within the play. A wacky individualist, a free spirit who treasures the adventures life offers, Camilla knows that one can deaden life by not living it the way one wants to; since time passes and one does not have many chances, one must take the opportunities that present themselves, as she did twenty years earlier during a summer romance with Aaron's father—who turns out to be Tucker Grogan and thus will be the father of the groom no matter what. Tucker had made Camilla feel attractive simply by wanting her, and for all these years the memory of that time, nurtured by imagination, has sustained her so that she has wanted no other man. She found her magic.

Norma's similarity to Camilla reveals itself in her penchant for tearing up calendar pages, an act symbolic of her desire to break free from the restrictions of a confined, regimented life. In the play's title passage, Camilla warns about all the marchers in the world who try to take away one's individuality, who want one to toe the line, to move in lockstep, as do those in the military. It is easier and safer to submit than to assert one's difference, but it is finally deadly dull to do so. Although Norma feels no guilt after her first night with Aaron, it takes some time before she can break free and dance by giving up the prospects of a secure and success-oriented life in suburbia with a lawyer-husband and replace that goal with her love for Aaron. Eventually, though, they do hear their waltz, and they do dance off.

Camilla makes no excuses for her conduct; what she did was right for her. If she has any guilt, it stems from her selfishness in letting Aaron love her so much that he finds it temporarily difficult to love another. Tucker is not perfect either; finding it awkward to communicate with other men, he has never made enough effort until now to reach out to Schuyler. Al-

though Schuyler, so much the prisoner of conventionality that he cannot respond to feelings, finds the shoe Norma kicks off before she dances away, he is no Prince Charming—in fact, he confesses to not believing in princes anymore—and so he symbolically falls asleep, a victim of the march, while his fully awakened and alive beauty waltzes off with another.

JOLSON SINGS AGAIN

Laurents revisited a political theme included in his initial movie script for *The Way We Were*. Having been briefly blacklisted himself, Laurents had wanted the film to examine the morality of informing about one's friends during Hollywood's blacklisting days in the late 1940's and early 1950's, but the director eliminated that theme, preferring to focus on the romance between the film's stars. The play's title refers to actor Larry Parks, star of the movie *The Jolson Story*, who testified about the activities of his comrades before the House Un-American Activities Committee investigating communists in Hollywood. Newsboys selling papers reporting Parks's testimony shouted, "Jolson Sings Again!"

In the play, four friends find their relationship damaged when subpoenaed to testify before the committee. The story explores the questions of where to draw the line against informing on one's friends and whether to associate with such informers. When Andreas testifies before the committee, Julian, a young gay playwright, breaks with Andreas, the director who had turned Julian's plays into major successes on stage and screen. Although Andreas is ashamed of what he has done, he defends his actions by asserting that making films was so important to him that the fear of blacklisting and being prevented from working in Hollywood overcame his feelings of guilt. Further he claims that he only named persons already named and, therefore, had not hurt anyone. Robbie, a Hollywood agent who is having an affair with Andreas, condones his behavior, but Robbie's husband Sidney, an uncompromisingly liberal screenwriter, condemns him.

Julian continues to have his plays produced on Broadway, where blacklisting did not apply, but when staged by other directors, his plays do not succeed. After having avoided Andreas for ten years, Julian finally turns to him with his latest play. Laurents's characters explore the complex interplay between personal principles and individual self-interest as each person faces the prospect of being blacklisted and prevented from pursuing a Hollywood career.

CLAUDIA LAZLO

The setting is a regional theater company rehearsing a play about an opera singer with a Nazi past in post-World War II Austria. The main play portrays the interactions of actors, director, and stage manager during the rehearsal. In the play-within-a-play, Claudia Lazlo is a brilliant soprano denied work in postwar Salzburg by a U.S. Army captain because she was a card-carrying Nazi. An admiring Jewish American lieutenant takes up her cause, offering to marry her to help her gain permission to resume her singing career.

As in *Jolson Sings Again*, Laurents examines the problem of where to draw the line between principle and self-interest. In the play-within-a-play, he asks what price an artist can morally agree to pay in order to pursue her career and questions how many political sins even a transcendent artist may be forgiven. The rehearsal scenes explore the way actors identify with the characters they portray, permitting Laurents to depict how directors, managers, and actors react to the text of a play.

OTHER MAJOR WORKS

LONG FICTION: *The Way We Were*, 1972 (novelization of his screenplay); *The Turning Point*, 1977 (novelization of his screenplay).

SCREENPLAYS: *The Snake Pit*, 1948 (with Frank Partos and Millen Brand); *Rope*, 1948 (with Hume Cronyn); *Caught*, 1949; *Anna Lucasta*, 1949 (with Philip Yordan); *Anastasia*, 1956; *Bonjour Tristesse*, 1958; *The Way We Were*, 1973; *The Turning Point*, 1977.

TELEPLAY: *The Light Fantastic: How to Tell Your Past, Present, and Future Through Social Dancing*, 1967.

RADIO PLAYS: *Now Playing Tomorrow*, 1939; *Western Electric Communicade*, 1944; *The Face*, 1945; *The Last Day of the War*, 1945.

NONFICTION: *Original Story By: A Memoir of Broadway and Hollywood*, 2000.

BIBLIOGRAPHY

Barnes, Clive. "Bad Idea Kills *Nick and Nora*." Review of *Nick and Nora*. *Post* (New York), December 9, 1991. According to Barnes, "a bad idea turned sour." He points at Laurents's multiple contribution as the main reason for the show's failure: "This is not a musical. It is a 'bookical'—a book with songs rather than a songbook."

"Decades Later, Naming Names Still Matters." *The New York Times*, March 14, 1999, Section 2, p. 7. Frank Rich interviews Laurents about *Jolson Sings Again*. Laurents describes his reasons for writing the play and explains his dislike for people whose testimony before the Un-American Activities Committee in the 1940's and 1950's destroyed the careers of their friends.

Guernsey, Otis L., Jr., ed. "An Ad Lib for Four Playwrights." In *Playwrights, Lyricists, Composers on Theater*. New York: Dodd, Mead, 1974. A conversation among Laurents, Sidney "Paddy" Chayefsky, Israel Horovitz, and Leonard Melfi, in which Laurents proves the most insightful regarding playwright expectations of directors and actors in production.

"*Gypsy* Stripped of Spirit." Review of *Gypsy*. *Post* (New York), November 17, 1989. This revival of *Gypsy*, with Tyne Daly in the role of Gypsy Rose Lee, was the second (a 1974 revival starred Angela Lansbury, and the original 1959 production starred Ethel Merman). Laurents directed this version and is here credited, with some reservations, for its success.

Kaufman, David. "When the Author Insists on Directing the Play, Too." *The New York Times*, February 11, 2001, Section 2, p. 5. Laurents explains how his dissatisfaction with other directors led him to undertake the task and discusses difficulties he discovered when directing his own plays.

Thomas P. Adler,
updated by Thomas J. Taylor and Milton Berman

RAY LAWLER

Born: Melbourne, Australia; May 23, 1921

PRINCIPAL DRAMA

Cradle of Thunder, pr. 1949
Summer of the Seventeenth Doll, pr. 1955, pb. 1957
    (commonly known as *The Doll*)
The Piccadilly Bushman, pr. 1959, pb. 1961,
    revised pb. 1998
The Unshaven Cheek, pr. 1963
The Man Who Shot the Albatross, pr. 1971
Kid Stakes, pr. 1975, pb. 1978
Other Times, pr. 1976, pb. 1978
The Doll Trilogy, pr. 1977, pb. 1978 (includes *Kid
    Stakes, Other Times, Summer of the Seventeenth
    Doll*)
Godsend, pr. 1982

OTHER LITERARY FORMS

Primarily known for his playwrighting, Ray
Lawler has written and adapted works for the British
Broadcasting Corporation.

ACHIEVEMENTS

Ray Lawler won first prize in a minor play competition in Melbourne, Australia, for his *Cradle of
Thunder* and wrote nine plays before becoming internationally famous with *Summer of the Seventeenth
Doll*. He shared first prize, worth about two hundred
dollars, for *Summer of the Seventeenth Doll* in a competition sponsored by the Playwrights Advisory
Board in 1955. *The Doll*, as it is known among Australian theater aficionados, was one of 130 plays submitted for judging. It shared first prize with a play by
Oriel Gray, *The Torrents*, and served as Lawler's cat-
apult to fame. With this play, he almost single-
handedly revolutionized Australian theater, bringing
it out of its previous lethargy.

Prior to the production of *Summer of the Seventeenth Doll*, there had been a feeling in Australia that
the homegrown dramatic product was inferior to foreign drama. It was largely because of the unparalleled
international success of *Summer of the Seventeenth
Doll* that Australian theater enjoyed a spectacular period of growth throughout the late 1950's and during
the next two decades. Today, Australian theater is
produced throughout the English-speaking world,
and even in non-English-speaking countries. With his
play, which won the *Evening Standard* Award for
Best Play in 1957, Lawler helped to stimulate Australians to a fuller appreciation of their own culture, not
only in terms of theater but also in other fields of artistic endeavor, such as literature, music, and the plas-
tic arts.

BIOGRAPHY

Raymond Evenor Lawler was one of eight children born to a tradesman in Melbourne, Australia. At
the age of thirteen, Lawler started work in an engineering plant and took lessons in acting in his spare
time. When he was twenty-three, he sold his first
play, which was never produced, to J. C. Williamson's theatrical company, known in Australia simply
as "the Firm." Lawler acted and wrote pantomimes
and scripts for revues, and when he was in his mid-
thirties, he became manager and director of the
Union Theatre Repertory Company. While in that position, he worked on the script of his masterpiece,
Summer of the Seventeenth Doll, in which he had
written a part for himself, that of Barney.

Lawler appeared in the original Australian production and in both the London West End and New
York Broadway productions, and his work as an actor
received high praise. After the early closing of the
Broadway production, he moved to Denmark; later,
he returned to London, then moved to Ireland in
1966. These moves were indirectly prompted by the
success of *Summer of the Seventeenth Doll*: Lawler
could not return to Australia, nor could he live in
London or New York, because of a tax situation resulting from productions of his play and the sale of
film rights. He took up residence in Ireland after
learning that he could obtain an income exemption
granted to writers in that country. Lawler is of Irish
descent and admires Irish writers. Lawler's wife, Jac-

queline Kelleher, is an actress originally from Brisbane; they have twin sons, born in 1957, and a daughter, Kylie, born in 1959.

Lawler returned briefly to Australia in 1971, after a lengthy absence, to assist with the production of *The Man Who Shot the Albatross*, a play about Captain William Bligh's rule as Governor of New South Wales. He moved back to Australia in 1975, and in 1977 assisted with the production of *The Doll Trilogy*, comprising *Kid Stakes*, *Other Times*, and *Summer of the Seventeenth Doll*. *The Doll Trilogy* relates the history of the protagonists of *Summer of the Seventeenth Doll* in the sixteen years prior to the time frame of that play. Both *Kid Stakes* and *Other Times* were written in the 1970's, some twenty years after Lawler's success with *Summer of the Seventeenth Doll*.

ANALYSIS

Summer of the Seventeenth Doll is by far Ray Lawler's most important work. Several of his early plays have not been published, and his subsequent plays do not have the same verve, although two of them, *The Piccadilly Bushman* and *The Man Who Shot the Albatross*, have both received critical acclaim.

Summer of the Seventeenth Doll is a seminal play in the development of contemporary Australian drama. It was written at a time when Australia was emerging from the domination of Great Britain and the United States, although both countries have retained a strong influence on the Australian way of life. Australia was subjected to a veritable invasion of British immigrants after World War II. By the time the play was written, more than one million Britons had moved to Australia. British and American films dominated the Australian market, and the most popular stage productions were from the West End or Broadway, often with second-rate British or American actors in the main roles and Australians in the secondary roles.

This problem had been recognized in Australia since at least 1938, when a number of Australians joined together to start the Playwrights Advisory Board (PAB), with a view to promoting the work of indigenous playwrights. The PAB was to have a lasting effect on Australian theater. One of its aims was to circulate plays among Australian producers, thereby seeking outlets for the playwrights, and it was responsible, during its existence from 1938 to 1963, for nurturing a great number of Australian playwrights. One of its methods for encouraging Australian writers was to develop competitions for Australian works. It was in one of these competitions that Lawler won first prize in 1955.

While Lawler was writing *Summer of the Seventeenth Doll*, the Australian Elizabethan Theatre Trust—"the Trust," for short—was being formed. This organization was begun at the instigation of H. C. Coombs, Governor of the Commonwealth Bank of Australia. The Trust was to be formed as a private enterprise, with the support of the public in the form of subscriptions. As Coombs wrote in 1954, in the literary magazine *Meanjin*, "The ultimate aims must be to establish a native drama, opera, and ballet which will give professional employment to Australian actors, singers and dancers and furnish opportunities for those such as writers, composers and artists whose creative work is related to the theatre." The Trust was to encourage such activities by offering financial support and guarantees to those producing Australian works. The initial appeal was for $200,000, and it was hoped that, once the Trust was established, the Australian federal government would lend its support to the cause of theater subsidies—which is precisely what happened. The federal government matched grants on a one-to-three basis, contributing one dollar for every three dollars raised by the Trust.

Both the PAB and the Trust played immensely important roles in Lawler's career. His sharing of first prize in the 1955 PAB-sponsored competition was a turning point for all involved. By 1954, the Trust had its own home, a former theater in the industrial Sydney suburb of Newtown, converted to a movie house and then restored to a theater. In January, 1955, it produced its first play, and then three more, not one of which was Australian. This was contrary to its founders' philosophy. On January 11, 1955, however, according to the official publication of the Australian Elizabethan Theatre Trust, *The First Year*, "a new page of theatrical history was written. . . . An Australian play by an Australian author, with an all-Australian cast, achieved at once a complete and re-sounding success." *Summer of the Seventeenth Doll* was the play, and with that success, Lawler's career was launched.

On November 28, 1955, Lawler's play opened at the Union Theatre at the University of Melbourne, where he was director. Although Lawler had felt somewhat diffident about having his play produced in the theater in which he was employed, fearing the production would lead to charges of favoritism, both the PAB and the executive director of the Trust pre-vailed on the vice-chancellor of the University of Melbourne to encourage the production.

The play opened to critical acclaim in Melbourne newspapers, as well as in other Australian and even British papers. It played for three weeks at the Union, earning for that theater the princely sum of $3,735.50, probably more money than the theater had hitherto made from any one play.

Once the play had gone through its tryout period as an experimental, university-produced play and had proved a success, the Trust was confronted with the problem of where to stage it in Sydney. The Trust owned the theater in Newtown, newly opened and re-named The Elizabethan. It was an immense barn of a theater, with some fifteen hundred seats, and it was almost solidly booked for its first year of operation. There was, however, a three-week gap in its book-ings, starting in mid-January: This period falls right in the middle of Australian summer, and the theater had no air-conditioning. Lawler's play was booked for this slot and once again received universal praise; Lawler's pioneering work was compared to that of Eugene O'Neill in the United States and John Millington Synge in Ireland, establishing a first-rate national theater.

After it completed its three-week booking at the Elizabethan, *Summer of the Seventeenth Doll* was taken on tour throughout New South Wales by the Arts Council of Australia. Other touring companies were formed, and some amusing anecdotes relate to those tours. Australia has vast distances, and the play

was touring the Northern Territory. One playgoer saw the production and thought that his wife should see it also. The following night, however, it had moved some six hundred miles, to the "neighboring" com-munity. The man took his wife to that community for the production and then returned home—a trip of twelve hundred miles to see a play.

After eighteen months, negotiations were under way to present the play in London, where Sir Lau-rence Olivier, who had read the script, became in-volved. It opened on the West End in April, 1957, with most of its original Australian cast from The Elizabethan, after tryouts in Edinburgh, Nottingham, and Newcastle. Lawler made a curtain speech in which he said: "The first play was produced in Aus-tralia in 1789. It was a convict production—and, need I add, it had an all-English cast. It has taken 168 years for an Australian company to pay a return visit."

During its run at the New Theatre in London, the film rights for the play were sold to an American company. Lawler shared in the profits, together with the Trust, Olivier, and a Broadway management firm. Arrangements were also made for a Broadway pro-duction, and after seven months at the New Theatre, the play was moved to New York. On opening night, there were seven curtain calls, but the press reviews were largely negative, and the production closed after three and a half weeks. Nevertheless, *Summer of the Seventeenth Doll* did find American success: Ernest Borgnine played the part of Roo in the film adapta-tion, and the play was very popular with summer stock companies. It was also presented in translation in Germany and Finland and was even translated into Russian.

SUMMER OF THE SEVENTEENTH DOLL

Summer of the Seventeenth Doll relates the story of two sugarcane cutters, Roo and Barney, who work seven months of the year in the Australian north and then have a five-month summer layoff in Melbourne, in the Australian south. Thus, they follow the sun. For the previous sixteen years, during their Mel-bourne sojourns, Roo and Barney have stayed in a boardinghouse, where they have taken up with Olive and Nancy, two barmaids whom they have known for the entire sixteen years. The play derives its title from

Roo's habit of bringing Olive a Kewpie doll each time he arrives for the layoff. Olive has collected and kept all of these dolls as symbols of the good times the foursome have had during the sixteen previous years.

This summer, the seventeenth, Nancy is no longer at the boardinghouse. She has decided to marry, and Olive has tried to replace her with a fellow barmaid, Pearl. Unfortunately, Pearl does not have the same disposition as Nancy, and Barney and Pearl do not hit it off. Matters are further complicated by the fact that Roo and Barney are getting old. Roo had a disastrous season and left the cane cutting early, being supplanted as the chief of his gang (the "ganger" in Australian idiom) by a younger man, Johnny Dowd. For his part, Barney has always had the reputation of being a "lady's man," having sired a number of illegitimate children, yet halfway into the play, the audience discovers that he had a disappointing season with women up north. This discovery is reinforced by his singular lack of success with Pearl.

Because Roo left the cane fields early, he was forced to seek employment in Melbourne, where he found work in a nearby paint factory. This is a vital point, for it is a complete loss of face for Roo to have to work in the city during the layoff. Barney brings Johnny, the new ganger, to the house and they discover Roo asleep in his paint-spattered clothes after a hard day's work. Roo is humiliated into making peace with Johnny but cannot forgive Barney for the humiliation, and this eventually leads to a fight between the two old friends.

Olive, meanwhile, has realized that the layoff romance has come to an end. Her "eagle, flying out of the sun to mate," has feet of clay. Still, she resists this realization, and when Roo offers to marry her, she has a tantrum and rages against the inevitability of the situation.

Summer of the Seventeenth Doll is a play about ordinary people. It is very simple in its construction. Its language is plain, studded with everyday expressions; it is not strained and does not strive for eloquence. The play develops in the customary three-act manner: exposition, development, a second-act climax, and a third-act resolution. There are no earth-shattering events, nothing startlingly out of the ordinary. It is a play that examines an Australian situation—a play that depends for its universality on the interrelations of men and women, ordinary working people who choose to live in a somewhat unorthodox manner but who have all the same needs and desires as the rest of the world: friendship, love, comfort, companionship.

Lawler recognizes Olive's need when Roo offers her marriage. Roo says tenderly: "Look, I know this is seventeen years too late, and what I'm offering is not much chop, but . . . I want to marry you, Ol." Olive responds emphatically: "No!" She says: "You can't get out of it like that—I won't let you." Roo is appalled. "Olive, what the hell's wrong?" Olive replies: "You've got to go back [to cane cutting]. It's the only hope we've got." "Give me back what you've taken," she says, to which Roo replies: "It's gone—can't you understand? Every little scrap of it—gone. No more flyin' down out of the sun—no more eagles. . . . This is the dust we're in and we're gunna walk through it like everyone else for the rest of our lives." Olive stumbles out of the house, and Roo, too inarticulate to weep, sees the seventeenth doll lying on a piano and crushes it. Barney leads him out of the house, their friendship perhaps restored, and the curtain falls.

Summer of the Seventeenth Doll is a truly indigenous play, firmly rooted in the Australian ethos, and it illustrates a world that was disappearing, even as the play was being written. The "mateship" that it espouses was eroding as rapidly as Australia was becoming an urban society, and it is this realization, more than any other, that shocks Roo into offering to marry Olive. Still, Lawler does indicate that life is cyclical. Johnny Dowd is introduced to Bubba, a neighbor in her twenties who has been friendly with Olive and Nancy all of her life. Bubba is determined to follow the same lifestyle, except that "things will be different"; she is sure that she will not suffer the same fate as Roo, Olive, Barney, and Nancy.

Lawler's mastery of the Australian vernacular was certainly responsible in part for the play's instant success with Australian audiences. Before the triumph of this play, most Australian playwrights had been careful to use a "cultured" or "refined" dialogue, with very few slang terms and little cursing. With one or two notable exceptions, such as Sumner Locke-Elliott's play *Rusty Bugles* (pr. 1948), which had audiences shocked by its use of the word "bloody," playwrights had eschewed the strong language so characteristic of everyday Australian speech. This caution was a reflection of the power wielded by the various State Chief Secretaries, analogous to the British Lord Chamberlain, with the right to remove plays from the stage because of perceived immoralities or offenses to public decency. Thus, Lawler's use of street language—which is employed in the play in the most natural way, not intrusively—had a great impact on Australian drama. Indeed, it has been suggested that the play failed on Broadway because of its use of Australian vernacular and dialect: The reviewer in the *New York Daily News* spoke of a "great invisible barrier of language between the United States and Australia."

THE PICCADILLY BUSHMAN

Lawler's next play was *The Piccadilly Bushman*. The term "Piccadilly Bushman" is a derogatory one and refers to a wealthy Australian who lives in the West End of London, in Earl's Court, known as "Kangaroo Court," not in the judicial sense but because of the large numbers of Australians ("kangaroos") living there. It was presented in 1959 in Melbourne, and in 1961 in Adelaide.

A savage portrait of a bitter man who has been unable to find his place in his homeland, the play examines the Australian feeling of inferiority that was instilled while Australia was a British colony. Australia was settled at the close of the eighteenth century as a substitute for the American colonies, at a time when Great Britain needed an outlet for the hundreds of convicts imprisoned in rotting hulks on British rivers. There were two classes of settler: On one hand, there was the convict, and on the other, his supervisors and those who, for one reason or another, believed that they would have a better chance at a new life in a new land. These two classes, the penal and the free, maintained a certain distance from each other for nearly two hundred years, and both classes always referred to Great Britain as "home." The supervisory and free-

settler class looked down on the emancipists, and British visitors looked down on the free settlers as colonials. By the end of the nineteenth century, when wealthier Australians began visiting Great Britain, they were lumped together with the descendants of the convicts and patronized by the British.

It was only in 1901, on federation, that Australia became independent, although retaining the status of membership in the British Commonwealth of Nations and recognizing the British monarch as titular head of the nation. The feeling of inferiority was pervasive in Australia, and it manifested itself in many different ways. Typical Australians referred to a British person as a "bloody Pommie," but they still regarded themselves as of British stock. It was only with the vast post-World War II immigration to Australia, at which time two million Britons as well as many hundreds of thousands of European migrants were attracted to the vastness of Australia from their own war-ravaged countries, that Australian attitudes began to change, and Australia began to come to terms with its own national ethos.

Lawler, who was himself an expatriate at the time of writing *The Piccadilly Bushman*, examines the motivations and feelings of an expatriate film actor who returns to Australia to star in a film and to try to save his marriage, or, if that is not possible, to take his son back to England with him. The play is written in three acts and is set in Sydney, in a spacious house overlooking Sydney Harbor. Alec, the protagonist, left Australia at the age of twenty-five, and he considers that his life up to that time had been a prison sentence. He has become successful and famous in Britain but has never overcome his sense of inferiority.

One of the secondary characters, O'Shea, is the writer of the film in which Alec is to star, and he is the foil to the expatriate. He realizes that Meg, Alec's wife, must stay with Alec. Meg has had a history of alcoholism and infidelity in England. It emerges that the men with whom she has been having affairs are the type categorized by O'Shea as misfits, that type of person who goes overseas but does not succeed in his chosen field. Meg does not understand that, while Alec is successful, he, too, is a misfit, and she consoles these other men rather than her husband.

O'Shea points out to her that it is Alec who is the greatest misfit of all.

Lawler tries, without much success, to address a number of questions in *The Piccadilly Bushman*. The play's central themes—the patronizing attitude of the British toward "colonials," homesickness, and the ambivalent attitudes of Australians toward Britain—were aimed at a rather small audience, and while the play attracted some praise, it was largely a failure, critically as well as financially.

Neither Alec nor O'Shea is drawn with great sympathy. Alec is shown to be something of an opportunist; he has used his wife as a stepping-stone in his career, and his attitudes throughout the play are essentially negative. O'Shea, supposedly the voice of reason, is long-winded and unpretentious almost to the point of naïveté.

THE DOLL TRILOGY

Of greater interest are the first two plays of *The Doll Trilogy: Kid Stakes* and *Other Times*. Though written many years after *Summer of the Seventeenth Doll*, as noted above, these two plays precede it in the internal chronology of the trilogy. Interestingly enough, the three plays worked very well together when first performed as a trilogy. After having been written separately and produced as self-contained plays, they were presented in repertory for two weeks in February, 1977, with two Saturdays devoted to productions in which all three plays were presented in sequence. The general slide from the joyous youth of *Kid Stakes* into the disillusionment of postwar Australia in *Other Times* and thence into the devastating finale of *Summer of the Seventeenth Doll* was accomplished with style and great success.

Kid Stakes had been presented for the first time in Melbourne in November of 1975. Reviews were not encouraging, and the play probably suffered because of comparisons with, and distant memories of, *Summer of the Seventeenth Doll*. Nevertheless, Lawler was encouraged to proceed with *Other Times* while *Kid Stakes* toured Australia. *Other Times* opened in December, 1976, at the Russell Street Theatre, to favorable reviews.

Kid Stakes begins immediately after the Depression. Barney and Roo have arrived in Melbourne for their first layoff, and they meet Olive and Nancy at the Aquarium. Also appearing is Bubba, here five years old, and the stage is set for the following sixteen years. Olive and Nancy quit their jobs as milliners to become barmaids, and Roo and Barney establish the pattern of the years to come. Olive's mother, Emma, is the owner of the boardinghouse where Olive and Nancy live. Emma is a crusty, middle-aged woman who accepts her daughter's lifestyle with some misgivings, feeling herself powerless to change things.

The setting for *Other Times* is the same boardinghouse, at the end of World War II. Barney and Roo have served in the Australian Army and are about to be demobilized. They are waiting to return north to resume their jobs as cane cutters, and they look forward to continuing their relationships with Olive and Nancy during layoffs. *Other Times* is the pivotal play in the series. In it, the characters become mature adults, whereas in *Kid Stakes* they were in their early twenties. Life is portrayed as no longer a game; Barney's practical jokes backfire for the first time during a poignant scene in which Emma's dreams of black-market profiteering are ridiculed.

Indeed, probably the turning point of the entire trilogy is the scene at the end of the second act of *Other Times*, which foreshadows the eventual breakup of the foursome. Nancy points out to Olive exactly what it has meant for Roo to stay together with Barney throughout the war. Roo rejected promotions, first, so that he and Barney would not be separated, and, second, so that he and Barney could go on leaves together and visit the girls. The audience understands that Nancy has outgrown the good-times philosophy of the layoffs and needs to put down more permanent roots. At the close of the play, her departure seems inevitable. *Other Times* is a melancholy and somber play, dramatizing a process of disillusionment that is thoroughly Australian in its particulars but universal in its import.

BIBLIOGRAPHY

Bartholomeuz, Dennis. "Theme and Symbol in Contemporary Australian Drama: Ray Lawler to

Louis Nowra." In *Drama and Symbolism*, edited by James Redmond. Cambridge, England: Cambridge University Press, 1982. The author believes that "the pronounced anti-intellectual strain in Australian life" is glamorized in *Summer of the Seventeenth Doll*; images of flying eagles are incongruous with the "drab necessities of urban employment." Cites Lawler's own comments on the de-emphasis of plot in favor of characterization. Sees the play as "the tragedy of those who are made inarticulate by words."

Brisbane, Katharine. "Beyond the Backyard." In *Australia Plays*. London: Walker Books, 1989. An anthology of five new Australian plays, all of which owe a debt, according to Brisbane's introductory essay, to Lawler's "*The Doll*, as it came to be called." Brisbane sees an irony that "the backbone of Australian drama is its Irish sensibility to language, rhythm, humour and logic." The play "is an almost perfect example of the conventional three-act form."

Fitzpatrick, Peter. *After "The Doll": Australian Drama Since 1955*. Melbourne: Edward Arnold, 1979. A strong chapter on Lawler sets out the argument for a decline in quality from *The Doll* to the two plays completing the trilogy, *Kid Stakes* and *Other Times*. While *The Doll* was precedent setting, it was not altogether "helpful," as it "left an inheritance which had partly to be lived down."

Hooton, Joy. "Lawler's Demythologizing of *The Doll: Kid Stakes* and *Other Times*." *Australian Literary Studies* 12 (May, 1986): 335-346. Examines the "retrospective" plays following *The Doll* and finds that the ambiguities of *The Doll* have been reconciled in the sequels. "Reformed text is much more thematically consistent, although far less richly suggestive" than the earlier play, the author states. Finds it less concerned with outback values, more a psychological than "a universally relevant study of the effects of time."

Rees, Leslie. *The Making of Australian Drama: A Historical and Critical Survey from the 1830's to the 1970's*. London: Angus and Robertson, 1973. In a chapter called "The Trust, *The Doll*, and the Break-through," the history of Lawler's relationship with the theater world is told. Photographs including ones of Lawler as Barney. Index and bibliography.

C. Peter Goslett,
updated by Thomas J. Taylor

HALLDÓR LAXNESS
Halldór Kiljan Guðjónsson

Born: Reykjavík, Iceland; April 23, 1902
Died: Mosfellsbær, near Reykjavík, Iceland; February 8, 1998

PRINCIPAL DRAMA
Straumrof, pr., pb. 1934
Snæfríður Íslandssól, pr. 1950
Silfurtúnglið, pr., pb. 1954
Strompleikurinn, pr., pb. 1961
Prjónastofan Sólin, pb. 1962, pr. 1966
Dúfnaveislan, pr., pb. 1966 (*The Pigeon Banquet*, 1973)

OTHER LITERARY FORMS

First and foremost a novelist and an essayist, Halldór Laxness published around fifty books, including seventeen novels, four collections of short stories, more than twenty nonfiction works, six plays, and a collection of poetry. He also translated into Icelandic a number of literary works, novels, plays, and memoirs. In addition, he edited four Icelandic sagas in modern spelling. Laxness wrote several essays on the theater and regularly wrote drama reviews for an Icelandic newspaper from 1931 to 1932.

ACHIEVEMENTS

Halldór Laxness was the most important Icelandic author of the twentieth century. He was a very prolific and versatile writer, constantly surprising his readers with new themes and literary genres. He always wrote in his mother tongue, Icelandic, but his works have been translated into more than forty languages. Many of his best-known novels are available in English translation. Laxness has left his mark on Icelandic theater. Apart from six original plays, eight of his novels have been successfully adapted for the stage. Moreover, nine of his novels and short stories have been filmed. As a dramatist Laxness is, however, almost unknown outside Iceland. Only one of his plays, *The Pigeon Banquet*, has been translated into English and produced on the stage in an English-speaking country (England). *The Pigeon Banquet* was also produced in Denmark in 1970, and in the 1950's *Silfurtúnglið* was staged in the Soviet Union (1955), Finland (1956), and Czechoslovakia (1956).

For most of his career, Laxness was a highly controversial writer because of his radical thoughts and artistic experiments. Nevertheless, many of his novels have become best-sellers, both in Iceland and on the international book market. In 1946, the novel *Sjálfstætt fólk* (1934-1935; *Independent People*, 1946) was introduced by the Book-of-the Month Club in the United States and sold more than 500,000 copies, and in 1977, *Independent People* and *Íslandsklukkan* (1943) were packaged as one volume in the Soviet Union and sold about 300,000 copies.

Laxness was granted various honors and awards for his writing and participation in public discussion. The most prestigious was the Nobel Prize in Literature, which he received in 1955 "for his vivid epic power, which has renewed the great narrative art of Iceland." Laxness received honorary doctorates from many universities, and in his last years, he was hailed as "the grand old man" in Icelandic and European literature.

BIOGRAPHY

Halldór Kiljan Guðjónsson, who later took up the name Halldór Kiljan Laxness, was of farming stock, born on April 23, 1902, in Reykjavík. In 1905 the family moved to a small farm near the city, Laxnes in Mosfellssveit (now Mosfellsbær), where the boy grew up. He was constantly writing as a child, and at the age of seventeen, he made his debut as a novelist with a neoromantic love story, *Barn náttúrunnar* (1919; child of nature). In the same year, he devoted himself to writing and made his first journey abroad. During the following decade, Laxness traveled widely in Europe and America, steeping himself in contemporary literature and culture in his search for ideological basis and personal style. In 1922-1923, he stayed at the Benedictine monastery of Saint Maurice de Clervaux in Luxembourg where he was converted to Roman Catholicism, and in 1923-1924, he studied at a Jesuit-run school in England with the intention of taking holy orders.

He made his breakthrough as a writer with the revolutionary novel *Vefarinn mikli frá Kasmír* (1927; the

Halldór Laxness (© The Nobel Foundation)

great weaver of Kashmir), a semiautobiographical work that portrays a young man and his spiritual turmoil. This novel, which bears the imprint of expressionism and Symbolism, marks the beginning of modernism in Icelandic literature.

In 1927-1929, Laxness stayed in the United States, learning about the cinema and writing in Hollywood. In the United States, he abandoned the Roman Catholic faith and became an ardent socialist. He acquainted himself with the American author Upton Sinclair and was influenced by his sociological novel. During the next twenty-five years, Laxness wrote a series of realistic novels marked by a radical socialistic view, in which he describes the social conditions in Iceland, past and present, and the people's struggle for survival and better life. Among these novels are *Þu vínviður hreini* (1931) and *Fuglinn í fjörunni* (1932; published together as *Salka Valka: A Novel of Iceland*, 1936), *Independent People*, *Heimsljós* (1937-1940; *World Light*, 1969), and *Íslandsklukkan*.

Laxness returned to Iceland in 1930, where he lived for the rest of his life, although he made numerous extended stays in other countries. In the 1950's, he gradually lost faith in socialism and declared his skepticism toward all totalitarian ideologies. Many of his late novels, as for example *Brekkukotsannáll* (1957; *The Fish Can Sing*, 1966), *Paradísarheimt* (1960; *Paradise Reclaimed*, 1962) and *Kristnihald undir Jökli* (1968; *Christianity at Glacier*, 1972), are marked by a philosophical relativism, partly based on Icelandic popular wisdom, partly on Daoism. In the 1960's, Laxness gave up novel writing for a while and devoted most of his time to the theater. In this period, he developed his own dramatical style, a mixture of realism, absurdism, farce, and satire. In the 1970's and 1980's, Laxness turned to essays and memoirs.

Laxness married twice and had four children. In 1945 he established a home in Mosfellssveit (now Mosfellsbær), close to his parents' farm, Laxnes. In this parish of his youth, he died on February 8, 1998.

ANALYSIS

Though Halldór Laxness always had close connections with the theater, his real career as playwright was relatively brief, from about 1960 to 1966. During this time, he wrote his three last plays, *Strompleikurinn* (the chimney play), *Prjónastofan Sólin* (the knitting workshop called "the sun"), and *The Pigeon Banquet*. The two other plays, *Straumrof* (short circuit) and *Silfurtúnglið* (the silver moon), were written during short breaks from other writing. Unlike most of Laxness's best-known novels, his plays focus on contemporary themes. Their setting is the materialistic urban world, where the old way of life, family ties, beliefs, and values are gradually giving way to individualistic desires to live according to one's own wishes and to pursue one's own dreams of happiness, fame, and wealth. All the plays are social dramas, in the sense that Laxness tries to reveal some great truth about Icelandic or Western society, especially its vital problems or failures. The two earliest plays are classical tragedies, written in realistic style and marked by the author's endeavor to move the audience. The last three plays are, on the other hand, pure comedies. They certainly deal with important questions but without giving any clear answers. These plays are commonly regarded as some of the earliest and most important Icelandic plays in the style of the Theater of the Absurd. As such, these plays are a milestone in Icelandic theater.

STRAUMROF

The first play by Laxness is a conventional psychological drama with close connections to the works of the Scandinavian dramatists Henrik Ibsen and August Strindberg. The play centers on a prosperous upper-class family, especially on the wife and mother, Gæa (mother Earth), who for years has led an isolated and sterile life inside the home. When her husband, Loftur (Sky), suddenly dies, she eyes a chance to escape from her prison. She begins to compete with her young and beautiful daughter, Alda (Wave), for a lover, setting the stage for catastrophe. As the names of the protagonists suggest, they are not only individuals but also mythological symbols or archetypes. Besides, it is in many ways natural to interpret them in the light of Sigmund Freud's ideas of the eternal conflict of id, ego, and superego. When the play was first produced in 1934, it created quite a shock because of its daring subject matter, and children were not admitted.

SILFURTÚNGLIÐ

A wife and mother is also the protagonist in *Silfurtúnglið*, a social satire with a tragic end. The play is set in postwar Iceland and describes the people's reaction to a flood of new and irresistible ideas and opportunities, which in many cases oppose traditional values. In *Silfurtúnglið*, the heroine must choose between her family (a husband and a child) and fame as an international entertainer. She is the inevitable loser because her conscience and desire are doomed to clash, and in the end, her life is in ruins. In spite of this, she refuses to give up, but as a free woman she is aware of her responsibility for what has happened. In this play, Laxness began to create his own dramatic style, by mixing realism and farce. Many critics have traced some influence here from the social realism and the dramatic theories of Bertolt Brecht, and Laxness was both a good friend and admirer of Brecht. The play was received with mixed feelings at its premiere in 1954. Some of the spectators were fascinated, whereas others criticized the pessimistic view expressed in the play.

STROMPLEIKURINN

Laxness's plays in the 1960's show clear signs of his changing political views and his skeptical attitude toward a literature whose main object is to solve some general social problems and to participate in the making of a better world. In Laxness's opinion, literature should be an autonomous world, free of any political ideology or propaganda. When *Strompleikurinn* first appeared on the stage, it surprised and puzzled most critics and audiences. No wonder, for the play violated in many ways the naturalistic tradition to which Icelanders were accustomed. It presents the home of a lower-class mother and her grown-up daughter, who for years have hidden the corpse of an old aunt in the chimney of their house so as to retain her pension. The daughter is mixed up in other kinds of fraud as well, and in the end, she has no other alternative than to disappear into the chimney. At the same time an Oriental spirit appears on the stage as a *deus ex machina* and saves the only person who has proved to be honest. Critics wondered what the author's intention was. Is the play a critical allegory, and if so, what do the chimney and the old aunt stand

for, or is the play only intended to amuse the audience with exaggerated characters and comical and improbable situations? When asked, Laxness gave no clear answer to these questions but merely hinted that he was trying to express his vision of the world.

PRJÓNASTOFAN SÓLIN

It is in no way easier to interpret *Prjónastofan Sólin* than *Strompleikurinn*. The author does not intend to tell a well-constructed story with convincingly motivated persons. Everything in this world is bizarre, symbolic, and haphazard. Most of the heroes' actions are illogical, useless, and absurd, and the protagonists are types rather than individuals. Some of them appear in disguise or change character and name constantly. The romantic beauty, La Belle Dame Sans Mercy, turns for a while into an urban guerrilla but ends up as the repentant sinner, Saint Mary Magdalene. Her main enemy is an invalid called Sine Manibus, a man without arms, who nevertheless turns out to be the character who has the strongest arms. Another interesting character is a strange philosopher who has the name and appearance of the Norwegian dramatist Ibsen but talks like a book or an oracle and seems quite unable to communicate with other persons. Is he the spokesperson for the author, as some critics think, or just a clown? *Prjónastofan Sólin* was poorly attended when it was first produced in 1966. However, many consider it to be Laxness's most ambitious play.

THE PIGEON BANQUET

Laxness's farewell to drama was much better received. Its main intention was to amuse people, and in this, it succeeded. *Dúfnaveislan* is written in the same style as the two previous plays, but its subject matter is more popular and more readily accessible. The play presents the world of a simple, middle-aged pants presser and his wife. They live and work in a small basement, nourish themselves on potatoes and fish, and do not like to charge their customers. All the same, money keeps pouring over the doorstep from highly satisfied people. To begin with, the couple tries to get rid of the money by stuffing it into the telephone, into the Bible, or under the threshold. It does not improve the situation when a helpful investor takes care of the money with the intention of buying a drop of milk for the couple's stepdaughter. Soon the presser is the owner of numerous apartment houses, cargo ships, and airplanes, according to a law of nature that says that if someone is trapped into owning a single apartment house, then there is nothing on God's earth that can save him from becoming owner of another twenty-four. This does not change the life of the presser and his wife, but all of a sudden, strange people appear, for example, a bankrupt millionaire who produces mouse feed for the whole world and gigantic haircombs for the bald. The play also enters into the world of farce or fairy tale, where everything can happen and only the masks are genuine. In the end, the millionaire disappears in a cloud of smoke, and the wealth of the presser is, to his great relief, deposed in an anonymous account in Switzerland.

Taken as a whole, Laxness's plays are not universally acclaimed. Some critics doubt that they will retain interest on the part of audiences or critics in the long term. Others claim that these experimental byproducts of the novelist Laxness are among the most interesting Icelandic plays of the twentieth century.

OTHER MAJOR WORKS

LONG FICTION: *Barn náttúrunnar*, 1919; *Undir helgahnúk*, 1924; *Vefarinn mikli frá Kasmír*, 1927; *Þu vínviður hreini*, 1931, and *Fuglinn í fjörunni*, 1932 (*Salka Valka: A Novel of Iceland*, 1936); *Sjálfstætt fólk*, 1934-1935 (*Independent People*, 1946); *Heimsljós*, 1937-1940 (*World Light*, 1969, includes *Ljós heimsins*, 1937; *Höll sumarlandsins*, 1938; *Hús skáldsins*, 1939; and *Fegurð himinsins*, 1940); *Íslandsklukkan*, 1943; *Hið ljósa man*, 1944; *Eldur í Kaupinhafn*, 1946 (collective title for previous 3 novels *Íslandsklukkan*); *Atómstöðin*, 1948 (*The Atom Station*, 1961); *Gerpla*, 1952 (*The Happy Warriors*, 1958); *Brekkukotsannáll*, 1957 (*The Fish Can Sing*, 1966); *Paradísarheimt*, 1960 (*Paradise Reclaimed*, 1962); *Kristnihald undir Jökli*, 1968 (*Christianity at Glacier*, 1972); *Innansveitarkronika*, 1970; *Guðsgjafaþula*, 1972.

SHORT FICTION: *Nokkrar sögur*, 1923; *Fótatak manna*, 1933; *Sjö töframenn*, 1942; *Sjöstafakverið*, 1964.

POETRY: *Kvæðakver*, 1930.

NONFICTION: *Kaþólsk viðhorf*, 1925; *Alþýðubókin*, 1929; *Í Austurvegi*, 1933; *Dagleið á fjöllum*, 1937; *Gerska æfintýrið*, 1938; *Vettvangur dagsins*, 1942; *Sjálfsagðir hlutir*, 1946; *Dagur í senn*, 1955; *Gjörningabók*, 1959; *Skáldatími*, 1963; *Upphaf mannuúðarstefnu*, 1965; *Íslendingaspjall*, 1967; *Vínlandspúnktar*, 1969; *Í túninu heima*, 1975; *Úngur eg var*, 1976; *Sjömeistarasagan*, 1978; *Grikklandsárinu*, 1980; *Af menníngarástandi*, 1986; *Sagan af brauðinu dýra*, 1987 (*The Bread of Life*, 1987); *Dagar hjá múnkum*, 1987.

TRANSLATIONS: *Vopnin kvödd*, 1941 (of Ernest Hemingway's *A Farewell to Arms*); *Birtíngur*, 1945 (of Voltaire's *Candide*); *Veisla í farángrinum*, 1966 (of Hemingway's *A Moveable Feast*).

EDITED TEXTS: *Laxdæla saga*, 1941; *Hrafnkels saga Freysgoða*, 1942; *Brennunjáls saga*, 1945; *Grettissaga*, 1946.

BIBLIOGRAPHY

Hallberg, Peter. *Halldór Laxness*. New York: Twayne, 1971. The first and only full-length study of Laxness in English. A comprehensive introduction, which focuses on the author's literary development and some of his most important novels. Contains a chronology, a brief introduction to the history of Iceland, a selected bibliography, and index.

Halldór Laxness, Maurice Maeterlinck, [and] Thomas Mann. Nobel Prize Library. New York: A. Gregory, 1971. Contains Laxness's presentation address and acceptance speech upon winning the Nobel Prize. Also contains a summary of his life and works.

Magnusson, Magnus. "Seeing the Truth." *New Statesman* 13, no. 637 (December 25, 2000-January 1, 2001): 91-92. Magnusson reflects on the reception in the United States of Laxness and his work, noting his early popularity. While concentrating on Laxness's fiction, he sheds light on the writer's character.

Scandinavica (May, 1972). Edited by Sveinn Skorri Höskuldsson. Special issue devoted to Laxness. It contains a number of critical essays on his work. Most of them are in English.

Thórir Óskarsson

NATHANIEL LEE

Born: Hatfield(?), England; c. 1653
Died: London, England; May, 1692

PRINCIPAL DRAMA

The Tragedy of Nero, Emperor of Rome, pr. 1674,
pb. 1675

Sophonisba: Or, Hannibal's Overthrow, pr., pb.
1675

Gloriana: Or, The Court of Augustus Caesar, pr.,
pb. 1676

*The Rival Queens: Or, The Death of Alexander the
Great*, pr., pb. 1677

Mithridates, King of Pontus, pr., pb. 1678

Oedipus, pr. 1678, pb. 1679 (with John Dryden)

The Massacre of Paris, wr. 1679, pr., pb. 1689

Caesar Borgia: Son of Pope Alexander the Sixth,
pr. 1679, pb. 1680

The Princess of Cleve, pr. 1680(?), pb. 1689 (based
on Madame de La Fayette's romance *La
Princesse de Clèves*)

Theodosius: Or, The Force of Love, pr., pb. 1680

Lucius Junius Brutus: Father of His Country, pr.
1680, pb. 1681

The Duke of Guise, pr. 1682, pb. 1683 (with
Dryden)

Constantine the Great, pr. 1683, pb. 1684

OTHER LITERARY FORMS

Although Nathaniel Lee published a few occasional poems, he is known primarily for his drama.

ACHIEVEMENTS

Nathaniel Lee was an extremely popular dramatist
of his time; many of his plays, including *Sophonisba*,
The Rival Queens, *Theodosius*, *Oedipus* (written with
John Dryden), and *Mithridates, King of Pontus* were
frequently revived and reprinted. These plays, five of
the most popular Restoration dramas, were produced
through the seventeenth century and occasionally revived in the next.

Lee wrote primarily heroic tragedy, characterized
by superhuman heroes torn between passion and

honor, a struggle that usually results in the hero's
death. Spectacle, battles, processions, and bombastic
language in rhymed couplets are common to this
form. Moreover, along with Dryden, with whom he
collaborated on two plays, *Oedipus* and *The Duke of
Guise*, Lee abandoned the use of rhymed couplets
and employed blank verse, which allowed for greater
expressiveness, realism, and emotive force.

Like the quality of his work, critical estimation of
Lee as a dramatist varies. Lee has been criticized for
his lack of balance and control, for allowing his
scenes to degenerate into mere spectacle and his dialogue into rant. Nevertheless, he created individual
scenes of great effect and passages of compelling
beauty and dramatic power. Many critics and historians of English drama have placed him in the first rank
of English dramatists and some have called him
great. Unfortunately, very little attention has been
paid to his work, which, according to the famous
critic George Saintsbury, has been "shamefully neglected."

BIOGRAPHY

Little is known about the early life of Nathaniel
Lee. The playwright was born to Richard and Elizabeth Lee about 1653. A minister thoroughly engaged
in the religious and political issues of the day, Richard Lee tended to the intellectual development of his
children, sending five of his six surviving sons to Oxford or Cambridge University. Therefore, Lee was
educated at the Charterhouse School in preparation
for Trinity College, Cambridge, where he received
his bachelor of arts degree in 1668-1669.

At the beginning of the next decade, Lee became
an actor, playing the Captain of the Watch in Nevil
Payne's *Fatal Jealousie* (pr. 1672) and Duncan in a
revival of Sir William Davenant's *Macbeth* (pr. 1663).
Although Lee was handsome and had a powerful
voice, he apparently suffered from stage fright, so
he retired and began playwriting. Lee's first play,
The Tragedy of Nero, Emperor of Rome, failed, but
Sophonisba was a success. *Gloriana* also failed, but

Lee recovered with *The Rival Queens*, which achieved a popularity that lasted into the eighteenth century. In the next few years, Lee saw plays such as *Oedipus*, *Theodosius*, and *Mithridates, King of Pontus* become successes.

Lee's last three plays did not match the success of *Theodosius*, and on November 11, 1684, he was admitted to the Bethlehem Royal Hospital, the insane asylum popularly known as Bedlam. The reasons for Lee's "distraction," as it was called, are not clear. He was evidently a heavy drinker and had a rather mercurial temperament. It is possible that, at the time of his confinement, he was suffering from the effects of poverty. Whatever the origins of his illness, Lee spent the next four years in Bedlam. He was discharged from the hospital in 1688, taking up residence on Duke Street. There is no solid evidence that Lee wrote any plays either during or after his stay at Bedlam, although he did compose some poetry. In the spring of 1692, he was found dead in the street and was buried on May 6, 1692, in an unmarked grave.

ANALYSIS

The plays of Nathaniel Lee are, for critic Allardyce Nicoll, "of inestimable importance in any attempt to divine the quality of tragedy of his age." From this glimpse into Lee's tragedy it is possible to see at work a serious search for a more comprehensive ethical perspective, despite staginess, special effects, and sensational events.

THE RIVAL QUEENS

Lee consistently used historical figures and events as his dramatic subjects. In *The Rival Queens*, Lee dramatized the fall of Alexander the Great, a larger-than-life figure who succumbs to his own passions and to the plots of others. His fall is truly tragic. When the play opens, Alexander is returning from his most recent exploits and is about to enter Babylon. Having committed some personal and political indiscretions, Alexander may not be warmly received by everyone. He has executed some of his most respected generals, imagining that they were trying to stage a coup. He publicly insulted Polyperchon, commander of the Phalanx, and Cassander, son of

the Macedonian governor, Antipater. Breaking a promise to his devoted Babylonian queen, Statira, he has returned to the bed of his hot-blooded first wife, Roxana. Finally, he has sanctioned the match between Parisatis, sister to Statira, and Hephestion, an unctuous courtier. Parisatis, however, is the lover of Lysimachus, a fearless soldier loyal to Alexander. Lysimachus believes that he is more deserving than Hephestion of Alexander's favor, as does Clytus, the conqueror's old and faithful adviser, who also served under Philip of Macedonia, Alexander's father.

Alexander enters Babylon triumphantly, but he is soon embroiled in the conflict between Hephestion and Lysimachus. Alexander tries to settle the issue by having Lysimachus thrown to a lion. The doughty warrior slays the lion with his bare hands, however, and Alexander, who cannot overlook such a marvelous feat, lets Lysimachus compete for the hand of Parisatis, deciding that the woman will go to the soldier who serves most impressively in battle.

At the same time, the rival queens are contending for Alexander's affections. On hearing that Alexander had bedded Roxana, Statira decides to remove herself from him. By this ploy, however, she risks losing him to Roxana, so she later entertains his impassioned lovemaking and forgives his recent intrigue with Roxana. Roxana witnesses the reunion and seeks revenge. Cassander convinces her to murder Statira as she awaits the conqueror's return from the banquet. Cassander, however, has arranged for Alexander to be poisoned at the feast.

At the banquet, a drunken Alexander becomes enraged at Clytus for his satiric barbs, and he kills the old man on the spot. Alexander's maudlin remorse for the impulsive deed is cut short by the news that Roxana and her band of thugs are threatening Statira. Alexander arrives just in time to see Roxana stab the queen. As she dies, Statira begs Alexander not to kill Roxana. He resists taking revenge, but only because his first wife is pregnant. The audience now discovers that Hephestion drank himself to death at the banquet. Alexander then begins to stagger from the poison poured into his drink. After hallucinating about his heroic past, the conqueror dies, leaving Lysimachus to apprehend the assassins and to claim, at last, Parisatis.

This play dramatizes the story and spectacle of a great man brought down by his own failures. If Alexander were merely the victim of an unfortunate series of events, as are many heroes of the Restoration's serious drama, the audience would not care about his fate, but Lee's Alexander is a tragic figure because he had the power to save himself. Poor judgment, not inescapable fate, causes him to fall. The play is made even more tragic because the audience can see his fall coming. The audience has more information than Alexander and knows that, by the conventions of tragedy, seemingly small lapses in judgment at the beginning of a play have large and damnable consequences toward the end.

Alexander's mistakes result from his letting passion overrule reason. Throughout the play, Alexander increasingly becomes the tool of his own passions. One of his first acts is to favor Hephestion by supporting his suit for Parisatis over that of Lysimachus. Like King Lear, Alexander elevates those who flatter him the most, rather than those who display quiet virtue: The glib court favorite is preferred over the silent but dutiful soldier. As the play continues, mistakes become misdeeds: At the banquet, Clytus is not merely ignored, he is slain. In the last scene of the play, Alexander loses his reason entirely and goes mad under the poison's influence.

The tension between Alexander's affective and intellectual faculties is dramatized by opposing pairs of characters. Roxana is a lusty, sensuous woman, intent on satisfying her sexual desires; Statira, in contrast, is a model of selfless devotion, ethereal, rather than earthy. On the side of passion is Hephestion, the sot; on the side of reason, Lysimachus, the soldier. Cassander is a scheming, sinister malcontent, willing to say what Alexander wants to hear, while he plots the conqueror's destruction; Clytus is a blunt, stoical adviser, who risks Alexander's wrath to criticize his indulgence in Persian luxuries. Lee polarizes the selfish character and the selfless, the scheming and the honest. The spiritual land of the first group is Babylon, the lap of decadent luxury; the spiritual land of the second group is Macedonia, the seat of austerity

and other martial virtues. Thus, the characterization and the very structure of the play reflect Alexander's inner conflict.

THE PRINCESS OF CLEVE

If *The Rival Queens* is quite clearly a tragedy, *The Princess of Cleve* defies precise generic description; Lee himself called the play "Farce, Comedy, Tragedy or meer Play." Set in Paris, the play focuses on the amorous exploits of Duke Nemours, a nobleman with a penchant and talent for seducing the wives of his compatriots. Despite his appetite for sexual sport, Nemours is betrothed to Marguerite, Princess of Jainville. Queen Catherine de Medici, however, wants to end the match so that the princess can marry the Dauphin, soon to be King Francis II.

To achieve her political ends, Catherine, who never appears in the play, persuades one of her ladies, Tournon, to sleep with Nemours and to find him other women to bed as well. Presumably, Marguerite will discover Nemours's faithlessness and welcome the Dauphin's attentions. In her campaign, Tournon first suggests to Marguerite that an amorous letter from a whore to her anonymous lover belongs to Nemours. She next attempts to involve Nemours with Celia and Elianor, the lusty wives of two fops, St. Andre and Poltrot. Tournon then spreads the news that the newly married Princess of Cleve is accepting Nemours's adulterous advances.

The action involving the two fops and their wives soon takes off without Nemours. St. Andre and Poltrot try intensely to be in style—which, by Restoration standards, meant betraying one's wife in a cavalier, offhand manner. Celia and Elianor, for their part, also engage in flirtations. All receive their proper reward: Celia and Elianor run off with Nemours (under the eye of Marguerite) and are eventually debauched by his cronies, Bellamore and Vidam; the husbands are unsuccessful in their own attempts, in effect receiving no compensation for the privilege of being cuckolded.

When the Prince notes a certain malaise in his wife, he implores her to reveal the origin of her low spirits, suspecting that she has taken a lover. She reluctantly confesses her passion for Nemours—a confession that eventually causes the Prince to die from heartbreak.

Nemours's association with the wives of the fops and with the Princess of Cleve arouses Marguerite's suspicion that he has not been faithful. She attends the ball in disguise and tries to arouse Nemours's passions as another woman. She succeeds, and when she doffs her disguise, Nemours can hardly deny his infidelity. Nemours, then, has presumably lost Marguerite, whose last words are "Monster of a Man," and he has lost the Princess of Cleve as well, even though she is now technically available: She has given him up forever. No sooner has she left the stage, however, when Nemours predicts that "I Bed her eighteen months three weeks hence, at half an hour past two in the Morning."

Nemours's prediction suggests the sleazy atmosphere and ethos of the play. He does not believe that the Princess of Cleve is as good as her word, but he does believe in his own sexual prowess. Indeed, any kind of oath in the universe of this play is meaningless. The Princess, Celia, Elianor, St. Andre, and Poltrot all do their best to violate their marriage vows. Because no character in the play is untainted by sin, the audience tends to judge them not by ethical standards but by sheer performance. Because there are no saints and no sinners, only winners and losers, the most impressive performer is Nemours.

Lee wanted to show his audience sexual libertinism unvarnished by witty rationalizations. When this play was composed, in about 1680, sexual promiscuity was almost a way of life for the English courtiers and their king, Charles II; George Villiers, the second duke of Buckingham and John Wilmot, the earl of Rochester, in particular, were infamous for their sexual adventures. The English court's rakish ways were reflected in plays such as John Dryden's *Marriage à la Mode* (pr. 1672), William Wycherley's *The Country Wife* (pr. 1675), and Sir George Etherege's *The Man of Mode: Or, Sir Fopling Flutter* (pr., pb. 1676). Lee's intention in *The Princess of Cleve* was to provide a corrective to the tacit acceptance of promiscuity often found in such works, whatever their explicit moral.

OTHER MAJOR WORKS

POETRY: "On the Death of the Duke of Albemarle," 1670; "To Mr. Dryden, on His Poem of Paradice," 1677; "To the Prince and Princess of Orange, upon Their Marriage," 1677; *To the Duke on His Return*, 1682; *On Their Majesties Coronation*, 1689; *On the Death of Mrs. Behn*, 1689.

BIBLIOGRAPHY

Armistead, J. M. *Four Restoration Playwrights: A Reference Guide to Thomas Shadwell, Aphra Behn, Nathaniel Lee, and Thomas Otway*. Boston: G. K. Hall, 1984. Provides extensive bibliographies of works by and relating to Lee, Thomas Shadwell, Aphra Behn, and Thomas Otway. Index.

_____. *Nathaniel Lee*. Boston: Twayne, 1979. After presenting the playwright and his milieu, Armistead marches straight through the plays, summarizing and identifying their themes. In a chapter entitled "Lee's Artistry," Armistead identifies Lee's "distinctive" style. Complemented by a genealogy tree and an excellent bibliography.

Canfield, J. Douglas. *Heroes and States: On the Ideology of Restoration Tragedy*. Lexington: University Press of Kentucky, 2000. A study of Restoration drama that covers Lee's *The Princess of Cleve*, among many other works from the period.

_____. *Tricksters and Estates: On the Ideology of Restoration Comedy*. Lexington: University Press of Kentucky, 1997. Canfield examines the characters known as tricksters in Restoration comedy. In his discussion, he focuses on lesser known playwrights, including Lee.

Ellison, Julie. *Cato's Tears and the Making of Anglo-American Emotion*. Chicago: University of Chicago Press, 1999. A study of public emotion that uses among its examples Lee's *Lucius Junius Brutus*.

Haggerty, George. *Men in Love: Masculinity and Sexuality in the Eighteenth Century*. New York: Columbia University Press, 1999. As part of his greater discussion of male "love," Haggerty examines the eroticized bonds of male friendship in Lee's *The Rival Queens*.

Hayne, Victoria. "'All Language Then Is Vile': The Theatrical Critique of Political Rhetoric in Nathaniel Lee's *Lucius Junius Brutus*." *ELH* 63, no. 2 (Summer, 1996): 337-350. Hayne provides a political interpretation of *Lucius Junius Brutus*.

Owen, Sue. "'Partial Tyrants' and 'Freeborn People' in *Lucius Junius Brutus*." *Studies in English Literature, 1500-1900* 31, no. 3 (Summer, 1991): 463.

Owen argues that *Lucius Junius Brutus* is not a Whiggish play but rather a somewhat radical work.

Douglas R. Butler,
updated by Frank Day

HENRI-RENÉ LENORMAND

Born: Paris, France; May 3, 1882
Died: Paris, France; February 16, 1951

PRINCIPAL DRAMA

Le Cachet rouge, pr., pb. 1900
La Grande Mort, pb. 1905, pr. 1909
Au Désert, pr., pb. 1905
Le Réveil de l'instinct, pr., pb. 1908
Les Possédés, pr., pb. 1909
Terres chaudes, pr. 1913, pb. 1914
Poussière, pr., pb. 1914
Le Temps est un songe, pr. 1919, pb. 1921 (*Time Is a Dream*, 1923)
Les Ratés, pr. 1920, pb. 1921 (*Failures*, 1923)
Le Simoun, pr. 1920, pb. 1921
Le Mangeur de rêves, pr., pb. 1922 (*The Dream Doctor*, 1928)
La Dent rouge, pr., pb. 1922
A l'Ombre du mal, pr., pb. 1924
L'Homme et ses fantômes, pr., pb. 1924 (*Man and His Phantoms*, 1928)
Le Lâche, pr., pb. 1925 (*The Coward*, 1928)
L'Amour magicien, pr., pb. 1926
Une Vie secrète, pr. 1929
Asie, pr. 1931, pb. 1938
Sortilèges, pr. 1932
Crépuscule du théâtre, pr. 1934 (*In Theatre Street*, 1937)
Arden de Feversham, pb. 1935, pr. 1938
Pacifique, pr., pb. 1936
La Folle du ciel, pr., pb. 1937
Terre de Satan, pb. 1942
La Maison des remparts, pb. 1942

OTHER LITERARY FORMS

Henri-René Lenormand's reputation rests almost exclusively on his plays, but during his career, he published collections of stories, novels, memoirs, and literary criticism. His memoirs, *Les Confessions d'un auteur dramatique* (confessions of a playwright) were published in two volumes, the first in 1949, the second in 1953, two years after his death.

ACHIEVEMENTS

Henri-René Lenormand deserves to be better known than he is at the beginning of the twenty-first century. Although copies of his plays are difficult to find, even in France, his plays were very popular in the 1920's and early 1930's—not only in France but also in England and in many European countries. His theater seemed to reflect the dark mood that gripped Europe after World War I. In the tone and ideas in his theater—the dreamlike ambience of his settings and his introspective, haunted characters—he represents the theatrical avant-garde of his day and prepared the way for such later twentieth century French playwrights as Jean Anouilh, Samuel Beckett, and Eugène Ionesco.

BIOGRAPHY

Henri-René Lenormand's artistic development drew much inspiration from his father, René, who was a composer. The work of both father and son was often unappreciated, especially by art patrons who were suspicious of the avant-garde.

Henri-René was an only child, born, raised, and educated in Paris, although he and his family spent considerable leisure time in the Norman countryside. Later, Lenormand traveled frequently and widely, visiting, either alone or with family, such places as Scotland, Polynesia, Russia, the United States, and Holland. These travels apparently made him sensitive to a kind of moral and cultural relativism.

Lenormand received his early education at the prestigious Lycée Janson Sailly. He went on to earn a degree in English literature from the Sorbonne, but he was greatly influenced by readings in other literatures as well—especially the works of Friedrich Nietzsche, Edgar Allen Poe, Fyodor Dostoevsky, and later Swedish playwright August Strindberg and Sigmund Freud. These writers' ideas heightened Lenormand's tendency to somber moods and thoughts and enhanced his notions, stimulated by travel and introspection, that some men are intellectually and morally superior to others—and therefore have greater moral freedom.

In 1905, Lenormand published a collection of stories and a play, *La Folie blanche.* Although he later published a bit more fiction, he soon committed himself to writing for theater. He married actress Marie Kalff in 1911 and was drafted into the army in 1915 but was deemed physically unfit (because of dysentery). He spent most of the years between 1915 and 1920 in Switzerland trying to regain his health. Here, he wrote most of the plays that were produced in Paris soon after the war. By 1924, he had established a worldwide reputation and oversaw productions of his plays in several countries.

He became active in movements against censorship of the arts, which had affected some of his works. As Lenormand grew older, his life and his ideas became darker and reflected personal and professional disillusionment. For example, his marriage was not stable, and he was apprehensive about the threat that cinema presented for the theater. He produced no plays after 1938, turned to teaching (he taught in the United States for a time), and died in 1951—having devoted several years to writing his memoirs.

ANALYSIS

In 1920, Henri-René Lenormand presented (at the Théâtre des Arts in Paris) a play called *Failures.* The title of this play could serve to describe the main characters in most of Lenormand's plays, which generally feature protagonists who are failures in some way: men and women who have failed to understand life or to take control of their lives and who are at the mercy of their instincts, their subconscious, or vague determining forces of which they are only remotely aware. Lenormand's plays often resemble Greek tragedy in that the lives of their despondent, lost characters frequently end in suicide or murder. However, Lenormand's theater lacks another important tradition of Greek tragedy in that there is not always a character who understands what has happened and attempts to explain the meaning of events.

Despite the bleak tenor of Lenormand's theater, Gabriel Marcel, the great French philosopher and critic, called him the most important French playwright of the period between World War I and World War II. His work was championed by such well-known impresarios and directors as Georges Pitoëff, Gaston Baty, and Charles Dullin; prominent actors and actresses appeared in productions of his plays. However, Lenormand never wrote or produced any plays after 1938, when World War II loomed on the European horizon.

When Lenormand's fame was at its peak, his plays were performed in several European countries and in New York City and Westport, Connecticut. His stature was still significant enough in the early 1960's that his *Failures* was included in an anthology of twentieth century French theater—alongside plays by more famous writers such as Paul Claudel, Jean-Paul Sartre, and Samuel Beckett—published in the United States and destined for use by American students. Although his work is rarely staged in the twenty-first century, his theater has not lost its power to create in the reader a fascination with his dreamy, even nightmarish settings and his dark, tormented characters who look for some reason to go on living—in creative work perhaps, or love, or benevolence.

TIME IS A DREAM

Time Is a Dream is one of Lenormand's first plays to enjoy a significant popular success. Its title expresses the play's focus, in that the fundamental philosophical tone of the play is nihilistic.

As the play's protagonist, Nico Van Eyden, comes to believe, it is impossible for humans to go beyond their subjective grasp of the world: People can never know "reality." Therefore, concludes Nico, life is essentially dream, fantasy, illusion—and has no meaning.

Early in the play, Nico's fiancée, Romée Cremers, tells Nico's sister, Riemke, of a strange vision. As she walked to meet Riemke and Nico on their estate, she saw a man apparently drowning in a pond. She—as well as Riemke and Nico—eventually realize that Romée's vision was of Nico. Her vision predicts the future (as Nico insists, past, present, and future are one and the same). The play ends with Nico's suicide—an idea inadvertently and tragically planted in his mind by Romée.

FAILURES

The title of *Failures* works on at least two levels. The characters are a troupe of struggling, poverty-haunted actors and musicians; their lack of success in avant-garde theater forces them to tour France, where they perform in dubious venues of several sorts. In addition though, the play's two main characters, husband and wife Lui ("he" in French) and Elle ("she" in French, although other characters sometimes refer to her as Juliette or Liette) desperately cope with their failures not only as actors but as husband and wife, and—ultimately—as human beings. Ironically, in this play about failed actors, Lui was played in the original Paris production by the very successful producer and director, Georges Pitoëff; Lenormand's wife, Marie Kalff played Elle; and the distinguished actor Charles Dullin appeared as Crouzols, a musician (perhaps modeled, it has been suggested, on Lenormand's father, composer René Lenormand).

So desperate do Lui and Elle become during their tour of the country that Elle sells her favors to a series of men who have seen her onstage and pursued her. She, of course, regrets this infidelity, and when Lui discovers what his wife has done, he has his own—rather desperate and vengeful—adulterous flings as well. He also starts to drink heavily. Eventually, both Lui and Elle come to the conclusion that their love was short-lived and that love does not suffice to keep

people from despair. After all, as Lui says at one point near the play's end, what is in fact the goal of life? What does it mean? Thus it becomes evident why Lenormand named his couple "He" and "She"—that is, in order to stress the universality of their situation. All lovers, Lenormand implies, will sooner or later see this same emptiness of their love and their lives. In a fit of drunken rage, convinced in his nihilism, Lui beats Elle to death, and when he is discovered by his fellow troupers, shoots himself in the presence of the police.

LE SIMOUN

The play's title, referring to a violent, hot, and destructive desert wind (the simoom), is relevant to the setting of the final tableau. In a broader sense though, the title hints at the heat and violence that besets several of the play's characters. *Le Simoun* is in fact about desire—particularly sexual desire—and people's inability to control or even satisfy it. Two minor characters provide indirect commentary on this theme. There is the Vérificateur, the local inspector of weights and measures, who recites aloud formulae from self-help books on self-control. At other times, a strange prophet appears briefly to argue that death is better than the tortures of desire.

The play's main character however is Laurency, a French businessman who fled France after a disastrous marriage. He now lives in the Algerian desert with his half-breed mistress, Aïescha. After his former wife's death, Laurency invites his adolescent daughter, Clotilde, to live with him. Unfortunately, her presence subjects her to danger—her own awakening sensuality, enhanced by the climate, and her father's quasi-incestuous feelings and subsequent guilt. Just as Clotilde is preparing to elope with a young Arab against Laurency's wishes, she is murdered by Aïescha, who has recognized Laurency's attention to Clotilde for what it is and is furious with jealousy.

A L'OMBRE DU MAL

A l'Ombre du mal is certainly one of Lenormand's best plays. It is among his most modern plays, with its main character, Rougé, a frighteningly lucid man who, like the hero of Albert Camus's *Caligula* (wr. 1938-1939, pb. 1944; English translation, 1948), questions the existence of objective moral values. Once again, as in *Le Simoun*, Lenormand explores what happens when sophisticated Europeans and their "civilized" culture are pitted against the harsh climates and unsettling customs and inhabitants of exotic locales. Here, the scene is French Equatorial Africa in 1905, and all the major male characters are French colonial officials, all of whom have been in Africa too long for their own good. There is Rougé, who represents his government in the village of Kadiéso. His subordinate is Le Cormier, who, along with his wife, misses France considerably. The Le Cormiers also frequently disagree with the way in which Rougé treats the natives, who are nevertheless an unpredictable group, with their own competing factions and primitive religion.

After enduring Africa's isolation, heat, and literal darkness (represented by the dense "forest" to which the characters refer repeatedly), Rougé has arrived at the conclusion that moral values—particularly the notion of "justice" as Europeans understand it, have no objective validity. Therefore, one can—quite simply—do what one wishes. Indeed, as Rougé sees things, doing injustice—deliberately punishing an innocent man rather than the guilty one—can be a source of pleasure. It is at this point in his development that Rougé strongly resembles the outrageous heroes of the Marquis de Sade's fiction.

In the play's third act, Rougé explains his ideas about goodness, evil, and justice to Préfailles, a former colleague whom he has not seen in years. Rougé's disposition to deliberate injustice was, he says, precipitated by Préfailles's treatment of him when he was the latter's subordinate years before. Because Préfailles was gratuitously cruel to him, Rougé has found the advantages of being deliberately cruel to others.

Rougé's dramatic foil is Madame Le Cormier, a kind woman who believes in goodness and doing good for others. She and Rougé come together briefly in act 3: She expresses her pity for Rougé, and Rougé is genuinely moved by her good will, but this emotional rapprochement never progresses.

A l'Ombre du mal climaxes in terribly logical style. Madame Le Cormier agrees to help an injured boy in the village, but she is seized by a rival group of natives and beheaded. The play's last lines, uttered by Rougé, are intriguingly ambiguous. Justice is done, proclaims Rougé when he learns what has happened to Madame Le Cormier. Yet, what exactly does he mean? Is he mocking people's concept of justice, which is in turn mocked by the death of the virtuous Madame Le Cormier? Or does he regret that the vicious cycle of cruelty that he has perpetuated has claimed an undeserving victim?

OTHER MAJOR WORKS

LONG FICTION: *Le jardin sur la glace*, 1906; *Une Fille est une fille*, 1949 (*Renée*, 1951); *L'Enfant des sables*, 1950; *Troubles*, 1950 (*The Rising*, 1952).

SHORT FICTION: *Déserts*, 1944; *Les Coeurs anxieux*, 1947.

NONFICTION: *Les Confessions d'un auteur dramatique*, 1949, 1953 (2 volumes).

BIBLIOGRAPHY

Dickman, Adolphe-Jacques, and Henriette Moussiegt. Introduction to *Le Temps est un songe*. New York: The Century Company, 1929. Also contains a brief preface by Lenormand himself and a brief bibliography of early Lenormand criticism. The book is a student edition, and despite its age, is a good point of departure for readers unfamiliar with Lenormand. Contains helpful notes and a student-level glossary.

Hyman, Ann. Introduction to *Les Ratés*. In *Anthology of Twentieth Century French Theater*, edited by Jacques Guicharnaud. New York: Paris Book Center, 1967. A fine succinct overview of Lenormand's life and career. Includes a brief analysis of *Les Ratés* and a good bibliography of Lenormand's work and a few secondary sources.

Jones, Robert Emmet. "Desire and Death in the Plays of Lenormand." *French Review* 30 (1956): 138-142. Essay on two important, perhaps fundamental themes in Lenormand's work.

_____. *H.-R. Lenormand*. Boston: Twayne, 1984. Still the definitive work in English on Lenormand. Essentially a convincing and fair defense of the playwright's contributions to drama. Jones comments on the weaknesses of Lenormand's work but insists that his drama has been unjustly neglected.

_____. "The Lower Depths." In *The Alienated Hero in Modern French Drama*, by Robert Emmet Jones. Athens: University of Georgia Press, 1962. Intelligent analysis of several of Lenormand's plays, especially in the context of alienation and rebellion. Extensive bibliography of works relevant to the artistic context within which Lenormand worked.

Palmer, John. "Lenormand and the Play of Psychoanalysis." In *Studies in the Contemporary Theatre*. Boston: Little, Brown, 1927. Looks at Lenormand's drama from a Freudian point of view.

Gordon Walters

JAKOB MICHAEL REINHOLD LENZ

Born: Sesswegen, Livonia, Russia (now Cesvaine, Latvia); January 12, 1751
Died: Moscow, Russia; May 24, 1792

PRINCIPAL DRAMA

Der Hofmeister: Oder, Vortheile der Privaterziehung, pb. 1774, pr. 1778 (*The Tutor*, 1972)

Der neue Menoza: Oder, Geschichte des cumbanischen Prinzen Tandi, pb. 1774, pr. 1963

Die Freunde machen den Philosophen, pb. 1776

Die Soldaten, pb. 1776, pr. 1863 (*The Soldiers*, 1972)

Der Engländer, pb. 1777, pr. 1916

OTHER LITERARY FORMS

Jakob Michael Reinhold Lenz was the author of one of the few lasting theoretical works to emerge from the Sturm und Drang (Storm and Stress) period in German literature. His *Anmerkungen übers Theater nebst angehängten übersetzten Stück Shakespears* (1774) served as a dramaturgy for the short-lived movement. Fully in line with the thinking of Johann Gottfried Herder, the young Johann Wolfgang von Goethe, and Friedrich Maximilian Klinger, Lenz rejected rules for drama composition. Like them, he attacked the French theater as superficial, disparaged the unities of time and place, and asserted that the greatest drama is conceived by emotion rather than reason.

Lenz wrote two volumes of poetry, two novellas, and a number of other theoretical essays; he also translated several plays by Plautus and made a substantial beginning on a novel. Yet his reputation as one of the leading writers of the Sturm und Drang movement and as a seminal drama theorist rests on the dramatic œuvre and on *Anmerkungen übers Theater nebst angehängten übersetzten Stück Shakespears*.

ACHIEVEMENTS

Jakob Michael Reinhold Lenz's contributions to German drama are best understood within the context of the Sturm und Drang movement, a movement mirrored not only in his plays but also in his life. The movement flourished during the 1770's as both a reaction to and a further development of the European Enlightenment. The latter movement was then well into late middle age, and its insistence on the primacy of reason in human affairs had become progressively more normative. Enlightenment ethics and poetics tended to be detailed and prescriptive. The Sturm und Drang movement countered with an assertion of the supremacy of the creative genius unfettered by sterile rules.

Lenz's dramas confronted a theater tradition based on French classicism and affirmed by the German Enlightenment with such innovations as the realistic depiction of everyday life, the use of short scenes in sequence, and the critical treatment of burning social issues that involved the ruling aristocracy. The works for which he is famous could not be understood as Aristotelian tragedies or comedies. In fact, modern scholarship often describes Lenz as the father of the German tragicomedy. Terminological nuances aside, Lenz was one of the first to experiment with a dramatic form better suited to the new middle-class audience for theater that had grown to maturity during the early and middle decades of the eighteenth century. His disavowal of tragedy—because its appeal was supposedly limited to a diminishing, aristocratic portion of the total audience—was one of the first suggestions that the genre itself might be anachronistic.

Lenz's original contribution to dramatic theory lies in his redefinition of comedy. He asserted the validity of the dramatic treatment of imbalance and tension within society. Only comedy presents such tension through its natural focus on events, whereas tragedy focuses on personalities. In the former genre, human destiny is a product of circumstance; in the latter, it is determined by high social station. By consigning tragedy to a stratum of the population with which most theatergoers had little empathy, Lenz was attempting to legitimate the comedy as the only true form of middle-class drama. In his eyes, the comedy should no longer be a lesson in ethics made palatable by humor; quite simply, it should be a depiction of everyday society. It was a definition that found application in his own plays.

Lenz was not a well-known dramatist during his lifetime. Few of his plays were performed, and acclaim, whether popular or critical, eluded those that were. When a contemporary mentioned his name, the focus of interest was usually his personality, not his work: Lenz the eccentric, the social misfit, and, later, the madman. His prominence in literary history is a product of reception by innovative, avant-garde writers and movements during the two centuries since his death. His reliance on sharp irony and his willingness to have both one-dimensional types and psychologically motivated characters on the same stage set a precedent for German Romanticism. His determination to use the stage as a forum for social protest would later serve as an example for Georg Büchner and Bertolt Brecht. It was only at the turn of the

twentieth century that Lenz became widely known—largely because of the efforts of the naturalists, who shared his desire to shock the theater audience by confronting it with uncomfortable realities that it preferred to forget. Lenz's slim œuvre has also been described as an ancestor of the "station-drama" and the epic theater of the 1920's and 1930's. Based on this reception history, one can acknowledge Lenz as the father of the non-Aristotelian tradition in German theater.

BIOGRAPHY

Born in 1751, Jakob Michael Reinhold Lenz was a pastor's son who attended school at Dorpat (later Tartu, Estonia). He studied at universities in Dorpat and Königsberg (later Kaliningrad Oblast, Russia). In 1771, he gave up the study of theology to accompany two young barons of the von Kleist family to Strasbourg, where he served as their private tutor. Soon Lenz had fallen in with Johann Wolfgang von Goethe, Friedrich Maximilian Klinger, and the other members of the Sturm und Drang circle around Johann Gottfried Herder. During his association with these other young writers, he produced the body of work for which he has become known: *The Tutor*, *The Soldiers*, *Anmerkungen übers Theater nebst angehängten übersetzten Stück Shakespears*, and the less influential *Der neue Menoza*.

Lenz's personal life was continually in a state of disarray, a circumstance that influenced the response to his work after his death. His advances were rejected by one woman after another, a wound further aggravated by the fact that the long list included Goethe's presumptive lovers Friederike Brion and Charlotte von Stein as well as Goethe's married sister. Soon after Goethe had taken up residence in Weimar, Lenz followed him to the court of Duke Karl August. There, Lenz's rather awkward and eccentric behavior amused members of the court. It was a well-intentioned condescension that turned into repugnance when the thoughtless guest wrote a parody that offended the duke. Lenz was expelled from Weimar in disgrace; he had been there eight months.

The literary establishment of his day, as well as earlier literary scholarship, tended to view Lenz as the reflection of young Goethe in a distorted mirror. Denigration of his work has usually been justified with references to the playwright's emotional instability. Often, such hostile reception has actually been prompted by Lenz's status as a socially "engaged" writer or as an innovator in dramatic form. Comparisons between the relatively sophisticated, upper-middle-class Goethe and the small-town provincial, however, are meaningless, and the fact that Lenz was attracted to women who were interested in writers is hardly surprising, particularly in the light of the small size of the towns in which he lived and the scarcity of educated young women at the time.

Shortly after Lenz's departure from Weimar, he began to show signs of progressive mental illness. For two years, friends cared for him, first in Switzerland, then in Strasbourg, and finally in Emmemdingen. In 1779, his youngest brother, Karl, took him home to his family, which had moved to Riga. Unable to get back on his feet there, he moved to Saint Petersburg and from there to Moscow in 1781. The details of his final years in Russia are sketchy at best. It is certain that he worked as a teacher in a private school and that he was at least partially supported by patrons. Yet attacks of insanity were becoming more frequent and his personal affairs, more confused. Lenz's wretched existence came to an end on a spring night in 1792, when he was found dead in a Moscow street.

ANALYSIS

Most of the significant plays written in German-speaking Europe during the eighteenth century are set far from the contemporary scene, distanced either in time or space, or both. Whether a writer belonged to the Enlightenment, to Sturm und Drang, or to classicism, any new publication was subjected to intense scrutiny by the censors of an absolutist prince who usually reacted swiftly and harshly to the very suggestion of criticism. It was typical of Jakob Michael Reinhold Lenz that he threw all caution to the winds and set his major plays in the here and now. They bring into sharp focus the venal, dehumanizing, exploitive organization of society in German-speaking Europe. Each play uses a family to provide both

formal structure and an empathetic touchstone for the writer's critique.

Other Sturm und Drang playwrights treat the tragic conflict between the dynamic, artistic genius and an insensitive, even hostile, social environment. The drama of German classicism teaches philosophical lessons based on ideals that transcend mere reality. This mild contempt for everyday society is unknown to Lenz and the Enlightenment, whose child he clearly is. Instead, the exposé is presented so thoroughly and in so pointed a fashion that the audience retains only a secondary interest in the fate of the characters. Those characters, far from being masters of their own destinies, are the inevitable products of a badly flawed society.

THE TUTOR

In Lenz's comedy *The Tutor*, the title figure is trapped between his physicality and society's contradictory expectations. A university student in theology, Läuffer takes a position as a tutor in the home of a nobleman, the Major von Berg. He is engaged to instruct the two children of the house, Leopold and Gustchen, in academic subjects and in the social graces. To the sophisticated, Francophile wife of the major, Läuffer seems clumsy, provincial, and, in the condescending sense, bourgeois. Even more dissatisfied with the appointment is the major's brother, Privy Councillor von Berg, who scolds the young tutor's father for having suggested the arrangement.

The action of the play begins when the privy councillor's son Fritz leaves to begin his studies at the university in distant Halle. Before leaving, he and Gustchen swear eternal fidelity to each other. It proves impossible for the fickle young Gustchen to keep her word; soon, she feels abandoned. Her pique, Läuffer's boredom, and long hours of contact lead to the inevitable liaison. When the girl discovers that she is pregnant, she and Läuffer flee to two separate hiding places. Gustchen bears her child in the forest hut of an impoverished, old, blind woman, and Läuffer finds lodgings with the simple, honest village schoolmaster, Wenzeslaus. Gustchen's melancholy descends into despair, and she is on the point of drowning herself when she is pulled from the water by Major von Berg. The distraught father has been searching for her since her disappearance. Meanwhile, blind Marthe takes the child to Wenzeslaus's schoolhouse, where Läuffer recognizes the child as his own. In a fit of guilt and depression, he castrates himself.

Throughout the action, Lenz inserts scenes from the riotous undergraduate life of Fritz von Berg and his fellow students. At the play's conclusion, Fritz returns to his family circle to forgive Gustchen and accept her child as his responsibility, while Läuffer remains in the remote village with the completely innocent Luise, who is content to be his life's companion.

The initial response to *The Tutor* was highly favorable, in part because the anonymously published work was thought to be the latest sensation from the pen of Johann Wolfgang von Goethe. The influence of William Shakespeare was detected in character development, in plot structure, and in the integrity of individual scenes. By 1774, the rejection of the unities of time and place by the Sturm und Drang movement was familiar to the small audience for drama in German-speaking areas. Readers and spectators had become accustomed to the use of many settings and extensive spans of time, and Lenz was able to introduce a range of empathetic characters into the epic panorama favored by the movement.

That the range itself was important to Lenz is evident in the title figure: Läuffer is not a hero whose personal crisis obscures the development of the other characters; rather, he serves as a catalyst whom forces beyond his control hurl into one web of interpersonal relationships after another. For his own family, for the von Berg family, for the teacher-pupil relationship with his charges, for the young couple, for Wenzeslaus and his pupils, for the nubile Luise and the children she will never have—for each set of interrelationships, he represents chaos and potential tragedy. His very name, which means "runner," suggests a lack of control as well as the frenetic pace of the action. The belief that social circumstance, instincts, and events themselves determine human happiness was a radical departure from Enlightenment philosophy with its naïve faith in the ultimate power of reason. Lenz takes his confrontation with the pos-

tulate of human perfectibility into the realm of the ironic by making his chaos-bringer a teacher, the very incarnation of the Enlightenment's hopes. Still, his grotesque, despairing act should not be viewed as symptomatic of complete pessimism. Lenz does have a lesson to teach; however, he is keenly aware of the obstacles in society's path.

One such obstacle is the mentality of the ruling class as represented by Major von Berg and his wife. Again, the name is significant: They act as though they are "from the mountain," lofty lords of all they survey. The woman is arrogant and supercilious; her French affectations serve only to accentuate her superficiality and stupidity. The major's one redeeming feature is his dogged devotion to his compromised daughter; otherwise, he conforms to the type of the miles gloriosus, the old braggart soldier whose greatest source of pride is his own unthinking obedience to his sovereign. His wife wants a private tutor for their children because people of rank are expected to have such a servant. The major is concerned that his son receive the amount of instruction necessary to follow in his father's footsteps. Whenever the two are together, the older man barks orders to keep the head high, the posture bolt upright. In the major and his lady, Lenz mounts a scathing critique of two major components of the upper class—the officer corps and the Frenchified lady of leisure. Yet the presence of the privy councillor indicates that the playwright was not prepared to dismiss the aristocracy as being completely without merit.

Nor was he content to give up on the teaching profession. Wenzeslaus is offered as an alternative to the half-educated, obsequious Läuffer. The village schoolmaster's dedication to his duties is made very apparent, as are the breadth and depth of his preparation. He is a solitary old bachelor who lives in rural simplicity, surrounded by books from which he loves to quote from memory—indeed, all too fluently. The price of isolation has been pedantry and self-centered ways. Still, Wenzeslaus's humanity and courage shine forth when he confronts a party of armed men who are in pursuit of the fugitive Läuffer.

The Tutor finds fault with several aspects of eighteenth century German society. The nobility supports an educational institution, the private tutor, that is actually deleterious to its children. The academic preparation and pedagogical ability of a tutor is unimportant as long as he is willing to accede to his employer's every whim. In the major, the hypermasculine loutishness of the blindly loyal officer corps is on display. In this context, what was at this point in the history of German literature a commonplace depiction of wild student life takes on added significance. The atmosphere in Halle cannot be counted on either to reform the aristocracy or to reorder society.

One major, pervasive problem is the ambivalent, and even pusillanimous worldview of the middle class. It is a tribute to the playwright's clear understanding of the complexity of the real world that he uses an aristocratic character to point out this state of affairs. The privy councillor's conversation with Läuffer's father in act 2, scene 1, is calculated to make Lenz's contemporary middle-class audience very uncomfortable. That social level prided itself on its university education. Not so secretly, it viewed itself as superior to a ruling class that was tied to a fading past and mired in superficial attitudes concerning human potential. The middle class longed for a truly meritocratic social order. Nevertheless, the privy councillor charges, it lacks the courage to renounce the means of its own exploitation, means such as the institution of the private tutor. Implicit in the critique is Lenz's belief that the stage should be used to effect change within society. His determination to remedy social ills is even more apparent in *The Soldiers*.

THE SOLDIERS

The final scene of *The Soldiers*, Lenz's other famous comedy, offers a discussion between two characters that have previously had choral functions. A countess who has tried to avert the tragic sequence of events speaks with the colonel of the regiment served by the officers referred to in the play's title. In the course of their conversation, the playwright offers one logical solution to the social problem he has dramatized. Then, shortly after completing work on *The Soldiers*, Lenz wrote a short essay that contains a second possible remedy.

The action of *The Soldiers* is set in three garrison towns in Flanders: Lille, Armantières, and Philippe-ville. Marie and Charlotte are the daughters of Wesener, who sells notions and fancy goods at his shop in Lille. The beautiful Marie is about to receive a marriage proposal from Stolzius, a cloth merchant in Armantières. The very first scene shows the young woman to be quite taken with the faddish love for all things French. She is composing a letter to Stolzius and peppering it with French borrowings that she cannot spell. The innocent pretentiousness of a teenage girl sets in motion a calamitous train of events when she attracts the attention of Baron Desportes, an army officer based at Armantières. While Desportes is callous, cynical, and self-aggrandizing among his peers, he knows how to turn the head of a naïve bourgeois girl with exaggerated flattery. Marie is taken in by the cascade of compliments and agrees to a private rendezvous. Although her father is outraged at first, he soon comes to look on the nobleman's attentions as a social coup in the making for Marie and the entire family; he even suggests that she hold off Stolzius while she determines the seriousness of Desportes's intentions. Soon, Stolzius has heard of Desportes's behavior and writes a mildly monitory letter to Marie. At first the girl is upset, but Desportes soon has her laughing at her former suitor in the course of the teasing and flirting that lead to her seduction.

From this point, the playwright accelerates the action by using short scenes that switch back and forth among the three towns. The third and fourth acts together boast twenty-one scenes, several of them consisting of a single speech. Desportes's fellow officers continue to indulge themselves in transient love affairs and to evince little or no concern for the feelings of others. Stolzius sinks into a state of despair. Leaving Marie to fend for herself, Desportes steals out of Lille to avoid his creditors. The officer Mary then tries to smooth the feathers that his friend has badly ruffled. Stolzius takes a job as adjutant to Mary. Soon it is clear that Mary has designs on Marie and that she is walking the path to sorrow for a second time. The Countess La Roche tries to engage her as a lady's companion with the avowed purpose of returning Marie to a virtuous, ordered existence. Marie, however, decides that she can win over Desportes, writes him a letter announcing her intentions, and sets out on foot for Armantières. Wesener also decides to find Desportes in order to force payment of heavy debts. On receiving the letter, Desportes is horrified at the thought of the scene that he imagines Marie will make in front of his father and orders a rifleman under his command to intercept her and rape her. Soon thereafter, Desportes and Mary have a conversation at lunch about Marie, to whom Desportes refers as a "whore." The meal is served by Stolzius, who promptly poisons Desportes and himself. Meanwhile, on the road to Armantières, Wesener is accosted by a shabby, starving woman whom he takes for a prostitute. Then comes the moment of recognition as father and daughter sink into each other's arms.

The problem discussed by Countess La Roche and the regimental colonel in the final scene is the regulation that officers remain unmarried. In order to protect innocent young girls during peacetime, the colonel suggests that the army might support groups of volunteer concubines, courtesans for the officers. In the later essay, Lenz suggested instead that officers be allowed to marry and that they be integrated into society as respected burghers.

Although the plot of *The Soldiers* is more complex than that of *The Tutor*, the tragic consequences for the middle class are the same: The lives of a young woman and a young man are destroyed. In both plays, the immediate cause is amorality within the aristocracy; neither Desportes and Mary nor Major von Berg and his wife display any sense of duty to the wider community. A specific practice—the institution of the private tutor, the rule of celibacy for commissioned officers—illuminates the absence of ethics among society's elite. The high degree of pathos in *The Soldiers*, the addition of a decidedly anticlimactic final scene, and the composition of a follow-up essay mark Lenz as an *écrivain engagé*. That commitment to progressive causes does not blind him to the faults of his own victimized stratum. The audience must finally decide whether the practical remedies suggested could have saved Stolzius and Läuffer from personal calamity. Their actions do suggest a posture of passivity in the face of the immuta-

ble dictates of destiny. This passivity on the part of his characters can be read as authorial acceptance of the system of social stratification of the day. All that could be hoped for would then be some amelioration of the crueler consequences of the system. Such a reading would stand in contrast to the posture of the typical Sturm und Drang hero with his brash self-confidence, his willingness to flaunt convention. The heroes of Klinger and Friedrich Schiller may succumb to irresistible forces, but they struggle mightily to the bitter end. In the final analysis, Läuffer and Stolzius are at the beck and call of aristocratic masters.

Are the events and attitudes portrayed intended as a lesson? Lenz's immediate predecessors in the genre of comedy were Enlightenment dramatists whose typical play is structured around a foolish central character. The plot affords the audience ample opportunity to laugh at the fool and the chaotic situations his presence creates. Whether the weakness in his personality is cured at the conclusion of the play is of secondary importance. The Enlightenment's primary concern is that the spectator return home more sensitive to the dangers of one pattern of behavior, whether it be furtiveness, greed, intolerance, or hypocrisy. While the amount of death in its final scene equals that present in many a tragedy, *The Soldiers* is faithful to the theory of comedy set forth in the *Anmerkungen übers Theater nebst angehängten übersetzten Stück Shakespears*: It is a study of social institutions and the actions and situations that they generate among everyday people. At the same time, Lenz makes use of spectator expectations nurtured during the Enlightenment in his presentation of negative examples. Wesener and his wife are fools worthy of derision for placing their desire for social advancement before Marie's virtue. Marie is herself a fool on several counts: Her ambition is less reprehensible than Wesener's only because of her age. A deficient education has left her with superficial concepts of refinement and maturity. In addition, she is insensitive to the feelings of one who is close to her, and she does not learn from her mistakes. Even Stolzius is guilty of a small measure of unreasoning behavior; after all, he has chosen to attach himself to this family of fools. Still, his tragedy is almost as unavoidable as it is undeserved. In the Weseners, Lenz shows a debt to the prescriptive stage of the Enlightenment; but in Stolzius, as in Läuffer, he presents a dimension of existence that is beyond the individual's power to control. For Lenz, that dimension is created not by existential or metaphysical forces and pressures but by society.

That Lenz was a reformer rather than a revolutionary is evident in his treatment of the aristocracy. The young officers are presented in the worst possible light; however, as is the case in *The Tutor*, it is left to members of the aristocracy to identify the social problem and suggest solutions. Lenz was content to see caring, creative nobles such as the colonel and the Countess La Roche at the apex of the social pyramid. The Sturm und Drang movement is often linked to the wave of egalitarianism most evident in the American and French Revolutions, but nascent republicanism should not be imputed to Lenz; he was satisfied with the class structure of his time.

DER NEUE MENOZA

Lenz's most wide-ranging critique of the *ancien régime* in Germany appears in his comedy *Der neue Menoza*. The play has enjoyed little success, either on the academic stage or in print, in part because the title is ill-conceived and in part because of flaws in plotting and character development. Tandi, Prince of Cumba, an imaginary realm in Central Asia, is traveling the world in search of true Christians. The play follows the motif of the noble savage who comes to Europe to behold the flower of human civilization but who discovers instead a mendacious, decadent reality. Tandi's European itinerary includes Germany, and he comes to stay with Herr von Biederling in Naumburg. Soon he falls in love with Biederling's daughter Wilhelmine, and they find their way past several complications to a happy ending. Among the complications is the depraved Count Camäleon, who has abandoned his old inamorata Donna Diana in order to woo Wilhelmine. The enraged Diana eventually exacts her revenge by disguising herself as Wilhelmine to attend a masked ball, where she stabs Camäleon as he tries to embrace "Wilhelmine." The consistent interest shown by the Sturm und Drang

movement in themes that would shock its audience is apparent in the other complication. Just as Camäleon crumples onto the ballroom floor, the possibility arises that Tandi and Wilhelmine are brother and sister. The close brush with incest completes Tandi's decidedly unfavorable impression of "civilization." The final revelation that, while he is indeed Biederling's long-lost child, Wilhelmine is actually not Biederling's daughter does little to mitigate the playwright's implicit charge that modernity is defined by such creatures as Camäleon and Diana.

Contemporary reviewers faulted *Der neue Menoza* for its reliance on exaggerated characters, caricatures with whom no empathy is possible. The playwright defended himself rather lamely with the observation that a certain amount of exaggeration is a necessity for effective drama. The comedy is structurally the most conservative of Lenz's three major plays; here, no permanent trauma touches the central characters. As in Enlightenment comedies, only fools suffer. The fact that the social critique is general and that it is offered by an "outsider" suggests a link with the Utopian writings of Albrecht von Haller and Johann Gottfried Schnabel, from the first half of the eighteenth century. Lenz is far more effective in *The Tutor* and *The Soldiers* because he focuses on specific abuses. In the absence of any revolutionary commitment, the perceptions of Prince Tandi must stand as the commonplace complaint of a young dramatist about a society whose diverse ills cannot possibly be loaded onto the shoulders of two characters.

OTHER MAJOR WORK

NONFICTION: *Anmerkungen übers Theater nebst angehängten übersetzten Stück Shakespears*, 1774.

BIBLIOGRAPHY

Diffey, Norman R. *Jakob Michael Reinhold Lenz and Jean-Jacques Rousseau*. Bonn: Bouvier, 1981. Diffey examines the influence of Rousseau on Lenz's work. Includes bibliography.

Guthrie, John. *Lenz and Büchner: Studies in Dramatic Form*. New York: Peter Lang, 1984. Guthrie compares the techniques used by Lenz and Georg

Büchner in their dramatic works. Includes bibliography.

Kieffer, Bruce. *The Storm and Stress of Language: Linguistic Catastrophe in the Early Works of Goethe, Lenz, Klinger, and Schiller*. University Park: Pennsylvania State University Press, 1986. Kieffer examines Lenz's work, along with that of Johann Wolfgang von Goethe, Friedrich Maximilian Klinger, and Friedrich Schiller, in the context of the Sturm und Drang movement. Includes bibliography and index.

Leidner, Alan C., and Helga S. Madland, eds. *Space to Act: The Theater of J. M. R. Lenz*. Columbia, S.C.: Camden House, 1993. A collection of essays about the Sturm und Drang playwright from a symposium on Lenz held at the University of Oklahoma in 1991. Includes bibliography and index.

Leidner, Alan C., and Karin A. Wurst. *Unpopular Virtues: The Critical Reception of J. M. R. Lenz*. Columbia, S.C.: Camden House, 1999. The authors look at the critical reception of Lenz's dramatic works. Contains bibliography and index.

Madland, Helga Stipa. *Image and Text: J. M. R. Lenz*. Atlanta, Ga.: Rodopi, 1994. Madland offers an interpretation and criticism of the Sturm und Drang playwright's works. Includes bibliography and index.

O'Regan, Brigitta. *Self and Existence: J. M. R. Lenz's Subjective Point of View*. New York: Peter Lang, 1997. O'Regan examines the dramatic works of Lenz with an eye to his portrayal of the self and the philosophy that pervades his works. Includes bibliography.

John Van Cleve

HUGH LEONARD
John Keyes Byrne

Born: Dublin, Ireland; November 9, 1926

PRINCIPAL DRAMA

The Italian Road, pr. 1954
The Big Birthday, pr. 1956
A Leap in the Dark, pr. 1957
Madigan's Lock, pr. 1958, pb. 1987
A Walk on the Water, pr. 1960
The Passion of Peter McGinty, pr. 1961
Stephen D, pr., pb. 1962 (adaptation of James Joyce's novels *A Portrait of the Artist as a Young Man* and *Stephen Hero*)
Dublin One, pr. 1963 (adaptation of Joyce's short-story collection *Dubliners*)
The Poker Session, pr., pb. 1963
The Saints Go Cycling In, pr. 1965 (adaptation of Flann O'Brien's novel *The Dalkey Archives*)
Mick and Mick, pr. 1966, pb. 1966 (as *All Nice People*)
The Au Pair Man, pr., pb. 1968
The Patrick Pearse Motel, pr., pb. 1971

Da, pr., pb. 1973
Summer, pr. 1974, pb. 1979
Irishmen, pr. 1975, pb. 1983 (as *Suburb of Babylon*; includes *A Time of Wolves and Tigers*, *Nothing Personal*, and *The Last of the Last of the Mohicans*)
Liam Liar, pr. 1976 (adaptation of Keith Waterhouse and Willis Hall's play *Billy Liar*)
Time Was, pr. 1976, pb. 1980
A Life, pr. 1979, pb. 1980
Kill, pr. 1982, pb. 1992
Scorpions, pr. 1983
Pizzazz, pr. 1984, pb. 1987
The Mask of Moriarty, pr. 1985, pb. 1987
Precious Memories, pr. 1988, pr. 1989, pb. 1991 (as *Unchanging Love*; adaptation of an Anton Chekhov short story)
Moving, pr. 1992, pb. 1994
Selected Plays of Hugh Leonard, pb. 1992
Magic, pr. 1997
Love in the Title, pr. 1998, pb. 2000

OTHER LITERARY FORMS

Home Before Night: Memoirs of an Irish Time and Place by the Author of "Da" (1979) is a charming, humorous memoir, which includes many of the characters, incidents, conversations, and witticisms in *Da*. *Out After Dark* (1989) is a sequel to his autobiography. Hugh Leonard has been a regular contributor of amusing topical commentaries in such Irish newspapers as *Hibernia*, the *Sunday Independent*, and the *Sunday Tribune*. He has also reviewed theater for *Plays and Players*. In 1991, he published a novel, *Parnell and the Englishwoman*, followed in 2001 by another novel, *A Wild People*.

ACHIEVEMENTS

Hugh Leonard is among the most widely produced of contemporary Irish dramatists. His plays have achieved commercial success in Ireland, Great Britain, and the United States. Exceptionally prolific and yet polished, Leonard has been a good journeyman author in various media. He honed his dramatic skills by writing extensively not only for the stage but also for radio, television, film, and newspapers, always with entertainment as a prime consideration. (His television play *Silent Song*, 1966, received the Italia Award.)

Leonard's reputation as an Irish Neil Simon suggests the aspects for which he has been both admired and criticized. His greatest asset as a playwright is essential to any commercially successful dramatist: He knows how to keep an audience entertained with humorous dialogue and situations. Conversely, his detractors have usually complained that his main weakness is a facile, glib superficiality. His best plays combine a theatrical flair for clever language and situation comedy with thoughtful depth of human understanding.

For example, his greatest achievement on the stage has been *Da*, which in 1978 won the Tony Award, New York Drama Critics Circle Award, Outer Critics Circle Award, and Drama Desk Award for Best Play. Mel Gussow of *The New York Times* claimed that *Da* is "in a class with the best of [Sean] O'Casey." Even the fastidious John Simon of *New York* magazine found it "complex and graceful" and

Hugh Leonard in 1978. (AP/Wide World Photos)

"entertaining, endearing and gently moving." Among Leonard's other honors, in 1967 *Silent Song* was awarded an award of merit from the Writers Guild of Great Britain and in 1974 *The Au Pair Man* won a Tony Award nomination for best play. He received a Harvey Award for *A Life*.

A new play by Leonard has often been a highlight of the Dublin Theatre Festival. At the same time, the theatrical facility and universal accessibility of his plays allow them to be transplanted with ease from Dublin's Abbey or Olympia theaters to London's West End and America's Broadway or regional companies.

BIOGRAPHY

Hugh Leonard is the pen name of John Keyes Byrne, who was born on November 9, 1926, in Dublin, Ireland. Leonard was adopted and reared by a couple in Dalkey, in south County Dublin, who were the prototypes for the foster parents in *Da*.

In 1945, at age eighteen, Leonard started work in the Land Commission for five pounds per week. He was always expecting to leave soon but remained for fourteen years, by which time his salary was ten pounds, eight shillings. In 1955, he married Paule Jacquet, a Belgian who lived in Moscow and Los Angeles during World War II. They had a daughter, Danielle.

To escape from the drudgery of his civil service job, Leonard joined a dramatic society. Amateur theater has been the seedbed for some of Ireland's best playwrights, and this was true for Leonard as well. *The Italian Road* was given an amateur production but was turned down by the Abbey Theatre. Then Leonard submitted *The Big Birthday* (which had an amateur production as *Nightingale in the Branches* in 1954), taking his pseudonym from the psychopath Hughie Leonard in the rejected play. *The Big Birthday* was produced in 1956 by the Abbey. He also wrote serial radio dramas, including the daily *The Kennedys of Castleross*, which was the main dramatic experience for the non-theatergoing, pretelevision majority in Ireland. He resigned from the Land Commission in 1959 to become a full-time professional writer.

Leonard wrote for Granada television in Manchester, England, and then moved there, and he later lived in London from 1963 until 1970, writing adaptations and original scripts for television. His numerous adaptations for television have included *Great Expectations* (1967), *Wuthering Heights* (1967), *The Hound of the Baskervilles* (1968), *Nicholas Nickleby* (1968), *Dombey and Son* (1969), *The Possessed* (1969), *A Sentimental Education* (1970), and *The Moonstone* (1972). He claimed that he could write an original television play in six to eight weeks or an episode of adaptation in two days. Leonard wrote the script for a major Irish television production in 1966, *Insurrection*, for the commemorations of the 1916 Easter Rising. He also wrote for film, including *Great Catherine* (starring and co-produced by Peter O'Toole) and *Interlude* (both 1968). Leonard's first play to open in London's West End was *Stephen D*, his adaptation of fellow Dubliner James Joyce's *A Portrait of the Artist as a Young Man* (1916) and *Stephen Hero* (1944). Before *Stephen D* was produced in New York in 1967, it had its American premiere at

the Olney Theater, near Washington, D.C., which has often introduced Leonard plays to the United States.

In 1970, Leonard returned with his family to Dalkey in south Dublin. Productions of *The Patrick Pearse Motel*, *Da*, *Summer*, *Irishmen*, *Time Was*, *A Life*, *Kill*, *Scorpions*, and *The Mask of Moriarty* attracted large audiences and generally favorable reviews. He continued to write for television, including the adaptation of *Strumpet City* (1981) for Radio Telefis Eireann with Peter O'Toole and Peter Ustinov featured in a major Irish production.

Leonard has been quite successful financially, and he especially benefited from a 1970's Irish tax law regarding artistic income as nontaxable. A segment of the television program *Sixty Minutes*, focusing on the Irish tax law, revealed that Leonard's large royalties from *Da* were not taxable whereas actors in Irish productions of Leonard's plays were taxed as usual. An article in the *Sunday Independent* titled "Leonard's 'Da' Gives Him £4,000 a Week!" quoted Leonard as saying that the Broadway production of *Da* was grossing eighty thousand dollars a week, of which he got 10 percent, amounting to £200,000 a year tax-free. He expected another two thousand pounds per week from United States touring productions. Moreover, he claimed to have sold the film rights for $150,000 with an extra $100,000 for writing the screenplay.

Some of his compatriots may have seen the prolific writer as a prodigal son, returned yet rich and unrepentant. Leonard has lived out much of his life in the public eye, particularly in the Irish newspapers. Whereas his new plays often appeared annually, his essays often appeared weekly, covering similar material in a different genre but containing what could be scenarios, scenes, themes, or quips from plays-in-progress. Leonard's humorous columns in Irish periodicals, such as *Hibernia*, the *Sunday Independent*, and the *Sunday Tribune*, have given his opinions high visibility, even notoriety. In his articles, private reminiscences have mingled with public declarations, winning him praise and blame as a wise man and a foolish egotist. He has used such extra-theatrical forums to sound off wittily and sometimes bitterly on diverse subjects, including Irish provinciality or modishness, contraception, narrow nationalism, prudery or vulgarity, Abbey Theatre policy, inefficient services, political shibboleths, demagoguery and skulduggery, and the violence of the Irish Republican Army, a daring target for ridicule. Indeed, few issues in Irish public life have gone unnoticed in Leonard's satirical essays. Allusions to "my present wife" in a country without divorce teased those who might regard this cosmopolitan author as a jet-set Don Juan contaminated by alien lifestyles and ideas. He has been among the celebrities that some Irish love to hate. While some would praise him as a brave clear voice with sharp barbs against deserving enemies, others would blame him for cheap, cynical, glib wisecracks. For example, his review of events in the year 1986 in the *Sunday Independent* (January 4, 1987) included sardonic put-downs of both God and an Irish prime minister in the same paragraph: "The Gobshite of the Year Award goes to God, for having His chance and missing it." Such comments, direct from the author rather than filtered through a mouthpiece in a play, add to Leonard's vivid public persona in Holy Ireland.

Leonard, whose work is better known in other parts of the world than the United States (although *Da* received considerable attention among American theater audiences and was made into a film starring Jack Lemmon), is less involved with political questions and more concerned with the family and small social groups of typical urban Irish life. His memoirs are rather more typical of his laconic humor and sometimes distancing technique.

Leonard remained with his wife and daughter in his home village of Dalkey, now an upscale suburb of Dublin, writing weekly humorous and satirical columns for various newspapers, according to Coílín D. Owens, "with scathing wit, denouncing political violence, extreme nationalism, provinciality, inefficiency, and the mores of Irish suburban social climbers."

ANALYSIS

As a playwright, Hugh Leonard is a dependable professional. He may not be of the first rank (few are), but unlike many a would-be dramatist, he can hold an audience. His plays are usually of some interest if not always of great depth. In short, his plays

show great talent but no genius, which is perhaps all an audience requires for the price of admission. In adapting Joyce's novels for the stage as *Stephen D*, Leonard showed a command over the special demands of theater as a genre. His play *The Poker Session* used a little humor, a staple of much of his work, but held the audience's attention with a Pinteresque menace, as a patient from a mental asylum takes revenge on his family with both method and madness. *The Au Pair Man* was an interesting allegory about the relationship between a dying British Empire and an emerging Ireland. *Summer* and *Irishmen* showed both Leonard's compassion for, and critique of, his compatriots. *Time Was* stretched Leonard's theatrical powers but did not really amount to a satisfying work. *The Mask of Moriarty* was a clever and original Sherlock Holmes story but did nothing more than tell a detective yarn with slick theatrical aplomb. Three plays that stand out among Leonard's large œuvre and that will be examined in his analysis are *The Patrick Pearse Motel*, *Da*, and *A Life*.

THE PATRICK PEARSE MOTEL

The Patrick Pearse Motel is a hilarious two-act farce meticulously constructed and cleverly written. This bedroom farce is in the style of Georges Feydeau, Eugène Labiche, or Alan Ayckbourn, with the unusual distinction that it is set in Ireland. It is not only an amusing sex romp but also an outrageous satire ridiculing the Dublin nouveau riche anxious to get more money and to forget their humble pasts. Set after the 1966 commemorations of the 1916 Easter Rising, the play portrays a new Ireland with a confused identity, invoking the pieties of nationalistic heroism while scrambling to assimilate with the worst of Anglo-American culture. The very title of *The Patrick Pearse Motel* suggests the contradictions of the new Ireland willing to peddle its devalued cultural icons as it enters the Common Market of international mediocrity and homogeneity.

Such a theme may seem rather heavy for a farce, but Leonard handles all aspects of his play with a light, sure touch. The setting is the upscale suburb of Foxrock in Dublin's "vodka-and-bitter-lemon belt," but the names of the characters are from Irish myths. There are three couples: Dermod and Grainne, Fintan and Niamh, and James Usheen and Venetia Manning. Usheen is obsessed with the English Miss Manning but is too full of self-love to share himself with any one woman. A talk-show host on British television, he is an outrageous parody of the modern celebrity whose character is profoundly shallow.

Dermod is a get-rich-quick businessman and social climber who, with Fintan, is opening the Patrick Pearse Motel in the Dublin mountains and the Michael Collins Motel in Cork. He and his beautiful wife, Grainne, have risen from a working-class housing estate to a Foxrock home with all the material goods that a *parvenu* couple could want. There is still something more, however, that Grainne desires: one "night of harmless innocent adultery." The man she is luring is Usheen, and the site for the consummation is to be the Patrick Pearse Motel, the setting for act 2.

The set for the motel is two bedrooms, which are mirror images of each other, with a corridor between. Nearly all the eighty-four rooms in the motel are identical (the Manchester Martyrs' room has three single beds), and all are named after the pantheon of Irish patriots, including Brian Boru, Thomas Davis, Michael Davitt, O'Donovan Rossa, and Bernadette Devlin. The action takes place in the Charles Stewart Parnell room (appropriate for adultery), where Grainne intends to have Usheen, and the Robert Emmet room, where her husband is being seduced by Venetia Manning.

Moreover, Fintan, who madly desires only his plain wife Niamh and wrongly suspects her of adultery, is trying to kill her as she hides in a wardrobe. The characters are not aware of the proximity of the other characters, because as one enters a space, another exits with split-second timing. A letter, wet trousers, a negligee, a fur coat, a shillelagh, and brandy, as well as husbands and wives, go astray and lead to all kinds of comic confusion. Despite the complications, the dramatist, like a master puppeteer, never loses control of the characters or the action, and as a social satirist, never loses sight of the thrust of the comedy to ridicule and correct human folly.

DA

Da is Leonard's most successful play both commercially and artistically. As much as in any other Leonard play, entertaining humorous dialogue and situations are mingled with a depth of compassion. In this autobiographical memory play, the humor is mirthful without malice and moves toward forgiveness. *Da* was conceived and premiered at the Olney Theater near Washington, D.C. Leonard's program notes for the 1973 world premiere at Olney said that during rehearsals for *The Patrick Pearse Motel* at Olney in 1972, someone (perhaps James Waring, the longtime American director of Leonard's plays) suggested that Leonard's stories about his father could be the basis for an amusing play. Within a year, Leonard had turned the suggestion into perhaps his best play. The original production, with John McGiver in the title role, was a success at Olney, in Chicago, and at the 1973 Dublin Theatre Festival. In 1978, *Da* featured Barnard Hughes in the successful Broadway production at the Morosco Theater and won many awards, including a Tony for best play.

"Da, in my part of the world, means father," writes Samuel Beckett in *Molloy* (1951; English translation, 1955). Leonard is also from Beckett's part of the world, south Dublin, but his treatment of his da is quite different from Beckett's stark, mordant style. Leonard's coming to terms with his dead father is bathed in a nostalgic, almost sentimental, glow. The tone of Charlie, the narrator, may indeed be resentful throughout the drama, but the overall tone of the play is light, generous, and forgiving. John Keyes Byrne the man may indeed have drawn on bittersweet personal experiences for this memory play, but Hugh Leonard the entertainer refined and altered that autobiographical material for the sake of a good yarn.

Charlie is a playwright in his early forties who has returned from London to Dalkey for his father's funeral in present time May, 1968. In the play as well as in Leonard's life, his "Da" and "Ma" were not his real parents but a couple who adopted him as a baby. As he is tidying up the house in which he was reared, he has flashbacks to his childhood and is haunted by the memories of his (foster) parents and by his own younger selves (played by a second actor). Unlike Thornton Wilder's *Our Town* (pr., pb. 1938), in which the dead observe the living and cannot communicate with them, Charlie observes those now dead and even argues with them. He quarrels even with his younger self.

The theatrical device of Charlie Now and Charlie Then, played by two actors, two decades apart but in lively debate, is more than a gimmick and is very effective for both humor and insight. It is interesting to note that Irish playwrights Brian Friel and Thomas Murphy have used similar antinaturalistic techniques in plays dealing with similar subjects. In *Philadelphia, Here I Come!* (pr. 1964), Friel split his main character into public and private selves played by two actors. In *A Crucial Week in the Life of a Grocer's Assistant* (pr. 1967), Murphy's protagonist slips from present time into fantasies of what might be. Such antinaturalistic techniques can use entertaining devices to reveal insight into interior life.

Another theatrical dimension that gives the play fluidity to move in time and place is the set. The main playing area in *Da* is the kitchen ("the womb of the play"), but this play is not the mere "kitchen-sink" realism of the stereotypical early Abbey drama, as there are several playing spaces. Moreover, as most of the characters now supposedly exist in the haunted mind of Charlie, they break the conventions of literal realism by walking through walls and crossing boundaries of playing areas, as well as moving forward and backward in their ages. The areas include a seafront and a hilltop. "On the other side of the stage is a neutral area, defined by lighting," to signify various locales.

In the opening scene, as Charlie Now meets his old friend Oliver (who can be played by the same actor who will play Oliver at a younger age), a remark about the dead father is the cue for Da to pass through the kitchen and contradict the remark. When Charlie is again alone, Da nonchalantly returns to comment on his own funeral. He disregards his son's order to "Piss off." About one of his catch phrases, "Yis, the angels'll be having a pee," Da says, "You ought to put that down in one of your plays." The protagonist playwright replies, "I'll die first." This irony is typical of how this reflexive play makes the playwright figure a target of humor, whereas Da, the "ignorant man," "lop-sided liar," "an old thick, a zombie, a mastodon," "a sheep," is the life of the drama. Charlie is learning that "love turned upside down is love for all that."

The dramatic conflict is not only between father and son but also within the son himself. In the fine scene that opens act 2, Charlie is berated by his younger self for not properly taking care of Da: "All the dirty bits over with when you got here." In fact, young Charlie finds the man he is to become "jizzless" and "a bit of a disappointment." In return, Charlie finds his younger self naïve and self-righteous.

An important theme in *Da* as in other Leonard plays is class differences. Having worked as a gardener for the upper-class Prynne family for fifty-four years, Da received a mere twenty-five pounds as severance pay. Charlie castigates Da for being so obsequious in accepting the mean, condescending patronage of the rich. In order to help his son, Da works for another four years for "Catholics with money, letting on they're the Quality." Charlie's debt to Da goes beyond the grave: The allowance that Charlie had been sending Da was saved as an inheritance. Da proclaims, "I didn't die with the arse out of me trousers like the rest of them—I left money!" The curtain falls as Da's ghost follows Charlie back to England.

A LIFE

Da's 1978 American success was followed by a 1979 sequel, *A Life*, premiered at the Abbey for the Dublin Theatre Festival and featuring Cyril Cusack. From *Da*, Leonard takes the thin, acerbic Mr. Drumm, the man who gets Charlie into the Irish civil service, the foil to Da, and makes him the central character of *A Life*. In the bittersweet *Da*, the sweetness of the title character gave the play its warm, even sentimental quality, triumphing over the bitter aspects of Charlie and Mr. Drumm. So it was a daring move to make the testy Drumm the chief protagonist of a sequel and yet retain the audience's interest in and sympathy for him. Mr. Drumm's attempts at humor are his cold caustic quips against his wife and few friends, and yet the play engages an audience's compassion for the dying central character despite his life of nastiness.

Desmond Drumm is described at various ages as "prickly," "a dry stick," "a nun," "a bitter old pill," with "a face on you like a plateful of mortal sins" (an Irishism also used by James Joyce and Brendan Behan). Foils to Mr. Drumm are his dotty wife, Dolly; exuberant, teasing Mary ("Mims"), whom Des loves when young but with whom he seems to be incompatible because she had "a mind like a mayfly"; and the man whom Mary marries instead, "feckless, good-humored" Lar Kearns. All four characters (Mr. Drumm, Dolly, Mary, and Kearns) are about sixty and have corresponding selves about forty years younger (Desmond, Dorothy, Mibs, and Lar) played by four other actors.

Like *Da*, *A Life* is set in May, but the mood is more autumnal and melancholy. Instead of looking forward to a well-earned retirement, Mr. Drumm is facing death and looking back on his life, with a sad realization of what was and what might have been. He visits Mary and Lar Kearns in order to redeem the time, perhaps not only the previous six years of silence but also a lifetime of opportunities for love wasted by selfish righteousness. As in *Da*, the set is inventively designed and lighted with various spaces to accommodate flashbacks to youth. As two older characters cross from a parlor into a kitchen, the scene jumps back forty years to their younger selves.

There are beautiful symmetries of comparison and contrast among the characters, the time periods, the stage areas, and various other mirror images. Such techniques are not only clever in themselves, but also, by distilling time and space, they reveal to the audience the importance of using well a life's short precious time. Drumm has such an epiphany in the play's last minutes: "Three hundred days a year for forty years . . . I've spent twelve thousand days doing work I despise. Instead of friends, I've had standards . . . Well, *I* failed."

OTHER MAJOR WORKS

LONG FICTION: *Parnell and the Englishwoman*, 1991; *A Wild People*, 2001.

SCREENPLAYS: *Great Catherine*, 1968; *Interlude*, 1968; *Da*, 1988; *Widow's Peak*, 1994; *Mattie*, 1998.

TELEPLAYS: *Insurrection*, 1966; *Silent Song*, 1966; *Great Expectations*, 1967 (based on Charles Dickens's novel); *Wuthering Heights*, 1967 (based on Emily Brontë's novel); *Nicholas Nickleby*, 1968 (based on Dickens's novel); *The Hound of the Baskervilles*, 1968 (based on Arthur Conan Doyle's story); *The Possessed*, 1969 (based on Fyodor Dostoevski's novel); *Dombey and Son*, 1969 (based on Dickens's novel); *A Sentimental Education*, 1970 (based on Gustave Flaubert's novel); *The Moonstone*, 1972 (based on Wilkie Collins's novel); *Strumpet City*, 1981 (based on James Plunkett's novel).

NONFICTION: *Leonard's Last Book*, 1978; *Home Before Night: Memoirs of an Irish Time and Place by the Author of "Da,"* 1979; *A Peculiar People and Other Foibles*, 1979; *Leonard's Log*, 1987 (diary); *Leonard's Log—Again*, 1988; *Out After Dark*, 1989 (autobiography); *Rover and Other Cats*, 1992; *Dear Paule*, 2000.

BIBLIOGRAPHY

Hogan, Robert. *After the Irish Renaissance: A Critical History of the Irish Drama Since "The Plough and the Stars."* Minneapolis: University of Minnesota Press, 1967. In a long chapter on the Dublin Theatre Festival, Hogan cites Leonard as "the most produced, most commercially successful playwright of the Festival." Contains a biographical sketch, followed by overviews of several plays, including *The Poker Session*, *Mick and Mick* (with a new title, *All the Nice People*, given it after its 1966 Festival opening), and *A Walk on the Water*.

Leonard, Hugh. *Out After Dark*. London: Andre Deutsch, 1989. Not only an autobiographical reminiscence of Leonard's beginnings in the theater (as an actor before a playwright), but also a full-length portrait of the life and energies of twentieth century Ireland, especially the Dalkey village life from which Leonard's humor and charming hardheadedness emerged. Leonard's first short pieces, such as "The Man on Platform Two" and "Nightingale in the Branches" (renamed *The Big Birthday*), were the seeds from which his successes grew.

Owens, Coílín D., and Joan N. Radner, eds. *Irish Drama, 1900-1980*. Washington, D.C.: Catholic University of America Press, 1990. This preface to Leonard's *Da* offers a biographical overview, covering the early plays, Irish radio, and television freelance writing. The authors quote Leonard on *Da* as "a monument to my father." Includes a select bibliography, a biography, criticism, and a good update on Leonard's journalistic endeavors and "upscale" suburban life in Dalkey.

Rollins, Ronald Gene. *Divided Ireland: Bifocal Vision in Modern Irish Drama*. New York: Lanham, 1985. Rollins pairs Brian Friel and Leonard in a "Fathers and Sons" chapter, whose thesis is that both focus on "the always awkward and ambivalent father-son relationship"; *Da*, like Friel's *Philadelphia, Here I Come!*, moves from objectivity to subjective memory and back.

Christopher Griffin,
updated by Thomas J. Taylor

MIKHAIL LERMONTOV

Born: Moscow, Russia; October 15, 1814
Died: Pyatigorsk, Russia; July 27, 1841

PRINCIPAL DRAMA

Tsigany, wr. 1830, pb. 1935
Ispantsy, wr. 1830, pb. 1935 (verse play)
Menschen und Leidenschaften, wr. 1830, pb. 1935
Stranny chelovek, wr. 1831, pb. 1935 (verse play; *A Strange One*, 1965)
Maskarad, wr. 1834-1835, pb. 1842, pr. 1917 (*Masquerade*, 1973)
Dva brata, wr. 1836, pb. 1880, pr. 1976 (*Two Brothers*, 1933)

OTHER LITERARY FORMS

Mikhail Lermontov's narrative poems include "Cherkesy" (1828; "The Circassians," 1965), "Kavkazsky plennik" (1828; "A Prisoner in the Caucasus," 1965), "Korsar" (1828; "The Corsair," 1965), "Ispoved" (1831; "A Confession," 1965), "Aul Bastindshi" (1832), "Sashka" (1834-1836), "Khadshi Abrek" (1835), "Boyarin Orsha" (1835-1836; "The Boyar Orsha," 1965), "Tambovskaya kaznacheyska" (1838; "The Tambov Treasurer's Wife," 1965), "Pesnya pro tsarya Ivana Vasilievicha i udalogo kuptsa kasashnikove" (1838; "Song of the Tsar Ivan Vasilievich and the Bold Merchant Kaksahnikov," 1965), "Mtsyri" (1839; "The Novice," 1965), "Skazka dlya detey" (1840; "A Fairy Tale for Children,"

1965), and *Demon* (1841; *The Demon*, 1875). Of these, the two best known and most important are "The Novice" and *The Demon*. They have strong dramatic overtones, especially in their use of dialogue. Both are set in the rugged mountains of the Caucasus, in a dreamlike world, and both deal with the problem of freedom versus fate and question the possibility of a free intellect devoid of moral considerations.

Although *The Demon* has remained more popular, "The Novice" is considered aesthetically superior. It is perhaps the most sustained piece of poetic rhetoric in Russian and abounds in lush descriptions of the wild Caucasian landscape. The wilderness of nature represents the untamed spirit of a novice, one who was adopted by the monks as a child but who yearns for the freedom of life and love. The rather vague plot tells of his escape from the monastery, his encounter with primitive natural elements, and his subsequent death. In this dream narrative, a journey through the unconscious, there is both a haunting musical quality and an overpowering sense of frustration expressed as a preference for death rather than the futility of a cloistered existence.

The Demon was to become the most popular poem in Russian in the second half of the nineteenth century. Its verbal music inspired an opera by Anton Rubenstein and paintings by Mikhail Vrubel. Later it was to become a source of inspiration for Aleksandr Blok and Boris Pasternak. Similar in content to "The

Mikhail Lermontov (Library of Congress)

Novice," it is unique in its presentation of the devil. Unlike John Milton's and Johann Wolfgang von Goethe's Lucifer, Lermontov's demon is not basically malicious. This demon yearns for his lost paradise and bemoans the fate that deprives him of it. He seems capable of genuine affection and invades a cloister to win the love of a beautiful Georgian princess, Tamara, whom he destroys with a fatal kiss. Lermontov was one of the first Russian authors to deal with the problem of evil, and his treatment of the demon shows a preoccupation with moral justification and fate.

Lermontov also composed more than three hundred lyric poems, many album verses, and verses of circumstance. With the exception of "Angel" (1831), perhaps the best Russian romantic lyric poem, his early verse is usually mediocre and in some cases verges on the obscene. He composed his best lyrics during the last few years of his life. Although often considered Alexander Pushkin's successor, Lermontov always remained vague and subjective. His verse

has a nervous, somewhat rugged style, with intermittent rhythm and hyperbolic images. Many of his works, however, are very popular, such as "Parus" ("The Sail," 1832) and "Testament" (1841).

Lermontov's prose fiction, possibly his most important literary contribution, includes two uncompleted novels, *Vadim* (written 1832-1834), a novel of St. Petersburg life, *Knyaginya Ligovskaya* (written 1836-1837; *Princess Ligovskaya*, 1965), and *Geroy nashego vremeni* (1839; *A Hero of Our Time*, 1854). *A Hero of Our Time*, Lermontov's only complete prose work, is considered the best Romantic novel in Russian. It consists of five tales and a preface, unified by the presence of Grigory Pechorin. A "superfluous man" in the tradition of François-René de Chateaubriand's René and Pushkin's Evgeny Onegin, Pechorin goes beyond them in his moral rebellion, defying ethical standards and looking for his own truth. His life has no purpose or goal. By using multiple narrators and points of view and Pechorin's own diary records, Lermontov maintains an objective stance while he leads the reader to a penetration of Pechorin's character. The novel is both semiautobiographical and a psychological portrait of an age. Pechorin, the child of his century, as Vissarion Belinsky described him, represents the social and political dissatisfaction of the 1840's with the conditions under Nicholas I.

Lermontov's prose and poetry are included in the five-volume *Polnoe sobranie sochinenii v piati tomakh* (1935-1937) in Russian. English editions include: *The Demon and Other Poems* (1965), *Selected Works* (1976), and several editions of *A Hero of Our Time*, of which one of the best is Vladimir Nabokov's edition.

ACHIEVEMENTS

Best known for his lyric and narrative poetry, especially *The Demon* and "The Novice," and for the only Russian Romantic novel, *A Hero of Our Time*, Mikhail Lermontov was nevertheless one of the few dramatic writers in Russia before Anton Chekhov. A child prodigy, he produced an extraordinary literary output before his death at the young age of twenty-six. He wrote all of his dramatic works before the age of twenty-two; he wrote most of them at age sixteen. Although generally considered as products of his youth, and not his mature literary output after 1837, Lermontov's plays are among the few examples of Romantic drama in Russia. This is especially important because in the 1830's there were practically no models for the theater in Russian. The only important dramas, Alexander Griboyedov's *Gore ot uma* (wr. 1824, uncensored pr. 1831, censored pb. 1833, uncensored pb. 1861; *The Mischief of Being Clever*, 1857) and Nikolai Gogol's *Revizor* (pr., pb. 1836; *The Inspector General*, 1890), were written after Lermontov's first plays.

Lermontov, however, grew up with a love for the theater. His maternal grandmother had presented plays in her home, the most notable being William Shakespeare's *Hamlet, Prince of Denmark* (pr. c. 1600-1601) on the occasion of her husband's suicide. As a child, Lermontov made wax marionettes and composed plays for them. While at the University of Moscow, the center of the theater in the 1820's and 1830's, he attended many theatrical performances. He was especially interested in Shakespeare and Friedrich Schiller, and the German Sturm und Drang became a major influence in his short dramatic career.

Because none of Lermontov's plays was presented or even published during his lifetime, they cannot be said to have influenced nineteenth century Russian drama. They are, however, valuable to the Lermontov scholar for the important autobiographical insights that they provide. They deal especially with the conflict between his grandmother and his father over his custody and with betrayed, lost, or impossible love. Soviet scholars point to the social implications of his works, noting his hatred of serfdom and his love of freedom, as evidenced by Gromova's iron hand in *Menschen und Leidenschaften* and the plea of the serfs in *A Strange One*.

An ardent member of St. Petersburg high society, Lermontov both longed for social acceptance and despised the empty aristocratic manners of his time. In the tradition of Molière, whom he knew and appreciated, he attacks the St. Petersburg nobility in a series of portraits reminiscent of the French comedian. His

contempt is especially evident in *Masquerade*, which Lermontov had projected as his most successful play, and which he hoped to see on the St. Petersburg stage. Disappointed at the refusal of the censors, he abandoned the theater and turned to lyric and prose works. This apprenticeship with five plays, however, served to sharpen his literary talent, to indicate the value of Romanticism, and to point the way to realism, the true manifestation of Russian literary greatness in the nineteenth century.

BIOGRAPHY

Mikhail Yurievich Lermontov was born on October 15, 1814, in Moscow, to an impoverished member of the petty nobility, Yury Petrovich Lermontov, and a wealthy but sickly mother, Mariya Arsenieva, the only daughter of a member of the illustrious Stolypin family. Lermontov's mother died in 1817, and his maternal grandmother, who hated her son-in-law, claimed custody of her grandson, assuming responsibility for his education and future career. While Lermontov was a child, his father left his son with the boy's grandmother and seldom met with him again before his death in 1831. Lermontov seems to have spent a happy childhood with his grandmother and cousins, especially Shan-Girei, at his grandmother's estate at Tarkhany. Twice they visited the Caucasus because of young Mikhail Yurievich's ailing health, an awesome experience later reflected in his verse and prose.

Lermontov was educated at Tarkhany by private tutors and showed a special aptitude for music, evident in the lyric quality of his verse, and for languages, in which he read widely. Foreign authors greatly influenced his writings, especially Shakespeare, Schiller, George Gordon, Lord Byron, and Molière. Lermontov began early to manifest a weakness for the affairs of the heart, and unhappy love affairs were to characterize his short life. His first serious involvement came in 1830 with Ekaterina Aleksandrovna Sushkova, who rejected him and, like Onegin and Tatyana, was herself to be rejected by him later. A rather mysterious young woman, Natalia Fedorovna Ivanova, was the inspiration for *A Strange One*, and Varvara Lopukhina was to become the angel and the muse of his life and his literary career.

In 1827, Elizaveta Arsenieva took her grandson to Moscow to prepare him for a university career. At first educated by private tutors, he attended the School for the Nobility from 1828 to 1830, when he was admitted to the University of Moscow, where he remained until 1832. Meanwhile, during that time, his father died. As an adolescent, Lermontov seems to have had rather cordial relations with his father, much to his grandmother's dismay, as reflected in the two autobiographical plays, *Menschen und Leidenschaften* and *A Strange One*. In 1832, Lermontov moved to St. Petersburg, at first planning to attend the university, but later entering the School of Guard Ensigns and Cavalry Cadets, from which he was graduated as cornet, or second lieutenant, in 1834. The period from 1834 to 1837, which he spent at Tsarskoe Selo as a Life Guard Hussar, was a time of frivolous living and writing, although Lermontov's last two plays date from this time.

In 1837, Pushkin died, killed in a duel. An unknown author circulated a poem entitled "Smert poeta" ("The Death of a Poet") and became famous overnight. He was soon identified as Lermontov. Less popular with the strict censorship of the day, he was sentenced to exile in the Caucasus, where he remained from March to December. Pardoned the following year, Lermontov returned to the capital, where he began to publish lyrics, including his best narrative poems, *The Demon* and "The Novice," in 1839. Portions of his novel *A Hero of Our Time* also began to appear that year. In 1840, a duel with Ernest de Barante again sent him to exile in the Caucasus. There he distinguished himself in hand-to-hand combat with rebel Caucasian tribes. After a two-month leave, Lermontov was to rejoin his regiment, and during his return journey, he wrote some of his best lyrics. With friends in Pyatigorsk, Lermontov chose to mock a certain Nikolay Martynov, who was an officer and former schoolmate at the Guards' School. Martynor challenged him to a duel. On July 27, 1841, Martynor shot Lermontov, killing him. Lermontov's poem on the subject of Pushkin's untimely death as the result of a duel thus ironically foreshadowed his own.

ANALYSIS

John Garrard, following Boris Eikhenbaum, lists several major themes in Mikhail Lermontov's juvenilia, which includes his five plays, written between 1830 and 1836. These themes include the tragic nature of love, the cult of Napoleon, the demoniac element, disillusionment, vengeance, passion for freedom, and original innocence. Of these, the most evident in the dramatic works are the tragic nature of love, disillusionment, vengeance, and the demoniac element. Lermontov reveals much autobiographical information in his plays, yet he also manifests in them the qualities of musical rhythm, ease of language, and facility with verse, along with talent for prose. Themes that were to characterize his lyric poems, such as friendship, vengeance, conquest of women, rivalry, and jealousy, are also present in his plays.

Particularly in his plays, Lermontov continues to seek an autobiographical hero. He is called Fernando in *Ispantsy*, Yury Volin in *Menschen und Leidenschaften*, Arbenin in both *A Strange One* and *Masquerade*, and both Alexander and Yury, in *Two Brothers*. Especially in the early plays, Lermontov's model is the Byronic hero. During the years from 1826 to 1832, and particularly from 1830 to 1832, Lermontov was strongly attracted by both the author and the person Byron. Yet most critics, following Lermontov himself, stress the difference between Byron and Lermontov. While the English poet used his works as a stage, Lermontov was totally sincere and actually experienced the frustrations and disillusionment he expressed in his plays. A morbid, fatalistic young man who yearned for social acceptance yet never failed to antagonize people by his intensity and cynicism, Lermontov suffered from the discord between the real and the ideal and was haunted by the desire for perfection.

Lacking in self-confidence, Lermontov's heroes consider themselves as victims of fate. In *Masquerade*, Kazarin speaks of the world as a deck of cards. The heroes, like their author, have a dual personality, very aptly described in the two brothers, Alexander and Yury, in Lermontov's unfinished drama, *Two Brothers*, or by the repeated theme of the angel and the demon in Lermontov's poetry. The brothers both respect and detest high society, desiring a social life as well as solitude. They are violent and intense men who are inclined to jump to conclusions. At the first sign of betrayal, their rage is uncontrollable and they seek immediate revenge. Arbenin of *Masquerade*, for example, poisons his wife at the slightest suspicion of infidelity, neither seeking proof nor heeding her protestations of innocence.

Lermontov was deprived of both mother and father during his childhood, growing up under the care of his domineering maternal grandmother, and thus his heroes express a longing for maternal and paternal affection. In *Ispantsy*, Lermontov's first drama, Fernando is reared by a foster parent and eventually meets his real father. Then, unknown to him, he falls in love with his sister. *Menschen und Leidenschaften* depicts a series of quarrels between a grandmother and a father for the possession of the son, ending with a rupture with the grandmother and a curse from the father. In *A Strange One*, the father is the villain, caring little for the son or the mother, and he even permits the mother to die without forgiving her for the infidelity she has acknowledged and repented. In *Two Brothers*, a father is tortured by the rivalry of his two sons for Vera Zagorskina, a married woman formerly beloved of both. In none of these plays is the conflict resolved, and the hero never receives the acceptance for which he yearns.

Not only are maternal and paternal love unrealized in Lermontov's plays, but also unrealized is romantic love. The desire for the love of a woman inevitably meets with frustration, and usually tragedy. Each play tells a story of unfulfilled love: Emilia and Fernando in *Ispantsy*, Yury and Lyubov in *Menschen und Leidenschaften*, Natasha and Arbenin in *A Strange One*, Nina and Arbenin in *Masquerade*, and Alexander and Yury for Vera in *Two Brothers*. The beloved woman is usually idealized, and she seems to represent either the mysterious Natalia Fedorovna Ivanovna or Varvara Lopukhina in Lermontov's own youth. Yet at the same time, the woman is either unfaithful or suspected of infidelity. The most striking example is *Masquerade*, in which the loss of a bracelet leads Arbenin to suspect his wife's involvement with his rival Zvezdich at a masquerade party.

Here the demoniac element comes into play. It is linked with a desire for vengeance, which seemed to characterize Lermontov himself, described by his friends as someone who always needed a victim. In their desire to avenge the betrayal—supposed or real—of a woman, Lermontov's heroes either destroy the woman or ruin themselves. Sorrini, the villain in *Ispantsy*, plans to trick Emilia for her refusal of his attentions, and she is actually killed by her real lover, Fernando. In *A Strange One*, Arbenin, suspecting Natasha's infidelity and distraught by his father's curse, poisons himself. *Masquerade* again remains the most violent example of vengeance, with the sadistic poisoning of Nina and the cruel revelation of the truth by the Stranger in Lermontov's second version of the play.

There is little variety in Lermontov's plays. He frequently borrowed from himself, and *Menschen und Leidenschaften* and *A Strange One* are merely variations on the same theme, the desire for paternal love. While very romantic in tone, his plays never reach a general subject, nor are they detached from their author. This is probably attributable both to Lermontov's youth and inexperience and to the fact that he had no Russian models. Most Russian theater in the 1830's consisted of vaudeville and melodrama of French origin, Lermontov, however, was strongly influenced by Shakespeare and Schiller. *Ispantsy* was inspired in large measure by Schiller's *Don Carlos, Infant von Spanien* (pr., pb. 1787; *Don Carlos, Infante of Spain*, 1798) and to some extent by Victor Hugo's *Hernani* (pr., pb. 1830; English translation, 1830). Lermontov's sympathetic treatment of the Jews was inspired by Gotthold Ephraim Lessing's *Nathan der Weise* (pb. 1779; *Nathan the Wise*, 1781) and Sir Walter Scott's *Ivanhoe* (1820).

Lermontov's first play, *Ispantsy*, is a historical melodrama, with long speeches, declamations, ponderous language, and a lack of decisive action. Although Lermontov abandoned foreign themes in his later works, he never fully lost his taste for melodrama, which is especially evident in the ghoulish death scene in *Masquerade*. He invariably sought a melodramatic ending for his plays: suicide, poisoning, or madness. The juxtaposition of a wedding and a funeral in *A Strange One* is a rather stylized but effective literary device. In most cases, the speech of the characters is bookish rather than natural, although the servants in *Menschen und Leidenschaften* and *A Strange One* do speak in a more informal style.

As Lermontov's plots are all similar, so his characters tend to resemble one another. They may be reduced to the autobiographical Byronic hero, the ideal woman, the unfaithful friend, and the father or mother figures. The fact that Lermontov uses the same names produces some confusion. Arbenin is the hero in two tragedies; Yury, in another two. Frequently the speeches of the characters do not flow from their personalities but are used by Lermontov to develop his ideas. In *Ispantsy*, the characters are arbitrarily stereotyped into heroes (the Jews) and villains (the Spanish Inquisition). The servants, however, seem to be more individualized and present a rather sympathetic portrait, attractive to Soviet literary critics who are anxious to emphasize Lermontov's social tendencies and hatred of serfdom.

The themes chosen by Lermontov—love and hate, jealousy, suspicion, murder, and violence—are rather Dostoevskian in nature, but they do not attain quite the same grandeur in Lermontov's hands because of his lack of integration and his narrow scope. In the works of Fyodor Dostoevski, the themes gain metaphysical stature. Lermontov indeed addressed philosophical issues in his mature works, especially dualism and the problem of evil, yet he did not attain to this level in his dramas, except in rare intervals, because he himself is the center of each one, and he did not learn to universalize autobiography.

Lermontov's plays show progress in dramatic technique. He shows greater control of his characters and his plot in *Menschen und Leidenschaften* and *A Strange One* than in *Ispantsy*. He varies the style and level of speech, places some important actions offstage, and widens the scope of his scenes. In *Masquerade*, he had an audience in mind for the first time, hoping to present the play before the St. Petersburg society he both admired and scorned—hence the satiric scenes that refer to them. More at home with Russian than with foreign themes, he was thus better in his later dramas. He was able to write in both po-

etry and prose, thus foreshadowing the dominance of prose in Russian literature, a development that was to mark its greatness. Unfortunately, Lermontov did not pursue his dramatic talents, which showed promise. His contribution to the Russian stage is what B. M. Eikhenbaum terms "theoretical experimentation."

While Lermontov's first full-length play, *Ispantsy*, is considered largely imitative and unoriginal, his next two, *Menschen und Leidenschaften* and *A Strange One*, are much more promising. They are called the autobiographical plays and were written in prose rather than poetry, as was *Ispantsy*. Because they are similar in tone and theme, they are usually considered together. Lermontov's first attempt at the theater, an opera based on Pushkin's play of the same name, called *Tsigany*, remained a fragment of a few pages.

MENSCHEN UND LEIDENSCHAFTEN

The plot of *Menschen und Leidenschaften* takes place on two levels, a family intrigue and a love triangle. The hero is Yury Nikolaevich Volin, whose father has come with his uncle to claim him after he has spent his youth with his grandmother, Marfa Ivanovna Gromova, whose violent personality corresponds to her name, which means "thunder." She rules her household with an iron hand and will stop at nothing to retain her grandson. Meanwhile, Yury decides to leave his grandmother and go with his father, who, he maintains, has the first claim on his affections. He is also in love with his cousin Lyubov, and addresses her as his consoling angel. His friend Zarutsky loves Lyubov's sister, Eliza, a rather flighty and unsteady young woman. Yury sees Lyubov in the company of Zarutsky and suspects infidelity. Actually, Zarutsky has come only to request Lyubov's assistance in arranging a meeting with Eliza.

As Marfa plots to keep her grandson with the collaboration of her servant Darya, Vasily Mikhailovich, Yury's uncle, tries to undermine the love of father and son by slander. Yury's father, believing his brother, curses his son. Yury is unable to bear the double burden of unrequited love and a father's curse, and so swallows poison. When death is imminent, he overhears Lyubov and Eliza talking and learns that Lyubov is innocent—and that his death is in vain.

Although the plot is overtly autobiographical, it lacks true unity. The character of Marfa Ivanovna is very powerful, and is probably inspired more by Denis Fonvizin's landowners than by Elizaveta Arsenieva, Lermontov's grandmother. In a charming scene before Yury swallows the poison, he inquires about his valet Ivan's family and children, and he advises him never to curse them. Thus Lermontov portrays the serfs with humanity and compassion, a point extolled by Soviet critics. Yury is a typical Byronic hero: melancholy, overwhelmed by a strange premonition, highly ebullient, and suspicious.

A STRANGE ONE

In the second play, *A Strange One*, Lermontov calls the hero Vladimir Arbenin. He also is torn by a family conflict, this time between his mother and his father, and an unfortunate love affair, but here the woman is actually guilty of infidelity. Arbenin's father is a cold, unsympathetic man, who has divorced his wife for a youthful flirtation of which she has long since repented. Arbenin pleads with him to visit his mother on her deathbed, but he consistently refuses. When she dies, he accuses his father of murder.

Meanwhile, Arbenin is in love with Natasha, modeled on Natalia Ivanova. Her cousin Sophia also loves him and by her slander succeeds in convincing Natasha to accept instead Arbenin's best friend Belinskoy, who knowingly betrays him and courts Natasha in order to make a rich marriage. Natasha accepts Belinskoy, and Arbenin, unable to endure the double tragedy, goes mad. As a final irony, Natasha and Belinskoy's marriage will take place on the day of Arbenin's funeral.

The hero of *A Strange One* also has a dual personality, tender yet cruel and vengeful. There is a tender scene in which the serfs ask Belinskoy and Arbenin to save them from their cruel mistress. On the whole, this play has a wider scope than Lermontov's other plays and shows his talent for satire and his use of varied styles because the servants are clearly distinguished from their masters. Again, Soviet critics see in the play an attack on serfdom. As dramatist, Lermontov is much better in *A Strange One*. His characterization has improved, his staging is varied, with

some important actions taking place behind the scenes, and his control of his material is much tighter. Yet neither *Menschen und Leidenschaften* nor *A Strange One* is considered highly successful drama.

MASQUERADE

Lermontov placed his highest hopes on *Masquerade*, planning it for the St. Petersburg stage, where he wished both to impress and to criticize the aristocracy of the times. In this play, he returned to poetry, using the *volny iamb*, or free iamb, an iambic meter with a varied number of feet. The hero is once again Arbenin, but this time the conflict of mother and father has disappeared, and only the love motif remains. Lermontov was by now quite familiar with St. Petersburg high society, so he used it as his setting and interspersed a highly emotional plot with satire.

At the beginning of the play, Arbenin generously uses his own mastery at cards to help a friend, Zvezdich, out of an embarrassing situation. Arbenin, a former dandy of loose morals, has married for money and surprisingly finds himself in love with his wife, Nina, modeled on Varvara Lopukhina, Lermontov's consoling angel. At a masquerade ball, Zvezdich meets a woman whom he believes to be Nina and tries to win her affection. When Nina's bracelet is missing, Arbenin accuses her of infidelity, although she steadfastly protests her innocence.

Meanwhile, the Baroness Stahl, who is actually guilty of soliciting Zvezdich's attention, spreads abroad the story of Nina's supposed guilt. She is in love with Zvezdich, "out of boredom, frustration, or jealousy." Arbenin tries to kill Zvezdich but is unable to do so. He does, however, humiliate Zvezdich at a card game by accusing him of cheating. Now convinced that his wife is guilty, Arbenin poisons her ice cream and then sadistically watches her die, cruelly repeating his accusations. She dies, protesting her innocence.

When Lermontov presented the play to the censors, in 1835, it was flatly rejected on the grounds of immorality. He then added a fourth act, in which Arbenin meets a man whom he had once humiliated at cards, who informs him of the truth about his wife and accuses him of murder. Arbenin goes mad as a result. This version, however, had no more success than the previous version. Lermontov then emasculated the entire play, but the censors still refused approval. Not until 1852 was the play approved, and it was not staged until 1917 by Vsevolod Meyerhold's theater. Lermontov, disappointed, abandoned the theater and became the author of other works that were to assure his fame, especially narrative and lyric poems and prose fiction.

OTHER MAJOR WORKS

LONG FICTION: *Vadim*, wr. 1832-1834, pb. 1935-1937 (in *Polnoe sobranie sochinenii v piati tomakh*); *Knyaginya Ligovskaya*, wr. 1836-1837, pb. 1935-1937 (in *Polnoe sobranie sochinenii v piati tomakh*; *Geroy nashego vremeni*, 1839 (serial), 1840 (book; *A Hero of Our Time*, 1854); *Princess Ligovskaya*, 1965).

POETRY: *Pesnya pro tsarya Ivana Vasilyevicha, molodogo oprichnika i udalogo kuptsa Kalashnikova*, 1837 (*A Song About Tsar Ivan Vasilyevitch, His Young Body-Guard, and the Valiant Merchant Kalashnikov*, 1911); *Stikhotvoreniya M. Lermontova*, 1840; *Demon*, 1841 (*The Demon*, 1875); *The Demon and Other Poems*, 1965; *Mikhail Lermontov: Major Poetical Works*, 1983.

MISCELLANEOUS: *Sochtsnentsya M. Ya. Lermontova*, 1889-1891 (6 volumes); *Polnoe sobranie sochinenii v piati tomakh*, 1935-1937 (5 volumes; includes all of his prose and poetry); *Polnoe sobranie sochinenii v shesti tomakh*, 1954-1957 (6 volumes; includes all of his prose and poetry); *A Lermontov Reader*, 1965 (includes *Princess Ligovskaya, A Strange One*, and poetry); *Michael Lermontov: Biography and Translation*, 1967; *Selected Works*, 1976 (includes prose and poetry).

BIBLIOGRAPHY

Briggs, A. D. P., ed. *Mikhail Lermontov: Commemorative Essays*. Birmingham, England: University of Birmingham, 1992. A collection of papers from a conference at the University of Birmingham in July, 1991, on Lermontov and his works. Bibliography and index.

Eikhenbaum, B. M. *Lermontov: A Study in Literary-Historical Evaluation*. Ann Arbor, Mich.: Ardis, 1981. A critical analysis of Lermontov's works that examines the historical context. Bibliography.

Garrard, John. *Mikhail Lermontov*. Boston: Twayne, 1982. A basic biography of Lermontov that covers his life and works. Bibliography and index.

Golstein, Vladimir. *Lermontov's Narratives of Heroism*. Evanston, Ill.: Northwestern university Press, 1998. A study of Lermontov's treatment of heroes in his literary works. Bibliography and index.

Vickery, Walter N. *M. Iu. Lermontov: His Life and Work*. München, Germany: O. Sagner, 2001. A biography of Lermontov that examines his life and work. Bibliography.

Irma M. Kashuba

ALAIN-RENÉ LESAGE

Born: Sarzeau, France; December 13, 1668
Died: Boulogne, France; November 17, 1747

PRINCIPAL DRAMA

Crispin, rival de son maître, pr., pb. 1707 (*Crispin, Rival of His Master*, 1766)
Turcaret: Comédie en cinq actes, pr., pb. 1709 (English translation, 1923)
Le Théâtre de la Foire: Ou, L'Opéra comique, pr. 1712-1738, pb. 1721-1737 (10 volumes; with d'Orneval, Louis Fuzilier, and others)
Œuvres de Lesage, pb. 1821 (volumes 11 and 12)

OTHER LITERARY FORMS

Author of translations, of dialogues, of varia, and of a great number of plays, Alain-René Lesage is best known as a novelist. His reputation as a novelist rests primarily on two works: *Le Diable boiteux* (1707;

The Devil upon Two Sticks, 1708, 1726), loosely adapted from Luis Vélez de Guevara's *El diablo cojuelo* (1641), and the highly original *Histoire de Gil Blas de Santillane* (1715-1735; *The History of Gil Blas of Santillane*, 1716, 1735; better known as *Gil Blas*). Both novels appear to deal with the Spain of the early seventeenth century, but in fact they are barely disguised satires of the mores of France a full century later. This was not a new procedure: It had been used as a basic ploy by the writers of imaginary voyages—of which Cyrano de Bergerac was perhaps the first to have achieved lasting renown. In fact, contrary to the claims of certain manuals of literary history, Lesage never saw Spain, and so a realistic description of the place and its mores would have been most difficult outside the realm of slavish imitation. In his two major novels—as in his *Histoire de Don Guzman d'Alfarache* (1732; *The Pleasant Adventures of Gusman of Alfarache*, 1812); *Le Bachelier de Salamanque* (1736; *The Bachelor of Salamanca*, 1737-1739), and *La Valise trouvée* (1740)—Lesage takes the basic plot from a Spanish author as well as many of his anecdotes, and adds a style and descriptions that, though somewhat derivative—owing more to French predecessors such as Jean de La Bruyère than to any Spanish influence—are highly original when the finished product is examined.

The Devil upon Two Sticks is a good case in point. Its first edition came out in mid-1707 and contained a fair number of anecdotes that can easily be traced to Guevara. Quickly and accurately judging the real source of its success, Lesage enlarged the work, adding numerous new anecdotes and countless allusions to his contemporaries for a second edition that appeared shortly thereafter. He repeated the process for a third edition, which also came out before the end of that year. The popularity of the work is confirmed not only by these three editions in rapid succession but also by two pirated ones (Amsterdam, same year) and by in excess of thirty more before the end of the century. Such was the success of the novel that in October, 1707, Florent Carton Dancourt, friend and protector of Lesage, put out two comedies, one entitled *Le Diable boiteux* and the other *Le Second chapitre du diable boiteux*. The plots in no way resemble that of Lesage's novel, but the debt is nevertheless substantial.

It was undoubtedly to cash in on the success of *The Devil upon Two Sticks* that Lesage's editor asked him for something in the same vein but more original and unabashedly contemporary. The first six books of *Gil Blas* appeared in 1715; the twelfth and last did not come out until twenty years later. Each installment was an immediate success, a verdict that has stood the test of time: The work is today considered the first French novel of mores and the first one that can truly be considered picaresque. Spanish picaresque novels had been very popular in France for some time, and there had been numerous translations. The influence of the Spanish picaresque can easily be seen in works such as Tristan L'Hermite's *Le Page disgracié* (1643) or Charles Sorel's *Histoire comique de Francion* (1623, enlarged 1633), but when all is said and done, there is no true French *picaro*—that resourceful young scoundrel whose amoral ways are the result of the unkind blows of fate and the evils of society, and who hops from one adventure to another merely to afford the reader a panoramic view of that society—before Gil Blas. In turn victim and *débrouillard*, Gil Blas is lackey, secretary, confidant of the powerful, rising quickly and falling with equal rapidity; he eventually manages to retire to a château that he has been able to acquire in spite of all the vicissitudes of his adventurous life and spends the rest of his years in peace. These adventures are but a framework, an excuse for the cynical and satiric commentary on the society the picaro traverses, and that society is definitely French, as viewed by Lesage mercilessly and with biting irony. Spain is the fiction, and it is this "unrealism" that allows the author to be all the more realistic about his contemporaries. Parisians and provincials; nobles, burghers, and peasants; intellectuals, clergymen, and rogues—the distinction is not always easy to maintain or to perceive—all are there in this vast tableau of mores, where vices and general corruption are the rule rather than the exception.

ACHIEVEMENTS

Whether one fully agrees with the verdict that Alain-René Lesage deserves his place in literary history more on the basis of his novels than on the basis of his plays, it is undeniable that his contributions to the development of eighteenth century French comedy are far from negligible. It is fashionable to dismiss all but two of his plays, *Crispin, Rival of His Master* and *Turcaret*, and to belittle the originality of these two in the bargain. Neither verdict is, however, fair.

Crispin, Rival of His Master is a delightful one-act curtain raiser whose outlandish *lazzi* provoke such laughter as to make one forgive the generally unsavory nature of all its characters. Those who have considered the play (and *Turcaret*) unpleasant because of its unlikable characters have done so because they took these characters out of the comedic *jeu* and reduced the play to pure literature. Having failed to revive romanesque comedy, with his close adaptations of Spanish drama, Lesage, with *Crispin, Rival of His Master* and eventually with *Turcaret*—brought life to the comedy of manners. Although his friend Dancourt had done much for the genre, Dancourt's comedies, populated by puppets, are sometimes funny but never really alive. Lesage's Crispin and Frontin owe much of their psychology to Molière's Scapin or Sganarelle, but these predecessors are characters created principally to make one laugh—at them, or at their tricks and trickery. Crispin and Frontin are closer to Figaro than to Scapin. Like the latter, they hold the reins of the intrigue, but like the former, they do so out of pride and ambition: pride in their social standing and their refusal to be denigrated solely on the basis of their lowly birth and condition; ambition, antithetically, to rise above that station thanks exclusively to their superior wit enhanced by their nearly total lack of scruples. With them, as with Figaro, one does not have characters wishing to change class—which is definitely the desire of a Jourdain—but deliberately challenging the entire notion of class, all the while making one laugh at those whose behavior is predicated on such notions. Comedy, particularly of mores, owes it to itself to be iconoclastic. *Crispin, Rival of His Master* and *Turcaret*, especially when seen (or read with the mind's eye on the physical aspects of stage business), are masterpieces of demystification. The critics have not always recognized this fact, but the theatergoing public has, and both these plays have maintained a more than honorable position in the repertoire of the Comédie-Française.

In spite of the impression given by school manuals, the French of the eighteenth century were even more avid theater devotees than their predecessors. Furthermore, they fancied themselves as connoisseurs, and this led to an era of specialization. Whereas the Comédie-Française, patronized mainly by the upper classes, restricted its offerings to more elevated genres defending the noble virtues and aspirations of its patrons, the more popular stages, particularly those of the fairs, gleefully responded to the plebeian demands of its *roturier* public. When Lesage, disappointed and hurt, left the Française for the Foire, he perforce changed his dramatic outlook, but he did not, for all that, give up all thoughts of coherent dramaturgy. Relying heavily on their legacy from the *commedia dell'arte*, the artists of the Foire had performed vaudevilles more remarkable for their isolated *lazzi* and disconnected burlesque scenes than for well-knit entities. Lesage single-handedly changed that—nine of the ten volumes of *Le Théâtre de la Foire* are taken up by plays that are entirely or partly by him. Toning down the excessively coarse tendencies of the Foire, he reduced the savagery of its political sallies for the sake of a less strident but more consistent and coherent comedy of manners. He also insisted on at least a semblance of structure and plot. The result is a light and lighthearted theater, highly topical and timely, with little or no thought given to tradition and verisimilitude, a forerunner of nineteenth century vaudeville.

BIOGRAPHY

Born in 1668 into an old Breton family, Alain-René Lesage had a very comfortable early childhood. In 1677, however, his mother died, and his father died five years later. Lesage was then adopted by his uncles, who promptly dispossessed him. The resulting penury was to be a major factor in his subsequent literary vocation. In an effort to continue the family tradition, Lesage began to study law, first at the Jesuit *collège* in Vannes—where Father Baschard gave him his first taste of and for theater—and later in Paris. Admitted to the bar, he was forced by contingencies to settle in the lowest strata of the legal profession. This did not prevent him from frequenting higher social and literary circles, and from meeting literary figures such as Dancourt, with whom he started a lifelong friendship and who encouraged his tastes for the stage. In 1694, he met and married Marie-Élisabeth Huyard, the daughter of a humble carpenter. Beautiful, pleasant, and totally devoted to René—a fully reciprocated devotion—she was to give him an element of stability and peace that he enjoyed all his life. She also gave him three sons and a daughter. Two of the sons were to become actors—one famous at the Comédie-Française, while the other disappeared into obscurity with a roving troupe in Germany—and the third became canon in Boulogne-sur-Mer.

In 1695, Lesage published his first literary endeavor, a translation of some letters from a Greek Sophist. The work of a careless hack, it went without reward of any kind. Some years later, Lesage met the Abbé de Lyonne, who became his protector, giving him a modest pension—which was to be paid until the death of that Maecenas in 1715—and urging him to learn Spanish so that he might translate some of the better plays of Pedro Calderón de la Barca and Lope de Vega Carpio. By 1700, Lesage had published his first translations from the Spanish. Two years later, the Comédie-Française accepted and played his *Le Point d'honneur*, an adaptation of *No hay amigo para amigo* (1636), by Francisco de Rojas Zorrilla. Originally in five acts, the adaptation was reduced to three by its author "to make it more lively," to use his own words. The change was of no avail: The play was lustily booed and withdrawn after two performances. Five years later, fate was less fickle with its bounty. In March, 1707, the Française performed his *Don César Ursin*, another adaptation from the Spanish (this time, of Calderón's *Mejor esta, que estaba*, 1630; *From Bad to Worse*, 1805)—and another utter failure—accompanied on the program by *Crispin, Rival of His Master*. During a performance at court, *Crispin, Rival of His Master* got the same treatment as *Don César Ursin*; not so in Paris, where it was

warmly applauded. Later that same year, *The Devil upon Two Sticks* appeared, and the success of the novel eclipsed that of the play.

The following year, Lesage presented a one-act comedy, *La Tontine*, to the Comédie-Française, which rejected it. It was eventually performed (in 1714) by the actors of the Foire under the title *Arlequin colonel*. The Comédie was not to follow suit until 1732. In the meanwhile, undaunted by the rebuff of the *comédiens*, Lesage gave them his dramatic magnum opus, *Turcaret*, which they also rejected. This time, Lesage did not accept the verdict. Sensing that the rejection stemmed from reasons other than artistic, he enlisted the aid of every powerful person he knew. Finally, in early 1709, following a direct order from the Dauphin, the five-act comedy was performed at the Comédie-Française. Even so, the powerful lobby of the financiers won out, and after only seven performances, the play was withdrawn. Lesage was a proud man. The gate for the seven performances had been more than respectable, and he never forgave the Comédie for having caved in to pressures having nothing to do with dramatic considerations. He turned his back on them, and from that day on wrote exclusively for the Foire.

The year 1715 was to be an important one in the career of Lesage. The first six books of *Gil Blas* were published and obtained an immediate and resounding success. That year, Louis XIV died, and the Regent, taking interest in the players of the Foire, protected them and even invited them repeatedly to court, thus giving them a degree of legitimacy and standing that they had never before enjoyed. Though their struggle against established rivals such as the Comédie-Française and the Opéra were far from over, this protection did earn for them a certain emancipation from artistic restrictions. In the ensuing years, the crises in that conflict spurred Lesage to lampoon his former collaborators of the Comédie in delightful works such as *La Querelle des théâtres* (1718) and *La Fausse Foire* (1721), both prologues, and *Le Rappel de la Foire à la vie* (1721), a lively one-act play. Also in 1721 appeared the first volume of *Le Théâtre de la Foire*. Three years later, a second volume of this collaborative effort appeared, almost simultaneously with the appearance of the second part (books 7 through 9) of *Gil Blas*.

In 1730, Lesage's oldest son (who, in spite of his father's remonstrances, had earlier joined the Comédie-Française, thus causing a temporary rift between father and son) played in a revival of *Turcaret*. The production must have had a certain success, since Montmesnil—the stage name of the son—was still playing the role a year later, a success which undoubtedly had much to do with the reconciliation of the two. That year, 1731, another successful volume of the *Théâtre de la Foire* was published. One year later, in 1732, *The Pleasant Adventures of Gusman of Alfarache* was published, followed by another novel, *Les Aventures de M. Robert Chevalier dit de Beauchesne* (*The Adventures of Robert Chevalier*, 1745). Both enjoyed popular favor, though contemporary critics saw, particularly in the latter, the work of a tiring hack. The actors of the Française, hoping perhaps to cash in on Lesage's popularity, finally decided to perform *La Tontine*; they proved only that their original rejection had not been without merit: The play was an utter failure.

This admixture of success and failure marks the years that follow. The volumes of the *Théâtre de la Foire* that came out in regular succession until 1734 owe much of their popularity to the contributions of Lesage; the last three volumes of *Gil Blas* (1735) were as popular as the preceding ones. On the other hand, *The Bachelor of Salamanca* did not get the same kind reception, and deservedly so. Lesage's last work of fiction, *La Valise trouvée*, was similarly dismissed, and with equal justification. The talents of the old man were definitely abandoning him. In 1743, Montmesnil died quite suddenly. Lesage, extremely grieved and aware of his failing ability to earn a decent living with his pen, decided to retire. With his wife, he went to live with his second son, then canon in Boulogne-sur-Mer. He spent his remaining years there in domestic tranquillity and died on November 17, 1747, in the arms of his wife.

ANALYSIS

Although Alain-René Lesage is probably best remembered for his novels, some critics argue that his dramatic works made a significant contribution to the French theater. His two best-known plays, *Crispin, Rival of His Master* and *Tucaret*, enjoyed popularity with audiences if not with critics.

CRISPIN, RIVAL OF HIS MASTER

Too much has been made of the debt which *Crispin, Rival of His Master* owes to Spanish drama. In fact, it owes much more to Molière—especially to the late Molière, the author of plays such as *Monsieur de Pourceaugnac* (pr. 1669; English translation, 1704) and the *comédies-ballets* from which long monologues have disappeared and in which rapid-fire dialogues give rise to a frenetic atmosphere of festive madness—and to Dancourt than to any foreign literature or influence.

Though the witty and sparkling dialogues and the astounding peripeteias are definite assets of this fast-paced one-act comedy, its originality lies in the creation of the titular hero, Crispin. He is not the only delineated character, but he does dominate. With quick, bold strokes, Lesage presents a broad array of pawns that Crispin will manipulate almost at will. One is quickly made to feel that one knows the gullible bourgeois, all the easier to fool because they think themselves to be keen judges of people and as shrewd as it is possible to be; the silly old mother-in-law-to-be, "between twenty-five and sixty," who believes any piece of flattery and sees the sense only of the last opinion she encounters, however much it may contradict what she has heard—and accepted—just before; the silly lover, Valère, without a cent or a conscience, who is readily tricked because he believes himself to be a consummate trickster; and Crispin's colleague, Labranche, who believes in honor among thieves, especially if one's fellow thief is as formidable as Crispin.

The notion of servants seconding the love interests of their young masters was already a comedic cliché at the time of the creation of *Crispin, Rival of His Master*; so was the idea of such servants acting like their masters, and even being caught up in the game. It had been a staple of the *commedia dell'arte* when Molière borrowed it for his *Les Précieuses ridicules* (pr. 1659, pb. 1660; *The Affected Young Ladies*, 1732). What is new in this play is that Crispin sees the possibilities of the role he is assigned and decides to emancipate himself from the inept tutelage of his master. From the outset, he plans to take his master's place, wooing the young lady coveted by that penurious employer, not so as to win her heart but her dowry, with which he plans to abscond before anyone is the wiser. Boastful of his quick wit, of his ability to turn any situation to his immediate advantage, and above all of his lack of morals and of conscience, he is more than the wearer of Scapino's mantle. He foreshadows Frontin and even the less brutal but more revolutionary Figaro. Cynical, irreverent, a skillful manipulator of people and of events, the resourceful Crispin talks himself into and out of one tight spot after another. Only the circumstances of a very cleverly contrived and resolved plot foil him (even so, he manages to survive). Only Figaro will have more brio, more wit used in the unequal fight with the powerful of his society. Like Figaro, Crispin is a survivor; just as amoral, but less grating, his immediate successor Frontin will do more than merely survive—he will conquer.

TURCARET

Insofar as the borrowings of Lesage for *Turcaret* are concerned, much the same can be said as for *Crispin, Rival of His Master*: The case, however legitimate, has been overstated. To be sure, one can find traces, in *Turcaret*, of La Bruyère's indignation, of the violent diatribes of the diverse pamphlets launched against financiers, as well as echoes of previous comedies, from those of Molière to the more contemporary ones of Dancourt. Such roots and echoes are inevitable in any work of art dealing with manners and character, and Molière is not considered a lesser dramatist for having borrowed from comedic predecessors. What matters is what Lesage did with his gleanings, and there his contribution is undeniable and sizable. *Turcaret* is a powerful synthesis of all the aforementioned elements, containing not the lifeless puppets that merrily flit through the dramas of Dancourt, but real, living characters. The situations and conditions are as vivid today as they were in 1708, though perforce some of the satire has lost the bite of its topicality. Most important of all, if one remains aware of what Molière called *le jeu du théâtre*,

then one sees that for all its topicality, *Turcaret* remains a fairly funny play. It is intended to moralize, to castigate mores, but through laughter, though it must be conceded that at times the authorial presence is too heavy and too ironically manifest to give free rein to uninhibited laughter.

For the modern reader, much of the humor has lost its edge; the topicality of the satire, an asset in 1708, has dated the work. At the time of the creation of *Turcaret*, the aristocracy was in decline, and the bourgeoisie, particularly the financiers, tax collectors, and speculators, were in full swing. Furthermore, the aristocracy had lost its values as well as its wealth: Politeness, the caricaturesque façade that Molière had mocked as the pretense of true nobility, had become the norm. It is this shallow, callous society, totally amoral and cynical, that *Turcaret* depicts. As such, it is a comedy of manners, or seems that way to the modern reader. To the contemporaries of Lesage, it was more, a *comédie d'actualité*, full of references to current events and situations, people and ploys. The expenses incurred by the crown had put it at the mercy of the financiers and tax farmers, who had become all-powerful. The wars of Louis XIV had made their rise possible: They were exploited by the aristocracy, but in exchange were given the right to exploit the people, and this they did ruthlessly. *Turcaret* is not simply a description of mores and manners; it is a polemical piece. Whereas *Crispin, Rival of His Master* is breathless in its dazzling speed, a string of delightful *lazzi* and witticisms ("Real justice is of such beauty that one should be willing to buy it at any price"), *Turcaret* is heavier, more massive in its caricature and its indictment. In form, it is a classical comedy; in intent, it is a vaudeville, as savage as any but not as lively. It elicits some genuine laughter; much of it must have grated at the time; some of it still does.

If the play has been able to survive in spite of its heavy steeping in topicality, that is in large part attributable to its fine structure. Some critics have blamed Lesage for applying a novelistic pattern to his drama, and indeed *Turcaret* displays the sort of linear narrative that one expects in a picaresque novel, though it is here open-ended: Turcaret is ruined—

more as a result of the vengeful intervention of an angry playwright than anything else, it would seem—and is replaced by Frontin; the world has not changed, only the players. For all its linearity, it is that structure that provides the *vis comica* of the play. Each act begins with a *coup de théâtre*, a sensational moment, and ends with a statement or situation that leaves the audience in suspense, speculating on what is to follow. As the tension is heightened by this coherent and fluid movement, one cannot help but sense that the entire play is a well-choreographed ballet, moving to music that is ever increasing in tempo and nervousness, and that not all the sorcerer's apprentices will be able to keep up with it. The characters are beautifully balanced for this frenetic dance: The Chevalier is the antithesis of the Marquis, as Frontin's cleverness is in stark contrast to Flamand's mental clumsiness. This is why there can be no denouement, no unraveling from within. The characters cannot by themselves bring about the crisis that the audience feels has been brewing for a long time. Caught in the tempo of their dance, they merely flow with the tide. Some are submerged by it, while others, such as Frontin, make good use of it. The crisis therefore leads to a change of cast, but one which has no bearing on the fundamental social order.

This flow is part of a dual rhythm. If the metaphor of a tide is to be used, it must be viewed as one with a multiplicity of currents—the two most obvious ones being the rise of Frontin and the fall of Turcaret—currents that may have been set in motion by the characters but that they cannot always control, though some adapt remarkably well. The play's reduced description of manners is the counterpoint of this demonic music. It reveals the characters and thus explains their balletic pantomime. The manners, in other words, are not there for the sake of realism but as a means of adding configuration to characters that in turn are expositors of a way of life, the ultimate expression of mores.

In this teeth-grinding comedy, all the characters are either insipid or distasteful, which is in itself a revelation. Turcaret is ridiculous; he is also odious. Above all, he is stupid and the architect of his own downfall. His success in business had been less a

question of brains than of ruthlessness, and in love, a one-on-one human relationship, he reveals himself to be a fool and ready prey. One might think that his downfall reflects an optimistic *Weltanschauung* (worldview) on the part of Lesage were it not for Frontin. Not as gratingly vicious as Crispin, Frontin is more efficiently amoral—rather than gleefully immoral—a no less chilling consideration. As a character, he is not an innovation; rather, this servant who is proud of his class and who offers apologies neither for his station nor for his methods of improving it is the perfection of a type, of a tradition, that of the cynical, devious, and self-serving valet. He has been called a future Turcaret; that is not entirely accurate. Turcaret is ruthless, but inept; Frontin has wit, even finesse. Turcaret is odious; Frontin superficially appeals, at least to those who admire quick-witted mordancy, but if one thinks of his amalgam of intelligence and amorality, the possibilities are chilling and test the limits of comicality. Turcaret's fall is caused in large part by his stupidity; one senses that Frontin will not make the mistakes of his predecessor. Throughout *Turcaret*, there are occasions for laughter; as the final echoes of Frontin's ultimate challenge—heralding the beginning of his reign—bring down the curtain, that laughter must yield to some rather sobering thoughts about the society of 1708—or of any other time.

THE ARLEQUIN PLAYS

In 1680, the two French theaters remaining in Paris merged to form the Comédie-Française and obtained a royal monopoly which only the Italian players, by virtue of their nationality, escaped. There were two major fairs in Paris at the time, that of Saint-Germain (February to Easter) and that of Saint-Laurent (August to September or October), and at both fairs the usual jugglers, tumblers, and marionette shows constantly tried to expand their dramatic activities beyond the restrictions imposed on them by varying edicts. When the Italian players were expelled in 1697, the *forains* tried to fill the void, unleashing an immediate war with the established players of the Comédie. Backed by the powers-that-be, the latter saw to it that the players of the *foires* were forbidden to use dialogue. The *forains* got around this by having a character leave the stage immediately after the delivery of his speech, to reappear when it was time for him to speak again; the play was thus a series of monologues, and within the law. The Comédie saw that its rivals would not yield as readily as it had hoped and spurred the police to greater severity. The result was that the *forains* were forbidden to use any words; they responded with panels unfurled from overhead, or simply pulled out of pockets, on which were printed words read by the public. Eventually, the actors began to sing what they could not speak, and when the Opéra objected, for it too had a monopoly, they again used the panels and mimed while the public sang the words on the panels to popular tunes, taking particular delight in those songs that satirized such petty restrictions. These "vaudevilles," also dubbed *opéra comique* (a title eventually sanctioned by the Académie Royale de Musique) became increasingly popular, a popularity enhanced by the savagery of the parodies of the more "serious" companies. Spoken dialogues did slip into the performances with fair frequency, the complaints of the Comédie and the surveillance of the police notwithstanding. In 1719, the *forains* were obliged to suspend their dramatic activities, but by 1721 they were flourishing again, with greater vitality than ever.

Originally, the theater of the fairs was a rather crude enterprise, appealing to the lowest instincts of a motley crowd. The first author really to see the potential of the limitations imposed on the *forains* was Lesage, and he can therefore be credited if not with giving birth to the *Opéra comique*, at least of raising it to a worthy artistic level. His first few efforts were as crude as any, but in 1713, he contributed *Arlequin roi de Sérendib*, in three acts, to the Foire Saint-Germain, and two one-act plays, *Arlequin Thétis* and *Arlequin invisible*, to the Foire Saint-Laurent, all three panel comedies sung by the audience. Most of his subsequent contributions to the fairs were sung on stage. Perhaps his greatest contribution to the genre is that he readily perceived that to keep within the restrictions imposed on the players and producers, the scenario had to be as simple as possible. Like Jean Racine, he saw that creativity would have to consist of "making something of nothing." His genius does

not reveal itself through intricate plots or profound characterizations, but by means of sparkling parodic wit and sharp social commentary. *Arlequin roi de Sérendib*, for example, must have obtained most of its laughter from the audience recognizing the parody of *Iphigénie en Tauride* (1704), a terrible opera by Joseph-François Duché de Vancy and Antoine Danchet, the implausible aspects of the original stretched ludicrously beyond the last possible shred of verisimilitude. He parodied not only opera but also the actors and works of the Comédie-Française, keeping in mind no doubt that this group had rejected him and that it was the major source of vexation for the *forains*—but conveniently forgetting that, when writing for the Comédie, he had been quite unkind to the *forains* with his scornful sallies.

Though Lesage added a few characters to those he inherited from the Italians, and though he toned down the vulgarity of the latter, it cannot be said that he was truly innovative in the realm of characterization. It is he, however, who must be credited with reducing the purely physical elements (juggling, tumbling, dancing) and making them subservient to the business of the play. Although the Théâtre de la Foire did not give posterity a single great masterpiece, it pleased a large audience, and a surprisingly varied one—which included the regent, who invited the *forains* to perform in his palace—and thus had a noteworthy influence on future dramatic currents. Though it was fused with the Théâtre Italien later in the eighteenth century, it must be credited with much of what went into the creation of nineteenth century vaudeville, and no less with softening the elitist tendencies of the Comédie-Française. To do that, it had to achieve a certain respectability; Lesage's works performed that service.

OTHER MAJOR WORKS

LONG FICTION: *Le Diable boiteux*, 1707 (*The Devil upon Two Sticks*, 1708, 1726); *Histoire de Gil Blas de Santillane*, 1715-1735 (4 volumes; *The History of Gil Blas of Santillane*, 1716, 1735; better known as *Gil Blas*, 1749, 1962); *Les Aventures de M. Robert Chevalier dit de Beauchêne*, 1732 (*The Adventures of Robert Chevalier*, 1745); *Histoire de Don*

Guzman d'Alfarache, 1732 (*The Pleasant Adventures of Gusman of Alfarache*, 1812); *Histoire d'Estévanille Gonzalès*, 1734 (*The Comical History of Estévanille Gonzalez*, 1735; also as *The History of Vanillo Gonzales, Surnamed the Merry Bachelor*, 1821-1824); *Le Bachelier de Salamanque*, 1736 (*The Bachelor of Salamanca*, 1737-1739).

SHORT FICTION: *Une Journée des Parques*, 1735 (*A Day of the Fates*, 1922); *La Valise trouvée*, 1740 (2 volumes).

MISCELLANEOUS: *Œuvres de Lesage*, 1821 (12 volumes); *Bibliothèque amusante*, 1865 (4 volumes; includes *Le Diable boiteux, Histoire de Gil Blas de Santillane, Histoire de Don Guzman d'Alfarache*, and *Histoire d'Estévanille Gonzalès*).

BIBLIOGRAPHY

Magruder, James. Introduction to *Three French Comedies*, edited by C. B. Coleman. New Haven, Conn.: Yale University Press, 1996. In the introduction to the collection, which contains a translation of *Turcaret*, translator Magruder describes both the work and Lesage.

Meglin, Joellen A. "*Le Diable boiteux*: French Society Behind a Spanish Facade." *Dance Chronicle* 17, no. 3 (1994): 263. A comparison of the 1836 ballet created by Jean Coralli and Edmond Burat de Gurgy and Lesage's novel, looking at the symbolism in the dance.

Claude Abraham

GOTTHOLD EPHRAIM LESSING

Born: Kamenz, Saxony (now in Germany); January 22, 1729

Died: Braunschweig, Brunswick (now in Germany); February 15, 1781

PRINCIPAL DRAMA

Damon: Oder, Die wahre Freundschaft, pb. 1747 (*Damon: Or, True Friendship*, 1878)

Der junge Gelehrte, pr. 1748, pb. 1754 (*The Young Scholar*, 1878)

Die alte Jungfer, pb. 1749 (*The Old Maid*, 1878)

Der Freigeist, wr. 1749, pb. 1755, pr. 1767 (*The Freethinker*, 1838)

Samuel Henzi, wr. 1749, pb. 1753 (verse play)

Die Juden, wr. 1749, pb. 1754, pr. 1755 (*The Jews*, 1801)

Der Misogyn, pb. 1755 (*The Woman-Hater*, 1878)

Miss Sara Sampson, pr., pb. 1755 (English translation, 1933)

Philotas, pb. 1759, pr. 1788 (English translation, 1878)

Minna von Barnhelm: Oder, Das Soldatenglück, pr., pb. 1767 (*Minna von Barnhelm: Or, The Soldier's Fortune*, 1786)

Emilia Galotti, pr., pb. 1772 (English translation, 1786)

Nathan der Weise, pb. 1779, pr. 1783 (verse; *Nathan the Wise*, 1781)

The Dramatic Works of G. E. Lessing, pb. 1878 (2 volumes)

OTHER LITERARY FORMS

Anyone who peruses the standard twenty-three volume set of Gotthold Ephraim Lessing's writings, *Sämtliche Schriften* (1886-1924), edited by Karl Lachmann and Franz Muncker, will readily see that plays are a very small part of Lessing's total literary output. Although Lessing worked in such diverse genres as the epigram, fable, and anacreontic verse, his most important nondramatic writings are to be found in the areas of art criticism, literary criticism, and theological studies. Most notable of his contributions to art criticism are *Briefe antiquarischen Inhalts* (1768; antiquarian letters) and *Wie die Alten den Tod gebildet* (1769; *How the Ancients Represented Death*, 1879). His treatise *Laokoon: Oder, Über die Grenzen der Malerei und Poesie* (1766; *Laocoön: An Essay on the Limits of Painting and Poetry*, 1836) deals with both art and literature. Other highpoints in literary criticism are the periodical *Briefe, die neueste Literatur betreffend* (1759-1760; letters on current literature) and *Hamburgische Dramaturgie* (1767-1769; *Hamburg Dramaturgy*, 1889). His publication of fragments from the writings of a recently deceased German Deist, Hermann Samuel Reimarus, during the years 1774-1778, triggered an acrimonious dispute with Pastor Johann Melchior Goeze. In 1778, in response to his adversary's attacks, Lessing produced a series of remarkable theological tracts, among which are numbered *Eine Duplick* (1778; a rejoinder), "Eine Parable" (1778; "A Parable from the German of Lessing," 1806), "Axiomata" (1778), and *Anti-Goeze* (1778). Soon after completing these tracts, he turned his attention to the fraternity of Freemasons and undertook an assessment of Masonic doctrines in a set of five dialogues entitled *Ernst und Falk: Gespräche für Freimaurer* (1778; *Masonic Dialogues*, 1927). The most profound expression of his religious outlook, however, is to be found in his last work, *Die Erziehung des Menschengeschlechts* (1780; *The Education of the Human Race*, 1858). In addition, Lessing conducted an extensive correspondence with other leading thinkers in Germany, and some of his most valuable ideas are found in the letters that he exchanged with men such as Moses Mendelssohn and Friedrich Nicolai.

Most of the aforementioned works, as well as the letters themselves, have a distinctly polemical tone that is the result of Lessing's intense passion for intellectual disputation. Lessing acknowledges this personality trait in article 70 of *Hamburg Dramaturgy*, where he offers the following advice to critical writers: "Let him first seek out someone with whom he can argue; thus, he will gradually get into his topic and the rest will come of its own accord." How fecund this polemical method was for Lessing himself is perhaps best attested by his critical treatise *Laocoön*, in which he uses some remarks made by Johann Joachim Winckelmann as a point of departure and, in the process of carrying on a running debate with this great art historian, succeeds in demonstrating the contradictions inherent in employing a temporal medium such as poetry for the purpose of static

description. In this way he shows that the proper domain of the poet lies in the depiction of progressive action. Addressing the way in which the argument in *Laocoön* unfolds, Eliza M. Butler writes that "the earlier Platonic dialogues alone perhaps in literature give the same exhilarating impression of participating personally in the quest for truth—of collaborating with the artist as a fascinating structure is built up, block by block, before one's eyes."

ACHIEVEMENTS

At the time that Gotthold Ephraim Lessing began his literary activity, Germany lacked a fully developed native theatrical tradition. The Thirty Years' War, which had ravaged the country during the first half of the seventeenth century, had retarded Germany's literary development to the extent that it had to rely on foreign models to an unhealthy degree. With respect to the theater, the most important playwright and dramatic critic during this period was Johann Christoph Gottsched, a Leipzig professor who championed the type of neoclassicism that flourished

Gotthold Ephraim Lessing (Library of Congress)

in neighboring France. As a youth, Lessing dutifully allowed himself to be indoctrinated with neoclassical theory, but he gradually grew dissatisfied with its conventions as he matured. Therefore, when the editor of a prominent literary journal wrote that nobody would deny that the German stage owed a great measure of its recent improvement to the efforts of Gottsched, Lessing responded by launching a vitriolic attack against the Leipzig professor in the periodical *Briefe die neueste Literatur betreffend*, which he, along with his friends Nicolai and Mendelssohn, had founded in January, 1759. Here, in the seventeenth letter, Lessing boldly announces: "I am that nobody; I deny it forthwith. It would have been better if Mr. Gottsched had never meddled with the theater."

He continues his assault by maintaining that the Germans have a greater spiritual affinity with the English than they have with the French and urges his countrymen to base their plays not on French models but on English ones. Lessing certainly meant to exclude neoclassical English playwrights such as Joseph Addison, whose *Cato* (pr., pb. 1713) he regarded as completely French in style. It should be stressed, however, that Lessing, in condemning French neoclassicism, was by no means rejecting the authority of Aristotle, whose *De poetica* (c. 334-323 B.C.E.; *Poetics*, 1705) he considered to be as infallible as the Stoicheia (compiled c. 300 B.C.E.; *Elements*, 1570) of Euclid; he simply contended that English authors such as William Shakespeare and other Elizabethan playwrights were far closer to the spirit of Greek tragedy than the French neoclassical dramatists. Indeed, not content with promoting among the German public a fuller appreciation of English drama, Lessing was also a tireless exegete of the *Poetics*, elucidating its doctrines in *Hamburg Dramaturgy* and in numerous other works of dramatic criticism.

Moreover, Lessing attempted to write plays that would embody the principles espoused in his critical works and thereby set a positive example for others to follow. In *Miss Sara Sampson*, Lessing created the first popular domestic tragedy in German literature, and in *Emilia Galotti*, his other middle-class tragedy, he paved the way for the plays of social protest soon to be penned by the angry young men of the Sturm und Drang movement. While he invented no radically new form of comedy, his comic masterpiece, *Minna von Barnhelm*, remains perennially popular. His play *Nathan the Wise* not only contains one of the most moving pleas for religious tolerance in world literature but also was the first German drama to make successful use of blank verse. By virtue of his pioneering efforts as playwright and critic, Lessing has rightly been called the founder of modern German literature.

BIOGRAPHY

Born on January 22, 1729, in a small town called Kamenz, located near the city of Meissen, in Saxony, Gotthold Ephraim Lessing was the second son and third child in a family of twelve children (five of whom died in childhood). His father, Johann Gottfried Lessing, shortly after earning a degree in theology from the University of Wittenberg, had obtained a modest position as assistant pastor in Kamenz and, in 1725, married Justina Salome Feller. Lessing's mother, although a loving and dutiful housewife, manifested little interest in either her husband's or her children's intellectual pursuits. It was, consequently, from his father that Lessing developed his own precocious appetite for reading. A frequently repeated anecdote relates that at the age of six Lessing refused to pose for a portrait holding a bird cage and insisted that the cage be replaced by a pile of books. (Interestingly, Lessing managed to collect a personal library of more than five thousand volumes in later life.) Lessing's father, despite some minor advancements in his career, remained an impecunious albeit respected clergyman throughout his entire life, but he nevertheless managed to find the wherewithal to send five of his sons to the university.

Lessing's own formal education began in a progressive Latin school at Kamenz, where he remained until the age of twelve. He then entered the Elector's School of St. Afra in Meissen, one of the three finest schools in Germany at that time, and proved himself such a gifted and eager pupil that his teachers described him as "a horse that requires double fodder." After five years of intensive study at St. Afra's, Lessing matriculated at the University of Leipzig as a student of theology, in deference to his father's wishes. Philology and literature, however, proved more congenial to him than did theology. At the same time, Lessing became involved in the lively social life of Leipzig, a city commonly referred to during this period as "a little Paris." It was in Leipzig that he became involved with the theatrical troupe headed by Professor Gottsched's protégée, Karoline Neuber, who encouraged him to make use of his literary talents to write original plays and who eventually produced one of his early works. Distressed by the academic indifference and general waywardness of his son, Lessing's father summoned him back to Kamenz, permitting him to return to Leipzig only on the condition that he would henceforth devote himself to the study of medicine. Before long, however, Lessing was obliged to flee from Leipzig because he was unable to make payment for debts incurred by some members of the Neuber troupe, for whom he had unwisely agreed to stand surety.

Except for about a year's time spent at the University of Wittenberg, from which institution he acquired a Master of Arts degree in 1752, Lessing worked as a translator and freelance journalist in Berlin from 1748 to 1755. Here he eventually came into close association with such leading thinkers as Mendelssohn and Nicolai, both of whom were to remain his lifelong friends. Unfortunately, Lessing was to forfeit the patronage of Frederick the Great, the king of Prussia, because of an incident involving his unauthorized possession of a manuscript by Voltaire, who was then staying at the royal palace at Potsdam. Voltaire took his complaint to the king, who consequently formed an unfavorable impression of Lessing and thereafter ruled out appointing him to the coveted position of royal librarian. Meanwhile, success crowned his activities as both author and critic. In 1755, after his play *Miss Sara Sampson* had been widely acclaimed, Lessing decided that he needed a change of scene and departed for a stay in Leipzig, a respite that lasted nearly three years. After his return to Berlin in 1758, he pursued his literary career with renewed vigor and produced such works as his play *Philotas* and the periodical *Briefe die neueste Literatur betreffend*.

Within three years, however, Lessing once again felt a strong desire to escape from the literary life in Berlin and was quick to accept a financially attractive offer to serve as private secretary to General von Tauentzien, commander of the Prussian forces occupying the Silesian city of Breslau as a result of military operations connected with the Seven Years' War. This direct experience in the "real" world inspired him to write his comedy *Minna von Barnhelm*. This play was published in 1767. While in Breslau, Lessing also enjoyed sufficient leisure to do extensive research in the realm of aesthetic theory, the results of which appear in his treatise *Laocoön*. In the course of this five-year sojourn in Breslau, he became restless from time to time and finally decided to return to Berlin. His stay in Berlin turned out to be relatively brief, since he soon agreed to serve in the position of dramatist and consultant to the newly founded German National Theater in Hamburg. This company, which had hopes of establishing itself as the first permanent repertory theater in Germany, failed after operating for a period of only two years. The weekly reviews and commentary that Lessing wrote for the project were gathered together and published in book form in 1769 under the title *Hamburgische Dramaturgie*. Many of these articles contain wide-ranging discussions on dramatic theory and technique that have earned for Lessing the reputation of being a dramatic critic second only to Aristotle in importance. Despite the demands of serving as adviser to the Hamburg company, he still found time to compose several other notable works, such as *Briefe antiquarischen Inhalts* and *How the Ancients Represented Death*.

Deeply in debt after the collapse of the Hamburg theatrical enterprise, Lessing, through the intercession of a friend, was offered the post of librarian at the Ducal Library at Wolfenbüttel, an institution where the philosopher Gottfried Wilhelm von Leibniz had once served the duke of Brunswick in a similar position. Although he was poorly paid and often found the enforced solitude of the library uncongenial, Lessing was to stay at this post for the remainder of his life. It was there, in 1772, that he wrote his second middle-class tragedy, *Emilia Galotti*. In October, 1776, he improved his personal life by marrying Eva König, the widow of a Hamburg merchant who had been a friend of long standing. His newly found happiness, however, was quite brief because his wife died in January of 1778, ten days after giving birth to a child who died within twenty-four hours of being delivered. Shortly after these tragic events, Lessing found himself the object of a virulent attack by pastor Goeze in connection with his publication of some deistically oriented manuscripts by the late Hermann Samuel Reimarus. He responded with a series of eleven scathing pamphlets directed at Goeze before being enjoined by the duke of Brunswick from any further publication on the subject of religion unless such material received prior approval by the official censors. Frustrated by this prohibition against replying to attacks directed at him, Lessing turned to writing his final play, *Nathan the Wise*, and by this means was able to make a moving plea for religious tolerance. The play was completed in 1779, but it was not actually performed until 1783, two full years after the author's death. Lessing died of a stroke on February 15, 1781, at the age of fifty-two, while visiting the city of Brunswick. He was buried there in a pauper's grave at public expense.

ANALYSIS

To some extent, all writing is autobiography, but the degree to which the autobiographical element manifests itself varies greatly from one author to another. Johann Wolfgang von Goethe was undoubtedly accurate when he called attention to the close relationship between his life and his work by stating that "all my writings are fragments of a great confession." On the other hand, such as statement as Goethe's could never have been made by Gotthold Ephraim Lessing because there is seemingly little overt connection between the fictive content of his major plays and his own personal life. In *Hamburg Dramaturgy*, Lessing goes as far as to reject the notion that he truly merits the title of creative writer and proceeds to assert:

Not everyone who takes a brush in his hand and lays on colors is a painter. The earliest of my attempts [at writing plays] were made in those years in which one is apt to regard desire and facility as genius. . . . I do not feel within me the living spring that works itself upward through its own native strength and breaks forth into such abundant, fresh, pure streams. I must

force everything out of myself by means of pressure and pipes.

If one bears in mind the difficulty that he had in transmuting life into art, one will more easily understand why it was necessary for Lessing to use so much material borrowed from other literary sources in order to write his own plays. In the same source cited above, he acknowledges the necessity of such borrowing with complete candor:

I would be so poor, so cold, so shortsighted if I had not, to some degree, modestly learned to borrow foreign treasures, to warm myself at foreign fires, and to strengthen my eyes through the glasses of art.

There is no sin in making use of vicarious experience obtained by reading the works of other writers; the degree to which Lessing was compelled to use the plots, the characters, and even the dialogue created by other authors, however, was so extreme that he drew on this source of inspiration almost as much as he drew on life. Indeed, in a book entitled *Leszing's Plagiate* (1888-1891), "Lessing's plagiarism," Paul Albrecht goes as far as to represent Lessing as an archthief, utterly devoid of originality. While this conclusion is extreme, the book is useful in that it makes one aware of the extent of Lessing's borrowing. In Lessing's defense, it should be noted that he allowed plenty of time for the material borrowed from other authors' works to simmer in his subconscious until a true synthesis had been achieved. Lessing's dramas were not, therefore, undigested episodes pasted together with the technical skill of a great critic, but rather unified creations that earn the right to be called original despite their secondhand inspiration.

How keenly Lessing felt his shortcomings as a playwright can be inferred from the fact that at the age of twenty-one he was already the author of seven complete plays, yet in the remaining thirty-one years of his life he was to write only five more. With respect to these five later plays, Lessing stated that whatever is tolerable in them he owed simply and solely to the critic in him. Accordingly, *Hamburg Dramaturgy* contains the following ringing endorsement of the value of criticism: "I am therefore always ashamed or vexed whenever I hear or read anything that disparages criticism. It is supposed to stifle genius, and I flattered myself into believing that what I gained from it enabled me to achieve something very nearly approaching genius. I am a lame man who finds it impossible to be edified by a calumny on the use of crutches." He hastens, however to add an important qualification: "But certainly, like the crutch that helps the lame man move from one place to another and yet cannot make him into a runner, so it is with criticism."

In light of the extreme critical temperament that informs all of Lessing's writings, it is imperative to recognize that each of his major plays is a concerted endeavor to solve a theoretical problem pertaining to dramatic form. Clearly, the playwright's chief motivation in writing *Miss Sara Sampson* was to extend the range of tragedy so as to include the middle class within its purview. Similarly, *Emilia Galotti*, in addition to being a protest against political tyranny, should also be viewed as an attempt to construct a model Aristotelian tragedy in accordance with the principles set forth in *Hamburg Dramaturgy*. In *Minna von Barnhelm*, Lessing not only pleads for a reconciliation between the Saxons and the Prussians in the aftermath of the hostility fostered by the Seven Years' War but also seeks to combine the serious and the comic in keeping with the suggestion of Denis Diderot concerning the feasibility of a mixed genre. Finally, in *Nathan the Wise*, his passionate advocacy of religious toleration is coupled with an attempt to work out the principles of writing a drama in verse form.

DAMON

As a youth, Lessing set himself the goal of becoming the "German Molière." Like Molière, who maintained that "the purpose of comedy is to correct men by entertaining them," Lessing held a didactic view on the function of literature. Not surprisingly, the didactic element in his early comedies is particularly strong. In his first play, a one-act comedy called *Damon: Or, True Friendship*, Damon and Leander are friendly rivals for the hand of a young widow, who devises a scheme involving a business venture to test the genuineness of their loyalty to each other.

Leander proves to be duplicitous, and the widow chooses to marry Damon because of his nobility of soul. Damon, for his part, forgives Leander and insists that his future wife do likewise.

THE YOUNG SCHOLAR AND
THE WOMAN-HATER

The Young Scholar, a play that Karoline Neuber first produced in Leipzig, is a three-act comedy with an extremely convoluted plot, the purpose of which is to ridicule pedantry. It is highly likely that there is an element of self-mockery in this work.

In *The Woman-Hater*, a one-act play that Lessing later expanded to three acts, a young woman disguises herself as a man in order to win over her fiancé's misogynistic father, who does not wish his son to marry. Although she does eventually succeed in winning the admiration of the father, he does not entirely abandon his misogyny after the unmasking. He consents to the marriage, but he goes on to declare that his son will have to learn about women the hard way.

THE OLD MAID AND THE FREETHINKER

In the one-act play *The Old Maid*, a wealthy unmarried woman of fifty is courted by a retired military man of dubious character. Their union is opposed by her dissipated nephew, who stands to lose his inheritance. The situation is resolved by the captain and the nephew agreeing to divide up the woman's money. Just why Lessing would want to reward roguery in this way remains a puzzle.

The plot of *The Freethinker* is derived from an obscure French source and involves an unpleasant atheist and a gentle minister who are respectively engaged to two sisters. The betrothal of the two sisters has been arranged by their father, and it soon turns out that each sister is in love with the other's fiancé. Before the appropriate exchange of partners is consummated, the minister has ample opportunity to display his sterling qualities. In doing so, he demonstrates to the atheist that, contrary to his expectations, virtue can be found in people who profess a belief in God. The atheist vows henceforth to model himself after the virtuous minister. It should be emphasized that none of these comedies would merit attention today if they were not part of the dramatic apprenticeship of one of the major figures in eighteenth century German literature.

THE JEWS

More important than any of the aforementioned plays is Lessing's comedy *The Jews* and the fragmentary tragedy *Samuel Henzi*. In *The Jews*, a nobleman narrowly escapes being robbed and murdered by two bearded assailants, whom he assumes to be Jews. His rescuer is an unknown traveler, who agrees to interrupt his journey to stay at the Baron's estate for a few days. During this visit, the Baron voices anti-Semitic views, to which the Traveler quietly demurs. By chance, the Traveler discovers false beards in the possession of the overseer of the Baron's estate. When confronted by this evidence, the overseer confesses to the assault on the Baron and reveals the identity of his accomplice. It is at this point that the Baron offers the Traveler his daughter's hand in marriage. The Traveler, however, declines on the grounds that such a union would be impossible in their society because he is a Jew. The Baron is now suitably perplexed. Although the Baron's daughter is still willing to enter into marriage with him, the Traveler states that the only reward he desires is to have his people judged fairly. This having been said, the Traveler departs.

SAMUEL HENZI

In the tragedy *Samuel Henzi*, Lessing turns to the topic of political oppression. His hero is a Swiss patriot who was executed in 1749 for attempting to overthrow the tyrannical government of Berne. Although Lessing managed to complete only the first act and part of the second, this fragment received much critical approbation when it was published by Lessing in 1753 as part of his *Kritische Briefe* (1753). Despite the topical nature of the play, Lessing chose to employ the rhymed Alexandrines of French classical tragedy to adhere strictly to the traditional dramatic unities.

MISS SARA SAMPSON

It is generally acknowledged that Lessing's prime objective in writing *Miss Sara Sampson* was to promote the acceptance of middle-class tragedy among his countrymen. Although this play is often described as the first German work in this genre, there is much to be said for according precedence to Andreas

Gryphius's tragedy *Cardenio und Celinde: Oder, Unglücklich Verliebte* (wr. c. 1647-1649, pb. 1657, pr. 1661). Lessing's inspiration, however, came from abroad. The chief influences were George Lillo's play *The London Merchant: Or, The History of George Barnwell* (pr., pb. 1731) and Samuel Richardson's novel *Clarissa* (1747-1748). In addition, Lessing also drew heavily from plays written by Thomas Shadwell, Charles Johnson, and Mrs. Susannah Centlivre for specific details of plot, character, and dialogue. It is, accordingly, highly appropriate for Lessing to have given an English title to his own middle-class tragedy.

The heroine of Lessing's play is an essentially virtuous woman who permits herself to be persuaded into living with a man out of wedlock. Although Sara's lover, Mellefont, faces disinheritance if he should marry her, the chief obstacles to consummating a marriage are psychological. Despite his love for Sara, Mellefont is unable to make the irrevocable commitment implied by the marital bond however much she may importune him to do so. At the opening of the play, the two lovers have been living together for several months at a country inn in a remote locality. Their whereabouts have, however, been discovered through the determined efforts of Mellefont's former mistress, Marwood. Shortly after discovering the location of the inn, Marwood appears on the scene and attempts to persuade Mellefont to leave Sara and resume the relationship that they had shared sporadically during a period of ten years. To play on his sympathies further, she brings along their illegitimate daughter, Arabella. When Mellefont refuses to leave Sara, Marwood attempts to stab him, but he promptly disarms her. Also on hand is Sara's father, Sir William Sampson, whom Marwood has apprised of the inn's location in order to create additional difficulties for the couple. When she learns that it is Sir William's intent to forgive his daughter, she arranges an interview with Sara for herself. Under a false identity, Marwood pleads her own case and that of her daughter, Arabella, but to no avail. She then poisons Sara. While Sara is dying, her father grants her parental absolution and accedes to her request that he adopt Arabella. Mellefont, full of remorse, commits suicide with the dagger that he had wrested away from Marwood a short time before. Despite the fact that audiences in Lessing's day would normally have regarded her as a fallen woman, Sara is otherwise so virtuous that her moral transgression is fully transcended and her death is genuinely tragic.

It is worth observing that, while extending the concept of tragedy to encompass the middle class, Lessing is careful to adhere to the traditional unities. The entire play takes place at the inn within a single day. It is somewhat implausible for Sir William to remain at the inn for several hours before attempting to see his daughter, but otherwise the plot works well within this framework. Lessing regarded the unities of time and place as useful devices, but he refused to consider them as essential parts of the Aristotelian method. He saw no need to hold on to the empty shell of the unities of time and place because the Greek chorus, which served as an idealized public and thus required the unities of time and place, had disappeared from European drama, and he charged that Voltaire and Pierre Corneille were able to retain them only through all sorts of twists and dislocations of the plot. Nevertheless, Lessing believed that it is advantageous for a dramatist to adhere to these unities whenever feasible, and he clearly believed that such was the case in *Miss Sara Sampson*.

A Faust Play

As part of his attack on French neoclassicism in the seventeenth installment of his *Briefe die neueste Literatur betreffend*, Lessing included a scene from a play dealing with the Faust legend on which he had intermittently been working for a number of years. The scene involves Doctor Faust's selection of a devil who is to serve as his assistant. After summoning seven devils, he asks each in turn to describe how swiftly his commands can be executed. He then chooses the one who claims that he is as swift as the transition from good to evil. Although the author of the scene is never identified, most readers would quickly conclude that it was Lessing himself. At the end of the excerpt he asks rhetorically: "What do you think of this scene? Would you like to have a German play that is made up exclusively of such scenes? Me too!" Unfortunately, only a few brief fragments of the play have survived. Nevertheless, Lessing deserves to be remembered as the first author to conceive of Faust as a positive figure worthy of redemption. To judge from the remarks that he made to his friends pertaining to his plans for a Faust play, Lessing appears to have rescued the protagonist from eternal damnation by presenting the entire action as a dream that serves as a providential warning to his hero against exceeding the limits of reason.

Philotas

Published in 1759, *Philotas*, a one-act prose tragedy, represents Lessing's attempt to create a Sophoclean drama treating the theme of patriotic self-sacrifice. In an endeavor to achieve "the noble simplicity and quiet grandeur" that Winckelmann held to be the most prominent characteristic of Greek art, Lessing limits himself to only four characters and a plot of undeviating unity. The play is set somewhere in the Greek world at the time of Alexander the Great. Philotas, the son of an unnamed king, has been captured by the enemy, along with a number of other soldiers whom his father had assigned to his command. The young prince deeply bemoans the fact that his wounds are slight and that he will survive. His father will, he believes, feel obliged to ransom him at the expense of the political interests of the state. As fate or chance would have it, it soon comes to light that his captor, King Aridäus, faces a similar predicament, for his own son was captured by the opposing side in the very same encounter. Hence, a simple exchange of the two captured princes seems to be the logical solution to the situation. Philotas, however, determines to kill himself so that his father will be able to exact full ransom from King Aridäus for the return of his son and thus advance the interests of his own state. To this end, Philotas persuades his captors to return his sword to him before the impending exchange and then inflicts a mortal wound on himself. While in his death throes, he conducts a dialogue with King Aridäus on the subject of patriotic self-sacrifice. The young prince argues that no sacrifice is too great for the sake of one's country. The king, for his part, places family above country and declares his intention of abdicating after the safe release of his son. Within this exchange, as well as elsewhere in the play, there are a number of topical references pertaining to Frederick the Great and the war between Prussia and Saxony that readers familiar with the history of Germany during the eighteenth century will readily discern. It is a bit difficult, however, to determine whether the author of the play is more inclined to share in the humanitarian sentiments expressed by King Aridäus or in the patriotic creed espoused by Philotas. The question remains the subject of debate among Lessing scholars.

MINNA VON BARNHELM

Published eight years after *Philotas*, *Minna von Barnhelm* may best be categorized as a comedy of high seriousness. Inspired by Diderot's speculations on the possibility of a mixed genre, Lessing endeavored to create a play midway between traditional comedy and bourgeois tragedy. In addition to the usual concerns of a writer of comedy, Lessing was also anxious to foster the emerging sense of a unified German national identity. To this end, he selected as his protagonists Minna von Barnhelm, a woman of gentle birth from his own native province of Saxony, and Major von Tellheim, a Prussian officer originally from one of the Baltic states. Through the symbolism of their marital union at the end of the play, Lessing urges his compatriots to suppress the animosities engendered by the recently concluded Seven Years' War and to embrace the cause of German unity under the aegis of the Prussian state.

The character of Major von Tellheim is generally believed to have been modeled after Lessing's close friend Ewald von Kleist, a Prussian officer and talented poet who died as a result of wounds incurred in a battle that took place in 1759. The major is a man of utmost probity, but his highly exaggerated sense of honor makes dealing with him extremely difficult. As the play opens, Tellheim is living in dire straits at a modest inn somewhere in Berlin. In addition to suffering from a shoulder wound, he has been discharged from the army on suspicion that he had solicited bribes from municipal officials in Prussian-occupied Saxony. In reality, the money in question was a loan to the municipality, and he has a legitimate legal claim to reimbursement. Being without funds and feeling himself dishonored, Tellheim has ceased writing to Minna, to whom he became betrothed while still in Saxony. She, however, seeks to resume contact with him and travels to Berlin with this object in mind. There, she and her maid Franziska check into the inn where Tellheim is lodging along with his own loyal servant, Just.

Despite Minna's passionate pleas that they proceed with their original plan for marriage, Tellheim refuses on grounds of personal honor. His reluctance to involve her in his plight comes as no surprise to the audience because he has already turned down several offers of financial assistance made by various individuals. Minna then devises a scheme to expose the folly of Tellheim's intransigence. She lets it be known, through Franziska, that she too is poor because her guardian, Count von Bruchsal, has disinherited her because he disapproved of her engagement to Tellheim. When Tellheim hears this, he rushes to Minna and attempts to get her back. Minna now turns Tellheim's former arguments against him and likewise rejects his offer on the basis of her own personal honor. Oddly enough, Tellheim does not appear to appreciate the irony of the situation in the slightest degree. At no time does he acknowledge the virtue of moderation or admit that his extreme concept of personal honor is injurious to the welfare of others. (One would expect such edification on the part of the protagonist to occur in a comedy by Molière.) Nevertheless, things turn out well for the major. He receives a letter informing him that, through the personal intercession of Frederick the Great, his monetary claims against the government will be honored and his commission in the army restored. Minna, after teasing him a bit longer, finally confesses that her alleged disinheritance was a ruse. Appropriately, her guardian appears on the scene and gives his full blessing to their marriage.

Two dramatic devices used in *Minna von Barnhelm* are worthy of note. First, much of the action in the play revolves around a pair of identical rings with which Minna and Tellheim had originally sealed their betrothal in Saxony. Hard-pressed for ready cash, Tellheim pawns his own ring to the innkeeper, who in turn sells it to Minna soon after she appears on the scene. Pretending to break off her engagement to

Tellheim, she returns it to him. He believes that it is her own ring that she is returning because she removes it from her own finger. After Tellheim receives the letter informing him of the king's intercession on his behalf, he attempts to redeem the ring that he had pawned with the landlord. He then makes the discovery that Minna had already done so and is also told that she refuses to give it up. Not realizing that he is already in possession of the ring, Tellheim concludes that it was Minna's intention from the very outset to break their engagement. On this basis, he is plunged into the depths of despair. It is at this point that Minna is moved to confess all, and her confession is supported by the opportune arrival of her guardian. Second, the intercession of Frederick the Great is another example of a dramatic technique that is analogous to the *deus ex machina* of Greek and Roman literature; since a king rather than a god comes to the rescue, this device has aptly been termed *rex ex machina*. Other important plays using this device are Lope de Vega Carpio's *Fuenteovejuna* (wr. 1611-1618, pb. 1619; *The Sheep Well*, 1936), in which Ferdinand and Isabella act on behalf of the beleaguered villagers of Fuenteovejuna, and Molière's *Tartuffe: Ou, L'Imposteur* (pr. 1664, rev. pr. 1667; *Tartuffe*, 1732), in which Louis XIV intervenes to save Orgon and his family from being dispossessed.

In addition to Minna and Tellheim, there are many other vivid characters in the play. Perhaps no other dramatic work of Lessing contains so many fully rounded supporting roles. There are, for example, Minna's resourceful maid and confidante, Franziska, and Tellheim's humorous, loyal servant, Just, who is constantly jousting with the greedy, prying innkeeper. There is also Paul Werner, Tellheim's loyal sergeant, who eventually becomes engaged to Franziska. Moreover, a disreputable French mercenary soldier, Riccault de la Marlinère, is introduced into the play to serve as a foil both to the uprightness of Major von Tellheim and as a warning against the pernicious influence of the Francophiles among Lessing's countrymen. One would like to believe that the superior characterization and dialogue in *Minna von Barnhelm* were the result of Lessing's having at last written a play based on personal experience. It therefore comes as a surprise to find that Curtis Vail makes the following statement in his exhaustive study of Lessing's English sources, *Lessing's Relation to the English Language and Literature* (1936): "If any work offers abundant material for those who wish to trace 'Lessing's plagiarism,' that work is *Minna von Barnhelm*."

EMILIA GALOTTI

There is considerable validity to the thesis that the importance of Lessing's next play, *Emilia Galotti*, stems from its social and political aspects. Lessing's primary intent in writing this work, however, lay elsewhere. His overriding purpose was to provide the German stage with an exemplary bourgeois tragedy embodying the principles of Aristotle. As Lessing makes abundantly clear in the seventy-seventh article in *Hamburg Dramaturgy*, a proper tragedy is a drama that evokes the emotions of pity and fear. The evocation of these emotions, he argues, is the exclusive prerogative of the dramatic method because it alone can dispense with narration entirely and depict events as occurring in present time. In order to demonstrate the potential inherent in the dramatic method pertaining to middle-class tragedy, Lessing decided to modernize an episode related by Livy in book 3 of his early history of Rome.

This episode, which had already been dramatized by the Spanish playwright Augustino de Montiano y Luyando, describes how a father kills his daughter in order to protect her chastity. As told by Livy, a well-known and brave centurion named Virginius had a daughter named Virginia. Despite the fact that she was engaged to a popular tribune, the powerful decemvir Appius Claudius arranged to have one of his men seize the girl and claim that she was the child of one of his female slaves. Virginia's father contested this claim vigorously, but Appius Claudius ruled against him at a public hearing. Utterly distraught, the father thereupon plunged a knife into his daughter's breast, exclaiming: "This is the only way, my child, to keep thee free." Escaping from the city unopposed, the father rallied his comrades and returned to Rome, where he charged the decemvir with violating the laws of the state and had him thrown into jail to await trial. Because he felt certain of being convicted, Appius Claudius killed himself.

After many years of deliberation, Lessing finally decided to omit the political ramifications of the story. He believed that the death of a daughter at the hands of her father, whose sole wish was to protect her virtue, was sufficiently tragic by itself and that the inclusion of political considerations would dilute its effect. In Lessing's version, the scene of the action is modern Italy, where Hettore Gonzaga presides over the principality of Guastalla. Hettore has become captivated by Emilia Galotti, as Lessing calls his "bourgeois Virginia," after meeting her at a soiree held in the house of Grimaldi. He instructs his chamberlain, the Marquis Marinelli, to contrive a plan through which he might satisfy his lust for the attractive commoner. Emilia, for her part, admits that she finds Prince Hettore to be a man of great charm. Marinelli nevertheless has several serious obstacles to overcome: Emilia's father, Odoardo, has a personal antipathy toward the libertine prince, and Emilia herself is about to be married to a young nobleman, Count Appiani. Marinelli and Appiani quarrel violently when the young count refuses to postpone his marriage in order to travel on business of state for the prince. Marinelli thereupon decides to resort to violence and arranges an attack on the carriage in which the betrothed couple will be riding on their way to the wedding. Appiani is killed by Marinelli's hirelings, and Emilia is ostensibly rescued by another agent of his, who then conducts her to Hettore's hunting lodge.

Emilia's father soon discovers her whereabouts and goes to the lodge. While there, Odoardo has a revealing conversation with Countess Orsina, a former mistress of Hettore. She informs Odoardo of the prince's complicity in the attack and hints that Emilia herself may have cooperated in the plot. Before departing, Countess Orsina gives Odoardo a dagger that she intended to use on her faithless lover and urges him to take revenge on the prince. When the prince finally appears, he poses as Emilia's benefactor, but he refuses to permit Odoardo to take his daughter home. The prince maintains that Emilia must remain in custody pending an investigation of the incident. Odoardo suspects the worst, but he decides against killing

the prince. Instead, he asks to see his daughter in private in order to explain matters to her.

Emilia now learns of Appiani's death, which until then she had merely suspected, and of her own helpless predicament. What appears to disturb her most is the possibility that she will be unable to resist Hettore's seductive advances and will surrender to him voluntarily. She now reminds Odoardo of the courageous example of Virginius and bemoans the fact that there are no such fathers anymore. Odoardo exclaims "There are, my daughter, there are!" and stabs her. The prince and Marinelli now enter. After asking Hettore whether he finds the dead body of Emilia enticing, Odoardo informs him that he will submit to the prince's judgment, but he reminds him that they both will one day answer to God for their deeds. His psyche completely shattered by the horrendous scene before him, the prince turns on Marinelli and orders him to depart forever.

If one compares Lessing's *Emilia Galotti* to its Roman source, several major differences readily appear. Emilia, for example, manifests a latent sexuality that makes her partially culpable for the calamitous denouement in the play. Perhaps it was to provide her with a tragic flaw that Lessing invested her with this trait. Sensuality itself is not necessarily a vice, but for Emilia to feel a strong attraction toward the prince at the very moment that she is about to marry Count Appiani must surely be viewed as a defect in an otherwise sterling character. Odoardo also differs from the Roman father in that he is much more passive in the face of tyrannical injustice than was the case with Virginius. Finally, Prince Hettore appears to have a greater quotient of personal charm than did Appius Claudius. The fact that the prince possesses a number of positive attributes does not diminish the element of social protest that many see in the play. It can indeed even be argued that the political system depicted here is so much the worse if such tragic events can occur under a ruler who is far from being a monster.

NATHAN THE WISE

Because the duke of Brunswick acceded to the demands of the clerical establishment that Lessing be enjoined from publishing anything on the subject of religion without prior approval from the official censors, he turned to drama as a means of continuing his debate with Pastor Goeze of Hamburg. "I must see," Lessing wrote to Elise Reimarus, "whether they will at least let me preach undisturbed from my old pulpit, the stage." In addition to being a moving plea on behalf of religious tolerance, *Nathan the Wise*, which is subtitled "a dramatic poem in five acts," was the first important work in German literature to employ blank verse. Henceforth, unrhymed iambic pentameter became the preferred verse form among German poets.

The key episode in the whole drama is the one in which the Jew Nathan relates the parable of the three rings to the Muslim ruler Saladin. This parable appears in many previous works of literature, among them Giovanni Boccaccio's *Decameron: O, Prencipe Galetto* (1349-1351; *The Decameron*, 1620). In the third story of the first day of *The Decameron*, Saladin, being hard-pressed for money, attempts to obtain a loan from a wealthy Jew named Melchizedek. After summoning the Jew into his presence, Saladin proceeds to use "force in the guise of reason" and asks him to state which religion he considers to be authentic: Judaism, Christianity, or Islam. The Jew extricates himself from this predicament by telling Saladin the story of a family in which the head of the household passed his position on to his favorite son irrespective of age. This selection was symbolized by the bestowal of a precious ring from the father to the son. After many generations, it came to pass that a father had three sons that he loved equally, so he secretly commissioned a master craftsman to make two more rings that were indistinguishable from the original, and when he was on the point of death, he took each son aside and privately gave one ring to each. After their father's death, each of them claimed to be the father's favorite son and produced a ring as proof thereof. Because the rings were so alike, the question as to who was the true and rightful heir could not be resolved and is still in abeyance. Thus it is with the three religions, Melchizedek claims. Impressed by the wisdom of the Jew's response, Saladin confesses all. Melchizedek, in the light of his host's candor, volunteers to make the loan, and the two become lifelong friends.

In Lessing's version of the ring parable, the three sons take their case before a judge, who, being unable to decide which of the rings is genuine, urges each of them to justify his claim to parental preference by behaving in a morally superior manner. Only in this way, the judge insists, can the genuine ring be determined. It is, however, extremely doubtful that Lessing himself viewed any of the three rings as authentic to the exclusion of the other two. It was his view that all revealed religions are true and false to an equal degree. Moreover, he preferred reason to revelation and genuinely enjoyed taking part in the quest for truth. This attitude is perhaps best explained by him in a passage in *Eine Duplick*:

The worth of a man does not consist in the truth he possesses, or thinks he possesses, but in the pains he has taken to attain that truth. For his powers are extended not through possession but through the search for truth. In this alone his ever-growing perfection consists. Possession makes him lazy, indolent, and proud. If God held all truth in His right hand and the singular incessant urge to strive after truth in His left hand, even though with the qualification that I must constantly fall into error, and said to me, "Choose," I would humbly choose the left hand and say, "Father, grant me this! Pure truth is for Thee alone!"

His own quest for truth eventually led him to question the validity of worshiping a Creator who is independent of his creation. While losing his faith in traditional religion, Lessing gradually moved closer to a belief in Divine Immanance. Thus, in the summer of 1780 he is reputed to have said, "There is no other philosophy than Spinoza's."

The fact that Lessing, at this point in his life, lacked any theological commitment to the doctrines of Christianity, Judaism, or Islam made him ideally suited to serve as a mediator for these mutually antagonistic religious communities. To put his plea for tolerance into dramatic form, he conjured up an exotic historical setting, somewhat reminiscent of Wolfgang Amadeus Mozart's *Die Entrung aus dem Serail* (1782; *The Abduction from the Seraglio*) in both scenery and costume, that provides a fitting backdrop for the recitation of the parable of the three rings by the noble Jew whose name, along with his accompanying epithet, gives the play its title. The scene is set in Jerusalem at the time of the Crusades. Nathan, returning home from a lengthy business trip to distant regions, learns that his foster daughter, Recha, had been rescued from a fire that nearly destroyed his home. The young man whose timely intervention has averted the catastrophe turns out to be a Knight Templar whose life had been spared by Saladin because of the Templar's striking resemblance to this Muslim ruler's late brother, Assad. Nathan seeks out the Templar immediately, and the two of them become friends at first meeting. The conversation between them is, however, interrupted by Saladin's summoning the Jewish merchant to his palace.

Saladin needs to borrow a substantial sum of money from Nathan for the purpose of financing his war against the Crusaders and, prompted by his sister Sittah, hopes to maneuver the Jewish merchant into making an adverse judgment about the genuineness of the Muslim faith in order to place himself in a more advantageous bargaining position. When Nathan arrives at the palace and is asked to declare which of the three monotheistic religions is the one true faith, he skillfully avoids entrapment by recounting the parable of the three rings and even manages to win the sultan's admiration by means of this shrewd response. The Templar and Racha have become better acquainted in the meantime, and on returning from the palace, Nathan is surprised to hear the young man ask for his foster daughter's hand in marriage. Nathan responds by requesting more time to consider the matter. In hope of facilitating the union of the young couple, Daja, a Christian woman who serves as Recha's companion, informs the Templar that her mistress had really been born a Christian and subsequently been raised in the Jewish faith by Nathan. Perplexed by this revelation, the Templar rushes off to seek counsel from the Christian Patriarch of Jerusalem. The Patriarch, whose character is said to mirror the bigotry of Lessing's adversary Pastor Goeze, insists that the penalty for subverting the faith of a Christian is no less than death at the stake. Shocked by this prospect, the Templar hastens to the palace in order to confer with Saladin. The Muslim ruler refuses to believe that Nathan would impose his own faith on a child that was abducted from its Christian parents and urges the Templar to exercise Christian forbearance by reserving judgment until all the facts become known.

As a result of inquiries initiated by the Patriarch of Jerusalem, it comes to light that Recha's father was a Crusader who bore the name of Wolf von Filneck. After the death of the mother in childbirth, the father asked a groom to deliver the infant into the care of Nathan, with whom the Crusader had earlier formed a friendship, so that he himself would be able to take part in a Christian attack on the Muslim stronghold of Gaza. The Jewish merchant readily accepted this new charge because of a personal tragedy that had befallen his family a few days before. A fact unknown to the Crusader, Nathan was at the time mourning the death of his own wife and seven children at the hands of Christian fanatics, and when he later reviewed news of the Crusader's death in the assault on Gaza, he decided to adopt Recha as a gift sent to him by God in compensation for his own tragic loss.

Further revelations come to light when a breviary that once belonged to Wolf von Filneck comes into Nathan's possession. On the breviary's first and last pages there is a list of Wolf von Filneck's kinsmen written in Arabic script by his own hand. It turns out that Wolf was originally a Muslim who converted to Christianity at the time of his marriage to a German woman. After a brief period of residence in Germany, the couple decided to return to the Holy Land for reasons that the playwright never makes explicit. Before leaving Germany, they entrusted their infant son to the care of the mother's brother, a Templar named Curt von Stauffen, who eventually adopted the boy as his own.

These facts make it clear that Recha and the young Templar are brother and sister: Leu and Blanda von Filneck. After recovering from their initial disappointment that they can no longer be lovers, the young man and woman are quick to accept their newly discovered sibling status. Nathan is astounded by this turn of events, since Wolf von Filneck, although acknowledging that he was neither German nor even European by origin, had never even hinted at his true identity or place of origin. Saladin, after hearing Nathan's description of his former friend's personal traits, asks to examine Wolf von Filneck's breviary and immediately recognizes the handwriting as that of his long-lost brother, Assad. Recha and the young Templar are, consequently, the sultan's niece and nephew. The effect of all these disclosures is to underscore the brotherhood of all people, and the play thus ends on a note of triumphant humanism. *Nathan the Wise* is the climax not only of Lessing's career as a playwright, but also of the Age of Enlightenment in Germany.

OTHER MAJOR WORKS

SHORT FICTION: *Fabeln*, 1759 (*Fables*, 1773).

NONFICTION: *Kritische Briefe*, 1753; *Abhandlungen vom weinerlichen oder rührenden Lustspiel*, 1754; *Vade mecum für den Hrn. Sam. Gotth. Lange*, 1754; *Theatralische Bibliothek*, 1754-1758; *Pope ein Mataphysiker!*, 1755; *Abhandlungen über die Fabel*, 1759 (*Treatises on the Fable*, 1773); *Laokoon: Oder, Über die Grenzen der Malerei und Poesie*, 1766 (*Laocoön: An Essay on the Limits of Painting and Poetry*, 1836); *Hamburgische Dramaturgie*, 1767-1769 (*Hamburg Dramaturgy*, 1889); *Briefe antiquarischen Inhalts*, 1768; *Wie die Alten den Tod gebildet*, 1769 (*How the Ancients Represented Death*, 1879); *Zerstreute Anmerkungen über das Epigramm*, 1771; *Zur Geschichte und Literatur*, 1773; *Von der Duldung der Deisten*, 1774 (English translation in *Theological Writings*, 1956); *Das Testament Johannis*, 1777; *Eine Duplick*, 1778; "Eine Parable," 1778 ("A Parable from the German of Lessing," 1806); "Axiomata," 1778; *Anti-Goeze*, 1778; *Ernst und Falk: Gespräche für Freimaurer*, 1778 (*Masonic Dialogues*, 1927); *Die Erziehung des Menschengeschlechts*, 1780 (*The Education of the Human Race*, 1858); *Theological Writings*, 1956.

TRANSLATION: *Das Theater des Hern Diderot*, 1759.

EDITED TEXT: *Briefe die neueste Literatur betreffend*, 1759-1760.

MISCELLANEOUS: *Selected Prose Works*, 1879; *Sämtliche Schriften*, 1886-1924 (23 volumes).

BIBLIOGRAPHY

Eckhardt, Jo-Jacqueline. *Lessing's "Nathan the Wise" and the Critics, 1779-1991*. Columbia, S.C.: Camden House, 1993. A long-term perspective of the literary criticism produced in response to Lessing's *Nathan the Wise*. Bibliography and index.

Gustafson, Susan E. *Absent Mothers and Orphaned Fathers: Narcissism and Abjection in Lessing's Aesthetic and Dramatic Production*. Detroit, Mich.: Wayne State University Press, 1995. A psychoanalytic study of the works of Lessing, with emphasis on his sense of aesthetics. Bibliography and index.

Hawari, Emma. *Johnson's and Lessing's Dramatic Critical Theories and Practice with a Consideration of Lessing's Affinities with Johnson*. New York: Peter Lang, 1991. An examination of the dramatic theories of Lessing and Samuel Johnson, as well as a comparison of their literary works. Bibliography and index.

Henriksen, Jan-Olav. *The Reconstruction of Religion: Lessing, Kierkegaard, and Nietzsche*. Grand Rapids, Mich.: Wm. B. Eerdmans, 2001. A study of the religious beliefs of Lessing, Søren Kierkegaard, and Friedrich Nietzsche as revealed by their lives and writings. Bibliography and index.

Redekop, Benjamin Wall. *Enlightenment and Community: Lessing, Abbt, Herder and the Quest for a German Public*. Montreal: McGill-Queen's University Press, 2000. An examination of the political and social views of Lessing, Thomas Abbt, an Johann Gottfried Herder as shown in their writings and lives. Bibliography and index.

Vallée, Gérard. *Soundings in G. E. Lessing's Philosophy of Religion*. Lanham, Md.: University Press of America, 2000. An examination of the religious philosophy of Lessing, as evidenced in his writings. Bibliography and index.

Victor Anthony Rudowski

MATTHEW GREGORY LEWIS

Born: London, England; July 9, 1775
Died: At sea, near Jamaica; May 14, 1818

PRINCIPAL DRAMA

Village Virtues, pb. 1796

The Minister, pb. 1797 (translation of Friedrich
  Schiller's play *Kabale und Liebe*)

The Castle Spectre, pr. 1797, pb. 1798

Rolla: Or, The Peruvian Hero, pb. 1799
  (translation of August von Kotzebue's play *Die
  Spanier in Peru: Oder, Rollas Tod*)

The Twins: Or, Is It He or His Brother?, pr. 1799,
  pb. 1962 (adaptation of Jean François
  Regnard's *Les Ménechmes: Ou, Les Jumeaux*)

The East Indian, pr. 1799, pb. 1800

Adelmorn the Outlaw, pr., pb. 1801

Alfonso, King of Castile, pb. 1801, pr. 1802

The Captive, pr. 1803 (dramatic monologue)

The Harper's Daughter: Or, Love and Ambition,
  pr. 1803 (revision of *The Minister*)

Rugantino: Or, The Bravo of Venice, pr., pb.
  1805 (two acts; revision of *The Bravo of
  Venice*)

Adelgitha: Or, The Fruits of a Single Error, pb.
  1806, pr. 1807

The Wood Daemon: Or, "The Clock Has Struck,"
  pr. 1807

Venoni: Or, The Novice of St. Mark's, pr. 1808, pb.
  1809 (adaptation of Jacques Marie de Monvel's
  play *Les Victimes cloîtrées*)

Temper: Or, The Domestic Tyrant, pr. 1809
  (adaptation of Sir Charles Sedley's translation,
  The Grumbler, of David Augustin Brueys and
  Jean Palaprat's play *Le Grondeur*)

Timour the Tartar, pr., pb. 1811

*One O'Clock: Or, The Knight and the Wood
  Daemon*, pr., pb. 1811 (music by Michael Kelly
  and Matthew Peter King; revision of *The Wood
  Daemon*)

Rich and Poor, pr., pb. 1812 (music by Charles
  Edward Horn; adaptation of Lewis's *The East
  Indian*)

OTHER LITERARY FORMS

Although Matthew Gregory Lewis was one of the most successful British dramatists of the Romantic era, his primary claim to fame today is his authorship of that most extravagant of gothic novels, *The Monk: A Romance*, which was originally published, in 1796, as *Ambrosio: Or, The Monk*. This was Lewis's first significant published work, and it created such a sensation among his contemporaries that he is still referred to more often by his nickname of "Monk" Lewis than by his given name. Despite the objections of moralists and literary critics alike, this lurid tale of human perversity, with its seductive demons and bleeding ghosts, sold prodigiously during Lewis's lifetime and remains standard reading for anyone studying the development of the English novel.

Two of Lewis's nondramatic publications were *The Love of Gain: A Poem Initiated from Juvenal* (1799), written in imitation of the Thirteenth Satire of Juvenal, and *Tales of Wonder* (1801), an anthology of horror poems. The former, an insignificant throwback to the subject matter and the style of the Age of Johnson, attracted little attention, but the latter stirred considerable interest, some of it admiring but much of it amused. *Tales of Wonder* was compiled in response to a vogue for gothic ballads that occurred after the publication in the 1790's of several translations of G. A. Bürger's *Lenore* (1773). Unfortunately, the vogue had begun to wane by the time the anthology appeared, and it was unmercifully parodied during the months following its publication. Nevertheless, it remains a work of considerable historical interest because of its inclusion of some of the early poetry of Robert Southey and Sir Walter Scott and because of its influence throughout the nineteenth century on poetic gothicism.

Much of Lewis's work was derived from or was influenced by German sources, and in 1805 and 1806, he published translations of a pair of German romances, one of which he subsequently dramatized. The first, *The Bravo of Venice: A Romance*, was based on J. H. D. Zschokke's *Aballino der Grosse*

Bandit, and the second, *Feudal Tyrants: Or, The Counts of Carlsheim and Sargans: A Romance, Taken from the German*, was a somewhat freer rendering of Christiane Benedicte Eugénie Naubert's *Elisabeth, Erbin von Toggenburg: Oder, Geschichte der Frauen in der Schweiz*. Suffice it to say of these works that they again show Lewis's fascination with the sensational and that both, especially *The Bravo of Venice*, achieved popular success.

Lewis was also an important writer of popular songs, many of which appeared first in his plays and a number of which were Lewis's original contributions to the works of his fellow playwrights. His nondramatic poetry, too, was sometimes set to music, and, collaborating with such people as Charles Edward Horn, Michael Kelly, and Harriet Abrams, Lewis was frequently able to catch the public's musical fancy. Such songs as "The Banks of Allan Water" (from *Rich and Poor*), "The Wind It Blows Cold" (from *Adelmorn the Outlaw*—both words and music by Lewis), "The Wife's Farewell: Or, Oh No My Love No!" and "The Orphan's Prayer" are unknown today, but in the early nineteenth century they were extremely popular. Lewis himself was a reasonably skillful melodist, and as the title of his most substantial song collection, *Twelve Ballads, the Words and Music by M. G. Lewis* (1808), indicates, he occasionally composed his own tunes.

Lewis published a mixed collection of poetry and prose, *Romantic Tales*, in 1808. This four-volume work contained one long narrative poem, five short stories, and seven ballads. Much of the material was translated or adapted from Continental originals, some of it again from the German. Although *Romantic Tales* shows frequent gothic touches reminiscent of much of Lewis's other work, the individual works vary considerably in tone and subject matter and belie the usual exclusive association of Lewis's name with the wondrous and the horrifying. Two other publications, *Monody on the Death of Sir John Moore* (1809) and *Poems* (1812), are even more remote from gothic extravagance and exhibit a neoclassical polish that would startle those who know Lewis only through *The Monk*, *Tales of Wonder*, and *The Castle Spectre*.

Matthew Gregory Lewis (Library of Congress)

Poems was the last volume of Lewis's work to be published during his lifetime, but two others appeared posthumously, *The Isle of Devils: A Metrical Tale* (1827) and *Journal of a West India Proprietor, Kept During a Residence in the Island of Jamaica* (1834). The former is a narrative poem in heroic couplets concerning a young woman who is pursued and victimized by monsters after a shipwreck. Critics have not treated it well. *Journal of a West India Proprietor*, on the other hand, has been praised more consistently than any of Lewis's other writings. It gives an engaging and unpretentious account of Lewis's two voyages to his estates in the West Indies, an account that Samuel Taylor Coleridge, generally one of Lewis's severest critics, found impressively well written.

Also of interest are Lewis's letters, many of which appeared in Margaret Baron-Wilson's *The Life and Correspondence of M. G. Lewis* (1839). Although he was not an important epistolary stylist, Lewis wrote letters that exhibit considerable charm and that, because of his extensive acquaintance with prominent persons, are sometimes of significance to the literary biographer and the historian.

ACHIEVEMENTS

Matthew Gregory Lewis is one of those delightful literary figures whose ability to appeal to the bad taste of the public brings them immense popularity during their own day and critical damnation forever after. In an age when most of Britain's greatest writers found themselves incapable of pleasing London audiences, Lewis brought immense sums into the coffers of the Drury Lane and Covent Garden theaters. He was a master of the sentimental and the sensational, and sentiment and sensation were what London audiences wanted. Although not all his plays, referred to by his biographer Louis F. Peck as "brainless stories," were popular successes, enough of them were to make Lewis the darling of the theater managers.

As one might expect of the author of *The Monk*, Lewis is primarily important for his contributions to dramatic gothicism. Indeed, Bertrand Evans, author of *Gothic Drama from Walpole to Shelley* (1947), writes that "the name of Matthew Gregory Lewis is perhaps the most important in the history of gothic drama." Lewis, Evans observes, drew together the "materials of his predecessors and contemporaries, English and German, and out-Gothicized them all." He did this most triumphantly in *The Castle Spectre*, which was an immediate and overwhelming theatrical sensation. According to Evans, its forty-seven performances made it "the most successful play of its time," a success achieved by ruthlessly sacrificing "consistency of character, probability of action, and forward movement of plot . . . to immediate sensational effect."

In order to appraise Lewis's approach fairly, however, it is necessary to know what was considered to be the height of fashion and of entertainment in his day—just at the beginning of the Regency period. The royal establishments at Blenheim and Bath set the tone for outrageous combinations of exaggerated Oriental borrowings mixed with every new fad that the empire builders had brought home from around the world. People went to playhouses more to see and be seen by others than to pay attention to the story

line of any play. The audiences in general were so preoccupied with finery and social scandals and made so blasé by experience at places such as Astley's Amphitheatre with fireworks, lakes filled with boats on which naval engagements were reenacted, and the like that it took a lot to get even a moment of their attention.

A man well suited to his time, Lewis was more skillful as an entertainer than as a dramatic artist, and his theatrical creations were so well attended because he had the capacity of engaging his audience's interest, often through unsubtle means. Whether by means of music, melodrama, or shameless spectacle, Lewis made his works impossible to ignore.

BIOGRAPHY

Matthew Gregory Lewis, the first child of Matthew Lewis and the former Frances Maria Sewell, was born in London, England, on July 9, 1775. His father served for a number of years as both chief clerk in the War Office and as deputy-secretary at war, positions whose salaries, in combination with the revenues from estates owned by the elder Lewis in Jamaica, rendered the Lewis household financially prosperous. Prosperity did not assure marital harmony, however, and his parents agreed to a permanent separation when young Matthew Gregory was seven or eight years old. According to a bill of divorcement that was never brought to enactment, the primary cause of his parents' estrangement was an adulterous affair carried on by Mrs. Lewis, which resulted in her giving birth to a child.

In addition to this illegitimate sibling, Lewis had two sisters, Maria and Sophia, and a brother, Barrington, all whom lived with their father. Young Matthew Gregory, who had begun his education at Marylebone Seminary, resided at Westminster College and Christ Church College, Oxford, during much of his childhood and adolescence and maintained affectionate contact with both of his parents. Throughout his lifetime, in fact, whatever slight cohesiveness existed within the Lewis family was largely the result of Matthew Gregory's efforts.

Although young Lewis was not a systematic, self-disciplined scholar, he did exhibit considerable talent in foreign languages, music, and literature, and by age sixteen, largely through the stimulation of a summer spent in Paris, he was busily at work as both writer and translator. His earliest efforts, about which he carried on a regular correspondence with his mother, who also had literary ambitions, were refused publication. Of the works that eventually made Lewis famous, however, a surprising number were completed, or at least begun, during his teens—a genesis that goes far to explain the adolescent feverishness of many of his most characteristic productions.

In Paris, Lewis became familiar with French drama, and there he may also have encountered translations of contemporary German literature. At any rate, he became thoroughly imbued with the spirit of the German Sturm und Drang movement during a stay in Weimar that began in July of 1792 when Lewis was seventeen. His father had sent him there to learn German so that he might enter the diplomatic service, and during his stay, he met Johann Wolfgang von Goethe and Christoph Martin Wieland, spent many hours translating German literary works, and continued to fashion a literary style of his own, a style heavily influenced by his experiences in both Paris and Weimar.

Lewis returned to Oxford in the early months of 1793 and was graduated in the spring of 1794, shortly before his nineteenth birthday. Between May and December of 1794, he held a minor diplomatic post at The Hague, where he found ample time to complete the novel that was to assure his fame. That novel, *The Monk*, was published in 1796 and made Lewis an immediate, and slightly infamous, celebrity. His presence was very much in demand at London social gatherings, a fact that delighted the gregarious young author.

In this same eventful year, Lewis became the parliamentary representative for Hindon in Wiltshire, a position he retained until 1802. His parliamentary duties and his literary fame brought him the acquaintance, during these and subsequent years, of many of the prominent men of England, a number of whom mention Lewis in their correspondence and other writings. The impression that these accounts give of Lewis is of a physically unattractive, dreadfully near-

sighted man, whose kindliness and affability made him difficult to dislike but whose boring garrulousness often made his company difficult to enjoy. A tone of amused, sometimes exasperated, affection suffuses many of these verbal portraits, especially those by Lord Byron.

As he had at The Hague, Lewis found sufficient time while a Member of Parliament to carry forward his literary projects. He was occasionally instrumental, too, in advancing the careers of other literary men, the most important of whom was Sir Walter Scott. In addition to inviting Scott, whom he had met in 1798, to contribute to *Tales of Wonder*, Lewis helped to arrange for the publication of Scott's 1799 translation of Goethe's *Götz von Berlichingen mit der eisernen Hand* (pb. 1773; *Götz von Berlichingen with the Iron Hand*, 1799). It is amusing to read Scott's account of the deference with which he, then almost entirely unknown as a writer, received Lewis's often imperious pronouncements concerning literary style.

During this same period, Lewis's talents as a playwright came to the public's attention, with *The Castle Spectre*, the third of his plays to be published but the first to be staged. *Village Virtues*, a social farce, and *The Minister*, a translation of Friedrich Schiller's *Kabale und Liebe* (pr., pb. 1784; *Cabal and Love*, 1795), had attracted little attention to Lewis's dramatic skills, but *The Castle Spectre*, which opened on December 14, 1797, earned eighteen thousand pounds for Drury Lane Theater in less than three months.

Lewis's next dramatic project, a translation of August von Kotzebue's 1794 play *Die Spanier in Peru: Oder, Rollas Tod* (pr. 1794, pb. 1795; *The Spaniards in Peru: Or, Rolla's Death*, 1799), appears originally to have been intended as a collaboration with Richard Brinsley Sheridan, but the pair found it impossible to work together, and Sheridan turned to another translator for assistance. Sheridan's version of the play, *Pizarro: A Tragedy in Five Acts*, opened in May, 1799, without acknowledgment of Lewis's initial contributions to the production, and achieved spectacular success. Lewis's version, *Rolla*, was published but not performed, and the ill will generated by this incident and by various other difficulties experienced by Lewis at Drury Lane eventually led to a temporary shift of his loyalties to Covent Garden.

Before this occurred, however, three more of his plays were presented at Drury Lane, *The Twins* and *The East Indian* in 1799 and *Adelmorn the Outlaw* in 1801, but none achieved any extraordinary success. The first two, a social farce and a sentimental comedy, were originally acted as benefit presentations for a pair of Drury Lane's veteran performers; although they served that purpose adequately, the critical and popular reception of the plays was at best lukewarm. Like his other attempts at comedy, they were neither great triumphs nor notable catastrophes. *Adelmorn the Outlaw* on the other hand, threatened to become an embarrassment of the first order. The stage set and the incidental music were well received, but the play itself was a critical failure. *Adelmorn the Outlaw* included many of the same melodramatic plot elements and gothic flourishes that had attracted enthusiastic audiences to *The Castle Spectre*, but *Adelmorn the Outlaw* was so absurdly and, at times, so tastelessly constructed that Lewis's utmost exertions were able to sustain it through a first run of only nine performances.

The reviewers treated Lewis's first Covent Garden production, *Alfonso, King of Castile*, with considerably more kindness. Although praise was not universal, some reviewers thought *Alfonso, King of Castile* the greatest tragic play of its age, and it was certainly Lewis's most concerted attempt at high dramatic art. The play is written in blank verse, occasionally with impressive poetic effect, but the plot is marred by a melodramatic intensity that makes it difficult for a modern-day reader to take seriously. *Alfonso, King of Castile* was published several weeks before its January 15, 1802, premiere, and though its first run of only ten performances suggests that it was a very modest popular success, it remained the play in which Lewis took the greatest artistic pride.

During 1803, Lewis's only new theatrical productions were *The Captive*, a dramatic monologue, and *The Harper's Daughter*, a shortened version of *The Minister*. They both appeared at Covent Garden, on March 22 and May 4, respectively, and each was successful after its own fashion. *The Harper's Daughter*

was a benefit presentation and drew a large enough audience to provide a tidy sum. *The Captive*, billed as a "mono-drama," was an extended speech by a young wife who had been consigned to a madhouse by her cruel husband. So effective was its presentation of the wife's gradual loss of sanity that several spectators experienced hysterical fits during and after the performance and the drama was withdrawn in order to preserve the mental health of Covent Garden's customers.

Lewis's next play, a melodrama in two acts entitled *Rugantino*, opened at Covent Garden on October 18, 1805, and was performed thirty times before enthusiastic houses. Lewis again caught the public's fancy by relying on spectacle rather than subtle art, and though an occasional viewer might complain of headaches brought on by the play's many pistol shots and thunderclaps, most were enthralled; nor did the dazzling costume changes and the gorgeous Venice scenery hurt the play's attendance. Lewis knew his audience well and gave it what it wanted.

Rugantino was followed on April 1, 1807, this time at Drury Lane, by the even more spectacular *The Wood Daemon*. Full of more gothic paraphernalia than any of Lewis's previous dramatic creations, *The Wood Daemon* is more truly a play of special effects than of plot and dialogue, and it was judged in such terms by contemporary reviewers: There was considerable praise for the production's visual impact but very little positive comment on the play as literary art. The visual impact was enough, however, to assure *The Wood Daemon* a first run of thirty-four performances.

Lewis's next three productions met with a more modest reception. *Adelgitha*, a play that Lewis had published in 1806, opened at Drury Lane in April of 1807 to favorable reviews. Centering on a character whose tragic life was meant to illustrate the fatal consequences of youthful sin, the play relies for its effect on melodramatic plot complication rather than visual spectacle, and although its nine first-run performances compare unfavorably with the thirty-four of *The Wood Daemon*, it was not nearly so ambitious a theatrical project and seems fully to have satisfied the expectations of those involved in its staging.

Venoni did not, at first, fare so well. The play, whose plot Lewis adapted from a French original, premiered at Drury Lane on December 1, 1808, and was immediately attacked by the reviewers. One scene in particular, in which a pair of lovers, unaware of each other's presence, speak alternating soliloquies from their adjoining dungeon cells, was judged especially ludicrous. The play required extensive rewriting, which Lewis undertook with some success, and *Venoni* had reached its eighteenth performance when a fire destroyed the theater. Lewis then provided the Drury Lane troupe, temporarily housed at the Lyceum Theater, with a farce entitled *Temper*, which opened on May 1, 1809, attracting so little attention that it was lost from Lewis's dramatic canon until 1942.

At this point, Lewis announced that he would write no more plays, a decision that, if he had adhered to it, would have denied posterity his most dubious contribution to British theater, the grand equestrian drama *Timour the Tartar*. *Timour the Tartar* was not the first play to introduce horses onto the British stage; that honor belongs to *Blue Beard*, whose cast of characters was horseless until February 18, 1811. On that date, the Covent Garden management made its initial test of the public's readiness to accept equestrian performers. The popular response was gratifying, and *Timour the Tartar*, whose equestrian elements were not extraneous interpolations but integral parts of the plot, was awaited with considerable anticipation. The play opened on April 29, 1811, to the howls of the critics and the applause of the paying customers. In the ensuing months, parodies and imitations abounded, one featuring a performing elephant, and *Timour the Tartar* itself was staged a profitable forty-four times.

Lewis's final two theatrical offerings were reworkings of old material. They do, however, illustrate Lewis's frequent use of songs to increase the entertainment value of his plays. Working with Michael Kelly and Matthew Peter King, Lewis transformed *The Wood Daemon* into "a grand musical romance" with the slightly altered title, *One O'Clock: Or, The Knight and the Wood Daemon*; collaborating with Charles Edward Horn, he extensively revised *The East Indian*, turning it into a comic opera entitled *Rich and Poor*. The musical romance premiered on August 1, 1811, and was performed twenty-five times during its first season by the company of the English Opera House; the comic opera opened on July 22, 1812, and was performed twenty-seven times by the same organization.

Lewis's literary endeavors had been made possible largely by a yearly allowance of a thousand pounds granted him by his father. This allowance was reduced for a time as a result of an argument between father and son over a sexual affair in which the elder Lewis had become involved, but the two managed to reconcile their differences before the father's death in May of 1812, and Lewis inherited all his father's considerable wealth. Very soon thereafter, he used a portion of the money to purchase a permanent home for his mother.

Another consequence of the inheritance was the first of Lewis's two voyages to Jamaica to inspect his island properties. The primary purpose of his visit, which occurred during the first three months of 1816, was to ascertain that slaves on his plantations were properly treated. Although Lewis made no provision for the freeing of these slaves, he did establish strict rules intended to make their lives more bearable. Also, to prevent a deterioration in their living conditions after his death, he added a codicil to his will insisting that any future heir to his estates visit the plantations every third year for the purpose of looking after the slaves' welfare. In addition, no slaves were to be put up for sale.

The alterations in Lewis's will were witnessed on August 20, 1816, by Lord Byron, Percy Bysshe Shelley, and Dr. John W. Polidori during a trip Lewis took to the Continent, a trip that lasted for more than a year. The most noteworthy literary events of that tour were his oral translation of Goethe's *Faust: Eine Tragödie* (pb. 1808, 1833; *The Tragedy of Faust*, 1823, 1838) for Byron, the latter's first direct experience with that work, and Lewis's telling ghost stories for the entertainment of Byron and the Shelleys. Although Lewis cannot be claimed to have inspired Mary Shelley's *Frankenstein* (1818) as she had begun her novel several weeks before Lewis's arrival in

Geneva, his enthusiasm for the gothic is likely to have encouraged her to continue the project.

After a short stay in England following his wanderings on the Continent, Lewis again set sail for Jamaica on November 5, 1817. During this second visit, he introduced further reforms to improve the plight of his slaves, and having assured himself that he had done what he could for them, he embarked for England on May 4, 1818. He was ill with yellow fever when the voyage began, and within two weeks, he was dead.

ANALYSIS

Despite considerable diversity in style and content. Matthew Gregory Lewis's plays are generally characterized by a melodramatic intensity that is often reinforced by visual spectacle. Dramatic subtlety was difficult to achieve in the huge theaters for which Lewis wrote, and Lewis's unsubtle ways were peculiarly suited to the physical environment in which his plays were performed. This is not to say, however, that Lewis presents no unified dramatic vision, that he has nothing to say about the state of human beings. On the contrary, his plays are surprisingly consistent in their expression of one particular theme—that the sanctity of human relationships should not and must not be violated.

Although the artistic merit of Lewis's plays is minimal, his contemporaries enjoyed them. The sensationalism and the melodramatic moralizing of his dramatic works are symptomatic of the bad taste that produced one of the most sterile periods in British theatrical history, and if Lewis cannot be accused of creating this bad taste, he can justly be said to have been the most adept playwright of his age at exploiting it.

THE CASTLE SPECTRE

The Castle Spectre, for example, relates the tale of the villainous Earl Osmond, who has sinned against the bonds of love at every opportunity and who pays the ultimate price for his crimes. Long before the action of the play begins, Osmond has already launched his egocentric career by overthrowing his own brother, the benevolent Earl Reginald, and inadvertently killing Lady Evelina, the woman whom he had

hoped to marry but who had married his brother instead. Evelina has martyred herself to love by throwing her body in the path of a dagger-thrust that Osmond intended for Reginald. Her sacrifice has not prevented the usurpation of her husband's power, but it has, as the audience is eventually informed, preserved her husband's life.

As one might expect of such a man, Osmond has shown no more respect for the relationship between a ruler and his subjects than he has for the ties of blood, and though he conceals the guilty secret of his rise to power, Osmond is universally hated as a tyrant. He surrounds himself with brutal henchmen who deal efficiently and savagely with any who would oppose their master. At the beginning of the play, there are no obvious threats to Osmond's continued dominion, but the isolation and loneliness that his actions have brought on him are soon to lead to his downfall.

Appropriately enough, the undoing of this sinner against the bonds of affection is the direct result of his falling in love. The unwilling object of his amorous attentions is his niece, the beautiful and virtuous Angela, daughter of Reginald and Evelina. To minimize Angela's threat to his power (as heir to the rightful lord), Osmond has placed her with a peasant couple who have reared her as their own child. He makes the fateful decision to call her back to the court, however, when her resemblance to Evelina inspires his passion. To legitimize Angela's sudden change in status, Osmond invents a story affirming her noble birth while concealing her actual parentage.

Like his obsession with Evelina, though, his interest in Angela is doomed to failure—again because the woman he has chosen has already selected a worthier man. During the last weeks of her peasant existence, she has fallen in love with the lowly Edric, whom she had met while she was living as a peasant, and even the opportunity to marry an earl is not temptation enough to shake her fidelity to this humble swain. Neither sweet words nor threats of imprisonment are sufficient to win her consent to become Osmond's wife.

As the audience soon discovers, Angela has chosen more wisely than she knows, because Edric is actually Percy, Earl of Northumberland, whose benevolent rule has earned for him the respect and affection of his people and whose purity of heart is suggested by the circumstances of his falling in love. Neither Percy nor Angela had been aware of the other's noble birth, but each has recognized the other's nobility of character. Percy and Osmond are spiritual opposites, and their rivalry for Angela is a clash between codes of behavior, between the ways of sentiment and the ways of selfishness.

One manifestation of this opposition is the method each uses to form alliances. Osmond surrounds himself with men who are motivated by fear and hatred or by self-interest. He enslaves his henchmen and awes them with his power, or he entices them with the hope of illusory rewards. His black slaves, like Hassan, have been stolen from their homelands and welcome every opportunity to wreak vengeance on the race that separated them from their loved ones. Others, like Kenric, have been promised worldly wealth and release from service in exchange for their fidelity, only to discover Osmond's intention to betray them. Percy's followers, on the other hand, eagerly join his effort to rescue Angela; they are motivated by love and remain faithful to their master at moments when Osmond's followers are most likely to become undependable. One in particular, Gilbert the Knave, has been the object of Percy's generosity during a period of personal crisis and shows his gratitude through his courageous support of his master at several key points in the play. As Percy himself says,

Instead of looking with scorn on those whom a smile would attract, and a favor bind forever, how many firm friends might our nobles gain, if they would but reflect that their vassals are men as they are, and have hearts whose feelings can be grateful as their own.

Osmond refuses to recognize this sentimental truth, and as a result, he loses the loyalty of a man who is in a position to reveal more about Osmond's perfidious nature than that noble cares for the world to know. When Kenric discovers that his master is plotting to kill him, he tells Angela the secret of her birth and that her father Reginald is alive, hidden away in a dungeon by Kenric himself so that he might blackmail Osmond if the need should ever arise. Unfortu-nately, Osmond overhears this conversation and goes in search of his hated brother, intending to carry to completion the fratricide that he had thought he had already committed.

Before the climactic arrival of the principal characters at Reginald's dungeon, the sympathy of the supernatural with the defenders of sentiment has been implied by the spectacular appearance to Angela of her mother's ghost. The specter of Evelina blesses Angela and directs her to rescue her father. Elements in this scene suggest the triumph of love over hatred, a triumph that occurs in the play's busy final moments. Osmond and Angela come on her father's darkened cell at almost the same time, and Osmond uses the occasion to threaten her with Reginald's death unless she acquiesces to their immediate marriage. This she is about to do when Reginald stops her by saying that he will take his own life rather than see his daughter dishonored. Enraged by this declaration and by news that Percy's forces have taken the castle, Osmond prepares to kill his brother but falls back in horror when Evelina's ghost repeats the self-sacrificing gesture of the living Evelina. Angela then strikes Osmond with the same dagger with which her mother had been stabbed, and the sinner against sentiment is carried away to die.

As one might imagine, despite the extraordinary commercial success of *The Castle Spectre*, it was not a universal favorite of the critics. This fact seems not to have concerned Lewis, however, who was especially cavalier in his response to one very particular objection to his play. When the critics pointed out that his inclusion of black slaves in the cast of characters of a gothic story was a patent absurdity, he defended himself by saying that he had done it to "give a pleasing variety to the characters and dresses" and that if he could "have produced the same effect by making my heroine blue, blue I should have made her."

ALFONSO, KING OF CASTILE

Obviously, Lewis did not take *The Castle Spectre* seriously as a work of art, but he did feel considerable artistic pride in *Alfonso, King of Castile*. Nevertheless, the two plays have essentially the same theme: The forces of sentiment are pitted against the forces of selfish ambition, and after the moral superiority of sentiment has been clearly displayed, ambition is defeated. In *Alfonso, King of Castile*, however, there are surprising twists of plot and characterization that create a greater sense of dramatic sophistication than is evident in the earlier play.

The curtain rises on a narrative situation that is already quite complex. Alfonso has been a good king, but he has been duped into committing one act of injustice. He has imprisoned his best friend, Orsino, on the basis of evidence fabricated by Orsino's enemies. As a result, Orsino's wife, Victoria, has died in poverty-stricken exile after swearing her son, Caesario, to avenge his father. Concealing his identity, Caesario has insinuated his way into the good graces of the king and has so successfully encouraged the rebellious spirit of the king's son that the son has defected to the king's foes. Caesario has also secretly won the love of and married the king's daughter, Amelrosa, but he has not managed, as the play begins, to break the filial bond between Alfonso and his daughter.

Ironically, it is love—for his parents—that causes Caesario to become filled with hatred. His hatred is directed against a man whose only fault is gullibility, and he attempts to make use of the innocent love of a virtuous woman to further his despicable ends. Like Osmond, Caesario is a sinner against the dictates of sentiment, and he, too, will pay with his life for his crimes.

That Caesario's actions are crimes is made clear in a number of ways. First, while courting Amelrosa, Caesario has shown his duplicitous nature by carrying on an illicit liaison with Ottilia, the vicious wife of Marquis Guzman, the man primarily responsible for his father's fall from grace. The difficulties of this situation cause him to weave a web of lies that suggest that his feelings toward neither woman are genuine. Furthermore, as the moment of Caesario's final vengeance against Alfonso approaches, it becomes increasingly obvious that a desire for personal power is at least as important in motivating Caesario as any wish to punish his father's persecutor. In fact, the killing of Alfonso is to be carried out in a way intended to alert any English audience to his murderer's villainy; a cache of explosives is to be detonated be-

neath Alfonso's palace, an obvious allusion to the infamous Gunpowder Plot.

During the course of the play, Orsino is discovered to be alive, and, despite his bitterness over the sufferings of himself and his family, he condemns Caesario's plans for the overthrow of Alfonso. When Alfonso has come to beg his forgiveness, his resentment has been too great to allow a reconciliation to occur, but when his son reveals his dastardly plotting, Orsino affirms the basic goodness of his former friend and allies himself with Alfonso rather than with Caesario. In a speech that summarizes the central idea of the play, he tries to draw his son back to the paths of virtue:

> True glory
> Is not to wear a crown but to *deserve* one.
> The peasant swain who leads a good man's life,
> And dies at last a good man's death, obtains
> In Wisdom's eye wreaths of far brighter splendour
> Than he whose wanton pride and thirst for empire
> Make kings his captives, and lay waste a world.

Unfortunately, Caesario's hatred and ambition blind him to the truth of his father's statement.

As they generally are in a Lewis play, the final scenes of *Alfonso, King of Castile* are almost overburdened with action. When the play ends, all the principals, with the exception of Alfonso himself, are either dead or dying, and Orsino, mortally wounded, has been forced to choose between killing his vicious son and watching the flawed but virtuous Alfonso be murdered. He chooses, in an odd affirmation of the laws of sentiment, to save the friend who had once betrayed him and to sacrifice the son.

TIMOUR THE TARTAR

Although it does call for the simulated detonation of a cache of gunpowder, *Alfonso, King of Castile* is less dependent for its success on sensational stage effects than are most of Lewis's plays. *Timour the Tartar*, for example, is unashamed stage spectacle from beginning to end. A play in which live horses take part in elaborate battle scenes and in which one particular equine performer leaps with its rider over a parapet into the sea could hardly be anything else. Nevertheless, the same thematic material that gives *Alfonso, King of Castile* some semblance of high seriousness is also to be found in *Timour the Tartar*, another tale of the triumph of sentimental virtue over egocentric vice.

Timour himself is the ruthless villain whose selfishness threatens the very existence of those whose actions are motivated by selfless love. Even his father, Oglou, fears for his life when in Timour's presence. As the code of sentiment dictates, however, he loves his son despite being afraid of him. Throughout the play, Oglou struggles to act in accordance with this love for his son while at the same time behaving properly toward two of his dearest friends, Agib and Zorilda, the most dangerous of Timour's enemies.

Agib is the son and Zorilda the widow of the murdered Prince of Mingrelia, and when the play opens, Agib is Timour's captive. Fortunately, Agib's jailer is the kindly Oglou, whose life was once saved by Zorilda. Oglou will protect Agib as best he can, but he lacks the courage to defy his son by setting Agib free. In a display of the deepest maternal fortitude, that task is undertaken instead by Zorilda.

Zorilda boldly enters Timour's palace disguised as his fiancée, the Princess of Georgia, a woman to whom Timour has become engaged without having met her. Her intention is to demand that Agib, a threat to their united power, be placed with her compatriots for safekeeping. Unfortunately, just as this plot is about to succeed, Oglou is forced to reveal Zorilda's true identity because he anticipates a similar revelation by Octar, Timour's messenger to the Georgian court.

In defiance of every rule of sentiment and decency, Timour proceeds to demand that the spirited Zorilda become his bride despite her obvious distaste for her husband's barbaric murderer; her son, Agib, is to be killed if she refuses. The necessity of making such a choice is obviated, however, when the faithful Oglou assists in getting Agib out of the palace. He asks only, as paternal sentiment demands, that mercy be shown to Timour if Agib and his allies succeed in overthrowing the tyrant. Out of respect for their friend's fatherly feelings, Zorilda and Agib agree.

By this point in the play, there have been illustrations of the sentiments appropriate to a number of hu-

man relationships: widow to deceased husband, son to deceased father, mother to son, father to son, and friend to friend. The play's final scene portrays, in rather spectacular fashion, the courageous love of a son for his mother. As Agib and his troops gather for their attack on Timour's stronghold, Timour, in full sight of the massed armies, attempts to kill the captive Zorilda. She flees and is forced to leap into the sea, at which point Agib spurs his horse over a parapet and rescues his mother from a death by drowning. The stage then becomes a battleground where the forces of virtuous sentiment defeat the forces of self-serving oppression with convincing finality.

ONE O'CLOCK

For his next theatrical effort, Lewis turned from the comparatively new equestrian drama to the more familiar gothic drama. He transformed his earlier *The Wood Daemon* into *One O'Clock: Or, The Knight and the Wood Daemon*, advertising this extraordinary concoction as "a grand musical romance." In keeping with this designation, it contains considerable singing and dancing, and its costumes, sets, and stage machinery are more extravagant than anything used in Lewis's previous productions. Nevertheless, *One O'Clock* is thematically consistent with Lewis's other plays in that it deals with the corrupting influence of egocentric ambition and the saving grace of sentimental virtue.

The power-mad villain of this particular piece is Hardyknute, a former peasant who has become the Count of Holstein by forming a pact with Sangrida, the Wood Daemon. Sangrida has granted him wealth, beauty, eternal youth, and invulnerability in battle in exchange for an annual sacrifice of a child. Each year, on the seventh of August, Hardyknute must spill innocent blood or become the Wood Daemon's perpetual slave. If he fails to accomplish his hideous task before Sangrida's clock strikes one in the morning, he will be subjected to everlasting torment. The play centers on Hardyknute's attempt to sacrifice a ninth child, Leolyn, and take possession of his reward, the beautiful peasant girl Una.

The representatives of virtuous innocence within the play are Leolyn, Clotilda, Oswy, and Una. Leolyn is the long-lost son of the former count, Ruric, whom

Hardyknute clandestinely murdered in order to seize power. Leolyn, who had been entrusted to Una's sister, Clotilda, was stolen by marauding Gypsies and reappears as the play opens, struck dumb and recognizable only by a birthmark on his wrist. Una, whose name suggests (among other things) the dreaded hour of sacrifice, is a young peasant maiden who has been so confounded by the magic of Sangrida that she is on the brink of marrying Hardyknute; her heart, however, belongs to Oswy. Oswy is the poor but faithful peasant who loves Una to distraction and would unhesitatingly lay down his life for her.

To an even greater extent than usual, Lewis concentrates the significant action of the play in the final scenes. The first two acts contain a painfully slow exposition of the plot, the introduction of sentimental subplots that are never satisfactorily integrated with the main plot, and the insertion of various entertainments and spectacles that are obviously intended to dazzle and divert the audience. Storms, secret passages, disappearing statues, and a miraculous bed are only a few of the special effects, with other diversions including a chorus of spirits, a procession of Gypsies, a triumphal march of troops leading a captured giant and dwarfs, a prophetic dream, and a ballet of the seasons, as well as intermittent outbursts of ballad-singing and guitar-playing. By the end of act 2, however, Hardyknute has come to realize, through the venerable device of the birthmark, that his predecessor's son is within the castle and that he must act if he is to preserve his power. He has also been reminded, by the terrifying voice of Sangrida, that only a few hours remain before he must make his annual sacrifice.

In the final act, the allegiance of the central characters to the laws of sentiment is tested, and only Hardyknute is found wanting. Clotilda, suspicious of Hardyknute's murderous intentions, guards Leolyn's bedchamber and is foiled in her vigilance only by a treacherous mechanism that lowers Leolyn's bed into a subterranean dungeon. At this point, Oswy is called on to seek help from the King of Denmark, a task he undertakes despite his worries concerning the wavering fidelity of his beloved Una. Una herself is tried most severely of all. After gaining access to the dun-

geon into which Leolyn has been caged and releasing him from his chains, she is confronted by Hardyknute, who reveals his dreadful secret and makes clear that he will spill her blood in place of Leolyn's if he can save himself from Sangrida in no other way. His love for her will make the murder difficult, but his self-love, being greater, will steel him to commit the crime. Faced with the choice of becoming Hardyknute's accomplice by revealing Leolyn's hiding place or of jeopardizing her own life, Una hesitates for a moment but then chooses to save the innocent young boy. Leolyn, in turn, proves himself worthy of Una's courageous selflessness by remaining in the dungeon and by finding a means of preventing her death. In full sight of Hardyknute, he climbs to Sangrida's clock and pushes the hands forward to the hour of one, thereby calling up the demon before Una can be killed. Sangrida appears immediately and, in a scene that is reminiscent of the conclusion of *The Monk*, four fiends drag Hardyknute away to his eternal punishment.

OTHER MAJOR WORKS

LONG FICTION: *The Monk: A Romance*, 1796 (also published as *Ambrosio: Or, The Monk*).

POETRY: *The Love of Gain: A Poem Initiated from Juvenal*, 1799; *Tales of Wonder*, 1801 (with Sir Walter Scott, Robert Southey, and John Leyden); *Monody on the Death of Sir John Moore*, 1809; *Poems*, 1812; *The Isle of Devils: A Metrical Tale*, 1827.

NONFICTION: *Journal of a West India Proprietor, Kept During a Residence in the Island of Jamaica*, 1834 (also as *Journal of a Residence Among the Negroes in the West Indies*, 1861).

TRANSLATIONS: *The Bravo of Venice: A Romance*, 1805 (of J. H. D. Zschokke's novel *Aballino der Grosse Bandit*); *Feudal Tyrants: Or, The Counts of Carlsheim and Sargans: A Romance, Taken from the German*, 1806 (4 volumes; of Christiane Benedicte Eugénie Naubert's novel *Elisabeth, Erbin von Toggenburg: Oder, Geschichte der Frauen in der Schweiz*).

EDITED TEXTS: *Tales of Terror*, 1799 (also as *An Apology for Tales of Terror*; includes work by Sir Walter Scott and Robert Southey); *Tales of Wonder*, 1801

(2 volumes; includes work by Scott, Southey, Robert Burns, Thomas Gray, John Dryden, and others).

MISCELLANEOUS: *Romantic Tales*, 1808 (4 volumes; includes poem, short stories, and ballads); *Twelve Ballads, the Words and Music by M. G. Lewis*, 1808; *The Life and Correspondence of M. G. Lewis, with Many Pieces Never Before Published*, 1839 (2 volumes; Margaret Baron-Wilson, editor).

BIBLIOGRAPHY

Blakemore, Steven. "Matthew Lewis's Black Mass: Sexual Religion Inversion in *The Monk*." *Studies in the Novel* 30, no. 4 (Winter, 1998): 521-539. This in-depth analysis of Lewis's *The Monk* examines his views as they manifested themselves in this work. In doing so, he sheds light on Lewis's dramatic works.

Frank, Frederick S. "The Gothic Romance, 1762-1820." In *Horror Literature: A Core Collection and Reference Guide*, edited by Marshall B. Tymn. New York: R. R. Bowker, 1981. Although Frank's primary concern is the gothic novel, with Lewis's *The Monk* mentioned prominently, he also gives accounts of several gothic plays, including Lewis's *The Castle Spectre, Adelmorn the Outlaw*, and *The Wood Daemon*.

Irwin, Joseph James. *M. G. "Monk" Lewis*. Boston: Twayne, 1976. Irwin's book is an excellent introduction to both the life and the literary career of Lewis. The chapter dedicated to Lewis's plays includes pertinent biographical facts, comments on the place of each drama in theatrical history, analyses of plots and themes, and accounts of the plays' popular and critical receptions.

Macdonald, David Lorne. *Monk Lewis: A Critical Biography*. Buffalo, N.Y.: University of Toronto Press, 2000. A biography of Lewis, covering his life and works. Bibliography and index.

Reno, Robert Princeton. *The Gothic Visions of Ann Radcliffe and Matthew G. Lewis*. New York: Arno Press, 1980. Although the focus of this study of the gothic works of Lewis and Ann Radcliffe, the book provides valuable information on Lewis's life and dramatic works.

Sandiford, Keith Albert. *The Cultural Politics of Sugar: Caribbean Slavery and Narratives of Colonialism*. New York: Cambridge University Press, 2000. Contains a discussion of Lewis's *Journal of a West India Proprietor, Kept During a Residence in the Island of Jamaica*. Bibliography and index.

Robert H. O'Connor

GEORGE LILLO

Born: London, England; February 4, 1693
Died: London, England; September 3, 1739

PRINCIPAL DRAMA
Silvia: Or, The Country Burial, pr., pb. 1730
The London Merchant: Or, The History of George Barnwell, pr., pb. 1731
The Christian Hero, pr., pb. 1735
Guilt Its Own Punishment: Or, Fatal Curiosity, pr. 1736, pb. 1737 (commonly known as *Fatal Curiosity*)
Marina, pr., pb. 1738
Britannia and Batavia, pb. 1740 (masque)

Elmerick: Or, Justice Triumphant, pr., pb. 1740
Arden of Feversham, pr. 1759, pb. 1762 (with John Hoadly)
The Works of Mr. George Lillo, pb. 1775 (2 volumes; Thomas Davies, editor)

OTHER LITERARY FORMS
George Lillo is known only for his plays.

ACHIEVEMENTS
Of George Lillo's seven plays, only *The London Merchant* was both a popular and critical success when first presented, and only it and *Fatal Curiosity*

continued to be performed long after most plays of their period had been forgotten. These homiletic domestic tragedies, which reflect their author's creed as a Dissenter, had a profound effect on the Continental drama of the late eighteenth century and early nineteenth century.

During a playwriting career that spanned less than a decade, Lillo tried his hand at most popular dramatic forms: ballad opera, heroic drama, masque, prose tragedy, blank-verse tragedy, even adaptations of Elizabethan domestic tragedy (*Arden of Feversham*) and Shakespearean romance (*Marina*, a reworking of the last two acts of William Shakespeare's *Pericles*). Lillo worked within the bounds of tradition but at the same time went beyond past practice. For example, his first play, *Silvia*, is a ballad opera of the sort that had become popular in the wake of John Gay's success with *The Beggar's Opera* in 1728. In it, Lillo follows Gay's pattern of punctuating the action with dozens of familiar tunes, and he includes burlesque and seriocomic elements. The pastoral motif dominates, however, and Lillo's announced intention—"to inculcate the love of truth and virtue and a hatred of vice and falsehood"—foreshadows the strong didacticism and sentimentalism of his two major plays that were to follow.

Lillo was a relatively inexperienced playwright when he offered *The London Merchant* to Theophilus Cibber, manager of a summer company acting at the Drury Lane. Though the famous actor David Garrick credited Lillo with "the invention of a new species of dramatic poetry, which may properly be termed the inferior or lesser tragedy," the drama of hapless George Barnwell is actually in the tradition of such Elizabethan domestic tragedies as the anonymously authored *Arden of Feversham* (1592) and *A Yorkshire Tragedy* (c. 1606). Further, earlier in the eighteenth century there were such middle-class forebears as Lewis Theobald's *The Perfidious Brothers* (pb. 1715) and Aaron Hill's *The Fatal Extravagance* (pb. 1720), the latter based on *A Yorkshire Tragedy*. Thomas Otway during the Restoration and Nicholas Rowe early in the eighteenth century also wrote plays whose sentimentalism and pathos verged on the melodramatic. Despite these predecessors, Lillo's achieve-

ment in *The London Merchant* is notable, for it is a realistic prose drama that consciously celebrates the virtues of middle-class life. It offered theatergoers (in its day, and for more than a century thereafter, as a Christmas and Easter entertainment for London apprentices) not a tale of "prinses distrest and scenes of royal woe," but the story of an honest merchant, his errant apprentice, and a conniving woman, characters with whom middle-class Londoners could identify and whose emotions they could share. Eschewing blank verse, Lillo chose to write in "artless strains," which emphasized both the realism and the bourgeois subject matter of the play and successfully accommodated his work "to the circumstances of the generality of mankind." Young men about town came to the first performance ready to scoff (having purchased from street hawkers copies of the Elizabethan ballad on which the play was based), but they soon "were drawn in to drop their ballads and pull out their handkerchiefs." Alexander Pope was at the first performance and reacted favorably. Queen Caroline asked for a copy of the play, and the royal family went to see it. Both *The Weekly Register* and *The Gentleman's Magazine* defended it enthusiastically against charges that its characters, "so low and familiar in Life," were therefore "too low for the Stage."

Enduringly popular as the play was, it did not start a trend on the London stage. There were some imitations, but only Edward Moore's *The Gamester* (pr. 1753) is noteworthy. On the Continent, however, it was both popular and influential. It was translated into French, German, and Dutch, and it was praised by Denis Diderot and Gotthold Ephraim Lessing, the latter of whom wrote, "I should infinitely prefer to be the creator of *The London Merchant* than the creator of *Der sterbende Cato*." Indeed, Lillo's play is a clear ancestor of Lessing's *Miss Sara Sampson* (pr. 1755), an early *Schicksaltragödie*, or German domestic drama.

Fatal Curiosity, another mercantile domestic drama but in blank verse, has been described by Allardyce Nicoll as the only tragic masterpiece produced between 1700 and 1750 and by William H. McBurney as a landmark play: "at once a climax to Restoration tragedy written according to 'the rules,' and a dramatic protest against the 'frigid caution' of an age in which 'Declamation roar'd whilst Passion slept.'" When first presented in 1736 at Henry Fielding's theater, it ran only seven nights, but when it was revived the following March as a curtain raiser for Fielding's *The Historical Register for the Year 1736*, it lasted for eleven nights. The play was revived again in 1741, 1742, and 1755. George Colman's pre-Romantic version was done in 1782, and Henry MacKenzie's reworking (called *The Shipwreck*) was presented in 1784. *Fatal Curiosity* clearly had continuing appeal to eighteenth century audiences, and its characterizations, moral sentiments, and theatricality withstood changing dramatic fashions. (Mrs. Elizabeth Inchbald, in *The British Theatre*, 1808, described a performance of Colman's version at which "a certain horror seized the audience, and was manifested by a kind of stifled scream.") In addition to its continuing presence on the English stage, the play was widely read, particularly in the aftermath of James Harris's enthusiastic comparison (in *Philological Inquiries*, 1781) of it to Sophocles' *Oidipous Tyrannos* (c. 429 B.C.E.; *Oedipus Tyrannus*, 1715), to William Shakespeare's *Othello* (pr. 1604) and *King Lear* (pr. c. 1605-1606), and to John Milton's *Samson Agonistes* (1671), and his description of it as "the model of a Perfect Fable." As in the case of *The London Merchant*, however, the enduring popularity of the play had very little effect on subsequent English tragedy. In Germany, however, where imitations, adaptations, and translations abounded between 1781 and 1817, it was as influential a forerunner of the *Schicksaltragödie* as was *The London Merchant*.

Though Lillo's other works were failures on the stage, and even though *The London Merchant* and *Fatal Curiosity* sometimes are dismissed as little more than sentimental melodramas, both are of lasting interest not only because they obviously addressed a need felt by audiences in England and on the Continent but also because they significantly influenced the course of German tragic drama.

BIOGRAPHY

George Lillo was born in London near Moorgate on February 4, 1693. His father was Dutch, his mother English. He was reared as a Puritan Dissenter. Lillo learned his father's trade as a jeweler, and the two were partners in London for some years until the son decided to become a playwright. Little else is known about Lillo's life; contemporary accounts by Thomas Davies and Theophilus Cibber are still the primary sources.

Davies says that though Lillo was a Dissenter, he was "not of that sour cast which distinguishes some of our sectaries." He further describes him as being "lusty, but not tall, of a pleasing aspect, though unhappily deprived of the sight of one eye." Of a meeting with Lillo during a rehearsal of *Fatal Curiosity* in 1736, Davies recalls:

> Plain and simple as he was in his address, his manner of conversing was modest, affable and engaging. When invited to give his opinion of how a particular sentiment should be uttered by the actor, he exprest himself in the gentlest and most obliging terms, and conveyed instruction and conviction with good nature and good manners.

Soon after the death of Lillo, Fielding wrote in tribute to him the following words of eulogy:

> He had the gentlest and honestest Manners, and, at the same Time, the most friendly and obliging. He had a perfect Knowledge of Human Nature, though his Contempt for all base Means of Application, which are the necessary Steps to great Acquaintance, restrained his Conversation within very narrow Bounds. He had the Spirit of an old Roman, joined to the Innocence of a primitive Christian.

On the evidence of these statements, one can conclude that Lillo patterned the character Thorowgood in *The London Merchant* after himself.

The prologue to *Elmerick*, his last completed play, suggests that near the close of his life Lillo was "Deprest by want, afflicted by disease . . . ," and the third performance of the play, at Drury Lane on February 26, 1740, was said to be "for the benefit of the author's poor relations. . . ." The evidence of his will, however, indicates otherwise (his primary beneficiary was a nephew, John Underwood, also a jeweler), and Davies reports that Lillo had accumulated a considerable estate from productions of his plays (*The London Merchant* alone was done seventy times between 1731 and his death) and through their publication by his friend John Gray, a London bookseller to whom Lillo sold the rights to all of his works.

Lillo died on September 3, 1739, and was buried three days later in the vault of St. Leonard's Church, in London's Shoreditch.

ANALYSIS

Largely because of *The London Merchant*, George Lillo is a playwright to be reckoned with in any consideration of middle-class or domestic tragedy, not only in England but also on the Continent, where his influence was more generally felt. He demonstrated once and for all that tragedy was not the exclusive province of princes, but that middle-class men and women possessed the necessary stature for tragic action. Although his plays are not of the first rank, they are worthy progenitors of a large body of later drama.

THE LONDON MERCHANT

"The Ballad of George Barnwell" (which was sung to the tune of "The Merchant"), the late Elizabethan song which became the source of Lillo's masterpiece, *The London Merchant*, was said to have been inspired by an actual murder case in Shropshire. The case concerned an apprentice who was seduced by an unscrupulous woman, embezzled funds from his master and gave them to the seductress, and then murdered an uncle in order to rob him. The authors of Elizabethan domestic tragedies often turned to accounts of murder cases for their sources, and Lillo was familiar with these sixteenth and seventeenth century middle-class plays (he wrote his own version of one, *Arden of Feversham*), so it is easy to understand the appeal of such a moralistic ballad to a young playwright who had been a shopkeeper and was a Calvinist Dissenter. It provided him with a substantive basis for a dramatized sermon on loyalty, honor, greed, and sexual morality—all of which he had touched on in his first play, *Silvia*.

Allusions early in *The London Merchant* date the action before the defeat of the Spanish Armada, but there is nothing else to detract from its contemporary realism (its original title included the words "A True History"), and Lillo's addition of the characters of Maria, Trueman, and Millwood's servants to the four in his source increased the possibilities for thematic development as well as dramatic conflict. He also made Millwood, the seductress, into a tragic figure through passages that recall Cleopatra and Lady Macbeth and by focusing on the reasons for her misanthropy.

The play opens with a dialogue between Thorowgood, the merchant, and Trueman, an apprentice, in which the master praises his country, its queen, and his fellow merchants, who "sometimes contribute to the safety of their country as they do at all times to its happiness." Thorowgood warns Trueman that if he "should be tempted to any action that has the appearance of vice or meanness in it," he should reflect "on the dignity of our profession," and then "may with honest scorn reject whatever is unworthy of it." When his only child, Maria, enters, the merchant recalls her many suitors, but she discounts "high birth and titles"; her melancholia, one suspects, is the result of unrequited love (for Barnwell, as it turns out).

The scene shifts to the home of Millwood, a malcontent who labels men "selfish hypocrites," hates other women, and supports herself by taking advantage "only of the young and innocent part of the sex who, having never injured women, apprehend no injury from them." Eighteen-year-old Barnwell, whom she has observed in financial transactions, is her latest intended victim, and Lillo prepares the audience well for his naïveté and easy distraction in the face of her advances. When she asks what he thinks about love, he talks about "the general love we owe to mankind" and his attachment for his uncle, master, and fellow apprentices. First addled and then smitten, Barnwell almost as quickly is miserable, having bought "a moment's pleasure with an age of pain." Conscience-stricken, he returns home, unable to reveal his transgression even to Trueman, his fellow apprentice and closest friend, but he is convinced that Millwood loves him. Thorowgood confronts but quickly pardons Barnwell for his unexplained absence ("That modest blush, the confusion so visible in your face, speak grief and shame") and then warns his charge: "Now, when the sense of pleasure's quick and passion high, the voluptuous appetites, raging and fierce, demand the strongest curb." Barnwell, though, is tempted anew, this time by Millwood's story of poverty. He seals his fate by giving her money taken from Thorowgood, but again is immediately tormented by remorse.

Asides and soliloquies are the means by which Lillo reveals Barnwell's recurring bouts of conscience, and they serve not only to develop his character but also to advance Lillo's didactic purposes, for almost all such speeches are brief exempla, parts of a play that scholar Stephen L. Trainor, Jr., describes as structured "according to the prescribed format for a Dissenting sermon."

Trueman, not present in Lillo's source, is a moral counterpart of the fallen Barnwell. He remains Thorowgood's willing student and loyal apprentice and illustrates the highest ideals of lasting friendship. Shaken as he is by Barnwell's flight and confession of embezzlement in a letter to him, Trueman plans with Maria to make up the losses and thus conceal all from her father. During their plotting, Maria turns to the audience: "In attempting to save from shame one whom we hope may yet return to virtue, to Heaven and you, the judges of this action, I appeal whether I have done anything misbecoming my sex and character." Lillo apparently wanted theatergoers to wrestle with the moral implications of the action not only after a play but also during it. Millwood's servants, like Trueman and Maria creations of Lillo, are the traditional helpmates and coconspirators of their mistress at the start, but they quickly become disillusioned and decide that "'Tis time the world was rid of such a monster" when Millwood convinces Barnwell to kill his uncle, for "there is something so horrid in murder that all other crimes seem nothing when compared to that." They resolve, therefore, to prevent the crime. The four characters Lillo has created thus dedicate themselves to saving a soul and eradicating evil. Representing several walks of life—apprentice, servants, daughter of a well-to-do merchant—they are role models for Lillo's audience, a substantial portion of which had been sent to the theater by masters and elders for edification as well as for entertainment.

The longest speech in the play is Barnwell's third-act soliloquy before the murder. Aware as he is of the "impiety" of his "bloody purpose" and sensing that nature itself trembles because of his "accursed design," he cannot fail to do Millwood's bidding: "She's got such firm possession of my heart and governs there with such despotic sway. . . . In vain does nature, reason, conscience, all oppose it." Hesitant to act, he finally stabs his uncle, who in his dying words asks the "choicest blessings" for his "dearest nephew" and forgiveness for his murderer. Barnwell's self-serving laments over the body have led many to echo Millwood's characterization of him as a "whining, preposterous, canting villain" who fails to evoke sympathy and lacks tragic stature. Lillo, however, was not influenced solely by classical tradition; his Calvinistic background also was probably a determining force in Barnwell's course of action. When he is seized as a result of Millwood's treachery, Barnwell complains: "The hand of Heaven is in it. . . . Yet Heaven, that justly cuts me off, still suffers her to live, perhaps to punish others. Tremendous mercy!" On the other hand, he recognizes the heinous nature of his crime ("This execrable act of mine's without a parallel") and accepts responsibility for what he has done: "I now am—what I've made myself." He also warns youths in the audience to "Avoid lewd women, false as they are fair. . . . By my example, learn to shun my fate." Such statements support Trainor's thesis that "Lillo seeks to bring the theatregoer to a sentient realization of the evil that exists within him for the purposes of confession and correction of that evil" and that this tragic concept evolved "from Puritan homiletic theory, which also seeks to achieve reformation by affective means."

The play as first presented and published has Millwood make her final appearance at the end of the fourth act as she is taken to prison, having been denounced by her servants. She lashes out at "men of all degrees and all professions . . . alike wicked to the utmost of their power," and as for religion, "War, plague, and famine have not destroyed so many of the human race as this pretended piety has done." Warped though her self-justification may be, she sees herself as a victim of society and is utterly unrepentant, as bitterly and uncompromisingly defiant as she was earlier in the play. There is not even a last expression of despair in the manner of Macbeth or Faustus.

Lillo originally had reunited Barnwell and Millwood at the gallows in a closing scene, "but by the advice of some friends it was left out in the representation," and not until the fifth edition (1735) was it included with the rest of the text. In addition to the highly charged drama of a meeting at the scaffold, the scene also softens a bit the sharp edges of Millwood's character because she laments the end of her "flattering hopes," admits to having "sinned beyond the reach of mercy," echoes Barnwell's Calvinism with her statement "And I was doomed before the world began to endless pains . . . ," and tells Barnwell that his prayers for her "are lost in air, or else returned perhaps with double blessing to your bosom, but they help me not." Her plaintive final cry recalls Christopher Marlowe's Faustus: "Encompassed with horror, whither must I go? I would not live—nor die! That I could cease to be—or ne'er had been!" These expressed doubts notwithstanding, Millwood remains unrepentant at the end, and as McBurney notes, "Millwood, rather than Barnwell, enacts the 'tragic' role of the Christian drama by dying in blasphemous despair."

The London Merchant is a play that must be considered from several vantage points. While the primary reason for its contemporary success was its middle-class realism and bourgeois morality, its newness was primarily a matter of degree and style, for Elizabethan domestic tragedies were equally homiletic and journalistically true to life. Lillo's occasional rhetorical excesses, however, tie it to the classical tradition, and his background as a Dissenter also is apparent.

GUILT ITS OWN PUNISHMENT

His only other noteworthy play is *Guilt Its Own Punishment: Or, Fatal Curiosity*, which was first presented in 1736 (when printed by Gray in 1737, its title was given as *Fatal Curiosity: A True Tragedy*). On this occasion as in 1731, Lillo based his domestic tragedy on an Elizabethan crime. Originally reported in a 1618 pamphlet, *News from Perin in Cornwall of a most Bloody and un-exampled Murther very lately*

committed by a Father on his owne Sonne (who was lately returned from the Indyes) at the Instigation of a mercilesse Step-mother . . . , the event was later recounted in Sir William Sanderson's *Compleat History of the Lives and Reigns of Mary Queen of Scotland, and of Her Son and Successor, James the Sixth, King of Scotland . . .* (1656), and this condensation of the pamphlet was included in *The Annals of King James and King Charles the First* (1681), known as *Frankland's Annals*. Lillo probably did not use the pamphlet as his source; he likely was familiar with one or both of the compendiums. In each of them, the wicked stepmother of the original has become the real mother of the victim, and preceding the murder account in each there is a discussion of Sir Walter Raleigh's fall from grace. In *Fatal Curiosity*, the real mother is the murderer, and early in the play, Old Wilmot and Randal, his young servant, discuss Raleigh's arrest.

Fielding's prologue spoken at the first performance was intended to justify this tragedy of "lower life," which also stood apart from most other plays of the period in that it had only three acts. Its pervasive didacticism, with love for country and the honorable nature of commerce again expressed, recalls *The London Merchant*. Loyalty to one's master and selfless love are also portrayed.

The action opens at the Cornwall home of Old Wilmot. Ruined by poverty and saddened by his son's failure to return from a voyage to India, the old man moves to discharge his loyal servant Randal from his "unprofitable service." Randal objects, but to no avail, and Old Wilmot suggests that he renounce "books and the unprofitable search/ Of wisdom there, and study humankind," for doing so will teach him how to "wear the face of probity and honor" as he proceeds to deceive people in order to take advantage of them for his own ends. The old man cynically instructs Randal: "Be a knave and prosper!" His own ruin, he says, has come about through his failure to treat humankind as they deserve. The world, he claims, "is all a scene of deep deceit," and the man "who deals with mankind on the square/ Is his own bubble and undoes himself." The lesson in villainy concluded, Randal bemoans the fall of his "High-minded . . . pitiful and generous" master, who once had honor as his idol. At the same time, though, Randal refers to Wilmot as improvident and pleasure-loving, the first of several such inconsistent and conflicting views of the protagonist of the play, whose tragic flaw is his misguided and untempered reason.

The scene shifts to the home of Charlot, who is engaged to the missing Young Wilmot. Charlot rejects overtures by other men and supports his parents, whom Maria, Charlot's maid, describes as gloomy, proud, and impatient. When Agnes, the mother, enters, Maria says that the old lady's "pride seems to increase with her misfortunes" and also refers to "her haughty, swelling heart." Thus, one is prepared for the emergence of Agnes as a villain who is destroyed by hubris and greed. Further, in conversation with Charlot, Agnes is scornful of "the common herd," to whose level she has been reduced by poverty. She is equally disdainful of her "wretched husband," whose "fixed love for me" is all that "withholds his hand" from "foul self-murder," a blasphemous desire that reveals the old man's loss of faith. Charlot attempts to counter Agnes's miseries by telling of a possibly prescient dream she had the night before in which Patience and Contemplation were joined by Young Wilmot and his parents. In the first two scenes, then, Lillo sets the stage for the return of the long-lost son and sows the seeds of the catastrophes to come.

Young Wilmot's appearance in the next scene is punctuated by a patriotic paean to England and a tedious speech of devotion to Charlot, to whose home he then repairs. Their reunion is marked by rhetorical bombast that the blank verse fails to ameliorate. Charlot, though a sentimental heroine in the tradition of Otway's Belvidera, is the most fully realized and believable person in *Fatal Curiosity*.

Soon after his reunion with Charlot, Young Wilmot has a chance meeting with Randal, and they scheme to hide the son's identity from his parents (his features having sufficiently changed during his long absence so they would not recognize him) to enable him to satisfy his curiosity by first meeting with them as a stranger. Lillo thus portrays him not only as a virtuous, loving, brave, and successful merchant but also as a self-indulgent adventurer who is very much his parents' son and is as much his own victim as he is Agnes's. He arrives at their home just as Agnes is leaving to sell a volume of Seneca to get money for bread. He gives them a letter of introduction ostensibly from Charlot, and they welcome him, talking of their lost son and listening to an account of his adventures. Fearful that his emotions will betray him into revealing his identity before Charlot arrives, he feigns a need for sleep and retires, giving into Agnes's care a casket with "contents of value." Alone, she is overtaken by curiosity and opens the box, which is filled with jewels, treasures that would end their "Base poverty and all its abject train. . . ." Old Wilmot enters; she shows him the jewels; and he senses her purpose: "Th' inhospitable murder of our guest!" What ensues is the most exciting dialogue in the play, as wife urges husband on, first gaining his tacit assent and eventually convincing him to commit the act. Her determination, persistence, and success are reminiscent of Lady Macbeth, while his reluctance and malleability recall Macbeth himself. No sooner is the deed committed than Agnes reacts in a manner that also recalls Shakespeare's play: "Inconstant, wretched woman!/ What, doth my heart recoil and bleed with him/ Whose murder you contrived?"

When Charlot and Randal arrive in the wake of the stabbing, the parents learn the full horror of their act, and Old Wilmot resolves that "Our guilt and desolation must be told/ From age to age to teach desponding mortals/ How far beyond the reach of human thought/ Heaven, when incensed, can punish." He then stabs Agnes, who asks forgiveness from her son and vows: "Had I ten thousand lives/ I'd give them all to speak my penitence,/ Deep, and sincere, and equal to my crime." Old Wilmot stabs himself, and before he dies proclaims that he and Agnes brought their ruin on themselves with their pride and impatience. "Mankind may learn . . . ," he says as he dies.

However serious the weaknesses of the first two acts may be, the tragic intensity of the third is overwhelming. Although the action of the entire play spans a period no greater than the time of presentation, there is a startling rapidity to the final progression toward the terrible catastrophes. This classical compression of time is as important to the effect as is Lillo's decision to have the murder done offstage, with Young Wilmot's muted "Oh, Father! Father!" and Agnes's reports and urgings providing all the immediacy that is needed. To avoid diluting the emotional impact, Lillo wisely brings the play to a rapid close after the father dies, while Randal delivers a choruslike coda: "Let us at least be wiser, nor complain/ Of Heaven's mysterious ways and awful reign."

BIBLIOGRAPHY

Burke, Helen. "*The London Merchant* and Eighteenth Century British Law." *Philological Quarterly* 73, no. 3 (Summer, 1994): 347. Burke presents an argument surrounding the final gallows scene of *The London Merchant* and relates the play to contemporary life.

Canfield, J. Douglas. *Heroes and States: On the Ideology of Restoration Tragedy.* Lexington: University Press of Kentucky, 2000. Canfield examines many Restoration tragedies, including Lillo's *The London Merchant.*

Faller, Lincoln B. *The Popularity of Addison's "Cato" and Lillo's "The London Merchant," 1700-1776.* New York: Garland, 1988. Faller attempts to explain why *The London Merchant*, which seems awkward and didactic to modern readers, achieved such success in the eighteenth century. He finds that the balance of sentimentalism, realism, and tragedy that went into establishing this domestic drama appealed to its contemporary audience.

Fields, Polly Stevens. "George Lillo and the Victims of Economics Theory." *Studies in the Literary Imagination* 32, no. 2 (Fall, 1999): 77-88. Fields theorizes that Lillo meant *The London Merchant* to be an argument against the dominant economic trend represented by John Law as well as a presentation of mercantile theory.

Haggerty, George. *Men in Love: Masculinity and Sexuality in the Eighteenth Century.* New York: Columbia University Press, 1999. Haggerty uses Lillo's *The London Merchant* to discuss the eroticized bonds of male friendship.

Gerald H. Strauss,
updated by Gerald S. Argetsinger

ROMULUS LINNEY

Born: Philadelphia, Pennsylvania; September 21, 1930

PRINCIPAL DRAMA

The Sorrows of Frederick, pb. 1966, pr. 1967

Goodbye Howard, pr. 1970, pb. 1984

The Love Suicide at Schofield Barracks, pr. 1972, pb. 1973

Democracy and Esther, pb. 1973 (adaptation of Henry Adams's novels *Democracy* and *Esther*; revised as *Democracy*, pr. 1974)

Holy Ghosts, pr. 1974, pb. 1977

The Seasons, Man's Estate, pr. 1974

Appalachia Sounding, pr. 1975

Old Man Joseph and His Family: A Play in Two Acts, pr. 1977, pb. 1978

Childe Byron, pr. 1977, pb. 1981

Just Folks, pr. 1978

The Death of King Philip, pr. 1979, pb. 1984

Tennessee, pr. 1979, pb. 1980

The Captivity of Pixie Shedman, pb. 1980, pr. 1981

El Hermano, pr., pb. 1981

April Snow, pr. 1983, pb. 1989

Laughing Stock, pr., pb. 1984 (includes *Tennessee*, *Goodbye Howard*, and *F.M.*)

The Soul of a Tree, pr. 1984

Why the Lord Come to Sand Mountain, pr., pb. 1984

Wrath, pr. 1985 (part of *The Show of the Seven Deadly Sins*)

Sand Mountain, pr., pb. 1985 (includes *Why the Lord Come to Sand Mountain* and *Sand Mountain Matchmaking*)

A Woman Without a Name, pr. 1985, pb. 1986

Pops, pr. 1986, pb. 1987 (six short plays; includes *Can Can*, *Clair de Lune*, *Ave Maria*, *Gold and Silver Waltz*, *Yankee Doodle*, and *Songs of Love*)

Heathen Valley, pr. 1987, pb. 1988 (adaptation of his novel)

Juliet, pr. 1988, pb. 1989

Pageant, pr. 1988 (with others; music and lyrics by Michael Rice)

Precious Memories, pr. 1988, pr. 1989, pb. 1991 (as *Unchanging Love*; adaptation of an Anton Chekhov story)

Three Poets, pr. 1989, pb. 1990 (3 one-act plays; includes *Komachi*, *Hrosvitha*, and *Akhmatova*)

Two, pr. 1990, pb. 1993

Can Can, pr., pb. 1991

Ambrosio, pr. 1992, pb. 1993

Romulus Linney: Seventeen Short Plays, pb. 1992

Spain, pr. 1993, pb. 1994

Six Plays, pb. 1993 (includes *F.M.*, *Childe Byron*, *Tennessee*, *Two*, *April Snow*, and *Heathen Valley*)

Shotgun, pr. 1994

Oscar over Here, pr. 1995, pb. 2000

A Christmas Carol, pr. 1995, pb. 1996 (adaptation of Charles Dickens's novel)

True Crimes, pr., pb. 1996

Mountain Memory: A Play About Appalachian Life, pb. 1997

Gint: A Play in Two Act from Henrik Ibsen's "Peer Gynt," pr. 1998, pb. 1999

Goodbye Oscar, pr., pb. 1999

A Lesson Before Dying, pr. 2000, pb. 2001 (adaptation of Ernest J. Gaines's novel)

Nine Adaptations for the American Stage, pb. 2000 (includes *Gint*, *Oscar over Here*, *True Crimes*, *Unchanging Love*, *A Woman Without a Name*, *The Unwritten Song*, *Lark*, *A Lesson Before Dying*, and *Strindberg*)

OTHER LITERARY FORMS

Romulus Linney is the author of novels—*Heathen Valley* (1962), *Slowly, by Thy Hand Unfurled* (1965), and *Jesus Tales* (1980)—as well as innumerable articles, reviews, poems, and short fiction, published in *The New York Times Sunday Book Review*, *New York Quarterly*, and elsewhere.

ACHIEVEMENTS

Romulus Linney's dramatic achievements are in two areas: historical biography and Appalachian mountain tales. He is ranked high among the few American playwrights writing historical drama for the contemporary theater. Without sacrificing theatricality, Linney brings to the stage the soaring language and large ideas that have been attributed to other great dramatic eras. In addition, through his folk plays dealing with Appalachian areas, he has become a voice for the rural lifestyles in danger of extinction in the United States. Like John Millington Synge in Ireland and Federico García Lorca in Spain, Linney captures the unique features of the speech of the rural areas of the Carolinas, Virginias, and Tennessee.

The much-produced Linney has been the recipient of virtually every major playwriting award and fellowship in the United States, including those of the National Endowment for the Arts (1974), the Guggenheim Foundation (1980), an Obie Award (1980), and a 1992 Obie Award for Sustained Excellence in Playwriting. In 1984, he was honored with an Award in Literature from the American Academy and Institute of Arts and Letters. He also holds two National Critics Awards (1988 and 1990). While his plays have been performed all over the United States and Europe, he has had a special relationship with the Whole Theatre in New Jersey and the Philadelphia Festival Theatre.

BIOGRAPHY

Romulus Linney was born in Philadelphia and reared in Madison, Tennessee. His father, a doctor and an avid outdoorsman, greatly influenced Linney's life but died when Linney was thirteen. He and his mother moved to Washington, where she taught public speaking. After he was graduated from Oberlin College in 1953, Linney attended the Yale School of Drama, where he received an M.F.A. degree in directing in 1958. He began his writing career as a novelist, writing *Heathen Valley* in 1962 and *Slowly, by Thy Hand Unfurled* in 1965. After some struggling, he wrote his first play, *The Sorrows of Frederick*, and found his true voice. After that time, Linney wrote many plays. He was a member of New Dramatists for seven years, and he continued to write, lecture, and conduct workshops at several colleges in the New York area, where he settled.

Linney's first attempt at Broadway, *The Love Suicide at Schofield Barracks*, while beautifully acted and staged, did not receive the necessary rave reviews to keep it running. Clive Barnes, in particular, complained of the script's improbability: "The play could not . . . ever make a particularly convincing or satisfying evening in the theater." Its subject matter, the double suicide of a general and his wife, was not palpable to the typical Broadway audience.

Romulus Linney (© Miriam Berkley)

An imaginative writer, Linney writes from two usually distinct points of view: the Tennessee-born background of such plays as *Sand Mountain* and *A Woman Without a Name*, and the cultured, historical perspective found in such works as *Childe Byron* and *Pops*, the latter being a series of short plays based on musical themes and reaching back in history to Hrosvitha, the tenth century German nun. *Sand Mountain*, actually two plays about the rural mountain life of Linney's youth, contains a Christmas celebration, *Why the Lord Come to Sand Mountain*, in which Jesus returns to earth to hear a mountain storyteller recount the story of the Nativity.

Linney has succeeded tremendously well in the regional theaters, where his plays are well received by non-New York audiences. In New York, his plays get fine reviews when produced on the League of Resident Theatres (LORT) stages, in workshop and showcase productions, and Off-Broadway. Returning to Oberlin College as a guest speaker in 1990, Linney read from several of his works. *A Woman Without a Name*, a diary play in which the main character's control of the English language improves as the play moves forward, was successful after various workshop productions. Linney has felt a continuing connection to the southeast. In 1996, Linney was in residence at Wake Forest University and earlier had taught or conducted workshops at other southern universities. His play *Three Poets*, three one-act plays centered on three female poets (Hrosvitha, Ono no Komachi, and Anna Akhmatova), was extremely successful in New York. In Louisville, at the Actors Theatre of Louisville, his play *Two*, about the second-in-command under Adolf Hitler, was well received in 1990; his six short plays gathered under the title *Pops*, and each having a musical theme, continued to be performed all over the United States in various venues.

Linney has served as professor of arts at Columbia University and adjunct professor of playwriting at the Actors Studio M.F.A. Program at the New School for Social Research.

From 1997 to 2000 he served on the Tony Award nominating committee. His memberships include the Council of the Dramatists Guild, the Ensemble Studio Theatre, The Fellowship of Southern Writers, the Corporation of Yaddo, and the Advisory Board of the Institute of Outdoor Drama.

ANALYSIS

Music, virtually always present in his work, is Romulus Linney's universal metaphor for the harmonies and cadences of human interaction. Linney has stated that, because his plays are often episodic, they fall into a natural structural rhythm, like music. His words are musical as well; Linney's works reveal his fine ear for dialogue, especially for the regionalisms embedded in folktales, old saws, and sayings, and figurative language born of the mountain life. An authenticity of expression, along with a sensitivity to linguistic rhythms, characterizes Linney's dialogue. From a position of healthy skepticism rather than cynicism, Linney sees a world of humor and warmth, in which the search for relationships based on mutual respect is never ending.

Despite his rural childhood, Linney is a sophisticated and very well-read author, drawing on his education and scholarly research as much as on his personal experiences to bring a surprisingly simple but authentic worldview to his work. Fascinated by the storytelling traditions of Appalachia, Linney finds a gold mine of material in the folktales of that region. Yet what separates his work from the anthropologist's is his ability to exploit the inherent dramatic qualities of the storytellers themselves.

APPALACHIAN PLAYS

In Linney's mountain plays, he makes use of the natural storytelling power of the stage to spin fascinating yarns about simple folk whose intuitive understanding of human relationships is expressed in superstitious old wives' tales. The action is often the dramatization of a story to witnesses—a play-within-a-play device that works well because the characters are natural storytellers. Linney's own storytelling powers are enhanced by this format because the characters, by their attitudes toward the value of tall tales, reinforce for the audience the magical qualities of theatrical reenactment. Yet Linney's work never descends to simple recitation; the personality of the storyteller, the reactions of the character-listener, and

the presence of "something at stake" for both always keep the dramatic tension intact.

SAND MOUNTAIN

The best illustration of the texture of Linney's mountain plays is the one-act play *Why the Lord Come to Sand Mountain*, which, together with *Sand Mountain Matchmaking*, constitutes the evening of drama *Sand Mountain*. An old mountain woman named Sang Picker (she gathers ginseng root for a living) asks the audience if they know any good "Smoky Mountain head benders," and proceeds to tell one of her own, a story that comes alive before her as the Lord and Peter enter, looking for Sand Mountain. When they find Jack, Jean, and Fourteen Children (played by one actor), the Lord and Peter are treated to another story: a reenactment of the conception, birth, and childhood of Jesus, reared by Joseph (acted by Jack) and Mary (acted by Jean), embellished with apocryphal details. "He'd come to Sand Mountain," Sang Picker tells the audience, "to hear tell about his Daddy, and Mary and hisself as a child, and he had." Jean supplies the moral (a favorite of Linney): "Hit ain't the ending whut's important. Hit's the beginning."

Sand Mountain Matchmaking pursues the dramatic potential of the courtship ritual. The widow Rebecca listens patiently to three suitors (in the traditional folktale format), then follows the bizarre but effective advice ("Cure a cold sore—kiss a dog") of an old mountain woman. The final match is an equal partnership based on mutual honesty.

HOLY GHOSTS

One early success, which has been re-created in many regional theaters, is *Holy Ghosts*, about a primitive Fundamentalist sect that uses snakes in its worship services. A convert to this religion, Nancy Shedman, leaves her husband, Colman, to marry the old father of the religion, Obediah Buckhorn; Colman follows her to the church and debunks her quasi-religious conversion. At the play's climax, however, Nancy chooses neither her husband nor her "savior"; she exercises a newfound independence from both and leaves for business school. Thematically, Linney deals with the shortcomings of unquestioning obedience (implied in Obediah's name), but Nancy's decision is a typical Linney signature: women turning their backs on men, the weaker sex.

IN A WOMAN WITHOUT A NAME

In *A Woman Without a Name* (based on Linney's novel *Slowly, by Thy Hand Unfurled*), serious in theme and tone, the nameless central figure keeps a journal, clumsily at first, but more and more articulately as the years pass. In the journal, she collects her feelings about the loss of her children one by one, the guilt she feels because she believes that she has somehow caused their deaths, and the indifference of the men in her life to her longing to express herself and to live a full life. The outcome of the play, partially drawing on historical fact, finds her the leader of a temperance society: "Anneal, Journal, Standard Dictionary: to put to the fire, then to freezing cold. To temper. To toughen. To make enduring. That is the word I understand now." The play bears a resemblance to *The Captivity of Pixie Shedman*, in which a young man reads the diary of his grandmother and learns of her exploitation by the men in her life, who treated her like property.

Two full-length dramas of the 1990's set in Appalachia reflect a dark mood. *Unchanging Love*, based on an Anton Chekhov story, sharply unveils the dishonest mendacity and lack of social compassion within a merchant family. *True Crimes*, adapted from Leo Tolstoy's *Vlast tmy* (pb. 1887; *The Power of Darkness*, 1888) exposes the degradation of a shiftless young backwoods lout whose lust and greed drives him to adultery, murder, and the rejection of confession of guilt so that a profitable marriage will not be impeded. Supportive of the play with reservations, critics praised Linney for not caricaturing or sentimentalizing his Appalachian figures.

HISTORICAL PLAYS

Linney's erudition and penchant for scholarly research are most clearly seen in his historical dramas, which in his hands become dramatic expressions of the chasm between the conceived ideal and the practical application of that ideal in an imperfect world. *Democracy and Esther*, later titled simply *Democracy*, is a dramatic combination of two Henry Adams novels. As in *Holy Ghosts*, the women in the play prove to be the strongest characters, declining offers of marriage from seemingly eligible men whose strength of character does not fulfill the women's expectations. Another historical drama, *Childe Byron*, deals with an imaginary meeting of Lord Byron and his estranged daughter, Ada, who challenges her father to justify his wretched life, in a mock trial at the moment of her death.

THE SORROWS OF FREDERICK

Frederick II, in *The Sorrows of Frederick*, abandons an important battle to attend the funeral of his dog; his greatest military triumphs are always marred by a personal loss. In Linney's portrait, Frederick is forceful, clearheaded, and single-minded in public affairs but almost pathetically inept in dealing with his personal life. His friendship with Voltaire, his unconsummated marriage to Elizabeth Christine, and especially his love for Fredersdorf, a childhood comrade, are all clumsily handled, while his military victories often come fortuitously, without effort. Linney dramatizes the complex career of Frederick through a series of time changes, moving backward and forward from pivotal public events to the significant personal events that exacerbate or ameliorate them.

THE LOVE SUICIDE AT SCHOFIELD BARRACKS

One of the most complex storytelling devices Linney has ever employed is used in the essentially antiwar play *The Love Suicide at Schofield Barracks*. Here, by the specific instructions of the General of Schofield Barracks, his own public suicide, along with his wife's, is reenacted by the officers and witnesses to the tragedy on the morning after the deaths. By means of disparate testimonies, which give a multiple perspective of the General's personality, the complex motives of his act are examined.

LAUGHING STOCK

Linney is perhaps most comfortable in the short-play format, where his storytelling abilities transform human relationships into entertaining yarns with warm-hearted morals. *Laughing Stock* consists of three fairly short pieces, at the same time comic and touching. *Tennessee* tells the story of a woman whose husband promised to take her to Tennessee, only to drive in circles until she was only seven miles from her childhood home. *Goodbye Howard*, despite its hospital setting, is a comedy in which three elderly sisters prematurely announce the death of their brother, only to discover that they have simply got off the elevator on the wrong floor. In *F.M.*, which takes place in a college writing class, a Faulkner-like novelist pours out his heart in the classroom, incidentally reminding the teacher of her own sidetracked talent and writing career.

POPS

The most ambitious collection of short plays, however, is *Pops*, a series of six short plays on the theme of love, designed to be performed by the ideal company of actors: juvenile, ingenue, leading man, leading lady, character man, and character woman. Sometimes working with historical material (as in "Ave Maria") and sometimes with the present (as in the delightful "Tonight We Love"), Linney finds the universal question in all love stories: whether two people fall in love through fate or through their own efforts.

SPAIN

Spain, another collection of three short plays (*Torquemada*, *Anna Rey*, *Escobedo de la Aixa*), forcefully compels a critical look at religiosity and crises of conscience in the fifteenth and twentieth centuries. The playlets are linked by the fifteenth century Abbot Escobedo, who humanely treats the insane and is persecuted by the Spanish Inquisition. His life furnishes an inspiring example that restores a despondent twentieth century psychiatrist to normalcy.

OTHER MAJOR WORKS

LONG FICTION: *Heathen Valley*, 1962; *Slowly, by Thy Hand Unfurled*, 1965; *Jesus Tales*, 1980.
TELEPLAY: *The Thirty-fourth Star*, 1976.

BIBLIOGRAPHY

DiGaetani, John L. *A Search for a Postmodern Theater: Interviews with Contemporary Playwrights*. New York: Greenwood Press, 1991. This interview with Linney (with photograph) concentrates on his influences (Pär Lagerkvist, the Swedish playwright and novelist among them) and on the relationship between language and writing for the theater. Includes good discussions of several works, including *Childe Byron*.

Disch, Thomas M. "Holy Ghosts." *The Nation* 245 (September 19, 1987): 282-283. Disch is much impressed with virtually all Linney's New York work; here, he claims that *Holy Ghosts* should be a standard like the works of Tennessee Williams or Henrik Ibsen. The essay provides an overview of Linney's work and addresses his Broadway problems and Clive Barnes's unfavorable review of *The Love Suicide at Schofield Barracks*.

_____. "Theater." *The Nation* 252 (March 18, 1991): 355-356. When Linney's play *Unchanging Love* moved from its premiere performance in Milwaukee in 1989, at the Milwaukee Repertory Theater, to its New York premiere at the Triangle Theatre Company, with the same director (John Dillon), Disch once again took the opportunity to speak highly of Linney's whole canon.

Rich, Frank. "Theater: *Holy Ghosts* Salvation for the Lonely." Review of *Holy Ghosts*, by Romulus Linney. *The New York Times*, August 12, 1987, p. C17. The Off-Broadway Theater 890 staged this production of *Holy Ghosts*, after two Off-Off-Broadway productions in the 1970's. In this visiting production of the San Diego Repertory Theatre, Rich finds that Linney "unfurls an arresting sensibility closer to that of Eudora Welty than Sinclair Lewis." He notes the script's shortcomings and the director's (Douglas Jacobs) failure to surmount them but says that "we find ourselves unexpectedly moved by the grace of lost souls who risk everything."

Tedford, Harold. "Romulus Linney on 'Sublime Gossip'" *Southern Theatre* 38 (Spring, 1997): 26-32. In his interview with Tedford at Wake Forest University, Linney discusses his background and motivations for the three types of plays he writes: historical, dramas about Appalachia, and a "grab-bag of personal plays" inspired by friends in the arts and Army experiences. He admits an interest in university theater training, and states his view that literature is more or less sublime gossip but has to be good gossip at its best. Includes a tersely detailed biographical profile and photograph.

Thomas J. Taylor,
updated by Christian H. Moe

HENRY LIVINGS

Born: Prestwich, England; September 20, 1929
Died: Delph?, England; February 20, 1998

PRINCIPAL DRAMA

Stop It, Whoever You Are, pr. 1961, pb. 1962
Big Soft Nellie, pr. 1961, pb. 1964
Nil Carborundum, pr. 1962, pb. 1963
Kelly's Eye, pr. 1963, pb. 1964
The Day Dumbfounded Got His Pylon, pr. 1963
    (radio play), pr. 1965 (staged), pb. 1967
Kelly's Eye and Other Plays, pb. 1964 (includes
    Big Soft Nellie)
Eh?, pr. 1964, pb. 1965
The Little Mrs. Foster Show, pr. 1966, pb. 1969
Good Grief!, pr. 1967, pb. 1968 (one acts and
    sketches: *After the Last Lamp, You're Free,
    Variable Lengths, Pie-eating Contest, Does It
    Make Your Cheeks Ache?, The Reasons for
    Flying*)
Honour and Offer, pr. 1968, pb. 1969
The Gamecock, pr. 1969, pb. 1971
Rattel, pr. 1969, pb. 1971
*Variable Lengths and Longer: An Hour of
    Embarrassment*, pr. 1969 (includes *The Reasons
    for Flying, Does It Make Your Cheeks Ache?*)
The Boggart, pr. 1970, pb. 1971
Conciliation, pr. 1970, pb. 1971
The Rifle Volunteer, pr. 1970, pb. 1971
Beewine, pr. 1970, pb. 1971
The ffinest ffamily in the Land, pr. 1970, pb. 1973
You're Free, pr. 1970, pb. 1968
Mushrooms and Toadstools, pr. 1970, pb. 1974
Tiddles, pr. 1970, pb. 1974
Pongo Plays 1-6, pb. 1971 (includes *The
    Gamecock, Rattel, The Boggart, Beewine, The
    Rifle Volunteer, Conciliation*)
This Jockey Drives Late Nights, pr. 1972, pb. 1972,
    1976 (adaptation of Leo Tolstoy's play *The
    Power of Darkness*)
Draft Sam, pr. 1972 (televised), pb. 1974, pr. 1976
    (staged)
The Rent Man, pr. 1972, pb. 1974

Cinderella: A Likely Tale, pr. 1972, pb. 1976
    (adaptation of Charles Perrault's story)
The Tailor's Britches, pr. 1973, pb. 1974
Glorious Miles, pr. 1973 (televised), pr. 1975
    (staged)
Jonah, pr. 1974, pb. 1975
Six More Pongo Plays Including Two for Children,
    pb. 1974 (includes *Tiddles, The Rent Man, The
    Ink-Smeared Lady, The Tailor's Britches, Daft
    Sam, Mushrooms and Toadstools*)
Jack and the Beanstalk, pr. 1974 (music by Alan
    Glasgow)
Jug, pr. 1975 (adaptation of Heinrich von Kleist's
    play *The Broken Jug*)
The Astounding Adventures of Tom Thumb, pr.
    1979 (children's play)
Don't Touch Him, He Might Resent It, pr. 1984
    (adaptation of a play by Nikolai Gogol)
*This Is My Dream: The Life and Times of
    Josephine Baker*, pr. 1987
Plays: One, pb. 1999

OTHER LITERARY FORMS

In addition to his plays for the stage, Henry Livings is known for his 1968 screenplay adaptation of *Eh?*, entitled *Work Is a Four-Letter Word*, and for his work as a television writer. He also was a prolific writer of television and radio drama, and in the 1980's he published two short-story collections, *Penine Tales* (1983) and *Flying Eggs and Things: More Penine Tales* (1986).

ACHIEVEMENTS

Usually clustered uncomfortably with the post-John Osborne playwrights of Great Britain, Henry Livings was perhaps more popular in the regional theaters than in London itself. An actor influenced by Joan Littlewood and her presentational approach to theater, Livings first confounded London audiences with *Stop It, Whoever You Are*, especially the industrial lavatory scene, the beginning of Livings's career-long interest in the workingman *in situ*. Along with successes at the Royal Court Theatre, London, Livings's plays were successful in Stratford, Manchester, Oxford, Lincoln, Birmingham, and Stoke-on-Trent. This appeal to the less sophisticated audience is what separated Livings from both critical approval and big-name notoriety in London theatrical circles. As for American productions, only the Cincinnati Playhouse in the Park showed continuing interest in Livings's work, having produced *Honour and Offer* as well as *Eh?*, his best-known play in the United States, which won a 1966 Obie Award for its production at New York's Circle in the Square Theatre. The value of Livings's contribution lies in his concentration on the fairly short entertainment segment, appealing directly to the working-class audience of every age, without concessions to more traditional dramatic considerations such as structure and psychological character studies. Combining the vaudevillian *lazzi* (the stock-in-trade of the British comic actor) with an uncanny insight into the real problems and delights of the British working class, Livings managed to make an evening at the theater the robust, titillating, hugely entertaining experience it was meant to be. His work added humor and linguistic virtuosity to the otherwise sober, even whining, "kitchen sink" school of British drama.

BIOGRAPHY

Born in Prestwich, Lancashire, on September 20, 1929, Henry Livings was not, as might be suspected from his work, reared in a working-class family, but in a white-collar family. Perhaps from visits to his father's place of work (George Livings was a shop manager), he began to look carefully at the lives of people at work. Livings's grammar-school years at Park View Primary School (1935-1939) and Stand Grammar School (1940-1945) put him in contact with the lives of his sturdy public-school classmates from Lancashire during the war years. After a brief enrollment (on scholarship) at Liverpool University (1945-1947), where he concentrated on Hispanic studies, Livings served as a cook in the Royal Air Force until 1950, when a series of jobs finally brought him to an acting career with the Century Mobile Theatre, in Leicestershire. Livings's association

with Joan Littlewood's company at the Theatre Royal, Stratford East, London, began with a role in Brendan Behan's *The Quare Fellow* (pr. 1954). It was Littlewood who encouraged Livings to continue writing, and, having married Fanny Carter, an actress with the company, in 1957, he wrote his first successful play, *Stop It, Whoever You Are*, produced at the Arts Theatre in London in 1961. Despite the furor it raised, and encouraged by the *Evening Standard* Award in 1961, Livings wrote busily during the next five years, a period that produced *Eh?*, *The Little Mrs. Foster Show*, *Kelly's Eye*, and several other plays. His audience, he found, was not in London but in the shires, where a more solidly working-class audience understood the world Livings was creating on stage, the language with which the characters communicated and failed to communicate, and the special defeats and triumphs of their social class. The anti-intellectual bias of Livings's vision naturally led him to radio and television; he was associated with the British Broadcasting Corporation's program *Northern Drift* and wrote several short radio works collected and published under the title *Worth a Hearing: A Collection of Radio Plays* (1967).

After 1970, Livings worked in shorter forms, writing short sketches centering largely on a picaresque but British working-class Scapin named Pongo. The Pongo plays have been collected in two volumes (1971 and 1974); the latter contains two plays for children, an important part of Livings's work, Livings finds his voice in the gathering places of the common worker, the lodge halls and Rotary clubs that recognize the veracity of his imagination and comprehend the language and life of his characters. Livings continued to write for the working class and children, with *Flying Eggs and Things* (1986) and the more serious *This Is My Dream: The Life and Times of Josephine Baker* (1987).

ANALYSIS

Quite a few of Henry Livings's plays begin with the entrance of a man at work or just from it, who addresses the audience directly, setting up the first confrontation, either with his environment or with the scabrous social system that put him somehow beneath the station he deserves, if wit and perception were the criteria. Henry Cash, beekeeper and bookkeeper in *Honour and Offer*, is typical:

> HENRY (*sombre and intense, to us*): This is where I contemplate. Later in the day, the bees murmur, and I'm able to contemplate even better.

This kind of opening, which violates traditional rules against addressing the audience directly, typifies the nature of Livings's relationship with the theater: It is a place where he goes to present himself in various disguises, to discuss in theatrical and humorous ways the dilemma of being in this world and happy at the same time. The signature of Livings's characters is whatever is opposite passivity, helplessness, anguish, and defeat. What separates the workingman from his pitiable superiors is that he works, while they merely swot at the free enterprise system as it is oddly practiced in England. Stanley, the lisping hero in *Big Soft Nellie*, defends his entire existence with the simple statement, "I am a man and I do a job."

The corollary to the dignity of work is the sanctity of the workplace. In Livings's world, a man's shop is his castle, and no interfering foreman or supervisor is going to taint it. Livings's best-known play, *Eh?*, takes place in the boiler-room of a mammoth dye factory, where someone upstairs shovels coal into the boiler while the hero, Valentine Brose, watches the gauges, at least in theory. Instead, Val commands his fortress like a baron, growing hallucinogenic mushrooms in the moist heat; bedding his new bride in the double bunk; confounding the works manager, the personnel officer, and the local environmentalist with startling vigor. Winning them over with his mushrooms does not save his castle, however, which is destroyed from within by a vigor of its own. "Once upon a time. There was a boiler. Once upon a time," recites Val as the boiler explodes, making the connection between children's tales and working-class life that Livings has claimed as his own invention.

For exploding or confounding, the best tool available to Livings's characters is the language. Just as Federico García Lorca captures the naturally poetic diction of the Spanish peasant and John Millington Synge re-creates the rhythms and cadences inherent in the Western Irish tongue, Livings reproduces the amazing language patterns of the working-class families of Liverpool, Yorkshire, Manchester, and Birmingham. It is a difficult tangle of near-communication, lost threads, subjective references, internal arguments going on underneath the normative conversation, subtexts overpowering the superficially civil correspondences, vague antecedents, and private vocabularies hinting at metaphoric connections long lost to logic. Miraculously, they understand each other—in fact, they are bonded by the commonality of their language, so that an argument shouted in the presence of strangers has all the secrecy of a family code. The reader may wish for more signposts through the labyrinth of utterances that seem to be attacks and ripostes but whose meaning is just out of reach; the signposts are there, but they are obscured by the lush undergrowth of Livings's imagination. If his characters are rather more loquacious than those of Harold Pinter, David Mamet, or Samuel Beckett, they share the same uneasy distrust of oversimplified exposition.

The comparison with Beckett does not end with the language. Livings finds great resources in the vaudeville skits and sight gags that find their way into Beckett's *En attendant Godot* (pb. 1952, pr. 1953; *Waiting for Godot*, 1954). In the opening scene of Livings's *The ffinest ffamily in the Land*, Mr. Harris spends a good five minutes at the elevator looking for his key in every possible nook and cranny of his outfit, while his wife and son look on. When Mrs. Harris takes a try, her hand goes through a hole in Mr. Harris's pocket and her wedding ring gets caught in the hair on his leg. Trapped in this ridiculous position, the Harrises take several elevator rides trying to avoid being seen by their lodger and her male companion. The short sketches collected as the Pongo plays (1971 and 1974) are essentially music-hall skits, featuring such visual tricks as walking in place, miming puddles and other impediments, exaggerated playing at saber and pistols, and mugging reactions. The broad appeal of this kind of humor calls on the talents of the actor, who must do considerably more than memorize his lines in order to bring the theatrical moment to life. Songs often introduce the plays, sung by a "Musician" visible onstage who often takes a small part in the stage business as well, as though the fictive stage intrudes on the real world at every turn. When, in *The Boggart*, the monster succeeds in scaring Pongo into wrestling with his daughter, the Musician joins in the fun with a song sung in harmony with the Boggart. In *Beewine*, however, an angry master, foiled in his pursuit of Pongo, takes out his wrath on the Musician, who must flee for his life as the skit ends.

While critics generally acknowledge Livings's debt to vaudeville and other popular forms, they find fault with his dramatic structure. Plots moving in one direction suddenly shift; pieces of business elaborately constructed are abandoned; characters introduced are left behind. Livings explains that he writes in short bursts, keyed to the attention span he perceives in the theater, and otherwise gives little attention to structure.

Taken together, Livings's plays constitute something more than just a variation on the "kitchen sink" or "dustbin" drama of the 1960's and 1970's. Livings's distinct contribution is a heartiness in the people dramatized in that era. They are harder-working, prouder, more robust than their counterparts in the hands of John Osborne, Arnold Wesker, or John Arden. They are more loving, more open, and more insistent that life give them their share. Also, like Livings himself, they are more content with being themselves and less charmed with the prospect of trying to be something they are not.

STOP IT, WHOEVER YOU ARE

A case in point is his first success, *Stop It, Whoever You Are*, actually a five-scene vehicle for a series of slapstick routines involving Perkin Warbeck and his attempts at simple survival. The play begins with a harmless flirtation between Warbeck (recently retired) and a buxom fourteen-year-old girl, and ends, after several visits to the factory lavatory, with the explosion of the leaking gas in the Warbeck household, peopled with Warbeck's ghost and Mrs. Harbuckle, medium extraordinaire, now bald and looking "like Warbeck in drag." The play resembles a meandering Sunday drive; it steps from point to point, and the sights are worth the trip.

THE LITTLE MRS. FOSTER SHOW

More serious in tone and more structurally sound is *The Little Mrs. Foster Show*, a nightmarish look not only at the decolonialization of Africa but also at the madness of war without zeal. Presented in the format of a touring lecture-with-slides on the adventures of Mrs. Foster's missionary work in Africa, the play deals with her relationship to a mercenary, Hook, who has been abandoned by his comrade, Orara, after his leg has been injured in a grenade blast. Stumbling on Hook in the jungle, Mrs. Foster submits to his charms but denounces him on their return to civilization, to save her reputation as a maiden. Orara imprisons and tortures Hook, but when an enterprising Mr. Clive convinces Mrs. Foster to take her story on the lecture circuit, they need Hook to help them dramatize those months together. Now sporting an artificial leg (but keeping the original one in a handy package on his lap), Hook joins the show. In an attempt to avoid the smell of the leg, Mrs. Foster splits her dress in half; now exposed, she "abandons the ruined dress and takes her place, brave and breathless, by Hook, to wave to us." Thus, her earlier modesty and refusal to face her own sensuality, which began Hook's troubles, now are abandoned in favor of a more honest admission of her complicity in the seduction. For critics who seek thematic consistency and structural integrity in Livings's work, this play provides a sufficiency of both.

KELLY'S EYE

The Hook-Mrs. Foster seduction contains a kind of vigor that typifies all the romances in Livings's work, especially those between husband and wife. Women here are demonstrative, even aggressive; they like to be tickled and chased; any sort of terrain will do, whether garden or workshop, and vows must be renewed and reinforced with deeds. Perhaps Livings's only purely serious full-length play, *Kelly's Eye*, is at base a love story. Fleeing the automobile of a young seducer, Anna finds the beach hut of Kelly, fugitive from the law for the murder of his best friend. Responding to their sudden attraction for each other but not wanting to reduce it to a simple sexual one, they agree to sleep apart, with Kelly protecting Anna while she reexamines her values. When Anna's father, Brierly, a typical Livings antagonist from the world of high finance, tries to return Anna to her country-club life, Kelly takes her away to a small seaside room, giving up his own anonymity and obscurity. A prying landlady and a nosy reporter ruin Kelly and Anna's substitute "honeymoon" by showing Brierly where they are hidden, and, in one of the most gruesome scenes in Livings's generally optimistic theater, Kelly swallows disinfectant and dies. Reminiscent of Eugene O'Neill or D. H. Lawrence, the play confused critics who expected the same kind of farce that Livings had produced before, and it did not receive favorable reviews. The starkness of the landscape in which this bizarre but honest love affair grows and the suddenness of the characters' willingness to expose themselves to one another mark this play as a significant work waiting only to be refound by a sensitive director.

A THEATRICAL FLAIR

For the reader, however, the delights of Livings's plays lie in their humor. This humor is almost always subtle when embedded in the language, but it is broad in the action. There is a kind of tension set up between the obvious, even childish, silliness of the stage business and the droll and obtuse humor of the dialogue, often understated, sardonic, in the ironic mode, and consequently available only to the careful reader. A particular habit of Livings is the elaborate stage direction, not unlike George Bernard Shaw's: Highly literate prose is inserted into the dialogue not only as a signal to the actor but also as a parenthetical comment by the playwright to the reader. As is always the case with irony, the sense of the line is apparent not necessarily in the words but in the tone, and Livings sees fit to assist the reader or actor in those moments. In a scene of conjugal bliss *al fresco*, from *Honour and Offer*, Livings prescribes this stage direction: "Doris shrieks with shocked glee, claps her hand to her mouth, glances toward the bench, and flees on tiptoe. They tiptoe hazardously round the savage beehive, excited as much by the need for silence and the danger of the malignant bees as by the prospect of one catching hold of the other." This sort of rhetorical insertion is not meant to get in the way of the director's task but to help the reader grasp the texture of the scene.

Conversely, Livings's ostensibly prose works contain the same theatrical flair that identifies his stage pieces. His work for the British Broadcasting Corporation, some of which is gathered in the collection entitled *Penine Tales*, straddles the boundary between prose and drama; their personal style and their obviously autobiographical content render them a sort of continuation of Livings's dramatic work, but reduced to words without pictures. "Twice-Nightly, Thursday Off to Learn It." "Fit-Up Touring, Also to Help in Kitchen," and "Will the Demon King Please Wear the Hat Provided?" all reflect Livings's early struggles as an actor. Although it is a mistake to take these short radio pieces as pure autobiography, it can be said, as a narrator admits in one of the stories about childhood, "The boy was me."

The 1986 volume *Flying Eggs and Things: More Penine Tales* continued in the same vein. The 1987 production of *This Is My Dream: The Life and Times of Josephine Baker*, however, examined the career of the celebrated expatriate African American singer and actress in more serious fashion.

OTHER MAJOR WORKS

SHORT FICTION: *Penine Tales*, 1983; *Flying Eggs and Things: More Penine Tales*, 1986.

SCREENPLAY: *Work Is a Four-Letter Word*, 1968 (adaptation of *Eh?*).

TELEPLAYS: *The Arson Squad*, 1961; *Jack's Horrible Luck*, 1961; *There's No Room for You Here for a Start*, 1963; *A Right Crusader*, 1963; *Brainscrew*, 1966; *GRUP*, 1970; *Shuttlecock*, 1976; *The Game*, 1977 (adaptation of Harold Brighouse's play); *The Mayor's Charity*, 1977; *Two Days That Shook the Branch*, 1978; *We Had Some Happy Hours*, 1981; *Another Part of the Jungle*, 1985; *I Met a Man Who Wasn't There*, 1985.

RADIO PLAYS: *Worth a Hearing: A Collection of Radio Plays*, 1967; *A Most Wonderful Thing*, 1976; *Crab Training*, 1979; *Urn*, 1981; *The Moorcock*, 1981.

NONFICTION: *That the Medals and the Baton Be Put on View: The Story of a Village Band, 1875-1975*, 1975; *The Rough Side of the Boards: A Rueful and Mendacious Theatrical Memoir*, 1994.

BIBLIOGRAPHY

Goorney, Howard. *The Theatre Workshop Story.* London: Methuen, 1981. Livings discusses his warm relationship with Joan Littlewood and her Theatre Workshop, where he worked and acted in the mid-1950's, "after an odd audition during which I was required to scythe hay across the stage." On his plays, Livings remarks, "I should like to think one play of mine could catch, just once, the rich texture and the tough purpose she displays again and again."

Hunt, Hugh, Kenneth Richards, and John Russell Taylor. *The Revels History of Drama in English, 1880 to the Present Day.* Vol. 7. London: Methuen, 1978. Livings took his place in modern drama "by virtue of the power and variety of his output, the striking individuality of his means of dramatic expression, alongside the major figures of the heroic days." Short but informative overview, from *Stop It, Whoever You Are* to *Honour and Offer.*

Rusinko, Susan. *British Drama, 1950 to the Present: A Critical History.* Boston: Twayne, 1989. Rusinko discusses Livings under the heading "Working Class Writers." She provides a brief biographical sketch, followed by informative outlines of *Stop It, Whoever You Are, Nil Carborundum,* and *Eh?* Discusses words and Livings's detailed instructions about how certain words are pronounced.

Taylor, John Russell. *The Angry Theatre: New British Drama.* Rev. ed. New York: Hill and Wang, 1969. An essential starting place for the study of Livings. Some critics, says Taylor, find his work "both profound and riotously funny [while] others determinedly find it neither." The important difference, he says, is that not only "does he come from the working class, but he writes principally for the working class." Good long discussions of several works, including *Jack's Horrible Luck* and more popular plays.

Thomson, Peter. "Henry Livings and the Accessible Theatre." In *Western Popular Theatre*, edited by David Mayer and Kenneth Richards. London: Methuen, 1977. An appreciation of the common appeal of Livings's work to the British housewife, "the bawdy mockery of respectable middle-class avarice." Considers the primacy of language, the convention of direct address, and other aspects of Livings's craft. Thomson says that Livings is "a man with a lot of plays in him, and hardly anywhere to put them."

Thomas J. Taylor

THOMAS LODGE

Born: London(?), England; 1558(?)
Died: London, England; September, 1625

PRINCIPAL DRAMA

The Wounds of Civill War, pr. c. 1586, pb. 1594
A Looking Glass for London and England, pr. c. 1588-1589, pb. 1594 (with Robert Greene)

OTHER LITERARY FORMS

Thomas Lodge is best known for his prose romances, which are among the precursors of the novel. The most famous of these prose romances, *Rosalynde: Or, Euphues Golden Legacy* (1590), was William Shakespeare's major source for *As You Like It* (pr. c. 1599-1600). Lodge also published several collections of poetry, a volume of poetic satire (*A Fig for Momus*, 1595), translations of Josephus (1602) and Seneca (1614), and a commentary on du Bartas (1621). Most of Lodge's works are available in the four-volume *The Complete Works of Thomas Lodge* (1883).`

ACHIEVEMENTS

Although Thomas Lodge is better known for his lyric poetry and his romances than for his drama, his two extant plays have an important place in the history of the English drama. Lodge was a competent if not a brilliant writer, and, more important, he was an innovative one. *The Wounds of Civill War* is one of the earliest dramas to be written principally in blank verse and may be the earliest extant example of an English drama based on classical history, a mode that became very popular with later Elizabethan playwrights. *A Looking Glass for London and England* provides almost a summary of the various strands of drama being woven together by Lodge and his contemporaries to form the framework of the drama of the Elizabethan period. Elements from both of the plays were borrowed by more successful playwrights whose works eventually overshadowed Lodge's. Lodge's drama remains important, however, from a historical standpoint and for its influence on his more brilliant contemporaries.

BIOGRAPHY

Because of the wide range of his abilities and interests, Thomas Lodge's biography is often offered as an example of the life of a typical Elizabethan gentleman and man of letters. Neither the date nor the place of his birth is known definitely, but he was probably born in 1558. He was the second son of a Lord Mayor of London. Lodge studied at the Merchant Taylors' School in London and entered Trinity College, Oxford, in 1573, completing his bachelor's degree in 1577. In April of 1578, he was admitted to study law at Lincoln's Inn, London.

Lodge's early years in London were marked by personal problems, the exact nature of which is unknown, but which led to an appearance in court and a brief period of imprisonment. He may have had some problems with debts, which may have led to the criticism of usury that appears in some of his works, including *A Looking Glass for London and England*, but it is unlikely that he was ever truly profligate. More likely, his personal difficulties resulted from his leanings toward and eventual conversion to Catholicism. Lodge's literary career began in 1579 with the publication of an epitaph for his mother. The next year, he became widely known for his reply to Stephen Gosson's *School of Abuse* (1579), a pamphlet attacking the arts on moral grounds. The quarrel be-

tween Lodge and Gosson continued for some years, with Lodge's final reply appearing in an epistle published with his *An Alarum Against Usurers* (1584).

Around 1585, Lodge made a voyage to the Canaries, during which he wrote his famous romance *Rosalynde*. Little is known of his activities during the next four years, but it is likely that he spent part of his time writing for the theater and that his two extant plays date from this period. He seems to have renounced the theater about 1589. In August of 1591, Lodge sailed to South America with Sir Thomas Cavendish. The expedition was plagued by misfortune, and Lodge was one of the few survivors to return safely to England.

Lodge continued to produce and publish a variety of nondramatic literature until 1596, when he turned to the study of medicine, receiving a degree from Avignon in 1598; the degree was recognized by Oxford in 1602. After studying law, enjoying a modestly successful literary career, and experiencing a brief stint as an adventurer, Lodge seems to have found his place in life as a physician. He married about 1601 and apparently developed a large practice in London, particularly among the Catholic population. Although the date of his conversion is unknown, he was definitely a professed Catholic by this time and had some difficulties with the law over his recusancy. He died in September, 1625, perhaps of the plague, which he may have caught while attending the poor in London.

ANALYSIS

Despite attempts to credit him with a number of early Elizabethan plays, especially the highly successful *Mucedorus* (pr. 1598), Thomas Lodge can be definitely identified as the author of only two extant plays, *The Wounds of Civill War* and *A Looking Glass for London and England*, the latter written with Robert Greene.

Neither of Lodge's plays can be dated with any precision, but both were probably written between 1585, when he made his first voyage to the Americas, and 1589, when he seems to have given up writing for the theater. Both *A Looking Glass for London and England* and *The Wounds of Civill War* were first published in 1594. Although published slightly later,

The Wounds of Civill War is believed to be the earlier of the two. Little is known of the stage history of either play. The title page of *The Wounds of Civill War* indicates that the play was performed by the Admiral's Men, but the records of the company do not mention the play. The early history of *A Looking Glass for London and England* is similarly blank, but there are records of a revival in 1592 and other indications that the play was successful. Allusions to Jonah and the whale and the story of Nineveh became popular on the puppet stage, and the influence of the play may have reached as far as Germany. Neither play has received much critical attention, nor has either play remained a living part of the English theatrical repertory.

Both of Lodge's dramatic works are experimental, which is at once their strength and their weakness. Like the other University Wits, Lodge was a dramatic pioneer, experimenting with new forms or with new uses for old theatrical materials. Unfortunately, he does not seem to have had the sense of dramatic form that allowed other writers, such as Shakespeare, to take the basic idea of the history play and create from it a much tighter and richer drama. Lodge's chief talent seems to have been as a lyric poet, but the verse of his plays shows his full lyric genius only rarely. Written at a time when blank verse first began to appear on the stage, Lodge's lines tend to be monotonous. He depends heavily on long set speeches rather than on true dialogue, which makes the plays seem rather stiff and sometimes unemotional. The plays also suffer from Lodge's tendency to moralize rather than let the action carry his moral concerns.

Lodge's work, however, should not be judged too harshly. While he was not a Shakespeare or a Marlowe, Lodge was a competent and sometimes daring dramatist. Despite his weaknesses, his influence on the English theater is significant and undeniable. *The Wounds of Civil War* and *A Looking Glass for London and England* remain important texts, the first for its pioneering role in the development of the history play and the second for its sophisticated combination of widely diverse literary elements, providing almost a summary of the most significant influences on the early English theater.

THE WOUNDS OF CIVILL WAR

The exact date of Lodge's first play, *The Wounds of Civill War*, is a matter of considerable critical discussion, principally because of its possible relationship with Christopher Marlowe's *Tamburlaine the Great*, Parts I and II (pr. c. 1587). *The Wounds of Civill War* has traditionally been dated later than Marlowe's tragedy. The two plays show a number of striking similarities, but while it seems probable that one play influenced the other, it is impossible to determine in which direction the influence moved. The argument for dating *The Wounds of Civill War* after 1587 is based primarily on the questionable assumption that the weaker playwright, Lodge, must have been influenced by the stronger writer, Marlowe. This assumption has been challenged by critics who offer strong evidence for an earlier date for Lodge's play. In his *Thomas Lodge: The History of an Elizabethan* (1931), N. Burton Paradise notes that similar scenes in the two plays could easily have begun with Lodge rather than with Marlowe, or could have been borrowed by both playwrights from other sources. The often-mentioned chariot scene in each play, for example—in which the hero enters in a chariot pulled by men—could have been derived from a similar scene in *Jocasta* (pr. 1566, pb. 1573), an earlier play that is a translation by George Gascoigne and Francis Kinwelmershe, which might have been familiar to both writers. It has also been noted that there are no verbal parallels between the two plays. It seems unlikely that Lodge, who shows in his other works a particularly sensitive ear for language, would have borrowed details from Marlowe's drama without picking up some of Marlowe's dynamic verse style. The verse in *The Wounds of Civill War* tends to be monotonous, with little flexibility or variety; most of the lines are end-stepped, with few feminine endings, suggesting that the play was written before Marlowe's important advances in the handling of dramatic blank verse. Finally, Lodge's play shows no influence of *The Spanish Tragedy* (pr. c. 1585-1589) by Thomas Kyd. Kyd's bloody tragedy seems to have initiated the Elizabethan interest in spectacular and often brutal special effects and had an immediate impact on the developing English drama. *The Wounds of*

Civill War contains many possibilities for such action. Had Lodge's chronicle been written after *The Spanish Tragedy*, one would expect its influence to appear in the staging of the battle scenes, at least, but Lodge's play makes little use of such sensational effects. The available evidence, then, suggests that *The Wounds of Civill War* might have been written about 1586, soon after Lodge's return from the Canaries but before the productions of Marlowe's and Kyd's popular and highly influential works.

If *The Wounds of Civill War* was written this early, it is the earliest English play based in classical history still extant. Even if it was written a few years later, it remains one of the first of a long series of history plays that were popular during the last years of Queen Elizabeth's reign. Lodge apparently used at least two sources for his chronicle: Appian's *Romaica* (n.d.; *History of Rome's Wars*, 1912-1913), translated in 1578, and Sir Thomas North's translation (1579) of *Bioi paralleloi* (c. 105-115; *Parallel Lives*, 1579), by Plutarch. In turning to the latter work, Lodge pointed the way for Shakespeare, who later used Plutarch as his major source for his Roman plays.

Although the title page of the first edition of *The Wounds of Civill War* identifies it as a tragedy, the play is more properly described as a chronicle or history play. It concerns the continuing conflict between Marius and Sulla during the Roman Civil Wars, beginning in 88 B.C.E. The story is episodic, covering a ten-year period of Roman history, and the play lacks unity, chiefly because Lodge followed his sources too closely. Although Lodge concentrates on the clash of personal ambitions between the major characters, the incidents are never quite drawn together with a central dramatic focus. The central conflict is one of ambition rather than of character, and the play lacks psychological depth, a fact that is particularly clear in the final act, when Sulla's remorse and subsequent death seem sudden and unmotivated. Despite numerous battle scenes, Lodge's chronicle remains rather static; its emphasis is on language rather than action. Fortunately, Lodge was a talented poet, and the verse, though often monotonous, is well-crafted and sometimes melodious.

The Wounds of Civill War, while imperfect, represents an important step in English dramatic history. The play is innovative and experimental rather than a polished achievement, and it should be judged accordingly. Lodge's writing tended to be better when he followed an established form, as in his prose romances. Lodge's experimentation with classical history may have produced a somewhat flawed work, but it provided other writers with an indication of the dramatic potential of the material.

A LOOKING GLASS FOR LONDON AND ENGLAND

A Looking Glass for London and England is similarly experimental and similarly flawed, but it is, for the most part, a tighter and more interesting drama than *The Wounds of Civill War*. Whether this is at all attributable to the influence of Lodge's collaborator, Robert Greene, is impossible to determine. The styles of the two writers are very similar, and in this play, they blend so smoothly that it is impossible to identify the authorship of the various parts.

The date of composition of *A Looking Glass for London and England* is most frequently given as 1588 or 1589. The play shows some influence of *Tamburlaine the Great* and *The Spanish Tragedy*, which suggests that it was written after 1587. The greater variety and flexibility of the verse suggests the influence of Marlowe, while the spectacular effects may have been designed to appeal to the taste for sensationalism primed by Kyd's tragedy. Lodge's renouncement of the theater in 1589 sets the latest possible date for the play, but it is likely that it was composed earlier because despite frequent references to contemporary events, it makes no mention of the Spanish Armada. This fact suggests that the play could have been written as early as 1587, just after the appearance of Marlowe's tragedy but before the threat of invasion by Spain.

A Looking Glass for London and England is a highly didactic work based loosely on the Old Testament book of Jonah. Lodge and Greene also probably used Josephus's history of the Jews, a work Lodge later translated. The authors exercised considerable freedom in expanding the story, particularly in the development of the character of Rasni, the King of

Nineveh, who does not appear in the sources, and in the addition and elaboration of a clown plot involving a smith and his servant.

Like *The Wounds of Civill War*, *A Looking Glass for London and England* is episodic, but it is held together by a clearer sense of dramatic purpose. Although the play's moralizing often seems naïve, it provides a central focus that holds the many disparate elements of the drama together. The final turn toward romantic comedy at the end is sudden, but it is prepared for by the biblical story and the basic moral stance of the work. *A Looking Glass for London and England* is innovative and traditional at the same time, blending together a variety of theatrical traditions into an original work. Its heavy didacticism suggests the influence of morality interludes. The basic story of the conversion of Nineveh is reminiscent of the plays of the mystery cycles, while the clown plot, with its devils, echoes the vice episodes of the morality plays. John Lyly's euphuistic style, which Lodge used quite seriously in his romances, is parodied in one scene. The characterization of the despot Rasni may be derived from Marlowe's *Tamburlaine the Great*, and the spectacular and sometimes violent effects suggest a debt to Kyd's *The Spanish Tragedy* as well as to the elaborate stage machinery of the mystery cycles. All of these elements are brought together in a kaleidoscopic form that possesses a surprising degree of unity and a distinct charm.

Other major works

LONG FICTION: *The Delectable History of Forbonius and Prisceria*, 1584; *Rosalynde: Or, Euphues Golden Legacy*, 1590; *Euphues Shadow*, 1592; *A Margarite of America*, 1596.

POETRY: *Scillaes Metamorphosis*, 1589; *Phillis*, 1593; *A Fig for Momus*, 1595.

NONFICTION: *A Reply to Gosson*, 1580; *An Alarum Against Usurers*, 1584; *The Famous, True, and Historicall Life of Robert Second Duke of Normandy*, 1591; *Catharos*, 1591; *The Life and Death of William Long Beard*, 1593; *The Divel Conjured*, 1596; *Prosopopeia*, 1596; *Wits Miserie and Worlds Madnesse*, 1596; *A Treatise on the Plague*, 1603; *The Poore Mans Talentt*, 1621.

TRANSLATIONS: *The Flowers of Lodowicke of Granado*, 1601; *The Famous and Memorable Workes of Josephus*, 1602; *The Workes of Lucius Annaeus Seneca*, 1614; *A Learned Summary upon the Famous Poeme of William of Saluste, Lord of Bartas*, 1625.

MISCELLANEOUS: *The Complete Works of Thomas Lodge*, 1883 (4 volumes; Sir Edmund Gosse, editor).

Bibliography

Allison, Antony Francis. *Thomas Lodge, 1558-1625: A Bibliographical Catalogue of the Early Editions (to the End of the Seventeenth Century)*. Folkestone, England: Dawsons of Pall Mall, 1973. A bibliography of early editions of the works of Lodge.

Helgerson, Richard. *The Elizabethan Prodigals*. Berkeley: University of California Press, 1976. A study of prodigal sons and repentance in Elizabethan literature that covers works of Lodge. Bibliography and index.

Paradise, N. Burton. *Thomas Lodge: The History of an Elizabethan*. 1931. Reprint. Hamden, Conn.: Archon Books, 1970. A substantial biography with a lengthy discussion of Lodge's two plays and of *Rosalynde*, the source of Shakespeare's *As You Like It*. Notes similarities between *The Wounds of Civill War* and George Gascoigne's *Jocasta*. Claims that Lodge was not influenced by Thomas Kyd's *The Spanish Tragedy*, for Lodge's plays lack many of the elements notable in Kyd's work. Bibliography.

Rae, Wesley D. *Thomas Lodge*. New York: Twayne, 1967. Covers the life and works and stresses the variety of Lodge's literary production. Bibliography, index.

Kathleen Latimer,
updated by Howard L. Ford

KENNETH LONERGAN

Born: New York, New York; 1961

PRINCIPAL DRAMA
The Rennings Children, pr. 1982
This Is Our Youth, pr. 1996, pb. 1999
Lobby Hero, pr. 2000, pb. 2001
The Waverly Gallery, pr., pb. 2000

OTHER LITERARY FORMS

Kenneth Lonergan achieved success in Hollywood with his screenplay, *You Can Count on Me* (2001). He also earned screenwriting credit for *Analyze This* (1999) and *The Adventures of Rocky and Bullwinkle* (2000); however, the film version of *Analyze This* does not correspond closely to Lonergan's draft.

ACHIEVEMENTS

Kenneth Lonergan's *You Can Count on Me* received an Academy Award nomination in 2001 for best original screenplay and was voted best screenplay by the New York Film Critics Circle and the Sundance Film Festival.

BIOGRAPHY

Kenneth Lonergan grew up in New York City and has lived there his entire life. He attended the Walden School in Manhattan and graduated from New York University. He began writing plays in high school and at age eighteen saw his play *The Rennings Children* produced by the Young Playwrights Festival in 1982. After graduating from college, he was affiliated with Naked Angels, an Off-Broadway troupe, while also working as a speechwriter and corporate scriptwriter.

Lonergan's father was a doctor and his mother a psychiatrist; after they divorced, his mother married another psychiatrist. Lonergan has a brother, half-brother, and several stepsiblings, and relationships among siblings are an important theme in his work. He also drew on personal experience in writing *The Waverly Gallery*, based on his observations of his grandmother's struggle with Alzheimer's disease.

The stage success of *This Is Our Youth* led Lon-

ergan to Hollywood to work on a variety of projects, including the box-office and critical failure *The Adventures of Rocky and Bullwinkle*. Although unhappy with the process of writing screenplays under studio control, Lonergan did not abandon screenwriting but instead sought independent production for *You Can Count on Me*. The play *Lobby Hero*, though produced after the film success in 2001, was written and contracted for production in 1998. In 2000, Lonergan married J. Smith-Cameron, an actress who appears in *You Can Count on Me*.

ANALYSIS

Kenneth Lonergan's work can be categorized as highly realistic, devoted to representing the language as well as the experience of characters thrust to the margins of society by age or social status. His work emphasizes character and situation over plot. In its realism, his style resembles that of his contemporary Rebecca Gilman, but his work is less driven by social issues. His focus is on intimate relationships, often between family members. His working process begins with a character, and he attempts to do justice to the inner life of those who may be perceived as inarticulate, whether they are teenagers, the elderly, or the uneducated. He finds myriad ways to dramatize the ambivalence and imprecision of many human situations and relationships. The success of his screenplay for *You Can Count on Me* brought Lonergan much publicity and a wider audience than most emerging playwrights ever expect to have. The production of *Lobby Hero*, shortly after the blast of publicity occasioned by the Academy Award nomination for *You Can Count on Me*, was covered in the New York newspapers as a major theatrical event, although the reviews were mixed. Some critics felt that the new play lacked the naturalness of Lonergan's earlier works and that its insights are handed directly to the audience rather than discerned. However, most audiences warmed to the ethical complexity in the quartet of characters sometimes behaving very badly indeed as they try to do the right thing.

The characters in Lonergan's plays often compare themselves to their own parents; this is true not only when characters are still close to childhood, as in *This Is Our Youth*, but also in the plays in which the protagonists are fully adult. Even William, the older security guard in *Lobby Hero*, reflects on the personality of his father. Elaine, the middle-aged psychiatrist in *The Waverly Gallery* finds her life still shaped by the temperament of her now-senile mother. This profusion of parents enhances the sense that Lonergan's characters do not believe themselves to be completely grown up; in particular, they may fail to see that the responsibility for their actions belongs only to themselves. The world of Lonergan's characters is a poignant one. Even the more corrupt of his characters appear lost rather than malicious, and good intentions certainly do not guarantee good outcomes.

Lonergan's working process is characterized by an obsessiveness about rendering the language of his characters with exactness, and his dialogue undergoes revision right into the rehearsal process. His goal is to capture how each character speaks, while also differentiating the characters from one another. James Joyce is a model for him in the creation of distinctive voices, and the title of an early unpublished play "Here Comes Everybody," alludes to Joyce's linguistically playful novel *Finnegan's Wake* (1939).

THIS IS OUR YOUTH

Set on the Upper West Side of Manhattan in 1982, this play concentrates entirely on several affluent college-aged characters, young people not only supported by their parents but also exploiting them: One of the young men, Warren, has just stolen fifteen thousand dollars from his father, a businessperson with Mafia ties. His self-aggrandizing friend Dennis proposes that they use the money to set up a drug deal. Dennis's father is a famous artist who has installed his son in his own apartment so that he will not have to live with him. Dennis has chosen not to attend college but believes he could be a fantastic success at whatever he chooses, for example, directing films. The young men are alternately profane and hysterical; almost everything about their language and personalities would offend the middle-class

theatergoers most likely to see the Off-Broadway production of this play.

However, Lonergan's play would not be very interesting if it merely set up these unlikable characters and exposed their all-too-obvious flaws. Its strength derives from the empathy Lonergan ultimately exacts for these characters, who are harshly critical of their fathers yet poised to have lives of lesser achievement and equal pain. Both of the young men imitate their fathers in their exploitative yet dependent relationship to women. Warren's sister was murdered some years before the play begins, and her death becomes a symbol of life's chaos and gives the lie to youth's illusion of invulnerability. The true vulnerability of youth is underlined when a drug-dealing friend dies of an overdose, launching Dennis into a tormented monologue that reveals the brittle shell of his self-esteem and his desperate need to project his failings onto others.

The end of the play is shaped by a startling miscommunication between Warren and Dennis, who takes seriously Warren's sarcastic remark that Dennis is his hero. Dennis urgently tells Warren that despite his sometimes cruel treatment of him, he is "on your side." In the last line of the play, Warren, in defeat, says he is going to go home. He is still too dependent on his parents and too immature to make any more inspired choices about the road ahead. His ambivalence about growing up is also revealed in the highly symbolic suitcase full of childhood toys and other items he brings with him to Dennis's apartment. At times he treats the vintage toys and sports memorabilia as valuable commodities to sell, but when offered actual opportunities to part with them for money, he finds that he is simply not ready to let any of them go.

The third character in *This Is Our Youth* is Jessica, described as a nineteen-year-old girl whom Warren finds attractive and whom Dennis thinks is out of Warren's league. A continual source of contention between the two men is Dennis's repeated mockery of Warren's luck with girls. Dennis and Warren think of women primarily in sexual terms, debating between calling Jessica and her friend Natalie for possible sex or taking the easy but expensive route and hiring prostitutes. As it turns out, Warren does spend the night with Jessica, but the evening is no financial bargain: He takes her on a date including a night at the Plaza Hotel that costs him a thousand dollars. Warren's exultation over his sexual success, which he immediately shares with Dennis, is flattened by Jessica's immediate ambivalence and inability to go forward with the relationship. The two part after a confrontation over one of the souvenirs lovingly kept in a suitcase: a baseball hat from the 1914 opening of Wrigley Field, given to Warren by his grandfather. Jessica, knowing its significance, asks Warren if she can have it, as a proof of his respect. He quickly agrees to give it to her, then plainly wants it back. He thus mirrors her ambivalence and the relationship falters.

THE WAVERLY GALLERY

In contrast to *This Is Our Youth*, *The Waverly Gallery* explores the language and dissolutions of age. Based on Lonergan's relationship with his grandmother, the play juxtaposes Daniel, the narrator, with his grandmother Gladys. For many years, Gladys, once an activist lawyer, has managed an art gallery (referred to in the play's title). Now she has become afflicted with Alzheimer's disease. Without condescending to the changes endured by the aging woman, Lonergan manages to make her situation both funny and heart-rending. The pathos of her decline is contrasted with the youthful naiveté of the earnest young artist whose work will be the last to be shown in her gallery. Gladys is also contrasted with her daughter Ellen, a woman in the prime of life, who reveals the fear that her own mind could one day slip into senility. Daniel, who lives next door to his grandmother and has been acutely aware of her decline, cannot bear to imagine such a fate for his mother. Like Lonergan's own mother, Ellen is a psychiatrist in her second marriage. Like Lonergan himself, Daniel is a speechwriter, although his grandmother persists in believing that he is a newspaper journalist.

This play, Lonergan's most autobiographical, shows his attention to the patterns of language and the poetry inherent in common speech of different kinds. That the daily language patterns of ordinary people demonstrate many of the same repetitions and reductions of Alzheimer's disease becomes evident when

these linguistic patterns are closely juxtaposed. Gladys constantly repeats the same questions and makes the same mistakes, but so, to a lesser extent, does Daniel's stepfather.

LOBBY HERO

This play, set, as the title hints, in the lobby of a hotel building, throws together two apartment building security men and two police officers in the aftermath of a crime. Bill, the more experienced police officer, is a morally slippery, self-admiring man who manipulates the naïve admiration directed toward him by his female partner, young Dawn. The security guards include Jeff, a well meaning but hapless fellow typical of Lonergan's earlier work, and William, his African American supervisor. The four are initially brought together by Bill's habit of visiting a friend called Jim who lives in the building, while Dawn waits for him downstairs. ("Jim" is eventually revealed to be a female prostitute). Both Dawn and Jeff are rookies, in the sense that their work and judgment is subject to review by a supervisor—the macho Bill and the fatherly William. Lonergan's dialogue allows the characters to pour out their feelings on a variety of topics including family values, the U.S. Navy, and loyalty to a boss.

The plot of *Lobby Hero* focuses on a murder investigation in which William's brother is a suspect. William is prepared to offer a false alibi for his brother, entangling Jeff in a moral dilemma and a peculiar opportunity to be a "hero." Both he and Dawn struggle to understand the relationship between honesty and pragmatism, something their elders seem to have resolved. Despite the crush she has on her married partner, Dawn is better able to articulate her discomfort than is Jeff, who manages only to be goofy and sluggish, yet yearns to be more. His lowly security job follows on being dismissed from the navy for smoking pot. He has much in common with Warren from *This Is Our Youth*, despite that character's affluence and education.

Ultimately each of the four characters is faced with complex ethical decisions. Painful aspects of human nature emerge, with sexuality, race, and police corruption all coming under scrutiny. Lonergan has never been naïve about the power of sexism, and here he couples that for the first time with an exploration of racial issues: William is the first African American character to appear in his dramas. Painfully proud of his rank of "captain" among the security guards, William is such a stickler for rules that he fired another guard for sleeping on the job and prevented the man from receiving a pension. Now he finds himself in the position of wanting to bend the rules for his own brother. Bill, the cop, is willing to lie on William's behalf but runs afoul of his own previous manipulation of Dawn. Each character is in trouble of some kind and could be in far deeper water if all the truth is told.

The plot of *Lobby Hero* goes beyond Lonergan's earlier plays in the depth of its plotting, but that does not reduce his reliance on character and dialogue as key elements in the way his work provides meaning. Ultimately the plot elements themselves are only important in giving the four characters opportunities to react.

OTHER MAJOR WORKS

SCREENPLAYS: *Analyze This*, 1999; *The Adventures of Rocky and Bullwinkle*, 2000; *You Can Count on Me*, 2001.

BIBLIOGRAPHY

Kushner, Rachel. "Kenneth Lonergan." *Bomb Magazine* (Winter, 2002). An interview with Lonergan, primarily about *Lobby Hero*.

Marks, Peter. "Artist at Work: Kenneth Lonergan." *The New York Times*, March 12, 2001. An analysis of Lonergan's career up to the rehearsal period for *Lobby Hero*. An interview with Lonergan is included.

Painter-Young, Jamie. "In the Driver's Seat." *Back Stage West*, November 2, 2000. Discusses the success of *You Can Count on Me* and its effect on Lonergan's subsequent career.

Diane M. Ross

FREDERICK LONSDALE
Lionel Frederick Leonard

Born: St. Helier, Jersey, Channel Islands; February 5, 1881
Died: London, England; April 4, 1954

PRINCIPAL DRAMA

Who's Hamilton?, pr. 1903
The Early Worm, pr. 1908
The King of Cadonia, pr. 1908 (libretto; music by Sidney Jones; based on Anthony Hope's novel *The Prisoner of Zenda*)
The Best People, pr. 1909
The Balkan Princess, pr. 1910 (libretto, with Frank Curzon; music by Paul Rubens)
Betty, pr. 1914 (libretto, with Gladys Unger; music by Rubens)
The Patriot, pr. 1915
High Jinks, pr. 1916 (libretto; music by Rudolph Friml)
Waiting at the Church, pr. 1916
The Maid of the Mountains, pr. 1917, pb. 1949 (libretto; music by Harold Fraser-Simson, lyrics by Harry Graham)
Monsieur Beaucaire, pr. 1919 (libretto; music by André Messager, based on a French libretto)
The Lady of the Rose, pr. 1921, pb. 1922 (libretto; music by Jean Gilbert, lyrics by Graham; adaptation of Rudolph Schanzer and Ernst Welisch's libretto)
Aren't We All?, pr. 1923, pb. 1924 (originally as *The Best People*)
Spring Cleaning, pr. 1923, pb. 1925
The Fake, pr. 1924, pb. 1927
Katja the Dancer, pr. 1924 (libretto, with Graham; music by Gilbert)
The Street Singer, pr., pb. 1924 (libretto; music by Fraser-Simson)

The Last of Mrs. Cheyney, pr., pb. 1925

On Approval, pr. 1926 (staged), pb. 1927, pr. 1982 (televised; originally as "The Follies of the Foolish")

The High Road, pr., pb. 1927

Lady Mary, pr. 1928 (libretto, with John Hastings Turner; music by Albert Sirmay and Philip Craig)

Canaries Sometimes Sing, pr., pb. 1929

Never Come Back, pr. 1932

Once Is Enough, pr., pb. 1938 (originally as *Half a Loaf*, wr. 1937, pr. 1958)

The Foreigners, pr. 1939

Another Love Story, pr. 1943, pb. 1948

But for the Grace of God, pr. 1946

The Way Things Go, pr. 1950, pb. 1951 (revised as *Day After Tomorrow*, pr. 1950)

Let Them Eat Cake, pr., pb. 1959 (revision of *Once Is Enough*)

Plays, pb. 2000

OTHER LITERARY FORMS

Frederick Lonsdale's success as a librettist for musical comedies and operettas was equal to his success as a playwright. His libretto for *The King of Cadonia* was clearly inspired by Anthony Hope's novel *The Prisoner of Zenda* (1894) and in its turn influenced Ivor Novello's operetta *King's Rhapsody* (pr. 1950). Lonsdale's most popular work in this vein was *The Maid of the Mountains*, which ran at Daly's Theatre, London, for a total of 1,352 performances. Lonsdale collaborated with other leading musical theater composers of the early twentieth century English stage, including Paul Rubens, who did the music for *The Balkan Princess* (written with Frank Curzon) and *Betty* (written with Gladys Unger). He also had a hand in a number of adaptations of European successes, such as *The Lady of the Rose* and *Katja the Dancer*, both with music by the German composer Jean Gilbert (pseudonym of Max Winterfield); *High Jinks*, with a score by the Hungarianborn Rudolf Friml; and *Monsieur Beaucaire*, with music composed by André Messager, the last major writer of French operetta. Lonsdale's last effort as a librettist was *Lady Mary*, which he coauthored with

John Hastings Turner to a score by Albert Sirmay and Philip Craig.

Generally, Lonsdale seems to have been sought out by the impresarios of musical theater for his ability to supply sprightly, well-constructed books that blended wit and sentimentality. The most convincing testimony to his skill in this area is *The Maid of the Mountains*, which was second only to Oscar Asche and Frederic Norton's *Chu Chin Chow* (pr. 1916) as the major musical success of London's West End theater during World War I.

After his major drawing-room comedies had achieved success in New York, Lonsdale's talents were also recognized and recruited by the film industry. He wrote, or had a hand in, several screenplays, including Alexander Korda's vehicle for Douglas Fairbanks, *The Private Life of Don Juan* (1934; with Lajos Biro), and Metro-Goldwyn-Mayer's episodic World War II tribute to British patriotism, *Forever and a Day* (1943; with Charles Bennett, C. S. Forester, John Van Druten, Christopher Isherwood, R. C.

Frederick Lonsdale in 1939. (AP/Wide World Photos)

Sherriff, and many others too numerous to mention). That he wrote so little for the screen can be attributed partly to his dislike of Hollywood ("I could never live in a film city because there is no conversation") and partly to his habit of breaking contracts.

ACHIEVEMENTS

Frederick Lonsdale reached his peak of acclaim in the 1920's and early 1930's, when his name was closely associated with sophisticated drawing-room comedies, such as those of Noël Coward, S. N. Behrman, and Philip Barry. During Lonsdale's long career as a playwright, which extended from the staging of *Who's Hamilton?* at the New Theatre, Ealing, in 1903, to the posthumous production of *Let Them Eat Cake* at the Cambridge Theatre, London, in 1959, his work was praised by such diverse theater critics as Henrik Ibsen's archenemy Clement Scott of *The Daily Telegraph*, Arthur B. Walkley of *The Times* (London), *The Sunday Times's* convivial James Agate, Heywood Broun of *New York World*, *The New Yorker's* resident wit, Robert Benchley, and the British eccentric, Hannen Swaffer of the *Daily Express*. Typical of such critics' comments was Benchley's on *Spring Cleaning's* New York production in 1923: "It is written with a respect for the audience's intelligence and has an easy humor that brought a pleasant glow to this sin-hardened heart." In the same vein, Agate, reviewing a revival of *On Approval* in London in 1933, observed that "time is powerless against true wit and diversion."

Lonsdale's reputation declined in the 1940's and 1950's, and indeed, in 1953, almost at the end of his life, he experienced the bitterness of an old established author being goaded by a critical wunderkind when Kenneth Tynan, writing in the *Evening Standard* about a revival of *Aren't We All?*, said: "Frederick Lonsdale's comedy, first produced thirty years ago, is what some would call gentle, others toothless: Where W. Somerset Maugham chews and digests his characters, Lonsdale merely mumbles them." Years later, however, interest in Lonsdale's work again arose. Though no innovator, Lonsdale was one of those artists who take a particular form and handle it with consummate skill and flair.

BIOGRAPHY

Unlike the heroes and heroines of his own plays, Frederick Lonsdale came from a decidedly humble background. Lonsdale was born Lionel Frederick Leonard on February 5, 1881, in St. Helier, the capital of Jersey in the Channel Islands. The third son of a local tobacconist and his wife, Frederick and Susan Leonard, Lonsdale was an unruly child who disappointed his family by refusing to attend school and by running off to Canada in his late teens on a romantic impulse. There he seems to have lived by his wits and, according to his own account, was not above perpetrating fraud to finance his passage back to England. On his return, he worked for some time on the Southampton docks and wrote plays in his spare time. When he moved back to Jersey in 1903, his first play had already been produced at a suburban London theater and had been noticed favorably by one of the leading British critics, Clement Scott, who had entered the theater by chance to shelter himself from the rain. The producing company brought the play to St. Helier that same year, and from that point Lonsdale began to be accepted into the more elevated reaches of Jersey society. His transformation from the "villainous and undisciplined child" of a small-town shopkeeper into an international celebrity whose smallest sartorial innovations made instant newspaper copy seems to have begun at about this time. Lonsdale was obviously a keen observer and a gifted mimic, and he rapidly assumed the manners and accent of the upper class, about which he was to spend much of his life writing.

In 1904, Lonsdale—still known in private life as Frederick Leonard—married Leslie Hoggan, the daughter of a retired colonel. For the first four years of their marriage, the young couple spent much of their time apart. Lonsdale had returned to England to pursue his career as a playwright and was not making sufficient income to provide a home for both of them there. Finally, however, he attracted the attention of a London impresario, Frank Curzon, who staged Lonsdale's first successful work, *The King of Cadonia*, at the Prince of Wales Theatre in September, 1908. The young couple were reunited and soon afterward changed their names by deed poll from Mr. and Mrs.

Frederick Leonard to Mr. and Mrs. Frederick Lonsdale, the name that the playwright had adopted as his nom de plume. From that time onward, Lonsdale's success was assured, and with *The Maid of the Mountains* in 1917, he achieved sufficient financial security to enable him to play the man-about-town for the next two decades.

By the mid-1920's, Lonsdale was equally celebrated in England and the United States. His marriage had failed, and he had separated from his wife and family. In the 1930's, he was invited to Hollywood to write screenplays, primarily for Metro-Goldwyn-Mayer. In that decade, his productivity as a playwright declined, and only three new works were staged between 1930 and 1940. With the advent of World War II, Lonsdale's criticism of the war effort and his voluntary exile in the United States lost him the respect of many of his compatriots. Nevertheless, when the war ended, he returned to England and resumed his career as a West End playwright. From 1950 onward, he spent much of his time in France, but by that time, his particular brand of witty drawing-room comedy had begun to fall out of favor, and his income declined steeply. Furthermore, age brought with it an increasing uncertainty of temper that made him unpopular with many members of the theatrical profession. Lonsdale died in London in 1954. He was survived by his former wife, Leslie, and three daughters.

ANALYSIS

Frederick Lonsdale's work, placed in historical perspective, occupies the midpoint in what might be called "the rise and fall of the drawing-room comedy," beginning not so much with Wilde as with Thomas William Robertson in the 1860's, continuing through such work in the late nineteenth and early twentieth centuries as Arthur Wing Pinero's *The Gay Lord Quex* (pr. 1899) and Maugham's *Lady Frederick* (pr. 1907), reaching a peak in the 1920's with *Private Lives* and *On Approval* and declining in the 1950's with such works as Terence Rattigan's *The Sleeping Prince* (pr. 1953), William Douglas Home's *The Reluctant Debutante* (pr. 1955), and Hugh and Margaret Williams's *The Grass Is Greener* (pr. 1958). The

shock waves that John Osborne's *Look Back in Anger* (pr. 1956) sent reverberating through the British theater made it difficult for any playwright thereafter to practice the art of light badinage among the denizens of Mayfair and Belgravia with quite such unselfconscious insouciance.

Comedy seldom gets a fair hearing from literary critics and historians, and writers who specialize in comedy must often be content with only the most condescending of acknowledgments. To point to Aristophanes and Molière, to Congreve, W. S. Gilbert, and George Bernard Shaw, will give pause only temporarily to those who regard comic playwriting as an inferior vocation. Yet, if one weighs Lonsdale's work against the "serious" work of his British contemporaries, the comparison is not altogether in Lonsdale's disfavor. J. B. Priestley's time plays and expressionist experiments, the attempts of W. H. Auden, Christopher Isherwood, Ronald Duncan, T. S. Eliot, and Christopher Fry to revive poetic drama, the bourgeois realism of R. C. Sheriff, John Galsworthy, St. John Ervine, and John Van Druten seem no likelier to hold the attention of future audiences and readers than Lonsdale's best comedies. The only British playwrights of the first half of the twentieth century who clearly surpass him are not the "serious" playwrights but other writers of comedy: Sir James Barrie, Shaw, and Coward.

With all his failing, his laziness, his self-plagiarism, his too-easy cynicism, and his occasional sentimentality, Lonsdale at his best possessed some distinct countervailing virtues, not least among them being a consummate sense of theater and a keen eye for the foibles of the upper class. Above all, his basic respect for human honesty and decency raised his most assured work to the level of critical comedy, an achievement that might very well have earned for him a nod of approval from both Aristophanes and Molière.

Lonsdale's plays were the product of an almost fatally facile talent. He wrote so easily and on the whole so successfully that he seems to have begun to regard his achievement as a species of confidence trick, similar to the one he claimed to have perpetrated as an adolescent in Canada. Peter Daubeney, the English director who staged *But for the Grace of*

God in 1946, has spoken of Lonsdale's "Olympian contempt for the theatre," calling him "an outstanding example of a man who despises the very medium where he excels." Clearly, though Lonsdale rivaled both Coward and Maugham in his ability to devise effective and amusing drawing-room comedies, he rarely attempted to extend his range. When he did—as in *The Fake* and *The Foreigners*—the result was invariably one of his rare failures at the box office. Maugham, on the other hand, though best in such high comedy as *The Circle* (pr., pb. 1921) and *The Constant Wife* (pr., pb. 1926), was able to write sardonic domestic comedies such as *The Breadwinner* (pr., pb. 1930) and effective melodramas such as *The Letter* (pr., pb. 1927). Coward, in whom sentimentality and romantic patriotism coexisted with cynicism and outrageousness, also stretched his talents to encompass not only the comedy of manners of *Private Lives* (pr., pb. 1930) but also the lower-class realism of *This Happy Breed* (pr. 1942), the suburban pathos of *Still Life* (pr., pb. 1936), and the epic social history of *Cavalcade* (pr. 1931). In itself, to be sure, such a narrow social range does not invalidate Lonsdale's work, any more than it does the work of Jane Austen, Henry James, Ivy Compton-Burnett, or, for that matter, of William Congreve, Marivaux, or Anton Chekhov. The question that remains is how far Lonsdale succeeded in using the essentially atypical milieu of the English upper class to reflect something beyond itself.

A close examination of Lonsdale's plays reveals not merely a fascination with the lives and manners of members of the English upper class but also a deeply divided attitude toward them. On the one hand, there is the apparent disdain for certain types who do not belong to the charmed circle—as in his occasional disparaging references to shop girls, Socialist politicians who never bathe, and illiterate Jewish theater managers. On the other hand, there is a moralizing tone in several of the plays in which the palms of honesty and worthiness are awarded to former chorus girls and women who live by their wits rather than to the aristocrats who patronize or exclude them. Another theme that emerges almost as consistently is that of the pleasures and perils of disguise. It

is difficult to resist the temptation to speculate that both of these themes attracted Lonsdale so powerfully because he had emerged from a world of shop girls, advanced by living on his wits, succeeded finally in making London society accept him by adopting an upper-class persona, and ever after feared that some day he would be unmasked.

MONSIEUR BEAUCAIRE

Lonsdale's love-hate relationship with the aristocracy and his preoccupation with disguise predate his first successful West End comedies. They go back, indeed, to his days as the librettist of such works as *The King of Cadonia* and *The Balkan Princess*. *Monsieur Beaucaire*, though an adaptation of a French libretto based on Booth Tarkington's novella (1900), illustrates the point almost perfectly. Lonsdale must have found it an appealing project because it attacks the hypocrisy and snobbishness of the upper class by unfolding the tale of a mysterious young French nobleman, the Marquis de Chateaurien, who is in love with an English noblewoman, Lady Mary Carlisle. His rival for Lady Mary's love, Lord Winterset, unmasks him as Monsieur Beaucaire, a common barber. Lady Mary then rejects him, only to discover to her chagrin that the common barber is, in reality, under the multiplicity of disguises, Louis XV's cousin, the Duc d'Orléans. Translated into the idiom of Lonsdale's later work, its message becomes that it is unwise to snub a shop girl, for she may turn out to have the soul of a duchess. Other possible propositions that might spring from this—that a duchess may turn out to have the soul of a shop girl, or that the souls of both duchesses and shop girls could be equally worthy of consideration—seem not to have interested Lonsdale to the same degree.

AREN'T WE ALL?

In his first really successful West End comedy, *Aren't We All?*, Lonsdale was still in his first flush of infatuation with the peerage. His depiction of Lord Grenham and his heir, Willie Tatham, of Lady Frinton, and of such representatives of the *jeunesse dorée* as Arthur Wells and Martin Steele is on the whole benign. Quite untypically, in fact, Lonsdale reserves his sharpest barbs for a Church of England clergyman who is married to Grenham's sister, Angela. Pompous, narrow-minded, hypocritical, and defensive, the Reverend Ernest Lynton is not so much a character as a caricature from *Punch*, and he clearly belongs to a world about which Lonsdale shows little knowledge or interest. His presence in the play, like that of his wife, is not essential to the main plot; he is there to provide an easily shocked target for Grenham's worldly cynicism and to set up the curtain line, which is also the title of the play:

> VICAR: . . . In answer to a simple remark I made last night, Grenham, you called me a bloody old fool! (*Puts his head in his hands as if crying.*)
> LORD GRENHAM: (*Puts his arm around his shoulder.*) But aren't we all, old friend?

To the degree that they are unable to separate appearance from reality, to penetrate disguises, or to refrain from leaping to conclusions, they are all indeed fools.

The play turns on a misunderstanding between two characters: Willie Tatham, Grenham's son, and Margot Tatham, Willie's wife. Willie is forced to wear the disguise of guilt, while Margot assumes the disguise of innocence. When the play opens, Willie has agreed to let Lady Frinton use his house to give a dance. Willie is worried and lonely. His wife has gone on a trip to Egypt, and he has not heard from her for more than a week. At the dance, a former actress with whom Willie is acquainted, Kitty Lake, is sympathetic to him, and they exchange a consoling kiss. Margot arrives home unexpectedly at that very moment and assumes immediately that Willie and Kitty are having an affair. Margot is unforgiving and proposes to leave Willie, but her very intransigence arouses the suspicions of her father-in-law, Lord Grenham. In an attempt to save his son's marriage, he unearths a secret alliance that Margot has formed in Egypt and arranges a confrontation between her and the young man concerned. His plan fails, however, when the young man gallantly pretends not to know Margot. Margot's mask remains secure, but her own confidence in her behavior toward her husband is shaken. Their peccadilloes cancel each other out, and at the end they go away together, reconciled.

The slightness of the plot is bolstered by two other concurrent actions: one in which Lord Grenham's sister, Angela, is gradually humanized as she learns to discard the appearance of grim, repressive "virtue" and to appreciate her brother's more flexible attitude toward life; the other in which Grenham is trapped into marriage with Lady Frinton by Margot, who, to revenge herself for his attempt to unmask her, places an announcement of their engagement in *The Times*. As in the main plot, changes are brought about in the circumstances of the characters as they are compelled to relinquish one set of attitudes for another.

Lonsdale's reputation for wit is not, on the whole, reinforced by the dialogue of this play. Lonsdale clearly intended Lord Grenham to be the main conduit of this quality, but at best he is able to rise to the sub-Wildean: "All my life I have found it very difficult to refuse a woman anything; except marriage." On the other hand, the dialogue generally is efficient, uncluttered, and has the rhythm, if not the content, of wit. Spoken, as it originally was, by first-rate light comedians, it seems to have persuaded audiences and critics alike that they had experienced the sensations of surprise and delight that true wit brings.

THE LAST OF MRS. CHEYNEY

In 1925, two years after the premiere of *Aren't We All?*, Lonsdale's most successful nonmusical play was staged. *The Last of Mrs. Cheyney* is, in a sense, an anomalous play because it resurrects the atmosphere and many of the devices of nineteenth century society melodrama. The echoes of, for example, Oscar Wilde's *Lady Windermere's Fan* (pr. 1892) are very strong, particularly during the second-act climax, which involves a woman being trapped in compromising circumstances with a man of dubious reputation. Lonsdale, however, amusingly inverts the formula to create a comedy drama with several well-placed *coups de théâtre*. The one that ends the first act is particularly effective. Mrs. Cheyney, apparently a wealthy widow from Australia, is holding a charity concert in the garden of her house. The concert is attended by various representatives of London society, including the upright Lord Elton, the disreputable Lord Dilling, and Mrs. Ebley, a woman who has grown rich on the attentions of other women's husbands. Lord Elton and Lord Dilling are both attracted to Mrs. Cheyney, but Elton's intentions are honorable whereas Dilling's are not. Rather unusually, Mrs. Cheyney's establishment seems to be staffed entirely by menservants; one of them, Charles the butler, strikes a chord in Dilling's memory. The butler is suspiciously gentlemanly, and Dilling suspects that they were at Oxford together. When the guests leave at the end of the concert, Mrs. Cheyney, who has represented herself as someone who neither smokes nor drinks nor swears, immediately lights a cigarette, burns her fingers on the match, and curses. Then, as she sits at the piano and begins to play, her menservants enter, sprawl on the furniture, and smoke. It becomes clear that they and Mrs. Cheyney are a gang of jewel thieves bent on relieving Mrs. Ebley of her pearls.

The play's second act builds to a similar bravura climax. It is set in Mrs. Ebley's house, where the characters from act 1 have assembled for the weekend. The plot to rob Mrs. Ebley is foiled by Lord Dilling, who, having recognized Charles as a jewel thief whom he had once encountered in Paris, switches bedrooms with Mrs. Ebley and catches Mrs. Cheyney as she comes in to steal the pearls. Dilling presents a proposition: Either Mrs. Cheyney can submit to him and remain undiscovered or he will ring the bell and turn her over to the police. Instead, Mrs. Cheyney rings the bell herself and, in front of Dilling, Elton, and the rest, hands back the pearls to Mrs. Ebley.

Act 3, adding a touch of Augustin Scribe and Victorien Sardou to the Wildean mix, revolves around a letter. Written by Elton to Mrs. Cheyney and containing a proposal of marriage, it also includes a number of painfully accurate pen portraits of the upper-class set in which Mrs. Cheyney has been moving and of which the stiff-necked Elton intensely disapproves. The possibility that Mrs. Cheyney might use this letter to cause a scandal prompts heavy bidding for its return. Elton writes Mrs. Cheyney a check for ten thousand pounds, and Mrs. Ebley promises to drop the charges of theft. Mrs. Cheyney accepts the check but then tears it up and informs them that she has already torn up the letter. The members of the house party, amazed by this, are even more amazed when they learn that it was she and not Dilling who rang the bell in Mrs. Ebley's bedroom. Their attitude to-

ward her changes; they see her as someone with a sense of good sportsmanship, which is their equivalent of honor. Somewhat surprisingly, she is willing to be reabsorbed into the set that has shown itself so eager to reject her, and, as the play closes, she agrees to become Dilling's wife.

Lonsdale's two chief themes echo throughout this play. Mrs. Cheyney is clearly more interested in being accepted by society than in thieving from it. As she says to Charles, her butler and coconspirator, toward the end of the first act: "I'm sorry, but I didn't realise when I adopted this profession that the people I would have to take things from would be quite so nice." Even when they have proved themselves not "quite so nice," she is willing to forgive and be forgiven by them. On the other hand, the flaws of the play's three main representatives of high society are repeatedly exposed to the audience. Lord Elton is priggish and pompous; Lord Dilling is a wastrel and a womanizer; Mrs. Ebley exploits her appeal for men. At the climax of the play, the unmasking of Mrs. Cheyney is paralleled by the unmasking of society itself. Lonsdale's ambivalence is amply demonstrated.

The pleasures and perils of disguise are illustrated chiefly in the characters of Mrs. Cheyney and Charles, though William the footman, Jim the chauffeur, and George the page boy are also implicated in the masquerade. Mrs. Cheyney and Charles, however, unlike the latter three, who are lower-class "Cockney" types, are represented as people of grace, wit, and charm, educated people who might well have made their way into society by legitimate means but who have chosen a more adventurous course. At the same time, their actions are given a moral color that verges on Lincoln green, inasmuch as the people they rob deserve it, having in their turn, morally speaking, robbed others:

> CHARLES: I'm not trying to persuade you, my sweet, but there is this to be remembered, the pearls we want from Mrs. Ebley were taken by that lady, without a scruple, from the wives of the men who gave them to her.

Mrs. Cheyney is persuaded, and she goes on to play a bold and dangerous game, seemingly courting exposure and disaster but winning through to acceptance and marriage into the peerage.

The Last of Mrs. Cheyney is a very skillful theatrical piece, with cleverly placed reversals, recognitions, crises, and climaxes. It is an admirable mechanism, like a fine example of a Swiss clockmaker's art, and as such it can still be persuasive on the stage. Yet in *The Last of Mrs. Cheyney*, Lonsdale had not yet achieved as sure a grasp of his themes as he did in his next play, *On Approval*.

ON APPROVAL

On Approval is in many respects the most economical of Lonsdale's comedies. It has only four characters, dispensing with the clutter of minor figures that in the earlier plays give substance and color to the milieu but contribute little to the action. The premise of the play is as self-consciously daring as that of Coward's *Private Lives*, to which it also bears a certain structural resemblance. The principal characters, Maria Wislak and the Duke of Bristol, are as monstrously egotistical as Coward's Eliot and Amanda, though they belong not so much to the smart set who honeymoon on the Riviera as to the landed gentry who grouse-shoot in Scotland. Like *Private Lives*, *On Approval* is a minuet of changing alliances. The action is initiated by the wealthy Maria, who decides that the pleasant but penniless Richard Halton may be a suitable candidate for her next husband. To try him out, she proposes to take him to her house in Scotland for a month. Her longtime enemy, the Duke of Bristol, decides that he will go, too, ostensibly to lend Richard moral support but actually to escape his creditors. The fourth member of the group is an attractive, good-natured pickle heiress, Helen Hayle, who follows in pursuit of the duke, with whom she is in love.

In the course of the action, Lonsdale leaves the audience in no doubt that the representatives of the ruling class are outrageously and comically tiresome. Not only do Maria and the duke berate and abuse each other incessantly, but also they treat the penniless Richard and Helen, the pickle-profiteer's daughter, like servants. The effect of this is to draw Richard and Helen closer together, and finally they conspire to sneak away in the only available automobile, just

as a massive snowstorm is beginning—a snowstorm that threatens to trap the monstrous Maria and the appalling duke together for several weeks. As Richard says: "It's the kindest thing that has ever been done for them. Such hell as a month alone here together will make them the nicest people in the world." This denouement recalls that of *Private Lives*, in which Eliot and Amanda tiptoe out of the Paris apartment to which they have eloped, leaving their respective spouses, Victor and Sybil, quarreling violently. Because *Private Lives* appeared two years later than *On Approval*, it is more than probable that Coward learned something from Lonsdale about the construction of sophisticated drawing-room comedies.

Clearly, in *On Approval*, Lonsdale has resolved his conflict with respect to acceptance/rejection by society. In this play, it is the upwardly mobile who are the "nice" people, unequivocally; the established members of society may yet become "nice" but only through undergoing an ordeal of isolation in uncongenial company. There is no falsely sentimental juxtaposition of gentlemen and jewel thieves, or duchesses and ex-chorus girls, with Lonsdale judiciously trying to hold the balance; here he rightly identifies with the aspiring middle class and asserts his own niceness against the arrogance of the upper class.

Lonsdale's other perennial theme, of masks and unmasking, is also present, though in a subtler form than in *The Last of Mrs. Cheyney*. Maria Wislak takes Richard Halton "on approval" to find out if he is as pleasant and congenial as he appears to be. She decides that he is, but meanwhile Richard has found out that Maria is not as she has appeared to him for twenty years, "too good, too beautiful, too noble" for him; indeed, she is "one of the most unpleasant of God's creatures." Like Lady Mary Carlisle in *Monsieur Beaucaire*, Maria is deeply chagrined at this turn of events: "To think I brought the brute here to find out if I like him, and he has the audacity the moment I tell him I do, to tell me he doesn't like me!" Similarly, Helen sees through the Duke of Bristol's charm to the spoiled schoolboy underneath: "To make him a decent man he needs six months before the mast as a common sailor." The misunderstandings and deceits that complicate the lives of the four characters in *On Approval* are much more character-based than in the somewhat mechanically contrived *Aren't We All?* and *The Last of Mrs. Cheyney*.

The dialogue, too, is more distinctive, more deft and more plausible. Instead of the secondhand epigrams of Lord Grenham and Lord Dilling, there is the genuine crackle and tension of strong-willed people using language as a weapon to penetrate their opponents' armor of conceit and self-absorption. The play's witty lines cannot be taken out of context to survive as freestanding aphorisms; their humor depends entirely on the audience's understanding of the characters of Maria, the duke, Richard, and Helen, and of the conflicts between them.

LET THEM EAT CAKE

On Approval is the high point of Lonsdale's achievement as a comic playwright. Though he continued to write sporadically for another quarter of a century and though none of the plays he wrote in that period (except *The Foreigners*) lost money, he never quite repeated the artistic and popular success he reached with his comedies of the mid-1920's. A typical example of his later work is *Let Them Eat Cake*, which like many of Lonsdale's plays is a revision, or a renaming at least, of an earlier one. *On Approval*, for example, was a substantial revision of an early, unproduced work, "The Follies of the Foolish," and *Aren't We All?* was a reworking of *The Best People*. *Let Them Eat Cake* was first titled *Half a Loaf* (written in 1937), was produced in 1938 as *Once Is Enough*, reappeared as *Half a Loaf* at the Theatre Royal, Windsor, in 1958, four years after Lonsdale's death, and finally opened at the Cambridge Theatre, London, in 1959, as *Let Them Eat Cake*. In it, Lonsdale reverts to the pattern of earlier plays such as *Aren't We All?* Indeed, its theme of marital misunderstanding is not dissimilar, and its cast list is even more replete with titled characters, including the Duke and Duchess of Hampshire, Lord and Lady Plynne, Lord and Lady Whitehall, Lord Rayne, and Lady Bletchley. The main action involves Johnny, the Duke of Hampshire, who becomes infatuated with Liz Pleydell, the wife of his friend Charles, and Nancy, the Duchess of Hampshire, who attempts to save their marriage. Johnny is prepared to leave his

wife and run away with Mrs. Pleydell to her orange plantation in South Africa. Nancy prevents them by the simple expedient of telling Mrs. Pleydell that she will not divorce Johnny, thereby rendering Mrs. Pleydell's social status, if she persists in going off to live with him, uncomfortably precarious. In the rather unconvincing denouement, Johnny realizes that Mrs. Pleydell's real object is not him, but his title, and that he has been suffering from the "temporary disease" of infatuation.

The main characters are even less attractive than those in *On Approval*, but in this case unintentionally so. There is also, as in *Aren't We All?* and *The Last of Mrs. Cheyney*, a superfluity of minor figures who have little function other than to provide a sort of living decor. Furthermore, the dialogue has the secondhand ring of reach-me-down epigrams, common in the earlier plays, as in this exchange:

> LADY BLETCHLEY: What actually is cirrhosis of the liver?
> REGGIE [LORD RAYNE]: A tribute nature pays to men who have completely conquered Teetotalism!

All in all, the play marks a regression in Lonsdale's technique: less economical and integrated than *On Approval* and less splendidly theatrical than *The Last of Mrs. Cheyney*.

OTHER MAJOR WORKS

SCREENPLAYS: *The Devil to Pay*, 1930; *Lovers Courageous*, 1932; *The Private Life of Don Juan*, 1934 (with Lajos Biro); *Forever and a Day*, 1943 (with Charles Bennett, C. S. Forester, John Van Druten, Christopher Isherwood, R. C. Sherriff, and others).

BIBLIOGRAPHY

Donaldson, Frances. *Freddy*. Philadelphia: J. B. Lippincott, 1957. This biography was written by the playwright's daughter, herself an actress and author. She paints an affectionate portrait of her father, being careful to discuss the weaknesses as well as the virtues of his character. She tells the remarkable story of a young man who was a shopkeeper's son and who had little formal education but who, because of his talent and native wit, transformed himself into one of the most successful authors of high comedy and chroniclers of England's upper class during the 1920's. She also notes that when one of his plays was revived in the 1950's, critics such as Kenneth Tynan dismissed him as irrelevant.

Kemp, Philip. "Cry Ho! The Eccentricities of . . . *On Approval*." *Film Comment* 35, no. 5 (September/October, 1999): 10-15. This essay on the 1947 film adaptation of Lonsdale's *On Approval* discusses the film and contrasts it with the play.

Nicoll, Allardyce. *English Drama*. Cambridge, England: Cambridge University Press, 1973. Nicoll believes that Lonsdale occupied the middle ground between W. Somerset Maugham and Noël Coward and was overshadowed by both. Lonsdale lacked Maugham's depth and Coward's cleverness, and although he enjoyed great success before and immediately after World War I, his lack of ideas soon dated him. Bibliography.

Stevens, Lianne. "Gaslamp's *On Approval* Gets Hearty Approval." Review of *On Approval* by Frederick Lonsdale. *Los Angeles Times*, August 19, 1986, p. 2. This revival of *On Approval* at the Gaslamp Quarter Theatre demonstrated Lonsdale's surge in popularity in the latter part of the twentieth century.

Anthony Stephenson,
updated by Mildred C. Kuner

EARL LOVELACE

Born: Toco, Trinidad; July 13, 1935

PRINCIPAL DRAMA

The New Boss, pr. 1962
My Name Is Village, pr. 1976, pb. 1984
Pierrot Ginnard, pr. 1977
Jestina's Calypso, pr. 1978, pb. 1984
The New Hardware Store, pr. 1980, pb. 1984
Jestina's Calypso and Other Plays, pb. 1984
    (includes *The New Hardware Store* and *My Name Is Village*)
The Dragon Can't Dance, pr. 1986, pb. 1989
    (adaptation of his novel)
The Wine of Astonishment, pr. 1987 (adaptation of his novel)

OTHER LITERARY FORMS

Earl Lovelace is better known for his novels than his plays. His first novel, *While Gods are Falling* (1965), won the 1963 competition for the British Petroleum Independence Literary Award as the best unpublished novel by a national of Trinidad dealing with West Indian themes. With the publication of *The Dragon Can't Dance* (1979) and *The Wine of Astonishment* (1982)—he later dramatized both novels—Lovelace was hailed as an outstanding Caribbean writer, and critical articles analyzing his novels appeared in literary journals. Lovelace also published a volume of short stories, *A Brief Conversion and Other Stories* (1988), based on his experiences as a civil servant in the Trinidad departments of agriculture and forestry.

ACHIEVEMENTS

After winning the $5,000 British Petroleum Independence Literary Award in 1964, Earl Lovelace received the Pegasus Literary Award in 1966 for outstanding contributions to the arts in Trinidad and Tobago. In 1977 *Pierrot Ginnard* won an award as best musical drama. Lovelace received a Guggenheim Fellowship in 1980, using it to attend the International Writing Program at the University of Iowa and the International Seminar Program of the Eastern Virginia International Studies Consortium. In 1986 Lovelace received a National Endowment for the Humanities grant as writer-in-residence at Hartwick College, Oneonta, New York. In 1997 Lovelace's novel *Salt* (1996) won the Commonwealth Writer's Prize.

BIOGRAPHY

Soon after his birth, Earl Lovelace moved with his mother to the island of Tobago, where they lived with his mother's parents. Lovelace credits his grandmother, Eva Whatley, of African and American Indian ancestry, and his mother, Jean Whatley Lovelace, as major influences during his youth. Although Lovelace attended Scarborough Methodist Primary School in Tobago before moving to Port of Spain, Trinidad, for his high school years, 1948 to 1953, he considers himself largely self-educated. Beginning in early childhood, Lovelace read American and English literature voraciously, especially admiring William Faulkner and Ernest Hemingway.

From 1953 to 1954 Lovelace worked as a proofreader for a Trinidad newspaper. In 1956 he became a forest ranger for the Department of Forestry, remaining in the Trinidad civil service as an agricultural assistant in the Department of Agriculture until 1966. During the 1961-1962 school year Lovelace attended the Eastern Caribbean Institute of Agriculture and Forestry. His work experiences deepened Lovelace's understanding of the land and people of Trinidad, informing the widely praised descriptive passages and the vernacular language of his books and plays.

Lovelace's first novel, *While Gods Are Falling* (1965) tells the story of Walter Castle, who migrated from his rural birthplace to the slums of Trinidad's capital city, Port of Spain. Castle's memories of his home village's supportive community contrast with the problems of poor families struggling against the destructive life of urban slums. The novel ends on a utopian note as Castle succeeds in uniting his neighbors to help young people survive the poisonous urban environment.

In 1966 Lovelace resumed his education, spending a year at Howard University in Washington, D.C. During the summer of 1967, he taught at Virginia Union University, in Richmond. Lovelace returned to Trinidad in 1967, becoming a columnist and editorial writer for the daily *Trinidad and Tobago Express* while continuing to write novels.

Lovelace's second novel, *The Schoolmaster* (1968), is set in a remote interior Trinidad village. It opens with a sentimental description of a rural village unified by strong traditions and stable families. A modernizing schoolteacher, who has no empathy for or understanding of the inhabitants, disrupts this Eden. Lovelace uses the villagers' everyday speech patterns to describe the tragic impact of modernization on the people of the village.

From 1971 to 1973 Lovelace taught at the University of the District of Columbia, Washington, D.C. The following year he entered the Johns Hopkins University writing program, earning an M.A. in 1974. When one of the instructors left for a Fullbright Fellowship, Lovelace took over his course. In 1977 he began teaching creative writing and literature at the University of the West Indies, St. Augustine, Trinidad.

Lovelace draws on his command of rural black colloquial speech effectively in the novels *The Dragon Can't Dance* and *The Wine of Astonishment*. In the latter, he successfully uses the voice of an uneducated protagonist to portray the destructive impact of religious persecution on the people of a rural village.

To illustrate problems of achieving national identity, Lovelace employs Trinidad folk tales in *Salt*. Alford George, an aspiring politician who embraces European ideals, fails in his attempts to carry out land reform. In contrast Bango, who kept in touch with the African culture of his ancestors, successfully inspires major ethnic groups of Trinidad with a new sense of communal understanding.

When he won a Guggenheim Fellowship in 1980, Lovelace returned to the United States and joined the Writers' Program at the University of Iowa. A National Endowment for the Humanities grant in 1986 took him to Hartwick College, Oneonta, New York, as writer-in-residence. Unlike some West Indian authors who moved to the United States or Europe after becoming famous, Lovelace remained faithful to Trinidad. He preferred to live with his wife and three children in the rural village of Matura, despite its lack of modern conveniences and distance from the capital city, Port of Spain.

ANALYSIS

Earl Lovelace's plays are frequently experimental, avoiding straight-line plot exposition and incorporating allegorical elements that signal their deeper relevance. In each play, singing and dancing exemplify traditional cultures resisting change.

Critics have correctly stressed the importance of achieving personhood in Lovelace's work. In every play, characters struggle to discover who they are and to gain individuality, despite the homogenizing pressures of an impersonal urban world. The plays explore the anxieties created by Trinidad's ethnic diversity and deplore the impact of urbanization and modernization on traditional Trinidadian life and culture.

Lovelace's plays clearly reflect the social tensions that divide Trinidad's ethnically varied population. Forty percent of the inhabitants are descended from African slaves imported during the eighteenth and early nineteenth centuries. After emancipation in 1838, the island's plantation economy faced a shortage of labor. In 1845 Great Britain agreed to permit importation of indentured laborers from India— always referred to as East Indians to differentiate them from nearly extinct original West Indians. In the twentieth century, East Indians became approximately equal in number to blacks. Some 18 percent of Trinidadians are of mixed heritage, while 2 percent are of European or Chinese descent. Although East Indians view themselves as culturally superior and maintain their own social and religious customs, blacks consider East Indians socially inferior, and the lightest skinned blacks join Europeans at the top of the social hierarchy.

Lovelace dramatizes the impact of modernization on traditional cultural and social practices. Trinidad's blacks transformed African patterns of singing and dancing into indigenous forms, notably calypso songs and the elaborate festivities of Carnival. However, as sugar plantations declined in importance, Trinidad's population shifted from rural areas to cities. By the end of the twentieth century, nearly three-quarters of the population lived in urban places. Few people had the skills to profit from the growing importance of the oil and petrochemical industries, and many families lived in poverty-stricken slums. The presence of United States troops during World War II introduced Trinidadians to American consumer goods and patterns of consumption. Leading characters in Lovelace's plays strive, with limited success, to maintain African-inflected customs against pressures for change.

MY NAME IS VILLAGE

The central action of the play concerns the struggle of Towntest with Roy Village. As the play begins, the older villagers come home from the fields singing work songs while four unemployed young men practice karate and break into a dance. Several high school girls arrive, joining Roy and his friends, Quickly and Smart, in singing and dancing. Towntest and two Yes Men, echoing everything he says, enter, revealing the urban world of pleasure and progress to the villagers. Towntest's enticements attract Roy. After Roy's father, Cyril Village, praises the beauty of their rural home, Roy rejects Towntest's blandishments. The play ends with everyone singing a hymn celebrating village life. For the first performance of the play in Port of Spain, in September, 1976, Lovelace used a cast consisting of neighbors he had rehearsed in his home village of Matura.

JESTINA'S CALYPSO

Jestina, the proprietor of a small retail store, is thirty-nine and unable to find anyone to marry her. She has been corresponding with an expatriate Trinidadian and has convinced him to return to Trinidad and marry her. Worried that she may be too black and ugly to please her suitor, Jestina sent him photographs of Laura, a younger and much lighter complexioned neighbor. Jestina dresses to go to the airport with Laura to meet the suitor, wondering how he will respond when he actually sees her. Neighbors sing derisive songs outside her window, mocking Jestina's unmarried state, and her ugliness. Jestina compares herself to Trinidad, with "breasts dragged down by centuries of bearing cane and coffee and cocoa" and "the marrow of my bones drained out like oil, pumped out, syphoned to infuse another's heart." Act two contains a play-within-a-play, in which the mocking neighbors re-enact Jestina's courtship and her rejection at the airport, interjecting calypso songs. At the close, Jestina returns, calling herself an ugly duckling whom only a prince's kiss can turn into a queen, but there is no man who has the courage to appreciate her. On one level the play calls on black men to recognize the diversity of black people and accept more than one standard of personal beauty. On another level it asks Trinidadians to develop a true sense of nationalism by appreciating their country and its land.

THE NEW HARDWARE STORE

As the audience passes through the lobby, Rooso, the store's advertiser, wearing placards on his chest and back, chants the praises of A. A. Ablack's hardware store. When the audience is seated, the play begins. Ablack, who took over the store after its white owner left the village during the Black Power demonstrations of the 1970's, faces discontent among his employees. His bookkeeper, Miss Calliste, requests that her vacation include time off she had earned, but not taken, under the white owner, but Ablack rejects her plea. Rooso refuses to carry out menial tasks assigned by Ablack. In the second act, Rooso sings calypso songs as everyone dances and turns into allegorical characters. Rooso is the embodiment of Carnival, Ablack the spirit of capitalism. Rooso also becomes a guerrilla leader reported killed during the Black Power protests. Miss Calliste transforms into the spirit of Trinidad and then into the lover of the guerrilla leader. She has been mourning his death and now celebrates his reappearance. At the end of the play the employees leave to sing calypsos during lunch, while Ablack contemplates replacing them with younger, more modern employees.

THE DRAGON CAN'T DANCE

The scene is Calvary Hill, a slum neighborhood in Port of Spain, where the residents and the local steel band are preparing for Carnival. Aldrick, leader of the area, is assembling his dragon costume. Young Sylvia would like to be with Aldrick, but he is unable to buy her a Carnival costume and she turns instead to Mr. Guy, the rent collector. Philo, a dark-skinned writer of calypso songs, loves lighter-skinned Cleothilda, queen of the yard, who snubs him. Pariag, an East Indian peddler, has moved to the Hill hoping for the inhabitants' friendship; they ignore him. When Pariag buys a bicycle to carry his merchandise, the neighborhood leaders are furious at his presumptuous acquisition of material goods superior to theirs; one morning, he finds his bicycle smashed. A Port of Spain corporation agrees to sponsor the Hill's steel band, providing uniforms bearing the company's logo. To be respectable and retain their sponsor, the steel band expels Fisheye, a street brawler.

Philo wins the Calypso Crown by abandoning the protest songs he previously wrote, substituting sexy lyrics; Cleothilda now views him favorably. Aldrick joins Fisheye in seizing a police car. When they name themselves the People's Liberation Army and call on the people of Calvary Hill to rise up and take power, no one follows them. Aldrick returns after five years in jail, musing that his rebellion and his Carnival dragon were nothing but masquerades. He realizes the dragon cannot dance again.

THE WINE OF ASTONISHMENT

In the interior village of Bonasse, Bee is the leader of the Spiritual, or Shouter, Baptists, who have added African ritual practices to Christianity. Using drums and bells to summon up the Spirit, they sing, shout, and talk in tongues when It appears, although the British government banned such behavior as devil worship in 1917. Following World War II, Trinidadians secured the right to vote, and Bee works hard to elect a local boy, Ivan Morton to the Governing Council, hoping he can bring religious freedom. Once in power, Morton does nothing. When Bee importunes him, Morton urges Bee to give up his superstitions, telling him that although Bee cannot become white, he can at least act white. When the congregation again violates the law, police raid the church and abusively arrest the people. Bolo, a champion stick fighter, frustrated by his inability to protect his friends, turns on the community, kidnaps two girls, and is shot by the police. When religious freedom is finally granted in 1951, the congregation finds that years of repression have tamed them. Ritual can no longer work its magic.

OTHER MAJOR WORKS

LONG FICTION: *While Gods Are Falling*, 1965; *The Schoolmaster*, 1968; *The Dragon Can't Dance*, 1979; *The Wine of Astonishment*, 1982; *Salt*, 1996.

SHORT FICTION: *A Brief Conversion and Other Stories*, 1988.

BIBLIOGRAPHY

Dance, Daryl Cumber. *Fifty Caribbean Writers: A Bio-Bibliographical Sourcebook.* New York: Greenwood Press, 1986. Devotes a chapter to Lovelace, analyzing his major works and listing scholarly articles concerning his books. Dance considers the quest for personhood (a term Lovelace prefers to manhood or identity), and the difficulty of achieving a true sense of self in an impersonal modern urban environment, as the major themes of his writings.

James, Louis. *Caribbean Literature in English.* New York: Longman, 1999. Provides a brief history of West Indian literature before turning to twentieth century writing dealing with the islands. One chapter discusses Trinidadian authors. James devotes another chapter to Lovelace, one of six major Caribbean writers granted separate chapters.

Taylor, Patrick. "Ethnicity and Social Change in Trinidadian Literature." In *Trinidad Ethnicity*, edited by Kevin A. Yelvington. Knoxville: University of Tennessee Press, 1993. Sees Lovelace as challenging ethnic stereotypes to open possibilities of building a more just society in Trinidad.

Thomas, H. Nigel. "From 'Freedom' to 'Liberation': An Interview with Earl Lovelace." *World Literature Written in English* 31 (Spring, 1991), 8-20. Lovelace describes his use of language and symbols within his novels and plays.

Milton Berman

CRAIG LUCAS

Born: Atlanta, Georgia; April 30, 1951

PRINCIPAL DRAMA

Marry Me a Little, pr. 1980 (with Norman René; music and lyrics by Stephen Sondheim)

Missing Persons, pr. 1981, pb. 1995

Reckless, pr., pb. 1983

Blue Window, pr., pb. 1984

Three Postcards, pr. 1987, pb. 1988 (music and lyrics by Craig Carnelia)

Prelude to a Kiss, pr. 1988, pb. 1990

Orpheus in Love, pr. 1992 (libretto; music by Gerald Busby)

God's Heart, pr. 1993, pb. 1999

The Dying Gaul, pr. 1998, pb. 1999

Stranger, pr. 2000, pb. 2002

This Thing of Darkness, pr. 2002

OTHER LITERARY FORMS

In addition to the plays listed above, Craig Lucas has written many one-act plays, five screenplays, and essays about theater for periodicals and anthologies. His best-known screenplays are for *Longtime Companion* (1990), one of the first major films to treat the subject of AIDS (acquired immunodeficiency syndrome), and *Prelude to a Kiss* (1992).

ACHIEVEMENTS

Craig Lucas's work has been given recognition in the form of prizes and fellowships, including Rockefeller, Guggenheim, and National Endowment for the Arts/Theater Communications Group awards. He has received a Tony nomination and been a Pulitzer finalist. Prizes won include George and Elisabeth Marton Awards (*Blue Window*, 1984), Los Angeles Drama Critics Award (*Blue Window*, 1985), Sundance Audience Award (*Longtime Companion*, 1990), Burns Mantle Best Musical (*Three Postcards*, 1987), the Excellence in Literature Award from the American Academy of Art and Letters (2000), and an Obie (2001) for his direction of *Saved or Destroyed* (pr. 2000) by Harry Kondoleon.

BIOGRAPHY

Craig Lucas was born in Atlanta, Georgia, in 1951 and attended Boston University where he studied with poet Anne Sexton and historian Howard Zinn. He credits Sexton with encouraging him to switch from poetry to plays; she also helped him get into Yale Drama School but then urged him to forego graduate school for a career in New York. Initially focused on acting and performing in the chorus of musicals, Lucas found another mentor in Stephen Sondheim and began his writing career by fashioning a show composed of discarded Sondheim songs. The revue, entitled *Marry Me a Little*, was produced with director Norman René, the first of many collaborations between the two. After some success writing for the New York stage, Lucas turned to screenwriting with *Longtime Companion* (1990), a film about a group of gay friends responding to the onset of the AIDS epidemic, and one of the first Hollywood vehicles to acknowledge the disease. A play written about the same time, *Prelude to a Kiss*, then became a film starring Meg Ryan and Alec Baldwin in 1992. Subsequently Lucas has focused both on dramas with a tragic focus, such as *The Dying Gaul*, and on works with music, such as his opera libretti with scores by Gerald Busby. His work has been nurtured by several not-for-profit theater groups, including South Coast Repertory, Berkeley Repertory, Playwrights Horizons, Circle Repertory, Atlantic Theater Company, and A Contemporary Theatre.

ANALYSIS

Craig Lucas is a versatile playwright with a serious sideline in musical theater. His work can be classified as postmodern in its playful disregard for realism and its emphasis on the uncertainty, even the absurdity, of modern life. In this respect, his work may be seen as influenced by Edward Albee, Eugène Ionesco, and even Samuel Beckett. On the other hand, some of his work, such as *Reckless*, has a lightness in the face of de-

spair that echoes the tone of such contemporaries as Stephen Sondheim and Caryl Churchill. In the early part of his career, Lucas did not treat gay themes directly or include many gay characters in his works. He has attributed this both to an initial reluctance to come out as a gay man to his family, to his belief that a playwright should create characters rather than model them on himself, and to the lack of models of effective gay drama when he was starting to write in the late 1970's. Nevertheless, it is possible to see a gay subtext in even his earliest plays, which do not mention AIDS but nonetheless treat the suffering that occurs when unexpected illnesses and death leave

Craig Lucas, left, with Norman René, director of Lucas's Prelude to a Kiss, *in 1990.*
(AP/Wide World Photos)

loved ones in shock and mourning. Thus his plays may be said to treat AIDS as representative of the kind of life-threatening calamity that men and women are vulnerable to at any time. Examples of such vulnerability include the many calamities in *Reckless*, the death of Libby's husband in *Blue Window*, and Rita's transformation in *Prelude to a Kiss*. With *God's Heart*, the tone of Lucas's work began to darken, a trend that continued with *The Dying Gaul* and *Stranger*.

RECKLESS

This play begins on Christmas Eve with the black comedy premise that a man, having second thoughts about the hit he ordered on his wife, Rachel, urges her to flee out the window before the killer arrives. Leaping in her nightdress, Rachel assumes a new identity that foists further confusion on her before she can reconcile herself to the past. First, she is taken in by Lloyd and his wife, Pooty, a paralyzed deaf woman. After Rachel has learned to communicate with the couple in sign language, Pooty reveals to her that the deafness is a charade designed to make Lloyd feel that she needs him. The three friends are visited by Rachel's now repentant husband, Tom, but before reconciliation can take place, Tom and Pooty are poisoned by a mysterious bottle of champagne left on the doorstep. In fear of being viewed as murderers, Rachel and Lloyd flee, but his deteriorating mental state leads him to subsist only on champagne and refuse to change out of the Santa suit he was wearing at the time of the poisonings. After Lloyd starves to death, Rachel ironically becomes a psychologist—ironic because throughout the play she has sought help from mental health professionals, only to have her concerns repeatedly trivialized or misunderstood. (One of her therapists turns out to be the school bus driver who ran over Rachel's mother when Rachel was six). In the final scene, Rachel realizes that her new client is her son, who believes she abandoned him and his brother on that Christmas Eve many years earlier. The play's last exchanges of dialogue imply the possibility of reconciliation for mother and son.

On the surface, *Reckless* takes its audience for a wild ride through Rachel's chaotic and violence-strewn experience. The often brutal world of this play

begins and ends in the context of Christmas, raising questions about the sentimental visions of family harmony associated with that holiday. Rachel's fellow sufferer, Lloyd, wears a Santa Claus suit through a crucial section of the play during which he is grieving the death of his wife and depriving himself of nutrition. Rachel's endurance amid the absurd coincidences and painful stripping away of human ties makes her resemble a suffering Beckett character. The last-minute reunion of mother and son, however, is a more hopeful gesture than we often find in Theater of the Absurd.

BLUE WINDOW

Blue Window is experimental in form on several levels. In this text, Lucas juxtaposes scenes of various guests getting ready for a dinner party against glimpses of the hostess's anxiety as she prepares to receive them. Lucas establishes a surface of trivial conversation while insinuating a subtext suggesting the great anxiety felt by the hostess Libby. The overlapping dialogue of the opening scene creates a feeling of absurdity as a lesbian couple practice arbitrary Italian phrases ("The highway is pink"), Libby's friend Griever performs lines from *A Streetcar Named Desire* (pr., pr. 1947) and mimics singer Diana Ross, and Tom attempts to compose the music of a song, worrying about the not-yet-written words. The play appears to have virtually no plot, other than the idea that Libby is very nervous about entertaining and relies on Griever to reassure her that the party will be successful. Over the course of the evening, the characters reveal their personal and professional preoccupations. Several are artists: Alice is a novelist, Griever a painter, and Tom a musician. Alice's female lover, Boo, is a family therapist. Norbert is Libby's skydiving instructor (though she has not yet jumped out of a plane). Only Emily, a secretary, pushes away all discussion of her work.

The structure of *Blue Window* can only be understood once Libby narrates the secret of her grief to Norbert, late in the play. She tells him of the terrible accident that sent her and her new husband, Marty, toppling over the side of the terrace of their seventh story apartment. Marty was killed; Libby survived with broken bones, ruined teeth, and a traumatized

Critical Survey of Drama

heart. Why does Lucas withhold Libby's story until so late in the play? The answer to that question lurks in the prior conversations characters have about the artistic choices made by musicians and writers. Alice talks of trying to capture the intangible and locate the resonant meaning behind the words of a play. Libby praises Alice for weaving characters together like music. Tom ponders the way that a favorite jazz musician can create the suggestion of a melody without actually playing a melody. Even Boo's work as a therapist is described in a way that seems relevant to Lucas's indirect method of revealing the heart of his plot. She gives the example of a child whose apparent learning disorder, indicated by a refusal to read, masks the deeper family problem of the father's illiteracy. With the source of Libby's grief revealed, the significance of earlier conversations emerges: Both Libby's story and the impossibility of conveying her story are the subtext of much of the preceding dialogue. The rest of the play forms a kind of coda in which the characters express their flawed love for one another in different ways, perhaps most movingly in the discovery that quiet Emily has, in fact, written the words for the song Tom has been trying to create.

PRELUDE TO A KISS

In this fantastical story, Rita, a young bride, is kissed by a mysterious old man on her wedding day and finds that she has traded her youth for his age. The story is told principally from the point-of-view of her husband, Peter, who gradually realizes that the body switch has occurred and who valiantly works to restore the spirit of Rita into the proper body. Obviously, this plot veers far from realism. It evokes stories as old as Geoffrey Chaucer's *Pardoner's Tale* (part of the *Canterbury Tales*, 1387-1400) in which an ancient wanderer tries to cheat death by regaining his youth in the form of some kind of trade. Peter's struggle is twofold: On the one hand, he wants to "fix" things by getting the original Rita back; on the other, he realizes that the Rita he loves exists in the old man's body, and that he can love her, if he has to, in that form.

An unexpected dimension of the body switch between Rita and the Old Man is that in some measure Rita also willed it to happen. She appears early in the

play as an endearing but very frightened character, so anxious about the state of the world that she cannot sleep and refuses to consider having children. Rita's view of the world as precarious accords with Lucas's presentation of random fates in his earlier works. Here, the risks of living are underscored by Peter's bemused account of the signs placed on roller coasters, "Ride at your own risk." His interpretation of the sign both mocks the likelihood of real risk in such a ride and acknowledges the fear that something mechanical or even supernatural will send the whole ride careening off the tracks. When Rita is confronted with the Old Man on her wedding day, she briefly fantasizes being at the end of life, having gotten past the terrors latent in a lifetime; she thinks of being close to death as a kind of victory. Given this, we might begin to wonder whether Rita has the will to return to her youthful self, knowing the risks of the years ahead. That her love for Peter finally motivates her to shed her fears and seek a full life is another one of Lucas's nods to a hope of happiness in spite of everything.

THE DYING GAUL

Lucas shocked many with the production of *The Dying Gaul* in 1998. The negative response was such that Lucas appended an afterward to the published text, objecting to the narrow-mindedness of critics who expected all his work to be in the playful vein of *Prelude to a Kiss*. *The Dying Gaul* does not have many light moments. The play directly addresses the grief of gay men for lovers lost to AIDS. Lucas acknowledges writing the play in twelve days shortly after the death of his lover and a series of other painful losses, including the deaths of his parents. The play foregrounds both the survivor's vulnerability and his anger, his guilt over helping his lover die, and his own persistent thoughts of suicide. Lucas's alter-ego in the play, Robert, is a writer currently negotiating with a Hollywood mogul over *The Dying Gaul*, a screenplay. Some of the play's few comic moments come as Jeffrey, the producer, explains to Robert why the studio loves his script yet wants him to make the AIDS-inflicted male character a woman, so as to appeal to a wider audience. Comedy gives way to a dark irony when Jeffrey, a married man with children, propositions Robert and reveals his avid bisexuality. Into the mix enters Elaine, Jeffrey's wife, whose apparent tolerance for his infidelity covers a wounded anger that erupts in the play's final scenes. Before the climax (with its report of offstage carnage worthy of Greek drama), an exchange takes place between Robert and Elaine resonant with both mysticism and modernity. With the help of some devious research (including a raid on the office of Robert's psychiatrist), Elaine manages to enter into an online relationship with Robert, hiding behind the screen name Arckangell. Robert, a student of Buddhism, has already confessed his tendency to see anonymous online messages as an opportunity for disembodied souls to communicate. Elaine exploits this receptivity by making Robert believe that his dead lover is contacting him from the other side, using the Internet as a kind of high-tech Ouija board. After gaining his trust, she leads him to reveal information that ultimately forces her rage at Jeffrey to the surface, precipitating the final catastrophe.

The Dying Gaul marks a shift in Lucas's work toward more direct confrontation with the specific horrors of contemporary life, a trend also visible in *God's Heart*, which tackles the reality of young African American men entrapped in the drug trade, and *Stranger*, inspired by a lurid crime. At the same time, some aspects of Lucas's earlier work structure *The Dying Gaul*, including fanciful or improbable plot twists that require the reader's suspension of disbelief. Early in the play, Jeffrey praises the film *Tootsie* (1982), for making an ideological, feminist point while at the same time managing to entertain rather than lecture the audience. However, Lucas does not follow that model. Rather, his play functions more like the statue Robert describes of a dying Gallic soldier, sculpted sympathetically by a Roman, his enemy. Robert suggests that if the enemy can empathize with his victim's suffering, then there is hope for reconciliation. Thus he presents his scathing play about the suffering caused by AIDS as a cry for attention from those who have not had reason to empathize with the victims of the disease.

OTHER MAJOR WORKS

SCREENPLAYS: *Longtime Companion*, 1990; *Prelude to a Kiss*, 1992 (adaptation of his play); *Reckless*, 1995 (adaptation of his play).

TELEPLAY: *Blue Window*, 1987.

BIBLIOGRAPHY

Schulman, Sarah. "Eyes Wide Open." *American Theatre* 18 (January, 2001): 36. A provocative interview that covers Lucas's personal life and professional career.

_____. *Stage Struck: Theater, AIDS, and the Marketing of Gay America.* Durham, N.C.: Duke University Press, 1998. Schulman discusses a variety of topics related to the portrayal of the gay experience in contemporary drama, asserting that works by straight writers conveyed a sanitized and false portrayal of gay life.

Sinfield, Alan. *Out on Stage: Lesbian and Gay Theater in the Twentieth Century.* New Haven, Conn.: Yale University Press, 1999. An analysis of gay theater in the context of contemporary culture.

Diane M. Ross

CHARLES LUDLAM

Born: Long Island, New York; April 12, 1943
Died: New York, New York; May 28, 1987

PRINCIPAL DRAMA
Big Hotel, pr. 1966, pb. 1989

When Queens Collide, pr. 1967, pb. 1989 (revised as *Conquest of the Universe: Or, When Queens Collide*, pr. 1979)
The Grand Tarot, pr. 1969, pb. 1989 (masque)
Bluebeard, pr. 1970, pb. 1971

Eunuchs of the Forbidden City, pr., pb. 1972

Camille: A Tear-Jerker, pr. 1973, pb. 1989

Hot Ice, pr., pb. 1974

Stage Blood, pr. 1975, pb. 1979

Caprice, pr. 1976, pb. 1989 (revised as *Fashion Bound*)

Der Ring Gott Farblonjet, pr. 1977, pb. 1989

The Ventriloquist's Wife, pr. 1978, pb. 1989

Reverse Psychology, pr. 1980, pb. 1989

Love's Tangled Web, pr. 1981, pb. 1989

Secret Lives of the Sexists, pr. 1982, pb. 1989

Le Bourgeois Avant-Garde, pr. 1983, pb. 1989

Galas, pr. 1983, pb. 1989

The Mystery of Irma Vep: A Penny Dreadful, pr. 1984, pb. 1987

Medea: A Tragedy, pr. 1984, pb. 1988

How to Write a Play, pr. 1984, pb. 1989

Salammbo, pr. 1985, pb. 1989

The Artificial Jungle: A Suspense Thriller, pr. 1986, pb. 1987

The Complete Plays of Charles Ludlam, pb. 1989

OTHER LITERARY FORMS

Charles Ludlam wrote several essays on the theater, some of which are collected in *Ridiculous Theatre: Scourge of Human Folly: The Essays and Opinions of Charles Ludlam* (1992), edited by Steven Samuels. In 1976 he was commissioned to write the book for *Isle of the Hermaphrodites: Or, The Murdered Minion*, but this musical about Catherine de 'Medici and the Saint Bartholomew's Day massacre never made it to Broadway. In 1977 he wrote "Aphrodisiamania," a scenario for the Paul Taylor Dance Company, and in 1980 he wrote a short opera, *The Production of Mysteries* (with resident composer Peter Golub) for Santa Fe Opera.

ACHIEVEMENTS

Charles Ludlam won critical plaudits and professional awards early, receiving his first Obie award in 1969 for distinguished achievement in Off-Broadway theater. The next year he won a Guggenheim Fellowship in Playwriting, and in 1971 second prize at BITEF International Avant-Garde Festival in Belgrade, Yugoslavia, for *Bluebeard*. In 1973 Ludlam collected an Obie for acting in both *Corn* and *Camille*. A special Obie followed in 1975 for *Professor Bedlam's Educational Punch and Judy Show*. In addition to a Playwriting award from the Rockefeller Brothers Foundation (1976), he won a Columbia Broadcasting System (CBS) Fellowship (1977) to coach graduate students in playwriting at Yale University and an Obie the same year for designing *Der Ring Gott Farblonjet*. Other awards included one for Excellence and Originality in Comedy from the Association of Comedy Artists (1978), two National Endowment for the Arts Fellowships in Playwriting (1982 and 1985), and a Drama Desk Special Award for Oustanding Achievement in Theater in 1983. *The Mystery of Irma Vep* won him a Maharam Foundation Award for Excellence in Design. In 1985 he won the Rosamund Gilder Award for distinguished achievement, and shortly before his death he was given an Obie for Sustained Achievement.

BIOGRAPHY

The middle son of Joseph William Ludlum (a master plasterer) and Marjorie Braun, Charles Ludlam showed his first interest in theater at age six after he was separated from his mother at the Mineola Fair. He wandered into a Punch and Judy show and later into a freak show. At home, he watched puppet shows on television and performed in his basement. He used to go trick or treating dressed as a girl on Halloween, but when he went to a school party in women's clothing, he caused a scandal. This led to his cross-dressing in secret, using his mother's clothes.

As a young boy, Ludlam liked the plays of William Shakespeare and the classics. He performed in school productions and had an apprenticeship at the Red Barn Theater (1958), a Long Island summer stock company. Inspired by Julian Beck and Judith Malina's Living Theater in Greenwich Village, he founded the Students' Repertory Theater, a thirty-two-seat space in an abandoned meeting hall above a liquor store. He was only seventeen at the time, but he directed and acted in obscure works by Japanese and Russian writers and in works by Eugene O'Neill. In 1961 he entered Hofstra University on an acting scholarship, graduating four years later, after writing (and destroying) his first full-length play, *Edna Brown*. By the time he graduated in 1965 with an education degree in dramatic literature, he had fully realized that he was gay and took to this lifestyle while feeding off the great cultural fermentation of rock-and-roll, happenings, experimental films, and burgeoning Off-Off-Broadway theater. He dressed in drag to play Mario Montez's lesbian lover in a brief scene in the 1965 underground film, *The Life, Death, and Assumption of Lupe Velez.*

Ludlam's New York stage debut came in 1966, when he played Peeping Tom in Ronald Tavel's *The Life of Lady Godiva*, a mixture of camp, drag, pageantry, and grotesquerie, directed by John Vaccaro at the Play-House of the Ridiculous in a loft on Seventeenth Street. He next transformed the role of Norma Desmond in Tavel's *Screen Test* into an extravagant star turn and went on to write *Big Hotel*, staged by Vaccaro. Their collaboration, however, came to an end in 1967 when Vaccaro was fired during rehearsals for Ludlam's *When Queens Collide*. Most of the cast walked out in support of him, and Ludlam founded his own troupe and staged the play, the first production of the Ridiculous Theatrical Company. Ludlam staged a midnight repertory with his first two plays at Tambellini's Gate on Second Avenue, going

on to broaden his techniques and interests and in 1969 to win the first of his numerous awards, despite an almost continual struggle with small budgets and sparse audience support. Before his first big commercial success in 1978 with *The Ventriloquist's Wife*, Ludlam supported himself by performing pranks for the television program *Candid Camera* (1960-1967) and by working in a health-food store or a bookstore.

However, with growing critical success, a cult following, and tours, Ludlam and his company were able to earn a down payment for a ten-year lease on what was to become their "permanent" home at One Sheridan Square. He had immense emotional support from his lover, Everett Quinton, who had made his stage debut in 1976 in Ludlam's *Caprice*. The two would live and work together for the rest of Ludlam's life. Ludlam entered the professional mainstream from time to time, winning a commission to write what proved to be an abortive Broadway musical in 1976, coaching students in playwriting at Yale and communications media at New York University, serving three years on New York State Council's theater panel, playing several nightclubs and the MGM Grand in Las Vegas, and even doing a little screen acting in such films as *Imposters* (1980) and *The Big Easy* (1987). However, his greatest legacy was as artistic director, playwright, director, designer, and star of his acclaimed company. As an actor with a strong face and bright eyes, he had many facial expressions. As a director, he was kind, fun, wild, erratic, and tough. As a designer, he would recycle any and all discarded items from trash cans and sidewalks. His small, independent movies that he directed (such as the 1981 silent, black-and-white film *Museum of Wax* or *The Sorrows of Dolores*, a black-and-white comedy-adventure whose filming lasted several years) were artistic indulgences, rather than commercial or critical successes.

By Thanksgiving, 1986, Ludlam knew he had AIDS (acquired immunodeficiency syndrome) but believed he

Charles Ludlam in 1978. (AP/Wide World Photos)

could beat it by taking up several hobbies and macrobiotics. He continued with his many projects: revising *Der Ring Gott Farblonjet* for Broadway, preparing *Titus Andronicus* for the New York Shakespeare Festival in Central Park, editing his film *The Sorrows of Dolores* for its premiere, and writing and planning the production of *Houdini*, as well as writing the documentary about the production of the play he was supposed to direct himself. The Houdini play was about the magician who tried to defeat death by daring it. Ludlam rehearsed the magician's death scene when he himself could not get out of a chair.

Ludlam was hospitalized on April 30, 1987, the same night that *The Sorrows of Dolores*, starring his lover and artistic partner, Quinton, as the heroine, opened at New York's Collective for Living Cinema. He died of complications from his disease on May 28. At his behest, Quinton assumed the artistic directorship of the Ridiculous Theatrical Company, producing the world premiere of Ludlam's *Medea*. In 1988 New York City renamed the street in front of the theater "Charles Ludlam Lane," and the next year Harper & Row published *The Complete Plays of Charles Ludlam*.

ANALYSIS

Charles Ludlam made an important contribution to stage comedy and gay and lesbian theater. Several of his thirty plays are thought-provoking entertainments that also happen to extend the boundaries of American theater. His comedy expresses its author's gay sensibility via gay characters and a style that incorporates drag, satiric excess, and parody. His comedy (known as The Ridiculous) is not simply low or merely saturated with foolish antics. Where the absurdists (such as Beckett, Jean Genet, Ionesco, and Alfred Jarry) sabotage seriousness and get bogged down in a cyclical structure, Ludlam revalues things held in low esteem by society and, by changing their context or scale, gives them new worth.

Ludlam studied the classics closely to understand their structures and techniques so that he could then invent his own through parody. For example, out of Shakespeare's *Hamlet, Prince of Denmark* (pr. c. 1600-1601) came *Stage Blood*; out of *La Dame aux camélias* (1848; *Camille*, 1857) by Alexandre Dumas, *fils*, came Ludlam's *Camille*; out of Richard Wagner's opera tetraology *Der Ring des Nibelungen* (1848-1876; known as the Ring Cycle) came *Der Ring Gott Farblonjet*; out of Molière's *Le Bourgeois Gentilhomme* (pr. 1670; *The Would-Be Gentleman*, 1675) came *Le Bourgeois Avant-Garde*; and out of Euripides' *Mēdeia* (431 B.C.E.; *Medea*, 1781) came Ludlam's *Medea*. However, Ludlam insisted that he was not pointing a finger at the classics to ridicule them: In fact, he and his fellow players were the buffoons who, nevertheless, were paradoxically serious about their humor. His games with plot were an attempt to realize his notion of an abstract plot or one that is filled with contradictions. This put him in the company of modernists, for it allowed him to experiment freely in order to draw attention to the antinaturalism of his writing. One of his biggest experiments was *Reverse Psychology*, which synthesized the epic form with the concentric. Although an epic play about a husband and wife, both of whom are psychiatrists who are having affairs with each other's patients who happen to be a married couple, this work has a concentric shape that is intensified by the plot device of an experimental drug that makes the characters fall in love with the person to whom they are least attracted.

Ludlam commented on his own links to classicism and modernism by pointing out how he used old things—plot, parody, and sexuality—to find new expressive possibilities and revalue techniques from various periods. He also pointed out that the tradition of plot and the use of incident in classical comedy was

> a little alphabet . . . a matrix of unseemly incident: inappropriate or contrary behavior which the clown exhibits; things falling out contrary to expectation, or propriety; things going wrong. . . . The abstract element in farce makes it the most modern dramatic medium. Its ability to reflect on the human condition is seemingly limitless.

Ludlam, therefore, envisioned The Ridiculous as a mode that freed the artist from having to conform to conventions, especially those of commercial theater.

BLUEBEARD

Billed as "A Melodrama in Three Acts,"*Bluebeard* became Ludlam's first critical success. In a concentric dramatic form, it uses melodrama, fantastic characters, and exotic locales to comment on sexual mores of its time (1970). Ludlam claimed to have been influenced by Anton Chekhov, explaining that, as in *Chayka* (pr. 1896, rev. pr. 1898; *The Seagull*, 1909), "Every character is perversely attracted to someone who doesn't like him." *Bluebeard* is an intellectual who tries to create a third sex out of a radical dissatisfaction with the two existing genders. The third genital represents the synthesis of the sexes. On one level, the play is an attack on the idea of altering people's bodies to gratify one's sexual urges.

CAMILLE

Recognizing that the Dumas story strikes an emotional chord with audiences no matter what its form (novel, play, opera, MGM film, or ballet), Ludlam adapted it to his own interests. The Dumas novel begins with a flashback after Marguerite's death, with the auction of the book that her lover, Armand, had given her. However, Ludlam did not think that a play would work as a flashback, so he reshaped Dumas's work to suit his own taste and production style. So, strictly speaking, it is an adaptation rather than an original creation. However, its value lies in its dedication to presenting something true from a ridiculous angle, such as a line made flamboyant or an action that is treated outrageously. Yet every gesture and line relates to the original romantic tragedy.

As envisaged by Ludlam, the role of Marguerite is not a drag queen act. The female impersonation makes the play profoundly feminist because it compels an audience to re-evaluate sexual prejudice and the American cultural taboo against cross-gender or transvestite interpretation. The female impersonation plays with the theme of illusion while also drawing attention to itself as a theatrical device.

DER RING GOTT FARBLONJET

Another example of Ludlam's exuberant, inflated theatricality, this play is a parody of opera in general, and of Wagner in particular. The jokes begin with characters' names: the Rhinemaidens are called Flosshilde, Woglinde, and Welgunde; the gods are known as Dunderhead, Froh, and Loga. Based on various libretti of Wagner's Ring Cycle (including Wagner's own libretto), Ludlam's comedy invents a special language, abandoning literal speech for a language that is often vaudevillian and German Yiddish. The new language reflects the evolution of human beings and thought in the tale. Characters speak different ways, echoing different periods of history, and are given linguistic leitmotifs: The Nihilumpens speak in a pidgin German; the Gibichungen speak an elevated Elizabethan diction; the heroic, chaste, lesbian Valkyries (dressed like motorcyclists) sound like Gertrude Stein; the Forest Bird speaks in plain English; and after he has tasted dragon blood, Siegfried suddenly understands birdsong and English.

THE MYSTERY OF IRMA VEP

Ludlam's biggest critical and popular success is a melodrama inspired by Victorian penny dreadfuls, cheap novels that combined lurid horror with inflated language and images. The play shamelessly steals plot devices, themes, and sometimes passages from Emily Brontë's *Wuthering Heights* (1847), Daphne du Maurier's *Rebecca* (1938), Bram Stoker's *Dracula* (1897), and the collage novels of Max Ernst, while using quick changes, double casting with gender transformations, and special effects. Servants Jane and Nicodemus welcome visitors to misty Mandacrest Manor where Lady Enid, second wife of Egyptologist Lord Edgar Hillcrest, has to cope with complications stemming from her husband's lingering attachment to memories of his first wife, Irma Vep. The result is an outrageously funny parody-collage with weird characters (such as a long-dead but strangely seductive Egyptian princess and a kindhearted werewolf). *The Mystery of Irma Vep* crystallizes Ludlam's highly self-conscious style that undermines sexual, psychological, and cultural categories in a structure that parodies classical or popular literary forms.

OTHER MAJOR WORK

NONFICTION: *Ridiculous Theatre: Scourge of Human Folly: The Essays and Opinions of Charles Ludlam*, 1992.

BIBLIOGRAPHY

Brecht, Stefan. *Queer Theatre*. New York: Methuen Books, 1986. Despite the pedantic jargon and generalized, pontifical tone, this book contains a useful discussion of the positive and negative aspects of Ridiculous Theater. Focusing on *Big Hotel* and *Conquest of the Universe*, Brecht argues that the ambiguity of sexual identity is a basic variant of the role-playing theme.

Dasgupta, Gautam. "Interview: Charles Ludlam." *Performing Arts Journal* (Spring/Summer, 1978): 69. A discussion of the origin and techniques of Ludlam's theater. Dasgupta distinguishes between Ridiculous and other comic forms such as lampoon, parody, and satire. Touches on the political aspect of the Ridiculous.

Romer, Rick. *Charles Ludlam and the Ridiculous Theatrical Company*. Jefferson, N.C.: McFarland, 1998. Offers a critical analysis of all the plays. Romer introduces Ludlam's work, mission, and artistic sensibility by starting with a brief biography, then delving into the roots of the Ridiculous and countercultural movements of the 1960's. Shows Ludlam as cultural scavenger with a penchant for "maximal art."

Keith Garebian

OTTO LUDWIG

Born: Eisfeld an der Werra, Thuringia (now in Germany); February 12, 1813

Died: Dresden, Germany; February 25, 1865

PRINCIPAL DRAMA

Hanns Frei, pb. 1843, pr. 1891

Die Torgauer Heide, pb. 1844

Die Rechte des Herzens, pb. 1845

Die Pfarrose, pb. 1847, pr. 1891

Das Fräulein von Scuderi, pb. 1848, pr. 1870 (based on E. T. A. Hoffmann's story "Mademoiselle de Scudéri")

Der Erbförster, pr. 1850, pb. 1853 (*The Hereditary Forester*, 1913)

Die Makkabäer, pr. 1853, pb. 1854 (verse play)

Der Engel von Augsburg, Agnes Bernauerin, wr. 1859, pb. 1870, pr. 1897

Marino Falieri, wr. 1860, pb. 1891 (fragment)

Tiberius Gracchus, wr. 1862-1865, pb. 1870 (fragment)

OTHER LITERARY FORMS

It was as a writer of fiction that Otto Ludwig achieved distinction as one of the foremost writers in nineteenth century German literature. He began by writing a series of stories on small-town life in Thuringia; with a graphic visual sense, he depicts social reality in his village tales. In 1856, he published an outstanding work, the novel *Zwischen Himmel und Erde* (*Between Heaven and Earth*, 1911), which was widely acclaimed as his best. In general, Ludwig's fiction is characterized by careful psychological analysis and attention to detail, showing at times even a cumbersome meticulousness. In addition to prose, Ludwig wrote some poetry, but his contribution was negligible.

Ludwig's major critical work is a collection entitled *Shakespeare Studien* (1871; Shakespearean studies). In addition to an analysis of William Shakespeare's technique, there are valuable reflections on many of the fundamental questions of poetry, especially of the drama, and they confirm Ludwig as a discriminating critic. Other critical writings are collected in *Dramaturgische Aphorismen* (1891; dramatic aphorisms). As a representative of *poetischer Realismus* (poetic realism), a term that he seems to have coined, Ludwig defines *künstlerischer Realismus* (stylized realism) as a balance between subjectively idealistic and objectively naturalistic art. Perhaps he admired Shakespeare so much precisely because he saw in Shakespeare's art the supreme embodiment of this principle.

ACHIEVEMENTS

Although Otto Ludwig's dramatic works are very uneven, he was one of the significant figures in nineteenth century German drama. According to Ludwig, modern drama must serve the common needs of the people. He regarded the theater as a place where people go to seek release from the burdens of life. His heroes, therefore, are often village people, his settings, frequently local. Within this framework, he continually emphasized the value of literature that was regional in inspiration. His reputation as one of Germany's outstanding representatives of regionalist literature seems secure. In his critical writings and choice of projects, Ludwig was dependent to an excessive degree on other examples, such as on E. T. A. Hoffmann's story "Das Fräulein von Scuderi" ("Mademoiselle de Scudéri"), on which he based one of his early comedies by the same name, or, the drama *Der Engel von Augsburg, Agnes Bernauerin* (the angel from Augsburg, Agnes Bernauerin), believed to be based on Friedrich Hebbel's theme of Agnes Bernauer. Ludwig is, nevertheless, accorded the praise due him as one of those dramatists who replaced with a greater variety of elementary human passions that rich, superficial life, which, through Friedrich Schiller's influence, had prevailed on the German stage. Ludwig attempted a faithful representation of reality. He demanded subjects suited to the times and wanted to reconcile art and life. Proceeding from a regional base, he showed that literature within a local framework need not be provincial.

BIOGRAPHY

Otto Ludwig, German dramatist, novelist, musician, and critic, was born into a patrician family at Eisfeld in Thuringia (now East Germany). His father, a middle-class city official, died when Otto was still a child. After his father's death, Ludwig attended the Gymnasium in Hildburghausen, but his mother withdrew him before he completed the course in 1828. Exposed early in life to music and poetry by his artistic mother, Ludwig continued his musical studies in his leisure time until economic considerations forced him to work for several years in the shop of his merchant uncle. After his mother died, Ludwig entered the Lyzeum in Saalfeld with the intention of completing his preparatory studies. Poor health, however, compelled him to abandon formal study at the school. Privately he continued his musical studies.

Although he was expected to follow a mercantile career, Ludwig preferred the arts and devoted the years from 1834 to 1838 to the study of music. Some of his operatic compositions were produced locally with great success. In 1837, *Die Geschwister* (the sisters), a *Liederspiel* (musical play), and in 1838, an opera, *Die Köhlerin* (the charcoal burner), attracted attention to him in musical circles in Meiningen, the nearby ducal residence. He was granted a stipend by the duke, which made it possible for him to study under Felix Mendelssohn in Leipzig in 1839. There, however, he became almost exclusively absorbed in literary plans, contemplating stories and dramas. Adverse criticism from Mendelssohn, poor health, and shyness finally led him to forsake his musical career, and he returned home, spending the years from 1840 to 1842 in Eisfeld. Hometown people regarded him as a failure. In 1842, he decided to return to Leipzig to devote himself to a literary career. He continued writing stories and dramas and made the acquaintance of Heinrich Laube and other literary celebrities. Later, he moved to Dresden, where he worked assiduously on a number of dramatic and novelistic ventures. *Die Makkabäer* (the Maccabees), a tragedy in blank verse, was completed in Dresden. After a brief stay, he retired to Meissen, where he lived, insular and somewhat privileged.

In 1850, *The Hereditary Forester*, a tragedy in five acts, made Ludwig famous. He emerged for a time from obscurity, formed more friendships, and, in 1852, he was married. In the late 1850's, he published his best works: *Die Heiterethei* and *Between Heaven and Earth* merit special praise. These years were the zenith of Ludwig's career, the height of his productivity as an artist and of his success and happiness as a man.

Ultimately, his inclination to measure modern drama by Shakespearean standards and his preoccupation with literary theory restrained his success as a creative writer. Excessive reflection caused him repeatedly to destroy what he had written. It is known that he made innumerable dramatic plans, some only sketched, others carried to various degrees of completion. Paralyzed by his own high standards, he was able to complete very little. Ludwig died in Dresden on February 25, 1865.

ANALYSIS

The name of Otto Ludwig evokes rich and varied images of a man considered by many to be one of the first modern realists in Germany. He has been more properly described, however, as a realist-idealist. Belonging to a period of transition from romanticism to realism, he tried to find the harmonious ideal of human existence. Despite his growing disillusionment, his work was never completely detached from this foundation.

THE HEREDITARY FORESTER

The Hereditary Forester made Otto Ludwig known and is by far his most frequently played drama. This domestic tragedy (*bürgerliches Trauerspiel*) was completed in 1850 with encouragement and suggestions from Eduard Devrient, manager of the Court Theatre in Dresden. It was produced the same year by Devrient, who played the title role. Although the play was at once proclaimed as a literary and theatrical event of great significance, only the first two acts were enthusiastically received; the audience seemed to be perplexed by the remainder of the drama. It was twice repeated before an empty house and not given in Dresden again until 1862. Some critics defended, more condemned, the tragedy. Laube produced it in Vienna in 1850, but in spite of a friendly reception, it was soon abandoned. It had considerable success in Weimar, and then various other stages. Ludwig intended the play to be "a declaration of war against unnaturalness and conventionalities of our latter-day stage literature." With true-to-life characters, unpretentiousness in language and gesture, and a carefully drawn milieu, he sought to capture a segment of middle-class life in Thuringia.

The protagonist, Christian Ulrich, is the hereditary forester of a large estate. For generations, his family has served the landed aristocracy well. Like his father and grandfather before him, he, too, associates his work with deep-rooted emotional values. His labor is

a duty imposed on him by tradition and entails obligations toward his heritage. His services have no mercantile value, for they are an extension of personality rather than a product that could be purchased with money.

After the estate has been purchased by his old friend Stein, Ulrich continues to exercise his "authority" as a "hereditary duty." Oblivious to the changes in ownership and the changes in the social order that have accompanied the beginning of urbanization, he repeatedly refuses to obey the new owner's directive to thin out the forest. Consequently, their long-standing friendship suffers. Although Stein persists in his efforts to persuade Ulrich to change his mind and save the friendship, the forester ignores all wishes and demands. Even threats of dismissal fail to convince him to oblige. He stubbornly believes that he cannot lose a position to which he has a hereditary right. Ultimately, abstract principles assume a greater importance than his own life. He dissociates himself psychologically, socially, and economically from the established order and adheres to the most rigorous and least sympathetic moral prescriptions of the Old Testament, thereby sacrificing his position and his happiness, as well as the happiness of his family.

A series of unfortunate incidents and schemes for revenge result in his accidentally shooting his own daughter, who was soon to be married to Stein's son. When he realizes his horrible mistake, he takes his own life.

Critics have noted several flaws in the construction of Ludwig's drama: The action depends too heavily on chance; moreover, Ludwig fails to connect the family tragedy with the broad movement of contemporary public life and the times. Although the revolutionary unrest of 1848 is in the background, he does not connect it in any way with the family tragedy. He offers, however, a vision of a changing world. He portrays a man who ignores at his peril important changes, a man with moral principles who fails to realize that his emotional values have been replaced by rational values such as adaptability, proficiency, and shrewdness, and that superficiality is a tendency of the times. This change of attitude even invades his private sphere, so that human relations deteriorate into alliances of convenience. Unable to reject his idealistic views, he loses his dignity as a man and becomes an object of calculation, a victim of circumstance. Ludwig shows the despair of a man who knows that the modern trend toward technical civilization has made him vulnerable because it has deprived him of his physical and spiritual stability.

DIE MAKKABÄER

The Hereditary Forester was followed by *Die Makkabäer*, which, though not attaining the popularity of *The Hereditary Forester*, contributed significantly to Ludwig's fame. The only other drama in addition to *The Hereditary Forester* performed on the stage during his lifetime, it is rarely, if ever, staged today. In this verse play, Ludwig transferred the realistic details of his Thuringian drama to a historical milieu: the revolt of the Maccabees in the first century B.C.E. against their Syrian oppressors.

The play is based on the Apocryphal book of the Maccabees. Under the leadership of Judas Maccabaeus, the son of a priest, Mattathias, and his wife, Leah, the Jews won victory over the Seleucid king Antiochus IV (called Epiphanes). Ludwig contrasts the Syrians and Jews in this drama. The Simonites are portrayed as opportunists without any deep religious feelings or national convictions. The Maccabees are people with spiritual aims who passionately fight and suffer for their ideals. Idealism is exemplified in Leah, who desires for one of her seven sons, Eleazer, the throne of Israel. Misguided by motherly devotion and excessive pride, she unwittingly becomes an accomplice in the martyrdom of her own sons. As prisoners of King Antiochus, they are ordered to become pagans or to die. When they refuse, they lose their lives. The sight of their martyrdom demoralizes Antiochus's army, and a victory is won.

Certain faults of construction are evident in this drama. In terms of psychological motivation, the victory of the Jews over the Simonites is not convincing, for it is only passive heroism that contributes to their defeat. In addition, the drama lacks unity of interest, in part because of the long process of development that the play underwent before completion. Nevertheless, there is the same attention to detail, convincing character portrayal, and in-depth psychological analysis that characterize Ludwig's prose.

OTHER MAJOR WORKS

LONG FICTION: *Die Emanzipation der Domestiken*, 1844 (novella); *Die Heiterethei*, 1855-1856 (novella); *Zwischen Himmel und Erde*, 1856 (*Between Heaven and Earth*, 1911); *Aus dem Regen in die Traufe*, 1857 (novella); *Die Heiterethei und ihr Widerspiel*, 1857 (includes *Die Heiterethei* and *Aus dem Regen in die Traufe*); *Thüringer Naturen*, 1857 (novella); *Die wahrhaftige Geschichte von den drei Wünschen*, 1891 (novella); *Aus einem alten Schulmeisterleben*, 1891 (novella); *Maria*, 1891 (novella).

NONFICTION: *Shakespeare Studien*, 1871; *Dramaturgische Aphorismen*, 1891.

BIBLIOGRAPHY

Thomas, Lionel. *Otto Ludwig's "Zwischen Himmel und Erde."* Leeds, England: W. S. Maney, 1975. Although this work focuses on Ludwig's novel *Between Heaven and Earth*, it sheds light on his dramatic work and life.

Turner, David. *Roles and Relationships in Otto Ludwig's Narrative Fiction.* Hull, England: University of Hull, 1975. An examination of Ludwig's prose that also provides insights into his plays.

Lieselotte A. Kuntz

JOHN LYLY

Born: Canterbury(?), Kent, England; c. 1554
Died: London, England; November, 1606

PRINCIPAL DRAMA

Campaspe, wr. 1579-1580, pr., pb. 1584 (also known as *Alexander, Campaspe and Diogenes*)

Sapho and Phao, pr., pb. 1584

Galathea, pr. c. 1585, pb. 1592

Endymion, the Man in the Moon, pr. 1588,
    pb. 1591

Midas, pr. c. 1589, pb. 1592

Mother Bombie, pr. c. 1589, pb. 1594

Love's Metamorphosis, pr. c. 1589, pb. 1601

The Woman in the Moon, pr. c. 1593, pb. 1597

Dramatic Works, pb. 1858 (2 volumes; F. W.
    Fairholt, editor)

OTHER LITERARY FORMS

John Lyly continues, unfortunately, to be most remembered for his early prose works, *Euphues, the
Anatomy of Wit* (1578) and *Euphues and His England*
(1580). These works uneasily combine the values of
moralistic Humanism with the erotic subject matter
and psychological potential of the Italian novella;
these two elements are overlaid and indeed overwhelmed by the famous style, subsequently labeled
"euphuism." Both Lyly's own contemporaries and
scholars have also assigned Lyly the authorship of
Pap with an Hatchet (1589), a turgid religious tract
published anonymously in the course of the Martin
Marprelate controversy.

ACHIEVEMENTS

Twentieth century readings have led to recognition of John Lyly as more than a quaint writer. Since
the initial work of Jonas Barish in 1956, Lyly's prose
style has been more highly (though still variously)
valued, and both Barish and, in 1962, G. K. Hunter
helped to enhance appreciation of Lyly's plays. Lyly
has been served by the freeing of Elizabethan drama
criticism in modern times from its earlier compulsion to consider its material in the light of William Shakespeare. Lyly can be seen now as, at his
best, a highly intelligent writer of comic psychological and philosophical allegory. He is important
not merely for his historical position or for his constructive skill but also for his insight—which is part
of the general Renaissance insight into human personality, informed by the newly experienced classics,
often expressed in a symbolic rather than a purely realistic mode.

BIOGRAPHY

Unsurprisingly for an Elizabethan, John Lyly's
date of birth cannot be ascertained. From college
records, it can be extrapolated back to some time in
the early 1550's, probably around 1554. Lyly was
brought up, perhaps also born, in Canterbury, where
his father was a cleric attached to the official service
of the archbishops. Lyly's near ancestors and family
included central figures in the tradition of Humanism
in England.

In the early 1570's, John Lyly appears on the
books of Magdalen College, Oxford. There is evidence that Lyly intended to pursue an academic career. On the other hand, some rather problematic testimony suggests that Lyly at Oxford was most noted
for his interest in the fashionable life and recreations
accessible to young men there. By the end of the
1570's, he had moved out of the academic setting
and was living in London. His two Euphues books,
which he wrote around this time, seem to reflect both
an affinity for a Humanistically colored academic
world and a certain distance from such a world. The
two books were immediately immensely popular, and
with their publication, Lyly's life rose clearly into a
new orbit, around the court of Queen Elizabeth I.

Lyly became attached to the household of Edward
de Vere, earl of Oxford, an important courtier; Lyly
may have been the earl's secretary. The connection
led into another one, crucial to Lyly's creative life. Oxford patronized the troupes of choirboy actors that
were based on the Chapel Royal and St. Paul's Cathedral. These troupes, carefully recruited and trained,
entertained the court during the major winter holidays, such as New Year's, and also, from the 1570's
on, performed for paying audiences at the indoor
"private" theater of Blackfriars in London. The
semicourtly, semiprofessional boys' theater was the
highly specialized medium in which Lyly worked
throughout the 1580's. Seven of his eight known
plays were written for boys; six of the eight are heralded on the title pages of their quarto editions as
having been performed before the queen.

Lyly's first play, *Campaspe*, had almost the same
phenomenal early popularity as his fiction. Lyly
clearly believed he was given reason during the

1580's to hope for regular employment under the queen. As the decade wore on, however, Lyly's court and theatrical career lost its promising rhythm.

The boys' companies' obstreperous participation in the Martin Marprelate controversy of 1588-1590 led to a ban on their productions throughout the 1590's, which all but shut down Lyly's theatrical work. His euphuistic style went rapidly from being in vogue to being the target of sophisticated ridicule. Although Lyly did serve in various parliaments throughout the 1590's, he never achieved the court office to which he aspired. At the time of his death in 1606, Lyly was burdened with a family whom he could not support and suits from his creditors that he failed to answer.

ANALYSIS

A sense of the Elizabethan literary environment suggests one appropriate overall comment on John Lyly's work. The 1580's, the decade of Lyly's principal achievements on the stage, were years of extraordinary literary ferment. Sir Philip Sidney and Edmund Spenser were decisively altering values in poetry. Almost doctrinaire neoclassic drama lingering from the 1560's gave way not only to Lyly but also to the violent tragedy of Thomas Kyd (1558-1594) and Christopher Marlowe. Lyly's drama corresponds to its transitional, eclectic times: His work made use of change as a chance for variety, instead of suffering from it as disorienting or disintegrating. Juxtapositions of Lyly to Shakespeare are likely to be odious, but Lyly may not be harmed by the recognition that, like Shakespeare, he profited from his historical moment. Lyly, like Shakespeare, grew toward a capacity to merge diverse elements in his plays and to hold together in suspension tints of different kinds of awareness and experience—Humanistic and Neoplatonic, lightly comic and seriously problematic. In Lyly's earlier works, the multiplicity of available influences helps create disunified writing; later, it yields writing that is rich and experimental.

Linking this literary-historical pattern mechanically with the content of the work would be a mistake, in Lyly's case as much as in Shakespeare's. Still, Lyly's greatest works celebrate change and

greet it as comic growth through which people become more fully human. *Galathea*, *Endymion, the Man in the Moon*, and *Love's Metamorphosis* especially should still be enjoyed for their adult gentleness, consciousness, and openness.

CAMPASPE

Campaspe, Lyly's first play, is closely related to the Euphues works in several respects, first of all in its Humanism. It shares with segments of the Euphues writings a typical Humanistic source, Plutarch. The work is to a large extent one of ethical counsel, specifically of counsel to the ruler. The boy actors produced the play before Queen Elizabeth, and much of it constitutes an image of wise conduct by an exemplary ruler from the past, Alexander the Great.

For critics such as Hunter and Peter Saccio, *Campaspe* is a major instance of lack of plot development or even sequence in Lyly's dramaturgy. Some scenes in the play, such as a meeting of Alexander with the philosophers of Athens, are detached set pieces not meant to advance any plot line, and involve characters who appear nowhere else in the play. Lyly regularly breaks the continuity of such actions as do develop in the play and thus denies the audience any steadily growing involvement with them. An action begun in one scene will not be resumed until several scenes later, after one's attention has been diverted and diverted again by different bits of other material. Characters' motives shift without explanation from one scene to another.

The point seems to be that Lyly's sense of construction is not based on the wholeness of a realistic action but, in this case, on a doctrinal picture. The interrelatedness of many of *Campaspe*'s scenes arises not from their placement in a plot but rather from their function as sections of the image of Alexander that the play is putting together. The scenes show the different characteristics (or characteristic modes of behavior) of Alexander as the good king: his benevolence toward the weak, his regard for the learned, and so on. Much of the play builds less by a process of sequential development, in which each new scene depends on previous ones for its full significance, than by additive composition, in which each scene is discrete, making its separate contribution to the total construction.

To the extent that *Campaspe* is more Humanistic picture than plot, it resembles the many images of model human figures in Renaissance literature such as Desiderius Erasmus's Christian knight in the *Enchiridion militis christiani* (1503), Baldassare Castiglione's *The Courtier* (1528), and Sir Thomas Elyot's *The Boke Named the Governour* (1531). Like much Humanistic writing, *Campaspe* is concerned with the function of the prince but also, as an important corollary, with the prince's relationship to his counselors (in Renaissance terms, to Humanistically educated subjects). *Campaspe*'s picture of Alexander is complemented by its picture of the Cynic Diogenes, an embodiment of an extreme claim for the virtuous counselor's status in the polity. One of Alexander's most exemplary decisions is his drafting of Diogenes for attachment to the court: Alexander wants to listen to a voice that speaks only for virtue, without regard for power.

In addition to these model figures, the Humanistic aspect of *Campaspe* involves sketches of moral tales. The prodigal-son narrative structure that critics have recognized in *Euphues, the Anatomy of Wit* also seems related to the rather minimal sustained sequence of actions in which Alexander does become directly involved: his experience of love for Campaspe, the realization that she loves the painter Apelles, and Alexander's final renunciation of her. Campaspe, humbly born, is clearly inappropriate as a match for Alexander; Hephastion moralizes on Alexander's love for her as a tempting detour from the course of honor.

Campaspe's resemblance to the Euphues books involves factors besides Humanism. Much of the play is overlaid by a euphuistic style; the style sometimes works positively to give dialogue epigrammatic pointedness. The love of Apelles and Campaspe is a very different matter from that of Alexander, and one that can be related not to the Humanistic but to the novella pattern lying behind *Euphues, the Anatomy of Wit*. Apelles and Campaspe's scenes, though other kinds of scenes are interspersed between them, themselves follow a perfectly regular rhythm, in which scenes of dialogue alternate with soliloquies by the

two lovers; dialogue and soliloquy were the major frameworks in which emotion could be explored in the Euphues books and the narrative tradition anterior to them. The love portrayed in the scenes is not a distraction from honor or serious matters; rather, it is personal feeling that seems to be central to the psychic lives of the two people involved, and it grows. Unlike the Humanistic picture scenes with their additive interrelation, the scenes of Apelles and Campaspe dramatize an intelligible development, through which the characters move continuously from the first sense of love toward more ample realization and expression of it.

As in the Euphues books, Humanism and this other narrative component coexist uneasily in *Campaspe*. The motif of Apelles and Campaspe's kind of love, virtually absent from the play's first two acts, weighs heavily in the last three, receiving about eight of their thirteen scenes. The large influx of romantic feeling produces an unbalancing shift in the whole mood of the play.

Along with the pictures of Alexander and Diogenes and the love story of Apelles and Campaspe, there is one further set of scenes in the play, which is of a kind different from anything in the Euphues books and which became increasingly important in Lyly's playwriting as it progressed. In *Campaspe*, there are only two or three scenes of high-spirited page comedy, in which servants of the play's major figures meet on some pretext, exchange jokes, mock their masters, and express unflagging appetites for food and drink. Such scenes sometimes culminate in the singing of drinking songs. It seems reasonable to relate this kind of material to two circumstances of the production of Lyly's plays. As court entertainment for holidays such as Christmas and Twelfth Night, Lyly's plays belonged to the Saturnalian context that C. L. Barber described in *Shakespeare's Festive Comedy* (1959), in which rule for the moment was to be made light of and appetite gratified even to excess. As plays performed by choirboys, Lyly's works gained dimensions when their comedy projected standard boys' appetites and smart-aleckism, and when they exploited the boys' musical talents. Among the other constituents of *Campaspe*, the festive, disrespectful page comedy attaches itself most strongly to the characterization of Diogenes, the disrespectful satirist, but the pages completely lack Diogenes' will to make moral judgments; their mockery is for the sake of having a good time. In fact, the page comedy seems extraneous both to the play's nobler Humanistic themes and, certainly, to Apelles and Campaspe's love.

Campaspe is a rich combination, but the continued lack of integration of the work's elements makes it a noticeably less impressive play than Lyly's more mature and mythic works. The play's proportion of success is connected with the appeal or impact of certain moments—bits of incisive dialogue such as that between Parmenio and Timoclea in the play's first scene, which, even more than the language of Diogenes, has the excitement of truth spoken to force; the last line, in which Alexander charmingly warns Hephestion that when he has no more worlds to conquer, then he may yet fall in love.

SAPHO AND PHAO

Sapho and Phao involved a new source for Lyly, Ovid, whose potential impact, however, was not fully realized until *Galathea*. Lyly was remarkably successful in adapting his source material to a generally Humanistic pattern. The Sappho of Ovid's *Heroides* (before 8 C.E.; English translation, 1567), whose whole character is that of a passionate lover, becomes in Lyly's play the queen of Syracuse, controlling a court and herself conditioned by social and political duties and norms. Phao becomes a figure like Campaspe, an inferior love. The play ultimately dramatizes Sapho's taking control of erotic power (personified as Venus and Cupid), which had sought to rule her. The parallel between Queen Elizabeth's chastity and Sapho's is obvious; the triumphant establishment of the latter becomes clear praise of the former.

GALATHEA

Roman mythography became a potent influence in Lyly's work in *Galathea*. Ovid was Lyly's source for this symbolic drama in which actions clearly have significance as they refer to an underlying dynamic pattern. Ovid's *Metamorphoses* (c. 8 C.E.; English translation, 1567) contains many incidents, through each and all of which the reader looks toward the un-derlying universal process of metamorphosis itself, the reality of change. Both *Galathea* and Lyly's later play, *Love's Metamorphosis*, consist of plots that are discontinuous—inconsequential if taken strictly on their own terms—but that imply a continuous line of allegorical meaning. This kind of writing clearly differs in several ways from the Humanistic modes that had more or less dominated Lyly's first two plays. It is truly dynamic, never static or additive as *Campaspe* was, even though the dynamic continuity does not appear on the literal plot level. It embodies truths (or visions) instead of encouraging conduct; therefore, it presents human life in a psychological rather than a hortatory manner, concerning itself with growth and health rather than with virtue and vice. Lyly's Ovidian drama is not set in an arena of social or political action, a historical or pseudohistorical court or city. The plots of *Galathea* and *Love's Metamorphosis* occur in the pastoral world, which traditionally has had symbolic value. Setting and symbolic purpose also differentiate this drama from the more realistic novella.

Love appears in *Galathea* not as a temptation countervailed by honor, but as a psychic presence experienced and accepted differently at different stages in a process of human growth. In other words, the play is a vision of adolescence. It takes its name from its adolescent girl heroine and ultimately from the nymph in *Metamorphoses* 13 whose lover changes before her eyes. As the play opens, young virgins are exposed to rumors of an incomprehensible savage force bent on attacking them. The allegorical progression begins as the play moves into the next scene, in which a better-understood, less terrifying, clearly erotic power, Cupid, is incited to show his power over virgins who are more mature at least in understanding. Thereafter, as the play meanders engagingly back and forth between its two main plots, love is presented in guise after different guise, but changing fairly steadily in a determinate direction, appearing in embodiments that are less frightening: Cupid assumes the disguise of a shepherd, is captured, and exercises his nature in a disarmed (and less external) state, as love develops as an emotion Galathea and Phyllida feel within themselves.

As love becomes understood as more acceptable, it also becomes more accepted. Through the course of the play, Galathea, Phyllida, and Diana's nymphs all succumb and come to enjoy this new part of their beings. The process is happy in its result. Neptune, who has become a mediator, effects a resolution in which love's power is recognized, not repressed, but in which it can be incorporated into intact human personalities rather than destroying them. Galathea and Phyllida are ready for healthy, mature, emotional life. With lovely precision, the play leaves them just ready, just at the verge, still within a semi-sexual stage that Lyly (like Shakespeare) dramatizes as involvement with someone not fully identifiable as one's sexual complement. As in *Twelfth Night: Or, What You Will* (pr. c. 1600-1602) and *As You Like It* (pr. c. 1599-1600), both produced about five years later, girls disguise themselves as boys and are fallen in love with as such: Galathea and Phyllida fall in love with each other, each under the misapprehension that the other is a boy. One is left uncertain at the end of the play which of the two a generous Venus is about to metamorphose into a male, to make full sexual life for them possible.

The delighted, smooth comic feeling of the play's ending is a point around which Lyly manages to orient a remarkable number of elements. *Galathea* is typical of Lyly's work inasmuch as it is a hybrid of diverse constituents—Lyly's first fully successful work in that these elements are fully integrated and mutually responsive. There is a good deal of euphuism in the style, but now delight in its neat working-out of syntax and sound can be subsumed in delight at the economy of growth that the play symbolizes (instead of jarring against a Humanistic message). Like the euphuistic aspects, the festive servant boys' subplot can now work to expand and prepare the audience for the joy to which the main plots are leading. In mood, the comedy of Rafe, Robin, and Dick represents a distinctive modulation away from Lyly's norm for such scenes: Instead of Lyly's usually loud, rambunctious, prank-playing boys, *Galathea*'s boys are gulls, and the resulting humor is somewhat quieter and very much in keeping with the whole play's trend, which is to settle into a smile more than to ex-

plode in laughter. At the end of the play, Venus welcomes the boys into direct contact with the main action. They are to serve as entertainers, enhancing the joy of the forthcoming marriage—which is exactly the role they have been performing throughout the play.

Galathea is in some ways Lyly's most characteristic success; it involves tendencies that were important in many of his other works. Like Ovid's *Metamorphoses*, it achieves a smooth unity among a diversity of coequal factors. The play marks the beginning of a mature phase of not invariably but usually unified dramatic works.

ENDYMION, THE MAN IN THE MOON

Endymion, the Man in the Moon dramatizes a Neoplatonic ascent through various levels of love and being to transcendent knowledge. Important details make the play's process congruent also with the general Christian concept of redemption.

The protagonist first appears caught in involvement with his immediate physical world, but also drawn by a reality beyond it. He loves Cynthia, with whom he is not yet in direct contact. The attraction seems bizarre and out of order, both to his friend Eumenides and to himself. Endymion's situation is complicated by his difficult and ambivalent relationship with Tellus. Low metaphysical status is represented here not only through the drama of Endymion's attitudes and problems, but also in the modes of description used: Cynthia at this point is, to all intents and purposes, the actual physical moon; Tellus is a very material, fecund earth goddess. Endymion's persistence on the earthly level appears in Tellus's power over him, which, however, has its limits. She cannot force Endymion's love back to herself, but she can hinder his rise. Through her agent Dipsas, she holds Endymion in sleep; he rests suspended, out of the worldly consciousness that has prevailed to this point in the play but unable to waken to the life that appears around his sleeping figure and that includes Cynthia as a directly present character.

As in *Galathea*, Lyly's allegorical line passes unbroken from one plot medium to another. As Endymion is sleeping, two surrogates, Corsites and Eumenides, act out the position that he occupies between two worlds. Both are deputized by Cynthia, Corsites to control Tellus, which he fails to do, thus continuing the dramatization of human weakness. Eumenides' mission is to find a way to help Endymion. He does so and reaches the height of purely human potential when, at some emotional cost, he puts aside the claims of human sexual love in favor of those of more purely spiritual friendship and of duty to Cynthia. The discovery he makes at this level is that further progress, in the form of the main protagonist's recovery from his trance, can come only through an act of condescension by Cynthia in the form of an act of love, a kiss. This is one of the points clearly suggestive of Christianity in the play, specifically of the Christian doctrine of human beings' need for God's loving gift of grace.

Cynthia's kiss arouses an Endymion who definitely has surpassed the passionate love in which he began. His altered language is noticeable, especially when one comes to this play from Lyly's earlier works. By the time *Endymion, the Man in the Moon* was written, euphuism, certainly of the kind found in the early narratives, was receding as a factor in Lyly's writing. By the play's end, Endymion is speaking in relatively even, straightforward sentences, reflecting his arrival at a definitely rational frame of mind. No longer so committed to a set style, Lyly could make language flexibly project action.

Endymion's appearances as an old man toward his play's end have a clear philosophical association. He resembles the old Platonic lover described by Pietro Bembo in Castiglione's *The Courtier*. Like the old lover, Endymion is no longer interested in physical love; instead, he is happy with the position he has achieved as a purified attendant in Cynthia's immediate presence. Endymion's final metamorphosis, back into a young man (he has slept and aged for forty years), may imply a Christian step beyond a philosophical one, a putting off of the old man and entry into a new life of redemption. Cynthia herself emerges as a benevolent supernatural figure near the play's close.

As a final image of hierarchy, Cynthia in the last scene brings love to fulfillment for several couples: herself and Endymion on down through pairs repre-

senting less exalted levels. The lowest in the line is the impersonal mating instinct of Sir Tophas, who earlier had wanted Dipsas, but—now that she is unavailable—reaches for her servant Bagoa. The play's low comedy is one of its liveliest elements. Sir Tophas is a new feature in such writing by Lyly—a sustained, gradually developed, low-comic character. His place in the play is somewhat indeterminate until he forces himself on the other characters' attention in the last scene, as the lowest level from which the hierarchical structure they have elaborated rises.

Endymion, the Man in the Moon is Lyly's most ambitious play. With its reach toward philosophy and religion, it embodies the continued expansiveness of Lyly's mind as well as the extent of his mature control.

MIDAS

Much of *Midas* is topical, political, and Humanistic. It is quite clear in the play, and accepted in the critical tradition, that discussion of an unsuccessful war by Midas's Phrygia against the island of Lesbos allegorically refers to Philip of Spain's attack on England with his Armada. Like its predecessors from *Sapho and Phao* on, *Midas* has its source in Ovid. The lighthearted Ovidian fables that provide *Midas*'s plot coexist rather uneasily with much of the dialogue's serious moral tone. The Humanistic lessons delivered by Midas's counselors are not responsive to the developing Ovidian plot. They stand apart as set pieces and tend simply to be repeated in one debate scene after another, instead of changing in any way corresponding to plot changes. In several respects, *Midas* is a rather unsatisfying reversion to Lyly's early dramatic pattern.

MOTHER BOMBIE

Neither hortatory nor Ovidian, *Mother Bombie* is instead a very pure experiment in neoclassic secular comedy. It is witty New Comedy of clever servants helping young people to overcome obstacles raised by their selfish elders; its ultimate ancestor is the Roman comedy of Terence. Within Lyly's work, there is a connection not to the kinds of dramatic writing that dominate his other plays as wholes, but instead to the usually secondary element of page comedy. In tone and action, the play is fairly firmly and neatly unified, although it seems thinner in meaning and less inventive than Lyly's plays based on mythography.

Love's Metamorphosis

Love's Metamorphosis is the most interesting of Lyly's later works, and probably his most underrated play. It is close to *Galathea* in several ways. As its title suggests, the whole play is Ovidian in feeling, although the main plots are actually not drawn from Ovid or from any other source. The play is a sequential allegory: It presents not only physical metamorphoses performed by the god Cupid but also, and much more important, like *Galathea*, changing visions of love (and of human relationships in general). The allegory is organized somewhat differently from that of *Galathea*. A distinct major vision is localized in each of the play's plots. The plot that gets first exposure, that of three amorous foresters' love for three nymphs, could be interpreted as a sane psychological critique of traditions of courtly love and Petrarchianism. The three lovers are met with refusals to love from the ladies to whom they are drawn. The ladies' refusals, instead of being idealized, are analyzed as various forms of sexual egotism. The ladies are punished by being metamorphosed into items of subhuman nature—a stone, a flower, a bird—symbolic of their different kinds of detachment from human involvement. Punishment in itself is not a solacing ending. The audience is left with a picture of one-sided adoration as a type of failed relationship.

On the other hand, instead of being an opposing figure who withdraws into himself and refuses contact (as the ladies themselves do to the foresters), Erisichthon emerges to attack the nymphs' own space, their sacred grove, and to prevent them from carrying out the activities proper to their natures. Relationships here are not exclusively erotic, but rather more well-rounded. The divinity to whom the maidens can appeal is Ceres, who suggests a broader (but less exalted, literally more down-to-earth) image of human experience than does the foresters' Cupid. Erisichthon is punished with famine, although again punishment is not resolution; he is brought before the audience later in the play, repentant of his actions but caught in punishment, unable to escape his actions' consequences.

The play's movement toward resolution begins when a third, clearly different vision of human relationships comes about, one that involves mutuality. Its protagonist, Protea, is constantly helping others and being helped by them. The pattern began in the character's past, when she yielded her virginity to Neptune and received his promise of future help in return. Neptune keeps faith, and Protea is saved through supernatural power in the various situations in which she finds herself during the play's course. At the same time, she is saving her father and her lover. She first avoids a relationship of pure (and not specifically erotic) dominance when she escapes from enslavement by a merchant. Then she destroys the alluring power of the selfish, isolated Siren over her lover Petulius. Thus, she has managed to eliminate from her life both of the dilemmas that the play's first two plots embody. Mutuality is allied to flexibility. Protea's name indicates her ability to change, and she defeats the bad versions of relationship through magical metamorphoses of her person. At the play's end, the vision associated with Protea expands over the play and redeems the other characters from their symbolic entrapment.

Although similar to *Galathea* as highly sophisticated psychological allegory, *Love's Metamorphosis* differs in tone. The play certainly remains a comedy, but it is a darker one than *Galathea* and allows at least as much awareness of difficulties and problems as any of Lyly's other works. The three ladies continue to resist love even in the play's last scene, long after (in the progress of the allegory) the benign concept of mutual, flexible interaction has become available. There is the suggestion of an egotism so profound that it cannot be brought into relationship to the external world except through coercion. *Love's Metamorphosis* does not include the page comedy that lightens up *Galathea* and tonally predicts a happy ending. One reaches the happy ending of *Love's Metamorphosis* with some feeling of relief, not through a play full of light or bland emotional ease. *Love's Metamorphosis* is also not very euphuistic. Instead of continuously providing symmetry, the play's language often conspicuously evades it. The description of the famine that will attack Erisichthon has some of the ruggedness and irregularity of seventeenth century "anti-Ciceronian" prose. The play in general experiments with asymmetry as a medium for its emotional, psychological conceptions.

The characterization of Protea involves a successful modulation for Lyly in the direction of genuine pathos. *Love's Metamorphosis* represents human beings' achievement of love against odds within themselves that must be taken seriously. Along with *Galathea* and *Endymion, the Man in the Moon*, this is one of the works by which Lyly ought to be remembered.

OTHER MAJOR WORKS

LONG FICTION: *Euphues, the Anatomy of Wit*, 1578; *Euphues and His England*, 1580.

NONFICTION: *Pap with an Hatchet*, 1589.

MISCELLANEOUS: *The Complete Works of John Lyly*, 1902, 1967 (3 volumes; R. Warwick Bond, editor).

BIBLIOGRAPHY

Alwes, Derek B. "'I Would Faine Serve': John Lyly's Career at Court." *Comparative Drama* 34, no. 4 (Winter, 2000):399-421. Alwes examines Lyly's dramatic works to see how they reflect on Lyly's career at court, especially how he portrays his relationship to Queen Elizabeth.

Fienberg, Nona. *Elizabeth, Her Poets, and the Creation of the Courtly Manner: A Study of Sir John Harington, Sir Philip Sydney, and John Lyly*. New York: Garland, 1988. An examination of Queen Elizabeth's relationship with several writers, including Lyly, and of British drama and poetry during her reign. Bibliography and index.

Houppert, Joseph W. *John Lyly*. Boston: Twayne, 1975. This general review of Lyly's career contains a brief discussion of euphuism and the prose period preceding dramatic involvement. The plays are analyzed as belonging to Lyly's early, middle, or late periods of development, and the scholarship is organized into negative and positive sections. Concludes with comments on Lyly's critical reputation and influence. Bibliography and index.

Pincombe, Michael, ed. *The Plays of John Lyly: Eros and Eliza*. New York: Manchester University Press, 1996. Describes the dramatic works of Lyly and details his relations with Queen Elizabeth. Bibliography and index.

Scragg, Leah. *The Metamorphosis of "Galathea": A Study in Creative Adaptation*. Washington, D.C.: University Press of America, 1982. An analysis of Lyly's *Galathea*, containing discussions of the play's relationship with the works of William Shakespeare and its source, the Greek deity of Galatea.

Wixson, Christopher. "Cross-dressing and John Lyly's *Galathea*." *Studies in English Literature, 1500-1900* 41, no.2 (Spring, 2001): 241-256. In his examination of cross-dressing in Lyly's *Galathea*, Wixson stresses that the phenomenon must be interpreted within the culture in which it existed, rather than interpreted according to the biases of modern times.

John F. McDiarmid,
updated by Howard L. Ford

M

CARSON MCCULLERS

Born: Columbus, Georgia; February 19, 1917
Died: Nyack, New York; September 29, 1967

PRINCIPAL DRAMA

The Member of the Wedding, pr. 1950, pb. 1951
    (adaptation of her novel)
The Square Root of Wonderful, pr. 1957, pb. 1958

OTHER LITERARY FORMS

Carson McCullers will be remembered primarily as a writer of fiction who experimented, with varying degrees of success, in the genres of drama, poetry, and the essay. She was one of the foremost of the remarkable generation of Southern women writers who, in addition to McCullers, included Flannery O'Connor, Eudora Welty, and Katherine Anne Porter. With her fellow women writers, and with such Southern male writers as William Faulkner, Truman Capote, and Tennessee Williams, McCullers shares an uncanny talent for capturing the grotesque. Her fictional world is peopled with the freaks of society: the physically handicapped, the emotionally disturbed, the alienated, the disenfranchised. This preoccupation with the bizarre earned for her a major place in the literary tradition known as the "southern gothic," a phrase used to describe the writers mentioned above and others who use gothic techniques and sensibilities in describing the South of the twentieth century.

Few have created a fictional South as successfully as has McCullers in her best fiction. Hers is a small-town South of mills and factories, of barren main streets lined with sad little shops and cafés, of intolerable summer heat and oppressive boredom. In her first and perhaps best novel, *The Heart Is a Lonely Hunter* (1940), she portrays a small Southern town from the points of view of five of its residents: Mick Kelly, the confused adolescent heroine; Doctor Cope-

land, an embittered black physician whose youthful idealism has been destroyed; Jake Blount, an alcoholic drifter with Marxist leanings; Biff Brannon, the sexually disturbed owner of the café, where much of the novel's action takes place; and John Singer, the deaf-mute whose kindness, patience, and humanity to the other characters provide the moral center of the novel.

The themes of *The Heart Is a Lonely Hunter* are ones that McCullers never completely abandoned in her subsequent fiction and drama: the loneliness and isolation inherent in the human condition, the impossibility of complete reciprocity in a love relationship, the social injustice of a racially segregated South, and adolescence as a time of horrifying emotional and sexual confusion. In *Reflections in a Golden Eye* (1941), she explored sexual tension and jealousy among the denizens of a Southern army post. *The Member of the Wedding* (1946), the novel she later adapted into the successful play of the same title, treats the delicate symbiotic relationship between a lonely adolescent girl, her seven-year-old cousin, and a black domestic. *The Ballad of the Sad Café*, first published in *Harper's Bazaar* in 1943 and later in a collection of McCullers's short works, is justifiably called one of the finest pieces of short fiction in American literature. It deals with another bizarre triangle, this one involving a masculine, sexually frigid, small-town heiress; her cousin, a hunchback dwarf; and her former husband, a worthless former convict with an old score to settle.

The four works of fiction mentioned above guarantee McCullers a permanent place among American writers of World War II and the postwar era. She also published more than a dozen short stories, most of which are not specifically set in the South. The best of them—"Wunderkind" (1936) and "A Tree. A

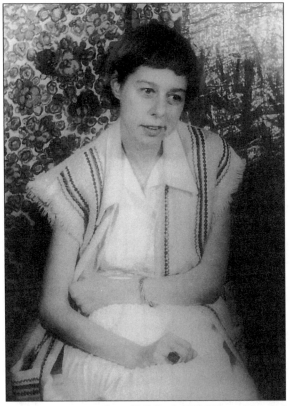

Carson McCullers in 1959. (Library of Congress)

Rock. A Cloud." (1942), for example—are proficiently executed exercises that demonstrate the sure control and balance so crucial to McCullers's longer fiction.

McCullers also wrote critical essays that betray a deep emotional and technical understanding of imaginative literature. Her small body of poetry, heavily influenced by the seventeenth century Metaphysicals, is consistently interesting. After McCullers's death, her sister, Margarita G. Smith, collected her previously uncollected short fiction, her literary criticism, and her poetry and essays in *The Mortgaged Heart* (1971).

ACHIEVEMENTS

Carson McCullers's reputation as a playwright rests solely on the phenomenal success of one play, *The Member of the Wedding*, which she based on her novel of the same title. Her only other play, *The Square Root of Wonderful*, was a critical and popular

failure and a professional disappointment from which McCullers never quite recovered. The very critics and theatergoers who hailed McCullers as a brilliant innovator in 1950 turned their backs on her in 1958. Flawed and uneven as her theatrical career was, however, McCullers deserves a special place among modern American playwrights, not only for what she achieved but also for what she attempted. With her friend Tennessee Williams, she was one of the first American playwrights to parlay a fragile, moody, nearly static vision of human frailty into solid commercial theater.

No one was more surprised by the success of *The Member of the Wedding* than McCullers herself. She had seen but a handful of plays in her life when Williams, with whom she was spending the summer of 1946 on Nantucket, suggested that she turn her novel into a play. Excited by the idea of writing in a new and unfamiliar genre and intrigued by Williams's sense that the novel had strong dramatic possibilities, McCullers spent that June calmly and steadily composing a draft of the play. Across the dining room table from her sat Williams, who was working on *Summer and Smoke*—it was the only time either of them was able to work with anyone else in the room. Despite Williams's willingness to help, McCullers steadfastly rejected her friend's advice, following instead her own creative instincts.

Though all odds were against it, the play was an immediate success when it opened on Broadway in January, 1950. Audiences gave the cast standing ovations, and the critics almost unanimously praised the work's grace, beauty, and timing. In the spring, *The Member of the Wedding* won two Donaldson Awards—as the best play of the season and as the best first Broadway play by an author—and the New York Drama Critics Circle Award for Best Play. McCullers was named Best Playwright of the Year and given a gold medal by the Theatre Club. *The Member of the Wedding* ran for 501 performances and grossed more than one million dollars on Broadway before enjoying a successful national tour.

This great acclaim, remarkable enough for a more conventional drama, is even more remarkable when one considers that *The Member of the Wedding* is a "mood play," dependent on emotion and feeling rather than on a standard plot. All three acts take place on one deliberately confining set, and much of the play's significant action happens offstage, "between acts," as it were. Indeed, even while praising the play, reviewers questioned whether it was a genuine drama at all. Like Williams's *The Glass Menagerie* (pr. 1944) and Arthur Miller's *Death of a Salesman* (pr. 1949)—significantly, the only two plays Carson McCullers had seen produced on Broadway before writing her hit—*The Member of the Wedding* is a play that subordinates plot to characterization, action to the almost poetic accretion of psychic detail. That audiences would even sit through, let alone cheer, such a slow-moving piece of drama was a revelation to the theater world of 1950.

The success of *The Member of the Wedding* solved McCullers's chronic financial problems and earned for her a reputation as a gifted and innovative dramatist, but seven years of ill health and personal tragedy ensued before her next play, *The Square Root of Wonderful*, opened on Broadway in October, 1957. Plagued from the outset by personnel changes and by McCullers's incompetence at the kind of last-minute rewriting required by the theater, the play failed almost immediately. Neither McCullers nor director Jose Quintero could do anything to save it, and it closed after only forty-five performances. The disaster of *The Square Root of Wonderful* left McCullers severely depressed, so anxious had she been to repeat the triumph of *The Member of the Wedding*. Various physical ailments by then made it difficult for her to write at all, and she never again attempted writing for the theater.

Biography

Carson McCullers's life was one beset by intolerable illnesses and complex personal relationships. The last twenty years of her life were spent in the shadow of constant physical pain, but like her fellow southerner Flannery O'Connor, she continued working in spite of her handicaps, seldom complaining. She was married twice to the same man, an emotional cripple who drained her financially and psychically and who ultimately killed himself. That she left behind her a

magnificent body of work and any number of devoted friends when she died at the tragically young age of fifty is a testament to the courage with which overwhelming obstacles can be overcome.

McCullers knew at first hand the small-town South that figures so prominently in her best writing. As the eldest of the three children of Lamar and Marguerite (Waters) Smith, Lula Carson Smith spent a normal middle-class childhood in the racially segregated mill town of Columbus, Georgia. Her father, like Mr. Kelly in *The Heart Is a Lonely Hunter* and Mr. Addams in *The Member of the Wedding*, was a jeweler who spent much of his time at work. Her mother, a lively, cultured woman and a strong influence throughout McCullers's life, encouraged her daughter's intellectual and artistic pursuits. By the age of fourteen, Carson Smith had dropped the Lula from her name and had announced her intention to become a concert pianist. She was by then practicing the piano several hours a day and taking lessons from Mary Tucker, the wife of an army colonel stationed at nearby Fort Benning. Her complex relationship with the Tucker family, at once giving her a sense of belonging and of estrangement, was later to provide material for the triangle theme of *The Member of the Wedding*. Like her heroine Frankie Addams, McCullers was fond of writing plays, casting them with family and friends, and staging them in her living room.

By the time she was graduated from high school, McCullers had already privately decided to become a writer rather than a musician. Inspired by the Russian realists and by the plays of Eugene O'Neill, McCullers had already tried her hand at both drama and fiction. The seventeen-year-old McCullers set out for New York City in September, 1934, with vague plans both to study music at the Juilliard School of Music and to study creative writing at Columbia University. By February, 1935, she had enrolled at Columbia, and the following September she enrolled in Sylvia Chatfield Bates's writing class at New York University.

During the summer of 1935, while she was vacationing in Georgia, a mutual friend introduced her to James Reeves McCullers, an army corporal stationed at Fort Benning. Reeves McCullers, like Carson, was interested in a career in letters. That he had neither the motivation nor the talent that enabled Carson to become a successful author was to be the source of much friction between them and a contributing factor to Reeves's eventual mental collapse. In 1936, Reeves left the army to join Carson in New York, and in September of 1937, they were married in the Smith home in Columbus.

By this time, McCullers had begun to undergo the cycles of illness and creativity that would characterize the rest of her life. Fatigued by the hectic pace of New York, she was forced to return to Georgia from time to time for peace and quiet, but her writing career had also taken off. Whit Burnett, with whom she had worked at Columbia, had published her story "Wunderkind" in the December, 1936, issue of his magazine *Story*, and she had begun to outline the plot of what would become her first novel, *The Heart Is a Lonely Hunter*. In the spring of 1939, while she was living with Reeves in Fayetteville, North Carolina, "The Mute" (as the novel was then called) was accepted by Houghton Mifflin. By autumn, she had completed a second manuscript, "Army Post" (later published as *Reflections in a Golden Eye*).

McCullers had long before vowed that when she would become a famous author, she would make New York her home. Feeling stifled in the South, their marriage in trouble, the McCullerses moved to New York only a few days after the publication of *The Heart Is a Lonely Hunter*, in June, 1940. The move, however, did nothing to improve their relationship. Carson, a sudden celebrity, was being courted by the literary world and making distinguished friends, among them W. H. Auden. That summer, as recipient of a fellowship to the Bread Loaf Writers Conference in Middlebury, Vermont, she came to know Wallace Stegner, Louis Untermeyer, and Eudora Welty. It was not only Carson's increasing fame and Reeves's continued obscurity that placed stress on their relationship. Both were sexually naïve at the time of their marriage, and both were given to infatuations with members of their own sex. Though most of their homosexual relationships remained unconsummated, Carson's crush on the brilliant young Swiss emigrant Annemarie Clarac-Schwarzenbach was difficult for

Reeves to tolerate. In September, 1940, Carson and Reeves separated. They were later divorced, only to remarry in 1945 when Reeves returned from action in World War II. For the rest of Reeves's life, they were to be alternately separated and reconciled. Their long and stormy relationship was ended only by Reeves's suicide in France in 1953.

When she separated from Reeves in the autumn of 1940, Carson accepted an invitation from her friend George Davis to move into a restored brownstone located in Brooklyn Heights. On establishing residence at 7 Middagh Street, she found herself in the midst of an unusual experiment in group housing; it later came to be known as February House. Besides her and Davis, the inhabitants included W. H. Auden, the striptease artist Gypsy Rose Lee, and, later, the composer Benjamin Britten and the writer Richard Wright and his family. McCullers made her home in this strange household intermittently for the next five years. When not traveling abroad, resting in Georgia, or spending time at Yaddo, the artists' colony in upstate New York, she played hostess in Brooklyn Heights to a distinguished group of celebrities from the literary and entertainment worlds, including Janet Flanner, Christopher Isherwood, Salvador Dalí, and Aaron Copland.

While in Georgia in February, 1941, McCullers suffered a stroke that left her partially blind and unable to walk for weeks. She would be victimized by such attacks for the rest of her life, and even after the first one, she never quite regained the kind of creative fervor of which she had once been capable. She was not to finish her next novel, *The Member of the Wedding*, until 1946, six years after she first started drafting it. Her final novel, *Clock Without Hands*, took her ten years to complete, not appearing until 1961. After 1947, as a result of the second severe stroke in a year, her left side was permanently paralyzed, and even the physical act of sitting at a typewriter was a challenge for her.

McCullers's Broadway career of the 1950's was, as has been noted, a source both of exhilaration and of disappointment for her. Nevertheless, her uneven career as a playwright brought her financial security, greater exposure than she had ever had before, and the fame she had craved since childhood. By the end of her life, she was an international literary celebrity, able to count among her personal friends the English poet Edith Sitwell and the Danish-born writer Isak Dinesen.

In 1958, severely depressed by Reeves's suicide in 1953, her mother's death in 1955, and the failure of her second play, McCullers sought professional psychiatric help from Dr. Mary Mercer, a therapist who was to care for McCullers until the author's death. Through the 1960's, McCullers was progressively less able and willing to leave the Nyack, New York, house that she had bought in 1951. She died there on September 29, 1967, of a cerebral hemorrhage.

ANALYSIS

Though Carson McCullers's reputation as a playwright will never approach her reputation as a writer of fiction, it is her uniqueness in both genres that accounts for both her successes and her failures. Her first play succeeded because it defied conventions of plot and action; her second play failed in part because it too often mixed the modes of tragedy, comedy, and romance. It is no accident that three of her novels have been made into successful films, nor is it accidental that no less a playwright than Edward Albee adapted her novella *The Ballad of the Sad Café* for the stage. McCullers's dramatic sense was in every way original, and both her hit play and her failure demand acceptance on their own terms, quite apart from the whims of current theatrical convention and popular tastes.

THE MEMBER OF THE WEDDING

Like the novel from which it was adapted, *The Member of the Wedding*, McCullers's first play, is a masterpiece of timing, mood, and character delineation. Insofar as there is a plot, it can be summarized as follows: Somewhere in the South, twelve-year-old Frankie Addams, a rebellious loner and a tomboy, secretly longs to belong to a group. Rejected by the girls at school, having recently lost her best friend, Frankie has no one to talk to except Berenice Sadie Brown, the black woman who cooks for Frankie and her father, and a seven-year-old cousin, John Henry. When she discovers that her brother, Jarvis, is going

to be married, Frankie decides to join him and his bride on their honeymoon and make her home with them in nearby Winter Hill, thus becoming once and for all a member—a member of the wedding. Though Berenice tries to make her come to her senses, Frankie persists in her plan and makes a scene during the ceremony, begging the couple to take her with them. When they refuse, an agonized Frankie vows to run away from home. Sticking her father's pistol into the suitcase that she has already packed for the honeymoon, Frankie does leave, but it is later disclosed that she has spent the night in the alley behind her father's store. Chastened and somewhat resigned, she returns home, admitting that she had thought of committing suicide but then had changed her mind.

By the end of the play, which takes place several months after the wedding, life has changed for all three main characters. John Henry has died of meningitis; Berenice has given notice to Mr. Addams; and Frankie, having largely outgrown the adolescent identity crisis of the previous summer, has acquired a best friend and a beau, both of whom she had earlier hated. Although Frankie is undoubtedly much happier than she was at the beginning of the play, she has become a pretentious teenager, bereft of the poetry and passion of childhood. Berenice has lost not only John Henry but also her foster brother, Honey, who has hanged himself in jail. As the curtain falls on the third act, Berenice is alone onstage, quietly singing "His Eye Is on the Sparrow," the song that she had sung earlier to calm the tortured Frankie.

Most of the "action" of the play takes place offstage and is only later recounted through dialogue. The wedding and Frankie's tantrum occur in the living room of the Addams house, but the scene never moves from the kitchen: The audience is told about the wedding and about Frankie's disgrace by characters who move back and forth between the two rooms. Both Honey's and John Henry's deaths occur between scenes, as does Frankie's night in the alley. By thus deemphasizing dramatic action, McCullers is able to concentrate on the real issue of the play, the relationship among Frankie, Berenice, and John Henry. By confining the action to one set, the kitchen and backyard of the Addams residence, the author effectively forces the audience to empathize with Frankie's desperate boredom and sense of confinement (and, perhaps, with Berenice's position in society as a black domestic). For much of the play, the three main characters are seated at the kitchen table, and this lack of movement lends the work the sense of paralysis, of inertia, that McCullers learned from the plays of Anton Chekhov and applied to the South of her childhood.

Frankie Addams is one of the most memorable adolescents in literature, at the same time an embodiment of the frustrations and contradictions inherent in adolescence and a strongly individual character. She yearns to belong to a group even as she shouts obscenities and threats to the members of the neighborhood girls' club. She is both masculine and feminine, a tomboy with a boy's haircut and dirty elbows who chooses a painfully vampish gown for her brother's wedding. McCullers skillfully exploits alternately comic and tragic aspects of Frankie's character. The audience must laugh at her histrionic declarations ("I am sick unto death!") but must also experience a strong identification with her sense of vulnerability and isolation ("I feel just exactly like somebody has peeled all the skin off me"). Caught between childhood and womanhood, she is curious about both sexual and spiritual love. She claims to have been asked for a date by a soldier, only to wonder aloud "what you do on dates," and she is still capable of climbing into Berenice's lap to hear a lullaby. Frankie's body is fast maturing, but her emotions are slow in catching up.

Berenice Sadie Brown serves in the play as Frankie's main female role model (Frankie's own mother has died in childbirth), an embodiment of fully realized adult sexuality. As complex a character as Frankie, Berenice is much more than a servant: She is confessor, nurse, and storyteller. At forty-five, Berenice has been married four times but truly loved only her first husband—the remaining three she married in vain attempts to regain the bliss she enjoyed with Ludie Maxwell Freeman. Her search for love closely parallels Frankie's own, and despite their often antagonistic relationship, they share moments of spiritual harmony, as when they discuss the nature of love, a "thing known and not spoken."

Berenice also represents the position of the black in a segregated South; indeed, the issue of racism is very much present in *The Member of the Wedding* (as it is in *The Heart Is a Lonely Hunter* and *Clock Without Hands*), a fact that has often been overlooked by critics of both the novel and the play. Though she is the most influential adult in the world of the two white children, she is treated as a servant by the white adults. Berenice must deal not only with Frankie's growing pains but also with problems ultimately more grave: the funeral of an old black vegetable vendor and the arrest, imprisonment, and suicide of her foster brother, Honey. Both Berenice and T. T. Williams, her beau, behave noticeably differently around white adults, while Honey, in a sense representative of a new generation of Southern blacks, refuses even to call Mr. Addams "sir." He is eventually jailed for knifing a white bartender who will not serve him. Honey's flight in the third act coincides with Frankie's own. Like Frankie, Honey is rebellious and frustrated, but unlike her, he is unable to find a place for himself in a hostile society. Death for Honey is preferable to confinement in the "nigger hole" or more "bowing and scraping" to white people.

If Honey's death in the third act symbolizes the end of Frankie the rebel, the death of John Henry represents the end of Frankie's childhood. Throughout the play, John Henry acts as a sort of idiot savant, uttering lines of great insight and demanding the plain truth from a hypocritical adult world. He asks Berenice why Mr. Addams has called Honey a nigger, and seems, ironically, incapable of understanding the nature of death. He is a link between Frankie and her childhood, a constant reminder of how recently she played with dolls (he gratefully accepts the doll that Jarvis has given Frankie as a gift after she rejects it). Frankie wants at once to be John Henry's playmate and to outgrow him. Though the transformed Frankie reacts coldly to John Henry's death, Berenice is devastated by it. She truly loved her "little boy," and she blames herself for having ignored his complaints of headaches in the first stages of his disease. John Henry dies a painful death, a victim who has done nothing to deserve his cruel fate.

The Member of the Wedding is a play about growing up, but it is also about the sacrifices that must be made before one can enter the adult world. Frankie is composed and even confident at the end of the play, but she has lost whatever sympathy she had for Berenice. Berenice is severely depressed by two deaths whose logic defies her. John Henry and Honey are dead, and the newlyweds are stationed in occupied Germany. When Berenice is left alone onstage at the end of the third act, holding John Henry's doll and singing a song whose truth the play has seriously questioned, the audience is forced to wonder with her whether the adult world of compromise and responsibility is worth entering.

THE SQUARE ROOT OF WONDERFUL

McCullers stated in the author's preface to the published version of *The Square Root of Wonderful* that the lives and deaths of her mother and her husband in part compelled her to write the play. Marguerite Smith's grace, charm, and love of life emerge in the character of Mollie Lovejoy, while Phillip Lovejoy embodies all the tragic contradictions that led Reeves McCullers to alcoholism and suicide. Like so much of McCullers's work, the play concerns a love triangle: Mollie Lovejoy, who lives on an apple farm in suburban New York with her twelve-year-old son, Paris, has twice been married to Phillip Lovejoy, an alcoholic writer now confined to a sanatorium. As the play opens, Mollie has only recently met John Tucker, a no-nonsense architect who is determined to wed her. Complications arise when Phillip Lovejoy unexpectedly returns to the farm, intent on a reconciliation with Mollie. His mother and his spinster sister are also on the scene, having come to New York from the South to visit Mollie and Paris and to see Phillip's new play (ironically, a failure).

The relationship between Phillip and Mollie has been a stormy one. The sexual attraction between them remains strong, and they sleep together on the night of Phillip's return, much to the chagrin of John Tucker. Still, Mollie cannot forget the years of drunken abuse she suffered at Phillip's hands. Physical abuse she could tolerate, but she decided to divorce him finally when he humiliated her by telling her that she used clichés. Mollie is clearly in a di-

lemma. In one of the play's most successful scenes, she admits to Paris that she loves both John and Phillip.

Phillip's problems, however, are manifold and insoluble. Clearly, he wants a reunion with Mollie so that she will protect him, as she once did, from his own self-destructive tendencies. When he at length realizes that Mollie will not return to him and, perhaps more important, that he will never again be able to write, he commits suicide by driving his car into a pond. With Phillip's death, Mollie is free to leave the apple farm and move to New York, and there is every reason to believe that she will eventually marry John Tucker.

Despite its commercial and critical failure, the play is perhaps worthy of more attention than it has received. At its best, it is a meditation on the nature of love. Mollie Lovejoy has always conceived of love as a sort of magic spell that is divorced from logic and free will. Her love for Phillip has brought her as much humiliation as happiness. From John Tucker, she learns that love can also be a matter of choice among mature adults. He uses the language of mathematics in describing his view of love to Paris: For John, humiliation is the square root of sin, while love is the square root of wonderful. The minor characters also provide interesting commentaries on the nature of love. Sister Lovejoy, the spinster librarian, lives in a world of fictional lovers drawn from the pages of books. Mother Lovejoy, while often a comic character, is at bottom a loveless woman who has spent her life humiliating her daughter.

The play's weaknesses, however, are many. The sure sense of timing that characterizes *The Member of the Wedding* is largely absent from *The Square Root of Wonderful*. The shifts in mood are less subtle than in the earlier play, and tragedy often follows too closely on the heels of comedy. The superb early morning scene in which Phillip Lovejoy says good-bye to his son, for example, is too rapidly undercut by a comic scene between Mother and Sister Lovejoy as they discuss Phillip's death. This tragicomic mixture of modes that McCullers executes so well in *The Member of the Wedding* goes awry in *The Square Root of Wonderful*, in part because none of the characters—except, perhaps, Phillip Lovejoy—is carefully enough drawn to elicit an audience's sympathy.

McCullers's best work is set in the South, not in upstate New York farmhouses. Her best work is also fiercely individual, completely defiant of convention and popular tastes. *The Square Root of Wonderful* fails largely because its author, in her eagerness to produce a second Broadway triumph, allowed producers, directors, and script doctors to strip it of the brilliant idiosyncracies that make *The Member of the Wedding* an American classic.

OTHER MAJOR WORKS

LONG FICTION: *The Heart Is a Lonely Hunter*, 1940; *Reflections in a Golden Eye*, 1941; *The Ballad of the Sad Café*, 1943 (serial), 1951 (book); *The Member of the Wedding*, 1946; *Clock Without Hands*, 1961; *Carson McCullers, Complete Novels*, 2001.

SHORT FICTION: *The Ballad of the Sad Café: The Novels and Stories of Carson McCullers*, 1951; *The Ballad of the Sad Café and Collected Short Stories*, 1952, 1955; *The Shorter Novels and Stories of Carson McCullers*, 1972.

CHILDREN'S LITERATURE: *Sweet as a Pickle and Clean as a Pig*, 1964.

MISCELLANEOUS: *The Mortgaged Heart*, 1971 (short fiction, poetry, and essays; Margarita G. Smith, editor).

BIBLIOGRAPHY

Bloom, Harold, ed. *Carson McCullers*. New York: Chelsea House, 1986. A collection of essays critically analyzing the works of McCullers. Bibliography and index.

Carr, Virginia Spencer. *The Lonely Hunter: A Biography of Carson McCullers*. New York: Carroll & Graf, 1985. A biography of McCullers that covers her life and work. Bibliography and index.

_____. *Understanding Carson McCullers*. Columbia: University of South Carolina Press, 1990. An examination of the works of McCullers. Bibliography and index.

Clark, Beverly Lyon, and Melvin J. Friedman, eds. *Critical Essays on Carson McCullers*. New York: G. K. Hall, 1996. Selected essays on McCullers that examine her life and work, with emphasis on her southern origins. Bibliography and index.

McDowell, Margaret M. *Carson McCullers*. Boston: Twayne, 1980. An analysis of McCullers's fiction and drama. Contains a brief chronology, a bibliography of works by and about McCullers, and an index.

Rich, Nancy B. *The Flowering Dream: The Historical Saga of Carson McCullers*. Chapel Hill, N.C.: Chapel Hill Press, 1999. An examination of McCullers's work, including her dramas. Bibliography.

Savigneau, Josyane. *Carson McCullers: A Life*. Boston: Houghton Mifflin, 2001. A biography of McCullers, looking at her works and her life, including her southern upbringing. Bibliography and index.

J. D. Daubs,
updated by Katherine Lederer

DONAGH MACDONAGH

Born: Dublin, Ireland; November 22, 1912
Died: Dublin, Ireland; January 1, 1968

PRINCIPAL DRAMA
Happy as Larry, wr. 1941, pr., pb. 1946
God's Gentry, pr. 1951
Step-in-the-Hollow, pr. 1957, pb. 1959
Lady Spider, pb. 1980

OTHER LITERARY FORMS
In addition to writing plays, Donagh MacDonagh collaborated with A. J. Potter in a ballet, *Careless*

Love, and an opera, *Patrick*, neither of which has been published. MacDonagh published two essays—one on his father, Thomas MacDonagh, in 1945, and one on James Joyce, in 1957—and was the author of several short stories. He often wrote new lyrics for old Irish ballads, some of which are collected in *The Hungry Grass* (1947) and *A Warning to Conquerors* (1968), two volumes of his poetry. With Lennox Robinson, MacDonagh coedited *The Oxford Book of Irish Verse* (1958) and, at the time of his death, was working on a dictionary of Dublin slang, which remains unfinished. The dictionary and the rest of MacDonagh's personal library and papers became the property of the Irish University Press.

Most important is MacDonagh's poetry, published in four volumes: *Twenty Poems* (1933), *Veterans and Other Poems* (1941), *The Hungry Grass*, and *A Warning to Conquerors*. Even his earliest poems are essentially dramatic and therefore foreshadow his later plays. Some, such as "Dublin Made Me" and "The Hungry Grass," are essentially mood pieces calculated to evoke in the reader precise feelings, such as patriotic allegiance to a proud, unbowed city or the nameless, all-encompassing fear of straying into a cursed area. Other poems are character sketches or dramatic dialogues apparently indebted to Alfred, Lord Tennyson.

Major themes of MacDonagh's drama also appear in his early poetry. In "Alleged Cruelty," for example, MacDonagh writes that we are all torn "with longings/ For something undefinable and wild," a recurrent thought in both the author's poems and his plays, often symbolized by the beauty of an unattainable woman. In contrast to such longings, our real lives, the poet asserts, are more like a horse, freighted with each passing year, endlessly running around the same track, or like "the changeless sound/ Of an engine running." This view leads MacDonagh to see past, present, and future as the same and therefore to accept and make the most of an inherently flawed world. Allied with this perception is a strong note of resignation, perhaps even fatalism, that creeps into MacDonagh's poetry from time to time, most notably in "The Veterans," one of his best poems. Like William Butler Yeats's "Easter 1916," "The Veterans" examines the famous Easter Rising of 1916. For his part in this rebellion, MacDonagh's father, Thomas MacDonagh, was executed on May 3, 1916. Whereas Yeats questions the human cost of this Irish rebellion, Donagh MacDonagh, one generation later, questions its legacy. Domesticated by time and history, the Easter Rising has become "petrified" and academic, at best a shadowy memory of what it once was.

Two other themes are worth mentioning, one traditional and the other radically modern. Like the Elizabethan sonneteers, especially William Shakespeare, MacDonagh sometimes envisioned life as a struggle between love and the ravages of time. In his poems and some of his best plays, "Joy" and "the heart's extravagance" are offered as experiences that temporarily halt the inexorable corrosion of time. More contemporary is MacDonagh's recognition that culture, knowledge, and thought are all "varnish," under which lurks the primitive beast in all of us, from which springs "all wild desirable barbarities" and "time's rat teeth."

ACHIEVEMENTS

Although Donagh MacDonagh was a poet, playwright, and scholar, a writer of ballads and short stories, the coauthor of a ballet and an opera, and a skillful and knowledgeable editor of Irish poetry, his real achievements are hard to gauge. This is true for two reasons. First, scholarly analysis of the Irish playwrights and poets who followed William Butler Yeats, John Millington Synge, George Russell (Æ), and Sean O'Casey is insufficient. Consequently, no complete history of modern Irish drama, no adequate bibliography, and few good anthologies exist. Indeed, many important plays of this period, at least one of which is by MacDonagh, remain unedited and unpublished. Other than a brief but trenchant study by Robert Hogan, the dean of modern Irish studies, few scholarly evaluations of MacDonagh have appeared. The second reason for the neglect of MacDonagh's work is more personal. His father, Thomas MacDonagh, has been the subject of numerous articles and two critical biographies, and the political and historical importance of the father has tended to overshadow the literary achievements of the son.

Some tentative judgments of Donagh MacDonagh, however, can be made. He was a better poet and playwright than his more famous father, and he, along with T. S. Eliot, deserves pride of place for attempting to resurrect poetic drama in the modern theater. In fact, MacDonagh's verse is more flexible and lively than Eliot's, and it has a much broader range, from ballad forms to rhyming couplets, from blank verse to colloquial Irish expressions, à la Synge. *Happy as Larry* is the best-known Irish verse play of recent memory, and some of MacDonagh's other plays, though almost completely unknown, are even better. His plays are notable for their deft characterization, whether sketched in detail or painted with a broad brush. Fame largely eluded MacDonagh during his lifetime, although he was elected to the Irish Academy of Letters, saw his verse play *Happy as Larry* translated into twelve European languages, and gained great popularity as a broadcaster on Radio Éireann, where he sang and recited folk ballads and ballad operas, often his own, and where he explained the significance and importance of Irish songs and poetry to a large and enthusiastic listening audience. Selected by Robinson to help edit *The Oxford Book of Irish Verse*, MacDonagh also contributed a learned and insightful introduction to the collection.

Biography

Born in Dublin on November 22, 1912, Donagh MacDonagh made the most of a life that was singularly unlucky and troubled. His father, Thomas MacDonagh, the great Irish patriot, was executed when Donagh was only three years old, and shortly afterward the young boy contracted tuberculosis. On July 9, 1917, only fifteen months after his father's death, Muriel MacDonagh, Donagh's mother, drowned while attempting to swim to an island off the shore of Skerries, an ocean resort close to Dublin. Thereafter, the custody of Donagh and his sister Barbara was contested for some time by the families of their father and mother, apparently in part because of a disagreement about whether the children should be reared as Catholics.

In time, Donagh was sent off to school, first to Belvedere College, where James Joyce had been a student some years earlier, and then to University College, Dublin, where he was part of a brilliant student generation that included such future notables as Niall Sheridan, Brian O'Nolan (who is best known under his pen names, Flann O'Brien and Myles na Gopaleen), Denis Devlin, Charles Donnelly—MacDonagh's close friend who died in 1937 during the Spanish Civil War—and Cyril Cusack, who later became an accomplished actor.

MacDonagh took both his bachelor of arts and master of arts degrees at University College, Dublin, and became a barrister in 1935. He practiced law until 1941, when he was named as a district justice for County Dublin, a post that required much traveling in the countryside.

At the time of his death on New Year's Day, 1968, MacDonagh was serving as a justice for the Dublin Metropolitan Courts. MacDonagh was twice married. His first wife drowned while she was taking a bath, and his second wife, who survived him, later choked to death on a chicken bone.

Analysis

Donagh MacDonagh's plays derive from three distinct sources. The first of these is the double heritage of the early Abbey Theatre: Yeats's romantic, poetic drama and the more realistic plays of Edward Martyn. All of MacDonagh's major works are comedies—even *Lady Spider* is technically a comedy—but in each one, the author offers a particular blend of realism and fantasy, with one or the other usually predominating. Another important source for MacDonagh's drama is his deep love of poetry and various verse forms. As a practicing poet, he attempted to revive the marriage of poetry and drama, experimenting with different types of verse that he thought were appropriate for and pleasing to theater audiences. The third source of MacDonagh's art is his great learning, above all his familiarity with Elizabethan and Jacobean drama, especially Shakespeare, and his scholar's interest in old Irish poetry and ballads and in various Irish dialects and slang.

Happy as Larry

All of these influences are present in MacDonagh's first published drama, *Happy as Larry*, his most popular and successful play. Technically accomplished, *Happy as Larry* has been described as "a ballad opera without music," and the definition is a good one. The rhythms of well-known Irish ballads and the use of homey Irish words and phrases provide a constant undercurrent of familiar patterns that make the verse easy to listen to or to read. MacDonagh employs short, medium, and long lines of verse, together with musical repetitions and refrains, to which he adds simplicity and clarity of diction. The result is a verse play of uncommon pleasure.

The plot of *Happy as Larry* is highly fanciful and melodramatic. Six tailors, one of whom is Larry's grandson, are located on the outer stage and introduce the story. Larry, a hard-drinking, fast-talking Irishman, happens on a young woman of about twenty who is kneeling by the grave of Johnny, her recently deceased husband. She is fanning the dirt on Johnny's grave, for her late husband made her promise not to marry again until the clay on his grave is dry. Intrigued and amused, Larry invites the young widow home to have a cup of tea. Meanwhile, at Larry's house, the local Doctor is attempting to seduce Mrs. Larry. Soon after Larry and the widow arrive, Seamus, the pharmacist, enters with a vial of poison, ordered by the evil Doctor, who puts it in Larry's drink. Poor Larry dies from the poison, and the shocked and bereaved Mrs. Larry quickly plans a wake, during which the nefarious Doctor presses his suit. Soon Mrs. Larry weakens and agrees to marry the Doctor, even though her husband's corpse is not yet cold.

Outraged, the six tailors, with the help of the three Fates, travel back in time to join the party at Larry's wake, where they decide to take a hand in events by using the Doctor's own poison against him. The unsuspecting Doctor toasts his future happiness and promptly dies. Seamus convinces Mrs. Larry to draw some blood from Larry's corpse in order to give the Doctor a transfusion, which, according to the pharmacist, will bring the Doctor back to life. Mrs. Larry agrees but faints and dies when she sees Larry's blood. Incredibly, the blood she drains from Larry contains the poison that killed him, so Larry revives, believing that he is the victim of a monumental hangover. The young widow consoles Larry over the loss of his wife and talks him out of a life of debauchery and dissipation. The second tailor ends the play by telling the audience that Larry will marry the young widow and live happily ever after.

MacDonagh provides a cast of wonderfully drawn comic types to complement his fantastic plot. Mrs. Larry talks too much, bosses her poor husband around, and is somehow capable of delivering a highly metaphysical eulogy for her dead husband: "Empty on their racks the suits are hanging,/Mere foolish cloth whose meaning was their wearer." Still, she is a loving and faithful wife until Larry's death. The Gravedigger, wholly superfluous to the plot, is right out of William Shakespeare's *Hamlet*; he is a comic reductionist and a walking, talking memento mori whose every line is a reminder that death is both unpredictable and unconquerable. The young widow is the Gravedigger's opposite number, healthy and buxom, good-humored and witty, and convinced that she can conquer death—as, in a way, she does, by marrying again and refusing to be a widow for the rest of her life. Larry is the archetypal henpecked husband, decent enough and faithful to his wife, but not above a little flirting on the side.

The star of the show is MacDonagh's evil Doctor, a hilarious combination of Oil Can Harry and Groucho Marx. MacDonagh endows the Doctor with the spurious eloquence of a first-class rake and with the persuasive powers of John Donne. Arguing at one point that love is religion because God is love, the Doctor slyly turns to Mrs. Larry and croons, "Let us pray/Together, Mrs. Larry." Later, this schemer touts the virtues of friendship to Mrs. Larry, arguing that since friendship transcends passion, his kiss should be allowed to linger. When the six tailors succeed in poisoning him, the audience is sure to cheer: He has been hoisted with his own petard.

The Doctor's fellow in crime, the unctuous pharmacist, spotlights MacDonagh's major theme in the play. Seamus's presence in this comedy is a kind of learned joke: The Greek *pharmakos* means both remedy and poison, just as the word "drug" even today carries both a positive and a negative sense. Thus, infusing this delightful comedy is a vision of the world in which nearly everything cuts two ways, and in which rigid views, either of proper conduct or of the opposite sex, need to be broadened and softened. Except for the Doctor and his henchman Seamus, everyone in *Happy as Larry* is a mingled yarn—both good and bad together.

The play gently asks us to support a widow's right to remarry. According to custom, especially in Catholic Ireland, widows do better to honor the memory of their dead husbands by not remarrying—Mrs. Larry makes exactly this point to the young widow—yet such expectations are both unrealistic and cruel, as Mrs. Larry discovers in the course of the play. MacDonagh endorses the young widow's wish to marry again rather than follow the outdated suicide of Dido or the self-immolation of Indian wives, both mentioned at the start of the play.

Allied to the theme of remarriage is MacDonagh's attempt to adjust male attitudes toward women. Though written twenty years before the rebirth of feminism in the 1960's, the play poses a key question about Larry's two wives: Which is bad and which is good? The answer is that both are essentially good. The play approves of Mrs. Larry's wish for companionship after Larry's death, though it does not approve of the way the Doctor manipulates her, and Mrs. Larry's attempt to save the Doctor, though it fails, stems from the reasonable premise that it is better to save a life than to let someone die. Likewise, the lusty young widow's wish to dry her husband's grave quickly is rewarded at the end of the play when MacDonagh allows her to marry Larry.

The second tailor, Larry's grandson, begins as a misogynist—"Woman curses every plan"—but ends by praising the many virtues of the young widow and by wishing that his own son "may be as happy as Larry." Like the second tailor, the audience learns the need for tolerance and empathy in an imperfect world.

Step-in-the-Hollow

Step-in-the-Hollow, like *Happy as Larry*, is an experimental play. Local dialects and lively, contemporary turns of phrase energize this comedy, which, again like its predecessor, contains a wide variety of verse forms. In both technique and construction, however, *Step-in-the-Hollow* is superior to *Happy as Larry* and was a great success when it premiered at the Gaiety Theatre, Dublin, on March 11, 1957. Parts of the play are written in rhyming couplets, a difficult and demanding form that MacDonagh uses with great skill and to good effect. The verse is flexible enough for the actors to avoid the singsong monotony that can vitiate a long series of couplets, and MacDonagh also employs the couplet form wisely: to highlight important moments in the play and as a device to underscore the character of Julia O'Sullivan, the local harridan who threatens to destroy Justice Redmond O'Hanlon, the main character.

The play is so well constructed that it moves along with great speed, full of interest and crackling with life and vitality. MacDonagh deftly uses the first act to introduce the main complications one by one. First, the audience learns that a government inspector is on his way to evaluate the courtroom procedures of Justice O'Hanlon. Then Julia O'Sullivan appears, with her daughter, aptly named Teazie, in tow, demanding that the Justice try Crilly Duffy, a local boy, for compromising her daughter's virtue. Throughout, the reactions of the Justice's cohorts—Molly, the Sergeant, and the Clerk—establish their essential characters for the audience, while MacDonagh holds back the main antagonists, Justice Redmond O'Hanlon and Sean O'Fenetic, the government inspector. When the Judge finally enters, MacDonagh adds a third complication: An old man, much like Redmond O'Hanlon, was in Teazie's room before Crilly Duffy entered.

Act 2 consists of two short scenes in which the case of O'Sullivan versus Duffy is argued and almost resolved. With the Inspector watching every move, Justice O'Hanlon tries as hard as he can to prevent the truth from being discovered, but Julia O'Sullivan discovers that O'Hanlon, not Duffy, is the real villain and storms into the courtroom to accuse the Justice. Overcome with emotion and gin, she builds to a climax at great length, allowing O'Hanlon to adjourn the court and whisk away the Inspector before Julia can name the man who compromised her little Teazie.

Act 3 belongs wholly to Molly Nolan, who conceives and executes a plan that saves the Justice, the Sergeant, and the Clerk, while ensuring her own future as the heir of Redmond O'Hanlon and the new wife of the Inspector. Skillful, effective, and satisfying, the conclusion to *Step-in-the-Hollow* is both unexpected and delightful.

The twin themes of this play are love and justice. The symbol of playful, worldly love is Sandro Botticelli's *The Birth of Venus*, prominently displayed in Justice Redmond O'Hanlon's apartment, the location for acts 1 and 3. During the play, MacDonagh examines different kinds of love: the May-December infatuation of the Justice for Teazie; the young love of Crilly and Teazie, who are to be married by the end of the play; the romantic, yet imprudent, love of the Sergeant for Molly; the lascivious love of the Justice for Molly; the liquor-induced love of the Clerk for Molly; and, finally, the birth of the Inspector's love for Molly, which she both induces and accepts in act 3.

In some ways, Molly is an unlikely heroine—as clever and resourceful as Shakespeare's comic heroines, whom she clearly resembles but with much less chastity. She took a tumble in the hay with the Sergeant once, and the full extent of her duties for the Justice clearly exceed those of a paid housekeeper. Moreover, Molly is no starry-eyed, empty-headed girl, such as Teazie; rather, she wants respectability and a good fortune, as well as the passion of first love, all of which the Inspector finally provides. Molly is not above asking, "What's in it for me?" and her mixture of love and prudence carries the day for herself and for others.

Molly's attitude toward love is highly practical, not extreme. The need for a practical, reasonable approach to justice is the play's complementary theme. Justice Redmond O'Hanlon and Inspector Sean O'Fenetic represent radical attitudes toward the law, neither of which can be accepted. Once a good scholar and student of the law, Justice O'Hanlon has been worn down by thirty years on the bench and has become the very embodiment of the Seven Deadly Sins that justice seeks to prevent and punish. On the other hand, the God-fearing Inspector, sworn to temperance, is an essentially innocent and sterile advocate of governmental rules and regulations that often hinder instead of promote the impartial administration of justice. Molly, rather than the Justice or the Inspector, leads the audience to a better understanding of justice and the law. She puts the Inspector in the same compromising position in which Crilly Duffy found Justice Redmond O'Hanlon. The point is simple and clear: Let him who is without sin cast the first stone. Mercy and forgiveness, and a second chance, are the better parts of justice.

As in his other plays, MacDonagh's characters are exceptionally well drawn—from the gin-soaked Julia O'Sullivan and the voyeuristic Mary Margaret Allen to the inhibited Inspector, who, with Molly's help, discovers at the end of the play that he has always been afraid of women. Above all, there is Justice Redmond O'Hanlon, an authentic triumph of the literary imagination. Old in years yet young at heart, limping after his last exploit with Teazie yet still chasing after women, this fat Justice is a liar, a cheat, and a scoundrel, but his cleverness and humor are endearing qualities that help him retain audience sympathy. He derives from Sir John Falstaff, as does the basic conflict of *Step-in-the-Hollow*: The clash between the Inspector and the Justice is an Irish version of the contest between the Lord Chief Justice and Falstaff in Shakespeare's *Henry IV, Part II* (pr. 1598). Moreover, some of the pathos and melancholy of Shakespeare's work creep into MacDonagh's play: Justice O'Hanlon's startling admission, "An old man knows what's lost," echoes Falstaff's frank confession in *Henry IV, Part II*, "I am old, I am old."

In part, however, O'Hanlon is an alter ego of the author himself, who also spent many years on the bench in Ireland. Though obvious differences exist between the playwright and his creation, a Justice who quotes T. S. Eliot and who displays above his bench the harp of Ireland, the symbol of old Irish poetry and music, shares something with MacDonagh. One suspects, for example, that O'Hanlon's wish to replace the rules of evidence with common sense echoes the wish of his creator, and the Justice's view that the law seems bent on mystifying common people may also have been shared by MacDonagh.

The Justice provides a sobering counterpoint to an otherwise happy ending. As the curtain is about to fall, O'Hanlon stands alone, looking out the window at Molly and the Inspector as they leave to get married. To grow old, the Justice muses, is to gain money, place, and power but to lose forever carefree youth and the chance to be in love again. "I can't complain" is O'Hanlon's last line, but the audience knows better.

LADY SPIDER

Lady Spider is MacDonagh's most daring and ambitious play, in which he offers his version of the Deirdre legend that has obsessed Irish poets and playwrights for more than one hundred years. The tragedy of Deirdre is to the Irish imagination as Homer's *Iliad* (c. 750 B.C.E.; English translation, 1614) is to the English, and it is fair to say that MacDonagh handles the love of Deirdre and Naoise much as Shakespeare treats the story of Troilus and Cressida. *Lady Spider* minimizes romance and fantasy by pushing comedy to the limits of realism. In short, MacDonagh demythologizes myth by making it modern, psychological, and political. The result is as brilliant as it is unsettling, a fable for modern times.

The story of Deirdre is part of the Red Branch Cycle of ancient Irish tales. During the reign of Conor, King of Ulster, a female child named Deirdre is born who, according to prophecy, will bring down the House of Usna and Emain Macha, the palace of King Conor. Conor refuses to kill the child; instead, he sends her into the wilderness to be brought up by Leabharcham, a nurse. Deirdre, whose name means "alarm" or "troubler," grows up to be so desirable that Conor intends to marry her, but she meets Naoise, a son of the House of Usna, and runs away with him and his two brothers, Ardan and Ainnle. After a few years, Conor sends Fergus to convince the lovers that all is forgiven. They accept Conor's offer to return to Ireland, whereupon the still lovesick king uses stealth and guile to kill Naoise and his brothers once they arrive at his palace. Three variant endings exist: Deirdre immediately kills herself, she quickly dies of sorrow, or Conor keeps her for a year, after which she commits suicide.

Three great Irish plays before MacDonagh's were based on the Deirdre legend, and each in its own way interprets Deirdre as a romantic symbol of female heroism and as a model of support, inspiration, and companionship for the Irish hero. In his *Deirdre* (1902), Æ depicts the heroine as the incarnation of the ancient Irish gods, who will one day return to validate the sacrifice of Deirdre and Naoise, made immortal by their escape into death. Images of sleep, dreams, and vision help establish a mystical context in which the world of myth and magic, not the everyday world, is the deepest reality and the most true. Yeats's *Deirdre* (pr. 1906) is an exercise in concentrated poetic imagery that accentuates the passion of the lovers and invites them to live forever in the Byzantium of art. The greatest of these three plays is Synge's *Deirdre of the Sorrows* (pr. 1910), written in simple, direct prose with a peasant dialect. Synge's version establishes a sympathetic connection between the lovers and nature; the lovers triumph over age and the mutability of earthly love by choosing the timeless immortality of death.

Just as Shakespeare wrote his *Troilus and Cressida* with Geoffrey Chaucer and Homer in mind, so MacDonagh composed his play as both a contribution to and a comment on the great plays that preceded his. He deromanticizes the story by using the technique of inversion. Unlike Æ, MacDonagh refers to no gods who wait in the wings, and mysticism gives way to a hard-nosed, deeply flawed world. Unlike Yeats, MacDonagh refuses to glorify the passion of Deirdre and Naoise; in fact, he purposefully degrades it into a sexual obsession that Deirdre must overcome. Like Synge, MacDonagh fills his play with nature imagery, but the effect is very different. Images of nature, animals, and food in *Lady Spider* accentuate the bestial side of man and his subjugation to appetites of all kinds. The blank verse that contains these images is tough, lean, and elemental, stunningly beautiful in its starkness.

The central purpose of *Lady Spider* is to criticize earlier versions of the Deirdre legend and to recover the basic meaning of the myth, which proves to be startlingly modern. This purpose may be seen by examining closely the way in which MacDonagh changes a scene that first appears in Synge's play. Synge invented the character of Owen, a grotesque peasant who values nothing but Deirdre's love. MacDonagh replaces Owen with Art, a Scottish king who promises Deirdre "honey words" and "truth," and who wishes to take her to the Palace of Art, the home of "sweet poetry," where all the bards and harpers will sing of Deirdre. She is singularly unimpressed with Art and threatens to cut out his tongue, the traditional punishment for poets who lie.

Literally, this exchange emphasizes Deirdre's desirability—wherever she goes, men lust after her. The scene also foreshadows the real reason that Conor wants her back in Ireland: Like King Art, King Conor is a lustful, unprincipled old man, as drawn to Deirdre as any young man. Symbolically, however, the ugly little Scottish king represents literary art, which has tried to appropriate Deirdre for its own purposes, oblivious to the beauty of the original myth. As MacDonagh sees it, Æ, Yeats, Synge, and many others are guilty of attempted rape, of forcing the legend into wholly alien significance. Soon after Deirdre first meets Art, he is killed while attempting to flee and lies sprawling in the middle of the stage at the end of act 2. This is poetic justice, so to speak, and the end, MacDonagh implies, of all of this romantic Deirdre nonsense in Irish art.

As this short explication illustrates, *Lady Spider* is richly artistic, despite its attitude toward art and poetry, and its characters are superbly realized. Naoise, Deirdre's lover, is the playboy of the Western world, cynical about women and sex and unable to get enough of either, a sort of Hotspur without young Percy's charm. Naoise is full of empty idealism and self-interest but unable to develop into anything better. His rival Conor is shrewder and more intelligent but has grown old without wisdom. A superb manipulator of men, he is in turn manipulated by his own glands, which make him as lecherous as a monkey. Buffeted between these two men, Deirdre is a quintessentially modern woman, blamed for being the source of all trouble yet in reality the victim of men's appetites and of her own.

Deirdre's development is the center of interest in the play. At first, MacDonagh's Deirdre dreams romantically about men. It is love she wants, but in Naoise she gets animal lust that makes her his sexual thrall. Desperate, she puts Naoise under *geasa*— magical bonds that are supposed to force consent—in an attempt to make Naoise marry her. After the couple flees to Scotland, Deirdre hardens with time, still

sexually captivated by her lover but increasingly aware of his faults, especially his promiscuity. Lured back to Ireland, Deirdre has outgrown Naoise, both mentally and physically, and she has frank admiration for the way in which Conor outwits and outmanipulates her and Naoise, causing the death of the latter. Seeing that manipulation is the necessary means to any end in this brutal, political world, Deirdre resolves to become Conor's wife, not out of love or even pity but to torment him with his sexual inadequacy, thereby becoming his master, driving him to despair, and securing his crown for her son, who is safe in Scotland. Deirdre's final goal will elude her, for the audience knows in advance that she will be the one to commit suicide.

The world of *Lady Spider* turns on negatives, on false hopes and Pyrrhic victories. MacDonagh has revealed the modern world in an ancient mirror, and it is a world in which all value has drained away, a world in which love is reduced to sex, in which supernature is replaced by nature, in which wisdom gives way to craft and guile, and in which human virtues are supplanted by animal appetites. This kind of world cannot support real tragedy, and so Deirdre remains alive at the play's end—doomed but denied the dignity of death. Paradoxically, however, the play itself is captivating, possessed of a hard, gemlike brilliance that simply overpowers the audience with the force of MacDonagh's vision. For all of these reasons, *Lady Spider* is the best of the Deirdre plays. However, it may not be MacDonagh's best play.

GOD'S GENTRY

Surprisingly, *God's Gentry* remained unpublished despite the fact that Robert Hogan, one of the few scholars to have seen it acted, calls *God's Gentry* "a much more colorful and theatrical show than *Happy as Larry*." The exact opposite of *Lady Spider*, *God's Gentry* pushes romance and fantasy to their limits in a story about a band of tinkers who invoke the help of an Irish god to turn County Mayo upside down. Tinkers and gentry trade places for a year until the god's power wears off. According to Hogan, *God's Gentry* is a perfectly delightful play, full of "dancing, singing, spectacle, and high spirits." It remains for some enterprising scholar to edit and publish this play—

and other inaccessible or unpublished plays by MacDonagh—so that this neglected modern playwright can begin to receive the critical attention and the wide audience that he deserves.

OTHER MAJOR WORKS

POETRY: *Twenty Poems*, 1933; *Veterans and Other Poems*, 1941; *The Hungry Grass*, 1947; *A Warning to Conquerors*, 1968.

EDITED TEXT: *The Oxford Book of Irish Verse*, 1958 (with Lennox Robinson).

BIBLIOGRAPHY

Browne, E. Martin, ed. Introduction to *Four Modern Verse Plays*. Harmondsworth, Middlesex, England: Penguin Books, 1957. One of the plays selected is MacDonagh's *Happy as Larry*. Browne discusses the play's particular sense of poetic drama in terms that provide a useful approach not only to the work in question but also to MacDonagh's distinctive language and dramaturgy. The discussion also draws attention to differences between Mac-Donagh and other modern writers of verse plays.

Hogan, Robert. *After the Irish Renaissance: A Critical History of the Irish Drama Since "The Plough and the Stars."* Minneapolis: University of Minnesota Press, 1967. MacDonagh's background and career are described in the context of experimentation in verse drama by the generation of Irish playwrights who immediately succeeded William Butler Yeats. All MacDonagh's important plays are examined, and their distinctive poetic origins and attainments are assessed. Contains bibliographical information concerning the plays.

MacDonagh, Donagh. "The Death-watch Beetle." *Drama*, no. 12 (February, 1949): 4-7. MacDonagh provides a succinct account of the rise, and what he considers the imminent fall, of the Abbey Theatre. His views are revealing in the light of his own status as a playwright, the orientation and tone of his plays, and the production of his works by companies other than the Abbey.

MacDonagh, Thomas. *Literature in Ireland: Studies Irish and Anglo-Irish*. Rev. ed. Tyone, Ireland: Relay Books, 1996. This volume by Donagh Mac-Donagh's father sheds light on MacDonagh's heritage and work.

Norstedt, Johann A. *Thomas MacDonagh: A Critical Biography*. Charlottesville: University Press of Virginia, 1980. A biography of Donagh Mac-Donagh's poet-patriot father, which is essential reading for a sense of MacDonagh's background and his work's relationship to his illustrious heritage. Includes limited information relevant to an evaluation of MacDonagh's work for the theater. Also contains a full bibliography.

Wickstrom, Gordon M. "Introduction to *Lady Spider*." *Journal of Irish Literature* 9, no. 3 (1980): 4-82. A first publication of MacDonagh's least-known work, based on the well-known Irish legend of Deirdre. The work's place in the canon of plays dealing with the Deirdre legend is evaluated, thereby providing a brief, instructive introduction to MacDonagh's dramatic imagination. The text comes complete with editorial annotations.

Edmund M. Taft,
updated by George O'Brien

MARTIN MCDONAGH

Born: London, England; 1970

PRINCIPAL DRAMA

The Beauty Queen of Leenane, pr., pb. 1996
The Cripple of Inishmaan, pr. 1996, pb. 1997
A Skull in Connemara, pr., pb. 1997
The Lonesome West, pr., pb. 1997
Plays, pb. 1999
The Lieutenant of Inishmore, pr., pb. 2001

OTHER LITERARY FORMS

Martin McDonagh's best-known works are his stage plays. Before turning to playwriting, he attempted a variety of literary forms, including screenplays and short fiction; however, his only early works to receive notice are two radio plays produced in Australia.

ACHIEVEMENTS

Martin McDonagh burst on the theatrical scene in the 1990's with a series of stage plays that earned instant acclaim in both Great Britain and the United States for their traditional style and provocative content. He emerged as a playwright of consequence at the same time that several other young British playwrights, including Mark Ravenhill, Patrick Marder, and Sebastian Barry, were mounting similarly controversial plays. Their unabashedly graphic texts and unflinching depictions of emotional and physical violence earned them comparisons to the Angry Young Man movement spearheaded by John Osborne that revitalized the conservative cultural climate of Great Britain in the 1950's.

When McDonagh's first four plays ran simultaneously in London's West End in a span of less than two years, it was a virtually unprecedented achievement, all the more remarkable for a previously unproduced playwright. After their initial stagings, all three plays in his Leenane Trilogy were staged in sequence as a marathon by the Druid Theatre in both Ireland and England.

In 1996, McDonagh won both the *Evening Standard* Theatre Award for most promising playwright for *The Beauty Queen of Leenane* and the Critics' Circle Theatre Award for most promising playwright. The Broadway production of *The Beauty Queen of Leenane* won Tony awards for best actor, best actress, best featured actress, and best director. It was also nominated for best play, as was *The Lonesome West* in 1997.

BIOGRAPHY

Martin McDonagh was born in England of Irish parents in 1970. His father, a construction worker, and mother, a part-time house cleaner, had moved from Connemara, Ireland, to London in the 1960's and raised Martin and his older brother, John, in Camberwell, a working-class neighborhood in the southern part of the city. He dropped out of high school at the age of sixteen and spent the next five years living partly on unemployment benefits.

McDonagh's ambition to write first emerged during these years, encouraged in part by his well-read brother, who aspired to be a screenwriter. He began to write in earnest when he turned twenty-one and his unemployment benefits ran out. McDonagh took a job as clerk at the Department of Trade and Industry to support himself and in his spare time tried his hand at a variety of literary forms: television scripts, short stories, and video scripts. None sold. He submitted twenty-two radio plays to the British Broadcasting Corporation, all of which were rejected. Eventually two were broadcast by a station based in Sydney, Australia.

Martin McDonagh in 1998. (AP/Wide World Photos)

McDonagh turned next to stage plays. After several unsuccessful scripts derivative of David Mamet's work, all of which he eventually discarded, he wrote *The Beauty Queen of Leenane*, reportedly in an eight-day burst of creativity. The story of an elderly woman and her caretaker spinster daughter trapped in bitter, brutal cohabitation in a small town in contemporary Ireland, it found favor with Garry Hynes, director of the Druid Theatre. The play opened to rave reviews in Ireland in 1996, and within a month was playing at the Royal Court Theatre in London. It transferred later that year to London's West End.

The Beauty Queen of Leenane was the first play in McDonagh's Leenane Trilogy, all of whose plays are set in Connemara and explore the lives of characters trapped in a stultifying small-town setting. The period drama *The Cripple of Inishmaan*, the first play in his Aran Islands Trilogy, opened in December of 1996 at the Royal National Theatre, where he had been appointed a writer-in-residence. By 1997, the Royal Court had also produced the other two plays in the Leenane Trilogy, *A Skull in Connemara* and *The Lonesome West*. *The Beauty Queen of Leenane* opened on Broadway in the United States in 1998 and garnered multiple Tony Award nominations, including best play. Within three years, McDonagh's first four plays all had been staged in New York, and he had earned critical notice as one of the most exciting new dramatists of the twenty-first century.

In a very short period of time, McDonagh established a reputation as one of the most provocative playwrights of his generation, a confrontational writer unafraid to explore the powerful, at times destructive emotions of his characters or tensions in relationships with the potential to explode in violence. The second play in his Aran Islands trilogy, *The Lieutenant of Inishmore*, a profile of an Irish terrorist, was deemed too controversial to stage and rejected by several theaters before it was mounted by the Royal Shakespeare Company in 2001.

Despite the acclaim for his playwriting and comparisons of his work to playwrights of the Irish Literary Renaissance, in interviews, McDonagh has professed indifference to the stage. He has rarely seen productions of other playwrights and has been more inspired by television and film, stating an interest in scripting, producing, and directing films.

ANALYSIS

Martin McDonagh's plays are set in rural Irish villages whose residents speak in a patois spiked with the coarse expressions of common people. As chronicles of small-town Irish life, they extend the literary tradition established by John Millington Synge, Sean O'Casey, and other writers of the Irish Literary Renaissance of the early twentieth century, who viewed the tensions and struggles within traditional Irish society as prognostic of greater social and political forces affecting the nation. McDonagh's dramas differ in their virtual avoidance of any overt political agenda and focus on fallible characters living lives shaped, and often malformed, by personal flaws and values peculiar to small-town life.

Loneliness is a common theme in McDonagh's plays. His main characters not only live in towns outside the social mainstream but also exist on the fringe of their society, set apart by personal inadequacies, physical afflictions, or criminal tendencies. Invariably, their efforts to integrate with their peers or flee to a fresh start in life meet with disappointment and disillusionment.

Though McDonagh's plays have a traditional style, they are notably modern in their quotient of violence. Characters mock one another in exchanges riddled with insults and obscenities that give the dramas a darkly comic edge. These verbal assaults sometimes culminate in physical assault and even murder. Usually, the most troubled and inevitably fatal relationships are those that should offer people the greatest comfort: between children and parents, husbands and wives, and siblings. The fragility of these familial bonds evokes a sense of moral instability and precariousness in the world of these plays.

The brutality of McDonagh's work is its most controversial aspect, and his plays have been criticized for pandering to tastes shaped by the violent excesses of television and film, the influence of which he openly acknowledges. If anything, McDonagh suggests that violence is actually an intimate form of social intercourse between his characters. As one character says in *The Lonesome West*, "It does show you care, fighting does." The violence of McDonagh's dramas contribute to their spirit of cynicism, which also is fueled by their mockery of traditional depictions of Irish life. McDonagh is very self-conscious of romantic images of Ireland in film and fiction and uses these as a measuring stick against which his grubby, realistic depictions of everyday life in ordinary towns fall woefully short.

The Beauty Queen of Leenane

McDonagh's first produced play, *The Beauty Queen of Leenane*, laid the groundwork for subsequent plays in the Leenane trilogy through its depiction of Connemara, the town in which it is set, as a dull and unfulfilling small village whose inhabitants are eager to escape it. With few opportunities in life, the indolent townsfolk indulge in drink, gossiping, self-destruction, and murder.

The play centers around the bitter, acrimonious relationship between Maureen Folan, a middle-aged woman who has never known romantic love, and her mother, Mag, an annoyingly needy woman who depends on Maureen for her care. Maureen's last chance for romance is an invitation from a potential lover to come with him to the United States. When busybody Mag intervenes to prevent it, Maureen kills her. Maureen is the archetypal character in McDonagh's dramas: the individual whose ordinary exterior conceals emotional turmoil with the potential to erupt in violence.

A critical and popular success, *The Beauty Queen of Leenane* was praised for its simple style and adherence to basic unities of drama. Its theme of the individual driven by desperation to violent extremes gives it a universality that transcends its contemporary Irish setting.

The Cripple of Inishmaan

McDonagh's second play is his most incisive look at the illusions and deceptions that sustain and motivate people trapped in unfulfilling lives. Billy Claven, a cripple since childhood, is desperate to leave the hometown that scorns and abuses him. To do so, he

must his lie his way onto the set of an American motion picture that is filming on location and engineer a trip to Hollywood for a screen test. Much of Billy's motivation stems from a misunderstanding of his past based on half-truths about his parents that were told to him by the villagers. Billy returns to Inishmaan, claiming to have turned down a job in Hollywood because he prefers being with the people he loves back home, when in truth he was turned down for the role, which was given to an able-bodied performer who could act crippled. By the play's end, nearly every character has revealed something duplicitous about himself or herself.

The story plays out against a real historical event, American director Robert Flaherty's filming of the renowned documentary *Man of Aran* in 1934. Ironically, this supposed exercise in cinema verité was artistically orchestrated to conjure a romantic image of the Irish isles. The play is sneeringly self-conscious of this rosy image of rural Ireland and methodically de-romanticizes it through the vulgar interactions of its characters.

A Skull in Connemara

The second play in McDonagh's Leenane Trilogy continues the exploration of the dark side of small-town life begun in *The Beauty Queen of Leenane* and is linked to *The Cripple of Inishmaan* in its depiction of social relations built on a foundation of lies. Its main character, Mick Dowd, is employed annually by the local church to exhume old bodies from the local graveyard to make room for the seemingly abundant supply of new corpses. Mick claims that he disposes of the remains he removes in a sacred fashion when in fact he pulverizes them and dumps them in the local river.

Years before, Mick's wife died in a suspicious car accident that the townspeople speculated was staged to cover up her murder. This year, guilt-ridden Mick is to dig up his wife's grave, and events build to the revelation that the people with whom he associates most closely have doctored evidence to prove he murdered her.

The play is an intricate tapestry of falsehoods, some harmless and amusing and some deadly serious, that keep the characters from knowing what to believe in. In one of its more ironic moments, Mick's confession of a crime he believes he did commit is dismissed by those who hope to frame him for the murder he did not commit. The uncertainty of truth as McDonagh depicts it contributes to the image of Connemara as a morally unstable landscape.

THE LONESOME WEST

The contentious relationship between two brothers, Coleman and Valene Connor, is the dramatic core of the third play in the Leenane Trilogy, which takes its title from a passage in Synge's *The Playboy of the Western World* (pr., pb. 1907) and is sometimes compared to Sam Shepard's drama *True West* (pr. 1980), another play in which siblings are engaged in a struggle for power over one another.

At the root of the troubles between the brothers is Coleman's murder of their father for a trivial insult. Valene has agreed to swear the murder was an accident if Coleman will sign over his share of their father's humble inheritance. Valene spends much of the play taking over the family house the two share and taunting Coleman for his pennilessness. Coleman boorishly disregards any of the house rules set down by Valene, and the two are usually at one another's throats. The violence of their relationship is so distressing to Father Welsh, the village priest who sees their conflict as one of several proofs that "God has no jurisdiction in this town," that he commits suicide, enjoining the brothers to make amends for the sake of his mortal soul. Coleman and Valene try to honor Father Welsh's request, but their reconciliation spirals into an outrageous contest of one-upmanship as each confesses to secret cruelties he inflicted on the other in the past. The play ends with a destructive battle between the two that shows violence is the only way the brothers know to deal with one another.

With its references to Roman Catholicism and appeal to a brotherly love that might heal the rift between two opponents, *The Lonesome West* is viewed by some as an allegory of the political struggle dividing contemporary Ireland. This interpretation of the play links it to McDonagh's *The Lieutenant of Inishmore*, which features characters overtly involved in the Irish war for independence.

THE LIEUTENANT OF INISHMORE

The most overtly political of McDonagh's plays, *The Lieutenant of Inishmore* is the first in which he directly references the political turbulence of contemporary Northern Island. Its main character, Mad Padraic, is a soldier in the INLA, a splinter group formed by radicals too violent to be accepted into the Irish Republican Army.

McDonagh uses the ideology of Ireland's rebel movement to expose the same self-interested and petty behavior shown by characters in his less politically focused plays. Padraic espouses a doctrine of liberation when committing crimes on behalf of the republic, but he is indifferent to the human suffering his acts cause. Angered when his beloved pet cat is killed, he concocts a political justification for killing his father, who had been caring for the cat. Padraic's warped sensibility is mirrored in Mairead, his lover, an animal rights activist who blinds cows in the misguided belief that this makes them less attractive to meat packagers. A vast moral no-man's land separates these flawed characters from the ideals they profess. The play's violence is so outrageously gruesome as to be comic. The matter-of-fact manner with which characters accept that violence, however, suggests an environment so accustomed to brutality that it has become inured to its excesses.

BIBLIOGRAPHY

Boles, William C. "Violence at the Royal Court: Martin McDonagh's *The Beauty Queen of Leenane* and Mark Ravenhill's *Shopping and Fucking*." *Theatre Symposium: A Journal of the Southeastern Theatre Conference* 7 (1999): 125-135. Explores the use of physical and emotional violence as an effective dramatic tool in the plays of McDonagh and a contemporary.

Brustein, Robert. "The Rebirth of Irish Drama." *The New Republic*, April 7, 1997. Discusses the plays of McDonagh and his contemporary, Sebastian Barry, as the first wave of a possible renaissance in Irish theater not unlike the Irish Literary Renaissance in the early twentieth century.

Lyman, Rick. "Most Promising (and Grating) Playwright." *New York Times Magazine*, January 25,

1998, p. 16-19. Biographic profile of the playwright on the eve of his stage debut in the United States. McDonagh discusses why he decided to become a writer and how he drifted into writing for the stage.

O'Toole, Finian. "Martin McDonagh." *Bomb* 63 (1998): 48-50. Interview in which McDonagh discusses his plays in the context of Irish culture and literature and the Irish storytelling tradition.

Stefan Dziemianowicz

JOHN MCGRATH

Born: Birkenhead, Cheshire, England; June 1, 1935
Died: Edinburgh, Scotland; January 22, 2002

PRINCIPAL DRAMA

Events While Guarding the Bofors Gun, pr., pb. 1966

Bakke's Night of Fame, pr. 1968, pb. 1973

Random Happenings in the Hebrides, pr. 1970, pb. 1972

Trees in the Wind, pr. 1971

Fish in the Sea, pr. 1972, pb. 1977 (music by Mark Brown)

The Cheviot, the Stag, and the Black, Black Oil, pr. 1973, pb. 1974, revised pb. 1981, pr. 1993

Little Red Hen, pr. 1975, pb. 1977

Yobbo Nowt, pr. 1975, pb. 1978 (music by Brown)

Joe's Drum, pr., pb. 1979

Swings and Roundabouts, pr. 1980, pb. 1981

Blood Red Roses, pr. 1980, pb. 1981

Behold the Sun, pr., pb. 1985 (opera libretto; music by Alexander Goehr)

Mairi Mhor: The Woman from Skye, pr. 1987

Border Warfare, pr. 1989, pb. 1996

John Brown's Body, pr. 1990

Waiting for Dolphins, pr. 1992

The Wicked Old Man, pr. 1992

The Silver Darlings, pr. 1992

Reading Rigoberta, pr. 1994

Half the Picture, pr. 1995 (with Richard Norton Taylor)

Ane Satire of the Four Estates, pr. 1996

The Last of the MacEachans, pr. 1996

Six-Pack: Plays for Scotland, pb. 1996 (includes *Border Warfare*, *The Cheviot, the Stag, and the Black, Black Oil*, *Blood Red Roses*, *Joe's Drum*, *Out of Our Heads*, and *Random Happenings in the Hebrides*)

OTHER LITERARY FORMS

John McGrath wrote dozens of scripts for television and film. *Z-Cars* (1962), which he cowrote with Troy Kennedy Martin, was one of the most popular series in the 1962 television season, and his *Diary of a Young Man* ran as a six-part television series in 1964. His films include *Billion Dollar Brain* (1967), *The Bofors Gun* (1968), and *The Dressmaker* (1988, shown again in 1992 on public television). Films have been made for television of several of his major plays—*The Cheviot, the Stag, and the Black, Black Oil* (1974), *Blood Red Roses* (1985), and *Border Warfare* (1989). His nonfiction works include *The Bone Won't Break: On Theatre and Hope in Hard Times* (1990).

ACHIEVEMENTS

Known as a socialist playwright, John McGrath wrote mainly for working-class audiences in rural and industrial-urban Great Britain. The key influences on his work begin with the approaches of the Unity Theatre of the 1930's, the Workers Theatre Movement formed in 1924, and the early Theatre Workshop of the 1950's, which combine popular tastes as defined by working-class culture with political themes. Furthermore, McGrath deeply admires the revolutionary theater of Vsevolod Meyerhold and Erwin Piscator, and films with a social conscience such as those produced by Jean Renoir and Sergei Eisenstein. Many of McGrath's plays employ skitlike agitprop techniques that feature humor, the songs and satire of the music-hall tradition, and folk, rock, and carnival music. Even so, the plays make new, challenging demands on their audiences with the serious underpinnings of ideological and ethical issues that endorse a revolutionary rather than a reformist perspective.

McGrath received the writers award from the British Academy of Film and Television Arts in 1994 and he also received the Writers Guild Lifetime Achievement award in 1997.

BIOGRAPHY

Although his father was a middle-class secondary-school teacher, John Peter McGrath identified with the working classes through his Irish Catholic immigrant grandparents and, especially, his paternal grandfather, who worked as a boilermaker in the Birkenhead yards. McGrath was reared in Merseyside (near Liverpool) until World War II, when the family was evacuated to a working-class district in North Wales, returning to Merseyside in 1951.

From 1953 to 1955, McGrath fulfilled his National Service as a gunner, bombardier, then artillery officer in the British army, which sent him to Germany and Egypt. His officer status helped to qualify him in 1955 as a student at the University of Oxford, where he took a Dip.Ed. in directing and writing in 1959.

McGrath gave up a promising career in commercial theater and the popular media to commit his talents to alternative groups. After being associated with the Royal Court Theatre and the Script Department at the British Broadcasting Corporation (BBC) from 1959 to 1965, he lent his energies briefly to Centre 42, the Writers' Action Group, and Everyman Theatre in Liverpool. One of the crucial turning points for McGrath was in 1968, when he went to Paris and was deeply influenced by the para-revolutionary fever during the May strike, when students joined nine million workers to shut down the French system.

In 1962, McGrath married Elizabeth MacLennan, a gifted actress who was also a 1959 graduate of the

University of Oxford. Their marriage produced three children. To make their own statement about mainstream theater, McGrath and MacLennan helped found the 7:84 Theatre Company in 1971 (known as 7:84), the name being a reminder that 7 percent of the population in Great Britain at that time owned 84 percent of the wealth. For seventeen years, the company played to packed houses, particularly in the Highlands of Scotland and around England. Moreover, McGrath's innovations in working-class theater inspired a new generation of political theater in Great Britain; many of the original members served as catalysts for other companies, such as the Belt and Braces Roadshow and the Monstrous Regiment.

In 1982, 7:84 began a series of revivals written by earlier playwrights called the Clydebilt Season. These shows, exploring the heritage of popular culture, complemented McGrath's own plays, which filled out the greater part of each new season. Despite 7:84's successful track record, or perhaps because of it, the conservative government of Margaret Thatcher, in 1985, withdrew the Arts Council grants for 7:84, England. In 1988, McGrath resigned as artistic director of the Scottish branch of 7:84 in response to fatal cuts announced by the Scottish Arts Council, and the company effectively died. After leaving 7:84, McGrath wrote for Wildcat, in Glasgow, and Freeway Films, a company that he founded in the late 1980's.

In 1979, McGrath became a Judith E. Wilson Fellow, a guest lecturer at the University of Cambridge. His lectures became the basis for *A Good Night Out: Popular Theatre: Audience, Class, and Form* (1981), a seminal work on the theory of working-class theater as a political forum. He returned to the University of Cambridge a decade later to discuss the problem of government subsidy for oppositional theater, a problem resulting from a clash in tastes between those who fund working-class theater and those who enjoy it. The lectures were published as *The Bone Won't Break: On Theatre and Hope in Hard Times*.

ANALYSIS

John McGrath's works, numbering more than forty plays, roughly fall into three periods—the plays written before he began to define working-class theater for the contemporary stage, the plays of the 7:84 years that applied his theories, and his direction in theater since the collapse of state-run socialism in the Soviet Union and Eastern Europe.

His earliest works feature lone, rebellious men who openly oppose middle-class institutions that stand for moneyed success, dehumanizing deference, and conformity. Though these rebels are able to define the system of values that they reject, they provide few practical solutions that might alleviate oppression of the individual spirit. Although positive about their own values and their attack on society, these loners never form adequate relationships, particularly with allies in causes that might help them create change, so their dissent remains fixed at a certain level. Being authentic—that is, living by their own principles—is more important to these men than joining others, lest they are forced to compromise. They have, therefore, a commitment largely to themselves and their own dissent. Nevertheless, they are compelling figures for the moral integrity that they articulate and the intensity of their resistance to mainstream values.

BAKKE'S NIGHT OF FAME

McGrath's early heroes in *Random Happenings in the Hebrides*, *Events While Guarding the Bofors Gun*, and *Bakke's Night of Fame* are thus best understood through the values of French existentialism, which influenced McGrath at the time. As an inmate on death row awaiting imminent execution, Bakke, in *Bakke's Night of Fame*, insists on defining his own humanity. He does this by drawing attention to himself as an individual unlike his predecessors on death row. He goads the attending priest, who tries to deal with him as yet another penitent parishioner, into consciously acknowledging Bakke as a person like any other, with contradictions, desires, fears, and whims. Bakke similarly toys with the guards and needles the executioner into catering to his mercurial moods. It is Bakke's way of struggling against the limitations of life itself and the humiliation of his fate. Teasing the priest into trying to guess whether he was guilty of his crime, Bakke attacks the traditional Christian notion of morality that judges human guilt.

It is never established whether Bakke committed a murder—some of the time he seems guilty and at other times he seems innocent—but the question of culpability is not important. Bakke wants to make it clear that he is a testament to the infinite mystery of human liberty. At the center of his being he has an inchoate but irreducible potential that gives him a freedom to assert his own autonomy. Whatever his fate, he attains dignity by virtue of his inviolable freedom to define himself as a human being and to amend that definition with each new act. The priest fails to grasp what Bakke is trying to teach him about life. He sees Bakke's patter as mere play-acting. Of course, that is what people around Hamlet accused him of doing too, and Bakke teases the priest with echoes from William Shakespeare that suggest that Bakke, like the Prince of Denmark, is conscious of being able to shape life's boundaries through each crucial decision and act.

For McGrath, *Bakke's Night of Fame* also provides an opportunity to protest the inhumanity of capital punishment, an issue that materializes the abstract nature of Bakke's struggle. Bakke insists on confronting his executioner and asking about the executioner's children, who might themselves have to face a death sentence some day. He is trying to force the person who will kill him to put a face on the man he will soon electrocute. Bakke makes no equivocation about capital punishment as an act of murder and the human life that is at stake.

THE 7:84 PERIOD

By contrast, McGrath's plays written during the 7:84 period deemphasize individualism. Their protagonists are likely to be female as well as male, and they stress solutions to topical issues of economic and social injustice through communal interests. Convinced that the sources of the working-class struggle could not be readily visualized and fully understood through the surface reality of everyday situations, McGrath rejected naturalism or realism as choices for dramatic forms. To reveal the underlying economic forces that are normally suppressed in the dominant culture, McGrath draws on Brechtian forms of art that attempt to force the audience to contemplate and question what they see. Specifically, his strategy is to draw on very stylized scenery and dialogue—often exaggerated, cartoonlike, and humorous—which creates some distance between stage and audience, inhibiting identification with the characters and situations.

McGrath wisely chose, however, not to adopt the full measure of audience alienation but to develop a modified form of Brechtian theater that would have a wide appeal among his audiences and still achieve the effect of revealing the hidden forces of capitalism, corporate monopoly, power, and greed. Noting that art's appeal is not universal and that most standards for art are determined by middle-class tastes, McGrath set out to discover what characterizes working-class entertainment in particular. He determined, above all, that he must be direct in his message for the working classes—that it must not be embedded in artistic form—and that he should use plenty of variety with comedy, music, and moment-by-moment change of effect. Working-class audiences like a fast pace, with a variety of emotion and rhythms defined by laughs, silence, song, and tears. He also decided to employ topical subject matter especially linked to local concerns and to work informally with the audiences using plenty of give-and-take with the crowds. Audiences are sometimes asked to join the actors on the stage with dancing and singing, as one of several ways audiences participated in 7:84's shows.

THE CHEVIOT, THE STAG, AND THE BLACK, BLACK OIL

The best-known play of this period is *The Cheviot, the Stag, and the Black, Black Oil*. The play protests the appropriation of Scotland's land over the centuries for raising sheep, hunting grouse, and exploiting oil reserves. It begins with the tragedy of the Clearances, a period in the 1800's when the crofters (tenant farmers) were thrown off their land at the whim of the large landholders, who wanted the land for recreation or income. So many of these people were burned out, chased to the sea, and put on ships for Canada that their number today is a mere fraction of what it once was. After repeated torture and harassment by the authorities, whole villages disappeared. Throughout *The Cheviot, the Stag, and the Black, Black Oil* are a parade of crofters who tell their sto-

ries with poignancy and humor, and their version of history contrasts with the aristocrats who, by their own words, reveal a profit motive and callousness. This history of the Clearances finds its analogue at the end of the play with the displacement of Scots in the Shetlands and Orkney islands by North Sea oil development. Because the cost of living has become too high for local inhabitants, they have had to sell out to developers.

The Cheviot, the Stag, and the Black, Black Oil was enormously popular on tour largely because it expressed the concerns of people in the Highlands, but also because it successfully employed the techniques that McGrath had earlier identified as characteristic of working-class theater. The scenery was a giant pop-up book, all the music—both rock and Highland fiddle tunes—was live, and the play drew on the Gaelic *Ceilidh* as a paradigm, a folk party with whiskey, storytelling, Scottish poetry, local music, and general entertainment.

BORDER WARFARE

With plays such as *The Cheviot, the Stag, and the Black, Black Oil*, McGrath found his voice in the issues defined by Scottish history, especially in celebration of folk heroes who protest colonization by outsiders and decry mistakes made by the Scots themselves, who have, in effect, relinquished control over their own affairs. These plays—among them *Little Red Hen*, *Joe's Drum*, and *Mairi Mhor*—point the way to *Border Warfare*, a work of epic proportions that brings together many of the themes of McGrath's earlier historic drama with themes on the nationalist cause. In this play, Scotland is the primeval land corrupted by cross-border raids between England and Scotland, diminished by foreign rule, and ennobled only by the contemporary hope of devolution (transfer) of power from the British parliament. All the key points of Scottish history concerning home rule are here—the battles over Northumbria, the clan rivalry that allowed the English an early foothold in Scotland, the scheming of King James I of Scotland and Mary Queen of Scots, the Union of 1707 that legalized absorption of the Scottish parliament by England, and the political infighting during the nineteenth century that has kept devolution almost within reach, but not quite. Once again, the play uses a combination of folk and contemporary music, stylized scenery, and a pageantlike structure that calls forth spokespeople from each generation. Despite the size of the production, *Border Warfare* was mounted without government subsidy.

WAITING FOR DOLPHINS

Waiting for Dolphins possibly marks a third shift in McGrath's writings because it is aimed more at middle-class leftists who feel alienated and isolated by the breakup of the world's largest Marxist government, the Soviet Union. With remarkable honesty, the play faces up to the destruction and mistakes of the Left and, with humor and acerbic commentary, takes on the demonization of socialism by reaffirming the leftist belief in a more just system. Its protagonist is Reynalda, a member of one of "the best English radical, non-conforming intellectual families," who runs a bed-and-breakfast place in North Wales and wonders how she will get along with her capitalist guests. While she reviews the contours of her activist years, she wonders what her response should become to the loss of socialist values. As an analogue, she recalls the dolphins she had once seen frolicking near Cyprus. They represent all that hangs delicately in the balance for both the environment and socialism. If future decisions do not consider their contribution to the world, they could become extinct. Her only recourse is to wait for the dolphins to resurface.

Waiting for Dolphins is an important departure for McGrath because it once again features an individual voice and addresses a new audience without the trappings of big production values. It turns to a more realistic dramatic form with well-developed characterization that invites audience sympathy and identification.

LATER PLAYS

McGrath's adaptation of *The Silver Darlings* from the popular Scottish novel of the same name by Neil M. Gunn was staged in 1994 by the Wildcat Theatre Company. It was produced on an "epic scale." McGrath's interest in political concerns was reflected in his production of *Reading Rigoberta*. Based on the life of the Nobel Prize winner, Rigoberta Menchu

Tum, the commanding one-woman play featured McGrath's wife as the renowned human rights activist whose family was brutalized by Guatemala's harsh dictatorship.

OTHER MAJOR WORKS

SCREENPLAYS: *Billion Dollar Brain*, 1967; *The Bofors Gun*, 1968; *The Virgin Soldiers*, 1969; *The Reckoning*, 1970; *The Dressmaker*, 1988; *The Long Roads*, 1991; *Mairi Mhor*, 1994.

TELEPLAYS: *Z-Cars*, 1962 (with Troy Kennedy Martin); *Diary of a Young Man*, 1964; *The Entertainers*, 1964 (documentary); *The Day of Ragnarok*, 1965; *Mo*, 1965; *Shotgun*, 1966; *Diary of a Nobody*, 1966; *Orkney*, 1971; *Bouncing Boy*, 1972, 1974; *The Cheviot, the Stag, and the Black, Black Oil*, 1974; *Once upon a Union*, 1977; *The Adventures of Frank*, 1980; *Sweetwater Memories*, 1984 (documentary); *Blood Red Roses*, 1985; *There Is a Happy Land*, 1987; *Border Warfare*, 1989; *John Brown's Body*, 1990; *Half the Picture*, 1995.

NONFICTION: *A Good Night Out: Popular Theatre: Audience, Class, and Form*, 1981; *The Bone Won't Break: On Theatre and Hope in Hard Times*, 1990; *Naked Thoughts That Roam About: Reflections on Theatre, 1958-2001*, 2002 (Nadine Holdsworth, editor).

BIBLIOGRAPHY

Cherns, Penny, and Paddy Broughton. "John McGrath's *Trees in the Wind* at the Northcott Theatre, Exeter." *Theatre Quarterly* 19 (September/October, 1975): 89-100. Although describing the workings of an early production, this article offers real insight into the 7:84 Theatre Company's rehearsal process and the special mix of ideology and theater that shapes the plays.

Craig, Sandy. "Unmasking the Lie." In *Dreams and Deconstructions: Alternative Theatre in Britain*. Ambergate, England: Amber Lane Press, 1980. A spirited account of the revolution in British theater beginning in 1968. Craig's discussion, which describes the whole range of theater in Great Britain, situates McGrath's work in the continuum between commercial and subsidized theater.

Itzin, Catherine. *Stages in the Revolution: Political Theatre in Britain Since 1968*. London: Eyre Methuen, 1980. An invaluable handbook that documents the work of the most important political writers and theater companies between 1968 and 1980. Arranged in chronological order, this book explains the sequence of events that shaped alternative theater and suggests a line of influence among the most creative people in theater at that time. Accurate and complete.

MacLennan, Elizabeth. *The Moon Belongs to Everyone: Making Theatre with 7:84*. London: Methuen, 1990. Heartwarming and informative, this book records the commitment and will of an entire family to the fulfillment of a dream. Especially valuable are MacLennan's details about the history of the 7:84 Theatre Company and the battle to keep it afloat financially once the Conservative government had targeted it for cuts. Most memorable are MacLennan's accounts of caring for the family while handling their many crises through many months on the road.

McGrath, John. "The Theory and Practice of Political Theatre." *Theatre Quarterly* 35 (Autumn, 1979): 43-54. McGrath's own article is the best theoretical discussion of 7:84's goals and ambitions.

McGrath explains these theories simply and elegantly.

Page, Malcolm. "John McGrath: NTQ Checklist Number One." *New Theatre Quarterly* 4 (November, 1985): 400-416. This bibliography is the place to begin serious research on McGrath and the 7:84 Theatre Company. It includes not only a brief chronology of McGrath's career and an annotated list of his plays up to 1985 but also an impressive catalog of the major articles written about McGrath and select reviews of his plays.

Stevenson, Randall, and Gavin Wallace, eds. *Scottish Theatre Since the Seventies*. Edinburgh, Scotland: Edinburgh University Press, 1996. A look at the development of the 7:84 Theatre Company, as well as other Scottish companies and theaters. Includes a separate chapter featuring an interview with McGrath.

Van Erven, Eugene. *Radical People's Theatre*. Bloomington: Indiana University Press, 1988. Covers popular theater around the world and uses the 7:84 Theatre Company to represent Great Britain. Especially good at providing a larger context for the theater company's politics and practices.

Reade W. Dornan,
updated by Andrea E. Miller

ANTONIO MACHADO

Born: Seville, Spain; July 26, 1875
Died: Collioure, France; February 22, 1939

PRINCIPAL DRAMA

Desdichas de la fortuna, o Julianillo Valcárcel, pr., pb. 1926 (with Manuel Machado)

Juan de Mañara, pr., pb. 1927 (with Manuel Machado)

Las adelfas, pr., pb. 1928 (with Manuel Machado)

El hombre que murió en la guerra, wr. 1928, pr. 1941, pb. 1947 (with Manuel Machado)

La Lola se va a los puertos, pr., pb. 1929 (with Manuel Machado)

La prima Fernanda, pr., pb. 1931 (with Manuel Machado)

La duquesa de Benamejí, pr., pb. 1932 (with Manuel Machado)

OTHER LITERARY FORMS

Among the most renowned Spanish poets of the twentieth century, Antonio Machado is the most prominent poet of the Generation of '98, the literary movement that developed from the political, cultural, and social crises affecting Spain that had culminated in the loss of its last colonial territories in 1898. Machado and other writers, including the philosopher and novelist Miguel de Unamuno y Jugo and playwright Ramón María del Valle Inclán, were united by their search for cultural identity and their reevaluation of Spain's place in the world after its loss of global dominance. Although he is best known as a poet, he also wrote essays, literary criticism, and other prose works.

ACHIEVEMENTS

Antonio Machado was elected a member of the Real Academia Española de la Lengua in 1927. He was honored with several posthumous international congresses, colloquia, and dedications. Machado organized the Homenaje a Valle-Inclán in 1932. He was also honored as Son of Soria for his service to the region.

BIOGRAPHY

Antonio Machado was born into a prominent bourgeois family of Seville. He was the second of five sons. His father, Antonio Machado Álvarez, studied law and philosophy, but his devotion to the study of native folklore gained him recognition as an eminent folklorist. He founded the journal *El folklore Andaluz* in 1882 and published several collections, including *Colección de cantes flamencos* in 1881 and the *Biblioteca de las tradiciones populares españoles* in 1884. Antonio Machado's grandparents lived with the family. The Machado patriarchs were intellectual and anticlerical positivists as well as liberal Republicans. One grandfather was the governor of Seville, and the other, dean of the School of Medicine at the Universidad de Sevilla, introduced Darwinism to Spain.

Antonio and his older brother Manuel studied under some of the greatest philosophers of the times. Among them were their father's friends, Francisco Giner de los Ríos and Francisco Quiroga. While in Puerto Rico serving as an attorney, their father fell gravely ill and died on his return to Spain in 1893. Three years later, their paternal grandfather died, and the entire family was dependent on their grandmother. Several of the sons tried unsuccessfully to make a life in the New World. The two older boys pursued translation and journalism as practical pro-

Antonio Machado

fessions. In 1899, Antonio joined his brother Manuel in Paris, where both of them worked as translators for the publisher Garnier. In the Latin Quarter, they met Oscar Wilde and other bohemian artists.

After returning to Madrid, Antonio Machado enrolled in the Universidad de Madrid. He published poems in *Electra*, a literary journal that promoted European modernism. His brother Manuel served as editor for the journal, which was directed by several founders of the Generation of '98: Pío Baroja (whom the brothers had met in Paris), Ramiro de Maetzu, and Francisco Villaespesa. Writers of note contributed to the journal, including Juan Ramón Jiménez and the founder of Latin American modernism, Rubén Darío.

Machado moved to Paris, where he maintained a friendship with Darío until the Nicaraguan's death. In 1902, he published his first poetry collection, *Soledades*, which was representative of the Generation of '98 mentality. Its stark images portray the individual lost in a landscape littered with the ruins of a crumbling society, a feeling Machado probably experienced as his own family suffered the consequences of the disintegration of the bourgeois stronghold on Spain's social structure.

Literary magazines such as *Helios*, *Blanco y Negro*, *Ateneo*, and the national newspaper *El país* published Machado's reviews and poetry from 1904 to 1907. He moved to Soria, the inspiration for his major collection of poetry, *Campos de Castilla* (1912; *The Castilian Camp*, 1982). There he met his future wife Leonor, and they married in 1909. They traveled to Paris but returned to Soria after Leonor developed tuberculosis. The publication of *The Castilian Camp* met with critical acclaim that established the poet internationally. Leonor died, and Machado left Soria for the seclusion of Baeza.

The Bolshevik Revolution of 1917 and World War I brought Machado out of seclusion, and he reestablished ties with his literary colleagues, including the philosopher Unamuno. Machado and Unamuno signed the manifesto of the *Liga antigermanófila*. Machado focused on journalism, writing reviews for the newspaper *El Sol* and literary journals *La Pluma* and *Índice*. He promoted the poetry of young writers, the future poets of the Generation of '27. He began his collaboration with one of the most important European literary journals, *Revista de Occidente*, founded by his colleague José Ortega y Gassett in 1923.

The Machado brothers made their foray into theater in 1924. They produced and directed an adaptation of *El condenado por desconfiado* (wr. 1615?, pb. 1634) by Tirso de Molina. Their staging was a critical and popular success. The positive reception inspired them to collaborate on other Golden Age productions, notably by Lope de Vega Carpio, in 1925. They were invited to perform at the Institución Libre de Enseñanza, their distinguished alma mater. The director of the college facilitated their next theatrical collaboration. In 1927, *Juan de Mañara* was staged in the Teatro de la Reina Victoria de Madrid. During the play's production, Antonio Machado was elected to the Real Academia Española.

In 1931, the Machado brothers wrote and produced *La prima Fernanda*. In 1933, La Barraca, the popular theater company founded by Federico García

Lorca, staged Machado's tragedy in verse *La tierra de Alvar González*. Machado mentored the brilliant young Lorca in his poetic as well as theatrical endeavors. Lorca, trained as a pianist, accompanied some of Machado's theatrical productions.

Antonio Machado died in 1939, of illness contracted while fleeing Barcelona, Spain, en route to the French border. Two years later, Manuel Machado produced and directed *El hombre que murió en la guerra*, written by the brothers in 1928.

ANALYSIS

Antonio and Manuel Machado's interest in drama was inspired by translations of classical French and British dramas and adaptations of Golden Age plays. They developed a theory of theater as they collaborated, from scriptwriting to staging. They respected the traditions of playwrights who set the standards for themes and structure, from Lope de Vega and Pedro Calderón de la Barca to William Shakespeare. Their staging demonstrates modern trends practiced in twentieth century theater. Frequent monologues and asides to the audience invite its participation and the dissolution of the third wall. As playwrights, they favored popular theater trends over classical approaches to staging, while their language and verse structure were erudite.

DESDICHAS DE LA FORTUNA, O JULIANILLO VALCÁRCEL

The brothers' first dramatic collaboration opened at the Teatro de la Princesa in Madrid on February 9, 1926. María Guerrero and her theater company, the most renowned Spanish theater company at the time, performed the drama. It was based on a legend about the illegitimate Julián, adopted by the duke of Olivares. He falls in love with Leonor but weds Juana according to the duke's wishes. Leonor disguises herself as Don César in order to befriend Julián, who does not discover her identity until his death.

The brothers' use of Golden Age plot twists, disguises, monologues, and asides, and references to stock characters and proverbs resulted in a play that was basically an updated version of the cape and sword play. The lines were written in eight-syllable verse, following classical Spanish versification. Contemporary audiences familiar with Golden Age drama responded favorably to Machado's dramatic adaptation.

JUAN DE MAÑARA

Antonio and Manuel Machado's second collaboration debuted in Madrid on March 16, 1927. The tragedy was based on a legend about a man who followed selfish desires until his spiritual transformation. In the Machado version, Mañara is symbolically a hunter as he is literally hunting for fulfillment. He is also deceived by a woman whom he helps escape from the law. *Juan de Mañara*'s plot and characters resemble those of the Romantic play *Don Juan Tenorio* (pr., pb. 1844; English translation, 1944) by José Zorrilla y Moral. The Juan depicted by the Machado brothers is more complex than that of Zorrilla; he questions his actions and motives as he undergoes the process of spiritual transformation. In addition, the female characters are more developed than those of the nineteenth century play, fluctuating between good and evil forces.

LAS ADELFAS

The play, a psychological drama in the style of Henrik Ibsen, opened in Madrid on October 22, 1928. The plot revolves around several complex characters, and dialogues and monologues explore psychoanalytic approaches to dreams and life experiences. Characters suffer from spiritual crises and interpersonal confrontations. The speech patterns incorporate foreign and invented vocabulary from scientific and dialectical usage. Telephone conversations and disjointed speech with noncorresponding dialogue refer to the disillusioned post-World War I European society. Although the drama won critical acclaim, its run was shortened by the lack of financial and popular success.

LA LOLA SE VA A LOS PUERTOS

The play debuted November 8, 1929, at the Teatro Fontalba in Madrid. Its popular appeal and long run made the play the most successful of all the Machado plays. It incorporated elements of the *andaluzada*, flamenco themes and plots popular in Andalucía. The brothers' expertise in versification elevated the dialogue to the satisfaction of Madrid's cosmopolitan audiences. A film version and later a *zarzuela*, or type of operetta, were inspired by the play. The influence of *La Lola se va a los puertos* on García Lorca can be seen in the Andalusian themes, folklore, and flamenco in his plays *La zapatera prodigiosa* (pr. 1930; *The Shoemaker's Prodigious Wife*, 1941) and *Bodas de sangre* (pr. 1933; *Blood Wedding*, 1939).

The play follows the classical model formulated by Lope de Vega. The plot and characters poeticize the theme of ideal love, and the dialogue follows the eleven-syllable verse structure common in Golden Age drama. Modernist elements work to blend Golden Age verse patterns with those of southern coastal Spain before the civil war. Several dialogues occur at once, and protagonists represent common *porteños*, not glamorized nobility. The set and characters merge twentieth century technology with patriotic and romantic traditions.

The setting for the play is a depressed Andalusian port town, home to Lola, who embodies the ideal woman and therefore is envied by Rosario, more representative of contemporary Andalusia. A father and son battle each other to win Lola's favor, but she prefers her constant companion, her guitar Heredia. Lola takes her guitar and leaves for Buenos Aires after the other characters have reconciled.

The verse structure allows the *cante hondo*, the deep song, to emerge from the dialogue, enabling actors to portray a wide range of emotions. The Machado brothers reveal their poetic expertise in lyrical dialogue and song segments that maintain the flow of action. They wrote the role of Lola for Lola Membrives, an internationally famous Argentine actress and flamenco singer. Her performance was widely regarded as the best of her long and successful career.

LA PRIMA FERNANDA

La prima Fernanda opened in Madrid's Teatro Victoria on April 24, 1931. It explores the issues arising from bourgeois and working-class conflicts as well as relationships thwarted by class inequity and societal expectations. In this play, the Machado brothers used dramatic verse to examine contemporary Spanish political and social issues. The drama addressed the dehumanized nature of artistic trends; the buying of influence by high-ranking military personnel, bankers, and unethical opportunists; monetary issues in marriage and divorce; and various aspects of the disintegration of Spanish society. However, the dramatic verse dialogue structure proved somewhat unsuitable for conveying contemporary themes. Critics expressed the view that modern prose would have been a better medium for the complex issues-oriented plot. The play's short run seemed to mark it a failure after the great success of *La Lola se va a los puertos*. The Machado brothers were concerned by the lack of critical success for *La prima Fernanda*, their first attempt to address contemporary themes in their drama.

LA DUQUESA DE BENAMEJÍ

La duquesa de Benamejí debuted at the Teatro Español in Madrid on March 26, 1932. The tragedy is set in Andalusia during the Napoleonic occupation. Its plot revolves around Lorenzo, a heroic character admired for deeds that resemble those of Robin Hood. After Lorenzo is captured and imprisoned, the Duchess of Benamejí pleads for his release, defending him before the Andalusian nobility. The jealous Rocío stabs her as she delivers Lorenzo's pardon. Lorenzo chooses to release all the other prisoners rather than free himself. As a consequence of his noble decision, he faces execution.

The three-act tragedy was the first of the Machado collaborations to combine verse with prose passages. The scenes rendered in prose are those that were used to maintain realism and thematic coherence and include battle scenes, conversations among peasants and military officers, and prison scenes. Scenes devoted to conversations involving royalty and formal affairs are rendered in eleven-syllable verse. The action of this romantic tragedy is propelled by its detailed characters rather than by the loosely defined plot. The protagonists follow the patterns of nineteenth century French Romanticism. As romantic heroes, they lose the opportunity to fulfill their mutual love because of their self-sacrificing and heroic deaths. The tragedy gained critical approval and audience support.

EL HOMBRE QUE MURIÓ EN LA GUERRA

Although *El hombre que murió en la guerra* was written in 1928, it was not performed until April 18,

1941, at the Teatro Español in Madrid. The play focuses on Juan, an orphan who joins the Spanish Legion to fight in France during World War I. He is listed among those killed in action, and the townspeople honor him with a yearly memorial. Juan, however, returns to the town in the guise of Miguel. Some townspeople believe his alias, while others accuse him of dishonoring their fallen hero or causing his death. Juliana loves him and knows his true identity. The townspeople force Juan to leave, and Juliana promises to accept him when he returns in a more honorable way.

Juan, the protagonist, has become disillusioned by the horror and futility of war. In the guise of a comrade who was not revered, Juan criticizes war for its stupidity and the waste of innocent and ignorant lives on both sides. This philosophical discussion of war is used to relate the Juan-Miguel character to the Spanish experience in World War I and the Spanish Civil War, which occurred two years before Manuel Machado produced the play. Machado used the play to honor his brother and mother, whose deaths resulted from illnesses contracted while fleeing war-torn Spain for the French border in 1939. The play served to heal some of his family's wounds as well as address the national condition. Manuel was a supporter of Fascist Francisco Franco during the Civil War, while Antonio was an outspoken Republican in his anti-Franco politics and writings.

OTHER MAJOR WORKS

POETRY: *Soledades*, 1902 (dated 1903); *Soledades, galerías, y otros poemas*, 1907 (*Solitudes, Galleries, and Other Poems*, 1987); *Campos de Castilla*, 1912 (*The Castilian Camp*, 1982); *Poesías completas*, 1917; *Nuevas canciones*, 1924; *De un cancionero apócrifo*, 1926; *Obras*, 1940; *Eighty Poems of Antonio Machado*, 1959; *Antonio Machado*, 1973; *Selected Poems of Antonio Machado*, 1978; *Selected Poems*, 1982; *Times Alone: Selected Poems of Antonio Machado*, 1983; *Roads Dreamed Clear Afternoons: An Anthology of the Poetry of Antonio Machado*, 1994.

NONFICTION: *Juan de Mairena*, 1936 (English translation, 1963).

MISCELLANEOUS: *Obras completas de Manuel y Antonio Machado*, 1946 (includes *De un cancionero apócrifo*).

BIBLIOGRAPHY

Cobb, Carl W. *Antonio Machado*. New York: Twayne, 1971. A concise overview of the life and works of Machado. Bibliography.

Krogh, Kevin. *The Landscape Poetry of Antonio Machado: A Dialogical Study of "Campos de Castilla."* Lewiston, N.Y.: Edwin Mellen Press, 2001. Although this work focuses on Machado's best-known work of poetry, it provides information on Machado's life and some of his literary themes. Bibliography and indexes.

Romero Ferrer, Antonio. *Los hermanos Machado y el teatro, 1926-1932*. Seville, Spain: Diputación de Sevilla, 1996. Criticism and interpretation of the Machado plays. In Spanish.

Walters, D. Gareth, ed. *Estelas en la mar: Essays on the Poetry of Antonio Machado*. Glasgow, Scotland: University of Glasgow, 1992. Although this collection of essays focuses on Machado's poetic efforts, it sheds light on his dramatic works. Bibliography.

Whiston, James. *Antonio Machado's Writings and the Spanish Civil War*. Liverpool, England: Liverpool University Press, 1996. An examination of Machado's literary efforts with emphasis on his treatment of the Spanish Civil War. Bibliography and index.

Carole A. Champagne

EDUARDO MACHADO

Born: Havana, Cuba; June 11, 1953

PRINCIPAL DRAMA

Worms, pr. 1981

Rosario and the Gypsies, pr. 1982 (one-act musical; book and lyrics by Machado, music by Rick Vartoreila)

The Modern Ladies of Guanabacoa, pr., pb. 1983

There's Still Time to Dance in the Streets of Rio, pr. 1983

Broken Eggs, pr., pb. 1984

Fabiola, pr. 1985, pb. 1991

When It's Over, pr. 1987 (with Geraldine Sherman)

Why to Refuse, pr. 1987 (one act)

Across a Crowded Room, pr. 1988

A Burning Beach, pr. 1988

Don Juan in New York City, pr. 1988 (two-act musical)

Once Removed, pr., pb. 1988, revised pr. 1994

Wishing You Well, pr. 1988 (one-act musical)

Cabaret Bambu, pr. 1989 (one-act musical)

Related Retreats, pr. 1990

Stevie Wants to Play the Blues, pr. 1990, revised pr. 1998 (two-act musical)

In the Eye of the Hurricane, pr., pb. 1991

The Floating Island Plays, pb. 1991, pr. 1994 (as *Floating Islands*; includes *The Modern Ladies of Guanabacoa*, *Fabiola*, *In the Eye of the Hurricane*, and *Broken Eggs*)

1979, pr. 1991

Breathing It In, pr. 1993

The Floating Islands, pr. 1994 (as cycle of four plays)

Three Ways to Go Blind, pr. 1994

Between the Sheets, pr. 1996 (music by Mike Nolan and Scott Williams)

Cuba and the Night, pr. 1997

Crocodile Eyes, pr. 1999

Havana Is Waiting, pr. 2001 (originally pr. 2001 as *When the Sea Drowns in Sand*)

OTHER LITERARY FORMS

Eduardo Machado is known primarily as a playwright but also works professionally in the theater as an actor and director, as a television writer and screenwriter, and as a filmmaker/director.

ACHIEVEMENTS

Eduardo Machado is in the vanguard of a generation of playwrights who, having immigrated with their families from various countries of Latin America, give voice to the experience of Latino displacement in North America. His best-known works are family dramas that chronicle the experiences of well-to-do Cubans as they awake to their betrayal by Fidel Castro's revolution, prepare for an exodus from the homeland, arrive in and adjust to the "new world," and reach their ultimate destinies. Machado dramatizes outward from the microcosmic domestic world to encompass the historical sweep of great social movements. His plays capture onstage the critical point at which momentous political events intersect with and influence intimate family crises. In so doing, he breaks iconoclastically with traditional dramatic form, attempting to lift naturalistic situations to a level of heightened theatrical poetry that may be called symphonic tragicomedy, synthesizing innovations of such precursors as Anton Chekhov, Federico García Lorca, and Maria Irene Fornes. Machado has received three National Endowment for the Arts fellowships for playwriting (1981, 1983, 1986), a Rockefeller Foundation fellowship (1985), and a Dorothy Chandler Pavilion Viva Los Artistas Award (1992). In 1993, Machado was awarded a Theatre Communications Group/Pew Charitable Trust grant for an artistic residency at the Mark Taper Forum in Los Angeles, and in 1995 he received one of the first new play initiative awards from the Nederlander organization and the Roundabout Theatre Company in New York City. In 2001, Machado received a playwriting award from the Berrilla Kerr Foundation. He was appointed in 1997 to the Theatre Arts faculty at New York's Columbia University to chair the graduate playwriting program in the School of the Arts. In addition to teaching and writing, he also serves as an associate artistic director of the Cherry Lane Theatre in New York City.

BIOGRAPHY

Eduardo Machado was born in Havana, Cuba, on June 11, 1953, the son of Othon Eduardo and Gilda (Hernandez) Machado. He was reared in the coastal town of Cojimar, in a large villa full of various relatives. His family members were of the class of landed businesspeople, and his father lived a life of leisure while residing in Cuba. Later, after immigrating to the United States, his father became an accountant. His grandfather owned a bus company. Machado attended a Catholic boys school in Guanabacoa, six miles from home, until the age of eight, when his family, fearing the radical social changes that Castro was implementing, sent him and his four-year-old brother to live with an aunt and uncle in Miami, Florida. Despite the boys' inability to speak English, they were immediately enrolled in an English-speaking public school. One year later, their parents followed them to Florida, and they soon resettled in Canoga Park, California, located in the San Fernando Valley, close to Los Angeles. He attended Van Nuys High School, then college for about four months, before going on to acting school.

Machado came to playwriting indirectly, first indulging an interest in acting, although at the age of twenty he managed a stage production of García Lorca's *La casa de Bernarda Alba* (pr., pb. 1945; *The House of Bernarda Alba*, 1947) at C. Bernard Jackson's Inner City Cultural Center in Los Angeles. His interest in acting led him to roles in plays by Fernando Arrabal, Bertolt Brecht, Franz Xaver Kroetz, and John Steppling at the Beverly Hills Playhouse, the Ensemble Studio Theatre, and the Padua Hills Playwrights Festival. It was at the latter that he first met Fornes, who was giving workshops in playwriting. He first became her assistant for her production of her own play *Fefu and Her Friends* (pr. 1977). Intuiting Machado's interest in playwriting, Fornes invited him to participate in a workshop. Fornes, also an expatriate Cuban, became the single most influential force on Machado's writing style and philosophy of theater. Machado followed her to New York, where he performed in her play *A Visit*, in 1982.

Machado started writing in 1980, and his first play, *Worms*, was given a reading at Ensemble Studio Theatre West in 1981. His subsequent plays were staged Off-Off-Broadway and in regional productions in rapid succession, appearing in such theaters as Ensemble Studio Theatre, Theatre for the New

City, Duo Theatre, Downtown Arts Company, and the American Place in New York; the Long Wharf Theatre in New Haven; the Mark Taper Forum and the Los Angeles Theatre Center in Los Angeles; the Actors Theatre of Louisville; the New Mexico Repertory; Stage One in Dallas; and the Magic Theatre in San Francisco. Several works were also mounted in Spanish translation at the Repertorio Español in New York City.

Machado married Harriet Marilyn Bradlin, a Jewish social worker, in 1972 at the age of nineteen and was divorced in 1989. His parents were divorced when Machado was twenty-one, and his father remarried soon after, an unusual occurrence among conservative Cubans. Machado lived on both coasts of the United States for many years but after his divorce settled in New York City. He is a flamboyant figure who likes grand public gestures; for example, he noisily submitted his resignation from Ensemble Studio Theatre in protest against its proclivity for naturalism. His plays *Broken Eggs*, *Fabiola*, *In the Eye of the Hurricane*, and *The Modern Ladies of Guanabacoa* were published together by Theatre Communications Group under the title *The Floating Island Plays*.

Following the publication of *The Floating Island Plays* in 1991, Machado received an artistic residency at the Mark Taper Forum in Los Angeles that engaged him with director Oskar Eustis, then artistic director of Trinity Repertory Theatre in Providence, Rhode Island, in the mammoth project to produce the four plays about the experiences of the Hispanic immigrant in a single production. *Floating Islands* was produced in 1994 to disappointing reviews, and Machado returned to New York City to work on an independent film and to restructure his playwriting career, writing five plays over the next seven years. In 1997 he became the head of the graduate program in playwriting at the School of the Arts at Columbia University. He continues to act and direct professionally and has created the independent film *Exiles in New York* (1999).

When Machado returned to Cuba in 1999 as a member of a Latin American film delegation, he was inspired to write a highly autobiographical play about a Cuban child exiled to the United States who returns to his homeland forty years later. First called *When the Sea Drowns in Sand* and later retitled as *Havana Is Waiting*, this work reverberates with Machado's familiar themes and characters that express his vision of the human condition with concern for memory, family, loss, politics, substance abuse, sexual ambivalence, and cultural divides. Produced in Cuba in December of 2002, *Havana Is Waiting* is Machado's first play to receive a production in the country of his birth.

ANALYSIS

Eduardo Machado is an openly homosexual Cuban American writer, teacher, and filmmaker who has written more than thirty plays both to encouraging and devastating reviews. Although his plays directly address Hispanic issues of displacement, identity, cultural divides, and sexual and ethnic stereotypes, he fervently argues that he writes not about a community but of the human condition.

Machado has most articulately woven a latter-day Chekhovian theater out of his and his family's experience of the Cuban Revolution in plays written before 1996. He has explored its dimensions in various styles. His forays into other subjects, such as AIDS (acquired immunodeficiency syndrome) and sexual ambivalence, are equally evocative. Machado succeeds in giving events of epic sweep a human face, without reducing their scale, and in daring to strive for fresh dramatic solutions to equally virgin thematic ground.

THE FLOATING ISLAND PLAYS

The four plays that form *The Floating Island Plays* represent the core of Machado's œuvre. These four plays depict the sequence of events that led members of the Cuban upper classes from complacent hegemony in their native land to exile and displacement in the United States. They depict key incidents in the lives of disparate members of the Marquez/Ripoll/Hernandez clan as they attempt to adapt to the cataclysmal changes that rain down on Cuba. It may be surmised that these families represent people about whom Machado heard through his own family and family members whom he actually knew.

The first play of the Floating Island series, *The Modern Ladies of Guanabacoa*, chronicles the Ripoll family in the years 1928 through 1931. While showing the romantic and sexual intrigues that beset the family, especially the leitmotif of sexual infidelity, Machado depicts in the background the first seeds of the social dissolution that would bear fruit in the later plays. Manuela, the young lady of the house, is being courted by Oscar Hernandez, a young man from a socially inferior household. Having survived a seven-year engagement with a fiancé who died, she is now considered "used goods" and undesirable by men of her station. Once Oscar and Manuela have fulfilled the proper steps of courtship and are married, Oscar wastes no time parlaying investments of his in-laws' money into a successful bus company, of which he becomes the head and through which he succeeds in displacing and marginalizing Manuela's brothers, the rightful heirs to the fortune, both of whom lack Oscar's drive and will. In an echo of Chekhovian drama, Oscar, like the merchant Lopakhin in *Vishnyovy sad* (pr., pb. 1904; *The Cherry Orchard*, 1908), benefits from the decadence of the upper classes and hoists himself up the social scale at their expense.

Arturo Ripoll, Sr., is a prosperous merchant who is prodigally using up the family fortune and his respectable name in a long-term, flaunted romantic liaison. In the play's climax, he is shot offstage, probably by his mistress's enraged husband. Oscar takes advantage of this turn of events to gain control of the family fortune and take a mistress for himself even as his wife, Manuela, is expecting a baby. Arturo's and Oscar's accepted adultery is juxtaposed with that of Adelita, Manuela's sister-in-law, who is viciously censured by the family for her infidelity to Ernesto. The prevailing sexual double standard for men and women in Cuban society is also reflected in the smaller daily rituals and mores among the Ripolls. Even as Manuela is straining to be more modern (and more American) by smoking, wearing low-cut dresses, and cutting her hair short, she and her mother still wait hand and foot on her two weak, pampered brothers, Ernesto and Mario. Whereas Maria Josefa, the family matriarch, agrees not to notice or mention her husband's unfaithfulness, all the family members complain vociferously about Adelita's conduct. In fact, the play is a compendium of the ceremonies that form their life together and to which they all cling as known, safe reality—ceremonies of courtship, adultery, eating, social hierarchy, and skin color. The Ripolls have a way of rating suitors according to the amount of Spanish as opposed to mulatto and Indian blood reflected in an individual's skin color. It is significant that Oscar, who gains economic ascendancy in the end, has a darker skin than the Ripolls, who boast of their Basque, European heritage.

The dialogue of *The Modern Ladies of Guanabacoa* is written in a typical Machado rhythm—short percussive lines that are reminiscent of Fornes. His scenes often turn on secrets that remain unspoken even as the characters weave a verbal skein of inessentials—food, servants, styles, and etiquette. Every so often a character will burst out with an unmediated, coarse exclamation that expresses the feelings that lurk at a primitive level and that formal surface of discourse is meant to hold in check.

Fabiola, the next play of the series, switches over to the Marquez family. Sonia Hernandez, a major character in *Fabiola* and presumably the daughter of Oscar and Manuela, the characters from *The Modern Ladies of Guanabacoa* (who do not appear in *Fabiola*), has married into the Marquez family. *Fabiola* gives the impression of greater passage of time, spanning the years 1955 to 1967, and is divided into six scenes. It encompasses the years of Castro's rise to power through his takeover and eventual embracing of Soviet-style communism. The Marquez family, prosperous factory owners, at first enthusiastically back Castro with money and strategy because he promises to stand up to the North American giant that has made of Cuba a puppet under Fulgencio Batista. Although they cheer when Castro takes Havana, they never count on having to make further sacrifices for the revolution. Castro's gradual conversion to communism ultimately forces them to flee Cuba in small groups, and in the last scene, they are made to vacate their home altogether and hand it over to the government.

In typical Machado fashion, the political action erupts onto the main action at first mutedly, as the lady of the house, Cusa, a sworn expert in the coming revolution, intently follows Castro's progress over the radio. Octavio, a cousin, intrudes at one moment, with his fingernails mutilated following a torture session by Batista's thugs. Ultimately, Castro's *milicianos* swarm through the house, triumphantly ordering about their social superiors. Machado furthermore epitomizes the brewing social transformation in the person of Sara, a servant. Sara is humiliated in the first act by a sister-in-law, Clara, a figure reminiscent of Natasha from Chekhov's *Tri sestry* (pr., pb. 1901; *The Three Sisters*, 1920), who spits in the loyal servant's face. This same servant joins the revolution and, in a tense scene in the second act, refuses to aid the family, much to their surprise as they had always considered her a family member and were blissfully oblivious to the inequities implicit in the master-servant arrangement.

In the play's foreground, once again, is a web of interpersonal conflicts among family members. Most prominent is the covert sexual relationship between the two Marquez brothers, Osvaldo and Pedro. Pedro's wife, Fabiola, has died before the curtain rises, and her body has mysteriously vanished from the crypt. Pedro, in reaction, is drinking heavily and enters a downhill emotional spiral, which ends only in the play's denouement, his suicide. He proposes to his married brother Osvaldo that they pick up where they left off with the sexual play in which they engaged when they were children. Osvaldo at first eludes him but then succumbs, and they have a protracted liaison, ending only with Osvaldo's immigration to the United States. His absence leaves Pedro bereft and serves as a catalyst for his total disintegration.

The brothers' incestuous relationship is played off against the other characters of the play: their father, Alfredo, who, like Arturo in *The Modern Ladies of Guanabacoa*, is having a long-term illicit relationship; their mother, Cusa, who takes refuge in politics and superstition; their high-spirited sister Miriam, who is enduring the clumsy wooing of the stiff Raulito and who ultimately consents to marry him against her better judgment; and Sonya, Osvaldo's wife, whose struggle is essentially intrapersonal, as

she longs unrequitedly to fulfill herself intellectually and make an impact on the world. Sonya suffers both from the marginality of living in Cuba and from the sense of her own uselessness in relation to a world in turmoil. She recalls, yet again, the Chekhovian archetype of the frustrated aristocrat who yearns for a self-significance never to be achieved.

Machado fashions a mosaic of characters, combining and recombining their encounters in brief two- and three-character scenes. The first act essentially focuses on the two Marquez brothers, whose cat-and-mouse game of attraction is repeatedly interrupted by intrusions from others but then is ultimately consummated as the curtain falls. Again, Machado's characters are aware of, but avoid discussing, the major issues that preoccupy them all: Osvaldo and Pedro's illicit relationship, one that everyone apparently knows about but that no one will openly discuss; Alfredo's kept woman; the growing dread of the family's exclusion from Cuban life; and Pedro's alcoholism and incipient disintegration. All these issues are swept under the carpet in a froth of music, dancing, fun, frolic, and, in the case of Cusa, political fanaticism.

The figure of Fabiola, the dead woman whose body at first disappears and then stubbornly refuses to decompose, stands for the dying aristocracy. She is decadence incarnate, and she literally haunts the house, causing records to start and curtains to flutter and preoccupying Pedro and all the others.

The action of *In the Eye of the Hurricane*, the third play in the series, is contemporaneous with that of *Fabiola*, occurring in the aftermath of Castro's rise to power. Built on a leaner, more linear crisis-drama structure than the sprawling, intricate *Fabiola*, it returns to the Hernandez and Ripoll families, now at the time of the Castro uprising. Oscar Hernandez is still head of the prospering bus company and is assisted by his wife, Manuela. Oscar has long ago deprived Manuela's brother, Mario, of his portion of the family wealth, and the latter now lives a dependent and subservient life with them. Maria Josefa, Mario and Manuela's mother, a severe woman and the repository of all the old values and manners, lives with them as well. The first act hinges on two unspeakable secrets that pierce the surface and dominate the action of the second act: The first is a letter that has arrived informing the family that Castro is planning to confiscate their buses, and the second is the news that Maria Josefa is dying. The play opens with Manuela speaking of safety as something to which to cling for dear life. Her mother rejoins that feeling safe is "the first step to violence and death." Defiant and in denial, the family goes on as though nothing unusual were in the wind; indeed, the spoiled daughter of the house, Sonia, is picking out a fancy sportscar at the very moment the *milicianos* appear with the confiscation order.

The two strands, the confiscation of the buses and the death of Maria Josefa, intersect in a curious fashion at the play's climax. This particular scene admirably illustrates Machado's tragicomic, ironic method at its most typical. Manuela and Oscar instruct their entourage to lie down in front of the buses to prevent Castro's men from taking the vehicles. Their unswerving certainty that they will save their property begins to crumble as many bus drivers disobey their orders and go out on their normal routes, only to have their buses taken from them. Those who remain on the premises do an about-face and refuse to lie down in front of the buses, with the exception of one loyal employee, Fulgencio, who caves in at the first sign of trouble. The crowd that the family called together to protest the *milicianos'* confiscation turns instead on the Hernandez family, who had oppressed them for decades, and chant rhythmically for the *milicianos* to go ahead and take the buses. In heroic desperation, Manuela and Oscar lie down in front of their buses, but the *milicianos* put them into reverse, a direction that the two had not anticipated, and drive them off, leaving their owners farcically lying on the ground.

Manuela tries to throw a lit cigarette into the motor of one departing bus but is restrained by Mario, who betrays his hated brother-in-law and shows himself fully prepared to go to work for Castro. Mario uses the social upheaval as an opportunity to correct the injustice perpetrated within the family. During the scene's greatest intensity, the old lady, Maria Josefa, comes back to life, again symbolic of the indomitable spirit of these proud, tenacious people. This crucial scene presents an occasion to reveal the family's courage and foolishness, their arrogance and blindness to the false premises on which their economic ascendancy rests.

The fourth play of the Floating Island series, *Broken Eggs*, is the most unremittingly comedic. Set in 1979 in Los Angeles, it shows what has become of the clan once transplanted to North America. The occasion is the wedding of Lizette, the young Americanized daughter, who is trying to leave her Latin roots behind her by marrying the scion of a Jewish family, the Rifkins. The setting is a waiting room of a "wedding mill," offstage, so to speak, from the main action—the wedding and banquet proper.

The family structure and traditional roles have now totally crumbled. Osvaldo (the same character from *Fabiola*, now middle-aged) has done the unthinkable: He was divorced from his wife, Sonya. He is now married to an Argentine woman whom they all hate. Their son, Oscar, is a homosexual and a cocaine addict. Osvaldo's sister Miriam, also from *Fabiola*, is addicted to alcohol and Valium. Sonya's mother, Manuela, is stolidly and ineffectually still holding the line of the old traditions, just as her predecessor, Maria Josefa of *The Modern Ladies of Guanabacoa*, did fifty years earlier, but with even less success.

Sonya's ultimately futile attempt to win back her wayward husband constitutes the main action of *Broken Eggs*. In the meantime, the comic preparations for the wedding and the way they go dizzyingly awry form a parade of quick scenes. Whatever should not happen does: The Argentine wife shows up and the Cuban family members taunt her, to their in-laws' consternation; they get drunk and high on drugs and hurl home truths at one another; and, as comic debacle, they run out of wedding cake and scurry to cut smaller pieces and give away their own slices to the Rifkins. *Broken Eggs*, the title of which represents the fate of the family displaced by the revolution and the saying "You can't make an omelette without breaking a few eggs," dramatizes the final gasp of the Cuban dynasty's grandeur and the varied choices the family members have made in California—assimilation, dissolution, and clutching the final vestiges of lost traditions.

ONCE REMOVED

Though not part of the Floating Island series, *Once Removed* is very much in keeping with Machado's theme of displaced Cubans. This work depicts a Cuban family summarily wrenched from their dignified existence in their homeland and dropped in an anonymous motel room in Hialeah, a place best known (as they ruefully remark) for dog races. *Once Removed* differs from the Floating Island plays chiefly for its pronounced boulevard tendencies. More than the other Machado plays, it is a well-made, Broadway-style comedy, full of one-liners about the Spam (canned meat) that the family is forced to ingest in a thousand different forms.

A BURNING BEACH

Also about Cuba, but a Cuba of the more remote past—the end of the nineteenth century—is *A Burning Beach*. It allegorically depicts the point in history during the Spanish-American War at which Cuba was wrested from Spain's domination and placed under American puppet rule. A jaunty American woman, Constance Buchanan, niece of one "Theodore" (who is meant to represent Theodore Roosevelt, hero of San Juan Hill), arrives at the home of a wealthy Cuban family. Although ostensibly a guest, she quickly shifts into business mode, figuratively seducing Ofelia, the maiden lady who is also the head of the house, and negotiating for the family's profitable sugar plantation. Constance succeeds in gaining hegemony, although the interracial son of the family, Juan, encounters the apparition of the liberator José Martí on the beach and swears to regain Cuba for Cubans. *A Burning Beach* is entirely schematic in its austere treatment of historical metaphor, and so it is a stylistic departure for Machado.

DON JUAN IN NEW YORK CITY AND STEVIE WANTS TO PLAY THE BLUES

Machado leaves his immigrant theme behind with such major works as *Stevie Wants to Play the Blues*, a musical about a female singer who transforms herself into a man, and *Don Juan in New York City*, which is chiefly about sexual ambivalence in the age of AIDS. The latter play, a work that is operatic in scope and amplitude, centers on D. J. (Don Juan), an experimental filmmaker, as a retrospective of his work is planned and executed. Apparently bisexual, D. J. is torn between a female singer-celebrity, Flora, and his trashy male lover, Steve. His conflict is enacted against the backdrop of the AIDS epidemic: D. J.'s good friend, Paul, a female impersonator, has taken refuge in the guise of Carole Channing and is preparing first for a concert of Channing's songs and subsequently for a successful suicide, as he eludes the depredations of AIDS. The baroque action is further complicated by actual film clips from D. J.'s creations and by passionate songs performed by two mysterious figures, Abuelo and Mujer, representatives of the world of traditional heterosexual love for which the classic Don Juan was known.

Machado has called *Stevie Wants to Play the Blues* a "gender-bender," a genre in which he examines premises about sexuality and takes the characters through surprising and unconventional revelations about their gender identifications. Other plays in which he toys with the notion of sexual identity are *Related Retreats*, about the lives of writers at an arts colony under the tutelage of a female guru, and *Breathing It In*, about a motley band of lost souls who congregate around a male/female guru couple who espouse the individual's embracing the woman-nature within. It at once satirizes groups such as Werner Erhard's individual, social transformation technique (EST) and the women's liberation movement of the 1970's and 1980's and concocts a string of variations on sexual transformation among its characters.

BETWEEN THE SHEETS

Machado wrote the book and lyrics for the musical *Between the Sheets*, an homage to Spanish playwright and poet Federico García Lorca. With music by Mike Nolan and Scott Williams, the 1996 musical was produced Off-Off-Broadway at the Playwrights' Collective to largely unfavorable reviews. Machado's musical book takes the Spanish Civil War as its setting and develops around Lorca's opposition to the fascism of Francisco Franco that leads to the writer's execution in 1936. The musical's themes show the oppositions of freedom and fascism, art and repression, with the homosexual poet as the central figure of contention in an actress's scheme (her husband had been Lorca's lover in the past) to use her seventeen-year-old son to seduce the playwright, thereby winning her a role in his play. The story amplifies betrayal as the central motif of personal and political warfare.

HAVANA IS WAITING

When the Sea Drowns in Sand (later retitled *Havana Is Waiting*) had its debut at the twenty-fifth annual Humana Festival of New American plays sponsored by the Actors Theatre of Louisville, Kentucky. Machado's three-character comedy blends autobiography, an emerging love affair, and the travail of the most famous Cuban child of the 1990's—Elian Gonzalez.

Called the most personal of Machado's works, *Havana Is Waiting* explores the universal need to "find home," to understand one's childhood and maturity, and to define one's adult self. The play was inspired by Machado's return to his homeland after forty years of "exile" in the United States that began when he was eight years old. Machado was one of thirteen thousand children of Cuba's elite families who were sent out of the country in 1960-1961 on Pan American flights to the United States with the tacit consent of Castro. In the early 1960's, Voice of America radio tried to convince Cuban parents that their children would be sent to Moscow by Castro for retraining if they did not avail themselves of the opportunity to send them to the United States. The exodus of children and the concomitant breakup of families followed. Machado did not return to Cuba until 1999, when he traveled there as part of the Festival International Del Nuevo Ciné Latino Americano. During the trip, Machado came to the realization that he was really an American and could no longer survive living in Cuba.

The play opens on a highly personal note as Federico (a thinly disguised Machado) reconsiders his decision to return to his native Cuba after thirty-eight years of exile following his parents' decision to send him to the United States. Nonetheless, Federico and his friend Fred begin the journey to Havana and arrive at the same time that Elian Gonzalez is found on the shores of Florida, having lost his mother at sea during their efforts to escape Castro's Cuba. Once in Cuba, and with the help of their taxi driver/guide,

who solicits their support to end the U.S. embargo against Cuba, the two men find in Federico's childhood home shifting emotions of longing, fear, and self-blame. The critic for the *Los Angeles Times* called the play "a tight, crafty, and exceptionally eloquent play about identity politics on every scale."

The retitled *Havana Is Waiting* opened Off-Broadway at the Cherry Lane Theatre in October of 2001. Machado said the new title refers to many things. "First, Havana is waiting for a forty-year-old embargo to end. Havana means waiting, for the people who live there. Waiting interminably in lines for anything from a bus to ice cream, but more importantly Havana, or as they say in Cuba, La Habana, was waiting for me to return."

OTHER MAJOR WORKS

SCREENPLAY: *Exiles in New York*, 1999.

TRANSLATION: *The Day You'll Love Me*, pr. 1989 (of José Ignacio Cabrujas's play *El día que me quieras*).

BIBLIOGRAPHY

Bigsby, C. W. E. *Modern American Drama, 1945-2000*. New York: Cambridge University Press, 2000. Bigsby writes succinctly of contemporary American drama and the diversity of Spanish-speaking communities and writers in the United States. Machado appears among the Cuban American writers.

Brand, Ulrika. "A Master Playwright Teaches His Discipline: An Interview with Eduardo Machado," *Columbia News* (June 28, 2001). On the occasion of the premiere of *When the Sea Drowns in Sand*, the public affairs office at Columbia University featured an interview with Eduardo Machado as director of the graduate playwriting program in the School of the Arts. He talks about his unique approach to teaching playwriting and the success of his students.

Brantley, Ben. "Eduardo Machado," *New York Times Magazine* (October 23, 1994): 38-41. Theater critic for *The New York Times* Ben Brantley discusses the four-play cycle of *The Floating Island Plays* as Machado's metaphor for political strife in

Cuba. As such, the plays address the experiences of the Hispanic immigrant in the United States; several generations of Machado's family become a mirror for a society in emotional, cultural, and economic flux.

Machado, Eduardo. "The Entire Canvas: An Interview with the Playwright." *American Theatre* 14, no. 5 (May/June, 1997): 15. Machado expresses concern that he often experiences the ultimate prejudice when he is treated exclusively as a Cuban American playwright by arts institutions. He argues that, despite the color of his skin and birthplace, he writes about the truth of the human condition.

Mayer, Oliver. "In the Political Soup." *American Theatre* 12, no. 1 (January, 1995): 17. Mayer examines Machado's Cuban American themes, which confront politics, sex, and race.

Palmer, Tanya, and Amy Wegener, eds. *Humana Festival 2000: The Complete Plays*. Lyme, N.H.: Smith and Kraus, 2001. The volume contains *When the Sea Drowns in Sand* and a brief biography of Machado.

Rubin, Don, and Carlos Solórzano, eds. *The World Encyclopedia of Contemporary Theater: The Americas*. New York: Routledge, 1996. Machado is included in the section on Cuban American theater.

Sterling, Kristin. "The Return to Cuba Helps Eduardo Machado Find Home and Inspiration." *Columbia News* (October 29, 2001). This feature article focuses on *Havana Is Waiting* and discusses the circumstances surrounding Machado's exile from Cuba and the play about his return forty years later to his homeland.

David Willinger,
updated by Milly S. Barranger

NICCOLÒ MACHIAVELLI

Born: Florence (now in Italy); May 3, 1469
Died: Florence (now in Italy); June 21, 1527

PRINCIPAL DRAMA

Andria, pb. c. 1517 (based on Terence's play; English translation, 1969)

La mandragola, pb. c. 1519, pr. 1520 (*The Mandrake*, 1911)

La Clizia, pr. 1525, pb. 1532 (based on Plautus's play *Casina*; *Clizia*, 1961)

OTHER LITERARY FORMS

Had Niccolò Machiavelli not written any of his other works, he would without doubt still be remembered today as one of the most innovative and perceptive playwrights of the sixteenth century, for he contributed much to revitalize the tradition of the Italian *commedia erudita*, combining classical and Boccaccean sources with contemporary themes and morals. Although Machiavelli's theatrical production is noteworthy for its satiric and biting treatment of societal attitudes, as well as (especially in his play *The Mandrake*) for its political overtones, Machiavelli is best known today for his political and historical writings, which mark one of the highest achievements in this sphere of intellectual pursuit. His best-known work, *Il principe* (wr. 1513; *The Prince*, 1640), that list of practical advice by means of which a prince, properly trained in the workings of politics, might acquire and maintain a state and muster enough *virtú* to overcome and keep in check *fortuna*, has had a profound impact on the development of political thought. Clearly implied in it is Machiavelli's tenet that politics and morality are independent of each other and that the behavior of people or the course of events is no longer necessarily determined by dogmas or fate; even the consequence of chance may be anticipated and confronted. Moreover, in chapter 26 of *The Prince*, Machiavelli reaches the highest expression of Italian nationalism and desire for political territorial integrity by exhorting the Italians to seek liberty and to unite against foreign invaders. Searching in ancient history for precedents that might offer solutions to the world in which he lived and explain the nature of human-kind, Machiavelli, in his *Discorsi sopra la prima deca di Tito Livio* (wr. c. 1513-1517, pb. 1531; *Discourses on the First Ten Books of Titus Livius*, 1636), attempted to analyze the proper functioning of a republican state so that the laws of ancient Rome could be successfully reapplied in a modern state in order to achieve national strength and unity. In addition, Machiavelli completed *Dell' arte della guerra* (1521; *The Art of War*, 1560), a dialogue on military tactics with examples drawn from both ancient and modern history, and *Istorie fiorentine* (1525; *The Florentine History*, 1595), the official history of Florence commissioned by Cardinal Giuliano de' Medici, which is noted for its political rather than purely historic tone, and in which Machiavelli had to reconcile his republican beliefs with a perfunctory pro-Medici posture.

Niccolò Machiavelli (Library of Congress)

ACHIEVEMENTS

Niccolò Machiavelli unquestionably belongs to the ranks of the most profound and original political theorists in history. This reputation not only rests on his most famous and influential work, *The Prince*, and on his other political works but also attests the political sophistication of such literary and dramatic efforts as *The Mandrake* and *Clizia*.

The considerable influence Machiavelli has had on political thought is evidenced by the several and varied reactions to his works throughout history. As a result of the Church's perception of his *ragione di stato* (reason of state) as a rejection of the connection of the state to Catholic teachings and as an obvious attempt to release rulers from religious compliance, Machiavelli was accused of impiety and his works were placed on the Index in 1559. Nevertheless, Machiavelli's works enjoyed great popularity while he was still alive, and even after his writings were banned they continued to be published—although, understandably, the publisher often chose to remain anonymous. The emperor Charles V, it is said, had only three books beside his bed: the Bible, Baldassare Castiglione's *Il cortegiano* (1528; *The Courtier*, 1561), and Machiavelli's *The Prince*. Ironically, among the greatest proponents of anti-Machiavellism

were also the French Huguenots, particularly Innocent Gentillet, who blamed Machiavelli for having provided Catherine de' Medici with the model of her unyielding statesmanship, which later culminated in the violent repression of French Protestants.

By the eighteenth century, however, despite some strong reservations on the part of such thinkers and rulers as Vico, Voltaire, and Frederic of Prussia, Machiavelli's works came to be viewed less critically through a so-called oblique interpretation. Jean-Jacques Rousseau, Giuseppe Parini, Giuseppe Baretti, and many others rejected the belief that Machiavelli propounded cunning and deception, and instead interpreted his writings as an attempt to show the immorality of political tactics, implying, at the same time, that through a proper application of politics it would also be possible to restore people's natural rights. Although at the beginning of the nineteenth century, as a result of his appeal for Italian unity, Machiavelli began to be considered a forerunner of the Risorgimento, his writings were later viewed unfavorably for their emphasis on the importance of the state rather than that of the individual quest for liberty and independence.

It is only in the twentieth century that an analysis of Machiavelli's works has been undertaken with proper consideration of the political, economic, and social circumstances present during Machiavelli's lifetime. It is only in this light that his realistic approach and personal concern for the forces at play in the society in which he lived, as demonstrated by the theories proposed in *The Prince*, and his criticism of Florentine social values, as reflected in his plays, may be properly understood.

BIOGRAPHY

On May 3, 1469, Niccolò di Bernardo dei Machiavelli was born in Florence, one of four children, to Ser Bernardo Machiavelli and Bartolomea de' Nelli. As the son of a rather poor branch of a noble family, Machiavelli later said that he learned to do without before he learned to enjoy what life had to offer. Little is known of Machiavelli's early years other than that he obtained a typical but substantial bourgeois education, also taking advantage of the extensive library that his father Bernardo had taken pains to create. It is known that as a young man he began to study Latin grammar under the guidance of a tutor named Matteo, and by the time he was twelve years old he was composing in Latin under the supervision of Paolo di Ronciglione. The Latin influence introduced him to such authors as Livy, Tacitus, Pliny, and Cicero, as well as Ovid, Lucretius, and Vergil, with whom he felt more familiar than the Greek historians and philosophers whose works he read in translation. From 1488 to 1498, he worked at the Rome office of the Berti bank, and at the age of twenty-nine, after the overthrow of the Medici rule in 1494 by Girolamo Savonarola's followers and the subsequent violent end of Savonarola's republican government in 1498, Machiavelli began his political career when he was elected secretary to the Second Chancery of Florence. This position, although not of major importance, allowed Machiavelli to go on frequent legations to other cities and towns in Italy, as well as to other countries, such as France, Germany, and Swit-

zerland. In addition, Machiavelli took on the position of secretary to the Dieci di Balia (the Ten of Power), a magistry that directed defense and diplomatic affairs. In 1501 or, according to some sources, 1502, he married Marietta Corsini, a devoted wife who eventually bore him six children.

In the course of his duties, Machiavelli's political philosophy began to develop. He was greatly influenced by his travel experiences, and he analyzed the strengths and weaknesses of the foreign nations he visited on his return from his legations, as evidenced by his *Rapporto delle cose della Magna* (wr. 1508; report on the state of Germany) and his *Ritratto di cose di Francia* (wr. 1512-1513; portrait of the state of France), among other works. One of the greatest influences on Machiavelli, however, was the ruthless Cesare Borgia, who was attempting to create his own principality in Italy and therefore threatened the fate of Florence. Machiavelli was sent on legation to Borgia twice, and he wrote an account of one of Borgia's brutal actions entitled *Descrizione del modo tenuto dal Duca Valentino nello ammazzare Vitellozzo Vitelli, Oliverotto da Fermo, il Signor Pagolo e il Duca di Gravina Orsini* (wr. 1503; on the manner adopted by the duke Valentino to kill Vitellozzo Vitelli, Oliverotto of Fermo, Sir Pagolo, and the duke of Gravina Orsini). Indeed, the methods of Borgia became the model on which Machiavelli based his idea of the prince, a ruthless, cunning ruler who would finally achieve the ultimate goal of uniting all of Italy. Machiavelli's pragmatic observations had the immediate effect of persuading the chief magistrate of Florence to create a state militia in 1505. In 1506, he was sent by the Florentine government to Rome to meet with Pope Julius II, who was then pursuing an expansionistic policy. Toward the end of the same year, Machiavelli added to his official duties the secretariat of the newly created Chancery of the Nine Officials of the Florentine Militia.

Machiavelli's political career changed course dramatically in 1512, when the Medici family returned to Florence after the defeat of the Florentine troops by the Spanish army led by Cardinal Giovanni de' Medici, the future Pope Leo X. Not only did he lose his position, but in 1513 he was also briefly imprisoned and tortured after having been wrongly accused of participating in a conspiracy against the Medici rule. After his release, Machiavelli lived in relative poverty for a number of years, but his forced inactivity enabled him to dedicate himself fully to his political and literary writings. In fact, some of his most famous works were produced during this time: *The Prince* was completed in 1513 (although it reached final form only in 1516, when Machiavelli dedicated it to Lorenzo de' Medici in the hope of obtaining a position), and most of the *Discourses on the First Ten Books of Titus Livius* was completed in 1517. Machiavelli's most famous play, *The Mandrake*, also dates from this period, as do a number of lesser works.

When Cardinal Giulio de' Medici, the future Pope Clement VII, came to govern Florence in 1520, Machiavelli's fortunes changed once again as the efforts of good friends to intercede on his behalf with the Medici family met with some success. The cardinal entrusted him with the duty of writing his opinions on the political conditions of Florence after the death of Lorenzo de' Medici (*Discursus florentinarum rerum post mortem iunioris Laurentii Medices*, wr. 1520), along with other minor tasks. His meeting with Francesco Guicciardini the next year began a warm and fulfilling friendship that lasted many years. Assigned the task of writing the official history of Florence, Machiavelli produced *The Florentine History* in 1525, which seemingly extolled the Medicean policies while at the same time reflecting his personal political views. *Clizia*, the second of his best-known dramatic works, was also finished in 1525, at the time of a tantalizing infatuation with a very young singer. Hoping to gain further favors from the Medici, Machiavelli sided with Giulio de' Medici—who, after many behind-the-scenes maneuvers, had become Pope Clement VII in 1523—against the Holy Roman Emperor Charles V. After much futile scheming, however, Clement was forced to witness from the castle of St. Angelo the fall of Rome and the ensuing sack of the city by the imperial troops in 1527. Florence, seeing again an opportunity to proclaim a Republic, banished the Medici family for the third time, and Machiavelli, who had returned to Florence in the hopes of re-obtaining his position at the Chancery, saw his candidacy rejected by his fellow Florentines because of his previous connection with the former rulers. Heartbroken and impoverished, Machiavelli died after an illness on June 21, 1527.

ANALYSIS

Aside from its worth as a literary genre, Italian comedy by the sixteenth century had become a vehicle for social and political criticism, a kind of *speculum mundi* by means of which the shortcomings and biases of communal society were exposed and ridiculed. Niccolò Machiavelli's theatrical production, especially *The Mandrake*, encompasses this satiric intent while interpreting the more popular sentiments of his fellow citizens, who still relished the storytelling tradition of Giovanni Boccaccio.

THE MANDRAKE

The Mandrake, one of the most successful plays of the Italian Renaissance, enjoyed great popularity even during Machiavelli's lifetime. Indeed, probably in 1522, during one performance the play had to be stopped at the end of the fourth act because of huge crowds that made its continuation unsafe. Although reference to certain historical events indicates that the action of *The Mandrake* takes place in Florence in 1504, the date of composition of the play has been disputed; it is most often considered to have been written during the late years of the author's exile— probably during the pre-Lenten festivities of 1518— and was first printed in Florence about 1519.

The structure of *The Mandrake* is patterned after that of a classic Roman play, with the plot following the traditional organization of protasis, epitasis, and catastrophe, and including paraskene, or transition, scenes. Quite evident in it are the classic comic drama's mocking tone and complicated plot structure, as well as the traditional five-act division and respect for dramatic unities; Machiavelli, however, has given these characteristics a new life, modifying and updating the classic model. The comedy embodies a greater realistic sense, and it is written in lively colloquial Florentine prose, revealing the influence of Boccaccio's storytelling. The sensuality and licentiousness of the plot closely resemble those of one of the tales of the *Decameron*, while the unfolding of the story also reveals a more direct satiric intent.

The Mandrake is introduced by a prologue that is divided into two sections. The first section describes the characters, the setting, and the plot. Machiavelli identifies the four main male characters as the lover, the gullible husband, the wicked friar, and the scheming parasite, and refers to the play as a *badalucco*, or joke. The second section of the prologue is used by Machiavelli to describe his relationship to society, portraying the author as unrewarded and unappreciated, as these well-known lines clearly indicate:

And if this subject is not worthy,
although I am trying to be light,
of a man who wants to seem wise and serious,
forgive him with this excuse: he is trying
with these trifle thoughts
to make his sad time more bearable,
for there is nowhere
where he can turn to;
he has been prevented from showing with other deeds
  his other virtues,
an unjust reward for his endeavors.

The plot of *The Mandrake* revolves around the efforts of Callimaco, who returns to Florence to seduce the most beautiful woman of the city, Lucrezia, the wife of a rich but obtuse doctor of laws, Master Nicia. Master Nicia, terribly distraught by his lack of children, will go to any lengths to help cure the supposed infertility of Lucrezia, but until now his efforts and expenses have been to no avail. Callimaco, driven by lust for the desirable Lucrezia, devises a scheme with the aid of his servant, Siro, and a local con man and parasite figure, Ligurio, to possess Lucrezia. Taking advantage of the foolish Nicia's obsession, Callimaco poses as a wise doctor who has the ultimate cure for Lucrezia's infertility: She need only drink a potion made of the mandrake root (hence the play's title), and she will conceive. Callimaco and Ligurio warn Master Nicia that the first man to sleep with Lucrezia after she has drunk this potion will die within one week. Thus, Callimaco easily persuades Nicia to permit Lucrezia to sleep with a young idler, whom, unknown to Nicia, he will pretend to be. With the aid of an unscrupulous friar, Fra Timoteo, who persuades her that the legitimate end of a Christian marriage is that of having children and that all means to reach this holy end are permissible, and of Lucrezia's calculating mother, Sostrata, Lucrezia is finally persuaded to take the potion. Once Callimaco confesses the plot to Lucrezia, she proclaims her love for him and her willingness to continue the conspiracy, saying that "some divine influence" must have willed this and that it is not for her to disobey "what heaven decrees."

The characters of *The Mandrake* reflect the Machiavellian perception of the Florentine society the author knew so well. Callimaco, the sensual protagonist, is driven only by his passions and is intent solely on seducing the married and virtuous Lucrezia, while Ligurio is the classic parasite who will do anything for a price. In Master Nicia, the representative of a particular wealthy class of Florentine society, the provincial, unprincipled bourgeois lawyer, Machiavelli indicates the most ridiculous and mocked character, the justly deserving victim of the joke that will ultimately make him a willing cuckold. It is perhaps the character of Fra Timoteo, the cynical and hypocritical confessor, however, that best reflects Machiavelli's bitter opinion of his fellow citizens and of their morals. Fra Timoteo, once he realizes that it is too late to abandon his role in the scheme, becomes entirely accommodating to Callimaco and Ligurio, and pockets without any qualms the bribe that the unwitting Nicia is forced to pay. Lucrezia, too, is finally swept into the conspiracy, for she admits that although she would have never agreed to the plan beforehand, once she has experienced the love of a younger man, she will go along with it.

Often described as the greatest dramatic work of the Italian Renaissance, this comedy also clearly represents a caustic and biting commentary on the mores of Florentine society. Although some critics have made attempts to demonstrate that the play is a political allegory, in which Callimaco represents Duke Lorenzo de' Medici, Lucrezia represents Florence, and Nicia represents Piero Soderini, Machiavelli's influential patron in the Florentine chancery, this reading has not gained wide acceptance, since Machiavelli's own contemporaries did not regard it as such.

Furthermore, *The Mandrake* is often considered a dramatic reflection of Machiavelli's political ideas, for it presents such recurrent Machiavellian themes as the end justifying the means, realism, and *virtú* as victorious over *fortuna*. Indeed, *The Mandrake* is a satiric treatment of human interaction in which *virtú*, or the use of cunning and intelligence to overcome *fortuna* and turn it to one's advantage, creates a new moral perception completely devoid of idealism and false morality.

CLIZIA

Of the other lesser dramatic works, *Clizia*, closely patterned after the *Casina* (English translation, 1774) of Plautus, occupies a distant second place in order of importance, while revealing some interesting glimpses into Machiavelli's life. Clizia, the abandoned daughter of a Neapolitan, is brought up as a member of the family by the Florentine Nicomaco, who has now fallen in love with her and has made plans to marry her off to one of his servants in order to finally possess her. His plans, however, are discovered by Nicomaco's son, Cleandro, who is also in love with but cannot marry Clizia because of her low birth and lack of dowry. Cleandro and his mother, Sofronia, attempting to thwart Nicomaco's plan and to gain time, insist on having her marry Cleandro's servant, Eustachio. After much debate, all agree to draw lots in order to decide whom Clizia should marry, but although Nicomaco wins the lot, Sofronia and Cleandro disguise a house servant as Clizia, and Nicomaco is humiliated when he enters the bride's chambers and discovers the trick. Cleandro eventually wins Clizia as his own bride when a rich Neopolitan, who claims to be Clizia's father, arrives and offers her in marriage to him, and the old, contrite Nicomaco goes back to his wife. In comparison to *The Mandrake*, *Clizia*'s tone is less acrimonious and only lightly moralizing, with an almost commiserating quality. Machiavelli's sympathetic tone toward Nicomaco's senile infatuation may be the result of his own love for the young and beautiful singer Barbara Fiorentina (or Salutati) when he was fifty-six years old. Nicomaco, in fact, is portrayed as an old yet dignified and vigorous man who, after leading an exemplary family life, is temporarily beset with amoral amorous desires. Indeed, the play ends with Nicomaco's ashamed return to societal mores, rather than with an acceptance of a new morality, as in the case of *The Mandrake*. The structure of *Clizia* is also different. While in *The Mandrake* the plot centers on two antithetical elements, that of love and that of mockery, here the two elements are unified in one character, Nicomaco, the mocked lover who finally returns to Sofronia, the symbol of concrete and moral bourgeois virtues. It almost appears that with *Clizia*, Machiavelli is warning his spectators that the time of political or moral nonconformism has passed, and that those who attempt to escape society's rules are destined for defeat.

OTHER MAJOR WORKS

LONG FICTION: *Novella di Belfagor Arcidiavolo*, 1516 (*The Novella of Belfagor Archdevil*, 1671)

POETRY: *Decennale primo*, 1504 (*First Decennial*, 1965); *Decennale secondo*, 1509 (*Second Decennial*, 1965); *Serenata*, 1513-1514 (*Serenade*, 1965); *L'asino d'oro*, 1517, 1549 (*The Golden Ass*, 1965); *Canti carnascialeschi*, 1523-1524 (*Carnival Songs*, 1965); *Lust and Liberty: The Poems of Machiavelli*, 1963.

NONFICTION: *Descrizione del modo tenuto dal Duca Valentino nello ammazzare Vitellozzo Vitelli, Oliverotto da Fermo, il Signor Pagolo e il Duca di Gravina Orsini*, wr. 1503; *Discorso dell'ordinare lo stato di Firenze alle armi*, 1507 (*Discourse on Florentine Military Preparation*, 1965); *Rapporto delle cose della Magna*, wr. 1508; *Ritratto di cose di Francia*, wr. 1512-1513; *Il principe*, wr. 1513, pb. 1532 (*The Prince*, 1640); *Discorsi sopra la prima deca di Tito Livio*, wr. 1513, pb. 1531 (*Discourses on the First Ten Books of Titus Livius*, 1636); *Discursus florentinarum rerum post mortem iunioris Laurentii Medices*, wr. 1520; *La vita di Castruccio Castracani*, 1520 (*The Life of Castruccio Castracani*, 1675); *Discorso delle cose fiorentine dopo la morte di Lorenzo*, 1520 (*Discourse on the State of Florence After the Death of Lorenzo*, 1965); *Dell' arte della guerra*, 1521 (*The Art of War*, 1560); *Istorie fiorentine*, 1525 (*The Florentine History*, 1595); *Discorso: O, Dialogo intorno alla nostra lingua*, 1525 (*Discourse: Or, Dialogue About Our Language*, 1961).

BIBLIOGRAPHY

Ascoli, Albert Russell, and Victoria Ann Kahn. *Machiavelli and the Discourse of Literature*. Ithaca, N.Y.: Cornell University Press, 1993. A study that provides critical analysis of Machiavelli's works. Bibliography and index.

Fischer, Markus. *Well-ordered License: On the Unity of Machiavelli's Thought*. Lanham, Md.: Lexington Books, 2000. An examination of Machiavelli's philosophies as they were expressed in his writings. Bibliography and index.

Kahn, Victoria Ann. *Machiavellian Rhetoric: From the Counter-Reformation to Milton*. Princeton, N.J.: Princeton University Press, 1994. An examination of Machiavelli's political and social views as expressed in his literary works. Bibliography and index.

Skinner, Quentin. *Machiavelli: A Very Short Introduction*. New York: Oxford University Press, 2000. A concise presentation of Machiavelli's life that focuses on his political and philosophical views. Bibliography and index.

Sullivan, Vickie B. *Machiavelli's Three Romes: Religion, Human Liberty, and Politics Reformed*. De Kalb: Northern Illinois University Press, 1996. A study of Machiavelli's religious, social, and political views as they appeared in his writings. Bibliography and index.

_____, ed. *The Comedy and Tragedy of Machiavelli: Essays on the Literary Works*. New Haven, Conn.: Yale University Press, 2000. A collection of essays that examine the literary works of Machiavelli. Bibliography and index.

Viroli, Maurizio. *Niccolò Machiavelli: A Biography of Machiavelli*. New York: Farrar, Straus & Giroux, 2000. A brief general-interest biography of Machiavelli focusing primarily on his career as a diplomat, secretary in the Republic of Florence, and writer.

Roberto Severino

ARCHIBALD MACLEISH

Born: Glencoe, Illinois; May 7, 1892
Died: Conway, Massachusetts; April 20, 1982

PRINCIPAL DRAMA

The Pot of Earth, pb. 1925
Nobodaddy: A Play, pb. 1926
Union Pacific: A Ballet, pr. 1934 (libretto; with Nicolas Nabokoff)
Panic: A Play in Verse, pr., pb. 1935
The Fall of the City: A Verse Play for Radio, pr., pb. 1937
Air Raid: A Verse Play for Radio, pr., pb. 1938
The States Talking, pr., pb. 1941
The Trojan Horse: A Play, pr. 1952 (broadcast), pb. 1952, pr. 1953 (staged)
This Music Crept by Me upon the Waters, pr., pb. 1953 (one act)
J. B.: A Play in Verse, pr., pb. 1958
Three Short Plays: The Secret of Freedom, Air Raid, The Fall of the City, pb. 1961
Herakles: A Play in Verse, pr. 1965, pb. 1967
Scratch, pr., pb. 1971 (inspired by Stephen Vincent Benét's short story "The Devil and Daniel Webster")
The Great American Fourth of July Parade: A Verse Play for Radio, pr., pb. 1975
Six Plays, pb. 1980

OTHER LITERARY FORMS

Critics concerned with the achievements of Archibald MacLeish unite in warning literary taxonomists against differentiating between his work as poet and as dramatist, for with only one exception, all his plays are composed in verse. Nevertheless, his poetic dramas form a group that can be considered separately from his poetry. Indeed, MacLeish's output in both genres is considerable; of the three Pulitzer Prizes he received, two were awarded for his poems.

As early as 1917, MacLeish published his collection of verse *Tower of Ivory*, bringing together his undergraduate efforts from his years at Yale, detached poems derivative in both tone and technique of the powerful nineteenth century British Romantic lyric tradition. The volume is significant, however, for introducing MacLeish's ubiquitous artistic themes: human beings' relation to God and the reality of human existence. No more of his poetry appeared until 1924, when *The Happy Marriage* was published. Here, MacLeish appears more influenced by the Metaphysical poets of the seventeenth century, and here he experimented with a number of more complex verse forms as well as with the difficulties inherent in paradox. Two other works of the 1920's, *The Pot of Earth* and *Nobodaddy*, have been included variously in discussions of either MacLeish's poetry or drama. In truth, they are embryonic verse plays, despite the author's reference to them as poems. Because they prefigure and resemble his fully developed plays, they should be included with that genre.

After continued exclusive attention to poetry, especially during his sojourn in France, MacLeish received his first major recognition as a poet for *Conquistador* (1932), a powerful lyric and descriptive epic in free terza rima form. Chronicling the heroic exploits of Hernando Cortés, as seen through the eyes of a Spanish soldier, the narrative poem was awarded the 1933 Pulitzer Prize in Poetry. MacLeish had personally visited Mexico in 1929, retracing by mule and on foot the route of the sixteenth century Spanish explorer and conqueror of Montezuma's Aztec empire. The poem expresses the ultimate hollowness of heroism, as both adversaries, Cortés and Montezuma, fall victim to corruption. Only the majestic landscape remains, the scene of monumental waste and loss.

Yet another facet of MacLeish's talent became evident in 1934, for then the poet became the librettist for a ballet, *Union Pacific*, celebrating the completion of the transcontinental railroad in 1869. A resounding critical and artistic success, the ballet was performed in New York and on extensive tours in both the United States and Europe by the Ballet Russe de Monte Carlo company, providing the rapidly maturing writer with his first experience on the professional stage.

Escapism into a more joyous and optimistic past was not, however, MacLeish's primary artistic thrust in the increasingly troubled 1930's, a decade that marked the poet's increased concern with social and political issues and his recognition of both the rapidly developing crisis in Europe and the infiltration into the United States of foreign ideologies, particularly Marxism. To give voice to his fears for the United States' ability to withstand these threats, MacLeish turned to prose, and by the time of World War II, he had published a number of volumes of patriotic political essays. Among the most influential was *A Time to Speak* (1941), followed by *A Time to Act* in 1943.

Since the early days of Franklin D. Roosevelt's New Deal, MacLeish had been an editor of *Fortune* magazine, using that journalistic forum to express his views on contemporary issues. Wartime public service claimed most of his creative energies, and it was not until 1948 that his next collection of poetry, *Actfive and Other Poems*, appeared. Although written as a play in three scenes and using the language of stagecraft, this work is usually considered a poem, one expressing disillusionment with American politics in action, for MacLeish had believed very strongly in Roosevelt's idealistic program for economic and social reforms.

In 1950, the first of MacLeish's two theoretical analyses of poetry appeared, *Poetry and Opinion*, followed eleven years later by *Poetry and Experience* (1961). In these essay collections, MacLeish expanded on his theories of "private" and "public" poetic worlds, extending his classroom work as a professor at Harvard to a larger reading audience. As if being a literary essayist, poet, playwright, and journalist were not challenge enough, MacLeish at this time in his career also wrote several screenplays and television scripts and made innumerable contributions to periodicals both in the United States and abroad. In 1966, he won an Academy Award for Best Feature Documentary for his 1965 screenplay *The Eleanor Roosevelt Story*.

Archibald MacLeish (Library of Congress)

ACHIEVEMENTS

Throughout his long and distinguished career, Archibald MacLeish's seemingly unlimited energies were spent in an amazingly broad range of activities directed at the reconciliation of literature and public service. He was an indefatigable lecturer in halls and on university campuses throughout the United States, exemplifying his informing belief that artists cannot indulge themselves by retreating exclusively to a private "tower of ivory" (the title of his first poetry collection) but must use their "gifts" (the title of his first published poem) by addressing themselves to current public issues in the larger world in which they all live.

In both his prose and poetry, MacLeish drew on his wide-ranging intellectual and aesthetic resources to recast the American legacy of myth, history, and folklore into powerful and moving parables for troubled times. The British critic John Wain has observed that "MacLeish . . . has certainly made it a central part of his business to 'manipulate a continuous parallel' between the immemorial and the modern." This

tendency is most evident in MacLeish's verse drama, and it is here that his achievement in twentieth century American literature is most significant. Until the appearance of *J. B.*, there had been little work of any importance in this genre, and the success of this monumental epic of philosophic rationalism encouraged others to explore new possibilities for poetic drama.

The popularity and critical acclaim earned by MacLeish's exemplary *J. B.* proves that he not only mastered the techniques of stagecraft but also, and more important, created a responsive, humanistic, yet classically theatrical work that speaks to common experience while at the same time engaging each member of his audience personally. In an age geared to mass audiences and noncontroversial, often mindless yet commercially successful productions, MacLeish's courage in refusing to compromise his beliefs and values is remarkable in itself.

BIOGRAPHY

The son of upper-middle-class parents, Archibald MacLeish was born in 1892 in Glencoe, Illinois, where he attended grammar school. His father, a Scot, was a prosperous department-store executive whose wealth allowed his son the privilege of a preparatory-school education at Hotchkiss School before his entrance into Yale University, where he took a B.A. degree in 1915. His mother, his father's third wife, was graduated from and taught at Vassar College and, before the birth of the poet, was president of Rockford College in Illinois. The young MacLeish was active in both literary and athletic groups at Yale and was elected to Phi Beta Kappa his junior year.

He enlisted for military duty in World War I, entering as a private in an army hospital unit and serving as a volunteer ambulance driver. After transfer to the artillery, he saw active duty at the front in France. He was discharged in 1918 with the rank of captain. In 1916, he married his childhood sweetheart, Ada Hitchcock, a singer. Four children were born to the couple, although one son died in childhood. After the war, he returned to Harvard Law School, which he had attended briefly before his military service. He taught government there for a year after he was graduated first in his class in 1919. Although avidly concerned with his developing poetic career, he practiced three years with a prestigious law firm in Boston.

By 1923, MacLeish had decided to give up the law, despite his election as a member of the firm. With his wife and children, he left for a five-year sojourn in France and Persia, and there he cultivated his artistic taste and talents by steeping himself in French literary culture. He also associated with the coterie of American expatriates then in Paris, among them Gertrude Stein, Ezra Pound, and Ernest Hemingway. MacLeish, however, had no intention of leaving his homeland permanently, and in 1929, he and his family returned, settling in the small New England village of Conway, Massachusetts, where the poet lived as a "gentleman farmer" for the rest of his life.

During these formative years abroad, the years MacLeish considered "the beginning of my more or less adult life," he matured rapidly as a poet and began to gain an audience for his work as well as critical acclaim. To support his family after his return, he joined the editorial board of *Fortune*, a new business magazine, work that brought him into intimate contact with influential leaders of business and government. This position provided him with a sense of focus for his increasingly liberal views concerning the destiny of the United States during the New Deal years of the Great Depression and the eve of global war.

In 1939, after holding office as the first curator of the Neiman Collection of Contemporary Journalism at Harvard, MacLeish accepted his first position in public life, serving as librarian of Congress until 1944. During the early war years, he also was a director of various branches of governmental information services and spoke and wrote effectively about the crucial issues of the day. In 1944-1945, he served as Assistant Secretary of State. After the war, he was one of the founders of the United Nations Educational Scientific and Cultural Organization (UNESCO) and, in 1946, became chairman of the American delegation at its first conference in Paris.

In 1949, MacLeish accepted an appointment as Boylston Professor of Rhetoric and Oratory at Harvard, holding this honored position until his retirement in 1962. In 1953, he received his second Pulit-

zer Prize in Poetry for *Collected Poems, 1917-1952*, and he was elected president of the American Academy of Arts and Letters. In 1959, he received another Pulitzer Prize for his verse drama *J. B.*, and in 1963, was named Simpson Lecturer at Amherst College, remaining there for four years.

Less than a month before his ninetieth birthday, MacLeish died in a Boston hospital. Even in the final months of his life, he was actively engaged in both writing and granting interviews, continuing to express both his unquenchable passion for art and his concern for justice.

Analysis

A critic observed in 1910 that "we cannot expect a rebirth of the poetic drama until our poets turn playwrights"; such an extended generic transition is obvious in the career of Archibald MacLeish. After publishing two early volumes of verse, he wrote two embryonic verse plays in the mid-1920's, *The Pot of Earth* and *Nobodaddy*, works often regarded as long poems. MacLeish himself included *The Pot of Earth* in his first anthology, *Poems, 1924-1933* (1933). All of this creative output resulted from his five-year sojourn in Paris.

Nobodaddy

Nobodaddy, the title of which came from William Blake's derisory name for the Old Testament God of vengeance and mystery, was written before *The Pot of Earth* but published a year after it. A short philosophical verse play in three acts, sometimes classed as a poetic essay or closet drama, *Nobodaddy* treats the Genesis story of the first family and prefigures MacLeish's use in *J. B.* of modernized Old Testament material to illuminate universal human dilemmas. In *Nobodaddy*, Cain and Abel struggle as adversaries, representing the conflict between the independent mind and the dogma of orthodoxy, a theme to which the poet would return in *J. B.*, three decades later.

The Pot of Earth

The Pot of Earth is also significant as a precursor of *J. B.*, for here too MacLeish used ancient myth as a vehicle for suggesting a reinterpretation of values—in this case Sir James Frazer's description, in *The Golden Bough* (1890), of fertility rites in the garden of Adonis as a metaphor for the disillusionment of a representative human being. In a series of dramatic scenes, an anonymous modern young girl realizes the lack of meaning and lack of free will in her existence as she, like the mythic symbolic plants, rapidly grows to sexual maturity, marries, reproduces, and dies, sacrificed in the endless pattern of ruthless natural forces directed by an indifferent and invisible Gardener, a figure previously evoked in *Nobodaddy*. Technically, *The Pot of Earth* offers evidence of MacLeish's mastery of a variety of verse patterns and other techniques of prosody such as complex assonance and alliteration, and has often been compared to T. S. Eliot's *The Waste Land*, which was published three years earlier. The two works do resemble each other in their mythic basis, although MacLeish's work is far more conservative stylistically; each emphasizes, in a manner typical of the 1920's, the transience of life.

PANIC

Returning to poetry, including *Conquistador*, MacLeish did not attempt drama for another decade, when *Panic* appeared. Together with two half-hour radio scripts provoked by MacLeish's concern for the seeming indifference of Americans toward the threatening world crisis, these plays were his only dramatic work until 1952, and they demonstrate the poet's exploration of the "underlying reality" beneath surface events. Shortly before his death, MacLeish recalled that he had "never seen anything that even remotely approached the misery and anguish and horror of the Great Depression"; this dark epoch in U.S. history was the background for *Panic*, his first play performed in a theater.

As in all of his poetry and prose during this period, MacLeish's theme in *Panic* is a warning against mindless acceptance of authoritarianism and a reminder of the threat to personal freedom in time of crisis. Here, the protagonist, McGafferty, a powerful and wealthy New York industrialist and financier, finds himself at the height of the American financial crisis, in February, 1933, elevated beyond his leadership abilities by the blind fear of those who look to him as their savior. These people, including his bank colleagues and the poor unemployed, perish. In the end, in the classical tradition, McGafferty perishes

helplessly along with them. The play, which has been seen as a hybrid—both Aristotelian tragedy and proletarian drama—drew heavily on the then voguish expressionist techniques. MacLeish was encouraged by the play's acceptance: When both workers and the unemployed responded enthusiastically, MacLeish stated, "Now I have found my audience."

This period piece of the Depression is highly significant in MacLeish's dramaturgic development, for in *Panic*, he experimented with a new verse form, accentual meter, responsive to the contemporary American speech rhythms. He continued to use this form, and not the popular blank verse, in all of his subsequent plays, with one exception, the prose *Scratch*. Briefly, accentual meter is a type of sprung rhythm; rather than counting syllables, one counts the number of stresses or accented syllables in a line. MacLeish's choice was a combination of five-accent lines (but unlimited syllables) and three-beat lines, both to underline conflict inherent in his plots and to avoid monotony.

THE FALL OF THE CITY AND AIR RAID

MacLeish's two vivid half-hour radio dramas in verse, *The Fall of the City* and *Air Raid*, followed his next poetry collection. Along with *Panic*, all three of his verse plays of the 1930's were evidence of his "public" poetry, generalizations of philosophical truths about human behavior focused on timely political issues. In the radio plays, which featured a collective protagonist, the seductive dangers of rampant totalitarianism as well as isolationism were presented by expressionist techniques. *The Fall of the City*, broadcast on the Columbia Broadcasting System (CBS) in 1937, included in its published version a foreword in which the playwright remarked on the effectiveness of radio for the presentation of verse drama to attract large audiences, claiming that "the imagination works better through the ear than through the eye." Here, MacLeish recalls that poetry is meant primarily to be heard, and thereby to stimulate the undistracted "word-excited imagination" into evocation of the depicted action. The advent of television eclipsed radio presentations of this sort, however, and MacLeish's advocacy came to little, as graphically visualized action rapidly captured popular taste.

In MacLeish's play *The Fall of the City*, the disembodied voice of an Announcer (as in classic expressionism, the characters lack personal names) objectively and dispassionately describes the collapse and destruction of a metropolis. A demoralized and terrified population has mindlessly refused to defend itself against the attack of the Conqueror, who promised a strong leadership for which they are willing to sacrifice personal freedom ("Freedom's for fools: Force is the certainty!"). The more digressive *Air Raid* does not exemplify the unity of place evident in the other radio drama, and therefore lacks the total immediacy and impact so vivid there but gains its effect by its topicality: Two years before *Air Raid*'s presentation on CBS, the ancient Basque town of Guernica had been destroyed by Nazi planes in a cruel demonstration of the blitzkrieg strategy of modern warfare. Again, in this play, MacLeish employed a callous and impersonal Announcer to describe the attack, underlining the grave dangers inherent in refusal by Americans to denounce this massacre of the innocent and the vulnerability of those who refuse to protect themselves against aggression. Ruthless and impersonal technical "progress" is thereby measured ironically against its price in human suffering. Together, these two verse plays, *The Fall of the City* and *Air Raid*, constitute American radio's major contribution to dramatic literature.

THE TROJAN HORSE

Not until the 1950's did MacLeish turn again to poetic drama. In six years, three plays appeared—*The Trojan Horse*, *This Music Crept by Me upon the Waters*, and his masterpiece in the genre, *J. B.*—each increasingly more complex both poetically and dramaturgically than anything he had previously attempted. *The Trojan Horse* continued MacLeish's indictment of mindless collective consent to self-destructive fear, in this case generated by the accusations of Joseph McCarthy. Recognizing that in the age of television, poetic drama written for radio was all but moribund, MacLeish indicated that his new one-act play would be performed on the stage, without scenery or other elements of stagecraft that might detract from the impact of the spoken word, as well as on radio. Indeed, the play was presented in both

forms, broadcast by BBC radio and included in a double bill with *This Music Crept by Me upon the Waters* by the Poets' Theatre in Cambridge, Massachusetts.

The Trojan Horse continued MacLeish's use of mythology as a vehicle for social criticism. Here he varied somewhat his use of accentual meter, combining a verse line of three accents with blank verse. MacLeish continued his expressionist technique of de-emphasis on individual characters by using nameless type characters, thereby focusing on the theme rather than on fully rounded characterization.

THIS MUSIC CREPT BY ME UPON THE WATERS

MacLeish's other one-act verse drama of this period, *This Music Crept by Me upon the Waters* (the title is from William Shakespeare's *The Tempest*, pr. 1611), uses the more conventional pattern of ten named cast characters to focus on an American proclivity to spoil whatever dreams and plans one has for achieving happiness. Because of the large cast, emphasis is on conversation, much in the manner of Eliot's *The Cocktail Party* (pr. 1949). Living on a contemporary paradisiacal Caribbean island, a group has gathered for dinner and falls into a discussion of what might constitute the good life—peace, order, simplicity—but each speaker reveals an inability to sustain such an idyllic existence. MacLeish implies that such idlers dream of the prelapsarian Edenic state without the willingness to assume the efforts that would earn it. In their despair, the antithesis of Job's fortitude, they inevitably "fumble happiness."

J. B.

MacLeish's major achievement in poetic drama, *J. B.*, fulfilled his own exhortation to poets to discover a metaphor for the truth they were moved to communicate. In the poetry of the Old Testament Book of Job, MacLeish found a metaphor for the eternal human dilemma: human beings' compulsion to know the meaning and cause of their afflictions and to be able to justify the works of God.

From one point of view, *J. B.* is two plays: the original script (the basis of the popular published version) produced at Yale University in April, 1958, and the revision that was produced and directed by Elia Kazan on Broadway in December of that year. The original is far more austere and poetic, although critics generally agree that the verse in *J. B.* does not represent MacLeish's finest poetry. When the drama was mounted for New York, a largely rewritten version developed during rehearsals, one that not only altered the play's structure (from eleven continuing scenes to two acts with an intermission) but also introduced new characters (such as the roustabouts), deleted others, and altered the roles of still others. Dramatically effective episodes of stage business were also developed in the Kazan production. Many of these changes resulted in little more than clarification for the stage of MacLeish's original ideas, but in the play's final scene, the entire philosophic resolution is altered by a shift in the protagonist's rationalization of his ordeal. In the New York version, as he is reunited with his wife, Sarah, he recognizes the value of his experience and affirms an almost Shelleyan belief in the strength and efficacy of love as a requisite for survival. In the original script, the play ends with Sarah's conviction that eventually the couple will achieve knowledge ("Blow on the coal of the heart and we'll know. . . . We'll know. . . ."). In the Kazan version, however, J. B. refutes her claim ("We can never *know*"), proclaiming that only by his suffering has he learned that one can "still live . . . still love."

Structurally also, *J. B.* is two plays, for the trials of the protagonist, the wealthy, powerful, and satisfied industrialist and banker, J. B., form a play within a play. J. B.'s story is framed by the drama of Zuss and Nickles, who appear to be "two broken-down actors" (MacLeish's own description of them) reduced to hawking balloons and popcorn at "a side show of some kind." As Zuss gradually assumes the role of a god (Zeus), metamorphosing into the imposing God of the biblical Job, Nickles assumes the role of the taunting Satan (Old Nick); together these two characters function as a Greek chorus, commenting on and participating in the trials of J. B. (Job).

MacLeish himself pointed out yet another aspect of duality in *J. B.* He saw his accomplishment as the construction of "a modern play inside the ancient majesty of the Book of Job," rather than as a distinct freestanding reconstruction, for he admitted the questions he probed in the play were "too large" to be

handled without the strong undergirding structure of the biblical story. Therefore, many of the original situations and characters appear in MacLeish's modernization: the specific details of Job's suffering (loss of fortune and family, as well as his physical afflictions), and the parade of his comforters, the ostensibly supportive Bildad, Eliphaz, and Zophar, who jargonize respectively Marxist, Freudian, and theological arguments that leave J. B., like his earlier counterpart, suffering even more acutely.

The original version of *J. B.* opens with a prologue: The elderly actors Zuss and Nickles are inspired to play an impromptu dialogue between "God in Job" and Satan, and they wear appropriate masks to facilitate their performance under the circus tent. By nature, Zuss is reluctant to attempt such a lofty role, but during the repartee with the cynical wit Nickles, he eventually assumes a highly orthodox religious posture that only goads his adversary to more audacious taunts. As they prepare for their "performance," they realize the need for someone to play Job, but foresee no difficulty, for, as Nickles observes, "Job is everywhere we go."

Now that the casting is complete, with Zuss as God and Nickles as "opposite to God," and mindful of the "they" who are the originals, the two actors gradually and unconsciously assume the actualities behind the roles they are playing. In effect, their play becomes the Book of Job. The satanic Nickles accuses God of being a creator who "fumbles Job" by giving him a mind that could "learn to wish" and be concerned with justice. As they continue, they discover that their masks have transformed them into the characters they have assumed; Nickles asks, "You really think I'm playing?" and from the darkness comes "A Distant Voice" that affirms their transformation into more than two seedy actors. The prologue ends with the voice beneath the Godmask speaking the words from the Bible that ask of Satan when he seeks a subject for his test of power "Hast thou considered my servant Job?" and the two begin their rivalry for supremacy over a contemporary counterpart.

Scene 1 follows with a joyful Thanksgiving dinner under way at J. B.'s house, where the family considers their good fortune ("we have so much!"). J. B. asserts seriously that "never . . . have I doubted God was on my side, was good to me," although his prescient wife, Sarah, is frightened: "It's not so simple as all that," for "God rewards and God can punish," because He is just, and J. B. agrees that indeed "a man can count on Him." Scene 2 returns to Zuss and Nickles, now controlled by their assumed roles, who rejoice that in the complacent J. B. they have found their "pigeon," and gloat that he will soon find out "what the world is like" as he becomes God's "victim of the spinning joke!"

In scenes 3 and 4, callous messengers come to the home of J. B. to tell him and his wife of the deaths of three of their five children in senseless accidents. In scene 5, Zuss and Nickles, who have been silently watching, return to centerstage to prophesy that J. B. is learning God's purpose for him—to suffer. The light on them fades as another messenger enters to report that J. B.'s youngest daughter has been abducted, sexually abused, and murdered by a psychopath, and Zuss and Nickles allude to the universality of their dramatized actions by recognizing that actually J. B. "isn't in the play at all," but is "where we all are—in our suffering."

Zuss and Nickles peer down in scene 6 as J. B. discovers that a bomb has destroyed his bank, taking with it his fortune as well as killing his last child. By now, Sarah is rebellious and hysterical and shrieks that God not only gives but also takes and "Kills! Kills! Kills! Kills!" Despite everything, J. B. continues to bless "the name of the Lord." In scene 7, Zuss and Nickles review the trials of J. B. and ridicule his endurance and refusal to despair. Zuss, as God, feels that he has triumphed over Nickles in J. B.'s test, but Satan refuses to concede, even though J. B.'s acceptance is "the way it ends" in the Bible. The two decide to continue his trials.

Scene 8 reveals that a worldwide nuclear holocaust has destroyed all but a few pitiful survivors, a rag-clad J. B. and his wife among them. His skin is blistered by the fire, the modern counterpart of Job's boils, but even now J. B. refuses to join Sarah in condemning God as their enemy, although he agonizes over why God is continuing their persecution. Sarah refuses to accept her husband's adamant defense of

God as just, and she vows to leave him, seeing his position as a betrayal of the innocence of their children. When he responds that he has "no choice but to be guilty," she challenges him to "curse God and die," and runs from him. Now totally alone, J. B. pleads "Show me my guilt, O God!" but experiences only an agonizing silence, just as Adam and Eve did after their Edenic transgression in *Nobodaddy*. Nickles, who has been watching, decides that this is the time to bring to J. B. the "cold comforters" who also appeared in the Book of Job, those dogmatists "who justify the ways of God to Job by making Job responsible."

The three appear in scene 9, with the same names as their biblical counterparts. When J. B. asks "My God! What have I done?" (to justify such suffering), Bildad, a Marxist, cries, "Screw your justice!" and praises collectivism as the ultimate solution to humanity's pain ("One man's suffering won't count"). J. B. insists that guilt matters, or all else is meaningless, but Bildad rants that "guilt is a sociological accident." The Freudian Eliphaz sees guilt as "a psychophenomenal situation," inciting Zophar, a religionist, to proclaim his belief that "All mankind are guilty always!," thereby negating any place for individual will in the matter. J. B. chides them all for squabbling and for mocking his misery, asserting that only in his suffering could he have found affirmation of his identity, by knowing it was "I that acted, I that chose."

J. B. again cries, "What have I done?" but there is still no answer from Heaven. Suddenly he hears the Distant Voice in a whirlwind; it rebukes and humiliates him for his arrogance in challenging God, and in the familiar biblical catechism reminds J. B. of God's many powers and accomplishments. The three glib comforters depart as J. B. is accused of desiring to instruct God. Not answered, only silenced, the humbled J. B. nevertheless proclaims that his eye has now seen God, and that because of this experience, "I abhor myself . . . and repent. . . ."

As scene 10 opens, Nickles and Zuss decide that they have had enough; Zuss is particularly distressed because, as Nickles observes, although he won the argument and was right about J. B., "being magnificent and being right don't go together in this universe."

Together they ridicule what they see as J. B.'s impotence, because he has "misconceived the part" and because he has given in and whimpered before the omnipotent voice of God. Outraged by his refusal to despair and by his utter subjection to God's will, the two old actors prepare to resume their circus jobs but recall that there is one more scene "no matter who plays Job or how he plays it," the restoration of his fortunes. Zuss reminds Nickles that when he is released from his suffering, J. B./Job will again assume his life, just as those of all generations do, so Nickles confronts J. B. directly to inform him of the resolution of his fate; signs of his deliverance appear, for J. B.'s blistered skin is healed and Sarah returns.

In the final lyric reconciliation scene, a new beginning from the ashes of destruction is evident as Sarah convinces J. B. that indeed there is no justice in the world, but there is nevertheless conjugal love, which, if strong enough, can triumph over heavenly tyranny. Even if God does not love, J. B. asserts, his existence suffices. In a final declaration, Sarah prophesies that when the heart is warmed by love, despite the loss of religious and societal support, "we'll see where we are" and "we'll know." They have no assurance of the truth of this claim yet no alternative but to accept its challenging promise, affirming, in MacLeish's words, "the worth of life in spite of life."

J. B. ran for 364 performances on Broadway. In its published form (the original version), it became a best-seller and was translated into several foreign languages. Some critics faulted MacLeish's attempt to portray modern people "in terms of a cosmic myth," while others pointed to excessive rhetoric. Although critical interpretations differed, all agreed that MacLeish's controversial modern morality play was a rarity on the American stage—a religious poetic drama that was a commercial and artistic success.

Herakles

MacLeish followed the triumph of *J. B.* with another verse play, *Herakles*, in 1965, and with the prose *Scratch* in 1971, in addition to the short *The Secret of Freedom* (1960), which was published together with two poetic radio dramas of the 1930's, *The Fall of the City* and *Air Raid*. *Herakles* ran for fourteen performances at the University of Michigan theater,

and *Scratch* ran for four in New York. *The Secret of Freedom* was written for television and was televised by the National Broadcasting Company (NBC).

Returning to Greek heroic myth and to Euripides for inspiration, MacLeish sought in *Herakles* to achieve the moral resonance of *J. B.* In this new parable, a monomaniacal American physicist is awarded the Nobel Prize for his Promethean achievement in finding new sources of energy but fails both as a humanist and as a husband and father in his mad pursuit of even greater glory and accomplishment. Like the labors of Herakles, Professor Hoadley's work benefits humankind, but he is an irresponsible individual and is forced to recognize the limits of his humanity. Less lyric than the original version of *J. B.*, *Herakles* is more tragically realistic in its portrayal of yet another victim of the sin of excessive pride. Whereas the essentially passive Job endured seemingly endless, meaningless suffering, the anti-Job Hoadley is a dynamic achiever, willing to sacrifice everything for the palpable rewards of his efforts.

Scratch

In *Scratch*, a drama suggested by Stephen Vincent Benét's popular short story "The Devil and Daniel Webster," MacLeish once again warned against the willingness to sacrifice personal freedom in exchange for controlled lives of comfort and stifling "law and order." Although relevant to the turmoil of the 1960's, *Scratch* was an artistic failure, dismissed by critics as ambiguous, too abstract, talky, and even tedious and incomprehensible. MacLeish never attempted full-length theatrical drama again. *The Great American Fourth of July Parade* (1975) was his final, somewhat nostalgic return to the form he had so ardently defended and so skillfully practiced.

Other major works

POETRY: *Songs for a Summer's Day*, 1915; *Tower of Ivory*, 1917; *The Happy Marriage*, 1924; *The Pot of Earth*, 1925; *Streets in the Moon*, 1926; *The Hamlet of A. MacLeish*, 1928; *Einstein*, 1929; *New Found Land: Fourteen Poems*, 1930; *Conquistador*, 1932; *Poems, 1924-1933*, 1933; *Frescoes for Mr. Rockefeller's City*, 1933; *Public Speech*, 1936; *Land of the Free*, 1938; *America Was Promises*, 1939; *Brave New*

World, 1948; *Actfive and Other Poems*, 1948; *Collected Poems, 1917-1952*, 1952; *New Poems, 1951-1952*, 1952; *Songs for Eve*, 1954; *The Collected Poems of Archibald MacLeish*, 1962; *The Wild Old Wicked Man and Other Poems*, 1968; *The Human Season: Selected Poems, 1926-1972*, 1972; *New and Collected Poems, 1917-1976*, 1976; *On the Beaches of the Moon*, 1978; *Collected Poems, 1917-1982*, 1985.

SCREENPLAY: *The Eleanor Roosevelt Story*, 1965.

NONFICTION: *Housing America*, 1932; *Jews in America*, 1936; *Background of War*, 1937; *The Irresponsibles: A Declaration*, 1940; *The American Cause*, 1941; *A Time to Speak: The Selected Prose of Archibald MacLeish*, 1941; *American Opinion and the War*, 1942; *A Time to Act: Selected Addresses*, 1943; *Poetry and Opinion: The "Pisan Cantos" of Ezra Pound*, 1950; *Freedom Is the Right to Choose: An Inquiry into the Battle for the American Future*, 1951; *Poetry and Experience*, 1961; *The Dialogues of Archibald MacLeish and Mark Van Doren*, 1964; *A Continuing Journey*, 1968; *The Great American Frustration*, 1968; *Champion of a Cause: Essays and Addresses on Librarianship*, 1971; *Riders on the Earth: Essays and Reminiscences*, 1978; *Letters of Archibald MacLeish, 1907-1982*, 1983 (R. H. Winnick, editor).

BIBLIOGRAPHY

Donaldson, Scott. *Archibald MacLeish: An American Life*. Boston: Houghton Mifflin, 1992. This exceptionally well-written biography has as its sources not only MacLeish's published poetry, essays, and plays but also his notebooks and journals. It is based on new accounts, articles, reviews, and letters from friends. The essence of the man, according to the author, was his multiplicity. His life was driven by two powerful and sometimes conflicting goals: He wanted to write great poetry, and he wanted to advance great causes. Numerous illustrations and a bibliography.

Drabeck, Bernard A., and Helen E. Ellis, eds. *Archibald MacLeish: Reflections*. Amherst: University of Massachusetts Press, 1988. This series of interviews done in the last five years of MacLeish's life, provide a look at the professional life of this dramatist and poet. The focus is on the writer; therefore, the work is like a memoir.

Ellis, Helen E., and Bernard A. Drabeck. *Archibald MacLeish: A Selectively Annotated Bibliography*. Lanham, Md.: Scarecrow Press, 1995. A bibliography of MacLeish's works and those about him. Contains an index.

MacLeish, William H. *Uphill with Archie: A Son's Journey*. New York: Simon & Schuster, 2001. William H. MacLeish, son of the famous dramatist and poet, had a somewhat troubled relationship with his father until later in life, but he produced a memoir that recalls the father with affection and portrays him as brilliant and talented. Sheds light on the famous man's personal life.

Maryhelen C. Harmon,
updated by Genevieve Slomski

TERRENCE MCNALLY

Born: St. Petersburg, Florida; November 3, 1939

PRINCIPAL DRAMA

The Lady of the Camellias, pr. 1963 (adaptation of a play by Giles Cooper, based on the novel of Alexandre Dumas, *fils*)

And Things That Go Bump in the Night, pr. 1962 (as *this Side of the Door*) pr. 1964, pb. 1966

Next, pr. 1967, pb. 1969 (one act)

Tour, pr. 1967, pb. 1968 (one act)

Botticelli, pr. 1968 (televised), pb. 1969, pr. 1971 (staged, one act)

¡Cuba Si!, pr. 1968, pb. 1969 (one act)

Here's Where I Belong, pr. 1968 (musical, book by McNally, music by Robert Waldman; adaptation of John Steinbeck's novel *East of Eden*)

Noon, pr. 1968, pb. 1969 (one act)

Sweet Eros, pr. 1968, pb. 1969 (one act)

Witness, pr. 1968, pb. 1969 (one act)

Bringing It All Back Home, pr. 1969, pb. 1970 (one act)

Where Has Tommy Flowers Gone?, pr. 1971, pb. 1972

Bad Habits: Ravenswood and Dunelawn, pr. 1971, pb. 1974 (two one-acts)

Let It Bleed, pr. 1972

Whiskey, pr., pb. 1973 (one act)

The Ritz, pr. 1974 (as *The Tubs*), pr. 1975 (staged), pr. 1976 (screenplay), pb. 1976

Broadway, Broadway, pr. 1978, revised pr. 1982, pb. 1986 (as *It's Only a Play*)

The Rink, pr. 1984, pb. 1985 (musical; book written by McNally, music by Fred Ebb, lyrics by John Kander)

The Lisbon Traviata, pr. 1985, pb. 1986

Frankie and Johnny in the Clair de Lune, pr., pb. 1987

Lips Together, Teeth Apart, pr. 1991, pb. 1992

Kiss of the Spider Woman, pr. 1992 (musical; book by McNally, music by Fred Ebb, lyrics by John Kander; adaptation of Manuel Puig's novel)

A Perfect Ganesh, pr., pb. 1993

Love! Valour! Compassion!, pr. 1994, pb. 1995

Collected Plays: Volume I, Fifteen Short Plays, pb. 1994

Andre's Mother and Other Short Plays, pb. 1994

Master Class, pr., pb. 1995

Collected Plays: Volume II, pb. 1996

Dusk, pr. 1996

Ragtime, pr. 1996 (musical; book by McNally, music by Stephen Flaherty, lyrics by Lynn Ahrens; adaptation of E. L. Doctorow's novel)

Corpus Christi, pr., pb. 1998

The Food of Love, pr. 1999 (libretto)

Dead Man Walking, pr. 2000 (libretto)

The Full Monty, pr. 2000 (musical; book by McNally, music and lyrics by David Yazbek)

The Visit, pr. 2001 (musical, book by McNally, music by Ebb, lyrics by Kander; adaptation of Friedrich Dürrenmatt's play)

A Man of No Importance, pr. 2002 (musical; book by McNally, music by Flaherty, lyrics by Ahrens)

OTHER LITERARY FORMS

In addition to his stage plays, Terrence McNally has written scripts and revised play scripts for screen, television, and radio. His teleplays include *Botticelli* (1968), *The Five Forty-eight* (1979, adapted from a John Cheever story), and *André's Mother* (1990). Among his screenplays are *The Ritz* (1976) and *Frankie and Johnny* (1991). McNally has also contributed several articles and interviews to *The Dramatists Guild Quarterly*.

ACHIEVEMENTS

Throughout his career, experimenting freely with style and technique, Terrence McNally has revealed a chameleonlike ability to adopt new comic guises. His earliest works, such as *And Things That Go Bump in the Night* and *Next*, reflect the influence of the Theater of the Absurd in their trenchant, black-humor ridiculing of a variety of social values and institutions. Moving toward a more sympathetic engagement in the plight of his characters, McNally has gradually muted his comic vision, producing plays such as *The Lisbon Traviata* and *Frankie and Johnny in the Clair de Lune*, which, though witty, are far more lyrical, sensitive, and forgiving.

McNally has been awarded two Guggenheim Fellowships and won an Obie Award (for *Bad Habits* in 1974) and an Emmy Award (for the teleplay *André's Mother* in 1991). He received citations from the American Academy of Arts and Letters and the National Institute for Arts and Letters for Achievement in Playwriting for *The Ritz*. He won the Tony Award for best book of a musical for both *Kiss of the Spider Woman* in 1993 and *Ragtime* in 1998. *Love! Valour! Compassion!* and *Master Class* won both the Tony Award and Outer Critics Circle Award for Best Play in 1995 and 1996, respectively. McNally also received a Pulitzer Prize nomination for *A Perfect*

Ganesh in 1994. He is a member of the American Academy of Arts and Letters and in 1981 became vice president of the Dramatists Guild.

BIOGRAPHY

Terrence McNally was born in St. Petersburg, Florida, in 1939, but he grew up in Corpus Christi, Texas, where he received his early education. His parents, both from New York, promoted his enthusiasm for theater by taking him to see both plays and musicals. In 1956, he entered Columbia University, where he took courses in writing and collaborated on variety shows. He completed his B.A. in English, Phi Beta Kappa, in 1960, and was named an Evans Traveling Fellow. With the fellowship, McNally went to Mexico, where he wrote a one-act play and sent it to the Actors Studio in New York. It piqued the interest of Molly Kazan, who appointed him stage manager there. Through his association with Kazan and

Terrence McNally in 1974. (AP/Wide World Photos)

her husband, Eli Kazan, McNally was hired as tutor to John Steinbeck's teenage sons, and in 1961 and 1962, he toured the world with the Steinbeck family.

Back in New York, McNally won an award for a one-act play, which, with revisions, would become *And Things That Go Bump in the Night*. In 1964, he received a grant for staging *And Things That Go Bump in the Night* at the Tyrone Guthrie Theatre in Minneapolis. The notoriety that surrounded the production induced producer Theodore Mann to try a New York staging in 1965, but it was met with extremely hostile reviews and closed within two weeks. The disheartened McNally briefly dropped playwriting and took up journalism, but prompted by theater friends, he returned to begin a prolific period in which he wrote several one-act plays produced either Off-Broadway or on public television. The best known, *Next*, ran for more than seven hundred performances and secured McNally's reputation as a talented writer of trenchant satire. Critics were generally less receptive to McNally's full-length plays, and the failure of *Broadway, Broadway* in 1979 sent the playwright into new creative doldrums. It was five years before he returned to the Broadway stage, with the musical *The Rink*, for which he wrote the book. Although received tepidly by critics, the work had a fairly long run, with large audiences.

With *The Lisbon Traviata* and *It's Only a Play*, McNally showed that he was back in high gear as a playwright and that he was capable of garnering important critical acclaim. The two plays were followed by *Frankie and Johnny in the Clair de Lune*, later revised for the screen, and by the Emmy-winning teleplay *André's Mother* and the play *Lips Together, Teeth Apart*, also a highly regarded work. Critical respect translated into award recognition for the three plays that followed: *A Perfect Ganesh* earned McNally his first Pulitzer Prize nomination, and *Love! Valour! Compassion!* and *Master Class* both received Tony Awards for Best Play, making McNally only the second playwright to win the award in successive years. The popular success of these plays notwithstanding, McNally has shown he is still not afraid to provoke audiences with controversial themes or approaches. In 1998, his play *Corpus*

Christi was nearly canceled before opening in New York when it drew criticism from outraged religious groups who objected to its depiction of Christ and his disciples as homosexuals. The play was picketed by protesters for much of its run, and a British Muslim organization, Defenders of the Messenger Jesus, issued a *fatwa* for McNally's death when the play opened in England two years later.

In his later works, McNally has revealed an increasing sympathy for his characters without sacrificing his acerbic wit, and although he has increased his comic range, there remains in all his work a residual sense of the absurd. Whereas topicality and the use of arcane references and in-jokes may have limited the appeal of his earlier plays, the universality of his mature work has proved him an artist of commanding range. Whether speaking in the voice of working-class stiffs, young urban professionals, aging women on holiday, or gay operas buffs, McNally articulates concerns and sensitivities that give shape to the human condition. His talent for mixing humor and pathos makes his most dramatic plays accessible, even as it makes him difficult to pigeonhole exclusively as either a comic or dramatist.

Although McNally devoted much of his time in the late 1990's and early part of the twenty-first century to writing librettos for the operas *The Food of Love* and *Dead Man Walking*, and books for musical versions of *The Full Monty* and *The Visit*, his heart is still very much in the dramatic stage. An ardent theater activist with a passionate belief in New York's Off-Broadway theaters, he has been an articulate spokesperson for the experimental theater, and in *The Dramatists Guild Quarterly*, he has been a forceful proponent for that movement. He has also championed regional theater for transforming the American stage into a national theater and refers to himself as "a regional theater playwright who just happens to live in New York." Regardless of how he is perceived at home or out of town, he is a profoundly witty writer who has mastered his craft.

Analysis

Terrence McNally's earliest plays, influenced by both avant-garde theater and Cold War anxieties, of-

fer savage criticism of society. Called by Harold Clurman "one of the most adept practitioners of the comedy of insult," McNally lashes out at various targets with an angry-young-man malice made palatable by his acerbic wit and solid stranglehold on a sense of the absurd.

And Things That Go Bump in the Night

Two prevalent, related themes that mark his early pieces are the dysfunction of the family and the alienation of the individual. His first major play, *And Things That Go Bump in the Night*, deals with a bizarre family living in a basement, exiled from normal society. An absurdist farce à la Samuel Beckett's *Fin de partie: Suivi de Acte sans paroles* (pr., pb. 1957; *Endgame: A Play in One Act, Followed by Act Without Words: A Mime for One Player*, 1958) and Arthur Kopit's *Oh, Dad, Poor Dad, Mamma's Hung You in the Closet and I'm Feelin' So Sad* (pr., pb. 1960), the work is a devastating critique on the perversion of values forced on human beings by modern exigencies. The plot, a series of sadomasochistic exercises accompanied by shrieks of fear and outrage, involves the ritual destruction of Clarence, the play's only "normal" character. He becomes a hapless victim in the sadistic and seemingly pointless games adroitly played by the "opera queen" Ruby and her children, Sigfrid and Lakme. Caring no more for their own kin, this trio mocks Grandfa, the grandfather who is about to be trundled off to an asylum for the insane. Love has simply degenerated into perverse carnality, care into apathy, and respect into derision. What remains are childish fears, such as the dread of the dark or solitude, that suggest an awful entropy in the human soul. There is no hope for humankind in this play's apocalyptic vision, but there may be some sort of retributive justice, symbolized by the persistent "thump" that grows in volume and frequency as the play draws to an end.

Although hostile to the play, critics did identify McNally as a disciple of black comedy. The family members are, after all, outrageously humorous in their grotesque fashion. The play is perplexing, however, in part because of the playwright's technique. It is a crazy quilt made up of nonsequiturs, arcane references, foreign phrases, musical oddments, and disconnected and, at times, obtuse behavior. Stung into clarifying his vision by the play's poor reception and after flirting with a career change, McNally began bringing his satire into sharper focus. In 1968, he had six plays in production, all one-acts Off-Broadway or teleplays on public television. In all of them, he takes a jaundiced look at dehumanizing and alienating aspects of American life. A favorite target is the Vietnam War and its eroding influence on values, a topic he treats in several works.

NEXT

The best-known example is *Next*, a one-act spoof about a middle-aged theater manager, Marion Cheever, who has been sent a draft notice by accident. The two-character play takes place at an induction center, during a humiliating physical examination conducted by a tough, no-nonsense female, Sergeant Tech. Cheever, who has no desire to be drafted into the army, tries to wheedle out of his situation, but his tormentor carries on with all the inexorable indifference of a federal meat inspector. Forced to strip, Cheever, ashamed of his plump body, wraps himself in the American flag, and despite his desire to evade the draft, is upset when he fails the ludicrous psychological portion of the examination and is ruled unfit. When the ritual is over, Cheever burlesques it in a monologue in which he apes Sergeant Tech and with increasing stridency attacks the dehumanizing way in which society sets its standards.

BRINGING IT ALL BACK HOME

Another example, *Bringing It All Back Home*, focuses on a dysfunctional family unable to grieve for the son killed in Vietnam and sent home in a wooden crate conveniently deposited in their living room. The dead soldier's sister and brother, engaged in a fierce sibling rivalry, verbally abuse each other, while their inept parents console themselves with inane observations, including the bromide that their son's death was quick and painless, even though a mine "tore his stomach right open." Selfish and vindictive, the nameless son and daughter excoriate each other while whining about their need for sex and drugs. The brother accuses his sister of being a slut; she accuses him of being a homosexual and a drug addict. The father offers simplistic parental advice, lecturing his son on

becoming a manly adult through self-discipline and learning to bowl. Meanwhile, he pets his daughter in an obvious display of repressed incest and, when left alone, makes obscene telephone calls to total strangers. His wife, perpetually under a hair dryer, is unable to surface and listen to the conversation. All seem to treat the son's death with stupefying indifference. At one point, that son pops up in his crate to protest, confiding that, contrary to what his family claims, his death "hurt like hell." Matters come to a head of sorts when a television crew shows up to tape a human interest segment for the news. Interviewed by Miss Horne, a "black troublemaker" who asks penetrating questions about the son's death, none of the family members can give a better answer than those provided by the worst self-serving apologists for the war. They are sorry human specimens, devoid of understanding, and numbed to uncaring by overexposure to daily horrors.

SWEET EROS AND WITNESS

In several of his plays of the late 1960's and early 1970's, McNally attacks such distressing complacency and insensitivity to human misery. *Sweet Eros* and *Witness*, produced as companion pieces on the same bill, both stress human beings' need to assume personal responsibility for action and passivity alike. Both are troubling allegories.

In *Sweet Eros*, a man abducts a girl, strips her, ties her to a chair, and then proceeds to tell her his life story. Although personable and glib, he has a massive ego and is principally interested in justifying his narcissism. At first, the girl struggles with moral outrage, but in the end, she becomes docile, finding it easier and safer to acquiesce before madness than to fight it. She symbolizes a society that indicts itself by entering into a silent partnership with evil.

Similarly, in *Witness*, another victim is tied to a chair, this time a salesman captured by a young man planning to kill the president of the United States. The would-be assassin wants a witness who can later testify to his sanity. Also invited to witness the act are a window washer and a female neighbor, neither of whom finds it the least bit odd that the bound and gagged salesman sits in their midst. Neither of them wishes to take any responsibility for what is planned, partly because, as the window washer complains, too much freedom has left them without any rules or moral imperatives. He thinks that shooting the president is all right in a doing-your-own-thing sort of way. In contrast, the young man plans the death of the president because he wants to demonstrate that such an act is futile, that it can change nothing.

Bad Habits

In two other one-acts, *Ravenswood* and *Dunelawn*, joined together as *Bad Habits*, McNally mocks two ways in which authority, represented by staff members at two contrasting sanatoriums, has dealt with asocial behavior. At Ravenswood, Dr. Jason Pepper encourages his patients to do whatever they want, even if it is demonstrably bad for them, while at Dunelawn, Dr. Toynbee and his two nurses drug unruly patients into silent stupors. As microcosms, the two sanatoriums suggest alternative ways in which governments have dealt with modern neuroses. At Ravenswood, Dr. Pepper panders to his patients' desires, even encouraging aggressive and aberrant behavior, whereas at Dunelawn, the patients are kept in wheelchairs and straitjackets and, if unruly, are drugged into docility. Neither solution to human problems is satisfying, though the therapy used at Ravenswood seems to promote at least an ephemeral happiness.

Ravenswood and *Dunelawn* reflect both the characteristic strengths and weaknesses of McNally's early satirical farces in the absurdist mode. Although much of the dialogue is humorous, the characters tend to be caricatures. Some are even reminiscent of cartoon characters. For example, Bruno, the groundskeeper in *Dunelawn*, is a variation on the cartoon Neanderthal at large in the modern world, as his "hubba hubba" tag phrase suggests. Both plays also have structural problems. They tend to dwindle away, more like skits than organic, complete pieces, which is a fault found even with *Next*, the playwright's most successful one-act.

McNally was well aware of the limitations and was sensitive to the criticism. He credits Elaine May, whose *Adaptation* (pr. 1969) was once staged with *Next*, with helping him rethink his ideas about character. She encouraged him to "write people instead of

symbols." Aware, too, that short one-acts were too restrictive for developing characters to their full potential, McNally turned increasing attention to writing full-length plays, including *Where Has Tommy Flowers Gone?*, which some consider his best early play.

Where Has Tommy Flowers Gone?

As critics have noted, the action of *Where Has Tommy Flowers Gone?* reflects the influence of Bertolt Brecht's epic theater. Using several episodic flashbacks, it chronicles the experiences that have shaped Tommy into an anarchist bent on destroying various art centers. Like other McNally antiheros, Tommy is an alienated but engaging young man drawn to violence as a last recourse in a stagnating, suffocating, and insensitive world. His story is presented in a stage collage, using pyrotechnics, photographic images, music, asides, and "news" vignettes to piece it all together. Tommy is drawn in the tradition of the picaresque rogue, part con artist, part pariah, wounded by an indifferent or hostile world. His personal hero is Holden Caulfield, from J. D. Salinger's novel, *The Catcher in the Rye* (1951). Like Holden, he sees the system as phony and is determined to destroy even the most noble and benign aspects of it, its art. As he wanders, he gathers a family of misfits around him, almost in a sacrilegious parody of an American ideal. An old drifter-actor, Ben Delight, who is full of self-aggrandizing lies, becomes his surrogate father, while Nedda, a girl encountered on his sexually promiscuous rampage, becomes a substitute wife. There is also Arnold, an ugly dog, that, loyal until Tommy's death, at curtain is led off on a new master's leash. The play's techniques sufficiently distance the audience to keep the whole mélange comical and innocuous. Although Tommy's outrageous romp involves wanton destruction, flimflam tricks, and petty thievery, it elicits neither sympathy nor condemnation, only laughter. McNally tries to make one think in the aftermath of that laughter, and to that end, as Brecht does, he constantly reminds his audience that what is before it is, after all, merely a fantasy.

The Ritz

Another energetic piece, free of polemic design, is *The Ritz*, wherein McNally demonstrates his mastery of high-speed, offbeat farce. It is set in a New York steam bath catering exclusively to homosexuals, where the pudgy protagonist, Gaetano Proclo, has sought refuge from his brother-in-law, Carmine Vespucci, who is out to kill him. As it turns out, Proclo has been set up by Vespucci, whose machinations have deliberately drawn Proclo to the place, an establishment owned and operated by Vespucci. Pursued by Michael Brick, a detective hired by Vespucci to hunt him down, Proclo dexterously but narrowly evades a series of comic disasters. Besides Brick, he is pursued by a homosexual "chubby chaser" whose taste in partners runs to the obese; a talentless female singer, Googie Gomez, who has it in her head that he is a producer; and, finally, his wife and Vespucci himself, who is hell bent on deceiving his sister into believing that her husband is a homosexual. It is a high-spirited, if silly, contrived plot, full of mistaken identities, misencounters, door-slamming and bed-hopping razzle-dazzle—pure nonsense with all hints of playwright as angry-young-man-with-a-message leached out of it. With it, the entertainer in McNally seems to score a total victory over the social critic.

For a time, McNally had difficulty following up *The Ritz* with a play that fulfilled its promise of future pieces crafted with an untroubled and detached comic vision. The poor reception of *Broadway, Broadway* and its first revival in 1982 as *It's Only a Play* dispirited the writer, sending his career into a temporary tailspin. His book for the musical *The Rink* was also panned as dated, lacking in both "bite" and "originality." McNally was obviously struggling to free himself of Cold War and free-speech demons that by the 1980's critics were dismissing as clichés.

THE LISBON TRAVIATA

Success came in 1985 with *The Lisbon Traviata* and a revival of *It's Only a Play*, both produced Off-Broadway by the Manhattan Theatre Club. The former play, revived in a critically acclaimed production of 1989, focuses on four homosexual men, two of whom, Stephen and Mike, are at a breakup point in their relationship. The demise of their "marriage" occurs in the second act, which in mood turns the play on end. The first act, which is uproarious, gives way to an acrimonious and sad conclusion.

The play opens in the apartment of Stephen's friend, Mendy, where Stephen has taken refuge because at home Mike is entertaining his new friend, Paul, in what Stephen hopes will be a one-night stand. Stephen and Mendy are opera buffs and devoted fans of the great diva Maria Callas, and they spend the evening bantering about opera lore. The crisis in Stephen's life is divulged almost offhandedly when Mendy pleads with him to return home to retrieve a recording of Callas as Violetta in Giuseppe Verdi's *La traviata* (1853). Stephen refuses, covering his anxieties with what for Mendy is a maddening insensitivity to Mendy's need to hear the legendary, Lisbon performance. In tormenting the desperate Mendy, Stephen reveals a keen verbal wit and seems totally in control of his emotions. That mask, however, comes off in the second act when he confronts Mike, who is moving out on him. It is now Stephen who is desperate and must do the pleading. His wit, though still with him, becomes sadly deficient, even hollow. It only angers Mike, who, before he leaves, punches Stephen to the floor and, at curtain, leaves him abandoned and miserable. (In an earlier, more operatic version of the play, Stephen stabs Mike and holds him dying in his arms as the curtain falls.)

McNally, himself an opera enthusiast, uses music of great passion in ironic counterpoint to the glib, "bitchy" wit of Mendy and Stephen, and although the playwright himself claims that his play is about "people with great passions," those passions at first seem to be sublimated in music; in the second act, however, Stephen's passion finally erupts in the futile confrontation with Mike. Stephen, who seems to need music as a continuous presence in his life, arrives home and immediately turns on the stereo receiver, tuning to a classical music station. When Mike appears, Stephen offers to put on music that Mike will like, something that will appeal to Mike's pedestrian tastes. Mike, as if to assert his total independence from Stephen, first tunes in a rock station, then later turns off the stereo. In the silence, Stephen is emotionally naked and extremely vulnerable.

IT'S ONLY A PLAY

In *It's Only a Play*, McNally ignores conventional advice against writing plays about the theater. Reflecting some of his own frustrations with the "system," epitomized by Broadway theaters and New York reviewers, he uses his talent for acerbic dialogue to puncture holes in its various pretensions and, in the process, creates an uproarious play with a simple premise. The piece is set in an upstairs bedroom in the townhouse of a wealthy woman who has just made her debut as a play producer and is now hosting an opening-night party. Most of the characters who parade in and out of the room are in some way connected with the play. The tension mounts as the moment of truth, the verdict of the reviewers, approaches. Unlike the offstage, famous guests who flit in and out of the party downstairs, those upstairs are short on talent and experience. They are, however, long on anxiety and ego. Included are the playwright Peter Austin, whose hopes for a second success will be crushed; James Wicker, a frantic actor whose television series gets cancelled; Frank Finger, a director, who, lucky but talentless, wants to salve his conscience with a flop; Julia Budder, the hostess; Virginia Noyes, a fading starlet; and Ira Drew, a minor critic and closet dramatist writing under the pseudonym "Caroline Comstock." Gus Washington, a streetwise black man who wants to be an actor and who is providing temporary help for the party, and Emma, an outspoken taxi driver, complete the *dramatis personae*. Offstage, in the bathroom, there is also Torch, a feisty dog that intimidates the unwary who attempt to use the facilities.

First-act hopes run high, as the initial reviews are favorable, but in the second act, reality in the form of a devastating review in *The Times* hits the hopefuls like acid sleet on a picnic. At the end, while the rest take new heart and excitedly plan to put another play into production, Peter Austin is left to his sullen self to ponder the fickleness of fortune and friends. Both witty and vitriolic, the play is merciless in its depiction of the New York theater scene. The backstabbing and name-dropping, threaded together with insincere flattery and a bravado that masks the characters' insecurities, are not that much of an exaggeration. McNally himself claims that the play comes as close to being a documentary as anything he ever wrote. It is, for all of its comic energy, a devastating indictment of a world that can be both fickle and cruel.

FRANKIE AND JOHNNY IN THE CLAIR DE LUNE

In two later plays, *Frankie and Johnny in the Clair de Lune* and *Lips Together, Teeth Apart*, McNally demonstrates that his comedy can never be pigeon-holed. The first of these is an erotic rhapsody on heterosexual love. Though just as witty, it is far more lyrical than any of McNally's earlier plays. It has only the two characters named in the title and focuses on Johnny's efforts to parlay his relationship with Frankie into something more than a one-night stand. She, worldly wise, resists, but by the end of the play, which is left inconclusive (a McNally characteristic), she seems, if not resigned to her fate, certainly more receptive to it. Johnny is the one with the old-fashioned notions about marriage and family. He verges on an anachronism, particularly in his unwavering insistence that fate has drawn them together. His mounting possessiveness annoys Frankie, who is not willing to leap into the commitment fire without a long, hard look. She meets his persistence with hurtful retorts that Johnny, always resourceful, deflects. In its comic duel, the play thus offers an ironic reversal of the relationship of the ballad characters of the same name.

Frankie and Johnny are unusual creations for McNally, whose focus in many plays is on a well-educated and culturally elite class, with mostly upstream sexual preferences. Frankie and Johnny are relative nobodies, born and reared in Allentown, Pennsylvania, but now living failed dreams in the Big Apple as coworkers in a short-order restaurant. Culture remains in the background of this two-part fugue on love.

LIPS TOGETHER, TEETH APART

In *Lips Together, Teeth Apart*, McNally sets the scene in Fire Island, a predominantly homosexual resort. John and Chloe Haddock and Sam and Sally Truman, two married couples, are celebrating the Fourth of July at a beach house, formerly the property of Sally's gay brother who has died of acquired immunodeficiency syndrome (AIDS). Against a background of a suicidal drowning, and fireworks and music from neighborhood parties, the characters try to work out their complex emotional problems. Chloe and Sam, who are brother and sister, know that John and Sally have had an affair, and they must sort through its implications for their friendships and marriages. Sally, meanwhile, deeply troubled by her brother's death, is trying to cope with the fact that he was homosexual and had a black lover. She is also determined to discourage any renewal of her brief affair with John, who presses with an urgency arising from the knowledge that he has an inoperable cancer of the esophagus.

Although the characters try to suppress their feelings, passions do flare up, erupting at one point in a fist fight between John and Sam. Their fears and anxieties are, however, buffered by the witty dialogue and some comic aspects of the situation. For example, all four are intimidated by the fact that on both sides of the house, in taller, more imposing beach houses, gay parties are in progress, and they have ridiculous fears about what their neighbors may assume about their sexual orientation. They also avoid the swimming pool, from the suspicion, Sally charges, that the water is infected with the AIDS virus.

The unhappiness of the situation comes in time-released doses. For example, knowledge of John's cancer is not disclosed to Sam and Sally until late in the third and final act. The pain is also blunted by McNally's technique of revealing the inner thoughts of his characters in quiet, unemotional asides to the audience that modulate what is otherwise often humorous dialogue. As in *The Lisbon Traviata*, in *Lips Together, Teeth Apart*, McNally elicits both laughter and compassion and puts them into a delicate comic alignment, a trick requiring a special kind of theatrical magic.

A PERFECT GANESH

By the 1990's McNally had clearly hit his stride as a playwright, with productions that were both popular and critical successes. His increasing versatility and range are typified in *A Perfect Ganesh* and *Love! Valour! Compassion!* Both explore the importance of love and the inherent risks of intimacy, but each takes a significantly different approach to its theme.

A Perfect Ganesh is the story of two aging female friends on vacation in India. Margaret Civil, the more reserved and controlling of the two, expects "to see India my way, from a comfortable seat, somewhat at a distance." Katharine Brynne, on the other hand, hopes to be "devoured" and "engulfed" by the vibrant life of the country. A variety of comic and dramatic experiences follow from their differing responses to the situations and people they encounter in their travels, and these give rise to revelatory moments of self-reflection.

Although the two women seem a study of contrasts they gradually reveal they are more alike than not. Katharine, who never accepted the homosexuality of a son who was murdered by gay bashers, is privately wracked with guilt. Her desire "to kiss a leper fully on the mouth and not feel revulsion" is not only a metaphor for her intended immersion in India but also an expression of her hope to reconcile herself with the son she cast out of her heart. Margaret also lost a child, in a moment when her rigid propriety superseded her willingness to show maternal affection, but she has never mentioned it to Katherine. She also keeps secret her recent discovery of a lump in her breast, one of several examples in McNally's plays of intimacy hindered by the prospect of death. McNally makes effective use of the Indian setting as a backdrop for Katharine and Margaret's inevitable transformations, particularly in a final scene on the River Ganges, where images of death, transfiguration, and resurrection provide a context for Margaret and Katherine's odyssey of "purgation and renewal." Presiding over events, and playing the role of many characters, is the elephant-headed god Ganesha, "the queller of obstacles," whose mythic origin as a child resurrected from the dead by a remorseful parent provides hopeful commentary on Katharine's quest.

LOVE! VALOUR! COMPASSION!

McNally turned from the exotic, richly symbolic landscape of *A Perfect Ganesh* to an ordinary terrain more suited to his witty urban sophisticates in *Love! Valour! Compassion!* Set in Duchess County New York, at a country home that one of the characters provides as a vacation retreat for his Manhattan friends, it follows the lives of eight gay men who regularly convene for three holidays—Memorial Day, Independence Day, and Labor Day—over the course of the summer. McNally organizes this unusually large (for him) cast into four distinct couples, each of whose relationship offers a different vantage point for exploring the theme of love. Gregory, a middle-aged ballet choreographer and the owner of the house, has been for some years the partner of Bobby, a young blind man with an almost ethereal personality. John, an egotistical and frustrated composer is involved in a brief fling with Ramon, a vibrant and attractive young dancer nearly half his age. Arthur and Perry, two young professionals in their early forties, have been together long enough to seem as comfortable with each other as an old married couple. Buzz, the comic spirit of the group and the most stereotypically flamboyant homosexual, is infected with AIDS, as is his lover, James, John's twin. A fifth couple forms under the circumstances of the household when Ramon and Bobby enjoy a brief tryst during one of the summer's retreats.

Discussions of love and sexuality flow naturally as the characters—both as couples and individuals—engage, confront, commiserate with, and combat one another over their different feelings and beliefs. Several express the wish for an unconditional love but each couple grapples with differences in lifestyle, careers, age, ethnicity, or temperament that make this nearly impossible. For example, Bobby is deeply in love with Gregory, even though he is not able to see Gregory's choreography, which his friends think of as the expression of Gregory's soul. However, Gregory is deeply hurt by Bobby's confession of an impulsive moment of infidelity, and thereafter his aging dancer's body is incapable of executing the dances he creates. Buzz and James come close to achieving the ideal of unconditional love in their commitment to one another even though they know that one must die and leave the other sick and alone. Death occurs or is imminent in each of the play's three acts, adding dramatic weight to the characters' witty repartee and humorous banter. At one stunning moment near the play's end, each character in succession directly tells the audience when and how he will die. As McNally presents it, the inevitability of death is not a reason to fear love but a reason to hunger more passionately for it.

Though several of McNally's plays have operatic casts, *Love! Valour! Compassion!* has the tight integration of a symphonic orchestration. Each of the characters is an instrument vital to the composition, alternating between humor and drama, past and present, dialogue and exposition, and internal and external geography to sound a variation on its theme. McNally weaves those variations mellifluously into a composition filled with harmony, counterpoint, and carefully timed crescendoes.

MASTER CLASS

With *Master Class*, McNally returned to the colorful world of opera and its passionate commentary on life. The play takes its inspiration from a visit opera diva Maria Callas made to Manhattan's Juilliard School of Music late in the early 1970's, several years before her death, and thus makes an appropriate bookend to *The Lisbon Traviata*. Here, Callas gives a master class in which she exhorts, intimidates, and humiliates the school's top students who have come to give recitals in private audience with her.

True to her reputation as a temperamental diva, Callas is stern and demanding, making jokes at the expense of the students—whom she refers to as her "victims"—and insulting them for anything less than total dedication to their art. She would seem cruel and unsympathetic but for the flashes of humanity that periodically break through her hard facade. Each aria the students sing is a touchstone for Callas's reflections on her own life, the difficulties she faced as an aspiring opera singer, her unfulfilling marriage to Giovanni Battista Meneghini, and her disastrous love affair with Aristotle Onassis. As she relives the drama of her life in reveries that are the dramatic equivalent of operatic solos, she assumes the persona of opera's classic heroines whose songs are the fullest expressions of their often tragic lives. Callas upbrades her pupils for not being able to provide details of the lives of the doomed characters whose songs they sing because she identifies totally with those characters. She is a greater artist than the students will ever be, not just because she has suffered for her craft, but because her suffering and her craft are indistinguishable. She is also the quintessential McNally character: someone for whom bravado and caustic wit are a cover for emotional vulnerability.

CORPUS CHRISTI

Awards bestowed on *Love! Valour! Compassion!* and *Master Class* were proof that McNally's talents were recognized by the theater establishment. Nevertheless, he ended the 1990's with a play that showed him still capable of producing controversy. *Corpus Christi* is in many ways a throwback to the polemical one-act plays of his early career. It presents the life of Jesus Christ (here named Joshua) as it might have played out in Corpus Christi, Texas, as McNally knew it growing up in the 1950's. Against a backdrop of teenage life at that time, Joshua comes to terms with his homosexuality, identifying with the rebellious characters played by James Dean because he feels different from everyone around him. The disciples he eventually gathers around him represent a cross-section of contemporary gay culture. McNally parallels society's persecution of gays with the historical persecution of Christ to illustrate Christ's important lesson that "all men are divine," regardless of their different orientations.

One of McNally's least complicated and artful plays, *Corpus Christi* received mixed reviews. However, well-publicized protests by Christian groups who took offense at his portrayal of Christ ironically underscored the play's theme and reinforced McNally's stature as a playwright not afraid to provoke a strong emotional response from his audience.

OTHER MAJOR WORKS

SCREENPLAYS: *The Ritz*, 1976; *Frankie and Johnny*, 1991; *Love! Valour! Compassion!*, 1994.

TELEPLAYS: *Botticelli*, 1968; *Last Gasps*, 1969; *The Five Forty-eight*, 1979 (from a story by John Cheever); *Mama Malone*, 1983 (series); *André's Mother*, 1990.

BIBLIOGRAPHY

Albee, Edward. "Edward Albee in Conversation with Terrence McNally." Interview by Terrence McNally. *The Dramatists Guild Quarterly* 22 (Summer, 1985): 12-23. As vice president of the Dramatists Guild, McNally has conducted interviews with fellow playwrights. This important example chronicles Albee's career with important parallels to McNally's own, with an emphasis on the new playwrights of the early 1960's.

Barnes, Clive. "Making the Most of *Ritz* Steam Bath." Review of *The Ritz* by Terrence McNally. *The New York Times*, January 21, 1975, p. 40. In this review of *The Ritz*, Barnes notes McNally's ability to write an engaging and zany farce based on situation. An even-tempered assessment by an important theater critic.

Bryer, Jackson R. "Terrence McNally." Interview with Terrence McNally. In *The Playwright's Art: Conversations with Contemporary American Playwrights*. New Brunswick, N.J.: Rutgers University Press, 1995. A long interview with the playwright conducted in 1991, when he was poised on the brink of wider recognition following the success of *Lips Together, Teeth Apart*. McNally reflects honestly on all aspects of his career and offers particularly pointed commentary on the state of theater in the United States.

De Sousa, Geraldo U. "Terrence McNally." In *American Playwrights Since 1945: A Guide to Scholarship, Criticism, and Performance*, edited by Philip C. Kolin. New York: Greenwood, 1989. This valuable aid to further study contains a brief assessment of McNally's reputation, a production history of his plays, a survey of secondary sources, a comprehensive bibliography through 1987, and suggested research opportunities.

Gurewitsch, Matthew. "Maria, Not Callas." *The Atlantic Monthly* 280 (October, 1997):102-107. Discusses the liberties McNally took with the life of Maria Callas to make his play "a highly personal, deeply perceptive meditation on the well springs and the consequences of supremacy in art." A respectful commentary on McNally's art and craft published in a leading magazine that reaches beyond the theater and drama communities.

Gussow, Mel. "Agony and Ecstasy of an Opera Addiction." Review of *The Lisbon Traviata* by Terrence McNally. *The New York Times*, June 7, 1989, p. C21. A review of the revised, nonviolent version of *The Lisbon Traviata*, this article offers a mixed appraisal of McNally's work and typifies the critical reception that the playwright garnered during the 1980's. Gussow relates the play to the influence of opera on McNally's life and art.

Hewes, Henry. "'Ello, Tommy." Review of *And Things That Go Bump in the Night* by Terrence McNally. *Saturday Review* 49 (May 15, 1965): 24. This piece is uncharacteristic of early critical assessments of McNally's work. It praises the playwright's talent and his willingness to tackle diffi-

cult themes. Hewes was one of the first to recognize McNally's great potential.

Zinman, Toby Silverman, ed. *Terrence McNally: A Casebook*. New York: Garland, 1997. A diverse and illuminating anthology of essays and interviews that cover the full range of McNally's career, with particularly solid contributions on his plays of the 1990's. Contains a bibliography of important secondary readings.

John W. Fiero,
updated by Stefan Dziemianowicz

IMRE MADÁCH

Born: Alsósztregova, Hungary; January 21, 1823
Died: Alsósztregova, Hungary; October 5, 1864

PRINCIPAL DRAMA

Mária királyn , wr. 1843, pb. 1880
Férfi és n , wr. 1843, pb. 1880
Csak tréfa, wr. 1843, pb. 1880
Csák végnapjai, wr. 1843, pb. 1880, pr. 1886
A civilizátor, wr. 1859, pb. 1880
Az ember tragédiája, wr. 1860, pb. 1862, pr. 1883
    (verse play; *The Tragedy of Man*, 1933)
Mózes, wr. 1860, pb. 1880, pr. 1888
Tündérálom, wr. 1864, pb. 1880 (fragment)
Madách Imre összes m vei, pb. 1880 (3 volumes)

OTHER LITERARY FORMS

Imre Madách wrote numerous poems, most of which were published posthumously. Only a few, including one slim verse collection, *Lantvirágok* (1840; lyre blossoms), appeared in print during his lifetime. He wrote five prose tales of scant literary significance. His newspaper articles, essays, speeches, and parliamentary addresses give evidence of his broad educational background and impressive rhetorical ability.

ACHIEVEMENTS

Most Hungarian critics consider Imre Madách their country's greatest philosophical dramatist. This

assessment is based almost exclusively on his most important play, *The Tragedy of Man*, frequently referred to as the "Hungarian *Faust*." His other works are important mainly in their relation to his one masterpiece or as historical and biographical documents. *The Tragedy of Man* is rightly seen as the culmination of various trends of European Romanticism. The drama gives an overview of the history of humankind within a wider metaphysical framework. Madách's work stands in the tradition of the *poème d'humanité* or *Menschheitsdrama* of the nineteenth century and shows the impact of various European writers and thinkers. Although the playwright chose a topic of universal significance and deliberately avoided specific references to his native culture, Hungarians have for many generations recognized the spirit of his drama as uniquely representative of their national experience. Since its first successful production at the Budapest National Theatre in 1883, it has remained a popular favorite on the Hungarian stage. Performances abroad as well as adaptations for radio and television in Europe and the United States, although frequently hampered by inadequate translations, have acquainted an international audience with Madách's play. In 1981, it even stimulated an opera, *Ein Menschentraum* (a dream of man), by the West German composer Peter Michael Hamel, in which the playwright's life and his drama are intertwined.

BIOGRAPHY

Imre Madách was born on January 21, 1823, at Alsósztregova in Northern Hungary. His family belonged to the landed gentry. Among his ancestors were warriors and poets, religious leaders and medical writers, legislators and lawyers. Madách's father married Anna Majthényi, a wealthy young woman from another aristocratic family, intelligent, strong-willed, and deeply religious. She bore her husband five children for whose upbringing she had to assume sole responsibility when he died in 1834.

The young Madách and his brothers and sisters enjoyed an excellent private education. In 1837, he was sent to Pest to complete his schooling and earn a university degree. He was very bright, sensitive, and serious, with a keen interest in art, literature, and philosophy. When he was only sixteen, his first poem appeared in a national magazine. Madách's constitution was weak: All through his life he would be plagued by health problems. His attachment to his mother was strong. In 1840, the seventeen-year-old author dedicated the slim volume of poetry he had printed to her, not to the girl for whom he had written it. Despite his interest in literature, he did not consider a writing career but intended to obtain a law degree. His formal studies in Pest came to an end in 1840, when he fell seriously ill, a condition possibly aggravated by psychological factors. He had fallen in love with a fourteen-year-old girl, and his mother insisted that she would never agree to their marriage. After a period of recuperation at home, he passed his bar examination in 1842 and then held a number of appointed and elected offices in his home county, but on several occasions, he had to resign for health reasons. He also became active in politics as a supporter of the "Centralist" movement of Baron József Eötvös and began contributing to a Pest newspaper. His first serious attempts at writing prose narratives and dramas also date to the period after 1842.

In 1845, Madách married Erzsébet (Erzsi) Fráter, a beautiful and vivacious seventeen-year-old girl, over the strong objections of his mother. The first years of their marriage were happy, but his mother's concerns had not been without foundation. Soon Erzsi became dissatisfied with married life, and even

their three children could not save their disintegrating relationship. His poor health prevented Madách from active participation in the 1848-1849 war against Austria, which claimed the lives of several of his family members. The sensitive and deeply patriotic poet was strongly affected by the national tragedy. Eventually, the war was to take an even more direct personal toll. In 1853, the Austrian authorities arrested him and imprisoned him for almost a year for having given shelter to a political fugitive. Erzsi's unbecoming behavior during and after his incarceration led to their divorce in 1854. For the next few years, Madách lived the life of a recluse. Eventually he started writing again, and his bitter experiences led to some of his best poetry. His 1859 comedy, *A civilizátor* (the civilizer), is a satiric description of Austria's attempts to "Germanize" Hungary. In 1860, he composed his masterpiece, *The Tragedy of Man.*

It was as if the writing of this play allowed him to break out of his self-imposed seclusion and to enter public life again. Madách won election as his county's representative to the 1861 Diet in Pest, where he soon gained a reputation as an outstanding orator. János Arany, then considered Hungary's greatest literary authority, agreed to review the manuscript of Madách's drama, which he initially rejected as an inferior imitation of Johann Wolfgang von Goethe's *Faust: Eine Tragödie* (pb. 1808, 1833; *The Tragedy of Faust*, 1823, 1838). Soon, however, he recognized the originality and importance of the work and became its most enthusiastic champion. The Kisfaludy Society, the country's leading literary association, published the play in 1862 and elected Madách a member. Almost overnight, the virtually unknown poet had become the nation's most famous playwright. To his disappointment, *Mózes*, completed in 1860, failed to meet with critical or popular acclaim. In 1863, he was made a corresponding member of the Hungarian Academy of Sciences, but his deteriorating health kept him from reading his inaugural address himself. His last dramatic attempt, *Tündérálom* (fairy dream), remained a fragment. On October 5, 1864, Madách succumbed to heart failure at his ancestral home.

ANALYSIS

Imre Madách's dramatic works testify to his keen interest in history and in social and political problems, to his acquaintance with traditional and contemporary trends in Western philosophy, to his concern with religious questions, and to his familiarity with world literature and with recent scientific discoveries and theories. His work is deeply personal and at the same time broadly universal. It reflects the culture of a country that had always considered itself part of the Western tradition while fiercely fighting any attempt from the outside to dominate or change its unique national character. The experience of a linguistically isolated people who over the centuries had continued to defend their political and cultural independence against overwhelming odds finds its philosophical expression in the ending of *The Tragedy of Man*: After a deeply pessimistic interpretation of world history, humankind is nevertheless encouraged to hope, to have faith, and to continue its struggle.

Madách's first dramatic ventures re-create episodes from the history of Hungary, as in *Mária királyn* (Queen Mary) or *Csák végnapjai* (Csák's last days); try to give a modern interpretation to an ancient myth, as in *Férfi és n* (man and woman), his Heracles drama; or castigate the injustices and shortcomings he had observed in contemporary society, as in *Csak tréfa* (only a joke). The plays demonstrate the immaturity of a twenty-year-old writer with no stage experience, fascinated by the European Romantic movement. Yet they also give evidence of his ability to bring history to life in dramatic scenes and to focus on important human concerns. The relationship between the sexes is one of his prominent themes.

A CIVILIZÁTOR

A civilizátor is the first of Madách's plays in which form and content blend well. Aristophanic satire is cleverly applied to Hungarian conditions. Stroom, the Hegel-spouting "civilizer," trying to bring the blessings of Germanic culture and of Austrian-style bureaucracy to Uncle István, the small landowner who represents the Hungarian people, is ultimately defeated. His army of cockroaches is no match for the fury of István and his farmhands, symbolizing the various ethnic minorities in Hungary

who had initially succumbed to Austrian attemps at dividing the nation. Madách's talent for satire and irony, already apparent in some of his poetry, is given an appropriate dramatic vehicle in this play. Thus, *A civilizátor* is also important in view of the characterization of Lucifer in *The Tragedy of Man*.

THE TRAGEDY OF MAN

In his most ambitious literary project, *The Tragedy of Man*, Madách attempted to present in fifteen dramatic scenes an overview of the history of humankind from the creation to the final days of the human race. Madách's iambic pentameter flows fairly easily, in part as a result of stylistic and metric corrections by Arany, and the drama's structure is clear and logical.

The exposition of the play appears to have been inspired by the biblical Book of Job and by the "Prologue in Heaven" of Goethe's *Faust*: The Lord has completed the noble task of creation and now accepts the praise of his angels. Only Lucifer refuses to join in. Instead, he mocks the Creator who made humankind as an act of self-admiration. Lucifer defiantly demands his share of the world that he helped create through his negativity. The two trees in Eden, scornfully granted him, will become his foothold in the effort to bring down the divine order just established. By persuading Adam and Eve to eat from the Tree of Knowledge, he begins to realize his plan. The first human beings lose their happy state of oneness with God. Outside Paradise, they will build their own world. In order to demonstrate his power, Lucifer conjures up the Earth Spirit but proves incapable of controlling the positive forces of nature that the spirit symbolizes. When Adam wants to know the future of the race whose founder he is to be, Lucifer shows him, in ten dream visions, selected phases from the history of humankind. Each one is designed to emphasize that all human progress is only an illusion, that all great ideals are bound to fail. In this way, Lucifer hopes to lead Adam into despair and to a renunciation of God.

Madách's ingenious idea to make Adam, the Faustian seeker for knowledge, the protagonist in each of the historic scenes gives the dramatic poem a unity and consistency lacking in another work written at almost exactly the same time and closely parallel-ing the aims of Madách's play: *La Légende des siècles* (1859-1883; *The Legend of the Centuries*, 1894), Victor Hugo's five-volume *poème d'humanité*. In each scene, Adam encounters Eve, Woman Eter-nal, in a different disguise, either inspiring him to reach for new ideals or attempting to pull him down into the dust. During his journey through history, he is accompanied by Lucifer, whose sarcastic com-ments provide a striking contrast to Adam's naïve idealism. Despite his devastating experiences, Adam continues to believe in a better future, spurred on by hope which is, quite in agreement with Arthur Schopenhauer's philosophy, a gift of the Devil.

The historical periods depicted are arranged in a dialectic pattern that appears to echo Georg Wilhelm Friedrich Hegel's view of the development of human-ity. Adam as Pharaoh represents despotic one-man rule. Through the encounter with Eve, he is persuaded to set his slaves free, and he moves into an era in which common interest supersedes the will of the in-dividual. As Miltiades in Athens, however, he falls victim to the excesses of a degenerating democracy. Madách's political experiences and his encounters with corruption and demagoguery are thus translated into a critical look at ancient Greece. In decadent Rome, Adam then tries to enjoy a life of leisure and luxury at the side of Eve, a beautiful courtesan. He remains dissatisfied until an encounter with Saint Pe-ter inspires him to pursue a new ideal. He hopes for a better future in a world where all people see their no-blest task in loving and serving their fellows. Yet the Christian era he enters in Constantinople at the time of the Crusades is not the age of love and brotherhood that he had envisaged. As Tancred, the Crusader, he enters a city torn by sectarian strife. Innocent people are killed for their beliefs. Eve as Isaura, in her inno-cent first love perhaps reminiscent of Madách's child-hood sweetheart, has to renounce her natural inclina-tions because she has been pledged to a convent. Adam asks his shield bearer, Lucifer, to take him to more restful times so that he may take a detached look at his surroundings from the peace of an ivory tower.

His wish is fulfilled: He finds himself as Johannes Kepler at the Imperial Court in Prague. He cannot reach inner peace, however, realizing that it is impos-sible to live outside society. His capricious and un-faithful wife, Barbara, another reincarnation of Eve, obviously modeled after Erzsi, has no understanding of his intellectual accomplishments and forces him to waste his time on horoscopes. Once again, Lucifer leads him into the future. Adam longs for an era that no longer hampers free intellectual pursuit through tradition and prejudice. As Georges-Jacques Danton in Revolutionary France, he soon discovers the darker aspects of this period. Eventually Maximilien Robes-pierre's jealousy as well as his own increasing doubts about the justness of his cause lead him to the guillo-tine. In this scene, Eve appears in two different roles, representing the dual aspect of womanhood as Madách outlines it in the drama. As a young aristocrat, con-demned to die, she inspires respect as she points to higher goals. As a coarse and bloodthirsty "woman of the people," she embodies everything Danton has come to loathe in the movement he is heading. Adam awakens from his dream once more as Kepler in Prague, where he has a conversation with a student seeking his advice. Although this dialogue is obvi-ously patterned after a similar encounter in Goethe's *Faust*, the intent is quite different, and Adam's warn-ings against obstructing one's view through theory and prejudice have nothing in common with the dev-ilish advice of Mephistopheles. Lucifer leads Adam into an age in which humankind's high ideals suppos-edly are rightly understood, and thoughts may be freely expressed.

With nineteenth century London, Madách is mov-ing into his own period. Significantly, Adam is no longer one of Hegel's "World-Historical Personal-ities," a mover of history; hereafter, he is merely a spectator. The dog-eat-dog atmosphere of early capi-talism, with its unfettered individualism, disgusts him. Eve appears as a typical representative of her age, quite willing to surrender for material gains. What ties her to her times falls off like a cloak, how-ever, in the *danse macabre* with which the scene concludes. Adam recognizes woman's role as the inspiration of searching man. The next station, the "Phalanstery," Charles Fourier's socialist utopian state, no longer has individuals fighting one another.

Instead, government takes care of everyone and makes all decisions. Science has solved many important problems, but the attempt to create life in a test tube fails as the Earth Spirit proclaims that humankind will never cross that threshold. Poetry, artistic creativity, family bonds, indeed, any remnants of individualism are banned or have already disappeared. Adam, a bemused visitor, witnesses the punishment of a few stubborn individuals who appear in the guise of great artists, thinkers, and fighters of the past. Lucifer leads him quickly away when, assuming an anachronistic stance of chivalry, Adam tries to come to the rescue of Eve, a mother whose child is to be taken away from her by the state.

The following brief scene marks a breach in the clear structure of Madách's drama. Adam and his diabolical companion fly through the vastness of space. Realizing that humankind's stubborn faith in a better future may foil his plans, Lucifer tries to push Adam out into emptiness. The Earth Spirit intervenes; humankind's ties to its natural abode are stronger than the negativity and cold intellectuality of Lucifer. The earth to which Adam returns, however, is not the hospitable environment that he had known. The sun has lost its power, and the few surviving human beings are reduced to the state of animals, fighting over what little food remains in their icy wasteland. When Adam recognizes his beloved Eve behind the coarse features of an Eskimo woman, he does not want to see any more and asks Lucifer to take him back from the future into the present. He is filled with despair, convinced that all human efforts will eventually lead into nothingness. Lucifer suggests suicide as the way out; thus, Adam can stop humankind's arduous and ultimately futile march through time before it has even started. That desperate step is made meaningless when Eve tells him that she is with child: Lucifer is defeated. Adam bows before the Lord, who restores his grace to the human race, points to woman as man's companion and inspiration, and even assigns an essentially positive role in the divine order to Lucifer: The Devil's continuing efforts to seduce and destroy will keep humankind from becoming idle and self-satisfied. Yet despite Adam's pleas, the Lord refuses to tell him whether Lucifer's presentation of hu-

man history is satanic distortion or objective truth. All he will say is that humankind ought to have faith and continue to struggle.

Much of the voluminous Madách scholarship of the last hundred years has—in addition to discussing the author's sources and possible influences—tried to pinpoint his philosophical position. Is the drama pessimistic, and the final scene merely a meaningless conventional gesture or an attempt to pacify critics who might object to the basic nihilism expressed in the historical overview? Because much of what Madách depicted in the individual scenes was based on his own reading of history and because he appeared impressed by the theories about the impending death of the earth, one cannot simply dismiss the main body of the drama as Lucifer's willful falsification of reality. Yet Madách seems to say that humankind knows only one aspect of that reality. In a sphere beyond human knowledge and comprehension, the fate of humankind may have been decided long ago. Neither Job nor Goethe's Faust nor Madách's Adam is aware of the fact that he may be only a pawn in a metaphysical struggle. Tertullian's paradoxical affirmation of faith, "Credo quia absurdum" ("I believe as it is unreasonable"), is what is demanded of Adam in the end, the same illogical faith that had sustained Hungarians over the centuries.

Madách's drama combines the concept of Goethe's Faustian hero with the melancholy of George Gordon, Lord Byron's Romantic loner and the universality of Victor Hugo. It owes much to the philosophies of Georg Wilhelm Friedrich Hegel and Arthur Schopenhauer. It deals with the claims and aspirations of the naïve materialists and the social utopists of the nineteenth century. In the details of the historical scenes, in his insights into economic and social conditions, Madách leans in the direction of the emerging realist movement in Europe. Still, *The Tragedy of Man* is essentially a Romantic work. Madách is a true Romantic in his use of literature as the vehicle to express his own feelings and record his struggles. His play depicts his efforts to overcome his bitterness and to arrive at a new assessment of womanhood. It is significant, though, that it is woman as mother, not as lover, who eventually foils the designs of the spirit of negation. The drama also shows Madách's attempt to define his religious position, moving from the Manichaean dualism of the first scene through a pantheism of sorts to the monotheistic concept of an almighty and omniscient God. This basically Christian, albeit nondogmatic, view has been overlooked by his many Catholic critics, who object not only to details in his description of Church history but also to the Kantian ethics of the final scene.

MÓZES AND TÜNDÉRÁLOM

The thematic richness and philosophical depth of *The Tragedy of Man* could not be duplicated in *Mózes*. Despite recent successful attempts to bring the play to life on the Hungarian stage, despite skillful characterizations, some adroit dialogue, and the tackling of important questions, particularly that of the relationship of the great heroic individual to the masses who do not understand him, *Mózes* seems little more than a vastly expanded scene from the previous drama. *Tündérálom*, Madách's last work, is very different. This fantasy, reminiscent of William Shakespeare's *A Midsummer Night's Dream* (c. 1595-1596) and Mihály Vörösmarty's *Csongor és Tünde* (1831),

combines a satiric look at the present with the Romantic longing for the past. The play, which demonstrates Madách's masterful handling of poetic language, was never completed. In the annals of world literature, Madách is and will remain the author of *The Tragedy of Man*.

OTHER MAJOR WORK
POETRY: *Lantvirágok*, 1840.

BIBLIOGRAPHY

Lotze, Dieter P. *Imre Madách*. Boston: Twayne, 1981. A basic examination of the life and works of Madách. Includes bibliography and index.

Madách, Imre. *The Tragedy of Man: Essays About the Ideas and the Directing of the Drama*. Budapest: Hungarian Centre of the International Theatre Institute, 1985. In addition to a translation by Joseph Grosz of *The Tragedy of Man*, this work contains a set of essays analyzing the play, discussing its reception, and describing and criticizing productions of the work. Contains bibliography.

Dieter P. Lotze

MAURICE MAETERLINCK

Born: Ghent, Belgium; August 29, 1862
Died: Nice, France; May 6, 1949

PRINCIPAL DRAMA

La Princesse Maleine, pb. 1889 (*The Princess Maleine*, 1890)

L'Intruse, pb. 1890, pr. 1891 (*The Intruder*, 1891)

Les Aveugles, pb. 1890, pr. 1891 (*The Blind*, 1891)

Les Sept Princesses, pb. 1890, pr. 1893 (*The Seven Princesses*, 1909)

Pelléas et Mélisande, pb. 1892, pr. 1893 (*Pelléas and Mélisande*, 1894)

Alladine et Palomides, pb. 1894 (*Alladine and Palomides*, 1896)

Intérieur, pb. 1894, pr. 1895 (*Interior*, 1896)

La Mort de Tintagiles, pb. 1894, pr. 1905 (music by Jean Nouguès; *The Death of Tintagiles*, 1899)

Aglavaine et Sélysette, pr., pb. 1896 (*Aglavaine and Selysette*, 1897)

Ariane et Barbe-Bleue, pr. in German 1901, pb. in French 1901, pr. in French 1907 (*Ardiane and Barbe Bleue*, 1901)

Sœur Béatrice, pr. in German 1901, pb. in French 1907 (*Sister Beatrice*, 1901)

Monna Vanna, pr., pb. 1902 (English translation, 1903)

Joyzelle, pr., pb. 1903 (English translation, 1906)

L'Oiseau bleu, pr. 1908, pb. 1909 (*The Blue Bird*, 1909)

Le Bourgmestre de Stilmonde, pr., pb. 1919 (*The Burgomaster of Stilemonde*, 1918)

Les Fiançailles, pb. 1922 (*The Betrothal*, 1918)

La Princesse Isabelle, pr., pb. 1935

L'Abbé Sétubal, pr. 1940, pb. 1959

Le Jugement dernier, pb. 1959

Théâtre inédit, pb. 1959 (includes *L'Abbé Sétubal*, *Les trois justiciers*, and *Le Jugement dernier*)

OTHER LITERARY FORMS

Maurice Maeterlinck, in his first published work, *Serres chaudes, poèmes* (1889; *Hot Houses*, 1915), demonstrated his substantial abilities as a poet. Throughout his life, he continued to write chansons (lyrics in a folksong style) for collections and for inclusion in his plays. Maeterlinck's prose, both in his plays and in his essays, always perches on the edge of verse in its rhythmic fluidity and rich imagery. Although he proved himself a lucid writer of expository prose with three scientific studies on bees, ants, and termites, it was in the realm of self-expression that he made his mark. Not since Ralph Waldo Emerson (whose works profoundly influenced Maeterlinck) has anyone been as able as Maeterlinck to combine the lyric with the metaphysical in essay form. The Belgian poet's essays constitute a major contribution to the genre.

The link between Maeterlinck's essays and his dramas is significant, especially in the essays in *Le Trésor des humbles* (1896; *The Treasure of the Humble*, 1897). For example, in the essays "Le Silence" ("The Silence"), "Emerson," and "L'Étoile" ("The Star"), he outlines an important aspect of his dramatic aesthetics—his belief in the insufficiency of words: "words fail in great part to express what they really should." Although various analyses have been written explicating the plays of Maeterlinck, none succeeds more revealingly than his own essays.

ACHIEVEMENTS

Until Maurice Maeterlinck appeared on the scene, Symbolism had created no viable theater—indeed, no drama at all except for a fragment by Stéphane Mallarmé and the hardly performable closet drama *Axël* (c. 1885-1886) by Villiers de L'Isle-Adam. In the five years between 1889 and 1894, Maeterlinck created several first-rate works that are in full accord with Symbolist aesthetics. Maeterlinck is inevitably cited by scholars as a playwright who is important primarily because of his historical significance and whose works are never performed. Nevertheless, one of his plays is still performed worldwide, almost intact, and usually untranslated from the language in which he wrote it. Indeed, his *Pelléas and Mélisande* may be performed more frequently throughout the world than any stage work by any other French playwright of Maeterlinck's generation. In 1902, Claude Debussy based his only completed opera on *Pelléas and Mélisande*.

BIOGRAPHY

Maurice-Polydore-Marie-Bernard Maeterlinck was born in 1862, in Ghent, a city rich in the old Flemish tradition. Much has been made of the influence that the cloudy and brooding atmosphere of the Low Countries exercised on Maeterlinck's more pessimistic works, an influence deriving from the constant tension between light and dark and expressed in the cloud-hung, sun-dappled landscapes of the seventeenth century Dutch painter Jacob van Ruisdael. An analysis of Maeterlinck's works demonstrates the importance of these alternations of light and dark.

The dramatist's father fit the stereotype of the materialistic Belgian burgher. Scholars have tended to read Maeterlinck's dramas as symbolic and spiritual works rejecting this bourgeois materialism, yet in the greatest of his dramas, Maeterlinck seeks to find and express what he called "the tragic in daily life." Maeterlinck seeks, like the Flemish and Dutch Masters, to illuminate in a domestic scene the eternal that lies beyond the surface of things. The subtle relationship between the metaphysical concerns of Maeterlinck and the materialistic milieu of the Belgian middle class is strikingly similar to that between Emerson's transcendentalism and the mercantile-centered world of nineteenth century Boston. Both men were drawn to the mystical, yet without neglecting the mundane. The works of both are filled with

Maurice Maeterlinck (© The Nobel Foundation)

attempts to strike a balance between otherworldly dreams and worldly concerns.

In 1885, Maeterlinck decided to move to Paris, if only for a year. He sat at the feet of the high priests of Symbolism—Villiers de L'Isle-Adam, Paul Verlaine, and Stéphane Mallarmé. His first play, *The Princesse Maleine*, met with astounding critical acclaim at the hands of the reviewer Octave Mirbeau, who hailed it as a masterpiece. It was not, but in the five years following, Maeterlinck wrote other plays that were. It was in Paris, too, that Maeterlinck met the dynamic actress-singer Georgette Leblanc, in 1895. She gave impetus to another phase in the playwright's development. For her, the playwright was to create his most forceful heroines, in a marked departure from the weak-willed victims he had created previously. This and other more forceful, even progressive, elements probably contributed greatly to his winning the Nobel Prize in Literature in 1911.

During this period, Maeterlinck also began to take an interest in politics. In a collection of essays entitled *L'Intelligence des fleurs* (1907; *Intelligence of Flowers*, 1907), he set forth a rarefied form of socialism. Although fearful of revolution, he suggested that it might be preferable to the perpetuation of social and political injustices. Far too timid and reclusive to have joined a revolutionary organization, Maeterlinck did contribute money to socialist unions and parties. Although a *pièce à thèse* seems antithetical to his meditative detachment, World War I and the German invasion of Belgium galvanized him into writing stage works on war.

For the most part, in his later years, Maeterlinck turned from the theater to expressive and expository prose. European and American theater of the later 1920's and the 1930's was moving in directions that he preferred to eschew. The stage trends were turning more and more to various manifestations of revived realism or naturalism. The man and the milieu had met briefly and transiently in the works that Maeterlinck had contributed to the Symbolist theater of the *fin de siècle*. Maeterlinck did not yearn to please crowds enough to adapt his style to a changing theater. Although Maeterlinck and Hollywood carried on a brief flirtation in 1920, they both soon recognized it as a misalliance. World War II did stir the latent playwright in Maeterlinck, resulting in several dramatic works—all of slight worth. Maeterlinck's death was fittingly dramatic. While a storm raged outside, he died in Orlamonde, his palatial home outside Nice. Then, in accordance with his belief that organized religion is a desecration of an infinite natural divinity, this most spiritual of poets was buried in a civil ceremony.

ANALYSIS

Maurice Maeterlinck's plays show him to be a craftsman of the highest integrity. His Symbolist plays are visual and tonal masterworks that draw on innovative stage techniques and scenic designs in ways that still seem modern. Maeterlinck also proves himself to be a thinker—if perhaps not a philosopher in the limited, specialized sense—of considerable merit. His plays, at their best, demonstrate an intellectual, and later social and political, import that continues to speak to modern audiences.

The French Symbolist aesthetic is expressed in Maeterlinck's plays. The concise form of the one-act play seems particularly appropriate for this aesthetic, relying as it does on the evocation of atmosphere through images with illusive and multivalent meanings. Therefore, most critics place *The Intruder* and *Interior* among the poet's well-regarded works. In *Pelléas and Mélisande*, his acknowledged masterpiece, Maeterlinck gives order to his moods and symbols by setting them in a tight five-act structure, which is based partly on the classical French drama of the seventeenth century and partly on the well-made play of the nineteenth century. Although *Pelléas and Mélisande* forms the crux of this consideration of Maeterlinck's finest stage works, several other works are considered as well.

The one-act, one-scene format of both *The Intruder* and *Interior* demonstrates a slowly but inevitably developing atmosphere, moving from light to dark over a set movement of real time that, to the eye insensitive to nuance, might seem static. Certainly, such sophisticated and expressive uses of light and other atmospheric effects were not new, but the concurrent emphasis on this temporal and visual mood progression was a characteristically *fin de siècle* contribution to the arts. The scenic conception of Maeterlinck's short plays—that of lighting that develops subtly over time—bears comparison visually with the Rouen Cathedral series of Claude Monet. Indeed, *The Intruder* and *Interior* are not only dramas but also theater in the full scenic sense of that word. Moreover, it is in these plays that Maeterlinck best embodied his theories concerning silence. In an essay on Emerson included in *The Treasure of the Humble*, Maeterlinck describes visiting an author whose works he had read but whom he had never met. In his works and during the conversation, this writer "has said many profound things concerning his soul; but in that small interval which divides a glance that lingers from a glance that vanishes, I have come to learn all that he could never say, and all that he was never able to cultivate in his intellect." These words sum up precisely the effect of the carefully

concerted stage pauses in the two one-act plays considered here.

THE INTRUDER

The Intruder moves from light to darkness, from life to death. A child has been born, but the mother is slowly dying in the next room. The play opens in a sitting room in an old château with a lighted lamp burning in the center. Throughout the play, the lamp flickers, as if in response to some supernatural presence, and eventually it goes out, as if in response to the unseen manifestation of death. At the outset of the drama, the stage directions say that the predominant color should be green—symbolic of a newborn life in the family. The play thus progresses from green to black—from life to death. A large Dutch clock reminds the audience of the flow of time. The members of the family present in the room are the uncle and father, representing the rational world of the five senses, and three little girls and their blind grandfather, representing in different degrees the otherworldly visionary. In the beginning, the adults, practical people with eyes that seem to see, dominate the dialogue—bullying the young and the old and blind. Yet in the end, when the lamp goes out, certainty is extinguished with it. The dialogue oscillates between the practical observations and platitudes of the uncle and father and, on the other side, the poetic apperceptions of the girls and old man. As the play moves toward its tragic conclusion, the dialogue is punctuated more frequently with Maeterlinck's simple but significant stage direction: "Silence." As the situation grows more solemn, words become more insignificant. Suddenly, a gleam of moonlight cuts the darkness, the sound of someone (death, perhaps) arising from an apparently empty chair, and the sudden cries of the now frightened infant in increasing gradations of terror. A door opens, and the audience perceives the silhouette of a Sister of Charity announcing the death of the child's mother; the family follows the sister into the death chamber, leaving the blind man groping his way in the dark, oblivious of the lighted door—an emblem of the blindness of even the most prescient among humanity.

INTERIOR

In Maeterlinck's *Interior*, an even more condensed

play than *The Intruder*, the audience sees a brightly lit domestic room being invaded by death. In the foreground of the stage are the people who have come to tell a family of the death of the daughter. In the background of the stage are windows through which the members of the family—played by miming actors—are visible. In short, the play focuses on what can only be termed a chorus downstage, commenting on the real drama taking place on the stage-within-a-stage. The chorus, which consists of a stranger, an old man, and his two daughters, are racing against time trying to get up enough courage to tell the family of the news before the procession of villagers arrives bearing the corpse of the daughter who has drowned. The audience sees tragedy poised on the outside, waiting to descend on the people inside—the distance at which they are set from the audience in the scenic concept allays any bathos. Outside, the members of the chorus coolly pose questions: Did the girl drown accidentally or was it suicide? Was she one of those who felt sorrow so deeply that she was unable to speak of it and had to bear it with a silence that became, in the end, too intense to bear? The old man asks the stranger to join him in breaking the news, because he is afraid of the silence that comes after the last word of bad news. The central characters, the mimes, most perfectly realize Maeterlinck's goal of mute eloquence.

PELLÉAS AND MÉLISANDE

While Maeterlinck demonstrates that he is master of the concise one-act drama, he shows himself equally a master of the full-length play with *Pelléas and Mélisande*. This work tightly fits the five-act structure, resembling closely the five-act structure of classical French drama—with the exception that, not the three unities, but the symbols with their subtle connection to the characters, unify Maeterlinck's drama.

Act 1 introduces the central images of the play. The act commences with maidservants opening the grand portals of the castle to wash the threshold—a ritual cleansing ceremony to celebrate the tragedy of life and death that is to be enacted beyond. One of the servants observes that "the sun is rising over the sea." Water imagery, either fountains, the sea, or both, per-

vades the play. Not only is the sea present in the first scene, but also, in the second scene, the middle-aged Golaud meets Mélisande by a fountain in a forest. On the shallow bottom of the pool is a golden crown belonging to Mélisande. In the fourth scene, the central image is that of a ship (the one that brought the newly married Mélisande and Golaud), which is leaving on a night when a storm is brewing. Immediately after the ship leaves, Mélisande and Pelléas, Golaud's younger half brother, have their first moments alone together. The scene ends with the two holding hands.

Maeterlinck reveals the symbolic implication of the images introduced during act 1 in the four remaining acts. In act 2, the young people go to a fountain. Mélisande says that this fountain, unlike the shallow one where Golaud met her, is "as deep as the sea," and it is by this basin that they realize how deeply in love they are. Mélisande loses her gold wedding ring in the fountain and, in the next scene, tells Golaud that she lost it in a cave by the sea. Ironically, her husband sends her, at night, to the cave with Pelléas to search for the lost ring. In scene 3 of act 3, Golaud, growing steadily more jealous, takes Pelléas into the crypt beneath the castle to view a deep pit with a "stagnant pool" at the bottom. With one hand he holds Pelléas's hand, so Pelléas can peer down into the pool; with the other, he holds a lantern. From the trembling light cast by the lantern, Pelléas (as well as the audience) senses that Golaud is sorely tempted to let his younger half brother fall over the edge. Scene 4 is one of complete contrast: The half brothers emerge from the cave with a sunlit sea before them. In act 4, Golaud catches the young couple in a nighttime tryst at the fountain where they met. He kills Pelléas and mortally wounds—more emotionally than physically—Mélisande. In act 4, the dying Mélisande asks that the windows be left open "until the sun extinguishes itself in the depths of the sea." The sun and the closing of the window correspond to the morning light and the opening of the door at the very outset of the play: In symbolic, if certainly not real time, the play moves from sunrise to sunset. Just as the sun moves in an eternal round, however, Mélisande dies, giving birth to a child, who like herself will live only to die.

The fatalistic vision of *Pelléas and Mélisande* leads scholars to see its characters as puppets entirely lacking in will. Certainly, the lovers are shadowy figures; they and their love resemble the stormy sea, the wounded boar, and the bolting horse found in the drama in that they are innocent and unself-motivated forces of nature. The human focus of the drama is on the old King Arkel and, above all, on the jealous husband Golaud. The levels of the emotional makeup of these men may be compared to soundboards, which resonate in response to, but also willfully act on, the youth, love, and destiny of the titular characters.

In speaking of Golaud, who is one of his grandsons, Arkel denies controlling his grandson's destiny, yet, only a few lines later, he stops Pelléas, his other grandson, from leaving on a long journey that would take him away from the castle and his fateful encounter with Mélisande; in so doing, he tampers with another's destiny. Later, Pelléas, perhaps realizing the danger of his love for Mélisande, asks again to leave, and Arkel again refuses permission.

Even more active in effect than King Arkel, Golaud, with his character as a jealous husband, is developed not only by the dialogue but also by the images in such a way as to transcend his conventional role. For example, the central scenes of act 3, which are pivotal to the entire drama, are representative of the two sides of Golaud's character. The dark, labyrinthine cavern of scene 3, with its pools of putrid water, symbolizes the irrational side of Golaud, which he tries his best to suppress throughout the play. The sunlit terrace of scene 4, on which Golaud tries to rationalize his jealousies and lectures Pelléas on the proper ways of comporting himself with his young sister-in-law, represents a temporarily recovered surface of behavior. The rational rhetoric comes to a close with Golaud calling Pelléas's attention to a flock of sheep on the way to the butcher, another symbol to which Maeterlinck will return in act 4, just before the scene in which Golaud commits murder.

Pelléas and Mélisande, as well as the two one-act plays, is darkly pessimistic. Maeterlinck structured them to move with taut linearity from light to darkness, from life to death. By contrast, Maeterlinck's later plays, different as each may be, all demonstrate a sense of optimism not found in his fatalistic works of the 1880's and 1890's. It is, certainly, a qualified optimism, extending hope to a happy few who have the innate will to attain their goals.

ARDIANE AND BARBE BLEUE

From among the plays after the 1890's, two show a different side of Maeterlinck as thinker than do his early plays: *Ardiane and Barbe Bleue* and *The Burgomaster of Stilemonde*. These plays indicate a poet facing the social and political problems of his day—if indeed very much on his own terms. *Ardiane and Barbe Bleue* centers on a strong woman who enters the legendary Bluebeard's castle to rescue the five women whom he is said to have killed but whom she believes are still alive. When Ardiane finds them, she tries to get them to leave the castle—but in vain. The other women, who are all named after Maeterlinck's earlier, weaker heroines, prefer a predictable existence as prisoners to the uncertainties of freedom. Ardiane is not merely an exceptional person who defies oppression in order to know and to act. As she opens the forbidden door of the castle where the women are hidden, she observes, "that which is permitted teaches us nothing."

THE BURGOMASTER OF STILEMONDE

The hero of *The Burgomaster of Stilemonde* resists political oppression of a superficially different sort. The play is set in Belgium during the German invasion at the outset of World War I. This work, which scholars have superficially dismissed as war propaganda, is in fact a drama about the ethical limits that must be placed both on military duty and on Christian forgiveness. Moreover, in this play as much as in *Interior*, Maeterlinck is able to show the transformation of a scene of mundane domesticity into one of starkest tragedy. At the beginning of the work, the audience sees the Burgomaster in all his middle-class complacency—a connoisseur of fine wines, rare orchids, and other material delights. In the end, he reaches heights of a secular martyrdom and a Christian forgiveness of the Prussian martinets who execute him. The Burgomaster's children, however, do not forgive, and the play ends on their defiance of the

German invaders. Although some might find in these later plays an unpleasant elitism, there is some truth in the fact that not all men or all women are able to sustain the heroic role or to bear the responsibility of freedom.

OTHER MAJOR WORKS

POETRY: *Serres chaudes, poèmes*, 1889 (*Hot Houses*, 1915); *Poésies complètes*, 1965.

NONFICTION: *Le Trésor des humbles*, 1896 (*The Treasure of the Humble*, 1897); *La Vie des abeilles*, 1901 (*The Life of the Bee*, 1901); *L'Intelligence des fleurs*, 1907 (*Intelligence of Flowers*, 1907); *Bulles bleues*, 1948.

BIBLIOGRAPHY

Courtney, W. L. *The Development of Maurice Maeterlinck and Other Sketches of Foreign Writers*. London: G. Richards, 1994. A collection of sketches on late nineteenth century and early twentieth century foreign writers that appeared in *The Daily Telegraph*.

Knapp, Bettina Liebowitz. *Maurice Maeterlinck*. Boston: Twayne, 1975. A concise examination of the life and works of Maeterlinck. Bibliography.

Lambert, Carole J. *The Empty Cross: Medieval Hopes, Modern Futility in the Theater of Maurice Maeterlinck, Paul Claudel, August Strindberg, and George Kaiser*. New York: Garland, 1990. Lambert examines the influences that Medieval thought had on the works of modern dramatists including Maeterlinck. Bibliography.

McGuinnes, Patrick. *Maurice Maeterlinck and the Making of Modern Theatre*. New York: Oxford University Press, 2000. McGuinnes discusses the influence of Maeterlinck on modern theater. Bibliography and index.

Mahony, Patrick. *Maurice Maeterlinck, Mystic and Dramatist: A Reminiscent Biography of the Man and His Ideas*. 2d ed. Washington, D.C.: Institute for the Study of Man, 1984. A biography of Maeterlinck that focuses on his concepts as expressed through his drama.

Rodney Farnsworth

FRANCESCO SCIPIONE MAFFEI

Born: Verona, Republic of Venice (now in Italy), June 1, 1675
Died: Verona, Republic of Venice (now in Italy), February 11, 1755

PRINCIPAL DRAMA

Merope, pr., pb. 1713 (English translation, 1740)
Le cerimonie, pr., pb. 1728
La fida ninfa, pb. 1730, pr. 1732 (libretto; music by Antonio Vivaldi)
Il Raguet, pr., pb. 1747
Teatro del Sig. marchese Scipione Maffei cilè la tragedia, pb. 1730

OTHER LITERARY FORMS

Francesco Scipione Maffei was a historian, theorist, antiquarian, archeologist, and literary critic. He campaigned vigorously for the reestablishment of a strong tradition of tragedy in the Italy of his day. He also wrote essays on archeology and antiquities. He helped found the literary journal, *Giornale dei Letterati d'Italia*, and wrote for its pages for many years. He is remembered as well for his work in archeology, especially that related to ancient Roman buildings and monuments, as in his essay on Roman amphitheatres, *Degli anfiteatri e singolarmente veronese* (1728; on amphitheatres and especially on that of Verona), and in his *Verona illustrata* (1732; Verona illustrated). He published a political tract addressed to the government of the Veneto region expressing the case against dueling: *Consiglio politico presentato al governo veneto* (1736; political advice to the Veneto government).

ACHIEVEMENTS

Francesco Scipione Maffei is chiefly remembered for his literary essays on tragedy, his collaboration with Luigi Riccoboni's theatrical company in developing a repertory of French and Italian tragedies, and most of all for his single tragedy, *Merope*, which was much imitated and admired.

BIOGRAPHY

Francesco Scipione Maffei came of a noble family and was himself a marquis. He studied with the Jesuits in Parma, then fought in the war of succession in 1704 in Bavaria. He returned to Verona for his studies but soon interrupted them for a long trip into France, England, Holland, and Belgium. He was a learned gentleman who published on a wide variety of subjects: literature, philosophy, theology, archeology, and dramatic arts. In this last connection, he was a champion of classical tragedy.

There were a number of theorists and playwrights in the very early years of the eighteenth century who wanted to establish tragedy in its purest form, and it was the mission of the Arcadian Academy founded in Rome in 1690. Maffei, who had spent time in Rome as a young man, was initiated into the Arcadian Academy in 1698, and in 1704 he established a Verona chapter of the academy. In 1700, the academy's president, Giovan Crescimbeni, published *La bellezza della volgar poesia* (the beauty of vernacular poetry), arguing that opera had spoiled the purer genres of comedy and especially tragedy. Gian Gravina, also a member of that academy, published five tragedies in 1712 followed by a critical defense, *Della tragedia* (on tragedy). Pier Martelli wrote several tragedies and is remembered for his special adaptation of the French Alexandrine verse that came to be called Martellian verse and was much imitated by other writers of serious drama of that day. There was palpable rivalry with France and an anxiety to match the triumphs seen in the work of Pierre Corneille and Jean Racine.

Maffei made himself a part of that cause. He joined forces with Luigi Riccoboni encouraging him to use his troupe to perform not only French tragedies but also such earlier distinguished Italian tragedies as Giangiorgio Trissino's *La Sofonisba* (wr. 1515, pb.

1524, pr. 1562), Torquato Tasso's *Il re Torrismondo* (pb. 1587), Muzio Manfredi's *Semiramis* (pr. 1593), and Orsatto Giustiniani's version of the Oedipus story, *Edipo tiranno* (pr. 1585). Maffei followed this by publishing an anthology of twelve exemplary Italian tragedies under the long title *Teatro italiano: O, Sia scelte di tragedie per uso della scene* (1723-1725, three volumes; the Italian theater or a collection of twelve tragedies for use on the stage). In answer to Maffei, the Dominican priest, Danele Concina, wrote a tract, *De spectaculis theatralibus* (pb. 1754), condemning all forms of theater. Maffei answered him much later in his essay *De teatri antichi e moderni* (1753; of ancient and modern theatres) published with the express approval of Pope Benedetto XIV, whom Maffei had known in Rome as Cardinal Lambertini.

Probably most important to this cause of reviving tragedy was the tragedy Maffei composed: *Merope*, his one well-known dramatic work. It opened in Modena, June 12, 1713, with Elena Balletti Riccoboni playing the title role and with the attendance of Duke Rinaldo and his court. It was a stunning success and went on to play in other cities before appearing at the Teatro San Luca in Venice, and each time enjoying great success, so much so that Maffei boasted of having finally trounced the French at the game of tragedy.

Despite this success, Maffei wrote very little for the theater thereafter. He concentrated on his studies for the remaining forty years of his life. Nevertheless, he had had an influence that was acknowledged much later in the century by such leading authors as Voltaire in France and Vittorio Alfieri in Italy, both of whom wrote plays based on the story of Merope. Indeed Alfieri, writing near the end of the eighteenth century, represents the realization of Maffei's hope for a significant Italian writer of tragedies.

ANALYSIS

Francesco Scipione Maffei's life was his work. As drama is concerned, he wrapped himself up in the vigorous campaign to give Italy a new tragic tradition based on the ancients. Between about 1710 and 1723, he was completely absorbed in this endeavor, then he gradually drifted away and took up other interests.

His convictions are clear both from his most famous play and from his writing on the subject of tragedy. He was convinced of the beauty of the ancient myths and history, which, in his view, have an inherent purity and universality. At the same time, he was equally convinced that the form tragedy would have to assume in the new age must be suited to the times. The classical qualities of economy of expression, tautness of plot, and rich suggestion of language must be retained, he argued. Nevertheless, slavish duplication of every practice and convention would be stultifying.

MEROPE

Maffei took the story of Merope from Greek mythology, a story that had been the basis for a lost play by Euripides. Merope, the widow of the deposed king of Messenia, is being wooed by the usurper, Polifonte, who fifteen years before had murdered her husband and two of her three sons and seized the throne. While he attempts to persuade her that he was justified in taking that act, a young stranger named Egisto is brought to court accused of murdering another young man. He wears a jewel that had belonged to Merope's lost son, Cresfonte, and she assumes the young man had murdered Cresfonte. She vows to take vengeance on him. She is on the point of stabbing him when she is stopped by Polidoro, the only person aware of the truth: Egisto is the lost son. At the time of the great carnage, Polidoro was entrusted with the little boy, took him away and raised him elsewhere. Even Egisto is unaware of his true identity. Once reunited as mother and son, they plot vengeance. She agrees to the marriage with Polifonte. In the midst of the wedding ceremony, Egisto/Cresfonte murders the tyrant, and the grateful populace rise up in jubilation and make him king.

This summary does not do justice to the play. It is written in a clear and compact manner and is a neat and tidy balance of ancient traditions and contemporary taste. There are no awkward conventions left over from the ancient Greek plays: It has no prologue, no messengers, no choral interludes (and no chorus), no confidants, and no soliloquies. It moves forward in a rapid-paced plot, catching the audience up in anticipation. The verse is lively and the revelations gripping. Psychologically, Merope is a complex and intriguing character who dominates the play in full naturalness. Alfieri's version years later fulfills the ideals Maffei pursued even better than Maffei's own effort.

OTHER MAJOR WORKS

NONFICTION: *Verona illustrata*, 1731-1732 (4 volumes, Vol. 4 translated as *A Compleat History of the Ancient Ampitheatres*).

MISCELLANEOUS: *Opere drammatiche e poesie varie*, 1928 (plays and prose).

BIBLIOGRAPHY

Carlson, Marvin. *The Italian Stage from Goldoni to d'Annunzio*. Jefferson, N.C.: MacFarland, 1981. Portrays the currents in eighteenth century Italian drama and devotes several pages to the effort to establish a tradition of classical tragedy in the new age with the work of Maffei as well as that of Vittorio Alfieri and others.

Kennard, Joseph S. *The Italian Theatre*. 2 vols. Reprint. New York: B. Blom, 1964. This is a full survey of the history of Italian theater from Roman times to the twentieth century. The section on eighteenth century drama devotes some attention to the work of Maffei.

Lessing, Gotthold Ephraim. *Hamburg Dramaturgy*. Translated by Helen Zimmern. New York: Bohn's Standard Library, 1890. Lessing's notes for the Hamburg National Theatre, written in the mid- to late eighteenth century, include commentary on Maffei's work.

Stanley Longman

JEAN MAIRET

Born: Besançon, France; May 10, 1604 (baptized)
Died: Besançon, France; January 31, 1686

PRINCIPAL DRAMA

Chryséide et Arimand, pr. 1625, pb. 1630 (based on Honoré d'Urfé's novel *L'Astrée*)

Sylvie, pr. 1626, pb. 1628

La Silvanire: Ou, La Mortevive, pr. 1630, pb. 1631 (based on d'Urfé's *L'Astrée*)

Les Galanteries du duc d'Ossonne, pr. 1633, pb. 1636

Virginie, pr. 1633, pb. 1635

Sophonisbe, pr. 1634, pb. 1635 (English translation, 1956)

Marc-Antoine: Ou, La Cléopâtre, pr. 1635, pb. 1637

Le Grand et dernier Solyman: Ou, La Mort de Mustapha, pr. 1637, pb. 1639

L'Illustre Corsaire, pr. 1637, pb. 1640

Roland furieux, pr. 1638, pb. 1640

Athénaïs, pr. 1639, pb. 1642

Sidonie, pr. 1640, pb. 1643

OTHER LITERARY FORMS

Jean Mairet published two slim collections of lyric poetry, much of it occasional verse, as addenda to the first editions of *Sylvie* and *La Silvanire*. A handful of poems composed in later years, left in manuscript, were published by his biographer Gaston Bizos. Mairet's prose writings, apart from a few surviving letters and diplomatic correspondence, consist of a treatise on poetic theory, published as the preface to *La Silvanire*, and several polemical pamphlets directed against Pierre Corneille. Mairet is remembered chiefly for his plays.

ACHIEVEMENTS

It is unfortunate that Jean Mairet has been traditionally remembered mainly for his role in the quarrel over Corneille's *Le Cid* (pr., pb. 1637; *The Cid*, 1637). In fact, he was one of the pivotal figures in the development of French classical drama and was among the most influential champions of what would become known as the three unities (those of time, place, and action). Revived interest in the Baroque stage has prompted a reevaluation of Mairet as a gifted representative of the preclassical sensibility who was unaware of the extent to which the new critical doctrine of classicism would conflict with that sensibility and ultimately banish his works from the Parisian stage. Mairet also deserves much of the credit for notable advances in the refinement of style, sophistication of characterization, and tightness of plot construction that occurred in the second quarter of the seventeenth century. Although he did not possess the genius of Corneille, Mairet had genuine dramatic talent. After more than three centuries, the best of his plays can still be read with pleasure and could conceivably be revived.

Despite his crucial role in the evolution of French classical doctrine, Mairet's exposition of theoretical issues is disappointing. His prefaces and polemics tend to be rambling and confused, with too much pedantic accumulation of sources and technical terms and too little original thought. A careful reading of these documents, however, reveals a number of innovations that would have a decisive impact. In the preface to *La Silvanire*, Mairet predicates the need for the unities, not on a slavish respect for Aristotle (whose work he probably never knew firsthand), but rather on the basis principle of verisimilitude. This last is justified in its turn as a prerequisite for aesthetic satisfaction. Because the principal aim of drama is the pleasure of the imagination, the play must conform to what the spectator can accept as believable. Mairet is careful to point out that an irregular play is not necessarily a bad one. What he does claim is that the rules are indispensable if one wishes to achieve perfection and equal the masterpieces of the past. By grounding the rules in pragmatic considerations, he helped move the debate away from the obsession with antiquity that had characterized early French poetic theory, and he undeniably hastened the acceptance of these rules among both playwrights and public. In the process, he anticipated the dictum espoused by (among others) Corneille, Jean Racine, and Molière: The primary rule is to please, and all further rules are derivable from it.

Another notable innovation was the principle known today as poetic justice, which Mairet helped introduce into French critical theory. Although he was mistaken in citing Aristotle as the inventor and champion of the "double ending" (that is, the good characters are rewarded and the villains are punished), Mairet, writing at a time when defenders of the stage were earnestly trying to demonstrate its high moral purpose, laid the groundwork for the adoption of this principle, albeit in a less rigorous form. Moreover, he appears to use poetic justice as a criterion to distinguish between the genres of tragedy and tragicomedy. The intermediate genre, featuring a clear polarization between good and evil characters, achieves its happy ending by the ultimate intervention of providential forces. Tragedy, on the other hand, shows the misfortunes of sympathetic characters, punished more harshly than they deserve, in order to instruct the audience to bear the vicissitudes of life with courage and resignation. This theory, pieced together from statements scattered throughout Mairet's prefaces and polemics, is a basically accurate reflection of dramatic practice in Mairet's time and is all the more remarkable in that French theorists showed little interest in discussing the intermediate genre.

BIOGRAPHY

Jean Mairet was descended from a staunchly Catholic family that had emigrated from Westphalia to Besançon during the Reformation. Baptized on May 10, 1604, he lost both parents at an early age. He began his studies in Besançon, later transferring, following an outbreak of the plague, to the Collège des Grassins in Paris. The plague, this time in Paris, interrupted his studies once again. At this point, Mairet seems to have gone to Fontainebleau to make contacts at court. He quickly won the favor of the duke of Montmorency, an enlightened patron of the arts, who invited him to his château. There Mairet met another of the duke's protégés, the poet Théophile de Viau, who became his friend and literary mentor. Although

Théophile spent most of his final years in prison, Mairet never disguised his admiration for the older poet and even edited a portion of his correspondence. In 1625, Mairet volunteered to join his patron in an expedition against the Protestants of La Rochelle and distinguished himself in two battles. When, upon the capture of the islands of Ré and Oléron, the campaign came to a speedy halt, the duke appointed Mairet his secretary and granted him a pension of fifteen hundred pounds.

It is not clear when Mairet began to write for the stage. In the dedicatory epistle to *Les Galanteries du duc d'Ossonne*, he claims to have written his first play at the age of sixteen, when barely out of school, and he gives dates for the composition of his other plays, as well. Because he deliberately misled the public about his age, however, claiming to have been born in 1610 (a statement generally accepted until later biographers located and published his baptismal certificate), his chronology must be viewed with suspicion. While trying to appear as more of a child prodigy than he really was, Mairet must have realized that readers of the dedication would remember the dates of the plays' premieres and the intervals between them. It is thus likely that the chronology he presents is accurate, provided that one adds six years to each of his figures. The resulting dates are closer to conformity with the dates of publication of the plays, for, except in the case of *Chryséide et Arimand*, which he later disavowed and which was printed without his authorization, there is no apparent reason why Mairet should have waited an average of six or seven years before publishing each successive play.

By the time he wrote his third play, Mairet had been considerably influenced by the duchess of Montmorency and her circle. The duchess, a cultivated patron of the arts like her husband, was a descendant of the powerful Orsini family and encouraged Mairet to study the masters of the Italian pastoral and to become involved in debates over the dramatic unities. In 1632, the duke was executed for treason, yet Mairet would never cease to extol the generosity of his former patron, however politically inexpedient this might seem. A period of financial difficulty followed, but Mairet was soon to find another generous and energetic protector in the count of Belin, who also surrounded himself with a group of gifted writers.

In the meantime, Mairet quickly established himself as one of the dramatic luminaries of his time. The eldest of a generation of playwrights who were to usher in French classical theater, Mairet managed to achieve at least a moderate success with all his plays through 1636. His *Sylvie* ranks alongside *The Cid* as the most popular play in the first half of the century. It was, in fact, the huge success of Corneille's tragicomedy that marked the beginning of Mairet's decline. Corneille's tactless decision to publish an autobiographical poem extolling himself as the foremost writer of his generation (a judgment that no one would dispute today but that was not so obvious in 1637) prompted the irate Mairet to print a sarcastic response, under the pseudonym Don Baltazar de la Verdad. This ballad, which denies Corneille any poetic ability whatsoever and claims that *The Cid* was plagiarized word for word from a Spanish source, provoked an equally scathing response from Corneille. This led to a long and vehement quarrel, involving many of the leading poets of the day and resulting in the publication of more than thirty polemical pieces for or against Corneille, most of which do little credit to the memories of their authors. It required the intervention of Cardinal Richelieu and the newly formed French Academy to bring the quarrel to a halt.

One beneficial result of the quarrel for Mairet was that he ingratiated himself with the cardinal, who provided him with a pension, despite the poet's earlier service to the cardinal's enemy, the duke of Montmorency. The cardinal's financial assistance became even more urgently needed when the count of Belin died in 1638. Mairet was not so fortunate, however, with his dramatic endeavors after 1637. Perhaps in response to the success of Corneille's irregular plays, Mairet composed a group of tragicomedies in the Baroque spirit that disregarded the unities he had worked so hard to promote. All were dismal failures. A final tragicomedy, *Sidonie*, returned to the unities but was an even bigger fiasco. The ever-mounting popularity of Corneille, combined with the cardinal's death in 1642, led Mairet to renounce the stage.

From 1645 to 1653, Mairet enjoyed a brilliant career as diplomatic representative of his native province of Franche-Comté (not yet part of France) in Paris. Mairet worked tirelessly to secure his province's neutrality in the prolonged war between France and Spain and was instrumental in negotiating two important treaties in 1649 and 1651. In 1653, Mairet's friends at the Spanish court were arranging to appoint him to an even more powerful post when Cardinal Mazarin, acting out of personal dislike for the poet and out of political expediency, exiled him to Besançon without warning. Mairet's attempts to appeal this order proved futile, and he could not return to Paris until the peace treaty of 1659. Although warmly received by the Queen Mother, who presented him with a sum of money in recognition of past services, he decided not to remain in the capital. The loss of his wife, who had died in 1658 leaving no children, combined with the realization that he had long outlived both his literary and his diplomatic reputation, prompted him to return to Besançon, where he lived in retirement until his death at the age of eighty-one.

ANALYSIS

During his lifetime, Jean Mairet helped establish the viability of the classical unities through his dramatic efforts. By placing believable personalities in plausible psychological conflicts, he avoided creating an aesthetic breach between dramatic theory and practice. Despite the inherent weaknesses in his works, he attained a level of believability during most of his career that furthered his primary desire, that of correctly interpreting the tastes of the audiences that he wished to please.

In the middle of the sixteenth century, the dramatic pastoral became a recognized genre in France, largely as a result of Italian influence. The refined portrayal of young love and the evocation of a delicious rustic fantasy world, free from material cares, where benevolent gods or magicians assured that all would turn out right, were among the principal attractions of the form. The 1620's, when Jean Mairet composed his three pastoral plays, marked the high point of the genre's popularity, soon to be eclipsed by that of tragedy. Already overly stylized and conventional, the pastoral had recently acquired a new vitality with the publication of Honoré d'Urfé's monumental novel, *L'Astrée* (1607-1628; *Astrea*, 1657-1658). Besides appealing to his countrymen's patriotism by setting his Arcadia in the Forez region of France, d'Urfé proved a model of stylistic excellence and a wide range of interesting plots and characters that would inspire the coming generation of playwrights. Mairet took the plots of his *Chryséide et Arimand* and *La Silvanire* directly from *Astrea*; *Sylvie*, based on a variety of literary sources, also shows the influence of d'Urfé.

SYLVIE

Sylvie, probably the finest of all French pastorals, was certainly the most popular. It went through twenty-two editions in Mairet's lifetime, fifteen of them in its first ten years, and remained in the active repertory for a number of years. Although much of the play's charm derives from the delicate grace of Mairet's poetry, its dramatic appeal results from a skillful mixture of elements from other dramatic genres. From the tragicomedy, Mairet took the chivalrous subplot of Prince Florestan, who falls in love with the beautiful Princess Méliphile upon viewing her portrait, undertakes a long and dangerous journey to meet her, is shipwrecked on the very island he seeks but is miraculously preserved, and finally wins the hand of his beloved by destroying a powerful magic spell. From the tragedy, Mairet took the cruel king who persecutes the young lovers and the moving episode in which the other pair of lovers, Thélame and Sylvie, each believing the other dead, pronounce a lament over the body of the beloved. These scenes were doubtless inspired by the tragedy *Pyrame et Thisbé* (1623) by Théophile and may well have been intended as Mairet's homage to his late friend. There are even comic episodes, such as the scenes involving Sylvie's materialistic parents, the delightfully witty repartee between the shepherdess and her rejected suitor Philène, and the stratagem whereby the latter tries to convince Sylvie of her prince's infidelity.

Although *Sylvie* predates Mairet's official acceptance of the three unities, it does try to observe the unity of place, at least in the flexible interpretation of the 1620's and 1630's. Apart from the opening scene

set in Candia, the action is limited to a forest overlooking the coast of Sicily, with the two nearby dwellings, the royal palace where the Princess Méliphile and her brother Prince Thélame live, and the hut of Sylvie's parents. Of more significance, though, is the presentation of the locale as an enchanted country blessed with exceptional fertility and beauty, conducive to blissful love and knightly adventure. Florestan, upon landing on the island, exclaims that this must be the abode of the gods. Thélame, revolted by the insincerity of life at court, goes there to seek not only love but also the purity and freedom of the natural order. This sense of exhilarating liberation is mirrored in the plot, which focuses on the indomitable love between a prince and a shepherdess, despite the opposition of a jealous rival, the irate fathers, and considerations of state. Although it requires the intervention of an oracle to ordain their marriage, it should be noted that Mairet does not utilize the customary last-minute recognition scene revealing his heroine to be of noble birth.

Mairet showed little regard for the unities of time and action here, although the first four acts span roughly twenty-four hours. Like earlier pastorals, *Sylvie* moves at a leisurely pace, with little attempt to create suspense. Certain episodes could be eliminated with no effect on the denouement. There is no real character development, although Mairet does try to motivate Philène's last-act change of heart (enabling him to marry the shepherdess Dorise, whom he has hitherto spurned). Finally, there is a note of unabashed sensuality, common to much of Mairet's theater but which would be anathema to the following generation. The characters freely give vent to their feelings, and spontaneity sometimes comes at the expense of dignity, as in Thélame's impetuous desire to enjoy Sylvie's body. The sensuality never becomes excessive, however, for Sylvie is perfectly capable of safeguarding her honor. At the same time, she maintains an ironic distance from the hyperbolic language of love and courtship, making the triumph of simplicity and sincerity one of the key motifs of the play.

LES GALANTERIES DU DUC D'OSSONNE

During the first three decades of the seventeenth century, comedy (as distinguished from farce) had virtually disappeared in France. Mairet contributed to the genre's remarkable revival in the 1630's with *Les Galanteries du duc d'Ossonne*, his sole comedy. Like his colleagues Corneille and Jean de Rotrou, he preferred to turn away from the comic stereotypes such as inept or scheming servants, pedants, elderly misers, and braggart soldiers to concentrate on the sentimental adventures of the leisure classes. The language is refined and chaste, even if the situations are not, the characters are more three-dimensional, and the lovers, rather than their intermediaries, are the active figures.

Mairet's comedy has often been attacked for its immorality. To be sure, the love affairs in this play are all outside the bonds of marriage, and there is a notoriously risqué scene in which the Duke gets into Flavie's bed after promising not to touch her. Nevertheless, compared to the novellas and comedies of the Renaissance, not to mention the real-life mores of the aristocracy in Mairet's day, the play is relatively tame. It is not even clear whether the work scandalized its audience at the premiere in 1633, since the only known denunciations come from Corneille and his allies during the quarrel over *The Cid* four years later. In any event, the play is set during the carnival season, as the opening lines indicate, and the actions of the Duke, and to a lesser extent those of the other principals, stem from a delight in game playing and adventure for their own sake.

Although the title character is historical (1579-1624) and did serve as viceroy of Naples, the plot of the comedy is purely fictional. The Duke, having seen the young and beautiful Emilie at the theater, falls in love with her (although his passions are never deep or lasting) and plans to seduce her. When her obsessively jealous husband, Paulin, is forced to flee Naples for having ordered the murder of his wife's beloved, Camille, the Duke offers him refuge in one of his country houses in order to keep him out of town. Paulin orders Emilie to stay with his widowed sister Flavie during his absence. The Duke, knowing that Flavie's house is directly across the square from his palace, pays it a nocturnal visit, despite the harsh winter weather, and finds Emilie, who reveals that she loves the supposedly dying Camille but esteems

the Duke. The Duke agrees to take her place in Flavie's bed while she goes to pay a final visit to her beloved. Meanwhile, Flavie, having overheard this conversation, resolves to inform the Duke of her own love for him by feigning to talk in her sleep when he enters the room. When the Duke discovers that the widow is a ravishing lady of twenty, he takes a romantic interest in her, while continuing to pursue Emilie. Some time later, Camille, having recovered from his wounds, also becomes attracted to Flavie and plans to court both ladies. The sisters-in-law discover these infidelities and vow revenge. A simultaneous nocturnal visit to the house by the two men, each of whom is mistaken in the dark for the other, leads to the revelation of all secrets and a general reconciliation. Camille returns to Emilie and the Duke to Flavie, with all four planning to feast and rejoice in Paulin's absence.

Because of its audacities, Mairet's play had no direct successor. Nevertheless, the cleverly constructed plot, the fast-moving stage action, the lifelike characters, and the adroit combination of serious and humorous scenes make this one of the most readable of the French Baroque comedies.

SOPHONISBE

Sophonisbe is a milestone in the history of French drama: the first tragedy composed in conscious conformity with the rules of classicism. The play's undeniable merits, reinforced by a superb production by the Marais troupe of Paris, was a huge popular and critical success, which contributed even more than Mairet's theoretical writings to the gradual acceptance of the rules and unities.

The subject of the courageous Carthaginian princess and her fierce determination to resist the domination of Rome had been treated by a number of earlier playwrights. Mairet's greatest innovation lay in the focus on internal, rather than external, conflicts and in the presentation of the protagonists as complex, three-dimensional characters who are neither totally innocent nor totally guilty, yet never lose the audience's sympathies. The conflict between duty and the destructive power of love is the central problem, as it would be in numerous other tragedies later in the century. Destiny (for the benevolent gods whom the characters frequently evoke fail to play any role in the action) seems to consist of two warring forces, the irresistible passion of love and the inflexible will of Rome, with the two lovers caught in the middle.

Mairet observes his cherished three unities without much difficulty. The action requires only twenty-four hours and, with the exception of a brief scene in Massinisse's camp, is confined to two adjoining rooms in Sophonisbe's palace. The plot moves swiftly toward the defeat and death of the principal characters and the total victory of the Romans. On the other hand, the rule of decorum (not fully codified at the time Mairet was writing) is sometimes violated. Syphax's denunciation of his wife as a harlot, the kiss that ends the first interview between Massinisse and Sophonisbe, and the repeated references to the consummation of their marriage (between acts 3 and 4) would not be tolerated a mere decade later. There are also occasional interjections of comic dialogue—another feature that classicism would later proscribe.

Because Mairet conceived of his protagonists not as moral exempla inspiring admiration, but as fallible human beings whose plight creates pathos, he made several significant changes in the historical material. Syphax, Sophonisbe's first husband, is, in this version, killed in the battle against the Romans so that her subsequent marriage to Massinisse appears more legitimate to a modern audience. Massinisse, unable to live without his beloved, commits suicide over her body at the end of the play. In Livy's account, both husbands survive her. Moreover, Mairet's Sophonisbe acts primarily out of love, and her patriotism and hatred of Roman tyranny rarely come to the fore. She thus appears as a fragile and delicate, rather than an aggressive and masculine, heroine. Finally, Mairet moves the decisive battle between the forces of Syphax and Massinisse to the area outside the city walls to guarantee the observance of the unities.

Throughout the play, the psychological struggles and transformations of the main characters provide the primary interest. The literal battle, which occurs offstage in act 2, is subordinated to the internal conflicts, and its outcome is determined by the characters' feelings and actions that precede it. Syphax goes into battle hoping for death, having discovered that his wife has been unfaithful to him and has betrayed her country by corresponding with the enemy general, Massinisse. Sophonisbe, torn between her love for Massinisse, to whom she had been promised before her marriage to Syphax, and her feelings of guilt and shame at her recent actions, clearly hopes for her husband's defeat, although she is far from confident about winning the victor's heart. It is her internal anguish that dominates act 2, during which she is onstage throughout, receiving reports about the course of the battle outside. The long and powerful interview between Massinisse and Sophonisbe in act 3 is one of the earliest uses of the *scène à faire* or obligatory scene (a climactic confrontation between the two most active characters, moving the action in a wholly new direction). Their decision to marry at once in order to present Rome with a *fait accompli* prepares the confrontation in act 4 with Scipion, the unfeeling and unyielding representative of Rome. The struggle is necessarily unequal, for the Numidian prince Massinisse has been thoroughly trained in Roman ways and is totally dependent on Rome politically and militarily. Because the greatest concession that he can obtain is to spare his bride the humiliation of a triumphal procession by making her take poison, the concluding scenes deal with the lovers' despair and suicides. Their steadfast devotion to each other and their courageous acceptance of death ultimately restore them to the dignity of tragic heroes.

BIBLIOGRAPHY

Bunch, William A. *Jean Mairet*. Boston: Twayne, 1975. A basic treatment of Mairet's life and works. Includes a bibliography and index.

Chadwick, C. "The Role of Mairet's *Sophonisbe* in the Development of French Tragedy." *Modern Language Review* 50 (1955): 176-179. Chadwick examines Mairet's *Sophonisbe* and how it helped developed the genre of tragedy in France.

Kay, Burf. *The Theatre of Jean Mairet: The Metamorphosis of Sensuality*. The Hague: Mouton, 1975. Kay analyzes the works of Mairet in terms of the sensuality employed in them. Includes a bibliography and index.

Perry Gethner

DAVID MAMET

Born: Chicago, Illinois; November 30, 1947

PRINCIPAL DRAMA

Camel, pr. 1968

Lakeboat, pr. 1970, revised pr. 1980, pb. 1981

Duck Variations, pr. 1972, pb. 1977

Sexual Perversity in Chicago, pr. 1974, pb. 1977

Squirrels, pr. 1974, pb. 1982

American Buffalo, pr. 1975, pb. 1977

Reunion, pr. 1976, pb. 1979

A Life in the Theatre, pr., pb. 1977

The Revenge of the Space Pandas, pr. 1977, pb. 1978 (one act; children's play)

The Water Engine, pr. 1977, pb. 1978

Dark Pony, pr. 1977, pb. 1979

The Woods, pr. 1977, pb. 1979

Mr. Happiness, pr., pb. 1978

Lone Canoe, pr. 1979 (music and lyrics by Alaric Jans)

The Sanctity of Marriage, pr. 1979, pb. 1982

Donny March, pr. 1981

The Poet and the Rent, pr., pb. 1981 (children's play)

A Sermon, pr., pb. 1981

Short Plays and Monologues, pb. 1981

Edmond, pr. 1982, pb. 1983

Glengarry Glen Ross, pr., pb. 1983

The Disappearance of the Jews, pr. 1983, pb. 1987 (one act)

Red River, pr. 1983 (adaptation of Pierre Laville's play)

Goldberg Street: Short Plays and Monologues, pb. 1985

The Shawl, pr., pb. 1985

A Collection of Dramatic Sketches and Monologues, pb. 1985

Vint, pr. 1985, pb. 1986 (adaptation of Anton Chekhov's short story)

The Cherry Orchard, pr., pb. 1986 (adaptation of Chekhov's play)

Three Children's Plays, pb. 1986

Three Jewish Plays, pb. 1987

Speed-the-Plow, pr., pb. 1988

Uncle Vanya, pr., pb. 1988 (adaptation of Chekhov's play)

Bobby Gould in Hell, pr. 1989, pb. 1991 (one act)

Three Sisters, pr., pb. 1990 (adaptation of Chekhov's play)

Oh Hell: Two One-Act Plays, pb. 1991

Oleanna, pr. 1992, pb. 1993

The Cryptogram, pr., pb. 1994

No One Will Be Immune: And Other Plays and Pieces, pb. 1994

Plays: One, pb. 1994

An Interview, pr., pb. 1995 (one act)

Plays: Two, pb. 1996

Plays: Three, pb. 1996

The Old Neighborhood, pr. 1997, pb. 1998 (includes *The Disappearance of the Jews*, *Jolly*, and *D.*)

Boston Marriage, pr. 1999, pb. 2001

Plays: Four, pb. 2002

OTHER LITERARY FORMS

While first and foremost a theatrician, David Mamet has also gained respect for his work in other literary forms. Perhaps Mamet's most popular contributions have been to Hollywood. His screenplays—*The Postman Always Rings Twice* (1981), *The Verdict* (1982), *The Untouchables* (1985), *House of Games* (1987), *Things Change* (1988), *We're No Angels* (1989), *Homicide* (1991), and *Glengarry Glen Ross* (1992)—have been praised for their intriguing plots and monologues of cruelty. Most scholars point to *House of Games*, with its ritualized forms of expiation, and *Glengarry Glen Ross*, with its dazzling repartee, as his best work in film. Finally, Mamet demonstrates his skill as an essayist in *Writing in Restaurants* (1986), a collection of essays that best spells out the playwright's theory of dramatic art as well as his sense of cultural poetics.

ACHIEVEMENTS

David Mamet, winner of a Pulitzer Prize in 1984 (for his play *Glengarry Glen Ross*), two Obie Awards

(1976, 1983), and two New York Drama Critics Circle Awards (1977, 1986) among many others, is regarded as a major voice in American drama and cinema. He animates his stage through language, a poetic idiolect that explores the relationship between public issue and private desires—and the effects of this relationship on the individual's spirit. He is known for his wit and comedy, but beyond the streetwise dialogues lie more problematic concerns. The typical Mamet play presents the near-complete separation of the individual from genuine relationships. Mamet replicates human commitments and desires in demythicized forms: commodity fetishism, sexual negotiations and exploitations, botched crimes, physical assaults, fraudulent business transactions enacted by petty thieves masquerading as business associates, and human relationships whose only shared features are the presence of sex and the absence of love. Although he varies his plays in terms of plots and themes, Mamet seems at his best when critiquing what he believes is a business ethic that has led to the corruption of both the social contract and his heroes' moral values. Mamet's major achievements, then, concern his use of language, his social examination of professional and private betrayals and alienation, and his ability to capture the anxieties of the individual—whether he or she is a small-time thief, a working-class person, or a Hollywood executive.

BIOGRAPHY

Born on the South Side of Chicago on November 30, 1947, David Alan Mamet became interested in the theater as a teenager. He worked at the Hull House Theatre and at Second City, one of Chicago's richest improvisational performance sites at the time, experiences that he recognized as having exerted an important influence on his language, characterizations, and plot structures. His mother, Lenore Silver, was a schoolteacher, his father, Bernard Mamet, a labor lawyer and minor semanticist, and though the parents' intellectual aware-

ness of language plainly influenced their son, their divorce seems to have affected the young Mamet even more greatly. Exiled to what Mamet saw as a sterile suburb of Chicago—Olympia Fields—his geographical move seemed all the more complicated because of his familial dislocations. His stepfather apparently (Mamet revealed in a 1992 essay entitled "The Rake") physically and psychologically abused the Mamet family, and it seems as if the world of the theater offered the playwright some form of reprieve and, later, recognition from a tension-filled youth. As a boy, Mamet also acted on television, an opportunity made possible by his uncle, who was the director of broadcasting for the Chicago Board of Rabbis. Mamet often was cast as a Jewish boy plagued by religious self-doubt and concerns.

After graduating from Francis Parker, a private school in downtown Chicago, Mamet attended Goddard College in Plainfield, Vermont, where he majored in theater and literature. At Goddard, he wrote his first play, *Camel*, which fulfilled his thesis requirement for graduation and was staged at the college in 1968. During his junior year (1968-1969), Mamet moved from Plainfield to New York City, where he studied acting at the Neighborhood Playhouse with Sanford Meisner, one of the founding

David Mamet (Brigitte Lacombe)

members of the Group Theatre in the 1930's. While his talents as an actor were minimal at best, Mamet's attention to idiolect and its cadence was greatly enhanced by Meisner. After earning his B.A. in literature in 1969, he worked in a truck factory, a canning plant, and a real estate office, and he labored as an office cleaner, a window washer, and a taxi driver. He also became a drama teacher for a year at the Marlboro College (1970-1971) and, after working at more odd jobs, returned to Goddard College as artist-in-residence (1971-1973). While at Goddard, he formed a group of actors that soon moved to Chicago as the St. Nicholas Theatre Company, for which he served as artistic director. Soon, Mamet's plays became regular fare within the burgeoning theater world in Chicago. Such small but influential theaters as the Body Politic, the Organic Theatre, and then the more established Goodman Theatre presented *Sexual Perversity in Chicago* and *American Buffalo*. In 1974, Mamet became a faculty member on the Illinois Arts Council and a year later a visiting lecturer at the University of Chicago. In 1976-1977, he became a teaching fellow at the Yale School of Drama.

Thus, the mid-1970's were pivotal years for the playwright. In 1975, *American Buffalo* opened at the Goodman Theatre and soon moved to the St. Nicholas Theatre; the play won a Joseph Jefferson Award for Outstanding Production, as did *Sexual Perversity in Chicago* that same year. Moreover, Mamet in 1975 finally saw his work staged in New York City: *Sexual Perversity* and *Duck Variations* opened at the St. Clement's Theatre and, in 1976, moved to the Off-Broadway Cherry Lane Theatre. In 1976, *American Buffalo* opened at the St. Clement's Theatre and Mamet won an Obie Award for *Sexual Perversity in Chicago* and *American Buffalo*. No fewer than nine Mamet plays appeared in 1977 in theaters in New Haven, New York, Chicago, and, among other cities, London. *American Buffalo*, for which Mamet received the New York Drama Critics Circle Award, premiered on Broadway in 1977, starring Robert Duvall. In 1980, Al Pacino starred in a revival of *American Buffalo* in New Haven. Such successes confirmed Mamet's reputation as a new and vital theatrical voice in the United States.

Mamet has written more than thirty plays, a number of sketches, poetry, essays, children's plays, several important Chekhov adaptations, a book concerning film directing, and more than a dozen screenplays. He has also garnered many awards, including a Pulitzer Prize for *Glengarry Glen Ross* in 1986. Mamet in the 1990's has been honored for his brilliant use of language and characterizations that capture important aspects of American cultural poetics. His play *Oleanna*, which opened at the Orpheum Theatre in New York City in October, 1992, and featured William H. Macy and Mamet's wife, British-born Rebecca Pidgeon, has only added to the dramatist's reputation for staging serious plays about serious matters.

ANALYSIS

David Mamet is an ethicist. From his initial plays—*Camel, Lakeboat*—to those pivotal works that first brought him notoriety—*Sexual Perversity in Chicago, American Buffalo*—and from *Glengarry Glen Ross* to *Oleanna*, Mamet explores a delicate moral balance between private self-interests and larger public issues that shape modern culture. Indeed, Mamet is at his best when critiquing the tensions between his heroes' sense of public responsibility and their definition of private liberties. Throughout his theater, Mamet presents a dialectic that, on the one hand, recognizes the individual's right to pursue vigorously entrepreneurial interests, but that, on the other, acknowledges that in an ideal world, such private interests should, but do not, exist in equipoise with a civic sense and moral duty. This underlying tension produces in Mamet's protagonists divided loyalties. Such tension also gives his theater its particular unity of vision and ambivalent intensity. Mamet has often mentioned that his views of the social contract have been greatly influenced by Thorstein Veblen's *The Theory of the Leisure Class* (1899), and such indebtedness in part accounts for Mamet's preoccupation with business as a sacramental world. Veblen's work, like Mamet's, underscores human action and response in terms of "pecuniary emulation," imperialist ownership, primitive sexual roles as first seen in ancient tribal communities, questions of honor, invidious comparisons, and the relationship between self-worth and wealth. Mamet is a theatrician of the ethical precisely because his characters, plots, and themes map out a predatory world in which only the fittest, and surely the greediest, might survive. Hence, Mamet's plays all are concerned with charting the moral relationship between the public issues of the nation and the private anxieties of its citizens.

Mamet seems at his best when dramatizing the way in which public issues, usually in the form of business transactions, permeate the individual's private sensibilities. "Business," for Mamet, becomes an expansive concept, including not only one's public, professional vocation but also one's private, personal existence—the problematic "business" of living itself. Under the guise of healthy competition and the right to pursue a contemporary version of the myth of the American Dream, Mamet's heroes too often conveniently twist such business savvy to suit their own selfish needs. Further, this examination of "business" suggests, for Mamet, that people live in a Macbethean world, where "fair is foul and foul is fair," where sharp business practice too often leads to corruption, where deception and stealing are simply regarded as being competitive within the American business world.

Mamet believes in the powers of the imagination and art to liberate, to create a liberal humanism. This is exactly what John in *A Life in the Theatre* and Karen in *Speed-the-Plow* believe. Such an attitude, however, clearly does not make sense, Mamet also implies throughout his theater, because there is little or no place for such romantic impulses in a hurly-burly business world. What makes Mamet's heroes so theatrically engaging to watch concerns an invisible inner drama, a subtextual crisis that haunts them: Underneath the character's hard-boiled, enameled public bravado lies a figure plagued with self-doubt and insecurities. If Mamet's heroes try to come to some higher consciousness, as do Don in *American Buffalo*, Aaronow in *Glengarry Glen Ross*, and Karen in *Speed-the-Plow*, such valiant impulses to come to awareness are not ultimately to be realized. Many of Mamet's best characters—Bernie in *Sexual Perversity in Chicago* or Teach in *American Buffalo*—simply seem unwilling or unable to understand what

Mamet believes are the regenerative powers implicit in self-awareness and self-responsibility. Some of his characters—most of the men in *Lakeboat*, for example—do not seem to understand that any form of transcendent consciousness even exists as a possibility. Perhaps this explains why many Mamet heroes lack the capacity to celebrate any experience external to the self. Instead, typical Mamet heroes seem motivated only in sexual and financial terms, blinding themselves to the larger personal or societal implications of their exploits. To be sure, some Mamet characters exude a deeper awareness, as do the Father and Daughter in *Dark Pony*, Aaronow in *Glengarry Glen Ross*, or Karen in *Speed-the-Plow*. Others, moreover, come tantalizingly close to understanding their own essential self and the reason for their existence in a world of diminished possibilities; Lang in *The Water Engine* and Edmond in *Edmond* possess some degree of self-awareness, ineffectual as such awareness turns out to be for them.

Mamet's works, however, show a grimly deterministic theater in which his heroes are victims. Their victimization stems from outer forces—a ruthless business associate, an opportunistic executive, a petty thief—as well as from inner forces: the failure of self-reliance, the exaggerated claim that proves false, and characters' obsession with money that they will never see and with relationships that will never be fulfilling. Thus, throughout his career, Mamet investigates the relatedness of one's job, sense of fulfillment, and morality. The problem facing his characters, however, is that they struggle (and usually fail) to take responsibility, choosing instead to avoid honest communication or anything that might lead to an authentic encounter. Instead, Mamet's heroes often commit ethically perverse deeds that only further contribute to their own marginalization. In their efforts not to confuse public and private issues, Mamet's characters ironically distort the social contract to such an extent that humane values, communication, and love are reduced to barely felt forces.

Mamet's theater, in sum, repeatedly returns to broader social questions about communication and community. To be sure, not every Mamet drama includes verbal tirades and physical if not psychological violence. *Duck Variations, A Life in the Theatre, Reunion, The Woods,* and *The Shawl*—to cite plays spanning much of Mamet's career—appear as relatively quiet, meditative works whose plots and themes seem more interiorized. On the other hand, the playwright seems most comfortable, and at the height of his aesthetic power, when he replicates anger and betrayal, mystery and assault, and when he deepens social satire into private loss. From *Sexual Perversity in Chicago* through at least *Speed-the-Plow,* relationships are as ephemeral as they are unsatisfying, and a brutalizing language seems to be an attempt by his heroes to mask, unsuccessfully, their primal insecurities. There are no villains in his theater—only individuals whose world of diminished possibilities and banalities defines and confines them. The detectable optimism found throughout much of *Writing in Restaurants,* a collection of essays that Mamet published in 1986 concerning his theory of art, seldom manifests itself in his theater. In a Mamet play, "things change" (to use the title of a Mamet screenplay), or perhaps things do not change, his characters remaining ossified spirits, divided against the self and the other, against home and their outer world. Mamet *is* a theatrician of the ethical. His characters, sets, and overall situations, however, map out a predatory world in which genuine communication and authentic love remain distant forces. Hence, Barker's lines in *The Water Engine* ratify, Mamet suggests, the gulf between idea and reality: "And now we leave the Hall of Science, the hub of our Century of Progress Exposition. Science, yes, the greatest force for Good and Evil we possess. The Concrete Poetry of Humankind. Our thoughts, our dreams, our aspirations rendered into practical and useful forms. Our science is our self." Such practicality, for Mamet, prefigures a kind of spiritual death on both a cultural and an individual level.

Mamet's following observation from *Writing in Restaurants* is hardly surprising: "As the Stoics said, either gods exist or they do not exist. If they exist, then, no doubt, things are unfolding as they should; if they do *not* exist, then why should we be reluctant to depart a world in which there are no gods?" This comment stands as the metaphysical question Mamet

raises, and refuses to resolve, in his theater. The resolutions, whatever they may be, are left for the audience to ponder.

DUCK VARIATIONS

Three early Mamet plays prefigure the issues discussed above. *Duck Variations* concerns Emil Varec and George S. Aronovitz, two men in their sixties sitting on a park bench, whose reflections and constant duologues reveal their attempt to come to terms with their own insignificance in the world. Built on numerous episodes, the play shows that the two men come too close to talking about their own finiteness, and so both replace honest conversation with banal talk, their way of avoiding their fear of death.

LAKEBOAT

In another early play, *Lakeboat,* Mamet presents life aboard the *T. Harrison,* a ship traveling through the Great Lakes. The men are leading death-in-life existences because their jobs have reduced their lives to deadening routines and habits. Built around fragments of conversation, the play presents ordinary men—Joe, Fred, and Fireman—leading desperate lives. To fill the void, they engage in endless talks that lead to no epiphany; like the ship, they simply sail through their lives.

SEXUAL PERVERSITY IN CHICAGO

Sexual Perversity in Chicago presents thirty-four scenes dealing with sex. The play opens in a singles' bar, where Bernard tells his friend Danny, in graphic detail, about his recent sexual encounter with a woman. Their conversations are carnivalesque dialogues filled with obscenities and dirty jokes. Deb and Joan, the central females in the drama, seem little better off, as Bernard's sexist remarks are matched by Joan's hostile response to Danny. Clearly in this play, Mamet outlines a world in which eros has been defleshed and a fundamental and anxiety-producing loneliness dominates. Near the end of the play, Danny and Bernard stare at women on the beach, and when one does not respond to Danny's coarse remarks, he screams obscenities, which outline the intensity of his frustration and his inability to deal with loss. Sexual encounters, devoid of any genuine love, account for the title and theme of this important work.

AMERICAN BUFFALO

These three earlier plays stand as examples of Mamet's interest in portraying people whose lives have almost been reduced to nothingness, a motif that he continues to refine in *American Buffalo, Glengarry Glen Ross, Speed-the-Plow*, and *Oleanna*, plays that most theatergoers and critics believe represent his best work.

American Buffalo concerns small-time thieves who find a buffalo nickel in Don's junk shop (where the play unwinds), motivating them to rob the man from whom Don supposedly purchased the coin. Don orchestrates the robbery plans, which the younger Bob, who eats sugar, soda, and drugs, will try to accomplish. Teach, a nervous man with a swagger, insists that he, a man, do the job; Teach cannot believe that Don would let Bob, a boy, try such a robbery. A long honor-among-thieves conversation ensues, in which Teach's lines brilliantly reflect Mamet's vision, a vision suggesting the extent to which ethics have been devalued and stealing has been elevated to the status of good business savvy. Free enterprise, Teach lectures Don, gives one the freedom "[t]o embark on Any . . . Course that he sees fit. . . . In order to secure his honest chance to make a profit." He quickly adds that this does not make him "a Commie" and that the "country's *founded* on this, Don. You know this." The robbery never takes place, but near midnight, Bob returns with another buffalo nickel. Don seems embarrassed, and Teach becomes agitated, hitting the boy several times. Bob reveals that he bought the coveted nickel, made up the story about a rich coin collector, and suggested the burglary. Suddenly, whatever friendships exist among the men temporarily evaporate: Teach attacks Bob and trashes the entire junk shop. A precarious friendship, however, still remains. The play ends when Teach regains his composure and readies himself to take the injured Bob to the hospital; Bob and Don exchange apologies, and the curtain falls. If the characters do not realize how much they have buffaloed one another, the audience certainly does.

GLENGARRY GLEN ROSS

Glengarry Glen Ross extends Mamet's preoccupation with business as a sacramental world. The play dramatizes the high-pressure real estate profession as seen through the plight of small-time salesmen. Greed lies at the center of the play, for the characters' directing force in life is to secure sales leads, to close deals with clients, and to rise to the top of the board, the chart announcing which man in the sales force wins the ultimate prize—the Cadillac. The losers will simply be fired. *Glengarry Glen Ross*, like *The Water Engine, Mr. Happiness*, and *American Buffalo*, relies on the myth of the American Dream as its ideological backdrop. The title refers to Florida swamps, not the Scottish Highlands, which indicates just how much the playwright wishes to make experience ironic in this drama. Whereas the characters in *Lakeboat, Reunion*, and even *The Shawl* lead lives of quiet desperation, those in *Glengarry Glen Ross* scream out two hours of obscenity-laced dialogue. Levene may be the most desperate, for his business failures of late lead him to crime: Through a Pinteresque unfolding of events, viewers learn that he robs his own office to secure precious sales leads. Moss is the most ruthless, masterminding the robbery while Aaronow simply seems bewildered by his cohorts' cheating. Williamson is the office manager, whose lack of sales experience and pettiness earn him the scorn of all. Ricky Roma, however, is different.

Roma emerges as the star of the sales team. He also appears as the most complex. Youthful, handsome, Roma exudes a certain panache that sets him apart from the others. Whereas the others talk about their past conquests and how, with luck (and deception), they will rise to the top of the sales board, Roma produces. If Levene and Moss radiate a frenetic pursuit of customers, Roma appears soft edged. Roma, indeed, nearly succeeds in swindling an unsuspecting customer, James Lingk, who nearly gets locked into buying suspect real estate. Ironically, Williamson reveals to Lingk the truth, and Roma loses his prized commission when Lingk cancels the deal. When Roma hears this, he screams obscenities at Williamson and adds: "You just cost me *six thousand dollars. (Pause.)* Six thousand dollars. And one Cadillac." More than losing a sale, Roma loses what ethical perspective, if any, he possesses. Roma, of course, cannot comprehend this. Like Levene and

Moss, Roma has no conscience, no sense of the boundaries of business ethics. Like the characters throughout Mamet's theater, Roma and his colleagues distort language and action to justify their work. The play ends with Levene's arrest; Mamet suggests that, after Levene's and perhaps Moss's arrests, life will go on, business as usual.

SPEED-THE-PLOW

Speed-the-Plow extends Mamet's business plays. Set in Hollywood, the play centers on Bobby Gould, the recently promoted head of production for a Hollywood film company, and Charlie Fox, a friend who shows him a "buddy prison" film script. They sense a hit because of a macho star who will fill the lead role. In a dialogue that by now is regarded as vintage Mamet, the two celebrate their future fame and money (that surely will be certified by casting the macho star in the film) through a litany of obscenities. The plot thickens when they have to read a serious novel for cinematic possibilities and when a temporary secretary, Karen, enters and Charlie bets five hundred dollars to see if Bobby can seduce her. Karen, however, preaches the truth to Bobby ("Is it a good film?" she asks), who decides to replace the "buddy prison" script with a film based on a novel on radiation. An outraged Charlie verbally and physically assaults Bobby when he hears this and rages at Karen. After Karen says that she would not have gone to bed with Bobby, Charlie throws Karen out, and he and Bobby become friends again and produce the banal "buddy" film. A lack of trust animates this play, in which these Hollywood men are the spiritual kin of the men in *American Buffalo* and *Glengarry Glen Ross*.

OLEANNA

Oleanna, a play that in part concerns sexual harassment, represents the playwright's response to the Anita F. Hill-Clarence Thomas controversy. In act 1, a male college professor, John, and a female student, Carol, are in his office, she there because of difficulties in understanding his class. John, who is under tenure review, offers to help. The complacent professor, who is happily married and is negotiating a deal on a house, listens as she confesses, "I don't *understand*. I don't understand what any-

thing means . . . and I walk around. From morning til night: with this one thought in my head. I'm *stupid*." He offers Carol some advice and a consoling hand. While the audience senses an impending catastrophe, act 1 gives little hint at—depending on one's point of view—just how distorted the interpretation of the seemingly innocuous events of the first act will become.

The hurly-burly of act 2, however, makes for sparkling drama. Carol registers a complaint, accusing the professor of sexism, classism, and sexual harassment. He calls her back to the office in a failed attempt to clear up any misunderstandings. For John, she is dealing with "accusations"; for Carol, he has to face "facts." A campus support group helps Carol, and the play presents her growing sense of power and John's loss of control over events for which he may or may not be responsible. By the final scene, John loses more than the house and tenure. The college suspends him, and he may be facing charges of rape. Reduced to a groveling, pathetic figure, John appears in stark contrast to the suddenly articulate and holier-than-thou Carol.

In *Oleanna*, Mamet returns to a world in which the gaps between words and deeds remain. The play is theatrically powerful precisely because its author never fills in such gaps. Instead, theatergoers might ask: Is Carol framing John? Are her accusations legitimate? Is Carol simply the first to have the courage to challenge a patronizing and, perhaps, womanizing male teacher? Is John so much a part of an inherently misogynistic world that he seems blithely unaware that his well-meaning actions are in fact highly sexist? Mamet invites viewers to respond to these and many other questions (issues of censorship, political correctness, battles of the sexes, representations of women in theater, and so on). Thus, this 1992 play continues Mamet's exploration of a world that remains a battleground of the sexes, where primal feelings of trust and rational human discourse between women and men remain problematic at best—if not impossible. The title of the play, taken from a folk song, alludes to a nineteenth century escapist vision of utopia. *Oleanna* reminds the audience of the impossibility of such vision.

THE CRYPTOGRAM

Mamet's *The Cryptogram* concerns John, a ten-year-old boy who is afraid to fall asleep and who wonders where his father is. Donny, John's mother, expresses frustration throughout the play because she has often tried in vain to persuade John to go to sleep. On the first night in the play, John refuses to go to sleep, making the excuse that he is awaiting his father, who has promised to take him camping. Del, a friend of the family, who seems to be romantically linked with Donny, tries to calm John down and coax him to go to sleep, yet he also appears to be distracting the boy, trying to hide from him the fact that John's father has left the family for good. Del tells Donny and John about a camping trip he took with John's father the previous week, yet Donny discovers subsequently that the camping trip never took place and that the father was actually using Del's abode to commit adultery. Donny feels betrayed by Del, thus terminating any opportunity for Del to have a permanent romantic relationship with Donny, which had been possible with Donny's husband out of the picture. A month later, feeling guilty that he has betrayed both Donny and John, Del gives John one of the boy's father's most prized possessions—his German pilot's knife. John, as usual, refuses to go to bed and only agrees to do so if he can sleep with a stadium blanket, which he cannot obtain because it is already packed (Donny, upset by her husband's decision to leave her and by Del's betrayal, is moving). Del gives John the knife as a memento of his father and also to cut the twine so that he can open the box containing the blanket. John takes the knife and walks toward the box, talking about voices that he hears in his bad dreams, voices that keep calling him. Hearing John say that the voices are calling him, Del hands him the knife and says, "Take the knife and go." The play ends chillingly as the audience is left to ponder what exactly John will do with the knife.

The play is entitled *The Cryptogram* because John keeps asking about his father and trying to solve the mystery surrounding his disappearance. Del and Donny refuse to tell him where his father is (actually, they, themselves, do not know) or that his father has left his mother, ending the marriage and breaking up the family structure. In fact, the conversations between Del and Donny are so cryptic that the audience experiences great difficulty in discerning what event has happened. The audience discovers that Del and Donny, the only characters who know what has transpired, keep secrets even from each other. However, it is Mamet's deft use of language that leads to the suspenseful nature of the mystery. Although Mamet is a dramatist, his plays manifest that he is a poet. His plays are very much about language itself. In *The Cryptogram* as well as his other dramas, Mamet excels in his use of dialogue; he exhibits an excellent ear for dialogue, whether it involves the two adults in this play who strive to maintain their secret from John about his father's decision to leave the family, the working-class dialogue of Teach, Bob, and Don in *American Buffalo*, or the middle-class realtors in *Glengarry Glen Ross*. Mamet adeptly uses dialogue to portray realistic characters with realistic language. In *The Cryptogram*, when Del asks John what he means when he mentions, "I could not sleep," John is confused because he believes that his comment is self-explanatory. Del denies that it is, remarking, "It means nothing other than the meaning you choose to assign to it." Del's comment concerns the power and the use of language, but it also is meant to confuse John. The dialogue between Del and Donny is also telling. As in many of Mamet's plays, the characters know each other so well that they finish each other's sentences and interrupt each other, which leads to the confusion and the cryptic and suspenseful nature of the events. Language becomes a code. Mamet leaves it for the audience to figure out different strands in the play, such as the mystery of the torn blanket. The intensity builds in the last scene, which is evident by the increasing wrath of Donny as she attempts to convince John to go to sleep and by John leaving with the knife, hearing voices that beckon him as he is without his male protector, his missing father.

REUNION

Two other Mamet plays that merit discussion are *Reunion*, a play whose title might better read as "disunion," and *Edmond*. In *Reunion*, Bernie tells Carol that, although he comes from a broken home, he is "a happy man" who works at "a good job," but his uneasiness remains, particularly when one sees the contemporary world in which he and Carol live: "It's a . . . jungle out there. And you got to learn the rules because *nobody's* going to learn them for you." Thus, true knowledge about the soul and the universe can, in Mamet's world, only be purchased, as the almost poetic lines continue: "Always the price. Whatever it is. And you gotta know it and be prepared to pay it if you don't want it to pass you by." Out of such everyday as well as sensory experiences, Mamet implies throughout his canon, emerge no epiphanies. Rather, his characters merely internalize the messy inconclusiveness of their misspent lives, without the reassurances of some higher consciousness.

EDMOND

In *Edmond*, the title character is a racist, sexist, homophobic who leaves his "safe" marriage and embarks on an urban quest to find meaning to his fragmented world. Encountering violence, murder, sexual frustration, and so on, he winds up in jail, sodomized by his black cell mate. If Edmond learns anything from his quest, it is that he accepts his own plight as an acquiescent victim in the jail cell. He becomes the compliant partner with his cell mate.

OTHER MAJOR WORKS

LONG FICTION: *The Village*, 1994; *The Old Religion*, 1997; *Wilson: A Consideration of the Sources*, 2000.

POETRY: *The Hero Pony*, 1990; *The Chinaman*, 1999.

SCREENPLAYS: *The Postman Always Rings Twice*, 1981 (adaptation of James M. Cain's novel); *The Verdict*, 1982 (adaptation of Barry Reed's novel); *The Untouchables*, 1985; *House of Games*, 1987; *Things Change*, 1988; *We're No Angels*, 1989; *Homicide*, 1991; *Glengarry Glen Ross*, 1992 (adaptation of his play); *Hoffa*, 1992; *Oleanna*, 1994 (adaptation of his play); *Vanya on 42nd Street*, 1994; *American Buffalo*, 1996 (adaptation of his play); *The Edge*, 1997; *The Spanish Prisoner*, 1997; *Wag the Dog*, 1997 (with Hilary Henkin; adaptation of Larry Beinhart's novel *American Hero*); *The Winslow Boy*, 1999 (adaptation of Terrence Rattigan's play); *State and Main*, 2000; *The Heist*, 2001.

TELEPLAYS: *Five Television Plays*, 1990; *A Life in the Theatre*, 1993 (adaptation of his play).

RADIO PLAYS: *Prairie du Chien*, 1978; *Cross Patch*, 1985; *Goldberg Street*, 1985.

NONFICTION: *Writing in Restaurants*, 1986; *Some Freaks*, 1989; *On Directing Film*, 1991; *The Cabin: Reminiscence and Diversions*, 1992; *The Village*, 1994; *A Whore's Profession: Notes and Essays*, 1994; *Make-Believe Town: Essays and Remembrances*, 1996; *True and False: Heresy and Common Sense for the Actor*, 1997; *Three Uses of the Knife: On the Nature and Purpose of Drama*, 1998; *Jafsie and John Henry: Essays on Hollywood, Bad Boys, and Six Hours of Perfect Poker*, 1999; *On Acting*, 1999.

CHILDREN'S LITERATURE: *The Owl*, 1987; *Warm and Cold*, 1988 (with Donald Sultan); *Passover*, 1995; *The Duck and the Goat*, 1996; *Bar Mitzvah*, 1999 (with Sultan); *Henrietta*, 1999.

BIBLIOGRAPHY

Bigsby, C. W. E. *A Critical Introduction to Twentieth-Century American Drama: Beyond Broadway*. Vol. 3. Cambridge, England: Cambridge University Press, 1985. Bigsby devotes about forty pages to Mamet, whom he considers "a poet of loss." His analyses are as sensitive as they are challenging, and they are compulsory reading for anyone interested in Mamet. Includes a bibliography.

_____. *David Mamet*. London: Methuen, 1985. This first book-length study of Mamet is essential reading. Bigsby examines twelve plays and sees Mamet as "a moralist lamenting the collapse of public forum and private purpose, exposing a dessicated world in which the cadences of despair predominate." Contains a brief bibliography.

Carroll, Dennis. *David Mamet*. New York: St. Martin's Press, 1987. Carroll's discussions of Mamet's language are excellent, and he considers the plays in terms of business, sex, learning, and communion. This slender volume also contains a useful bibliography and chronology.

Dean, Anne. *David Mamet: Language as Dramatic Action*. Rutherford, N.J.: Fairleigh Dickinson University Press, 1990. In this perceptive study, Dean suggests that language describes, prescribes, defines, and confines Mamet's characters.

Hudgins, Christopher C., and Leslie Kane, eds. *Gender and Genre: Essays on David Mamet*. New York: Palgrave, 2001. This significant essay collection contains chapters on mothers in *American Buffalo* and *Speed-the-Plow*, gender and desire in *House of Games* and *Speed-the-Plow*, the women in *Edmond*, teaching in *Oleanna*, language and violence in *Oleanna*, and several other chapters. The book is very useful considering that the essays are very good and gender is a prevalent theme in Mamet's drama.

Kane, Leslie. *Weasels and Wisemen: Ethics and Ethnicity in the Work of David Mamet*. New York: Palgrave, 1999. This book, by a major authority on Mamet, covers issues such as morality and vice, as well as the influence of Jewish culture in his drama. Kane's book analyzes the theme of power in Mamet's drama, such as the relationship between power and ethics in his plays.

_____, ed. *David Mamet: A Casebook*. New York: Garland, 1992. The volume contains Kane's introduction, her two interviews, and her bibliography in addition to twelve essays by Ruby Cohn, Dennis Carroll, Steven H. Gale, Deborah R. Geis, Ann C. Hall, Christopher C. Hudgins, Michael Hinden, Pascale Hubert-Leiber, Matthew C. Roudané, Henry I. Schvey, and Hersh Zeifman. Contains a detailed annotated bibliography, an excellent chronology, and a thorough index.

_____. *David Mamet in Conversation*. Ann Arbor: University of Michigan Press, 2001. This book consists of interviews that Mamet has given, including some that have never appeared before in print. In these interviews, Mamet discusses his plays and films, as well as various themes such as sex, theatre, and dialogue. The interviews with Jim Lehrer and Charlie Rose are among the best in the book.

_____. *David Mamet's "Glengarry Glen Ross"*: Text and Performance. New York: Garland, 1996. This essay collection is essential for scholars and students who study this play. The essays concern the play as a detective story, the film version, anxiety, money, nostalgia, Levene's daughter, identity, and morality (this chapter also covers *Edmond*), and other themes. The book concludes with a very useful bibliography.

Matthew C. Roudané,
updated by Eric Sterling

GÓMEZ MANRIQUE

Born: Amusco, Tierra de Campos, Spain; c. 1412
Died: Toledo, Spain; c. 1490

PRINCIPAL DRAMA

Momos al nacimiento de un sobrino suyo, wr. c. 1440

Momos de doña Isabel para su hermano don Alfonso, pr. 1467

Lamentaciones hechas para la Semana Santa, wr. 1467-1481

Representación del nacimiento de Nuestro Señor, wr. 1467-1481

OTHER LITERARY FORMS

During his lifetime, Gómez Manrique was known simply as a poet, the word "dramatist" having little or no relevance in fifteenth century Spain. His *cancionero* consists of 108 compositions conserved in manuscript form through the efforts of his good friend, Don Rodrigo Pimental, the count of Benavente. In addition to the courtly love poetry typical of his generation, his most famous works are moral treatises and elegies clearly within the tradition of Juan de Mena and Iñigo Lopez de Mendoza, marqués de Santillana. In fact, the great Spanish critic Marcelino Menéndez y Pelayo was of the opinion that Manrique was the third best poet of his time after Santillana and Mena.

His best work is undoubtedly *Coplas para el Señor Diego Arias de Ávila*. Dedicated to one of the favorites of Henry IV of Spain, it is both an elegy and an impassioned plea for the judicious and moderate use of power by one who had been injured by its abuse. In its lyricism and careful elaboration of the *Ubi Sunt* theme, it is clear that it served as a model for its more famous counterpart, *Las coplas que fizo para la muerte de su padre*, written by his nephew and admirer, Jorge Manrique.

ACHIEVEMENTS

To Gómez Manrique belongs the honor of being the first known dramatist in the Spanish language. There has been much speculation about the origins of the Spanish theater, but aside from a few Latin religious plays and a fragment of the *Auto de los reyes magos* of the twelfth century, little or nothing is known about the early Spanish theater until Manrique's *Representación del nacimiento de Nuestro Señor*. Much has been surmised, however, from the scanty evidence, and *Representación del nacimiento de Nuestro Señor* has become one of the focal points in a growing controversy. Many critics have pointed to it as evidence for the existence of at least a flourishing religious medieval theater. In this theory, Manrique's work is only the last link in a chain, most of whose other links have unfortunately been lost. Others such as A. D. Deyermond deny such a relationship and insist that *Representación del nacimiento de Nuestro Señor* must stand alone and cannot be attached so arbitrarily to any dramatic tradition. Nevertheless, one fact remains unchallenged. *Representación del nacimiento de Nuestro Señor* is a real play and was designed for a real audience and was almost certainly performed.

As more facts concerning the daily life of early Renaissance Spain have come to light, attention has shifted to Manrique's other religious work, *Lamentaciones hechas para la Semana Santa*. Given the static nature of *Lamentaciones hechas para la Semana Santa*, scholars always had assumed that it was never intended for performance, but now some evidence seems to indicate that brief religious dramatic works were performed as part of the ceremonial processions of Holy Week, much like the much more elaborate *autos sacramentales* of the following decades. Manrique, *corregidor* of Toledo and in charge of all civic demonstrations in a city famous for its religious spectacles, could have written *Lamentaciones hechas para la Semana Santa* essentially for its performance through the streets and plazas of Toledo on Good Friday.

BIOGRAPHY

Little is known of the life of Gómez Manrique; even the year of his birth is uncertain. His family was a prominent one: The Manriques were proud of the fact that they were men of both "armas y letras," and the artistic endeavors of the Manrique family itself constitute a brief summary of the literary life of late medieval and early Renaissance Spain.

Manrique's uncle and mentor Iñigo López de Mendoza, marqués de Santillana, following a family tradition, was famous for his *serranillas* as well as his didactic and allegorical *decires*. Always an innovator, he prematurely tried to introduce the Italian sonnet into Spain and can be considered the first Spanish literary critic. His *Carta* to Dom Pedro (1449) essentially deals with the nature of poetry but also gives a critical overview of European and Spanish poetry. His nephew Jorge Manrique, for whom Gómez himself served as teacher and role model, immortalized his father, Rodrigo Manrique, the *maestre* of Santiago, and himself in the aforementioned *Las coplas que fizo para la muerte de su padre*. Gómez Manrique, in addition to writing poetry and drama, was one of the foremost orators of his day, an art that he freely and openly used to further the political ends of his family. If in the twentieth century, the name Manrique calls to mind literary associations, in the fifteenth, it meant only one thing—power. The Manriques were the most powerful warlords of their time. With their participation, kings and queens were made and broken. In a distinct departure from the prevailing practice of the century, however, they were also known for their honor, and they were men of their word. Gómez himself was often called on to act as witness or arbitrator in important legal and political decisions.

Although much about the life of Gómez Manrique remains uncertain, the chronicles of his time are full of his exploits, which have the flavor of a chivalric novel. Deploring the inept rule of John II, he became the sworn enemy of Don Álvaro de Luna, the king's favorite, whom he fought and eventually helped depose. Later he turned against Henry IV, John's son, and allied his family to the cause of the young prince Don Alfonso and eventually to that of his sister, the infanta Isabel. In fact, his one dramatic work of which the exact date of performance is known, the *Momos de doña Isabel para su hermano don Alfonso*, was written at the request of the princess to honor her younger brother Alfonso on the occasion of his fourteenth birthday. It is a bittersweet little work whose exuberance is marred by the fact that the young boy would never live to celebrate another birthday. Later, Manrique would also be the man chosen to stage and direct another "political" drama; the escorting and protecting of the disguised Ferdinand of Aragon on his journey to Castile to marry Isabel against the wishes of her brother, the king. Henry, enraged by the marriage, declared his daughter Juana as his legitimate heir and Isabel to be the usurper, and again there was civil war.

During this war, Manrique, acting as knight-champion of Castile, was chosen by Ferdinand to challenge the king of Portugal to combat in the name of all Spain when the latter refused to acknowledge Isabel's right to the throne. Also, Manrique, as the military governor of Toledo, saved that pivotal city for Isabel not only by his military prowess but also by the force of his powerful oratory. Realizing that because of the disaffection of the nobility and the archbishop, the city was in great danger of being lost, Manrique, standing alone in the great square, pleaded with his fellow citizens to remember their oaths and their duty to the city they loved. He carried the day and later used his experiences in Toledo to write one of his more important poems, traditionally called *Coplas de mal qobierno de Toledo*, but whose true title is *Exclamación y querella de la gobernación*.

Manrique died in Toledo around 1490. He had lived through and participated in most of the important events of his time. He continued to deprecate his literary endeavors, telling friends that although he had learned the art of warfare from his brother, Don Rodrigo, he had never had any formal literary training and considered himself only a scribbler. It was only the pressure of his friends that forced him to duplicate his manuscripts, although what has been lost and what saved will never be known.

ANALYSIS

Although Gómez Manrique is the first known Spanish dramatist, he does not have the distinction of being the "father" of Spanish theater. That honor belongs to Juan del Encina. Manrique brought the theater one step closer to its glory of the Golden Age, however, and his contributions to Spanish literature were not only important but also beautiful.

MOMOS AL NACIMIENTO DE UN SOBRINO SUYO

Manrique owes his fame as the first-known Spanish dramatist to four brief works with dramatic possibilities. Of the four, the least known is the *Momos al nacimiento de un sobrino suyo*. The *momos*, or mumming, was a very popular entertainment in the palaces and great houses of the fifteenth century. It was a mixture of dancing, singing, poetic recitation, and gift giving, whose only requirement was that the mummers had to be disguised.

One type of *momos*, generally associated with a baptism or a birthday, was the *hados* in which the person honored was endowed with great gifts by various supernatural, allegorical, or mythological beings. In *Momos al nacimiento de un sobrino suyo*, the mummers grant to Manrique's nephew the virtues they are dressed to represent: justice, prudence, temperance, fortitude, faith, hope, and charity.

MOMOS DE DOÑA ISABEL PARA SU HERMANO DON ALFONSO

If the least is known about *Momos al nacimiento de un sobrino suyo*, the most is known about the *Momos de doña Isabel para su hermano don Alfonso*, because Isabel, the young instigator of the work, was later to become the great queen of Spain, and Don Alfonso, her brother, was the boy who had been proclaimed king in a rebellion directed in great part by the Manriques only two years before. It is definitely known that the work was performed in 1467, and the names of mummers are known. Even the time of its performance, in the evening, after supper, is recorded in the Castilian court annals. The *Momos de doña Isabel para su hermano don Alfonso* opens with Isabel, covered with tufts of fur, giving a rather flowery discourse on the reason for the disguise. She informs the prince that she and her eight sister "muses" have come by mysterious devices from their home in the sacred mountain of Helicon to offer him their greatest "hados." Her eight ladies-in-waiting, dressed copiously in feathers, now appear to musical accompaniment. They dance around the prince offering him his heart's desires. He will be a great warrior, he will be lucky in love, and finally, Isabel wishes him greatness not only in this life but also after death. The *Momos de doña Isabel para su hermano don Alfonso*, a happy prophecy for a lad from whom much is expected, from all accounts was a great success, but read today it has tragic undertones. The last words of the play that deal with death are prophetic irony. Within a few months, Alfonso would be dead. The "muses" were wrong. They could not see the future.

LAMENTACIONES HECHAS PARA LA SEMANA SANTA

Lamentaciones hechas para la Semana Santa is a completely lyric work. There is no real evidence, although there are suggestions, that it was ever performed. "Performed" in this case means chanted or sung, because there is no action in this work. It is simply a tragic *llanto*, a lament, a secular imitation of the *Planctus Mariae* with three characters, the Virgin Mary, Saint John, and Mary Magdalene, who never speaks. It is a moving and beautifully written work, whose repeated refrain, "¡Ay dolor!" echoes like a throbbing heartbeat. It demonstrates to great effect the poetic skill of Manrique, but it is not theater, at least not in the form in which it has come down.

REPRESENTACIÓN DEL NACIMIENTO DE NUESTRO SEÑOR

Representación del nacimiento de Nuestro Señor is theater. Manrique composed it at the request of his sister, who was the assistant mother superior at the monastery of Calabozanos, where it was almost certainly performed. *Representación del nacimiento de*

Nuestro Señor follows the story of Christ's birth according to the Gospel of Saint Luke with the addition of some very special touches. The play begins with a doubting and very confused Joseph unsure of what or whom to believe. Joseph was often depicted as a comic figure in medieval tradition, and an angel appears and derides him, denouncing him as "el más loco de los locos." The customary obligatory nativity scenes follow, the adoration of the child by its mother, the angel appearing to the shepherds, the shepherds coming to the stable to adore, but even in the midst of rejoicing, a warning note is sounded. Manrique wants his audience never to forget that the reason for this divine birth was a terrible mortal death. Joy is allied to sorrow in Mary's first speech, and no Magi bearing beautiful gifts appear. Instead, robed figures, symbolizing the scenes of Christ's Passion, present to the child the instruments of his death: the chalice, the rope with which he is tied to the pillar, the whips, the crown of thorns, the cross, and the nails and lance. The drama, a blend of liturgical tradition and *momos*, juxtaposes the concepts of life and death. The final scene returns to the joyous theme of birth with the nuns singing a beautiful lullaby to the Christ child. It is one of Manrique's most beautiful poetic songs, and a fitting ending to his most ambitious dramatic work.

OTHER MAJOR WORKS

POETRY: *Exclamación y querella de la gobernación: Regimiento de principes*, 1495; *Coplas para el Señor Diego Arias de Ávila: Cancionero*, 1885 (2 volumes).

NONFICTION: *Carta*, 1449.

BIBLIOGRAPHY

Deyermond, A. D. *The Middle Ages*. New York: Barnes and Noble, 1971. A study of the literary history of Spain during the period in which Manrique wrote.

Scholberg, Kenneth R. *Introducción a la poesía de Gómez Manrique*. Madison, Spain: Hispanic Seminary of Medieval Studies, 1984. This Spanish-language volume on Manrique's poetry sheds light on his dramatic works.

Charlene E. Suscavage

PATRICK MARBER

Born: London, England; September 19, 1964

PRINCIPAL DRAMA
Dealer's Choice, pr., pb. 1995
Closer, pr., pb. 1997
Howard Katz, pr., pb. 2001

OTHER LITERARY FORMS

Patrick Marber is known principally as a dramatist, but he has written extensively for British radio and television programs such as *On the Hour*, *After Miss Julie*, *The Day Today*, *Knowing Me Knowing You*, *Paul Calf Video Diary*, and *Pauline Calf Video Diary*. Marber has also written for periodicals such as the daily newspaper the *Observer*, for which he wrote opinion and editorial columns.

ACHIEVEMENTS

Patrick Marber's first play, *Dealer's Choice*, was first produced in the Cottesloe Auditorium of the Royal National Theatre in London in February of 1995. *Dealer's Choice* won the *Evening Standard* Theatre Award for Best Comedy and the Writer's Guild Award for Best West End Play. In May of 1997, Marber's second play, *Closer*, premiered at the Royal National Theatre. *Closer* won the *Evening Standard* Theatre Award for Best Comedy and the Critics' Circle Best Play Award. In 1997, *Closer* received the prestigious Laurence Olivier Award given out by the Society of West End Theatre for the best new play. In March of 1999, *Closer* premiered on Broadway in New York, where it won the New York Drama Critics Circle Award for Best Foreign Play. *Closer* was nominated for a Tony Award.

BIOGRAPHY

Patrick Marber attended Wadham College in Oxford, England, before beginning his career as a writer, dramatist, and actor for television and the theater. Marber's father was a financial analyst, but the young Marber knew early on that he wanted to be involved in comedy and acting, writing, and producing plays.

Marber had a stint as a stand-up comic doing shows in clubs, which provided him with material for some of his plays. In the past, he has admitted to a fondness for gambling, a theme that shows up in his plays. He worked for several years as a writer and performer for British radio, television serial programs, and made-for-television movies.

Marber has an extensive list of appearances as an actor in television serials and made-for-television movies. He appeared in the television series *Saturday Zoo* in 1993, as Peter O'Hanarha-Hanrahan, Jaques-Jaques Liverot, and Chapman Baxter in *The Day Today* in 1994, and in *Knowing Me Knowing You with Alan Partridge* in 1994. Marber also took roles as Christian de Neuvillette in *Cyrano de Bergerac* on the Bravo channel in 1985, as Niall in *Cadfael* on the Public Broadcast System in 1998, as Dr. Piper in "The Curator" episode of *Coogan's Run* in 1995, as Max Cone in the "Thieves Like Us" episode of *Boon* in 1995, and as Sergeant Sayers in *Mike and Angelo* in 1996. Marber appeared as Tom Stirling in the made-for-television movie *Dreams Lost, Dreams Found* on the Showtime channel in 1987. Marber's other television appearances include the role of Humphrey Devize in *The Lady's Not for Burning* in 1987, as the Dealer in *Private Prince* in 1993, as John Trevanion in *Poldark* in 1996, and as Hamish in the miniseries *Big Women* in 1998.

Marber also acted on the stage as a Mariner in the Royal Shakespeare Company Theatre's production of *The Tempest* in Stratford-upon-Avon in 1982. Marber had the role of Second Billy in *Shining Souls* at the Old Vic Theatre in London in 1997.

ANALYSIS

Patrick Marber's three plays are unique in style; he writes using few sustained monologues or lengthy speeches. The playwright does not like set dramatic speeches and prefers improvisation, wit, and zippy exchanges. In his plays, Marber portrays back-and-forth interactions and the give-and-take quickness of relationships among close groups of friends, lovers, family members, and business partners. He has a dark, comedic, and pessimistic view of human nature and relationships. The playwright's background as a stand-up comic and television writer and actor give a freshness and clarity to his plays. His plays come with explicit words and shocking frankness and are not appropriate for younger audiences because of their explicit sexual discussions and use of profanity. However, Marber's plays have touched a nerve in their accurate account of the lives of working-class young urbanites struggling to find meaning in the modern world.

DEALER'S CHOICE

In the preface to the published edition, Marber comments that he wrote the first draft of *Dealer's Choice* at night in one week of early January, 1994. At the time he wrote the play, Marber did not answer the telephone, and he left his apartment only to walk the dog or buy cigarettes, rarely speaking to anybody. Then, the playwright spent a year revising, rewriting, and re-creating the play with the assistance of other actors, stage managers, friends, and theater patrons. The play emerged from improvisational work Marber did with a group of actors at the National Theatre in London. The published version that appeared in 1995 was the seventh draft of the original play, and Marber planned to revise the play when it was produced again.

Dealer's Choice is a somber and bleak comedy about a father and son, compulsive gambling, relations among friends, business deals, deceit, and human trust. Poker is the metaphor for life that runs throughout the play. The six characters Mugsy, Sweeney, Stephen, Frankie, Carl, and Ash appear in a split set in Stephen's restaurant in London. On the stage, the characters' interaction is divided between a kitchen and the restaurant itself. Stephen owns the restaurant, Sweeney is the cook, and Mugsy and Frankie are the waiters. Carl is Stephen's happy-go-lucky son, and they have had a troubled relationship over the years.

The play takes place one Sunday evening and the following Monday morning. The joking and jesting friends discuss the art of card playing with the necessary wisecracking, bluffing, gamesmanship, and boasting that goes along with working-class men enjoying their pastimes. In many ways, the play is about male power relationships and how men attempt to recruit and deceive others, even their friends and family, to realize their dreams and win the game. These men have difficulty expressing emotions openly, so they hide behind the bravado and tense emotions of the poker game.

The friends have gathered every Sunday night for years for a ritual game in the basement beneath Stephen's restaurant. There is a special intensity and uneasiness to the card game on this particular night. The professional gambler Ash shows up to collect Carl's unpaid gambling debt of four thousand pounds that Ash lent to Carl for poker, roulette, and blackjack. Carl had asked his father Stephen for money so that he could start his own restaurant business, but Carl is too much of a compulsive gambler and a malcontent to actually run a restaurant. Stephen is unaware that Carl has incurred large debts, and he tries to talk Carl into continuing to work for him. The climax of the play takes place during the emotional power struggle between Stephen and his directionless son. Stephen tells Mugsy, "I have to tell you that I think my son is the last person in the world anybody should go into business with." Stephen has tried to counsel his son and make him part of the family business while Carl has tried to lead the life of a professional gambler. When Ash confronts Carl, he says he cannot pay the debt. Stephen loses his temper over his son's bad fortunes, but Ash offers to flip a coin to decide on the debt. Ash flips the coin and wins the money. Carl yells at his father for trying to protect him and living in the illusion of power with his little weekly poker game. As Carl leaves, he asks if the poker game will be at the same time next week. Nothing has changed except for the characters gaining some insight into the power relationships around them.

CLOSER

Marber's second play concerns the state of sexual relationships in late twentieth century London. The central issue of *Closer* is the difference between superficial lust and unconditional love between men and women. All the major characters experience a complex web of love, physical intimacy, desire, and betrayal. The play describes an emotional and sexual battleground and the disturbed and confused emotions that come out of being deceived. For mature audiences only, *Closer* holds nothing back with its detailed accounts of adulterous relations and computer chat room pornography. Marber's play confronts, shocks, and cajoles the audience into accepting the barren reality that modern "morality" has produced.

The four main characters are Dan, a newspaper reporter responsible for the obituary section; Alice, a professional adult entertainer; Anna, a photographer; and Larry, a physician who specializes in dermatology. Each character ends up betraying at least one other person because of lust. Dan meets Alice when he sees her sitting on a park bench with a wounded, bleeding leg. Alice has been hit by a taxicab. While waiting at the hospital with Dan, Alice inspects the contents of Dan's briefcase and notices that the crusts of his sandwich have been cut off. She asks him if his mother used to cut off his crusts, and she falls in love with Dan as she relates her own family history to him. Alice tells Dan about her career as a professional stripper who knows why men are drawn to exotic entertainment clubs. Dan leaves his girlfriend, Ruth, for Alice over the course of a year, and then Dan writes a novel about Alice's colorful past life. However, when Dan meets the photographer Anna, who has been hired to take a photo for the jacket of his book about Alice, he is instantly smitten by Anna and asks to see her again. Dan and Anna kiss each other and try to experience some emotional intimacy while Alice is traveling to the studio in order to meet Dan. Next, Alice overhears the emotion-laced conversation between Dan and Anna, and she confronts Anna, whom she accuses of trying to steal Dan away.

Frustrated by the turbulent emotions that he is feeling and torn between Alice and Anna, Dan pretends to be a woman in a pornographic computer chat room exchange. Using the skills that Alice has taught him, Dan meets Larry and convinces Larry to meet him in a public park. Larry thinks that he is about to meet a woman named "Anna." The real Anna, the photographer, coincidentally happens by the same park, and she meets Larry in place of Dan. While

married to Larry, Anna has an affair with Dan for almost a year before telling her husband. The chaos and attempts at normalcy do not work. The title of the play, *Closer*, becomes ironic as the audience realizes that modern people with superficial ties to each other do not have the ability to experience intimacy. Because she is unable to live with the truth, Alice commits suicide at the end of the play. The other characters discover that Alice had stolen her name and biography from a memorial to someone else. Alice could not get "closer" to anyone because she was living a lie.

HOWARD KATZ

Marber's third play continues with the dark, spare, and combative dialogue style of his earlier work. The main character, Howard Katz, is a Jewish entertainment executive who has recently turned fifty, an event that has signaled a major downturn in his life. The play centers on the psychological decline of the protagonist, whose mental torment and anguish spills over from his work to his family. This is more than a routine midlife crisis. Howard is detached, depressed, and unable to find meaning in his work. He denounces the shallow values of the entertainment world and his dislike for egotistical managers and untalented performers. Howard questions the value of the relationships that have defined his life. The eponymous hero falls deeper and deeper into a self-destructive downward spiral, seemingly unable to explain the object of his search. Howard's existential anguish is similar to Willy Loman's self-doubt in Arthur Miller's classic play *Death of a Salesman* (pr., pb. 1949).

The play is enacted inside Howard's head as he sits on a nondescript park bench contemplating suicide. The gloomy attraction of flirting with self-destruction is a theme right out of *Dealer's Choice* and *Closer*. This spare set of *Howard Katz* resembles Samuel Beckett's *En attendant Godot* (pb. 1952, pr. 1953; *Waiting for Godot*, 1954), a classic of the Theater of the Absurd. While reviewing the course of his life, Howard gets angry with his wife, father, mother, and brother, and he has flashback conversations with them. When Howard's wife explains that she is content with everything they have in their marriage and home, he backs away in disgust, unable to give voice to his numbness and anger. Howard begins to vent his frustration at everyone around him, putting his career at risk and alienating his friends and family. Howard's descent into the abyss of doubt and depression is a strange kind of search for faith that he resolves at the end of the play, finally saying that he wants to learn how to live. He does not commit suicide to rid himself of his internal demons. Howard Katz emerges from his deep depression in trying to reconstruct his life.

OTHER MAJOR WORK

TELEPLAY: *After Miss Julie*, pr. 1995, pb. 1996.

BIBLIOGRAPHY

Brustein, Robert. "Two Moral X-rays." *The New Republic* (June 28, 1999): 36. This critic submits that Marber's *Closer* is the most interesting new British play since Harold Pinter's first productions. *Closer* portrays the manipulation and shallowness of four characters attempting to find new meaning through switching partners and experimenting with new identities.

Iverne, James. "Closer to the Bone." *Time International* 157 (June 25, 2001): 64. Argues that Marber's new play, *Howard Katz*, should earn him a ranking as the most promising young British playwright to come along in many years. The new play has less humor and is a more direct, raw confrontation with the issues that define human struggle.

Kellaway, Kate. "Closer." *New Statesman* 127 (May 1, 1996): 51-52. Claims that Marber is an outstanding writer of dialogue like earlier playwright Harold Pinter, who introduced an original style when he slowed dialogue down, skimming fat from it. Pinter's characters were often inarticulate and repetitive, but in the silence between the lines there was a world. Marber speeds dialogue up and shows how this is a mirror of modern life.

Kroll, Jack. "Porn o' Plenty." *Newsweek* 133 (April 5, 1999): 70-71. This regular theater critic laments the fact that explicit language and sexual themes have found their way into mainstream theater productions on Broadway. In the critic's view, Marber's play *Closer* brought the most graphic dialogue ever heard on a Broadway stage to New York, although it is a darkly funny and a powerful statement about the lack of love to be found among modern intimates.

Jonathan L. Thorndike

DONALD MARGULIES

Born: Brooklyn, New York; September 2, 1954

PRINCIPAL DRAMA

Luna Park, pr. 1982, pb. 2001
Resting Place, pr. 1982
Gifted Children, pr. 1983
Found a Peanut, pr., pb. 1984
What's Wrong with This Picture?, pr. 1985, pb. 1988
Zimmer, pr. 1988
The Model Apartment, pr. 1988, pb. 1990
The Loman Family Picnic, pr., pb. 1989, (music by David Shire)

Pitching to the Star, pr. 1990, pb. 1993
Women in Motion, pr. 1991
Sight Unseen, pr. 1991, pb. 1992
Pitching to the Star and Other Short Plays, pb. 1993
July 7, 1994, pr. 1995, pb. 1997
Collected Stories: A Play, pr. 1996, pb. 1998
Broken Sleep: Three Plays, pr. 1997 (music by Michael-John La Chiusa)
Dinner with Friends, pr. 1998, pb. 2000
God of Vengeance, pr. 2000

OTHER LITERARY FORMS

Although Donald Margulies' reputation is based on his stage plays, he has also written for the following television series: *Divorced Kids' Blues* (1986), *Baby Boom* (1988), and *Once and Again* (1999). His adaptation of *Dinner with Friends* was produced in 2001 for Home Box Office (HBO). Two important nonfiction works are an autobiographical article in *The New York Times* (1992) and the transcript of his participation in a Dramatists Guild-sponsored panel discussion with fellow playwrights Wendy Wasserstein and Chris Durang on ethics and responsibilities in modern theater (1986).

ACHIEVEMENTS

Donald Margulies has experienced critical success and major honors in regional theater and Off-Broadway. His 1989 black comedy *The Loman Family Picnic* was a Drama Desk Award nominee and was selected as a best play in the Burns Mantle Theater Yearbook. His play about a Jewish American painter, *Sight Unseen*, was a huge breakthrough; for this play, Margulies received the Obie Award for Best New American Play and the Dramatists Guild/Hull-Warriner Award and was nominated for a Drama Desk Award and Pulitzer Prize. In 1996, Margulies' poignant play about the betrayal of a writer by her protégée, *Collected Stories*, won the Los Angeles Drama Critics Circle Award for Outstanding New Play and the Drama-Logue Award; it was also nominated for the Drama Desk and Dramatists Guild/Hull-Warriner Awards and Pulitzer Prize.

Margulies' most commercially successful play, *Dinner with Friends*, a bittersweet meditation on modern marriage, won the American Theater Critics Association's New Play Award, Dramatists Guild/Hull-Warriner Award, Lucille Lortel Award, Outer Critics Circle Award, and 2000 Pulitzer Prize in Drama.

Margulies was elected to the Dramatists Guild Council in 1993 and has received grants from Creative Artists Public Service, the New York Foundation for the Arts, the National Endowment for the Arts, and the John Simon Guggenheim Foundation. He received the 2000 Sidney Kingsley Award for Outstanding Achievement in the Theater.

BIOGRAPHY

The second son of Robert and Charlene Margulies, Donald Margulies was born on September 2, 1954, in Brooklyn (Coney Island), New York. His father was a wallpaper salesperson who unhappily worked long hours for forty years at the same company yet was always frightened of being fired. His mother was a positive, education-oriented woman who worked in various offices when her children were young.

An exception to Robert Margulies' often withdrawn nature was his love of Broadway musicals. He enjoyed listening to original-cast recordings during his rare free time, and when his son was nine, he took his family into Manhattan for a Broadway vacation. Although the young boy loved musical comedies, he felt privileged to enjoy Herb Gardner's *A Thousand Clowns*. This comedy introduced Donald Margulies to art as a representation of life, specifically the complex relationship between fathers and sons that would eventually inhabit his early work.

Another seminal work in Donald Margulies' intellectual evolution was Arthur Miller's *Death of a Salesman* (pr., pb. 1949), which he read at age eleven. Miller's deeply moving drama of a frightened father, mother, and two sons in Brooklyn resonated loudly with Margulies as a reflection of his own life. Other inspiring literary "fathers" were J. D. Salinger, who understood the youngster's adolescent angst and confusion, and Philip Roth, whose writings honestly taught Margulies about being a Jewish man.

Margulies got an odd bit of encouragement about his own writing abilities in 1972 when his school principal censored a short story the John Dewey High School senior had written, only to have the U.S. District Court rule in favor of young Margulies. Art was another great talent and interest for Margulies. He earned an art scholarship to the Pratt Institute, where he studied for eighteen months. He found that his favorite medium and the process of its creation—collage—was not unlike playwriting.

When Margulies transferred to the State University of New York at Purchase, the works of writer/collagist Kurt Schwitters, portrait artist Alberto

Giacometti, and mixed-media artist Robert Rauschenberg served as artistic influences. However, the theater still intrigued him. Theater critic and professor Julius Novick became his literary mentor, and Margulies discovered more literary "fathers" in novelist William Faulkner and dramatist Harold Pinter.

After graduating from college, Margulies supported himself briefly as a graphic designer. Concurrently, he worked with Jerry Stiller, Anne Meara, Jeffrey Sweet, and others in a writing group called the New York Writer's Bloc, from which Margulies derived great creative inspiration.

Pals (1978) was Margulies' first theatrical examination of his relationship with his father. In 1982, *Resting Place* (his only play written in free verse) and *Luna Park*, adapted from a short story by Delmore Schwartz (an author Margulies admired) were produced. In 1983, the Jewish Repertory Theatre produced his play *Gifted Children*, which grew from the Writer's Bloc experience.

While *Gifted Children* and the subsequent *Found a Peanut* were not critical successes, Margulies moved on with *What's Wrong with This Picture?*, in which he dealt with his relationship with his father after his mother's death in 1978. The play was produced Off-Broadway in 1985 and 1990 and on Broadway in 1994. Margulies continued with the black comedies *The Model Apartment* in 1988 and *The Loman Family Picnic* in 1989; between the two, he briefly wrote and produced a television series, *Baby Boom*. His 1990 one-act play, *Pitching to the Star*, is a savagely funny satire on Hollywood hypocrisy.

His first major critical success that broke in setting and theme from his earlier work, *Sight Unseen*, was an outgrowth of a 1988 autobiographical play called *Heartbreaker*, commissioned by South Coast Repertory. In 1994, the Mark Taper Forum in Los Angeles commissioned Margulies' one-act musical *Broken Sleep* (music by Michael-John La Chiusa), and *July 7, 1994* was commissioned by the Actors Theatre of Louisville. The two one-act plays premiered together at Louisville's 1995 Humana Festival of New American Plays. With a third play added, *Broken Sleep: Three Plays* opened at the Williamstown Theatre Festival in 1997.

Margulies has also enjoyed great success with *Collected Stories*, which was revived in 1998 starring famed actress and acting coach Uta Hagen, and the Pulitzer Prize-winning *Dinner with Friends*, which began at the 1998 Humana Festival followed by a successful Off-Broadway run. In 2000, Margulies reimagined Sholem Asch's controversial 1906 Yiddish play *God of Vengeance* (concerning the difficult relationship between parent and child) and reset the drama, moving it from eastern Europe to the lower east side of New York City. The play premiered at Seattle's A Contemporary Theatre.

Margulies, professor of playwriting at Yale University, married Lynn Street, a geriatrician, in 1987; in 1992, they had a son, Miles.

ANALYSIS

Like the contemporary playwrights he admires—Caryl Churchill, David Mamet, John Guare, Tom Stoppard, and Harold Pinter—Donald Margulies uses a wide variety of plot lines and imaginative, dramatic techniques with economy, insight, and an unerring ear for the rhythms of human speech. In writing his plays, Margulies takes snippets of human experience in many colors, sizes, shapes, and textures and places them like scraps of paper in a collage, adjacent to, over, under, and around each other, objectively, satirically, humorously, or ironically, sometimes to conceal, sometimes to reveal, and always to depict life and human behavior provocatively.

As a modern playwright, Margulies has his plays explore contemporary social issues such as divorce, art and commerce, alienation, betrayal, despair, and personal loss. As a Jewish American playwright, he also concerns his plays with the aftermath of the Holocaust, cultural assimilation, pressure for happy marriage and economic success, and characters who feel like outsiders. However, Margulies universalizes his characters' lies, hypocrisies, yearnings, and confusion so that they transcend ethnic stereotypes, and he is writing about all people.

Although his early plays deal mostly with the complicated relationship between parent and child, Margulies' body of work is most compelling because of his refusal to cheat audiences and readers by simplifying such enormously complex issues as the profound and contradictory dynamics of human motivation and interaction. Like classic playwright Anton Chekhov, Margulies touches the very essence of life and loss by boldly exploring shocking truths with humanism and humor.

THE LOMAN FAMILY PICNIC

With sharp echoes of Arthur Miller's *Death of a Salesman* and subtler ones of Eugene O'Neill's *Long Day's Journey into Night* (pr., pb. 1956), Sam Shepard's *True West* (pr. 1980), and John Cheever's short stories, *The Loman Family Picnic* is a scathing, surreal, somewhat autobiographical black comedy about a hopelessly dysfunctional and despairing middle-class Jewish family in 1960's Brooklyn.

Parallels with Miller's classic include desperately frustrated and unhappy Herbie, who is anxious to be appreciated at work, and his two lonely sons. The oldest, Stewie, is disgusted that the rabbi will not explain the meaning of the Scripture he must learn for his upcoming bar mitzvah, while the youngest, Mitchell, is exasperated that he receives citywide recognition for his artwork only to be ignored by his father. Another Miller parallel is a ghostly character that provokes a living one; the ghost of wife/mother Doris's eternally youthful twenty-three-year-old aunt (who killed herself) is an ironic contrast to Doris's frustration with aging.

Margulies' collagelike dramatic technique is original and startlingly ironic. Doris's private monologues chronicling her marital misery are juxtaposed with her public protestations of happiness. This dramatic contrast overlays Mitchell's writing of a musical comedy called *Willy!* (based on *Death of a Salesman*), in which he yearns for impossible family harmony at one picnic. Also, Mitchell's fantasy is superimposed over Herbie's furious choice of chocolate ice cream over low-calorie tuna.

Irony abounds as the family masks its real unhappiness by intermittently smiling mechanically at a series of flashbulbs in the bar mitzvah scene. To underscore Herbie and Doris's horrific sadness, the couple fantasizes about each other's deaths while three illusory resolutions before the chilling real end ironically return the audience to the couple's noncommunicating start.

Margulies' savagely funny and heartbreaking attack on dysfunctional families and their empty rituals; social pretensions and hypocrisies, and the illusion that marriage solves personal problems or cures loneliness transcends time, place, and ethnic stereotypes in honestly dealing with personal and familial loss.

SIGHT UNSEEN

In *Sight Unseen*, a memory play, Margulies uses forward and backward time sequencing and multilayered, psychological perspectives to create a kaleidoscopic work about loss of love and self, artistic and personal integrity, and ethnic identification.

Jewish American painter and spoiled media hound Jonathan Waxman paints now only for those who commission paintings "sight unseen." To resurrect his faded inspiration, Waxman visits his former lover (Patricia) and her archaeologist husband (Nick). The archaeological metaphor is apt because Waxman visits Patricia to find out what was there for him then as well as what is there now. His excavation of the past provides only opposite perceptions of a portrait of Patricia that Jonathan had painted long before. For her it is a symbol of their shared love and past; for him it is a moneymaker.

Waxman's shrinking from—then grabbing opportunistically for—his Jewish identity serves as a metaphor for his emotional dishonesty, the lies he tells himself to justify his self-defeating behaviors and choices. Margulies has written a cautionary tale, an indictment of the commerce of art and the cult of celebrity, twin infections that lead from the death of idealism and love to the selling and loss of self.

DINNER WITH FRIENDS

Like an earthquake's aftershocks, Margulies' Pulitzer Prize-winning *Dinner with Friends* sensitively and objectively explores the subtler, complex emotional tremors that fan out from the epicenter of divorce.

Couples Karen and Gabe and Beth and Tom are best friends. Food writers Karen and Gabe are stunned when, after a delicious dinner in their kitchen, Beth confesses that Tom is leaving her for another woman. As Beth and Tom end their marriage, Margulies takes the audience back to their awkward first meeting and ahead to their new lives and relationships. Feeling destabilized as a couple, Karen and Gabe are left to examine their comfortable (but stagnant?) marriage and their confused feelings about Tom and Beth. Without favoring any character's position, but with compassionate insight for each, Margulies elucidates the essential fragility of all the interdependent relationships that people mistakenly believe to be constant. *Dinner with Friends* is about the loss of comfortable certainty.

Because much of the play transpires around the preparation and consumption of a meal, Margulies uses the metaphor of food as nourishment to characterize the couples. Gabe and Karen enjoy food together and share it with friends. For Tom and Beth, talk of food deflects more serious subject matter, while for Karen and Gabe such talk facilitates communication.

Margulies extends the theme of infidelity so that it is not only Gabe and Karen, the couple, who feel betrayed by their friends' marital breakup, but individually Gabe fears that his friendship with Tom, and Karen fears that hers with Beth, have also been shams. The death of trust and its metamorphosis into self-doubt echo through the play. Is divorce freedom from suffocation or failure? Are responsibility and loyalty admirable or cowardly? Margulies gives no simplistic answers.

OTHER MAJOR WORKS

TELEPLAYS: *Dinner with Friends*, 2001 (adaptation of his play); *Collected Stories*, 2002 (adaptation of his play).

BIBLIOGRAPHY

Bossler, Gregory. "Donald Margulies." *The Dramatist* (July/August, 2000): 4-14. Bossler's sweeping interview covers Margulies' art background, his contributions to theater, and his work as a professor of playwriting.

Coen, Stephanie. "Donald Margulies." *American Theatre* (July/August, 1994): 46-47. This insightful interview focuses on the Jewish elements in Margulies' early works.

Durang, Christopher, Wendy Wasserstein, Donald Margulies, and Jeffrey Sweet. "Ethics and Responsibilities." *The Dramatists Guild Quarterly* (Summer, 1986): 15-23. Margulies makes valuable contributions to a discussion with other young playwrights about the responsibilities of artists regarding ethics in society.

Margulies, Donald. *Sight Unseen and Other Plays*. New York: Theatre Communications Group, 1996. In addition to *Found a Peanut*, *Sight Unseen*, *The Loman Family Picnic*, *What's Wrong with This Picture?*, and *The Model Apartment*, this edition contains Margulies' "Afterword," an invaluably insightful essay about his early life, originally published as "A Playwright's Search for the Spiritual Father," June 21, 1992, in *The New York Times*. Critic Michael Feingold's useful essay, "Donald Margulies, or What's an American Playwright?," is also included.

Schlueter, June. "Ways of Seeing in Donald Margulies' *Sight Unseen.*" *Studies in American Drama, 1945-Present* 8, no. 1 (1993): 3-11. Schlueter emphasizes perception of self and others as an important layer in this complex play.

Howard A. Kerner

MARIVAUX
Pierre Carlet

Born: Paris, France; February 4, 1688
Died: Paris, France; February 12, 1763

PRINCIPAL DRAMA

Le Père prudent et équitable: Ou, Crispin l'heureux fourbe, pr. c. 1709, pb. 1712

Arlequin poli par l'amour, pr. 1720, pb. 1723 (*Robin, Bachelor of Love*, 1968)

La Surprise de l'amour, pr. 1722, pb. 1723 (*The Agreeable Surprise*, 1766)

La Double Inconstance, pr. 1723, pb. 1724 (*Double Infidelity*, 1968)

Le Prince travesti: Ou, L'Illustre aventurier, pr. 1724, pb. 1727

L'Île des esclaves, pr., pb. 1725 (*Slave Island*, 1988)

Le Triomphe de Plutus, pr. 1728, pb. 1739 (*Money Makes the World Go Round*, 1968)

Le Jeu de l'amour et du hasard, pr., pb. 1730 (*The Game of Love and Chance*, 1907)

L'École des mères, pr., pb. 1732

L'Heureux stratagème, pr., pb. 1733 (*The Wiles of Love*, 1968)

Les Fausses Confidences, pr. 1737, pb. 1738 (*The False Confessions*, 1961)

L'Épreuve, pr., pb. 1740 (*The Test*, 1924)

La Femme fidèle, pb. 1746, pr. 1755

Théâtre complet, pb. 1878, revised pb. 2000

Théâtre de Marivaux, pb. 1929-1930, 1951

Seven Comedies, pb. 1968

OTHER LITERARY FORMS

Marivaux was, among other things, a journalist, specializing in articles on literary and moral questions. During two periods in his life (1717-1720 and 1751-1755), he collaborated on the *Nouveau Mercure*, a periodical that featured and reviewed the "Moderns." He founded several periodicals as well: *Le Spectateur français* (1722-1723, 1727, 1761), whose title was borrowed from Joseph Addison and Richard Steele's *Spectator; L'Indigent Philosophe* (1728); and *Le Cabinet du philosophe* (1734).

Another genre in which Marivaux achieved considerable success was the novel. Beginning in his youth with parodies of the "precious" novel, he developed an appreciable sense for realism and psychological and sociological truth in *La Vie de Marianne* (1731-1741; *The Life of Marianne*, 1736-1742) and *Le Paysan parvenu* (1734-1735; *The Fortunate Peasant*, 1735).

ACHIEVEMENTS

Marivaux's genius was most evident in his come-

dies. More than half of them were written for the Théâtre Italien, which had reopened in 1716, and were admirably interpreted by one of the Italian actresses, Gianetta Benozzi, called Silvia. During a period of about twenty-five years, Marivaux wrote some twenty-seven plays in prose, in one or three acts, frequently influenced by the Italians, whose freedom and fantasy coincided well with his own individualistic tendencies. Despite considerable variety in style, Marivaux excelled in comedies of love, with final analyses of that emotion developed in all its nuances and set in clever plots. His plays are salon comedies, *divertissements*, almost ballets, through which the secrets and surprises of the human heart are revealed in all their truth and poetry.

In these psychological comedies, the obstacle to love is neither exterior (as in Molière) nor insurmountable (as in Jean Racine). It always arises from a case of self-love, a bias, a disappointment, a misunderstanding; there is an appeal to reason, but reason does not govern love. Love must have its way, usually aided by a wily servant with well-intentioned ruses, and there is a happy ending, to be sure. In such a comedy, the lovers are amusing but never ridiculous, although the servants and some of their antics often are. The principal characters do not have a comic vice or flaw, as in Molière. What is humorous is the struggle in their hearts, which is always authentic, however artificially conceived.

Marivaux does not have the power of either Molière or Racine, but he is closer to the latter through his keen understanding of love, its subterfuges, its charms, and its irresistible appeal. Above all, he is a master of feminine psychology. He always knows exactly when to stop, however, to keep love from becoming tragic. Moreover, he includes many details that Racine merely suggests. Throughout his plays, Marivaux remains a witness to his characters' reactions, sometimes as an ironic spectator, sometimes as a sympathetic confidant.

Marivaux's fine analyses require a similar subtlety in language. His audience must be sensitive to the greatest refinement in terms and intonations, as are the characters themselves. Although their masters speak the language of the salons, the servants re-create *préciosité ridicule*. Yet the virtuosity in language known as *marivaudage* is never an affectation, for it is not merely a style. Marivaux's vivid imagination constantly creates new situations and perceives the most delicate reactions in his characters. He depicts them faithfully, not by ordinary, but by extraordinary means. It is the solidity of his content that sustains the fragility of his form.

BIOGRAPHY

Pierre Carlet de Chamblain de Marivaux was baptized in Paris, in the parish of Saint-Gervais, on February 8, 1688. The traditional date of his birth, February 4, is therefore probably correct. Some time between 1699 and 1702, his father, Nicolas Carlet, was made director of the Mint at Riom, the former administrative capital of Auvergne. The post brought with it a small apartment and a modest income. The father occupied this post until his death on April 14, 1719, and his widow requested and obtained a temporary authorization to continue in his place.

Little else is known of Marivaux's childhood, including his schooling, although he said later that he had a fair knowledge of Latin and none of Greek. He was in Paris in 1710, where on November 30 he registered in the Faculty of Law as Pierre de Carlet. From 1710 to 1713, there are traces of his career at the faculty, but finally they disappear. He did not become a brilliant law student. Marivaux must have had a strong sense of his true vocation, for he was already writing voluminously. His registrations in law were very likely camouflage for his family, which probably would not have approved of his career as a writer.

Marivaux's early works reveal him as full of ideas and projects, eager to experiment, yet still unsure of himself, his talent, his future role in the literary life of the day, or even of the name that he was to use. *Le Père prudent et équitable*, probably written in a week to win a bet and privately performed in Limoges, was signed M*** (Marivaux?). A young law student from Paris on holiday with a friend, Marivaux may not have cared to pose as a writer, but he must have taken satisfaction in following up his local success by having the play published.

Marivaux (Hulton Archive by Getty Images)

Marivaux's career was launched primarily with parodic and polemical novels directed against the partisans of the Ancients; he had become associated with Antoine Houdar de La Motte and Bernard le Bovier de Fontenelle, who were influential in favoring the Moderns. Although Marivaux's *Homère travesti: Ou, L'Illiade en vers burlesques* (1716) did not amount to much, it was reviewed at length in the *Nouveau Mercure* and the *Nouvelles littéraires*. Moreover, Marivaux was introduced in the salon of Mme Lambert, among others, where he was appreciated as a brilliant conversationalist. Like his contemporary Voltaire, the young bourgeois writer of genius now believed that he would never have to practice a safe but boring career in law.

A few months after the appearance of the *Homère travesti*, the notorious author of twenty-nine contracted a very respectable marriage with Colombe Bologne, aged thirty-four and possessed of a substantial dowry. Although he had known other young women, Marivaux's courtship of Colombe had been a long one, and their marriage was probably based on inclination as well as convenience.

There is some evidence that Marivaux began writing for the Théâtre Italien as early as 1717, with an edition of *The Agreeable Surprise*, approved for the censors by La Motte in that year but not staged until 1722, when Luigi Riccoboni's company produced it. The Italians began to use French plays only in 1718, and Marivaux made his début with them in 1720 with *L'Amour et la vérité*, coauthored by the chevalier Rustaing de Saint-Jorry. Most of the text of this unsuccessful play has been lost.

More serious was Marivaux's financial loss a few months later when the famous speculative enterprise of John Law collapsed. Exactly how much Marivaux and his wife lost or how they subsisted immediately thereafter is unknown. Legend has it that this event determined Marivaux to write for a living. This determination is unlikely, however, given not only Marivaux's temperament but also the fact that it was rare for an author to earn much from his work. In 1720, he had won a marked success at the Hôtel de Bourgogne with a distinctively Italian play, *Robin, Bachelor of Love*, proving that by himself he could write the kind of play that only Riccoboni's company could perform, and one that was worthy of their best efforts. This was a very critical time for the Italians, too, however, and in 1721 they closed the Hôtel de Bourgogne to set up at the Foire Saint-Laurent, engaging Alain-René Lesage and his collaborators in the hope of recouping their fortunes with a proven type of spectacle having wide popular appeal.

After trying his hand unsuccessfully at his first and only tragedy for the Théâtre Français, *Annibal* (1720), Marivaux revised *The Agreeable Surprise*, which was a great success as staged by the Italians in 1722. It was at this time that, with Marivaux's assistance in interpreting the text, Silvia went from *seconde* to *première amoureuse*, and that a lasting relationship was formed between author and actress. This work not only established the nature and style of the Marivaux comedy but also often served as the vehicle for testing candidates for promotion through the ranks of the company.

It is not difficult to explain the great affinity that Marivaux felt with the Italians. Not only was he in sympathy with the wide range of possibilities afforded by their stagecraft—some of which were already a part of the *théâtres de la foire*—but he also understood from the beginning the human qualities that informed their work. Their style depended essentially on teamwork—that is, on the profound sense of mutual respect between persons of proven talent who work together to create something new. The Italians had an exciting art form, centered on love interest, but, of equal importance, they practiced respect in the daily exercise of their profession and had a strong sense of personal and professional integrity. They lacked a repertoire, but Marivaux in large measure remedied this lack with plays that were French in content but Italian in structure and style.

While he was creating his brilliant comedies, Marivaux was engaged also in other writing, notably *Le Spectateur français*. He had planned to publish it every two weeks, but, much more of an artist than a journalist, Marivaux was at best able to produce a number only once a month. Some of his pieces illustrated the "natural" style of the journalist, for whom observation, a sense of actuality, ease in finding topics, and an interest in daily events were the most important qualities. Marivaux was excited by Addison and Steele's *Spectator*, for in many respects he shared their views on human conduct, but his "Spectator" was essentially an artist. More than half his collection consists of pieces to which observation contributed something, yet which are much more than spontaneous reflections of what chance put in his path. The least-interesting material today is a collection of carefully composed pieces worked up by Marivaux to move readers to share his indignation over various kinds of human behavior and to share his sympathy for their victims. The most interesting pieces are those in which, responding to personal criticism, the Spectator hotly defends his right to be himself. This important series deals largely with the relations of writer, critic, and public, and it reveals Marivaux to be very much a partisan of the Moderns.

For the period from 1725 to 1730, very little is known for certain concerning Marivaux. His "Italian period" had come to a close, and he made three attempts to establish himself at the Théâtre Français. The plays of this period, including those written for

Riccoboni's troupe, are less Italian in nature, and they are marked by a critical, philosophical character that makes them less interesting today. Marivaux continued to experiment with new ideas, and his work was not always readily accepted. Voltaire was a partisan of the Ancients in matters of art; he had no personal contact with Marivaux and not much contact with his work, it seems, but he could not refrain from commenting to others about his lack of naturalness and unconventional notions on form.

Marivaux's peak period seems to have been from 1730 to 1735. Although it is difficult to know when or in what stages he composed them, a number of major works were published during that time: *The Game of Love and Chance*, the whole of *The Fortunate Peasant*, the continuation of *The Life of Marianne*, and *Le Cabinet du philosophe*, in eleven numbers composed of a miscellany so varied as to have no unity or interest for his contemporaries, and to make one think that his finances were such that he felt compelled to publish anything and everything. As always, he examines every idea, new or old, from every perspective and with the utmost subtlety. After 1736, there was a gradual slackening in the tempo if not in the quality of Marivaux's production. *The False Confessions* was his last full-length play and, along with *The Game of Love and Chance*, constitutes Marivaux's chief glory today. This was not always the public's judgment, nor was it the author's judgment, and others of his works have enjoyed more constant popularity.

Marivaux was elected to the French Academy in 1743. The event seems to have marked a turning point in his life. His creative activity, already on the wane, declined sharply. He wrote no more for the Théâtre Italien. He started no new novels and left two of them unfinished. It has been conjectured that he experienced a religious conversion or merely one to respectability. Nevertheless, the works that he produced in his semiretirement, although minor, were far from negligible.

Marivaux was for the most part not taken seriously by his contemporaries. An author who did not practice the noble genres or a dramatist who was not regularly produced by the Théâtre Français was not to be taken seriously. With rare exceptions, neither the social nor the intellectual elite of his day appreciated Marivaux's originality or understood the significance of his work. A few clichés regarding him, coined early in his career, have continued to be applied. Like the Italians, like Silvia, of whom the public never tired, Marivaux was considered an entertainer both in public and in private. He was much appreciated for his personal qualities—his charm, his wit, his high standards of morality—but professionally he was misunderstood by almost everyone. Mme de Tencin decided that he should be a member of the Academy, and after ten years she succeeded in 1743 in having him elected. His acceptance speech was modest enough, for he knew the opinions of his new colleagues. The reception speech, delivered by Archbishop Languet de Gergy, a very slight talent, must have been more than usually frustrating and humiliating; it made passing reference to Marivaux's many works as popular, however impure in content and style, but made it clear that he had been elected primarily because he was such a good fellow. Nevertheless, Marivaux was a faithful academician, believing that the creative writer was the one best qualified to judge matters of language and literature. He was rarely absent except for reasons of health, which became an increasingly serious problem for him. In 1750, he was appointed chancellor of the Academy, and in 1759 its director.

Marivaux had lost his wife, for whom he grieved, and his daughter, Colombe Prospère, became a nun in 1746. His finances were always in a confused state, partly because of excessive generosity and partly because of mismanagement. He lived with and found consolation in the company of Mlle de Saint-Jean, but the exact nature of their relationship is unknown. He continued to write and, as noted above, although his later pieces are relatively brief and of minor importance, all are interesting because of their originality. He continued to see old friends and to frequent the fashionable salons. More and more, however, he seems professionally to have become a forgotten man. Marivaux's death on February 12, 1763, passed almost unnoticed in print. Several contemporary evaluations of his life's work give condescending praise for the qualities that were to make him great for posterity in the nineteenth and twentieth centuries and, as when he was alive, damn him for not adhering to classical literary conventions.

ANALYSIS

Although Marivaux sometimes repeated himself from one work to the next, he strove above all to be original. His highly personal art, composed almost entirely of nuances, served his observation of matters of great human value. The sometimes maligned *marivaudage* holds profound, universal significance. Marivaux's psychology is as refined as that of the *précieux*, but it is in no way based on conventions. Despite their fanciful framework, his comedies generally have a simple plot, with little that is improbable, and the portrayal of life is always true. Similarly, with the exception of some of the lower-class characters, Marivaux's expression is elegant without the excesses of *préciosité*. It is thus that his theater teaches truth, the inner truth of classicism. Marivaux was to be emulated by dramatists of comparable ambition, dramatists such as Alfred de Musset, Jean Giraudoux, and Jean Anouilh, original, modern, and yet in the classical French tradition.

SLAVE ISLAND

Slave Island is an early play that exhibits all of Marivaux's characteristic strengths. Following a shipwreck, two masters (Iphicrate and Euphrosine) and their slaves (Arlequin and Cléanthis) reach an island of former slaves, where they are forced to exchange roles. The slaves are emancipated and the masters are enslaved until each regains his former station by undergoing the prescribed treatment. Trivelin, the magistrate of this island republic, states the moral of the adventure: The difference in social positions is the way the gods test us.

This one-act "philosophical" play as produced by the Italians was the finest immediate success of Marivaux's life, especially coming as it did after a fiasco at the Théâtre Français. Despite the seriousness of his message, conveyed quite directly, Marivaux had not forgotten that he was a dramatist. The subject and theme are well integrated and were perfectly suited to the talents of the Italian actors, among

whom was Silvia, and the construction is careful, with a good progression and balance of emotions.

Although the idea of the play is Marivaux's, expressed also in *Le Spectateur français*, it continues the line of social criticism found in other works of the day, including those of Marivaux, generally pursued by the actor Thomassin in the character of Arlequin. At first jokingly, then quite seriously, the latter tells his master some plain truths. The same happens with their feminine counterparts, except that, realistically, the mistress clings more desperately to her class distinction, and her slave has a greater need for revenge. The masters must hear themselves described by their former slaves and confess that the highly critical portraits, excessively lengthy in the case of Euphrosine and Cléanthis, brief and to the point in that of Iphicrate and Arlequin, are accurate. Next the former slaves imitate the gallantry of their masters, but despite Cléanthis's skill, Arlequin prefers to take advantage of his new station to make love to Euphrosine and orders Iphicrate to woo the willing Cléanthis. Both former slaves play their parts to the limit, so much so that the sensitive and confused Euphrosine is on the verge of being truly hurt.

In the fast-paced conclusion, both former masters try emotional blackmail on their former slaves, with whom they have always lived in close association. There are varying results, but finally compassion triumphs, Iphicrate and Euphrosine are pardoned, and presumably everyone will behave differently in the future. The play's success was short-lived, however, for obviously it could not please either the extreme Right, the court, or the extreme Left, the militant philosophes. A modern reader who does not understand that Marivaux, neither a would-be revolutionary nor a socialist, was merely preaching fraternity or human solidarity, cannot be pleased by the play. *Slave Island* was one of his favorites because of its moral.

L'ÉCOLE DES MÈRES

The one-act play *L'École des mères* shows Marivaux in a different mode. Its premise is familiar comic material: The tyrannical Mme Argante is rearing her daughter, Angélique, with the utmost strictness and would like her to marry M. Damis. Angélique, however, loves Eraste, M. Damis's son, and she rebels. Love finally triumphs over the authority of a mother and the pretensions of a father who, unknowingly, is his son's rival.

This play reminds the viewer of several of Molière's works on a theme that had become commonplace, and of pieces more typical of the French stage than of the Italian. Again, however, the source is material written by Marivaux for *Le Spectateur français*, and it was the Italians who produced the play, again with Silvia in the lead. Whereas the tyranny of which the girl in the original piece complained was based on her mother's excessive piety, a subject considered taboo on the stage, the tyranny of Angélique's mother is stated in broadly human terms. Moreover, Angélique is much more discerning, much more aware of the complexities of human behavior than Agnès; she is much more "modern" in the social context of Marivaux's day. Despite the constraints placed on her, she knows that others lead a freer life, and at times she is eager to risk freedom and take responsibility for her own decisions. Although her mother tells her that girls of good family do not need to do anything of the kind because their experienced mothers know better, Angélique wants to become experienced on her own.

Marivaux successfully put forward Angélique's case in terms acceptable to the enlightened public of his times, a relatively small number as in any age. The tendency now, however, is to see *L'École des mères* as a play dealing with a problem that has lost its urgency; like any thesis play, it is regarded by some as a museum piece. Nevertheless, Angélique remains an attractive and living character.

DOUBLE INFIDELITY

Double Infidelity is a more substantial work, subtle and brilliantly plotted. A prince, required by law to marry a countrywoman and charmed by the beauty of Silvia, one of his subjects, has her abducted. Silvia, however, intends to remain faithful to her fiancé, the peasant Arlequin, and refuses to see the prince. He therefore decides to pass as an officer of the royal household in Silvia's presence. Neither external pressures nor material inducements move her. Meanwhile, the clever Flaminia, daughter of one of the prince's courtiers, manipulates Arlequin, who has

been called to the palace and unsuccessfully offered blandishments to give Silvia up, and wins his heart. Revealing himself as extremely considerate and refined, the prince finally manages to stir Silvia, Silvia and Arlequin's love having died for lack of constant mutual concern, the importance of which Marivaux had pointed out in the number of *Le Spectateur français* that immediately preceded the creation of the play. Silvia and Arlequin at last discover their "double inconstancy," and the prince makes known his true rank; he will wed Silvia, and Flaminia will wed Arlequin.

This play leads the short list of Marivaux's favorite works. As in *The Fortunate Peasant*, there is such a rich texture formed by the author's intentions and the complex human action that it is not always easy to grasp the work as a whole. Performed by the Italians, *Double Infidelity* was a success at the same time that it gave rise to the first of the clichés—he was a practitioner of *la métaphysique du coeur*—henceforth applied to Marivaux to imply that his psychological action was too complicated for the public to follow. His plays were appreciated merely for the entertainment value of their plots, while their fine psychological analysis and social criticism were largely overlooked. Clearly, Marivaux meant the work to be useful as well as entertaining.

The play is a sequel to *Robin, Bachelor of Love* and has the same moral lesson to offer. Flaminia's somewhat frightening artfulness, learned at court, is applied to winning an artless peasant for her husband. Silvia, polished by love, gladly accepts the life of her prince's court instead of a simple, uncomplicated one with Arlequin. Acted by the great Thomassin, Arlequin was ever the protean figure that could become whatever the author wanted him to be; the play belongs to him.

THE GAME OF LOVE AND CHANCE

The Game of Love and Chance is regarded by many critics as Marivaux's masterpiece. In act 1, Silvia obtains permission from her father, M. Orgon, to disguise herself as her maid, Lisette, who in turn will take her place when they meet Silvia's suitor, Dorante. Meanwhile, unknown to Silvia, Dorante has determined to change roles with his valet, Arlequin.

At their first meeting, both Silvia and Dorante, each taking the other for a servant, are astonished to find such distinction and refinement in a person of low birth.

In act 2, Lisette and Arlequin make clear their attraction for each other, while Silvia feels an inclination for Dorante, as he does for her. Troubled, he speaks of leaving, whereupon Silvia suggests her feeling for him, then, ashamed, wishes to abandon her disguise. Her father, however, is opposed. At last, Dorante, determined to put an end to the hoax, reveals himself. Reassured and delighted, Silvia continues the game.

In act 3, M. Orgon's son, Mario, seeking to provoke Dorante by arousing his jealousy, pretends to love Silvia. Lisette and Arlequin make their positions known to each other. Bitter, Dorante acts as though he is going to depart. Silvia is alarmed, but he returns and finally asks for her hand. Silvia has achieved her objective and may now reveal herself.

Although very successful when produced by the Théâtre Italien, this play was not immediately recognized as the classic that it has become. It is true, however, that *The Game of Love and Chance* replaced *The Agreeable Surprise* as a work in which the Italians could test new actors, and that the *Nouveau Mercure* published a long review that has been republished many times as the play acquired its present reputation.

Of all Marivaux's comedies, it draws on the largest number of obvious sources and contains the largest number of allusions to well-known works of the preceding century. The culmination of a particular theatrical tradition, it realizes the possibilities of a cluster of ideas and devices that earlier dramatists had been unable to develop fully and forms a perfect vehicle for the author's personal vision of human relations. The chief traditional device exploited by Marivaux is that of the disguise. Disguises, though they do not fool the spectator, realistically speaking, as the characters' true social and personal qualities cannot be disguised, work very well dramatically. The chief idea developed by Marivaux and traditional from the time of Pierre Corneille and Molière is that of free choice in marriage, especially for the woman,

who must have a clear picture of what men in general and her man in particular are like before she consents. Partly through coquetry, partly to gratify her *amour-propre*, but principally for that reason must Silvia prolong her disguise almost to the end of the play.

By its formal perfection, the richness and definitive quality of the text, the complexity and truth of the characters, and the variety of the action—alternating emotional tension with youthful exuberance and comic verve, blending the real and the ideal—*The Game of Love and Chance* has proved itself to be a masterpiece of comedy. A happy fusion of the Italian and the French styles, it serves to illustrate the concept of pure theater, by which is meant the representation of human action transposed into a world at once close enough to and far enough removed from everyday life to permit insights that cannot otherwise be portrayed in such a short length of time.

THE FALSE CONFESSIONS

The False Confessions was Marivaux's last full-length play and his last major work for the stage. Dorante, a young man of good family who is, however, financially ruined, is in love with Araminte, a young, wealthy widow. Advised by his former valet, Dubois, he enters her household as her business manager. Dubois, too, is in the service of Araminte, and he confides to his mistress that her manager loves her, as though it were a secret, although Dorante and he have arranged for him to do so. As a clever psychologist, however, he recommends that she not respond to Dorante's passion. These "false confidences" have the desired effect: They arouse love in Araminte, who will wed Dorante.

No doubt it would surprise Marivaux to know that this play, like *The Game of Love and Chance*, is now considered one of his most characteristic and one of his greatest works. He thought of it as simply another of his plays and another, too, that was not as successful in its first run as in later ones. Yet *The False Confessions* has perhaps even a richer dramatic texture than that of *The Game of Love and Chance*, with a greater number of conflicting desires and interests, all contributing directly to the denouement. It is the play that most harmoniously unites Marivaux's Italian and French styles as it deals with a familiar problem in human experience in strictly contemporary terms.

All scholarly criticism notwithstanding, the basic problem in the play is a very simple, universal one, and it is resolved perfectly. Men often fall in love with women who are inaccessible because of their superior social status, and the challenge of this inaccessibility contributes greatly to their desirability. Men react in different ways to the challenge, with different results. The few who win their love are those who, for all their passion, retain some wit to enable them to use all their resources and luck to bridge the social gap. Dorante is this type of man, the most interesting for Marivaux's audience as for most audiences. According to a long cultural tradition, the French tended to believe that a lady should be won, and that initiative and genius on the part of the gentleman deserved to be rewarded, if he was honorable and sincere.

Marivaux had to steer a tricky course between a romantically ideal solution, which would have appeared insipid in 1737, and a crudely realistic solution in order to arrive at an acceptable stage presentation of this rather elementary situation. He also had to contend with the convention of the unity of time. Fortunately, Marivaux could draw on other conventions, those of Italian dramatic practice, to remove the action from the plane of simple realism to which his subject tended. Against the forces of realism, represented chiefly by minor but important characters, a balance is struck by the principals, Dubois, who loves Araminte vicariously and is therefore Dorante's alter ego, and Araminte. Dubois-Dorante's stratagem of the false confidences has as its objective both the fortune and the person of the young widow; if she responds as expected, it is not merely because she is duped by the stratagem but also because she knows that Dorante will be a good husband.

OTHER MAJOR WORKS

LONG FICTION: *Les Effets surprenants de la sympathie*, 1713-1714; *La Voiture embourbée*, 1714; *La Vie de Marianne*, 1731-1741 (*The Life of Marianne*, 1736-1742; also as *The Virtuous Orphan: Or, The Life of Marianne*, 1979); *Le Paysan parvenu*, 1734-1735 (*The Fortunate Peasant*, 1735); *Le Télé-* maque travesti, 1736; *Pharsamon*, 1737 (*Pharsamond: Or, The New Knight-Errant*, 1750).

SHORT FICTION: *Le Bilbouquet*, 1714.

POETRY: *Homère travesti: Ou, L'Illiade en vers burlesques*, 1716.

NONFICTION: *Pensées sur la clarté du discours*, 1719; *Le Spectateur français*, 1722-1723, 1727, 1761 (includes *L'Indigent Philosophe* and *Le Cabinet du philosophe*); *Réflexions*, 1744-1755; *L'Éducation d'un prince*, 1754; *Le Miroir*, 1755 (essay); *Journaux et œuvres diverses*, 1969; *Œuvres de jeunesse*, 1972.

BIBLIOGRAPHY

Badir, Magdy Gabriel, and Vivien Elizabeth Bosley, eds. *Le Triomphe de Marivaux: A Colloquium Commemorating the Tricentenary of the Birth of Marivaux, 1688-1988*. Edmonton: Department of Romance Languages, University of Alberta, 1989. A collection of papers on Marivaux, covering various aspects of his life and work. Bibliography.

Brady, Valentini Papadopoulou. *Love in the Theatre of Marivaux: A Study of the Factors Influencing Its Birth, Development, and Expression*. Geneva: Droz, 1970. A critical examination of Marivaux's dramatic works, with emphasis on his treatment of love. Bibliography.

Cismaru, Alfred. *Marivaux and Molière: A Comparison*. Lubbock: Texas Tech Press, 1977. Cismaru compares and contrasts the dramatic works of Marivaux and Molière. Bibliography and index.

Culpin, D. J. *Marivaux and Reason: A Study in Early Enlightenment Thought*. New York: Peter Lang, 1993. An examination of the Marivaux's philosophy and the early Enlightenment. Bibliography and index.

Haac, Oscar. *Marivaux*. New York: Twayne, 1973. A basic biography of Marivaux that covers his life and works. Bibliography and index.

Pucci, Suzanne L. *Sites of the Spectator: Emerging Literary and Cultural Practice in Eighteenth Century France*. Oxford, England: Voltaire Foundation, 2001. A look at Marivaux's contributions to *Le Spectateur français* and the literary climate of the times. Bibliography and index.

Richard A. Mazzara

CHRISTOPHER MARLOWE

Born: Canterbury, England; February 6, 1564
Died: Deptford, England; May 30, 1593

PRINCIPAL DRAMA

Dido, Queen of Carthage, pr. c. 1586-1587, pb.
  1594 (with Thomas Nashe)
Tamburlaine the Great, Part I, pr. c. 1587, pb. 1590
  (commonly known as *Tamburlaine*)
Tamburlaine the Great, Part II, pr. 1587, pb. 1590
Doctor Faustus, pr. c. 1588, pb. 1604
The Jew of Malta, pr. c. 1589, pb. 1633
Edward II, pr. c. 1592, pb. 1594
The Massacre at Paris, pr. 1593, pb. 1594(?)
Complete Plays, pb. 1963

OTHER LITERARY FORMS

Christopher Marlowe translated Lucan's *Bellum civile* (60-65 C.E.) as *Pharsalia* (1600) and Ovid's *Amores* (c. 20 B.C.E.) as *Elegies* (1595-1600) while still attending Cambridge (c. 1584-1587). The renderings of the *Elegies* are notable for their imaginative liveliness and rhetorical strength. They provide as well the earliest examples of the heroic couplet in English. *Hero and Leander* (1598), a long, erotic poem composed before 1593, is also indebted to Ovid. It is the best narrative of a group that includes William Shakespeare's *Venus and Adonis* (1593) and John Marston's *The Metamorphosis of Pigmalion's Image* (1598). The vogue for these Ovidian epyllions lasted for more than a decade, and Marlowe's reputation as a poet was confirmed on the basis of his contribution. He completed only the first two sestiads before his death, after which George Chapman continued and finished the poem. Marlowe's brilliant heroic couplets create a world, in Eugene Ruoff's words, of "moonlight and mushrooms"; his lovers are the idealized figures of pastoral works, chanting lush and sensual hymns or laments. A sophisticated narrator—viewed by most critics as representing Marlowe's satiric viewpoint—manages to balance the sentimentalism of the lovers, giving the poem an ironic quality that is sustained throughout. This tone, however, is not a feature of Marlowe's famous lyric, "The Passionate Shepherd to His Love." First published in an anthology entitled *The Passionate Pilgrim* (1599), the poem is a beautiful evocation of the attractions of the pastoral world, a place where "melodious birds sing madrigals." Technically called an "invitation," "The Passionate Shepherd to His Love" became an extremely popular idyll and was often imitated or parodied by other writers. One of the most intriguing responses, "The Nymph's Reply," was composed by Sir Walter Raleigh and published in *The Passionate Pilgrim*. Its worldly, skeptical attitude offers a contrast to the exuberance of Marlowe's lyric. Without a doubt, this pastoral piece, along with *Hero and Leander*, would have ensured Marlowe's reputation as a major literary figure even if he had never written a work intended for the stage.

ACHIEVEMENTS

It is difficult to overestimate the poetic and dramatic achievement of Christopher Marlowe. Although his career was short (about six years), Marlowe wrote plays that appealed to an emerging popular audience and that strongly influenced other dramatists. The heroes of the plays have been called "overreachers" and "apostates," figures whom many critics believe reveal the defiance and cynicism of Marlowe himself. In addition to introducing these controversial, larger-than-life protagonists, Marlowe was also instrumental in fusing the elements of classical—and especially Senecan—drama and native morality plays, thereby establishing a style that would be followed by many subsequent playwrights. *Doctor Faustus* is the prime example of Marlowe's talent for combining classical satire and a conventional Elizabethan theme of humanity in a middle state, torn between the angel and the beast. The vitality of *Doctor Faustus*, *Tamburlaine the Great*, and Marlowe's other works can be traced as well to his facility for writing powerful yet musical blank verse. Indeed, so regular and forceful is his style that his verse has been described as "Marlowe's mighty line," and his achievement in blank verse no doubt influenced Shakespeare. It is apparent in such plays as *Richard II* (pr. c. 1595-1596), *The Merchant of Venice* (pr. c. 1596-1597), and *Othello, the Moor of Venice* (pr. 1604, rev. 1623) that Shakespeare was also inspired by certain of Marlowe's themes and plots.

Marlowe did not possess a patriotic spirit; his heroes are not Prince Hals but rather men similar to Shakespeare's Richard III. Yet he was sensitive to the range of passion in human nature. Many of Marlowe's characters reflect a true-to-life, even psychological complexity that preceding English playwrights had been incapable of demonstrating. Doctor Faustus's fear on the night he will lose his soul is beautifully portrayed in the memorable Latin line, adapted from Ovid's *Amores*, "O lente, lente currite noctis equi!" ("O slowly, slowly, run you horses of the night"). Barabas, villain-hero of *The Jew of Malta*, displays almost the same intensity of feeling as he rhapsodizes over his gold, his "infinite riches in a little room." Over the short span of his career,

Christopher Marlowe (Hulton Archive by Getty Images)

Marlowe moved away from the extravagant declamatory style of *Tamburlaine the Great* to a blank verse—notably in *Edward II*—that echoed the rhythm of elevated speech. It is difficult to predict what further advances there would have been in his style had he lived as long as Shakespeare. It is doubtful, however, that he would have changed so radically as to achieve universal popularity. His vision was satiric and therefore narrow; the themes and characters that he chose to write about lacked widespread appeal. Nevertheless, "Kit" Marlowe transformed the English stage from a platform for allegorical interludes or homespun slapstick into a forum for exploring the most controversial of human and social issues. Marlowe also established the poetic medium—vigorous blank verse—that would prove to be the dominant form of dramatic expression until the close of the Elizabethan Age.

BIOGRAPHY

Christopher Marlowe was born in Canterbury, England, in February, 1564. His father was a respected member of the tanners' and shoemakers' guild. Marlowe attended the King's School of Canterbury in 1579 and 1580 and in 1581 began study at Corpus Christi College, Cambridge. He was the recipient of a scholarship funded by Matthew Parker, archbishop of Canterbury. As a foundation scholar, Marlowe was expected to prepare for a post in the Church. In 1584, he took his bachelor of arts degree, after which he continued to hold his scholarship while studying for his master of arts degree. It appears that he would not have been granted his degree in 1587 except for the intervention of the queen's Privy Council. This body declared that Marlowe had done the government some service—probably as a spy in Reims, home of exiled English Catholics—and ordered that he be granted his M.A. at the "next commencement." Marlowe had no doubt been writing poetry while at Cambridge, and he probably decided to make his way in this profession in London. It is certain that he was there in 1589, because he was a resident of Newgate Prison during that year. He and a man named Thomas Watson were jailed for having murdered another man, although it appears that Watson actually did the killing. Three years later, in 1592, Marlowe was again in trouble with the law, being placed under a peace bond by two London constables. Clearly, the young writer and scholar did not move in the best of social circles, even though his patron was Thomas Walsingham and Sir Walter Raleigh was his close friend. One of Marlowe's colleagues, a man with whom he once shared a room, was Thomas Kyd, who in May of 1593 was arrested, charged with atheism, and tortured. Kyd accused Marlowe of atheism, claiming that the heretical documents found in their room belonged to the latter. The Privy Council sent out an order for Marlowe's arrest (he was staying at the Walsingham estate), but instead of imprisoning him, the Council simply required that he report every day until the hearing.

That hearing never took place: Marlowe died within two weeks after his detainment. On May 30, after a bout of drinking at a tavern in Deptford, Marlowe quarreled with a companion named Ingram Frizer, who settled the account by stabbing the playwright. Those who believed the charge of atheism brought against him saw Marlowe's end as an example of God's justice. Others, however, speculated on the possibility that he was the victim of an assassination plot, spawned to eliminate a spy who may have known too much. This theory seems fanciful, but it had many contemporary adherents, as the details surrounding the murder do not adequately explain the facts. Whatever the cause, Marlowe's death marked the tragic end of a meteoric career on the public stage. As an innovator—and rebel—he challenged his fellow playwrights to achieve greater heights of creativity, and he left behind a rich legacy of plays and poems.

ANALYSIS

Taken as a whole, Christopher Marlowe's canon represents a crucial step forward in the development of Elizabethan dramaturgy. Without him, there could not have been a Shakespeare or a John Webster, both of whom learned something of the art of popular melodrama from this master. It is lamentable that Marlowe's early death deprived audiences and subsequent critics of more examples of his poetic drama, drama that stirs both the heart and the mind.

DIDO, QUEEN OF CARTHAGE

Marlowe probably began writing plays while he was a student at Cambridge. *Dido, Queen of Carthage*, which appeared in quarto form in 1594, was composed in collaboration with Thomas Nashe and was first performed by the children's company at the Chapel Royal. How much Nashe actually had to do with the work is conjectural; he may have only edited it for publication. The tragedy shows little evidence, however, of the playwright's later genius. It is closely tied to Vergil's *Aeneid* (c. 29-19 B.C.E.; English translation, 1553), with much of its blank verse qualifying as direct translation from the Latin. The characters are wooden and the action highly stylized, the result of an attempt to translate the material of epic into drama. The play impresses mainly through the force of its imagery.

TAMBURLAINE THE GREAT, PART I

Sections of Marlowe's first popular theater success, *Tamburlaine the Great, Part I*, were probably sketched at Cambridge as well. First produced around 1587 (probably at an innyard), this exotic, bombastic piece won for its author considerable fame. His name was quickly cataloged with other so-called University Wits—men such as Robert Greene, John Lyly, and George Peele, whose dramas dominated the Elizabethan stage in the late 1580's. Marlowe's great dramatic epic was roughly based on the career of Timur Lenk (1336-1405), a Mongolian fighter who had led an army that defeated the Turks at Ankara in 1402. The defeat meant the salvation of Europe, an event that doubtless stimulated Marlowe's ironic vision. The playwright could have found the account of the audacious Scythian's career in many Latin and Italian sources, but his interest may have been first aroused after reading George Whetstone's *The English Mirror* (1586).

Tamburlaine emerges as an Olympian figure in Marlowe's hands. He begins as a lowly shepherd whose physical courage and captivating, defiant rhetoric take him to victories over apparently superior opponents. Although episodic, the plot does achieve a degree of tension as each successive opponent proves more difficult to overcome. Tamburlaine's first victim is a hereditary king named Mycetes, who underrates his adversary's strength and persuasiveness. The lieutenant who is sent to capture the upstart is suddenly and decisively won over to the rebel's side. Tamburlaine next outwits Cosroe, Mycetes' brother, who thinks he can use this untutored fighter to consolidate his own power. As the "bloody and insatiate Tamburlaine" kills him, Cosroe curses the turn of Fortune's Wheel that has cast him down. Even so, Marlowe believes not in the capricious goddess as the chief ruler of humankind but in a kind of Machiavellian system directed by the will of his larger-than-life hero.

A major test of Tamburlaine's will comes in his confrontation with Bajazeth, emperor of the Turks. Before the battle between the two warriors, there is a boasting bout between their two mistresses, Zenocrate and Zabina. The former, daughter to the Soldan of Egypt and in love with Tamburlaine, praises her beloved's strength and his destined glory. Both women also pray for the victory of their men, parallel actions that invite a comparison between the pairs of lovers. When Tamburlaine defeats Bajazeth, he takes the crown from Zabina's head and gives it to his queen—and "conqueror." Marlowe thereby demonstrates that the play qualifies as a monumental love story as well. Bajazeth is bound up and later thrown into a cage with his defeated queen; this contraption is then towed across the stage as part of Tamburlaine's victory procession. Before the final siege of Damascus, the city that houses Zenocrate's father, the Soldan, Tamburlaine unveils a magnificent banquet. During the festivities, he releases Bajazeth from his cage in order to use him as a footstool from which he will step onto his throne. This audacious touch of spectacle verifies Marlowe's aim of shocking his audience and displays contempt for the pride of rulers.

In the midst of this banquet, Tamburlaine orders his lieutenants to "hang our bloody colors by Damascus,/ Reflexing hues of blood upon their heads,/ While they walk quivering on their walls,/ Half dead for fear before they feel my wrath!" These threatening, boastful words are followed quickly by a change of colors to black, which signifies Tamburlaine's intention to destroy the city. He underscores this pur-

pose by condemning four virgins, suppliants sent to assuage his anger, to their deaths on the spears of his horsemen. The destruction of the city soon follows, although the Soldan and the King of Arabia (to whom Zenocrate is still betrothed) lead out an army to do battle with their oppressor. While this battle takes place offstage, Bajazeth and Zabina are rolled in to deliver curses against their torturers. Wild from hunger and despair, Bajazeth asks his queen to fetch him something to drink; while she is away, he brains himself against the bars of the cage. Zabina, returning from her errand, finds her husband's battered corpse and follows his lead. The horror of this double suicide no doubt satisfied the popular audience's appetite for gore, an appetite that Marlowe fed lavishly in this play.

The finale of the first part depicts Tamburlaine's victory over the Soldan, who is spared because the victor plans to crown Zenocrate Queen of Persia. Meanwhile, her betrothed, the King of Arabia, dies from battle wounds; his death causes little conflict, however, in Zenocrate, who follows Tamburlaine as if he were indeed her conqueror, too. Now the lowly shepherd-turned-king declares a truce, buries his noble opponents with solemn rites, and prepares to marry his beloved in pomp and splendor. He appears to stand atop Fortune's Wheel, a startling example of the Machiavellian man of iron will to whom no leader or law is sacrosanct. There is little sense here that Tamburlaine is intended as an example of pride going before a fall. He has achieved stunning victories over foes who are as immoral as he is; most of them, including Bajazeth, emerge as fools who miscalculate or underrate Tamburlaine with fearful consequences. No doubt the popularity of the play is traceable to this fact and to the truth that most people nurture an amoral desire for fame or power that this hero fulfills with startling success.

TAMBURLAINE THE GREAT, PART II

Part II shows Tamburlaine continuing on his road to conquest, securely characterizing himself as the scourge of God. As the play opens, Sigismund, Christian king of Hungary, and the pagan monarch Orcanes agree to a truce. This ceremony strikes one as ironic, as pagans and Christians swallow their pride in order to challenge and defeat the half-god who threatens them. In the meantime, Tamburlaine proudly surveys the fruits of Zenocrate's womb: three sons through whom he hopes to win immortality. One of the brood, however, is weak and unattracted by war; Calyphas seems devoted to his mother and to the blandishments of peace. His effeminate nature foreshadows Tamburlaine's decline and fall, revealing that his empire cannot survive his own death. Even though his two other sons exhibit natures cruel enough to match their father's, the flawed seed has obviously been planted.

The hastily forged truce is suddenly broken when Sigismund tears the document and turns his forces on Orcanes. Though Marlowe appears to be attacking the integrity of Christianity, he was in fact appealing to his audience's anti-Catholic sentiments. When Sigismund is wounded and dies, moreover, Orcanes announces that Christ has won a victory in defeating one so treacherous as Sigismund. While these events transpire on the battlefield, another death is about to take place in Tamburlaine's tent. Zenocrate has been in failing health, and her imminent death causes her husband to contemplate joining her. That he should entertain such a gesture at the height of his power confirms the depth of his love for Zenocrate. Her imploring words—"Live still, my lord! O, let my sovereign live!"—manage to stay his hand, but his pent-up rage cannot be restrained at her death. Shifting from a figure of gentleness and compassion in a moment's time, Tamburlaine orders the town in which she dies to be burned to the ground.

With the defeat of Sigismund, Orcanes emerges as a kingmaker, leading the grand procession at which Callapine, the avenging son of Bajazeth, vows to use his new crown as the means to conquer the lowly Scythian. This scene is succeeded by another ceremonial pageant, this one led by the mournful Tamburlaine and his sons carrying the coffin of Zenocrate. Her body will remain with the company wherever they go in battle. Determined to teach his sons the arts of war, Tamburlaine commences a lesson in besieging a fort. When Calyphas balks, afraid of wounding or death, an angry father lances his own arm and orders his sons to dip their hands in his

blood. All of them comply, although Calyphas is moved to pity at this horrid sight. With this ritual, Marlowe underscores the tribal nature of his hero's family but at the same time implies that the letting of blood by Tamburlaine will not necessarily cure the "defect" in it.

The central battle in the second part pits Tamburlaine and his sons against Callapine and his crowned kings before Aleppo. In a preliminary verbal skirmish, Tamburlaine belittles Almeda, a traitor, who cowers behind Callapine's back when invited to take his crown. The scene is seriocomic as Almeda proves himself a coward before his kingly followers; his weakness is meant to parallel that of Calyphas, Tamburlaine's son. The latter remains behind in a tent playing cards while his two brothers earn martial honors on the battlefield. When they and their father enter, trailing the conquered Turkish monarchs behind them, Tamburlaine seizes his weakling son and stabs him. Among the many scenes of bloodshed Marlowe presents in the play, this is probably the most shocking and repulsive. Although he cites his role as God's scourge and this deed as "war's justice," Tamburlaine here reveals a self-destructive side of his nature that has not been evident before.

The audience does not have long to ponder the murder; the scene of horror is quickly followed by one of pageantry. Trebizon and Soria, two pagan kings, enter the stage drawing a chariot with Tamburlaine holding the reins. This spectacle is accompanied by the superhero's disdaining words: "Holla, ye pamper'd jades of Asia!/ What can ye draw but twenty miles a day,/ And have so proud a chariot at your heels,/ And such a coachman as great Tamburlaine?" The monarch-prisoners hurl curses at their captors as, like Bajazeth and Zabina, they are taunted unmercifully. Tamburlaine's soldiers are rewarded with Turkish concubines, after which the royal train heads toward Babylon for yet another bloody siege.

Before the walls of this ancient city, Tamburlaine calls on its governor to yield. (The scene recalls the negotiations before the walls of Damascus in Part I.) When he refuses, the lieutenants Techelles and Theridamas lead their soldiers in scaling the city's walls. The victory is quickly won, and Tamburlaine, dressed in black and driving his chariot, proudly announces the city's defeat. A quaking governor promises Tamburlaine abundant treasure if he will spare his life, but the conqueror disdains such bribes and has his victim hanged in chains from the walls. Theridamas shoots the governor while Tamburlaine proceeds to burn Muhammadan books in an open pit. Defying Mahomet to avenge his sacrilege if he has any power, Tamburlaine suddenly feels "distempered"; he recovers quickly, however, when he hears of Callapine's army advancing. Does Marlowe mean to imply that his hero's unexpected illness is punishment for his act of defiance? Although such an explicit moral lesson seems uncharacteristic, the connection between the two events appears to be more than a passing one.

The weakened Tamburlaine manages a final victory over Bajazeth's son, after which he produces a map that represents the extent of his conquests. With a trembling finger, he also directs his sons' attention to the remaining countries that they will be expected to conquer. Giving his crown to Theridamas (who later bestows it on Amyras) and turning his chariot over to his sons, Tamburlaine then calls for Zenocrate's hearse, beside which he stretches out to die. Before the mighty general's body is carried off, Amyras delivers the fitting eulogy: "Meet heaven and earth, and here let all things end,/ For earth hath spent the pride of all her fruit,/ And heaven consum'd his choicest living fire:/ Let earth and heaven his timeless death deplore,/ For both their worths will equal him no more." The death of the Scourge of Heaven follows no particular event; its suddenness only serves to underscore Tamburlaine's mortality. The audience is reminded of Alexander's demise in the midst of his glory. Because the chariot becomes such a dominant prop in the second part, Marlow may have likewise meant to suggest a parallel between his hero and Phaëthon, who in his pride fell from Jove's chariot because he could not control its course. Whatever the interpretation of this hero's fall, there can be little doubt that his mighty feats and his Senecan bombast made him an extremely popular—and awesome—figure on the Elizabethan stage.

THE JEW OF MALTA

For his next play, *The Jew of Malta*, Marlowe also chose an antihero who poses a threat to the orderly rule of European society. As Tamburlaine had ruled by martial strength, Barabas (named to recall the thief whose place on the Cross was taken by Christ) hopes to dominate the world by his wealth. Although Marlowe depicts him as a grasping, evil man (to the delight of the anti-Semitic Elizabethan audience), Barabas holds one's interest as Richard III does—by the resourcefulness of his scheming. Just as Tamburlaine's audacity appeals to an unconscious desire for power, so Barabas's scorn for Christian morality probably appealed to the audience's wish to defy authority. He is not portrayed, however, as a sympathetic character, even though in the early stages of the play, the behavior of his Christian opponents toward him reveals their hypocrisy. Faced with a threat from the powerful Turkish fleet, Ferneze, the Maltese governor, turns to Barabas for help in raising tribute money. While three of his colleagues agree to give up half of their estates and consent to baptism, Barabas refuses this arrangement, miscalculating the power and determination of the governor. Accompanied by a chorus of anti-Semitic remarks by the knights, Ferneze announces that he has already sent men to seize Barabas's property. He also declares that he intends to transform the Jew's mansion into a nunnery; this news further enrages Barabas, who curses them: "Take it to you, i' th' Devil's name." This scene highlights the hypocrisy of the Maltese; it also reveals the extent of Barabas's hatred for those among whom he has lived and worked. The audience has learned from the prologue spoken by Machiavel that the hero is one of his disciples and soon realizes that the subsequent action will show him "practicing" on his enemies.

When his daughter Abigail comes to recount angrily the takeover of their house, Barabas counsels patience, reminding her that he has hidden a fortune beneath its floorboards. In order to recover the money, he spawns a daring plan that requires his daughter to take vows as a means of entering the newly founded nunnery. In a heavily theatrical confrontation staged by Barabas, father accuses daughter of deserting him and their religion, while in an aside he tells her where to find the money. As Abigail is hurried into the mansion, she is spied by two young men, Mathias and Lodowick, both of whom fall in love with her—a rivalry that Barabas will later turn to his advantage. Later that night, Abigail appears on a balcony with Barabas's bags in her hands; she throws these down to him as he sees her and shouts: "O girl! O gold! O beauty! O my bliss!" This outburst illustrates the Jew's seriocomic nature, as he employs such impassioned speech to praise his gold. Eight years later, Shakespeare incorporated this trait into his characterization of Shylock in *The Merchant of Venice*.

In the square the next day, Barabas begins to practice in earnest against Ferneze. Ferneze's son Lodowick expresses his love for Abigail and is invited by Barabas to supper for a meeting with his "jewel." This dinner will prove Lodowick's undoing, as Barabas tells the audience in an aside. The Jew then proceeds to purchase the slave Ithamore, who will serve his master's will no matter what the command. In order to test the fellow, Barabas lists a remarkable catalog of evil deeds—including poisoning wells in nunneries—that he has supposedly committed. Ithamore responds by declaring himself in a league of villainy with the Jew: "We are villains both!—Both circumcised, we hate Christians both!" The slave aids his master by taking a forged challenge from Lodowick to Mathias, with whom Abigail is truly in love, even though her father has forced her to display affection for Lodowick. When the rivals meet to engage in a duel, Barabas is positioned above them, watching with pleasure as they kill each other.

Now, however, Ithamore and Abigail, whom he has told of the feigned challenge, know the extent of Barabas's treachery. In melodramatic fashion, the Jew decides that his daughter must die or she will reveal his deed. To kill her, he has Ithamore prepare a poisoned pot of rice to be "enjoyed" by all the nuns. To secure Ithamore's loyalty, Barabas promises him the whole of his inheritance, and he seems to adopt him as his son. The audience, however, knows from another aside that Barabas intends to kill his slave

as well when the time is right. Ithamore does his master's bidding, but before Abigail dies, she gives proof of her father's guilt to Friar Bernardine (depicted as a lustful clown), who vows to confront the Jew with it, accompanied by Friar Jacomo. Barabas outwits these two fellows, assuring them that he wishes to be converted; as he did with Lodowick and Mathias, he starts the two men quarreling with each other. By means of a clever ruse devised with the aid of Ithamore, he also eliminates these potential enemies. As each of his schemes proves successful, Barabas celebrates more openly and melodramatically. In this play, unlike *Tamburlaine the Great*, the audience senses that the hero-villain will soon go too far, tripping up on some unforeseen obstacle. The audience is meant to experience this sense of impending doom, especially after the murder of the innocent Abigail, who converted to Christianity before her death. This deed establishes a parallel between Barabas and the biblical Herod, another murderer of innocents.

Meanwhile, Ithamore, aided by a pimp and his whore, tries to blackmail his master to feed the whore's expensive tastes. Barabas resolves to kill them all. Disguised as a French musician, he comes to the party at which Ithamore and the others are drunkenly planning to destroy the Jew. Barabas plays and sings, then tosses to the revelers a bouquet that he has dusted with poison. They smell it and go ahead boldly in their plan to expose the Jew's actions. Before they die, they manage to tell Ferneze of Barabas's treachery; he and the others are led off-stage, from where an officer quickly comes to tell of *all* of their deaths. The audience quickly learns, however, that Barabas has taken a sleeping potion and thus has deceived his enemies. Now intent on revenge, he joins forces with the besieging Turks, showing them a way into the city through a hidden tunnel.

With a suddenness of movement that imitates the Wheel of Fortune, Ferneze is defeated and Barabas is appointed governor of the island by the Turks. Rather than torturing and killing the former governor, as might be expected, Barabas offers to return his power and destroy the Turks if Ferneze will pay him, which

Ferneze agrees to do. The Jew then invites Calymath to a feast in celebration of their great victory. Hard at work in the hall, Barabas constructs an elaborate trap that he plans to spring on Calymath with Ferneze's help. When the moment arrives, however, the Maltese governor cuts a rope that causes Barabas to fall into the trap, a large cauldron filled with boiling liquid. Ferneze then arrests the Turkish leader, telling him that his troops have been surprised and killed in the monastery where they were housed. Amid the shouts and curses of the Jew—"Damn's Christians, dogs, and Turkish infidels!"—the play ends in triumph for the Maltese citizens.

The Jew of Malta ends in the defeat of Machiavellian plotting. Even though he is a scheming villain throughout most of the action, however, Barabas might also be considered a near-tragic figure if one regards him as a man who degenerates in reaction to the evil done to him. In part, this reaction must follow from the behavior of Ferneze and Calymath; neither is morally superior to Barabas. He must honestly be described as the Elizabethan stereotype of a Jew, given to melodrama and sardonic humor. The audience feels no sympathy for him in his death, only a kind of relief that his destructive will has been defeated by someone capable of outwitting him. Although he finally overreaches himself, Barabas emerges as a totally fascinating villain, matched only by Shakespeare's Iago and Richard III.

THE MASSACRE AT PARIS

In *The Massacre at Paris*, Marlowe depicts the episodic adventures of another antihero, the Guise, who is distinguishable from his predecessors only in representing the power of the Papacy. The character is based on a historical figure who was assassinated in 1588; the action recounts the infamous Saint Bartholomew's Day debacle of 1572, when hundreds of Huguenots were murdered by Catholic forces. The succession of victims, whom the Guise orders murdered ostensibly to please the Church, makes the audience recoil from the character and his motives. Lacking any comic element in his nature, he qualifies as a parodied Machiavel intent on disrupting the reign of Henry III, a lecherous and inept leader. The Guise's soliloquies show him to be in quest of an

"earthly crown," which he believes he deserves because of his superior will and intelligence. What makes him different from Tamburlaine is his inability to control his passions and the behavior of those closest to him. In critical situations, his rhetoric fails him. His wife's affair with the king's favorite cuckolds the Guise. Henry delights in making the sign of the horns at him in public. Enraged at being made a figure of public ridicule, he arranges to kill his rival, an act that all but ensures his fall.

The man who stands in opposition to both the Guise and Henry III is King Henry of Navarre. Although his speeches lack the fire and melodrama that mark the Guise's outbursts, Navarre champions a Catholicism that is anticlerical, even fundamentalist. He also defends the principle of king and country, which the Guise and Henry seem to have forgotten in their quest for power. To prove his antipapal views, Navarre joins forces with Queen Elizabeth in an alliance the rightness of which Marlowe underscores by having a dying Henry III embrace it. This bit of manipulation has led some critics to argue that with this play, Marlowe was returning to his own Christian faith and was rejecting the amoral position taken by Tamburlaine. It is dangerous, however, to infer an author's beliefs from those held by his characters; there is no corroborating evidence in this case. There can be little doubt that Navarre is intended to be seen as a heroic character unlike any encountered in the other plays. If he is not Prince Hal, he is certainly Bolingbroke, a man who acts on principle and proves effective.

Even though the confrontation between Navarre and the Guise has about it all the elements of exciting drama, *The Massacre at Paris* is ultimately disappointing. The Guise's philosophy of seeking out perilous situations in order to test his strength of will does hold one's attention for a while, but the play offers none of the heroic bombast of a Tamburlaine or witty audacity of a Barabas. There is a great deal of bloodshed on the stage and off, but there is no clear purpose for the murders, no sense in which they forward some particular end in the plot. To complicate matters, the text that has survived is garbled; no amount of reconstructing can account for the missing links. While Marlowe may have been attempting a new dramatic design (some textual critics suggest that the original version was twice as long), *The Massacre at Paris* in its present form cannot be regarded as achieving the degree of pathos necessary to call it a successful tragedy.

EDWARD II

In *Edward II*, however, such pathos can be found in the fateful careers of two men whose wills and hearts are sorely tested. Edward is presented as a man who is required to rule as king even though his weak nature disqualifies him from the task. As misfortune hounds him, he acquires humility and insight, which help to give him a more sympathetic personality than he has at the play's opening. He progresses toward self-understanding, and this transformation distinguishes him from more static characters such as Tamburlaine and Barabas. On the other hand, Mortimer, a man like Navarre who starts out professing deep concern for the destiny of his country, gradually loses the audience's sympathy as he becomes driven by ambition for the crown. This pattern of characterization charges *Edward II* with pathos of the kind Shakespeare would achieve in his tragedy *Richard II*, which was based on Marlowe's play and appeared a year after it.

Like Shakespeare, Marlowe turned to Raphael Holinshed's *Chronicles* (1577) to find the source material for *Edward II*. While earlier playwrights had attempted to transform the stuff of chronicle history into drama, Marlowe was the first to forge a dramatic design that is coherent and progressive. He presents a single theme—the struggle between Edward and his nobles—modulating it by means of the hero's victories and defeats. When Edward is finally overcome and the crown falls to his heir, he pursues Mortimer and his deceitful queen until revenge is won. In an ending unlike those of Marlowe's earlier plays, the accession of Edward III brings with it the promise of happier, more prosperous days. This exuberance at the close is a far cry from the condition of the state when the action begins. Gaveston, Edward's minion, seeks to divide his lover from the nobles not only for sexual reasons. He shows that he is ambitious and disdainful of his superiors. In an

opening-scene confrontation (which Gaveston overhears), Edward defies the lords, announcing his intention to appoint Gaveston Lord High-Chamberlain. Edward's brother Kent at first supports him, telling the king to cut off the heads of those who challenge his authority. Yet by the close of the scene, when Edward has alienated the lords, the commons, and the bishops, Kent begins to wonder openly about his brother's ability to rule.

Mortimer, a man possessed by brashness, stands as the chief opponent to the king. He is begged by Queen Isabella not to move against the crown, even though she has been displaced by Gaveston. Mortimer is not alone in his opposition to the king's behavior. The archbishop of Canterbury joins the peers in composing a document that officially banishes Gaveston. Although Edward rages against this rebellious act, he soon realizes that to resist might well lead to his own deposing. He is trapped because he has placed love for his minion above his concern for England. It is significant in this regard that Gaveston is both low-born and a Frenchman, which qualified him as a true villain in the eyes of Elizabethan Englishmen. Before the two men part, expressing vows that sound like those of heterosexual lovers, Edward turns to Isabella, accusing her (at Gaveston's prompting) of being involved in an affair with Mortimer. Tortured by her husband's harsh, and for the moment untrue, words, Isabella approaches the lords and, with Mortimer's aid, convinces them to rescind the banishment order. Edward rejoices, suddenly announcing plans to marry Gaveston to his niece; his enthusiasm is not shared by Mortimer and his father, who see this as another move to entrench Gaveston in royal favor. The minion's success also breeds Machiavellian ambition in younger courtiers, the audience learns from a short interlude involving Young Spencer and Baldock. This mirroring technique, by which lesser characters are observed copying the traits of the central figures, serves Marlowe's moral or instructive purposes in other plays as well.

When Gaveston returns in triumph, he expresses contempt for the "base, leaden earls" who greet him with a mocking recital of his newly acquired titles. Lancaster, then Mortimer and others, draw their swords and threaten Gaveston, an action that prompts Edward to order Mortimer from his court. A shouting match follows, sides are taken, and the earls set about planning how they will murder Gaveston. Fuel is added to the fire when Edward childishly refuses to ransom Mortimer's uncle, who has been captured by the Scots. (One can see in this episode parallels with the Hotspur-Henry IV quarrel in Shakespeare's *Henry IV, Part I*, pr. 1598.) Rejecting his brother Kent's sound advice to seek a truce with the lords, Edward declares his intention to be revenged on them all, plotting openly with Gaveston to be rid of his enemies. By allowing himself to be driven by anger, Edward exhibits his political naïveté: His threat against Mortimer also alienates the people, to whom he is a hero. Furthermore, as Marlowe makes clear, the lords frequently express their desire to expel the king's favorite, not the king. It is important to realize that the playwright does not present the homosexual affair in an exploitative way; rather, he wants the audience to understand how Edward's blind defense of his "friendship" makes it easy for his enemies to rally to the cause.

The lords finally decide to move openly against Gaveston, whose whereabouts Isabella reluctantly reveals. Isabella's position has been made increasingly difficult by the king's claim that she and young Mortimer are lovers. Now her action seems to confirm Edward's suspicions, even though she affirms her love for the king and her son. When Gaveston is overtaken by his enemies—one of whom compares him to Helen of Troy—he is accused of being a common thief, then given over to Warwick's custody, an act that ensures his death. Rather than solving the country's problems, however, the removal of Gaveston exacerbates them. Edward quickly embraces the support of Young Spencer and Baldock, his new favorites, while continuing to ignore the incursions of Scots marauders and of the French King Valois, who has invaded Normandy. Marlowe here paints a vivid picture of the collapse of the body politic from internal and external forces. Yet when the inevitable civil war breaks out, Edward wins, proceeding quickly to take revenge against those "traitors" who opposed him. In his rage, however, he makes another mistake;

rather than killing Mortimer, he imprisons him in the Tower, where his ambition (or *virtu*) has an opportunity to flower. With the aid of Edward's disgruntled brother Kent, Mortimer escapes to France to seek aid—along with Isabella—to restore England to her former health. It now appears that Isabella and Mortimer have joined forces to place Prince Edward on the throne. Yet as they leave the French court with promises of support, the queen and the young climber appear to have their own interests, not those of the kingdom, at heart.

Not surprisingly, Edward is easily defeated in a second encounter with the lords, bolstered as they are by the troops of Mortimer and Isabella. Isabella immediately proclaims Prince Edward the new "warden" of the realm, then turns the question of Edward's fate over to the lords. It is at this point that Marlowe begins portraying the deposed king in a more sympathetic light. When he is captured by Leicester, Edward, along with Young Spencer and Baldock, is disguised and begging sanctuary from an abbot. In these perilous straits, he still refuses to denounce his friendship with obvious parasites. As the bishop of Winchester asks for his crown, deeming the act for "England's good," Edward suddenly refuses to take it from his head, accusing Isabella and Mortimer of outright rebellion. What makes Edward such a pitiful figure here is his inability to comprehend his part in creating the circumstances of his fall. He regards himself as a wronged innocent surrounded by wolfish traitors; this self-blindness prevents him from acting wisely and in the country's best interests. Although he lacks the spiritual dimensions of Shakespeare's King Lear, his jealous possession of the crown represents the same childlike faith in the object, not in the qualities which it represents. This attitude and the behavior that it engenders—a self-dramatizing resignation—lead to Edward's death.

References to the Wheel of Fortune fill the final scenes of *Edward II*. Mortimer and Isabella appear to have reached the Wheel's top, as both actively plot Edward's death. Isabella emerges, however, as a mother determined to see her son ascend the throne, while Mortimer clearly plots to seize power for himself. He determines that the deposed king must die, but he will act through subordinates rather than directly. Mortimer's tactics represent the victory of Machiavellianism, as he proceeds to rule through plotting and hypocrisy. He has Prince Edward crowned, declaring himself to be protector, then sends Lightborn and Matrevis to murder Edward. In a sad yet gruesome scene, the disheveled Edward is murdered in his jail bed when Lightborn places a table on top of him and jumps up and down on it. This horrible deed is quickly answered by Edward III, who arrests Mortimer, has him hanged and beheaded, and then places the head on his father's hearse. Isabella is sent to the Tower as the new king demonstrates the traits of strength and decisiveness that assure England's future glory. Edward III is a monarch who, like Shakespeare's Henry V, restores not only peace but also the values of patriotism and justice, which are necessary to the peaceful progress of the state.

In *Edward II*, Marlowe scores several successes. He creates a coherent play out of strands of historical material, lending pathos and poetic strength to the main character. He explores the depths of human emotions and depicts skillfully the ambiguous personalities of figures such as Isabella with consummate talent. He also reveals the effects of Machiavellianism in a personage, Mortimer, whose nature is more believable, less stereotyped, than those of Barabas or the Guise. These advances in dramaturgy not only lent tragic potency to *Edward II* but also prepared the way for Marlowe's most spectacular tragic achievement, *Doctor Faustus*.

DOCTOR FAUSTUS

A major obstacle in the path of critics of Marlowe's most popular melodrama, however, is the state of the text. Not published until eleven years after the playwright's death, the play was modified by "doctors" who were paid to add certain effects and delete others. To complicate matters further, an enlarged quarto edition was published in 1616; this version features alterations that suggest it may have been printed from the promptbook. Today's text is largely the work of Sir Walter Greg, who attempted a reconstruction of the play based on the extant quartos. The tragedy bears some resemblance to English morality

interludes dealing with damnation and salvation. By selecting the Faustus myth, however, Marlowe was committed to portraying a story of damnation alone, with a hero who realizes too late the terrible consequences of selling his soul to the Devil. Indeed, the most impressive aspect of *Doctor Faustus* is its incisive treatment of the protagonist's tortured state of mind, which could easily be construed as an object lesson to sinners in the Elizabethan audience. Yet Marlowe was not preparing an interlude for the edification and instruction of simpleminded rustics. He was a daring, provocative artist exploring the character of a man who was legendary for his intellectual curiosity and for his intense desire to break the bonds of human knowledge and experience. However, *Doctor Faustus* does not contain any praise for the Christian religion and, therefore, is not a Christian morality play. The character Doctor Faustus is closely related to Tamburlaine, another Marlovian hero whose desire for knowledge and power sent him on a spectacular quest. While Tamburlaine, however, is able to win the prize—if only for a brief time—Doctor Faustus in fact falls from the position of social and spiritual prominence he holds at the play's opening. He is a victim of a system he chooses to defy. In that act of defiance, he begins almost immediately to deteriorate into a fool. The stages of that decline are carefully, ironically traced by Marlowe, who seems to want the audience to regard his hero's striving as a futile gesture. The play's ending, with Faustus being led away by devils who torture and then dismember him, offers no optimistic vision to the audience. *Doctor Faustus* thus stands as Marlowe's most pessimistic play, a tragedy that instructs its spectators in the dangers and ultimate limitations of the human imagination.

The play's opening (after an induction by a Senecan Chorus) finds Faustus in his study rejecting the orthodox or conventional disciplines and hungering for the demigod status of a magician. Even though he is cautioned against incurring God's anger by the Good Angel, Faustus invites two magicians, Valdes and Cornelius, to dine with him. In an effective bit of mirroring, Marlowe invents a servant named Wagner, who mimics the behavior of his master by behaving condescendingly toward two scholars who have come to warn Faustus about practicing the "damn'd art." One is struck throughout the play by the concern shown for the hero by his friends.

When Doctor Faustus manages to cast a spell and call up his servant Mephostophilis, the audience should quickly realize that he has made a bad bargain. Lucifer's messenger tells him directly that he desires the magician's soul and that Faustus will possess only the power the devils choose to give him. Unfortunately, Faustus's pride blinds him to the reality of the contract, which he signs with his own blood. He must forfeit his soul after twenty-four years of magic. In a humorous parallel scene, Wagner, too, calls up spirits and purchases the services of a clown, the burlesque counterpart of Mephostophilis. The slapstick underplot makes clear the ironic point: The servants control their masters and not vice versa.

While the Good Angel urges Faustus to repent, he instead boldly defies God and mocks the existence of Hell. His haughtiness begins to weaken, however, when second thoughts about the contract start to plague him. Supposing himself to be beyond salvation, Faustus instead turns to Mephostophilis for answers to questions about the creation of humanity and the world. In place of answers, Mephostophilis offers evasions and sideshows, such as the procession of the Seven Deadly Sins. Again a comic scene echoes the main action as Robin the Clown steals his master's conjuring books and invites Dick to turn invisible with him, in which state they plan to visit the tavern and drink all they wish without paying. References to bills and nonpayment throw into relief the predicament of the hero, whose "bill" must be paid with his life. When the audience next encounters Faustus, he is in fact supposed to be invisible as he visits a papal banquet, where he daringly strikes the pope and plays sophomoric tricks on the cardinals. The appeal of such anti-Catholic skits to a Protestant audience is obvious; Marlowe reinforces that point when he has Faustus help rescue the rival Pope Bruno from imprisonment. Yet even though he succeeds in puncturing the vanity of Rome, Faustus also reveals himself to be a second-rate showman rather than the demigod

he had hoped to become. Marlowe accomplishes this effect by depicting his hero first in the papal setting; then in Emperor Charles's court, placing the cuckold's horns on the heads of three courtiers; and finally in a tavern, where he tricks a horse-courser into believing he has pulled off Faustus's leg.

This foolery has been heavily criticized by commentators as nothing more than an attempt to divert the mechanicals. Some have argued that the scenes involving Robin and the other clowns were in fact added by subsequent playwrights. There can be little doubt, however, that many of these scenes are intended to underscore the hero's decline and to foreshadow later events. The horse-courser's pulling off of Faustus's "leg" and the subsequent purchase of a mare that turns out to be a bale of hay foreshadow the hero's final dismemberment and comment on the bad bargain that Faustus has made with Lucifer. As in plays such as Shakespeare's *Henry IV, Part I*, burlesque business in the underplot of *Doctor Faustus* provides a more informal way of appreciating the thematic significance of the main action.

Marlowe also exhibits his expertise in using conventions of the Elizabethan stage to reinforce his main themes. At the court of Emperor Charles, Faustus creates a dumb show that depicts Alexander defeating Darius, then giving the defeated king's crown to his paramour. (While this action is taking place, Mephostophilis places the cuckold's horns on the head of Benvolio, one of the courtiers who has challenged Faustus's authority.) The dumb show celebrates the victory of a great warrior and is obviously intended as an elaborate compliment to the emperor. Yet it also suggests how distant Faustus himself is from the noble stature of an Alexander; instead of performing great deeds—his original purpose—he can function only in the medium's role. This identity is reinforced in the climactic scene of the play, when Faustus requires Mephostophilis to conjure up Helen of Troy. She crosses the stage quickly, leaving Faustus unsatisfied. He is then approached by an old man who urges him to repent before it is too late. Stricken by these words and by his conscience, Faustus nearly commits suicide with a dagger that the invisible Mephostophilis conveniently places in his hand. The old man returns to stop him, but when he leaves the stage, Mephostophilis materializes and berates Faustus for his desperate attempt. Now believing himself beyond redemption and driven by desire, the magician calls again for Helen of Troy, whom he praises, kisses, and then leads away.

Several commentators believe this act of intercourse with a spirit (a succuba) damns Faustus unequivocally. His soul has become so corrupted as a result that it shares the demoniac spirit with the other devils. Marlowe, however, clearly wants his audience to believe that Faustus could save himself at any time should he decide to repent and ask forgiveness. The dilemma he faces is that he is torn between despair and faint hope; he never manages to decide on a course of action and take it. This depiction of man as a battleground for the forces of good and evil looks back to the morality plays and ahead to plays of psychological complexity such as Shakespeare's *Hamlet, Prince of Denmark* (pr. c. 1600-1601). In the case of *Doctor Faustus*, the failure to repent allows Lucifer, Mephostophilis, and other devils to conjure up yet another vision, this time of a horror-filled Hell. Left alone on the stage, Faustus makes a pitiful attempt to slow the passage of time—"O, lente, lente, currite noctis equi!"—but now his magic has left him. This speech highlights one of the play's chief ironies: Twenty-four years have passed as quickly as twenty-four hours, the last one ticking away toward Faustus's doom. When the scholars who were Faustus's friends next enter, they find only his limbs, the grim remains of a man who thought himself to be a god. Hell turns out to be no fable for the damned hero. The hero of *Doctor Faustus*, Marlowe's major artistic and popular success, belongs with Marlowe's others by virtue of his defiance and his compelling rhetorical style.

OTHER MAJOR WORKS

POETRY: *Hero and Leander*, 1598 (completed by George Chapman); "The Passionate Shepherd to His Love," 1599 (in *The Passionate Pilgrim*).

TRANSLATIONS: *Elegies*, 1595-1600 (of Ovid's *Amores*); *Pharsalia*, 1600 (of Lucan's *Bellum civile*).

MISCELLANEOUS: *The Works of Christopher Marlowe*, 1910, 1962 (C. F. Tucker Brooke, editor); *The Works and Life of Christopher Marlowe*, 1930-1933, 1966 (R. H. Case, editor); *The Complete Works of Christopher Marlowe*, 1973 (Fredson Bowers, editor).

BIBLIOGRAPHY

Downie, J. A., and J. T. Parnell. *Constructing Christopher Marlowe*. New York: Cambridge University Press, 2000. This scholarly study contains essays on Marlowe's life and works. Includes bibliography and index.

Grantley, Darryll, and Peter Roberts, eds. *Christopher Marlowe and English Renaissance Culture*. Aldershot, Hants, England: Scholar Press, 1996. This collection of essays covers topics such as Marlowe and atheism and the staging of his plays and provides in-depth analysis of most of his plays. Bibliography and index.

Hopkins, Lisa. *Christopher Marlowe: A Literary Life*. New York: Palgrave, 2000. A study of Marlowe's career and what is known of his life. Hopkins focuses on Marlowe's skepticism toward colonialism, family, and religion.

Simkin, Stevie. *Marlowe: The Plays*. New York: Palgrave, 2001. Simkin provides in-depth analyses of Marlowe's dramas, major and minor. Bibliographical references and index.

_____. *A Preface to Marlowe*. New York: Longman, 2000. In addition to providing a biography of Marlowe, Simkin analyzes his major and minor plays, concluding with a chapter on Marlowe's influence on the theater. Bibliography and index.

Tauton, Nina. *Fifteen-nineties Drama and Militarism: Portrayals of War in Marlowe, Chapman, and Shakespeare's Henry V*. Aldershot, England: Ashgate, 2001. Tauton looks at war in the works of Marlowe, William Shakespeare, and George Chapman, writing in the late sixteenth century. Bibliography and index.

Tromly, Fred B. *Playing with Desire: Christopher Marlowe and the Art of Tantalization*. Buffalo, N.Y.: University of Toronto Press, 1998. Tromly discusses the dramatic works of Marlowe from the playwright's use of tantalization. Bibliographical references and index.

Trow, M. J., and Taliesin Trow. *Who Killed Kit Marlowe? A Contract to Murder in Elizabethan England*. Stroud, England: Sutton, 2001. This discussion focuses on Marlowe's mystery-shrouded death, providing both the evidence that is available and the many theories that exist. Bibliography and index.

Robert F. Willson, Jr.,
updated by Glenn Hopp

JOHN MARSTON

Born: Near Coventry, England; October 7, 1576 (baptized)
Died: London, England; June 25, 1634

PRINCIPAL DRAMA

Histriomastix: Or, The Player Whipt, pr. 1599, pb. 1610
Antonio and Mellida, pr. 1599, pb. 1602
Antonio's Revenge, pr. 1599, pb. 1602
Jack Drum's Entertainment, pr. 1600, pb. 1601
What You Will, pr. 1601, pb. 1607
The Dutch Courtesan, pr. c. 1603-1604, pb. 1605
The Malcontent, pr., pb. 1604
Parasitaster: Or, The Fawn, pr. 1604, pb. 1606 (commonly known as *The Fawn*)
Eastward Ho!, pr., pb. 1605 (with George Chapman and Ben Jonson)
The Wonder of Women: Or, The Tragedie of Sophonisba, pr., pb. 1606 (commonly known as *Sophonisba*)
The Insatiate Countess, pr. c. 1610, pb. 1613 (completed by William Barksted)
The Plays of John Marston, pb. 1934-1939 (3 volumes; H. Harvey Wood, editor)

OTHER LITERARY FORMS

John Marston's satiric bent is apparent in his first publications: *The Metamorphosis of Pigmalion's Image and Certaine Satyres* (1598) and *The Scourge of Villanie* (1598). Indeed, the Pigmalion poem, ostensibly in the Ovidian amatory mode fashionable in the 1590's, is most interesting and effective as a satiric commentary on the very tradition that it purports to embrace. Underlying the familiar romantic paradigm of the sculptor's infatuation with his creation is the portrayal of an artist beset by what Marston calls a "fond dotage," a form of insanity. Pigmalion's inability to separate shade from substance is an obvious target for the unremitting satire that informs nearly all of Marston's work. Moreover, the poem's lurching oscillations between the genres of erotic epyllion and verse satire point to the stylistic confusion that mars several of Marston's plays.

Certaine Satyres and *The Scourge of Villanie* broaden the field of satire to include an entire world of corruption and decay, of dissolving social ties and religious values. Emotionally forceful, if not always structurally coherent, the satires parade a motley cast of characters representative of the assorted vices and foibles of fallen humanity. This dramatization of moral states, as well as an overriding obsession with sexual depravity and hypocrisy, carries over into Marston's plays.

ACHIEVEMENTS

A ceaseless experimenter, John Marston invested a variety of dramatic forms with the satiric, even mordant, worldview that originated in the late 1590's and came to define Jacobean drama. To study Marston, therefore, is to study the structural varieties of Elizabethan and Jacobean drama: the morality play in *Histriomastix*, revenge conventions in the Antonio plays, romantic comedy in *Jack Drum's Entertainment*, tragicomedy in *The Malcontent*, classical tragedy in *Sophonisba*. Marston's recurring dramatic strategy pits individual integrity against worldly corruption under hysterically theatrical conditions. His protagonists are often conscious role players, gambling for survival in a world not of their making, which they bitterly condemn. Fascinated by theatrical artifice, by shadings of illusion and reality, and by the interplay between actor and role, Marston speaks to the twentieth century as clearly as he did to his own. Despite the relatively infrequent performance of his plays, even in his own day, Marston's influence on his contemporaries was profound, his uniquely strident voice echoing through the plays of John Webster, Cyril Tourneur, and John Ford, among others.

BIOGRAPHY

John Marston, the son of a prominent and prosperous lawyer, was christened on October 7, 1576. The exact date and place of his birth are unknown, although he surely passed his youth in Coventry, where his father, a distinguished member of the Middle Temple, was town steward from 1588 until his death in 1599. Little is known of Marston's early life until he matriculated at Brasenose College, Oxford, in 1592. After completing his bachelor of arts degree in 1594, he resided in London at the Middle Temple, sharing his father's chambers and beginning to study law. That Marston would never practice law was apparent by 1599, when his father cautioned him "to foregoe his delighte in playes, vayne studdyes, and fooleryes." A resigned yet plaintive note creeps into the final version of his father's will, when, leaving his law books to his son, the dying man recalls his hope "that my sonne would have proffetted in the studdye of the lawe wherein I bestowed my uttermost indevor but man proposeth and God disposeth." Marston nevertheless continued to live in the Middle Temple, a not uncommon practice at a time when fewer than 15 percent of the residents actually embraced law as a profession. No better place for witty companionship, lively debate, and satiric mockery could have been found; the influence of Middle Temple life was to shape Marston's entire literary output.

That output, as well as its early cessation, was perhaps regulated by the religious and political climate of the era. The bishops' ban on satiric and erotic poems in 1599 may have prompted Marston's shift to playwriting in the same year. In 1605, Ben Jonson and George Chapman were jailed for their jibes in *Eastward Ho!* against James I and the Scots, although the offending material might as easily have been Marston's. When the king, insulted by attacks against him in two plays, one of which may have been Marston's *The Fawn*, closed all London theaters in March, 1608, he vowed that the offending playwrights should "never play more but should first begg their bred and he wold have his vow performed." This time Marston could not avoid the punishment he had luckily escaped in 1605; he was committed to Newgate Prison. He wrote no plays thereafter.

From the time of his 1606 marriage to Mary, daughter of the Reverend William Wilkes, one of King James's favorite chaplains, Marston had given up his Middle Temple lodgings to reside at the Wiltshire residence of his father-in-law. Whether it was that churchman's influence, the fear of the king's wrath, or the natural evolution of a moral habit of mind that led Marston into holy orders is unclear. In any event, the playwright severed his theatrical connections in 1608 by selling his shares in the Blackfriars Theatre. He was ordained as a deacon in September, 1609, and as an Anglican priest later that year, on Christmas Eve. Thereafter, Marston surfaced from his provincial clerical duties only briefly in 1633 to demand the withdrawal of an unauthorized collection of six of his plays. Marston died in London on June 25, 1634. His epitaph, *Oblivioni Sacrum*, recalls his early dedication "To Everlasting Oblivion" from *The Scourge of Villanie*. By the time of his death, Marston had long since put behind him that "delighte in playes, vayne studdyes, and fooleryes" of which his father had despaired.

ANALYSIS

John Marston's entire dramatic career can be read as an attempt to adapt the materials of Renaissance formal satire to the stage. Although his output reveals no neat gradations of development, it falls conveniently into two general divisions: those plays from *Histriomastix* through *What You Will*, crowded into the years between 1599 and 1601, and those that followed, ending with Marston's retirement from the theater. Perhaps the 1601-1604 hiatus constituted a period of artistic reflection and consolidation for Marston; in any event, the later plays seem clearly more successful in their integration of satiric materials and dramatic form.

Whatever their relative success as dramatic vehicles, Marston's plays characteristically advance his moral vision by means of a potent mixture of satiric denunciation and exaggerated theatricality; the grotesque savagery of his early imagery was remarkable even in an age in which harsh rhetoric was the norm. Although Marston's satirists never lose their hard-edged scorn, they are gradually transformed from irresponsible railers lashing out at anyone or anything that angers them into responsible critics of people and manners. Marston's targets are legion, but they all inhabit the world of city or court.

The crucial task for Marston the dramatist is to find appropriate modes of theatrical expression for his essentially mordant worldview. Because no single attitude is proof against the rapacious onslaughts of human wickedness, the playwright is forced into constant shifts of rhetoric and tone. These, in turn, produce a drama of wrenching extremes in which tragedy is forever collapsing into melodrama and comedy into farce. At the heart of the drama is usually found Marston's mouthpiece, a satiric commentator living painfully in a fallen world whose vices he condemns and whose values he rejects. Often disguised, the satirist proceeds by seeming to embrace, even to prompt, the very crimes and foibles that he savagely denounces. His disguise symbolizes the chasm between being and seeming wherein lies the hypocrisy to be discovered and exposed; moreover, it allows the fitful starts and stops, the aesthetic and moral twists embodied in the deliberate theatricality of Marston's seriocomic vision.

The dangerously insecure and deceptive worldview of the plays invites the growing misanthropy of Marston's satire. Feelings of guilt and revulsion define bodily functions and poison sensual delights. Marston includes many images of the body and its functions in his works, perhaps suggesting the dramatist's unconscious thoughts. Dramatic action takes place in a nightmare world of brutal lust and violent intrigue in which darkness cloaks venal and shameful deeds. Women, once incidental factors in man's degeneracy, increasingly become repositories of perverted desire, culminating in the animalistic Franchischina of *The Dutch Courtesan*. Social intercourse consists mainly of manipulations and betrayals from which Marston's dramatic persona finds refuge only in the impassive self-containment of stoicism. When neither stoicism nor withdrawal can protect Sophonisba from the spreading stain of worldly corruption, Marston's last heroine elects the only remaining moral refuge: suicide. It is an ironically apt solution to the problem of acting in a depraved world, and it highlights the central theme of Marston's plays: the moral cost of living in such a world.

Marston's early plays experiment with various dramatic forms: the morality play in *Histriomastix*, romantic comedy in *Jack Drum's Entertainment*, the revenge play in *Antonio's Revenge*. Chiefly interesting as attempts to find appropriate vehicles for satiric commentary, they contain many of the theatrical ingredients but little of the dramatic power of Marston's masterpiece, *The Malcontent*.

THE MALCONTENT

The Malcontent depicts the morally debilitated world of *What You Will* and the Antonio plays. Here, however, the characters are neither the mere labels for the commonplace ideas of *What You Will* nor the tenuous projections of the satiric background of the Antonio plays. In the central figure of Malevole-Altofronto, Marston has created the perfect objective correlative for his worldview. That view is embedded in the structure of *The Malcontent*, which continues and amalgamates *Antonio and Mellida* and *Antonio's Revenge*. Eddying between comedy and tragedy, *The Malcontent* employs all the Senecan sordidness, theatrical self-consciousness, and satiric commentary of its predecessors. Ostensibly, *The Malcontent* is a revenge play at the heart of which Altofronto, deposed duke of Genoa, assumes the disguise of Malevole in order to regain his dukedom from the usurper Pietro, who, in turn, is the tool by which the scheming Mendoza advances his own ducal ambitions. Unlike the typical revenge play, which culminates in the hero's bloody reprisals, *The Malcontent* achieves a fragile harmony based on the hero's modified goals, for this revenger seeks to reform rather than to destroy. Undeniably bitter at his dispossession, Altofronto is nevertheless driven as much by the will to rejuvenate his enemies as to reclaim his rule. A victim of deception and intrigue, Altofronto must learn to deceive his deceivers. The mask of Malevole becomes a strategy for survival in the ridiculous yet hazardous world created by fallen humanity. That world is defined by the sexual corruption of Aurelia, Pietro's unfaithful wife; of Ferneze, her lustful lover, who competes with Mendoza for her favor; of Biancha, who distributes her favors wholesale; and of Maquerelle, the overripe procuress, no less than by the sinister plotting of Pietro and Mendoza.

Altofronto's mask is so firmly in place from the outset that a considerable portion of the first act transpires before Malevole reveals his true identity to the "constant lord," Celso. By this time, he has already tortured Pietro by disclosing Aurelia's adultery with Mendoza. Liberated by the traditional role of the malcontent, Malevole will continue to castigate the corruption that he exposes. Malevole shapes the play even as he is shaped by its demands: It is in the service of reform that he spotlights human vice and folly. The essentially passive satirist, periodically intruding into other characters' stories, now emerges as the hero of the play whose still biting commentary is crucial to its action. When Malevole, who has been hired by Mendoza to solicit Altofronto's "widow," Maria, and to murder Pietro, reveals the depth of Mendoza's perfidy to the horrified Pietro, the latter disguises himself as a hermit and returns to court to announce his own death. Mendoza now moves swiftly to consolidate his rule, banishing Aurelia, sending Malevole off to urge his case to the imprisoned Maria, and hiring the hermit to poison Malevole, who in turn is ordered to poison the hermit. Forced into a horrified recognition of the depraved world that he has helped create, Pietro is not even permitted the solace of Aurelia's sincere repentance

before Malevole's savage castigation of earth as "the very muckhill on which the sublunarie orbs cast their excrement" and man as "the slime of this donguepit." This episode at court and its aftermath typify Malevole's practice of moral surgery: positioning characters first to confront their own depravity, then to repent of it, and finally to excise it. Malevole's manipulations fittingly culminate in the court masque that ends the play. Ordered by Mendoza to celebrate his accession to power, the masque becomes the vehicle of his undoing. The masquers reveal themselves as Mendoza's apparent murder victims, and Malevole, again Altofronto, reclaims Maria and his dukedom. Such characters as Pietro, Aurelia, and Ferneze, truly contrite and repentant, are freely pardoned; others, such as Maquerelle and the knavish old courtier, Bilioso, are banished from court. Mendoza, reduced to cravenly begging for his life, is contemptuously, and literally, kicked out.

Altofronto's intricate role-playing and manipulations have brought concord out of discord. By consciously delimiting his revenge, by constantly pointing to the absurdity of human action, and by the consummate theatricality not only of his gestures but also of his double role, he transforms the revenge play into a vehicle for social conciliation.

THE DUTCH COURTESAN

In *The Dutch Courtesan*, Marston abandons the satiric furor and Italianate intrigues of *The Malcontent* for exuberant comedy. Although its dramatic material is undeniably lighter, *The Dutch Courtesan* is equally successful in its depiction and analysis of human nature. The play's moral center is Freevill, who plans one last visit to Francischina, the courtesan of the title, before settling down to married life with the angelic Beatrice. Outraged by Freevill's loose conduct, Malheureux goes along in order to admonish Francischina and dissuade his friend. A chilly, puritanical, and inexperienced young man, Malheureux is jolted from his moral complacency at first sight of the courtesan, whom he immediately longs to possess. When Francischina demands Freevill's murder as the price of her favors, the distressed Malheureux confesses his plight to his friend. Concluding that only strong medicine can restore Malheureux to his senses, Freevill concocts a bizarre plot. The friends stage a quarrel, after which Freevill goes into hiding. Claiming Francischina's favors as his promised reward for killing Freevill, Malheureux is deceived when she betrays him to the law. Meanwhile, Freevill has vanished, and with him, the corroborating evidence of the hoax. Condemned to hang, Malheureux is saved only at the gallows by Freevill, who justifies his friend's anguish as the price that must be paid for moral enlightenment.

The Dutch Courtesan is a comic morality play whose end is psychological and social, rather than religious, salvation. It proceeds by establishing a dialectic between love and lust, defined at the outset by Freevill, who sees no moral inconsistency between his former lust for Francischina and his present love for Beatrice. Whoring, no less than marriage, is a valid expression of man's nature. This Malheureux denies, arguing for a rigid line of demarcation between virtue and vice and thereby against the reality of the human condition. A "snowy" man of cloistered virtue, Malheureux must be brought face-to-face with an exemplum of his folly in the alluring person of Francischina. Undeniably a good man, as evidenced by his refusal to betray Freevill at Francischina's behest, Malheureux must be brought to the foot of the scaffold to attain self-knowledge. Regarding himself as above passion, he becomes "passion's slave"; proffering himself as Freevill's moral tutor, he becomes his moral pupil. One of Marston's most effective characterizations, he mirrors the playwright's moral torment. Regarding lust as the deadliest sin, his imagination nevertheless dwells on the loose sexuality he abhors. Shocked by the moral degeneracy of the beautiful Francischina, he eddies between frantic desire and consuming guilt. In this drama of initiation, Malheureux, like his creator, must learn to recognize and control his natural desires, not to annihilate them.

These lessons are farcically reinforced in a brilliant subplot that features Cocledemoy's gulling of the affected pseudo-Puritans, the Mulligrubs. By causing Mulligrub's false arrest for thievery and effecting his victim's release only at the point of execution, Cocledemoy, like Freevill, exposes and cauter-

izes moral absolutism. This subplot, combined with Tysefew's bantering wooing of Beatrice's sister, Crispinella, also functions to preserve the play's light tone.

By introducing a purely comic subplot, by inflating Malheureux's rhetoric, by layering Francischina's diatribes with a thick Dutch accent, and by establishing Freevill's beneficent control of the action, Marston invokes a world of comic absurdity as he dissipates its potential tragedy. A perceptive study in sexual psychology, *The Dutch Courtesan* balances and expands its author's moral vision.

THE FAWN

The Fawn, Marston's frothiest comedy, recapitulates that vision and its modes of achievement. Like *The Dutch Courtesan*, it treats the perverted natural instincts resulting from repressed or misdirected sexuality; it also employs a double plot no less sophisticated than its predecessor's. Like *The Malcontent*, it is set in an Italian court corroded by folly and flattery, and its hero is a disguised duke bent on reform. *The Fawn*'s lighter tone stems primarily from its unthreatened duke and its more farcical than sinister court intrigues.

Hercules, duke of Ferrara, appears at the court of Gonzago, duke of Urbin, disguised as Faunus, the consummate flattering courtier and a member of his son Tiberio's retinue. Tiberio's ostensible mission is to negotiate the marriage of Gonzago's fifteen-year-old daughter, Dulcimel, to his sixty-four-year-old father. Actually, Duke Hercules hopes that Dulcimel's charms will arouse his unnaturally aloof son to woo the girl for himself. To ensure that end, he monitors the action as Faunus. Because Dulcimel immediately falls in love with Tiberio and sets out to awaken the young man's latent feelings, Faunus is freed to deal with the corruption and hypocrisy of the court; nearly half the play is devoted to providing him with appropriate occasions to practice the art of flattery on the unsuspecting courtiers. Lulled into freely confessing their follies, Faunus's victims indirectly satirize themselves. Because vanity rather than Machiavellian intrigue marks Urbin's court, Faunus contents himself with exposing grotesqueries rather than reviling corruption. The stuff of satire—Nymphadora's claim to be the world's great lover, Herod's assertion of superiority, Dosso's impotence and his wife Garbetza's adultery with his brother, Zuccone's jealousy of his estimable wife Zoya—takes the form of sexual foibles. That these sins are merely skin-deep allows Marston to turn his satiric commentator from savage railer to witty practitioner of the courtly games he plans to expose. Moreover, the sexual waywardness of the minor characters functions as an implicit comment on the sexual backwardness of Tiberio. The double plot of *The Fawn* therefore proceeds along parallel tracks, Faunus dealing with sexual excess, Dulcimel with sexual indifference. Successful resolution depends on the ability of Faunus and Dulcimel to awaken Gonzago to the folly around him—his own as well as his court's.

Gonzago, duke of Urbin, is one of Marston's most inspired comic creations. Delighting in words and garrulous in conversation, he imagines himself the consummate rhetorician. His several long-winded speeches, studded with odd bits of classical lore, are designed to bolster his self-image of a learned man of ripe wisdom; instead, they reveal him as an unknowing self-flatterer and, therefore, as a potential gull. Dulcimel plays on her father's vanity to promote the very affair he would frustrate, using him as a go-between to inform the slow Tiberio of her interest. Shamelessly flattered by his daughter, Gonzago becomes her unwitting instrument; "hee shall direct the Prince the meanes the very way to my bed." Through four acts, Dulcimel, like Faunus, wields the weapon of flattery. In the fifth act, Faunus exploits her actions, trapping the duke in the same way that he has trapped others.

The final act is played on a two-level stage: Tiberio climbs a "tree" to join Dulcimel above, while Hercules remains below. The marriage of the young lovers presumably coincides with the several judgments rendered by Cupid's Parliament. Symbolic of healthy and natural love, the union of Dulcimel and Tiberio implicitly condemns the courtiers, who have violated Cupid's laws. Paraded before the court and arraigned on Faunus's evidence, they are exposed and released. Finally, Gonzago is indicted for his pretensions to wisdom and, more serious, for his attempts to

obstruct life's natural flow. "What a slumber have I been in," cries the duke, whose court promises to be healthier hereafter.

In its comic characterizations, in its tonal consistency, and in its technical assurance, *The Fawn* is a masterly achievement. Marston's fusion of satiric force and content, apparent in *The Malcontent* and *The Dutch Courtesan*, is no less perfect in *The Fawn*.

SOPHONISBA

Sophonisba is Marston's attempt at high Roman tragedy. Full of high moral sentiment expressed in consistently lofty verse, it impressed T. S. Eliot as Marston's best play. Its purpose, implicit in its alternate title, *The Wonder of Women*, is to portray human perfection in the person of its heroine, Sophonisba. To evoke her ideal virtue, Marston employs his characteristic tactic of pitting individual honor and integrity against a corrupt world. It is in the altered relationship between character and context, however, that *Sophonisba* embodies Marston's tragic design. Earlier protagonists manipulated adversaries and events; Sophonisba is victimized by them. A Malevole or a Hercules recognized surrounding evil, satirically castigated it, and finally dispersed or reformed it. Sophonisba, no less perceptive, can only reaffirm her virtue in a world whose evil she cannot alter and can evade only by suicide. The wildly chaotic settings for court intrigues have yielded to a harder, more frightening world of realpolitik.

Before the end of the second act, the main characters and the political world they inhabit are sharply defined. A note of discord is struck early, when the news that Carthage has been invaded disrupts the nuptials of Sophonisba and the famed Carthaginian general Massinissa. When she selflessly postpones marital consummation in the face of her husband's martial duty, she elicits the first of his many expressions of awe at her character: "Wondrous creature, even fit for Gods, not men . . . a pattern/ Of what can be in woman." Much of the remainder of the play consists of tableaux that present repeated assaults on Sophonisba's unassailable virtue, each designed to spotlight her moral grandeur. In similar fashion, political evil surfaces in the scene immediately following Massinissa's departure for battle. No sooner does he leave than the senators of Carthage plot to betray him and Sophonisba for an alliance with the powerful Syphax. Their treachery backfires when Syphax, driven by lust for Sophonisba, who had earlier rejected him, deserts his army in his frenzy to reach her. Syphax's forces defeated, Massinissa and Sophonisba are reunited. Their happiness is, however, as illusory as it is brief. Syphax, his lust frustrated by Sophonisba's virtue and his prestige tarnished by Massinissa's victory in single combat, conceives a final act of vengeance. Arguing, ironically, that Sophonisba's virtues of loyalty to Carthage and constancy to Massinissa will tempt the latter to break his oath of allegiance to Rome, Syphax convinces the Roman general Scipio to demand that she be delivered up to Roman captivity. Confounded by the excruciating choice of betraying his allies or his wife, Massinissa crumbles. No such dilemma exists for Sophonisba, whose immediate decision to commit suicide implicitly condemns her husband's failure to do so. A good and courageous man, albeit Sophonisba's moral inferior, Massinissa is reduced to mixing the poisoned wine for her supremely stoic gesture. Eulogizing her—"O glory ripe for heaven"—he measures her distance from ordinary mortals.

The meaning of Sophonisba's suicide transcends its dramatic function of saving Massinissa by eliminating his moral dilemma. For Marston's heroine, suicide is a welcome escape from "an abhord life" of Roman captivity; it has become virtue's only possible response to the world's depravity. For the playwright, her death creates a dramatic impasse. An obsessive moralist from the outset of his literary career, Marston found in satiric comedy the means of exposing, castigating, and reforming evil. Abandoning satire for pure tragedy, he traps Sophonisba in a world of omnipresent evil that she can recognize but not alter. Thus, the final outcome of the struggle of individual integrity against the corrupt world is martyrdom. After *Sophonisba*, Marston's eventual desertion of the stage for the pulpit may have been the only viable extension of that struggle.

OTHER MAJOR WORKS

POETRY: *The Metamorphosis of Pigmalion's Image and Certaine Satyres*, 1598; *The Scourge of Villanie*, 1598.

BIBLIOGRAPHY

Caputi, Anthony. *John Marston, Satirist*. Reprint. New York: Octagon Books, 1976. By treating Marston primarily as a satirist, Caputi's book demonstrates the unity of thought between Marston's verse satires and his drama, both comic and tragic. Caputi offers important background information on the companies that performed Marston's plays, though sometimes overemphasizing their importance for interpreting Marston's drama.

Geckel, George L. *John Marston's Drama: Themes, Images, Sources*. Rutherford, N.J.: Fairleigh Dickinson University Press, 1980. Geckel analyzes Marston's plays, looking closely at his sources and themes. Bibliography and index.

Ingram, R. W. *John Marston*. Boston: Twayne, 1978. The best introduction to Marston available, this general book covers all of his works, including the nondramatic. Its analysis of the plays, however, is thorough and integrates earlier criticism. Its annotated bibliography evaluates selected books and articles, including general sources on the period and on the genre of satire.

Tucker, Kenneth. *John Marston: A Reference Guide*. Boston: G. K. Hall, 1985. The most complete annotated bibliography available for Marston, listing, in chronological order, all significant studies of Marston's work from his time to 1985.

Wharton, T. F. *The Critical Fall and Rise of John Marston*. Columbia, S.C.: Camden House, 1994. Wharton examines the literary criticism of Marston's works over the years, placing them in historical perspective.

_____, ed. *The Drama of John Marston: Critical Re-Visions*. New York: Cambridge University Press, 2000. A quadcentennial tribute to the heretofore neglected playwright.

Lawrence S. Friedman,
updated by John R. Holmes

RHODODENDRON PORTRAITS

RHODODENDRON PORTRAITS

by

D. M. van Gelderen

and

J. R. P. van Hoey Smith

Translated from the Dutch language by
Nancy Handgraaf and Ton Handgraaf

TIMBER PRESS

Published in cooperation with the
ROYAL BOSKOOP HORTICULTURAL SOCIETY

ISBN 0-88192-194-7
Printed in Hong Kong

TIMBER PRESS, INC.
9999 S.W. Wilshire, Suite 124
Portland, Oregon 97225

Library of Congress Cataloging-in-Publication Data

Gelderen, D. M. van.
    [Rhododendron atlas. English]
    Rhododendron portraits / by D.M. van Gelderen and J.R.P. van Hoey
Smith ; translated from the Dutch language by Nancy Handgraaf and
Ton Handgraaf.
        p.   cm.
    "Published in cooperation with the Royal Boskoop Horticultural
Society."
    Translation of: De rhododendron atlas.
    Includes bibliographical references (p.   ) and index.
    ISBN 0-88192-194-7
    1. Rhododendron. 2. Rhododendron--Pictorial works. I. Hoey
Smith, J. R. P. van. II. Royal Boskoop Horticultural Society.
III. Title.
SB413.R47G4513 1992
635.9'3362--dc20   91-23264
                                                    CIP

CONTENTS

'Scarlet Wonder' and 'Bengal'. This type of classification was never practiced in Boskoop. Pioneers of rhododendron hybridizing at Boskoop were the nurseries C. B. van Nes and Sons, M. Koster and Sons, L. J. Endtz & Co., and H. den Ouden and Sons. C. B. van Nes and Sons bred a large number of excellent cultivars from a cross between 'Stanley Davies' and 'Queen Wilhelmina'. Among these are the beautiful red hybrids 'Britannia', 'C. B. van Nes', 'Earl of Athlone', 'Trilby', 'Langley Park', and 'Unknown Warrior'.

One of the most striking successes of the last 25 years in rhododendron hybridizing was made with the crosses with *R. yakushimanum* and *R. wardii* as parents, largely pioneered by nurserymen in northern Germany. These crosses brought dozens of good and hardy hybrids into the trade. H. Hachmann was very successful with *R. yakushimanum* and *R.*

wardii, producing hybrids 'Morgenrot', 'Silberwolke', and 'Goldkrone', the last a beautiful yellow color.

Notable North American breeders include D. G. Leach, C. Dexter, and H. Lem. They produced many large-flowering and winter-hardy hybrids by using *R. fortunei.* A. Shammarello introduced a line of very winter-hardy *R. catawbiense* hybrids. A good example is 'Belle Heller', one of the best white cultivars available.

A number of British horticulturists and gardeners have been quite active in hybridizing, including Lord Aberconway, who bred 'Elizabeth' and 'Fabia', and Lionel de Rothschild and his son, Edmund, with 'Loderi' and 'Carmen'. Knap Hill Nursery, Hydon Nurseries, and the nursery of the Waterer family have been key players.

Rhododendron, Clematis alpina.

This book encompasses the elepidote rhododendrons (those without scales); these are the large-flowered, evergreen species and hybrids. The plants in this volume are divided into 18 groups. Alphabetical order would make it easier to locate specific names, but the natural sequence would be lost.

Group 1	1a. *R. ponticum* and hybrids
	1b. *R. caucasicum* and hybrids
	1c. *R. smirnowii* and hybrids
Group 2	2a. *R. catawbiense* and hybrids
	2b. *R. maximum* and hybrids
Group 3	3a. *R. yakushimanum* and hybrids
	3b. *R. degronianum* (*metternichii*) and hybrids
	3c. *R. makinoi* and hybrids
Group 4	4a. *R. arboreum* and hybrids
Group 5	5a. *R. insigne* and hybrids
Group 6	6a. *R. facetum* (*eriogynum*) hybrids
	6b. *R. elliottii* and hybrids
	6c. *R. strigillosum* and hybrids
Group 7	7a. *R. griersonianum* and hybrids
Group 8	8a. *R. griffithianum* and hybrids
	8b. *R. orbiculare* and hybrids
Group 9	9a. *R. fortunei* and hybrids
	9b. *R. fortunei* ssp. *discolor* and hybrids
	9c. *R. decorum* and hybrids
Group 10	10a. *R. campylocarpum* and hybrids
Group 11	11a. *R. wardii* and hybrids
Group 12	12a. *R. thomsonii* and hybrids
	12b. *R. viscidifolium* and hybrids
Group 13	13a. *R. williamsianum* and hybrids
Group 14	14a. *R. neriiflorum* and hybrids
	14b. *R. haematodes* and hybrids
	14c. *R. sanguineum* and hybrids
Group 15	15a. *R. dichroanthum* and hybrids
Group 16	16a. *R. forrestii* and hybrids
Group 17	17a. Subsection Taliensia, species and hybrids
	17b. Subsection Campanulata, species and hybrids
	17c. Subsection Fulgensia, species and hybrids
	17d. Subsection Maculifera, species and hybrids
	17e. Subsection Glischra, species and hybrids
Group 18	18a. Subsection Barbata, species and hybrids
	18b. *R. calophytum/sutchuenense* and hybrids
	18c. *R. auriculatum* and hybrids

DEFINITIONS

The following terms are used throughout the text.

Genus: *Rhododendron.*
Subgenus: A division of a genus.
Species: (example) *R. ponticum.*
Subspecies: Divisions within species.
Section: A group of related species.
Subsection: A division of a section.
Series: A group that is part of or equal to one subsection.
Subseries: Division of one series.
Variety: Division of a species or subspecies. May be a population of wild plants that survives on its own but does not differ enough to qualify as a separate species. This is also true for a subspecies.
Forma: A division of a variety.
Cultivar: Cultivated variety.
Population: A population of seedlings from a single crossing with similar characteristics, but individual differences.
Clones: Vegetatively propagated, identical plants.
Motherplant (Seed parent)/Fatherplant (Pollen parent): When the parents of plants are listed, the seed parent is listed first, the pollen parent second.
Breeder: Person or institution that selected or developed the plant.
Year of Introduction: Year the plant was introduced, not the year of selection or development.
Year of Registration: Year the plant was registered with the Registration for Rhododendrons at the Royal Horticultural Society Gardens, Wisley, GB (Dr. A. C. Leslie).
Lepidote: With scales. The leaves, pedicels, bark of the branches, and sometimes the flowers have scales.
Elepidote: Without scales. All the plants in this book belong to this group.
Indumentum: Densely covered with feltlike hair, mostly on the undersides of the leaves.
Chinese Provinces: The names of Chinese provinces are written in Pinying handscript as mandated by the People's Republic of China—Sichuan = Szechuan, Anhui = Anhwei, Hubei = Hupeh, etc.

A NOTE ON THE PHOTOGRAPHS

The photographs for this book were selected from 3000 taken since 1960. We wanted to show rhododendrons in their most natural states, and therefore most of the photographs were taken in gardens, arboreta, parks, and nurseries without artificial lights or tripods.

A few words are necessary about flower color in photographs. A photograph is never a perfect copy of that which is seen by the human eye. The film is a factor; the ideal film, able to reflect true colors, is not yet available. This is especially true with the colors of lilac to dark purple; there always seems to be too much red in these colors. The time of day a photo is taken also affects the outcome. Experience has proven that there is too much yellow light in the early morning or evening. One might think that the blue light would be dominant in midday, but that is not the case. Full sun is suitable only for landscape shots or photographs of complete shrubs or where the surfaces are not flat to reflect the light. Further, some of the flowers, especially pinks, have a reflective waxy layer. Days with slightly overcast skies are ideal.

EXPLANATION OF CAPTIONS

Format:

'**Plant name**' (synonym). Grower/introducer, year of introduction; year of registration. Female parent × male parent. Awards. Height in meters or centimeters, or centimeters, month(s) in bloom [in roman numerals], hardiness zone △[A, B, C, etc.].

Plant sequence is based on the Cullen-Chamberlain system which is described later. All hybrids within a group are listed in alphabetical sequence. Beginning each sequence are any mutants or selections. These appear along with the species name. Plant names in parentheses immediately following the hybrid name are recognized synonyms.

The name of the person, nursery, or institution that selected and bred the plant is given next (when known). However, it has been impossible to trace the breeder on some of the hybrids.

Breeder information precedes the name of the introducer. When only one name appears it is always that of the breeder. A question mark indicates the breeder and raiser are both unknown. A list of breeders representing all *Rhododendron* in this volume follows.

22 8500 ft.). It was described by Trautvetter in 1885.

When full grown, *R. smirnowii* is a fairly large shrub up to 4 m (13 ft.) tall and often wider. The shrub is densely foliated; leaves are dark green, oblong-lanceolate, with round tips. The undersides of the leaves are densely covered with silver-white indumentum. The flower buds are also covered with white hair and offstanding bud scales. The shape of the flowers is similar to that of *R. caucasicum*; the color is lilac pink.

Rhododendron ungerii looks much like *R. smirnowii* and grows in the same area. Both species are able to cross pollinate. *Rhododendron ungerii* leaves are longer and widest in the middle. The plant is larger, sometimes treelike in habit, reaching a height of 7 m (21 ft.).

The German nursery T. R. J. Seidel used *R. smirnowii* frequently for hardiness and beautiful leaf color; in recent years it has been crossed with *R. yakushimanum*.

GROUP 2

Group 2a. *R. catawbiense* and hybrids
Photographs on pages 83–137.

Rhododendron catawbiense, along with *R. ponticum*, is one of the most well-known species, named for the Catawba River in North Carolina. It is native to the Alleghany Mountains of Virginia, in the northeastern United States, and is found there in great abundance.

Anyone who has traveled the famous Blue Ridge Parkway has admired *R. catawbiense* at its finest. In the wild, *R. catawbiense* is a large, open shrub. The leaves are broadly oval, dark green, 5–15 cm (2–6 in.) long and 3–7 cm (1.5–3 in.) wide; the undersides are covered with light green down. The funnel-shaped flowers are borne in densely packed trusses of 15–20 corollas. Their color is lilac-purple, rose to white, with a yellow-green basal blotch.

Rhododendron catawbiense was imported to Europe about 1800, and to England in 1809 by J. Fraser. The French botanist Michaux described this species in 1803, and it was being used at that time for breeding. The T. R. J. Seidel Nursery in Germany used *R. catawbiense* to a large extent. They introduced many hybrids between 1880 and 1914; the new cultivars from any single year were given names beginning with the same letter from the alphabet. In England, crosses were made with *R. arboreum* to improve hardiness in the red-flowered hybrids.

After 1945, A. Shammarello hybridized with *R. catawbiense* on a large scale to produce hybrids that could survive temperatures in the midwestern part of the United States. Some of his crosses became quite famous, but were not worthy of planting in milder climates. The Dutch contribution to the *R. catawbiense* hybrids is limited; one good example is 'Nova Zembla', introduced by M. Koster and Sons. This is a very beautiful winter-hardy cultivar with red flowers and strong foliage. H. den Ouden and Sons also introduced some very good *R. catawbiense* hybrids such as 'Dr. V. H. Rutgers' and 'Van der Hoop'.

Rhododendron catawbiense is rarely used nowadays for new crosses, as most of the possibilities have been tried. The hybrids are easily recognized by their convex, shiny green leaves. *Rhododendron catawbiense* hybrids are free-flowering, and the flower trusses are well built. The typical flower color of these hybrids is lilac with variations of lilac-pink, lilac-red, reddish purple, wine-red, red, or yellow. Hachmann, from Germany, introduced some true red, winter-hardy hybrids.

Group 2b. *R. maximum* and hybrids
Photographs on pages 138–140.

Rhododendron maximum is rarely found in collections and is, therefore, rarely used for breeding. Near the end of the last century, some hybridizing was done with this North American native, but because the flowers are mediocre and the foliage pale there was not much interest. It is mainly native to the Virginias mainly but extends north to Nova Scotia. The growth habit is very dense and can reach 3 m (10 ft.). The plant is very hardy but does not qualify as a desirable garden plant. *Rhododendron maximum* 'Roseum' has no connection with *R. maximum*; the correct name is *R. ponticum* 'Roseum'.

GROUP 3

Group 3a. *R. yakushimanum* and hybrids
Photographs on pages 141–172.

Rhododendron yakushimanum is currently a very popular species. It is a slow-growing, moderately sized shrub which usually does not exceed 1.5 m (5 ft.)—perfect for the small garden. The leaves are 5–10 cm (2–3 in.) long and 2–3 cm (0.75–1.25 in.) wide and covered with soft brown indumentum on the undersides. New spring leaves are covered with white hairs, giving the new growth a whitish grey coloring. The top surfaces of the leaves lose this pubescence during the summer. The flower buds are formed in late summer and are very hairy. The flowers are borne in dense trusses, are trumpet- to funnel-shaped, and are apple blossom pink and fading to pure white.

Rhododendron yakushimanum was described by Prof. Nakai, a Japanese botanist, in 1921. At that time the spelling was "R. yakusimanum," but the present spelling has been used since 1960. The reason for this is unclear, as the island of Yakushima, to which *R. yakushimanum* is native, has always, in literature, had the same spelling. The island is one of the most southern in Japan, approximately 150 km south of Kyushu, at 30 degrees latitude (it is surprising that *R. yakushimanum* is so winter-hardy). The species is protected in its native habitat by the Japanese government; the area is small, but well maintained.

Two plants were first exported in 1934 from K. Wada in Japan to Lionel de Rothschild for the Exbury Gardens, UK. It took some 15 years before plants found their way to Germany and the Netherlands. One of the Rothschild plants was taken to Wisley Gardens, where it won an FCC award in 1947. It was vegetatively propagated, and the clone was given the name 'Koichiro Wada' in 1970. It is compact with small, dark green leaves, slightly convex and covered on the undersides with a thick indumentum. 'Koichiro Wada' is widely used for hybridizing; possibly only *R. griersonianum* is used more.

Significant selections include 'Ken Janeck', white flowers with large leaves; 'Overstreet', also white with grayish olive leaves and a thick indumentum; and 'Esveld Select', pink in bud, later turning to white. The last grows rather quickly, is very hardy, and stays compact. A few cultivars show variation from the light-pink-to-white coloring of the species: 'Dusty Miller', dark salmon-pink fading to soft yellow; 'Bambi', orange-pink fading to pink; and 'Coral Velvet', also with this color variation. When stronger, nonfading colors appear, other desirable characteristics, such as the indumentum, seem to disappear. A few hybrids are able to retain the desirable *R. yakushimanum* characteristics but still have rather stable colors: 'Morgenrot' is blood-red in bud and dark pink in bloom; 'Anuschka' and 'Fantastica' belong to the same category.

The German nurseryman H. Hachmann spent a large part of his life hybridizing rhododendrons. He bred particularly for hardy plants with beautiful flowers, often using *R. yakushimanum* and particularly 'Koichiro Wada'. Dozens of hybrids were named by him, and they are among the finest introduced in the last 30 years.

In England, Waterer, Sons, and Crisp were active hybridizers. They introduced the series of hybrids named for Snow White's seven dwarfs.

Group 3b. *R. degronianum* (*metternichii*) and hybrids
Photographs on pages 173–176.

Rhododendron degronianum is a relatively unknown species and one that has not been used much for hybridizing. The nomenclature for *R. degronianum* and its close relatives is very complicated. *Rhodo-dendron metternichii* is better known as *R. degronionum* and is now considered a subspecies, *heptamerum*. *Rhododendron degronianum* and ssp. *heptamerum* vary mainly in the number of petals, five and seven respectively.

Von Siebold and Zuccarini described *R. metternichii* in 1835. The name was accepted until it was discovered that the same plant had already been described in 1826 by Blume as *Hymenanthes japonica*. As a result, *R. metternichii* was changed to *R. japonicum* (Blume) Schneider. Later it was determined that *R. japonicum* (Gray) Suringar was the correct name for the well-known Azalea Mollis. A thorough revision of this complicated species resulted in a change of status for *R. metternichii* to a subspecies of *R. degronianum* with the name ssp. *heptamerum*. Yet this name was already being used by Maximowicz since 1870 for the variety name of the same plant. The double use of *R. japonicum* was then dropped. *Rhodo-dendron degronianum* ssp. *heptamerum* is a broad shrub growing to 2 m (7 ft.) tall and 3–4 m (10–13 ft.) wide. The leaves are stiff, light green, smooth edged, and have a thin white indumentum. The flowers are borne in fairly dense trusses, 8–12 corollas per truss, with seven petals and 14 stamens, an unusual characteristic in this subsection. The color is non-fading light pink. *Rhododendron degronianum* ssp. *degronianum* is more compact, flowers earlier (April), and has 5-petaled flowers and 10 stamens. The flowers are light pink and do not fade. The leaves are fairly small, 4–7 cm (1.75–3 in.) long and 2–4 cm (1–2 in.) wide with a light brown indumentum. These plants are endemic to Japan, in the hills of Honshu and Kyushu islands.

In the beginning of this century, Seidel in Germany crossed the species with other rhodo-dendrons for hardiness, low compact growth, and the pink color. Not many plants survived. After World War II, Dietrich Hobbie made crossings with *R. degronianum* ssp. *heptamerum* and some close selections and varieties. Vuyk van Nes of Boskoop introduced 'Rijneveld'; it is a very rich blooming plant, pure pink, but could have better foliage.

Group 3c. *R. makinoi* and hybrids
Photographs on pages 177–179.

Rhododendron makinoi has beautiful leaves, but is, unfortunately, rarely found. It has dense foliage and grows to about 2 m (6.5 ft.) high and 3 m (10 ft.) wide. The leaves are knife-shaped, 20 cm (8 in.) long and only 1–2 cm (0.5-0.75 in.) wide. The flowers resemble those of *R. degronianum*: they are fairly small, light pink, have five petals, and are borne in dense trusses. This species is winter-hardy. In spring, the plants look like they are covered with snow; the new growth is covered with white hairs that disappear in summer.

Group 14a. *R. neriiflorum* and hybrids
Photographs on pages 357–358.

Subsection Neriiflora consists of approximately 25 species and their subspecies. This subsection is closely related to Subsection Thomsonia. All species are native to Bhutan, the Chinese provinces of Yunnan and Xizang, and the border area of Upper Burma. Most are not seen in parks or gardens as they are not hardy enough for general planting and grow best in conditions of high rainfall and uniform temperatures. Three species are described in this group: *R. neriiflorum*, *R. haematodes*, and *R. sanguineum*.

Rhododendron neriiflorum was discovered by Father Delavay and described by Franchet in 1886. The species is variable and divided into several subspecies of little horticultural importance.

It is a fairly large, not very dense shrub growing to 3–4 m (10–13 ft.) and about the same in width. The leaves are elliptical to narrow-oval, 5–8 cm (2–3.25 in.) long and 2–3 cm (0.75–1.5 in.) wide, light green with gray-white indumentum on the undersides. The sturdy flowers are mostly blood-red, sometimes transparent, with a few black dots; they are borne in loose, hanging trusses. The plant is difficult to maintain in cultivation and therefore used very little for hybridizing outside Great Britain. Lord Aberconway and Lionel de Rothschild produced 'F. C. Puddle' and 'Nereid'. Lord Swaythling introduced 'David', a vivid red.

Group 14b. *R. haematodes* and hybrids
Photographs on pages 359–361.

Rhododendron haematodes is native to Yunnan, Xizang, and northern Burma, with the Tali Mountains and the basin of the Salween River being the most important areas of distribution. Father Delavay discovered the species, and Franchet described it in 1886 along with *R. neriiflorum*. The name *haematodes* ("bloodlike") refers to the blood-red color of the flowers. *Rhododendron haematodes* is a dwarf shrub that can grow up to 2 m (7 ft.) tall, but usually it is only 75 cm (32 in.), and much wider. The shrub is very compact with dense branches and leaves. The leaves are 4–6 cm (1.5–2.25 in.) long, 2–3 cm (0.75–1.25 in.) wide, and a shiny, dark green; the undersides are covered with a thick orange indumentum. The flowers are borne in small trusses of 2–4, are blood-red, broad, bell-shaped, and substantial. The calyx is often red and can be 2.5 cm (1 in.) wide.

This species is used for hybridizing on a limited scale in Great Britain and Germany. 'Grosclaude' is a nice hybrid previously mentioned with the *R. facetum* hybrids. Lord Aberconway, Lionel de Rothschild, and others used *R. haematodes* to produce such hybrids as 'Choremia', 'Marshall', 'May Day', 'Hiraethlyn', and 'Humming Bird'. In Germany, George Arends developed 'China Boy' and 'Gnom'. Young plants of all these hybrids have poor bud set.

Group 14c. *R. sanguineum* and hybrids
Photographs on pages 362–365.

Rhododendron sanguineum is variable in growth habit, leaf shape, flower color, and adaptability in the garden; it has been divided into two subspecies, from which come a number of varieties. The true *R. sanguineum* is a sturdy, upright shrub 1.5–2 m (5–6.5 ft.) tall; usually its flowers are red, but occasionally they are pink. The variety *haemaleum* is smaller and has conspicuous dark, black-red flowers. These shrubs seldom grow higher than 1 m (3 ft.) and have sparse foliage. The variety *didymoides* grows somewhat taller and has red flowers and sparse foliage. *Rhododendron sanguineum* ssp. *didymum* has a creeping habit, and its flower color is like that of var. *haemaleum*, a dark blood-red. The well-known cultivar 'Carmen' is a hybrid of this subspecies (× *R. forrestii*).

GROUP 15

Group 15a. *R. dichroanthum* and hybrids
Photographs on pages 366–380.

Rhododendron dichroanthum is variable and divided into five subspecies. All are native to southern China in Yunnan Province and to the southern part of the Himalayas to Burma at elevations up to 3000 m (9000 ft.). It was discovered by George Forrest and described by Diels in 1912.

This species is very attractive to hybridizers because of its striking flower colors of orange, orange-yellow, salmon-pink, salmon-yellow, and orange-red. The calyx is often colored the same as the corolla, which enhances the effect. The flowers are born in loose trusses of 3–7, and are funnel- or bell-shaped. The plants are rarely taller than 2 m (7 ft.); the habit is open and loose, but can also be densely branched and dwarf, depending on the subspecies. The leaves are leathery, oval, 3–6 cm (1.3–2.25 in.) long and 2–3 cm (0.75–1.25 in.) wide. The undersides are covered with gray indumentum. Winter hardiness is only moderate.

As mentioned, *R. dichroanthum* has been used for hybridizing because of the attractive colors. Unfortunately, its less desirable characteristics—small number of flowers per truss, sloppy growth, and marginal winter hardiness—are rather dominant.

In Great Britain, Lionel de Rothschild produced a number of hybrids, including 'Golden Horn', 'Felis', and 'Jasper'. The nursery G. Reuthe introduced 'Sonata', a peculiar mixture of orange, salmon-yellow, and purple-lilac; it is a hybrid with 'Purple

Splendour'. W. C. Slocock bred 'Goldsworth Orange', one of the best *R. dichroanthum* hybrids. In Germany, Hachmann and Bruns crossed 'Goldsworth Orange' with other hardy hybrids to develop the hardy 'Bernstein', 'Gloria', 'Silvia', and 'Diana'. In the United States, Lem introduced 'Brinny', an orange-salmon dwarf form; 'Hello Dolly'; and 'Jingle Bell'. A Dutch hybrid of *R. dichroanthum* "blood" is 'Dr. Ans Heyting'.

The subspecies are rarely used for hybridizing; only *R. dichroanthum* ssp. *scyphocalyx* is worth mentioning. It is a low-growing, densely branched shrub up to 1 m (3 ft.) tall. The leaves are smaller than those of the species, and the flower colors are softer, mostly cream-salmon. The cultivar 'Golden Gate', from the United States, is a rich, multicolored selection. 'Medusa', introduced by Lord Aberconway, was selected from a crossing with ssp. *scyphocalyx*, and has good foliage.

GROUP 16

Group 16a. *R. forrestii* and hybrids
Photographs on pages 381–393.

This famous rhododendron is better known as *R. repens*. However, this name is no longer allowed due to the priority principles in nomenclature; it has been proven that *R. forrestii* and *R. repens* are one and the same species. The basic difference between them is the coloration on the undersides of the leaves: purple-lilac for *R. forrestii* and green for *R. repens*, not sufficient enough of a difference to maintain two species.

Rhododendron forrestii is native to the Chinese provinces of Yunnan and Xizang, and the bordering area of Burma at high elevations of 4000–6000 m (12,000–18,000 ft.). The species is named after one of the greatest plant hunters to ever travel China, George Forrest (1873–1932).

The plant is valued for its very low, creeping growth habit—it rarely exceeds 20 cm (8 in.) in height. The leaves are small and broadly egg-shaped, 1–3 cm (0.5–1.25 in.) long and 1–2 cm (0.5-0.75 in.) wide, shiny, green, stiff, with deeply recessed veins. The flowers are bell-shaped, alone or in pairs, and flaming red in color. Despite its well-known name, *R. forrestii* is seldom found in cultivation. The species is difficult to transplant and prefers rock gardens; the rock garden in the Rhododendron Park in Bremen, Germany, is an example of this ideal environment.

The brilliant red flower color is dominant, making this species popular for hybridizing. It is most often the fatherplant (pollinator). D. Hobbie of Germany was a pioneer in hybridizing with *R. forrestii*; his most important cross was with 'Essex Scarlet'. About 25 cultivars have been named from the hundreds resulting from that one cross; 'Scarlet Wonder' is the most important, along with 'Mannheim', 'Bengal', 'Juwel', and 'Aksel Olsen'—all are very good dwarf rhododendrons. The flower colors differ only slightly, but the habits and foliage types differ considerably. Lord Aberconway of Great Britain introduced 'Carmen', a creeping plant with dark red flowers; 'Elizabeth', also red; and 'Ethel'. Scarse Dickinson introduced two miniature plants, 'Little Ben' and 'Little Bert'. Nurserymen in the United States introduced 'Fireman Jeff', 'Martha Robbins', and 'Peekaboo'.

GROUP 17

Group 17a. Subsection Taliensia, species and hybrids
Photographs on pages 394–397.

Subsection Taliensia contains dozens of species, all of which have beautiful leaves. The flowers are not often spectacular—mostly white, pink, or lilac. The plants flower only when mature, sometimes not until 20 years of age, and the trusses are small. Not much hybridizing has been done with these species despite their beautiful foliage and winter hardiness.

Rhododendron roxieanum, the most spectacular species in this subsection, is a very hardy, slow-growing shrub up to 2 m (7 ft.) tall and wide. The dark green leaves are small and lanceolate with dense brown hair on the undersides and recessed veins on the tops. The flowers are white or pale pink and borne in small trusses. Dawyck Gardens, Peebles, Scotland, has a planting demonstrating the variations within this species; all the variations are interesting for their foliage.

Rhododendron bureavii, from which have come several available clones, grows to 3 m (10 ft.) tall and wide. The leaves and twigs are covered with a very attractive, dense, brown-red indumentum. The white flowers are small, funnel-shaped, and borne in small trusses, but the plants seldom flower. In the United States this species was crossed with 'Fabia', producing a few very nice, winter-hardy hybrids with orange-pink flowers and beautiful foliage: 'Hansel' and 'Gretzel' are much alike; 'Hazel', a pink, grows somewhat larger.

Rhododendron clementinae forms a dense shrub 2–2.5 m (7–8 ft.) tall and somewhat wider. The leaves are broadly egg-shaped, blue-green on top with orange-brown indumentum underneath.

Rhododendron taliense is the species for which the subsection is named. It is a shrub about 3 m (10 ft.) tall and wide with stiff, dark green, egg-shaped leaves with olive-colored indumentum. Its white, often

R. ponticum, Turkey.

R. ponticum.

R. ponticum f. *album.*

R. ponticum **'Cheiranthifolium'**.

R. ponticum **'Imbricatum'**.

R.   ponticum   **'Roseum'**.   ?,
<1890. *R. ponticum* × ?. 4+ m,
VI, △AA.

R. ponticum **'Aureovariegatum'**. ?, <1900. 3 m, V, △B.

R. ponticum **'Variegatum'**. ?, <1900. 3 m, V, △B.

'Alice Heye'. ?, <1940; reg. 1958. ? × *R. ponticum* hyb. 2 m, V, △A.

'Chionoides'. J. Waterer, <1871; reg. 1958. *R. ponticum* hyb. × *R. ponticum* hyb. 3 m, V, △A.

'Clementine Lemaire'. P. Moser & Fils, <1925; reg. 1958. *R. ponticum* hyb. × ?. 3 m, V, △B.

'Concessum' ('Alphonse'). J. Bijls, <1854; reg. 1958. ? × ?. 1.5 m, V–VI, △B.

'Countess Fitzwilliam'. Fisher, Son & Sibray, <1900; reg. 1958. ? × ?. 3 m, V, △B.

al
6:
R.

'Dandy'. ?, <1980. ? × ?. 2 m, V, △A.

'Edeltraud' ('Eleonore'). H. Hachmann, <1987; reg. 1989. 'Hachmann's Ornament' × 'Furnivall's Daughter'. 2 m, V, △A.

'Hamilcar'. ?, <1940; reg. 1958.
? × ?. V, △B.

'Herbstfreude'. H. Hachmann, <1987. 'Hachmann's Ornament' × 'Furnivall's Daughter'. 4 m, V–VI, △A.

'Hillcrest'. B. Esch, <1980. ? × ?. 2 m, V, △B.

'Hyacinthiflorum Plenum'. ?,
<1950. *R. ponticum* hyb. × *R.
ponticum* hyb. 2 m, V–VI, △A.

'Hymen'. T. J. R. Seidel, 1906;
reg. 1958. 'Boule de Neige' ×
'Everestianum'. 3 m, V–VI, △A.

'Jeanne d'Arc'.

'**Jeanne d'Arc'**. M. Koster & Sons, <1940; reg. 1958. ? × ?. 2 m, V, △B.

'**John Spencer'**. A. Waterer, <1870. ? × ?. 3 m, VI, △A.

'**Joseph Whitworth'**. J. Waterer, <1867; reg. 1958. *R. ponticum* × ?. 3 m, V–VI, △A.

'Kokardia'. H. Hachmann,
1978; reg. 1983. 'Humboldt' ×
'Direktoer E. Hjelm'. 3 m, V,
△A. (Grp. 2a.)

'Lady Strangford'. C. Noble,
<1875; reg. 1958. ? × ?. 2 m, V,
△B.

'Marcel Menard'. Croux & Fils, <1924. ? × ?. 2 m, V–VI, △A.

'Marie Stewart'. Stewart & Son,
<1957; reg. 1961. ? × ?. 2 m, V,
△B.

'Martin Hope Sutton'. A.
Waterer, <1915; reg. 1958. *R.
ponticum* hyb. × ?. 2 m, V, △B.

**'Memoire de Dominique Ver-
vaene'**. D. Vervaene, <1950;
reg. 1958. *R. ponticum* hyb. × ?. 3
m, V, △A.

'Merveille de Boskoop'. Felix & Dijkhuis, 1966; reg. 1966. 'Mrs. Charles S. Sargent' × 'Britannia'. 3 m, V, △B.

'Minnie'. Standish & Noble, <1858; reg. 1958. ? × ?. 1.5 m, V, △B.

'Mme Jules Porges'. P. Moser & Fils, <1900; reg. 1958. ? × ?. 4 m, V, △B.

Grp. 1a.
R. ponticum & hyb.

'Pygmalion'. J. Waterer, Sons & Crisp, <1933; reg. 1958. ? × ?. AM 1933. 3 m, IV–V, △B.

'Ronkonkoma'. A. A. Raustein, 1976; reg. 1977. 'Blue Peter' × 'Purple Splendour'. 2 m, V, △A.

'Royal Purple'. Standish & Noble, 1860; reg. 1958. ? × ?. 2 m, V, △A.

'Sappho'. A. Waterer, <1847; reg. 1958. *R. ponticum* hyb. × ?. AGM 1969, AM 1974. 3 m, V, △B.

'Snowflake'. A. Waterer, <1875; reg. 1958. *R. ponticum* hyb. × ?. 2 m, V, △A.

'Sweet Simplicity'. J. Waterer, Sons & Crisp, <1922; reg. 1958. *R. ponticum* × ?. 3 m, V, △B.

68 Grp. 1b.
    R. caucasicum & hyb.

'Albert Schweitzer'. Adriaan van Nes, 1960; reg. 1961. ? × ?. 4 m, V, △B.

'Baccarat'. Adriaan van Nes, <1960; reg. 1961. ? × 'Max Sye'. AM Boskoop 1960. 3 m, V, △B.

'Boskoop'. Adriaan van Nes, <1958; reg. 1961. ? × 'Max Sye'. AM Boskoop 1960. 2 m, IV–V, △B.

'Boule de Neige'. Oudieu, 1878; reg. 1958. *R. caucasicum* × *R. catawbiense* hyb. 3 m, V, △A.

'Calliope'. T. J. R. Seidel, <1894. *R. caucasicum* × ?. 2 m, V, △A.

'Cheer'. A. M. Shammarello, <1955; reg. 1958. 'Cunningham's White' × *R. catawbiense* hyb. 2 m, IV, △B.

'Erna'. T. J. R. Seidel, 1903; reg. 1958. *R. smirnowii* × 'Mrs. Milner'.
3 m, VI, △AA.

'Kinloss'. Knap Hill Nurseries,
<1968; reg. 1968. *R. smirnowii* ×
?. 2 m, V, △A.

'Lunik'. J. Scholz, 1961. *R.
smirnowii* × 'C. S. Sargent'. 3 m,
V–VI, △AA.

'Margret'. D. Heinje, <1954. *R. smirnowii* × ?. 2 m, V–VI, △A.

'Rosel

'Mrs. Prain'. Kew, RBG, reg. 1958. ? × *R. smirnowii*. 2 m, V–VI, △A.

'Nathalie'. W. Nagel, 1982. 'Elizabeth' × *R. smirnowii*. 2 m, V, △A.

88 Grp. 2a.
R. catawbiense & hyb.

'**Anton**'. T. J. R. Seidel, 1906; reg. 1958. 'Everestianum' × 'Everestianum'. 4 m, V–VI, △AA.

'**Arnim**'. T. J. R. Seidel, 1906. ? × ?. 3 m, V, △AA.

'**Arno**'. T. J. R. Seidel, 1906; reg. 1958. 'Everestianum' × ?. 3 m, V–VI, △AA.

'Aronimink'. C. O. Dexter/Scott Hort. Foundation, 1940; reg. 1980. 'Pygmalion' × (*R. haematodes* × 'Wellfleet'). 1.5 m, V, △A. (Grp. 1a.)

'Atrosanguineum'. H. Waterer, <1851; reg. 1958. *R. catawbiense* × ?. 4 m, V–VI, △AA.

'Ballet'. ?, <1950. ? × ?. V, △A.

'Bas de Bruin'. A. Waterer, <1935; reg. 1958. *R. cataw-biense* × ?. 3 m, V, △B.

'Beauty of Surrey' ('Beauty of Berry Hill'). A. Waterer, <1872; reg. 1958. ? × ?. FCC 1872. 2 m, V, △B.

'Belle Heller'. A. M. Sham-marello, <1958; reg. 1958. 'Catawbiense Album' × *R. catawbiense* hyb. 3 m, V–VI, △A.

'Bismarck'. T. J. R. Seidel, 1900; reg. 1958. 'Viola' × 'Everestianum'. 4 m, V–VI, △A.

'Blandyanum'. Standish & Noble, 1850; reg. 1958. 'Altaclarensis' × *R. catawbiense*. 3 m, V, △A.

'Blanka'. H. Hachmann, <1988; reg. 1989. 'Babette' × 'Perlina'. 2 m, V, △A.

'Blinklicht' ('Sparkling Light').
H. Hachmann, <1982; reg.
1983. 'Nova Zembla' × 'Mars'. 3
m, V–VI, △A.

'C. S. Sargent'. A. Waterer,
1888; reg. 1958. *R. catawbiense* ×
?. 4 m, V, △A.

'Caractacus'. A. Waterer, 1865;
reg. 1958. *R. catawbiense* × ?.
FCC 1865. 4 m, VI, △AA.

'Catalgla'. J. Gable, <1958; reg. 1958. *R. catawbiense* f. *album* 3 m, VI, △AA.

'Catherine van Tol'. J. C. van Tol, <1913; reg. 1958. *R. catawbiense* × ?. 3 m, V–VI, △AA.

'Charles Dickens'. A. Waterer, 1865; reg. 1958. *R. catawbiense* × ?. FCC 1865. 3 m, V–VI, △A.

'**Charles   Noble**'. C. Noble,
<1940; reg. 1958. ? × ?. 3 m, V,
△A.

'**Claudine**'.   H.   Hachmann,
<1987; reg. 1989. 'Sammet-
glut' × 'Daisy'. 2 m, V, △A.

'**Cosima**'. T. J. R. Seidel, 1893;
reg. 1958. 'Everestianum' ×
'Everestianum'. 4 m, V–VI,
△AA.

'Countess of Athlone'. C. B. van Nes & Sons, 1923; reg. 1958. 'Geoffrey Millais' × 'Catawbiense Grandiflorum'. 4 m, V, △B.

'Countess of Derby' ('Eureka Maid'). H. White, Sunningdale, 1913; reg. 1958. 'Pink Pearl' × 'Cynthia'. AM 1930. 4 m, V, △B.

'Countess of York' ('Catalode'). J. Gable, 1936. 'Catawbiense Album' × 'Loderi King George'. 3 m, V, △A.

'Cynthia', *Quercus rubra* 'Aurea', Kew.

'Cynthia' ('Lord Palmerston'). Standish & Noble, <1856; reg. 1958. *R. catawbiense* × *R. griffithianum* hyb. AGM 1969. 3 m, V, △B.

'Delta'. Boot & Co, <1965; reg. 1965. *R. catawbiense* hyb. × *R. ponticum* hyb. 3 m, V–VI, △AA.

'Dr. H. C. Dresselhuys'. H. den
Ouden & Sons, 1920; reg. 1958.
'Atrosanguineum'   ×   'Don-
caster'. 4+ m, V–VI, △AA.

'Duftauge'. W. Wuestemeyer,
1985. ? × ?. 2 m, V, △A.

'Dr. V. H. Rutgers'. H. den
Ouden & Sons, 1924; reg. 1958.
'Charles Dickens'   ×   'Lord
Roberts'. 3 m, V–VI, △A.

'Edward S. Rand'. A. Waterer, 1870; reg. 1958. *R. catawbiense* × ?. 3 m, V, △A.

'Elie'. A. M. Shammarello, <1955; reg. 1958. 'Cunningham's White' × *R. catawbiense* hyb. 3 m, V, △AA.

'English Roseum'. A. Waterer, <1900; reg. 1958. *R. catawbiense* × *R. catawbiense* hyb. 4+ m, VI, △AA.

'Erich'. T. J. R. Seidel, 1903; reg. 1958. 'Mrs. Milner' × *R. cataw-biense*. 3 m, V, △AA.

'Ernst Graf Silva Tarouca'. ?, 1987. ? × ?. 1.5 m, V, △A.

'Everestianum'. A. Waterer, <1850; reg. 1958. *R. cataw-biense* × ?. 4+ m, V–VI, △AA.

'**Germania**'. Dietrich Hobbie, <1979. 'Antoon van Welie' × 'Catherine van Tol'. 2 m, V, △A.

'**Gomer Waterer**'. J. Waterer, <1900; reg. 1958. *R. catawbiense* × *R. griffithianum* hyb. AM 1906. 3 m, V, △A.

'**Graf Zeppelin**'. C. B. van Nes & Sons, <1940; reg. 1958. 'Pink Pearl' × 'Mrs. Charles S. Sargent'. 3 m, V, △B.

'**Grandezza**'. H. Hachmann, <1985; reg. 1989. 'Furnivall's Daughter' × 'Roseum Elegans'. 1.5 m, V, △A.

'**Gudrun**'. T. J. R. Seidel, 1905; reg. 1958. 'Eggebrechtii' × 'Mme Linden'. 3 m, V, △A.

'**Hachmann's Constanze**' ('Constanze'). H. Hachmann, <1975; reg. 1984. 'Humboldt' × 'Kluis Sensation'. 3 m, V, △AA.

'Hildegard'. T. J. R. Seidel, <1950. *R. catawbiense* hyb. × ?. 3 m, V, △A.

'Himalaya'. Felix & Dijkhuis, <1965. 'Everestianum' × ?. 3 m, V, △A.

'Holbein'. T. J. R. Seidel, 1906; reg. 1958. 'Alexander Adie' × 'Carl Mette'. 4 m, V–VI, △A.

'Holden'. A. M. Shammarello, <1958; reg. 1958. *R. catawbiense* hyb. × 'Cunningham's White'. 3 m, IV–V, △A.

'Holger'. T. J. R. Seidel, <1916; reg. 1958. 'Eggebrechtii' × 'Mme Linden'. 3 m, V, △A.

'Holstein'. H. Hachmann, 1978; reg. 1983. 'Humboldt' × 'Catawbiense Grandiflorum'. 3 m, V, △AA.

'Homer'. T. J. R. Seidel, 1916;
reg. 1958. 'Kaiser Wilhelm' ×
'Agnes'. 4 m, V–VI, △A.

'Humboldt'. T. J. R. Seidel, 1926;
reg. 1958. *R. catawbiense* × ?. 3m,
V–VI, △AA.

'Ice Cube'. A. M. Shammarello,
1961; reg. 1972. 'Catalgla' ×
'Belle Heller'. 3 m, V, △A.

'Ignatius Sargent' ('The Boss').
A. Waterer, <1900; reg. 1958. *R. catawbiense* × ?. 4 m, V–VI, △AA.

'Isar' ('Purple Hill'). Dietrich Hobbie, <1983. *R. brachycarpum* var. *nikomontanum* × 'Giganteum'. 2 m, V–VI, △A.

'James Bateman'. A. Waterer, 1865; reg. 1958. ? × ?. 1.5 m, V, △B.

Grp. 2a.
       R. catawbiense & hyb.

'James Brigham'. ?, <1950; reg.
1958. ? × ?. 3 m, V, △A.

'James Marshall Brooks'. A.
Waterer, 1870; reg. 1958. ? × ?.
1.5 m, V, △B.

'John Waterer'. J. Waterer,
<1860; reg. 1958. *R. cataw-
biense* hyb. × ?. 3 m, V–VI, △B.

'Kate Waterer'. J. Waterer,
<1865; reg. 1958. *R. cataw-
biense* × ?. 3 m, V, △B.

'King Tut'. A. M. Shammarello,
1958; reg. 1958. (*R. smirnowii* ×
'America') × *R. catawbiense* hyb.
2 m, V, △AA.

'Kleefeld'. A. W. Backhus,
<1947. ? × ?. 2 m, V–VI, △A.

'Leopold'. T. J. R. Seidel, 1909; reg. 1958. *R. catawbiense* × 'Mira'. 3 m, V, △A.

'Lord Fairhaven'. Knap Hill Nurseries, 1955; reg. 1958. ? × ?. 2 m, V, △B.

'Lord Roberts'. B. Mason, <1900; reg. 1958. *R. catawbiense* hyb. × ?. 3 m, V, △A.

'Maria Stuart'. A. Waterer,
1875; reg. 1958. ? × ?. 2 m, V,
△A.

'Marie Forte' ('Mademoiselle
Marie Forte'). ?, <1935; reg.
1958. *R. catawbiense* hyb. × ?. 3
m, V, △A.

'Marion' ('Dutch Marion'). Felix
& Dijkhuis, <1953; reg. 1958.
'Catawbiense Grandiflorum' ×
'Pink Pearl'. 3 m, V, △B.

'**Mrs. A. Stirling**'. ?, <1925. ? ×
?. △A.

'**Mrs. Davies Evans**'. A.
Waterer, <1915; reg. 1958. *R.
catawbiense* hyb. × ?. AM 1958. 3
m, V, △B.

'**Mrs. Helen Koster**'. M. Koster
& Sons, reg. 1958. 'Mrs. J. J.
Crosfield' × 'Catawbiense
Grandiflorum'. 3 m, V–VI, △B.

'**Mrs. Milner**' ('Bibber'). A.
Waterer, <1900; reg. 1958. *R.*
catawbiense × ?. 3 m, V, △AA.

'**Mrs. P. den Ouden**'. H. den
Ouden & Sons, 1925; reg. 1958.
'Atrosanguineum' × 'Doncas-
ter'. 3 m, V–VI, △A.

'**Mrs. R. S. Holford**'. A. Waterer,
1866; reg. 1958. *R. catawbiense*
hyb. × ?. 3 m, V–VI, △B.

124   Grp. 2a.
       R. catawbiense & hyb.

'Old Port'. A. Waterer, 1865; reg. 1958. *R. catawbiense* hyb. × *R. ponticum* hyb. 3 m, V–VI, △B.

'Oratorium'. H. Hachmann, 1985; reg. 1989. 'Hachmann's Feuerschein' × 'Thunderstorm'. 1.5 m, V–VI, △A.

'Parker's Pink'. C. O. Dexter, 1959; reg. 1973. ? × ?. AE 1973. 3 m, V, △A.

'Parson's Grandiflorum'. A. Waterer, <1875; reg. 1958. *R. catawbiense* × ?. 4+ m, V–VI, △AA.

'Parson's Gloriosum'. A. Waterer, <1860; reg. 1958. *R. catawbiense* × ?. 3 m, V–VI, △AA.

'Pelopidas'. J. Waterer, <1865; reg. 1958. *R. catawbiense* × ?. 3 m, V–VI, △A.

'**Renata**'. T. J. R. Seidel, 1915; reg. 1958. 'Annedore' × 'Mrs. Milner'. 3 m, V, △A.

'**Rochelle**'. G. Nearing, 1969; reg. 1970. 'Dorothea' × 'Kettledrum'. 1.5 m, V, △A.

'**Romeo**'. A. M. Shammarello, 1958; reg. 1972. *R. catawbiense* hyb. × *R. catawbiense* hyb. 2 m, V, △A.

'**Roseum Elegans**'. A. Waterer, <1851; reg. 1958. *R. cataw-biense* × ?. 4+ m, V–VI, △AA.

ismu
erer,
18:

'**Roslyn**'. P. Vossberg, 1972; reg. 1973. 'Purpureum Elegans' × 'Everestianum'. 3 m, V–VI, △AA.

'**Salvini**'. Young, <1883; reg. 1958. *R. catawbiense* hyb. × ?. 3 m, V, △A.

'Spring Dawn'. A. M. Shammarello, <1970. *R. catawbiense* hyb. × 'Mrs. Charles S. Sargent'. 3 m, V, △A.

'Stella' ('Stella Waterer'). A. Waterer, 1865; reg. 1958. *R. catawbiense* × ?. 3 m, V, △A.

'Sultana'. A. Waterer, <1858; reg. 1958. *R. catawbiense* hyb. × ?. 3 m, V, △A.

'Sylph'. A. Waterer, 1915; reg. 1958. ? × ?. 2 m, V, △A.

'The General'. A. M. Sham-marello, 1955; reg. 1958. *R. catawbiense* hyb. × *R. catawbiense* hyb. 3 m, V–VI, △AA.

'Titania'. H. Hachmann, 1987. ? × ?. 1.5 m, V, △A.

'Tuerk'. T. J. R. Seidel, 1917. *R. catawbiense* hyb. × *R. catawbiense* hyb. 3 m, V, △A.

'Ute'. ?, ? × ?. 3 m, V, △A.

'Vauban'. A. Waterer, reg. 1958. *R. catawbiense* × ?. 3 m, V, △B.

'Van der Hoop'. H. den Ouden
& Sons, 1925; reg. 1958.
'Atrosanguineum' × 'Doncas-
ter'. 4 m, V–VI, △A.

'Von Oheimb Woislowitz'. T. J.
R. Seidel, 1906; reg. 1958. 'Ever-
estianum' × 'Carl Mette'. 3 m,
V–VI, △AA.

'Van Weerden Poelman'. H. den
Ouden & Sons, <1925; reg.
1958. 'Charles Dickens' × 'Lord
Roberts'. 3 m, V, △A.

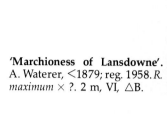

'Marchioness of Lansdowne'.
A. Waterer, <1879; reg. 1958. *R. maximum* × ?. 2 m, VI, △B.

'Mum'. J. Waterer, <1897; reg. 1958. *R. maximum* × ?. 1.5 m, V, △B.

'Tintoretto'. C. Frets & Son, <1939; reg. 1958. *R. maximum* × ?. 2m, V, △A.

R. yakushimanum.

R. yakushimanum.

142 Grp. 3a.
R. yakushimanum & hyb.

R. yakushimanum.

R. yakushimanum.

R. yakushimanum.

'Andre'. R. de Belder, <1978; reg. 1979. 'Britannia' × *R. yakushimanum*. AM Boskoop 1978. 1.5 m, V, △B.

'Ann Lindsay'. H. Hachmann, 1985; reg. 1989. 'Blinklicht' × ('Mars' × *R. yakushimanum*). 1 m, V, △A.

'Anni'. A. Behrens, <1988. *R. yakushimanum* hyb. × 'Polar Star'. 1 m, V, △A.

'Bashful'. J. Waterer, Sons & Crisp, 1971; reg. 1971. *R. yakushimanum* × 'Doncaster'. 1.5 m, V, △B.

'Chelsea Seventy'. J. Waterer, Sons & Crisp, 1972; reg. 1972. *R. yakushimanum* hyb. × ('Eclipse' × 'Fusilier'). 1.5 m, V, △B.

'Clivia'. W. Stoeckmann, <1981. 'Manderley' × *R. yakushimanum*. 1.5 m, V, △A.

'Cup Cake'. B. & M. Thompson, <1980. *R. yakushimanum* × 'Medusa'. 1.5 m, V, △B.

'Daniela' ('Deleilah'). H. Hachmann, 1984; reg. 1989. 'Nachtglut' × ('Mars' × *R. yakushimanum*). 1 m, V, △A.

'Doc'. J. Waterer, Sons & Crisp, 1972; reg. 1972. *R. yakushimanum* × 'Corona'. 1.5 m, V, △B.

'Dolcemente'. H. Hachmann, <1987. *R. yakushimanum* 'Koichiro Wada' × ?. 1 m, V, △A.

'Dopey'. J. Waterer, Sons & Crisp, 1971; reg. 1971. (*R. facetum* × 'Fabia') × (*R. yakushimanum* × 'Fabia'). AM 1977, FCC 1979. 1.5 m, V, △B.

'Dusty Miller'. J. Waterer, Sons & Crisp, 1975; reg. 1975. *R. yakushimanum* × ?. 50 cm, V, △B.

'Edelweiss'. Joh. Wieting, <1985. *R. yakushimanum* × *R. yakushimanum.* 1 m, V, △A.

'Excelsior'. D. Heinje, <1981. *R. yakushimanum* 'Koichiro Wada' × 'Kluis Sensation'. 1 m, V, △A.

'Fantastica'. H. Hachmann, 1983; reg. 1985. 'Mars' × *R. yakushimanum* 'Koichiro Wada'. 1 m, V, △A.

150 Grp. 3a.
R. yakushimanum & hyb.

'Fruehlingserwachen'. Joh. Bruns, <1987. 'Kluis Triumph' × *R. yakushimanum*. 1.5 m, V, △A.

'Golden Torch'. J. Waterer, Sons & Crisp, 1972; reg. 1972. 'Bambi' × ('Grosclaude' × *R. griersonianum*). AM 1984. 1 m, V, △B.

'Grumpy'. J. Waterer, Sons & Crisp, 1971; reg. 1971. *R. yakushimanum* × ?. AM 1979. 1 m, V, △B.

'Hachmann's Belona' ('Belona'). H. Hachmann, 1982; reg. 1983. *R. yakushimanum* 'Koichiro Wada' × 'Britannia'. 1 m, V, △A.

'Hachmann's Marlis' ('Marlis'). H. Hachmann, 1985; reg. 1989. 'Mars' × *R. yakushimanum* 'Koichiro Wada'. 1 m, V, △A.

'Hachmann's Polaris' ('Polaris'). H. Hachmann, 1978; reg. 1984. *R. yakushimanum* 'Koichiro Wada' × 'Omega'. 1 m, V, △A.

'Loreley'. Joh. Bruns, <1987. (*R. yakushimanum* × 'Doncaster') × (*R. dichroanthum* ssp. *scyphocalyx*). 1 m, V, △A.

'Lumina'. H. Hachmann, 1982. 'Kokardia' × ('Mars' × *R. yakushimanum*). 1 m, V–VI, △A.

'Manuela'. H. Hachmann, 1985; reg. 1989. 'Blinklicht' × ('Mars' × *R. yakushimanum*). 1.5 m, V, △A.

'Martina'. H. Hachmann, 1987.
? × ?. 1 m, V, △A.

'Mist Maiden'. D. G. Leach,
<1983; reg. 1984. *R. yakushi-*
manum × *R. yakushimanum*. 1 m,
V, △A.

'Molier'. Wisley, <1987. *R.*
yakushimanum × ?. 1.5 m, △B.

'Percy Wiseman'. J. Waterer, Sons & Crisp, <1971; reg. 1971. *R. yakushimanum* × 'Fabia Tangerine'. AM 1982. 1.5 m, V, △B.

'Pink Cherub'. J. Waterer, Sons & Crisp, 1968; reg. 1969. *R. yakushimanum* × 'Doncaster'. AM 1968. 1 m, V, △B.

'Rendez-Vous'. H. Hachmann, 1983; reg. 1985. 'Marinus Koster' × *R. yakushimanum* 'Koichiro Wada'. 1 m, V–VI, △A.

'Renoir'. RHS Gardens, Wisley, <1961; reg. 1963. 'Pauline' × *R. yakushimanum*. AM 1961. 1.5 m, V, △B.

'Samsonite'. H. Hachmann, 1987. *R. yakushimanum* 'Koichiro Wada' × ?. 1 m, V, △A.

'Santana'. H. Hachmann, 1987; reg. 1989. 'Mars' × *R. yakushimanum* 'Koichiro Wada'. 1 m, V, △A.

'Silver Lady'. G. Horstmann/ J. Wieting, 1985. *R. yakushimanum* × *R. smirnowii*. 1.5 m, V, △A.

'Silvetta'. H. Hachmann, 1985; reg. 1989. 'Humboldt' × *R. yakushimanum* 'Koichiro Wada'. 1.5 m, V–VI, △A.

'Sleepy'. J. Waterer, Sons & Crisp, 1971; reg. 1971. *R. yakushimanum* × 'Doncaster'. 1.5 m, V, △B.

'Sparkler'. J. Waterer, Sons & Crisp, <1971; reg. 1971. (*R. facetum* × 'Fabia') × (*R. yakushimanum* × 'Britannia'). 1 m, V, △C.

'Sneezy'. J. Waterer, Sons & Crisp, 1971; reg. 1971. *R. yakushimanum* × 'Doncaster'. AM 1986. 1.5 m, V, △B.

'Stanley Rivlin'. A. F. George, Hydon Nurseries Ltd., 1971; reg. 1972. *R. yakushimanum* × 'Royal Blood'. 2 m, V, △B.

'Streatly'. Crown Estate Comm., Windsor, <1964; reg. 1965. *R. aberconwayi* × *R. yakushimanum*. AM 1965. 1.5 m, V, △A.

'Surrey Heath'. J. Waterer, Sons & Crisp, 1975; reg. 1975. (*R. facetum* × 'Fabia') × (*R. yakushimanum* × 'Britannia'). AM 1982. 1.5 m, V, △B.

'Tatjana'. H. Hachmann, 1983; reg. 1985. 'Nachtglut' × ('Mars' × *R. yakushimanum*). 1 m, V, △A.

'Timothy James'. J. Waterer, Sons & Crisp, 1971; reg. 1972. *R. yakushimanum* × 'Fabia Tangerine'. 1.5 m, V, △B.

'Titian Beauty'. J. Waterer, Sons & Crisp, 1971; reg. 1971. (*R. facetum* × ˙ 'Fabia') × (*R. yakushimanum* × 'Fabia'). 1.5 m, V, △B.

'Tolkien'. P. Wiseman, 1958; reg. 1985. (*R. facetum* × 'Fabia') × (*R. yakushimanum* × 'Britannia'). 1.5 m, V, △B.

174 Grp. 3b.
R. degronianum
(*metternichii*) & hyb.

R. hyperythrum.

'Baron van Dedem'. Vuyk van
Nes, <1975; reg. 1989. 'Rijneveld' × ?. AM Boskoop 1975. 2
m, V, △A.

'Daphne'. T. J. R. Seidel, 1902;
reg. 1958. *R. degronianum* ssp.
heptamerum × ?. 1.5 m, V, △A.

'**Eidam**'. T. J. R. Seidel, 1903; reg. 1958. *R. degronianum* ssp. *heptamerum* × 'Alexander Adie'. 2 m, V, △A.

'**Erika**'. T. J. R. Seidel, 1903; reg. 1958. *R. degronianum* ssp. *heptamerum* × ?. 2 m, V, △AA.

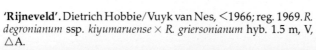

'**Rijneveld**'. Dietrich Hobbie/Vuyk van Nes, <1966; reg. 1969. *R. degronianum* ssp. *kiyumaruense* × *R. griersonianum* hyb. 1.5 m, V, △A.

Grp. 4a.
R. arboreum & hyb.

180

R. arboreum, Stonefield Castle.

R. arboreum, Himalayas.

R. arboreum ssp. *arboreum.*

R. arboreum ssp. *arboreum.*

R. arboreum ssp. *arboreum.*

R. arboreum ssp. *arboreum.*

188 Grp. 4a.
R. arboreum & hyb.

'Bulstrode Park'. C. B. van Nes
& Sons, <1922; reg. 1958. *R.
griffithianum* hyb. × 'Sefton'. 4 m,
V, △C.

'C. B. van Nes'. C. B. van Nes &
Sons, 1921; reg. 1958. 'Queen
Wilhelmina' × 'Stanley Davies'.
3 m, IV, △C.

'Clivianum'. Iveson, 1849; reg.
1958. *R. catawbiense* × *R.
arboreum* ssp. *cinnamomeum* f.
album. 3 m, IV, △C.

'**Corry Koster**'. M. Koster & Sons, 1909; reg. 1958. 'Doncaster' × 'George Hardy'. 3 m, IV–V, △B.

'**Dame Nelly Melba**'. Sir Edmund Loder, 1926; reg. 1958. 'Standishii' × *R. arboreum* ssp. *arboreum*. AM 1926. 4 m, V, △D.

'**Doncaster**'. A. Waterer, <1900; reg. 1958. *R. arboreum* ssp. *arboreum* × ?. 2 m, V, △B.

'Kluis Sensation'. A. Kluis, 1946; reg. 1958. 'Britannia' × *R. griffithianum* hyb. 2 m, V, △B.

'Lamplighter'. M. Koster & Sons, <1955; reg. 1958. 'Britannia' × 'Mme F. J. Chauvin'. FCC Boskoop 1955. 3 m, V, △C.

'Langley Park'. C. B. van Nes & Sons, 1922; reg. 1958. 'Queen Wilhelmina' × 'Stanley Davies'. 4 m, V, △C.

'Lee's Scarlet' ('Lee's Early Scarlet'). Lee & Kennedy, <1850; reg. 1958. *R .caucasicum* × *R. arboreum* ssp. *arboreum*. 3 m, II–III, △B.

'Leopardi'. T. Methven & Sons, 1868; reg. 1958. *R. arboreum* ssp. *cinnamomeum* f. *album* × ?. 4 m, V, △A.

'Louis Pasteur'. L. J. Endtz & Co, 1923; reg. 1958. 'Mrs. Tritton' × 'Viscount Powerscourt'. 3 m, V, △B.

'Markeeta's Prize'. Flora Markeeta Nurseries, 1967; reg. 1969. 'Loderi Venus' × 'Anna'. 3 m, V, △B.

'Mevrouw P. A. Colijn'. M. Koster & Sons, <1910; reg. 1958. 'Mme de Bruin' × 'Mrs. E. C. Stirling'. 3 m, VI, △B.

'Michael Waterer'. J. Waterer, Sons & Crisp, <1894; reg. 1958. *R. ponticum* × *R. arboreum* ssp. *arboreum*. 3 m, V–VI, △B.

'Mme de Bruin'. M. Koster &
Sons, 1904; reg. 1958. 'Doncaster' × 'Prometheus'. 3 m, V, △B.

'Mona Lisa'. Joh. Bruns, 1961.
('Goldsworth Orange' × R.
wardii) × 'Kluis Triumph'. 3 m,
V, △A.

'Mrs. A. M. Williams'. Otto Schulz/C. B. van Nes, 1892; reg.
1958. R. griffithianum × R. arboreum ssp. arboreum. AM 1926, AM
1933, AM 1954. 3 m, V, △B.

'Peter Koster'. M. Koster & Sons, 1909; reg. 1958. ? × 'George Hardy'. 2 m, V, △B.

'Princess Elizabeth'. J. Waterer, Sons & Crisp, 1928; reg. 1958. 'Bagshot Ruby' × ?. AM 1933. 3 m, V–VI, △B.

'Professor J. H. Zaayer'. L. J. Endtz & Co, <1940; reg. 1958. 'Pink Pearl' × 'Langley Park'. 2 m, V, △B.

'Red Admiral'. J. C. Williams, <1958; reg. 1958. *R. arboreum* ssp. *arboreum* × *R. thomsonii* ssp. *thomsonii*. 4 m, IV, △D.

'Red Jack'. Proefstation Boskoop, 1987; reg. 1991. *R. forrestii* × ('Wilgen's Ruby' × 'May Day'). AM Boskoop 1987. 3 m, V, △B.

'Red Riding Hood'. W. C. Slocock, 1933; reg. 1958. 'Atrosanguineum' × *R. griffithianum*. 3 m, V, △C.

Grp. 5a.
R. insigne & hyb.

R. insigne.

'Anneliese'. Joh. Bruns, 1961. *R. insigne* × 'El Alamein'. 1.5 m, V, △A.

'Ariane'. Joh. Bruns, <1986. 'Graf Zeppelin' × *R. insigne*. 1.5 m, V–VI, △A.

'Bad Zwischenahn'. Joh. Bruns, 1984. *R. insigne* × ?. 1.5 m, V, △A.

'Brigitte'. H. Hachmann, 1980; reg. 1983. *R. insigne* × 'Mrs. J. G. Millais'. 2 m, V, △A.

'Duchess of Cornwall'. R. Gill & Son, 1910; reg. 1958. ? × ?. AM 1974. 3 m, V, △C.

'Hachmann's Diadem'. H. Hachmann, 1983. 'Furnivall's Daughter' × 'Hachmann's Ornament'. 2 m, V, △A.

'Johann Bruns'. Joh. Bruns, <1986. (*R. insigne* × 'Graf Zeppelin') × (*R. wardii* × *R. fortunei* ssp. *discolor*). 1 m, V, △A.

'Kings Ride'. Crown Estate Comm., Windsor, 1971; reg. 1972. *R. insigne* × *R. yakushimanum*. 2 m, V, △B.

'Nofertete'. Joh. Bruns, <1983.
'El Alamein' × *R. insigne*. 1.5 m,
V, △A.

'Oberschlesien'. G. Luettge/D.
Hobbie, <1966. *R .insigne* × *R.
yakushimanum*. 1 m, V–VI, △A.

'Seestadt Bremerhaven'. H.
Nosbuesch/Joh. Bruns, 1983;
reg. 1985. 'Graf Zeppelin' × *R.
insigne*. 1.5 m, V, △A.

210 Grp. 6a.
R. facetum (eriogynum)
& hyb.

R. kyawii.

R. facetum (eriogynum).

R. venator.

'**Carmania**'. L. de Rothschild,
1935; reg. 1958. 'Souvenir of
Anthony Waterer' × *R. facetum*. 3
m, V, △B.

'**Dukeshill**'. Crown Estate
Comm., Windsor, <1972; reg.
1973. 'Kiev' × 'Lady Digby'. AM
1973. 3 m, V, △C.

214   Grp. 6b.
      R. elliottii & hyb.

R. elliottii.

'Billy Budd'. F. Hanger, 1954;
reg. 1958. 'May Day' × *R. elliottii.* AM 1957. 1 m, V, △C.

'Beefeater'. RHS Gardens,
Wisley, 1958; reg. 1961. *R. elliottii* × 'Fusilier'. AM 1958, FCC
1959. 3 m, V, △D.

'Fusilier'. L. de Rothschild, <1938; reg. 1958. *R. elliottii* × *R. griersonianum*. AM 1938, FCC 1942. 3 m, V–VI, △D.

'Gibraltar'. L. de Rothschild, 1939; reg. 1958. 'Bibiani' × *R. elliottii*. 3 m, IV, △D.

'Grenadier'. L. de Rothschild, 1943; reg. 1958. 'Moser's Maroon' × *R. elliottii*. FCC 1943. 4 m, VI, △C.

'Shadow Secretary'. M. A. C. Noble, 1966; reg. 1966. *R. elliottii* × 'Sarita Loder'. 3 m, V–VI, △D.

'Tornado'. Proefstation Boskoop, 1978; reg. 1979. ('Wilgen's Ruby' × 'May Day') × 'Billy Budd'. AM Boskoop 1978. 2 m, V, △B.

R. strigillosum.

R. strigillosum.

'Crossroads'. H. L. Larson,
<1980. *R. strigillosum* × ?. 3 m, V,
△B.

R. griersonianum.

'**Anna Rose Whitney**'. Th. van
Veen, 1954; reg. 1958. *R. grier-
sonianum* × 'Countess of Derby'.
AM Boskoop 1971, PA 1954,
AM 1987. 4+ m, V, △B.

'**Amaura**'. Lord Aberconway,
1933; reg. 1958. 'Penjerrick' × *R.
griersonianum.* AM 1933. 3 m, VI,
△C.

'Annie Dalton' ('Degram'). J. Gable, 1960; reg. 1961. *R. griersonianum* hyb. × 'America'. 2 m, V–VI, △A.

'Betsie Balcom'. Th. J. McGuire, 1974; reg. 1977. 'Princess Elizabeth' × 'Elizabeth'. 2 m, V, △C.

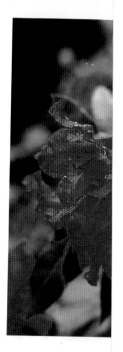

'Bonfire'. J. Waterer, Sons & Crisp, 1928; reg. 1958. (*R. fortunei* ssp. *discolor* × 'Mrs. R. G. Shaw') × *R. griersonianum*. AM 1933. 3 m, V–VI, △C.

'Sunrise'. Lord Aberconway, <1942; reg. 1958. *R. griffithianum × R. griersonianum*. AM 1942. 4 m, V–VI, △C.

'Eliz
<19
forre
1939
△C.

'Eliz

'Susie'. Crown Estate Comm., Windsor, <1987. *R. griersonianum × R. souliei*. 1.5 m, V, △C.

'Tortoiseshell   Champagne' ('Champagne'). W. C. Slocock, 1945; reg. 1958. 'Goldsworth Orange' × *R. griersonianum*. 2 m, V, △C.

'Vanessa'. Lord Aberconway, 1924; reg. 1958. 'Soulbut' × *R. griersonianum.* FCC 1929. 2 m, V, △C.

'Vanessa Pastel'. Lord Aberconway, 1946; reg. 1958. 'Soulbut' × *R. griersonianum.* AM 1946, FCC 1971. 2 m, V, △C.

'Vulcan'. J. Waterer, Sons & Crisp, 1938; reg. 1958. 'Mars' × *R. griersonianum.* AM 1957. 3 m, V–VI, △B.

'Whitney's Dwarf Red'. W. Whitney/De Sather, <1980. ? × *R. griersonianum* hyb. 1.5 m, V, △B.

'Winsome'. Lord Aberconway, 1939; reg. 1958. 'Humming-bird' × *R. griersonianum*. AM 1950. 1.5 m, V, △B.

'Woodcock'. RHS Gardens, Wisley, <1971; reg. 1972. 'Elizabeth' × *R. hyperythrum*. AM 1986. 1.5 m, V, △B.

R. griffithianum.

R. griffithianum.

'Alice'. J. Waterer, <1910; reg.
1958. *R. griffithianum* × ?. AM
1910. 4 m, V, △C.

'Annie E. Endtz'. L. J. Endtz & Co, 1939; reg. 1958. 'Pink Pearl' × ?. 4 m, V, △B.

'Angelo'. L. de Rothschild, 1930; reg. 1958. *R. griffithianum* × *R. fortunei* ssp. *discolor*. AM 1935. 4 m, VI, △C.

'Antoon van Welie'. L. J. Endtz & Co, <1930; reg. 1958. 'Pink Pearl' × ?. 4 m, V, △A.

'Beauty of Littleworth'. C. Mangles, Farnham, <1884; reg. 1958. *R. griffithianum* × *R. campanulatum* hyb. FCC 1904, FCC 1953. 4+ m, V, △C.

'Aristocrat'. M. Koster & Sons, <1965; reg. 1965. ? × ?. 3 m, V, △B.

'Eileen'. J. Waterer, Sons & Crisp, <1958; reg. 1958. 'Duchess of Teck' × *R. griffithianum*. 2 m, V, △B.

'Gauntlettii'. ?, <1934; reg. 1958. *R. griffithianum* × *R. maximum*. 4 m, V, △D.

'General Eisenhower'. A. Kluis, 1946; reg. 1958. *R. griffithianum* × ?. 3 m, V, △B.

'**Geoffrey Millais**'. Otto Schulz/
C. B. van Nes & Sons, 1892; reg.
1958. *R. griffithianum* × ?. AM
1922. 3 m, V, △B.

'**George Hardy**'. J. H. Mangles,
1922; reg. 1958. *R .griffithianum*
× *R. catawbiense*. 3 m, V, △B.

'**Hurricane**'. W. Whitney/De
Sather, 1969; reg. 1976. 'Mrs.
Furnivall' × 'Anna Rose Whit-
ney'. 3 m, V, △B.

'Irene'. Gebr. Guldemond, <1950; reg. 1958. *R. griffithianum* hyb. × ?. 3 m, V, △B.

'Isabella Mangles'. J. H. Mangles, <1880; reg. 1958. *R. griffithianum* × ?. 4 m, V, △B.

'Lady Decies'. J. Waterer, <1922; reg. 1958. *R. ponticum* hyb. × *R. griffithianum* hyb. 3 m, V, △B.

'Lady Stuart of Wortley'. M. Koster & Sons, 1909; reg. 1958. 'Coombe Royal' × *R. griffithianum* hyb. AM 1933. 3 m, V, △C.

'Lem's Monarch' ('Pink Walloper'). Halfdan Lem, 1971. 'Anna' × 'Marinus Koster'. 4 m, V, △B.

'Loderi'. Sir Edmund Loder, 1901; reg. 1958. *R. griffithianum* × *R. fortunei* ssp. *fortunei*. 4+ m, V, △C.

'Loderi Dairymaid'. Sir Edmund Loder, 1901; reg. 1958. *R. griffithianum* × *R. fortunei* ssp. *fortunei*. 3 m, V, △C.

'Loderi King George'. Sir Edmund Loder, 1901; reg. 1958. *R. griffithianum* × *R. fortunei* ssp. *fortunei*. AM 1968, FCC 1970. 4+ m, V, △C.

'Loderi Patience'. Sir Edmund Loder, 1901; reg. 1958. *R. griffithianum* × *R. fortunei* ssp. *fortunei*. 3 m, V, △C.

'Loderi Pink Diamond'. Sir
Edmund Loder, 1901; reg. 1958.
R. griffithianum × *R. fortunei* ssp.
fortunei. FCC 1914. 4+ m, V,
△C.

'Loderi Pink Topaze'. Sir
Edmund Loder, 1901; reg. 1958.
R. griffithianum × *R. fortunei* ssp.
fortunei. 4 m, V, △C.

'Loderi Sir Joseph Hooker'. Sir
Edmund Loder, 1901; reg. 1958.
R. griffithianum × *R. fortunei* ssp.
fortunei. AM 1973. 4+ m, V, △C.

'**Mrs. Lindsay Smith**'. M. Koster & Sons, 1910; reg. 1958. 'George Hardy' × 'Duchess of Edinburgh'. AM 1933. 4 m, V–VI, △B.

'**Mrs. Lionel de Rothschild**'. A. Waterer, <1931; reg. 1958. *R. griffithianum* hyb. × ?. AM 1931. 3 m, V, △B.

'**Mrs. Tom H. Lowinsky**'. A. Waterer, <1919; reg. 1958. *R. griffithianum* × 'Halopeanum'. AM 1919. 3 m, V, △C.

'Peggy Bannier'. Adriaan van Nes, <1960; reg. 1961. *R. griffithianum* hyb. × 'Antoon van Welie'. AM Boskoop 1960. 3 m, V, △B.

'Penjerrick'. S. Smith of Penjerrick, <1923; reg. 1958. *R. campylocarpum* (Elatum Grp.) × *R. griffithianum*. AM 1923. 4 m, IV, △C.

'Pink Bride'. Sir Giles Loder, <1931; reg. 1958. *R. griffithianum* × 'Halopeanum'. AM 1931. 3 m, V, △D.

'Rosy Morn'. Sunningdale
Nurseries, <1931; reg. 1958.
'Loderi' × R. souliei. AM 1931. 3
m, V, △B.

'Shangri La'. L. de Rothschild,
<1965; reg. 1966. 'General Sir
John du Cane' × R. grif-
fithianum. AM 1965. 3 m, VI,
△C.

'Snow Queen'. Sir Edmund
Loder, 1926; reg. 1958. 'Halo-
peanum' × 'Loderi'. AM 1934,
AM 1946. 3 m, V, △C.

'The Strategist'. J. Waterer, <1900; reg. 1958. *R. griffithianum* × ?. 3 m, V, △B.

'Topsvoort Pearl'. Topsvoort Nursery, <1935; reg. 1958. 'Pink Pearl' × ?. 4 m, V, △C.

'Trude Webster'. H. E. Greer, <1960; reg. 1961. 'Countess of Derby' × 'Countess of Derby'. PA 1963, PA 1971. 3 m, V, △B.

R. orbiculare ssp. *orbiculare*.

R. orbiculare red form, Bremen.

'Elfin'. Sir James Horlick, 1933; reg. 1958. 'Dr. Stocker' × *R. orbiculare* ssp. *orbiculare*. 2 m, V, △C.

'Leuchtkugel'. Joh. Bruns, 1958. 'China' × 'Bremen'. 1.5 m, V, △A.

'Robin Redbreast'. J. C. Williams, 1933; reg. 1958. *R. orbiculare* ssp. *orbiculare* × *R. fortunei* ssp. *discolor* (Houlstonii Grp.). 2 m, V, △B.

'Silk'. Evans, <1956; reg. 1958.
R. orbiculare ssp. *orbiculare* × *R.*
souliei. 2 m, V, △B.

'Temple Belle'. RBG Kew, 1916;
reg. 1958. *R. orbiculare* ssp.
orbiculare × *R. williamsianum*. 1.5
m, IV–V, △B.

'Thomasine'.   Rosemoor?,
<1967. *R. orbiculare* ssp. *orbicu-*
lare × ?. 2 m, V, △B.

R. fortunei ssp. *fortunei.*

R. fortunei ssp. *fortunei.*

'Aristide Briand'. L. J. Endtz & Co, <1930; reg. 1958. 'Pink Pearl' × ?. 4 m, V, △B.

'China'. W. C. Slocock, 1936;
reg. 1958. *R. wightii* × *R. fortunei*
ssp. *fortunei*. AM 1942, AM
1948, FCC 1982. 3 m, V, △B.

'Cotton Candy'. R. Henny &
Wennekamp, 1958; reg. 1961.
'Marinus Koster' × 'Loderi
Venus'. 4 m, V, △C.

'David Gable'. J. Gable, <1960;
reg. 1961. 'Atrosanguineum' ×
R. fortunei ssp. *fortunei*. 3 m, V,
△B.

'Dexter's Appleblossom'. C. O.
Dexter/Sandwich, Mass.,
<1960; reg. 1977. *R. fortunei*
hyb. × *R. fortunei* hyb. 4 m, V,
△A.

'Dexter's Orchid'. C. O. Dexter,
<1960. *R. fortunei* hyb. × *R. for-
tunei* hyb. 3 m, V, △B.

'Dexter's Purple'. C. O. Dexter/
P. Vossberg, <1960. *R. fortunei*
hyb. × *R. fortunei* hyb. 4 m, V,
△A.

'**Direktoer E. Hjelm**'. D. A. Koster, <1955; reg. 1958. *R. fortunei* hyb. × ?. 4 m, V, △B.

'**Disca**'. J. Gable, 1944; reg. 1958. *R. fortunei* ssp. *discolor* × 'Caroline'. 4 m, IV, △C.

'**Double Date**' ('Whitney's Double Pink', 'Toandos'). W. Whitney/De Sather, 1975; reg. 1977. *R. fortunei* hyb. × ?. 2 m, V, △B.

'**Dr. Tjebbes**'. C. A. van den Akker, 1966; reg. 1969. ? × *R. fortunei* hyb. AM Boskoop 1967. 3 m, V–VI, △B.

'Dr. Arnold W. Endtz'. L. J. Endtz & Co, <1927; reg. 1958. 'Pink Pearl' × *R. catawbiense* hyb. 3 m, V, △B.

'**Duchess of York**'. G. Paul, <1894; reg. 1958. *R. fortunei* ssp. *fortunei* × 'Scipio'. AM 1894. 3 m, V, △B.

'Elizabeth de Rothschild'. Edmund de Rothschild, <1965; reg. 1965. 'Lionel's Triumph' × 'Naomi'. AM 1965. 3 m, V, △C.

'Faggetter's Favourite'. W. C. Slocock, <1933; reg. 1958. *R. fortunei* ssp. *fortunei* × *R. fortunei* hyb. AM 1933, AM 1955. 3 m, V, △C.

'Fiona'. L. E. Brandt, 1952; reg. 1961. 'Bow Bells' × 'Loderi Pink Diamond'. 3 m, V, △C.

'Fred Wynniatt'. Edmund de Rothschild, <1963; reg. 1964. *R. fortunei* ssp. *fortunei* × 'Jalisco'. AM 1963, FCC 1980. 4 m, V, △C.

'Friesland'. L. J. Endtz & Co, <1940; reg. 1958. 'Pink Pearl' × *R. catawbiense* hyb. 3 m, V, △B.

'Gloxineum' ('Gloxinia'). C. O. Dexter, 1955; reg. 1958. *R. fortunei* ssp. *fortunei* × ?. 3 m, V, △B.

'Hollandia' ('G. Stresemann'). L. J. Endtz & Co, <1939; reg. 1958. 'Pink Pearl' × 'Charles Dickens'. 4 m, V, △B.

'Humoreske'. B. Kavka, 1959. 'Pink Pearl' × 'Peter Koster'. 3 m, V, △A.

'Ice Cream'. W. C. Slocock, <1960; reg. 1961. 'Dido' × *R. fortunei* hyb. AM 1960. 3 m, VI, △B.

'Lady Bessborough'. L. de Rothschild, <1933; reg. 1958. *R. fortunei* ssp. *fortunei* × *R. campylocarpum* (Elatum Grp.). FCC 1933. 4 m, VI, △C.

'Ice Cream Flavour'. L. de Rothschild, <1970. *R. fortunei* hyb. × ?. 3 m, V, △B.

'Lady Horlick'. Sir James Horlick, 1930; reg. 1961. *R. campylocarpum* ssp. *campylocarpum* × 'Loderi'. 3 m, V, △C.

'Isabel Pierce'. Halfdan Lem, 1975; reg. 1976. 'Anna' × 'Lem's Goal'. 3 m, V, △C.

'Jan Dekens'. L. J. Endtz & Co/J. Blaauw & Co, 1940; reg. 1958. *R. fortunei* hyb. × ?. 3 m, V, △B.

'Lavender Girl'. W. C. Slocock, <1950; reg. 1958. *R. fortunei* ssp. *fortunei* × 'Lady Grey Egerton'. AM 1950, FCC 1967. 3 m, V, △B.

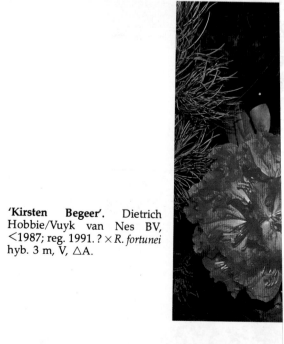

'Kirsten Begeer'. Dietrich Hobbie/Vuyk van Nes BV, <1987; reg. 1991. ? × *R. fortunei* hyb. 3 m, V, △A.

'Lem's Cameo'. Halfdan Lem, 1962; reg. 1976. 'Dido' × 'Anna'. 1.5 m, V, △B.

'Luscombei'. T. Luscombe, 1880; reg. 1958. *R. fortunei* ssp. *fortunei* × *R. thomsonii* ssp. *thomsonii*. 4 m, IV, △C.

'**Marinus Koster**'. M. Koster & Sons, <1937; reg. 1958. *R. griffithianum* hyb. × ?. AM 1937, FCC 1948. 3 m, V, △B.

'**Marlene Vuyk**'. Vuyk van Nes, <1975; reg. 1989. 'Direktoer E. Hjelm' × ?. 3 m, V, △B.

'**Mary Tasker**'. H. R. Tasker, 1979; reg. 1979. 'Jalisco' × 'Fawn'. 1.5 m, V, △C.

'Naomi Early Dawn'. L. de Rothschild, 1926; reg. 1958. 'Aurora' × *R. fortunei* ssp. *fortunei*. 4 m, IV–V, △B.

'Naomi Exbury'. L. de Rothschild, 1933; reg. 1958. 'Aurora' × *R. fortunei* ssp. *fortunei*. 4 m, V, △C.

'Naomi Glow'. L. de Rothschild, 1926; reg. 1958. 'Aurora' × *R. fortunei* ssp. *fortunei*. 4 m, V, △B.

'Naomi Hope'. L. de Rothschild, 1926; reg. 1958. 'Aurora' × *R. fortunei* ssp. *fortunei*. 4 m, V, △B.

'Ruby Bowman'. P. Bowman, 1953; reg. 1958. *R. fortunei* ssp. *fortunei* × 'Lady Bligh'. PA 1951. 3 m, V, △C.

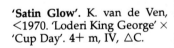

'Satin Glow'. K. van de Ven, <1970. 'Loderi King George' × 'Cup Day'. 4+ m, IV, △C.

'Naomi Paris'. Edmund de Rothschild, <1960; reg. 1970. 'Aurora' × *R. fortunei* ssp. *fortunei*. 3 m, V, △B.

'Naomi Pink Beauty'. L. de Rothschild, 1926; reg. 1958. 'Aurora' × *R. fortunei* ssp. *fortunei*. 3 m, V, △C.

'Queen Souriya'. W. C. Slocock, 1937; reg. 1958. *R. fortunei* ssp. *fortunei* × *R. campylocarpum* hyb. AM 1957. 2 m, V, △C.

'White Glory'. Dowager Lady Loder, <1937; reg. 1958. 'Loderi' × *R. irroratum*. AM 1937. 4+ m, V, △C.

'Romfort'. W. Wuestemeyer, 1985. 'Rombergpark' × *R. fortunei* hyb. 3 m, V, △A.

'Wissahickon'. C. O. Dexter, 1970. 'Pygmalion' × (*R. haematodes* × 'Wellfleet'). 3 m, V, △B.

'Rosy Dawn'. J. J. Crosfield, 1939; reg. 1958. *R. fortunei* hyb. × *R. thomsonii* ssp. *thomsonii*. 3 m, V, △C.

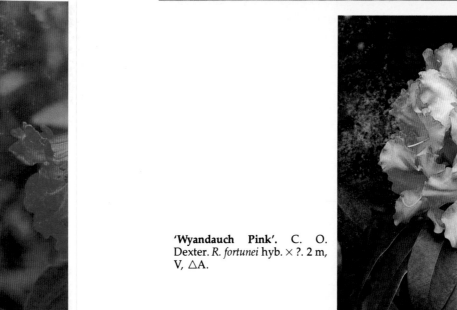

'Wyandauch Pink'. C. O. Dexter. *R. fortunei* hyb. × ?. 2 m, V, △A.

R. fortunei ssp. discolor.

R. fortunei ssp. discolor.

R. oreodoxa ssp. oreodoxa.

R. fortunei ssp. *discolor* & hyb.

'Platinum Pearl'. H. E. Greer, 1982. 'Trude Webster' × *R. fortunei* ssp. *discolor*. 3 m, V–VI, △B.

'Repose'. Edmund de Rothschild, 1950; reg. 1958. *R. fortunei* ssp. *discolor* × *R. lacteum*. AM 1956. 3 m, V, △C.

'Silver Sixpence'. J. Waterer, Sons & Crisp, <1975; reg. 1975. *R. discolor* hyb. × *R. yakushimanum* hyb. 1.5 m, V, △B.

'Sir Frederick Moore'. L. de Rothschild, 1935; reg. 1958. *R. fortunei* ssp. *discolor* × 'Saint Keverne'. AM 1937, FCC 1972. 3 m, V, △C.

'Thomas Messel'. Th. Messel, <1985. *R. fortunei* ssp. *discolor* × ?. 4 m, V, △C.

'Wilhelm Schacht'. Dietrich Hobbie, 1973. *R. fortunei* ssp. *discolor* × 'Professor Hugo de Vries'. 2 m, V, △A.

R. campylocarpum & hyb.

R. campylocarpum **ssp.** *campy-locarpum*, Inverewe.

R. campylocarpum **ssp.** *campy-locarpum*.

R. campylocarpum **ssp.** *campy-locarpum* (Elatum Grp.).

R. campylocarpum **ssp.** *calo-*
xanthum.

'Adriaan Koster'. M. Koster &
Sons, 1920; reg. 1958. 'Mrs.
Lindsay Smith' × *R. campylo-*
carpum hyb. 2 m, V, △B.

'Anita'. Lord Aberconway,
1941; reg. 1958. *R. campylo-*
carpum ssp. *campylocarpum* × *R.*
griersonianum. 2 m, V, △C.

'Carita Inchmery'. L. de Rothschild, 1935; reg. 1958. 'Naomi' ×
R. campylocarpum ssp. *campylocarpum*. 2 m, V, △B.

'Chaste'. J. J. Crosfield, 1930;
reg. 1958. *R. campylocarpum* ssp.
campylocarpum × 'Queen o'the
May'. 3 m, V, △C.

'Chinmar'. K. Sifferman, 1960;
reg. 1984. 'China' × 'Margaret
Findlay'. 3 m, V, △C.

'Cornish Cream'. Col. Bolitho,
<1937; reg. 1958. *R. campylo-
carpum* ssp. *campylocarpum* ×
'Fortorb'. 3 m, V, △C.

'Creamy Chiffon'. W. Whitney,
<1980. *R. campylocarpum* hyb. ×
?. 1.5 m, V, △B.

'Cremorne'. L. de Rothschild,
1947; reg. 1958. *R. campylocarpum* ssp. *campylocarpum* ×
'Luscombei'. AM 1947. 3 m, V,
△C.

'Dairymaid'. W. C. Slocock, 1930; reg. 1958. *R. campylo-carpum* hyb. × ?. AM 1934. 2 m, V, △B.

'Damaris'. E. J. P. Magor, 1926; reg. 1958. 'Dr. Stocker' × *R. campylocarpum* ssp. *campylo-carpum*. 3 m, V, △B.

'Diane'. M. Koster & Sons, 1920; reg. 1958. 'Mrs. Lindsay Smith' × *R. campylocarpum* ssp. *campylocarpum*. AM 1948. 2 m, V, △B.

'Eclipse'. L. de Rothschild, 1948; reg. 1958. 'Lady Bessborough' × 'Dido'. 2 m, V, △C.

'Elsie Straver'. M. Koster & Sons, <1966; reg. 1969. *R. campylocarpum* ssp. *campylo-carpum* × ?. 2 m, V, △A.

'Emerald Isle'. RHS Gardens, Wisley, 1956; reg. 1958. 'Idealist' × 'Exbury Naomi'. AM 1956. 3 m, V, △B.

'Flashlight'. L. de Rothschild, 1938; reg. 1958. *R. callimorphum* × *R. campylocarpum* ssp. *campylocarpum*. 2 m, V, △B.

'Gladys'. S. R. Clarke, <1926; reg. 1958. *R. campylocarpum* ssp. *campylocarpum* × *R. fortunei* ssp. *fortunei*. AM 1926, AM 1950. 3 m, V, △C.

'Goldsworth Yellow'. W. C. Slocock, 1925; reg. 1958. *R. campylocarpum* ssp. *campylocarpum* × *R. caucasicum*. AM 1925. 1.5 m, IV–V, △B.

'Harvest Moon'. M. Koster &
Sons, <1948; reg. 1958. 'Mrs.
Lindsay Smith' × *R. campylocarpum* ssp. *campylocarpum.* AM
1948. 2 m, V, △B.

'Koster's Cream'. M. Koster &
Sons, 1945; reg. 1958. *R. campylocarpum* hyb. × ?. 2 m, V, △B.

'Lady Primrose'. W. C. Slocock,
<1933; reg. 1958. *R. campylo-
carpum* ssp. *campylocarpum* × ?.
AM 1933. 2 m, V, △C.

'Letty Edwards'. S. R. Clarke, <1946; reg. 1958. *R. campylocarpum* (Elatum Grp.) × *R. fortunei* ssp. *fortunei*.

'Logan Damaris'. K. McDouall, 1926; reg. 1958. *R. campylocarpum* ssp. *campylocarpum* × 'Dr. Stocker'. AM 1948. 3 m, V, △B.

'Maharani'. H. Hachmann, 1978; reg. 1983. 'Harvest Moon' × 'Letty Edwards'. 3 m, V, △A.

'Manor Hill'. Crown Estate Comm., Windsor, 1974; reg. 1974. 'Dido' × ('Jalisco' × *R. yakushimanum*). AM 1974. 50 cm, V, △C.

'Marcia'. Lord Swaythling, <1944; reg. 1958. *R. campylocarpum* ssp. *campylocarpum* × 'Gladys'. FCC 1944. 1.5 m, V, △B.

'Mariloo'. L. de Rothschild, 1941; reg. 1958. 'Dr. Stocker' × *R. lacteum*. 3 m, IV–V, △D.

R. *campylocarpum* & hyb.

'Queen Elizabeth II'. Crown Estate Comm., Windsor, <1967; reg. 1968. 'Idealist' × 'Crest'. AM 1967, FCC 1974. 3 m, V, △C.

'Ripe Corn'. W. C. Slocock, 1967; reg. 1967. 'Goldsworth Orange' × 'Naomi Exbury'. 3 m, V, △B.

'Simona'. H. Hachmann, 1978; reg. 1983. 'Harvest Moon' × 'Letty Edwards'. 2 m, V, △A.

'Souvenir of W. C. Slocock'. W. C. Slocock, <1928; reg. 1958. *R. campylocarpum* ssp. *campylocarpum* × ?. AM 1935. 2 m, V, △B.

'Vondel'. M. Koster & Sons, <1940; reg. 1958. *R. campylocarpum* hyb. × 'Mrs. Lindsay Smith'. 2 m, V, △C.

'Zuiderzee'. M. Koster & Sons, 1936; reg. 1958. 'Mrs. Lindsay Smith' × *R. campylocarpum* hyb. AM 1936. 3 m, V, △B.

310 Grp. 11a.
R. *wardii* & hyb.

R. *wardii* ssp. *wardii.*

R. *wardii* ssp. *wardii.*

R. *wardii* ssp. *wardii* (Litiense Grp.).

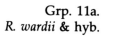

R. wardii ssp. *puralbum.*

'Cool Haven
Hillier & S
1970. 'Chaste
wardii (Litien
△C.

'Alice Street' ('Miss Street'). M.
Koster & Sons, 1953; reg. 1958.
'Diane' × *R. wardii* ssp. *wardii*. 3
m, V, △B.

'Allegretto'. H. Hachmann,
<1988. ? × ?. 2 m, V, △A.

'Hachmann's Marietta'. H. Hachmann, 1986; reg. 1989. 'Tosca' × *R. yakushimanum* 'Koichiro Wada'. 50 cm, V–VI, △A.

'B
19
×
△

'Hachmann's Marina'. H. Hachmann, <1978; reg. 1978. 'Omega' × *R. wardii* ssp. *wardii*. 3 m, V, △A.

'
w
'
ss
△

'Haida Gold'. R. M. Bovee, 1986. *R. wardii* ssp. *wardii* × 'Goldfort'. 1.5 m, V, △B.

'Hotei'. K. Sifferman, 1968; reg. 1970. 'Goldsworth Orange' × (*R. souliei* × *R. wardii* ssp. *wardii*). PA 1968, AM 1974. 2 m, V, △A.

'**Idealist**'. L. de Rothschild, <1941; reg. 1958. 'Naomi' × *R. wardii* ssp. *wardii*. AM 1945. 3 m, V, △C.

'**Ightham Yellow**'. G. Reuthe Ltd., 1952; reg. 1958. *R. wardii* ssp. *wardii* × *R. decorum*. 3 m, V, △C.

'Mancando'. H. Hachmann,
1985. 'Hachmann's Marina' ×
('Omega' × *R. wardii* ssp. *wardii*).
1.5 m, V, △A.

'Marinella'. H. Hachmann,
1988. *R. wardii* hyb. × ?. 1.5 m, V,
△A.

'Moonshine Bright'. RHS
Gardens, Wisley, 1952; reg.
1958. 'Adriaan Koster' × *R.
wardii* ssp. *wardii* (Litiense
Grp.). 3 m, V, △C.

'**Moonshine Crescent'**. RHS Gardens, Wisley, <1960; reg. 1961. 'Adriaan Koster' × *R. wardii* ssp. *wardii* (Litiense Grp.). AM 1960. 3 m, V, △C.

'**New Comet'**. RHS Gardens, Wisley, 1957; reg. 1958. 'Idealist' × 'Naomi'. AM 1957. 3 m, V–VI, △C.

'**Nippon'**. Dietrich Hobbie, <1980. *R. wardii* hyb. × *R. catawbiense* hyb. 1.5 m, V, △A.

'Orchard Road'. ?. 'Pacific
Queen' × *R. wardii* ssp. *wardii*. 3
m, V, △?.

'Peeping Tom'. A. O. Wright,
1965; reg. 1966. *R. wardii* ssp.
wardii × 'Mrs. Furnivall'. 2 m, V,
△C.

'Primula'. Dietrich Hobbie,
<1981. *R. wardii* hyb. × *R. wardii*
hyb. 1.5 m, V, △A.

'Rosa Regen'. Dietrich Hobbie, <1975. *R. wardii* hyb. × *R. wardii* hyb. 3 m, V, △A.

'Roza Stevenson' ('Roza Harrison'). J. B. Stevenson, 1951; reg. 1970. 'Loderi Sir Edmund' × *R. wardii* ssp. *wardii*. FCC 1968. 3 m, V, △C.

'Sandra'. H. Hachmann, 1982; reg. 1983. (*R. wardii* ssp. *wardii* × 'Alice Street') × 'Hachmann's Marina'. 1.5 m, V, △A.

'Stadt Delmenhorst' ('Neptun'). Joh. Bruns, <1975. 'Berryrose' × *R. wardii* ssp. *wardii* (Litiense Grp.). 1.5 m, V, △A.

'Stadt Westerstede'. G. D. Boehlje, <1982; reg. 1984. 'Letty Edwards' × *R. wardii* hyb. 1.5 m, V, △B.

'Trompenburg'. Dietrich Hobbie/Trompenburg Arboretum, <1980; reg. 1991. *R. wardii* hyb. × *R. wardii* hyb. 1.5 m, V, △A.

'Vienna'. Knap Hill Nurseries, 1962; reg. 1964. 'Naomi' × *R. wardii* ssp. *wardii*. 3 m, V, △C.

'Virginia Richards'.

'Virginia Richards'. W. Whitney/De Sather, 1965; reg. 1976. (*R. wardii* ssp. *wardii* × 'F. C. Puddle') × 'Mrs. Betty Robertson'. PA 1962, AM 1985. 3 m, V, △B.

R. thomsonii ssp. *thomsonii*,
Nepal.

R. thomsonii ssp. *thomsonii*.

R. thomsonii ssp. *thomsonii*.

R. thomsonii **ssp.** *thomsonii.*

'Aries'. Sir J. Ramsden, 1922; reg. 1958. *R. thomsonii* ssp. *thomsonii* × *R. neriiflorum* ssp. *neriiflorum.* AM 1932, FCC 1938. 1.5 m, V, △C.

R. × *candelabrum.*

'**Ascot Brilliant**'. J. Standish, Bagshot, 1861; reg. 1958. *R. thomsonii* ssp. *thomsonii* × 'Blandyanum'. 4 m, IV–V, △C.

'**Aurora**'. R. Gill, 1922; reg. 1958. 'Kewense' × *R. thomsonii* ssp. *thomsonii*. AM 1922. 4 m, V, △C.

'**Bagshot Ruby**'. J. Waterer, 1900; reg. 1958. *R. thomsonii* ssp. *thomsonii* × *R. catawbiense* hyb. AM 1916. 3 m, V, △B.

'Betty'. Sir Giles Loder, 1927; reg. 1958. *R. fortunei* ssp. *fortunei* × *R. thomsonii* ssp. *thomsonii*. AM 1927. 4 m, V, △C.

'Cavalier'. R. Henny, 1958; reg. 1958. 'Pygmalion' × 'Tally Ho'. 4 m, VI, △D.

'Chanticleer'. L. de Rothschild, 1935; reg. 1958. *R. thomsonii* ssp. *thomsonii* × *R. facetum*. 2 m, V, △C.

'Cornish Cross'. S. Smith,
<1920; reg. 1958. *R. thomsonii*
ssp. *thomsonii* × *R. griffithianum*.
4 m, IV, △C.

'General Sir John du Cane'. L.
de Rothschild, 1933; reg. 1958.
R. thomsonii ssp. *thomsonii* × *R.
fortunei* ssp. *discolor*. 3 m, V, △C.

'J. G. Millais'. J. Waterer, 1915;
reg. 1958. 'Ascot Brilliant' ×
'Pink Pearl'. 3 m, IV, △B.

'Little Paddocks'. Sir James Horlick, 1940; reg. 1958. *R. campylocarpum* ssp. *campylo-carpum* × *R. thomsonii* ssp. *thomsonii*. 1.5 m, V, △C.

'Maroze'. J. B. Stevenson, 1937; reg. 1958. *R. meddianum* × 'Red Admiral'. 2 m, V, △C.

'Mrs. James Horlick'. Sir James Horlick, 1940. *R. thomsonii* ssp. *thomsonii* × 'Dr. Stocker'. 4 m, IV, △B.

338 Grp. 13a.
       R. williamsianum & hyb.

R. williamsianum.

R. williamsianum.

'Ammerlandense'.   Dietrich
Hobbie, 1946; reg. 1958. 'Britan-
nia' × *R. williamsianum*. 1.5 m, V,
△A.

'April Glow'. A. C van Wilgen, 1965; reg. 1969. *R. williamsianum* × 'Wilgen's Ruby'. AM Boskoop 1965, AM 1975. 1.5 m, IV–V, △B.

'Bad Zwischenahn'. Dietrich Hobbie, 1968. *? × R. williamsianum.* 1.5 m, V, △A.

'Berlin'. Dietrich Hobbie/Joh. Bruns, 1964. 'Mme de Bruin' × *R. williamsianum.* 1 m, V, △B.

'Boccia'. Dietrich Hobbie/ Hachmann, <1987; reg. 1989. *R. catawbiense* 'Compactum' × *R. williamsianum.* 1.5 m, V, △A.

'Bow Bells'. L. de Rothschild, 1934; reg. 1958. 'Corona' × *R. williamsianum*. AM 1935. 1.5 m, V, △B.

'Brocade'. L. de Rothschild, 1934; reg. 1958. 'Vervaeniana' × *R. williamsianum*. 2 m, V, △C.

'Brickdust'. R. Henny, 1959; reg. 1961. *R. williamsianum* × 'Dido'. 1 m, V, △B.

'Cowslip'. Lord Aberconway, 1930; reg. 1958. *R. williamsianum* × *R. wardii* ssp. *wardii*. AM 1937. 2 m, V, △B.

'Caroline Spencer'. Dietrich Hobbie/Adams-Acton, 1950; reg. 1958. *R. fortunei* ssp. *fortunei* × *R. williamsianum*. 1.5 m, V, △B.

'Dr. Schlapper'. Dietrich Hobbie, <1970. 'Doncaster' × *R. williamsianum*. 1.5 m, IV–V, △B.

Grp. 13a.
R. williamsianum & hyb.

'Elfenbein'. Dietrich Hobbie, <1975. 'Adriaan Koster' × *R. williamsianum*. 1.5 m, V, △A.

'Elizabeth Lockhart'.

'Elizabeth Lockhart'. R. D. Lockhart, 1964; reg. 1965. *R. haematodes* ssp. *haematodes* × *R. williamsianum*. 1 m, V, △B.

'Gartendirektor Glocker'.
Dietrich Hobbie, <1952; reg.
1958. 'Doncaster' × *R. williamsianum.* 1.5 m, V, △A.

'Gartendirektor Rieger'. H.
Robenek/D. Hobbie, <1971.
'Adriaan Koster' × *R. william-
sianum.* 2 m, IV–V, △A.

'Georg Stipp'. Dietrich Hobbie/
Hesse, <1960. 'Mme de Bruin'
× *R. williamsianum.* 1.5 m, V, △A.

'Goerlitz'. V. von Martin/Joh. Bruns, <1964; reg. 1972. 'Rinaldo' × *R. williamsianum*. 1 m, V, △A.

'Hachmann's Evelyn' ('Evelyn'). H. Hachmann, 1976; reg. 1989. 'Oudijk's Sensation' × 'Daisy'. 2 m, V, △A.

'Hallelujah'. H. E. Greer, 1976; reg. 1976. 'Kimberly' × 'Jean Marie de Montague'. AE 1983. 1.5 m, V, △B.

'Hebe'. E. J. P. Magor, 1923; reg.
1958. 'Neriihaem' × *R. william-*
sianum. 1.5 m, V, △B.

'Hummingbird'.

'Hummingbird'. J. C. Williams,
1933; reg. 1958. *R. haematodes*
ssp. *haematodes* × *R. william-*
sianum. 1 m, V, △B.

Grp. 13a.
R. williamsianum & hyb.

'Irmelies'. H. Hachmann, 1987;
reg. 1989. 'Oudijk's Sensation' ×
'Marinus Koster'. 1.5 m, V, △A.

'Jock'. Stirling Maxwell, 1939;
reg. 1958. *R. williamsianum* × *R.
griersonianum*. 1.5 m, IV–V, △B.

'Karin'. Proefstation Boskoop,
1966; reg. 1969. 'Britannia' × *R.
williamsianum*. AM Boskoop
1958. 2 m, IV–V, △B.

'Kimberly'. H. E. Greer, <1963; reg. 1964. *R. williamsianum* × *R. fortunei* ssp. *fortunei*. PA 1963. 1.5 m, IV–V, △B.

'Kimbeth'. H. E. Greer, <1979; reg. 1979. 'Kimberly' × 'Elizabeth'. 1 m, V, △B.

'Libelle'. Dietrich Hobbie, 1952; reg. 1958. 'Faggetter's Favourite' × *R. williamsianum*. 1.5 m, V, △B.

'Linda'. Proefstation Boskoop, 1968; reg. 1969. 'Britannia' × *R. williamsianum*. AM Boskoop 1968. 1.5 m, V, △A.

'Lissabon'. V. von Martin/Joh. Bruns 1972, 1964; reg. 1972. 'Nova Zembla' × *R. williamsianum*. 1.5 m, V, △A.

'Mission Bells'. B. Lancaster, 1958. *R. williamsianum* × *R. orbiculare* ssp. *orbiculare*. 1.5 m, V, △A.

'Moerheim's Pink'. Dietrich Hobbie/Moerheim BV, 1972; reg. 1973. 'Genoveva' × *R. williamsianum*. AM 1972. 1.5 m, V, △B.

'Moonstone'. J. C. Williams, 1933; reg. 1958. *R. campylocarpum* ssp. *campylocarpum* × *R. williamsianum*. 1 m, V, △B.

'Oldenburg'. Dietrich Hobbie, 1953; reg. 1958. *R. fortunei* ssp. *discolor* × *R. williamsianum*. 2 m, V, △A.

'Pink Pebble'. E. G. Harrison, 1954; reg. 1958. *R. callimorphum* × *R. williamsianum.* AM 1975. 1 m, V, △B.

'Pipaluk'. E. G. Harrison, 1968; reg. 1969. 'Dr. Stocker' × *R. williamsianum.* 1.5 m, V, △B.

'Pook'. ?, <1980. *R. williamsianum* × ?. 1.5 m, V, △B.

'Psyche'. Dietrich Hobbie, 1950; reg. 1958. 'Sir Charles Butler' × *R. williamsianum.* 2 m, V, △B.

'Rose Point'. L. Pierce, 1972; reg. 1980. 'Dido' × *R. williamsianum.* 1 m, V, △B.

'Rothenburg'.

'Rothenburg'. V. von Martin/
Joh. Bruns, <1968; reg. 1972.
'Diane' × *R. williamsianum*. 3 m,
V, △B.

'Royal Pink'. Dietrich Hobbie/
Le Feber, <1964; reg. 1965.
'Homer' × *R. williamsianum*. 2 m,
V, △B.

'Stadt Essen'. Dietrich Hobbie,
1978. 'Louis Pasteur' × *R.
williamsianum*. 2 m, V, △A.

'Stockholm'. D. G. Leach, 1972;
reg. 1974. 'Catalgla' × *R. William-*
sianum 3 m, V, △A.

'Thomwilliams'. E. J. P. Magor,
1927; reg. 1958. *R. thomsonii* ssp.
thomsonii × *R. williamsianum*. 1.5
m, V, △B.

'Tibet'. Dietrich Hobbie/Gebr.
Boer, 1966; reg. 1969. 'Bis-
marck' × *R. williamsianum*. 1.5 m,
V, △B.

'Treasure'. J. J. Crosfield, 1937;
reg. 1958. *R. forrestii* ssp. *forrestii*
× *R. williamsianum.* 1 m, V, △B.

'Willbrit'. Dietrich Hobbie/Le
Feber & Co, <1964; reg. 1965.
R. williamsianum × 'Britannia'. 2
m, V, △A.

'Willy-Nilly'. Collingwood In-
gram, 1971; reg. 1972. 'Harold
Heal' × *R. williamsianum.* 1.5 m,
V, △C.

R. neriiflorum ssp. *neriiflorum.*

R. neriiflorum ssp. *neriiflorum*
(Euchaites Grp.).

'Atroflo'. J. Gable, 1940; reg.
1958. 'Atrosanguineum' × *R.
floccigerum*. 3 m, VI, △B.

'Choremia'. Lord Aberconway, 1933; reg. 1958. R. *haematodes* ssp. *haematodes* × R. *arboreum* ssp. *arboreum*. AM 1933, FCC 1948. 2 m, IV–V, △C.

'Fandango'. L. de Rothschild, 1938; reg. 1958. 'Britannia' × R. *haematodes* ssp. *haematodes*. 1 m, V, △B.

'Fireman Jeff'. L. E. Brandt, 1970; reg. 1977. 'Jean Marie de Montague' × 'Grosclaude'. 1.5 m, IV–V, △B.

'Fuego'. Dietrich Hobbie, <1970. 'Mme de Bruin' × *R. haematodes* ssp. *haematodes*. 1.5 m, V, △A.

'Gnom'. G. Arends/G. D. Boehlje, 1959; reg. 1964. *R. haematodes* ssp. *haematodes* × *R. catawbiense* hyb. 2 m, V, △A.

'Ovation'. W. Nagel, 1983. 'Mars' × *R. haematodes* ssp. *haematodes*. 2 m, V, △A.

'Iphigenia'. E. J. P. Magor, 1934;
reg. 1958. *R. haematodes* ssp.
haematodes × 'Red Admiral'. V,
△B.

'Impi'. L. de Rothschild, 1945;
reg. 1958. *R. sanguineum* ssp.
didymum × 'Moser's Maroon'.
AM 1945. 1.5 m, V, △B.

'Oporto'. Collingwood Ingram,
1953; reg. 1968. *R. sanguineum*
var. *haemaleum* × *R. thomsonii*
ssp. *thomsonii*. AM 1967. 1 m, V,
△C.

'Red Cap'. J. B. Stevenson, 1935; reg. 1958. *R. sanguineum* ssp. *didymum* × *R. facetum*. 1.5 m, V, △C.

'Thomaleum'. Collingwood Ingram, 1958; reg. 1958. *R. thomsonii* ssp. *thomsonii* × *R. sanguineum* var. *haemaleum*. 1 m, V, △?.

'Thomsang'. ?, <1960. *R. thomsonii* ssp. *thomsonii* × *R. sanguineum* ssp. *sanguineum*. 1.5 m, V, △B.

Grp. 15a.
R. dichroanthum & hyb.

R. dichroanthum ssp. *dichroanthum.*

R. dichroanthum ssp. *scyphocalyx.*

'Abendsonne' ('Vorwerk
Abendsonne'). Dietrich Hobbie, <1976. 'John Walter' × *R.
dichroanthum* ssp. *scyphocalyx*.
1.5 m, V, △A.

'Amaretto'. H. Hachmann, <1987; reg. 1989. *R. dichroanthum* hyb. × 'Hachmann's Marina'. 1.5 m, V, △B.

'Apricot Nectar'. Marshall Lyons, 1971; reg. 1972. *R. dichroanthum* hyb. × 'Jalisco'. 1 m, V, △B.

'Bernstein'. H. Hachmann, 1978; reg. 1983. 'Goldsworth Orange' × 'Mrs. J. G. Millais'. 3 m, V, △A.

'Berryrose'. L. de Rothschild, 1934; reg. 1958. 'Doncaster' × *R. dichroanthum* ssp. *dichroanthum*. AM 1934. 1.5 m, VI, △C.

'Brinny'. W. Graves, <1964; reg. 1965. ('Day Dream' × 'Margaret Dunn') × ?. 2 m, V, △B.

'Brookside'. Crown Estate Comm., Windsor, <1962; reg. 1963. 'Goshawk' × *R. griersonianum*. AM 1962. 3 m, V–VI, △C.

'C. I. S.'. R. Henny, 1952; reg. 1958. 'Loder's White' × 'Fabia'. PA 1952, AM 1975. 3 m, V, △C.

'Coral Reef'. RHS Gardens, Wisley, <1954; reg. 1958. 'Fabia' × 'Goldsworth Orange'. AM 1954. 3 m, V–VI, △C.

'Creminrose' ('Salome'). H. Hachmann, <1979; reg. 1989. 'Fruehlingszauber' × 'Letty Edwards'. 2 m, V, △A.

Grp. 15a.
R. dichroanthum & hyb.

'Diana'. Joh. Bruns, <1975. 'Professor J. H. Zaayer' × 'Goldsworth Orange'. 1.5 m, V–VI, △A.

'Donna Hardgrove'. D. L. Hardgrove, 1978; reg. 1979. *R. fortunei* ssp. *fortunei* × (*R. wardii* ssp. *wardii* × *R. dichroanthum*). 2 m, V, △A.

'Edward Dunn'. E. Ostbo, 1958; reg. 1958. (*R. dichroanthum* × *R. neriiflorum*) × *R. fortunei* ssp. *discolor*. PA 1958. 2 m, V, △B.

'Fabia'. Lord Aberconway, 1927; reg. 1958. *R. dichroanthum* ssp. *dichroanthum* × *R. griersonianum*. AM 1934. 2 m, V, △C.

'Gloria'.

'Gloria' ('Christiane'). Joh. Bruns, <1980. 'Goldsworth Orange' × 'Professor F. Bettex'. 2 m, V–VI, △A.

'**Golden Gate**'. ?, <1975. *R. dichroanthum* ssp. *scyphocalyx* × ?. 2 m, V, △C.

'**Golden Horn**'. L. de Rothschild, 1939; reg. 1958. *R. dichroanthum* ssp. *dichroanthum* × *R. elliottii*. AM 1945. 1.5 m, V–VI, △C.

'**Goldsworth Orange**'. W. C. Slocock, 1938; reg. 1958. *R. dichroanthum* ssp. *dichroanthum* × *R. fortunei* ssp. *discolor*. AM 1959. 2 m, V, △B.

'Hachmann's Bananaflip' ('Bananaflip'). H. Hachmann, 1987; reg. 1989. *R. brachycarpum* ssp. *fauriei* × 'Goldsworth Orange'. 1 m, V, △A.

'Hachmann's Libelle' ('Libelle'). H. Hachmann, 1981; reg. 1985. 'Goldsworth Orange' × 'Mrs. J. G. Millais'. 1.5 m, V, △A.

'Hello Dolly'. Halfdan Lem, 1973; reg. 1974. 'Fabia' × *R. smirnowii*. 2 m, V, △B.

'Sweet Sue'. J. Waterer, Sons & Crisp, <1961; reg. 1972. (*R. facetum* × 'Fabia') × (*R. yakushimanum* × 'Fabia'). 1.5 m, V, △B.

'Tidbit'. R. Henny, 1957; reg. 1958. *R. dichroanthum* ssp. *dichroanthum* × *R. wardii* ssp. *wardii*. PA 1957. 2 m, V, △B.

'Tokaija'. H. Hachmann, 1987. ? × ?. 1 m, V, △A.

R. forrestii ssp. *forrestii.*

R. forrestii ssp. *papillatum.*

'Baden Baden'. Dietrich Hobbie, 1956. 'Essex Scarlet' × *R. forrestii* ssp. *forrestii*. 2 m, V, △AA.

'Bengal'. Dietrich Hobbie, <1960. 'Essex Scarlet' × *R. forrestii* ssp. *forrestii*. 1 m, V, △A.

'Bremen'. G. Arends/Boehlje, 1959; reg. 1964. *R. forrestii* ssp. *forrestii* × *R. catawbiense* hyb. AM Boskoop 1970. 1.5 m, V, △B.

'Brilliant'. J. Waterer, <1950;
reg. 1958. *R. thomsonii* ssp.
thomsonii × ?. 3 m, V, △C.

'Buketta' ('Hachmann's Buketta'). H. Hachmann, 1979; reg.
1983. 'Spitfire' × 'Fruehlingszauber'. 1 m, V, △A.

'Burning Love' ('U. Siems').
Dietrich Hobbie, 1973. 'Essex
Scarlet' × *R. forrestii* ssp. *forrestii*.
1 m, V, △A.

'Fruehlingszauber' ('Spring Magic'). Dietrich Hobbie/ Bruns, 1962; reg. 1970. 'Essex Scarlet' × *R. forrestii* ssp. *forrestii*. 1 m, V, △A.

'Gertrud Schaele'. Dietrich Hobbie, 1951; reg. 1958. 'Prometheus' × *R. forrestii* ssp. *forrestii*. 2 m, V, △B.

'Graefin Kirchbach'. V. von Martin/Bruns, 1966; reg. 1972. 'Scharnhorst' × *R. forrestii* ssp. *forrestii*. 1.5 m, V, △A.

'Juwel'. Dietrich Hobbie, <1960. 'Essex Scarlet' × *R. forrestii* ssp. *forrestii*. 1.5 m, IV–V, △A.

'Linswege' ('Linswegeanum'). Dietrich Hobbie, 1946; reg. 1958. 'Britannia' × *R. forrestii* ssp. *forrestii*. 1 m, IV, △B.

'Little Ben'. C. R. Scrase-Dickins, <1937; reg. 1958. *R. forrestii* ssp. *forrestii* × *R. neriiflorum* ssp. *neriiflorum* (Euchaites Grp.). FCC 1937. 30 cm, IV, △B.

'Little Bert'. C. R. Scrase-Dickins, <1939; reg. 1958. *R. forrestii* ssp. *forrestii* × *R. neriiflorum* ssp. *neriiflorum* (Euchaites Grp.). AM 1939. 30 cm, IV, △B.

'Moerheim Jubilee'. Dietrich Hobbie/Moerheim Nurseries, 1965; reg. 1969. 'Essex Scarlet' × *R. forrestii* ssp. *forrestii*. 1.5 m, VIII, △A.

'Monica'. Dietrich Hobbie, 1973; reg. 1989. 'Dr. H. C. Dresselhuys' × *R. forrestii* ssp. *forrestii*. AM Boskoop 1975. 1.5 m, V, △A.

'Parkjuwel'. Joh. Bruns/Bruns, <1969. 'Essex Scarlet' × *R. forrestii* ssp. *forrestii*. 1.5 m, IV, △A.

'Pruhonice'. Res. Station Pruhonice/Boot & Co BV, <1970; reg. 1989. *R. forrestii* ssp. *forrestii* × ?. 1.5 m, V, △A.

'Ruth Otte'. Dietrich Hobbie, 1953. ('Ammerlandense' × *R. wardii*) × *R. forrestii* ssp. *forrestii*. 1 m, V, △A.

R. adenogynum (Adenophorum Grp.).

R. bureavii.

R. bureavii.

'Burfield'. ?, <1985. *R. bureavii*
× 'Renoir'. 2 m, V, △B.

'Hansel'. Halfdan Lem, 1979. *R.
bureavii* × 'Fabia'. 1.5 m, V, △B.

'Hazel'. H. E. Greer, 1979; reg.
1979. *R. bureavii* × ?. 3 m, V, △A.

R. lacteum.

R. roxieanum ssp. *roxieanum.*

R. roxieanum ssp. *roxieanum*
(Oreonastes Grp.).

R. taliense.

R. wasonii.

'Herkules'. T. J. R. Seidel, <1894. *R. campanulatum* hyb. × *R. catawbiense* hyb. 3 m, V, △AA.

'John Barr Stevenson'. J. B. Stevenson, <1960; reg. 1961. *R. lacteum* × 'Logan Damaris'. AM 1971. 2 m, V, △C.

'Susan'. J. C. Williams, <1930; reg. 1958. *R. campanulatum* ssp. *campanulatum* × *R. fortunei* ssp. *fortunei*. AM 1930, AM 1948, FCC 1954. 3 m, V, △B.

R. fulgens.

R. fulvum.

R. fulvum.

R. mallotum.

Grp. 17d.
Subsection Maculifera,
spp. & hyb.

R. *maculiferum* ssp. *maculiferum.*

R. *maculiferum* ssp. *anhweiense.*

R. *aberconwayi.*

**R. aberconwayi 'His Lord-
ship'.** Crown Estate Comm.,
Windsor, <1945; reg. 1961. *R.
aberconwayi* × *R. aberconwayi.*
AM 1945. 2 m, V, △B.

'Enborne'. Crown Estate
Comm., Windsor, <1966; reg.
1967. *R. aberconwayi* × *R.
maculiferum* ssp. *anhweiense.* AM
1966. 2 m, V, △B.

R. irroratum.

R. smithii.

R. smithii (Argipeplum Grp.).

R. barbatum.

'Duchess of Portland'. Fischer, Son & Sibray, <1903; reg. 1958. *R. barbatum* × 'Handsworth White'. AM 1903. 2 m, IV, △C.

'Fireball'. R. Gill & Son, 1925; reg. 1958. *R. barbatum* × 'Ascot Brilliant'. AM 1925. 3 m, V, △B.

'Calfort'. Collingwood Ingram, <1932; reg. 1958. *R. calophytum* ssp. *calophytum* × *R. fortunei* ssp. *fortunei*. AM 1932. 4 m, V, △B.

'Calrose'. Lord Aberconway, <1939; reg. 1958. *R. calophytum* ssp. *calophytum* × *R. griersonianum*. 4 m, V, △C.

'Nimrod'. Edmund de Rothschild, 1963; reg. 1964. *R. irroratum* × *R. calophytum* ssp. *calophytum*. 4 m, V, △B.

R. sutchuenense.

'Geraldii'. ?, reg. 1958. *R. praevernum* × *R. sutchuenense.* AM 1945. 3 m, III–IV, △B.

'Kordesa'. W. Kordes, 1985. 'Progres' × *R. sutchuenense.* 2 m, IV, △A.

R. auriculatum.

'Aladdin'. J. J. Crosfield, 1930; reg. 1958. *R. griersonianum* × *R. auriculatum*. AM 1935. 4+ m, VI, △C.

'Argosy'. L. de Rothschild, 1933; reg. 1958. *R. fortunei* ssp. *discolor* × *R. auriculatum*. 4 m, V, △C.

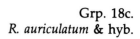

'Polar Bear'. J. B. Stevenson, 1926; reg. 1958. *R. diaprepes* × *R. auriculatum*. FCC 1946. 4+ m, VII–VIII, △B.

R. diaprepes.

R. diaprepes.